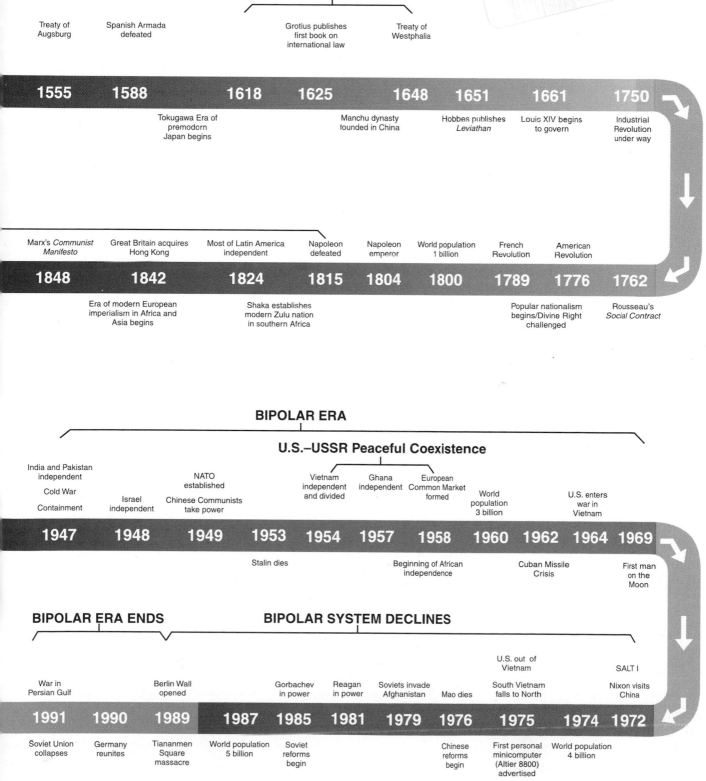

THIRTY YEARS' WAR

Treaty of Augsburg — Spanish Armada defeated — Grotius publishes first book on international law — Treaty of Westphalia

1555 | **1588** | **1618** | **1625** | **1648** | **1651** | **1661** | **1750**

Tokugawa Era of premodern Japan begins — Manchu dynasty founded in China — Hobbes publishes *Leviathan* — Louis XIV begins to govern — Industrial Revolution under way

Marx's *Communist Manifesto* — Great Britain acquires Hong Kong — Most of Latin America independent — Napoleon defeated — Napoleon emperor — World population 1 billion — French Revolution — American Revolution

1848 | **1842** | **1824** | **1815** | **1804** | **1800** | **1789** | **1776** | **1762**

Era of modern European imperialism in Africa and Asia begins — Shaka establishes modern Zulu nation in southern Africa — Popular nationalism begins/Divine Right challenged — Rousseau's *Social Contract*

BIPOLAR ERA

U.S.–USSR Peaceful Coexistence

India and Pakistan independent
Cold War
Containment — Israel independent — NATO established / Chinese Communists take power — Vietnam independent and divided — Ghana independent — European Common Market formed — World population 3 billion — U.S. enters war in Vietnam

1947 | **1948** | **1949** | **1953** | **1954** | **1957** | **1958** | **1960** | **1962** | **1964** | **1969**

Stalin dies — Beginning of African independence — Cuban Missile Crisis — First man on the Moon

BIPOLAR ERA ENDS   ## BIPOLAR SYSTEM DECLINES

U.S. out of Vietnam
SALT I

War in Persian Gulf — Berlin Wall opened — Gorbachev in power — Reagan in power — Soviets invade Afghanistan — Mao dies — South Vietnam falls to North — Nixon visits China

1991 | **1990** | **1989** | **1987** | **1985** | **1981** | **1979** | **1976** | **1975** | **1974** | **1972**

Soviet Union collapses — Germany reunites — Tiananmen Square massacre — World population 5 billion — Soviet reforms begin — Chinese reforms begin — First personal minicomputer (Altier 8800) advertised — World population 4 billion

John T. Rourke, Ph.D., is a professor in the Department of Political Science at The University of Connecticut. He is a coauthor with Mark A. Boyer of *World Politics: International Politics on the World Stage, Brief,* Fourth Edition (McGraw-Hill/Dushkin, 2002); the author of *Presidential Wars and American Democracy: Rally 'Round the Chief* (Paragon House, 1993); a coauthor of *Direct Democracy and International Politics: Deciding International Issues Through Referendums* (Lynne Rienner, 1992); the editor of *Taking Sides: Clashing Views on Controversial Issues in American Foreign Policy, Second Edition* (McGraw-Hill/Dushkin, 2002) and *Taking Sides: Clashing Views on Controversial Issues in World Politics,* Tenth Edition (McGraw-Hill/Dushkin, 2002), the author of *Making Foreign Policy: United States, Soviet Union, China* (Brooks/Cole, 1990), *Congress and the Presidency in U.S. Foreign Policy-making* (Westview, 1985), and numerous articles and papers. He enjoys teaching introductory classes, and he does so each semester at the university's Storrs and Hartford campuses. His regard for the students has molded his approach of conveying scholarship in a language and within a frame of reference that undergraduates can appreciate. Rourke believes, as the theme of this book reflects, that politics affect us all, and we can affect politics. Rourke practices what he propounds; he is involved in the university's internship program, advises one of its political clubs, has served as a staff member of Connecticut's legislature, and has been involved in political campaigns on the local, state, and national levels.

International Politics on the World Stage

NINTH EDITION

JOHN T. ROURKE

University of Connecticut

The McGraw·Hill Companies

Book Team
Vice President and Publisher   *Jeffrey L. Hahn*
List Manager   *Theodore Knight*
Developmental Editor   *Ava Suntoke*
Director of Production   *Brenda S. Filley*
Director of Technology   *Jonathan Stowe*
Art Editor   *Pamela Carley*
Designer   *Charles Vitelli*
Typesetting Supervisor   *Juliana Arbo*
Typesetting   *Jocelyn Proto*
Proofreaders   *Robin N. Charney, Cynthia Gross*
Graphics   *Laura Levine, Tom Goddard, Eldis N. Lima*
Permissions Editor   *Rose Gleich*

McGraw-Hill/Dushkin

A Division of The **McGraw-Hill** Companies

Cover © 2002 Digital Vision
Cover Design *Kristin Schwarz*

The credit section for this book begins on page 631 and is considered an extension of the copyright page.

Library of Congress Control Number 2002106285

ISBN 0-07-282804-8

Printed in the United States of America
10 9 8 7 6 5 4 3 2 1

http://www.mhhe.com/

Preface

This Edition: Changes and Organization   As a result of this text's view that our lives are inescapably affected by world politics, *International Politics on the World Stage,* Ninth Edition, stresses the impact that world events and international interdependence have on your students' lives. In addition to highlighting the effect that the world has on them, this approach points out to students the connection between the events of current history and the theories of international politics that have been conceived and refined by political scientists.

Each time I revise this text I think to myself, "The world will settle down and the next edition will be easier." Wrong! This edition proved to be a major challenge and effort. You will see that there is a continued emphasis on being current in order to engage the students without being journalistic. The traumatic terrorist attacks on September 11, 2001, marked the day as one of those few that almost everyone will remember with a vivid recollection of where they were when they learned of the horrific news. That tragedy, the ensuing U.S.-led operation against al-Qaeda and the Taliban regime in Afghanistan, and the other events related to what has become known simply as 9-11 understandably dominate our perspectives of 2001 and 2002, but there were many other important changes in the action on the world stage. President George W. Bush assumed the U.S. presidency, and his unilateralist approach to world politics led to the U.S. rejection of the Kyoto Treaty (1997) to control greenhouse gases, the Anti-Ballistic Missile Treaty (1972) that barred either Washington or Moscow from building a ballistic missile defense system, and the treaty that led to the creation of the International Criminal Court (ICC) in 2002. Elsewhere in the world, the violence between Israelis and Palestinians went from bad to worse, nuclear weapons-armed Pakistan and India teetered on the edge of war, Argentina descended into economic chaos, and other unsettling events beset the world. There were also a number of attempts to improve the state of the world. These included the World Conference Against Racism (2001), in Durban, South Africa; the International Conference on Financing for Development (2002), in Monterrey, Mexico; and the World Summit on Sustainable Development (2002) in Johannesburg, South Africa. The newest country, East Timor, was "born" on May 20, 2002; most of the world's leaders hailed the creation of the ICC in July 2002; and Switzerland joined the United Nations in the fall. All these and other recent events are extensively detailed. It is also important to be as current as possible with the massive amount of changing data that details economic performance and capacity, weapons levels and transfers, and other statistical aspects of world politics. I have used original sources for my data when possible so that students will have the most recent information available.

The organizational scheme reflecting this text's view that the world is at a juncture brings to mind Robert Frost's poem, "Two Roads Diverged in a Wood." One road is the traditional way of sovereign states pursuing their self-interests in an often inequitable and conflict-filled world. The alternative, less-traveled-by path is the way of cooperation in a system in which states are less sovereign and international organizations play a wider and more authoritative role.

The text begins with an introduction to the importance of world politics to students and to the methods, theories, and purposes of political science (chapter 1), the evolution of and current instability in the world political system (chapter 2), and the three levels of analysis that need to be studied simultaneously—the system, state, and individual levels (chapters 3, 4, and 5). Then, beginning with chapter 6, the two roads theme organizes the remaining chapters of this edition, with usually alternating discussions of national conflict and international cooperation in successive chapters. In this way, equal attention can be given to the two roads without losing sight of the fact that they lead in divergent directions.

The substantial changes in this edition make it reflect more accurately the changing nature of world politics. The more I study the subject, the more I am impressed with the idea that the world is a primitive political society. As such, it is a political system that is marked by little organization, frequent violence, and a limited sense of global responsibility. It is a world of conflict. But there is also a world of cooperation, a countertheme, based on a still-limited desire among states and their people to work together globally as they begin to realize that their fates are inextricably entwined with one another and with the political, economic, social, and environmental future of our planet.

Data and Graphics   Many new tables, figures, photographs, maps, and other graphics have been added to emphasize, expand, and give visual life to ideas. Full-color maps with geographical, historical, and statistical information that students should find especially relevant to the text's discussion are placed throughout the text. Also, significant revisions have been made to both the instructor's manual and to the extensive testbank, which are available from the publisher in both printed and computerized versions. These are further explained in the paragraph on Supplements on the next page.

Research, Citations, Bibliography, and Suggested Readings   One of the aims of this text is to bring together a representative sampling of the latest research in international relations. Scholarly articles, so often ignored in survey texts, are particularly emphasized. This research is documented by extensive references using the "in-text" style and by a significant bibliography. In addition to recognizing my intellectual debt to a host of scholars, the references and bibliography also serve as a reading list for students, as explained to them in the "To the Students" section of this preface. As such, references are often meant to serve as suggestions for further reading and do not necessarily mean that the cited author(s) propounded what is being said at the point of reference. Using this approach instead of the end-of-chapter placement gives inquisitive students immediate thoughts for additional reading.

For those instructors whose organization differs from mine, care has been given to the table of contents and to the index in order to facilitate integrating the text with your syllabus. You will find, for example, that:

> **Economics** is discussed in chapter 1 (how it affects students), 9 (as a basis of power), 14 (general global conditions) and 15 (national economic competition), 16 (international economic cooperation), and 18 (sustainable development).
> **Terrorism** is addressed in all or in parts of chapters 1, 7, 11, 12, and 13.
> **Moral and humanitarian issues** are taken up extensively in chapters 11 and 17 and also form an important part of the discussions of national interest, coercion, and economic challenges in, respectively, chapters 6, 12, 16, and 17.

The organization of the text flows from this conception of the world as a primitive, but developing, political system. The text not only analyzes world division and conflict but also focuses on cooperation both as a goal and in practice.

The Parts   Part I, which includes chapters 1 through 5, discusses how to study international politics. Students will read in chapter 1 that there are realists and idealists and will, I hope, be prompted to think about where they, their professors, and others with whom they may discuss politics stand on the realist-idealist scale. Although I began as a realist, I find myself less sure of my own wisdom on this point as time goes by. In fact, I have become convinced that substantial changes have to be made in the way international politics is conducted. Perhaps "realism with a nagging idealist conscience" would be an apt description of this text's orientation.

Part I also addresses levels of analysis. As students will soon discover, academics disagree about the proper focus of study. Three levels (system, state, and individual) are presented here. The text primarily utilizes state-level analysis (how countries make foreign policy) as discussed in chapter 4, but, here again, my views have evolved and changed since the first edition. The more I learn, the more I have become impressed with the role of system-level analysis (how the nature of the world system influences politics); there are two full chapters on this subject. Chapter 2 outlines the evolution of the world political system, and chapter 3 discusses system-level theory. Both of these chapters pay particular attention to the profound system change that is now occurring. Chapter 4 discusses the analysis of world politics from the level of the nation-state. Since it is unwise to ignore the human factor in international politics, that level is explored in chapter 5.

Part II, which includes chapters 6 and 7, deals with two divergent political orientations. The traditional orientation is nationalism. The alternative orientation is made up of transnational ideas, identifications, and processes.

Part III, consisting of chapters 8 and 9, examines the alternative ways that the world can be organized politically. In this part, I alternate between national and international approaches, with discussions of the state in chapter 8 and international organizations in chapter 9.

Part IV, which includes chapters 10 and 11, explores divergent approaches to the conduct of world politics. Chapter 10 covers the traditional approach, national diplomacy; chapter 11 examines the alternative road of international law and morality.

Part V, consisting of chapters 12 and 13, introduces two approaches to physical security in the world political system: national security (chapter 12) and international security and other alternative approaches (chapter 13).

Part VI, chapters 14 through 16, describes in detail global economic conditions and trends (chapter 14), then turns to a chapter on national economic competition (chapter 15) and contrasts that with international economic cooperation (chapter 16).

Part VII looks into current conditions and ways to preserve and enhance human rights and dignity (chapter 17) and the environment (chapter 18).

Supplements There are several supplements that have been created to assist both instructors and students in the use of this text. The instructor's manual *Teaching and Testing From International Politics on the World Stage* outlines and discusses the text's objectives, contains several analytical exercises, and gives several other teaching supports, in addition to providing approximately 1,800 multiple-choice and essay questions organized by chapter and degree of difficulty. These examination questions are also available on the Brownstone Diploma Testing computer disk. PowerPoint slides for each chapter are available at the Web site and offer the instructor an easy-to-use and effective visual aid in the classroom.

Online Learning Center With PowerWeb This is a new online site that offers online current course-specific articles by leading authorities in the field, daily news updates, weekly updates by content experts, interactive exercises, research links, and student study tips. This learning tool is free to students with a new copy of the text, at the text Web site, http://www.dushkin.com/rourke.

🌐 To the Student

The world, familiar to us and unknown.

Shakespeare, *Henry V*

The world is changing at breathtaking speed! That reality is one of the most important things for you to understand about international politics. Yet I have found that most undergraduate students, having been born into this era of warp-speed change, consider it normal. It is not. Recorded history dates back over 30 centuries. A great deal of what we will discuss in this text has happened in the last century, even within your lifetime. But truly understanding this rate of change—maybe *feeling* the rate of change is a better way to put it—is hard without perspective.

As a way of trying to convey the dramatic pace of change, I introduce you to Elizabeth "Ma Pampo" Israel in chapter 6. This amazing woman, who lives in Dominica, a Caribbean island country, was born in 1875, has lived in three different centuries, and is 127 years old as this book is being written. Among other things, Ma Pampo gives us a sense of how quickly the world is changing.

When she was born in 1875, Ulysses S. Grant was president of the United States. There was an emperor in China, an Ottoman Empire ruled by a sultan, a czar in Russia, a kaiser in Germany, and an emperor in Austria-Hungary who ruled much of Central Europe. Most of Africa and Asia were still colonies of European powers. There were less than 1.5 billion people in the world; only birds (and insects and bats) could use wings to fly, and the world's most ferocious weapons were the Gatling gun and the long-range artillery piece.

The communist revolution in Russia occurred when she was 42; the Soviet Union disappeared when she was 116. For me, communism and the cold war were the totality of my historical experience; for Ms. Israel they were mere interludes.

If you think about events, trends, and technology in this way-in terms of what one person has seen and experienced-you can begin to grasp how fast they are moving. When Ma Pampo was born people were basically earthbound. She was 28 when the first airplane flew, 69 when the first jet plane took off, 86 when Soviet cosmonaut Yuri Gagarin became the first human in space, and 94 when Neil Armstrong stepped onto the Moon's surface. There are many other things to consider. Ma Pampo is more than twice as old as atomic weapons; the world's population has quadrupled during her life; she is older than three-quarters of the countries that exist today. Radios, televisions, computers, and some of the other technological innovations that affect us so profoundly now did not exist when Ma Pampo was born.

One of the strong themes in this book is the challenges that face the world and the alternative approaches to addressing those challenges. Use Ma Pampo to help you think about these issues. If, for example, it took all of human history-tens of thousands of years-to reach a world population of less than 1.5 billion in 1875, and if, during her life, we have added another 4.5 billion people, then how much time do we have to get the world population under control? If you live as long as Ma Pampo (and you might, given modern medical technology), then what will the world population be when you are 127 years old?

In this sense of contemplating the future by pondering the past, thinking about Ma Pampo is really more about tomorrow than about yesterday or even today. When I talk about her, my thoughts are on our twenty-first century more than on her nineteenth and twentieth centuries.

Using this Text   The text that follows is my attempt to introduce you to the complex and compelling study of international politics. Prefaces are often given scant attention, but they can be a valuable learning tool for you. They let you in on the author's conceptions, the mental pictures of a text. What is the author's approach? What are the author's orientations and biases? Does the text have one or more basic themes? How is the text organized? In this preface I have addressed these issues. I hope you'll read it.

In writing this text I have tried to use straightforward prose and have assumed that students who take this course know little about international politics. To help you further, I have included an outline and objectives at the beginning of each chapter. Before you read the chapter, pay attention to its outline and objectives. It is axiomatic that if you know where you are going, you will find it a lot easier to get there! Additionally, I have written a numbered summary at the end of each chapter to help you quickly review the scope of the chapter. This, of course, is no substitute for carefully studying the chapter.

There are many figures, tables, maps, and photographs in this book. Pay close attention to them. You will find that they graphically represent many of the ideas presented in the text and will help you understand them. But if you really want to know all about something, you will have to read a lot more than just this book and to involve yourself in more than just the course for which it has been assigned. To make it easier for you to do this, I have chosen an "in-text" reference system that gives you citations as you read. Thus (Hobbes, 2000: 171) refers to page 171 of the book or article written by (in this case, Professor Heidi) Hobbes in 2000, which is listed alphabetically in the references and bibliography.

I have also noted studies that helped me think about and organize various topics and those that might be informative to you. I encourage you to utilize the references and bibliography to advance your knowledge beyond the boundaries of this text. You will find a list of the abbreviations that I have used throughout the book on page 600. Explanations for terms set in **boldface** will be found in the glossary at the end of the text.

Some note should be made of this book's title, *International Politics on the World Stage,* and the Shakespearean quotations that begin each chapter and are used from time to time to highlight a point. The idea behind this motif is to convey some of the sweep and complexity of the world drama. No one who has ever read William Shakespeare can dismiss his masterpieces as easily understood or inconsequential. The events on the world stage are similar—complex, full of drama, sometimes hopeful, often tragic, and always riveting. But you, the reader, would be mistaken to assume that the play analogy means that, as a member of the audience, you can be content to sit back and watch the plot unfold. Quite the contrary, part of what makes the world drama so compelling is that the audience is seated on stage and is part of, as well as witness to, the action that is unfolding. And that is one reason why I have also quoted more recent world players. Shakespeare's plays are of the past; the world drama is ongoing. Furthermore, as in an improvisational play, you in the audience can become involved, and, given the consequences of a potentially tragic rather than a happy ending, you ought to become involved. If there is anything that this text proposes, it is that each of us is intimately affected by international politics and that we all have a responsibility and an ability to become shapers of the script. As we shall see, our play has alternative scripts, and what the next scene brings depends in part on us. There is wisdom, then, in Shakespeare's advice in *All's Well that Ends Well* that, "Our remedies oft in ourselves do lie."

I am sincerely interested in getting feedback from the faculty members and students who use this text. My pretensions to perfection have long since been dashed, and your recommendations for additions, deletions, and changes in future editions will be appreciated and seriously considered. People do write me, and I write them back! You are encouraged to join this correspondence by writing to me. E-mail is probably easiest, and I am at: john.rourke @uconn.edu. This book, just like the world, can be made better, but its improvement depends heavily on whether or not you are concerned enough to think and act.

John T. Rourke

Acknowledgments

Over the earlier editions of this text, I have been glad not only to thank my faculty colleagues from around the country who have reviewed the last edition, but to list as well all those who contributed through their comments to previous editions. Alas, sheer space constraints no longer permit this. Still, I gratefully acknowledge those who contributed so much to the past editions. Also, beginning the list of reviewers anew, I wish to thank those faculty members from around the country who have taken the time to give their suggestions for the following editions. I have tried to make adjustments wherever possible. Some contributors have pointed out specific concerns about matters of fact or interpretation, and a number of corrections have been made. On a larger scale, comments on the ever-changing staging and script of world drama leads me to constantly revise the structure of the book and the balance of its coverage in ways great and small. For these contributions, I would like to thank the following for their perspicacity:

Lance W. Bardsley
 Santa Fe Community College

E. Donald Briggs
 University of Windsor

Jon D. Carlson
 Arizona State University

Jose A. da Cruz
 Ozarks Technical Community College

Paul Haber
 University of Montana

Donald L. Hafner
 Boston College

Kent J. Kille
 Ohio State University

Thomas Louis Masterson
 Butte College

Joe Mac McKenzie
 San Diego Mesa College

Charles McCloy
 Trident Technical College

Chaldeans Mensah
 Grant MacEwan College

John R. Queen
 Glendale Community College

Donald Roy
 Ferris State University

Karrin Scapple
 Southwest Missouri State University

Jaroslav Tir
 University of Illinois at Urbana-Champaign

Primo Vanicelli
 University of Massachusetts, Boston

I also owe a debt to each author listed in the bibliography of this and the previous editions. The work that these scholars have done on specific subjects provides the intellectual building blocks that are a significant part of the final structure of this, or any worthwhile, introductory textbook. This text is also evolutionary, and I want to continue to express my appreciation to all those who read and commented on the previous editions. Additionally, I also want to thank the colleagues who called, wrote, or e-mailed me or have taken the time at International Studies Association meetings or other conferences to give me the benefit of their views. I have even, on occasion, taken off my name tag and helped the staff at the publisher's booth at professional meetings. The comments I have received in this anonymity have been sometimes encouraging, sometimes humbling, but always helpful.

Best of all, I have received many good suggestions from students. My own students have had to both read the text and listen to me, and their often obviously candid comments have helped the generations of students who will follow. My favorite was a sophomore who did not do well on his first exam and came to my office to lay blame on that blankety-blank textbook. As we talked, he made some interesting observations. It was also clear that he had not connected the author's name on the front of the book with his professor. You can image how surprised, not to mention disconcerted, he was when it finally dawned on him that he was grumping about the book to its author!

I owe special thanks to Kimberly Weir of the University of Connecticut, who served as a research and editorial assistant during the preparation of this edition. Kimberly has proven to have an extraordinary ability to not only comment on my handling of the big University of Connecticut substantive topics but to also ferret out the smallest substantive and technical errors that bedevil all authors. For this attention to detail she has frequently earned one of my most laudatory margin comments, "good eye."

Michael Butler, University of Connecticut, is responsible for revising the instructor's manual, *Teaching and Testing From International Politics on the World Stage*. He shouldered the task of preparing, revising, and updating the test items for the ninth edition of the instructor's guide, as well as adding to the list of readings for each chapter in the text. I greatly appreciate his diligence.

Then there is the staff of McGraw-Hill/Dushkin. They have encouraged me and supported me. Ava Suntoke is my editor, and I am delighted with her expertise and patience. Robin Charney and Cynthia Goss's proofreading, and their amazing eye for technical detail and substantive consistency, added to the process of ensuring accuracy. I also want to thank the McGraw-Hill/Dushkin typesetters, Juliana Arbo and Jocelyn Proto, for their diligence and for not threatening my life through innumerable changes.

One of the things I like best about this edition is "its look." Pamela Carley has assembled photographs and editorial cartoons that bring powerful visual life to the concepts I express in words. Charles Vitelli not only performed the difficult, but crucial, task of arranging text and illustrations; he drew the original cartoons in this book. He and his able associates (Tom Goddard, and Eldis Lima) took my raw mental images and turned them into wonderful representations of the issues being discussed in the text. In the same area, Laura Levine did an extraordinary job with the exacting art of creating the text's many tables, figures, and maps, and Kristin Schwarz designed this edition's striking cover. I owe a great debt to those who have created such a visually attractive, educationally effective package for my words. Thanks are also due to Alice and Will Thiede of Carto-Graphics in Eau Claire, Wisconsin, for their standard of excellence in producing the maps that appear in the textbook. Another feature of this text is the accompanying Web site with supplementary material and exercises. For this I thank Jonathan Stowe, Marcuss Oslander, and Chris Santos.

Finally, anyone who has written will recognize that it is an intensely personal, as well as professional, experience. I am fortunate to have people around me who understand when I am seemingly glued to my computer for long periods of time and who sometimes insist that I shut it off. My son and friend John Michael helps me endure the ups and downs of the New York Giants and UConn athletic teams, shares the frustrations of fishing, and occasionally tries to interpret X-generation culture for me.

To all of you:

I can no other answer make but thanks, thanks, and ever thanks.

Shakespeare, *Twelfth Night*

Visit the Online Learning Center With PowerWeb at

http://www.dushkin.com/rourke/

Contents in Brief

Contents

Part I: Approaches to World Politics

Part II: Two Roads: Divergent Political Orientations

🌐 Part III: Two Roads: Divergent Organizational Structures

🌐 Part IV: Two Roads: Divergent Approaches to Conduct

Part VI: Pursuing Prosperity

Part VII: Pursuing Preservation

Chapter 1

Thinking and Caring About World Politics

An honest tale speeds best being plainly told.

Shakespeare, *Richard III*

Be not too tame neither, but let your own discretion be your tutor: suit the action to the word, the word to the action.

Shakespeare, *Hamlet*

We will have to repent in this generation not merely for the vitriolic words and actions of the bad people, but for the appalling silence of the good people.

Martin Luther King Jr., "Letter From Birmingham City Jail"

We are entering a new millennium, a new world, a global economy. [The world] is shrinking all the time.

Secretary of State Colin Powell, Senate confirmation hearings, 2001

Chapter Objectives

After completing this chapter, you should be able to:

- Explain the interconnection of all the actors in the international system and the effects that events taking place in one country have on other countries.
- Describe some of the effects of world politics on individuals.
- Describe how the world is interconnected economically.
- Analyze how world politics affects the way countries distribute their economic resources.
- Consider how global problems and challenges, such as population increases, pollution, and resource depletion, affect individuals and their living space.
- Discuss the role of political cooperation as a response to environmental degradation.
- Consider how individuals can make a difference in world politics.
- Summarize realist beliefs and assess their impact on the world political system.
- Understand the tenets and goals of idealism as a present and future force in world politics.
- Identify the analytical orientations of political scientists.
- Identify the goals and research methods of political scientists.
- Understand the three levels of analysis used in the study of world politics.

All the world's a stage, and all the men and women merely players," William Shakespeare (1564–1616) wrote in *As You Like It*. The Bard of Avon was a wise political commentator as well as a literary giant (Alulis & Sullivan, 1996). Shakespeare's lines are used here because they help convey the drama of world politics. The characters are different, of course, with Canada, China, Germany, Japan, Russia, and the United States replacing those of his time and imagination. Beyond that, though, there are remarkable parallels between international relations and the master's plays. Both are cosmic and complex. The characters are sometimes heroic; at other times they are petty. The action is always dramatic and often tragic. As with any good play, the audience was drawn into the action at The Globe, the London theater where Shakespeare staged his works. Similarly, the global theater of international politics draws us in. Indeed, we are seated on the stage, no matter how remote the action may seem or how much we may want to ignore it. Like it or not, we and the world are stuck with each other. The progress of the play, whether it continues its long run or closes early, is something we will all enjoy or endure.

Another quotation from Shakespeare—this time from *Macbeth*—is also worth pondering. Macbeth despairs that life "struts and frets his hour upon the stage" in a tale "full of sound and fury." Again the playwright hits the mark! The global drama has a cast of national actors (countries) that are often at odds with one another. It is true that many examples of cooperation and humanity can be found in them. But they are also full of ambition, self-serving righteousness, and greed, and it is a rare day when some of the countries are not in open conflict. And even when they are not threatening one another, they are forever calculating what is good for themselves and taking action based on their national interests.

⊕ The Importance of Studying World Politics

The last line from Macbeth's soliloquy is where this text and Shakespeare part company. The Bard pessimistically pronounces the action of life as "signifying nothing." That thought has a certain fatalistic appeal. "What the hell," we can say, "why bother with a complicated subject about faraway places that have little to do with me?"

If they did not know it already, Americans learned on September 11, 2001, that world politics can dramatically impact them, as the box, The End of Illusion, discusses.

Whether the tragic events surrounding 9-11 will permanently increase Americans' interest in and knowledge about world affairs remains uncertain. In the past Americans have normally paid little or no attention to world events and issues. Earlier studies have found that only about 20 percent of Americans follow foreign news and that most Americans have little information about global politics.[1] This lack of information is particularly startling for a relatively well-educated populace with easy access to an impressive array of broadcast, print, and other news sources. One survey asked four factual questions of people in eight countries. As Figure 1.1 details, the study found that the percentage of correct responses by Americans was higher than only those from Mexico, where only about 60 percent of children get as far as high school. Indeed, the average American was unable to answer any of the four questions correctly.

Is this widespread lack of information about or interest in world events justifiable? The answer is no! This text does not often try to tell you what to think or do. But one message is stressed here: The world drama is important and deserves our careful attention. We are more than mere observers. We are all on the stage along with everybody else, and, whether we like it or not, we are all caught up in the tidal ebb and flow of global events.

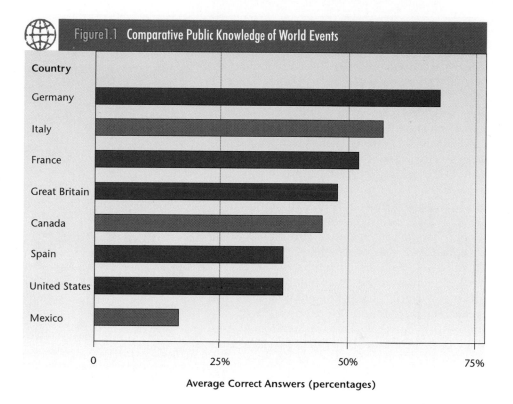

Figure1.1 Comparative Public Knowledge of World Events

Country

Germany

Italy

France

Great Britain

Canada

Spain

United States

Mexico

0   25%   50%   75%

Average Correct Answers (percentages)

Data source: Time, March 28, 1994, p. 22.

How much people know about world politics varies greatly from country to country. This figure shows the average percentage of correct answers given by people in different countries to four relatively easy questions about who was fighting in the Balkans, what group Israel was trying to achieve peace with, the name of the president of Russia, and the name of the UN secretary general. Most Germans could correctly answer each of the four questions; most Americans could answer none of them correctly.

This does not mean, though, that you are stuck with the world as it exists or as it is evolving. The Irish literary lion, Oscar Wilde (1854–1900), once observed wryly that "the world is a stage, but the play is badly cast." If you agree, do not stand idly by. You can play an active part; you can make a difference! The script is not set. It is an improvisational play with lots of room for ad-libbing and even for changing the story line. We do not have to accept playing the role of a walk-on with no lines. We can speak up if we so wish and join the action if we try. Capturing center stage is difficult, and even the great have not held it for long, but we can all play a part. The important message of this text is that your efforts to become knowledgeable about the world and to try to shape its course to your liking are worthwhile because international politics does matter. It plays an important role in your life, and you should be concerned. To understand that further, let us turn to a number of ways, some dramatic, some mundane, in which international politics affects your economic life, your living space, and, potentially, your very existence. Then we will turn to the pivotal question: Can we make a difference?

WORLD POLITICS AND YOUR FINANCES

World politics affects each of our personal economic conditions in many ways. The human toll of the attacks of September 11, 2001, on those who died, their families, and their friends was, of course, the most devastating impact. But there were also monumental economic costs, as detailed in the box, The Financial Toll of 9-11.

THE END OF ILLUSION

The morning of September 11, 2001, dawned clear in New York City. At daybreak the temperature was already 66°F and would climb to an unseasonal 80°F. People soon began arriving in their offices in Manhattan, and the volume of air traffic at New York's airports increased as travelers headed around the country and the world. The morning in Boston, Washington, D.C., and elsewhere on the U.S. east coast was similar, with people working, flying the friendly skies of United and other airlines, and otherwise going about their day. Few were giving any great thought to world politics, and almost no one would have replied "yes" if asked whether they thought global politics would affect them intimately that day.

Yet it did. Unbeknownst to all but the terrified passengers and crews, four commercial airliners had been hijacked by terrorists directed by al-Qaeda. This shadowy Islamic radical group was led from Afghanistan by Osama bin Laden, the son of a wealthy Saudi businessman.

At 8:45 A.M., American Airlines Flight 11, scheduled to fly from Boston to Los Angeles with a crew of 11 and 81 passengers, including 5 terrorists, crashed into the north tower of the World Trade Center about 100 floors up. The news of the disaster spread quickly, and many Americans at their television screens watched when, sickeningly, just 18 minutes later, United Airlines Flight 175 flew into the south tower. On board, 9 members of the crew, 51 innocent travelers, and another 5 terrorists were incinerated in the immense fireball. Inside the twin towers and in the surrounding

The end of the illusion of safety that many, perhaps most, Americans had enjoyed is symbolized by this woman, who is fleeing the horror of the terrorist attacks that brought devastating destruction on the World Trade Center in New York City and to the Pentagon near Washington, D.C., on September 11, 2001.

streets, the scene was horrific. Nearly 3,000 people died, many of them instantly. Others perished from fire and smoke, from collapsing steel, and from plummeting to earth in desperate acts to escape the flames. Outside, hundreds of rescue workers lost their lives amid the rain of debris and bodies from above.

More routinely, the impact of international economics on individuals continues to expand as world industrial and financial structures become increasingly intertwined. Indeed, as we shall see, the ties between national and international affairs are so close that many social scientists now use the term **intermestic** to symbolize the merger of *inter*national and do*mestic* concerns. To illustrate the increasingly ubiquitous connections between your own personal financial condition and world politics, we will briefly explore three aspects of that relationship: how international trade, the flow of international capital, and defense spending all affect your finances.

International Trade and Your Finances

The global flow of goods (tangible items) and services (intangible items such as revenues from tourism, insurance, and banking) are important to your financial circumstances. An example is U.S. dependence on foreign sources for vital resources. That reality was brought sharply into focus in 2000 as crude oil prices rose to more than $30 a barrel, driving up the prices of gasoline, heating oil, and other petroleum products, which skyrocketed by as much as 70 percent in the United States. Then in 2001, the upward trend reversed, and by early 2002, crude oil was selling on the

The nation went on alert, but the day's tragedies had not ended. At 9:40 A.M., American Airlines Flight 77, originally bound from Dulles International Airport in Virginia to Los Angeles, dived into the Pentagon located in Arlington, Virginia, just across the Potomac River from the nation's capital. All 6 crew members, 53 passengers, and 5 hijackers were killed, as were 189 civilian and military workers in the building. It was the first successful attack on the nation's capital by a foreign enemy since the British had burned it during the War of 1812.

The final act in this ghastly drama took place at 10:00 A.M. in a field near Pittsburgh, Pennsylvania. Four hijackers had seized United Airlines Flight 93 bound from Newark, New Jersey, to San Francisco. They had turned the plane around, and were heading, it is thought, for the White House. On board, several passengers had made calls on their cell phones and were aware of the other attacks. Their conversations with the ground tell of a heroic decision by the passengers to rush the hijackers and attempt to retake control of the plane. A switchboard supervisor whom Todd Beamer, a passenger, had reached heard the passengers recite the Lord's Prayer. Then Beamer said, "Are you guys ready? Let's roll." The cockpit voice recorder picked up the sounds of a furious struggle. The valiant effort did not save those who took action. The plane spun out of control and crashed, killing the 7 crew members, 34 passengers, and 4 hijackers. But the brave refusal of the passengers to accept their fate probably saved the lives of an untold number of people in and around the White House.

Certainly, the people who died in the World Trade Center, including rescue workers, at the Pentagon, and on the four doomed flights were affected most directly that tragic day by world politics. They were not the only ones though. Indeed, all Americans and, subsequently, many people around the world who thought that they had little or nothing to do with global affairs were affected. The thousands who died left behind tens of thousands of bereaved family members and friends. The attack and the U.S. response to it also has staggering economic ramifications. The country's already limping economy sank even lower. People lost jobs, and the financial markets plunged. Soon, the war in Afghanistan, the increase in domestic security, significant additions to the U.S. defense budget, and numerous other related events and policies added to the financial and human costs of 9-11.

The impact of the terror attacks on Americans and on people around the world is highlighted in many places in this text. What is important here is to see that we are all on the world stage where the ebb and flow of the action affects us all every day in ways large and small. It is hard to find a proverbial silver lining in the 9-11 tragedy. If there is one, though, it is columnist Robert J. Samuelson's view that there has been an end of illusion. More Americans now truly comprehend that the world cannot be ignored. Perhaps, as Samuelson put it, "What was destroyed was not just the World Trade Center and part of the Pentagon but also Americans' dreamlike feeling [of being] insulated from the rest of the world."[1]

international market for just over $16 dollar a barrel, and gasoline prices had dropped by over 40 percent in the United States.

Trade also wins and loses jobs. There is a steadily increasing likelihood that international trade and your job are related. Exports create jobs. The United States is the world's largest exporter, providing other countries with $1.1 trillion worth of U.S. goods and services in 2000. Creating these exports employed some 16 million Americans, about 13 percent of the total U.S. workforce. Employment in many other countries is even more reliant on exports. For example, about 25 percent of Canadian workers depend on exports for their jobs.

While exports create jobs, other jobs are lost to imports. The clothes, toys, electronics, and many other items that Americans buy were once produced extensively in the United States by American workers. Now most of these items are produced overseas by workers whose wages are substantially lower.

Jobs are also lost to service imports. Experienced computer programmers in India command a monthly salary about one-fourth the salary paid to American programmers. India's software exports grew from $219 million in 1993 to $5.1 billion in 2001, and now more than 300,000 Indians create computer programs, mostly for the

U.S. market. This work is sometimes done over links established between programmers' computers in India and servers in the United States and elsewhere.

Lost jobs are a serious matter, but before you cry "Buy American!" and demand barriers to exclude foreign goods, it is important to realize that your standard of living is improved by inexpensive foreign products. The United States annually imports over $60 billion worth of clothes and footwear. What Americans pay for these shirts, sneakers, and other items of apparel would be much higher if they were made by American workers earning American wages and bore the label, "Made in the U.S.A."

The Flow of International Capital and Your Finances

The global flow of international finance affects you in more ways than you probably imagine. *Investment capital* is one aspect of this flow. Many familiar U.S. companies that provide jobs for Americans are owned by foreign investors, and the product and marketing decisions that they make have a wide impact. For example, the textbooks that are available to American college students are, in part, produced by foreign corporations, which have bought up American publishing companies in a quest to capture the $23 billion U.S. book market, including the $3 billion in textbook sales. Among the largest academic presses, the British media conglomerate Pearson P.L.C. acquired Simon & Schuster (the owner of Prentice Hall and other academic imprints), and St. Martin's is a subsidiary of Holtzbrinck of Germany. Reference book giants Encyclopedia Britannica and Merriam-Webster are both controlled by Switzerland's Safra Group. In some cases, companies are facing economic difficulty, and they and the jobs they provide are saved by the infusion of foreign capital. In other cases, the inflow of foreign investment capital creates jobs for Americans. This is true, for example, for American workers who make Nissan automobiles in Tennessee, Hondas in Ohio, Toyotas in Kentucky, and Mitsubishis in Illinois.

Did You Know That:
Tourist services are considered a service export and provide considerable revenue for Americans. During 1999, 46 million foreign visitors spent over $91 billion in the United States, more than twice as much as in any other country and 20 percent of the world total.

International financial markets are yet another connection between your pocketbook and the global economy. The percentage of American families owning individual stocks, bonds, or mutual fund shares, either directly or through their pension plans, jumped from 32 in 1989 to 49 in 1998. Furthermore, 60 percent of all mutual fund shares are owned by households with earnings under $75,000. Such statistics mean that the stock and bond markets are no longer the concern of just the rich. Thus it was not only wealthy Americans whose finances were severely, in some cases permanently, damaged by the al-Qaeda terrorist attacks, as noted in the box, The Financial Toll of 9-11.

Even under normal conditions, there are numerous connections between the value of stocks and bonds that Americans hold and the world economy. One way is that the companies that make up the Standard & Poor's 500, a key index of the U.S. stock market, do 40 percent of their business overseas. When the world economy is good, the profits they earn result in part in dividends and capital gains for American investors and for the pension funds of American workers. Additionally, institutions also invest heavily in stocks and bonds in other countries. Sometimes, such as with retirement earnings, individuals may be directly affected. Other times, you may be indirectly affected. To cite just one example, your college or university, especially if private, may invest part of its endowment in foreign securities. How they do will affect areas such as scholarship aid and tuition.

Defense Spending and Your Finances

The budget of your national government and the taxes it raises to fund the budget are yet another way that world politics affects you economically. At the very least,

(Continued on page 8)

THE FINANCIAL TOLL OF 9-11

The financial impact on the United States and its citizens of the terror attacks of September 11, 2001, was astronomical. The economic damage caused directly by the attacks and the resulting financial shock waves across the country and the world were so extensive that it will be years before a final estimate is possible.

Business and commerce virtually stopped for two days after the attack, creating an estimated loss of $35 billion. Damage and financial losses to U.S. businesses sent the unemployment rate spiraling upward from 4.9 percent in August to 5.4 percent in October, a loss of about 500,000 jobs. Layoffs were particularly high in the airlines industry (81,000 lost jobs) and the travel industry (58,000 lost jobs). The International Monetary Fund estimates that the drop in consumer spending, delays in shipping due to tighter security, and other factors resulting from the attack slowed the U.S. economy by about 0.5 percent, which annualizes to about $50 billion.

The following $80.9 billion in relative immediate costs during the last quarter of 2001 are far from all the losses and are meant to convey only a sense of the financial devastation to Americans caused by the attacks.[1]

Although the loss of human life was by far the most grievous cost of the 9-11 terror attacks on the United States, there were also huge economic losses. This surreal landscape of the rubble of what had been the twin towers of the $4 billion World Trade Center gives a small sense of the physical and financial damage that Americans suffered.

The Attack Itself: At least $16 billion

Destruction of the World Trade Center complex	$4.0 billion
Damage to the Pentagon	$0.7 billion
Cleanup of rubble from crash sites	$1.3 billion
Four passenger jets	$0.4 billion
Damaged N.Y.C. equipment, streets, utilities, etc.	$2.0 billion
Corporate property	$3.2 billion
Death benefits, medical costs, etc.	$2.6 billion
Workers' Compensation	$1.8 billion

Immediate Economic Aftermath (September):
At least $12.4 billion

Lost airline and cargo revenues	$4.7 billion
Lost hotel industry revenue	$0.7 billion
Lost advertising revenue	$1.0 billion
Lost retail sales	$6.0 billion

Permanent Investment Losses: Approximately $40 billion
The value of stocks sold on the New York, Nasdaq, and Amex stock exchanges dropped collectively nearly $1.7 billion. The markets recovered this loss by year's end, but the thousands of Americans who, for one reason or another, had to sell stock in the weeks after 9-11 permanently lost tens of billion of dollars.

Air Transportation Security (First Year):
At least $5.5 billion

Increased inflight security officers	$2.0 billion
Increased airport security	$3.0 billion
Antiterrorist devices on airlines	$0.5 billion
Increased state and municipal security costs (September–December)	$2.5 billion
Cost of war in Afghanistan (October–December)	$4.5 billion

The costs of responding to the acts of terror will also extend into the future. A preview of those came in January 2002 when President George W. Bush unveiled his budget proposals for FY2003. He called for a $48 billion increase in military spending, including a $10 billion reserve fund to pay for antiterrorism operations abroad. The president also requested that the homeland security budget be doubled to almost $38 billion. This included $3.5 billion for local police, fire, and medical emergency responders, $11 billion for border security, $6 billion for bioterrorism prevention, $5 billion for aviation security, $1 billion for intelligence operations, and over $11 billion for other programs, such as improving security at government buildings. "This is a two-front war," Bush told listeners. "Overseas we're fighting, and at home we're fighting.[2]" The increases alone (+$48 billion for the military, +$19 billion for homeland security) represent $240 for each American that will have to be paid for in higher taxes, less spending on other programs, or higher deficits.

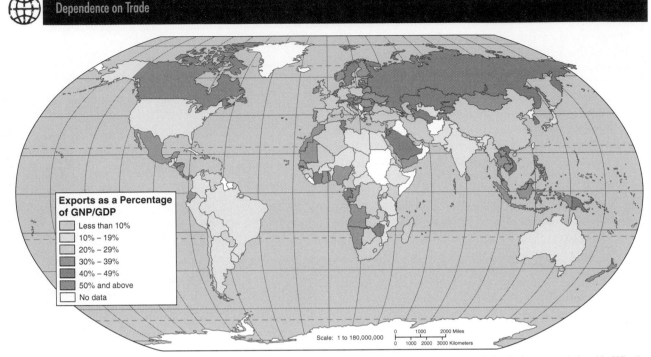

Dependence on Trade

Exports as a Percentage of GNP/GDP

- Less than 10%
- 10% – 19%
- 20% – 29%
- 30% – 39%
- 40% – 49%
- 50% and above
- No data

Scale: 1 to 180,000,000

All countries, even the most economically powerful ones, are becoming increasingly dependent on trade for their economic health. Whether you are American or Zimbabwean, there is a good chance that your job, the price you pay for the goods you buy, and other factors in your economic well-being are dependent on global trade.

you pay taxes to support your country's involvement in world affairs. In FY 2001 the U.S. government spent $1.9 trillion (that's right, trillion, not billion). Spending on general foreign affairs (such as foreign aid) was minor, accounting for only $18 billion, about 1 percent of the budget. Defense spending was considerably more important. It amounted to $306 billion, approximately 16.1 percent of the U.S. budget. This equals about $1,100 per American for national defense.

The more of a country's wealth that is devoted to military spending, the less is available for private use and for domestic government spending. Table 1.1 compares countries by a number of defense spending criteria. As you can see, some countries devote huge sums to defense; others spend little. Countries also vary widely in their defense expenditures compared to such economic measures as their **gross domestic product** (GDP: a measure of all goods and services produced within a country).

One way to think about defense spending and to relate it to yourself is to compare defense spending with federal spending on higher education. With about 5 percent of the world's population, the United States accounts for 37 percent of the world's military spending. Even after the 9-11 attacks, some people question the need to spend more than a quarter trillion dollars a year with no hostile, extraordinarily powerful country facing the United States. Yet, the government has now built twenty-one B-2 bombers at a cost of over $2.1 billion each, and has begun to develop the next generation of fighter aircraft, which may eventually cost $1 trillion to deploy.

Did You Know That:

Even limited military operations are very costly. Recent U.S. interventions and their costs are:

Grenada	1983	$76 million
Panama	1989	$164 million
Persian Gulf	1990–1991	$61 billion
Somalia	1992–1994	$675 million*
Haiti	1994–1995	$427 million
Bosnia	1996	$1.3 billion*
Kosovo	1999–2000	$5.2 billion*
Afghanistan	2001–	$10 billion*

*first year of multiyear operation

Table 1.1 Comparative Military Expenditures

Country	Total (US$ Billions)	As Percentage of Budget	As Percentage of GDP	Per Capita (US$)
Canada	7.5	6.0	1.2	192
China*	39.8	+30.0	5.4	32
India	14.9	26.0	3.4	14
Israel	8.7	21.8	9.4	1,489
Japan	42.9	9.2	0.9	319
Kenya	0.3	6.7	3.1	11
Mexico	4.3	3.3	0.9	42
Russia*	56.8	+50.0	5.1	380
Sweden	5.2	4.6	2.3	588
United States	306.1	16.1	3.1	1,036

Data sources: CIA (2002), World Almanac (2002).

*Defense spending figures tend to be less reliable than most other data. The data for China and Russia are especially controversial. The + sign before the percentage of budget for China and Russia denote that with both expenditures and overall budget uncertain, the percentages are at least that high.

The range of government spending on defense as an overall amount, as a percentage of a country's budget or of its gross national product, and as a per capita expenditure varies widely. Whatever the exact figures, defense spending affects your economic conditions in a number of ways, such as jobs, taxes, and budget choices.

Although there is no one-to-one relationship between reduced defense spending and increased higher education spending, it is worth thinking about what would be possible if some defense spending were reallocated to higher education. In 2000 about 15 million students were enrolled in U.S. colleges. The annual cost of room, board, and tuition at the average four-year private college was $22,630; at the average public college it was $9,808. If, for example, the Pentagon deleted just one B-2 bomber (a saving of $2.1 billion), that money would be enough to give an all expenses-paid scholarship at the average private college to 92,797 students or at the average state university to 214,111 students.

Such concerns are not confined to the United States. Some 40,000 German students protested in Bonn over what they considered to be gross underfunding of higher education. A particular point of ire was the $13 billion that Germany had committed to develop the joint European warplane, the Eurofighter. "For a billion marks, 6.5 Eurofighters or 6,481 smart students—which do we need more in the future?" one protest placard read.[2]

Yet the reallocation of defense spending that might bring economic relief to some people, such as college students, would harm the economic circumstances of other people. Many national economies, industries, and workers are heavily dependent on defense spending. Defense spending in the United States declined from about 6.2 percent of the GDP in 1985 to 2.9 percent in 2001. Many jobs have been lost. In the late 1980s there were some 8 million people employed in military uniform, as civilian employees of the Department of Defense, or as defense industry workers. This combined uniformed and civilian U.S. workforce has now declined by 38 percent, or about 3 million wage earners. The lost jobs have created tremendous pressure from negatively affected individuals, communities, and businesses to maintain defense spending. As former assistant secretary of defense Lawrence J.

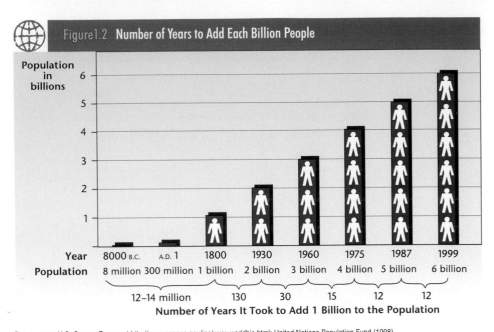

Figure 1.2 Number of Years to Add Each Billion People

Data sources: U.S. Census Bureau at http://www.census.gov/ipc/www.worldhis.html; United Nations Population Fund (1998).

The world population is growing at an alarming rate. In October 1999 it passed the 6 billion mark and is expanding at a rate of about 210,728 people a day, 8,764 an hour, 146 a minute, 2.4 a second. You can go to a world population clock at http://metalab.unc.edu/lunarbin/worldpop and enter the day you were born to see how much the world population has grown in the intervening years.

Korb has commented, to some degree, "Both the administration and Congress… view defense as a federal jobs program."[3]

WORLD POLITICS AND YOUR LIVING SPACE

International politics can affect far more than your pocketbook. It can determine the quality of the air you breathe, the water you drink, and many other aspects of the globe you inhabit.

The growth of the world's population and its pressure on resources threaten to change the quality of life as we know it. It took 100,000 years of human existence for the world population to reach 6 billion, a dubious mark that, according to UN calculations occurred on October 12, 1999. The increase of 77 million people in 1999 alone is the equivalent of a new U.S. population every 3.5 years or a new Canadian population every 147 days. The UN Population Fund (UNFPA) predicts that by 2050 the population will have exploded to 9 billion people, a 50 percent increase in only half a century. Figure 1.2 depicts the population explosion.

Americans and Canadians will not be immune to this avalanche of humanity. The burning of fossil fuels to warm and propel this mass and to supply it with material goods creates emissions of over 6 billion tons a year of carbon dioxide and other gases that, most scientists worry, are causing global warming. The decade of the 1990s was the warmest in recorded history, with 1998, at an average of 62.46° F, the warmest year since records were first kept in 1856. The global temperature in 2000 was the sixth warmest on record, and stood at 0.7° F above the long-term (1880–1999) average.

Warmer temperatures may be welcome to some, but the ramifications are worrisome. Among other things, many scientists claim that the warming is melting the polar ice caps, thereby raising sea levels and threatening to flood coastal areas of the world. There are some Pacific island countries that worry about virtually disappearing

Changes in the environment are one concern that the world must solve collectively. Global warming is thought to be related to the growing intensity and frequency of the El Niño phenomenon, in which abnormally warm waters in the mid-Pacific Ocean bring torrential rains to some areas and severe drought to others. The human impact of this drastic weather is evident in the face of this frantic Ecuadorian woman who is being helped by rescue workers, after her home was swept away in one of the El Niño–associated storms that inundated the U.S. and Latin American west coasts in 1999. Like 30,000 other Ecuadorians, she was left homeless; unlike 200 Ecuadorians, she survived.

under the rising seas. Scientists project that global warming will also increase the frequency and intensity of torrential rainfall, hurricanes and other windstorms, and other forms of violent weather. The annual World Disasters Report issued by the International Red Cross in 2000 said that during the six previous years, the number of people who needed aid after natural disasters like floods and earthquakes had risen, from fewer than 500,000 a year to more than 5.5 million. A significant majority of them were victims of weather-related catastrophes, including the El Niño/La Niña conditions that originate in the Pacific. This phenomenon, with a range of damaging climatic effects, including torrential rains in some areas and droughts in others, is due to global warming. Among its other effects in the last few years have been torrential rains and horrendous flooding in Central and South America, which cost billions of dollars in damage and killed thousands, and, conversely, one of the worst droughts in 50 years in Southeast Asia with resultant widespread forest fires, crop failures, and other damage.

The chemicals we spew into the air also cause disease. Among other things, they attack the Earth's ozone layer, which helps shield the Earth from the Sun's deadly ultraviolet rays. Higher exposure to ultraviolet rays increases your risk of developing melanoma, the deadliest form of skin cancer, whenever you enjoy yourself at the beach or are otherwise outdoors. It is well established that the ozone layer has thinned considerably during recent decades. Concomitantly, the rate of new melanoma cases has grown dramatically from 1,168 of every 100,000 Americans to 3,650. This 213 percent increase means that 47,700 Americans were diagnosed with melanoma in 1999, and a projected 9,600 of these victims will die of the disease.

There are numerous other proven or suspected deleterious environmental trends that are despoiling our living space. The United Nations Environment Programme (UNEP) reports that in addition to the perils already mentioned, erosion destroys 25 billion tons of topsoil each year, 900 million urban dwellers breathe dangerous levels of sulfur dioxide, and 25 percent of the Earth's animal and plant species may become extinct by the year 2020. "The environment is worse now than 20 years ago," declared UNEP head Mustafa K. Tolba. "Time is running out. Critical thresholds may already have been breached."[4]

It is true that most environmental problems have not been caused by world politics. It is also true, however, that we humans are unlikely to be able to stem, much less reverse, the degradation of the biosphere without global cooperation. That has begun, but only slowly and somewhat uncertainly, as detailed in chapter 18.

WORLD POLITICS AND YOUR LIFE

Plants and animals may be joined by humans on the endangered species list. International politics now has the potential of extinguishing most or all of the human race. Unlike most of history, when the vast majority of war deaths were soldiers, civilian casualties in the twentieth century rose drastically as civilians increasingly became a target of military operations. Nearly as many civilians as soldiers were killed during World War II. Now more civilians than soldiers are killed. According to the UN, civilians accounted for 75 percent of everyone killed during wars in the 1980s and 90 percent of all war deaths during the 1990s. Most tragically, these casualties included 2 million children, who died from wounds and other war-related causes. In a nuclear war or act of nuclear terrorism, military casualties would be a mere footnote to the overall death toll.

The attacks of September 11, 2001, also brought into sharp focus the reality that violent international attacks are not confined to those launched by countries using their military forces. Americans on that morning found that they were not safe in their offices, traveling around the country, or, by extension, in their homes from terrorists. It must also be said that this unsettling reality has long been felt more acutely in other parts of the world that, for much longer, have been subjected to or the scene of more frequent acts of international terrorism (Heymann, 2002).

The possibility of war is a special concern for college-age adults because they are of prime military age. An examination of the ages of U.S. Marines killed during the Vietnam War shows that of those who died, 84 percent were aged 18 to 22. Some soldiers killed in war are volunteers, but not all are. Many countries have a draft to staff their military services. The United States abandoned the draft in the early 1970s, but draft registration is still required of all military-age males.

It is also the case that military combat is a matter that increasingly affects women directly as well as men. In the United States and elsewhere, the types of combat units in which women are allowed to serve are expanding. Either by volunteering or by being required to go, many more women may fight and die in future wars.

Such an idea is not farfetched. American women now serve as combat pilots and as officers on warships. Women in some other countries are also pressing their governments for equal access to all military units. The Supreme Court of Israel, for instance, ruled in favor of a woman who contested the military's refusal to allow her and other women to become combat pilots. Public attitudes are moving slowly toward accepting the idea of women in combat. A poll of Americans in December 2001 found that 52 percent were willing to see women serve in ground forces, such as the infantry. When asked if women should be subject to the draft, 46 percent of Americans said yes, 50 percent said no, and 4 percent were undecided.[5]

Even if they are not allowed into ground combat units, women are serving in military roles that bring more of them ever closer to the fighting. Thirty-five thousand women served in the Persian Gulf during the war against Iraq in 1991. Others have served since then in Somalia, Haiti, Bosnia, Kosovo, Afghanistan, and

World politics can affect your life if you join or are drafted into your country's military. This is increasingly true for women as well as men. Among the soldiers from many countries who have been dispatched to Afghanistan is Marlis Sure. She is pictured here in Kabul, where she was one of the first contingents of German paratroopers assigned to serve in the International Security Force in Afghanistan.

every other combat zone in which U.S. forces have been deployed. The story of one of those women, Cindy Beaudoin, is told in the box on page 14.

Don't be surprised, then, if you, female or male, someday find yourself directly involved in world politics by way of the draft and an all-expenses-paid government trip to some exotic corner of the world. You can try to ignore world politics, but it may not ignore you.

World politics, then, does count. We are all involved economically and environmentally. Furthermore, it can threaten our very lives. Wars have continued and will continue to happen. Young men—and probably young women—have been and will be drafted. Some will die—perhaps you. In the worst possible circumstance, nuclear war, it will not matter whether you were drafted or not. Terrorism is no longer a remote event for Americans (Posner, 2002). As President Bush put it in his January 2002 State of the Union address, "Our discoveries in Afghanistan confirmed our worst fears.... We have seen the depth of our enemies' hatred in videos where they laugh about the loss of innocent life. And the depth of their hatred is equaled by the madness of the destruction they design." Moreover, the president continued, "We have found diagrams of American nuclear power plants and public water facilities, detailed instructions for making chemical weapons, surveillance maps of American cities and thorough descriptions of landmarks in America and throughout the world."[6]

CAN WE MAKE A DIFFERENCE?

The next logical question is, Can I make a difference? The answer is, Yes, you can make a difference! It is true that we cannot all be president or secretary of state, but we can take action and we can make our views known.

Direct action is one way to influence global relations. This happens in routine and, on occasion, in dramatic ways more frequently than we think, as shown in a recent study that examines the myriad ways in which people in Duluth, Minnesota,

Cindy Marie Beaudoin arrived at the University of Connecticut as a first-year student in September 1990. Just a month earlier, Iraq had invaded Kuwait. Cindy enrolled in the usual liberal arts courses, facing the terrors of college calculus and chemistry. On November 17, her life turned a corner. Cindy was also Specialist Beaudoin, a soldier in the 142nd Medical Company of the Connecticut National Guard. Her company was called up to active duty. Specialist Beaudoin, at age 19, was on her way to the war that waited in the Persian Gulf. Cindy withdrew from classes rather than opt to make up the work when she returned. "I probably won't remember half the stuff I've learned when I get back," she explained.[1]

On Sunday, January 13, 1991, just four days before the war began, her unit left for Saudi Arabia. The 142nd moved forward behind advancing combat units when the ground war began on February 24.

1972–1991

Specialist Beaudoin penned a two-line stanza on her helmet that read: "Look at this place that we have found. No one knows where we are bound."

Four days later, Iraq's army had been routed, and President Bush declared a cease-fire. The war was not over yet for Specialist Beaudoin. The 142nd's journey had taken it north from Saudi Arabia into Iraq and then east to just across the border into Kuwait. There, at about 3:00 P.M. on February 28, an explosion rocked the 142nd's convoy. "God-damn," trooper Beaudoin shouted as she tumbled from her truck; "They're firing at us." A moment later she realized that she had been hit. The cause of the blast is still uncertain. It hardly matters. Cindy Beaudoin's leg was gone; shrapnel had torn her abdomen. Three hours later she was in a medivac helicopter headed for the rear. It wasn't soon enough; Cindy died during the flight. There is, in war and death, a grim equality.

serving as "citizen diplomats," interact with others from around the globe (Sharp, 2001). Students have also often been important agents of political change through direct action. The sum of millions of individual actions—ranging from burning draft cards, to massive demonstrations in front of the White House, to students protesting and even dying on U.S. campuses—helped end American involvement in Vietnam. Consumer boycotts can also play a part. Individuals have made a difference by refusing to eat tuna fish that does not bear the "dolphin safe" label. Even more recently, students on many U.S. college campuses have participated in protests and brought consumer pressure to bear on clothing and footwear companies that sell products manufactured in so-called sweatshops in Asia and elsewhere. These manufacturers pay little, require long hours, and have poor safety records. Adding to the pressure, colleges began to follow the lead of their students. The University of Notre Dame, for one, announced in 2000 that it would ban the manufacture of its licensed products in 13 countries that have unfair labor standards. As a result of these efforts, Nike and other companies have joined the Fair Labor Association (FLA), a coalition organization of human rights groups, manufacturers, and activists at over 130 universities and colleges, who work together to help protect the rights of factory workers worldwide.

Voting for candidates is another way to affect policy. Elected leaders do not always follow their campaign promises, but, in a broad sense, who gets elected does influence policy. It made a difference in Israeli foreign policy and, potentially in global politics, when in 2001 conservative candidate Ariel Sharon defeated and replaced liberal prime minister Ehud Barak.

The U.S. presidential election in 2000 was waged primarily on domestic issues, but there were still important foreign policy differences between candidates George W. Bush and Al Gore. President Bush has pushed to build an antiballistic missile defense system, has not supported the Kyoto Treaty on global warming, and has taken a number of national security and foreign policy stances that, almost certainly, are different than what a President Gore would have done.

We can all take an active role in the world political drama instead of being part of the passive audience. There is an increasing number of people who oppose globalization. For them, the phenomenon is symbolized by the privately organized annual gathering of the World Economic Forum, which brings together world business and political leaders. One of those who chose to act rather than just watch is Beka Economopolos, an organizer for what protestors dubbed the "Anti–World Economic Forum." She is shown here speaking at a news conference in January 2002 just before the World Economic Forum began its four-day session at the Waldorf Astoria Hotel in New York City.

Direct voting on international questions is also possible in some countries (Setala, 1999; Rourke, Hiskes, & Zirakzadeh, 1992). In 2000, Danish voters rejected replacing their traditional currency, the krone, thus declining to join most other countries in the European Union that have adopted the new common currency, the euro. During the 1990s, East Timorese, Croatians, Ukrainians, and several other nationalities voted to declare independence from the countries of which they had been a part. Also during the decade, and taking an opposite view, Puerto Ricans rejected independence (or statehood), and citizens of Quebec also voted against autonomy (Conley, 1997). The Swiss voted by referendum to join the World Bank and the International Monetary Fund. They had rejected proposals to join the UN, but in March 2000 changed their mind and voted to become a UN member. Citizens in Austria, Finland, and Sweden voted in favor of joining the European Union; voters in Norway rejected membership. Hungarians voted to join the North Atlantic Treaty Organization (NATO). Finally, expressing your opinion orally, or in writing, or even having your opinion sampled in a poll, can have an impact. Public opinion polls are widely published, and political leaders in many countries keep a weather eye on public attitudes (LeDuc, 2000).

> **Did You Know That:**
> With an average turnout of just 35 percent during five presidential elections between 1980 and 2000, Americans aged 18 to 24 had the lowest voting turnout of any age group. A young adult is about half as likely to vote as an adult aged 45 to 64. This gap affects whose voices are heard by politicians.

The point is that you count—by voting, protesting, joining issue-oriented groups, donating money to causes you support, or even by having your thoughts recorded in a political poll. Few individual actions are dramatic, and by themselves few significantly change world politics, but the sum of many smaller actions can and does make a difference. Do not consider politics a spectator sport. It is more important than that. Treat politics as a participant—even a contact—sport.

The World Tomorrow: Two Roads Diverge

The imperative to be active is particularly important as the world begins a new millennium. It is not too strong to argue that we have arrived at a crucial junction in the paths by which we organize and conduct our global politics. Contemplation of that junction brings to mind Robert Frost and his famous poem, "The Road Not Taken" (1916). Frost concluded his poem with the thought that

> I shall be telling this with a sigh
> Somewhere ages and ages hence:
> Two roads diverged in a wood, and I—
> I took the one less traveled by,
> And that has made all the difference.

Like the works of Shakespeare, Frost's lines are timeless and challenge the reader's intellect and emotions. We can build on Frost's imagery of two roads, one the traditional, "more traveled-by" road, the other an alternative, "less traveled-by" road, to discuss two possible paths for the future. The traditional road is a continuation of the path that world politics has mostly followed for at least five centuries. This route has been characterized by self-interested states struggling to secure their self-interests in a largely anarchistic international system.

The alternative direction entails significant changes in the way that politics is organized and conducted. Those who favor the alternative path argue that states need to abandon the pursuit of short-term self-interest and take a more cooperative, globalist approach. From this perspective, the advent of nuclear weapons, the deterioration of the global environment, and other looming problems create worries that time is running out, unless the world finds a new way to govern itself.

Some of those who advocate this road see, and even favor, a decline in the central role played by states in the international system. These analysts also see, and often favor, a rise of global institutions, such as the UN, and regional organizations, such as the European Union (EU), as authoritative actors capable of constraining individual countries. At its extreme, this process would lead to regional governments or even to a global government, as discussed in chapter 9. Such ideas are not new, but they represent the road less traveled by in world politics.

Frost leaves his reader with the thought that choosing the less familiar road "made all the difference." What is unknown is whether Frost's "sigh" was one of contentment or regret. Frost wisely left that to the reader's imagination and judgment. Similarly, a major challenge that this text presents to you is deciding which road you think the world should travel by.

REALISM AND IDEALISM: SOME TRAVEL NOTES ON TWO ROADS

To help you begin to make your choice, the following section describes and contrasts the two paths and discusses those who advocate each direction. Those who favor adhering to the traditional road are often associated with the philosophical approach to politics called realism. Those who favor charting a new course along the alternative road are frequently identified with the philosophical approach to politics called idealism.

Before we detail these two approaches, some comments on the terms are appropriate. First, realism and idealism is not an "either-or" choice. Rather, the terms characterize two ends of a spectrum of attitudes, and there are few people who are either unswerving realists or unmitigated idealists.

Second, there are a variety of names applied to both approaches. The traditional path is variously associated with words such as realist (realism, realpolitik), balance of power, national (nationalist), conservative, and state-centered (state-centric, state-based). The alternative approach is associated with such words as idealism (idealist), globalism, (new) world order, liberal, liberal institutionalism, and internationalist. You will also find the prefix "neo" attached to some of these words (as in neorealism or neoliberalism) to designate recent variations on the more classic concepts (Beer & Harriman, 1996).

Third, there are a number of related orientations, such as feminism, political economy, and constructivism, that vary from general realism and idealism in part because they have different assumptions about what is important and, therefore, focus on different things. *Feminist scholars*, one notes, place "gender—which embodies relationships of power inequality—as [their] central category of analysis" (Tickner, 1997:614). *Political economy* scholars focus on wealth as the key unit of analysis (Burch & Denemark, 1997). *Constructivist scholars* focus on individuals and groups and how they construct their identities in relation to one another and to countries and other political structures (Kubalkova, Onuf, & Kowert, 1998). Each of these theoretical orientations is important and multifaceted, and each deservedly receives extended attention later in this text (Locher & Prügl, 2001).

Fourth, do not get fooled by the connotations of realism and idealism. The terms are used here because they are the common names for their schools of thought in international relations theory. But the sobriquets are flawed. "Realists" are not necessarily those who see things as they "really" are. Nor are "idealists" a bunch of fuzzy-headed dreamers. As you will see, perhaps a better name for realists would be "pessimists." Conversely, "optimists" is probably a more enlightening, if not more precise, label for idealists. The point is not to prejudge books by covers or theories by labels.

For all these subtleties, realism and idealism are distinct views, and they present a choice that this book asks its readers to consider, Which road should we take: realism or idealism?

To help decide this question, the following sections compare realism and idealism according to their respective views about the fundamental nature of politics, the roles of power and justice in the conduct of political affairs, and the prospects for international competition and cooperation (Sterling-Folker, 1997; Rosenau & Durfee, 1995).

THE NATURE OF POLITICS: REALISM AND IDEALISM

The disagreement between **realists** and **idealists** about the nature of politics is perhaps the most fundamental division in all of political discourse. The two schools of thought disagree over the very nature of *Homo politicus* (political humankind), and their respective views govern their approaches to domestic as well as to international politics. At root, realists are pessimists about human nature; idealists are optimists about human nature. The following sections will explore various schools of thought about the nature of politics (Beitz, 1999; Osiander, 1998; Rose, 1998; Schmidt, 1998). Realists portray politics in somber hues (Spegele, 1996). They believe that political struggle among humans is probably inevitable because people have an inherent dark side. Many realists would trace their intellectual heritage to such political philosophers as Thomas Hobbes (1588–1679). He believed that humans possess an inherent urge to dominate, an *animus dominandi*. Hobbes argued in *Leviathan* (1651) that "if any two men desire the same thing, which nevertheless they cannot both enjoy, they become enemies and… endeavor to destroy or subdue one another." Taking the same point of view, one leading realist scholar,

There are occasional junctions in the course of international events when the world has the opportunity to make fundamental decisions about the future. We are now at such a fork in the road. The cold war has ended, and the new world order is yet to be determined. The paths suggested by realists and idealists are very different. The realist path is more familiar; the idealist path is less traveled by. Which one we choose could make all the difference.

Hans Morgenthau, wrote that an "ubiquity of evil in human actions" inevitably turns "churches into political organizations… revolutions into dictatorships… and love of country into imperialism" (Zakaria, 1993:22).

A relatively more recent variation on realism is the neorealist school of thought (Schweller & Priess, 1997). *Neorealists* focus on the anarchic nature of a world system based on competition among sovereign states, while classic realists stress human nature as the factor that shapes world politics. As one neorealist puts it, the international system based on sovereign actors (states), which answer to no higher authority, is "anarchic, with no overarching authority providing security and order." The result of such a self-help system is that "each state must rely on its own resources to survive and flourish." But because "there is no authoritative, impartial method of settling these disputes—i.e. no world government—states are their own judges, juries, and hangmen, and often resort to force to achieve their security interests" (Zakaria, 1993:22). What unites both realists and neorealists is that they doubt whether there is any escape from conflict. Classical realists believe human nature is immutable, and neorealists are skeptical about the ability of interdependence or international organizations to promote cooperation (Cox, 1997). As one scholar argues, "Even in a world that is clearly become more interconnected, the game *is* domestic politics for national policymakers" who continue to make policy based on national interests. As for the impact of interdependence and the role of international organizations, the scholar contends that, "Far from transposing the practice of autonomy and unilateral policy-making, cooperation in interdependent conditions can serve merely as an avenue for policy makers to continue business as usual." In the end, she concludes, "Anarchy trumps us in every social act" (Sterling-Folker, 2002:231).

Idealism and the Nature of Politics

Idealists reject the notion that all or most humans are inherently political predators. Instead, idealists are prone to believe that humans and their countries are capable of achieving more cooperative, less conflictive relations. In this sense, idealists might trace their intellectual lineage to political philosophers such as Jean-Jacques Rousseau (1712–1778). He argued in *The Social Contract* (1762) that humans had joined together in civil societies because they "reached the point at which the obstacles [to bettering their existence were] greater than the resources at the disposal of each individual." Having come to that point, Rousseau reasoned, people realized that their "primitive condition can then subsist no longer; and the human race would perish unless it changed its manner of existence." Like Rousseau, contemporary idealists not only believe that in the past people joined together in civil societies to better their existence; they are confident that now and in the future people can join together to build a cooperative and peaceful global society (Moravcsik, 1997).

There is also a neoidealist (often called neoliberal) school of thought (Mansbach, 1996). *Neoidealists*, like neorealists, ascribe much of world conflict to the same cause: the anarchic world system based on competition among sovereign states (Jervis, 1999; Legro & Moravcsik, 1999). Like all idealists, neoidealists believe that humans can cooperate in order to achieve mutual benefits. Therefore, since neoidealists also hold that the anarchic system hinders cooperation, they further believe that the best path to cooperation is through building effective international organizations. This prescription is why neoidealists are often also called liberal institutionalists. Typically, two theorists of this school contend that "when states can jointly benefit from cooperation,… we expect governments to attempt to construct" international organizations to facilitate cooperation. The two scholars go on to argue that, in turn, international organizations add to the growth of cooperation by providing various benefits to member-states that "facilitate the operation of reciprocity" (Keohane & Martin, 1995:42).

THE ROLES OF POWER AND JUSTICE: REALISM AND IDEALISM

Realists and idealists also disagree in how they describe the roles of power and justice as standards of international conduct, and the two schools are even more at odds over the role that these standards should play. Realists could be styled the "might makes right" school of thought. Idealists would contend that "right makes right."

Realism: An Emphasis on Power

Realists believe that struggles between states to secure their frequently conflicting national interests are the main action on the world stage. Since realists also believe that power determines which country prevails, they hold that politics is aimed at increasing power, keeping power, or demonstrating power. This is hardly a new thought. Over 2,000 years ago, Kautilya, minister to the first Maurya emperor of India, wrote, "The possession of power in a greater degree makes a king superior to another; in a lesser degree, inferior; and in an equal degree, equal. Hence a king shall always endeavor to augment his own power."

Given the view that the essence of politics is the struggle for power, realists maintain that countries and their leaders, if prudent, are virtually compelled to base their foreign policy on the existence of what realists see as a Darwinian, country-eat-country world in which power is the key to the national survival of the fittest. In the words of one scholar, "In an environment as dangerous as anarchy," those who ignore realist principles "would ultimately not survive" (Sterling-Folker, 1997:18). From this point of view, the national interest can be defined for the most part as whatever enhances or preserves the state's security, its influence, and its military and economic power. In the world that exists and probably has always existed, realists would argue, might makes right—or at least it makes success.

Morgenthau (1986:39), for one, reasoned that it is unconscionable for a state to follow policy based only on morality because "while the individual has a moral right to sacrifice himself" in defense of a moral principle, "the state has no right to let its moral disapprobation... get in the way of successful political action, itself inspired by the moral principle of national survival." This does not mean that realists are amoral (Murray, 1996). Indeed, they argue that the highest moral duty of the state is to do good for its citizens. More moderately, many other realists argue that surviving and prospering in a dangerous world requires that morality be weighed prudently against national interest. One scholar has summed up this realist rule of action with the maxim, "Do 'good' if the price is low" (Gray, 1994:8).

Idealism: An Emphasis on Justice

Idealists do not believe that acquiring, preserving, and applying power must be the essence of international relations. Idealists argue that, instead of being based on power, foreign policy should be formulated according to cooperative and ethical standards. President Bill Clinton regularly expressed his idealist philosophy while he was in office. He asked Americans to support sending U.S. troops to Bosnia because "it is the right thing to do." He called up images of "skeletal prisoners caged behind barbed-wire fences, women and girls raped as a tool of war, [and] defenseless men and boys shot down in mass graves.... We cannot save all these people," Clinton declared, "but we can save many of them..., [so] we must do what we can."[6]

When Bill Clinton campaigned for president in 1992, his idealist leanings led him to strongly criticize President George H. W. Bush for maintaining normal relations with China despite its poor human rights record. As president, Clinton learned to better appreciate Bush's realist views, and the policies of the two presidents toward China differed little. The change in Clinton's stance is captured in this photo of an obviously amiable Clinton and President Jiang Zemin of China together at a press conference during the November 2000 meeting of the Asia-Pacific Economic Forum in Bandar Seri Begawan, the capital of Brunei.

The views of Clinton and other idealists do not mean that they are out of touch with reality. When, for example, Clinton sought the presidency in 1992, he assailed President George H. W. Bush for his realpolitik approach to relations with China and other autocracies. Clinton castigated Bush, charging that, "From the Baltics to Beijing, from Sarajevo to South Africa, [he has] sided with the status quo instead of democratic change, with familiar tyrants rather than those who would overthrow them." Clinton promised that he would "assert a new [more idealist] vision for our role in the world."[7] As president, though, Clinton learned that his power to change China's behavior was limited and that he could not afford to overly antagonize another major power. As a result, necessary realism tempered his idealism, and, as he admitted near the end of his first term, "it would be fair to say that my policies with regard to China have been somewhat different from what I talked about in the [1992 presidential] campaign."[8]

Idealists also dismiss the realists' warning that pursuing ethical policy often works against the national interest. The wisest course, idealists contend, is for Americans and others to redefine their interests to take into account the inextricable ties between the future of their country and the global pattern of human development.

PROSPECTS FOR COMPETITION AND COOPERATION: REALISM AND IDEALISM

The previous two sections have examined how realists describe the nature of politics and the respective roles of power and justice. This section addresses the even more important question of whether countries follow the dictates of realpolitik or strive to establish a new world order based on greater international cooperation.

Realism and the Competitive Future

There are many implications to the view of most realists that the drive for power and conflict are at the heart of politics and that there is "little hope for progress in international relations" (Brooks, 1997:473). Based on this view, realists advocate a relatively pragmatic approach to world politics, sometimes called *realpolitik*. One principle of realpolitik is to secure your own country's interests first and worry about the welfare of other countries second, if at all, on the assumption that other countries will not help you unless it is in their own interest. This makes realists very wary of what is sometimes termed *idealpolitik*. Self-sacrificing policies are not just foolish but dangerous, according to Morgenthau (1986:38), because countries that shun realpolitik will "fall victim to the power of others."

A second tenet of realpolitik holds that countries should practice balance-of-power politics, which is explained further in chapter 3. This tenet counsels diplomats to strive to achieve an equilibrium of power in the world in order to prevent any other country or coalition of countries from dominating the system. This can be done through a variety of methods, including building up your own strength, allying yourself with others, or dividing your opponents.

A third realist policy prescription is that the best way to maintain the peace is to be powerful: "Peace through strength," as President Ronald Reagan was fond of saying. President George W. Bush is very much of that school. "We will build our defenses beyond challenge, lest weakness invite challenge," was the way he put it during his January 20, 2001, inaugural address. Thus, realists believe that it is necessary for a country to be armed because the world is dangerous. Idealists would reply that the world is dangerous because so many countries are so heavily armed.

It is important to say that this does not cast realists as warmongers. Instead, a fourth realist tenet is that you should neither waste power on peripheral goals nor pursue goals that you do not have the power to achieve. This frequently makes realists reluctant warriors. It is worth noting, for instance, that Morgenthau was an early critic of U.S. involvement in the war in Vietnam. He thought it was a waste of U.S. resources in a tangential area: the wrong war, with the wrong enemy, in the wrong place. Prudence, then, is a watchword for realists.

Idealism and the Cooperative Future

Idealists believe that humanity can and must successfully seek a new system of world order. They have never been comfortable with a world system based on sovereignty, but they now argue that it is imperative to find new organizational paths to cooperation. Idealists are convinced that the spread of nuclear weapons, the increase in economic interdependence among countries, the decline of world resources, the daunting gap between rich and poor, and the mounting damage to our ecosphere mean that humans must learn to cooperate more fully because they are in grave danger of suffering a catastrophe of unparalleled proportions.

Idealists are divided, however, in terms of how far cooperation can and should go. Classic idealists believe that just as humans learned to form cooperative societies without giving up their individuality, so too can states learn to cooperate without surrendering their independence. These idealists believe that the growth of international economic interdependence or the spread of global culture will create a much greater spirit of cooperation among the world countries.

Neoidealists are more dubious about a world in which countries retain full sovereignty. These analysts believe that countries will have to surrender some of their sovereignty to international organizations in order to promote greater cooperation and, if necessary, to enforce good behavior. "The fundamental right of existence," Pope John Paul II told the UN General Assembly, "does not necessarily call for sovereignty as a state." Instead, the pontiff said, "there can be historical circumstances in which aggregations different from single state sovereignty can… prove advisable."[9]

As for the future, idealists are encouraged by some trends in recent years. One of these is the growth of interdependence. Idealists also support their case by pointing to the willingness of countries to surrender some of their sovereignty to improve themselves. The European Union (EU), for instance, now exercises considerable economic and even political authority over its member-countries. They were not forced into the EU; they joined it freely. This and other indications that sovereignty is weakening will be discussed at length later in the text.

Idealists also condemn the practice of realpolitik. They charge that power politics leads to an unending cycle of conflict and misery, in which safety is temporary at best. They look at the last century with its more than 111 million deaths during two world wars and innumerable other conflicts and deride realists for suggesting that humanity should continue to rely on a self-help system that has failed to provide safety so often and so cataclysmically. Idealists further assert that the pursuit of power in the nuclear age may one day lead to ultimate destruction.

This does not mean that idealists are unwilling to use military force, economic sanctions, and other forms of coercion. They are not so naive as to think that the potential for conflict can be eliminated, at least in the foreseeable future. Therefore most idealists are willing to use coercion when necessary to halt aggression or to end oppression. The use of coercion to restore right is especially acceptable to idealists if it is accomplished through cooperative efforts such as UN peacekeeping forces or sanctions.

ASSESSING REALITY: REALISM AND IDEALISM

Before we leave our discussion of realism and idealism, it is worth pausing to ask which theory better explains how the world has operated and how it operates now. On balance, it is safe to say that throughout history competition rather than cooperation has dominated international relations. Not being at war is not necessarily the same as being at peace in a cooperative way, and suspicion, tension, and rivalry, rather than cooperation, have been the most common traits of what we euphemistically call international peace.

It is also the case that realpolitik is still usually the order of the day, especially where important national interests are involved. Most political leaders tend toward realism in their policies, and even those who lean toward idealism often take the realpolitik road (Elman, 1996). As we noted earlier, Bill Clinton was an idealist as a candidate but moved toward a more realist policy as president. Saying that does not mean, however, that idealism is a view that only those without power can hold, because the realities of the world can also modify realist attitudes. Two scholars examining the new presidency of George W. Bush commented astutely, "Don't be surprised if the 'new realism' [of the Bush administration] starts to look a bit different this autumn. Newborn administrations tend to exhibit steep learning curves," and as a result, "practical solutions to complex global realities displace simple campaign promises." The scholars predict that "if the Bush administration remains attuned to global reality, it is likely to… expand tactical options beyond decisive and unilateral military action, just as the Clinton administration moved in the opposite direction, pulling back from some bold [idealist] international rhetoric" (Legro & Moravcsik, 2001:80).

The short answer to the "what is" question almost certainly is that both realism and idealism influence policy. Realpolitik self-interest has been the dominant impulse of countries. Still, it is also true that countries can be cooperative and even altruistic at times. Moreover, it may well be that the idealist approach is gaining ground as states recognize that competition and conflict are increasingly dangerous and destructive and that peaceful cooperation is in everyone's self-interest. It would be naive to argue that the world is anywhere near the point of concluding that self-interest and global interests are usually synonymous. But it is not fatuous to say that an increasing number of people have come to the conclusion that working toward the long-term goal of a safe and prosperous world is preferable to seeking short-term national advantage. Thus, while the question "what is" should engage our attention, the far more important questions are "what should be" and "what will be." What should be is for you to decide after reading this book and consulting other sources of information. What will be is for all of us to see and experience.

How to Study World Politics

"Well, OK," you may say, "international politics is important and it affects me. And, yes, there are important choices to make. So I'll agree that I should know more about it and get active in the world drama. But where do I start?" Ah, I am glad you asked!

The first thing you should do, if you have not already, is to read the preface. This will tell you how I have structured this text and will help you understand what follows. The next chapter will give you more help in establishing a base to understanding world politics by laying out a brief history of and the current trends in the world system.

POLITICAL SCIENTISTS AND WORLD POLITICS

Before getting to the chapter on global history and trends, it is important that you understand something about what political scientists are attempting to do and how they go about doing it. This knowledge is important to help understand the efforts and goals of the many studies that are cited in this text and others that you may read. Evaluating the research of scholars may also help you construct and conduct your own studies of international relations or any other subject.

Why Political Scientists Study World Politics

There is a long history of international relations as an intellectual focus, and concepts such as anarchy and sovereignty were at its core long before realism, idealism, and other schools of thought were articulated and labeled (Schmidt, 1997). Like all political scientists, scholars study world politics in order to formulate theories—generalizations—about politics. Therefore, what concerns political scientists is understanding patterns that occur over time or that occur in many places at the same time. There are many ways to acquire this understanding, but, whatever the approach, theory is at the heart of political science (Hermann, 1998; Lepgold, 1998).

Within this emphasis on theory, international relations scholars have three subsidiary goals in mind: description, prediction, and prescription. *Description* is the oldest and most fundamental of these three goals. This task sounds a whole lot easier than it is. Not only are events complex and information often difficult to obtain, but political science description should focus on patterns. When a political scientist studies a single event (a case study) or, better yet, a series of events across time or over space, the object is not to just describe the event(s). Instead, the goal is to relate them to a pattern of other events. One illustrative area of political science research has been to try to prove or disprove the hypothesis, "Democracies do not fight each other" (Gartzke, 1998; Gleditsch & Hegre, 1997; Thompson & Tucker, 1997). By studying history, many political scientists have concluded that, indeed, democracies tend not to go to war with one another. This research is discussed fully in chapter 8.

Prediction is even more difficult than description because of the complexity of human nature. Nevertheless, political scientists can use careful research as a basis for "analytical forecasting [by which to] give a reasoned argument for what they expect to happen" (George, 1994:172). If, for instance, we believe the descriptive studies that conclude that democracies are peaceful toward one another, then it is possible to predict that a democratic Russia will be less likely to be antagonistic toward the United States and other democracies than the nondemocratic Soviet Union.

Prescription is a third goal. Some political scientists go beyond their objective studies and come to normative (what is right or wrong) conclusions and prescribe policy (Kelman, 2000). Those who believe that democracies have not been (description) and will not be (prediction) aggressive toward one another, may wish

Political scientists sometimes practice world politics, as well as study it. Before heading to Washington to become the president's national security adviser in 2001, Condoleezza Rice was provost at Stanford University, where she also taught political science. She holds a Ph.D. in political science from the University of Denver.

to advocate (prescription) policies that promote the adoption or preservation of democracy. Such advocates might, for example, urge extending massive economic aid to Russia in order to avoid the economic turmoil that is so often associated with a slide toward authoritarian government.

Political scientists, it can be added, do more than talk to students and write about their theories. Some political scientists enter directly into the policy-making realm. Among them is Condoleezza Rice, who left her position as a professor of political science at Stanford University to become the national security adviser to President George W. Bush. In the preceding administration, President Bill Clinton, Vice President Al Gore, and Secretary of State Madeleine Albright all had one or more degrees in political science. Other political scientists try to influence policy indirectly through such methods as serving in so-called think tanks dedicated to policy advocacy, writing op-ed pieces in newspapers, and testifying before legislatures.

How Political Scientists Conduct Research

The most fundamental thing that political scientists need to gather is evidence. They do so by three basic research methodologies: logic, traditional observation, and quantitative analysis. All research should apply logic, but valuable contributions can be made by relatively pure logical analysis (Bueno de Mesquita & Morrow, 1999). Aristotle and the other great political philosophers who are mentioned in this book relied primarily on logical analysis to support their political observations. This technique is still important. Some of the best work on nuclear deterrence has been done by analysts who employ deductive logic (from the general to the specific) to suggest specifically how nuclear deterrence works.

Did You Know That:
The first political scientist to become U.S. president was Woodrow Wilson, who received his Ph.D. (1886) from Johns Hopkins University and taught political science at several colleges. The second was Bill Clinton, who graduated with a specialization in international relations from Georgetown University (1968). Of the two major party candidates in 2000, Al Gore had a B.A. in government from Harvard University (1969), while George W. Bush inexplicably majored in history instead of political science at Yale University.

A second methodology, traditional observation, uses a variety of techniques to study political phenomena. One method is historical analysis, using sources such as archives, interviews, and participant observation. Traditional observation is an old and still valuable methodology. There are many modern studies of why wars occur, but we can all still learn much by reading *The Peloponnesian War*, written by the Greek historian Thucydides in about 410 B.C. Realists, for instance, are persuaded by his analysis that a struggle for power caused the Peloponnesian War (intermittently between 460 and 404 B.C.) between Athens and Sparta. "What made war inevitable," Thucydides wrote, "was the growth of Athenian power and the fear which this caused in Sparta" (Genest, 1994:71). What the historian did is called a case study, and many modern studies use this method to look at one or more events or other political phenomena in order to add to what we can say about international relations theory.

Quantitative analysis is a third methodology. Political scientists who use this method are interested in measurable phenomena and use mathematical techniques. The studies on war and democracy cited in chapter 8 are able to use quantitative methods because countries and wars are relatively measurable.

WHAT TO STUDY: LEVELS OF ANALYSIS

Another major division among analytical approaches used by political scientists has to do with the level of focus. The essential question here is, What do we study? One approach by political scientists has been to divide the study into **levels of analysis**. These refer to the level of the factors that affect international politics. Scholars have suggested anywhere from two to six possible levels to analyze world politics. Most commonly, analysts use three levels, and that number will be used here. The three levels are:

1. **System-level analysis**—a worldview that takes a "top-down" approach to analyzing global politics. This level theorizes that the world's social-economic-political structure and pattern of interaction (the international system) strongly influence the policies of states and other international actors. Therefore, understanding the structure and pattern of the international system will lead to understanding how international politics operates.
2. **State-level analysis**—a view in which the concern is with the characteristics of an individual country and the impact of those traits on the country's behavior. This level theorizes that states (countries) are the key international actors. Therefore, understanding how states as complex organizations decide policy will lead to understanding how international politics operates.
3. **Individual-level analysis**—a view in which the focus is on people. This level argues that in the end people make policy. Therefore, understanding how people (individually, in groups, or as a species) decide policy will lead to understanding how international politics operates.

Focus on one level of analysis does not mean exclusion of the others. Indeed, it would be best to think of the levels as occurring along a scale from the general (system-level analysis) to the specific (individual-level analysis). It is possible to focus on one level and still use elements of the others. In the following four chapters, we will examine extensively the implications of each of these levels. After chapter 2 and its discussion of the history of and current trends in the international system, chapter 3 takes up system-level analysis, including the evolution of the world system and theories about how systems operate. Then chapter 4 discusses state-level analysis, followed by chapter 5 on individual-level analysis.

Chapter Summary

1. This book's primary message is captured by Shakespeare's line, "All the world's a stage, and all the men and women merely players." This means that we are all part of the world drama and are affected by it. It also means that we should try to play a role in determining the course of the dramatic events that affect our lives.
2. Economics is one way that we are all affected. The word *intermestic* has been coined to symbolize the merging of *inter*national and d*omestic* concerns, especially in the area of economics. Countries and their citizens have become increasingly interdependent.
3. Economically, trade both creates and causes the loss of jobs. International investment practices may affect your standard of living in such diverse ways as determining how much college tuition is, what your income is, what interest rate you pay for auto loans and mortgages, and how much you can look forward to in retirement. The global economy also supplies vital resources, such as oil. Exchange rates between different currencies affect the prices we pay for imported goods, the general rate of inflation, and our country's international trade balance.

4. Our country's role in the world also affects decisions about the allocation of budget funds. Some countries spend a great deal on military functions. Other countries spend relatively little on the military and devote almost all of their budget resources to domestic spending.

5. World politics also plays an important role in determining the condition of your living space. Politics has, for the most part, not created environmental degradation, but political cooperation will almost certainly be needed to halt and reverse the despoiling of the biosphere.

6. Your life may also be affected by world politics. You may be called on to serve in the military. Whether or not you are, war can kill you.

7. There are many things any one of us can do, individually or in cooperation with others, to play a part in shaping the future of our world. Think, vote, protest, support, write letters, join organizations, make speeches, run for office—do something!

8. There are demands for and predictions of a new world order. The future path of the world can be thought about as analogous to Robert Frost's poem about two roads diverging in a wood. The poet wrote that the path he chose made all the difference. So too will the road that the world chooses make all the difference. Therefore it is important to think about the direction in which you want the world to go.

9. One road is the traditionalist approach, which focuses on the continuing sovereign role of the state as the primary actor in the international system. The traditionalist approach is associated with many terms; "realism" is perhaps the best known. Realism focuses on the self-interested promotion of the state and nation. Realists believe that power politics is the driving force behind international relations. Therefore, realists believe that both safety and wisdom lie in promoting the national interest through the preservation and, if necessary, the application of the state's power.

10. The second, alternative road is advocated by those who stress the need for significant change, including both a restructuring of power within states and international cooperation and global interests. Of the terms associated with this approach, "idealism" is used herein. Idealists believe that realpolitik is dangerous and outmoded. They believe that idealpolitik should be given greater emphasis and that everyone's "real" interest lies in a more orderly, more humane, more egalitarian world.

11. Political scientists have numerous orientations, including realist, idealist (and their variations neorealist and neoidealist), feminist, and political economist.

12. Political scientists study international relations to describe and predict political phenomena, and to prescribe courses of action. In their studies, scholars use a variety of methodologies, including logic, traditional observation, and quantitative techniques, to analyze phenomena and test hypotheses. Scholars also have several orientations, which include focusing on power, human social relations, and economics.

13. There are three levels of analysis from which world politics can be studied. They are system-level analysis, state-level analysis, and individual-level analysis. They are not mutually exclusive. Each of these levels is discussed in detail in the next several chapters.

Chapter 2

The Evolution of World Politics

I am amazed, methinks, and lose my way among the thorns and dangers of the world.

Shakespeare, *King John*

Whereof what's past is prologue, what to come, In yours and my discharge.
Shakespeare, *The Tempest*

All true histories contain instruction; though, in some, the treasure may be hard to find.

Anne Brontë, *Agnes Grey*

We have need of history in its entirety, not to fall back into it, but to see if we can escape from it.

José Ortega y Gasset, *The Revolt of the Masses*

Chapter Objectives

After completing this chapter, you should be able to:

- Recognize major trends in the evolving world system from the birth of states to the present.
- Understand the origin of the current world system and the importance of the Treaty of Westphalia (1648).
- Identify the changes that occurred during the eighteenth and nineteenth centuries and continue to have an important impact on the international system.
- Discuss the pace of world political evolution at the beginning of the twentieth century and describe the weakening of the multipolar system.
- Discuss the transition from a bipolar system to the most likely form of a modified multipolar system.
- Analyze the potential shift in the international system away from a strictly Western orientation.
- Identify both international and domestic challenges to the authority of the state.
- Discuss the implications of following either the traditional national security or alternative international security approach in the quest for peace.
- Understand the implications of economic interdependence and the counterpressures to pursue more traditional national economic policies.
- Discuss the implications of the growing economic disparity between the North and South.
- Analyze the future of human rights and environmental issues in the face of national resistance to international solutions.

This chapter has two purposes. The first is to establish a historical foundation on which to build our analysis of international relations. To this end the following pages give a brief historical narrative that emphasizes the themes and events you will encounter repeatedly in this book.

The second goal of this chapter is to sketch the evolution of the current, rapidly evolving world political system (Robertson, 1997). The concept of an **international system** represents the notion that the world is more than just a sum of its parts, such as countries, and that world politics is more than just the sum of the individual interactions among those parts. The idea of an international system is also based on the belief that there are general patterns of actions among the system's actors. These patterns and their causes are explored in chapter 3.

It is advisable to be patient as you read through the following overview of the evolution of the international system. You will find that this chapter will often introduce a topic briefly and then hurry on to another point. "Wait a minute," you may think, "slow down and explain this better." Hang in there! Other chapters fill in the details.

It would also be wise to keep your mind open to change. The current international system evolved relatively slowly for several centuries, then shifted rapidly during the twentieth century. Warp-speed technological innovation is the most important source of change. It has brought benefits, such as nearly instantaneous global communications, less disease, and enhanced material well-being. Hyperspeed technological change has also created or intensified many problems, such as global warming, the expanding population, and nuclear weapons. In short, as one scholar has written, there is "turbulence in world politics" as "Spaceship Earth daily encounters squalls, downdrafts, and windshears as it careens into changing and uncharted realms of experience" in the twenty-first century (Rosenau, 1990:4, 7).

The Evolving World System: Early Development

There have been numerous global and regional international systems, with some scholars dating them back to the southern Mesopotamian region of Babylon some 7,500 years ago (Cioffi-Revilla, 2000). For our purposes, we can pick up this evolutionary tale beginning in about the fifteenth century. It was then that modern states (countries) began to coalesce. The emergence of states as the focus of political authority involved two contradictory trends—integration and disintegration—that transfigured the system that had existed for the preceding millennium.

The *integration process* began in part as the result of the weakening of small feudal units (such as baronies, dukedoms, and principalities) and city-states (such as Venice), which could no longer maintain their political viability and autonomy. They declined because of a series of changes in technology and economics that diminished their strength. As these small units faltered, kings gained enough power to consolidate their authority and to end the virtual independence of the feudal states and city-states.

The *disintegration process* involved the growing unwillingness of people to accept distant, overarching authority. Some of this had to do with the secularization of politics, especially the resistance in Europe to the political authority of the pope and the Roman Catholic Church. Disintegration also included revolts against, and the eventual collapse of, huge multinational empires. This was a long process that began in Europe with the decline and fall of the Holy Roman Empire in the sixteenth and seventeenth centuries and arguably also included the collapse of the Soviet Union in 1991. More than any other event, the **Treaty of Westphalia** (1648) has come to symbolize this eclipse of overarching authority and the founding of modern states. This treaty ended the Thirty Years' War and established the independence of the Netherlands, several German states, and a number of other Protestant political entities from the secular authority of the Holy Roman Empire and its Roman Catholic dynasty (the Hapsburgs) and, by extension, from the religious authority of the pope in Rome.

The story of the origins of the modern state is told in greater detail in chapter 8, but it is appropriate to make a few essential points here about the growth of states and their place in the international system. First, in the post-Westphalia system, states became the primary actors in the international system. This leading role remains today. A great deal, although not all, of the action on the world stage is about states and groups of states interacting with one another.

Second, the operation of the post-Westphalia system is partly the result of the fact that states came to possess **sovereignty**. This means that they do not recognize any higher legitimate authority. The pivotal role of the sovereign state has had a defining influence on the international system because the system has no central authority to maintain order and dispense justice. As such, international relations occur within an **anarchical political system**. This does not mean that the international system is a scene of unchecked chaos. To the contrary, the system operates with a great deal of regularity. It exists, however, mostly because countries find it in their interest to act according to expectations. But when a state decides that it is in its interests to break the largely informal rules of the system, as Iraq did in 1990 when it invaded Kuwait, there is little to stop it except countervailing power. Similarly, there was no global police force in the anarchical system to prevent the al-Qaeda terrorists from launching the attacks on the United States on September 11, 2001. The point is that in the international system, anarchy does not mean chaos; it means the lack of a central authority.

Did You Know That:
The word *anarchism* is derived from the Greek *anarchos* (without ruler), which is a combination of the Greek negative prefix *an* (no, against, without) and the Greek word *archos* (ruler).

The Evolving World System: The Eighteenth and Nineteenth Centuries

The emergence of the sovereign state as the primary actor was just the beginning of the evolution of the modern international system. The pace of change began to quicken in the eighteenth century. Many of the events that occurred between 1700 and 1900 and many of the attitudes that developed during this time helped shape the structure and operation of the international system as it exists currently. Three themes stand out: the coming of popular sovereignty, the Westernization of the international system, and the culmination of the multipolar system.

Popular Sovereignty The establishment of the concept of **popular sovereignty** marked a major change in the notion of who owned the state and how it should be governed. Prior to the late 1700s and early 1800s, the prevailing principle of governance was the theory of the divine right of kings, which held that the monarch was the sovereign and that the people in the sovereign's realm were subjects. The political identification of individuals tended to have a local orientation. It was the monarch, not the people, who owned the state and in whom legitimate political authority rested (Guibernau, 1996). The American (1776) and French (1789) Revolutions challenged this philosophy. *Democracies* were established on the principle that sovereign political power rests with the people rather than with the monarch. The notion of popular sovereignty also changed and expanded the concept of *nationalism* to include mass identification with and participation in the affairs of the state

(Continued on page 32)

World Countries

The international system includes many types of actors. Of these, states (or countries) are the most important. National boundaries are the most important source of political division in the world, and for most people nationalism is the strongest source of political identification.

Scale: 1 to 125,000,000

Note: All world maps are Robinson projection.

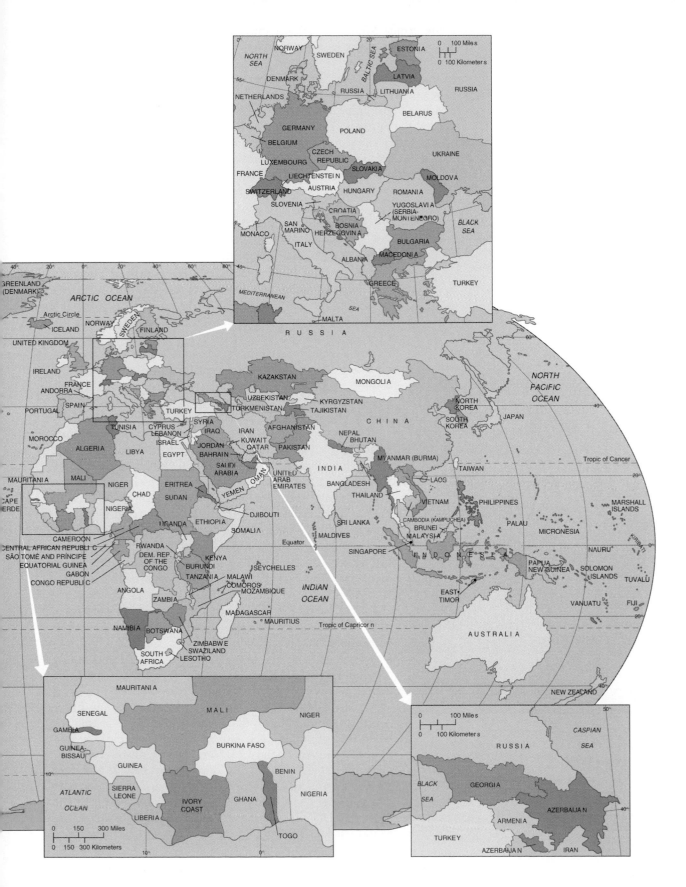

(country). If the people owned the state, then they had both a greater emotional attachment to it and a greater responsibility to support it. One symbol of this change was that Napoleonic France (1799–1815) was the first country to have a true patriotic draft that raised an army of a million strong.

From its beginnings in America and, particularly, in France, democratic nationalism spread throughout Europe and steadily undermined monarchical government and its concept of divine right. The collapse of the dynasties in China, Germany, Austria-Hungary, Russia, the Ottoman Empire, and elsewhere early in the twentieth century marked the real end of strong monarchical government. The multiethnic, in some cases colonial, empires held by several of these monarchies also disintegrated, and the British, French, and other empires would not last much longer.

The French Revolution was a key event in the growth of democratic nationalism. This is the idea that the state is a possession of the people and, therefore, that all political authority resides with the people rather than with the monarch. Here, French fighters fly over the Arc de Triomphe in Paris trailing smoke colored to resemble the red, white, and blue of the Tricolor, the flag adopted during the French Revolution to replace the gold *fleur-de-lis* on a white background standard of the royal house of Bourbon. The celebration was taking place on Bastille Day, which commemorates July 14, 1789, the date of the fall of the Bastille prison in Paris and the beginning of the French Revolution.

Westernization of the International System The domination and shaping of the international system by the **West** was a second important characteristic of the eighteenth and nineteenth centuries. Somewhat earlier, the growth of European power had enabled Great Britain, France, and other European countries to thrust outward and take control of North and South America and some other regions. The Arab, Aztec, Chinese, Incan, Mogul (Indian), Persian, and other non-European empires or dynasties began to decline and fall. The process accelerated in the nineteenth century, with Europeans coming to dominate the globe and to see themselves "as forming an exclusive club enjoying rights superior to those of other political communities" (Bull & Watson, 1982:425).

One reason for the **Westernization of the international system** was the scientific and technological advances that sprang from the Renaissance (about 1400–1650) in Europe. This sparked the **industrial revolution**, which began in the mid-1700s in Great Britain and then spread to the rest of Europe, Canada, and the United States. The rapid industrialization of the 1800s also occurred elsewhere, such as Japan. Mostly, though, industrialization was a Western phenomenon, and in the few non-Western countries where it did occur, industrialization came later and usually much less completely.

Industrialization and associated advances in weaponry and other technology had a profound impact on world politics. The European powers gained in strength compared with nonindustrialized Asia and Africa. Since the industrialized countries needed to find resources and markets to fuel and fund their economies, industrialization promoted colonialism. Many industrialized countries also coveted colonies as a matter of prestige. The result was an era of Euro-American **imperialism** that subjected many people to colonial domination. The fate of Africa is graphically displayed in the map on page 33. Many Asian cultures were similarly subjected to **Eurowhite** domination. China, it should be noted, was never technically colonized, but after the 1840s it was divided into spheres of influence among the Western powers, and it lost territories to Great Britain (Hong Kong), Japan (Taiwan/Formosa), and Russia (parts of Siberia).

(Continued on page 33)

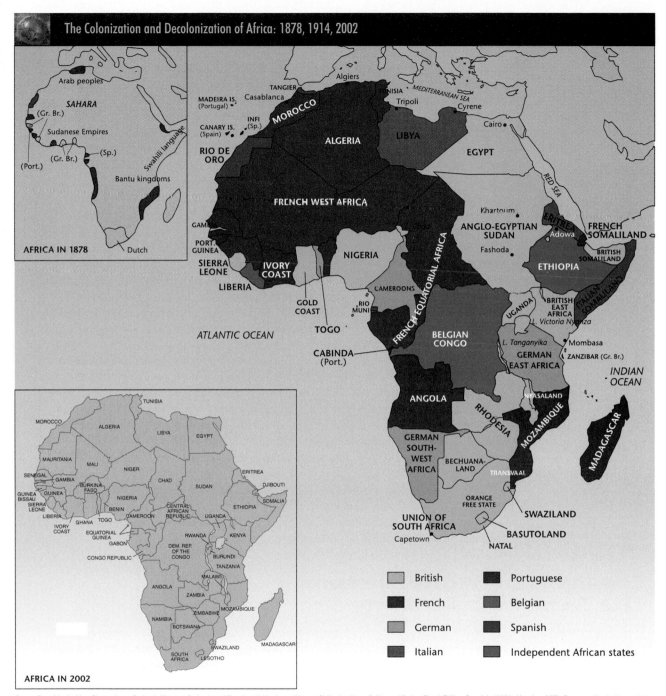

The Colonization and Decolonization of Africa: 1878, 1914, 2002

AFRICA IN 1878

Arab peoples
SAHARA
(Gr. Br.)
Sudanese Empires
(Port.)
(Gr. Br.)
(Sp.)
Swahili language
Bantu kingdoms
Dutch

MADEIRA IS. (Portugal)
CANARY IS. (Spain)
TANGIER
Casablanca
INFI (Sp.)
MOROCCO
ALGIERS
TUNISIA
MEDITERRANEAN SEA
Tripoli
Cyrene
Cairo
ALGERIA
LIBYA
EGYPT
RIO DE ORO
FRENCH WEST AFRICA
RED SEA
Khartoum
ANGLO-EGYPTIAN SUDAN
Adowa
ERITREA
FRENCH SOMALILAND
Fashoda
BRITISH SOMALILAND
GAMBIA
PORT. GUINEA
NIGERIA
ETHIOPIA
SIERRA LEONE
IVORY COAST
LIBERIA
GOLD COAST
CAMEROONS
RIO MUNI
FRENCH EQUATORIAL AFRICA
UGANDA
BRITISH EAST AFRICA
L. Victoria Nyanza
ITALIAN SOMALILAND
TOGO
CABINDA (Port.)
BELGIAN CONGO
L. Tanganyika
Mombasa
GERMAN EAST AFRICA
ZANZIBAR (Gr. Br.)
ATLANTIC OCEAN
INDIAN OCEAN
ANGOLA
NYASALAND
RHODESIA
MOZAMBIQUE
MADAGASCAR
GERMAN SOUTH-WEST AFRICA
BECHUANA-LAND
TRANSVAAL
ORANGE FREE STATE
SWAZILAND
UNION OF SOUTH AFRICA
Capetown
BASUTOLAND
NATAL

AFRICA IN 2002

MOROCCO, TUNISIA, ALGERIA, LIBYA, EGYPT, MAURITANIA, MALI, NIGER, SENEGAL, GAMBIA, BURKINA FASO, GUINEA BISSAU, GUINEA, SIERRA LEONE, LIBERIA, IVORY COAST, GHANA, TOGO, BENIN, NIGERIA, CHAD, SUDAN, ERITREA, DJIBOUTI, SOMALIA, ETHIOPIA, CENTRAL AFRICAN REPUBLIC, CAMEROON, EQUATORIAL GUINEA, GABON, CONGO REPUBLIC, DEM. REP. OF THE CONGO, RWANDA, BURUNDI, UGANDA, KENYA, TANZANIA, ANGOLA, ZAMBIA, MALAWI, MOZAMBIQUE, ZIMBABWE, NAMIBIA, BOTSWANA, SWAZILAND, SOUTH AFRICA, LESOTHO, MADAGASCAR

Legend:
- British
- French
- German
- Italian
- Portuguese
- Belgian
- Spanish
- Independent African states

Source: Perry Marvin, Myra Chase, James R. Jacob, Margaret C. Jacob, and Theodore H. Von Laue, *Western Civilization: Ideas, Politics and Society*, Fourth Edition. Copyright 1992 by Houghton Mifflin Company. Used with permission.

The industrialization of the West was one factor that caused the colonization of Asia and Africa in the late 1800s and early 1900s. This map and its insets show that Africa was largely controlled by its indigenous peoples in 1878 (inset) but had, by 1914 (larger map), become almost totally subjugated and divided into colonies by the European powers. Then, after World War II, the momentum shifted. Independence movements led to decolonization. Now there are no colonies left in Africa. Thus the West's domination of the world has weakened.

Americans soon joined in the scramble for colonial possessions. The United States acquired such Pacific territories as Hawaii and Samoa in the 1890s. Victory in the Spanish-American War (1898) added Guam, Puerto Rico, and the Philippines. Additionally, during the next several decades, U.S. domination over many of the Caribbean and Central American countries became so strong that their true independence was in doubt.

As noted earlier, these colonial empires were, for the most part, not long-lived. Still, they had a major and deleterious impact on the subjugated areas that continues to affect world politics. The imperialist subjugation of Asians, Africans, and others by Europeans and Americans set the stage for what became the **North-South Axis**. Indeed, in the overlapping currents of history, the anticolonial movement had begun. An earlier imperial era, which had brought European control to the Western Hemisphere, began to crumble rapidly. In 1804 Haiti won its independence from France, and by 1824 all of Spain's colonies in Central and South America as well as Portugal's colony of Brazil had thrown off colonial rule. The North-South Axis had begun to form.

Growth of the Multipolar System A third characteristic of the 1700s and 1800s is that the **multipolar system** reached its zenith. The multipolar system, which governed political relations among the major European powers from the Treaty of Westphalia in 1648 through the mid-twentieth century, peaked in the 1700s and 1800s because of the global dominance of the European powers. The international system was multipolar in the sense that political affairs were dominated by numerous major powers. For example, in the century between the final defeat of Napoleon (1815) and the outbreak of World War I (1914), the major powers were Great Britain, France, Prussia/Germany, Austria-Hungary, Russia, and to a lesser extent Italy and the Ottoman Empire/Turkey.

The multipolar system that existed between 1648 and 1945 was characterized by shifting alliances designed to preserve the **balance of power** by preventing any single power or combination of powers from dominating Europe and, by extension, the world. Prime Minister Winston Churchill once clearly enunciated balance-of-power politics as a governing principle of British foreign policy when he explained that "for four hundred years the foreign policy of England has been to oppose the strongest, most aggressive, most dominating power on the Continent" (Walt, 1996:109).

The balance-of-power process succeeded for three centuries in preventing any single power or coalition from controlling Europe and perhaps the world. It did not, however, persist or keep Great Britain and the other dominant European countries from falling from the ranks of major powers.

⊕ The Evolving World System: The Twentieth Century

The twentieth century was a time of momentous and rapid global change (Chan & Weiner, 1998; Keylor, 1996). The *rapid pace of change* in our time is an important theme for you to keep in mind as you read the balance of this chapter and, indeed, of this book. It is hard for almost any of us to grasp how rapidly things are changing compared to the earlier pace of social, political, and technological evolution. When the twentieth century began there were no airplanes; monarchs ruled Russia, Germany, Italy, and most other countries; there were no important global organizations; uranium was a little-known metallic element; and there were about 1.5 billion people in the world. By the time the century ended, humans could rocket into space and deliver their weapons by intercontinental ballistic missile; elected officials governed most countries; the United Nations, World Bank, World Trade Organization, and other international organizations came to play important roles in the world; nuclear energy powered city lights and industrial production, while simultaneously threatening the environment and our very lives through nuclear weapons; and the world population quadrupled to 6 billion people. All this has happened in just one century, a time period that represents only about 3 percent of the approximately 3,500 years of recorded human history.

Technology has been the prime mover of this rapid change. The twentieth century saw the creation of radio, television, and Internet communications, nuclear power, computers, power chain saws, air and space travel, intercontinental ballistic missiles, effective birth control, antibiotics, crack cocaine, and a host of other innovations that can benefit or bedevil us—keep us together or tear us apart. The world's economy has expanded vastly. Some of the changes have been positive. Many of us have material possessions that a person living a century ago would not have been able even to imagine. But economic expansion has also brought ills, including pollution, deforestation, ozone buildup, and the extinction of untold animal and plant species.

It seems that the world is evolving much faster than ever before. That is evident in part in Figure 2.1, which shows the increased pace of technological and scientific innovation. Technology is both creating and solving problems. Whether the positive or negative results predominate depends in part on our ability to address the issues in a politically responsible way. But with the accelerated pace of change, there is not time for a leisurely, evolutionary search for solutions.

THE TWENTIETH CENTURY: THE YEARS TO WORLD WAR II

The pace of world political evolution began to speed up even more by the beginning of the 1900s. Democracy was rapidly eroding the legitimacy of dynastic monarchs. In 1900 there were still czars and kaisers; they would be gone in less than two decades. **Nationalism** increasingly undermined the foundations of multiethnic empires. World War I was a pivotal point. Two empires, the Austro-Hungarian and Ottoman, were among the losers. The result was the (re)establishment of countries such as Czechoslovakia, Poland, and Yugoslavia. Other countries like Jordan, Lebanon, Syria, and Palestine/Israel came under the mandate (control) of the League of Nations and finally became independent after World War II.

The end of the balance of power that had governed European relations during the 1800s was marked by the tragedies of two world wars. The reasons for the end of the multipolar system are still subject to dispute. We can say, however, that the European system changed from being one that was fluid and permitted shifting alliances and pragmatic cooperation to a system dominated by two increasingly rigid and hostile alliances. In World War I (1914–1918) the Central Powers included Germany, Austria-Hungary, and Turkey. The Allied Powers consisted of France, Russia, and Great Britain, which were joined by Italy just after the outbreak of the war. After its defeat in the war, Germany was at first treated severely, but the multipolar system soon led to a **realpolitik** attempt to reestablish balance by allowing Germany in the 1930s to rebuild its strength. With Germany defeated, the British worried that France might once again dominate Europe and threaten them as it had under Napoleon. Therefore, the British tried to offset French power by acquiescing to German rearmament and diplomatic demands. It was, for the British, a near-fatal mistake.

Events in Russia also prompted the British and, especially, the French to tolerate German revitalization. The seizure of power by Lenin's Bolsheviks in 1918 evoked horror in the West. Communist ideology combined with Russian military might seemed to threaten the Western powers. Some saw a rearmed Germany serving as a bulwark against the "Red menace."

The grotesqueness of World War I was another reason why Great Britain and France did not seriously try to restrain resurgent Germany. The two victors had each

The overthrow of the czarist government in Russia in March 1917 was applauded widely in the West. But when the Bolsheviks, as the early communists were called, came to power in November of that year, the specter of communism alarmed many Europeans and Americans. This early cartoon (1920) depicts the frightening image of Soviet communism common in the West at the time.

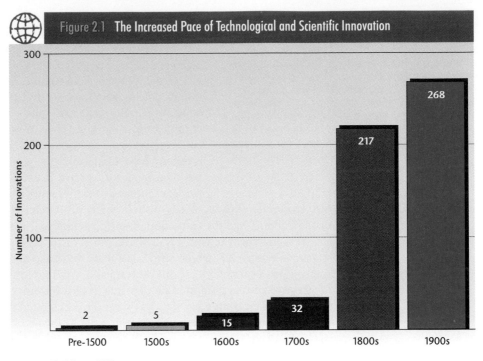

Figure 2.1 The Increased Pace of Technological and Scientific Innovation

Data source: World Almanac (2002).

The escalating pace of technological and scientific change has had a major impact on human beings in general and on world politics in particular. This figure depicts important innovations whose dates of discovery or invention are known. As you can see, only about 10 percent of these occurred before 1800. Another 40 percent occurred in the 1800s, and about 50 percent during the 1900s.

lost almost an entire generation of young men. When Adolf Hitler came to power (1933) and rearmed his country, they vacillated timorously over taking action. The **Munich Conference** (1938) became synonymous with this lack of will when Great Britain and France gave way to Hitler's demands for the annexation of part of Czechoslovakia. British prime minister Neville Chamberlain and other leaders held the false hope that an **appeasement policy** toward Germany would maintain peace.

While all this was occurring in Europe, the rest of the world community expanded and changed during the first 40 years of the twentieth century. Some states gained independence; other existing states, especially Japan and the United States, gradually began to play a more significant role and to undercut European domination of the international system. China began the century saddled with a decaying imperial government and foreign domination, but it overthrew its emperor in 1911 and started a long struggle to rid itself of foreign domination and to reestablish its role as a major power. Also during the first four decades of the century, the League of Nations was established, and many other non-European countries joined world diplomacy through membership in the League. Although international relations still focused on Europe during the first four decades of the 1900s, a shift was under way. The voices of Africa, Asia, and Latin America began to be heard on the world stage.

THE TWENTIETH CENTURY: THE COLD WAR BEGINS AND ENDS

World War II was a tragedy of unequaled proportions. It also marked major changes in the nature and operation of the world political system. This section will focus on the shifts in the polar structure of the system through the end of the cold war. There are a number of other changes that began or accelerated during this period that continue to affect us all in the early twenty-first century. These will be taken up in the following section that discusses the issues and choices that lie before us.

On the political front, a series of shifts in the system occurred in the decades after 1945 that involved the actors and, indeed, the polar structure of the system itself. World War II finally destroyed the long-decaying, mostly European-based multipolar structure. It was replaced by a bipolar system dominated by the Soviet Union and the United States. To those who experienced its anguished intensity, East-West hostility seemed to augur an unending future of bipolar confrontation and peril. As is often true, the view that the present will also be the future proved shortsighted. The bipolar era was brief. Significant cracks in the structure were evident by the 1960s; by 1992 the bipolar system was history.

The Rise and Decline of the Bipolar System

World War II devastated most of the existing major actors. In their place, the United States emerged as a military and economic **superpower** and the leader of one **power pole**. The Soviet Union, though incredibly damaged, emerged as leader of the other pole. The USSR never matched the United States economically, but the Soviets possessed a huge conventional armed force, a seemingly threatening ideology, and, by 1949, atomic weapons. The **East-West Axis** was established.

The exact causes of the confrontation, termed the **cold war**, are complex and controversial. It is safe to say, however, that varying economic and political interests and the power vacuum created by the collapse of the old balance-of-power structure created a bipolar system in which a great deal of world politics was centered on the confrontation between the two superpowers.

The American reaction to the perceived world Soviet/communist threat was the **containment doctrine**. This principle transformed U.S. foreign policy from a prewar norm of isolationism to a postwar globalism, opposing the Soviet Union (and later Communist China) diplomatically and militarily around the world. The United States sponsored a number of regional alliances, most notably the North Atlantic Treaty Organization (NATO, established in 1949). The Soviets responded in 1955 with the Warsaw Treaty Organization (or Warsaw Pact). Both sides also vied for power in the developing countries, and both Soviet and American arms and money flowed to various governments and rebel groups in the ongoing communist-anticommunist contest.

Despite intense rivalry marked by mutual fear and hatred, the reality that both superpowers possessed nuclear weapons usually led them to avoid direct confrontations. There were a few, however, including the scariest moment of the bipolar era, the Cuban missile crisis of 1962. The Soviets had begun building nuclear missile sites in Cuba, and President John F. Kennedy risked nuclear war to force them out.

The containment doctrine also led to the U.S. involvement in Vietnam. Vietnamese forces led by nationalist/communist Ho Chi Minh defeated France's colonial army in 1954 and achieved independence. But the country was divided between Ho's forces in the north and a pro-Western government in the south. The struggle for a unified Vietnam soon resumed, and the United States intervened militarily in 1964. The war, though popular at first, quickly became a domestic trauma for Americans as casualties mounted on both sides. Perhaps the most poignant symbol of opposition to the war was the death in May 1970 of four students at Kent State University during clashes between antiwar demonstrators and Ohio National Guardsmen. War-weariness finally led to a complete U.S. disengagement. Within a short time Ho's forces triumphed and Vietnam was unified in 1975.

Vietnam caused a number of important changes in American attitudes. One was increased resistance to the cold war urge to fight communism everywhere. Second, Americans saw more clearly that the bipolar system was crumbling, especially as relations between the Soviet Union and China deteriorated.

Beginning approximately with the administrations of Soviet leader Leonid I. Brezhnev (1964–1982) and American president Richard M. Nixon (1969–1974), East-West relations began to improve, albeit fitfully. Nixon accurately assessed the changing balance of power, especially the rise of China, and he moved to better relations through a policy of **détente** with Moscow and Beijing. They came to similar realpolitik conclusions about the changing power configuration of the international system and sought improved relations with Washington.

The End of the Bipolar System

During the 1970s and early 1980s, East-West relations continued to warm, although there were cool periods. Then relations began to change more rapidly. Mikhail S. Gorbachev became the Soviet leader in 1985 and moved to ease the Soviet Union's oppressive political system and to restructure the country's cumbersome bureaucratic and economic systems. While Gorbachev's goals were limited, he opened a Pandora's box for the communist Soviet Union and unleashed forces that were beyond his control.

Gorbachev also sought better relations with the West in order to allow him to reduce the military's burdensome share of the USSR's economy, to receive more favorable trade terms, and to accrue other economic benefits. With this in mind, Gorbachev, among other things, announced that the USSR was willing to let Eastern Europeans follow their own domestic policies. Eastern Europeans moved quickly to escape Moscow's orbit. This was symbolized most dramatically in East Germany, where the communist government fell rapidly apart. East Germany dissolved itself in October 1990, and its territory was absorbed by West Germany into a newly

The end of the bipolar system and the accompanying demise of communism in the Soviet Union and Eastern Europe is symbolized by these school children playing on a toppled statue of former Soviet dictator Josef Stalin in a Moscow park in late 1991. Soon thereafter, on Christmas night 1991, the Soviet Union ceased to exist.

reunified Germany. Other communist governments in the region also fell, and the Warsaw Pact dissolved in early 1991.

It was hard to believe then, but the Soviet Union was next. The USSR soon collapsed, as its constituent republics declared their independence. On December 25, 1991, Gorbachev resigned his presidency of a country that no longer existed. That evening, the red hammer-and-sickle Soviet flag was lowered for the last time from the Kremlin's spires and replaced by the red, white, and blue Russian flag. Few novelists could have created a story of such sweep and drama. The Soviet Union was no more.

⊕ The Twenty-First Century Begins: Changes and Choices

"What is past is prologue," Shakespeare comments in *The Tempest*. That is as true for the real world of today and tomorrow as it was for the Bard's literary world of yesterday. One hopes that no future historian will be able to write a history of the coming century under the title *The Tempest*. Titles such as *As You Like It* or *All's Well That Ends Well* are more appealing possibilities for histories yet to be.

Whatever the future will bring, we are in a position similar to that of Banquo in *Macbeth*. He sought to know the future, and we can sympathize with him when he pleads with the Witches of Endore, "If you can look into the seeds of time, And say which grain will grow and which will not, Speak then to me." In Banquo's case, the witches gave him a veiled prophecy that he neither understood nor was able to escape. We are luckier; we have an ability to shape the harvest if we mind another bit of advice that Shakespeare gives, this time in *Much Ado About Nothing*. Our ability to achieve a favorable future, he advises, is determined "by the fair weather that you make yourself: it is needful that you frame the season for your own harvest."

The sections that follow are meant to help you determine your harvest during the coming decades by examining the factors and trends that will benefit or beset the world during your lifetime and beyond that into the future. To facilitate the discussion here, these topics are divided into four areas of changes and choices: political structure and orientation, security, international economics, and the quality of life.

POLITICAL STRUCTURE AND ORIENTATION: CHANGES AND CHOICES

There are a number of important changes occurring in the political orientation and organization of the international system. A new polar structure is emerging, the Western orientation of the system is weakening, and the authority of the state is being challenged from without and from within.

The Emerging Polar Structure

For all the significance of the collapse of the Soviet Union and the bipolar structure, an even more important change is the structure of the new international system. Scholars do not fully agree on how to characterize the system, in part because it is still evolving.

To a degree, the system resembles a *traditional multipolar system*, one that is structured and operates much like the system that existed until World War II. A few major powers dominate, with the power poles including the United States, China, Germany, Japan, and Russia. A few other countries, most notably India, with its huge population and nuclear weapons, may join that group. As chapter 3 explains, multipolar systems are characterized by patterns of alliances that are more fluid and

The international system has become less Westernized in the last several decades as more and more African, Asian, and other countries have gained independence and strength, and as they and their leaders have taken on increasingly important roles on the world stage. Fifty years ago the countries of both men with President George W. Bush in the White House Rose Garden in May 2001 were colonies of Great Britain. Olusegun Obasanjo, to the left, is president of now-independent Nigeria, and now-sovereign Ghana's Kofi Annan, to the right, is secretary-general of the United Nations.

complicated than the relationships in the bipolar system. Who is allied with whom and in opposition to whom will depend more on individual issues and on shifting circumstances than on fixed alliance systems. Russia and China vehemently oppose the U.S. plan to build a ballistic missile defense system, but Muslim discontent in their countries helped strengthen Moscow and Beijing's support of the U.S. antiterrorist campaign in the aftermath of the 9-11 attacks. The dominance of the United States in the current system also gives it characteristics of what might be termed a **limited unipolar system** (Huntington, 1999). In a unipolar system, a single **hegemonic power** dominates the system and plays the central role in both making and enforcing system rules. That is too strong to characterize the U.S. role in the current system, but it is also true that the United States is, by far, the strongest of the poles.

Yet other scholars believe that the system is evolving toward becoming a *modified multipolar system.* They think that it will not look or operate like a traditional multipolar system because states and alliances are now being joined by regional and global international organizations, such as the European Union and the United Nations, as major power centers. Analysts believe that these new types of major actors will change the dynamics of the international system in ways that are discussed in chapters 3 and 9.

The Weakening Western Orientation of the International System

The dominant Western orientation of the international system is weakening as a result of the expansion of the number and power of non-Western states. The colonial empires established by the imperial Western powers collapsed after World War II, and in the ensuing years over 100 new countries have gained independence (more than tripling the previous number). The vast majority of these new countries are located in Africa, Asia, and other non-Western regions. Wherever they are, non-Western countries have become a stronger voice in international affairs, and a few, especially China, have achieved enough power to command center stage. These countries have joined together in such movements and organizations as the Group of 77 in order to promote their causes. Moreover, they have also gained considerable sway in other international organizations. For example, non-Western countries now command a majority in the United Nations General Assembly (UNGA).

While these countries have many differences, they share several commonalities. Most are not well-off economically, earning them the commonly used sobriquet of less developed countries (LDCs). Most of these countries have an ethnic or racial makeup that is not Eurowhite, and they share a history of being colonies of or being dominated by Eurowhites. Furthermore, many of these countries have value systems that differ from the Western values that form the basis of current international law, concepts of human rights, and other standards in the international system (Neuman, 1998).

It should not be surprising, then, that many of these new or newly empowered countries support extensive changes in the international system. The result of all this is that the perspectives and demands of these countries are considerably changing the focus and tone of world political and economic debate.

Challenges to the Authority of the State

While the dynamics of the emerging international system are being determined in part by the changing polar configuration of states and by the rise in importance of non-Western states, the system is also being affected by the fact that states are no longer virtually the only important actors in the world drama. Instead, as Benjamin Barber (1996) contends in a book entitled *Jihad vs. McWorld: How Globalism and Tribalism Are Reshaping the World*, national states and the state-based structure of the world are being eroded by antithetical forces, some of which are splintering states into fragments (jihad, tribalism) and others of which are merging states into an integrated world (McWorld, globalism). As Barber (p. 4) puts it, if the first set of forces prevail, there is a "grim prospect of a retribalization of large swaths of humankind by war and bloodshed: a threatened balkanization of nation-states in which culture is pitted against culture, people against people, tribe against tribe, a Jihad in the name of a hundred narrowly conceived [identifications and loyalties]." The other trend, if it triumphs, melds "nations into one homogeneous global theme park, one McWorld tied together by communications, information, entertainment, and commerce." For now, Barber believes, "Caught between Babel and Disneyland, the planet is falling precipitously apart and coming reluctantly together at the very same moment."

The Forces of McWorld Many analysts believe that there are political, economic, and social pressures, the forces of **McWorld**, which are breaking down the importance and authority of states and moving the world toward a much higher degree of political, economic, and social integration.

Political integration, for example, is evident in the increasing number and importance of international organizations, such as the United Nations and the World Trade Organization (WTO). When there are trade disputes, countries are no longer free to impose unilateral decisions. Instead, they are under heavy pressure to submit disputes to the WTO for resolution.

Economic interdependence, the intertwining of national economies in the global economy, means that countries are increasingly less self-sufficient. As noted in chapter 1, national governments have a decreasing ability to manage their own economies. Instead, global trade, international monetary exchange, and other financial flows in the global marketplace play a strong part in determining the jobs we have, whether our investments rise or fall, our country's inflation rate, and many other economic matters. This loss of economic controls diminishes the general authority of a state. There is a lively debate over what this means for the future of states (Hout, 1997; Strange, 1997; Hirst & Thompson, 1996). But some scholars believe that, as one puts it, "Globalization will markedly constrain the autonomy and effectiveness of states and, at a minimum, raise serious questions about the meaning of internal and external sovereignty" (Korbin, 1996:26).

Social integration is also well under way in the view of many scholars. They believe that the world is being integrated—even homogenized—by the habits of cooperation and cross-cultural understanding that result from rapid travel and communication and from increased economic interchange of goods and services. People of different countries buy and sell each other's products at an ever-increasing rate; Cable News Network (CNN) is watched worldwide; the World Wide Web gives us almost instant global access to a wealth of information; e-mail has revolutionized communications; English is becoming something of a lingua franca for diplomacy, business, and other forms of international interaction. At a less august level, it is possible to travel around the world dining only on Big Macs, fries, and shakes at the 29,000 McDonald's outlets in 120 countries serving fast food to over 16 billion customers each year and taking in over $40 billion a year (of which 52 percent was earned outside the United States). Thus, amid some worrisome culinary trends, there are indications that we, the world's people, are moving toward living in a more culturally homogenized global village. This outward trend works to weaken inward-looking nationalism, the primary basis of identification with and loyalty to one's country.

The Forces of Tribalism States are also being tested by and are sometimes collapsing because of a number of pressures, including erosive ethnic rivalries. Barber's main title refers to this as *jihad* (an Arabic word that means struggling to spread or defend the faith), but because of the particular meaning of jihad, this text will use his other term, **Tribalism**, to refer to the process of disintegration.

The important point is that whatever one calls the process, the world has recently seen an upsurge of states splintering and collapsing under the pressure of secessionist forces. The Soviet Union dissolved into 15 independent countries in 1991, and some of them are ethnically unstable. Similarly, Yugoslavia broke apart, and one of its new republics, Bosnia, itself collapsed in ethnic warfare. In 1998 what was left of Serb-dominated Yugoslavia further convulsed when ethnic Albanians, who are a majority in Kosovo Province, rose up against Serb control. Elsewhere, what was Czechoslovakia is now two countries; the people of East Timor declared independence from Indonesia; Turkey's army wages war against separatist Kurds; the Hutu massacre in 1994 of hundreds of thousands of Tutsis exposed the myth of a single Rwandan people; the list could go on.

At the extreme, fragmented states can become what some observers called **failed states**. These are unified only in name, and in practice are a shell for a number of competing groups, none of which can govern effectively or long. Somalia is such a country and so is Afghanistan, as most Americans and others found out in 2001. The country is divided ethnically, linguistically, and religiously among Pashtuns (38 percent), Tajiks (25 percent), Uzbeks (6 percent), Hazaras (19 percent), and a host of even smaller groups (Aimaks, Baluchis, Brahuis, Kirghiz, Kipchaks, Kazakhs, Nuristanis, Turkmen, Wakhi, and others). Furthermore, most of these groups have subgroups, many of which are armed and controlled by individuals described accurately as warlords. "We are dealing with a failed state, a state with no working institutions, its infrastructure in ruins, many of its best brains in exile," is how Christopher Patten, the external relations commissioner of the European Union, described the situation.[1]

The example of Afghanistan also provides, according to one scholar, "a useful point of departure for understanding how failed and failing states, through the very ills that are brought about or exacerbated by their weakness, can have such disproportionate influence in regional and international politics in the new millennium." The lesson to draw, the scholar adds, is that "Afghanistan needs to be made into a functioning state if it is going to be kept from [once again] infecting the outside world."[2] The same could be said of other failed states.

SECURITY: CHANGES AND CHOICES

Military security in today's world is provided primarily by individual countries. Each state is responsible for its own protection and tries to maintain a military capability to defend its national interests. Other countries normally come to the aid of a country that has been attacked only if they find it in their national interest to become allies of that country or to otherwise support the beset country. Kuwait provides a good example. The United States came to Kuwait's aid mostly because of oil. If Kuwait produced tropical fruit, it is unlikely that a half-million U.S. troops would have rushed to defend the world's banana supply.

Whatever the advantages of national security based on self-reliance may be, there are also disadvantages. One is the cost. During the 10 year period 1991–2000, total world military expenditures amounted to $9 trillion, about one-third of which was U.S. military spending. A second drawback to the traditional way of providing security is that it is hard to say that it works very well when, during the twentieth century alone, over 111 million people were killed in wars. That is almost 6 times as many people as were killed in the nineteenth century and approximately 16 times the number of people slain during the century before that. Even more ominously, the advent of nuclear weapons, heralded by the atomic flash over Hiroshima on August 6, 1945, means that the next war could bring down the final curtain on humankind.

The limited ability of the forces provided by traditional military spending to provide security were also highlighted by the terrorist attacks of September 11, 2001, on the World Trade Center and the Pentagon, the headquarters of the U.S. military. The devastation raised global awareness of what has been termed **asymmetrical warfare**. As one analyst explained, "Pentagon and military intellectuals have long talked about a revolution in military affairs and the notion of 'asymmetrical warfare'—using unconventional tactics in combat rather than using forces of comparable size and employing similar tactics in battle. Terrorism takes the concept of asymmetrical warfare to another level by not even engaging military forces in battle."[3]

Did You Know That:
Total world military expenditures in 2000 were $804 billion. That was about equal to the year's combined GDPs of the following 21 countries: Albania, Bulgaria, Cambodia, El Salvador, Ethiopia, Finland, Hungary, Ireland, Malta, New Zealand, Oman, Peru, Rwanda, Somalia, Sri Lanka, Tanzania, Togo, Uganda, Uruguay, Zambia, and Zimbabwe.

The nature of the forces that use asymmetrical warfare also means that even after an attack they are difficult to defeat. President George Bush recognized this during his State of the Union address in January 2002 when he noted that despite the decisive U.S. victory in Afghanistan, "thousands of dangerous [terrorist] killers, schooled in the methods of murder, often supported by outlaw regimes, are now spread throughout the world like ticking time bombs, set to go off without warning."[4]

In the face of these realities, the world is beginning to work toward new ways of providing security, which chapter 13 details. *Arms control* is one trend. The high cost of conventional war and the probable cataclysmic result of a war using weapons of mass destruction (nuclear, biological, chemical) have forced the political system toward trying to avert Armageddon. During the last decade alone, new or revised treaties have been concluded to deal with strategic nuclear weapons, chemical weapons, land mines, nuclear weapons proliferation, and several other weapons issues.

International security forces are another relatively new thrust in the quest for security. United Nations peacekeeping forces provide the most prominent example of this alternative approach to security. In 1948 there were none, and there never had been a UN peacekeeping mission. In 1988 there were 5; in 2002 there were 15 under way, with over 47,000 military and police personnel deployed. Using such forces is in its infancy, but they may eventually offer an alternative to nationally based security. There are even calls for a permanent UN army that would be available for immediate use by the UN.

The Bush administration came to office in 2001 with a skeptical view of international security cooperation. The events of 9-11 did much to change that. The president and his top advisers quickly realized how little they could do, especially outside the immediate military sphere, without global support. "We are creating a coalition to go after terrorism," Secretary of State Colin Powell told an audience two days after the attack. "We are asking the United Nations and every other organization you can think of—NATO, the European Union, the Organization of Islamic Countries, the OAS, everybody—to join us once and for all in a great coalition to conduct a campaign against terrorists who are conducting war against civilized people."[5]

INTERNATIONAL ECONOMICS: CHANGES AND CHOICES

The years since World War II have included a number of trends in international economics that will continue to affect the international system as it moves through this century. Economic interdependence and economic disparity between the wealthy North and the relatively less developed South are two matters of particular note.

Economic Interdependence

One important economic change in the international system that has gained momentum since World War II is the growth of economic **interdependence**. The trade in goods and services during 2000 exceeded $7.6 billion; Americans alone own more than $7.1 trillion in assets (companies, property, stock, bonds) located in other countries, and foreigners own more than $8.7 trillion in U.S. assets; the flow of currencies among countries now exceeds $1.5 trillion every day.

This increasingly free flow of trade, investment capital, and national currencies across national borders has created such a high level of economic interdependence among countries that it is arguably misleading to talk of national economies in a singular sense. The impact of interdependence on virtually every citizen in every country is discussed briefly in chapter 1 and in depth in chapter 14. Suffice to say here, then, that whether you realize it or not, global finance affects everything from the price of the clothes that you wear, through the jobs that are available (or not) to you, to the interest you will pay on mortgages, car loans, and other debts.

To deal with this interdependence, the world during the last half-century has created and strengthened a host of global and regional economic organizations. The three most important global economic organizations are the World Bank, the International Monetary Fund (IMF), and the World Trade Organization (WTO). Additionally, there are numerous economic agencies associated with the UN and several regional organizations, such as the Association of Southeast Asian Nations (ASEAN), the European Union (EU), and Mercosur in South America that both respond to and further interdependence.

Before leaving our discussion of economic interdependence, it should be noted that the road to integration is neither smooth nor is its future certain. There are numerous difficulties. Trade and monetary tensions exist among countries. Many people are opposed to surrendering any of their country's sovereignty to the UN, the WTO, or any other international organization. Other people, concerned about workers' rights, product safety, and the environment, worry

Multinational corporations dominate the world economy. Coca Cola, which is organized into two companies (Coca Cola Corporation and Coca Cola Enterprises), had combined revenues in 2000 of $35.25 billion, and well over 100,000 employees. During the 1970s, Coke advertising featured a song, "I'd Like to Buy the World a Coke." That has become almost literally true. Coca Cola estimates that 6 billion of its products are bought each day globally, which means that, on average, every human on Earth samples a Coca Cola product daily. If this picture of a monkey in Thailand taking a Coke break is to be believed, humans are not the only ones worldwide who have acquired a taste for Coke and made the company into an international financial powerhouse.

It is often difficult for people in the United States and other economically developed countries to fully comprehend the depth of poverty that grips many people in the less developed countries. This picture of children scavenging in a garbage dump would be a scandal in one of the EDCs. The scene is unfortunately commonplace in many LDCs, including Iraq, where this picture was taken.

that free trade has allowed multinational corporations to escape effective regulation (Cutler, Haufler, & Porter, 1999). As one analyst puts it, the move to create an unfettered global economy "pulls capital into corners of the globe where there is less regulation, which in turn makes it harder for advanced nations to police their capital markets and social standards" (Kuttner, 1998:6). Indeed, these and other worries have sparked a growing opposition to and occasionally violent protests against further interdependence. There are, in short, significant choices to be made in how to order financial relations among countries.

Economic Disparity Between North and South

There is a wide disparity in economic circumstance between the relatively affluent life of a small percentage of the world population who live in a few countries and the majority of humanity who live in most countries. The terms North and South are used to designate the two economic spheres. The North symbolizes the wealthy and industrialized **economically developed countries (EDCs)**, which lie mainly in the Northern Hemisphere. By contrast, the South represents the **less developed countries (LDCs)**, the majority of which are near or in the Southern Hemisphere. The acronyms EDC, LDC, and associated designations are discussed in Explanatory Notes on page 571.

The economic and political ramifications of the North-South divide are discussed extensively in chapters 14, 15, and 16, but a few basic points are appropriate here. One is that the economic circumstances of countries are not truly dichotomized. Instead they range from general opulence (the United States) to unbelievable poverty (Bangladesh). There are some countries of the South that have achieved substantial industrialization and whose standards of living have risen rapidly. These countries are called **newly industrializing countries (NICs)**. Moreover, there are some wealthy people in LDCs and numerous poor people in EDCs.

(Continued on page 46)

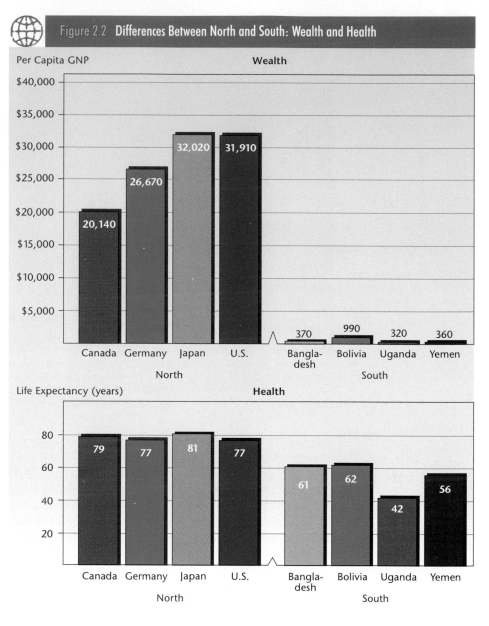

Figure 2.2 Differences Between North and South: Wealth and Health

Data source: World Bank (2002).

The difference between the lives of people in the North and those in the South is measured by per capita GNP wealth and life expectancy. By these, and many other standards, the people of the South are severely disadvantaged compared to those who live in the North.

Yet, it is also the case that such details cannot disguise the fact that there is a vast economic gap between North and South. The per capita **gross national product (GNP)** in 1999 of the North was $26,440. At $1,240, the per capita wealth of those in the South was a mere 4.7 percent of that of their contemporaries in the North. This immense gulf in wealth has devastating consequences for the poor. Their children, for instance, suffer an unconscionable mortality rate that is almost 7 times greater than the infant mortality rate in the wealthiest countries. As Figure 2.2 shows, and as the box The 6 Billionth Baby relates, by economic and health measures, the countries of the North and those of the South live in virtually different worlds. The North is predominantly a place of reasonable economic security, literacy,

(Continued on page 48)

THE 6 BILLIONTH BABY

October 12, 1999, was a Tuesday, and for the most part, it was not an unusual day. The twelfth of October was Columbus Day in many Spanish-speaking countries in the Americas and had once also been in the United States until the holiday had been shifted by law to the nearest Monday to stretch out the weekend. Elsewhere the people of Equitorial Guinea and Spain were celebrating their respective national days. Individually, the day marked the birthdays of some 16,438,356 people, give or take a few, around the world.

For all the prevailing "just another day" sense of October 12, though, it was a day of importance to humans and the Earth they inhabit. Somewhere in the world on that day, a first cry heralded the arrival of the baby who brought the global population to 6 billion. Carol Bellamy, executive director of UNICEF, dubbed the infant, the "6 Billionth Baby."[1]

When the world population reached 5 billion just 12 years, 3 months, and 1 day earlier on July 11, 1987, the UN decided to designate a child born on that date as the 5 billionth baby. The chosen symbol was Matej Gaspar, an infant born in Zagreb, in what was then Yugoslavia and what is now the capital of Croatia. One hopes that Matej is now a teenager and escaped the killing that engulfed Yugoslavia soon after he was born.

In the intervening 12 years, the UN thought better of bestowing what is not necessarily an accolade of being the next billionth baby on another child. Thus there was no symbolic baby named, and, in truth, there is no way to tell which of the approximately 358,988 babies born on October 12, 1999, was, indeed, the 6 billionth baby.

Thus it is impossible to know for sure if the child was a boy or a girl, whether he or she was born to wealth or poverty, or even if the baby lived or died quickly. Statistically, however, we can conclude that the chances are that the child's health, educational, economic, and other prospects are not very good. How could they be when only about 15 percent of the world's population lives in the relatively prosperous North and 85 percent lives in the less economically developed South? In fact, so many of the people in the South are so poor—often living on less than two or three dollars a day—that there is a 30 percent chance the 6 billionth baby was born into extreme poverty.

If in the birth lottery the baby was born in the South, then he or she, compared to a child in the North, is half as likely to have been delivered by a health professional, is twice as likely to have had a dangerously low birth weight, and is four times more likely to die before age 5. The baby is also 16 times more likely to have had his or her mother die from pregnancy or delivery complications, is 30 percent less likely to learn how to read and write, and, even if he or she does survive infancy, is still likely to live 11 years less than if he or she had been born in the North.

Whoever the 6 billionth baby is, then, we should all wish him or her luck. He or she will probably need it given the vast gap between the economic, health, educational, and other conditions in the North and South.

The world population reached 6 billion on October 12, 1999, according to UN calculations. The child, who might be called the "6 Billionth Baby," marked a 400 percent increase in the world population during the twentieth century alone. Perhaps the baby, one of about 359,000 born that day, came to an economically secure family. But with 85 percent of the world population living in less developed countries, the odds are great that the child, like the Cambodian baby in the picture, was born to a family who has to struggle against poverty and disease.

and adequate health care. By contrast, the lives of the people of the South are often marked by poverty, illiteracy, rampant disease, and early death.

One ramification of the weakening Western orientation of the international system discussed earlier is that this economic inequity is causing increased tension along the so-called North-South Axis. The LDCs are no longer willing to accept a world system in which wealth is so unevenly distributed.

Many people in the LDCs blame much of their poverty on past colonialist suppression and on what they believe are current efforts by the EDCs to continue to dominate the system by keeping the LDCs economically and politically weak. While such feelings do not justify terrorism, it is important to understand that the widespread grinding poverty among the LDCs is one of the factors that led to the rage behind the September 11, 2001, attacks on the United States. President Bush indirectly acknowledged that in his 2002 State of the Union speech, when he said he would take such actions as doubling the size of the Peace Corps so that it could "join a new effort to encourage development and education and opportunity in the Islamic world," with the goal of "eliminating threats and containing resentment" in order to "seek a just and peaceful world beyond the war on terror."[6]

The point, whether or not you believe that the EDCs oppress the LDCs, is that choices must be made in the face of the changes that are occurring. One option for the wealthy countries is to ignore the vast difference in economic circumstances between themselves and the LDCs. The other option is to do more, much more, to help. Both options carry substantial costs.

THE QUALITY OF LIFE: CHANGES AND CHOICES

The last few decades have spawned several changes involving the quality of human life that will continue to affect world politics in the new century and the choices we must face. Preserving human rights and the environment are two matters of particular note.

Human Rights

It borders on tautology to observe that violations of human rights have existed as far back into history as we can see. What is different is that the world is beginning to take notice of human rights violations across borders and is beginning to react negatively to them.

The change involves the **norms** of behavior that help regulate and characterize any political system. Behavior in virtually all political systems is governed by a mix of coercion and voluntary compliance. Norms, or values, are what determine voluntary compliance. For example, the values about the conduct of war are changing, and attacks on civilians are losing whatever legitimacy they may once have had. There are international tribunals trying individuals accused of war crimes and crimes against humanity in Rwanda and in the Balkans, including the former Serbian president of Yugoslavia, Slobodan Milosevic. Such prosecution may become even more common now that the treaty to establish a permanent International Criminal Court has been adopted.

There are numerous other areas in which the demand for the protection of human rights is louder and stronger. The rights of women are just one of the subjects that have recently become a focus of international concern and action, and women have become increasingly active in defense of their rights around the world. Women are "no longer guests on this planet. This planet belongs to us too. A revolution has begun," is how Gertrude Mongella, a Tanzanian diplomat, has put it with considerable accuracy.

During the past several decades, human rights has become an increasingly important theme of the global dialog. One of the consequences of the Taliban government in Afghanistan being ousted was that women were no longer required to wear the head-to-toe burqa, and the Taliban ban on their holding jobs and going to school was lifted. As this January 2002 picture indicates, it is taking the women of Afghanistan a while to accept that they will not be beaten if they show their faces in public, but at least one obviously pleased woman has decided to risk being liberated.

One of the many impacts of the U.S.-led action against the Taliban regime of Afghanistan is the relief it brought to the women of that country. Under the fundamentalist regime headed by religious leader Mullah Mohammad Omar, women were not allowed to work, go to school, travel unescorted, or appear in public except wearing a burqa, which is a head-to-toe draped garment with only a mesh opening to see through. It was symbolic that Sima Samar, Afghanistan's new minister of women's affairs, was seated in the visitors' gallery in the Capitol during President Bush's 2002 State of the Union message. She had long lived in exile in Pakistan, but had she returned to Afghanistan less than six months earlier, she would not have been allowed to appear in public with her face visible, much less serve in the country's cabinet.

As with many of the other issues that challenge us, it would be naive to pretend that the end of human rights abuses is imminent or that progress has not been excruciatingly slow. Yet it would also be wrong not to recognize that there is movement. Leaders at least discuss human rights concerns; that was virtually unheard of not many years ago. Sometimes, if still not usually, countries take action based on another country's human rights record. Human rights conferences are no longer unnoticed, peripheral affairs. A significant number of human rights treaties have been signed by a majority of the world's countries. In sum, what was once mostly the domain of do-gooders has increasingly become the province of presidents and prime ministers.

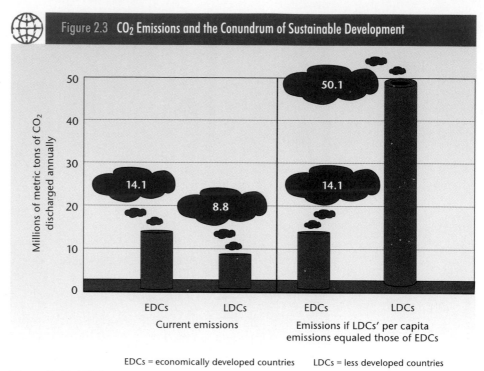

Figure 2.3   CO$_2$ Emissions and the Conundrum of Sustainable Development

EDCs = economically developed countries   LDCs = less developed countries

Data source: World Bank (2002).

The small percentage of the world's population who live in EDCs currently produce 63 percent of the carbon dioxide (CO$_2$) emissions. If the LDCs were to reach the same level of development as the EDCs, their CO$_2$ emissions would increase 569 percent and total world emissions would increase 280 percent. That would be an environmental disaster. The conundrum of sustainable development is how to help the LDCs develop in an environmentally acceptable way.

The Environment

The mounting degradation of the biosphere has its origins in the industrial revolution and, therefore, like the abuse of human rights, is not new to the world stage. Like human rights, what has changed is the attention that is now being paid to the subject and the international efforts to protect the environment that have begun.

The greatest challenge is to achieve **sustainable development**, that is, to (a) continue to develop economically while (b) simultaneously protecting the environment. As with human rights, progress on the environment has been slow, but progress is being made, as discussed in chapter 18. Among other advances, the subject has shifted from the political periphery to presidential palaces. What leaders have come to realize is that their national interests are endangered by environmental degradation, as well as by military and economic threats. As a White House national security report released in 2000 characterized the problem, environmental problems can "compromise our national security.... These threats respect no national boundary." The report went on to warn, "We face potentially... devastating threats if we fail to avert irreparable damage to regional ecosystems and the global environment. Other environmental issues, such as competition over scarce fresh water resources, are a potential threat to stability in several regions."[7]

The need to balance economic development and environmental protection is recognized, even by those countries that are struggling to alleviate widespread poverty and its associated ills. Yet achieving sustainable development will not be easy. Among other challenges, the LDCs need extensive assistance to develop in an environmentally responsible way. UN officials have placed that cost as high as $125 billion a year, and many observers believe that the North should bear a great deal of the cost for three reasons. One is that the North is much wealthier than the South. The second reason is that the North has historically emitted 70 percent of the carbon dioxide (CO_2) and a majority of most other pollutants, despite having less than one-quarter of the world population. "You can't have an environmentally healthy planet in a world that is socially unjust," Brazil's president Fernando Collor de Mello noted at one point.[8]

Third, even if you do not agree with the social justice view, it is arguable that the North should assist the South out of sheer self-interest. To better understand the North's stake in LDC development and its impact on the environment, consider Figure 2.3. On the left you can see that with about four times as many people, the LDCs only produce a little more than half as much CO_2 as the EDCs. On the right you can see that if the LDCs produced on a per capita basis the same amount of CO_2 as the EDCs, then the annual discharges of the LDCs would soar to 50.1 billion tons, an environmental disaster.

 Chapter Summary

1. This chapter has two primary goals. One is to establish a reference framework from which the historical examples used in this book can be understood in context. The second goal is to sketch the evolution of the current world political system.

2. The current world system began to develop in about the fifteenth century, when modern states started to form due to a process marked by both integration and disintegration of earlier political authority. The Treaty of Westphalia (1648), more than any other event, demarcated the change between the old and the new systems. With the sovereign state at its center, the newly evolving system is anarchical.

3. Several changes occurred during the 1700s and 1800s that had an important impact on the international system. The emergence of the concept of popular sovereignty involved a shift in the idea of who legitimately controls the state. The divine right of kings gave way to the notion that political power does, or ought to, come from the people. During these two centuries, the system also became Westernized and the multipolar configuration reached its apogee.

4. The twentieth century witnessed the most rapid evolution of the system. The multipolar system tottered, then fell. The bipolar system declined as other countries and transnational actors became more important, as the expense of continuing confrontation strained American and Soviet budget resources, and as the relative power of the two superpowers declined. The bipolar system ended in 1991 when the Soviet Union collapsed.

5. During the twentieth century, nationalism also undermined the foundations of multiethnic empires. European contiguous empires, such as the Austro-Hungarian Empire, disintegrated. The colonial empires dominated by Great Britain, France, and other Eurowhite countries also dissolved.

6. There are numerous new trends, uncertainties, and choices to make as we enter the twenty-first century. One significant question is what will follow the bipolar system. The most likely possibility is some form of modified multipolar system. But even though there are likely to be four or more major powers, as in a multipolar system, the system is unlikely to parallel earlier multipolar systems because of the other significant changes that have occurred in the international system. One such change is that international organizations have become much more numerous and more central to the operation of the international system.

7. Another shift in the international system is its weakening Western orientation. The number and strength of non-Western countries have grown substantially, and the strength of these states will almost certainly continue to grow in this century. These countries often have values that differ from those of the Western countries.

8. Challenges to the authority of the state represent a third shift in the international system, which has strong implications for the twenty-first century. There are both disintegrative internal challenges to the state and integrative external challenges.

9. The pursuit of peace is also at something of a crossroad. The destructiveness of modern weaponry has made the quest for peace even more imperative. There are two overriding issues. One is how to respond to the challenge that asymmetrical warfare presents to traditional national defense strategies. The second is whether to seek overall security through the traditional approach of self-reliance or to place greater emphasis on international peacekeeping, arms control, and other alternative international security approaches.

10. The international economy is also changing in ways that have important implications for the twenty-first century. Economic interdependence has progressed rapidly. The transnational flow of trade, investment capital, and currencies has economically entwined all countries. There are, however, counterpressures, and countries have important choices to make in the near future. One is whether to continue down the newer path to economic integration or to halt that process and follow more traditional national economic policies. If the decision is to continue toward greater economic integration, then a second choice is how to regulate the global economy to deal with the legitimate concerns of those who are suspicious of or even outright opposed to greater globalization.

11. The effort to resolve the wide, and in many ways growing, gulf between the economic circumstances of the countries of the economically developed North and the less economically developed South is also a mounting issue in the new century.

12. A final set of issues that must be addressed in the new century involve the quality of life: human rights and the environment. Both issues have become the subject of much greater international awareness, action, progress, and interaction. Yet ending the abuses of human rights and protecting the environment are still distant goals.

System-Level Analysis

Mad world! Mad kings! Mad composition!

Shakespeare, *King John*

If you live among wolves you have to act like a wolf.

Soviet leader Nikita Khrushchev, 1971

Chapter Objectives

After completing this chapter, you should be able to:

- Describe what international systems are and how they help the political scientist understand the world.
- Analyze systemic factors and understand their application to international politics.
- Characterize national and supranational actors in the international system.
- List the types and characteristics of transnational actors, including intergovernmental and nongovernmental organizations.
- Understand the international system's scope and level of interaction.
- Distinguish among the kinds and operations of the different system poles and discuss the effects of varying relative power concentrations.
- Explain how power assets, norms of behavior, and geographic characteristics affect the distribution and exercise of power in the system. Address how changes in the number or power of major actors can alter the international system.
- Discuss how changes in power are related to system stability.
- Understand how a system's economic patterns affect the operation of the system.
- Understand the norms that help determine patterns of behavior and system stability and why those norms may be changing.
- Explore some possible directions of the future international system.
- Understand the strengths and shortcomings of a system-level analysis.

The discussion in chapter 1 of how to study international politics introduces levels of analysis as an analytical concept. The issue is where to focus our study of world politics. Is it most fruitful to study the nature of the world (system-level analysis), to study how countries make foreign policy (state-level analysis), or to study people as individuals or as a species (individual-level analysis)? The best answer is to understand all three levels. Chapter 2 surveys system-level analysis through a brief overview of the evolution of the current world system. This chapter examines system-level analysis by discussing it as a theory. Chapter 4 takes up state-level analysis, and chapter 5 focuses on individual-level analysis.

System-level analysis is a "top-down" approach to studying world politics. It begins with the view that countries and other international actors operate in a global social-economic-political-geographic environment and that the specific characteristics of the system help determine the pattern of interaction among the actors. Systems analysts believe that any system operates in somewhat predictable ways—that there are behavioral tendencies that the actor countries usually follow.

Political systems are an ever-present part of our lives. Although each of us has free will, each of us is also part of many overlapping systems that influence our behavior and make it reasonably, although far from perfectly, predictable. These systems range from very local ones, such as your family and school, to much larger systems, such as your country and the world. Whatever its size, though, how a political system operates is based on four factors: structural characteristics, power relationships, economic realities, and norms.

Structural Characteristics of the International System

All systems have identifiable structural characteristics. These include how authority is organized, who the actors are, and what the scope and level of interaction among the actors is.

THE ORGANIZATION OF AUTHORITY

The authority structure of a system for making and enforcing rules, for allocating assets, and for conducting other authoritative tasks can range from very hierarchical to anarchical. Most systems, like your university and your country, are hierarchical. They have a **vertical authority structure** in which subordinate units answer to higher levels of authority. Vertical systems have central authorities that are responsible for making, enforcing, and adjudicating rules that restrain subordinate actors. Other systems have a **horizontal authority structure** in which authority is fragmented. The international system is one such system with a mostly horizontal authority structure. It is based on the sovereignty of states. *Sovereignty* means that countries are not legally answerable to any higher authority for their international or domestic conduct (Jackson, 1999). As such, the international system is anarchic; it has no overarching authority to make rules, settle disputes, and provide protection.

To see how horizontal and vertical structures operate differently, ask yourself why all countries are armed and why few students bring guns to class. The reason is that states in the international system (unlike students in your college) depend on themselves for protection. If a state is threatened, there is no international 911 number that it can call for help. Given this self-help system, each state feels compelled to be armed.

While the authority structure in the international system remains decidedly horizontal, change is under way. Many analysts believe that sovereignty is declining and that even the most powerful states are subject to an increasing number of authoritative rules made by intergovernmental organizations (IGOs) and by international law. In 2002, for example, the World Trade Organization (WTO) appeals board ruled in favor of the European Union (EU) in a complaint the EU brought against the United States, charging that the U.S. practice of giving tax breaks to U.S. companies for goods they sold in Europe and elsewhere abroad amounted to a government subsidy of exports, a violation of world trade rules. Offsetting the sting of such losses, the United States has prevailed at other times in the WTO. One of these victories came in 2000, when the WTO found in favor of a U.S. complaint that Canada was illegally infringing on U.S. patent rights. Countries still resist and often even reject IGO governance when it touches on sensitive political issues, but that does not negate the slowly growing authority of IGOs in the international system.

Countries are also no longer totally free to make internal policy on even purely domestic matters. For example, the United Nations (UN) condemned the military overthrow of democracy in Haiti and authorized the U.S.-led intervention in 1994 that toppled the military junta. International tribunals sitting in Tanzania and the Netherlands are trying, respectively, individuals for atrocities committed within Rwanda and in the Balkans. The trial of Slobodan Milosevic, the former president of Yugoslavia, is one of those taking place. Sovereignty certainly continues as a cornerstone of the authority structure of the international system. There is, however, a growing view among many that sovereignty is and ought to be limited. This sense was captured by Pope John Paul II, who told the UN General Assembly that while every country has "the right to shape its life according to its own traditions," this sovereign authority excluded "of course, every abuse of basic human rights and in particular the oppression of minorities."[1]

THE ACTORS

Another characteristic of any system is its actors. What organizations operate in the system, and what impact do they have on the course of international relations? We can answer these questions by dividing actors into three general categories: national actors, international actors, and transnational actors.

States as Actors

Countries (states) are the principal actors on the world stage. A **state** is a tangible, sovereign political entity that possesses territory as well as a number of other characteristics detailed in chapter 8. States can generally be identified by such objective criteria as having a defined territory and a government.

Before discussing states as actors, it is important to note that this book and many other works in political science differentiate the term state from two other important terms, nation and government. As detailed in chapter 6, a **nation** is a group of people who identify with one another politically because of common characteristics, such as shared history, language, culture, religion, or race. Americans are a nation; the United States is a state. The term **government** can be used in two ways. It can refer to a type of government, such as the democratic system in Canada or the authoritarian system in China. Government can also designate the specific regime, such as the government of Prime Minister Jean Chrétien in Canada or that of President Jiang Zemin in China.

Because states are the most important actors, the current configuration is termed a **state-centric system**. The leading role that states play in the international system is determined by several factors, including state sovereignty, the state's status as the primary focus of people's political loyalty, and the state's command of the preponderance of economic and military power.

Inasmuch as the nature and operation of states and their governments are dealt with extensively in chapters 8 and 4 respectively, we will not detail them here. What is important for this discussion, though, is that states dominate the action and act with independence. Yet for all this talk of the pivotal role of sovereign states in a largely anarchical international system with a horizontal authority structure, it is also true that states are not the only system-level actors. Moreover, there are significant centralizing forces in the system that are slowly moving it, at least somewhat, toward a vertical authority structure.

International Governmental Organizations as Actors

A second group of system-level actors are made up of an array of international organizations. These actors are also called **intergovernmental organizations (IGOs)**. Almost all IGOs have a central administrative structure. The UN is headquartered in New York City and has an administrative staff headed by a secretary general.

A significant thing to remember about IGOs is that more and more in the past century, states have come to share the stage with this relatively new type of actor (Tarrow, 2001). One indication of the enhanced role of IGOs is the steep rise in their number. In 1900 there were 30 IGOs. That number has increased approximately tenfold, with nearly 300 IGOs now in existence. Chapter 9 deals extensively with IGOs. Therefore, here we can confine our preview of IGOs to considering their membership, roles, and authority.

The United Nations is an important example of the many international organizations that have come on the world scene since 1945. Their roles, importance, and authority in the international system have increased greatly.

IGO Membership The key characteristic of IGOs that distinguishes them from other types of international organizations is that IGOs have individual countries as members. Some IGOs, such as the UN, have member-countries from all parts of the world and, in fact, are approaching universal membership. The membership of other IGOs is regional, with a more limited geographic scope; for example, regional location is the basis of membership in the Organization of African Unity (OAU). Yet other IGOs have membership based on a common interest among members. An example is the Organization of Petroleum Exporting Countries (OPEC), which includes such oil-producing and exporting countries as Indonesia, Nigeria, and Venezuela, in addition to its members from the Middle East.

IGO Roles IGOs are involved in a wide array of activities and some IGOs have multiple functions. The UN, for one, is a general-purpose IGO that works to protect or improve the environment, human rights, and economic conditions, as well as to promote peace and to address other more traditional political matters. Other IGOs are more specialized—the World Health Organization (WHO) is an example, as is Interpol, whose activities are outlined in the box, World's Top Cop. In Table 3.1, take note of the wide range of IGO activities, the diversity of the locations of their headquarters, and the various nationalities of the administrators who head them.

Table 3.1 Sample Intergovernmental Organizations, 2001			
Organization	Members	Headquarters	Chief Officer
International Atomic Energy Agency	132	Austria	Egyptian
International Civil Aviation Organization	187	Canada	Brazilian
International Fund for Agricultural Development	162	Italy	Swedish
International Maritime Organization	158	United Kingdom	Canadian
International Monetary Fund	183	United States	German
United Nations	189	United States	Ghanaian
World Bank	183	United States	American
World Health Organization	191	Switzerland	Norwegian
World Meteorological Organization	185	Switzerland	Nigerian
World Trade Organization	144	Switzerland	Thai

Intergovernmental organizations perform a wide variety of functional, or nonpolitical, tasks in the world today, whether they concern themselves with tracking down criminals, regulating civil aviation, or promoting health.

Alliances are a special type of IGO. Most alliances are merely military treaties, but a few also have organizational structures and have taken on roles beyond their original military purpose (Bennet, 1997; Mansfield & Bronson, 1997). Indeed, it is possible for alliances to survive even after the reason for their formation has been eliminated. A prime example is the North Atlantic Treaty Organization (NATO), which is altering both its functions and its geographic scope (Borawski & Young, 2001; Mattox & Rachwald, 2001). These changes are discussed in the box, The New NATO Marches East (pages 60–61).

IGO Authority A key issue for IGOs is the basis of their authority. Are they merely shells for national diplomacy and policy or do IGOs make policy independently? Traditionally, IGOs have had little independent authority. Instead they have been and remain primarily vehicles for the diplomacy of their member-states (Sterling-Folker, 2002). Countries try to build a coalition IGO in order to garner enough votes to have it pursue a particular policy. This is called parliamentary diplomacy and is discussed in chapter 10. Iraq and the United States, for example, vie within the UN to loosen or retain the UN economic sanctions on Iraq that were imposed after the Persian Gulf War (1990–1991).

Many observers believe, however, that the authority of IGOs is growing and that they are beginning to constitute a centralizing force in the international system by becoming important actors that exercise authority in their own right. It can even be said that some IGOs demonstrate early signs of becoming **supranational organizations**. Such organizations are those whose authority, at least in theory, supersedes the sovereignty of their individual members. We noted earlier, for instance, that at the global level the WTO has the ability to review the laws and policies of the United States and other member-countries to ensure that they meet the standards of the world's most important trade treaty, the General Agreement on Tariffs and Trade (GATT).

(Continued on page 58)

WORLD'S TOP COP

If anyone can rightfully claim the title of world's top cop it is Ronald K. Noble, who in November 2001 became the secretary-general of the International Criminal Police Organization, better known as Interpol. He will play a key role in fighting transnational crime.

Globalization has many benefits, but it has its drawbacks also. One of the negatives is the globalization of crime. Whether the criminals are garden-variety white-collar embezzlers, organized mob members, drug runners, or terrorists, there is a rapid increase in how they can and do operate across national boundaries. Interpol is an important IGO in the global effort to control transnational crime.

The organization was founded in 1923, and the United States joined in 1938. Initially Interpol's headquarters were located in Vienna, Austria, but it relocated to Paris after World War II and then to Lyon, France. It currently has 179 member-states and an annual budget of over $26 million. Its overall policy is set by its assembly, which includes all members. Interpol's staff number just under 400, of whom about one-third are police experts, with the rest being technical and administrative support personnel.

The agency's new head, Secretary-General Noble, is American, and he brought impressive qualifications to his job as the world's top cop. He graduated from Stanford University Law School and became an assistant U.S. attorney general in Philadelphia, where he never lost a case. During 1988 and 1989, Noble was the chief of staff of the Criminal Division, U.S. Department of Justice. He served from 1994 to 1996 in the U.S. Treasury Department as undersecretary for enforcement, a position that included supervision of the Secret Service, Customs Service, and Bureau of Alcohol, Tobacco and Firearms. When named the new head of Interpol, Noble was a professor of criminal law at New York University Law School.

Interpol does not have armed officers or arrest powers like most local and national police forces. Instead, it acts as an international clearinghouse for information by maintaining records and helping countries exchange information about criminals (such as the location of known international criminals as well as fingerprint, DNA, and other information) and about a wide variety of crimes (such as counterfeiting

The activities of the International Criminal Police Organization (Interpol) have drawn more attention since the terror attacks on the World Trade Center and the Pentagon. The agency formed a September 11 Task Force to fight international terrorism. Indicative of that effort, Interpol director, Ronald K. Noble, a former U.S. assistant attorney general, is holding up a document containing a photograph of Osama bin Laden during an Interpol meeting in Madrid three days after the attacks.

and drug trafficking). In more recent years, cyber crime, including transmitting viruses, and terrorism have become an increasing part of Interpol's focus. The events of September 11, 2001, sharpened that focus. Secretary-General Noble was an expert at combating money laundering in the United States, and he has pledged to put that expertise to use. As he noted, "Interpol is committed to both the fight against terrorism and the funds that make such heinous acts possible. We are dedicated to the task of shutting down funds earmarked for terror."[1]

At the regional level, the 15-member EU has evolved further than any other IGO toward supranational authority. In addition to achieving a high degree of economic integration, including a new common currency called the euro, which went into general circulation on January 1, 2002, the EU has created a quasi-government with limited decision-making authority. Some Europeans favor the development of the EU into a true federal European government. For example, Germany's chancellor Gerhard Schröder proposed in April 2001 a plan that would so significantly strengthen the authority of the EU relative to its member-states that, as one newspaper commented, "if accepted in an EU constitutional convention in 2004, [it] would lay the foundations for what the most ardent integrationists see as an eventual United States of Europe."[2] Not all Europeans agree, and the future is uncertain. Despite such reservations, it is remarkable how far the once divided, often warring countries of Europe have moved toward a truly supranational European Union (Calleo, 2001; Preston, 1998).

Transnational Organizations as Actors

A third category of actors in the international system is **transnational actors.** These are organizations that operate internationally, but whose membership, unlike IGOs, is private. The two most numerous and most organized types are nongovernmental organizations and multinational corporations. In the post–9-11 world, we must also take note of terrorist groups as another type of transnational actor.

Nongovernmental Organizations Like IGOs, **nongovernmental organizations (NGOs)** operate across borders. Unlike IGOs, NGO membership consists of private individuals and groups. Amnesty International and Greenpeace are examples of NGOs. Both the number and importance of NGOs is increasing on the world stage. In 1900 there were 69 NGOs. Since then the number of NGOs has expanded 70-fold to approximately 5,000. Furthermore, the influence and range of activities of these transnational actors are growing as their numbers increase and as technological advances allow them to operate more effectively across political boundaries. The most important aspect of NGOs, according to one analyst, is that their "role in global negotiations and global governance has been emerging stealthily and slowly over the last quarter century" (Phan, 1996:2). This role most commonly occurs when numerous NGOs that have an interest in one aspect or another of global society link together with supportive national organizations, sympathetic government agencies, and IGOs to form what one study refers to as **transnational advocacy networks (TANs).** The IGOs that constitute a TAN have "shared values" and exchange "information and services" related to their mutual concern with human rights, the environment, or some other subject (Keck & Sikkink, 1998:2; Hawkins, 1999).

The place of NGOs on the world stage has become so established that they have achieved a degree of formal recognition by the UN and other international actors (Raustiala, 1997; Weiss, 1998). For example, major UN conferences on world problems now have two centers. One is the IGO meeting itself, to which countries send delegates. The other is a parallel NGO meeting attended by representatives of private groups. This practice began with the UN-sponsored Earth Summit held in Brazil in 1992, and it is now a part of virtually all major UN-sponsored conferences. For example, when the United Nations World Conference Against Racism met in Durban, South Africa, during September 2001, the

International nongovernmental organizations (NGOs) are important global actors. Like most UN-sponsored official conferences, the World Conference Against Racism held in Durban, South Africa, during September 2001 had a parallel conference of NGOs meeting nearby. In this picture a delegate to the NGO conference shows opposition to the U.S. decision to leave the official conference to protest what the Bush administration considered unfair charges of racism against Israel.

THE NEW NATO MARCHES EAST

The North Atlantic Treaty Organization was formed in 1949 to save Western Europe from what many believed to be a threat from the Soviet Union. Then, after NATO had stood guard for 45 years, the USSR collapsed. The end of NATO's original purpose did not mean, however, that the alliance disappeared. Instead, NATO is undergoing a metamorphosis in which it is expanding both its role and its membership.

The first way that NATO has sought new life is by expanding its mission to include crisis intervention and peacekeeping (Yost, 1999). Bosnia provided the first example of the new mission. After several years of ineffective attempts to end the fighting there, NATO finally moved militarily in 1995. NATO air strikes against the Bosnian Serbs helped bring them to the peace table. The multinational Implementation Force (IFOR) that moved into Bosnia, and remains there, is essentially a NATO operation.

Four years later, NATO once again found itself using force to restore peace in the Balkans. In this case, Kosovo was the focus of NATO action. It is important to know that the reason NATO intervened was not because of a military threat to the alliance. Rather, according to NATO's secretary general, there was a "shocking picture of a planned campaign of violence against Kosovar Albanian civilians." Between March and June 1999, NATO warplanes and cruise missiles conducted over 10,000 strikes that pummeled targets in Serbia, Montenegro, and Kosovo (all provinces in Yugoslavia) in an effort to force the Serbs to end their attempt to ethnically cleanse Kosovo of its majority Albanian ethnic population. Once that succeeded, approximately 45,000 troops (mostly from NATO, with small contingents from other countries)

The North Atlantic Treaty Organization has transformed itself from an alliance to deter a Soviet attack to a more general security organization that primarily keeps peace in Europe. NATO forces have intervened since the mid-1990s in Bosnia, in Kosovo, and most recently in Macedonia. This picture shows German soldiers on patrol in an armored tank near Skopje, the capital of Macedonia, in late 2001, as part of NATO's efforts to prevent further fighting between the country's ethnic Albanian minority and its ethnic Macedonian-dominated government.

formed the Kosovo Force, or KFOR, entered Kosovo, and remain there to maintain order.

A third NATO crisis intervention in the Balkans occurred in September 2001 when 3,500 NATO troops moved into Macedonia. The goal was to stabilize the country, which had been torn by fighting between its ethnic Macedonian majority (66 percent) and its sizable ethnic Albanian minority (23 percent).

official governmental conference was attended by 30 heads of state and delegations from more than 150 countries. The parallel NGO Forum drew some 7,000 representatives from approximately 1,000 NGOs. A sense of the diversity of these NGOs can be gained from a sampling of them, including Amnesty International, Black Parent Speaks, B'nai Brith Canada, European Women's Lobby, Grupo de Lesbianas Feministas (de Peru), Human Rights Watch, Inter-Church Committee for Refugees, Physicians for Human Rights, and the Tibetan Centre for Human Rights and Democracy.

In addition to making their views known to officials and through the media to the world community, such NGO conferences also help to build TANs by expanding the network of contacts, organizations, and knowledge that delegates can use to promote their efforts. "I don't think the world will ever be the same again," predicted Brownie Ledbetter, an American delegate. "Here we have women networking from all over the world, across incredible barriers. And with faxes and the Internet, it will grow even more."[3]

NATO's most recent call to action came in September 2001. In the immediate aftermath of the attacks on the World Trade Center and the Pentagon, NATO invoked Article 5 of its charter. This article declares that an attack on any member-state is an attack on all the members of the alliance, implying automatic European backing for U.S. retaliation. By doing so, NATO for the first time its 52-year history committed each member-state to take "such action as it deems necessary, including the use of armed force, to restore and maintain the security of the North Atlantic area." Certainly an attack had occurred on the United States. But one has to wonder what the leaders who established NATO in 1949 to counter the Soviet threat would have thought. Could they have foreseen that NATO's first act of self-defense would be a response to an attack launched by a multiethnic terrorist organization headquartered in Afghanistan, using civilian aircraft as weapons?

The second aspect of NATO's evolution involves expanding its membership. The designation "North Atlantic" is being strained by the admission of states in Eastern Europe. The first step came in 1999 when the Czech Republic, Hungary, and Poland joined the alliance. Also that year, in the words of a NATO fact sheet, leaders of the member-countries meeting in Washington, D.C., "reaffirmed... their enduring commitment to NATO's Open Door policy, pledging that this round of NATO enlargement will not be the last." According to the fact sheet, nine countries (Albania, Bulgaria, Estonia, Latvia, Lithuania, Macedonia, Romania, Slovakia, and Slovenia) have declared their wish to join NATO, and the alliance intends to "help those states build the strongest possible candidacy for future membership."[1]

President George W. Bush, despite some early skepticism about the U.S. involvement in NATO in particular and multilateralism in general, supports NATO's continued expansion. Speaking in Poland at the University of Warsaw, the president declared, "All of Europe's new democracies, from the Baltic to the Black Sea and all that lie between, should have the same chance for security and freedom, and the same chance to join the institutions of Europe [including NATO], as Europe's old democracies."[2] Read literally, this invitation would ironically include Russia and several other former Soviet republics.

What remains unclear is what the expansion of NATO's role and membership will mean in the future. The change in role may well mean that American, Canadian, and European forces will engage in more peacekeeping missions, like the ones in Bosnia, Kosovo, and Macedonia. In this sense, NATO is no longer exclusively, or even primarily, an alliance designed to ward off an outside threat. Instead, at least for now, it is a regional peacekeeping organization dedicated to keeping stability within its region by intervening in civil wars and other internal disturbances.

The expansion of NATO's membership also means that the United States and other members are now required to come to the defense of Poland and other states far from the North Atlantic. Nine other countries are seeking admission to NATO, and the inclusion of some of those will bring the NATO (and, therefore, the U.S.) defensive commitment to the very border of Russia. How Americans will react if the need arises to defend Poland from an invasion by the Russians or some other aggressor or, under Article 5, to assist a European country that has suffered a terrorist attack masterminded from afar remains to be seen.

Multinational Corporations A second important type of transnational actor consists of **multinational corporations (MNCs)**, also sometimes referred to as **transnational corporations (TNCs)**. By whatever name, the expansion of international trade, investment, and other financial interactions has brought with it the rise of huge MNCs. These businesses have production and other operations that extend beyond mere sales in more than one country. The role of MNCs is discussed in detail in chapter 14, but suffice it to say here that the economic power of these corporate giants gives them a substantial role in international affairs. Some idea of the economic power of the MNCs can be gained from comparing their gross corporate product (GCP: sales, and other revenues) to the **gross national product (GNP:** a measure of all goods and services produced by a country's citizens and businesses) of various countries (Figure 3.1). The largest MNC in 2000, ExxonMobil, had a GCP of $210.4 billion that was about equal to the GNP of Austria ($204.2), more than twice Egypt's GNP ($95.2 billion), about 3 times the GNP of Chile ($69.9 billion),

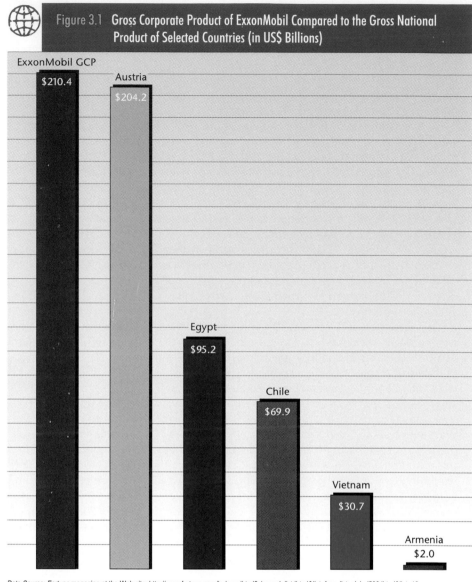

Figure 3.1 Gross Corporate Product of ExxonMobil Compared to the Gross National Product of Selected Countries (in US$ Billions)

Data Source: Fortune magazine at the Web site: http://www.fortune.com/indexw.jhtml?channel=list.jhtml&list_frag=list_global500.jhtml&list=19.

Multinational corporations (MNCs) are one category of NGO. Some idea of the enormous economic power of MNCs can be gained by comparing the 2000 gross corporate product (revenues) of Exxon-Mobil, the world's largest MNC, to the gross national product (earnings) of selected countries.

almost 7 times greater than Vietnam's GNP ($30.7 billion), and about 110 times Armenia's GNP ($2.0 billion).

Terrorist Groups A third type of transnational actor with which we must deal is **terrorist groups**. The U.S. State Department's "2001 Report on Foreign Terrorist Organizations" lists 28 such groups, including al-Qaeda.[4] Even more ominously, the Federation of American Scientists list of 370 such groups in its report on "Liberation Movements, Terrorist Organizations, Substance Cartels, and Other Para-State Entities."[5] The combined membership of these organizations is uncertain, but it is in the tens of thousands.

Terrorist organizations bring together private individuals who attack civilians and use other methods to inflict pain on an opponent. The goal of the terrorists is to gain compliance with their wishes by undermining the opponent's morale and by making it seem better that opponents give in to the demands of the terrorists than risk further suffering. Terrorism is discussed extensively in chapter 12, but we should note here that a number of changes in the international system have made it easier for such groups to operate. Increasingly, terrorist groups are able to travel and communicate globally with ease. Through their networks (cells) scattered all over the globe, they can also readily move funds from country to country, sometimes as easily as by using a charge card or an ATM card.

All these and other elements of the transnational aspect of terrorism came to the fore as the world learned about the activities of al-Qaeda. Osama bin Laden, the leader of al-Qaeda, was born in Saudi Arabia; his chief deputies, Dr. Ayman al-Zawahiri and Muhammed Atef, both came from Egypt. Of the 19 suicide hijackers who perished aboard the four U.S. airlines on September 11, 15 were Saudi, 2 were from the United Arab Emirates, 1 was from Lebanon, and 1 was from Egypt. Most of al-Qaeda's members were Saudis, Egyptians, Pakistanis, and people from other predominantly Muslim countries. But individuals from Canada, France, and Great Britain were also among al-Qaeda's members, which for that matter additionally included an American, John Walker Lindh, who was captured during the fighting in northern Afghanistan.

Did You Know That:
The term "al-Qaeda" (or "al Qa'ida") is Arabic for "the base."

SCOPE AND LEVEL OF INTERACTION

A third structural characteristic of any political system is the range (scope) of areas in which the actors interact and the frequency and intensity (level) of those interactions. One key to understanding the evolution of the international system is to see that the scope and level of international interaction are very much higher now than they were during the 1800s or even in the first half of the 1900s.

Economic interdependence provides the most obvious example of the escalating scope and level of interaction. It is nonsense today to imagine that any country can go it alone in splendid isolation. Even for a powerful country like the United States, a "fortress America" policy is impossible. Without foreign oil, to pick one obvious illustration, U.S. transportation and industry would literally soon come to a halt. Without extensive trade, the U.S. economy would stagger because exports are a key factor in economic growth. American exports of goods and services in 2000 accounted for 7.3 percent of the U.S. GNP that year, which makes them an important factor in the health of the U.S. economy.

Data about expanding trade and other forms or international economic interchange does not, however, capture fully the degree to which the widening scope and intensifying level of global financial interaction is increasing transnational contacts among people. Modern telecommunications and travel, for example, are making once relatively rare personal international interactions commonplace. Foreign travel is just one telling indication of this change. Between 1990 and 2000 the number of foreign visitors to the United States jumped 29 percent from 39.4 million to 50.9 million. During the same period, the number of Americans traveling overseas increased 35 percent from 44.6 million to 60.2 million. People used to talk about the "mysterious Orient" or "darkest Africa." Now Americans by the millions visit these places, and people from abroad are regular visitors to the United States.

It is important to note that the range and intensity of interaction has important political implications. Some theorists argue that large-scale, extended war is becoming difficult or impossible between economically interdependent countries. According to this theory, for example, the world should be safe from the intrastate warfare in Europe that earlier led to two world wars. A related theory holds that the chance of war has decreased because of increased cultural contact among countries through modern travel and communications. Insofar as either of these theories is true, interdependence will bring greater peace. But it may be that the converse is also true: If conflict does erupt in an interdependent world, it will be harder to stand apart from the fray, as the Persian Gulf War demonstrated in 1991. It is also the case, as noted, that the degree to which the world has become interconnected has increased the global reach of terrorists and, to a degree, their motivation to strike.

Power Relationships in the International System

Having examined the structural characteristics of the international system, we can turn our attention to another key factor: power relationships. The central idea to understand here is that the distribution of power within a system affects the way that the system operates. To see this, we can look at three topics: the number of poles, the concentration of power, and the causes and effects of changes in power.

NUMBER OF SYSTEM POLES

Many analysts believe that a pivotal determinant of how any given system operates is the number of major power poles that it has. Traditionally, a **power pole** in a system has consisted of either (1) a single country or empire or (2) a group of countries that form an alliance or a bloc. It is possible that in the future a global IGO, such as the UN, or a regional IGO, such as the EU, might acquire enough power and independence from its member-states to constitute a pole. While we will concentrate on global polar relations, it is worth noting that regions also have more localized polar structures. In the words of one study, "the international system is composed of multiple, overlapping systems. The global system encompasses all the states in the world, while regional systems comprise only local members" (Lemke & Warner, 1996:237). China, Japan, and the United States, for instance, constitute what has been termed a "triad of another kind" in the Asia-Pacific region (Zhang & Montaperto, 1999). It also may be that a country such as India can be a regional pole without being a global power.

There are several ways that the number of poles affects the conduct of the international system. To see this, we can examine two factors that may vary according to the number of poles in a system. One is the rules of the game of power politics. The second is the propensity of a system for instability and war.

The Rules of the Game

Some political scientists believe that the pattern of interaction varies according to the number of poles that a system has. It is possible, for example, to identify patterns or rules of the game for unipolar, bipolar, tripolar, and multipolar systems. It is especially interesting to compare bipolar and multipolar systems in order to contrast the rules of the system that has just passed with the rules of the system that is now evolving. Figure 3.2 displays four types of system structures and ways in which the patterns of interaction differ across them.

Unipolar Systems There are two ways an international **unipolar system** could occur. One would be if one country or group of countries were able to dominate the system. The second way would be through the establishment of a world government.

Domination by a **hegemonic power** or hegemonic alliance has never really happened, although in ancient times the Roman, Mongolian, and Chinese empires incorporated or controlled all or most of the established societies in the world. There have been times, however, when one country came close to dominating international relations. Great Britain stood as a hegemonic power for a good part of the

(Continued on page 66)

Figure 3.2 Models and Rules of the Game of Various International System Structures

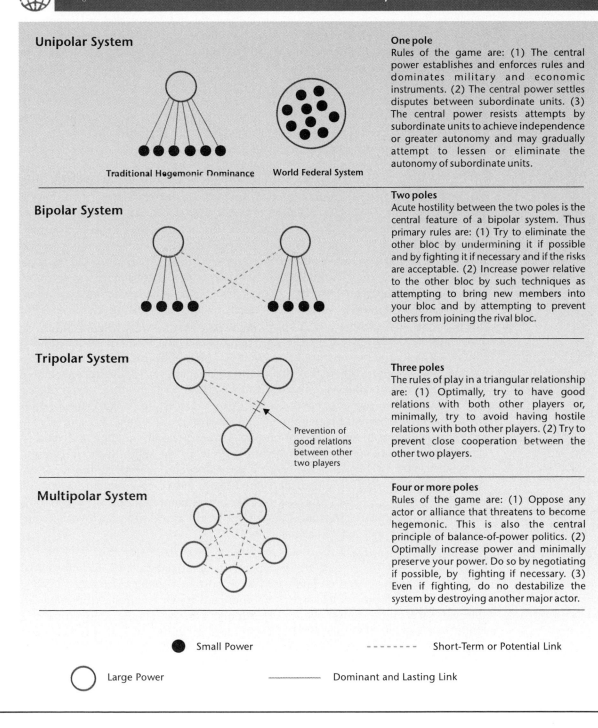

Unipolar System

Traditional Hegemonic Dominance   World Federal System

One pole
Rules of the game are: (1) The central power establishes and enforces rules and dominates military and economic instruments. (2) The central power settles disputes between subordinate units. (3) The central power resists attempts by subordinate units to achieve independence or greater autonomy and may gradually attempt to lessen or eliminate the autonomy of subordinate units.

Bipolar System

Two poles
Acute hostility between the two poles is the central feature of a bipolar system. Thus primary rules are: (1) Try to eliminate the other bloc by undermining it if possible and by fighting it if necessary and if the risks are acceptable. (2) Increase power relative to the other bloc by such techniques as attempting to bring new members into your bloc and by attempting to prevent others from joining the rival bloc.

Tripolar System

Prevention of good relations between other two players

Three poles
The rules of play in a triangular relationship are: (1) Optimally, try to have good relations with both other players or, minimally, try to avoid having hostile relations with both other players. (2) Try to prevent close cooperation between the other two players.

Multipolar System

Four or more poles
Rules of the game are: (1) Oppose any actor or alliance that threatens to become hegemonic. This is also the central principle of balance-of-power politics. (2) Optimally increase power and minimally preserve your power. Do so by negotiating if possible, by fighting if necessary. (3) Even if fighting, do no destabilize the system by destroying another major actor.

● Small Power   - - - - - - - - Short-Term or Potential Link

○ Large Power   —————— Dominant and Lasting Link

The relationships that exist among the actors in a particular type of international system structure vary because of the number of powerful actors, the relative power of each, and the permitted interactions within the system. This figure displays potential international system structures and the basic rules that govern relationships within each system. After looking at these models, which one, if any, do you think best describes the contemporary international system?

eighteenth and nineteenth centuries. The United States currently holds a similar position. "The United States of America predominates on the economic level, on the monetary level, on the military level, on the technological level, and in the cultural area in the broadest sense," France's foreign minister, Hubert Védrine, commented. "It is not comparable, in terms and power of influence, to anything we know in modern history."[6] Most analysts classify the current system as a multipolar (four or more major power centers) system. Yet the reality that one of those, the United States, is so much more powerful than any of the others leads some observers to believe that something approaching a limited unipolar system, with the United States as the sole hegemonic power, has existed from the 1990s through the present. Reflecting the current system's somewhat dual-personality structure, one scholar has characterized it as "uni-multipolar" (Huntington, 1999:36).

A unipolar system could occur through the establishment of a **world government**. In this case, subordinate actors, such as the current states, might have a level of autonomy, but they would not be sovereign. One variation would be a *centralized world government*, in which the subordinate units had little or no independent authority. A second possibility is a *federal world government*. In a federal system the central government is the "supreme law" of the land, as the U.S. Constitution puts it, but the subordinate units (such as U.S. states) have considerable autonomy in some areas. The exact rules of a unipolar system, whether established through hegemony or a world government would depend on the degree of autonomy of subordinate units. In rough approximation, though, and depending on how dominant the hegemonic power or other power center was, the rules might be: (Rule 1) The central power plays a dominant role in establishing and enforcing rules for matters that affect the system. The central power especially dominates or even monopolizes military and economic instruments. (Rule 2) The central power plays a key role in settling disputes between subordinate units. (Rule 3) The central power resists attempts by subordinate units to achieve greater autonomy or, especially, to create a rival pole. Indeed, the central power may gradually attempt to lessen or eliminate the autonomy of subordinate units. (Rule 4) The subordinate units, especially if their status is involuntary, seek to lessen or even escape the authority of the hegemonic power. The view that the United States has or could attain hegemonic power has prompted France's foreign minister to comment that one of his country's primary foreign policy objectives is ensuring that "the world of tomorrow [is] composed of several poles, not just a single one."[7]

Bipolar Systems This type of system is characterized by two roughly equal actors or coalitions of actors. There may be important nonaligned actors, but they are neutral and do not threaten the two dominant poles. Acute hostility between the two poles is the central feature of a **bipolar system**. Thus primary rules are: (Rule 1) Eliminate the other bloc by techniques including war, if it is necessary and the risks are acceptable. (Rule 2) Increase power relative to the other bloc by such techniques as bringing new members into your bloc and preventing others from joining the rival bloc.

One way to see how bipolar systems operate is to compare two that existed almost two and one-half millennia apart: The first is the bipolar system centered on the Athenian Empire and on Sparta and its allies. The second is the struggle between the two blocs led by the United States and the Soviet Union, which dominated the last half of the twentieth century.

Did You Know That:
The Punic Wars (264–146 B.C.) between Rome and Carthage typified the intense hostility in bipolar systems. The Roman war cry was *Carthago delenda est!* (Carthage must be destroyed!) And so it was. When Rome finally vanquished Carthage, the victors razed the city to the ground, sold its citizens into slavery, and decreed that no one could ever again live where Carthage had once stood.

Predictably, relations between the two blocs were bitter in both systems. The Greek historian Thucydides wrote in his *History of the Peloponnesian War* (400 B.C.), which chronicled the struggle between the two Greek city-states from 432 B.C. to 404 B.C., that "what made war inevitable was the growth of Athenian power and fear which this caused Sparta." The fear and counterfear was also evident in the United States and USSR, which, atomic scientist J. Robert Oppenheimer wrote, were like "two scorpions in a bottle, each capable of killing the other" (Jones, 1988:523).

Also, in the way that bipolar systems operate, both eras saw an either-you're-for-us-or-against-us intolerance of neutralism. In a segment of his epic work called the "Melian Debate," Thucydides reports that the Athenians are pressing a small city-state, Melos, to subordinate itself to Athens. The Melians ask, "So, you would not agree to our being neutral... allies of neither" Athens or Sparta? "No," the Athenian ambassador replies, because "our subjects would regard that as a sign of weakness in us." When Melos refused to submit, the Athenians attacked, and when the Melians surrendered, "slew all the men of military age... and sold the women and children as slaves." This ancient hostility toward neutralism was expressed in more modern times by, for one, U.S. secretary of state John Foster Dulles (1953–1959), who condemned neutrality as an "immoral and shortsighted concept" (Paterson, Clifford, & Hagen, 2000:279).

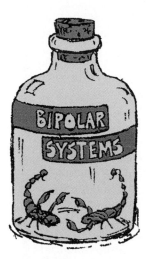

Bipolar systems are often characterized by intense conflict between the two major powers, which has been equated to the death struggle of two scorpions trapped together in a bottle.

Tripolar Systems Among the various permutations of a triangular relationship, one analysis postulated that the ideal position for any country is to be the "pivot player" in the triangle. This occurs when the country has good relations with both other countries, which, in turn, are hostile toward one another. In this position, the other two need you, and you can gain concessions for your continued friendship. The least favorable position is to be the "odd country out" in a triangle, where the other two players are friendly, and both are hostile toward you. Based on these calculations, the rules of play in a triangular relationship are: (Rule 1) Optimally, try to have good relations with both other players or, minimally, try to avoid having hostile relations with both. (Rule 2) Try to prevent close cooperation between the other two players.

There has not been an exact historical example of a **tripolar system**, but many observers believe that from the late 1960s through the beginning of the 1990s, a "strategic-triangle" system existed. The players were the United States, the Soviet Union, and China, which the two superpowers perceived as an emerging superpower. To a degree, the interaction of these three adhered to the rules of a tripolar system. Rule 1, for example, may explain why two strongly anticommunist U.S. presidents, Richard M. Nixon and Ronald Reagan, moved to better relations with Communist China. The reasoning was that China's growing strength created a strategic triangle that left the U.S. presidents little choice if they did not want to risk the simultaneous enmity of China and the Soviet Union.

Multipolar Systems As the number of poles in a system increases, the dynamics of the system become concomitantly more complex. A **multipolar system** containing four or more major powers is a relatively fluid and competitive system in which the countries involved form shifting alliances. Since the amassing of too much power by any one actor or alliance threatens all the other actors, there is a tendency to form counterbalancing alliances and to try to win allies away from the predominant coalition. This type of system is also sometimes characterized as a **balance-of-power** system, a concept discussed in the box of the same name.

The rules of the multipolar game are: (Rule 1) Oppose any actor or alliance that threatens to become hegemonic. This is also the central principle of balance-of-power

BALANCE OF POWER

Any discussion of how international systems operate must address the concept of balance of power. There are variations in the way that scholars use the term and there is broad disagreement between realists and idealists about the degree to which balance-of-power politics does and should affect world politics (Vasquez, 1997; Waltz, 1997; Christensen & Snyder, 1997; Elman & Elman, 1997; Schweller, 1997; Walt, 1997). In essence, realists believe that the practice of balance-of-power politics is necessary and proper; idealists disagree on both counts.

Whatever one's views, though, it is important to look at basic balance-of-power politics and its impact on world politics. Fundamentally, those who believe in the efficacy of balance-of-power theory assumes that:

1. There is a possibility, and perhaps a natural tendency, for some states to seek regional or even global hegemony.
2. Other states will seek to prevent hegemony by strengthening themselves or entering antihegemonic alliances with other threatened states.
3. A balance of power, therefore, is desirable because it (a) preserves the independence of countries and (b) creates an equilibrium that promotes order and peace.

Balance-of-power theory is applicable to any of the polar configurations, but it is most often associated with multipolar systems. Advocates of balance-of-power politics also believe that leaders will be well advised to continue to practice its principles in the evolving multipolar system. These realists reject the idealist contention that power politics is outmoded because of such factors as the growth of international organizations and independence and that power politics is a failed and increasingly dangerous way of trying to achieve stability and peace. Henry Kissinger, for one, counsels that "in the next century American leadership will have to articulate for their public a concept of the national interest and explain how that interest is served—in Europe and in Asia—by the maintenance of the balance of power."[1]

politics. (Rule 2) Increase power or, at least, preserve your power. Do so by negotiating if possible but by fighting if necessary. (Rule 3) Even if fighting, do not destabilize the system by destroying another major actor. Therefore, permit defeated major actors to maintain/regain their status. This third rule is based on the recognition that today's opponent may be tomorrow's partner in a coalition to block the hegemonic ambitions of today's ally. Among other things, the flexibility of a multipolar system also means that major actors can rise or fall without significantly changing the basic multipolarity of the system. In the European multipolar system that extended roughly from 1648 to 1945, there were occasional shifts in which countries were poles. Spain and Sweden were early major powers. They eventually declined to secondary status but were replaced by other rising powers, such as Prussia (later Germany). Other countries, such as Great Britain and France, remained powers throughout the period. In this case, the number of major powers remained above four, and, therefore, the system continued to operate as a multipolar system.

One way to see how these rules of the game are affecting policy in the evolving international system is to consider this question: Why, after opposing the Soviet Union for over 40 years during the bipolar era and finally seeing it fall, has the United States been willing, even eager, to aid Russia? For system-level analysts, the answer is that the West has extended billions of dollars in aid to Russia and taken other steps to prop it up because the hostility dictated by bipolar system Rule 1, "try to eliminate the other bloc," has been supplanted by multipolar system Rule 3, "do not destabilize the system by destroying another major actor."

The fluidity that Rule 3 promotes does not just mean keeping an open mind about one's adversaries. It also means not assuming that one's allies cannot become opponents. This is very unlike the rigid alliances of a bipolar system. Indeed, the fluidity of who is friend and foe at any given time can also lead to what almost seems contradictory policies, a tale that is told in the box, Japan: A Rising Sun? on pages 70–71.

CONCENTRATION OF POWER

A pole is a major power center, but not all major powers are equal. This inequality affects how the system operates because system stability varies in part according to the degree to which power is concentrated or diffused among the various poles. This finding leads to questions about the stability of the system when two or more poles (countries or alliances) are in a condition of relative *power equality* or *power inequality* (Schweller, 1998; Gochman & Hoffman, 1996; Schampel, 1996).

Some scholars argue that war is more likely when antagonistic poles have relative *power equality*, creating "a situation in which [every power] can perceive the potential for successful use of force" (Geller, 1993:173). By this logic, war is less likely when power is concentrated in one camp, because the weaker poles will be deferential. Other scholars disagree. They believe that conflict is more likely between countries of relative *power inequality*. The reasoning is that when two antagonists are equal in power, they are deterred from war by the fear of being defeated or by the mauling they will take even if they are victorious. Why, you might ask, would an obviously weaker country fight rather than compromise or give way? One reason is that an aggressor may attack and leave the country no choice. Emotions are another reason. "Live free or die," as the New Hampshire license plate proclaims. What occurs, research shows, is that decision makers are willing to accept much greater risks to prevent losses than to gain an advantage.

Still other scholars conclude that conflict is least likely when power is equal or very unequal and most likely when there are moderate power differences between antagonists (Powell, 1996). Less dramatic differences may lead countries either to miscalculate their power relative to that of their opponent or to gamble.

POWER CHANGES: CAUSES AND EFFECTS

The power equation in the international system is seldom stable for very long. The power of countries rises and falls. Major powers sometimes decline to the point that they are no longer a pole. They may even cease to exist, as did the USSR. Other countries may come into existence and later rise to the rank of major power, as did the United States. New power poles could even be an alliance or an international organization, as suggested in the map on page 73, NATO and the EU March East.

There are a number of highly debated general theories about power-based changes in the international system. Some scholars propound "cycle theories," which hold that power cycles occur over a period of a few decades, or even as much as a century (Pollins, 1996). The cycles are demarcated by great-power or "systemic" wars that reflect strains created by power shifts within the system. They might be equated to earthquakes in the geological system. The systemic wars, in turn, further alter the system by destroying the major power status of declining powers and elevating rising powers to pole status. Then the process of power decay and formation begins anew. Another study uses the idea of "chaos theory" to argue that while there is an evolution of power in the system, "this evolution is *chaotic* [in that] the patterns of global power are not strict chronological cycles, but variable patterns influenced by... small random... effects" that can change the timing and impact of the cycle (Richards, 1993:71).

Whatever their view, analysts agree that the international system does change and that the shifts are important. Therefore, how power changes is a key concern. Since the current polar structure of the international system is clearly in flux, it is especially timely to consider the causes and effects of power transitions (Tammen et al., 2000).

(Continued on page 72)

JAPAN: A RISING SUN?

In a world in which only the United States has both the economic and military strength to warrant the title "superpower," Japan is one of the few countries with the potential to achieve that rank in the foreseeable future. Despite its recent travails, Japan's economy and advanced technological capabilities create a base from which it could expand on its already considerable, if highly restrained, military capabilities. The question is whether it can and wants to assert itself and acquire the military tools to do so.

There are several factors at work against the possibility of Japan rebuilding and using its military. Internally, the horrific suffering, including atomic bomb attacks, that the Japanese endured in World War II has left them profoundly pacifistic. One indication is that Japan unofficially limits spending on the Self-Defense Force (SDF) to no more than 1 percent of the GDP. Although this is one of the world's largest military budgets, the SDF has neither long-range offensive systems such as bombers or aircraft carriers, nor nuclear weapons. There is also a clause (Article 9) in Japan's constitution that bars the "use of force as a means of settling international disputes." The continuing strength of opinion among the Japanese against using force was evident in an April 2001 survey, which found that 74 percent of all Japanese want Article 9 left unchanged.[1]

For all this aversion to militarism, changes in the balance of power in the international system and in Japanese attitudes are creating a new assertiveness that could lead to an increase in the size and capacity of the SDF. While "Japan's reemergence as an independent military power would be unsettling," notes one commentator, "it may not be preventable" (Menon, 1997:34).

First, the Japanese worry that isolationist pressures in the United States are weakening its commitment to defend Japan and, more generally, to promote the stability of Asia. There is a "nagging feeling," one Asian diplomat has commented, "that after the cold war America isn't going to have the will or the wallet to make the sacrifices that a superpower has to make."[2] Similarly, polls have found that between 1992 and 1997 the percentage of Japanese who believe that the United States would honor its alliance and defend Japan against an aggressor fell from 68 percent to 53 percent.[3]

A second factor affecting Japan's international policy is growing nationalism. The passage of time since World War II and an increased sense of national pride are changing Japanese attitudes. Many of the changes are small, but still give a sense of the shift in views. For example, in 1999 the Education Ministry directed schools to display the flag and sing the national anthem ("Kimigayo," His Majesty's Reign) during ceremonies, practices hitherto unusual.

Some observers worry about the rise of "revisionists" who contend that Japan was trying in the 1930s and early 1940s to liberate Asia from Western colonialism and that, therefore, Japan should shed its guilt for the war. This faction is still small, but, as one Japanese observer warns, "The revisionists are rapidly increasing their influence on public opinion" (Kunihiro, 1997:36). The strength of this revisionist opinion is arguably what led Prime Minister Junichiro Koizumi to visit the Yasukuni Shrine in August 2001, on the anniversary of Japan's surrender in World War II. Among others, 14 of the country's leaders who were either hanged or sentenced to prison for war crimes are enshrined there. The move outraged many of Japan's neighbors that had suffered from the crimes committed during World War II. China's Foreign Ministry protested, "The Chinese government and people lodge their fierce anger and dissatisfaction." South Korea's government added its dismay, saying that it could not "find the words to express our concern that a Japanese prime minster would pay homage to war criminals."[4] Polls showed that opinion was fairly evenly divided among Japanese who favored the visit, opposed it, or were uncertain.[5] The view of one Japanese scholar is that Koizumi had a good sense of public opinion. While most Japanese "do not explicitly endorse Koizumi's decision," the scholar commented, "implicitly they applaud [it]. They know very well it will be criticized, but at the bottom of their heart many ordinary Japanese people say, 'Koizumi, you did good.'"[6]

A third factor promoting a more assertive military policy by Japan is U.S. pressure. In what amounts to a somewhat inconsistent stand, American policy makers sometimes fret about a possible remilitarization of Japan. American officials are usually loath to say it, but one reason for U.S. reluctance to confront China over the many issues that divide Washington and Beijing is the prospect that a more assertive, even remilitarized, Japan might become a Pacific region antagonist. It is revealing that President George H. W. Bush defended his forgiving posture toward Beijing less than a year after the Tiananmen Square massacre

Japan is slowly moving away from its policy of not having long-range military capability or deploying its forces away from Japan itself. Among the changes that have raised concerns internationally and within Japan was Tokyo's decision to militarily support the U.S.-led operations against Afghanistan. In this photograph, relatives of the crew of the Japanese naval vessel *Uraga* wave rising sun flags, as the ship sails from Yokosuka naval base near Tokyo in November 2001, to join two other Japanese warships en route to the Indian Ocean. The deployment marked Japan's first combat operation in 56 years.

in 1989 on the grounds that, "I want to retain contacts [with China] because, as you look around the world.... Take a look at Japan. Take a look at a lot of countries in the Pacific. China is a key player."[7]

Yet despite this concern, American policy makers also have encouraged Japan to build up its forces and take a more assertive stance. Part of this, according to the logic of balance-of-power politics, is to offset Chinese strength in Asia, just as Chinese strength balances Japan's.

American officials have also wanted Japan to give greater support to U.S. military efforts. During the Persian Gulf War, U.S. officials expressed impatience with Japan's refusal to commit troops to the war. Although Japan contributed $11 billion to the war effort, U.S. Secretary of State James Baker told the Japanese, "Your checkbook diplomacy... is clearly too narrow."[8] "First the Americans taught us that pacifism was a good thing, and then they called us cowards when we did not send troops," a Japanese official complained with justification.[9]

A similar scenario occurred in 2001 during the war against the Taliban and al-Qaeda in Afghanistan. U.S. Deputy Secretary of State Richard Armitage called on Japan to "show the flag" in support of the military campaign. Howard Baker, the U.S. ambassador to Tokyo, similarly expressed the opinion that the "reality of circumstance in the world is going to suggest to the Japanese that they reinterpret or redefine Article 9." At least partly in response to this pressure, Japan's Prime Minister Junichiro Koizumi moved to send forces. "If we say, 'no, we can't do this and that' at a time when everyone is gearing up to crush terrorism," Koizumi told parliament, "Japan will never get respect among the international community."[10] Japanese legislators agreed, and on November 9, 2001, two Japanese destroyers, the *Kurama* and the *Kirisame,* and a supply ship, the *Haman,* left their home ports in Japan en route to the Indian Ocean. Japan had in 1992 sent noncombat forces to support the UN peacekeeping force in Cambodia, but the departure of the three warships marked the first time in 56 years that Japanese combat forces had been deployed outside the immediate area of the homeland.

Many observers applauded Japan's willingness to act. Others worried. The step "sets a precedent," fretted scholar Motofumi Asai. "People will get used to the idea, and then [Japan] will take the next step toward engaging the military with the world," Asai predicted. "I don't think that's to the advantage of the United States or other countries. Eventually they will find out," he concluded ominously.[11]

How far Japan will go in building and using its military forces cannot yet be predicted, but there is no question that it continues to consider its options. For many years "it was a taboo to discuss" enhancing Japan's forces and their role, former prime minister Yasuhiro Nakasone has commented. "But now it is not a taboo, and people are thinking about it seriously."[12] Even the possibility of acquiring nuclear weapons is beginning to be occasionally discussed. As political scientist Seizaburo Sato notes, "Russia is still there [powerful and near Japan]. If the U.S. did withdraw [from the Western Pacific], if China continues to mobilize its military forces, if North Korea goes nuclear, then Japan would go nuclear. You would have to prepare yourselves against Japanese forces. And we are pretty efficient."[13]

The Causes of Changes in Power

Power changes in three ways. First, change may occur in the sources of power or in their relative importance. Second, power shifts may occur when conditions change within the major actors. Third, the dynamics of balance-of-power politics prompts countries to try to prevent dominance by others and to build their own power.

The Sources of Power Power is based on many factors. Developments in any one of them can affect the international system. Occasionally, the change may be sudden. For example, nuclear weapons and missiles that can carry them rapidly to strike anywhere in the world dramatically changed the system in the decade after World War II. More recently, it is possible to argue that the power equation of the international system is rapidly being changed by the reality that second- and third-rank powers such as Iraq, or even terrorist organizations, have or can acquire nuclear, biological, and chemical weapons of mass destruction and the means to deliver them.

More often, sources of power and their importance evolve slowly. For all the revolutionary impact of nuclear weapons, a more important evolutionary change may be the gradual decline of the usefulness of military might. Some analysts believe that military power is becoming less important because of the astronomical economic costs of wars and their potential cataclysmic effect. The decrease in the importance of military force as a policy instrument has, according to this line of thought, increased the importance of economics as a source of power. Most observers would agree, for instance, that Japan is a major power even though its military forces remain very limited. Russia still possesses a fearsome nuclear arsenal, yet its economy and society are in such disarray that its status as a major power has plummeted.

Advancing interdependence may also mean that even other forms of coercive power, such as economic sanctions, are gradually becoming less relevant. The reasoning for this is that a country that applies the sanctions may do as much harm to itself as to the country it is trying to punish. Certainly military might and economic capacity remain the cornerstones of state power, but such factors as technological sophistication and leadership capacity may be growing in importance.

Conditions Within Major Actors While the system influences the actions of states, conditions within countries and the resulting policy decisions made by them can also change the system. The fate of the Soviet Union provides a dramatic example of the impact of domestic factors on foreign policy and, in turn, on the international system. The disintegration of the Soviet Union stemmed in part from such domestic factors as its inefficient economic and political system, separatist demands by the national groups within it, and a crushing military budget.

Conditions within a state may also cause it to act "abnormally," that is, not play an expected role in global affairs. Sometimes, for example, countries are abnormally aggressive, as were Japan and Germany leading up to World War II. This can upset or even transform the system, as occurred when World War II shattered most of the major powers and led to the bipolar era.

At other times, major powers can act with abnormal passivity, which can also "undermine the global balance of power" (Cederman, 1994:528). Some people believe, for example, that the United States does not have the political will to fulfill its superpower role in the post–cold war world. When Americans are asked whether the United States should play an active role in the world, most say yes. Americans, however, are less willing to support involvement when they are asked more specific questions that bring to light the costs and dangers of being involved. On the economic front, one study found that 35 percent more Americans favored cutting economic foreign aid than favored expanding it. The percentages were even stronger for military aid, with 47

(Continued on page 74)

NATO and the EU March East

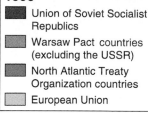

1990
- Union of Soviet Socialist Republics
- Warsaw Pact countries (excluding the USSR)
- North Atlantic Treaty Organization countries
- European Union

2001
- North Atlantic Treaty Organization countries
- European Union
- European Union applicant countries
- North Atlantic Treaty Organization applicant countries
- North Atlantic Treaty Organization and European Union applicant countries

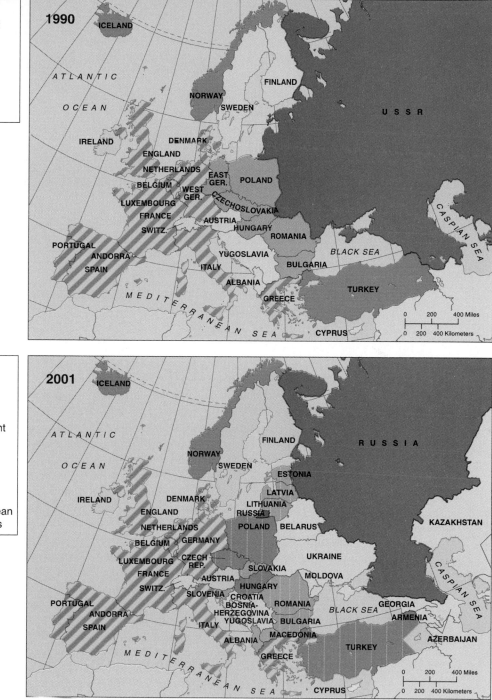

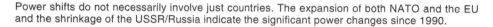

Power shifts do not necessarily involve just countries. The expansion of both NATO and the EU and the shrinkage of the USSR/Russia indicate the significant power changes since 1990.

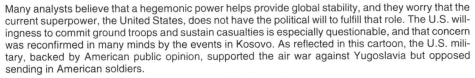

VICTORY PARADE

Many analysts believe that a hegemonic power helps provide global stability, and they worry that the current superpower, the United States, does not have the political will to fulfill that role. The U.S. willingness to commit ground troops and sustain casualties is especially questionable, and that concern was reconfirmed in many minds by the events in Kosovo. As reflected in this cartoon, the U.S. military, backed by American public opinion, supported the air war against Yugoslavia but opposed sending in American soldiers.

percent more Americans in favor of decreasing it than in favor of increasing it. On the military front, Americans are also reluctant warriors. Prior to the United States taking action, only a minority of Americans favored sending ground forces to Haiti in 1994, to Bosnia in 1995, or to Kosovo in 1999.[7] A thin majority of Americans favored sending U.S. ground forces to Somalia in 1992, but that support collapsed once casualties began to occur, as told in the 2002 movie, *Black Hawk Down*.

Polls in early 2002 did show that Americans supported military action against Iraq, Iran, and North Korea after President Bush called the three countries the "axis of evil" in his State of the Union address. It is arguable, however, that this somewhat unusual bellicosity on the part of the public was a result of the short time that had elapsed since the 9-11 attacks and also the fact that the president made it clear that no military action was imminent. How the public would react to the actuality of war with any of the three countries is an entirely different matter.

Such responses have persuaded some foreign observers that Americans no longer have the will to lead. André Fountain, the editorial chief of the French newspaper *Le Monde*, has contended that the United States "no longer has the money or the public backing to play a prominent role abroad."[8] American officials share this worry. President George W. Bush expressed it when he told a reporter in December 2001, "I do believe there is the image of America out there that we are so materialistic that we're almost hedonistic, that we don't have values, and that when struck we wouldn't fight back. It was clear that [Osama] bin Laden felt emboldened and didn't feel threatened by the United States."[9]

Some scholars also worry that the United States is not willing to play its expected role as the hegemonic power (superpower) in the international system (Wohlforth, 1999). Richard Haass (1997) depicts the United States as "The Reluctant Sheriff" and writes that "what the United States does and does not do can help determine history."[10] What many realists like Haass contend is that according to the balance-of-power theory, the United States should exercise its formidable power to preserve stability and to shape the world system to the U.S. design. "There can be no peace in the Balkans unless Washington is fully engaged," a French diplomat commented.[11] Expressing the same view from the Middle East, a former Israeli diplomat opined that in the search for peace, "Nothing can happen without the Americans. Everything can happen with them."[12] And in Asia, a diplomat explained, "We cannot antagonize the Chinese by saying it publicly, but everybody will be more comfortable with American ships in place [in the Pacific]."[13] This desired U.S. role also extends to socioeconomic issues. When President Clinton decided not to attend the UN-sponsored conference on human welfare held in Copenhagen, the head of the UN Development Programme complained that "this summit without Clinton will be like staging Hamlet without the Prince of Denmark."[14]

Did You Know That:
The hegemonic position of the United States is evident statistically. With less than one-twentieth of the world's population, the United States accounts for about one-fifth of the world's combined GDPs, one-fifth of total world trade, and one-third of world military expenditures.

Such concerns need to be viewed with some caution, however. One recent study of post–cold war changes concludes, "Put simply, the relative decline of American power has not led to a prolonged, across-the-board decrease in efforts to maintain the stability of the international system" (Bobrow & Boyer, 1998:286). Thus there seems to be no immediate danger of general system instability.

Balance-of-Power Politics As the box Balance of Power notes, countries resist the domination of others and may seek to establish themselves as a power pole. This dynamic of resisting the power of others and seeking power for yourself can be pursued unilaterally or in alliance with others. In either case, however, the dynamic, if successful, shifts the power equation. It may be that diplomats from around the world recognize that U.S. power is important to system stability, but it is also true that the governments of these diplomats will struggle to undermine U.S. hegemony. German chancellor Gerhard Schröder has warned, "That there is a danger of unilateralism, not just by anybody but by the United States, is undeniable."[15] These concerns were heightened when George W. Bush became president in 2001. A number of his policies, such as his unilateral rejection of the Kyoto treaty on global warming and his decision to build a ballistic missile defense system, drew criticism from some of even the staunchest U.S. allies. So did his designation of Iraq, Iran, and North Korea as an axis of evil, and his expressed willingness to take military action against them alone if necessary. The reaction of German foreign minister Joschka Fischer was, "Without compelling evidence, it will not be a good idea to launch something that will mean going it alone. The international coalition against terror does not provide a basis for doing just anything against anybody—and certainly not by going it alone. This is the view of every European foreign minister."[16]

The Effects of Changes in Power

There are many ways that changes in power affect the system. System-level analysts examine both the specific effects of alterations in the sources and distribution of power and the degree to which power transitions create dangerous instability in the system.

Specific Effects of Changes in Power Any significant change in the *sources of power* or the distribution of power among the major actors is likely to alter the operation of a system. The development of nuclear weapons provides an example of the impact that a change in the sources of power has on the system.

Nuclear weapons altered, perhaps permanently, which states could claim to be a hegemonic power, or in more modern terms, a superpower. Another impact of nuclear weapons and the development of missiles to deliver them, systems analysts would say, was to compel the United States to abandon its isolationist stance and become an active internationalist actor. Americans realized that whatever their preferences might be, they could no longer be secure behind their flanking oceans.

Nuclear weapons technology may have also shifted the rules of the game by which a system operates. Three earlier bipolar systems—those that pitted Athens against Sparta, Macedonia against Persia, and Rome against Carthage in ancient times—were marked by warfare between the two "superpowers" and the eventual defeat of one by the other. Yet the recent, cold war bipolar system did not result in the military death struggle that has characterized earlier bipolar systems. The nuclear devastation that each superpower could wreak on the other worked to keep the two powers from attacking each other directly because the outcome was predictable: mutual annihilation.

Changes in the *distribution of power* also affect the system. This occurs when the system shifts from one polar configuration to another. The recent move from a bipolar to a multipolar configuration is an example. Another way that the changing distribution of power is affecting the system is in the weakening of the system's Western orientation. Until well into the twentieth century, most power in the international system was held by European and European-heritage countries. This resulted in a system based mainly on European organizational, legal, and normative traditions. The way that democracy is defined in terms of a legal procedure, rather than by equitable outcome, and the elevation of individual rights over community welfare are both, for instance, much more strongly rooted in Western tradition than they are in other cultures.

Power Transitions and System Stability "Great powers are like divas. They enter and exit the stage with great tumult," one analyst observes (Zakaria, 1996:37). What this means, and many studies have concluded, is that the world is most prone to violence during times of system transitions (Kugler & Lemke, 1996). That is, wars between major powers are most likely when the power of one or more of them is declining and the power of the other(s) is rising. In such situations it is harder for antagonists to judge their relative power. Furthermore, the declining power may try to maintain its dominant position by attacking the rising power before it becomes too powerful. Simultaneously, the rising power, dissatisfied with its secondary status, may try to improve it by confronting the dominant but declining country. One recent study has concluded that war is most likely when the power of a rising, dissatisfied country nears or becomes equal to that of a dominant state. Then, "power parity provides the opportunity to act for those who are committed to changing the status quo" (Lemke & Warner, 1996:256).

The origins of World Wars I and II provide, in the estimate of some social scientists, a historical example of the effect of power transitions. Early in the twentieth century, power was shifting rapidly. As the twentieth century began, Germany was newly united, and its power was increasing. So was American power, although the country remained largely isolationist. Japanese power was also beginning to grow. Other great powers were beginning to fade. Imperial China, the Austro-Hungarian Empire, and the Ottoman Empire were in states of terminal decay. Russia was also tottering, although the communists would eventually reestablish the power that the czarist government was losing. Germany and Austria-Hungary provide apt illustrations of the calculations of a rising and a declining power. By the beginning of the twentieth century, Germany was ready to challenge the previously dominant states, primarily Great Britain, for ascendancy. By contrast, Austria-Hungary was trying desperately to preserve a shadow of its former glory as the Holy Roman Empire. The result of these two opposite motives was that Germany and Austria-Hungary joined in an alliance that turned aggressive in 1914 and helped ignite World War I. Alas, the "war to end all wars" wasn't the end of war at all; it was just the first round in a power transition. World War II was the second round. It broke out after a breathing space, and it finally spelled an end not only to the power of most of the remaining major European actors but to the multipolar system itself.

A final thought on transitional systems is that they tend toward instability when hegemonic powers are no longer able or willing to control events in countries that were once part of their bloc or in their sphere of influence. Some scholars believe, for example, that the collapse of Soviet/Russian power allowed the simmering ethnic tensions in the formerly communist-dominated Balkans to erupt into the violence that occurred during the 1990s.

By the same logic, according to one study, "increased hegemonic control is associated with fewer wars [and] crises" (Volgy & Imwalle, 1995:819). This may help explain why a settlement was achieved in the Balkans in the mid-1990s once the United States exerted itself there. The reality, commented former British foreign secretary David Owen, is that "when the most powerful country in the world decides to lead the negotiations and adopt a realistic posture, it's just a different ballgame."[17]

Economic Patterns in the Political System

How the international system works is based in part on its economic patterns. We can gain a sense of the impact of these patterns by touching on just three of them: economic interdependence, natural resource production and consumption, and the maldistribution of development.

Economic interdependence is one pattern that we have noted repeatedly (Jones, 1999). There is some controversy over whether or under what conditions interdependence promotes peace or creates tensions. One study concludes, for instance, that established powerful states (status quo powers) are most likely to join together to deter aggression "when there are extensive ties among the status quo powers and few or no such links between them and the perceived threatening powers." By contrast, "When economic interdependence is not strong between status quo powers or if the status quo powers have significant links with threatening powers, [status quo] leaders' capacities to balance are limited," which leads to "weak responses" and "a greater likelihood of aggression by the [threatening] power" (Papayoanou, 1997:135).

Whatever the specific impacts of economic interdependence may be, there is no disagreement that it profoundly affects the international system. This is evident, among other ways, in the refusal of President Clinton to use economic sanctions to pressure China to improve its checkered human rights record. Commenting on the president's stand, the *New York Times* wrote with only some hyperbole that Clinton was recognizing "the underlying shift evident in all the industrial democracies today: economic concerns have taken center stage in foreign affairs decision-making. This is the age of the Finance Minister.... The game of nations is now geo-Monopoly, and it is first and foremost about profits, not principles."[18]

The pattern of *natural resource production and consumption* also influences the operation of the system. The strong reaction of the industrialized (and petroleum import-dependent) countries to Iraq's aggression in 1990 was based on the distribution of resources. Turmoil in the Persian Gulf region threatened vital oil supplies. While the Bush administration could have decided not to intervene, a system-level analyst would point out that it had little choice. American presidents as far back as Harry S. Truman had pledged U.S. protection of the West's primary petroleum source. Even the usually conciliatory Jimmy Carter had declared during his January 1980 State

Even though this magazine cover is over 25 years old, it aptly portrays the power of big multinational corporations (MNCs) in the economically interdependent world. Exxon, whose corporate symbol was the Exxon tiger, was immense in 1974. Since then it has merged with Mobil, and the combined company was the world's largest MNC in 2000 with a gross corporate product (earnings) of $210.4 billion.

of the Union message that any attempt "to gain control of the Persian Gulf will be regarded as an assault on the vital interests of the United States of America." Given the distribution of system resources, then, Iraq's invasion of Kuwait and threat to Saudi Arabia and other oil producers brought what a system-level analyst would say was a predictable reaction from the powerful petroleum-importing states. Led by the United States, they moved militarily to end the threat to their supplies because, as U.S. secretary of state James A. Baker III explained to reporters, "The economic lifeline of the industrial world runs from the gulf, and we cannot permit a dictator… to sit astride that economic lifeline."[19]

The *maldistribution of development* is a third economic pattern that has consequences for the international system. States, which are the main actors in the system, are divided into relative haves and have-nots. At the most general level, this economic division pits the less developed countries (LDCs) of the South and their demands for equity against the economically developed countries (EDCs) of the North along the North-South Axis. More specifically, as we shall see, there is a connection between the poor economic conditions in LDCs and such problems as rapid political oppression and instability, population growth, and environmental degradation. These problems harm the people of the South and, by their spillover effect, are detrimental for the people of the North as well. An economic pattern in which a small minority of people and countries enjoy high standards of living while the vast majority of people and countries are relatively impoverished both creates a drag on the world economy and is morally questionable. The disparity also creates resentments rooted in desperation, fertile ground that could one day yield systemic violence—a reminder of Abraham Lincoln's maxim that "a house divided against itself cannot stand."

As the immediate shock of the terror attacks that occurred on September 11, 2001, has ebbed, many analysts have begun to examine the underlying causes that gave rise to the fanaticism of the 19 suicide hijackers and those who supported them. It does not excuse the act to say that one possible cause is the economic gap between most Muslim countries and people and the West. The "anger and… intolerance of anything American… should… give us pause," a former staff member of the U.S. National Security Council sagely commented. "We don't have to agree with it or to think that all this is due to our own behavior to think about where we go from here. We have got to deal with the underlying anger," he concluded. "It is real, it's not just a figment of someone's imagination, and it's a clear warning signal that we have to pay attention to."[20]

Norms of Behavior in the International System

The widely accepted standards that help regulate behavior are the fourth major element of any system. These standards of behavior, or values, constitute the **norms** of a system. A caveat is that to be valid, norms must be generally recognized and followed, but they need not be either accepted or practiced universally.

Systems develop norms for two reasons. First, various psychological and social factors prompt humans to adopt values to define what is ethical and moral. Second, humans tend to favor regularized patterns of behavior because of the pragmatic need to interact and to avoid the anxiety and disruption caused by the random or unwanted behavior of others. Over the centuries, for instance, pragmatism led to norms (now supplemented by treaties) about how countries treat each others' diplomats even in times of war. When conflict broke out in the Persian Gulf in 1991, U.S. and other enemy diplomats in Baghdad were not rounded up and executed. Iraqi diplomats in Washington, D.C., and elsewhere were similarly safe from official reprisal.

Changes that occur in the norms of the international system are an important aspect of how the system evolves. What is evident in the current system is that norms are becoming more universal while they are simultaneously being challenged.

The uniformity of norms is the result of the McWorld effect, the homogenization of global culture because of economic interdependence, global communications, and other factors. It would be a vast overstatement to contend that capitalist (free-market) economies, democracy, and the precepts of individual human rights reign triumphant throughout the world. But these and other beliefs about the "right way" to do things have certainly become the dominant theme.

Yet it is also true that the exact nature of these precepts is being modified as a result of the de-Westernization of the international system. Norms that have heretofore influenced the system were established by the dominant countries of the West. Now the countries of Asia, Africa, and elsewhere have become more assertive, and they sometimes disagree with and challenge some of the established values (Lensu & Fritz, 1999). For example, some cultures in Asia and elsewhere stress the good of society, whereas American and some other political cultures emphasize the rights of the individual. Reflecting this, the rights of the accused are less extensive and punishments are often harsher in Asia and other countries that take the more communitarian view. Punishment in Singapore, for one, can be quite draconian by American standards and range from $100 fines for failing to flush a public toilet, through being beaten on the buttocks with a bamboo cane for vandalism, to death sentences for 20 different offenses. Many Americans find such standards of crime and punishment extreme. Yet the view is different from that part of the world. "We believe that the legal system must give maximum protection to the majority of our people," says Shanmugan Jayakumar, Singapore's foreign minister. "We make no apology for clearly tilting our law and policy in favor of the majority."[21]

Another important change in the nature and role of norms is that the international cast of actors is more willing than it used to be to take action to enforce changing norms. The strengthening norms of democracy and human rights, for one, prompted global economic sanctions and other pressures that eventually forced South Africa's white government to end apartheid and eventually to turn political power over to the black majority (Klotz, 1997). Changing norms about how we use the biosphere also persuaded Japan to pledge to end drift-net fishing because it kills all forms of marine life caught up in the giant nets. After a UN debate on the issue, a Japanese official explained that his country gave way because, "Since no other country sided with us, we have to consider Japan's position in international society and yield."[22]

The willingness to countenance war, especially unilateral action by an individual country, is also weakening. Wars still occur, but they are being perceived as less legitimate and are more widely condemned in principle. The unilateral U.S. invasion of Panama in 1989 was, for example, condemned by both the UN and the Organization of American States (OAS). Since then, the United States has sought the support of the United Nations and also often that of a regional organization, such as the OAS or NATO, for its military actions in Somalia, Haiti, Bosnia, Kosovo, and even in Afghanistan. In the most recent case, the United States called for an urgent session of the UN Security Council and persuaded it on September 12, 2001, to unanimously pass Resolution 1368, which recognized "the inherent right of individual or collective self-defense," and called "on all States to work together urgently to bring to justice the perpetrators, organizers and sponsors of these terrorist attacks," stressing that in addition to the terrorists themselves, "those responsible for aiding, supporting or harboring the perpetrators, organizers and sponsors of these acts will be held accountable."

System-Level Analysis: Predicting Tomorrow

We have, in the preceding pages, examined the international system and how it is shaped by its characteristics: global authority structure, power relationships, economic patterns, and norms of behavior. We have also seen that all these factors are in flux. The question is, then, whether system-level analysis can give us some clues about the world we will experience tomorrow. What do these changes portend for the system during the twenty-first century?

The changes that we have been discussing seem to be simultaneously pulling the international system in different directions. One direction is along the traditional, state-centric road that the system has traveled for centuries. Nationalism, as we shall see, remains the most potent political idea in the world today, and the number of sovereign states has tripled since 1945.

Then there is the alternative road. For all the strength of states as the principal actors in the international system, many scholars conclude that the dominance of states as the focus of political authority is in decline. The issue is what will fill this power vacuum. For the moment, one scholar sees "a ramshackle assembly of conflicting sources of authority" and argues that "The diffusion of authority away from national governments has left a yawning hole of nonauthority" (Strange, 1997:199, 14). If this is true, where does the alternative road take us?

The answer is uncertain because the state-centric system is in some disarray due to pressures from two directions (Hoffmann, 1998; Kaufman, 1997). Some pressures are pushing the system toward greater international cooperation and even supranational governance. This movement toward more global structures is the McWorld tendency that is explored in chapter 2. It is based on the buildup of economic and ecological forces that demand cooperation and integration and, thus, are pressing us all into one commercially homogenous global network tied together by technology, ecology, communications, and commerce.

Other pressures, the tribalism tendency toward fragmentation, are promoting subnational or transnational political organizations that are vying for the loyalty of individuals and, therefore, undermining the state. Most obviously, there is a strengthening of subnational movements such as **ethnonational groups** that demand autonomy or even independence from the states in which

Globalization has arguably increased the power of multinational corporations and to a degree has homogenized world culture. Some people are uneasy that they are losing political control and that their culture is being diluted. This has sparked increasing protests in recent years. Obvious symbols of global business and acculturation, such as McDonald's outlets, often bear the brunt of this dissatisfaction. In this photo, Ronald McDonald has been symbolically toppled by an avalanche of apples dumped by French farmers in Cavaillon, France, who were angered over their loss of sales to imported food.

they reside. This is evident, as detailed in chapter 6, in the breakups of Czechoslovakia, the Soviet Union, and Yugoslavia; the secession of East Timor from Indonesia in 1999; and the literally dozens of ethnonational conflicts that are under way on every continent. There is also, as chapter 7 discusses, an increase in the appeal of such transnational identifications as religion and even gender as the primary political identification of some individuals.

Where will all this lead? There is broad disagreement (Modelski & Thompson, 1998; Neumann & Weaver, 1997). Some analysts believe that states will remain strong, integral units and that the system will remain state-centric. Another school of thought believes that the world's complex interdependence will result in a much higher level of global authority. Barber (1995:20) agrees that "in the long run, the forces of McWorld... may be unstoppable." A third school of thought argues that disintegration, not integration, will prevail (Enriquez, 1999). At the pessimistic extreme, an article entitled "The Coming Anarchy" predicts that the current system "is going to be replaced by a jagged-glass pattern of city-states, [poor] shanty-states, [and] nebulous and anarchic regionalisms," a virtual nonsystem in which "war and crime become indistinguishable" as "armed bands of stateless marauders clash with the private forces of the elites" (Kaplan, 1994:72). Yet another pessimistic view envisions a future in which there is a "clash of civilizations," as religious, ethnic, and cultural conflict replace state rivalries (Huntington, 1996).

The estimation of most scholars incorporates both views. According to this synthesis, states will still be important, but so too will be supranational and subnational structures. Scholars have not settled on a name for what they foresee. Chapter 2 used the term "modified multipolar." The term "modified" reflects the belief of many scholars that the state will have to compete for political legitimacy and power with rising subnational, transnational, and international actors (Rosenau, 1997). This view has led some scholars to envision a "postinternational" era in which the **politics of identity** will make traditional national political identification just one of many ways that people define their primary sense of political identity (Hobbes, 2000).

 # Chapter Summary

1. System-level analysis is an approach to the study of world politics that argues that factors external to countries and the world political environment combine to determine the pattern of interaction among countries and other transnational actors.

2. Countries are often compelled to take certain courses of action by the realities of the world in which they exist.

3. Many factors determine the nature of any given system. Systemic factors include its structural characteristics, power relationships, economic patterns, and norms of behavior.

4. One structural characteristic is how authority is organized. The international system is horizontal, based on state sovereignty, and therefore it is anarchical. There are, however, relatively new centralizing forces that are changing the system toward a more vertical structure.

5. Another structural characteristic is determined by who the major actors in the system are. Currently these are sovereign states, but intergovernmental actors and transnational actors are becoming more numerous and important.

6. A third structural characteristic is a system's scope and level of interaction. The current system is becoming increasingly interdependent, with a rising number of interactions across an expanding range of issues. Economic interdependence is especially significant.

7. Among power relationships, an important factor is the number of poles in a system. Bipolar systems, for instance, may operate differently and be more or less stable than multipolar systems.

8. The pattern of concentration of power is another system characteristic. Whether poles are relatively equal or unequal in power, the shifts in relative strength influence behavior in the system.

9. Power changes in the system when there are shifts in the sources of power or when conditions within major actors affect their tangible or intangible power assets.

10. A system's economic patterns also affect its operation. For instance, the inequitable distribution of wealth among the countries of the world has created tension along what is known as the North-South Axis.

11. Changes in power cause specific changes; for example, the development of nuclear weapons may have directed the United States away from its isolationist stance. Changes in power are also related to system instability.

12. Norms are the values that help determine patterns of behavior and create some degree of predictability in the system. The norms of the system are changing. Many newer countries are, for instance, challenging some of the current norms of the system, most of which are rooted in Western culture.

13. It is clear that there are significant changes occurring in all the determining elements (structural characteristics, power relationships, economic patterns, and norms of behavior) of the international system. What is not clear is exactly what the new system will look like and how it will operate. Scholars use terms such as uni-multipolar, modified multipolar, and postinternational to describe the system that is currently evolving.

14. The view of this book is that system-level analysis is a valid approach to the study of world politics. It must, however, be used in conjunction with other approaches in order to understand world politics fully.

Chapter 4

State-Level Analysis

An old man, broken with the storms of state, Is come to lay his weary bones among ye; Give him a little earth for charity.

Shakespeare, *Henry VIII*

Oh, that lovely title, ex-president.

Dwight D. Eisenhower, just before leaving office

Chapter Objectives

After completing this chapter, you should be able to:

- Understand the major emphases of state-level analysis.
- Understand various factors affecting foreign policy, including the type of government, domestic factors, gender, and the type of situation and issue.
- Explain how a state's internal dynamics influence foreign policy.
- Understand the importance of political culture on foreign policy.
- Evaluate the role and influence of various subnational actors, including political leaders, bureaucratic organizations, legislatures, political parties, interest groups, and the people.

State-level analysis, a second approach to understanding world politics, emphasizes the national states and their internal processes as the primary determinants of the course of world affairs. As such, this approach focuses on midrange factors that are less general than the macroanalysis of the international system but less individualistic than the microanalytical focus of human-level analysis.

Understanding State-Level Analysis

State-level analysts, like system-level analysts, believe that states have long been and continue to be the most powerful actors on the world stage. The two approaches differ, however, on how much freedom of action states have.

Unlike system-level analysts, who believe that the international system pressures states to behave in certain ways, state-level analysts contend that states are relatively free to decide what policies to follow. A state-level analyst would say, "Yes, all countries must deal with the realities of the world system," but, "No, not even the least powerful state is a puppet on the string of the international system." In sum, state-level analysts concentrate on what countries do and how they decide which policy to follow (Bueno de Mesquita, 2002).

Studying what countries do is based on the view, as one study puts it, that "much of what goes on in world politics revolves around interactions between governments—two or more states trying to gauge the rationales behind the other's actions and anticipate its next move" (Hermann & Hagan, 1998:133). These interactions are called events, and these events and subsequent events (reactions and counter-reactions) are studied through **event data analysis**. This approach is useful for analyzing matters such as reciprocity between countries. For example, if country A upgrades its military (event), how will country B respond (event)? Will an arms race occur?

Decision-making analysis, or investigating how countries make policy choices, is the second concern of state-level analysts. Once again to contrast system- and state-level analyses, a system-level analyst would contend that, for example, the U.S. military response to Iraq's invasion of Kuwait was almost inevitable, given the realities of where oil was produced and consumed in the system. A state-level analyst would differ strongly and insist that the U.S. response depended on the presidential-congressional relations, the strength of public opinion, and other factors internal to the United States. Therefore, state-level analysts would conclude that to understand the foreign policy of any country, it is necessary to understand that country's domestic factors and its foreign policy–making processes (Chittick & Pingel, 2002; Milner, 1997). These factors, state-level analysts say, combine to determine how states act and, by extension, how the international system works as a sum of these actions.

Making Foreign Policy: Types of Government, Situations, and Policy

Most people do not think much about how foreign policy is made, and when they do, many imagine that presidents or prime ministers decide, and it is done. In reality, decision making is usually a complex process. Sometimes the national leader may be pivotal, but more often the leader does not play a decisive role. One way to begin to see the limits of even powerful leaders is to examine the authority of President Franklin Delano Roosevelt and the power of Lilliputians.

Roosevelt was an epic leader who led his country to victory over both the Great Depression and Hitler. Historians have rated him as one of the three best American presidents. To us, FDR seems to have been very much in charge. Roosevelt was, however, less assured. He often felt fettered by the restraints put on him by the bureaucracy, Congress, public opinion, and other factors.

FDR grumbled often about the bureaucracy, especially the N-A-A-A-V-Y, as he sometimes pronounced it derisively. "To change anything in the N-A-A-A-V-Y," Roosevelt once lamented, "is like punching a feather bed. You punch it with your right and you punch it with your left until you are finally exhausted, and then you find the damn bed just as you left it before you started punching" (DiClerico, 1979:107). Sometimes the Navy would not even tell him what it was up to. "When I woke up this morning," FDR fumed on another occasion, "the first thing I saw was a headline… that our Navy was going to spend two billion dollars on a shipbuilding program. Here I am, the Commander-in-Chief of the Navy, having to read about that for the first time in the press" (Sherill, 1979:217).

Congress also restrained Roosevelt. Isolationist legislators hampered his attempts to aid the Allies against the Axis powers before Pearl Harbor. Toward the end of the war, Congress threatened to block his dream of a United Nations. Diplomat Charles Bohlen (1973:210) has recalled FDR bitterly denouncing senators as "a bunch of obstructionists" and declaring that "the only way to do anything in the American government [is] to bypass the Senate."

Public opinion was also isolationist and further restrained Roosevelt in his desire to help the Allied powers. As late as October 1941, FDR warned the British ambassador that if "he asked for a declaration of war, he wouldn't get it, and opinion would swing against him" (Paterson, Clifford, & Hagan, 2000:182).

Roosevelt did not see himself, then, as the dominant figure that we remember him to be. He knew that to lead the country he had to get it to follow him and that getting it to do so could be difficult and take time. Speaking of his desire to move Americans away from isolationism and toward ever greater support of Great Britain, Roosevelt told one confidante, "The government… cannot change [directions] overnight.… Governments, such as ours, cannot swing so far or so quickly" (Paterson, Clifford, & Hagan, 2000:112). Indeed, he might have compared himself to Gulliver in Jonathan Swift's classic tale. The shipwrecked Gulliver was washed ashore in Lilliput. Although the Lilliputians were only a few inches high, Gulliver awoke to find himself bound by countless tiny ropes. He could have broken any one of them, but he could not free himself from all of them.

The point is that, like Gulliver, the freedom of all foreign policy decision makers, whether in democratic or dictatorial states, is limited by an intricate web of governmental and societal restraints. To understand this web, we will explore three general aspects of foreign policy making: (1) how differences in the type of government, the type of policy, or the type of situation influence the policy process; (2) the impact of political culture on foreign policy; and (3) the roles of the various political actors in making foreign policy.

TYPES OF GOVERNMENT

One variable that affects the foreign policy process is a country's type of domestic political system. Classifying political systems, such as democratic and authoritarian governments, is an important preliminary step to studying how they vary in policy and process because there is strong evidence that differences in the process (how policy is decided) will result in differences in policy substance (which policy is adopted).

Democratic and Authoritarian Governments

The line between **democratic governments** and **authoritarian governments** is not precise. One standard that differentiates the two types, however, is *how many and*

One thing that marks a country as authoritarian is severe restrictions on political participation. China considers members of the Falun Gong spiritual group dangerous because they represent a possible rallying point against the government. The people in this photograph are in Hong Kong protesting the arrest of over a thousand Falun Gong members in China. Because of international agreements, China allows somewhat greater freedoms in Hong Kong than elsewhere in the country. Police would have arrested these people if the protest had been held in Beijing.

what types of people can participate in making political decisions. In countries such as Canada, political participation is extensive, with few adults formally excluded from the political process. In other countries, such as China, participation is limited to an elite based on an individual's political party, economic standing, or some other factor (Nathan, 1998).

How many forms of participation are available is a second criterion for judging forms of government. Political dissent in the United States is public, frequent, often strident, and touches on issues ranging from the president's foreign and domestic policies through his personal life. China, by contrast, tolerates very little open disagreement with policy. During recent years, the government in Beijing has tried to present a somewhat less authoritarian image, but there are still regular instances of the arrest of dissidents, the oppression of minorities (especially Muslims and Tibetans), the lack of democracy, and other restrictions on political and civil rights. Some individuals have even been arrested for downloading criticism of China's government from the Internet. The Falun Gong, a spiritual movement that blends traditional exercises with Buddhism and Taoism, has been a particular target of government ire over the past few years, with many of its members being arrested on charges such as endangering state security. Wary of the growth of any popular organization, President Jiang Zemin warned, "We must not underestimate it, and even more so, should not be gullible. If this problem is not swiftly solved, it will become a major social disaster."[1]

Democracy and Foreign Policy Choices

To say that democracies allow greater participation in the political process than do autocracies does not mean that political influence is equally shared in a democracy. Indeed, what policies are adopted in any form of government, including a

democracy, is heavily influenced by how many and what types of people can participate effectively in making political decisions. Research on participation and
influence reveals "gaps," which are important because *who* makes decisions has an
important influence on *what* policy is adopted. To explore one aspect of the difference between the ideal of "we the people" and the reality of varying participation
and influence, we will explore two gaps: the leader-citizen opinion gap and the
gender opinion gap.

The Leader-Citizen Opinion Gap One standard of democracy is the degree to
which the views of the citizenry are reflected in policy. This is important because
in the United States and other countries, the opinions of those who are the leaders
of government, business, and other areas often vary from the opinions of the citizens who make up the general public, creating a **leader-citizen opinion gap**.
According to one survey taken in 1998, most Americans, for instance, would
permit their government to assassinate terrorist leaders; most leaders would not. A
majority of leaders would give more U.S. funds to the International Monetary
Fund to help it react to international financial crises; most of the public would not.
Most of the public would impose economic sanctions on China for its human
rights abuses; most of the leaders opposed the idea (Rielly, 1999).

Another series of questions in the 1998 survey asked whether U.S. troops
should be used to counter invasions of Israel, Poland, Saudi Arabia, South Korea,
and Taiwan. A majority of the leaders favored using troops in each scenario; a
majority of the public opposed intervention. Thankfully, these questions remained
matters of theory since no such invasions occurred. In one case, however, the relative significance of the opinions of leaders and citizens was put to the test. A survey
asked whether the United States should intervene militarily if Serbian forces killed a
large number of ethnic Albanians in Kosovo. A majority of American leaders favored
a military response; only a minority of citizens agreed. The following year, the
United States and its allies had to decide whether to intervene to stop the ongoing
slaughter. Soon U.S. warplanes were bombing Yugoslavia.

The Gender Opinion Gap Gender provides another relevant standard of democracy.
Despite some progress by women, males continue to dominate political decision
making globally. Opinion polls often find that the percentage of men and women
who support or oppose a policy differs. Indeed, sometimes a majority of one sex
favors a policy or a candidate, and a majority of the other sex takes the opposite
view. Because of this **gender opinion gap**, some scholars argue that the underrepre-
sentation of women in the political process has substantive impacts on policy. It is
appropriate to ask, for instance, how balanced the views of the leaders of the G-8
(the seven most powerful industrialized countries plus Russia) are, given the fact
that they are all males, as the photograph on page 88 shows.

Another interesting ramification of the continuing dominance of the political
arena by males relates to the issue of whether, on average, men are more bellicose
than women. There is at least some empirical evidence to support this view. In the
United States, for example, polls going back as far as World War II have consistently
found that women are less ready than males to resort to war or to continue war
(Rourke, Carter, & Boyer, 1996:376). Among the most recent crises, the gender difference was evident in 1999 as the United States debated whether to launch air
strikes against and even send ground troops to attack Yugoslavia over its ethnic
cleansing policy in Kosovo. Neither option was supported by either American men
or women, but 49 percent of men favored air strikes, while only 38 percent of women
did; and 46 percent of men favored using ground forces, while only 36 percent of
women did.[2] Opinion in the aftermath of the terrorist attacks of September 11, 2001,

What is missing from this photograph of world leaders? Women! There are real, if not legal, restrictions on political participation by women in even the most democratic governments. This is a photograph taken in 2001 of the leaders of the G-8, the seven major economic powers and Russia, gathered in Genoa, Italy, at their annual summit meeting. All are men. From right: Chancellor Gerhard Schröder (Germany), Prime Minister Jean Chrétien (Canada), President Vladimir Putin (Russia), Premier Silvio Berlusconi (Italy), President Jacques Chirac (France), President Bush, Prime Minister Tony Blair (Great Britain), and Prime Minister Junichiro Koizumi (Japan).

once again found women less ready than men to endorse military action, although in this case a majority of both men and women did support such a response. When asked whether the United States should retaliate militarily against the terrorists even if it meant that "many thousands of innocent civilians may be killed," 74 percent of men but only 62 percent of women said yes. A question that put the stakes of a military response at "thousands of American military personnel [being] killed," found 79 percent of American men but only 65 percent of American women still favoring action.[3]

This gender opinion gap was not confined to Americans. A survey in late September 2001 that asked the British about whether they would support sending British troops to Afghanistan recorded 53 percent of men and only 36 percent of women answering yes.[4] An earlier, even more extensive, survey in 1990 that studied the opinions of men and women in another 11 countries about the Persian Gulf War found that, with one exception, a greater percentage of men than women favored using force. This pattern is shown in Figure 4.1. Take note of several things in this figure. One is the gender opinion gap. The men in all but one of the countries, Turkey, were more likely to favor war than were the women. Second, notice the variations between countries. Women, on average, cannot be described confidently as antiwar, nor can men be characterized as pro-war. Both men and women favored war in three countries (and arguably also in Germany, where 60 percent of men and 50 of women favor action). In three countries men supported and women opposed military action, and in four neither women nor men favored war. Americans were not included in this poll, and the exact level of support for war by men and women varied considerably during the five months between Iraq's invasion of Kuwait in August 1990 and the beginning of the U.S.-led military action against Iraq in January 1991. Whatever the exact levels

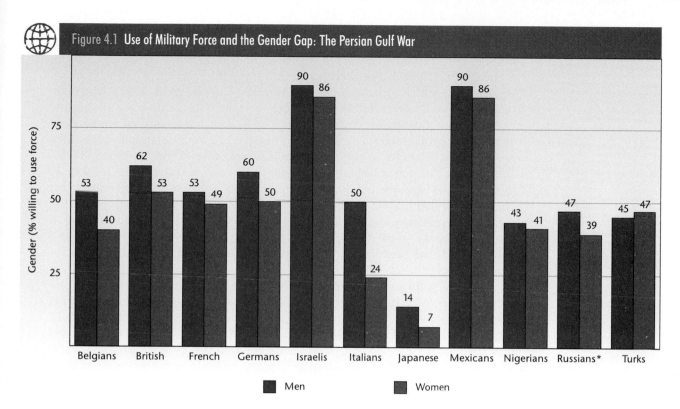

Figure 4.1 Use of Military Force and the Gender Gap: The Persian Gulf War

Data source: Wilcox, Hewitt, & Allsop (1996).

The question was: Should UN soldiers fight if the [economic] embargo [on Iraq] fails?
*The Soviet Union still existed, but the survey was taken in Moscow. Respondents were almost certainly Russians.

Women are less likely than men to favor the use of military force. This was true for each of the 11 nationalities shown here except the Turks, when asked about going to war against Iraq in 1991. It was also true for Americans. Also note the considerable variations among countries in the willingness to endorse war.

of support, however, the pattern of greater male bellicosity held true. For example, just before the counteroffensive began in January 1991, there was a 20-point gender opinion gap, with 62 percent of men surveyed in favor of military action, compared with only 41 percent of women.[5] Indeed, the gender gap preceding the war was so wide, ranging up to 25 percent, that famed pollster Louis Harris noted that "decisively, women oppose a war" and called the male-female difference in opinion a "gender gulf."[6]

Clearly, then, a gender opinion gap exists. It is also the case, however, that the pattern between countries also shows the possible impact of other factors. For example, national interest may account for the fact that war was favored by both men and women in Israel, which was threatened and then attacked by Iraq. Cultural beliefs may have also played a role. The pacifistic leanings of the Japanese are probably the reason that a vast majority of both Japanese men and women opposed using the military. The fact that, like Iraqis, most Turks are Muslims may help explain why a majority was unwilling to support the use of force in the Persian Gulf.

TYPES OF SITUATIONS

Whatever the form of government, the policy-making process is not always the same (Amadife, 1999; Astorino-Courtois, 1998). Situation is one variable that determines the exact nature of the foreign policy process. There are a number of ways that political scientists have classified situations to try to study variations in the foreign policy process. Of these classifications, the most widely studied are the differences in policy making that can be observed in **crisis situations** compared to noncrisis situations. A crisis is a circumstance in which decision makers are (1) surprised by an event, (2) feel threatened (especially militarily), and (3) believe that they have only a short time in which to make a decision (Brecher & Wilkenfeld, 1997). The more intense each of the three factors is, the more acute the sense of crisis.

One trait of the policy process during a crisis is that decisions tend to be made by relatively small groups of high-level political leaders. Public opinion is apt to rally in support of whatever action the political leaders take (James & Rioux, 1998). During noncrisis policy making, other subnational actors (such as the legislature, interest groups, and the public) are more likely to be active and influential. This characteristic was evident during U.S. decision making in the aftermath of the terrorist attacks of September 11, 2001. The key decisions were made by a handful of people whom the press sometimes referred to as President Bush's "war cabinet." These include the president and the seven other individuals shown in the photograph below.

A second pattern evident during crises is that legislators, most other leaders, and public opinion will tend to rally behind the head of the country's executive branch. Again, this was evident during the tense period immediately following the 9-11 attacks, as is discussed later in this chapter under the heading Political Executives and illustrated in Figure 4.2. Indeed, during crises the political system creates considerable pressure not to dissent from executive actions. Almost six months after the terrorist attacks of September 11, the U.S. Senate majority leader Thomas Daschle commented, "Before we make commitments in resources, I think we need a clearer understanding of what the direction [of the war in Afghanistan] will be." That seemingly reasonable remark brought an angry response from the Senate minority leader, Trent Lott. "How dare Senator Daschle criticize President Bush while we are fighting our war on terrorism," Lott asked rhetorically. A member of the House, who like Lott had apparently lost track of the positive role of debate in a democracy, used the definition of treason to castigate Daschle for "giving aid and comfort to our enemies." Aware of the perils of opposing the president at such times, Daschle had a spokesperson quickly issue assurances that he meant "no criticism of President Bush or his campaign against terrorism."[7]

Also, leaders usually strive during a crisis to make rational decisions, but their ability to gather and analyze information is hampered by the exigency of time. This and the anxiety or anger engendered by a crisis often increase the emotional content of decisions. With limited information, little time to think, and with elevated emotions, decision makers rely heavily on preexisting images. "During fast-moving events those at the center of decision are overwhelmed by floods of reports compounded of conjecture, knowledge, hope, and worry," Henry A. Kissinger (1979:627) has recalled from his years as U.S. national security adviser and secretary of

During a crisis situation, it is common even in a democracy for policy to be made by a small group, usually centered around the country's chief executive. This photograph shows the principal U.S. decision makers gathered in the White House on Wednesday, Sept. 12, 2001, the day after the terrorist attacks on the World Trade Center and the Pentagon. From left to right are CIA Director George Tenet, Attorney General John Ashcroft, Secretary of Defense Donald Rumsfeld, Secretary of State Colin Powell, President George Bush, Vice President Dick Cheney, Chairman of the Joint Chiefs of Staff General Henry Shelton, and National Security Adviser Condoleezza Rice.

state. "These must then be sieved through [the decision makers'] preconceptions. Only rarely does a coherent picture emerge."

What this means is that decision makers will respond to a situation according to the images they already have. If leaders perceive another country as aggressive and if that country mobilizes its forces during a crisis, then decision makers will probably see that act as preparation for attack rather than as preparation for defense. The onset of World War I, for example, can be traced in part to the series of mobilizations and countermobilizations by Austria-Hungary, Germany, Great Britain, France, and Russia. Most of these calls to arms were arguably defensive, but they resulted in a spiral of hostility based on misperceptions. Each country steadily increased its readiness in the belief that it must mobilize to defend itself, while, simultaneously, other countries were viewing the increased readiness as preparations to strike.

TYPES OF POLICY

How foreign policy is decided also varies according to the nature of the **issue area** involved. This type of analysis rests on the idea that issues that address different subject areas will be decided by different decision makers and by different processes. One theory about policy making holds that presidents and other leaders have greater power to decide foreign policy than they do to determine domestic policy. The latter area is one in which legislatures, interest groups, and even public opinion play a greater role. Agreement on whether this theory is true or not has so far eluded scholars.

One explanation for this lack of consensus may be that many policies are neither purely domestic nor purely foreign. Instead they have elements of both policy types and constitute a third type called **intermestic policy**. Foreign trade is a classic example of an intermestic issue because it affects both international relations and the domestic economy in terms of jobs, prices, and other factors. The influence of political leaders is less on such intermestic issues because they, like domestic issues, directly impact and activate interest groups, legislators, and other subnational actors more than do foreign policy issues. It follows that presidential leadership is strongest on *pure foreign/defense policy issues*, weaker on *mixed (intermestic) issues*, and weakest on *pure domestic issues.*

🌐 Making Foreign Policy: Political Culture

To repeat an important point, the state is not a unitary structure. Even authoritarian states are complex political organisms. Therefore, as one scholar notes, "All foreign policy decisions occur in a particular domestic context. This environment includes the... political culture... of a society" (Gerner, 1995:21).

Political culture refers to a society's general, long-held, fundamental practices and attitudes that are slow to change. It has two main sources. One is the national historical experience: the sum of events and practices that have shaped a country and its citizens. The fact that the United States has been invaded only once (in 1812) while China has been invaded many times makes American and Chinese attitudes about the world very different. The second source of political culture is the national belief system: the ideas and ideologies that people hold. Whether it is capitalism in the United States, Shiism in Iran, Sinocentrism in China, Zionism in Israel, or Russia's sense of its greatness, these intellectual orientations are important determinants of how a country defines itself and decides its policy (Cooper, 1999; Hudson, 1997; Lapid & Kratochwil, 1996).

Even those who study political culture are apt to concede that "demonstrating in a convincing fashion the independent influence of culture on political behavior is difficult" (Gaenslen, 1997:272). To begin to overcome this challenge and to ascertain its impact on policy, we can divide political culture into attitudes about (1) protecting and enhancing the national core, that is, the country's territory and population; (2) creating and maintaining a favorable world order; and (3) projecting values, that is, judging others by and converting them to those values. These three categories can be used to examine the role of any country's political culture in its foreign policy. But for the sake of illustration, the impact will be clearer if we focus on just one country: China.

NATIONAL CORE

An official publication of China proclaims that its first foreign policy principle is "Maintaining Independence, Self-Reliance and National Sovereignty" (China, 1993:3). This encapsulation of China's attitudes toward its national core reflects a number of interrelated traits of Chinese political culture, including Sinocentrism, insistent sovereignty, and a sense of being beset.

Sinocentrism

The notion of Sinocentrism is an expression of the tendency of the Chinese to see themselves as the political and cultural center of the world. The Chinese word for their country is "Zhong Guó." It means "middle place" and symbolizes the Chinese image of themselves.

One aspect of political culture that affects China's foreign policy is Sinocentrism, the tendency of the Chinese to see themselves and their country as the center of the political and cultural world. This self-image is represented by these Chinese characters. They are Zhong Guó, the Chinese name for their country, which translates as middle (Zhong, on the left) place (Guó, on the right).

China has been relatively weak and in turmoil for most of the last century, and Chinese assertions of their centrality have been and remain muted. President Jiang Zemin has reassuringly pledged, "China will never seek hegemony" (May, 1998:52). Some analysts worry, however, that such assurances are merely tactical, and that the middle kingdom complex can be seen in statements such as those of General Mi Shenyu, who counsels, "For a relatively long time it will be absolutely necessary that we quietly nurse our sense of vengeance. We must conceal our abilities and bide our time" (Bernstein & Munro, 1997:22). These pessimistic analysts also believe China's intentions are evident in its mounting defense expenditures. Most experts agree that Beijing grossly underreports what it spends on its military, but even by the government figures, China's increases of almost 13 percent for the year 2000 and more than 17 percent each for 2001 and 2002 were large, especially given that they had been preceded by a decade of double-digit increases in defense spending.

Sinocentrism also leads the Chinese to consider their principles immutable and not subject to negotiation or compromise. "Traditionally, other nations and people were expected to conform with China's norms and values," one study comments. That "basic attitude that the rest of the world should conform has changed little" (Wilhelm, 1994:25).

Some observers suspect that Sinocentrism will also prompt a rejuvenated China to seek to once again dominate its traditional sphere of influence in neighboring areas, especially Southeast Asia. In the view of one scholar, "From Beijing's post-cold war perspective, Asia is the center of Chinese power and influence, the calculus of ever-expanding circles radiating outward in all directions" (Kim, 1997:248). Beijing has alarmed other capitals in the region by claiming sovereignty over the Paracel Islands and the Spratly Islands in the South China Sea, by slowly building structures and communications capabilities on them, and by occasionally sending military units to these islands in what the defense minister of the Philippines has called a "creeping invasion."[8] Indeed, China claims control over almost all of this sea, an

China has moved gradually to reassert its authority over its former territories and over areas that once fell within China's sphere of influence. Its claims include the Paracel Islands and the Spratly Islands. Both island groups are also claimed by neighboring countries. Such claims have convinced many observers that China seeks regional dominance.

area extending southward nearly 1,500 miles from the Chinese mainland. These claims, one scholar writes, are part of a "remarkable and potentially dangerous" new Chinese concept of *haiyang guotu guan*, or "sea as territory" (Kim, 1997:248). What creates the peril is that the Paracels are also claimed by Vietnam and Taiwan. The Spratly Islands are also claimed by Brunei, Malaysia, the Philippines, Taiwan, and Vietnam.

Insistent Sovereignty

Chinese political culture is also marked, in the words of former U.S. secretary of state Henry Kissinger, by a "prickly insistence on sovereignty."[9] The stress that China puts on its sovereign control over what it defines as its territory stems from the fact that during the 1800s and early 1900s China was coerced into surrendering considerable territory to European countries and to Japan. Those countries and the United States also established de facto control over extensive areas in China. China never lost its theoretical independence, but in practice it was divided and dominated by outside powers. "This was a period of humiliation that the Chinese can never forget," a Chinese general explained during an address to the U.S. Army War College. The sense of humiliation, he went on to explain, "is why the people of China show such strong emotions in matters concerning our national independence, unity, [and] integrity of territory and sovereignty" (Kane, 2001:46).

That intensity has been evident, among other places, in China's determined effort to regain the territories it lost during its period of weakness. Tibet, which had earlier escaped all but technical Chinese suzerainty and which claims to have become fully independent in 1911, was invaded by and incorporated into China in 1950. Great Britain's Hong Kong reverted by treaty to China in 1997 and Portugal's Macau followed suit in 1999. Other claims related to the 600,000 square miles China had earlier lost to Russia were settled in 1997, with some territory restored to Beijing. These territorial changes leave the status of Taiwan as the sole remaining "lost territory." The issue of what Taiwan is to be or not to be is detailed in the box of that name.

The Chinese sense of sovereignty also has ramifications beyond territory. They reject, for example, the right of the United States or anyone else to comment on human rights in China. Exemplifying this, President Jiang has depicted the international calls for human rights reform by China as part of a neoimperial plan by "certain big powers for encroaching on the sovereignty of others under the pretext of promoting human rights and democracy."

Sense of Being Beset

A sense of being beset by foreign peril is a third core orientation of Chinese political culture. This trait springs from a combination of Zhong Guó's sense of being the middle place and a history marked by foreign invasions. These include the conquest by Mongols under Ghenghis Khan (1167–1227) and the establishment of the Yuan dynasty (1260–1368) by his grandson, Kublai Khan. The Ming dynasty (1368–1644) reestablished Han Chinese control, but it was toppled by the Manchus, who invaded from the north and ruled China until the fall of the last emperor in 1911.

All of this and more has created a mind-set among the Chinese that they are beset by potentially hostile outsiders. The country's most famous symbol, the Great Wall of China, epitomizes the Chinese sense of being besieged. The wall stretches 1,500 miles, is on average 25 feet high, and is the only human-made structure visible from outer space. It was begun under the Chin dynasty in the third century B.C., and it was periodically extended and reinforced over the next 1,800 years to wall out the marauding "barbarians" to the north.

(Continued on page 94)

TAIWAN: TO BE OR NOT TO BE

"To be or not to be, that is the question," Prince Hamlet muses in one of Shakespeare's oft-quoted lines. It is also what President Chen Shui-bian and the other citizens of Taiwan might ask of themselves.

Taiwan (also formerly called Formosa) is located 100 miles to the east of south-central China, has a total land area of 13,969 square miles (about the size of Maryland and Delaware combined), and a current population of 22.37 million. The island was part of China until it was seized by Japan in 1895. China regained the island after World War II, but Taiwan again became politically separated when the Nationalist government led by Chiang Kai-shek fled to Taiwan in 1949 after being ousted by the communist forces of Mao Zedong. Both Mao's government and Chiang's government agreed that there was only one China and that Taiwan was an integral part of China. The two disagreed about which government legitimately represented China. For years, the United States and most other countries recognized Taiwan (Nationalist China, the Republic of China) as the legitimate government of all China, and Taiwan held the China seat in the United Nations.

Over time, though, most countries shifted their diplomatic recognition to Beijing. The UN seated Beijing's representative and, in effect, expelled Taiwan's in 1972; Washington shifted its recognition to the mainland in 1978. Still, Taiwan has continued to exist independently, even though, in essence, it had become a vague diplomatic entity.

For about two decades after the shifts in the 1970s, the issue of Taiwan's status remained relatively moot. More recently, though, two factors have heightened tensions as Taiwan flirts with seeking recognition as a sovereign, separate state and China threatens war, if necessary, to stop any such move. One factor is the growing confidence of Taiwan. It has prospered. Taiwan's $343 billion GDP makes it the world's nineteenth largest economy; its combined merchandise exports and imports of $288 billion make it the world's eleventh largest trader. Taiwan also has a formidable military, spending some $8 billion a year on its approximately 375,000 troops and an impressive array of armaments. "The realities are that Taiwan is large, does exist, and is a force to be reckoned with in economic terms," an Asian diplomat has commented. "Now they feel they should be given some international space. It is an emotional, psychological thing. They feel inferior. They feel they are being treated as pariahs."[1]

The passage of time has also changed attitudes in Taiwan. The country has two ethnic groups: the traditional Taiwanese, who make up 85 percent of the population, and the closely related mainland Chinese, many of whom arrived in 1949 and who, thereafter, dominated politics. Among the Chinese, the old guard from the mainland has given way to Chinese born on Taiwan. Their attachment to the mainland is less pronounced than that of their elders. Also, the ethnic Taiwanese have become more prominent politically. In 1988, Lee Teng-hui became the first president of Taiwan of ethnic Taiwanese heritage. Lee, however, was the leader of the Nationalist Party, which was established by those who had fled China in 1949. The March 2000 presidential election marked yet another step away from China. The Nationalists lost the power they had held for over a half century when opposition candidate Chen Shui-bian was elected. Like his predecessor, Chen is Taiwanese; but unlike Lee, Chen, who was born in 1951, is the first president of the post-separation generation: those who have lived neither in China itself nor in Taiwan during a period when it was united with the mainland.

Over the past decade or so, there have been numerous signs that Taiwan is cautiously seeking legal independence. President Lee sought to promote UN membership for Taiwan and took a number of other actions to try to enhance Taiwan's image of independence. Lee was regularly condemned by Beijing, but he seemed relatively palatable compared to President Chen, the leader of the pro-independence Democratic Progressive Party.

Any move toward independence is anathema to Beijing. China has repeatedly vowed to use force to reincorporate Taiwan if the island declares its independence. This stand and candidate Lee's leanings toward independence sparked a crisis in the months preceding Taiwan's March 1996 presidential election. In an attempt to intimidate Taiwan, China conducted large military maneuvers in the Taiwan Strait that included firing missiles into "test areas" near Taiwan's main ports. In the end, China's fear campaign failed. The United States sent two aircraft carrier–led flotillas

More recently, the Chinese feeling of peril was given substance when much of China fell under de facto colonial domination by Japan and several European powers during the period of humiliation beginning in the mid-1800s, as noted earlier. Then, from 1949, China's sense of being beset was further reinforced by the communist

The uncertain status of Taiwan—somewhere between part of China and an independent country—has the potential to become an explosive issue. China has repeatedly said it will invade the island if its government declares independence; President Bush has pledged to defend Taiwan from China, as the April 26, 2001, headline in the English-language *Taiwan News* proclaims.

to the area. Washington warned Beijing not to be rash and simultaneously cautioned Taipei not to be provocative. The election proceeded peacefully.

Tension soared again as the 2000 election approached. In February, the mainland government released a report entitled "The One-China Principle and the Taiwan Issue" that, for the first time, implied ominously that China would not wait forever for reunification. If Taiwan refuses "indefinitely" to agree to "reunification through negotiation," the report warned, "then the Chinese government will be forced to adopt all drastic measures possible, including the

use of force."[2] Further raising the heat, an editorial in the *Liberation Army Daily* forecast "a blood-soaked battle" if Taiwan formally declared independence.[3]

Such threats brought a series of counterwarnings from U.S. officials. Undersecretary of State William B. Slocombe, for example, cautioned China that it faced "incalculable consequences" if it took military action. What ensued was a complex, three-sided, Beijing-Taipei-Washington negotiation, which is detailed in chapter 10. What is important here is that the key elements involving Taiwan's status included U.S. assurances to China and warnings to Taiwan that it did not support independence; the willingness of candidate, then newly elected president, Chen to back away from his pro-independence stand and at least rhetorically adhere to the principle of One-China and peaceful negotiations on reunification; and China toning down its rhetoric about moving militarily against Taiwan if it did not soon agree to reunification. Unlike what occurred in 1996, there were no overt demonstrations and counterdemonstrations of Chinese and American military muscle.

Thus, the waters in the Taiwan Strait calmed. Pro-independence talk and activity has been muted in Taiwan, and China seems willing, at least for now, to wait. "We don't need to threaten Taiwan anymore," a foreign policy official in Beijing recently observed hopefully. "Our economy is our best weapon. We won't attack them. We will buy them. It's very Chinese."[4] Indeed China has become so muted on the future of Taiwan that it barely reacted to a statement by President George W. Bush that "the Chinese must understand" that he would do whatever it took to "help Taiwan defend herself" if attacked by China. Earlier that almost certainly would have brought a sharp reply from Beijing. Instead, a foreign ministry spokesperson merely observed, "We have noted this point."[5] While this lull in the storms in the Taiwan Strait is welcome, the issue is far from resolved and remains potentially dangerous. Taiwan remains an international oddity, neither a state nor a dependent territory. China's determination to regain all its lost territories remains unfulfilled. The reversion to China's control of Hong Kong in 1997 and of Macau in 1999 leaves Taiwan as the last remaining unreclaimed territory. Now, as China's Foreign Ministry spokesman Chen Jian has said, "the settlement of the motherland" is "on the top of the agenda."

ideological view that the imperialistic capitalists would inevitably attempt to destroy the communist movement before it could bring about capitalism's downfall.

From Beijing's perspective, the end of the cold war has not lessened the international threat to China (Shambaugh, 2000). A frequently heard charge from Beijing is that the United States is worried about the growth of China's power and is trying to contain it by encircling it with a series of bases and alliances. As James Lilley, former U.S. ambassador to Beijing, has explained, "China sees America snuggling up to India…, recognizing Vietnam, selling F-16s to Taiwan, walking hand in hand with Japan into the 21st century, wanting a united Korea under Seoul allied with the U.S." What that looks like to the Chinese, Lilley concludes, is "a ring around China."[10]

This sense of threat persists strongly in Chinese thought, although there are some indications that it may be dissipating in part as China grows strong. As U.S. forces built up in the area and long-term U.S. bases were established in Afghanistan, Kyrgyzstan, Uzbekistan, and other areas near China, some Chinese strategists viewed them as a threat. "These developments give those people stronger evidence to argue that the war in Afghanistan is part of a plot, a strategic ploy, aimed at encircling China," commented Chu Shulong, an observer at Tsinghua University. That suspicious view met with unusual, less pessimistic counterarguments. For example, University of Beijing professor Ye Zicheng wrote that China needs "to walk out of the shadow of the past 100 years of our diplomacy of humiliation… and instead face the world like a big country." Remarkably, Beijing's policy seemed to follow this less suspicious view; China supported the U.S. intervention. "The quick, clear support that Jiang Zemin gave to the United States was unprecedented. Never before had China endorsed a U.S. military action against a Third World state," Chu noted accurately.[11]

FAVORABLE WORLD ORDER

China is a curious mixture of a former great power that once dominated its region, a currently developing and still officially communist country, and a country whose economic and military power is growing so rapidly that it has superpower potential (Karmel, 2000; Johnston & Ross, 1999; Murray, 1998). All these factors dispose China toward favoring changes in the status quo. One shift that China is seeking is an *enhanced world role* for itself. As its power has grown, one analyst comments, "recent Chinese thinkers have defined the defense of Chinese sovereignty to include defense of an international order that supports China's political system" (Kane, 2001:47).

Given this view, China's diplomatic activity has expanded considerably in recent years, and Beijing's focus has extended beyond its region to include a greater array of global concerns. The regular increases in China's military spending noted above have emphasized power-projection forces designed to apply military power at a distance. For example, as Lieutenant General Liu Shunyao has put it, China's air force is striving to "realize as soon as possible a change from territorial defense to a combination of defense and offense."[12] Some analysts view such statements with foreboding; others see them merely as a burgeoning great power asserting its status, much as other powerful countries have and that "the likelihood of Chinese aggression is close to zero" (Berry, 2001:40).

China's view of the proper world order leaves some leaders in Southeast Asia and other observers to suspect that Beijing may try to reassert Zhong Guó's historical geopolitical domination over the Southeast Asian **sphere of influence**. As Lee Kuan Yew, a former prime minister of Singapore, has observed, "Many medium and small countries in Asia are uneasy that China may want to resume the imperial status it had in earlier centuries and have misgivings about being treated as vassal states having to send tribute to China, as they used to in past centuries" (Bernstein & Munro, 1997:20).

Another aspect of China's worldview is increased *international economic interchange*. China is intent on modernizing itself economically and has come to realize that it needs Western technology and investment to do so. As a result, China has moderated some of its disputes with the capitalist-industrial countries and has established "special economic zones" to promote greater trade and foreign investment, and even now has decidedly capitalist stock exchanges in Shanghai and Shenzhen, as well as in the recently acquired territory of Hong Kong. China is also a member of the IMF, the World Bank, and other international economic institutions that it once condemned as tools of capitalist imperialism. This is a fairly recent orientation, and it conflicts somewhat with China's traditional self-reliance. China also campaigned to become a charter member of the World Trade Organization (WTO), and after long being blocked by the United States and other countries, the way for Beijing's membership was cleared by agreements with the United States and the European Union, and China became a member of the WTO in December 2001.

PROJECTING VALUES

The political culture of a nation determines the degree to which it applies its own values to judge others. For example, Americans have a missionary zeal to reshape the world in the American image, in the belief that the more other countries resemble the United States the better off they will be (Latham, 1997). This can lead to cultural imperialism. It also means that, more than most other countries, the United States champions human rights (albeit its own interpretation of rights) and, to some degree, applies those standards in making foreign aid and other foreign policy decisions. In the words of one study, national security interests play "the most prominent role" in determining U.S. aid policy, but "human rights do [also] play a role in the decision of who receives U.S. bilateral foreign assistance and how much aid they are allotted" (Apodaca & Stohl, 1999:195).

Chinese political culture attitudes about projecting values are very different from those of Americans. Despite China's immense pride in its culture, there is no history of trying to impose it on others. Even when communist ideology (with its element of exporting the revolution) was a much stronger part of China's foreign policy, Beijing was much less active than was Moscow in trying to convert others. This is a long historical orientation that existed even when China dominated much of the world that it knew. The orientation is based in part on Confucianism's tenet of leading by example rather than by forceful conversion. It also has to do with the Sinocentric attitude that the "barbarians" are not well suited to aspire to the heights of Chinese culture and are best left to themselves as much as possible. Among other current ramifications, this nonmissionary attitude makes it very hard for the Chinese to understand why Americans and some others try to insist that China adopt what it sees as foreign values and standards of behavior on human rights and other issues. Instead of taking these pressures at face value, the Chinese see them as interference or, worse, as part of a campaign to subvert them.

Making Foreign Policy: Actors in the Process

No state (national actor) is a unitary structure, a so-called black box. Instead, the state is more of a "shell" that encapsulates a foreign policy process in which a variety of subnational actors take part. These **subnational actors** include political executives, bureaucracies, legislatures, political opposition, interest groups, and the people. It is the pattern of cooperation and conflict among these subnational actors that constitutes the internal foreign policy–making process.

POLITICAL EXECUTIVES

The beginning of this chapter showed President Franklin Roosevelt's frustrations with the limitations on his authority. Yet it can also be said that **political executives** (officials whose tenure is variable and dependent on the political contest for power in their country) are normally the strongest subnational actors in the foreign policy process. These leaders are located in the executive branch and are called president, prime minister, premier, chancellor, or perhaps king or emir.

Whatever their specific title, political executives have important **formal powers**, those granted by statutory law or the constitution. Most chief executives are, for example, designated as the commanders in chief of their countries' armed forces. This gives them important and often unilateral authority to use the military. President Bush was relying on his authority when on the night of September 11, 2001, he told Americans and the world that the U.S. response to the attacks that morning "will make no distinction between the terrorists who committed these acts and those who harbor them." He made that clear when he informed Congress that he had commenced military actions against not only the al-Qaeda terrorists but also against the Taliban government of Afghanistan, "pursuant to my constitutional authority to conduct U.S. foreign relations as Commander in Chief and Chief Executive."[13]

Political executives also frequently possess important **informal powers**. Their personal prestige is often immense, and skillful leaders can use their public standing to win political support for their policies. As noted earlier, the informal standing of the chief executive as leader can be particularly powerful during times of crisis when other national leaders, legislators, and public opinion tend to rally in support of the chief executive and whatever policy that leader has chosen to respond to the crisis.

This **rally effect** was very pronounced in the United States in the aftermath of the 9-11 attacks. Congress quickly passed a $40 billion dollar antiterrorism package and a resolution supporting President Bush's potentially far-reaching policy of attacking not only the terrorists but also any country that gave them safe haven. There were some voices in Congress that warned against giving the president too broad a mandate to wage war and that urged the president to consult more fully with Congress. The majority, however, almost certainly agreed with the view expressed by one member that, "To be honest, at a time like this, Congress needs to be careful not to assert itself too much in a military and intelligence global operation." Other members even criticized their colleagues who pressed for greater congressional involvement. The administration "should keep focused on what's important, not holding hands with crybabies up here in Congress," one member grumbled.[14]

Also, as is normal during a crisis, public opinion rushed to offer support to the president personally and to the actions he was undertaking in response to the attacks. The personal support is evident in the public's response to the polls that a number of polling organizations regularly conduct, asking the public to rate how well the president is doing in office. This rating will typically improve dramatically during a crisis, and the pattern held true during the post–9-11 crisis, as Figure 4.2 demonstrates. Often the rush of support drops off almost as quickly as it went up. Bush's popularity remained high for an unusual amount of time, but as evident in the figure, the president's approval rating had begun to ebb by early 2002.

While the chief executives in most democratic countries possess formal and informal foreign policy powers that are greater than their domestic authority, presidents and premiers are not absolute monarchs. The spread of democracy and the increasingly intermestic nature of policy in an independent world mean that political leaders must often engage in a **two-level game** in which "each national

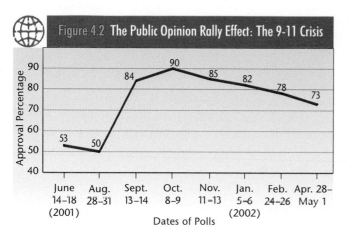

Figure 4.2 The Public Opinion Rally Effect: The 9-11 Crisis

Data source: CBS News/*New York Times* Poll found on the PollingReport.com Web site at: http://www.pollingreport.com/BushJob.htm

Fluctuations in President Bush's ratings before and after September 11, 2001, are typical of many crisis events. Crisis/noncrisis is one situational variable that influences foreign policy making. During a crisis, it is normal for public opinion to become much more favorable to the overall job a leader is doing, as this figure shows. Public opinion will also normally support whatever policy the president has announced or taken. Then the rally effect ebbs, sometimes quickly.

leader plays both the international and domestic games simultaneously" (Trumbore, 1998:546; Boyer, 1996). The strategy of a two-level game is based on the reality that to be successful, diplomats have to negotiate at the international level with the representatives of other countries and at the domestic level with legislators, bureaucrats, interest groups, and the public in the diplomat's own country. The object is to produce a "win-win" agreement that satisfies both the international counterparts and the powerful domestic actors so that both are willing to support the accord. Reflecting this reality, one former U.S. official has recalled that "during my tenure as Special Trade Representative, I spent as much time negotiating with domestic constituents (both industry and labor) and members of the U.S. Congress as I did negotiating with our foreign trading partners" (Lindsay, 1994:292).

BUREAUCRACIES

Every state, whatever its strength or type of government, is heavily influenced by its **bureaucracy**. The dividing line between decision makers and bureaucrats is often hazy, but we can say that bureaucrats are career governmental personnel, as distinguished from those who are political appointees or elected officials.

Although political leaders legally command the bureaucracy, they find it difficult to control the vast understructures of their governments. That was true in the past for President Franklin Roosevelt and the N-A-A-A-V-Y and other agencies, and it is true today for leaders such as President Vladimir Putin of Russia and President George W. Bush. Their wariness of their respective bureaucracies was evident during a joint press conference they held during a meeting of the Asia-Pacific Economic Cooperation meeting held in Shanghai, China, in October 2001. The two presidents were optimistically expounding on a new spirit of U.S.-Russian cooperation when a reporter asked them if they could "say with certainty that your teams will act in the same spirit?" Amid knowing laughter, Bush replied, "It's a very good question you ask, because sometimes the intended [policy] doesn't necessarily get translated throughout the levels of government [because of] bureaucratic intransigence." President Putin agreed. "Of course, there is always a bureaucratic threat," he conceded.[15] To understand this power, our discussion of the role of bureaucracies will focus on two points: bureaucratic perspective and bureaucratic methods.

Did You Know That:
Because of the respect for authority that is part of Japanese political culture, the country's bureaucrats are especially revered and powerful. Some 45,000 of Japan's best young professionals applied recently for just 780 positions in the senior civil service.

Bureaucratic Perspective

Bureaucrats often favor one policy option over another based on their general sense of their unit's mission and how they should conduct themselves. How any given policy will affect the organization is also an important factor in creating bureaucratic perspective. Often what a given bureaucracy will or will not favor makes intuitive sense. The military of any country will almost certainly oppose arms reductions or defense-spending cuts because such policies reduce the military bureaucracy's resources and influence. But the stereotypic view that the military is always gung ho to go to war is not accurate. Whether the area was Kosovo, Bosnia, Haiti, or elsewhere, the U.S. military has been a main center of opposition to intervention within the government, and especially to the use of ground forces. A common view, expressed by then former chairman of the Joint Chiefs of Staff, General (and later secretary of state) Colin Powell, is that "politicians start wars. Soldiers fight and die in them."[16]

The military's wariness about being sent into action in Afghanistan provides at least some evidence of the persistence of this bureaucratic perspective. President George W. Bush recalling his demand that the military give him options including the use of ground forces, remarked, "I think that General [Henry] Shelton [chairman of the Joint Chiefs of Staff] wasn't sure about [me as] the commander in chief at this point in time. He was a little uncertain as to whether or not we were going to create expectations [the military] couldn't live up to."[17]

Bureaucratic Methods

An organization's perceptions will cause it, consciously or not, to try to shape policy according to its views. Bureaucracies influence policy decisions by filtering information, tailoring recommendations to fit the bureaucracy's preference, and implementing policy in ways that alter policy direction.

Filtering information is one method that bureaucracies use to influence policy. Decision makers depend on supporting organizations for information, but what they are told depends on what subordinates believe and what they choose, consciously or not, to pass on. Occasionally, for example, a bureaucracy suppresses information that would embarrass the agency or undermine its policy preference. One of the notable disasters in U.S. foreign policy was the Bay of Pigs operation of 1961. The plan, which was formulated and supervised by the CIA, entailed a landing of anti-Castro Cuban exiles at La Bahía de Cochinos in Cuba. The operation was a disaster, with most of the invaders killed or captured by Cuban forces. One reason, according to declassified information, is that not only did the Soviets and presumably the Cubans know the exact date of the invasion, but the CIA knew that the Soviets knew. Yet the CIA did not warn either the White House or the Cuban exiles, because, it is reasonable to argue, doing so would have probably meant canceling the CIA-supported operation and admitting that the CIA had almost certainly been penetrated by Soviet agents.

Subordinates also filter information because they may be afraid that unwelcome news will endanger their careers. In the 1960s, amid the anticommunist consensus of the cold war, one U.S. official recalls, "candid reporting of the strengths of the Viet Cong and the weaknesses of the [U.S.-backed South Vietnamese] Diem government was inhibited" by the fear that any diplomat or intelligence analyst who suggested that the communists might win would be dismissed as weak-minded or, worse, as "soft on communism" (Thompson, 1989:593).

Recommendations are another source of bureaucratic influence on foreign policy. Bureaucracies are the source of considerable expertise, which they use to push the agency's preferred position. One scholar, after analyzing bureaucratic recommendations in several countries, concluded that leaders often faced an "option funnel." This means that advisers narrow the range of options available to leaders by presenting to them only those options that the adviser's bureaucratic organization favors. The options and capabilities developed according to the bureaucracy's "cultural penchant," the analyst continued, "often decided what national leaders would do even before they considered a situation" (Legro, 1996:133).

Bureaucracies can also "sell" a policy to a leader by intentionally or unintentionally overestimating the chances of success. During the first days after the terrorist attacks on the World Trade Center and the Pentagon, President Bush was intent on taking meaningful action. There were, however, neither existing contingency plans nor easy answers as to what to do. That created an opportunity for the CIA to become a leading player in operations instead of being confined to just intelligence gathering. CIA director George Tenet and the head of his counterterrorist center, Cofer Black, pressed the president to authorize CIA operations teams to work in Afghanistan with the Northern Alliance forces there and to hunt down al-Qaeda and Taliban leaders. According to reports, Black enthusiastically threw his fist into the air and urged the president, "You give us the mission," assuring him that "we can get 'em." "We'll rout them," Black predicted, leaping from his chair, "They'll have flies on their eyeballs." To Bush, who had already said he wanted the terrorist and Taliban leaders "dead or alive," and who was being assured by the CIA that the agency could deliver just that, it seemed like a perfect solution. An agency covert operations team was soon on its way. To say that the CIA's assurances were overly optimistic is a matter of history. The year 2001 passed into 2002, with al-Qaeda's Osama bin Laden, the Taliban's Mullah Omar, and much of the rest of the leadership of the two groups neither captured nor with flies on their eyeballs.

Implementation is another powerful bureaucratic tool. There are a variety of ways that bureaucrats can influence policy through the manner in which they carry it out. To a substantial degree, bureaucrats have discretion to carry out policy within broad parameters set down by decision makers. When they have options, it is normal for an official to choose the one that fits with his or her policy outlook. That implementation may inadvertently vary from what policy makers might have wished. At times, however, a bureaucrat can consciously attempt to delay, change, or ignore a decision or try to seize the initiative and act on their own. A fascinating example of both options occurred in Kosovo in 1999. Russia was attempting to play a role in the Balkans at the same time the largely NATO (North Atlantic Treaty Organization) force was taking up peacekeeping duties in Kosovo after Yugoslavia had capitulated. When the Russians landed a force at the airport in Pristina, the capital of Kosovo, the NATO commander, American general Wesley Clark, responded by ordering Lieutenant General Mike Jackson, the British commander in the area, to move his tanks to the airport and to block the runways to prevent Russia from landing supplies or reinforcements. Jackson refused, telling Clark, "No, I'm not going to do that. It's not worth starting World War III."[18]

These events demonstrate several aspects of implementation. One was the initiative of General Clark. Washington and the other NATO capitals were negotiating with Moscow about the Russian role when Clark, on his own initiative, decided to try to force the Russians to leave Kosovo and made a move that could conceivably have led to combat between Russian and NATO troops. Second, and adding another bureaucratic twist to the tale, Clark's initiative was trumped when his subordinate, General Jackson, refused to implement the order. One wonders whether Jackson should have been court-martialed, hailed for averting World War III, or both. In any case, whatever the political leaders might have wished, it was the generals in the field who made policy.

LEGISLATURES

In all countries, the foreign policy role of legislatures is less than that of executive-branch decision makers and bureaucrats. This does not mean that all legislatures are powerless. They are not, but their exact influence varies greatly among countries. Legislatures in nondemocratic systems generally rubber-stamp the decisions of the political leadership. China's National People's Congress, for example, does not play a significant role in foreign policy making.

Even in democratic countries, however, legislatures are inhibited by many factors. One of these is tradition. The leadership has historically run foreign policy in virtually all countries, especially in time of war or other crises. Second, there is the axiom that "politics should stop at the water's edge." The belief is that a unified

(Continued on page 103)

THE LONE DISSENTER

Immediately after the terrorist attacks on the World Trade Center and Pentagon, Congress moved toward passing a joint resolution authorizing President Bush to do what he had already decided to do: to take retaliatory military action. At a meeting in the White House just before passage of the resolution, the longest-serving U.S. senator (since 1958), Robert Byrd, told Bush that he could not expect the same open-ended authority that President Lyndon Johnson had received in 1964. Byrd remembered that Congress had later come to regret the Tonkin Gulf Resolution that preceded the full-scale U.S. entry into the war in Vietnam. "We still have a Constitution," the senator told the president, pulling a copy from his pocket.[1]

Yet, despite this note of caution, Congress quickly passed a joint resolution permitting the president "to use all necessary and appropriate force against those nations, organizations, or persons he determines planned, authorized, committed, or aided the terrorist attacks that occurred on September 11, 2001, or harbored such organizations of persons, in order to prevent any future acts of international terrorism against the United States by such nations, organizations or persons." The president could use the language, if read literally, to support an attack on any one of the "axis of evil" countries of Iraq, Iran, and North Korea or, indeed any country in the world that he believes is guilty of aiding or abetting terrorism.

Casting caution aside, Senator Byrd and the rest of the Senate passed the resolution by a vote of 98 to 0; the House agreed by the lopsided margin of 420 to 1. The lone dissenter in either house of Congress was Representative Barbara Lee, a Democrat from the California district around Oakland. The congresswoman agreed that "We must bring the perpetrators of this horrific action to justice." "But" she cautioned, "during this period of grief, mourning, and anger, the U.S. Congress has a responsibility to urge the use of restraint so that the violence does not spiral out of control and to consider all of the implications of our actions."[2]

Lee's vote sparked a torrent of verbal assaults. One arch conservative commentator wrote that "Barbara Lee is not an antiwar activist, she is an anti-American communist who supports America's enemies."[3] Others said worse; there were even threats of physical assault, and security agents were assigned to protect her.

Those who leap to condemn such a principled stand might well remember that only two members of Congress voted against the Tonkin Gulf Resolution and the broad authority it gave the president in 1964 "to take all necessary measures to repel any armed attack against the forces of the United States and to

Congresswoman Barbara Lee of Oakland, California, was the only member of Congress to vote against authorizing President George Bush to use force in Afghanistan and elsewhere after the 9-11 terrorist attacks on the United States. Like the two senators who in 1964 voted against using force in Vietnam, Representative Lee was castigated for being un-American. Time proved the two senators to be wise; only time will tell whether Lee or the rest of Congress had the greater wisdom.

prevent further [North Vietnamese] aggression [in the region]." The House of Representatives passed the resolution by a vote of 416 to 0, and the Senate added its support by a margin of 88 to 2, with Democratic senators Wayne Morse of Oregon and Ernest Gruening of Alaska the two dissenters. Morse predicted that "within the next century, future generations will look with dismay and great disappointment upon a Congress which is now about to make such a historic mistake."[4] The senator's only mistake was that he far overestimated the time it would take for dismay to be felt. Within a few years, most members of Congress regretted their vote and their tendency, as William Fulbright, chairman of the Senate Foreign Relations Committee put it, to revert to "a kind of tribal loyalty when war is involved" (Rourke, 1993:144). In 1970, Congress repealed the resolution, but it was too little, too late.

The lesson is that rallying to the president's support in time of crisis is not necessarily wise. Nor is dissent synonymous with lack of patriotism. Time proved Morse and Gruening correct and the 424 members who voted the other way wrong. It will take time to be sure whether in 2001, the 508 yea votes or Lee's one nay vote was based on the greater wisdom.

Legislatures and even individual legislators can play a strong foreign policy role in the United States and other democratic countries. The influence that Congress will have over long-term U.S. policy toward Afghanistan made it prudent for Afghanistan's interim leader, Hamid Karzai (second from right), and the country's minister of women's affairs, Sima Samar, to meet with Senator Joe Biden (right), chairman of the Senate Foreign Relations Committee, and its ranking minority member, Senator Jesse Helms. Karzai and Samar had come to Washington to attend President Bush's State of the Union address in 2002.

national voice is important to a successful foreign policy. This is particularly true during a crisis, which is highlighted in the box, The Lone Dissenter. Third, the tradition of executive dominance has led to executives normally being given extensive constitutional power over foreign policy. In Great Britain, for example, a declaration of war does not require the consent of Parliament. And even in the United States, where only Congress can declare war, presidents regularly take military action without a declaration of war or any other form of congressional consent. Fourth, legislators tend to focus on domestic affairs because, accurately or not, voters perceive domestic issues as more important and make voting decisions based in part on the legislator's domestic record rather than on his or her foreign policy stands. Indeed, paying too much attention to international affairs leaves legislators open to the electoral charge that they are not sufficiently minding their constituents' interests.

None of this means that legislatures do not sometimes play an important role in foreign affairs and have a range of potent powers, such as the ability to appropriate or withhold funds (Bacchus, 1997). Legislative activity is especially likely and important when a high-profile issue captures public attention and public opinion opposes the president's policy.

Even more commonly, intermestic issues are involved that directly affect constituents and interest groups in the legislators' electoral districts and spark legislative activity. As one member of the U.S. Congress put it, "Increasingly all foreign policy issues are becoming domestic issues. As a reflection of the public input, Congress is demanding to play a greater role."[19]

POLITICAL OPPOSITION

In every political system, those who are in power face rivals who would replace them, either to change policy or to gain power. In democratic systems, this opposition is legitimate and is organized into political parties (Breuning, 1996; Noël & Thérien, 1996). Rival politicians may also exist in the leader's own party. Opposition is less overt and/or less peaceful in nondemocratic systems, but it exists nonetheless and in many varied forms. One distinction divides opposition between those who merely want to change policy and those who want to gain control of the government. A second division is between those who are located inside and outside of the government. Just one example of how political opposition can influence foreign policy is contained in the box entitled Frustration-Aggression Analysis and the Rise of Vladimir Putin, in chapter 5.

INTEREST GROUPS

Interest groups are private (nongovernmental) associations of people who have similar policy views and who pressure the government to adopt those views as policy. Traditionally, **interest groups** were generally considered to be less active and influential on foreign policy than on domestic policy issues because foreign policy often had only a limited effect on the groups' domestic-oriented concerns. The increasingly intermestic nature of policy is changing that, and interest groups are becoming a more important part of the foreign policy–making process. We can see this by looking at several types of interest groups.

Cultural groups are one type. Many countries have ethnic, racial, religious, or other cultural groups that have emotional or political ties to another country. For instance, as a country made up mostly of immigrants, the United States is populated by many who maintain a level of identification with their African, Cuban, Irish,

Cultural groups can play a strong role in foreign policy. Latinos, especially Mexican Americans, are a rapidly growing demographic group, and it is probable that they will exercise increasing influence on immigration and other aspects of U.S. policy toward the homelands of their heritage. This photo shows Mexican Americans in Santa Ana, California, calling on Governor Gray Davis to end what the protesters consider unfair restrictions on Mexican immigrants getting a driver's license. The mask to the left of the picture represents Mexico's president Vicente Fox, who was scheduled to visit with Davis soon after this photograph was taken in March 2001.

Mexican, Polish, and other heritages and who are active on behalf of policies that favor their ancestral homes (Saideman, 2001; de la Garza, & Pinchon, 2000; Henry, 2000). The growing political importance of Mexican Americans, for example, has helped make the administration of George W. Bush open to immigration reform. Jewish Americans urge U.S. support of Israel. African Americans are active on a variety of issues that would benefit Africa, such as in pressing the U.S. government to ease patent protections on medicine needed to combat the astronomically high levels of AIDS in southern Africa. The sentiments of many Cuban Americans plays a strong role in the continuing U.S. refusal to recognize or even permit most trade with the government of Fidel Castro in Cuba. The list of groups and their influence need not continue to underline the importance of these political identity groups in the foreign policy process of the multicultural United States.

Economic groups are another prominent form of interest activity. They make contradictory demands for both protection from foreign competition and for pressure on other governments to open up their markets (Chrystal, 1998). As international trade increases, both sales overseas and competition from other countries are vital matters to many companies. They lobby their home governments for favorable domestic legislation and for support when a company is having a dispute with the government of a host country in which it is operating. Strong pressure from a generally united business community, for example, was the key element in the passage of the law that in 2000 ended the annual review by Congress of U.S. trade relations with China and secured U.S. support of China's entry into the WTO. Business leaders lined up solidly for the proposal, which they believed would bring them better sales and investment opportunities and spent an estimate $10 million on an advertising campaign advocating the change. Individual legislators were visited by hordes of economic leaders lobbying for the bill. "It seems like there have been hundreds of them," one congressman sighed.[20]

Did You Know That:

The score: 25–0. The 25 business leaders and 0 human rights leaders invited to the White House state dinner for President Jiang Zemin of China demonstrate the relative influence of business groups and human rights groups on U.S. policy toward China. Among the business guests were representatives of American International Group, Apple Computers, Asea Brown-Boveri, AT&T, Atlantic Richfield, Bell Atlantic, Boeing, DreamWorks, Eastman Kodak, General Electric, General Motors, IBM, International Corporation, Oracle, PepsiCo, Proctor & Gamble, U.S. China Business Council, United Technologies, Viacom, Westinghouse, and Xerox.

Certainly, there was opposition to the bill from human rights groups and others, but they were far outgunned. "A few thousand people bused to Washington… can't change the fact that the sky is blue, the earth is round and trade is the key to [American prosperity]," commented Representative David Dreier of California.[21] He might have added, "Or that even in a democracy, money equals influence."

Labor unions also affect trade issues and some other types of foreign policy. For example, labor unions are at the forefront of the forces in the United States that oppose rapid expansion of free trade and the empowerment of international economic organizations, which, according to AFL-CIO president John Sweeney, represent the "capstone of the corporate-dominated world marketplace."[22] Union members were among those who demonstrated against the WTO meeting in Seattle, Washington, in late 1999, against the IMF and World Bank in Washington, D.C., in April 2000, and against the World Economic Forum meeting in New York City in 2001.

Another economic group, farmers and other agricultural producers, are active in many countries in vigorous opposition to policies that would open their countries to increased competition from foreign agricultural sources. The North American Free Trade Agreement (NAFTA) has farmers worried. Mexican milk producers feel engulfed by a flood of milk from American cows. "If something isn't done about this soon," said Maria Teresa Berisain, a dairy farmer, "in three to four years no [Mexican] milk producers will be left."[23] To the north, brussels sprout farmer Steve

Bontadelli worries at his farm in central California, "It's simple math. In Mexico, they pay workers $6 a day. That's what we're paying per hour. We just can't keep up."[24] And yet further to the north, the National Farmer's Union of Canada claims that "NAFTA and [other free trade] agreements... have led to lower and more volatile [agricultural] prices. It is unacceptable that these agreements also limit Canada's ability to deal with those low and volatile prices through the design and implementation of effective safety net programs."[25]

Issue-oriented groups make up another category of interest group. Groups of this type are not based on any narrow socioeconomic category such as ethnicity or economics. Instead they draw their membership from people who have a common policy goal. The concerns of issue-oriented groups run the gamut from the very general to the specific. Some groups concentrate on one or a few specific issues. The United Nations Association of the United States brings together Americans who support the UN. At the general end of the spectrum, the Council on Foreign Relations draws together some 1,500 influential (elite) Americans who hold an internationalist point of view, and the council's journal, *Foreign Affairs*, serves as a forum for circulating the view of the elite. As Deputy Secretary of State Strobe Talbott said of the journal, "Virtually everyone I know in the foreign policy/national security area of government is attentive to it."[26]

Transnational interest groups also deserve mention. Some of these are nongovernmental organizations (NGOs) of like-minded individuals from many countries who pool their resources to press their own and other governments to adopt policies desired by the group. Transnational corporations also conduct extensive lobbying efforts in countries where they have interests. Many foreign countries also try to influence specific policy in other countries or, more generally, to project a positive image. And during late 2001, the military campaign against the Taliban was not the only one waged by the Northern Alliance of Afghanistan. The coalition also hired a U.S. lobbying firm, spending at least $150,000 to have Philip S. Smith & Associates help persuade official Washington to grant the Northern Alliance a strong role in the post-Taliban government of Afghanistan.

THE PEOPLE

The vast majority of citizens in any country do not have a direct say in policy making. Yet they play a role. This role is obviously more important in democratic systems than in authoritarian systems, but there is no system in which the public is totally ignored by leaders. To discuss the people's role, we will look at four factors: variations in interest in foreign affairs, dimensions of public opinion, the quality of public opinion, and the influence of public opinion on foreign policy (Powlick & Katz, 1998).

Variations in Interest in Foreign Affairs

International events and issues do not consistently command the attention of most citizens. Insofar as people are concerned with politics, they are normally focused on domestic pocketbook issues such as unemployment and taxes or social issues such as abortion. This domestic focus means, among other things, that foreign affairs issues do not normally determine how the average citizen votes. The U.S. presidential election of 2000 was no exception. One poll asked Americans how important each of five issues (education, health care, Social Security and Medicare, the economy and jobs, and America's role overseas) would be in their deciding whom to support for president. More than 75 percent of the respondents said that each of the four domestic issues would be very important; only 43 percent said that the U.S. global role would be very important.[27]

Sometimes, however, the broad public focus is on foreign policy. There is also a segment of the public, the "attentive public," that regularly pays attention to world events (Krosnick & Telhami, 1995). It is accurate to say, then, that public opinion runs the gamut from being interested in to being oblivious to foreign policy, depending on the situation and the issues. Crises will engage a significant segment of the population's attention. So will intermestic policies. Pure foreign policy issues that are not crises will engender much less attention.

Dimensions of Public Opinion

It is also important to note that the generic term public opinion disguises many variations in opinion. *Ideology* is one source of division. Public opinion ranges across ideology or values scales, such as isolationism-internationalism, militancy-cooperativeness, and multilateralism-unilateralism. Each of these ideological orientations strongly influences the individuals who hold them. One study of the ideological dimensions of American public opinion over 20 years (1974–1994) found Americans fairly evenly divided among four groups it termed isolationists, hardliners, accommodationists, and internationalists. *Isolationists* are individuals who favor a very limited U.S. role in foreign affairs. *Hardliners* are militant internationalists who favor unilateral U.S. action, especially military action, to support U.S. national interests. *Accommodationists* are cooperative internationalists who prefer multilateralism and the support of global justice and stability even beyond immediate U.S. national interest. *Internationalists* are comfortable with both the militant unilateralism and narrow definition of national interest favored by hardliners and the less militant multilateralism and more expansive definition of U.S. concerns favored by the accommodationists (Wittkopf, 1990, 1994).

Demographic groups, categorized by economic circumstance, gender, age, and other characteristics, are also the source of variations in public opinion. Gender is one important demographic characteristic that was discussed in the earlier section on the gender opinion gap.

A third variation involves the *leader-citizen public opinion gap* discussed earlier in this chapter. Among other differences between the two groups, the public tends to be less internationalist than is the group made up of the country's social-economic-political leaders, the elite (Murray, 1997). This difference is made clear in Figure 4.3. It is important to understand that these differences have an impact on policy because which policy is adopted sometimes depends on whether the views of the leaders or the citizens prevail. Note, for example, that the U.S. public would not be willing to support using U.S. troops to defend Taiwan if it were invaded by China. But the leadership would, and that view is supported by President George W. Bush, as discussed in the box, Taiwan: To Be or Not To Be, earlier in this chapter.

The Quality of Public Opinion

Another important aspect of public opinion to consider is its quality (Holsti, 1997). Some analysts dismiss the public as uninterested in and ignorant about foreign policy. They contend that, if too closely heeded by policy makers, the uninformed whims of public opinion create dangerous instability in foreign policy. Others disagree and hold that public opinion is both reasonable and stable.

The resolution of this disagreement depends in part on the questions that are asked. Some studies indicate that the public is apathetic, uninformed, and cannot answer specific questions about world politics. Figure 1.1 on page 3, for instance, shows that when people in eight countries were asked if they knew four specific facts

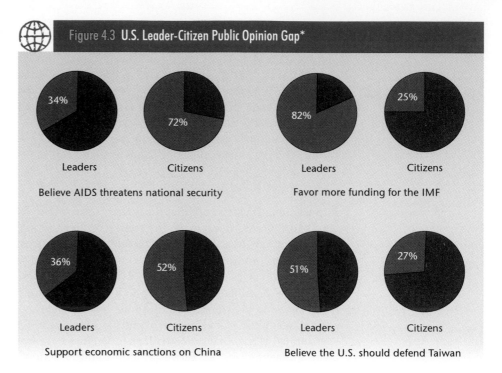

Figure 4.3 U.S. Leader-Citizen Public Opinion Gap*

Leaders 34% / Citizens 72% — Believe AIDS threatens national security

Leaders 82% / Citizens 25% — Favor more funding for the IMF

Leaders 36% / Citizens 52% — Support economic sanctions on China

Leaders 51% / Citizens 27% — Believe the U.S. should defend Taiwan

Data sources: "American Public Opinion and U.S. Foreign Policy, 1999," Chicago Council on Foreign Relations Web site, http://www.ccfr.org/publications/opinion/opinion.html.

*Questions: Do AIDS and other diseases pose a vital threat to the United States? Should the United States give more funds to the IMF to meet world financial crises? Should the United States impose economic sanctions on China for human rights abuses? Should the United States send troops if China invaded Taiwan?

Even in a democracy, the policy preferences of the citizenry and its leaders often differ. This figure shows that, compared with U.S. leaders, the American public is more apt to see AIDS as a national security threat, less inclined to fund the IMF, more favorable to sanctions against China in response to its human rights abuses, and less willing to commit U.S. troops to the defense of Taiwan. Whose opinion should usually prevail? Whose opinion usually does?

related to world affairs, an average of only 45 percent of the respondents were able to supply the correct answer to any one of the questions. The data also shows, though, that what people know varies significantly among countries. Germans were the most knowledgeable, with a 68 percent correct response rate. Two other nations, the French and the Italians, also scored better than 50 percent. The British, Canadians, Spaniards, Americans, and Mexicans were, in descending order, all under 50 percent.

Research that takes a broader perspective is more charitable about the quality of public opinion. Studies that examine long-term trends in public opinion and studies that compare shifts in opinion to events in order to see if opinion moves in a reasonable way find that public opinion is neither erratic nor unreasonable. For example, a review of studies of American opinion on the use of military force found that "the public evaluates the use of America's armed forces pragmatically and in a way consistent with fundamental international principles regarding sovereignty and self-determination.... The public is 'pretty prudent'" (Oneal, Lian, & Joyner, 1996:274).

The Influence of Public Opinion on Foreign Policy

Whatever the divisions or quality of public opinion may be, the key matter is its impact on foreign policy. To a degree, the interest of the public and impact of its opinion rise and fall according to the situation and the policy issue, and the type (democratic, authoritarian) of government, as discussed earlier. There are direct and indirect channels of public influence on policy, as noted in chapter 1.

The public in a few countries can decide foreign policy through direct democracy techniques such as referendums. Since the UN was founded, the Swiss have declined to join the world organization for fear that membership would violate Switzerland's traditional neutrality. The question of UN membership was once again presented to Swiss voters in a March 2002 referendum. The poster on the left and to the near right (with the ax) ask people to vote *non* (no), while the second poster from the left and the one on the far right advocate a *oui* (yes) vote on UN membership. In a 1986 referendum on the question, 75 percent of voters had said *non*, but 55 percent said *oui* in 2002, and Switzerland applied for UN membership beginning in mid-2002.

Direct Democracy Occasionally, the public gets to decide an issue directly through the use of referendums. Use of **direct democracy** is still limited, but it is growing. The people of Switzerland decided by direct vote in 2002 to join the United Nations. During the decade before that, voters in Austria, Finland, and Sweden voted to join the EU; Norwegian and Swiss voters rejected membership; and Danish voters rejected replacing the kroner with the euro. Australians decided to continue to recognize the British monarch as their head of state; the people of East Timor voted for independence from Indonesia; a majority of Hungarians cast ballots in favor of joining NATO; residents of Quebec voted against seeking autonomy or independence from Canada; a majority of voters in Nevis cast ballots in favor of their island seceding from the federation of St. Kitts and Nevis, but failed to get the required two-thirds vote for independence; the Swiss voted against a proposed ban on exporting arms; and there have been a variety of other referendums in which citizens, rather than legislatures, decided policy.

Indirect Democracy All democracies, even those that sometimes decide policy or make laws by using a referendum, are basically republican forms of government in which policies and laws are made by elected officials and their appointees. Therefore, it is more common for public opinion to have an indirect influence on policy through voting for officials and through the sensitivity of those officials to public attitudes.

Voting is one channel of indirect influence. First, voters sometimes get to choose among candidates who have different foreign policy goals and priorities. The changes of Israeli prime ministers in recent years—from liberal Shimon Peres to conservative Benjamin Netanyahu in 1996 to liberal Ehud Barak in 1999 to conservative Ariel Sharon in 2001—have had a great deal to do with the candidates' divergent views about how to deal with security and with the Arab world.

Decision makers' beliefs account for a second channel of indirect influence. Whatever the exact level of public interest may be, politicians are prone to believe that the public is watching and that if they ignore it or have it turn against them, they will suffer during the next election. At one point during the debates within the Bush administration about how to respond to the 9-11 terrorist attacks, Secretary of Defense Donald Rumsfeld raised the question about whether military action should be taken against Iraq in addition to Afghanistan. Secretary of State Colin Powell argued vigorously that it should not, in part because Americans would not support it. "Any action needs public support," Powell asserted.[28]

Decision makers also tend to believe that the chances of foreign policy success overseas are enhanced by public opinion support at home. "I knew full well that if we could rally the American people behind a long and difficult chore, that our job would be easier," President Bush commented about ordering military action against Afghanistan in 2001. "I am a product of the Vietnam era," the president explained. "I remember presidents trying to wage wars that were very unpopular, and the nation split."[29] Most decision makers in a democracy also believe that public opinion is a legitimate factor that should be considered when determining which policy is to be adopted. For all these reasons, public opinion does count, particularly when the people are strongly for or against a policy (Foyle, 1997; Powlick, 1995).

Chapter Summary

1. States are traditionally the most important political actors. States are political organizations that enjoy at least some degree of sovereignty.

2. Foreign policy is not formulated by a single decision-making process. Instead, the exact nature of that process changes according to a number of variables, including the type of political system, the type of situation, the type of issue, and the internal factors involved.

3. Many scholars believe that the fact that democracies include a greater diversity of subnational actors in the foreign policy arena has an impact on policy. It is also the case that as current democracies become more democratic by, for example, ensuring more and more authoritative participation of women, this will also affect policy.

4. States are complex organizations, and their internal, or domestic, dynamics influence their international actions.

5. One set of internal factors centers on political culture, which is the fundamental, long-held beliefs. China is used to illustrate how political culture attitudes toward the national core influence what is perceived as a favorable world order, and about the degree to which a nation should project its values.

6. Another set of internal factors centers on the policy-making impact of various subnational actors. These include political leaders, bureaucratic organizations, legislatures, political parties and opposition, interest groups, and the public. Each of these influences foreign policy, but their influence varies according to the type of government, the situation, and the policy at issue. Overall, political leaders and bureaucratic organizations are consistently (though not always) the strongest subnational actors.

Chapter 5

Individual-Level Analysis

There is history in all men's lives.

Shakespeare, *Henry IV, Part II*

Be not afraid of greatness. Some are born great, some achieve greatness, and some have greatness thrust upon 'em.

Shakespeare, *Twelfth Night*

My mind-set is Munich; most of my generation's is Vietnam.

U.S. secretary of state Madeleine Albright

Toughness doesn't have to come in a pinstripe suit.

U.S. senator Dianne Feinstein

Chapter Objectives

After completing this chapter, you should be able to:

- Define what is meant by individual-level analysis in world politics and outline the nature-of-humankind approach.
- Identify the roles of psychological and biological factors in the nature-of-humankind approach.
- Discuss the humans-in-organizations approach and consider role factors in this context.
- Explain how group-behavior factors function in the humans-in-organizations approach.
- Describe the psychological focus of the idiosyncratic-behavior approach.
- Consider how political and personal history can shape political leaders' decision making.
- Outline major sources and characteristics of decision makers' perceptions and assess the impact of those perceptions.
- Understand the impact of operational reality.

111

This chapter analyzes humans as actors on the world stage. The focus on humans lies at the micro end of the scale that ranges from macroscopic, system-level analysis detailed in chapter 3, through mid-range, state-level analysis discussed in chapter 4, to this chapter's microscopic, individual-level analysis.

The fundamental task of this chapter is to identify the characteristics of the complex process of human **decision making**. This includes gathering information, analyzing that information, establishing goals, pondering options, and making policy choices.

The human role in the world drama can be addressed from three different perspectives: human nature, organizational behavior, and idiosyncratic behavior. *Human nature* involves the way in which fundamental human characteristics affect decisions. *Organizational behavior* looks at how humans interact within organized settings, such as a decision-making group. *Idiosyncratic behavior* explores how the peculiarities of individual decision makers affect foreign policy.

Individual-Level Analysis: Human Nature

Leaders are not cybernetic decision-making machines. Instead, their decisions are affected by human emotions. In the aftermath of the terrorist attacks on the United States on September 11, 2001, President Bush was sometimes angry and sometimes incredibly sad. Here, tears are visible in the president's eyes in a photograph taken two days after the attack. He had just completed a call to New York City's Mayor Rudolph Giuliani and was overcome by the mayor's description of the devastation and loss of life at the World Trade Center.

The central question is this: How do fundamental human characteristics influence policy? To answer that, a first step is to understand that humans have limited and flawed decision-making abilities because people are unable intellectually and physically to learn and process all the information required to make fully rational decisions. Moreover, we humans have emotions that warp our judgment. Sometimes, for instance, presidents simply get angry. Soon after the terrorist attacks on the World Trade Center and Pentagon, President George Bush was in Air Force One consulting with Vice President Dick Cheney. "We're going to find out who did this," the president angrily exclaimed, "and we're going to kick their asses."[1] At other times leaders become overwhelmed with human emotion and cry, and more than once President Bush did that too, as the accompanying photograph shows. To study the limiting effects of human nature on rationality, we can examine cognitive, psychological, and biological factors in decision making.

COGNITIVE FACTORS

Decision making is one of the most complex things that political scientists study (Vertzberger, 1998). At its most abstract, decision-making analysis is involved with cybernetics, which is the study of control and communications systems. Since no human even approaches being a perfect cybernetic system, another important term to note is **cognitive decision making**. This means that humans necessarily make decisions within the limits of what they consciously know and are willing to consider (Geva & Mintz, 1997). Since there are many external and internal barriers or boundaries to what a decision maker knows or even can know, cognitive decision making is also called "bounded rationality." External boundaries include such factors as missing or erroneous information and the inability of any decision maker to know for sure what decision makers in another country are thinking or how they will react to various policy options. Internal boundaries that account for cognitive limits include every decision maker's intellectual and physical limits. No decision maker has the vast intellectual or physical capacity to analyze completely the mass and complexity of information that is available. Emotions are another all-too-human internal restraint on rational decision making. People regularly ignore information that they find emotionally unacceptable.

To see the difficulty of making a purely rational decision, recall your decision about which college to attend. Surely you did not just flip a coin, but did you consider all colleges worldwide, analyzing each according to cost, location, social atmosphere, class size, faculty qualifications, living arrangements, and program requirements? Did you consult a wide range of experts? Did you ignore such emotional factors as how far away from home the school was and how that interacted with your desire to be near, or perhaps far away from, your family, friends, or romantic partner? The answer, of course, is that you did not do all these things fully. Instead, you probably conducted a relatively limited rational review of information and options, then factored in irrational emotional considerations. You also relied on fate, because part of your happiness and success at college depends on things (such as with whom you would share your dorm room) that were unknowable when you applied. Thus you made one of the more important decisions of your life within a significant degree of bounded rationality.

Foreign policy decisions are also made within the limits of bounded rationality. Therefore, a key issue involves how policy makers cope with various cognitive limits on rational decision making. Four of the many mental strategies for coping with cognitive limits are seeking cognitive consistency, wishful thinking, limiting the scope of the decision, and using heuristic devices.

Seeking Cognitive Consistency Decision makers tend to seek cognitive consistency by attempting to suppress ideas and information that run counter to accepted interpretations of events and actors or counter to the policy path that a policy maker is determined to follow. Avoiding uncomfortable information is one way to do this. Later in this chapter we will look at the disastrous attempt by the Carter administration to rescue U.S. hostages from Iran in 1980. What is revealing is that there was information that the mission would probably fail. Its commander put the probability of success at "zero." The CIA estimated that at least 60 percent of the hostages would be killed, and one observer reported that a dress rehearsal for the rescue attempt was "the sorriest display of professionalism I've ever seen" (Smith, 1984:118). Carter and most of his aides ignored the foreboding signs because they were frustrated by deadlocked negotiations and concerned over the president's political vulnerability. Because they could not simultaneously favor a rescue attempt and believe that it would fail, they achieved cognitive consistency by discounting negative information.

Wishful Thinking A second mental strategy to cope with cognitive limits is wishful thinking. To justify in their minds decisions that they have made or wish to make, humans tell themselves that their choice will succeed. President Carter's chief of staff, Hamilton Jordan, later wrote that he and others at the White House were so desperate for the hostage rescue mission to succeed that "I couldn't even contemplate failure.... I couldn't get my mind off the helicopters lifting off from the embassy grounds with the hostages. I wanted desperately for this Godforsaken crisis to be over and done with" (Vandenbroucke, 1991:419).

Arguably President George W. Bush also engaged in some wishful thinking when he accepted the CIA's optimistic assurances that if he would authorize the agency to insert its paramilitary operatives into Afghanistan, the leaders of al-Qaeda and the Taliban would be either captured or dead—have "flies on their eyeballs," as the CIA's head of counterterrorism put it. Caught between an urgent desire to do something and the reality that there was little quick action that he could take effectively, the president was perhaps too willing to believe what he was told. As one journalistic account reported Bush's decision to authorize the CIA operation, "It was never quite as quick or as simple as [the agency] made it sound, but at that moment it was what the president wanted to hear." Bush was tired of rhetoric, Secretary of State Colin Powell thought; "The president wanted to kill somebody."[2]

Limiting the Scope of Decisions A third way that decision makers cope with cognitively complex problems is by limiting the scope of decisions. Deciding small things is easier than deciding big ones. Incrementalism is one way to limit what must be decided. Because they cannot know everything, decision makers will most often make what seems to be the safest choice by following established policy or only making small (incremental) changes. "Satisficing" is a related strategy. This means adopting the first option that is presented that minimally meets your goals rather than continuing to search for an optimum solution.

Using Heuristic Devices The use of heuristic devices is a fourth strategy to deal with cognitive limits. A heuristic device is a mental tool or frame of reference that helps an individual sort and evaluate information. In this sense, people use heuristic devices as shortcuts that allow them to skip long and detailed gathering and analyses of information and come to decisions quickly.

There is a wide variety of **heuristic devices** that humans use to reach decisions quickly. We will discuss three: national belief systems, stereotypes, and analogies.

National belief systems are based in political culture. Part of U.S. policy during the cold war stemmed from the fact that most Americans shared a national belief system that saw the authoritarian, communist, and officially atheistic Soviet Union as antithetical to everything they valued. This cold war consensus made decisions easy: oppose any advance by the communists. For example, Americans went to war in Vietnam with relatively little dissent. As then Secretary of Defense Robert McNamara later explained, there was a widespread belief that "the loss of Vietnam would trigger the loss of Southeast Asia, and conceivably even the loss of India, and would strengthen the Chinese and the Soviet position across the world, weakening the security of Western Europe and weakening the security of North America.… I'm not arguing [we viewed it] correctly—don't misunderstand me," McNamara conceded, "but that is the way we viewed it."[3]

Stereotypes are a second heuristic device that sometimes stem from political culture. For example, Western attitudes toward the Middle East are shaped in part by stereotypes. It is relatively easy to identify with the distinctly Western-looking, often English-speaking Israelis. Most people would be hard pressed, for example, to pick out any of the recent Israeli prime ministers from among a gathering of Western business people. It is harder to relate to Arabs, who often speak English less fluently and who are more apt to wear non-Western garb. It would be less difficult to distinguish these business people from Yasser Arafat, wearing his trademark black and white checkered *kaffiyeh* on his head.

During the tense months after the September 11, 2001, terrorist attacks, most leading American political figures were admirably careful to warn Americans against viewing all Muslims, especially American Muslims, in the same light as the terrorists. But there were incidences of stereotyping in official Washington. For instance, Attorney General John Ashcroft reportedly told a columnist, "Islam is a religion in which God requires you to send your son to die for him. Christianity is a faith in which God sends his son to die for you."[4] Ashcroft's office later complained that his remark was misconstrued, but it did not deny that he had made it.

Analogies are a third heuristic shortcut. We make comparisons between new situations or people and situations or people that we have experienced or otherwise have learned about (Peterson, 1997). How decision makers use analogies will be discussed in depth later, but, in essence, what happens is this: An issue, such as Saddam Hussein threatening Kuwait in 1991, is associated with a known historical event, such as Adolf Hitler threatening Czechoslovakia in 1938. Given the analogy, the course of action is clear: stand up to Iraq, just as we should have stood up against Nazi Germany. The trick, of course, is selecting the right analogy.

PSYCHOLOGICAL FACTORS

Theories that focus on the common psychological traits of humankind also help explain political behavior. **Frustration-aggression theory** is one such approach. It contends that frustrated societies sometimes become collectively aggressive. It is possible to argue, for example, that mass frustration promoted the rise of Adolf Hitler and German aggression in World War II. Germany's capitulation at the end of World War I left many Germans bewildered. They had defeated Russia earlier, and their army was still in France when the war ended. Germans were embittered further by the harsh economic and political terms imposed by victors, the resulting 1,700 percent inflation and economic devastation of Germany during the 1920s, and the treatment of the country as a political pariah. Entering this turmoil, Hitler capitalized on the Germans' pent-up anger by telling them that their defeat in the war and their subsequent plight were caused by Jewish and Bolshevik conspirators. Rearm and reclaim your proud heritage! Hitler told the Germans. There are only two choices, he proclaimed in *Mein Kampf*: "Germany will be either a world power or it will not be at all." The frustrated German people rallied behind the call to conquest, and World War II ensued.

In a very different context and time, it is possible to argue that frustration-aggression analysis can give us some insight into what would cause many in the Muslim world to hate the United States and some to become terrorists, driven by such intensity that they are willing to commit suicide in the act of wreaking death and destruction on the United States and its citizens. This connection between emotion and action is discussed in the box, Why Do They Hate Us?

BIOLOGICAL FACTORS

Various biological theories provide yet another way to explain human behavior (Somit & Peterson, 1997). One of the most important issues in human behavior is the so-called nature-versus-nurture controversy. The question is the degree to which human actions are based on animal instinct and other innate emotional and physical drives (nature) or based on socialization and intellect (nurture). With specific regard to politics, **biopolitics** examines the relationship between the physical nature and political behavior of humans. Biopolitics can be illustrated by examining two approaches: ethology and gender.

Ethology

The comparison of animal and human behavior is called **ethology**. Konrad Lorenz (*On Aggression*, 1969), Desmond Morris (*The Naked Ape*, 1967), Robert Ardrey (*The Territorial Imperative*, 1961), and some other ethologists argue that like animals,

(Continued on page 116)

WHY DO THEY HATE US?

"Americans are asking, 'Why do they hate us?'" President Bush told Congress on September 20, 2001. The answer the president provided was, "They hate what we see right here in this chamber—a democratically elected government.... They hate our freedoms—our freedom of religion, our freedom of speech, our freedom to vote and assemble and disagree with each other."

Perhaps, but many analysts believe that the president's explanation should have addressed the conditions that have spawned the hatred that led to the 9-11 attacks. One distinguished American analyst put the source of rage in a very different light. Instead of a hatred for freedom, he suggested that "the disproportionate feelings of grievance directed at America have to be placed in the overall context of the sense of humiliation, decline and despair that sweeps the Arab world." He warned that Osama bin Laden and his al-Qaeda followers "are not an isolated cult... or demented loners."[1]

The analyst's view of widespread negativity among Muslims toward the United States was confirmed by a Gallup poll conducted in nine Muslim countries in January 2002. The survey results showed 53 percent of Muslims in these countries having an unfavorable opinion of the United States, with only 22 percent having a favorable view and the rest undecided. Frank Newport, the editor-in-chief at Gallup, summed up the results as finding that most Muslims viewed the United States as "ruthless, aggressive, conceited, arrogant, easily provoked, [and] biased.... The people of Islamic countries have significant grievances with the West in general and with the United States in particular."[2]

One way to try to understand the rage is to contemplate the words of Osama bin Laden. It is easy to dismiss them as the ravings of a fanatic, even a lunatic. Yet it is important to see that the essence of his views are echoed widely in the Muslim world.

The fate of the Palestinians is one source of anger. "We struggle... in order to end the injustice inflicted on the oppressed in Palestine," bin Laden told a video camera in a tape that was aired in late December 2001.[3] Muslims, particularly Arab Muslims, view Jews as modern-day intruders who, with the support of the West, especially the United States, have oppressed the Palestinians. The turmoil between Jews and Palestinians is detailed in chapter 6, and it is not necessary to try to fix blame for the region's torment to understand that television in Muslim countries bombards its viewers with images of attacks by Israeli security forces on Palestinians. "You see this every day, and what do you feel?" asks Rafiq Hariri, Lebanon's prime minister. "It hurts me a lot. But for hundreds of thousands of Arabs and Muslims, it drives them crazy."[4]

A sense of Islam being beset by Eurowhites, first from Europe and now from the United States, is a second flash point. Bin Laden spoke of what he sees as the current oppression of fellow Muslims as "the most dangerous and fiercest crusade against Islam." In this he echoes a sense of many Muslims about historical animosity against them that, in their view, goes back nearly a thousand years. The sensitivity of Muslims was highlighted by the intense reaction when President Bush referred to the campaign against terrorism as a "crusade." The *Egyptian Gazette* editorialized that Muslims "feel they are the target of a latter-day crusade. Bush himself fueled these feelings when he vowed to launch a 'crusade,' a term that conjures up images of military expeditions undertaken by European Christians against the Muslim world in the twelfth and thirteenth centuries."[5]

Bin Laden also expressed anger because, as he sees it, "A nation of 1,200 million Muslims is being butchered from east to west every day—in Palestine, in Iraq, in Somalia, in southern Sudan, in Kashmir, in the Philippines, in Bosnia, in Chechnya and in Assam—and we do not hear anything from them [the Americans]." This view reflects what one former U.S. secretary of state depicted as a "constant undercurrent in a lot of the Muslim world" that the United States "doesn't care about preventing [atrocities] against Muslims, but we will go out of our way to hit the Iraqis when they do things."[6]

Resentment is also fostered by the vast economic gulf between the relative wealth of most Americans compared to the poor conditions of most people living in Muslim countries. From this perspective, the tapes showed a gaunt bin Laden justifying his cause as an effort to destroy the "international, usurious, damnable economy—which America uses along with its military power to impose infidelity and humiliation on weak people."

To capture the depth of feeling among Muslims, it is worth reflecting on a verse published on the front

humans behave in a way that is based partly on innate characteristics. Ardrey (pp. 12–14), for example, has written that "territoriality—the drive to gain, maintain, and defend the exclusive right to a piece of property—is an animal instinct" and that "if man is a part of the natural world, then he possesses as do all other species a

The banner carried by this group of Pakistanis in Islamabad on September 15, 2001, urges Americans to think about why they are hated by some people. That question, "Why do they hate us?" was also asked rhetorically by President Bush during a speech to the nation after the 9-11 attacks. Bush said it was because the United States represents freedom. Many observers have suggested that there are other reasons. What is important is to understand the views of others, even if they hate you.

page of *Al-Hayat*, a Pan-Arab newspaper published from London. The poet wrote:

> Children are dying, but no one makes a move.
> Houses are demolished, but no one makes a move.
> Holy places are desecrated, but no one makes
> a move....
> I am fed up with life in the world of mortals.
> Find me a hole near you.
> For a life of dignity is in those holes.[7]

In addition to capturing the sense of frustrated humiliation, the source of the poem is important. It was not penned by a potential suicide bomber seeking martyrdom. Rather, it was written by Saudi Arabia's ambassador to Great Britain, a member of the arch-conservative Saudi royal family.

Islam in all its complexities is treated in greater detail in chapter 7. Still, three things need to be stressed here. One is that nothing justifies the attacks on the World Trade Center and the Pentagon. The second is that although bin Laden's view is shared by most Muslims in the United States and around the world, a poll of Muslims in nine countries revealed that 67 percent of the respondents would characterize the attacks as "morally unjustifiable." A tiny 15 percent felt the attacks were justified, with the remainder unsure. Nevertheless, the third point is that it is important to contemplate the views of Osama bin Laden and other terrorists. If the old maxim that "an ounce of prevention is worth a pound of cure" has any worth, then an efficacious way of reducing the chances of future terrorism may well be to address the root causes and not to simply build defenses.

genetic... territorial drive as one ancient animal foundation for that human conduct known as war."

It is clear that territorial disputes are a common cause of war. To begin with, one study points out, "Most interstate wars are fought or begin between neighbors"

(Vasquez, 1995:277). Furthermore, another study concludes that since 1945, "war is a highly probable event in cases where contiguous states... disagree about the location of their shared boundary" (Kocs, 1995:173).

There are some territorial clashes that might seem rational to an outsider, but other disputes defy rational explanation. One war that was hard to comprehend by anyone but those involved was the fighting in 1998 and again in 2000 between two desperately poor countries, Ethiopia and Eritrea, over tiny bits of territory along their border. The land was described in one press report as "a dusty terrain of termite mounds, goatherds, and bushes just tall enough for a camel to graze upon comfortably."[5] It was, said one observer, "like two bald men fighting over a comb."[6] Even the leaders of the two countries could not explain why war was waged. "It's very difficult to easily find an answer," Eritrea's president, Isaias Afwerki, admitted. "I was surprised, shocked, and puzzled," added a perplexed Meles Zenawi, the prime minister of Ethiopia.[7]

Waiting in the wings to escalate is the dispute over a group of five islets and three barren rocks 200 miles off China's central coast. Japan calls the islets Senkakus; China calls them Diaoyu. Japan has controlled the islands since the 1895 Sino-Japanese war, but China asserts that they "have been Chinese territory since ancient times." It is tempting to treat such contretemps with amusement, and, to paraphrase a game, ask, "Where in the World Is Senkakus?" Unfortunately, it is no joke. One person has already drowned, as contesting groups of Japanese and Chinese patriotic zealots have planted their country's respective flags on the tiny dots of land. Also, the rhetoric between Tokyo and Beijing has heated up, with, for instance, China declaring that the "Chinese people are outraged and want to issue a strong

It may be that primordial territorial instincts sometimes cause humans to fight wars over virtually useless territory. Here we can see two Ethiopian militiamen in the barren landscape that is typical of the area over which Ethiopia and Eritrea waged a war in 2000 that killed thousands. Was fighting over barren land rational or was it based on animal territorial instincts?

protest" against Japanese flag-waving on the islets.[8] It is possible, of course, to offer various rationales for every territorial war that has occurred. Still, one has to wonder whether many such confrontations are not prompted by some primordial impulse about territory that growls "Mine!" from deep within the human psyche.

Gender

A second biopolitical factor that interests many analysts is the possibility that some differences in political behavior are related to gender. An adviser to President Lyndon Johnson has recalled that once when reporters asked him why the United States was waging war in Vietnam, the president "unzipped his fly, drew out his substantial organ, and declared, 'That is why.'"[9] Such earthy sexual explanations by male leaders are far from rare in private, and they lead some scholars to wonder whether they represent gender-based aggressiveness to policy making or are merely gauche.

The connection, according to some analysts, is that power seeking is a particularly male sexual impulse. One study of primates has commented on the "remarkable parallels in male primate behavior" and on the "observed pattern of power seeking or status striving that appears to hold across species among males." The reason, the study continues, is that "males tend to act to increase power as a means of increasing their reproductive success." Moreover, the connection with politics is that "statesmen, who think and act in terms of interests defined as power, should be no exception" to this primordial drive (Schubert, 1993:29, 21). From this perspective, Napoleon's claim that "power is my mistress," or Henry Kissinger's confession that "power is a great aphrodisiac," can be construed as deep-seated revelations rather than mere rhetorical flourishes.[10]

Political scientists are just beginning to examine the questions of whether or not gender makes a difference in the political attitudes and actions of policy makers. A related, more general question is whether any gender differences that do exist are inherent (biological, genetic) or the product of differences in male and female socialization (Ember & Ember, 1996). The ultimate question is whether an equal representation (or perhaps dominance) of women in foreign and defense policy making would make an appreciable difference in global affairs. Many scholars answer yes and say that the change would be for the good. Francis Fukuyama (1998:33), for one, contends that political violence is a product, in part, of male-dominated politics because, "statistically speaking it is primarily men who enjoy the experience of aggression and the camaraderie it brings and who revel in the reutilization of war." By contrast, Fukuyama believes, a world dominated by women "would be less prone to conflict and more conciliatory and cooperative than the one we inhabit now." Other scholars classify such views as part of the "myth of women's pacifism," and contend that a future world dominated by women "would not be as rosy as Fukuyama suggests" (Caprioli, 2000:271; Ehrenreich & Pollitt, 1999). Certainly there is good evidence, as noted in the discussion in chapter 4 about the gender opinion gap, that women in the mass public are less likely to countenance war than men. The attitudes of women in positions of authority may be much different, though. So far only a relatively few of them have been elected to lead countries, although that number is slowly growing, as is evident in the map on p. 120. Yet, even when past queens who had real power—such as Elizabeth I of England and Catherine the Great of Russia—are included, the relative scarcity of female international leaders makes comparisons with their male counterparts difficult. There can be no doubt, though, that able, sometimes aggressive, leadership has been evident in such modern heads of government as Israel's Golda Meir, India's Indira Gandhi, and Great Britain's Margaret Thatcher.

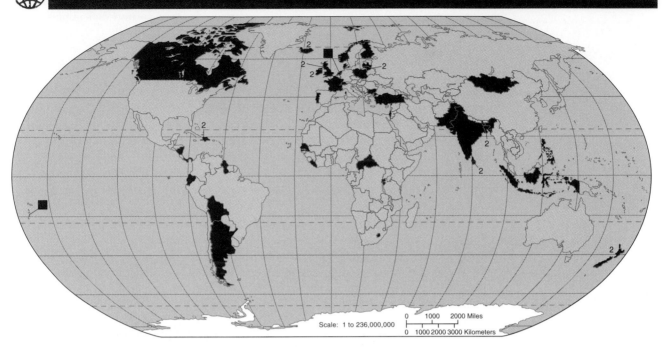

Female Heads of State or Government Since 1950

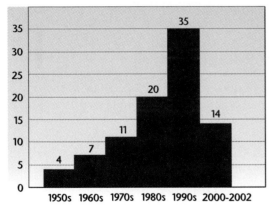

Some analysts believe that gender influences policy attitudes. One limit on the ability to be certain about this issue is the fact that relatively few women have led their countries. Still, that number is growing. This map and bar graph demonstrate across time the increase in the number of women leaders as heads of state and heads of government (such as presidents, prime ministers, and queens). During the 1950s, only 4 women led their countries. Since then, there has been a steady increase in the number of countries with women leaders. By the 1990s, the number had increased almost ninefold to 35. With 14 countries having women leaders already through the first two-and-a-half years of the first decade of the twenty-first century, it appears that this decade will set yet another new record for the number of countries being led by women.

The so-called **nature-versus-nurture** debate will undoubtedly continue far into the future and presents some fascinating questions. One of these is the basis of the box, "So Say the Mamas": A Feminist World. Whatever the exact role of biological factors may be, though, it is important to bear in mind that no one argues that biology is the sole cause of behavior or even that most human behavior is instinctual rather than learned. Furthermore, learning can modify behavior even if it is partly genetic. This is demonstrated by the basically peaceful conduct of interpersonal relations in most societies.

Individual-Level Analysis: Organizational Behavior

A second approach within individual-level of analysis examines how people act in organizations. Just as our overall cultural setting influences how we behave, so do the more specific pressures of our positions and the dynamics of group interaction

"SO SAY THE MAMAS": A FEMINIST WORLD

The assignment for my undergraduate honors course in international relations one semester was to do a project that involved almost anything but the standard 15-page, go-to-the-library, don't-forget-the-bibliography research paper. The results were fascinating. Among others, the submitted projects included a short story entitled "So Say the Mamas" by one of the women students.

The year was 2050 as "So Say the Mamas" opened. A number of women from around the world decided that the violence and inequality of the male-dominated world would never change and that it would be easier to forge a new civilization than try to fix the existing one. So they gathered a racially and ethnically representative group of women from around the world, acquired a spaceship, and left Earth, bound for the uninhabited, but habitable, planet of Xylos.

The women landed on Xylos and set about establishing a new society. Among the other provisions that they had brought from Earth, the women possessed a large quantity of frozen sperm that they could use for artificial insemination. By analyzing the sperm before implantation, the women could ensure that only female babies were born, thereby preserving forever an all-female population on Xylos.

At first, with relatively few women, the society on Xylos was governed by the "founding mothers" who had initiated the interplanetary move. This group was universally called the Mamas, and the rules that they established were promulgated with the declaration, "So Say the Mamas."

In time the women of Xylos multiplied and moved beyond their initial political structure and, by dint of sheer numbers, beyond their original, close-knit society. The author of "So Say the Mamas" went on to consider the nature of Xylos a millennium after its founding. Had the women established a world in which racial and ethnic differences had disappeared or were irrelevant? Or had racial and ethnic divisions built up? Was there equality on Xylos? Or had women established hierarchies based on race or some other characteristic? Was there a global government of Xylos? Or had the women divided themselves into sovereign states? Was there cooperation and peace on Xylos? Or had competition and warfare overtaken the planet? In short, was Xylos a brave new world, or had it become just like male-dominated Earth, which the Mamas had fled a thousand years earlier?

What the woman who wrote the story concluded is not as important here as what you think. The year is 3050. How does humanity fare on Xylos?

affect how we behave. Thus the **organizational behavior** of humans significantly influences the decision-making process of governments, as well as the operation of clubs, businesses, and other types of groups. Two concepts, "role behavior" and "group decision-making behavior," are useful to discuss how humans act in organizational settings.

ROLE BEHAVIOR

We all play a variety of roles. They are based on the attitudes and behaviors that we adopt given the position that we hold. Your attitudes and how you act—whether you are in class, on the job, or in a family situation—depends on your role, on whether you are the professor or a student, a manager or a worker, or a parent or child.

Presidents and other policy makers also play roles. The script for a **role** is derived from two sets of expectations about how an actor should think and behave. Self-expectations are one important source of role. Behavior in a given position is based partly on what an individual expects of himself or herself. Expectations of others are the second important source of role behavior. We behave in certain ways because of what others expect of us in a particular role. Such expectations are transmitted by cues that leaders receive from advisers, critics, and public opinion about how they, in the role of leader, should act. One common role expectation is that leaders be decisive and do things. A leader who approaches a problem by saying "I don't know what to do" or "we can't do anything" will be accused of weakness.

Whatever President Bush's thoughts about his own safety may have been in the hours immediately after the attacks on the morning of September 11, 2001, his sense of his role as president soon took over. He was in Florida when the attack occurred, and was soon aloft in Air Force One heading for a more secure location, first at one, then another Air Force base. Before long, however, he demanded that he return to Washington, irritably telling his chief of staff, "I want to go [back to the White House] ASAP. I don't want whoever did this holding me outside of Washington." The senior Secret Service agent objected that the situation was "too unsteady still" to risk returning to Washington. Bush disagreed. "I'm coming back," he told the vice president over the phone. Among other things, Bush felt it was his job to be in Washington and to speak reassuringly to the American public. "One of the things I wanted to do was to calm nerves," he later said. "I felt like I had a job as the commander in chief," he continued, and he also wanted to assure the country "that I was safe... not me, George W., but me the president."[11]

It is probable that overriding the concerns of the Secret Service was a wise decision by Bush in this instance. But there are also times when the role creates pressure to take action even when it might be better to wait or not to act at all. Reflecting this, former secretary of state Dean Rusk (1990:137) recalled, "We tended then—and now—to exaggerate the necessity to take action. Given time, many problems work themselves out or disappear."

A last point about role is that it is not immutable for any given position. Instead, there is "a more complex, less rigid relationship between role and issue position" than is implied in the old maxim "Where you stand depends on where you sit" (Ripley, 1995:91); roles are just one of a range of factors that determine how an individual acts in a position.

GROUP DECISION-MAKING BEHAVIOR

People behave differently in organizations than they would act if they were alone (Hagen, 2001; Hermann, 2001). There are complex and extensive theories about decision making in a group setting, but for our purposes here, the most important aspect of organizational decision making is the tendency toward **groupthink** (Schafer & Crichlow, 2002; Hart & Stern, 1997).

Causes of Groupthink

The primary cause of groupthink is pressure within decision-making groups to achieve consensus. Consensus may be a true meeting of minds, but it also may be the product of leaders and groups ignoring or suppressing dissidents, discordant information, and policy options, or of subordinates being afraid to offer discordant opinions or information.

Ignoring or Suppressing Dissidents, Discordant Information, and Policy Options
Groupthink creates an atmosphere in which discordant information or advice is rejected or ignored. Furthermore, dissenters risk rejection by the group and its leaders. This pattern was evident in the Carter administration during the hostage crisis with Iran (1979–1980). Carter and his aides were so intent on trying to rescue the hostages that the opposition of Secretary of State Cyrus Vance only earned him their contempt and soon cost him his job. White House chief of staff Hamilton Jordan has remembered "feeling sorry for Cy." National security adviser Zbigniew Brzezinski's evaluation of Vance was even more patronizing: "A good man who has been traumatized [and made weak] by his Vietnam experience." And the president wrote Vance off as "extremely despondent lately" and "deeply troubled and heavily

burdened." It did not matter that the disastrous raid proved Vance right. Within a month he was forced out of office, and Carter announced that he was appointing a new, "more statesmanlike figure" as secretary of state (Glad, 1989:50–56).

Reluctance of Subordinates to Offer Discordant Opinions While the Vance case shows that subordinates sometimes do dissent, it is not the norm. Usually they are careful not to contradict what they know or think to be the preferences of the group and, especially, their superiors. Experienced officials understand that dissenting, especially once the leader has taken a position, is risky. Therefore, they avoid it.

The U.S.-backed Bay of Pigs operation in 1961 to topple Fidel Castro ended quickly in utter disaster. A number of advisers thought the plan highly dubious, but remained silent. Admiral Arleigh Burke recalled that the military was skeptical of the CIA operation, but President Kennedy told the service chiefs, "You're not involved in this." This rebuff, according to Burke, had "a very strong effect on the whole damn thing. We *did* keep our hands off"(Vandenbroucke, 1991:110). Similarly, Assistant Secretary of State Thomas Mann later lamented that despite his doubt he also supported the invasion "because I did not wish to leave the impression that I would not support whatever the president decided to do" (Gleijeses, 1995:32).

There are some indications of groupthink during the White House decision making about how to respond to the 9-11 attacks. President Bush has recalled that when he heard about the second aircraft hitting the World Trade Center and, thus, knew it was terrorism and not an accident, "I made up my mind at that moment that we were going to war."[12] That left little room for advisers to safely suggest diplomacy. An aide remembers that Bush's attitude was that "we weren't going to dither and study [the situation] to death." As a result, "There wasn't a lot of soul-searching [among advisers]." At least one adviser has expressed the opinion that the president's single-minded determination to take rapid action also suppressed information. "The president finds out what he wants to know," the adviser commented, "but he does not necessarily find out what he might need to know."[13]

Effects of Groupthink

The urge for consensus that characterizes groupthink limits the policy choices available. It also decreases the chances that the policy chosen will prove successful.

Limited Policy Choices Anthony Lake, who served as national security adviser to President Clinton, recognized that "there is a danger that when people work well together [that] you can take the edge off options." This can lead, Lake says, to "groupthink... [with] not enough options reaching the president."[14] One way that groupthink may limit policy choices is through **incremental decision making**, which adheres to established policy or makes only marginal changes. One of Lake's predecessors, Zbigniew Brzezinski, has compared foreign policy to "an aircraft carrier. You simply don't send it into a 180-degree turn; at most you move it a few degrees to port or starboard" (Paterson, Clifford, & Hagan, 2000:414).

Lowest Common Denominator Policy Another way that groupthink's drive for consensus limits policy choices is that decision makers often adopt the policy that is least objectionable rather than the optimal policy. During the Cuban missile crisis, President Kennedy and his advisers did not decide to blockade Cuba because they thought it was the best thing to do. In fact, few of the decision makers really liked the idea of a blockade. Instead, it was a compromise between those who wanted to use military force to destroy the missiles and those who preferred to use diplomacy to persuade Moscow to withdraw the missiles.

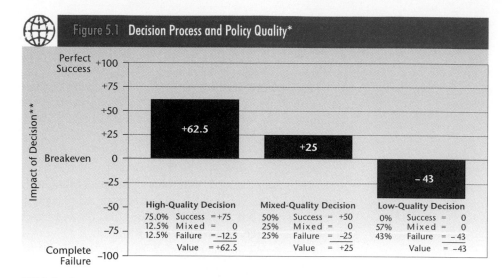

Figure 5.1 Decision Process and Policy Quality*

* High Quality = 0 or 1 symptom of defective decision making.
Medium Quality = 2 or 3 symptoms of defective decision making.
Low Quality = 4 or more symptoms of defective decision making.

** Success = Experts agreed that outcome was favorable for U.S. interests = +1.
Mixed = Experts disagreed on whether or not outcome was favorable to U.S. interests = 0.
Failure = Experts agreed that outcome was unfavorable for U.S. Interests = –1.

Data sources: Herek, Janis, & Huth (1987:217). Also see Purkitt (1990) and Welch (1989).

The quality of the decision-making process affects the quality of the decisions, as this figure shows. For this figure, successes were assigned an abstract value of +1, mixed results received a null value of 0 (zero), and failure received a value of –1.

Poor policy A review of the decisional inadequacies brought on by groupthink leads to the question, Do poor decisions result in policy failures? The answer is yes. Decision making that falls victim to groupthink invariably does not achieve optimal foreign policy. This was confirmed by three scholars who studied nineteen crisis decisions and rated them for evidence of 7 different symptoms of defective decision making (Herek, Janis, & Huth, 1987). Eight decisions had either 0 or 1 symptom and were rated "high quality." Four decisions with 2 or 3 symptoms were rated "medium quality," and seven decisions with 4 or more symptoms were rated "poor quality." The researchers then asked experts to evaluate the impact of each decision as positive or negative in its effects on U.S. national interest. As Figure 5.1 indicates, there is a distinct relationship between the quality of the decision process and the effectiveness of the policy adopted.

Individual-Level Analysis: Idiosyncratic Behavior

A third approach to individual-level analysis focuses on humans as individuals. This approach holds that the choices made by individual leaders are important in shaping events (Hermann, *et. al*, 2001). Therefore it emphasizes the idiosyncratic characteristics of political leaders. Note that idiosyncratic means individual, not odd. **Idiosyncratic analysis** assumes that individuals make foreign policy decisions and that different individuals are likely to make different decisions. In its simplest form, this approach includes examining biographies and memoirs as political histories. More recently, analysts have written sophisticated "psychobiographies" that explore the motivations of decision makers. Scholars are also using increasingly sophisticated methodologies such as content analysis, which involves analyzing the content of a decision maker's statements and writings to understand the basic ways he or she views the world.

Whatever the specific methodology of such studies, the point is not what a leader decided. Rather, the fundamental question is why the leader chose certain paths. What are the internal factors that motivated the decision maker? The list of possible psychological factors is long, but for our discussion we will consider five basic characteristics of individual decision makers: personality, physical and mental health, ego and ambition, political history and personal experiences, and perceptions.

PERSONALITY

The study of personality stems from the belief that, in the end, decisions are made by individuals and that the personalities of those decision makers affect what they do. One scholar has concluded after long study that "the personalities of the leaders... have often been decisive.... In all cases [studied], a fatal flaw or character weakness in a leader's personality was of critical importance. It may, in fact, have spelled the difference between the outbreak of war and the maintenance of peace" (Stoessinger, 1998:210).

When studying personality types and their impact on policy, scholars examine a leader's basic orientations toward self and toward others, behavioral patterns, and attitudes about such politically relevant concepts as authority. There are numerous categorization schemes. The most well known of these places political personality along an active-passive scale and a positive-negative scale (Barber, 1985). Active leaders are policy innovators; passive leaders are reactors. Positive personalities have egos strong enough to enjoy (or at least accept) the contentious political environment; negative personalities are apt to feel burdened, even abused, by political criticism. Many scholars favor active-positive presidents, but all four types have drawbacks. Activists, for example, may feel compelled to try to solve every problem even though not doing something might be preferable. That was arguably true in some cases for President Clinton, whom most political psychology studies categorize as an extremely activist personality, and who himself admitted to being "almost compulsively overactive" (Renshon, 1995:59).

President George W. Bush, in the view of one political scientist, "is positive, but toward the passive end of the scale." In a description that would also fit Ronald Reagan and other passive-positive presidents, the analyst writes that Bush "likes people and spends a great deal of time being social. He masters briefs, but he does not do much homework. Beyond a few issues that he cares about, he has no drive to dominate the domestic political process, or the Executive branch, or the world."[14]

Whatever the best combination may be, there is wide agreement that the worst is active-negative. The more active a leader, the more criticism he or she encounters. Rather than taking criticism in stride, though, the leader assumes that opponents are enemies and may withdraw into an inner circle of subordinates who are supportive and who give an unreal

This torn poster is symbolic of the destruction caused by Bosnian Serb wartime leader Radovan Karadzic. The words that cannot be read are, "Don't Touch Him," a warning to Serbs not to shelter Karadzic, who has been indicted for war crimes. The atrocities he ordered against Bosnian Muslims were arguably the product of a personality of a man who in 1971 wrote a poem entitled, "Let's Go Down to the Town and Kill Some Scum."

view of events and domestic and international opinion. Adolf Hitler and Josef Stalin and, to a lesser degree, Lyndon Johnson and Richard Nixon were all active-negative personalities who showed symptoms of delusion, struck out at their enemies, and generally developed bunker mentalities.

PHYSICAL AND MENTAL HEALTH

A leader's physical and mental health can be important factors in decision making (Park, 1994). In a book entitled *The Dying President* (1998), noted historian Robert Farrell details the diplomacy of Franklin Delano Roosevelt toward the end of World War II. Farrell concludes that the president was so ill from hypertension that he was "in no condition to govern the republic." This period included such critical junctures as Roosevelt's meeting with British prime minister Winston Churchill and Soviet leader Josef Stalin at Yalta in February 1945. Some analysts believe that the ailing president, who by then could not concentrate for long or work more than four hours a day, was too debilitated to resist Stalin's demands for Soviet domination of Poland and the rest of Eastern Europe. Less than two months later, the president suffered a massive brain hemorrhage and died.

A few leaders may even have acute mental problems. A psychiatrist who studied Adolf Hitler had concluded that he was "very disturbed," although not legally insane.[15] To make matters worse, drugs further destabilized him. As World War II turned against the Germans, Hitler's drug intake for a panoply of real and imagined illnesses reached epic proportions. Barbiturates, laxatives, cardiac stimulants, opiates, steroids, hormones from female placentas and from the testes and prostates of young bulls, caffeine, methamphetamine, and Eukodal (a morphine equivalent) all coursed through his blood. After mid-1944 Hitler also received multiple daily cocaine treatments for sinusitis. One analysis notes, "The precise effects of this pharmaceutical cocktail on Hitler's mental state [are] difficult to gauge. Suffice it to say, in the jargon of the street, Hitler was simultaneously taking coke and speed."[16] The drug combinations Hitler used would almost certainly generate a high-low cycle, producing euphoria and delusions of grandeur followed by paranoia and irrational anger. This bizarre pattern closely resembles Hitler's wildly inconsistent moods and decisions late in the war. It is probably too much to argue that a more lucid Hitler would have won the war or achieved a stalemate, but the conflict would almost certainly have gone on longer (L'Etang, 1970).

Alcohol abuse can also lead to problems. For example, there are persistent stories that President Richard Nixon, who Secretary of State Henry Kissinger once called "my drunken friend," alarmed advisers with his drinking and was once incapacitated during an international crisis with the Soviet Union (Schulzinger, 1989:178). Alcohol also impaired President Boris Yeltsin's ability to govern. His bouts with alcohol led to a number of incidents of bizarre public behavior, such as loudly singing a song that was different from what the band was playing at a public ceremony. Fortunately, especially for a man who had command over nuclear weapons, there were no major incidents. Still, the alcohol plus Yeltsin's heart condition (which required quadruple bypass heart surgery in 1996), so weakened the president that Russia was virtually leaderless during his second term.

EGO AND AMBITION

The egos and personal ambitions of political leaders can also influence policy. Ego, especially the male variety, sometimes works to make leaders want to appear tough. This trait may well have figured in the onset of the Persian Gulf War. There is something revealing in the name of Iraq's president, Saddam Hussein. His original name was Hussein al-Takrit, but once in power, he dropped al-Takrit and added Saddam, an Arabic word that means "one who confronts." The ego of Saddam Hussein's nemesis, George H. W. Bush, also may have influenced policy. Bush came to office with a reputation for being wishy-washy, and the "wimp factor" became a regular subject of journalistic comment. *Newsweek* magazine, for example, ran a picture of Bush and a banner, "The Wimp Factor," on the cover of a 1989 issue. It is possible that an ego-wounded Bush responded by being too tough. He soon invaded Panama, and the following year, during the Persian Gulf crisis, some analysts argued that Bush's fierce determination not to negotiate with Iraq left Baghdad little choice but to fight or capitulate. Certainly, it would be outrageous to claim that Bush decided on war only to assuage his ego, but to ignore the possible role of this factor would be naive. In fact, even after defeating Panama and Iraq, Bush remained testy about the wimp image. Addressing a California audience in June 1991, Bush expostulated with prickly pride, "You're talking to the wimp... to the guy that had a cover of a national magazine, that I'll never forgive, put that label on me" (Rourke, 1993:31).

Ambition is another driving force that sometimes affects decision makers (Renshon, 2000). The ambition to remain in power is, according to two scholars, "the very essence of the office-holding *homo politicus*" and can influence foreign policy (Bueno de Mesquita & Siverson, 1993:30). The policy of President John F. Kennedy toward the USSR and other communist nations was driven, in part, by Republican charges that he and other Democrats were "soft on communism." The president was determined not to let such accusations hurt his reelection chances. Soviet leader Nikita S. Khrushchev recalled that at his first meeting with Kennedy (in Vienna, Austria, in 1991), Kennedy had pleaded, "Don't ask for too much. Don't put me in a bind. If I make too many concessions, I'll be turned out of office." "Quite a guy," was Khruschev's sarcastic evaluation of Kennedy. "He comes to a meeting but can't perform. What the hell do we need a guy like that for? Why waste time talking to him?" (Fursenko & Naftali, 1997:134).

POLITICAL HISTORY AND PERSONAL EXPERIENCES

The past is a fourth factor that shapes a political leader's approach to world problems. Philosopher George Santayana wrote in *The Life of Reason* (1905) that "Those who cannot remember the past are condemned to repeat it." Contemporary policy makers frequently echo that sentiment. "History is a strange teacher," Secretary of State Madeleine Albright mused. "It never repeats itself exactly, but you ignore its general lessons at your peril."[17] The trick of letting history be one's teacher is learning the right lesson. The ability of decision makers to wisely apply the lessons of history is not, however, always evident, as we will see by examining lessons drawn from political history and personal experience.

Political History

Historical analogies that are based on how individuals or even societies interpret historical events and apply their supposed lessons are a regular part of policy making. The **Munich analogy** is one such history lesson that figures frequently in policy debates and rationale. When Germany threatened Czechoslovakia in 1938, France and Great Britain were unwilling to confront Hitler to risk war on behalf of what Prime Minister Neville Chamberlain told the British was "a faraway country about which we know little." The British and French therefore agreed at the Munich Conference to appease the Germans by letting them annex the Sudetenland region of Czechoslovakia. The traumatic events of World War II followed, and that experience "taught" that compromise with aggressive dictators would only encourage them.

During the intervening years leaders have repeatedly cited the lesson of the 1930s as justification for confronting international opponents and, if necessary, going to war. "If history teaches us anything, it is that... appeasement does not work," President H. W. Bush declared to the American people when Saddam Hussein's forces attacked Kuwait. "As was the case in the 1930s," Bush instructed, "we see in Saddam Hussein an aggressive dictator threatening his neighbors. Half a century ago the world had a chance to stop a ruthless aggressor and missed it. I pledge to you: We will not make that mistake again" (Rourke, 1993:30). War followed.

Similarly, George W. Bush viewed the terrorist attacks in 2001 partly through the perspective of the Munich analogy. During his State of the Union message on January 29, 2002, the president alluded to the three-country (Germany, Italy, Japan) Axis powers of World War II when he said that another three countries, Iraq, Iran, and North Korea, "constitute an axis of evil, arming to threaten the peace of the world." Even more directly during another speech, the president called Osama bin Laden and other terrorists "the heirs to fascism. They have the same will to power, the same disdain for the individual, the same mad global ambitions. And they will be dealt with in just the same way," Bush promised. "Like all fascists," the president continued, "the terrorists cannot be appeased: they must be defeated."[18]

Lessons of history often fade as those who remember them become fewer and as more recent history teaches new lessons. One such new lesson for Americans is the **Vietnam analogy**. This is almost the antithesis of the Munich syndrome. Now when there is the possibility of an intervention, especially in a civil war, the cry "no more Vietnams" is heard (Simons, 1998). The image of Vietnam was, for instance, raised frequently by those who opposed U.S. intervention in Bosnia. "Most of us hark back to Vietnam and have faint enthusiasm for punching somebody to see what happens," one senior U.S. military officer commented on the possibility of sending U.S. troops to the Balkans.[19]

Two subsidiary comments about the use of historical analogies are important. First, as a heuristic device, historical analogies are too often used to avoid thinking rather than to inform decisions. Both Saddam Hussein and Osama bin Laden are certainly odious individuals, just as Hitler was. Neither the Persian Gulf in 1990 nor Afghanistan in 2001, however, had much resemblance to Europe in 1938. Nor, it can be added, did the difficult terrain and the irregular forces in the Balkans in the 1990s mean that it was like Vietnam in the 1960s. The point is that a historical analogy should be the beginning, not the end, of a political discussion, and it is the responsibility of the individual using the analogy to demonstrate its applicability.

Second, policy makers sometimes make a decision, then select a likely historical analogy to justify their position. A study of the congressional debate on the Persian Gulf War resolutions in 1991 found that almost all foreign policy conservatives and Republicans (who were predisposed toward military action) used the Munich example to argue for war. By contrast, almost all foreign policy liberals and Democrats (who were predisposed to continue economic sanctions) used the Vietnam example to argue against quick military action. The data led to the conclusion that the Munich and Vietnam analogies were "used by members of Congress as post-hoc justifications for policy choices and [did] not help determine them" (Taylor & Rourke, 1995:467).

Personal Experiences

Decision makers are also affected by their personal experiences. One might think that General Colin Powell would have been an advocate of using military force in crises he had to face as chairman of the Joint Chiefs of Staff under presidents George H. W. Bush and Bill Clinton, and as secretary of state under President George W.

The personal experiences of leaders can affect their perceptions and decisions. Secretary of State Colin Powell was a young Army officer in Vietnam. Many analysts believe that Powell's reluctance to use military power when he was chairman of the Joint Chiefs of Staff (1989–1993) and as secretary of state reflects that bitter experience. This picture shows General Powell laying a wreath in 1991 at the Vietnam Veterans Memorial in Washington, D.C.

Bush. The reality is that he has proven to be a very reluctant warrior. Powell was one of the generation of junior officers who served in Vietnam and who were frustrated, even traumatized, by their sense of political restraints denying them the chance to achieve victory, by seeing their men die in an ultimately futile war, and by the opprobrium heaped on the military by many critics of the war. Arguably as a result, Powell has been consistently wary of committing U.S. troops to action. This has been especially so in situations such as Panama (1989), Somalia (1992), and the Balkans (early 1990s) in which the U.S. goal was achieving political change (not defeating an enemy force as such) and, therefore, in which the U.S. political leaders were not willing to commit massive numbers of U.S. troops and give U.S. military commanders free rein in deciding how to "win" the war. In Powell's words, "The American military has constantly been nailed about the so-called Vietnam syndrome. Does it affect our thinking? Sure it was the most definitive military event in our lives and in our career.... What those of us in the military are trying to do is... to make sure that our political leaders understand the consequences of going to war and how to go to war well and do it well."[20]

Powell was also cautious about using military force too broadly in response to the 9-11 attacks. One option, pushed by Deputy Secretary of Defense Paul Wolfowitz with some support from his boss, Secretary of Defense Donald Rumsfeld, was to extend the targets of attack beyond al-Qaeda and the Taliban in Afghanistan to Iraq. They voiced this opinion both to the president and in public. They considered Iraq a terrorist state and a threat to national security, as did the president, who later named Iraq as part of the axis of evil. Powell vigorously opposed the Iraq option. "What the hell, what are these guys thinking about?" Powell at one point asked General Henry Shelton, chairman of the Joint Chiefs of Staff. "Can't you get these guys back in the box?" It is indicative of the intensity of Powell's opposition that he even publicly aired his disagreement with the Defense Department. "Ending terrorism is where I would like to leave it," Powell told reporters. "Let Mr. Wolfowitz speak for himself."[21]

PERCEPTIONS

A decision maker's images of reality constitute a fifth idiosyncratic element that influences their approach to foreign policy. These images are called **perceptions**. Images and reality may be the same; they may be dramatically different. Some factors in world politics, such as the existence of Kashmir in Asia, are in the realm of objective reality. Other factors are subjective. India perceives Kashmir as an integral and proper part of the country. Pakistan perceives Kashmir to be a territory whose largely Muslim population has been illegally annexed by India—a territory that should be part of Pakistan. Since India's and Pakistan's perceptions are mutually exclusive, it follows that perceptions sometimes distort reality.

Perceptions have a multitude of sources. Many, such as belief systems and historical analogies, are related to the cognitive limits discussed earlier in this chapter or to the idiosyncratic characteristics of decision makers that we have been analyzing in this section. The information that decision makers receive from their bureaucracies or elsewhere, as discussed in chapter 4, is another important source of perceptions. Whatever their source, though, perceptions have a number of characteristics and impacts that are important to world politics (Blanton, 1996).

Characteristics of Perceptions

There are numerous common perceptual characteristics that influence policy making. To demonstrate this, we can take a look at five common characteristics of perceptions.

We often assume that others see the world the same way that we do. George H. W. Bush dealt with Saddam Hussein, and with Arabs in general, on the assumption that they operated from the same mental framework that he had. When, for example, the U.S.-led coalition amassed a huge military force and gave Iraq an ultimatum to get out of Kuwait or suffer the consequences, Bush assumed that the Iraqis could count, would realize that they would be flattened, and would give way. Just three weeks before that perception was proven false by the onset of war, a reporter asked President Bush if he thought that Iraq would quit Kuwait. "Some leaders tell me [that Iraq] cannot get out," he replied. "I do not have much of a feel" for the Arab point of view, Bush conceded, but, he went on, Saddam Hussein "must understand what he is up against in terms of power.... Oh God," Bush concluded hesitantly, "my gut says he will get out of there" (Rourke, 1993:37).

We are apt to perceive other countries as more hostile than our own. This tendency is particularly strong when there is a lack of knowledge about others. When Ronald Reagan took office in 1981 he was prone to demonizing the USSR, once even calling it an evil empire. Similarly, soon after Soviet president Mikhail Gorbachev came to power in 1985 he characterized President Reagan as a prisoner of the military-industrial complex who "couldn't make peace if he wanted to."[22] Neither Reagan's nor Gorbachev's image was especially accurate. History records that as they learned more about one another and about each other's country through a series of summit meetings, the views of the two leaders moderated substantially. By the end of Reagan's tenure the two had met so often and so cordially that they were dubbed the Ron and Gorby Show.

We tend to see the behavior of others as more planned and coordinated than our own. During the cold war, both the Americans and the Soviets imagined that the other side had a carefully planned, well-executed master strategy to expand its power and influence and to frustrate and defeat its opponents. By contrast, each side saw itself as on the defensive and as responding on a piecemeal basis to the aggressive thrusts of the other side. Former secretary of state Henry Kissinger (1979:1202) has described the two superpowers as behaving like "two heavily armed blind men feeling their way around a room, each believing himself in mortal peril from the other whom he assumes to have perfect vision." Each, according to Kissinger, "tends to ascribe to the other side a consistency, foresight, and coherence that its own experience belies. Of course, over time even two armed blind men in a room can do enormous damage to each other, not to speak of the room."

We find it hard to understand why others dislike, mistrust, and fear us. President George W. Bush captured this overly positive sense of oneself when at a press conference he asked a rhetorical question, "How do I respond when I see that in some Islamic countries there is vitriolic hatred for America?" In response to his own question, the president pronounced himself "amazed that there's such misunderstanding of what our country is about that people would hate us. I am—like most Americans, I just can't believe it because I know how good we are."[23]

Perceptions play a major role in decision making. One common characteristic of perceptions is that we tend to assume that others see our good intentions and are not afraid of us. When President George W. Bush labeled Iran, Iraq, and North Korea as the axis of evil, many people feared that the rhetoric presaged a U.S. attack. When President Bush traveled to South Korea in February 2002, he met protesters, including these Roman Catholic nuns in Seoul, displaying a sign that indicates their perceptions of the president and his views.

Others are less sure of Americans' innate goodness. For example, the deputy director of Al Ahram, Egypt's respected think tank, contends that "America should spread its culture, rather than weapons or tanks.... They can't just project an image of contempt for those they wish to lead." In much the same vein, an Indonesian sociologist comments that the U.S. global "military presence and power looks like swagger to some in the Muslim world.... You are a superpower, you are a military superpower, and you can do whatever you want. People don't like that, and this is dangerous." From this perspective, the campaign against Afghanistan, the announced U.S. intention to topple Saddam Hussein, the characterization of Iran as well as Iraq as evil, and other U.S. actions and attitudes can be perceived as part of a larger hostility toward Islam. "When Bush talked of a Crusade... it was not a slip of the tongue. It was a mindset. When they talk of terrorism, the only thing they have in mind is Islam," is how one retired Pakistani Air Force general put it.[24]

We and others tend to have similar images of one another. During the cold war, for example, Americans and Soviets each saw the other as implacably hostile. This **mirror image perception** spawned nearly a half century of tension, arms, and danger. "Peace through strength," is how President Ronald Reagan put it. The Soviets felt the same way: imperiled and defensively armed. "We have to conduct our policies from a position of strength," Nikita Khrushchev told a Soviet audience. "There can't be any other policy. Our opponents don't understand any other language.... If I took any other view," Khrushchev concluded, "I'd be a jellyfish" (Fursenko & Naftali, 1997:134).

In a more contemporary setting, whatever the real wishes, peaceful or bellicose, that Jewish Israelis and Palestinian Arabs may have in the Middle East, the operational reality of conflict is based on a mirror image perception of one another as violent and untrustworthy. If Prime Minister Ariel Sharon is asked who is responsible for the tragedy that has befallen the region, his answer is clear and simple: "The one who is responsible is Yasser Arafat and the Palestinian Authority.... After calm is restored, we start negotiations."[25] Arafat's view is equally straightforward, if very different. The source of conflict, he believes, is Sharon and Israel's determination "to deprive our people, to force us to our knees in order to continue perpetrating occupation and racial discrimination."[26]

The Impact of Perceptions

The most obvious impact of perceptions is that they form a "lens" or "prism" through which we perceive reality. When our perceptions are inaccurate they distort our images both of ourselves and of others. Try borrowing a pair of glasses from a friend. Look at the world around you. It becomes distorted, with the degree of distortion depending on how thick the lenses are. Similarly, the degree of perceptual distortion relates to the strength of the beholder's beliefs. Such misperception can cause us to misjudge the actions of others and to fail to understand how our own actions are perceived by others. If this were the only extent of the impact of perceptions, their role would be limited, but it is not. Perceptions affect how we act on the world stage.

The link between perception and policy is the concept of **operational reality**. Policy makers tend to act, or operate, based on perceptions, whether they are accurate or not. For example, the operational reality of perceived communist hostility led the United States to intervene in Vietnam in the mid-1960s, to spend billions of dollars, and to sacrifice tens-of-thousands of lives in a place of such marginal strategic value that even President Lyndon Johnson once called it "a raggedy-ass fourth rate country."[27] History sometimes provides a test of whether a perception is true, and in the case of Vietnam the unification of that country under communism in 1975 turned out not to have the disastrous consequences for the rest of Asia and beyond that Americans once feared. Now, the U.S. government cares relatively little about the form of Vietnam's political system (still communist), and it is hard to imagine even a foreign invasion (say, by China) causing the United States to send in a half-million troops, as it did in the 1960s.

There is a related perceptual phenomenon called an **operational code**. This idea describes how any given leader's worldview and "philosophical propensities for diagnosing" how world politics operates influence the "leader's... propensities for choosing" rewards, threats, force, and other methods of diplomacy as the best way to be successful (Walker, Schafer, & Young, 1998:176). To some degree, for example, a leader's operational code reflects whether that leader leans toward the idealist or the realist end of the spectrum, as discussed in chapter 1.

President Bill Clinton viewed the United States as operating in a complex, technology-driven, interconnected world, in which conflict was more likely to result from countries' internal conditions (such as poverty, civil strife, and autocracy) rather than from traditional power rivalries between states. This led him to push democratization, to favor U.S. support of multilateral cooperative efforts, to be most comfortable using force when it was done in support of human rights (such as in Haiti, Bosnia, and Kosovo), and to act with considerable restraint even when he did use force (Harnisch, 2001; Jewett & Turetzky, 1998).

Presidents who have a realpolitik orientation are, for example, less likely to use military force for humanitarian reasons. They are more likely to see the world as a political contest in which they are in competition with other powers, to countenance force when they perceive a threat to the U.S. strategic position, and to use less restraint when using force. President Nixon, for instance, believed that foreign relations "are a lot like poker—stud poker with a hole card. The hole card

The cold war perception in the 1960s was that a communist victory in Vietnam might have a domino effect, leading all of Southeast Asia, and perhaps beyond, to fall to communism. This brought the United States to war in the region. The communists won, but the perception proved false. Instead, Vietnam and the rest of the region have become increasingly capitalist and, to a degree, Western-ized. That is captured in this picture, where a Vietnamese farmer and his cow head for rice fields past a giant billboard advertising a luxury hotel on the outskirts of Hanoi. Many of the patrons of such hotels are visiting businessmen and, increasingly, those Vietnamese who are amassing wealth de-spite the country's continued official adherence to communism.

is all-important because without it your opponent… has perfect knowledge of whether he can beat you. If he knows he will win he will raise you. If he cannot, he will fold and get out of the game." Nixon thought, therefore, that a diplomatic strategy of keeping an opponent uncertain was necessary because "the United States is an open society. We have all but one of our cards face up on the table. Our only covered card is the will, nerve, and unpredictability of the President—his ability to make the enemy think twice about raising the ante" (Rogers, 1987:31).

That operational code helps explain why Nixon raised the ante in Vietnam by, for example, unleashing in 1972 such a tremendous "Christmas bombing" offensive against North Vietnam's cities that one U.S. official described it as "calculated bar-barism" (Paterson, Clifford, & Hagan, 2000:392). Nixon believed that these actions would help persuade the North Vietnamese and their Soviet backers to cash in their chips and agree to more serious negotiations. Actually, the terms Nixon got after the bombing were not much different from those offered before. Be that as it may, the point is that the president's crisis-operational code caused his violent reaction, which he later claimed was a major turning point to end the war.

Although it is a bit early to evaluate the operational code of George W. Bush, the indications are that it fits the realist mode. He never directly criticized President Clinton for only using cruise missiles to respond to incidents such as the al-Qaeda–directed attacks on U.S. embassies. Still, he expressed his belief that "the antiseptic notion of launching a cruise missile into some guy's, you know, tent, really is a joke," he said. "I mean, people viewed that as the impotent America… of a flaccid, you know, kind of technologically competent but not very tough country that was willing to launch a cruise missile out of a submarine and that'd be it."[28] Instead, Bush ordered more extensive military action, and he vowed repeatedly to take Osama bin Laden and other terrorist leaders "dead or alive."

⊕ Chapter Summary

1. Individual-level analysis studies international politics by examining the role of humans as actors on the world stage.

2. Individual-level analysis can be approached from three different perspectives. One is to examine fundamental human nature. The second is to study how people act in organizations. The third is to examine the motivations and actions of specific persons.

3. The human nature approach examines basic human characteristics. Cognitive, psychological, and biological factors influence decision making. Cognitive factors include cognitive decision making, cognitive consistency, wishful thinking, limiting the scope of decision, and using heuristic devices. Frustration aggression is the primary psychological factor considered, while biological factors include ethology and gender.

4. The organizational-behavior approach studies role factors, that is, how people act in certain personal or professional positions. The approach is also concerned with how groups behave and how the interactions affect decisions.

5. Groupthink is one possible outcome of organizational behavior, in most cases leading to bad decisions. Ignoring or suppressing dissidents, discordant information, and policy options are all causes of groupthink. Another is the reluctance of subordinates to offer discordant opinions. Among the effects of groupthink are limited policy choices, lowest common denominator policy, and poor policy.

6. The idiosyncratic-behavior approach explores the factors that determine the perceptions, decisions, and actions of specific leaders. A leader's personality, physical and mental health, ego and ambitions, understanding of history, personal experiences, and perceptions are all factors.

7. Perceptions are especially important to understanding how leaders react to the world. These spring from such sources as a group's or an individual's belief system, an individual's values, and the information available to the individual.

8. Perceptions can be explained by exploring operational reality. How a group or an individual perceives a situation, another individual, or another country is often a distortion of reality. Distorted perceptions are important because leaders act on what they perceive to be true rather than on what is objectively true.

Nationalism: The Traditional Orientation

I do love My country's good with a respect more tender, More holy and profound, than mine own life.

Shakespeare, *Coriolanus*

If he govern the country, you are bound to him indeed; but how honourable he is in that, I know not.

Shakespeare, *Pericles, Prince of Tyre*

Our country! In her intercourse with foreign nations may she always be in the right; but our country, right or wrong.

Stephen Decatur, 1816

You're not supposed to be so blind with patriotism that you can't face reality. Wrong is wrong, no matter who does it or who says it.

Malcolm X, *Malcolm X Speaks*, 1965

Chapter Objectives

After completing this chapter, you should be able to:

- Define nationalism.
- Identify the elements that make up a state.
- Describe how a nation differs from a state.
- Identify and explain the ideal concept of nation-state and its relationship to nationalism.
- Discuss why nationalism may be said to be both a cohesive and a divisive force.
- Understand nationalism as the product of historical development.
- Identify arguments predicting the end of nationalism and the demise of the territorial state, and note post–World War II trends that have contradicted these predications.
- List and discuss positive and negative aspects of nationalism.
- Identify the ideal and actual relationships between nation and state.
- Define multistate nationalities and explain when they occur.
- Understand the origins of microstates and the problems that their existence presents to the state-centric system.
- Explain the place of nationalism and the nation-state in today's world where transnational and other structures and identifications are also increasing in scope and intensity.

Aliens fascinate us. Not the aliens that immigration officials worry about, but the ones that come from other planets. Whether it is the comical others in *3rd Rock From the Sun* or the aggressive aliens in the sci-fi thriller *Independence Day*, our entertainment media are filled with "others." These others can do more than amuse or scare us; they can tell us something. For instance, take E.T.— the extraterrestrial being. Now, there was one strange-looking character. He—she?— had a squat body, no legs to speak of, a large shriveled head, saucer eyes, and a telescopic neck. And the color! Yes, E.T. was definitely weird. Not only that; there was presumably a whole planet full of E.T.'s—all looking alike, waddling along, with their necks going up and down.

Or did they all look alike? They might have to us, but probably not to one another. Perhaps on their planet there were different countries, ethnic groups, and races of E.T.'s. Maybe they had different-length necks, were varied shades of greenish-brown, and squeaked and hummed with different tonal qualities. It could even be that darker-green E.T.'s with longer necks from the country of Urghor felt superior to lighter-green, short-necked E.T.'s from faraway and little-known Sytica across the red Barovian Sea. If E.T. was a Sytican, would the Urghorans have responded to the plaintive call, "E.T., phone home"?

We can also wonder whether E.T. could tell Earthlings apart. Was he aware that some of his human protectors were boys and some were girls and that a cross section of racial and ethnic Americans chased him with equal-opportunity abandon? Maybe we all looked pretty much the same to E.T. If he had been on a biological specimen-gathering expedition and had collected a Canadian, a Nigerian, and a Laotian, he might have thrown two of the three away as duplicates.

The point of this whimsy is to get us thinking about our world, how different from and how similar to one another we humans are, and how we categorize

Nationalism tends to make us view people from other cultures and countries as different from ourselves. Many would see each of these five babies as culturally different, just as we perceive as different the people from the countries represented by the flag quilt on which the babies are resting. One has to wonder whether a being from another world, such as E.T., would see these babies as different or basically all the same.

ourselves. What we will see is that we do not have an image of ourselves as humans. Rather, we divide up ethnically into Chinese, Irish, Poles, and a host of other "we-groups." Despite our manifest human similarities, we usually identify and organize ourselves politically around some "we-group" subdivision of humanity. If you think about it, you see yourself politically as a citizen of the United States, or some other country. You might even be willing to fight and die for your country. Would you do the same for your hometown? Or Earth?

Nationalism is the political identity focus that makes most people feel patriotic about their country, but not their hometown or their planet. This identification is our traditional political orientation. It has helped configure world politics for several centuries and will continue to shape people's minds and affairs in the foreseeable future. Few would argue with the observation that nationalism reigned as "the nineteenth and twentieth centuries' most powerful political idea" (Taras & Ganguly, 1998:xi). Despite its strength, however, nationalism today is not as unchallenged as it once was. Some even doubt whether it will or should continue and predict or advocate various transnational alternative orientations.

This juxtaposition of the traditional nationalist orientation and the alternative transnational orientation represents one of this book's main themes: that the world is at or is approaching a critical juncture where two roads diverge in the political wood. The two paths to the political future—traditional and alternative—are mapped out briefly in chapter 1.

This chapter and those that follow will explore the two roads, usually by comparing them in successive chapters. This chapter, for example, takes up nationalism, the traditional way we identify ourselves politically. Then, in chapter 7, we will turn to alternative, transnationalist orientations.

Understanding Nations, Nation-States, and Nationalism

Three concepts will help explain the divisions that characterize traditional global politics. Those three concepts are: nation, nation-state, and nationalism (Mortimer & Fine, 1999; Barrington, 1997).

NATIONS

A nation is a people who mutually identify culturally and politically to such a degree that they want to be separate and to control themselves politically. As such, a nation is intangible. A **nation**, of course, includes tangible people, but the essence of a nation is its less tangible elements, such as similarities among the people, their sense of connection, and a desire of the people to govern themselves. A state is an institution; a nation is "a soul, a spiritual quality," a French scholar once wrote (Renan, 1995:7).

Demographic and Cultural Similarities The similarities that a people share are one element that helps make them a nation. These similarities may be demographic characteristics (such as language, race, and religion), or they may be common culture or historical experiences. When such commonalities are strongly present, the formation of the nation precedes that of the state. In Europe, nations generally came together first and only later coalesced into states. Germans, for instance, existed long before they came together as Germany in the 1860s and 1870s. Germany was again divided in 1945, but Germans, both east and west, felt that there should be *ein Deutschland*, one Germany. Eventually the East German Communist regime collapsed

Nationalism comes from many sources, including undergoing common experiences. The terrorist attacks on September 11, 2001, strengthened American nationalism. The burst of patriotism is captured here in this photograph of rescue workers after raising the Stars and Stripes over the rubble of the World Trade Center. It is an image reminiscent of the U.S. Marines raising the American flag over Mount Suribachi, Okinawa, in February 1945 near the end of World War II.

because its legitimacy among the East German people evaporated. Beginning on October 3, 1990, there was once again *ein Deutschland.*

In other regions and circumstances, the formation of the state comes first. In such cases, a critical task of the state is to promote internal loyalty and to create a process whereby its diverse citizens gradually acquire their nationalism through common historical experiences and the regular social/economic/political interactions and cooperation that occur among people living within the same state (Barkey & von Hagen, 1997). This form of **state building** is very difficult. For example, many states in Africa are the result of boundaries that were drawn earlier by colonial powers and that took in people of different tribal and ethnic backgrounds. These former colonial states often do not contain a single, cohesive nation, and the diverse cultural groups find little to bind them to one another once independence has been achieved. Rwanda and Burundi are neighboring states in which Hutu and Tutsi people were thrown together by colonial boundaries that, with independence, became national boundaries, as depicted in the map of Africa on page 33. The difficulty is that the primary political identifications of these people have not become Rwandan or Burundian. They have remained Hutu or Tutsi, and that has led to repeated, sometimes horrific, violence.

It should be added that nation-building and state-building are not necessarily locked in a strict sequential interaction, where one fully precedes the other (Cederman, 1997). Sometimes they evolve together. This approximates what occurred in the United States, where the idea of being American and the unity of the state began in the 1700s and grew, despite a civil war, immigration inflows, racial and ethnic diversity, and other potentially divisive factors. The point is that being within a state sometimes allows a demographically diverse people to come together as a nation through a process of *e pluribus unum* (out of many, one), as the U.S. motto says. It could be said that the American nation is the outcome of Valley Forge, Martin Luther King, the interstate highway system, McDonald's, CBS, the Super Bowl, Gloria Estefan, enduring the trauma of the 9-11 terrorist attacks, and a host of other people, events, and processes that make up the American experience.

Feeling of Community A second thing that helps define a nation is its feeling of community. Perception is the key here. For all the similarities a group might have, it is not a nation unless it feels like one. Those within a group must perceive that they share similarities and are bound together by them. Unfortunately, groups also often define themselves by how they differ from other groups of "strangers" (Guibernau, 1996:49). Whether a group's sense of connection comes from feeling akin to one another or different from others, it is highly subjective.

Desire to Be Politically Separate The third element that defines a nation is its desire to be politically separate. What distinguishes a nation from an ethnic group is that a nation, unlike an ethnic group, has a desire to be self-governing or at least autonomous. In the United States there are many groups, such as Italian Americans, who share a common culture and have a sense of identification. They are not, however, nations because they are not separatists. In nationally divided states (like Cyprus, with its majority-Greek and minority-Turkish communities), the minority nationalities refuse to concede the legitimacy of their being governed by the majority nationality.

Sometimes the line between ethnic groups and nations is not clear. In many countries there are so-called **ethnonational groups** that either teeter on the edge of having true nationalist (separatist) sentiment or that have some members who are nationalists and others who are not. Canada is one such country where the line between ethnic group and nation is uncertain. There is an ongoing dissatisfaction among many French Canadians in the province of Quebec about their status in the Canadian state. Some Québécois favor separation, others do not.

NATION-STATES

A second element of our traditional way of defining and organizing ourselves politically is the **nation-state**. This combines the idea of a nation with that of a state.

A nation-state (more commonly called a state or country), is a tangible entity. It has territory, people, organization, and other reasonably objective characteristics. Canada and China are states.

Did You Know That:
Flags as national symbols are relatively modern inventions. Earlier, most countries' flags were really those of the royal dynasties. The French tricolor, for example, dates only to the time of the French Revolution, when it replaced the white flag with *fleur-de-lis* of the royal house of Bourbon.

The nation-state is the ideal joining of nation and state, the notion of a unified people in a unified country. There are two ways in which this can occur. One is where a state is created by a nation that wishes to govern itself independently. A second scenario for the creation of a nation-state is when once-diverse people within a state learn to identify with one another and with the country in which they reside.

The nation-state is represented by many symbols, such as flags, national anthems, or animals (eagles, bears, dragons). It is the object of patriotic loyalty, and most people view it as the highest form of political authority.

In practice the nation-state concept diverges from the ideal in two ways. First, many states, such as Canada, contain more than one nation. Second, many nations overlap one or more international borders and may not even have a state of their own. The presence of Palestinians in Egypt, Israel, Jordan, and elsewhere is a current illustration. This lack of "fit" between nations and states is often a source of international conflict, as discussed later. Indeed the gap between the theory of nation-states and the reality of ethnically and nationally divided states is so great that some scholars prefer the term national state to emphasize the idea of a state driven by nationalism.

NATIONALISM

The third aspect of our traditional political orientation is **nationalism** itself. It is hard to overstate the importance of nationalism to the structure and conduct of world politics (Beiner, 1999). Nationalism grows from the sense of community and turns it into "a principle of political loyalty and social identity" (Gellner, 1995:2). Nationalism does this by merging the three concepts of state, nation, and nation state in a way that is personally related to citizens. The transformation occurs when individuals (1) "become sentimentally attached to the homeland," (2) "gain a sense of identity and self-esteem through their national identification," and (3) are "motivated to help their country" (Druckman, 1994:44). This merging of the three concepts means that nationalism is an ideology that holds that the nation, embodied in its agent, the sovereign nation-state, should be the paramount object of the political loyalty of individuals.

The Evolution of Nationalism

The evolution of nationalism and the development of the state-centric international system are intertwined. Neither states nor nationalism nor the state-centric system have always existed. This is important because if something has not always been, it does not necessarily always have to be. It is also important to note that nationalism has evolved and continues to do so. Understanding the historical dynamics of nationalism will assist you in evaluating its current status and its value and will help you to form preferences about the future of nationalism.

THE RISE OF NATIONALISM

Nationalism is such a pervasive mindset in the world today that it may be difficult to believe that it has not always existed. It has not. Indeed, most scholars contend that nationalism is a relatively modern phenomenon. It is certainly the case, one scholar notes, that "there have always… been distinctive cultures." It is also the case that in some very old societies the "upper classes have had some sense of shared ethnic solidarity." What is modern, the scholar continues, is the "nationalist idea," the belief that people who share a culture should "be ruled only by someone co-cultural with themselves" (Hall, 1995:10).

Early Nationalism It is impossible to precisely establish when nationalism began to evolve, but one early step occurred in Europe toward the end of the Dark Ages. Charlemagne became king of the Franks in 768, and during his long reign he gained control over most of western and central Europe. The extent of his empire was recognized officially in 800 when Pope Leo III proclaimed him emperor of Romans, a symbolic title denoting the universal empire that had been Rome's. Whatever unity Charlemagne brought to the West did not long exist after his death in 814. What followed was a fragmentation of the empire into different cultures. The use of Latin as a language spoken by all elites across Europe declined. Localized languages took Latin's place and divided the elites. This was but the first step in a process that eventually created a sense of divergent national identities among the upper classes.

The growth of nationalism became gradually intertwined with the development of states and with their synthesis, the national state. We will review the history of states in chapter 8, but we can say here that some of the earliest evidence of broad-based nationalism occurred in England at the time of King Henry VIII (1491–1547). His break with the centralizing authority of the Roman Catholic Church and his establishment of a national Anglican Church headed by the king were pivotal events. The conversion of English commoners to Anglicanism helped spread nationalism to the masses, as did the nationalist sentiments in popular literature. In an age when most people could not read, plays were an important vehicle of culture, and one scholar has characterized the works of William Shakespeare (1564–1616) as "propagandist plays about English history" (Hobsbawm, 1990:75). "This blessed plot, this earth, this realm, this England," Shakespeare has his *King Richard II* exalt. In another play, *Henry VI*, Shakespeare notes the end of the authority of the pope in Rome over the King in London by having Queen Margaret proclaim, "God and King Henry govern England." This sounds commonplace today, but omitting mention of the authority of the papacy was radical stuff 450 years ago (Alulis & Sullivan, 1996).

Modern Nationalism The evolution of nationalism took an important turn in the 1700s and began to change into its modern form based on the close association of the people and the state. Until that time, the link between the states and their inhabitants was very different. Most people were emotionally unconnected to the state in which they lived. As one study points out, "The Medieval Frenchman was a subject of the… monarch, not a citizen of France" (Guibernau, 1996:52). This changed once the people took control of the state and, therefore, identified with it. **Popular sovereignty** had been evolving slowly in Switzerland, England, and a few other places. But it accelerated when the American and French Revolutions dramatically shifted the basis of theoretical political authority in states away from the divine right of kings and toward the idea, as the American Declaration of Independence proclaimed, that governments derive their "just powers from the consent of the governed." While the impact of the American Revolution took time to spread from the isolated United States, the French Revolution's doctrine of "liberty, equality, fraternity" was more immediate. The pens of such French philosophers as Rousseau, Voltaire, and Montesquieu spread the idea of popular sovereignty far beyond France's borders. Soon France's powerful legions added the sword to the tools that spread the philosophy of the national state throughout Europe.

From these beginnings, the idea of popular sovereignty and the belief in the right to national self-determination began to spread around the globe. Some countries were formed when a nation coalesced into a national state. This was true for Germany and Italy in the 1860s and 1870s. In other cases, national states were established on the ashes of empire. The Spanish empire fell apart in the 1800s, and the Austro-Hungarian and Ottoman empires collapsed after World War I. By the mid-twentieth century, nearly all of Europe and the Western Hemisphere had been divided into nation-states, and the colonies of Africa and Asia were beginning to demand independence. The doomed British and French empires soon vanished also. Only the Russian-Soviet empire survived—but not for long. Nationalism reigned virtually supreme around the world.

These developments were widely welcomed. An image of "populist-romantic nationalism" appealed to liberals on two grounds (Gellner, 1995:6). First, the idea of a nation contains an implied equality for all members. Liberal philosophers such as Thomas Paine in *The Rights of Man* (1791) depicted the nation and democracy as inherently linked in the popularly governed nation-state. Liberals also welcomed nationalism as a destroyer of empires. Among other important expressions of this view is Article 55 of the United Nations Charter, which states that "the principle of… self-determination of peoples" is one of the "conditions of stability and well-being which are necessary for peaceful and friendly relations among nations."

Some analysts predicted after World War II that nationalism was dying. The obituary notice proved premature, and nationalism continues to determine most people's political identification. Now, however, there are signs that nationalism and the related concept of sovereignty are weakening.

THE PREDICTED DEMISE OF NATIONALISM

World War II marked a sharp change in liberal philosophy about nationalism. Fascism and other forms of virulently aggressive nationalism helped bring about the horrors of the war and cast a pall on the concept of nationalism. Some observers believed that the war demonstrated that the state system was not only anachronistic but dangerous. The development of nuclear weapons, in particular, led some analysts to conclude that the sovereign state could no longer carry out the primary task of protecting the nation and therefore was doomed. The emphasis on free trade and growing economic interdependence also seemed to augur an end to the nationalist

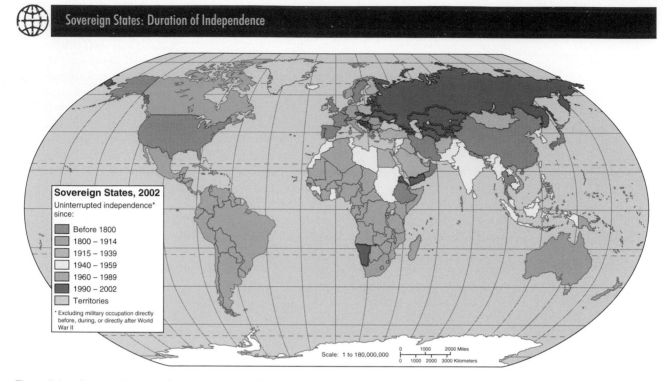

Sovereign States: Duration of Independence

Sovereign States, 2002
Uninterrupted independence*
since:

- Before 1800
- 1800 – 1914
- 1915 – 1939
- 1940 – 1959
- 1960 – 1989
- 1990 – 2002
- Territories

* Excluding military occupation directly
before, during, or directly after World
War II

Scale: 1 to 180,000,000

Figure 6.1 on the opposite page gives you a sense of the recent rapid growth in the number of countries. This map gives you an opportunity to see the geographic dimensions of that growth. Notice that Asia and Africa have seen the most change. Most of the countries that now exist on those continents were colonies of a European country in 1940.

age. Indeed, the newly established (1945) United Nations symbolized the desire to progress away from conflictive nationalism and toward cooperative globalism.

The thrust of this thinking led numerous scholars to predict the imminent demise of the national state or, at least, its gradual withering away. As it turned out, such retirement announcements and obituaries proved reminiscent of the day in 1897 when an astonished Mark Twain read in the paper that he had died. Reasonably sure that he was still alive, Twain hastened to assure the world: "The reports of my death are greatly exaggerated." Rather than retire or die, nationalism gained strength as a world force.

PERSISTENT NATIONALISM

The continued strength of nationalism is summarized in Figure 6.1, which shows that between 1940 and 2002 the number of states increased 272 percent. This growth is also evident in the color map, Sovereign States: Duration of Independence. For most of this time, the primary force behind the surge of nationalism was the anti-imperialist independence movements in Africa, Asia, and elsewhere. More recently, nationalism has reasserted itself in Europe. Germany reemerged when West Germany and East Germany reunited. More commonly, existing states disintegrated. Yugoslavia dissolved into 5 countries and Czechoslovakia became 2 states. Soon another state became 15 countries when the last great multiethnic empire, the vast realm of Russia, then the USSR, sank under its own ponderous weight like a woolly mammoth in the La Brea tar pits. Except for East Timor, Eritrea, Namibia, and Palau, all of the states that have achieved independence since 1989 are in Eastern Europe or are former Soviet republics (FSRs). There are also nationalist

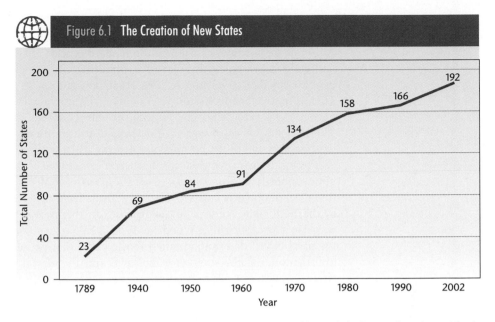

Figure 6.1   **The Creation of New States**

This figure and the map on the opposite page portray the rapid growth in the number of countries in the international system. From the beginning of the sovereign state about 500 years ago, it took until 1940 for 69 states to evolve. In the intervening 60 years, that number has nearly tripled.

stirrings—in some cases demands—among the Scots, Irish, and Welsh in Great Britain; the Basques and Catalans in Spain; and among other ethnonational groups elsewhere in Europe (Caplan & Feffer, 1996).

It may seem contradictory, but the continuing strength of nationalism does not mean that those who earlier predicted its demise were wrong. It may only mean that they were premature. For all the continuing strength of nationalism, there are numerous signs that nationalism is waning and that states are weakening. In the last section of this chapter we will turn to the future course of nationalism. To help evaluate the current role of nationalism and to decide whether it is a good standard for the future, we should consider the positive and negative roles that nationalism plays in world politics.

Nationalism: Builder and Destroyer

When Pope John Paul II addressed the UN General Assembly in 1995, he spoke of the "difference between an unhealthy form of nationalism which teaches contempt for other nations or cultures, and... proper love of one's country."[1] What the pope could see about nationalism is that, like the Roman god Janus, it has two faces. Nationalism has been a positive force for political democratization and integration. It has also brought despair and destruction to the world. It is, in essence, both a uniting and a dividing force in international politics (McKim & McMahan, 1997).

THE BENEFICENT FACE OF NATIONALISM

Most scholars agree that in its philosophical and historical genesis, nationalism was a positive force. It has a number of possible beneficial effects.

Nationalism promotes democracy. The idea that the state is the property of its citizens is a key element of nationalism. This idea received a strong boost from the American and French Revolutions. If the state is the agent of the people, then the people should decide what policies the state should pursue. This is democracy, and, in the words of one scholar, "Nationalism is the major form in which democratic consciousness expresses itself in the modern world" (O'Leary, 1997:222). In short, nationalism promotes the idea that political power legitimately resides with the people and that governors exercise that power only as the agents of the people. Therefore, two Spanish scholars conclude, "Democracy is unimaginable without the notion of a sovereign people" (Cardús & Estruch, 1995:352).

Nationalism encourages self-determination. In modern times, the notion that nationalities ought to be able to preserve their cultures and govern themselves according to their own customs has become widely accepted. The English utilitarian philosopher John Stuart Mill's essay *On Liberty* (1859) argued that "where the sentiment of nationality exists... there is a prima facie case for unity of all the members of the nationality under... a government to themselves apart." Self-determination was also a key element of Woodrow Wilson's Fourteen Points (1918). Most recently, the ideal of self-determination led to the belief that people in colonies and those in multinational states such as Yugoslavia and the Soviet Union should be able to choose whether or not to become independent.

Nationalism discourages imperialism. A related impact of nationalism is that it strengthens resistance to outside occupation. One example is the recent history of the Chechens related in the box, The Chechens: Death or Freedom.

Nationalism allows for economic development. Many scholars see nationalism as both a facilitator and a product of modernization. Nationalism created larger political units in which commerce could expand. The prohibition of interstate tariffs and the control of interstate commerce by the national government in the 1787 American Constitution are examples of that development. With the advent of industrialization and urbanization, the local loyalties of the masses waned and were replaced by a loyalty to the national state.

Subordinate nations have usually been shortchanged economically. This has been true in colonial empires, like those once controlled by the British and French, and in theoretically integrated multiethnic empires, such as the Soviet Union. This economic exploitation of colonized peoples is one cause of the poverty that persists in much of the world today. Similarly, many of the FSRs are, by political experience and economic circumstance, also less developed countries (LDCs). Most of the non-Russian peoples were conquered by and incorporated into Russia. Their languages, customs, and religions were often suppressed. Like other people in LDCs, their socioeconomic standards are lower than those in the country that once controlled them. The six predominantly Muslim FSRs (Azerbaijan, Kazakhstan, Kyrgyzstan, Tajikistan, Turkmenistan, and Uzbekistan) have an average per capita GDP that is only about 37 percent of Russia's. By another telling standard, the infant mortality rate in the six Muslim republics is 62 percent higher than it is in Russia. It is certain that these new countries face years of economic hardship, but, from their perspective, at least their efforts will be devoted to their own betterment.

Nationalism allows diversity and experimentation. It has been argued that regional or world political organization might lead to an amalgamation of cultures or, worse, the suppression of the cultural uniqueness of the weak by the strong. By contrast, diversity of culture and government promotes experimentation. Democracy, for instance, was an experiment in America in 1776 that might not have occurred in a one-world system dominated by monarchs. Diversity also allows different cultures to maintain their own values. Political culture varies, for example, along a continuum on which the good of the individual is on one end and the good of the society is on the other end. No society is at either extreme of the continuum, but Americans and people in some other nations tend toward the individualism end and its belief that the rights

(Continued on page 146)

THE CHECHENS: DEATH OR FREEDOM

That nationalism discourages imperialism is well demonstrated by the Chechens. The approximately 1 million Chechens are a largely Islamic people living in the northern Caucasus region just west of the Caspian Sea. Chechnya (or the Chechen Republic) encompasses about 6,000 square miles (a bit larger than Connecticut). Imperial Russia began a campaign in 1783 to conquer the Chechens that went on for so long and was so fierce that the Russian poet Mikhail Lermontov wrote in 1832 of the Chechens, "Their god is freedom, their law is war." Even after Russia finally established control in the mid-1800s, rebellions persisted. It seemed, as one military governor warned, that the Russians and their czar "would find no peace as long as a single Chechen remains alive."[1]

During World War II, Moscow deported the entire Chechen population to the east and away from the invading Germans. Stalin suspected the Chechens might assist the Germans under the old theory that my enemy's enemy is my friend. Even though one-third of all Chechens died during their time in the

One benefit of nationalism is that it encourages people to resist outside domination. Yet that resistance is also a source of violence. This photograph taken amid the rubble of Grozny, Chechnya's capital, depicts that duality. This Chechen boy playing with a crude, make-believe wooden machine gun is probably aiming it at imaginary Russian soldiers. When he grows up, it is very possible that this 7 year old will be aiming a real machine gun at real Russian troops who will be really shooting back.

gulag (an acronym for "Main Directorate of Corrective Labor Camps"), they remained defiant. As Aleksandr Solzhenitsyn wrote in *The Gulag Archipelago* (1973), "There was one nation that would not give in... [to] submission—and not just individual[s]..., but the whole nation to a man. These were the Chechens.... And here is an extraordinary thing—everyone was afraid of them. No one could stop them from living as they did. The [Soviet] regime which had ruled the land for thirty years could not force them to respect its laws."[2]

The Chechens were allowed to return to their native land in the mid-1950s but remained restive. Once the USSR dissolved, their quest for self-rule redoubled. Amid often ferocious fighting that has cost between 60,000 to 100,000 lives, they achieved a level of autonomy in 1996, then lost it in early 2000 when they were again overrun by Russian arms. The struggle continues, however, with a Russian attack on the Chechens in early 2002 so severe that the U.S. State Department rebuked Russia on the grounds that its "operations in Chechnya indicates a continuation

of human rights violations and the use of overwhelming force against civilian targets."[3] Russia maintains a tenuous hold on Chechnya, but current Russian leaders, like czars and commissars before them, are finding it daunting to subdue a people whose national anthem goes in part:

We were born at night, when the she-wolf whelped.
In the morning, as lions howl, we were given our names.
In eagles' nests, our Mothers nursed us,
To tame a stallion, our Fathers taught us....
Granite rocks will sooner fuse like lead,
Than we lose our Nobility in life and struggle....
Never will we appear submissive before anyone,
Death or Freedom—we can choose only one way....
We were born at night, when the she-wolf whelped.
God, Nation, and the Native land.

of the individual are more important than the welfare of the society. The Chinese people and those in some other countries tend more toward the communitarian end of the continuum and hold that the rights of the individual must be balanced against those of the society and sometimes even be subordinated to the common good.

THE TROUBLED FACE OF NATIONALISM

The benevolent view of nationalism that dominated the earlier part of this century is no longer commonly held. President Woodrow Wilson may have promoted national self-determination as a basic political principle, but recent American presidents have warned of the ills of unrestrained nationalism. "Militant nationalism is on the rise," President Clinton cautioned, "transforming the healthy pride of nations, tribes, religious, and ethnic groups into cancerous prejudice, eating away at states and leaving their people addicted to the political painkillers of violence and demagoguery."[2] Clinton's warning was based on fact. The number of ongoing ethnonational conflicts over self-determination rose steadily from 4 in 1956 to 40 in 1990, then declined to 26 in 2000. It is possible that ethnonational conflict has peaked and will continue to decline, but it is too early to tell whether the drop since 1990 is an anomaly or a positive sign. Unfortunately, whatever the number of conflicts, the intensity and magnitude of ethnonational conflicts remain high, as evident in Figure 6.2 (Gurr, Marshall, & Khosla, 2001; Saideman, 1997). The ills that nationalism brings can be subdivided into how we relate to others and the lack of fit between states and nations.

How We Relate to Others

By definition, nationalism is feeling a kinship with the other "like" people who make up the nation. Differentiating ourselves from others is not intrinsically bad, but it is only a small step from the salutary effects of positively valuing our "we-group" to the negative effects of devaluing the "they-group." Four aspects of negative nationalism are xenophobia, internal oppression, external aggression, and lack of concern for others.

The earlier, multinational state of Yugoslavia collapsed because it did not command the internal loyalty of most of its people. Instead, Yugoslavia atomized amid deadly conflict into the states and restive provinces shown here.

Xenophobia One too-frequent product of nationalism is **xenophobia**, the suspicion, dislike, or fear of other nationalities. Negative nationalism also often spawns feelings of national superiority and superpatriotism, and these lead to internal oppression and external aggression (Kateb, 2000). It is this reality that moved Voltaire to lament in 1764 that "it is sad that being a good patriot often means being the enemy of the rest of mankind."[3]

Feelings of hatred between groups are especially apt to be intense if there is a history of conflict or oppression. Past injuries inflicted "by another ethnic group [are] remembered mythically as though the past were the present," according to one scholar.[4] For Serbs, this heroic lore centers on the battle of Kosovo in 1389, in which the Ottoman Turks defeated Serbia's Prince Lazar, thus beginning five centuries of Muslim domination. The battle, according to one commentary, is "venerated among the Serbs in the same way Texans remember the Alamo." Adds Serb historian Dejan Medakovic, "Our morals, ethics, mythology were created at that moment, when we were overrun by the Turks. The Kosovo cycle, the Kosovo myth is something that has permeated the Serbian people."[5]

It is a tragic irony that the symbolic battle of Kosovo is now entwined with the future of Kosovo Province in what is left of Yugoslavia. As a result of the ethnic ebb and flow over the centuries in the region, 90 percent of Kosovo is made up of ethnic Albanians, who are mostly Muslims, rather than the predominately Christian Orthodox Serbs.

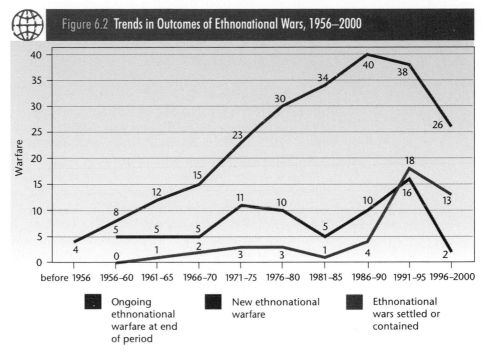

Figure 6.2 Trends in Outcomes of Ethnonational Wars, 1956–2000

Legend:
- Ongoing ethnonational warfare at end of period
- New ethnonational warfare
- Ethnonational wars settled or contained

Data source: Gurr, Marshall, & Khosla (2001).

The number of ethnopolitical conflicts within countries rose steadily from the 1950s to 1990, and these conflicts were much more common than conflicts between countries. Then domestic strife began to decline in the 1990s. Notice that the number of new wars reached a five-year high of 16 in 1991–1995, but 18 existing conflicts were settled or contained, reducing the overall number slightly at the end of the period. With only 2 new conflicts in the 1996–2000 period, and with 13 settled or contained, the number of conflicts existing at the end of the period dropped markedly. Whether this trend represents a short-term anomaly or a new period of much reduced domestic conflict remains to be seen.

Internal Oppression Nationalism can frequently lead to internal oppression. It is rare to find a multinational country in which the dominant ethnonational group does not have political, economic, and social advantages over another group or groups. Perhaps inevitably, this inequality of circumstance leads the disadvantaged groups to become restive. But the complaints of the oppressed are not easily resolved because, as UN secretary general Kofi Annan has pointed out, the minority group's social and economic inequality "tends to be reflected in unequal access to political power that too often forecloses paths to peaceful change."[6] As a result, open rebellion and ethnonational warfare often erupt.

Nationalist intolerance can also lead to conflict when, as one scholar notes, it becomes "a scavenger [that] feeds upon the pre-existing sense of nationhood" and seeks "to destroy heterogeneity" by trying to suppress the culture of minority groups, or by driving them out of the country (Keane, 1994:175). The ethnic cleansing frenzy in Bosnia-Herzegovina between 1992 and 1995, the genocidal attacks on the Tutsis by the Hutus in Rwanda in 1994, and the attacks on ethnic Albanian Kosovars by Serbian Kosovars and Serbian Yugoslav troops in 1998 and 1999 are the most recent horrific outbreaks of xenophobic violence, but there are many other lesser instances.

At its farthest extreme, nationalism engenders the sense of superiority and hatred of the kind that festered in Nazi Germany. The Germans thought that their "Aryan nation" was at the top of a ladder that descended downward to where, at the bottom, Slavic peoples were considered marginal humans and were to be kept as virtual and expendable slaves in segregated and degrading conditions. Jews and Gypsies were "nonpeople" and "racial vermin" to be exterminated, along with the insane and homosexuals. "The highest purpose of a *folkish* state," Hitler preached in *Mein Kampf*, is "preservation of those original racial elements which bestow culture and create the beauty of a higher humanity. We, as Aryans, can conceive of the state only as a living organism of [German] nationality."

External Aggression This sense of superiority and devaluing of other people, which is so often part of fervent nationalism, can also become an excuse for the conquest and domination of neighbors. Underneath its ideological trappings, the Soviet Union was a classic multiethnic empire built on territories seized by centuries of czarist Russian expansion and furthered by Soviet arms. From its beginning 500 years ago as the 15,000-square-mile Duchy of Moscovy (half the size of Maine), Russia, and then the USSR, ultimately grew to be the world's largest country. This expansion is shown in the map on page 149.

Many of those territories have been lost, but there are strong suspicions that a rejuvenated Russia will try to reclaim them. Such concerns have been heightened by a number of actions or statements, including the 1996 passage by Russia's parliament, the Duma, of a resolution expressing the view that the dissolution of the Soviet Union had been illegal and, by inference, that all the now-independent FSRs should once again come under Moscow's control.

For now Russia's economic and other travails mean that it is not in a position to even consider trying to reassert the earlier domination of its neighbors that it had in the days of czars and comrades. Indeed, old-fashioned imperialism may have become too costly economically and diplomatically to pursue in the future. Yet there is gnawing concern that the German theoretician Karl Marx was prescient when he warned long ago that "the policy of Russia is changeless. Its methods, its tactics, its maneuvers may change, but the polar star of its policy—world domination—is a fixed star."[7]

Did You Know That:
Russians have traditionally seen themselves as the successor to the earlier great Western empires centered in Rome and Constantinople. In fact the Russian royal title of czar (tsar) is a derivative of Caesar.

Lack of Concern for Others The mildest, albeit still troubling, trait of negative nationalism is a lack of concern for others. Because we identify ourselves as the we-group, we tend to consider the they-group as aliens. Our sense of responsibility—of even human caring—for the "theys" is limited. People in most countries accept the principle that they have a responsibility to assist the least fortunate citizens of their national we-group. All of the economically developed countries (EDCs) have extensive social welfare budgets, and the people in those countries engage in countless acts of charity, from donating blood to distributing toys for tots. The key is that we not only want to help others in our we-group, we feel that we have a duty to do so.

Internationally, most of us feel much less responsible. Horrendous conditions and events can occur in other countries that evoke little notice relative to the outraged reaction that would be forthcoming if they happened in our own country. Few Americans, for example, cared much about conditions in Afghanistan before the fall of 2001. Then Americans became greatly alarmed. Great distress was voiced over the Taliban government not allowing women to work, to go to school, or to appear in the street without wearing the head-to-toe garment, the *burqa*. During his 2002 State of the Union address, President Bush even saluted the head of Afghanistan's new Ministry of Women, Sima Samar, who was seated in the congressional gallery. The outside world also decried the Taliban's religious oppression, including the arrest of Christian missionaries and the destruction of two giant Buddha statues carved from a cliff in central Afghanistan some 1,400 years ago. Once the Taliban were toppled, the media was full of upbeat stories about how people could now listen to music and even dance, how men could shave their beards if they wished, and how people could once

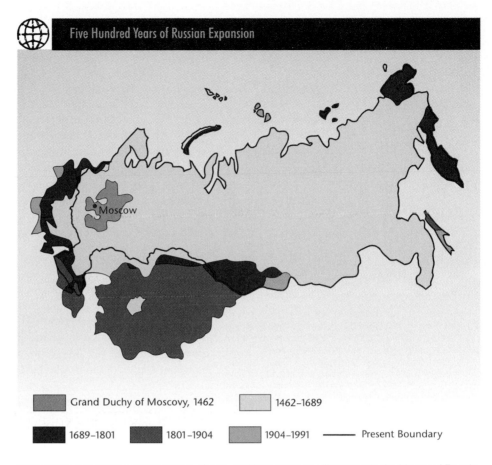

Five Hundred Years of Russian Expansion

Moscow

| | Grand Duchy of Moscovy, 1462 | | 1462–1689 |
| | 1689–1801 | 1801–1904 | 1904–1991 | ——— Present Boundary |

Nationalism has positive and negative effects, and both these are illustrated in the history of Russia. Among the negative effects, nationalism often prompts expansionism. The Grand Duchy of Moscovy was about half the size of Maine when it was founded in about 1480. It expanded under Russian czars and then Soviet commissars to become what was the world's largest country.

again watch television and access the Internet without censorship. Governments rushed aid to feed and shelter the Afghanis during the coming winter, and countries attending a special International Conference on Reconstruction Assistance to Afghanistan in Japan pledged over $2 billion to reconstruct Afghanistan.

The reality, of course, was that what focused Americans and others on the travails of Afghanistan was not so much empathy for other human beings as fear and anger over terrorism. Until then, the "we-they" lines created by nationalism left most outsiders unconcerned about the deprivations that most Afghanis experience. Oppression had existed at least since the Taliban takeover in 1996, and in many ways long before that. The violence that accompanied the U.S.-led attack was also a continuation of the experiences that the people of Afghanistan have suffered since at least the mid-1970s, when a military coup overthrew the monarchy, setting off an ongoing power struggle among various groups and nonstop outside interference, ranging from a massive Soviet intervention (1979–1988) to the supply of arms to one group or another by India, Iran, Pakistan, the United States, and other countries. Well over 2 million Afghanis were killed between the 1973 coup and the beginning of the 2001 U.S. intervention, and more than 6 million had fled to refugee camps in Pakistan and elsewhere. For a country with a population of about 26 million, that is the equivalent of over 21 million Americans dead and 64 million American refugees, given the U.S. population of 278 million.

One negative aspect of nationalism is that it causes a lack of concern for people of other nationalities. In addition to dropping tons of bombs on Afghanistan, the United States dropped tons of food packages containing beans with tomato sauce, bean and potato vinaigrette, and other items on the country to demonstrate the goodwill of Americans toward Afghanis. One has to wonder whether a massive U.S. program years ago to help Afghanistan might have eased the conditions that, in part, led the country to become a safe haven for the al-Qaeda terrorists.

For most of those who stayed in Afghanistan and managed to survive the warfare, life was and remains a grim struggle. Data from Afghanistan is scant, but the average per capita income is about $400; only about one-third of all Afghanis are literate; the average Afghani lives only 46 years; 2 percent of all women who are giving birth die; and about 16 percent of all the country's children die before they reach age 5. All or most of these conditions, even if somewhat eased, are likely to continue into the foreseeable future in Afghanistan. The question is whether the concern that the terrorist attacks engendered among the economically developed countries will remain as time passes.

The Lack of Fit Between Nations and States

The spaces occupied by nations and states often do not coincide (MacIver, 1999). In fact, most states are not ethnically unified, and many nations exist in more than one state. This lack of "fit" between nations and states is a significant source of international (and domestic) tension and conflict. There are four basic disruptive patterns: (1) one state, multiple nations; (2) one nation, multiple states; (3) one nation, no state; (4) multiple nations, multiple states.

One State, Multiple Nations The number of **multinational states** far exceeds that of nationally unified states. Indeed, only about 10 percent of all countries truly fit the nation-state concept. The rest of the countries fall short of the ideal by at least some degree, with, at the extreme, 30 percent having no national majority. The map on page 151 showing the degree of demographic unity of each country indicates racial and ethnic, as well as national, diversity. Most of these minority groups do not have separatist tendencies, but many do or could acquire them.

Canada is one of the many countries where national divisions exist. About 27 percent of Canada's 31 million people are ethnically French (French Canadians) who identify French as their "mother tongue" and first language (Francophones). The majority of this group reside in the province of Quebec, a political subdivision rather like (but politically more autonomous than) an American state. Quebec is very French; of the province's 7.4 million people, 81 percent are Francophones, Catholic, and culturally French.

Many French Canadians have felt that their distinctive culture has been eroded in the predominantly English-culture Canada. There has also been a feeling of economic and other forms of discrimination. The resulting nationalist sentiment in the province gave rise to the separatist Parti Québécois and to a series of efforts in the 1980s and 1990s to obtain autonomy, even independence, for the province. The most recent of these was a referendum on separation held in 1995. The voters in Quebec rejected independence, but this time with only a razor-thin majority of 50.6 percent voting *non* to sovereignty and 49.4 percent voting *oui*.

It is too early to tell when, or even if, another referendum will occur (Seymour, 2000). Nationalist feelings continue in Quebec, but they have eased based on better economic and cultural conditions for the Francophones and, perhaps, the (at least temporary) reluctance to continue an unsuccessful struggle. A poll conducted in 2001 that presented Québécois with the exact question that was on the 1995 referendum and asked them how they would vote found that support had dropped to 42

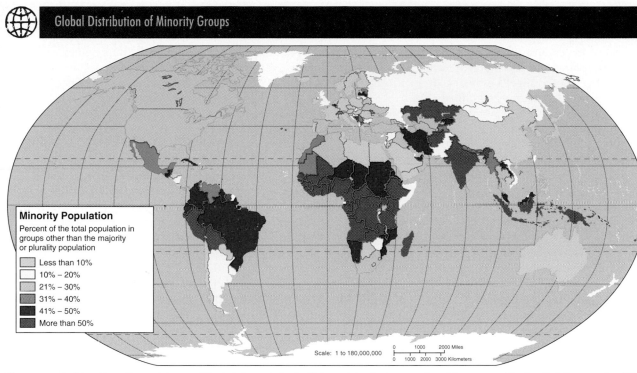

Global Distribution of Minority Groups

Minority Population
Percent of the total population in groups other than the majority or plurality population

- Less than 10%
- 10% – 20%
- 21% – 30%
- 31% – 40%
- 41% – 50%
- More than 50%

Scale: 1 to 180,000,000

The concept of a nation-site envisions political states, each of which contains just one nation. Moreover, virtually all of the people of that nation would live within the state. In reality, few countries fit this ideal. As this map shows, most countries are ethnically and nationally diverse. Because they do not have aspirations for independence or autonomy, not all minority populations are nations, but many are.

percent.[8] "The sense of anger that allowed Quebecers to contemplate a break with Canada just isn't there any more," comments one observer. "The movement is a little bit stalled," concedes the editor of the pro-independence newspaper. "Even a lot of [separatist] organizers are asking themselves publicly whether it is possible to win. That's quite a change."[9]

Many multinational states have not been as fortunate as Canada, which has largely avoided bloodshed over its national division. Other states have suffered extraordinary violence. In 1994, the death and destruction spawned by clashing ethnonationalist groups in Rwanda was given voice by Prime Minister Agathe Uwilingiyamana when the killing began: "There is shooting. People are being terrorized. People are inside their homes lying on the floor. We are suffering," she said in a broadcast from the capital, Kigali, appealing for help.[10] Those were her last public words; soon after, she was dragged from her refuge in a UN compound and murdered by marauding Hutus.

One Nation, Multiple States A second departure from the nation-state ideal occurs when nations overlap the borders of two or more states. When a **multistate nation** exists, nationalist sentiments create strong pressures to join the politically separate nation within one state. This impulse has frequently played a role in recent international politics when a nation was divided into two states, as indicated by the examples of North and South Vietnam, North and South Korea, East and West Germany, and the two Yemens. Ireland and Northern Ireland provide another possible example, although the Scottish heritage of many of the Protestants in the North makes the existence of a single Irish nationality in two states controversial. In any case, a single nation that dominates two states has an urge to unite the states and,

(Continued on page 154)

PALESTINIANS: A NATION WITHOUT A STATE

Two nations, Israeli and Palestinian, have both long existed in the same area. Most of that territory is now controlled by Israelis; the Palestinians mean to get enough of it back to create a Palestinian state.

The dispute goes back to Abraham and his sons, Isaac, who founded the Jewish nation, and Ishmael, the symbolic father of all Arabs. Such biblical stories are important because the Jews base their claim to Israel partly on Jehovah's promise to Moses to deliver the Hebrews out of Egypt to "a land flowing with milk and honey" (Exodus 3:8). The catch is that God directed the Hebrews "unto the place of the Canaanites"—occupied territory. Jewish fortunes changed, though, and after a millennium the last vestige of their control in the region was ended by the Romans in A.D. 70. During the diaspora that followed, most Jews were scattered throughout the world (Farsoun, 1997).

The Palestinians have existed in the region for centuries and may date back to the pre-Hebrew tribes in the area. In any case, Palestinian Arabs were the area's primary inhabitants for many centuries and comprised 90 percent of the population in 1920. Most Palestinians are Muslims, but many are Christians.

In Europe, however, Zionism gathered strength in the nineteenth century. **Zionism** is the nationalist, not strictly religious, belief that Jews are a nation that should have an independent homeland (Shlaim, 1999). After the British captured Palestine from Turkey during World War I, they allowed limited Jewish immigration into the area. The trickle became a flood when those fleeing Nazi atrocities swelled the Jewish population in Palestine from 56,000 in 1920 to 650,000 by 1948 (compared to nearly 1 million Arabs). In rapid succession, fighting for control erupted, Britain turned the issue over to the UN, and Arab leaders rejected a UN plan to partition Palestine into a Jewish state and an Arab state. Israel won the ensuing war in 1948 and acquired some of the areas designated for the Arab state. At least 500,000 Palestinians fled to refugee camps in Egyptian-controlled Gaza and elsewhere; another 400,000 came under the control of Jordan in an area called the West Bank (of the Jordan River).

Since then, Israel has fought and won three more wars with its Arab neighbors. In the 1967 war Israel captured considerable territory, including the Sinai Peninsula and Gaza from Egypt, the Golan Heights from Syria, and the West Bank (including East Jerusalem) from Jordan. Victory, however, did not bring Israel peace or security. The most important reason is the unresolved fate of the West Bank, which is central to the quest of Palestinians for their own autonomous, even independent, homeland.

Security is one reason that Israel has retained control of the West Bank. It thrusts far into Israel's central region, and Israel has refused to withdraw before peace is fully achieved. Part of the full-scale peace, the Israelis say, is the cessation of terrorist acts against them. Israel is also reluctant to quit the West Bank because the territory is emotionally central to many, especially very conservative Jews, who call the West Bank by its biblical names of Judea and Samaria. Israel would find it especially difficult to surrender control of East Jerusalem, which is a holy city for Jews, as it also is for Muslims and Christians.

The fate of Israel, the Palestinians, and the occupied territories has created an explosive mix that has defied resolution for over a half century. Surely, there have been times of hope and progress, when pressures from outside countries and war weariness among both Israelis and Arabs created the incentive to try to settle their differences. Peace agreements were reached between Israel and Egypt in 1979, after meetings with President Jimmy Carter at the presidential retreat at Camp David, and between Jordan and Israel in 1994.

Progress has been made toward ending a few sources of Israeli-Palestinian tension. Most Palestinians no longer advocate the dissolution of Israel and are willing to settle for their own state in more limited areas. An increasing number of Israelis are willing to admit that the Palestinians cannot be kept a stateless people in perpetuity. Talks held in Norway between Israel and the Palestine Liberation Organization (PLO) resulted in the Oslo Agreement in 1993 whereby (1) Israel recognized the PLO as "the representative of the Palestinian people"; (2) the PLO renounced violence and recognized Israel's right to exist; and (3) the two sides agreed to a plan to create Palestinian self-rule in the West Bank and Gaza by century's end. Soon thereafter, Israel turned over some of its authority in Gaza and parts of the West Bank to the Palestinians, and Yasser Arafat became the first head of the Palestinian National Authority (Robinson, 1997).

Alas, peace was not at hand. Each step toward peace has been followed by a retreat to hatred and violence. Each side, Israeli and Palestinian, charges the other with bad faith and with fostering conflict. These mutual accusations reached a crescendo as violence mounted throughout late 2001 and into 2002, and they were reflected by public opinion on both sides. An opinion survey of Palestinians in November 2001

The possibility of peace in the Middle East teeters on the knife edge of Israeli-Palestinian relations. During the past few decades there have been times of great hope, such as after the Camp David accords (1978) and Oslo accords (1993). During 2002 and at other times, peace has seemed impossible, as symbolized by this photograph of a Palestinian policeman and an Israeli soldier angrily confronting each other in the West Bank city of Hebron.

that asked, "Do you think that there is a chance for peaceful coexistence between Palestinians and Israelis?" found only 33 percent of Palestinians said yes.[1] Israelis were equally pessimistic. After Arafat promised to curb the violence, a December 2001 a poll found that only 11 percent of Israelis believed he was sincere.[2]

Rather than trying to untangle blame in this convoluted tragedy, the most important issue is how to end it. Achieving that goal will be extraordinarily difficult. There are a number of specific, seemingly intractable issues to resolve. The two that are the most difficult involve the status of Jerusalem and the fate of the Jewish settlements in Gaza and the West Bank. Both Israelis and Palestinians claim Jerusalem as their capital, and for either side to surrender all or part of its claim to the city will be emotionally, and, therefore politically, wrenching. The matter of the settlements is almost as insoluble. Over the years, the Israeli government has allowed Jewish "settlers" to build enclaves in Gaza and the West Bank. If these areas became part of a Palestinian state, either the Jewish settlers would become citizens, or at least residents, of Arab-controlled independent Palestine, or the settlements would remain islets of Israeli sovereign territory within Palestine. The first option is unacceptable to the Israelis; the second is anathema to the Palestinians.

Beyond these two issues, the larger need is almost certainly for two things to occur. One is the establishment of an independent Palestinian state. The other is an end to Palestinian attacks on Israel.

As for the goal of creating an independent Palestine, that has long been the goal of the Palestinians. Moreover, most of them are now willing to accept a more limited territory encompassing Gaza and the West Bank instead of all of what was old Palestine. Much of the international community has also come to support an independent Palestine. "The idea of a Palestinian state has always been part of a vision, so long as the right of Israel to exist is respected," President George W. Bush commented in late 2001.[3] Even Israelis are coming to accept a Palestinian state as a necessary part of ending the violence. One recent poll found 51 percent of Israelis in favor of a Palestinian state, 43 percent opposed, and 6 percent unsure.[4]

President Bush's commitment to supporting a Palestinian state "so long as the right of Israel to exist is respected" is the crux of the greatest difficulty in achieving that goal. From the Palestinian perspective, ending the violence is difficult because most Palestinians do not trust the Israelis and believe that the violence is a key to forcing concessions by Israel. Operating from the opposite side of that mirror image of duplicity, many Israelis are convinced that an independent Palestine will become a safe haven from which terrorists can launch even more and deadlier attacks on them. That fear was sharpened throughout 2001 and into 2002 when the bloodletting was especially horrific with Israeli civilians dying at parties, on buses, in cafes, and elsewhere at the hands of gunmen and suicide bombers. Indeed the cycle of attack and retaliation reached such a level that President Bush issued a blunt warning: "The signal I am sending to the Palestinians is stop the violence and I can't make it any more clear," Bush told reporters at the White House. "I hope that Chairman Arafat hears it loud and clear."[5]

What the future will hold cannot be foretold with confidence. The strife in the region from Gaza to the West Bank is part of the ancient as well as current history of the Middle East. One can but hope that the leaders on both sides will step away from the precipice and, instead, look to antiquity to remember the words of the book of Isaiah (52:7): "How beautiful upon the mountains are the feet of him that bringeth good tidings, that publisheth peace."

thus, itself. Today only Korea (and arguably Ireland) remains as an example of such a division, and the two Koreas have begun a dialogue that may eventually erase first their hostility and then their border. But there is often conflict over union, a tension that led to fighting between the two halves of the nation in four of the examples (Vietnam, Korea, Ireland, and Yemen).

Another recipe for trouble is where most members of a nation live in their own state while other members of the nation live as a minority population in one or more adjoining states. This creates conflict when those minority populations wish to join the motherland or when the motherland claims the area in which they live. This demand is called **irredentism**. Even if a nation-state is not (yet) seeking to incorporate all the members of the nation, surrounding states with minority segments of that nationality may react with worried hostility.

The long-standing instability in the southern Balkans is based in large part on such overlapping ethnonational and state boundaries. One reason for concern about the fate of Kosovo Province, given its majority Albanian population and the Serb-dominated government of Yugoslavia, is that if fighting were to resume, neighboring Albania might be drawn into the conflict on the side of the Kosovar Albanians. This concern has been intensified by events in neighboring Macedonia, where the country's 22 percent Albanian minority has clashed bloodily with the Macedonian-dominated government . "We must also fight for our freedom in Macedonia, just as Albanians are fighting for their freedom in Kosovo," proclaimed one ethnic Albanian in Macedonia.[11] For the moment, a NATO peacekeeping force has brought a modicum of stability to the country, but it is not certain whether that calm would last if NATO's forces were to withdraw.

To complicate matters further, the Macedonians themselves might be the source of irrendentist conflict with Greece. The Macedonians in Yugoslavia declared their independence in 1991 and, reasonably, named their country Macedonia. This, however, angered and worried Greece, just to the south. The most northern part of Greece is its Macedonian region, and Athens is worried that independent Macedonia might have irredentist designs on the Macedonians in Greece. The Greeks and the Macedonians also squabble over which culture can properly claim to trace part of its lineage to ancient Macedon and its hero Alexander the Great (356–323 B.C.).

One Nation, No State A third pattern where the state and nation are not congruent occurs when a national group is a minority in one or more states, does not have a nation-state of its own, and wants one. The Palestinians are a familiar example of a **stateless nation**; their status is detailed in the box, Palestinians: A Nation Without a State on pages 152–153.

Yet another stateless nation is that of the Kurds, an ancient, non-Arab people of the Mesopotamian region, who are mostly Sunni Muslims. The most famous of all Kurds was Saladin, the great defender of Islam who captured Jerusalem from the Christians (1187) and who then defended it successfully against England's King Richard I (the Lion-Heart) and the other invading Christians during the Third Crusade (1189–1192). Estimates of the Kurdish population range between 14 million and 28 million. About half the Kurds are in Turkey; Iran and Iraq each have another 20 to 25 percent; and smaller numbers reside in Syria and Armenia. Sporadic and continuing attempts to establish an independent Kurdistan have caused conflicts with the countries in which the Kurds live. These disputes also sometimes involve outside countries, such as when the United States launched cruise missile attacks on Iraq in September 1996 after Baghdad's forces attacked one of the Kurdish groups in northern Iraq. Also, concern that Turkey is sometimes brutal in its campaign to quell its restive Kurds is one factor standing in the way of Turkey's wish to join the European Union.

Multiple Nations, Multiple States A fourth pattern emerges when one examines the global demographic and political map closely: the most common configuration of nations and states is a complex one in which several states and several nations overlap. Afghanistan, the countries around it, and the ethnonational groups in the country and the region provide a prime example of a country where this pattern of overlapping borders among nations and states has created a volatile mix.

Afghanistan is far from the only example. India is so divided among various religious, ethnic, language, and social groups that it is a wonder that the country exists at all. Moreover, some of India's many ethnonational groups overlap its borders with neighboring countries. One of those groups is the Hindu Tamils, who are split between India (where most live in the southern state of Tamil Nadu) and Sri Lanka. The Tamils in Sri Lanka have fought a long, bloody guerrilla war against the Buddhist Sinhalese majority that has left over 60,000 dead and perhaps 800,000 others displaced as Tamils and Sinhalese civilians each fled to areas controlled by their group. Many of the former Soviet republics (FSRs) also constitute a hodgepodge of nations and states that frequently resemble a *matryoshka*, the classic nested Russian folk art doll in which each doll has a smaller one inside. As noted in the box Afghanistan: Fact or Fiction, that country has significant populations of Tajiks and Uzbeks, who also have their own national states in Tajikistan and Uzbekistan. To cite just one more example, the Moldovan ethnic majority in Moldova, another FSR, is ethnically akin to the Romanians. Therefore, there is some urge for closer association between, even the unification of, neighboring Romania and Moldova. Not everyone in Moldova feels that way, however, and the ethnic Russian- and Ukrainian-dominated region in western Moldova has formed a breakaway area styled the Transdniester Republic. The catch is that if that region actually became independent, it would contain 40 percent Moldovans, who would have irredentist ties to greater Moldova or, perhaps, a greater Romania that had incorporated Moldova.

 # Nationalism and the Future

Now that we have seen the benign and malevolent faces of nationalism past and present, we can turn to the future of nationalism. We should ask ourselves (a) whether we favor the spread or curtailment of nationalism and (b) whether it will persist or wane as the primary focus of political identity for most people.

SELF-DETERMINATION AS A GOAL

One way to examine your feelings about nationalism is to extend the concept to every group that wishes to be sovereign (Moore, 1997). If being a proud member of a nation is good for you, and if the nationalistic urge of your people to govern itself in its own nation-state is laudable, then should not that privilege—or perhaps right—be extended to everyone? Americans, for one, asserted in 1776 that their nation had a right to have its own state, and they have fiercely defended it ever since.

Although it is impossible to determine exactly where the ultimate limits of national identification are, one study estimates that "there are over 5,000 ethnic minorities in the world" (Carment, 1994:551). Each of these groups has the potential to develop a national consciousness and to seek independence. Before dismissing such an idea as absurd, recall that political scientists widely recognize the existence of Barber's (1996) tribalism tendency: the urge to break away from current political arrangements and, often, to form into smaller units. World politics during

(Continued on page 158)

AFGHANISTAN: FACT OR FICTION

Certainly Afghanistan is a fact. It is on every map of south Asia, it is a member of the United Nations, it has a flag and a capital, and it possesses all the other legal and symbolic characteristics of a state.

Yet it would also be accurate to term Afghanistan a **failed state**. It is a country that, despite its legal and symbolic trappings, is so fragmented that it cannot be said to exist as a unified entity. In this sense, Afghanistan is an operational fiction, even if it is a legal and geographic fact.

The history of Afghanistan is one of frequent conquest going back to Persia's Darius the Great (522 B.C.), Macedonia's Alexander the Great (330 B.C.), Genghis Khan and the Mongols (1221), India's Moghul Empire (1504), and other invaders. The origins of Afghanistan in its present state begin in 1747, when the leader of one of the Afghan Pashtun (or Pathan) tribes in the region around Kandahar in the south began to expand his power to the north and east. This brought

Afghanistan may be viewed as the crossroads of many nations. As the map indicates, the people of Afghanistan belong to various ethnonational groups that are often in conflict with one another. Whether it will be possible to create a united Afghanistan or whether it will persist as a failed state remains to be seen.

the Pashtuns into conflict with Russian imperial expansion to the north in the areas that are now Tajikistan, Turkmenistan, and Uzbekistan, and with British imperial expansion in what is now India and Pakistan. Eventually, Russia prevailed in the north, and the British invaded Afghanistan in 1839, establishing fitful control until the repeated Afghan uprisings finally forced them out in 1919.

The following years saw a series of ethnic Pashtun monarchs rule uncertainly until the last of them, Muhammad Zahir Shah, was overthrown in 1973. During this time Russia and Britain, followed later by India, Iran, and Pakistan, all often interfered in the country. Five years after the last king was toppled, a leftist government was established, followed by a massive Soviet intervention in 1979 to protect it. Being the cold war era, that sparked U.S. support of

anti-Soviet *mujahedin* (holy warrior) groups, some of which later were part of the Taliban forces.

The origins of the word "Afghan," which dates back over 1,000 years, is uncertain, although some scholars believe that it is derived from an ancient Turkic word meaning "between." Certainly that makes intuitive sense, given Afghanistan's history of being invaded from every quarter and often being a political buffer zone between the larger empires and countries around it. This sense of being at the crossroads helps to explain the ethnonational complexity of the country, with most of its larger groups linked to the countries around Afghanistan. The diversity has also meant that there is only a limited degree to which the people in the territory called Afghanistan have identified as Afghans. There have certainly been times when a degree of unity has been achieved in the face of invaders or during the relatively brief periods of time under strong rulers. Even in those times, however, the sense of being an Afghan has been much less central to the political identification of most people in the country than their ethnic identification. Certainly, it could not be said that there is any such thing as an ethnic Afghan.

Most reference sources list Afghanistan's ethnic groups (and their percentage of the population) as Pashtun (38 percent) Tajik (25 percent), Hazara (19 percent), and Uzbek (6 percent), with smaller groups making up the remaining 12 percent. In fact, the ethno-demographic structure is much more complex than that. To begin, there are 10 million Pashtuns in Afghanistan and another 18 million members in neighboring, Punjabi-dominated Pakistan. Together this stateless Pashtun nation has some aspirations to found its own state, Pashtunistan. It is also the case, though, that the Pashtuns, an Indo-Aryan people, are divided into some 60 clans or tribes, such as the Durrani and the Ghilzay. Each has a traditional territory, and there is a history of rivalry and armed clashes among many of them.

Further to the north are the Tajiks, who are of Persian stock, and the Uzbeks and a smaller number of Turkmen, who are Turkic people. All these groups are also linked respectively to their ethnic brethren in the neighboring countries of Tajikistan, Uzbekistan, and Turkmenistan. These ethnonational groups formed the core of the Northern Alliance that the United States supported in its war against the largely Pashtun Taliban regime. The Hazaras differ from most other groups in Afghanistan in several ways. They claim descent from Genghis Khan and the Mongols. Also, whereas most other Afghans are Sunni Muslims, a majority of Hazaras are Shi'ite Muslims, which gives them links to Iran to the west. The Hazaras, who claim that they have been persecuted by the Pashtuns, were also part of the Northern Alliance and harbor some dreams about an independent Hazarajat (or Hazaristan).

Beyond these groups there are the Nuristani, an Indo-Aryan people centered in northwestern Afghanistan; the Aimaks of Turco-Mongolian origin who live in the west central mountain region; the Balochi who are in Pakistan and Iran as well as Afghanistan; and a number of other ethnonational groups that differ from one another in a variety of demographic ways.

It is also worth noting that Afghanis speak some 31 different languages and dialects. Pashto is the language of the Pashtuns, while Tajiks, Hazaras, Aimaks, and some other groups speak variations of Dari, a language akin to Farsi, the language of Iran. The Nuristani and some other groups speak Western Dardic, the Balochi have their own Indic-related dialect, and the Uzbeks and Turkmen speak different, but related, Turkic dialects.

What all this means politically is that defeating the Taliban and al-Qaeda was far easier for the U.S.-led coalition than will be the task of stabilizing the country. "We do have an interest in the kind of stability in Afghanistan that will make it less likely that Afghanistan will become a base for terrorist operations against us in the future," commented Douglas J. Feith, U.S. under secretary of defense for policy. "We want the current Afghan political experiment to succeed." Then Feith added, "We are not involving ourselves in internecine politics, including the politics backed by guns, as the definition of our military mission."[1]

Achieving those two goals, stability and staying above internecine rivalries, has proved difficult. The process of establishing a post-Taliban interim government was a difficult negotiation that only succeeded under intense pressure from the United States. Within weeks, however, old rivalries began to emerge. In the northwest, for example, Ismail Khan, a warlord of Tajik origin known as the "Lion of Herat," began to carve out an autonomous fiefdom. Although he proclaimed loyalty to the government in Kabul, one central government official's view was that "Ismail Khan is a man who wants to be powerful."[2] Among other things, Khan is said to have provoked a U.S. attack on a rival warlord by supplying false information that the targeted force was Taliban. It is also the case, as has been true for a millennium or more, that outside powers may well support one side or another. Iran has links to Khan. India and Pakistan have supported various groups for reasons that have to do with the two countries' rivalry over Kashmir.

Continuing this tale of ethnonational diversity, overlapping national boundaries and state borders, and divisive big-power rivalries in Afghanistan is not necessary to underline the point that the country is at demographic and political crossroads. Surely Afghanistan exists in a formal way, but it does not exist as the primary focus of political identification and loyalties of its multiple ethnonational groups. "You don't have a functioning state [in Afghanistan]," is how one expert on Central Asia put it. "There is no sense of nationhood.... Blood [kinship] is much more important."[3]

recent decades has been marked by strong nationalist movements (Musgrave, 1997). Many of these have waged bloody campaigns of separation, and the incidence of protest, rebellion, and communal conflict, and the magnitude and intensity of these conflicts, rose markedly during most of the past half-century, as Figure 6.2 demonstrates.

There are numerous good reasons to support **self-determination**. In addition to the benefits of nationalism noted earlier, self-determination would end many of the abuses that stem from ethnic oppression. If all ethnic groups were allowed to peacefully found their own sovereign units or join those of their ethnic brethren, then the tragedies of Bosnia, Chechnya, East Timor, Kosovo, Rwanda, and many other strife-torn peoples and countries would not have occurred.

There are also, however, numerous problems associated with the unlimited extension of self-determination. *Untangling groups* is one problem. Various nations are intermingled in many places. Bosnia is such a place; Bosnian Muslims, Croats, and Serbs often lived in the same cities, on the same streets, in the same apartment buildings. How does one disentangle these groups and assign them territory when each wants to declare its independence or to join with its ethnic kin in an existing country?

The *dissolution of existing states* is a second problem that the principle of self-determination raises for many states, ranging from Canada about Quebec, through Great Britain about Scotland, to Spain about the Basque region and Catalonia (Keating, 1996). Americans also need to ponder this problem. They have long advocated the theory of a right of self-determination. The Declaration of Independence asserts just this when it declares that "When in the course of human events, it becomes necessary for one people to dissolve the political bands which have connected them with another" and to assume "separate and equal" status, then it is the "right of the people to alter or to abolish [the old government] and to institute [a] new government." President Woodrow Wilson made much the same claim when he told Congress in 1918 that "self-determinism is not a mere phrase. It is an imperative principle of action."[12] One has to wonder, however, how Wilson would have applied this principle to national minorities in the United States. Do, for instance, Wilsonian principles mean that all Americans should support those native Hawaiians who claim correctly that they were subjugated by Americans a century ago and who want to reestablish an independent Hawaii?

Did You Know That:
There is an active native Hawaiian independence movement. Haunai-Kay Trask, who heads Kalahui Hawaii, the largest Hawaiian nationalist group, contends that her group's aim is "decolonization in the last area of the world to decolonize—the Pacific Basin."[1] The state of Hawaii held a referendum in 1996 among native Hawaiians to determine their preferences for the future. The result was a resounding 73 percent "yes" for independence.

In other places, creating ethnically homogeneous states would have multiple complexities. To create nation-states out of the various enthnonational groups in Afghanistan would require disentangling many places where the groups overlap. It would also include some groups joining neighboring countries such as Tajikistan and Uzbekistan. But then what would happen to the Tajiks who live in Uzbekistan and the Uzbeks who live in Tajikistan? And in the case of the Pashtuns, a Pashtunistan would have to be created by pieces taken out of Pakistan and Iran, as well as Afghanistan.

Microstates present a third problem related to self-determination. The rapidly growing number of independent countries, many of which have a marginal ability to survive on their own, raises the issue of the wisdom of allowing the formation of what have been called **microstates**. These are countries with tiny populations, territories, and/or economies. Such countries have long existed, with Andorra, Monaco, and San Marino serving as examples. But in recent years, as colonialism has become discredited, many more of these microstates have become established.

Many microstates lack the economic or political ability to stand as truly sovereign states. One set of measures can be seen in Table 6.1's comparison of a tiny

Table 6.1 Characteristics of a Micostate, a U.S. State, and a U.S. City			
	Kiribati	Rhode Island	Glendale
Population	94,149	1,048,319	194,973
Territory (sq. mi.)	226	1,545	30.6
Per Capita Wealth*	950	26,528	25,719

*Per capita GDP for Kiribati; per capita personal income for Rhode Island and Glendale, California.

Data source: World Almanac (2002).

Some analysts worry about instability associated with the limited ability of microstates to sustain themselves economically or to defend themselves. The sovereign state of Kiribati is smaller in most ways than the geographically smallest U.S. state, Rhode Island, and Glendale, California, the U.S. city with only the one-hundredth largest population.

Western Pacific island country, the smallest U.S. state, and the one-hundredth most populous U.S. city. There are 40 microstates, countries with populations of less than 1 million. These microstates comprise about one-fifth of all the world's countries. In fact, as Figure 6.3 depicts, if you added up all their populations, they would amount to just 12.3 million people, smaller than Cambodia's population; about 46 percent that of Tokyo, the world's most populous city; and only 36 percent of California's population.

The perplexity about microstates is that one can simultaneously support the theory of self-determination and worry about the political liability that microstates cause. This quandary is exacerbated by the fact that larger predatory powers, not the microstates, are the real source of danger. In a perfect world, the military and economic strength of a state would not matter. But the world is not perfect, and therefore it is reasonable to evaluate microstates within the reality of the international system that exists. Most microstates have scant ability to defend themselves against internal or external attack. That was amply demonstrated in 2000 when a handful of indigenous Fijians led by a failed insurance salesman managed to seize the country's prime minister and a number of ministers, to force the resignation of the president, and to force an agreement barring Fijians of ethnic Indian descent from political power. After a prolonged crisis, the rebel leader was arrested, but some of his oppressive actions stood. This was evident in the fact that he was charged with treason for overthrowing the ethnic Fijian president, but no charges were filed for ousting the Indo-Fijian prime minister.

Many microstates also lack a sustainable economic base. The sovereign state of Nauru, a tiny (8 square miles) island country of some 10,000 people, which lies 300 miles to the northeast of Papua New Guinea, bases virtually its entire economy on the export of phosphates, used for fertilizer. This product is derived from guano, the droppings of seabirds, which covered most of the island and has provided Nauruans with considerable income. Unfortunately, 80 percent of the island has been strip-mined to its rock base, leaving it, in one description, "a pitted, ghostly moonscape." Worse, what is left of the guano will soon be gone, and Nauru will have no economy at all. Nauruans may have to accept Australia's offer to resettle them on an island off its east coast. "It would be very

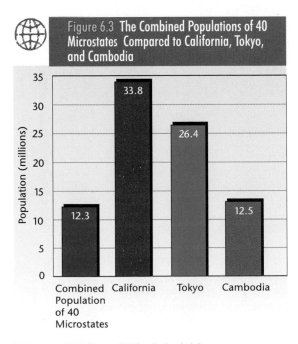

Figure 6.3 **The Combined Populations of 40 Microstates Compared to California, Tokyo, and Cambodia**

Data sources: World Almanac (2000), author's calculations.

(Continued on page 160)

THE NEWEST COUNTRY

East Timor, the world's newest country was officially "born" on May 20, 2002. The newest country occupies about half the island of Timor, which is located between Indonesia (which controls West Timor) and Australia to the south.

East Timor was one of the last remnants of the more than 450-year-old Portuguese empire when the East Timorese declared their independence in 1975. That independence was stillborn when the Indonesian military annexed both West Timor (which had been a Dutch colony) and East Timor in a bloody intervention that cost some 60,000 East Timorese lives.

Continuing East Timorese desires for independence and considerable international pressure finally persuaded Indonesia to allow a referendum on independence in 1998. Elements of the Indonesian military stationed on Timor tried to intimidate the East Timorese into staying away from the polls. Then, when that did not happen, and there was a 79 percent vote in favor of independence, irregular forces armed by the military went on a rampage, killing thousands and destroying schools, roads, and other parts of the infrastructure. The human and economic devastation was finally stopped when Australia, followed by the United Nations, intervened militarily. After the referendum and the final expulsion of Indonesia's forces, the United Nations Transitional Administration for East Timor took control as an interim step to preparing for independence.

Certainly, the travails of the East Timorese and the general appeal of the high-minded principle of self-determination make it attractive to welcome this newest of all countries. Yet East Timor also presents a near classic case of all the drawbacks of microstates. Both its territory, some 7,334 square miles (about the size of New Jersey), and its population, 770,000 (about equal to Indianapolis, Indiana), are small. The ability of East Timor to defend itself against outside attack by Indonesia or another outside threat is near zero. Impoverished is the best word to describe its economy. The countries annual per capita gross domestic product (GDP) is about $405, one of the lowest in the world. Its only significant export is coffee. One bright spot is that Australia has agreed to begin paying East Timor $180 million in annual oil and gas royalties once energy begins to flow from undersea drilling in the so-called "Timor Gap" between the two countries. Even those revenues, however, would only increase the per capita income to $639.

Many social conditions reflect East Timor's profound poverty. Life expectancy is only 55 years. Over 12 percent of East Timorese children die before they reach their fifth birthday. There are only about 30 physicians and another 400 or so health professionals in the country.

The question then is, Apart from emotion, is the global community better off with yet another microstate?

The world's newest country, East Timor, became fully independent on May 20, 2002, after a UN transitional administration had helped it for two-and-a-half years to transform itself from a territory of Indonesia to a sovereign state. This joyful woman celebrates amid others waving the country's new flag in the capital city of Dili on independence day.

sad to leave our native land; but what else can we do?" grieves 84-year-old James Aingimea. "The land of our ancestors has been destroyed."[13]

Thus the exigencies of the real world suggest that some standard has to be applied to independence movements. There is a large array of ethnonational groups with aspirations that arguably are just as legitimate as were American goals in 1776. Should they all be supported, and, if not, which independence movements should be favored and why? There are critics of self-determination who charge that "liberalism's embrace of national self-determination [has] raised more questions than it [has] answered" (Hoffmann, 1995:163). Or, as another scholar puts it, "Self-determination movements... have largely exhausted their legitimacy.... It is time to withdraw moral approval from most of the movements and see them for what they mainly are—destructive" (Etzioni, 1993:21).

By contrast, some commentators advocate broad support of self-determination, which one analyst calls "the most powerful idea in the contemporary world" (Lind, 1994:88). Between these two ends of the spectrum of opinion, many seek a set of standards by which to judge whether or not a claim to the right of secession is legitimate. One such standard is whether a minority people is being discriminated against by a majority population (Hannum, 1999). Perhaps it would be wiser for the international community to guarantee human and political rights for minority cultural groups than to support self-determination to the point of reductio ad absurdum. Whatever the standard though, it is certain that applying the principle of self-determination is difficult in a complex world (Ramet, 2000; Talbott, 2000).

NATIONALISM: WILL THE CURTAIN FALL?

A critical question in the future of nationalism, and indeed the course of world politics, is whether nationalism will significantly weaken or even die out. The answer is unclear. The existence of divergent identities based on language and other cultural differences extends as far back into time as we can see. From a biblical perspective, there may have been a single people at the time of Adam and Eve and their immediate descendants. But later in the first book of the Bible, God reacts with dismay by the attempt of humans to build the Tower of Babel up to the heavens in an effort to elevate themselves to the deity's level. To defeat that pretentious plan, God creates different languages to complicate communication. "Behold," God commands, "the people is one, and they have all one language.... [L]et us go down, and there confound their language, that they may not understand one another's speech" (Genesis 11:6-7).

Whether this tale is taken literally or symbolically, the point is that diverse cultural identities are ancient and, some analysts would say, important, perhaps inherent, traits of humans that stem from their urge to have the psychological security of belonging to a we-group. One scholar contends, for example, that being a member of a nation both "enables an individual to find a place... in the world [in] which he or she lives" and, also, to find "redemption from personal oblivion" through a sense of being part of "an uninterrupted chain of being" (Tamir, 1995:432). Yet it must also be said that group identification and nationalism are not synonymous. The sense of sovereignty attached to cultural identification is relatively modern. "Nationalism and nations have not been permanent features of human history," as one scholar puts it (O'Leary, 1997:221). Therefore, nationalism, having not always existed, will not necessarily always be the world's principal form of political orientation.

What does the future hold? Some scholars believe that nationalism will continue to flourish as the main source of political identification; other scholars expect nationalism to eventually cease to be an important political phenomenon. The most common view among political scientists is a middle position that holds that nationalism will persist for the foreseeable future as a key sense of the political identification of most people, but that it will not enjoy the unrivaled center stage presence it has had for several hundred years (Ishiyama & Breuning, 1998; Eley & Suny, 1996).

Also unclear is what would follow if state-centric nationalism were to die out. Some scholars believe that it will be replaced by culture, religion, or some other demographic characteristic as the primary sense of political self. Yet another group of scholars argues that a sense of global nationalism could emerge based on the similarities among all humans and their common experiences, needs, and goals. One such scholar envisages "a nation coextensive with humanity" that would then come together in a "United States of the World" (Greenfeld, 1992:7).

What can we conclude from this scholarly disagreement? Will nationalism persist "until the last syllable of recorded time," to borrow words from Shakespeare's *Macbeth*? The answer is that the script for tomorrow's drama on the world stage is still being written by the world's political playwrights. If we think the world drama important, each of us should lend a hand to establishing the plot, casting the actors, and writing the dialogue.

Chapter Summary

1. Nationalism is one of the most important factors in international politics. It defines where we put our primary political loyalty, and that is in the nation-state. Today the world is divided and defined by nationalism and nation-states.

2. Nations, nation-states, and nationalism are all key concepts that must be carefully defined and clearly differentiated and understood.

3. The political focus on nationalism has evolved over the last five centuries.

4. After World War II, some predicted an end to nationalism, but they were wrong. Today nationalism is stronger, and the independence of Afro-Asian countries, the former Soviet republics, and other states has made it even more inclusive.

5. Nationalism has both positive and negative aspects.

6. On the plus side, nationalism has promoted democracy, self-government, economic growth, and social/political/economic diversity and experimentation.

7. On the negative side, nationalism has led to isolationism, feelings of superiority, suspicion of others, and messianism. Nationalism can also cause instability when there is a lack of fit between states and nations. Domestic instability and foreign intervention are often the result of such national instability. Nationalism has also led to a multiplicity of microstates.

8. There are many enthnonational groups that are seeking or may seek independence. Among other considerations, this could lead to the further multiplicity of microstates.

9. In a world of transnational global forces and problems, many condemn nationalism as outmoded and perilous. Some even predict its decline and demise. Such predictions are, however, highly speculative, and nationalism will remain a key element and powerful force in the foreseeable future.

Chapter 7

Transnationalism: The Alternative Orientation

A speedier course than lingering languishment
Must we pursue, and I have found the path.

Shakespeare, *Titus Andronicus*

Not all those that wander are lost.

J. R. R. Tolkien, *The Fellowship of the Ring*

An invasion of armies can be resisted, but not an idea whose time has come.
Victor Hugo, *Histoire d'un Crime*, 1852

Chapter Objectives

After completing this chapter, you should be able to:

- Understand the concept of transnationalism.
- Examine and discuss transnational ideas and ideologies.
- Understand the underpinnings of transnationalism.
- Understand the origins of globalism and how it relates to idealism, postmodernism, and postinternationalism.
- Identify evidence for the increasing level of transnational interaction.
- Discuss the growth of transnational movements and organizations.
- Understand the transnational women's movement philosophy.
- Identify transnational activity of the women's movement and trace its progress.
- Discuss the transnational elements of religion.
- Examine both the positive and negative roles of religion in world politics.
- Analyze, as a case study, the role of Islam in world politics.
- Examine the cohesive and divisive effects of transnational culture.
- Discuss the future role of global political and cultural organization.

Breathtaking change has been a constant theme in books about international politics written during the last decade. We are in a period of "sweeping and revolutionary changes," one study begins (Klare & Chandrani, 1998:vii). "We have entered into a period of turbulent transitions," another study concurs (Mansbach & Rhodes, 2000:xi).

One direction of change, as discussed in chapters 6 and 8, is the fragmentation of existing large states into ever smaller units as minority nations within the states seek their own independent homelands. The rise in the willingness of ethnonational groups to demand—and even fight for—self-determination has created what might be called **micronationalism**. This trend toward the fragmentation of political identities, Benjamin Barber's (1996) "Tribalism," is associated with the increased number of microstates (such as East Timor), that have established their independence during the past few decades.

The other direction of change is taking humankind on a path toward a broader, more inclusive view of humanity. This call for change reflects frustration with the traditional way that we humans have organized ourselves politically, by making our nation and its associated sovereign territorial state the primary focus of our political identity. Whether that political organization is the modern nation-state or some earlier micronational form, such as the city-state or the feudal estate, there have been critics who urge that we look beyond such territorially bounded structures and political identities and adopt transnational affiliations as an alternative to traditional identification with and loyalty to the nation-state. Exploring the possibility of **transnational political identity** is the focus of this chapter. As we shall see, a growing number of people view themselves as politically connected to a variety of groups, such as religion, that transcend the traditional political boundaries of nation and state. Therefore, transnationalism presents an alternative route to the future, or as Robert Frost might put it, a political road less traveled by.

The Origins and Evolution of Transnationalism

The concept of **transnationalism** includes a range of political identities, activities, and other phenomena that connect humans *across nations and national boundaries*. Transnationalism is, therefore, inherently counternationalist in that it undermines nationalism (and its tangible manifestation, the national state) by promoting cross-national political activity. These interactions, in turn, raise the possibility of people adopting a sense of primary **political identification** that does not focus on the nation-state.

Transnationalism springs from two sources. Global interaction is one. The degree to which economic interdependence, mass communications, rapid travel, and other modern factors are intertwining the lives of people around the world is a constant theme of this book. Human thought is the second source of transnationalism. The philosopher René Descartes argued in *Discourse on Method* (1637) that intellect is the essence of being human. "I think, therefore I am," he wrote. People can think abstractly, can conceive of what they have not experienced, and can group ideas together to try to explain existence and to chart courses of action.

TRANSNATIONAL THOUGHT

Our ability to think beyond our personal experiences is important in understanding current transnationalism because until recently it has persisted on the periphery of world politics. Therefore we need to spend time examining transnational ideas and ideologies. Whether or not it is literally true that, as Ecclesiastes (I:9) tells us, "There is no new thing under the sun," it is often profitable to understand that many very modern ideas have very ancient origins.

Early Transnational Thought

Transnational thought in Western culture can be traced to the Stoics of ancient Greece and Rome. Stoicism flourished from about 300 B.C. to A.D. 200, a period marked by the eclipse of the small Greek city-states and the rise of the large Macedonian, then Roman, empires. This expansion of political boundaries was accompanied by a new school of thought founded in about 300 B.C. by the Cypriot philosopher Zeno.

The word stoicism has come to mean accepting one's burdens without complaint, but the philosophy of classical Stoicism embodies much more. Stoicism portrayed people as individuals who are part of humanity, not as members of one or another smaller political community. As such, Stoic outlook was cosmopolitan, a word derived from combining the Greek *cosmos* (world) and *polis* (city). Thus it is not too much of a stretch to say that Stoics had a sense of themselves as global citizens. Reflecting this, the Roman emperor Marcus Aurelius wrote of himself in *Meditations*, "my... country, so far as I am [the emperor], is Rome, but so far as I am a man, it is the world."

In time, Stoicism declined, but its influence did not vanish. To the contrary, the writings of the Stoic philosophers influenced later thinkers, as we shall see. Also, some elements of Stoicism were incorporated into early Christian thought in the West. These Christians often passively resisted the Romans and other persecutors; they practiced a communitarian lifestyle; they held a universal view of humankind.

It is important to note that other ancient, non-Western great philosophical traditions contain teachings that are similar to the cosmopolitan thrust of Stoicism. Philosophies such as Confucianism and religions such as Buddhism and Hinduism all contain transnational elements that parallel those in Stoicism. For example, Siddhartha Gautama (ca. 563–483 B.C.), who became known as the Buddha, urged that we adopt a universal perspective. "Whatsoever, after due examination and analysis, you find to be conducive to the good, the benefit, the welfare of all beings," he taught, "that doctrine believe and cling to, and take it as your guide."

Later Transnational Thought

The idea of transcending local political structure and power remained alive over the centuries. "We have it in our power to begin the world over again," the revolutionary Thomas Paine proclaimed in *Common Sense* (1776). We remember Paine as an American patriot, but that is an ill-fitting description. Instead, Paine was committed to a philosophy, not to any country. He described himself as a "citizen of the world" and was dubious about countries because they "limited citizenship to the soil, like vegetation." It is true that Paine's writing helped galvanize Americans during their struggle for independence, but of that effort, Paine wrote in 1779 that he would have "acted the same part in any other country [if] the same circumstances [had] arisen there which have happened here."[1] Paine supported the American Revolution not to establish yet another narrow nationality but because he believed, as he wrote in *The Rights of Man* (1779), that it represented a "new method of thinking" and was "in great measure the cause of mankind." Paine also supported the French Revolution, which he saw as continuing the work of its American counterpart and leading a "march on the horizon of the world" that "neither the Rhine, the [English] Channel, or the ocean... can arrest" (Fitzsimons, 1995:579). That transnational march, Paine predicted, would lead to free trade and to establishing an international congress to resolve differences among states. Thus today's trend toward globalism would have neither surprised nor dismayed Paine.

During the same revolutionary period in which Paine was writing, the philosopher Immanuel Kant took the idea of international cooperation for peace even further. Kant wrote in *Idea for a Universal History From a Cosmopolitan Point of View* (1784) that countries should abandon their "lawless state of savagery and enter a federation of people in which every state could expect to derive its security and rights… from a united power and the law-governed decisions of a united will."

The thinking of nineteenth-century German communist philosophers such as Friedrich Engels and Karl Marx also contained a strong element of transnational thought. They stressed the commonality of humankind and foresaw a global community. Marx and Engels also believed that the economic classes inherent in capitalism were the source of human divisions and that states were capitalist tools that the wealthy class, the bourgeoisie, used to keep control of the working class, the proletariat. The "history of all hitherto existing society is the history of class struggles," *The Communist Manifesto* (1848) explained; "workingmen have no country." What Engels foresaw was that once communism was triumphant, "as soon as class rule… [is] removed, nothing more remains to be repressed, and a special repressive force, a state, is no longer necessary." This means, Engels reasoned, that the state becomes "superfluous, and then dies out of itself."

Contemporary Transnational Thought

After existing on the periphery of political thought during the halcyon days of nationalism, transnational thought came increasingly to the fore in the twentieth century. The main thrust of this perspective was covered in the extensive discussion of idealism in chapter 1. As noted there, idealists contend that a transition from a conflictive, state-centric system to a cooperative, interdependent system is both under way and is desirable.

Another perspective that is related to transnationalism is called **postmodernism**. At its core, postmodernism contends that reality is subjective rather than objective. This view holds that reality is created by the ways that we think and by our discourse (writing, talking) about our world. Postmodernists believe that we have become trapped by stale ways of conceiving of how we organize and conduct ourselves.

As such, postmodernism is especially important for transnationalism because it seeks to examine the ways we organize ourselves politically. Postmodernists believe that organizing ourselves politically around a geographically defined country is only an image in our mind reinforced by the way that we discuss politics. Postmodernists believe, for instance, that political identity is structured by such national identities as American or Mexican, and they want to change the discourse on political identity so that it could also include, for instance, being a woman or a human as a focus of political identity.

A closely related concept is **postinternationalism** (Hobbes, 2000). This idea holds that in a turbulent world, people have begun to change their political identity and, in many cases, are giving much greater weight to subnational political identities, such as their ethnic group, or to transnational political identities, such as their gender. From this perspective, we are entering an era where "international" is becoming an outmoded concept that misses the multiple levels, from local to global, with which people identify and around which they organize themselves politically.

Such seemingly radical ideas have often alarmed those who trod the traditional path. Paine's revolutionary fervor was welcomed by Americans in rebellion, but once the United States was established, Paine seemed dangerous to many. Former president John Adams wrote in 1807 that he doubted that "any man in the world has had more influence on its inhabitants or affairs for the last thirty years than Tom Paine." That worried Adams, who condemned Paine's efforts to revolutionize the world as being "a career of mischief" conducted by "a mongrel between pig and puppy, begotten by a wild boar and a bitch wolf" (Fitzsimons, 1995:581).

Despite the fulminations of Adams and other traditionalists about the alternative path propounded by philosophers such as Zeno and Paine, the idea has persisted. "Nationalism is an infantile disease. It is the measles of the mind," Albert Einstein wrote in 1921. Such ideas remained on the periphery, however, until the years following World War II. Since then, theory has begun to assume at least limited reality. In fact, it may be that the ideas of Paine and similar thinkers, no matter how much they were dismissed in their own eras as odd, even dangerous, have better stood the test of time than the views of their detractors.

TRANSNATIONAL EVOLUTION

It can be said with certainty that the transnational evolution of the world is occurring rapidly. The exact course that evolution will take, how far it will proceed, and how tranquil or turbulent the evolutionary path will be all remain to be seen. It is possible, for instance, that the transnational path will lead to greater global harmony. Or it may be that transnationalism may serve only to add to the dimension of conflict that exists in the current international system.

Transnationalism as a Path Toward Greater Harmony

There are some elements of transnationalism that involve greater interdependence and harmony as we move toward globalism and becoming citizens of what Barber refers to as McWorld. This type of transnationalism is very much in accord with the vision of the idealist school of political thought discussed in chapter 1. The evolution of transnationalism toward greater global harmony is also the path on which this chapter concentrates. As you will see, the world is being brought together by powerful transnational trends in economics, communications, and transportation and by the rapid growth of transnational organizations and movements.

Transnationalism as a Path Toward Greater Conflict

There is also a less welcome road down which transnationalism may take us. This involves an antithetical, negative image of transnational culture, one that envisions a world divided and in conflict along cultural lines. Those who see transnationalism in this light tend to be realists, many of whom would strengthen the national state as a bulwark against the dangers of hostile transnational alignments.

The best-known thesis of this view is Samuel P. Huntington's (1996, 1993) image of a coming "**clash of civilizations**." Huntington's (1993:22) thesis is that "the fundamental source of conflict" in the future will "be cultural" and that "the battle lines of the future" will pit "different civilizations" against one another. He projects (p. 25) that world politics will be driven by the "interactions among seven or eight major civilizations," including "Western, Confucian, Japanese, Islamic, Hindu, Slavic-Orthodox, Latin American, and possibly African."

Like many analysts, Huntington (p. 26) believes that various modern forces work to "weaken the nation-state as a source of identity" and that new cultural identifications will emerge "to fill this gap" and to group countries into cultural blocs. His prediction for such alignments is dark. "Over the centuries," according to Huntington (pp. 25–27), "differences among civilizations have generated the most prolonged and the most violent conflicts," because "cultural characteristics and differences are less mutable and hence less easily compromised and resolved than

Transnationalism is not necessarily a path to greater world harmony. Scholar Samuel Huntington has predicted that transnational cultures, including Western and Islamic, will someday engage in a "clash of civilizations." Although they probably had never heard of Huntington, the image of a cultural conflict is how this group of Pakistanis viewed the continuing presence of U.S. and other Western troops in neighboring Islamic Afghanistan.

political and economic ones." What should we make of this image of a future world torn asunder by the clash of civilizations?

Clashes along transnational religious lines provide one unsettling sign that Huntington's theory is not totally unthinkable. This phenomenon is most closely associated in the minds of many people with Islamic fundamentalism since the terrorist attacks on the United States on September 11, 2001. In reality, the growth of religious fundamentalism as a political force involves most of the world's great religions. One example is provided by the coming together of Hinduism and nationalism in India and that country's clashes with Muslim Pakistan, all of which is related in the box, India, Pakistan, Religion, and the Bomb on pp. 182–183. Yet other aspects of religious fundamentalism are discussed later in this chapter.

Persistent racism and other forms of xenophobic intolerance are another cultural reality that lend credence to Huntington's culture-clash thesis. People from the United States, Canada, Europe and other predominantly Eurowhite cultures often angrily reject charges that the policies of their countries sometimes have a racist tinge, but there is at least some evidence to support the indictment.

The inaction of Western powers, while Christians were slaughtering Muslims in Bosnia during the early 1990s; the barring of Muslim Turkey from the mostly Christian EU; and the vigorous opposition of the largely Christian West to Muslims (or Hindus) getting nuclear weapons, while ignoring the Israeli nuclear stockpile, all cause some Muslims to suspect that racism is the cause of such policies. Such views are not confined to Muslims. Just before his death, Richard Nixon wrote, "It is an awkward but unavoidable truth that had the [mostly Muslim] citizens of Sarajevo [the capital of Bosnia] been predominantly Christian or Jewish, the civilized world would not have permitted [the atrocities that occurred]."[2]

Similarly, latent racism may account for the near nonresponses by the West to many crises in Africa and other non-Eurowhite regions and countries. UN secretary-general Boutros-Ghali (1992–1997) once charged that "Eurocentrism" prompted the major powers to leave Africans to the "cruelties of fate." When his comments brought angry protests, especially in the British press, Boutros-Ghali retorted that he was being attacked "because I'm a wog" (a British pejorative for a nonwhite colonial subject).[3] Reacting similarly to the West's unwillingness to try to stop the unimaginable slaughter in Rwanda in 1994 and a number of other tragedies that have beset Africa in recent years, Ghanaian diplomat Victor Gbeho observed, "If I were paranoid, I would say the delays [in getting a response by the big powers] we always face here are due to the fact that we are dealing with Africa."[4]

Divisions along traditional cultural lines also arguably provide support to the culture-clash thesis. For example, some observers also see a rebirth of "Slavophilism," or the support of Slavic-Orthodox culture to which Huntington refers. This impulse helped set off World War I when Slavic Russia sided with Slavic Serbia against Austria-Hungary. More recently, Russia was more sympathetic during the fighting in Bosnia and, later, in Kosovo to the Serbs than were most other countries. Russia's foreign minister charged the Western media with focusing only on abuses by the Serbs and described a "mirror situation" in which the Russian media was stressing "the hardships suffered by the Serbs." The result, he said, is that "when I deliver mild criticism of Serbs here [in Russia], I am seen as a betrayer of our Slavic brotherhood."[5]

Whether such evidence presages a future that fits with Huntington's prediction is highly speculative. Numerous analysts disagree with Huntington (Walt, 1997). Some point out that while racism, ethnic and religious intolerance, and other forms of culturalism are unsettling, they have persisted throughout human history and, thus, do not augur increased cultural clashes. Other analysts believe that the forces that are bringing the world together will overcome those that are driving it apart. Another scholar contends that "the real clash of civilizations will not be between the West and one or more of the Rest," but will occur within Western civilization as it struggles with itself over the postmodernist tendency toward "marginalizing Western civilization" as the work of "dead white European males" and other "boring clichés of the deconstructionists" (Kurth, 1994:14–15).

🌐 Transnational Interaction

Whether its manifestations are positive or negative, transnationalism is occurring at a quickening pace in the international system. The growth of transnationalism is more than a matter of intellect; it stems from myriad interactions across national borders. Such contacts have certainly always existed, but they have grown at an explosive rate during the past fifty years or so. What is even more significant is that the scope and level of these international interactions will continue to expand exponentially in the foreseeable future. The change is being driven or made possible by a range of factors—economics, communications, transportation, and organizations. You will see, among other things, that each of these factors both promotes and is dependent on the others.

TRANSNATIONAL ECONOMICS

Economic interchange across borders is bringing the world together in many ways. The intensifying reality of economic interchange and interdependence is addressed in chapters 1, 2, and 14 and, thus, need not be reiterated beyond two basic points. The first is that the international economy affects each of us through our jobs, what we pay for the goods and services we consume, and many other economic aspects of

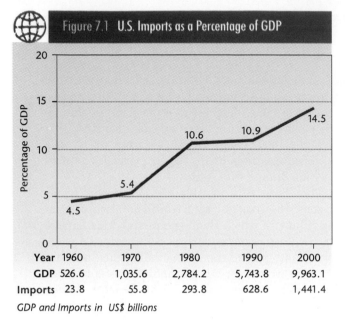

Figure 7.1 U.S. Imports as a Percentage of GDP

Year	1960	1970	1980	1990	2000
GDP	526.6	1,035.6	2,784.2	5,743.8	9,963.1
Imports	23.8	55.8	293.8	628.6	1,441.4

GDP and Imports in US$ billions

Data sources: World Almanac (2002); IMF (2002).

An increasing percentage of the wealth produced in the United States (GDP) is spent on goods and service imports, which means that more and more of what Americans own and consume and the services they use come from abroad. The mounting expenditures on imports are an example of the increase in transnational economic interchange and interdependence.

our lives. Second, as economically intertwined as we are today, it is likely that the connections will grow even more complex and comprehensive.

What is important to see here is that economic interchange has a transnational impact that extends beyond dollars and cents. Many analysts believe that economic interchange is bringing people together transnationally through a familiarity with each other and each other's products. Some of these contacts are interpersonal; more have to do with the role of international economics in narrowing cultural differences and creating a sense of identification with trading partners. About half of Japan's annual foreign trade is with the Western industrialized countries. The impact of this trade flow is evident in Japan's sense of affinity with others. One study found that when Japanese people were asked whether they more closely associated with Asian or Western countries, 54 percent of those willing to make a choice replied "Western countries." When asked why they identified with Western countries, 89 percent said it was because of "economic interaction" (Namkung, 1998:46). The degree to which we are absorbing each other's products is evident in Figure 7.1, which shows the increased amount of the wealth that Americans produce that is spent on imported goods and services.

TRANSNATIONAL COMMUNICATIONS

It is almost impossible to overstate the impact that modern communications have had on international relations (Tehranian, 1999; Vlahos, 1998; Deibert, 1997). In only a century and a half, communications have made spectacular advances, beginning with the telegraph, followed by photography, radio, the ability to film events, telephones, photocopying, television, satellite communications, faxes, and now computer-based Internet contacts and information through e-mail and the World Wide Web. It is also the case that more and more people around the globe are getting their news from the same sources. The most obvious omnisource is CNN, which now reaches virtually every country in the world.

Rapid global communications also allow political leaders, governments, and movements to transmit messages, even propaganda, around the world. This aspect of mass communications is often controversial. As part of the U.S. response to the 9-11 terror attacks, the Pentagon moved to establish an Office of Strategic Influence to plant false stories (euphemistically labeled "disinformation") in the media, designed to undermine the credibility of U.S. opponents. Fortunately, in the view of many, a torrent of criticism from within the United States and abroad killed the proposal. "The office is done. What do you want, blood?" an angry Secretary of Defense Donald Rumsfeld asked reporters who continued to press him with questions about the abortive propaganda effort.[6]

At least equally controversial was the ability of Osama bin Laden to transmit messages through the mass media to the world. The first of these was the result of an October 2001 interview of bin Laden conducted by Al-Jazeera (The Peninsula), a television network that is based in Qatar and watched by an estimated 35 million Arabs. The Bush administration objected to Al-Jazeera airing the tape. "We didn't

Modern technology has made transnational communications an important factor in global politics. Even though he was hiding in the mountains of Afghanistan, al-Qaeda leader Osama bin Laden was able to use videotapes transmitted via Al-Jazeera television network in Qatar and CNN to carry his message to the entire world as late as December 2001.

want them to help bin Laden and his merry band of freaks," a U.S. official explained. Increasing the pressure, Vice President Dick Cheney told the emir of Qatar that broadcasting the video would subject the emirate to being labeled "Osama's outlet to the world."[7] The network gave in to Washington's wishes, but U.S. media outlets soon acquired a copy of the tape and decided to air at least excerpts. Perhaps unwilling to risk confrontations with the major U.S. media outlets, the White House only asked, according to a presidential spokesperson, "the networks to exercise judgment about how these... messages will air," while recognizing that "editorial decisions can only be made by the media." The tapes were soon broadcast in the United States and, indeed, around the world. "I don't see any conflict between patriotism and good journalism," said the president of CBS News, Andrew Heyward.[8]

Another impact of global communications is that they undermine authoritarian governments. As such, the rapid mass communications that are taken for granted in the industrialized democracies are still greeted with suspicion by authoritarian governments. In China, those with Internet access must register with the police, and China's State Bureau of Security warns that "All organizations and individuals are forbidden from releasing, discussing, or transferring state secret information on bulletin boards, chat rooms, or in Internet news groups."[9] Penalties include imprisonment and heavy fines for the use of the Internet to "split the country" (air dissent). Whatever Beijing's hopes are to control "leaks" in and out of the country, they are probably roughly akin to Peter trying to hold back the sea by putting his finger in the dike.

In a process that has been labeled "democratic internationalism," transnational communications have also provided citizens from different countries with the ability to interact, exchange views, organize political activity, and undertake political action (Gilbert, 1999). There are now so many examples that are facilitated through modern communications, especially the Internet, that it is tempting to say that almost any cause you might think of has a transnational network. To get some sense of this, try going to a Web search engine such as Google and keyboard in "Students for a Free Tibet," "Students United for a Responsible Global Environment," "Students for Peace Awareness," "United Students Against Sweatshops," or virtually any other political cause, and you will find college student groups organizing themselves and communicating across the world on behalf of their beliefs.

Modern communications are also bringing the gruesome realities of war into people's living rooms and the earlier sanitized, even sometimes heroic, image is largely a thing of the past. While televised pictures of starving Somalis helped propel U.S. troops into Somalia in 1993, subsequent television images of a slain, nearly naked U.S. soldier being dragged by a rope through the dusty streets of Mogadishu, the basis of the movie *Black Hawk Down*, created a public uproar that soon forced President Clinton to withdraw the troops.

TRANSNATIONAL TRANSPORTATION

Just as transnational communication rapidly transmits our images and thoughts across national borders, transnational transportation carries our products and people with a speed that would have been incomprehensible not very long ago. This point about the advent of rapid, mass transnational transportation makes it worth thinking about the life of Elizabeth "Ma Pampo" Israel of Dominica, who church records indicate was born in 1875, making her the world's oldest documented person.

One thing that modern transportation has done during the life of this modern Methuselah is to make the world more familiar and interdependent by creating the ability to move huge amounts of what we produce across borders and oceans. Just before she was born, the most famous merchant vessel of its time, the *Flying Cloud* (1851–1874), was 229 feet long. Now if Ma Pampo gazed seaward from the shores of her island country, she might spot the modern tanker *Seawise Giant*, which at 1,504 feet long (almost one-third of a mile) is so large that crew members often use bicycles on board to travel from one point to another. This ship is part of the world merchant fleet that is made up of almost 28,000 freighters and tankers, which have a total capacity to carry, at any one moment, over 733 million tons of goods.

Air transportation also brings our national products to one another, but it is even more important as a way of carrying people between countries. When Ma Pampo was 20 years old, Lord Kelvin, president of the Royal Society, Great Britain's leading scientific advisory organization, dismissed as "impossible" the idea of "heavier-than-air flying machines."[10] Just eight years later, in 1903, Orville and Wilbur Wright proved Lord Kelvin wrong. Now international air travel has become almost routine and each year rapidly carries hundreds of millions of travelers between countries. Caracas, Venezuela, is closer in travel time to New York than is Los Angeles, and London is not much farther. In 1997 about 24 million Americans flew overseas, and about an equal number of other people flew to the United States. It strains the imagination, but given the speed of the supersonic transport (SST) and the time-zone differences, it is possible to fly across the Atlantic from London to New York, and when you land, the local time in New York will be earlier than the time in London when you took off.

TRANSNATIONAL ORGANIZATIONS

As discussed in chapter 3, the last half century has seen a phenomenal growth in the number and activities of private transnational organizations, called nongovernmental organizations (NGOs). What is important here about this growth is that it reflects a

Did You Know That:
When the first bootlegged copies of the 2002 film *Black Hawk Down* were shown in Mogadishu, Somalia, where the events portrayed in the film occurred in 1993, most Somalis rooted against the Americans. Said one man who had paid the equivalent of 10 cents to see the film, "As you can see, Somalis are brave fighters. If the Americans come back to fight us, we shall defeat them again."[1]

disenchantment with existing political organizations based in or dominated by states. "Stifled by the unwillingness of nations and international organizations to share decision making, and frustrated by the failure of political institutions to bring about reform," one study explains, "political activists began to form their own cross-border coalitions in the 1970s and 1980s" (Lopez, Smith, & Pagnucco, 1995:36). These coalitions born of frustration led to an upsurge in the founding of NGOs to act as the organizational arm of transnational social movements, such as those that promote women's rights, nuclear disarmament, or environmental protection.

The global women's movement provides an illustration of the process. First, as with many causes, the advances that women have made internationally have not generally come at the initiative of national governments. Instead, the place of women's issues on the international political agenda is largely the result of women's groups pressing governments and international organizations to address their concerns.

Second, NGOs facilitate the building of networks of contacts and interaction across borders. The networks of NGOs and national organizations that share an interest in a specific aspect of global society are called transnational advocacy networks (TANs). This networking function was one of the valuable benefits for the approximately 30,000, mostly female delegates from some 2,000 NGOs who met in Huairou, China. The meeting paralleled the **fourth UN World Conference on Women (WCW)**, which met in Beijing in 1995. "The real action here," said Sri Lankan delegate Hema Goonatilake, "is hearing and learning, forming networks."[11]

Third, NGOs bring pressure on governments to support the NGOs' various transnational programs. Reviewing the impact of the successive World Conferences on Women, the New York-based Women's Environment and Development Organization (WEDO) reported recently that 70 percent of the world's national governments have now drawn up plans to advance women's rights, and 66 countries have established national offices of women's affairs. "What's happened… could not have happened without Beijing," one scholar notes. "The energy, the activity of Beijing has not gone away."[12]

Modern transnational trade, communications, transportation, and organizations would not be relevant here if they merely brought people into contact and had no political impact. The fact is, though, that these transnational phenomena are important politically. They facilitate links among people that transcend state boundaries and help establish identifications that supplement or sometimes even take the place of nationalism. Some of these connections are global; others are narrower. But they are all transnational and are creating a different political mind-set. To explore these transnational links further, we can look in more depth at the transnational women's movement and also explore transnational religion and transnational culture.

The Transnational Women's Movement

It strains the obvious to point out that women globally have been and remain second-class citizens economically, politically, and socially. Historical data is scant, but there are stark current statistics. No country has achieved socioeconomic or political gender equality. There are relative differences between countries, with the gap between men and women generally greater in less developed countries (LDCs) than in economically developed countries (EDCs). Still, the country-to-country differences are not all explained by economics. Socioeconomic gender differences are represented in the color map on page 174.

We will say much more about the status of women later, but for now consider the following barrage of facts: Women constitute 70 percent of the world's poor and two-thirds of the world's illiterates. They occupy only about 1 in 7 of the managerial

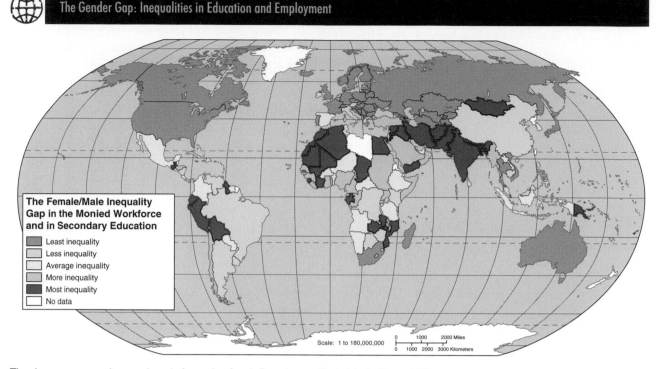

The Gender Gap: Inequalities in Education and Employment

The Female/Male Inequality Gap in the Monied Workforce and in Secondary Education

Least inequality
Less inequality
Average inequality
More inequality
Most inequality
No data

Scale: 1 to 180,000,000

The day may come when each end of a scale of male/female equality is labeled "equal." That time has not arrived yet, and this map classifies countries on a scale of relative inequality, ranging from least inequality to most inequality. All societies are held back by legally or socially restricting the educational and work opportunities of females, who make up half the population. While every country does this, the less developed countries, those that need "people power" the most, tend to be the most restrictive and to waste the talents of their women.

and administrative jobs and constitute less than 40 percent of the world's professional and technical workers. Worldwide, women are much less likely to have access to paid employment, and the average women who does have a job earns only about half of what the average man does.

Life for women is, on average, not only hard and poorly compensated; it is dangerous. "The most painful devaluation of women," the UN reports starkly, "is the physical and psychological violence that stalks them from cradle to grave" (UNDP, 1995:7). Among other signs of violence against women is the fact that about 80 percent of the world's refugees are women and their children. Statistics also show, the UNDP report (p. 44) continues, that annually "an estimated 1 million children, mostly girls in Asia, are forced into prostitution. And an estimated 100 million girls suffer genital mutilation." The national incidence of women who have been the victim of abuse by an intimate partner averages 25 percent and ranges up to 58 percent.

Such economic, social, and political abuses of women are not new. What has changed is women's ability to see their common status in global terms through transnational communication and transportation. What is also new is the focused determination of women and the males who support the cause of gender equality to work together through transnational NGOs to address these issues. As the UNDP report (p.1) points out, "Moving toward gender equality is not a technocratic goal—it is a political process."

The global women's movement is the driving force in this political process. We can examine this effort by looking first at the feminist philosophy and goals, then turning to the efforts of the women's movement.

THE TRANSNATIONAL WOMEN'S MOVEMENT: PERSPECTIVES AND GOALS

The first thing to note about the women's movement is that whether it is termed feminism or some other name, its adherents share some common views but also vary considerably in their attitudes and emphases. Indeed, even the term feminism is an issue; for a variety of reasons, some women find what they see as the feminist ideology to be fully relevant to their experiences. Others are put off by the unfortunate stereotype of feminism as necessarily radical. "I think [women do] not feel as passionately militant thirty years later," one woman comments.[13] Also, the genesis of the feminist movement is rooted mostly in the United States and other industrialized, Western countries. As such, many of its primary concerns and values (such as individualism) understandably spring from the dominant Eurowhite cultures of those countries. For example, at the meeting in 2000 of the so-called **Beijing + 5 Conference** at the UN in New York City, to review progress since the 1995 Beijing conference, one group of women from LDCs complained that the agenda was too Western dominated and did "not reflect the reality of [some LDC] women's concerns nor the very real challenges they have to meet on a daily basis in trying to work for the implementation of the Beijing recommendations."[14]

It is also the case, however, that these criticisms are rejected by some feminists. "The oft-heard argument that feminism (read the struggle for women's equality) is a struggle pursued primarily by elite women is simply another example of the traditional demeaning of women," one study argues (Fraser, 1999:854). "History is replete with examples of male leaders who are not branded with this same charge, even though much of history is about elite men."

Perspectives of the Transnational Women's Movement

It is not the place of this text to attempt to settle this dispute among women. Instead we will adopt the strategy of a feminist author and use the term feminism "in its original meaning: the theory of, and the struggle for, equality for women" (Fraser, 1999:855). From this perspective, it is possible to highlight a number of common points in feminist thought about world politics. First, those in the women's movement feel left out of the process and even the conceptualization of world politics. Feminist scholars maintain that the definition of what is relevant to the study of international relations, as presented in textbooks and most other scholarship written by men, is a product of the male point of view and ignores or underrepresents the role of women, their concerns, and their perspectives (Scott, 1996). The problem, women's equality advocates say, is that the scholarly definition of international relations has "excluded from that conception, quite comprehensively,… the [lives] of most women," who "experience societies and their interactions differently" than do men (Grant & Newland, 1991:1).

Concepts such as peace and security are prime examples of how, according to feminists, men and women perceive issues differently. One feminist scholar suggests that "from the masculine perspective, peace for the most part has meant the absence of war and the prevention of armed conflict" (Reardon 1990:137). She terms this "negative peace." By contrast, Reardon (p. 138) continues, women think more in terms of "positive peace," which includes "conditions of social justice, economic equity and ecological balance." Women, more than men, are also apt to see international security as wider than just a military concept; as also including security from sexism, poverty, domestic violence, and other factors that assail women (Razavi, 1999). Women favor this more inclusive view of security because, according to another study, "the need for human security through development is critical to

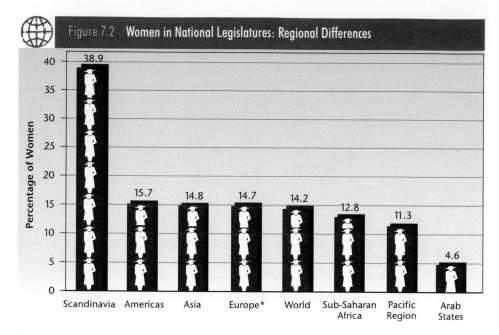

Figure 7.2 Women in National Legislatures: Regional Differences

*Excluding Scandinavia

Data source: International Parliamentary Union Web site at http://www.ipu.org/.

By one measure, women have come a long way, increasing their global share of national legislative seats from 3 percent in 1955 to 14.2 percent in 2002. But there is a long way, 35.8 percent, to go to reach 50 percent and equality. Clearly this goal is closer in some regions than in others.

women whose lives often epitomize the insecurity and disparities that plague the world order" (Bunch & Carillo, 1998:230).

Goals of the Transnational Women's Movement

A second central point about the transnational women's movement is that it is normative and includes an agenda for change. One obvious goal is to increase the participation of women in the political process and the positions they hold at all levels. In mid-2002, only 11 women were serving as the presidents or prime ministers of their countries, just 8 percent of all cabinet ministers were women, and women made up a scant 14 percent of the members of the world's national legislatures and 9 percent of the world's judiciary. Moreover, these overall figures do not reveal that women have an even smaller political presence in some regions, as Figure 7.2 indicates.

International organizations are no less gender skewed. No woman has ever headed the UN, the International Monetary Fund (IMF), the World Trade Organization (WTO), or the World Bank, and women occupy only about 15 percent of the senior management positions in the leading IGOs. Like male political leaders, some females have been successful in office; others have not. Yet, as the longtime (1980–1996) president of Iceland, Vigdis Finnbogadottir, has remarked, the stereotype remains that "women are not competitive enough or women do not understand economics." "If you do something wrong," she warned other women at a conference, "you will be attacked with the strongest weapon—mockery."[15]

The derogatory whisper campaign that women make weak leaders has been repeatedly disproved by the records of female leaders such as Prime Minister (1966–1977, 1980–1984) Indira Gandhi of India, Prime Minister (1969–1974) Golda Meir of Israel, and Prime Minister (1979–1990) Margaret Thatcher of Great Britain, each of whom led her country to victory in war (with, respectively, Pakistan in 1971, several Arab states in 1973, and Argentina in 1982). Similarly, women who have served among the ranks of such key international relations officials as foreign minister and defense minister have also proven their mettle when necessary. Madeleine Albright, the first woman to serve as U.S. secretary of state, provides an example. She proved to be more willing to use military force than the chairman of the Joint Chiefs of Staff, Colin Powell. The general has recalled that at one point when he expressed reluctance to send U.S. troops to Bosnia, Albright asked him heatedly, "What's the point of having this superb military… if we can't use it?" General Powell recorded thinking he "would have an aneurysm."[16]

Advocates of women's political activism see their goal as more than simply a drive for power. They also see power for women as a way to change policy based on the view of at least some feminists that, overall, women have somewhat different values than men on a variety of issues. While the governance of Margaret Thatcher and other women demonstrates that women leaders can and have used military force, it is also the case, as discussed in chapter 4, that women have been generally less inclined to advocate force than men have been. There also are other differences. A recent poll found, for instance, that American women consistently place more emphasis than do men on international social and economic programs. One illustrative question asked men and women to prioritize whether countries should get U.S. foreign aid based on whether the recipient was important to U.S. security, was important as a U.S. trading partner, or was poor.[17] The rankings (and percentages) were:

Men	Women
1. Security (37%)	1. Poverty (35%)
2. Trade (34%)	2. Security (34%)
3. Poverty (25%)	3. Trade (26%)

The transnational women's movement additionally addresses the normative issue of how to improve the lot of women—and everyone else—in the international system. As such, the concern extends beyond sexism's deleterious effect on women to include the impact of discrimination on the entire society. Feminists point out correctly that keeping women illiterate retards the entire economic and social development of a society. It is not a coincidence, for example, that the percentage of women in the paid workforce is lowest in those countries where the gap between male and female literacy is the highest. Educating these illiterate women would increase the number of ways that they could contribute to their countries' economic and social growth. Beyond this, there is a correlation between the educational level of women and their percentage of the wage-earning workforce, on the one hand, and restrained population growth, on the other. In other words, one good path to population control is creating a society of fully educated men and women who are employed equally in wage-earning occupations.

THE TRANSNATIONAL WOMEN'S MOVEMENT: PROGRAMS AND PROGRESS

Programs to promote gender equity are making progress, but they also have a long way to go. As the concluding report of the Beijing + 5 Conference put it, "Even though significant positive developments [during the last five years] can be identified, barriers remain, and there is still the need to further implement the goals and commitments made in Beijing."[18] While reviewing the progress and the distance yet to go, it is important to remember that just 30 years or so ago, gender equality was not even a prominent political issue in the various countries, much less on the world stage. Inasmuch as chapter 17 of this book will spend considerable time discussing the progress of women in the area of human rights, we will focus in this section on political advances that women are making.

Programs of Transnational Women's Organizations

Women have been and are politically active in a large number of national and transnational organizations that focus all or in part on women's issues. These organizations and their members have interacted transnationally at many levels ranging from the Internet through global conferences. Individually, women with Internet access can now, for instance, find out more about their common concerns through such sites as the home page of WomenWatch: The UN Internet Gateway on the Advancement and Empowerment of Women at http://www.un.org/womenwatch/. Collectively, women are now frequently gathering in such global forums as the UN Conference on Population and Development (UNCPD), held in Cairo in 1994, the fourth WCW, and the Beijing + 5 Conference. Beyond the substantive proceedings of such conferences, they facilitate transnational contacts among women. Parma Khastgir, a Supreme Court justice in India and a delegate to the 1995 WCW, stressed this contribution in her observation that "what appealed to me most [about the WCW] was that people overcame their ethnic barriers and were able to discuss universal problems. They showed solidarity."[19]

It is difficult to measure the precise impact that transnational communications are having through individual interactions, world and regional conferences, and the mass media (Shaheed, 1999). There is evidence, however, that cultural differences among women relating to their roles are narrowing. Figure 7.3 shows, for example, that the views of Japanese women, who have been very traditional, are beginning to parallel the attitudes of American women.

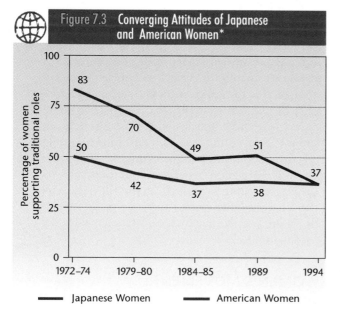

Figure 7.3 **Converging Attitudes of Japanese and American Women***

Japanese Women ———
American Women ———

*This figure incorporates data from surveys that asked similar, but not always the same, questions about accepting or rejecting traditional roles for women and men. Questions were not always asked in the same year in both countries.

Data source: Ladd and Bowman (1996).

Transnational communications help create similar values across national boundaries. Changes in attitudes about the roles played by women began earlier in the United States, Canada, and Europe than elsewhere. Feminist attitudes have, however, spread globally to even very traditional societies, such as Japan's, as this figure shows.

Advances of Women in Politics

Another standard by which to judge the impact of the transnational feminist movement is the advancement of women in politics. "Never before have so many women held so much power," writes one scholar. "The growing participation and representation of women in politics is one of the most remarkable developments of the late twentieth century" (Jaquette, 1997:23). Both these statements are certainly factual, but it is also the case that progress is slow and that women are a distinct political minority. As former Norwegian prime minister Gro Harlem Brundtland commented dryly, "I was the first woman in 1,000 years [to head Norway's government]. Things are evolving gradually."[20]

To add a bit of historical perspective: women only began to be able to vote in national elections a little more than a century ago. In 1893 New Zealand was the first country to recognize the right of women to vote. Other countries followed suit slowly. Switzerland in 1971 was the last EDC to allow female suffrage. Now, almost all countries do, although there are still some exceptions, such as Bahrain, Kuwait, Saudi Arabia, and the United Arab Emirates.

Voting was a significant political step for women, but access to political office has come more slowly. Australia in 1902 became the first country to constitutionally assure

This is a rare photograph indeed. Normally, pictures of world leaders are made up entirely, or nearly so, of men. This photograph of world leaders gathered at Harvard University is composed exclusively of women, all but two of whom have been prime ministers of their countries. From left to right, those standing (and their country) are: Tansu Ciller (Turkey), Hanna Suchocka (Poland), Kazimiera Prunskiene (Lithuania), Benazir Bhutto (Pakistan), Mary Eugenia Charles (Dominica), and Kim Campbell (Canada); seated are Violetta de Chamorro (Nicaragua), Vigdis Finnbogadottir (president, Iceland), and Laura Liswood (executive director, Council of Women World Leaders). That there are enough women leaders to form a council represents change and progress.

women the right to stand for election, and the world's first elected female national legislators took their seats in Finland's parliament in 1907. The first woman other than a monarch to become a head of state was President of the Presidium Yanjamaa Nemendeyen Sbaataryn of Mongolia in 1953, and the first woman prime minister, Sirimavo Ratwatte Dias Bandaranaike of Ceylon (now Sri Lanka), did not take office until 1960. From these beginnings, the ranks of female political leaders have grown, as the map on page 120 in chapter 5 demonstrates. Still, their limited numbers reflect the continuing formidable barriers to leadership and full political participation by women (Reynolds, 1999).

The path to political power in international organizations has also been an uphill climb (Meyer & Prügel, 1999). The UN Charter pledges equal opportunity for men and women. The reality a half century after the Charter was adopted is that women hold only 36 percent of the professional staff positions and only 15 percent of all top UN administrative posts. Just 6 percent of the ambassadors to the UN are women. "We are a collection of all the world's chauvinisms," one UN staff member has commented bluntly.[21] Still, progress is being made. The secretary general has appointed a number of women to high UN posts. Most notably, Kofi Annan in 1998 named Canadian diplomat Louise Fréchette as deputy secretary-general, the UN's second highest post. Other recent additions to the ranks of women in top UN posts include American Carol Bellamy (director of the UN Children's Fund, or UNICEF); Norwegian Gro Harlem Brundtland (director general of the World Health Organization); Irish Mary B. Robinson (UN High Commissioner for Human Rights), and Saudi Thoraya Ahmed Obaid (executive director of the UN Population Fund (UNFPA). Thus, things are changing. Former UN executive Nafis Sadik has recalled that in the 1970s, when she first came to work at the UN, "Western men saw me as an Asian woman; very decorative, but I couldn't possibly have any ideas."[22] When she retired in 2000 after 13 years as head of UNFPA, no one saw Executive Director Sadik any longer as an adornment.

The accomplishments of these women have been, of course, personal. Many of the other advances of women have been made through national efforts. It is also the case, however, that the progress of women almost everywhere has been facilitated by and, in turn, has contributed to the transnational feminist movement. Women have begun to think of themselves politically not as only American, or Canadian, or Zimbabwean women, but as women with a transnational identity and ties. This is both transforming national politics and weakening the hold of nationalism.

Transnational Religion

Most of the world's great religions have a strong transnational element. Religions are not political ideologies in the strictest sense. Nevertheless, many religions have all the characteristics of an ideology and have an impact on the secular world as well as on spiritual life. This is particularly true when the adherents of a spiritual concept actively apply their beliefs to secular political goals.

This occurs when a religion, which is a basis of spiritual identity, becomes a source of political identity among its members. When religion and political identity become intertwined, the members of a religion may take a number of political actions. One is to try to transform their religious values and laws into the laws of their country. Individuals who identify politically with their religion may also be moved to politically support the causes of people of the same religion in other countries or even regions of the world. This sense of support is why, for example, Jews from around the world are likely to support Israel and Muslims from around the world are apt to support the Palestinians. A sense of religious unity also helps explain why Osama bin Laden, a Saudi, was able to recruit Egyptians, Pakistanis, Chechens, and Muslims from many other countries to the ranks of al-Qaeda and to find a base for the organization in Afghanistan.

RELIGION AND WORLD POLITICS

"You're constantly blindsided if you consider religion neutral or outside world politics," cautions international relations scholar the Reverend J. Bryan Hehir of Harvard. It is "better to understand the place that religion holds in the wider international framework," the Roman Catholic theologian observes wisely.[23]

Religion has played many roles in world politics. Certainly, it has often been and continues to be the source of peace, humanitarian concern, and pacifism. It is also true, though, that religion has been at the center of many bloody wars. The establishment and expansion of Islam beginning late in the sixth century and the reaction of Christian Europe set off a series of clashes, including the eight Crusades (1095–1291), between the equally combative Islamic and Christian worlds. The Protestant Reformation (1517) divided Christianity, and the resulting rivalry between Protestants and Catholics was one cause of the Thirty Years' War (1618–1648) and other conflicts. Religion also played a role in the imperial era. Catholic and Protestant missionaries were early European explorers and colonizers. Whatever the missionary movement's good intent and works were, it also often promoted and legitimized the political, economic, and cultural subjugation of local people by outsiders.

Religion-based political conflict continues. It is an element of the conflict between Israelis, who are mostly Jewish, and Arabs, who are mostly Muslim. When Great Britain gave up its colonial control of the Indian subcontinent in 1947, that area was divided between the Hindus and the Muslims. Countless members of each faith were killed in the ensuing conflict and in the subsequent wars between India and the newly created state of Pakistan. That tension continues, with a particular focus on India's predominantly Muslim border territory of Kashmir.

Religion also causes or exacerbates conflict within countries. What was Yugoslavia disintegrated in part along religious lines. The people living in Bosnia-Herzegovina were of the same Slavic stock and spoke the same Serbo-Croatian language, but being Catholic Croats, Muslim Bosnians, and Eastern Orthodox Serbs divided them into fratricidal factions. More recently, religion plays a role in the cultural divide between Serbs and Muslim Albanians in Yugoslavia's Kosovo Province and between Macedonians and Muslim Albanians in Macedonia. Yet another example is the long struggle between the Roman Catholics and Protestants of Northern Ireland that killed over 3,000 people between 1969 and the establishment in 1998 of a still tenuous peace.

Organized religion also plays a range of intermediate roles as a transnational actor, projecting its values through a range of intergovernmental organizations (IGOs). Among Christians, the World Evangelical Alliance, founded in 1846, is an early example of a Protestant NGO.

The Roman Catholic Church is by far the largest and most influential of current religion-based NGOs. The Vatican itself is a state, and the pope is a secular as well as a spiritual leader. The political influence of Roman Catholicism, however, extends far beyond the Vatican. Under John Paul II, the Church has been active on a variety of fronts. Early in the pope's reign, this included attempts to weaken communist governments in Poland and other countries in Eastern Europe with a Roman Catholic heritage. More recently, the Church has played a role in preventing the inclusion of language that specifically advocates abortions, homosexual unions, or other practices in the programs supported by UN conferences on women held in Egypt in 1994, in China in 1995, and in New York City in 2000. Additionally, John Paul II has made over 100 apostolic visits to countries outside the Vatican, and he has been active on such issues as seeking an end to economic sanctions against Iraq and Cuba as injurious to civilians, pressing for nuclear arms restraint, and calling on the world's wealthy countries to do more to aid the developing countries.

THE STRENGTH OF RELIGIOUS FUNDAMENTALISM

One aspect of religion that appears to have gained strength in many areas of the world is **fundamentalism**. This phenomenon is also called religious traditionalism and religious nationalism. At least in the way that it is used here, a religious fundamentalist is someone who holds conservative religious values and wishes to incorporate those values into otherwise secular political activities, such as making laws that would apply not only to the faithful who agree with them, but to everyone. There is also a transnational element to some fundamentalists, who believe that loyalty to the religion should supersede patriotism and that all adherents of their religion should be united politically. That may mean bringing people together across borders; it may also mean driving out people of another or no faith or suppressing their freedoms within borders.

There is considerable debate over whether the rise of fundamentalism is a series of isolated events or related to a larger global trend. Taking the latter view are scholars who believe that at least part of the increase in the political stridency of religion is based on two factors: first, the mounting failure of states to meet the interests of their people, and, second, a resistance to the cultural blending that has come with modern trade, communications, and transportation. This leads people to

(Continued on page 182)

INDIA, PAKISTAN, RELIGION, AND THE BOMB

Relations between India and Pakistan have been a volatile mix of religion and nationalism that has led to three wars and numerous smaller armed skirmishes for more than a half century. The area that now comprises the two countries plus Bangladesh was part of the British Empire until 1947. As the British withdrew, amid horrific religious riots and killing that left hundreds of thousands of people dead, many Muslims living in Hindu areas fled to the two halves of Pakistan: West Pakistan (current Pakistan) and East Pakistan (now Bangladesh), while Hindus in Muslim areas sought safety in India.

War immediately broke out between the two new countries over Kashmir, a large area along the northern part of the two countries' 1,800-mile border. The traditional ruler of the region was Hindu and opted to join India; most of the residents were Muslim and wished to become part of Pakistan. The war continued for two years, with India retaining most of the territory.

A second Indo-Pakistani war erupted along the northern frontier in 1965, with each country escalating the border fighting by launching air strikes against the other's cities in the region. China threatened to join the fighting on Pakistan's side and was only deterred by U.S. and British opposition. Once again, as it had in 1949, the United Nations–sponsored cease-fire restored an uneasy peace.

The third war between India and Pakistan broke out in 1971 when the Muslim Bengalis living in East Pakistan (and otherwise much akin to Hindu Bengalis in India) demanded greater autonomy from the central government in Karachi located in West Pakistan. West Pakistani troops moved with exceptional brutality to oppress the movement, the Bengalis in East Pakistan declared themselves an independent Bangladesh, India intervened on the side of Bangladesh, and fighting raged in that area and spread to Kashmir. In the end, Pakistan was soundly defeated, and Bangladesh gained independence.

Since then there have been periodic clashes and continual tension, especially over Kashmir. Occasionally, there have been scares of full-scale war as occurred in May 2002 when both countries mobilized along the border. What has made prospects in the region even worse is a combination of two related factors—nuclear weapons and religion. They have changed what has long been a perilous situation into what is arguably the world's most dangerous flash point between two countries.

Nuclear war became a horrendous possible consequence of a fourth war on May 11, 1998, when India had exploded its first nuclear weapon in a test series. Seventeen days later, Pakistan answered with its own tests. "I cannot believe that we are about to start the twenty-first century by having the Indian subcontinent repeat the worst mistakes of the twentieth century," a distressed President Clinton said.[1]

Religion has also increased as a source of tension with religious fundamentalism on the rise in both Pakistan and India. The change in Pakistan has been part of the general increase in religious traditionalism throughout the Muslim world as discussed in other parts of this chapter. The government of Pakistan has remained relatively secular, but large parts of the Pakistani population have become more fundamentalist. For this reason as well as strategic reasons, Pakistan was a primary supporter of the Taliban regime of Afghanistan, and was the world's only country to maintain diplomatic relations with Kabul even after the terror attacks on the United States in September 2001.

There has been a parallel rise of nationalist religious traditionalism in India, politically represented by the Bharatiya Janata Party (BJP), which came to power in 1998 amid frustration over general government ineffectiveness and continued nationalist sentiment. Statistically, the BJP won only 26 percent of the popular vote and one-third of the seats in the Lok Sabha, the dominant chamber in India's parliament. That was enough, however, to establish a coalition government and install its leader, Atal Behari Vajpayee, as prime minister.

Muslims and many Hindus fear that a government controlled by the BJP might try to suppress religious and cultural diversity in India. Vajpayee has regularly tried to dispel such concerns, and BJP policy has been restrained by the fact that it heads an unstable coalition government. Still, many Hindu nationalists are virulently strident and wish to create *Hindutva*, a theocratic Hindu India, or even *Akband Bharat* (Old India), a mythical concept of a unified Indian subcontinent

seek a new source of primary political identification. Frequently, that is with their religion and with their coreligionists across national borders.

As part of this process, political conservatism, religious fundamentalism, and avid nationalism often become intertwined. For example, Israel's politics are strongly influenced by the role of orthodox Jewish groups. With respect to international

The rise of militant Hindu nationalism in India and the clashes between Hindus and Muslims within India are worrisome. A recent round of bloody fighting began in February 2002. Muslim train passengers claimed that they were being beset by Hindu thugs on board. When the train arrived at a station in a Muslim area, the Hindus on the train were trapped on board. It was set ablaze and 58 people burned to death in the fire that this grisly picture shows. This led to Hindu retaliation against Muslims elsewhere in a round of killing during which more than 500 people, mostly Muslims, died.

(Bangladesh, Bhutan, India, Nepal, and Pakistan) under Hindu Indian leadership (Bouton, 1998). According to one nationalist leader, "Muslims are converted Hindus, but they have forgotten their Hinduness. So we will awake them to their Hinduness."[2] Prime Minister Vajpayee is a moderate by BJP standards, but even he has warned that "appeasement" of Muslims and other minorities in India would "injure the Hindu psyche."[3] Also, there are unsettling instances of the government promoting religious bias. The education minister, for example, recently rejected history texts with a secular image of India and mandated the use of texts that present Indian history from a Hindu perspective.

Recent events have once again underlined the danger that the mix of religion and politics has created on the Indian subcontinent. Sectarian violence broke out in February 2002 within India between Hindus and the country's sizable (14 percent) Muslim minority over the plan of Hindu fundamentalists to build a temple on the site of a Muslim mosque that had earlier been destroyed by Hindu extremists. Hundreds of people, mostly Muslims, were killed in the fighting. Muslims burned several railway cars full of Hindus, incinerating those inside; Hindus roamed the streets killing Muslims. "There is a fire inside us. Our blood is boiling. There is a volcano of anger," one marauder raged.[5] Whether the rioters were Muslim or Hindu is irrelevant; both sides felt the same.

Confrontation also turned to violence once again, with India and Pakistan teetering on the edge of war after Pakistani Muslim extremists attacked India's parliament building on December 13, 2001, setting off a gun battle that resulted in the death of nine Indian security officers and a civilian and all five terrorists. This was followed by clashes in Kashmir that brought the two nuclear powers close to all-out war. Fortunately, a strong diplomatic push by the United States, China, Russia, and other countries persuaded both sides to exercise restraint, and the crises ended by mid-2002. Nothing was settled, though, and it may only be a matter of time before the world once again watches anxiously as the mix of India, Pakistan, religion, and the bomb edges the region toward a potential catastrophe.

affairs, the religious right in Israel tends to favor a hard-line stance with the Palestinians, no compromise on the status of Jerusalem, and the continuation of Jewish settlements in Gaza and the West Bank. Indeed, this political faction claims that the West Bank and the Golan Heights are part of the ancient land given in perpetuity to the Jewish nation by God. Among other things, the conservative parties pushed legislation through the Knesset that requires a national referendum to approve the return of any portion of the Golan Heights to Syria. Whether the policy ramifications are domestic or international, "The issue," according to a Hebrew University scholar, "is whether Israel will shape a way of life according to Western, democratic concepts, or one infected by Middle Eastern fundamentalism and theocratic impulse." Others dismiss such concerns. "We're not going to make a second Iran in the Middle East," a rabbi who also heads a religion-oriented political party assures listeners.[24] Ordinarily, like people who are fervent in all religions, those on the right wing of Jewish politics are peaceful. But again, like among zealots of every conviction, there are violent elements and individuals. For example, Prime Minister Yitzhak Rabin, who took a very moderate approach to the Palestinians, was assassinated in 1995 by a fanatical Israeli, who denounced his victim for "setting up a Palestinian state [in the West Bank] with an army of terrorists... [that Israelis soon] will have to fight."[25]

India has also seen the rise of religious traditionalism. This has led to the rise of a Hindu nationalist party to power in India. Unlike some of the religions being discussed here, the vast majority of Hindus live in one country, India. Indeed, tiny Nepal is the only other country with a Hindu majority. As such, the Hindu traditionalism of the Bharatiya Janata Party (BJP) has a strong nationalist content. The tensions, regular border clashes, and several instances of all-out war between largely Muslim Pakistan and Hindu-dominated India have a number of sobering ramifications, which are discussed in the box, India, Pakistan, Religion, and the Bomb.

While a number of the world's major religions illustrate the intersection of religion and global politics, more can be gained from a closer examination of one religion. To that end, we can turn our attention to Islam because of its growing sociopolitical impact and because its history and tenets are too often unknown or misrepresented in the Western world.

ISLAM AND THE WORLD

Islam is a monotheistic religion founded by Muhammad (ca. 570–632). The word *Islam* means "submission" to God (Allah), and *Muslim* means "one who submits." Muslims believe that Muhammad was a prophet who received Allah's teachings in a vision. These divine instructions constitute the Koran (or Qur'an), meaning "recitation."

It is the political application of Islam by Muslims that interests us here (Esposito, 1997). A traditional Islamic concept is the *ummah*, which encapsulates the idea that Muslims are or should be a united spiritual, cultural, and political community. Muhammad was the first leader of the ummah. Muslims distinguish between Muslim-held lands, which they call *dar al-Islam* (the domain of Islam), and non-Muslim lands, which are termed *dar al-harb* (the domain of unbelief). One of the tenets of Islam is the jihad, "struggle" in the name of Allah. Those who struggle to defend or promote Islam are sometimes called *mujahedin*. It is important to stress that jihad does not necessarily mean either expansionist or armed struggle. It can also mean peacefully spreading Islam or defending the faith (Johnson, 1997). This reality has too often been lost in false stereotypes of Islam, a problem that became even more prevalent in the aftermath of the terror attacks on the United States in September 2001. Not atypically, for instance, television evangelist Pat Robertson told his audience that the Koran instructs Muslims "if you see an infidel, you are to kill him," and that Islam "is not a peaceful religion that wants to coexist. [Muslims] want to... control, dominate and then, if need be, destroy."[26] Apart from displaying ignorance, it was a surprising view from someone whose own religion, Christianity,

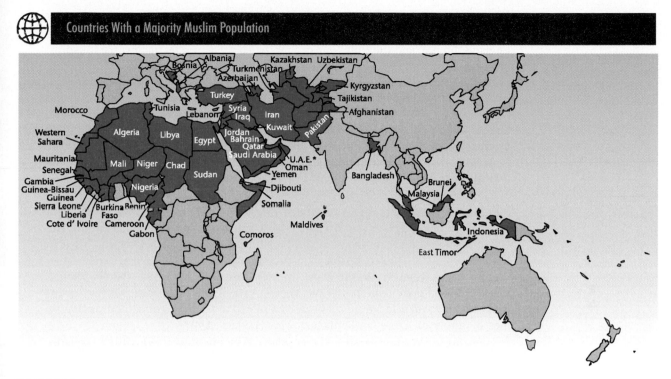

Countries With a Majority Muslim Population

*United Arab Emirates

This map of the countries in which Muslims constitute a majority of the population illustrates that Islam is not confined to the Arab states in the Middle East. In fact, most Muslims are not Arabs. The largest predominantly Muslim state is Indonesia, where 87 percent of the country's 228 million people are Muslims. The people of Pakistan and Iran, the second and third most populous predominantly Muslim countries, are also not Arabs.

has at one time or another been distorted by fanatics committing almost every imaginable atrocity, including burning people at stakes.

The political ramifications of Islam are important because there are over 1 billion Muslims spread widely over the world, as demonstrated by the above map of countries in which Muslims are more than half of the population. They are a majority among the Arabs of the Middle East and also in non-Arab countries like Algeria, Bangladesh, Iran, Pakistan, Sudan, Turkey, several of the former Soviet republics (FSRs: Azerbaijan, Kazakhstan, Kyrgyzstan, Tajikistan, Turkmenistan, and Uzbekistan), and Indonesia (whose 228 million people make it the most populous Muslim country). There are other countries, such as Nigeria, Tanzania, and the Philippines, in which Muslims constitute an important political force. Indeed, only about one of every four Muslims is an Arab. To explore political Islam, we can examine five factors: the political heritage of Muslims, Islam and nationalism, Islam and the non-Islamic world, Islamic sectarianism, and Islamic traditionalism and secularism.

The Political Heritage of Muslims

The attitudes of Muslims toward the non-Muslim world are shaped by three historical elements (Lewis, 1996). A *triumphant past* is the first element. During Islam's early period, Muslim zeal sparked rapid religious and political expansion by peaceful conversion and violent conquest. This drive was led at first by Arabs, then by Ottoman Turks and other Muslim dynasties. At their farthest, the boundaries of Muslim domination encompassed the Middle East, North Africa, southwestern Asia to the Ganges River, Spain, and central Europe to just south of Vienna.

Conflict with Christian powers, especially those of Europe, is a second element of Muslim political heritage. At the urging of Catholic popes, the Christian kings of England, France, and the Holy Roman Empire led the Crusades against the Muslims. Muslims also clashed for hundreds of years with Christianity's Orthodox emperors of Byzantium and later with the Orthodox czars of Russia. Later still, most Muslim lands fell under the colonial rule of Christian European powers. Even today, in the view of many Muslims, Christian powers still dominate the world and beset them. Many Muslims are dismayed, for example, by the fact that all of the UN Security Council's permanent members except China are countries with a Christian heritage. Moreover, two council members, Great Britain and France, are the same countries that led the Crusades and later colonized a good portion of the Muslim world.

The domination of Muslims by others is the third key historical element of Muslims' political heritage. After about the year 1500, Muslim secular strength declined slowly over the centuries. A variety of European powers had by the late 1800s come to dominate many of the Muslim areas from Mauritania in Africa to Indonesia in Asia. The last vestige of Muslim power was eclipsed when the Ottoman Empire was defeated in World War I. In the aftermath, the British and the French became the colonial overlords of the Middle East. As a result, most Muslim countries, whatever their location, share an experience of recent colonial domination by mostly European, Christian-heritage powers (Lustick, 1997).

During the last half century, direct political domination ended with the collapse of colonialism. New countries came into being; others moved from autonomy to full independence. As with most new countries, the Muslim states fiercely guard their sovereignty. Most Muslims also chafe under the foreign control that has frequently persisted through economic dominance and other neocolonialist practices exercised by the Western powers. In recent years, this indirect domination has been eased by the growth of oil power, and there has been a concurrent growth of Islamic fundamentalism, pride, and militancy that has interacted with and supplemented the nationalism of Islamic countries.

Islam and Nationalism

There are elements of the reawakening of Muslim assertiveness that support the unification in the ummah. After centuries of outside political, economic, and cultural domination, the people in the region that stretches from Morocco to Afghanistan have begun to reclaim their heritage in what might be called a "Muslim pride" movement.

The resurgence of Islam also includes international support for the strengthening of Muslims. Islamic solidarity efforts have ranged from coordination in protecting Islamic holy places, through support of the Palestine Liberation Organization, to support of Pakistan's possession of nuclear weapons. Among Arab Muslims, the common tie of Islam has helped promote Pan-Arab sentiment. This Pan-Arab feeling has led to the establishment of some regional cooperation (the Arab League, for example) and even attempts to merge countries.

Despite all of these elements of Pan-Muslim and Pan-Arab sentiment, it is unlikely that Muslims will reestablish the ummah in the foreseeable future. Ethnonationalism is one factor that will prevent this. Many Muslim countries have sharp differences and vie with one another for regional influence (Tibi, 1997; Lefebvre, 1996). Some Muslims, notably the Kurds who live in Turkey, Iraq, Iran, and elsewhere, want to form their own countries. Further solidifying nationalism, there are major ethnic differences within Islam. Culturally, Indonesians are no more like Syrians than are Canadians.

Indeed, Indonesians are ethnically not even like one another, and their political views are more strongly tied to ethnicity and other factors than to religion.

According to a study of Indonesia's 1999 elections, there was a "lack of strongly positive relationship between religion, especially Muslim variants, and partisan choice." By contrast, the identification of voters as Javanese, Sudanese, Batak, Balinese, Malay, or one of the other linguistically and culturally distinct groups in Indonesia "played a larger independent role" in the elections than expected (Liddle & Mujani, 2000:37, 25).

Islam and the Non-Islamic World

The political history of Muslims influences their current attitudes toward *dar al-harb*, the domain of unbelief, in several ways. One is the frequent evidence of anti-Western feeling. In the eyes of many Muslims, the United States is the most recent dominant Euro-Christian power. Americans have therefore inherited Muslim resentment based on what one Arab leader describes as "Western behavior over centuries that has been unfair to Muslims."[27] Muslims also see the struggle with Israel and what they perceive as U.S. bias toward Israel as part of a long, ongoing history of attempted Western domination of their region. "There is a deep feeling that when it comes to the Arabs, it's always very harsh treatment, and when it comes to the Israelis, it's easy," notes an Egyptian analyst.[28]

The degree to which these feelings are held widely among Muslims was confirmed by a poll of nine Muslim countries conducted during January 2002. Of the Muslims surveyed, 53 percent had an unfavorable opinion of the United States; only 22 percent expressed a positive opinion. Just 12 percent of Muslims thought the West respects Islamic values. As for the question of Israel and the Palestinians, as few as 1 percent of Muslims in some countries (Kuwait and Morocco) and at most 12 percent of Muslims in any country (Indonesia) felt that the United States was dealing fairly with the Palestinians.[29] The same sense of alienation from the West also influenced Muslim attitudes toward the U.S.-led attack on Afghanistan in 2001

It is a vast error to imagine that most Muslims are radical militants. Like people everywhere, the overwhelming number of Muslims wish simply to live in peace, a sentiment expressed in this photograph of a "Solidarity Day" rally, September, Sept. 27, 2001, in Peshawar, Pakistan. The Muslims at this gathering felt that Islam had been blamed unjustly for the terrorist attacks on the United States and that individuals, not religions or cultures, were the culprits.

and 2002. Opinion polls in Muslim countries found strong condemnation of the terror attacks on the World Trade Center and Pentagon, but the surveys also showed that 67 percent of those Muslims surveyed considered the U.S. campaign in Afghanistan to be unjustified. A mere 9 percent thought it was justified, with the balance unsure.[30]

Before leaving this topic of perceptions, it is worth noting that Americans held a negative mirror image of Muslims. Only 24 percent of the Americans polled in early 2002 held a favorable opinion of Muslim countries, while 41 percent expressed an unfavorable view. The poll also confirmed that most Americans have little respect for Muslim culture, with about two-thirds of Americans saying Muslim countries would be better off if they adopted U.S. and Western values.[31]

Islamic Sectarianism

Religion is not always a source of Islamic unity. Instead, religious conflict has been sparked by sectarian splits. The most important of these separates the majority Sunnis and the minority Shiites (Francke & Fuller, 2000). The issues between the two sects involve doctrinal matters beyond our scope of inquiry here. What is important here is that the sometimes quiescent Sunni-Shiite rivalry was reignited in 1979 when the Ayatollah Ruhollah Khomeini led fundamentalist Shiites to power in Iran. One of Khomeini's proclaimed goals was to reestablish Islamic unity under Shiite leadership by displacing Sunni control of Saudi Arabia (which controls Mecca, the holiest of Muslim places) and other countries. The most serious clash was Iran's war with Iraq (1980–1988). There were territorial and other nationalistic causes behind the war, but Khomeini's determination to overthrow Iraq's Sunni-dominated regime was also a cause of the war and of the millions of casualties that occurred.

The death of Khomeini in 1989 eased, but did not end, Sunni-Shiite strife. Among other places, Muslim sectarianism has spelled continuing tragedy for Afghanistan. Various rebel factions fought together in a 14-year effort to evict the Soviet invaders and to oust Afghanistan's communist government. Then, with victory in 1992, rebel unity dissolved, and the various factions have continued to fight a civil war that has taken countless lives and utterly destroyed the country's cities and infrastructure. Ethnic divisions were one source of the trouble, but these intermingle with and are supplemented by the contest for power between Sunni and Shiite factions. The Sunni Taliban government of Afghanistan has also had numerous border clashes with Shiite Iran, and the Iranians supplied arms and other support to anti-Taliban forces, especially the Shiite Hazara ethnonational group. There have also been persistent reports since the fall of the Taliban that Iran is continuing to support some factions within Afghanistan, especially the forces of Ismail Khan, the warlord who controls the heavily Shiite area around Herat (the city in Afghanistan closest to Iran). These Shiites and other ethnonational groups of Afghanistan are discussed in the box, Afghanistan: Fact or Fiction, in chapter 6.

Islamic Traditionalism and Secularism

A second point of division within Islam separates Muslim traditionalists and secularists. Traditionalist (fundamentalist) Muslims want to preserve or, in some cases, resurrect many of the cultural traditions, such as banning alcohol and having women cover their faces in public, which have been weakened under the influence of Western culture. Fundamentalists also want to establish legal systems based on the *shari'ah* (the law of the Koran) rather than on Western legal precepts. The traditionalists also look forward to the reestablishment of the ummah. "The notion that a majority should rule and the notion of the political party are all Western notions," explains one ranking Muslim theologian. What "Islam calls for," he continues, is "obedience to the ruler, the unification of the nation and advice by religious scholars."[32]

Secularists, by comparison, believe that within Islam there can be many Muslim states and that religious and secular law should be kept separate. A top Arab jurist argues, for example, that "politicized Islamic groups proclaim Islam to be a nation when in fact Islam is a religion."[33] Whatever may be theologically correct, the fact is that traditionalist Muslim movements during the 1990s gained strength in Algeria, Iran, Turkey, and several other Muslim countries.

Does any or all of this mean that there is a "green peril," a term that relates to the traditional association of the color green with Muslims? Not necessarily. Just as it would be wrong to ignore the role of religion in politics, it would be misleading to make dire predictions (Faksh, 1997). One limit is that there is an ebb and flow of the strength of traditionalism and secularism. Moreover, as one study argues, "Democracy itself and Islam are not mutually exclusive," although there are often cultural differences about how democracy is understood and implemented (Midlarsky, 1999:504). For example, the balance has begun to shift away from traditionalism in Iran, which for more than 20 years was dominated by conservative Shiite clerics. The parliamentary elections in Iran in 2000 resulted in serious losses for religious conservatives and gains for the more secular opposition. The moderates both gained control of the parliament and also captured the presidency when the moderate Mohammad Khatami won 70 percent of the votes cast, trouncing his conservative opponent.

Another reason to be wary about alarmist views of religious traditionalism is that mixing any religion, including Islam, with politics is not inherently explosive. Religion most often promotes peace. Certainly, as with any movement, there are extremists who have lost their sense of proportion. But there are also many devoutly religious people who think and act with moderation. It should also be remembered that, where it exists, fanaticism is often a by-product of deprivation, frustration, and other ills. To a substantial degree, Muslims are merely reacting against what they believe are the wrongs of the recent past and are attempting to uplift the circumstances of Muslims everywhere. Perhaps the best lesson to draw is that religion is a significant factor in international relations. Like any set of coherent ideas, religion helps define who is on which side and thus often plays a powerful role in shaping the perceptions of political leaders and the actions of the countries they command.

Transnational Culture

Having examined the transnational aspects of the specific identifications of gender and religion, we can now turn our attention to the transnationalization of culture (Iriye, 1997). It is too early to speak of a world uniculture, but we have in the last half century moved quickly and substantially in that direction. It is also the case, though, that there is substantial resistance to the movement toward what Barber (1996) termed McWorld.

Discussions of the evolution of an amalgamated global culture inevitably include a great deal about McDonald's, basketball, rock music, e-mail, and other such aspects of pop culture as well as commentary about more overtly political transnational phenomena such as the global reach of CNN. It would be an error to suppose that such a discussion of the impact of burgers and the Chicago Bulls on global culture is an attempt to trivialize the subject. Instead, there is a long line of political theory that argues that the world will come together through myriad microinteractions rather than through such macroforces of political integration as the United Nations. This school of thought believes that political communities are built by social communities and that those social communities come together through a process of interaction, familiarization, and amalgamation of diverse existing communities. Scholars who examine this bottom-up process look for evidence in such factors as the flow of communications and commerce between countries and the spread across borders of styles of dress, similarities in what people eat, and what people do for recreation.

THE SPREAD OF COMMON CULTURE

There is significant evidence of cultural amalgamation in the world. The leaders of China once wore "Mao suits"; now they wear Western-style business suits. When dressing informally, people in Shanghai, Lagos, and Mexico City are more apt to wear jeans, T-shirts, and sneakers than their country's traditional dress. A young person in Kyoto is more likely to be listening to Incubus than to traditional Japanese music. Big Macs, "fries," and milk shakes are consumed around the world.

Before looking further at the evidence, one caution is in order. You will see that a great deal of what is becoming world culture is Western, especially American, in its origins. That does not imply that Western culture is superior; its impact is a function of the economic and political strength of Western Europe and the United States. Nor does the preponderance of Western culture in the integration process mean that the flow is one way. The West is being influenced by material things and philosophical values from other parts of the world. The United States, for example, is influenced by many "imports," ranging from pasta, through increasingly popular soccer, to Zen Buddhist meditation.

Language One of the most important aspects of converging culture is English, which is becoming the common language of business, diplomacy, communications, and even culture. President Jiang Zemin of China and many other national leaders can converse in English. Indeed, a number of them, including Jacques Chirac of France, learned or improved their English while enrolled at U.S. universities. UN secretary-general Kofi Annan received his B.A. and M.S. degrees from U.S. universities.[33] A bit more slowly, English is spreading among common citizens. This is evident in differences among various age groups in the percentages of people who can speak English. Among Europeans, for instance, 89 percent of all school children now have English instruction, and 67 percent of those between 15 and 24 speak at least some English compared to only 18 percent of Europeans over age 55 who can do so. Modern communications are one driving force in the spread of English. Whether you watch CNN in Cairo or Chicago, it is broadcast in English. There are certainly sites on the World Wide Web in many languages, but most of the software, the search engines, and information in the vast majority of Web sites are all in English. One estimate is that 90 percent of all Internet information and traffic is in English. As the Webmaster at one site in Russia comments, "It is far easier for a Russian… to download the works of Dostoyevsky translated in English to read than it is for him to get [it] in his own language."

Business is also a significant factor in the global growth of English. The United States is the world's largest exporter and importer of goods and services, and it is far more common for foreign businesspeople to learn the language of Americans than it is for Americans to learn Chinese, German, Japanese, and other languages. A report issued by the Japanese government declared that "achieving world-class excellence demands that all Japanese acquire a working knowledge of English."[34] There are similar demands in Europe. "English is an imperative," according to Didier Vuchot, chairman European operations for the executive recruiting firm, Korn/Ferry International.[35]

In a related way, the current ascendancy of capitalism on the world stage is bringing vastly increased numbers of foreign students to the United States to study

The global popularity of American movies is one of the many ways that the world is being homogenized culturally. This picture taken in Tokyo shows a Japanese couple passing by a movie poster announcing the July 2001 opening of the movie *Pearl Harbor*. Despite the movie's plot, it was a hit, opening in 430 theaters, grossing more than $5 million its first week in Japan, and ending the year as the country's third most popular movie, measured in earnings.

business, with students taking bachelor of business and MBA degrees constituting 21 percent of all foreign students enrolled in U.S. universities and colleges. Moreover, the fact that U.S. higher education attracts many foreign students helps spread English and the American culture. Some 515,000 foreign students are now studying in the United States, with Japan's 47,000 students being the most numerous.

Consumer products The interchange of popular consumer goods is another major factor in narrowing cultural gaps. American movies are popular throughout much of the world. Hollywood is pervasive, earning 50 percent of its revenue abroad—a 20 percent jump in twenty years. American movies dominate many foreign markets, earning 50 percent of all film revenues in Japan, 70 percent in Europe, and 83 percent in Latin America. By contrast, foreign films account for just 3 percent of the U.S. market. It is not surprising, then, that at one point in early 2002, some countries (and their most popular movies) for the week were: Brazil (*Ocean's Eleven*), Finland (*Monsters, Inc.*), Hong Kong (*Black Hawk Down*), Japan (*The Lord of the Rings*), Mexico (*Shallow Hal*), and Russia (*Vanilla Sky*). Joining the tidal wave of visual common culture, American television programming is also increasingly omnipresent. For example, only about 30 percent of all television programs in Latin America originate in that region, while 62 percent come from the United States, and 8 percent are made elsewhere.

Older American movies are available, among other places, through the more than 2,600 stores that Blockbuster Video has in 26 countries outside the United States. And if non-Americans want to look authentic at an American movie, they can get a pair of jeans distributed through Levi Strauss's 34 regional headquarters, which employ about half the company's workers and earn Levi Strauss about one-third of its annual sales. Even if the product is not Western, the style often is. Kuwaiti radio now airs a call-in show called *Love Line*. Host Talal al-Yagout tells listeners in a soothing voice that "we get to talk about love, broken hearts, getting married."[36] This is not a translation from Arabic; the host and his callers converse in English. Chinese culture has also succumbed to many things American, as related in the box, And Never the Twain Shall Meet: Until Now.

To return to and reemphasize the main point here, there is a distinct and important intermingling and amalgamation of cultures under way. For good or ill, Western, particularly American, culture is at the forefront of the beginning of a common world culture. The observation of the director-general of UNESCO, that "America's main role in the new world order is not as a military superpower, but as a multicultural superpower," is probably an overstatement, but it captures some of what is occurring (Iyer, 1996:263).

What is most important is not the specific source of common culture. Rather it is the important potential consequences of cultural amalgamation. There are, as noted, analysts who welcome it as a positive force that will bring people and, eventually, political units together. There are other people who see transnational culture as a danger to desirable diversity.

AND NEVER THE TWAIN SHALL MEET: UNTIL NOW

"Oh, East is East, and West is West, and never the twain shall meet." Perhaps these words seemed true when Rudyard Kipling penned them in *The Ballad of East and West* (1889), but they hardly apply anymore.

As in many countries, Western pop culture is making significant inroads in China. Children there successfully pester their parents into buying 180,000 Mi Loushu (Mickey Mouse) comic books each month, and the mayor of Shanghai traveled to Los Angeles to ask Disney officials to build a Disneyland in his city. Kentucky Fried Chicken is also winning many converts to its American specialty with 475 outlets in more than 121 cities. McDonald's, with 377 outlets in 67 cities, is the second largest fast-food company in China, and it and KFC dominate the market (Watson, 2000). Together they serve up, for instance, an estimated 70 percent of the french fries sold annually in China. An order of fries costs an average $1.20, equal to about a half-day's pay for the average Chinese worker. "It's a bit expensive to eat here," one diner commented about McDonald's, "but I guess for a high-fashion restaurant like this, the prices are O.K."[1] After indulging in a *jishi hanbao* (cheeseburger), hungry Chinese might go to Dairy Queen to get a *sheng dai* (sundae) for dessert. Following such a gastronomic tour de force, the calories can be worked off by dancing at Beijing's Hard Rock Cafe to rockers such as Cui Jian and his top single "Rock on the New Long March." Finally, exhausted by the night's adventures, revelers might choose to get some rest at Beijing's Hilton, Holiday Inn, Radisson, or Sheraton hotel.

While at the hotel relaxing, patrons can turn on the television and watch CNN in English or change channels to catch a National Basketball Association (NBA) game. Finding one will be easy, because state television often carries two NBA games each weeknight and more on the weekends.

American YMCA missionaries brought basketball to China in the late 1890s, soon after the game was invented in the United States, which arguably makes China the second oldest basketball-playing country. Chinese fans are intense. They shout *pee-ow liang*! (pretty) for 3-point jump shots, but their favorite is the awesome *kou qui* (slam dunk). Even though he is past his glory days with the Chicago Bulls, "The most famous American in China is Michael Jordan," contends one observer, who cites a survey that reportedly found that Jordan was more popular among Chinese than Chairman Mao Zedong.[2] It might be added that

One place that East has met West is on the basketball court. The American-originated sport is so popular in China that one recent poll found that basketball superstar Michael "Air" Jordan was more popular than Chinese political superstar Mao "Chairman" Zedong. It is likely that this stand in Beijing does a brisker business selling Air Jordan posters than Chairman Mao posters.

the basketball trade does not all flow toward China. In 2001, the first Chinese player joined the NBA when 7-feet-1-inch Wang Zhizhi donned a Dallas Mavericks jersey. He was followed by potential superstar Yao Ming, the 7-feet-5-inch center of the Shanghai Sharks, who entered the NBA's June 2002 draft.

China's enthusiasm for "roundball" had spurred the NBA to team up with sneaker producers Nike and Reebok to ride the popularity of present and past NBA stars in China. Michael "Air" Jordan and others promote the sport to sell a bonanza of merchandise to what they hope will be more than 1 billion fans. "We are really bullish—if you'll excuse the term—on basketball in China," says an NBA executive stationed in Hong Kong.[3]

THE RESISTANCE TO A COMMON CULTURE

Those who resist a common culture in the world worry about what Barber (1995) refers to as the "yawn" of cultural homogeneity—McWorld—that may accompany globalization. Consider, for example, the plight of France as it struggles to preserve its cherished and concededly glorious culture in the face of the engulfing tide of foreign culture, especially of Anglo-Saxon origin. The French worry, for instance, that the 570 McDonald's outlets in France represent what an editorial in the newspaper *Le Figaro* called gastronomic "new terrorism." "America, imperial power, doesn't just intend to stuff our heads with its diplomatic obsessions," the editorial complained, "It also means to cram our bellies in its own way."[37] This sense has led to numerous attacks in France on the McDonald's outlets. One such "culture commando" is José Bové, a French sheep farmer, who in 1999 bulldozed a McDonald's outlet in the region in the south of France famous for its sheep's milk–based Roquefort cheese. "McDonald's is one culture—in Singapore in Texas and in France—and we don't want that," Bové explained. "Each people have the right to eat what it wants."[38] Unimpressed, a French court in September 2000 sentenced Bové to six months in prison.

The French also worry that their language is under siege, and French president Chirac has condemned the rising English-language domination of the Internet and other forms of international communication as a "major risk for humanity" through "linguistic uniformity and thus cultural uniformity."[39] There are even those guardians of all that is French who view the invasion of alien words as more than a simple linguistic sacrilege. "The use of a foreign language is not innocent," France's minister of culture has warned. In reality, he has declared, it is part of the "considerable efforts" to infiltrate French culture by the "Anglo-Saxons" as one prong of attack in their "hegemonic drive."[40]

French traditionalists have fought back (Carruthers, 1998; Grantham, 1998). France has amended its constitution to declare: "The language of the republic is French."[41] The national Assembly has enacted laws requiring that English words not be used in teaching, business, or government, and to assist in modernizing French, numerous agencies work to find French substitutes. The Ministry of Finance, for example, has decreed *non* to "e-mail" and *oui* to *message electronique*. One is tempted to wish the defenders of all things French a hearty *la bonne chance avec la défense de votre langue*, good luck with the defense of your language. Still, it may be too late to stem the English tide. About one-third of all French people already speak English, and the percentage is rising.

Lest one think that such nationalistic attempts to protect cultural diversity is all a matter of silliness about invasions of Anglo-Saxon hamburgers and the like, consider the fact that delegates from 19 countries met in Ottawa, Canada, in 1998 to discuss how to distinguish culture from commerce so that countries could protect their cultures from exported American movies, CDs, and similar items. The worry that these delegates and others have, according to one scholar, is that "if national identities are indeed being eroded, what is likely to take their place is not rich cultural pluralism..., but a world market as the distributor of cultural resources" that will tend toward "a lowest-common-denominator mass culture exemplified by Disney, McDonald's, and Australian soap operas." That, he concludes, "will be bad news" (Miller, 1995:187).

Thus, fear of cultural erosion is not limited to France. It exists broadly. It was further evident in the Russian who characterized the English-dominated Internet as "the ultimate act

Did You Know That:
The basic unit of the metric system, the meter, was named and defined by the French in 1793 as one ten-millionth of the distance between the Equator and the North Pole. To increase accuracy using atomic clocks, the meter was redefined by the International Bureau of Weights and Measures in 1983 as the distance that light will travel through a vacuum in one-299,792,458th of a second. For those who are without an atomic clock, a meter is equal to 39.37 inches.

of intellectual colonialism."[42] Similar concerns about cultural amalgamation can be found in Asia. China in 2002 announced that it was requiring McDonald's to remove its trademark golden arches and billboards on the grounds that they were "visual pollution." Similarly in India, the campaign platform of the BJP attacked the inroads of foreign culture. Kentucky Fried Chicken outlets became the centerpiece of what Indian newspapers dubbed "The Chicken War" when government health inspectors shut down the KFC in New Delhi after two flies were found on the premises. Flies, of course, were not the issue. Rather it was the sense that tandoori chicken, a classic Indian dish, and the rest of Indian culture is being eaten away by fried chicken and the rest of American culture. As the BJP campaign slogan went, "Send us microchips, not potato chips."

Transnationalism Tomorrow

It is impossible to predict how far transnationalism will progress. It is not inconceivable that a century from now humans will share a common culture and perhaps even a common government. That is, however, far from certain. There are those who doubt that the trend of today toward transculturalism will continue into the future. Some analysts believe, for example, that English will cease to be the common language of the Internet as more and more non-English-speaking people gain access. "Be careful of turning astute observations about the current state of the Web into implications for the future," one observer cautions wisely.[43]

E Pluribus Unum?

Moreover, nationalism, as we saw in the last chapter, is proving to be a very resilient barrier to globalization and to such transnational movements as Islam. Whether it is based on political nationalism or on simple cultural familiarity, there is also strong resistance to cultural homogenization. However rational it might be to use the metric system, the bulk of Americans still seem to agree with the publisher of the anti-metric newsletter *Footprint*, who rejects "the folly of adopting faddish European units of measure."[44]

It is also very evident, however, that nationalism organized in the nation-state is under assault. One direction of attack is from the various jihad movements, secular and religious. Nation-states are splintering as people increasingly identify with smaller national units, ethnic groups, religions, and other demographic units. From the opposite direction, the forces of globalization press nations to assimilate with one another economically, socially, and politically. "We have to learn to push our politics in two directions at once: upward beyond the nation-state and downward below the nation-state," writes one scholar who advocates diminished nationalism. "For purposes of dealing with global issues [such as the environment], we need to inspire a large sense of global citizenship, because these are global problems with only global solutions." He adds, though, that people are seeking smaller units of political reference because they realize that "the planet is no substitute for a neighborhood," and that it is only in associations smaller than states, much less the globe, that "people can have a direct hand in exercising responsibility for their communities."[45]

Chapter Summary

1. This chapter explores the bases and evidence of transnationalism in the world. Transnationalism includes a range of loyalties, activities, and other phenomena that connect humans across nations and national boundaries.

2. Some streams of transnational thought are referred to as globalism, cosmopolitanism, or some other such encompassing word. Other transnational movements, such as religion and gender, have a more limited focus.

3. The development of transnationalism springs from two sources: human thought and global interaction.

4. The lineage of the globalist strain of transnational thought extends in Western culture back to the Stoics of ancient Greece and Rome and to Buddhism in Eastern culture. Transnationalist thought is evident today in idealism, postmodernism, and postinternationalism.

5. Many observers believe that transnationalism will lead to greater harmony in the world. There are other analysts, however, who think that we are not moving toward a common culture but, instead, toward a future in which people will identify with and politically organize themselves around one or another of several antagonistic cultures or so-called civilizations.

6. Transnational interaction is increasing, as evident in changes in economics, communications, transportation, and organizations. International economic interdependence, mass communications, the ease of travel across borders, and the growth of transnational organizations are all helping to break down national barriers.

7. An important modern trend in international relations is the growth of transnational movements and organizations that are concerned with global issues. This includes the transnational women's movement and its associated organizations.

8. Though women's attitudes and emphases may vary, the transnational women's movement shares a similar philosophy and goals. These center on the idea that women around the world should cooperate to promote gender equality and to transform the way we think about and conduct politics at every level, including the international level.

9. Feminists, both women and the men who support gender equity, are pursuing numerous projects and making progress. The fourth World Conference on Women and its follow-up Beijing + 5 Conference are just examples of activity in this area.

10. Most religions have a strong transnational element. Some religions assert universalistic claims; other religions create an urge to unite all the members of that religion across countries.

11. Religion has played many roles in world politics. The roles have been both positive and negative. The current rise in religious fundamentalism in many areas of the world is worrisome.

12. To understand the role of religion in world politics, a case study of Islam discusses the global impact of a transnational religion.

13. Transnational culture is both bringing the world together and dividing it. The movement of goods, ideas, and people across national boundaries is helping to create what is perhaps the beginning of a common global culture. Some people see this as a positive development; others oppose it.

Chapter 8

National States: The Traditional Structure

For the whole state, I would put mine armour on,
Which I can scarcely bear.

Shakespeare, *Coriolanus*

Something is rotten in the state of Denmark.

Shakespeare, *Hamlet*

Who saves his country, saves himself, saves all things, and all things saved
do bless him! Who lets his country die, lets all things die, dies himself igno-
bly, and all things dying curse him!

Senator Benjamin H. Hill Jr., 1893

Man exists for his own sake and not to add a laborer to the state.

Ralph Waldo Emerson, *Journals*

Chapter Objectives

After completing this chapter, you should be able to:

- Understand how states as political organizations are defined.
- Examine the origins of states.
- Understand various theories of governance.
- Analyze forms of authoritarian governance.
- Analyze standards of democracy.
- Discuss the importance of balancing individualism and communitarianism in democracies.
- Examine the drive to institute democracy globally and the related implications for global and national security.
- Understand various types of interests in determining international activity.
- Discuss the future of states as principal actors in the world system.
- Understand the democratic peace thesis.

This chapter and the next one examine two divergent roads that we can take toward politically organizing the world stage. This chapter will take up the traditional organization: the state. Then, chapter 9 will examine the alternative type of organization: international governmental organizations.

The Nature and Origins of the State

In considering states, it is important to understand how their existence as sovereign actors affects world politics and also what their political future is. Discussing these matters, however, requires that we first establish a foundation of knowledge about what states are and how they came into being and have evolved.

THE STATE DEFINED

States are territorially defined political units that exercise ultimate internal authority and that recognize no legitimate external authority over them. States are also the most important units in defining the political identity of most people. When an Olympian steps atop the ceremonial stands to receive his or her gold medal, the flag of the victor's country is raised and its national anthem is played. States are also the most powerful of all political actors. Some huge companies approach or even exceed the wealth of some poorer countries, but no individual, company, group, or international organization approaches the coercive power wielded by most states. Whether large or small, rich or poor, populous or not, states share all or most of six characteristics: sovereignty, territory, population, diplomatic recognition, internal organization, and domestic support.

Sovereignty

The most important political characteristic of a state is **sovereignty**. This term means that the sovereign actor (the state) does not recognize as legitimate any higher authority. Sovereignty also includes the idea of legal equality among states. As we shall discuss further, sovereign states developed late in the Middle Ages (ca. 500–1350) from a consolidation and simultaneous expansion of political power. First, the rulers of Europe expanded their political authority by breaking away from the secular domination of the Holy Roman Empire and the theological authority of the pope. Second, the kings also consolidated political power by subjugating feudal estates and other competing local political organizations within their realms. The resulting states exercised supreme authority over their territory and citizens; they owed neither allegiance nor obedience to any higher authority.

It is important to note that sovereignty, a legal and theoretical term, differs from independence, a political and applied term (James, 1999). Independence means freedom from outside control, and in an ideal, law-abiding world, sovereignty and independence would be synonymous. In the real world, however, where power is important, independence is not absolute. Sometimes a small country is so dominated by a powerful neighbor that its independence is dubious at best. Especially in terms of their foreign and defense policies, legally sovereign countries such as Bhutan (dominated by India), the Marshall Islands (dominated by the United States), and Monaco (dominated by France) can be described as having only circumscribed independence (Clapham, 1999).

While independence has always been relative, the weakening of the doctrine of state sovereignty is more of a recent phenomenon. It is one of the most important changes under way in the international system (Hashmi, 1997). The world community

Holland's Scheveningen prison provides a solid symbol of the erosion of absolute sovereignty for states and their leaders. The prison houses numerous individuals on trial for war crimes before the UN-established tribunal in The Hague. Among those incarcerated is Slobodan Milosevic, who is charged with numerous violations of international law allegedly committed while he was serving as president of Yugoslavia.

is beginning to reject sovereignty as a defense for a government's mistreatment of its citizens. During the early 1990s, global condemnation coupled with economic and other forms of sanctions forced the Eurowhite-dominated government of South Africa to end the apartheid system of oppression of its non-European-heritage citizens, especially its blacks. The UN also rejected the sovereignty defense when in 1994 it condemned the military overthrow of Haiti's elected president and authorized UN members "to form a multinational force... [and] to use all necessary means" to topple the military junta. Soon thereafter, a U.S.-led force sent the generals packing into exile. The international community in the late 1990s demanded that the Yugoslav government cease its brutal attacks on rebellious towns in Kosovo, even though that province is clearly part of Yugoslavia. When diplomacy and sanctions failed, NATO warplanes went into action. The Serbs were driven from Kosovo, and the province was occupied by KFOR, the multinational Kosovo Force.

A related and dramatic demonstration of the diminution of sovereignty is the trial of Slobodan Milosevic, the former president (1989–2000) of Yugoslavia, on war crimes charges. The action marks the first time in history that an elected president has had to answer in an international court for actions taken while in office. The 29-count indictment against Milosevic includes genocide, murder, torture, and other crimes against humanity and violations of the Geneva Conventions (1949) and characterizes him as having "participated in a joint criminal enterprise" that led to the death and inhumane treatment of tens of thousands of people in Bosnia, Croatia, and Kosovo during the 1990s. If convicted by the International War Crimes Tribunal for the Balkans, which is located in The Hague, the Netherlands, Milosevic could be sentenced to life in prison.

Expressing a widespread view, one human rights advocate hailed the prosecution of Milosevic as evidence that "even the highest government officials are vulnerable to international prosecution for the most heinous human rights crimes.... It will begin to force would-be tyrants to think twice before replicating Milosevic's atrocities."[1] Other observers worried, however, that whatever crimes Milosevic may

	San Marino	China	Ratio
Table 8.1 San Marino and China: Sovereign Equals			
Territory (sq.mi.)	24	3,705,400	1:154,392
Population	26,937	1,261,832,482	1:46,844
GDP	$210,000,000	$1,064,500,000,000	1:5,069
Military Personnel	0	2,800,000	1:∞
Vote in UN General Assembly	1	1	1:1

China includes data for now-incorporated Hong Kong. San Marino has a police force with an annual budget of about $37 million.

∞ = infinity

Data sources: World Almanac (2002); CIA (2002).

The legal concept of sovereign equality is very different from more tangible measures of equality, as is evident in this comparison of two countries: San Marino and China.

have committed, putting him on trial before a UN-sponsored tribunal and similar actions have, as one U.S. senator put it, "turned the principle of national sovereignty on its head."[2] Taking a similar view, a member of the U.S. House of Representatives asserted that "the prosecution of Milosevic, a democratically elected... leader of a sovereign country.... threatens U.S. sovereignty." The representative went on to explain, "We cannot have it both ways. We cannot expect to use [war crimes tribunals] when it pleases us and oppose [them] where the rules would apply to our own acts of aggression."[3]

What should we make of these restraints on internal sovereignty in South Africa, Haiti, and Yugoslavia? It would be naive to imagine they mean that in the foreseeable future the world community will regularly ignore sovereignty to take a stand against racism or authoritarianism whenever and wherever they occur. It would be equally wrong, however, not to recognize that the actions against racial oppression, military coups, ethnic cleansing, and neofascism were important steps away from the doctrine of unlimited state sovereignty.

Sovereignty also implies legal *equality* among states. That theory is applied in the UN General Assembly and many other international assemblies, where each member-state has one vote. Are all states really equal, though? Compare San Marino and China (Table 8.1). San Marino lies entirely within Italy and is the world's oldest republic, dating back to the fourth century A.D. After years of self-imposed nonparticipation, the San Marinese decided to seek membership in the UN. "The fact of sitting around the table with the most important states in the world is a reaffirmation of sovereignty," explained Giovanni Zangoli, the country's foreign minister.[4] The General Assembly seated San Marino in 1992 as a sovereign equal. Nevertheless, it is obvious that whatever sovereignty may mean legally, in many ways the two countries are not equal.

Territory

A second characteristic of a state is territory. It would seem obvious that a state must have physical boundaries, and most states do. On closer examination, though, the question of territory becomes more complex. There are numerous international disputes over borders; territorial boundaries can expand, contract, or shift dramatically; and it is even possible to have a state without territory. Many states recognize what they call Palestine as sovereign, yet the Palestinians are scattered across other countries such as Jordan. An accord that the Israelis and Palestinians signed in 1994 gave the Palestinians a measure of autonomy in Gaza (a region between Israel and Egypt) and in parts of the West Bank, and these areas have been expanded through subsequent negotiations. Therefore, depending on one's viewpoint, the Palestinians have some territory, no territory, or have been expelled from the territory now occupied by Israel. It is also possible to maintain, as the United States and most other countries currently do, that the Palestinians still have no state of their own.

Population

People are an obvious requirement of any state. The populations of states range from the 880 inhabitants of the Holy See (popularly referred to as the Vatican) to China's approximately 1.3 billion people, but all states count this characteristic as a minimum requirement.

What is becoming less clear in the shifting loyalties of the evolving international system is exactly where the population of a country begins and ends. Citizenship has become a bit more fluid than it was not long ago. For example, a citizen of one European Union (EU) country who resides in another EU country can now vote in local elections and even hold local office in the country in which he or she resides. Similarly, a reform accord reached in 1996 by the political parties of Mexico allows Mexicans who have emigrated to the United States to vote in Mexican presidential elections.

Diplomatic Recognition

A classic rhetorical question is, If a tree fell in the forest and no one heard it, did it make a sound? The same question governs the issue of statehood and the recognition by others. If a political entity declares its independence and no other country grants it diplomatic recognition, is it really a state? The answer seems to be no.

How many countries must grant recognition before statehood is achieved is a more difficult question. When Israel declared its independence in 1948, the United States and the Soviet Union quickly recognized the country. Its Arab neighbors did not extend recognition and instead attacked what they considered to be the Zionist invaders. Was Israel a state at that point? It certainly seems so, because which countries, as well as how many of them, extend recognition is important.

Yet a lack of recognition, even by a majority of other countries, does not necessarily mean a state does not exist. Diplomatic recognition by most countries of the communist government of Mao Zedong in China came slowly after it took power in 1949. U.S. recognition was withheld until 1979. Did that mean that the rechristened People's Republic of China did not exist for a time? Clearly the answer is no because, as one scholar comments, "power capabilities are equally or more important than outside recognition" in establishing the existence of a state (Thompson, 1995:220).

The issue of recognition remains a matter of serious international concern. Taiwan is for all practical purposes an independent country, and it is recognized by more than two dozen countries. Yet, Taiwan itself does not claim independence from China, and thus is a *de facto* (in fact) but not *de jure* (in law) state. Tibet provides another example in the region of what might be called a state-in-waiting, as the box, The Wisdom of Patience, on p. 202 explains.

Another contemporary issue involves the Palestinians. Many states recognize a Palestinian state and did so even before the Palestinians acquired any autonomous territory in Gaza and the West Bank beginning in the mid-1990s. Currently, according to the Palestine National Authority (PNA), almost 100 countries (including China and India) recognize an "independent State of Palestine," some 79 (including the United States) accept Palestinian passports, and 22 countries maintain representative missions in Gaza or the West Bank. Moroever, the United Nations Security Council passed a resolution in March 2002 calling for a separate Palestinian state. Yet since the PNA has not declared an independent Palestine, it would be hard to construe these diplomatic ties as recognizing Palestinian sovereign statehood. When the final steps toward independence come, as seems increasingly likely to occur, the degree to which countries recognize that independence and establish full diplomatic relations will have important legal and political ramifications for the nascent state of Palestine.

Did You Know That:
Countries other than the United States, where the Internet started, have a national "domain" designation of the state's cyberspace territory. An indication of evolving statehood for Palestine is that in March 2000 the Internet Corporation for Assigned Names and Numbers granted a domain designation ".ps" to the Palestinian National Authority (PNA). Fighting has delayed the implementation of the .ps designation, so for now the PNA's site remains http://www.pna.org/. Soon, however, you will probably be able to visit the Web site of the PNA at http://www.gov.ps/.

Certainly, the standard of diplomatic recognition remains hazy. Nevertheless, it is an important factor in the international system for several reasons. One is related to psychological status. History has many examples of new countries and governments, even those with revolutionary ideology, that have assiduously sought outside recognition and, to a degree, moderated their policies in order to get it. Second, external recognition has important practical advantages. Generally, states are the only entities that can legally sell government bonds and buy heavy weapons from another state. Israel's chances of survival in 1948 were enhanced when recognition allowed the Israelis to raise money and purchase armaments in Europe, the United States, and elsewhere. Also, it would be difficult for any aspirant to statehood to survive for long without recognition. Economic problems resulting from the inability to establish trade relations are just one example of the difficulties that would arise. The case of Taiwan shows that survival while in diplomatic limbo is not impossible, but it is such an oddity that it does not disprove the general rule.

Internal Organization

States must normally have some level of political and economic structure. Most states have a government, but statehood continues during periods of severe turmoil, even anarchy. Afghanistan, Liberia, Sierra Leone, Somalia, and some other existing states dissolved into chaos for an extended time during the last decade and had no functioning national government. Yet none of these "failed states" ceased to exist legally. Each, for instance, continued to sit as a sovereign equal, with an equal vote, in the UN General Assembly. In the case of Afghanistan, the United Nations never recognized the de facto control of most of the country by the Islamic Emirate of Afghanistan, the Taliban's name for the country from 1995 through 2001. Instead, the United Nations continued its recognition of the Islamic State of Afghanistan, the country's pre-Taliban name, and to seat the representation sent, after 1995, by the political wing of the rebel Northern Alliance.

An associated issue arises when what once was, and what still claims to be, the government of a generally recognized or formerly recognized state exists outside the territory that the exiled government claims as its own. There is a long history of recognizing governments-in-exile. The most common instances have occurred when a sitting government is forced by invaders to flee. A current and controversial example of what claims to be a government-in-exile involves Tibet, as explained in the box on the next page.

Domestic Support

The final characteristic of a state is domestic support. At its most active, this implies that a state's population is loyal to it and grants it the authority to make rules and to

THE WISDOM OF PATIENCE

The issue of Tibet's status presents an interesting case study for what constitutes a state. Tibet is large (471,000 square miles, almost twice the size of Texas) and sits 15,000 feet high in the Himalayas between India and China. There are about 3 million Tibetans and an equal number of Chinese in Tibet. Another 2 million or so Tibetans live in adjacent areas in China or are refugees in northern India. China claims them as Chinese, but the Mongolian-stock Tibetans are distinct from the Han, the dominant Chinese ethnic group. Also, the Tibetan language is related more to Burmese than it is to the major Chinese dialects (Mandarin, Cantonese, Fukienese). Moreover, while Tibetans are Buddhists, their form of Buddhism has its roots in India, not China. Tibetan Buddhism and Tibetan ethnonational identity are closely connected. For over a thousand years, Tibet was a theocracy, ruled spiritually and politically by the Dalai Lama and other lamas. The current, fourteenth Dalai Lama was just five years old when he was enthroned in 1940.

Tibet was an independent kingdom from the 800s to the 1300s. It then came under the sway of Ghengis Khan and the Mongols. Later, as Mongol power ebbed, Tibet exercised increased autonomy, and in 1577 the Mongol emperor Altan Khan recognized the reality of Tibet's self-governance by first calling its theocratic leader as the Dalai Lama (lama of all within the seas). Soon, however, Tibet's autonomy was eclipsed. Chinese influence grew, and a massive invasion by China in 1751 established the Chinese emperor's suzerainty over Tibet.

Thus Tibet was independent for about 600 years, then for another 600 years was in a political twilight zone, not fully sovereign but often exercising considerable autonomy from Mongol and, later, Chinese rule. A new era of independence began in 1911, when imperial China collapsed, and lasted until 1950, when Chinese forces again seized control. At first, the Dalai Lama remained in Tibet and exercised some authority. Then in 1959 the Tibetans revolted against China. They were bloodily crushed, China revoked Tibet's autonomy, and the Dalai Lama and his supporters fled south to India and established a government-in-exile at Dharamsala.

Tibet's connection with China is important because Beijing traces its authority back through centuries of Chinese emperors and the ebb and flow of their political control over Tibet (Goldstein, 1997). The Tibetans concede that they were subjects of the imperial dynasties but maintain that Tibet was autonomous. Moreover, Tibetans argue that they were under the suzerainty of the emperor, not China. They note that in an earlier era, emperors ruled subjects in various lands, but that rule was personal. Thus, according to the Tibetans, the fact that the Chinese emperor ruled Tibet did not make Tibet part of China.

For the moment, Tibet is firmly under the control of Beijing, but the cause of Tibetan independence or autonomy is very much alive. Recent Dalai Lamas have also worked diligently to win official international support for Tibet. So far, however, none have enjoyed much success. For instance, in 1909, with the

govern (legitimacy). At its most passive, the population grudgingly accepts the authority of the government. For all the coercive power that a state usually possesses, it is difficult for any state to survive without at least the passive acquiescence of its people. The dissolution of Czechoslovakia, the Soviet Union, and Yugoslavia are illustrations of multinational states collapsing in the face of the separatist impulses of disaffected nationalities.

It is important to note for our discussion of the future of states that domestic support is based on pragmatic considerations as well as on emotional attachment to the national state. Those who study the origins of the sovereign state point out that states developed in part "as the result of a social coalition based on the affinity of interests and perspective" between emerging kings and important elements of the population (Spruyt, 1994:79). The point is that states are political organizations created to perform tasks, to "establish Justice, insure domestic Tranquillity, provide for the common defense, promote the general Welfare, and secure the Blessings of Liberty," as the Preamble to the U.S. Constitution puts it. Because states are meant to provide such benefits, states derive part of their domestic support from their ability to deliver the proverbial goods. When states are unable to meet important needs

Whether or not a territorial entity is or is not a state is not always precisely clear. Tibet and Taiwan are two territories that exist in something of a twilight. Each has some characteristics that are necessary to being a state; but neither is a state. Thus when, as shown here, the exiled head of Tibet, the Dalai Lama (left), and the president of Taiwan, Chen Shui-bian (right), meet, they do so as leaders of political entities and perhaps potential states, but not as heads of state.

have the efforts of the current Dalai Lama to build support. President George W. Bush had only been in office four months before the Dalai Lama visited him at the White House in May 2001. During the meeting, the Dalai Lama emphasized, "I am not seeking independence, I am seeking genuine autonomy." That did not assuage China, which characterized the Dalai Lama as "a political exile engaged in separatist activities" and warned that "official meetings and contacts between him and the U.S. administration" constituted "rude interference" in China's internal affairs.[1]

For his part, President Bush was very cautious. Through a White House press release, he declared his "strong support for the Dalai Lama's tireless efforts to initiate a dialogue with the Chinese government" and expressed his "hope that the Chinese government would respond favorably." The press release also noted that "the President and the Dalai Lama agreed on the importance of strong and constructive U.S.-China relations" and that Bush commended "the Dalai Lama's commitment to nonviolence."[2] The meaning of this language is that Washington would not threaten to upset relations with Beijing by pressing it too hard on the status of Tibet and was discouraging any resort to violence by the Tibetans.

Thus, as they have been for most of the last eight centuries, the Tibetans continue to be dominated by a powerful neighboring nationality and unable to gain diplomatic recognition or other expressions of support from the established states. It is likely, though, that the Dalai Lama and other Tibetans will persist, mindful of the Buddha's teaching that "Tolerance, patience and understanding are the highest virtues."[3]

Chinese imperial court in its death throes, the thirteenth Dalai Lama appealed to Great Britain for support. This was rejected by London, according to a British document, on the grounds that Tibet was a "worthless piece of territory" (Heberer, 1995:303). The British were not alone in this view. During the 1911–1950 period of Tibetan independence, no country extended diplomatic recognition to Lhasa.

That diplomatic isolation has continued, but so

(and some analysts say states now cannot do so), the domestic support of the state weakens. This observation about the founding and evolution of the sovereign state leads to a further discussion of origins of the modern state.

THE ORIGINS OF THE STATE

In the last chapter we noted the decline of the Greek city-states as the center of political organization in the West and the eventual domination of the universalistic Roman Empire. After more than five centuries as the hub of the known Western world, Rome fell in 476. Thereafter, secular political power in the West was wielded for almost a millennium by two levels of authority—one universal, the other local. On the universalistic **macrolevel**, international organizational authority existed in the form of the Roman Catholic Church. Christianity as interpreted by the Catholic Church and its pope served as the integrating force in several ways. The Church kept Latin alive, which provided a common language among intellectuals. Christian doctrine underlay the developing concepts of rights, justice, and other political norms. Even kings were theoretically (and often substantially) subordinate to the pope. It was, for example, Pope Leo III who crowned Charlemagne "Emperor of the Romans" in 800. Charlemagne's empire did not last, but the idea of a new Christian-Roman universal state was established, and was strengthened further when in 936 Otto I was crowned head of what became known as the **Holy Roman Empire**.

Centuries later, the overarching authority of the Catholic Church was supplemented and, in some cases, supplanted, by great multiethnic empires. These political conglomerations came to exercise control over many different peoples. The Austro-Hungarian, British, Chinese, Dutch, French, German, Ottoman, Russian, Spanish, and other empires controlled people in their immediate continental areas and on other continents. Most of the people within these empires did not feel a strong political identification with or an emotional attachment to them. Many of these empires lasted into this century; but the collapse of the Soviet Union, which had inherited the Russian empire, marked the end of the last of the great multiethnic empires that had provided an earlier degree of macrolevel integration.

The local, *microlevel* of authority centered on political units that were smaller than the states that would one day evolve. The **feudal system** was characterized by principalities, dukedoms, baronies, and other such fiefdoms, which were ruled by minor royalty who provided local defense. This warrior elite was largely autonomous, even though individual nobles were theoretically vassals of a king or an emperor.

It is important to understand here, as one scholar explains it, that systems of governance "had vastly different characteristics" than they do today. "They were nonterritorial, and sovereignty was, at best, disputed" (Spruyt, 1994:35). Certainly rulers, from emperors to barons, controlled specific pieces of territory. The land that a feudal lord controlled, though, was mostly a function of his individual power and his relationship to other feudal lords and, thus, was not fixed. The Church and the Holy Roman Empire by definition sought to include all Christians, not a defined territory. Furthermore, the very nature of the feudal system, in which vassals were theoretically subservient to kings and kings were theoretically subservient to emperors and popes, meant that sovereignty did not exist legally and often did not exist in fact.

By the thirteenth century the fabric of universalism and feudalism had begun to fray. In the words of one scholar, "At the end of the Middle Ages, the international system went through a dramatic transformation in which the crosscutting jurisdictions of feudal lords, emperors, kings, and popes started to give way to territorially defined authorities" (Spruyt, 1994:1). The existing nonterritorially defined, hierarchical system was replaced by a system based on territorially defined sovereign states.

The Decline of the Feudal System

The forces of change in the Middle Ages that eroded the feudal system were many. Of these, two factors stand out—military technology and economic expansion.

Military Technology Advances in military capabilities, especially the introduction of gunpowder, diminished the ability of the relatively small feudal manors to provide security. The first mention of guns in Europe is contained in a manuscript written in Florence in 1327. Thereafter, an armored knight, the

States became the dominant form of political organization for several pragmatic reasons. One of these was that with military uses of gunpowder from the 1300s, territorially larger states proved more defensible than were feudal realms and their castles.

epitome of the feudal warrior elite, could be shot off his horse by a quickly trained commoner armed with a primitive firearm; the castle, the centerpiece of feudal defense, could be demolished easily by cannons. These and other factors meant that static defenses of small territories needed to be replaced by defense based on the ability to maneuver, which could be provided only by a territorially larger unit, the state.

Economic Expansion The growth of Europe's economy undermined the feudal system and promoted the state system. *Improved trade* was one factor. The decline of the Viking maritime menace to the north of Europe and the easing of Muslim barriers to trade with Asia increased trade with lands to the east of Europe and brought in new wealth. This in turn led to the building of larger ships, which created even greater possibilities for trade. The journeys of Marco Polo to China and other lands far from his native Venice between 1271 and 1295 were an early manifestation of this new commercial activity. Soon thereafter, the search for trade was a major focus of Europeans and led, among other things, to the journey of Christopher Columbus to the Caribbean in 1492.

The beginning of early *mass production* was a second factor driving economic expansion. Individual craftsmen began to give way to primitive factories. The full-scale **industrial revolution** did not take place for several hundred more years, but by the 1200s the early stages of this new mode of production already required larger markets and larger sources of supply for raw materials than the limited territory of the feudal realm provided.

The rise of trade and manufacturing and, consequently, the accumulation of new wealth resulted in important changes in political power. Increased trade and manufacturing added to the size, wealth, and, therefore, power of the commercial class, the burghers. In the same way, the need for trading centers and manufacturing centers led to the increase in the size and importance of towns. Neither burghers nor towns fit with the feudal system, which was based on the authority of the local lord over mostly agricultural peasants. The economic needs of the burghers and towns led them to support the creation of larger political units more suited for uninterrupted commerce. In this desire the burghers found ready allies in kings. The kings wanted to increase their control over their often-fractious feudal lords but needed money to finance the men and arms to overcome local resistance. The burghers wanted to destroy local restraints and had the money to loan the kings. The resulting alliance helped create the modern state. In fact, the burghers became so powerful in their own right that, much later, they were part of the elite that resisted the king and launched democracy in the United States and elsewhere.

In sum, changes in military technology rendered the feudal manor obsolete as a defensive unit and changes in manufacturing and commerce rendered the feudal manor obsolete as an economic unit. Larger political units were needed to provide protection and to operate efficiently. Furthermore, improved communications and transportation made people more aware of and cooperative with their ethnic kin in other areas. The feudal system was doomed.

The Decline of Universalistic Authority

At the same time that the micropolitical feudal system was decaying, the macropolitical claims of universalistic authority by the pope and the Holy Roman emperor were also being increasingly challenged. In part, political-religious authority began

> **Did You Know That:**
> The most successful of the new economic elite of the Middle Ages was the Italian family founded by Giovanni di Bicci de' Medici (1360–1429). The immense wealth gained by this family of bankers and merchants led to political power. They dominated the city-state of Florence from the 1400s until 1737 as dukes and duchesses; two de' Medicis became queens of France (Catherine in 1547, Marie in 1610); and three de' Medicis became popes (Leo X in 1513, Clement VII in 1523, and Leo X in 1605).

to decline as the authority of kings grew through the just-discussed process of subduing feudal manors and incorporating them into their kingdoms. As kings became more powerful, they began to reject the real, or even titular, political authority of the pope.

The decline of papal authority and the increase in royal power were reinforced by a period of cultural and intellectual rebirth and reform called the **Renaissance** (about 1350–1650). Educated people looked to the classical Hellenic and Roman cultures as models and developed a concept of personal freedom that ran counter to the authority of the Church.

One significant outcome of this secular movement was the **Protestant Reformation**. Influenced in part by Renaissance thinking, Martin Luther rejected the Catholic Church as the necessary intermediary between people and God. In 1517 Luther protested Catholic doctrine and proclaimed his belief that anyone could have an individual relationship with God. Within a few decades, nearly a quarter of the people of Western Europe became Protestants.

The first great secular break with the Catholic Church occurred in England, where King Henry VIII (1509–1547) rejected papal authority and established the Anglican Church. The Reformation also touched off political-religious struggles elsewhere in Europe. The ostensible issue was religious freedom, but there were also important political causes and consequences. When the century-long struggle between the imperial and Catholic Holy Roman Empire and the nationalist and Protestant ethnic groups ended with the **Treaty of Westphalia** (1648), centralized political power in Europe was over. The Holy Roman Empire had splintered into two rival Catholic monarchies (Austria and Spain); a number of Protestant entities (such as Holland and many German states) gained independence or autonomy; and other countries, such as Catholic France and Protestant England, were more secure in their independence. Thus, many scholars regard 1648 as marking the births of the modern national state and of the world political system based on sovereign states as the primary political actors (Philpott, 1999).

The Victory of the Sovereign State

The breakdown of the feudal-universalistic systems did not, however, lead immediately to the uncontested growth and political dominance of states. Instead, the people of the Middle Ages experimented with several types of political organizations to see how well they met the security and economic needs of the time.

The Early State and Its Competitors The revival of city-states, such as Florence and Venice, was one alternative scheme of political organization. Another was the formation of loosely confederated city-leagues based on common economic interests. The most famous of these mercantile alliances was the Hanseatic League (*hanse*, German for "merchant guild"). Founded in 1358 to protect commerce against piracy, and eventually including 70 north-central European cities such as Hamburg and Lübeck, the city-league became a major economic force.

Neither the city-league nor city-state form of organization persisted; the state did. The Hanseatic League ended in 1667, when its council met for the last time. The fortunes of Florence and other city-states ebbed more slowly, but they eventually faded also. What is important is that states bested city-states and city-leagues to become the successor of the feudal-universalistic system of political organization. This occurred for identifiable, pragmatic reasons. A review of the complex factors involved in this victory of the state is beyond our telling here, but the essential point, as one scholar puts it, is that in time "sovereign states displaced city-leagues and city-states… because their institutional logic gave them an advantage in mobilizing

One of the events that secured the future of the evolving sovereign state system occurred when the Spanish Armada dispatched in 1588 by Phillip II, king of Spain and ruler of the Holy Roman Empire, failed in its attempt to conquer Protestant England in the name of the Roman Catholic empire. The naval battles in the English Channel between the 125-ship Armada and the smaller, but ultimately victorious, English fleet are represented in this painting, which hangs in the British National Maritime Museum in Greenwich.

their societies' resources" (Spruyt, 1994:185). States were best equipped to conduct commerce and to provide defense.

We can see two key points from the foregoing. First, sovereign, territorial states as we know them have not always been the basis of international political organization (Opello & Rosow, 1999). Second, states did not succeed earlier systems and prevail over competing systems or organizations because states were inevitable or because they had some special moral or philosophical claim as the ultimate expression of human political organization. Rather, states won out because they worked better at a particular time in history. Remembering this point about the pragmatic origins of the state will be crucial to judging the contemporary argument about the future of the state when we take that matter up later in the chapter.

Evolution of States Toward Democracy To round out this survey of the founding and evolution of the state, we can note that during the several centuries that followed the Peace of Westphalia, the genesis of national states continued as economic and social interaction grew and monarchs such as Louis XIV of France (1643–1715), Frederick II of Prussia (1740–1786), and Peter the Great of Russia (1682–1725) consolidated their core domains and even expanded them into empires. In the development of the modern national state, however, one key element was yet to come. Missing was the concept that the state is an embodiment of the nation (the people). Kings claimed to rule their realms by "divine right"; thus France's Louis XIV could proclaim, "*L'état, c'est moi*" (I am the state). Perhaps it was so then, but in 1793 another French king, Louis XVI, lost his head over this presumption, and the people claimed the state for themselves.

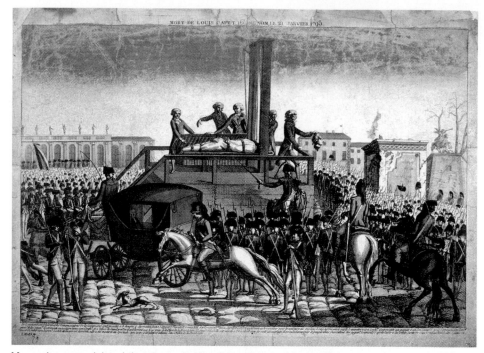

Monarchs once claimed that they ruled by divine right and "owned" the state. Through the French Revolution (1789) and the execution of Louis XVI, the French people claimed France for themselves. This 1793 painting, *Mort de Louis Capet 16e du Nom, le 21 Janvier 1793*, shows the crowd cheering as the executioner displays the king's head.

The coming of democracy, exemplified by the American (1776) and French (1789) Revolutions promoted the creation of the national state. The fixed territory of modern states and their sense of sovereign singularity had already begun to create a spirit of nationalism in England and elsewhere. Still, the attachment of most individuals to the state was limited by the theory that the state was the property of the monarch and the people were the crown's subjects. Democracy changed the theory of who owns the state from monarch to citizen, and that solidified nationalism. Now the state was the possession of the people, who, therefore, were obliged to support it emotionally and materially.

Once this occurred, all the basic parameters for the modern state that exists today were in place. Certainly, new states continued to evolve into being as older systems slowly disintegrated. Important states like Germany and Italy did not exist a century and a half ago; other states like Vietnam did not exist 50 years ago; still other states like Ukraine did not exist a decade ago. The idea that people own and are tied to their countries also continued to evolve. A century ago, monarchs ruled nearly everywhere. Now they rule almost nowhere, and even authoritarian governments claim power in the name of the people.

The State as the Core Political Organization

Having explored the evolution of states, our next task is to look at the state as our primary political organization. Chapter 4 pointed out that the anarchical nature of the international system stems from the fact that the sovereign state is the key actor in the system. Then chapter 5 looked inside the state to illuminate the foreign policy–making process. What we can add here are examinations of differing theories of governance and of national and other interests.

THEORIES OF GOVERNANCE

It is possible to divide theories of governance into two broad categories. One includes types of **authoritarian government**, which allow little or no participation in decision making by individuals and groups outside the upper reaches of the government. The second category includes **democratic government**, which allows much broader and more meaningful participation. As with many things we discuss, the line between authoritarian and democratic is not precise. Instead, using broad and meaningful participation as the standard, there is a scale that runs from one-person rule to full, direct democracy (or even, according to some, to anarchism). The map on p. 212 provides one way to order types of government, with the countries in shades of green being generally democratic and the countries in other colors being generally authoritarian.

Authoritarian Theories of Governance

The world has witnessed the coming, dominance, and the passing of a number of nondemocratic political theories about how societies should be organized and governed. These can be grouped under general authoritarian theory and a number of more specialized theories. Before turning to them it should be noted that many garden-variety dictatorships are based on an urge to power by an individual or a group, not by any overarching theory of how societies are best governed. That said, it is also the case that democracy has not always appealed to all political theorists.

General Authoritarian Theory Political theorists who have favored one or another form of authoritarian rule share a skeptical view of the intellectual or moral ability of the mass to govern itself. They believe, therefore, that people and their political structures (such as states) are best governed either by dictators or other forms of one-person rule or by oligarchies, which means rule by the few. Oligarchies can include hereditary aristocracies, plutocracies (rule by the wealthy class), or one-party rule (such as the Communist Party), among other schemes.

Authoritarian theory dates back to the beginning of political theory. The Greek philosopher Plato (circa 428 B.C.–347 B.C.) in his famous work *The Republic* dismissed democracy as "full of... disorder and dispensing a sort of quality of equals and unequals alike." He contended that the common citizenry trying to direct the state would be analogous to sailors on a ship "quarrelling over the control of the helm; each thinks he ought to be steering the vessel, though he has never learned navigation...; what is more, they assert that navigation is a thing that cannot be taught at all, and are ready to tear in pieces anyone who says it can." Plato's conclusion was that ships needed strong captains and crews that took orders and that "all those who need to be governed should seek out the man who can govern them."

In more contemporary times, Juan Donoso Cortés (1809–53), a Spanish legislator and political theoretician, well outlined authoritarian theory in his "Speech on Dictatorship" (1849) to Spain's parliament. According to one study, "Donoso viewed human beings as essentially and naturally depraved and irrational." Therefore, he believed that the order and, indeed, the survival of civilization depend on "the will of those who rule to demand and impose obedience... as well as upon the willingness of subjects to obey and believe their rulers."[5]

Specific Authoritarian Theories **Theocracy**, the idea of theocratic rule by spiritual leaders, is ancient. Now, however, it has almost disappeared, and the Holy See (the Vatican) is the world's only pure theocracy. There are, however, some elements of theocracy left in the popular, if not the legal, status of Japan's emperor, Thailand's king, and (most strongly) Tibet's exiled Dalai Lama. Iran's government also contains an element of theocracy, as did the Taliban government of Afghanistan before it was toppled in 2001. Furthermore, the increased strength of religious fundamentalism in many places means that it is not unthinkable that a rejuvenation of theocracy might occur.

Monarchism, a system of governance through hereditary rulers, is another ancient theory of governance that continues. It has faded greatly, however, and strong monarchism, which rests on the theory of the divine right of kings, has declined almost to the point of extinction. There are only a few strong monarchs (such as Saudi Arabia's king) scattered among a larger number of constitutional monarchies that severely restrict the monarch's power.

Communism as it originated in the works of Friedrich Engels and Karl Marx is essentially an economic theory. As applied, however, by Vladimir Lenin and Josef Stalin in the USSR, by Mao Zedong in China, and by other Communist leaders in those countries and elsewhere, communism also falls squarely within the spectrum of authoritarian governance. Even Marx expected that a "dictatorship of the proletariat" over the bourgeoisie would follow communist revolutions and prevail during a transitional socialist period between capitalism and communism. Lenin institutionalized this view. His concept of dictatorship meant, in the words of one study, "the dictatorship of the Communist Party over the proletariat, since [Lenin] had little faith that the working class had the political understanding or spontaneous organizational ability to secure the existence and expansion of a communist state" (Ebenstein, Ebenstein, & Fogelman, 1994:125). Stalin further concentrated political authority in his person and in a small group of associates. Even the Communist Party lost its control, and, another study explains, "After 1930, not a single protest was raised; not a single dissenting voice or vote expressed" any difference with what Stalin decided (Macridis & Hulliung, 1996:117). Indeed the encompassing social, economic, and political control that Stalin claimed was termed "totalitarian."

Fascism is another authoritarian political philosophy that in some of its manifestations embraces totalitarianism. The term fascism is often used loosely to describe almost anyone far to the right. That approach is wrong, for the term should be used with some precision. Modern fascism can be traced to Italy and the ideas of Benito Mussolini and to a variant, National Socialism and Adolf Hitler and his Nazi followers in Germany. Its basic tenets include (1) rejecting rationality and relying on emotion to govern; (2) believing (especially for Nazis) in the superiority of some groups and the inferiority of others; (3) subjugating countries of "inferior" people; (4) rejecting individual rights in favor of a "corporatist" view that people are "workers" in the state; (5) demanding that economic activity support the corporatist state; (6) viewing the state as a living thing (the organic state theory); (7) believing that the individual's highest expression is in the people (*volk* in German); and (8) believing that the highest expression of the *volk* (and, by extension, the individual) is in the leader (*führer* in German, *duce* in Italian), who rules as a totalitarian dictator.

This approach, which we will generically call fascism, spread beyond Italy and Germany to include such other countries as Spain under Francisco Franco (1939–1975) and Argentina under Juan Perón (1946–1955). What makes fascism of more contemporary interest is that it is again astir in a variety of countries. The term fascist is so tainted by history that few concede to being fascist. That does not, however, diminish the worry, expressed by an official of the UN Commission on Human Rights, that "neo-fascism and neo-Nazism are gaining ground in many countries—especially in Europe."[6]

There are many recent areas of concern in Europe, but just three—Austria, France, and Italy—will suffice to make the point. In Austria, the Freedom Party led by Jörg Haider won 27 percent of the vote in the 1999 parliamentary elections in a campaign based in part on virulent anti-immigrant rhetoric. Freedom Party posters warned against *überfremdung*, a term coined in Nazi Germany, which translates as "foreign infiltration." Among Haider's views: "The Africans who come here are drug dealers and they seduce our youth. We've got the Poles who concentrate on car theft. We've got the people from the former Yugoslavia who are burglary experts. We've got the Turks who are superbly organized in the heroin trade. And we've got the Russians who are experts in blackmail and mugging."[7]

Neofascism also exists in France, where in April 2002 Jean-Marie Le Pen, head of the ultra right-wing National Front Party, finished second in the first round of presidential voting. Le Pen advocates xenophobic, anti-immigrant policies and has dismissed the extermination of 6 million Jews and others in the Holocaust as a mere "detail of history."[8] Although Le Pen received only 17 percent of the vote in the election round that had 16 candidates, his second-place finish behind President Chirac (who received 20 percent of the vote) stunned France and, indeed, much of the rest of the world. Chirac easily beat Le Pen in the second round of voting in early May, but Le Pen's strong showing was ample proof of the strong rightist sentiment in Europe.

Italy is also flirting with the fascism that gripped it before and during World War II. The government of Prime Minister Silvio Berlusconi includes numerous members of such neofascist parties as the Italian Social Movement (MSI) and the National Alliance (NA). These individuals include Gianfranco Fini, the head of the NA, who serves as deputy premier. Among other things, and in words that Benito Mussolini would have approved, Berlusconi has urged Europeans to "be confident of the superiority of our civilization," and he has expressed the conviction that "the West will continue to conquer peoples, like it conquered communism."[9]

Did You Know That:
Some Italian neofascists believe that J. R. R. Tolkien's work promotes fascist values. The right-wing National Alliance (NA) has run so-called Hobbit camps for youngsters and acclaimed the 2002 opening of the movie *The Lord of the Rings*. "There is a deep significance to this [movie] as a parable about the battle between community and individuality," explained one NA leader.[1]

Thus, in the first years of the twenty-first century, it is possible to give only a mixed report on the prospects for the end of authoritarian government. Generally democracy has progressed in recent decades, and, despite a few relapses, **authoritarianism** has been held in check. Yet, it is also the case that retrograde political philosophies are far from extinct. As one analysis notes gloomily, "ideologies often go through a process of ebb and flow. Right-wing extremism and authoritarianism have deep roots" (Macridis & Hulliung, 1996:183). Democracy has become more prevalent, but it is also far from triumphant.

Democratic Theories of Governance

The existence of democratic government (which is derived from the Greek word *demos*, meaning "the citizenry") dates from the ancient Greek city-states circa 500 B.C. For more than 2,000 years, however, democracy existed only sporadically and usually in isolated locations. The gradual rise of English democracy, then the American and French Revolutions in the late eighteenth century, marked the change of democracy from a mere curiosity to an important national and transnational political idea. Still, the spread of democracy continued slowly. Then, during the late 1980s and early 1990s, dictatorship fell on hard times, and many observers tentatively heralded the coming of a democratic age. This view was captured by Francis Fukuyama's (1989:3) essay, "The End of History?" In it he suggests that we may have come to "the end of mankind's ideological evolution and the universalization of Western liberal democracy as the final form of government." Other observers are less optimistic about democracy's strength or the future spread of democracy (Attali, 1997).

Whoever is correct in the long run, data shows that for now the spread of democracy has not stalled. One periodic study has found that both the number and

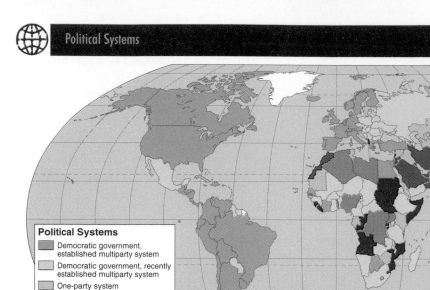

Political Systems

Political Systems
- Democratic government, established multiparty system
- Democratic government, recently established multiparty system
- One-party system
- Military government
- Monarchy or theocracy
- Disordered state

Scale: 1 to 180,000,000

The democratization of the world's countries, which began symbolically with the American (1776) and French (1789) Revolutions, progressed slowly for 150 years, then accelerated after World War II. Now, as this map and Figure 8.1 on the next page indicate, the majority of countries are full-fledged- or quasi-democracies.

percentage of democratic countries increased between 1989 and 1999. At the same time, the number and percentage of authoritarian countries declined, with most of those that changed transitioning to the mixed category. The current status of global democracy is evident in the map above and Figure 8.1 on page 213.

STATE GOVERNANCE AND WORLD POLITICS

How states are governed has a number of ramifications for world politics. We will explore two: the drive to institute democracy globally and the related implications of democratization for global and national security.

The Drive for Universal Democracy: Issues

When President Woodrow Wilson asked on April 2, 1917, for a declaration of war against Germany, he told Congress that America should fight because, among other reasons, "The world must be made safe for democracy." Clarion calls to defend and expand democracy continue. Yet, without denying the benefits of democracy, several issues exist with regard to the efforts to export it. Three such difficulties relate to the standards of democracy, the possibility of democracy, and the impact of democracy on domestic security.

Standards of Democracy One difficulty with promoting democracy is that it is not always clear what is democratic and what is not. Americans, Canadians, Western Europeans, and some others tend to emphasize **procedural democracy**. If citizens periodically choose among competing candidates and follow other such procedures, then there is democracy. Many other cultures in the world stress **substantive**

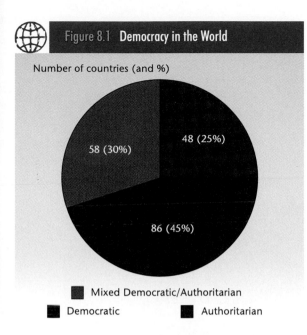

Figure 8.1 **Democracy in the World**

Number of countries (and %)

58 (30%)

48 (25%)

86 (45%)

■ Mixed Democratic/Authoritarian
■ Democratic   ■ Authoritarian

Note: Freedom House uses the designations free, partly free, and not free. Freedom House uses two scales of 1 (most free) to 7 (least free) each to designate the degree of civil liberties and political rights in countries. Countries with a combined score of 5 or less are considered free (democratic); countries scoring 6 through 10.5 are considered party free (mixed); countries scoring 11 and above are considered not free (authoritarian).

Data source: The Web site URL is: http://www.freedomhouse.org/research/survey2002.htm

Despite progress, democracy is not as fully rooted or as widespread as we might wish. Less than half the world's countries are fully democratic. A quarter of all countries are still strongly authoritarian; and the rest are mixed systems with some democratic and some authoritarian aspects.

democracy. They see democracy as a substantive product associated with equality.

Critics of American-style democracy comment, for example, that a country has failed democratically if, despite meeting procedural requisites, it produces a perpetual socioeconomic underclass based on race, ethnicity, gender, or some other factor, such as exists in the United States. Such a system, they contend, although going through the motions of democracy, in the end, denies the most important element of democracy: the substantive human right to equality. Critics further argue that any system with such vastly different economic circumstances is inherently undemocratic because the theory of government "of, by, and for the people" is undercut by the ability of wealthy individuals, groups, and corporations to spend large sums to hire professional lobbyists, to wage public relations campaigns, to donate money to electoral campaigns, to pay attorneys to sue opponents in court, and otherwise to use economic muscle unavailable to most citizens. This, the critics say, makes the contest unfair and undemocratic, no matter what the theory may be.

Defining democracy is also complicated by a second set of standards. **Individualism** argues that the rights and liberties of the individual are paramount. By contrast, **communitarianism** contends that the welfare of the collective (the community, the society) must be valued over any individual's benefit. Leaders of economically disadvantaged countries often argue that their struggle to feed, clothe, and otherwise attend to the needs of their people does not allow the "luxury" of Western-style democracy, with its incessant political bickering and its attention to the individual.

The Possibility of Democracy Yet another conundrum when promoting democracy as a norm in the international system involves whether democracy is always possible. In most of the West, where democracy has existed the longest and seems the most stable, it evolved slowly and often fitfully. More recently, other parts of the world have experienced increased degrees of democratization, but the likelihood that any single country will adopt democratic values and practices is at least partly linked with internal factors, such as attitudes about democracy and a country's educational and economic level.

With regards to attitudes, it would be a mistake to assume that everyone, everywhere is yearning to be free or that leaders in a democracy do not have autocratic tendencies. The box, Russia: Precarious Democracy, looks at one country where democratic principles hang in the balance.

There is a strong relationship between democracy and economic development. This is evident in Figure 8.2, which shows that democratic countries have a much higher per capita gross domestic product than do mixed democratic/authoritarian countries and authoritarian countries. As for economic and education level, it may be that attempting to promote full-fledged democracy in countries with poor economic and educational conditions is tantamount to trying to impose an alien political system on a socioeconomic system that is not ready for it. Doing so may even prove counterproductive. As one analyst has put it, "The

RUSSIA: PRECARIOUS DEMOCRACY

Russia's democratic heritage is extraordinarily limited. During most of its history of over 600 years, the country was ruled by a long line of autocratic czars in a political system that was often exceptionally despotic even in an age of kings and emperors. Then in March 1917, Nicholas II, the last of the czars, was overthrown and a fledgling democracy was established under the leadership of Alexander Kerensky. After a brief moment of abortive democracy, however, Russia once again descended into autocracy when in November 1917 the Bolshevik Communists lost a vote in the Russian parliament and responded by seizing power. What followed was a dictatorship that sometimes surpassed the oppressive excesses of the czars, particularly during the long rule of Josef Stalin (1924–1953). Democracy was once again—really for the first time—established when the USSR collapsed in December 1991. The question now is whether democratic governance will survive.

At first Russia's new president, Boris Yeltsin, seemed to be both a dynamic leader and a champion of democracy. Both images proved false. Russia's infrastructure collapsed amid economic chaos, and Yeltsin showed himself to be increasingly intolerant of criticism. With his health failing, he resigned under pressure. He was succeeded as president by Vladimir Putin, who had spent most of his professional career in the KGB (the Soviet secret police), and who had headed its successor organization (Russia's FSB).

The question at hand here is what the future of democracy is in Russia, especially with Putin in the presidency. The answer to that question rests in substantial part on both the attitudes of Russians

Concern about the future of democracy in Russia increased in 2002 when President Vladimir Putin's government seized the last independent television station, TV6. That left the station's news anchors, pictured here, protesting on one of the country's independent radio stations. In the background is an image of Putin on a calendar called "The 12 Moods of the President." He seems to be glancing at the station's bull's-eye-like logo. One hopes that it is coincidental and not an omen of the radio station also becoming the target of a government takeover.

toward democracy and also on Putin's willingness to abide by the rules of democratic governance.

With regards to the attitude of the Russian people, it cannot be said that they have developed an ingrained commitment to democracy. One indication is a recent survey that asked Russians to indicate which

democracy we are encouraging in many poor parts of the world is an integral part of a transformation toward new forms of authoritarianism" (Kaplan, 1999:178). Or, in another scholar's succinct phraseology, "Democracy can be bad for you" (Hobsbawm, 2001:25)

There are other scholars who take exception to this view and argue that democracy enhances development. The recipient of the 1998 Nobel Prize in economics, for one, contends that democracy promotes economic growth by pressing leaders to invest their countries' capital in education, consumer production, and other areas that will build economic strength and stimulate production instead of in military spending and other less productive economic paths (Sen, 1999).

Democracy and Domestic Security Some observers also contend that the move from authoritarian to democratic government can produce very negative side effects. It is possible to argue, for example, that the turmoil that has engulfed what was once of 10 things (ranging from good health to life without war) was most important to them. Only 6 percent of the respondents ranked "freedom" as most important, and that quality placed a poor eighth. When asked which of the 10 was least important, freedom ranked third at 20 percent.[1]

Such findings about Russians' values have a real impact on what they are willing to support. Vladimir Putin, the president of Russia, has proclaimed, "Democracy in Russia has been established forever."[2] Most observers are less certain than he is. For example, Freedom House, an organization that monitors civil rights and political liberties around the world, contends in a report, *Nations in Transit 2001*, that Russia has "regressed significantly in [its] democratization indicators over the last five years." The report goes on to say that while reasonably free elections "take place at regular intervals," it is also true that "elite manipulation and irregularities abound." Furthermore, "The rule of law remains weak. Democratic institutions are underdeveloped. The accountability of state officials to the citizens is minimal. And the legislature and the judiciary have little control over the executive." As for the citizenry, the report comments, "Society is more passive in the political sphere, and [self-] survival—more than any other factor—promotes public activism."[3]

These conditions have done little to harm Putin's stature among Russians, who still give him approval ratings above 70 percent. This lofty standing reflects the fact that Putin has brought some relief to the economic desperation that plagued Russia during the 1990s, and he also has reestablished an image of a strong leader in the Kremlin after years of ineffectual governance by the evermore feeble and erratic President Boris Yeltsin. These changes have made the average Russian willing to ignore what some see as Putin's restraints on Russia's democracy. "I could never imagine," commented Professor Andrei Zorin of the Russian State University, that "there is such a strong desire [among Russians] for a powerful leader." There is an "incredible consensus."[4]

That desire for strong leadership, and the Russians' willingness to accept restrictions on their civil liberties that goes with it, was very evident when, for example, Putin's government took over the country's last independent major television station in January 2002. A survey found that many Russians agreed that it was a "political move," yet the same poll recorded more than 70 percent of Russians continuing to express the belief that the president remains an advocate of democratic change. The reason for these conflicting views, one liberal Russian commentator lamented, is that "the public does not want to defend its interests."[5]

At least in the near term, the future of democracy in Russia rests in part on the degree to which President Putin supports or undermines it. One expert comments that Putin is "indifferent to democracy. He did not come to power with a grand master plan to re-create Soviet dictatorship—but when push comes to shove, and when it's in his interests, he's willing to transgress the democratic rules of the game." The future direction of Russian democracy also depends in part on the strength and skill of those Russians who are committed to supporting it. "We're going to see in the next coming months a real struggle between forces for democracy and Mr. Putin's government. And who wins that battle, I think, is still an open question," another analyst concludes.[6]

a much larger Yugoslavia is a result of the end of the authoritarian control of the communist government. Once that control was relaxed, the multiple ethnonational rivalries that had been dormant soon erupted into bloody conflict. Similar patterns can be seen in several African countries, in the former Soviet Union, and elsewhere in cases where independence or the coming of democracy has unleashed bloody ethnic clashes.

To this contention, supporters of global democratization respond that any bloodshed that it brings pales when compared to the brutality inflicted by authoritarian regimes. One study of "democide," the killing of unarmed residents by governments, demonstrates that the degree to which a government is totalitarian "largely accounts for the magnitude and intensity of genocide and mass murder" committed by that government. Therefore, the study reasons, "the best assurances against democide are democratic openness, political competition, leaders responsible to their people and limited government. In other words, power kills, and absolute power kills absolutely"(Rummel, 1995:25).

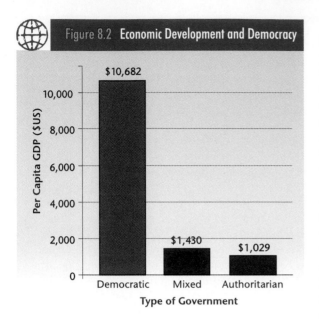

Figure 8.2   Economic Development and Democracy

Economic development and democracy are strongly related. Virtually all countries of even moderate levels of economic development are democratic. With the exception of a few Arab oil-producing states (such as Saudi Arabia), almost all authoritarian countries are quite poor. It may well be that helping countries develop economically is a necessary step toward helping them to achieve and maintain democratic political systems.

Democracy and International Security Formulating what has come to be termed **democratic peace theory**, the German philosopher Immanuel Kant argued in *Perpetual Peace* (1795) that the spread of democracy to all countries would eliminate war. Kant reasoned that a democratic peace would occur because "if the consent of the citizens is required in order to decide that war should be declared..., nothing is more natural than that they would be very cautious in commencing such a poor game, decreeing for themselves all the calamities of war."

Modern scholarship tends to confirm Kant's theory (Chan, 1997; Elman, 1997). Using empirical methods, contemporary studies have established, as one scholar puts it, that "democracies are unlikely to engage in any kind of militarized disputes with each other or to let any such disputes escalate into war. They rarely even skirmish" (Russett, 2000:232; Oneal & Russett, 1999; Schultz, 1999). This view is accepted by many scholars "as 'the closest thing to an empirical law' in world politics" that exists (Henderson, 1999:482; Thompson & Tucker, 1997).

Several caveats about democratic peace theory should be noted. First, democracies do go to war, although only with autocracies. The easy example is the United States, which is both a leading democracy and the country that has most often been at war since 1945. Second, not all scholars agree with the theory of democratic peace (Caprioli, 1998). For example, some analysts are skeptical that the absence of war between democracies is anything more than a historical anomaly that may not persist in the future (Gartzke, 1998). It may be then that future history will prove democratic theory wrong. For now, though, there is broad, albeit not complete, agreement among scholars that democracies have more peaceful relations with each other than do democracies with authoritarian states or authoritarian states with one another. From this perspective, even if a world in which all countries were democratic did not produce perpetual peace, as Kant thought, it might produce preponderant peace and, thus, should be promoted (Huntley, 1998).

NATIONAL AND OTHER INTERESTS

Whatever the system of governance of any state, a key factor that governs its affairs and interactions on the global stage are its interests. The concept of national interest is used almost universally to argue for or against any given policy. Most political leaders and citizens still argue that it is paramount. Certainly, most Russians thought it laudable when President Boris Yeltsin proclaimed that "the main goal of our foreign policy is consistent promotion of Russia's national interests."[9] Indeed, it is hard to imagine a national leader announcing that he or she had taken an important action that was counter to the national interest but in the world's interest. Even if such an aberration occurred, it is improbable that the leader would remain in office much longer.

National Interest as a Standard of Conduct

The use of national interest as a cornerstone of foreign policy is a key element of the road more traveled by in world politics. Realists contend that it is a wise basis for foreign policy. Henry Kissinger (1994:37), for one, regrets what he sees as the current U.S. "distrust of America's power, a preference for multilateral solutions and a reluctance to think in terms of national interest. All these impulses," Kissinger believes, "inhibit a realistic response to a world of multiple power centers and diverse conflicts."[10]

Realpolitik nationalists further contend that we live in a Darwinian political world, where people who do not promote their own interests will become prey for those who do. Nationalists further worry about alternative schemes of global governance. One such critic of globalism notes that in intellectual circles "anyone who is skeptical about international commitments today is apt to be dismissed as an isolationist crank." Nevertheless, he continues, globalization should be approached with great caution because "it holds out the prospect of an even more chaotic set of authorities, presiding over an even more chaotic world, at a greater remove from the issues that concern us here in the United States" (Rabkin, 1994:41, 47).

THE ISOLATIONIST
"AM I MY BROTHER'S KEEPER ?"

AMERICA WILL NEVER ACCEPT
THE CURSE OF CAIN!

Critics of the concept of national interest claim that it makes people indifferent to the world around them. There is a strong U.S. strain of isolationism that persuades some Americans that their country has few global interests or responsibilities. That persistent feeling is epitomized by this 1924 poster reacting to U.S. losses during World War I, in which, presumably, the United States had unwisely tried to be its brother's keeper. Showing some ignorance of the book of Genesis (4:11), the poster misses the point that God did not curse Cain for being his brother's keeper, but for killing him and then lying to God. The Creator had asked Cain where his brother Abel was, and had been told by Cain, "I do not know; am I my brother's keeper?" One has to wonder why anyone would imagine that God or nature considers allowing one's brothers (and sisters) to die by refusing to help to be a curse.

There are other analysts who reject the use of national interest as a guide for foreign policy. Their objections are:

There is no such thing as an objective national interest. Critics say, what is in the national interest is totally subjective and "approximates idiosyncrasy" (Kimura & Welch, 1998). Analysts can accurately point out that national interest has been used to describe every sort of good and evil. As used by decision makers, it is a projection of the perceptions of a particular regime or even a single political leader in a given international or domestic environment. Consider again the 1994 U.S. invasion of Haiti. President Clinton told the American people that what happens in Haiti "affects our national security interests" and it was therefore imperative that "we must act now" to "protect our interests."[11] A majority of the American people disagreed with Clinton. A survey just before Clinton's speech found that only 13 percent of respondents believed that "U.S. interests are threatened" and that only 34 percent favored U.S. participation in a multinational invasion.[12]

Using national interest as a basis of policy incorrectly assumes that there is a common interest. The contention here is that every society is a collection of diverse subgroups, each of which has its own set of interests based on its political identity (Chafetz, Spirtas, & Frankel, 1999). Furthermore, the concept of national interest inherently includes the assumption that if a collective interest can be determined, then that interest supersedes the interests of subgroups and individuals. Writing from the feminist perspective, for example, one scholar has noted that "the presumption of a similarity of interests between the sexes is an assumption" that cannot be taken for granted because "a growing body of scholarly work argues that... the political attitudes of men and women differ significantly" (Brandes, 1994:21).

National interest is inherently selfish and inevitably leads to conflict and inequity. The logic is simple. If you and I both pursue our national interests and those objectives are incompatible, then one likely possibility is that we will clash. Another possibility is that the interest of whichever of us is the more powerful will prevail. That is, power, not justice, will win out. Certainly, we might negotiate and compromise, as countries often do. But in an anarchical international system that emphasizes self-interest and self-help, the chances of a peaceful and equitable resolution are less than in a hierarchical domestic system that restrains the contending actors and offers institutions (such as courts) that can decide disputes if negotiation fails.

The way that national interest is applied frequently involves double standards. This criticism of the idea of national interest charges that countries often take actions that they would find objectionable if applied to themselves. President George W. Bush came into office advocating a fairly unilateralist U.S. policy. Yet he has bridled when other countries have insisted on their own unilateral interpretations of policy and have refused to support Washington on such issues as a proposed military campaign against Iraq. France's Prime Minister Lionel Jospin, for one, warned Washington against the "strong temptations of unilateralism" and criticized Bush for trying to "reduce the world's problems to the single dimension of the fight against terrorism" and for thinking "one can rely on solving them through the dominance of military means."

National interest is often shortsighted. This line of reason argues, for example, that because economically developed countries (EDCs) are mostly concerned with their immediate, domestic needs, they give precious little of their wealth to less developed countries (LDCs) in the form of foreign aid. This is shortsighted, some analysts contend, because in the long run the EDCs will become even more prosperous if the LDCs also become wealthy and can buy more goods and services from the EDCs. Furthermore, the argument goes, helping the LDCs now may avoid furthering the seething instability and violence born of poverty.

Alternatives to National Interest

Global interest as a standard of conduct is one alternative to national interest. Proponents of this standard contend that the world would be better served if people defined themselves politically as citizens of the world along with, or perhaps in place of, their sense of national political identification. One such advocate writes, "The apparent vast disjunction between what humankind must do to survive on the planet in a reasonably decent condition... and the way world society has typically worked throughout history... points to the need... for substantial evolution of world society in the direction of world community" (Brown, 1992:167).

Those who advocate a more global sense of our interests do not reject national interest as such. Instead, they say that national interest is usually defined in a counterproductive, shortsighted way, as noted above. In the long run, globalists argue, a more enlightened view of interests sees that a nation will be more secure and more prosperous if it helps other states also achieve peace and prosperity. This is the line of reasoning taken by those who contend that if the economically developed countries (EDCs) do more now to help less wealthy countries develop economically, the EDCs will win in the long run through many benefits, such as better trade markets and less political instability and violence. That is essentially the point that Han Seung-soo, president of the UN General Assembly, made in March 2002 to world leaders who had gathered in Monterrey, Mexico, to discuss world economic and political development. Especially "in the wake of September 11," the South Korean diplomat told the conference, it is imperative to recognize "that development, peace and security are inseparable," because the poorest countries are "the breeding ground for violence and despair."[13]

Individual interests are another alternative to national interest. Virtually all individuals are rightly concerned with their own welfare. To consider your own interests could be construed as the ultimate narrow-mindedness, but it also may be liberating.

It may be that your interests, even your political identification, may shift from issue to issue.

It is appropriate to ask, then, whether your individual interests, your nation's interests, and your world's interests are the same, mutually exclusive, or a mixed bag of congruencies and divergences. Only you, of course, can determine where your interests lie.

States and the Future

Sovereign, territorially defined states have not always existed, as we have noted. Therefore, they will not necessarily persist in the future. The questions are, Will they? Should they? The future of the state is one of the most hotly debated topics among scholars of international relations. As one such analyst explains, "Central to this future is the uncertain degree to which the sovereign state can adapt its behavior and role to a series of deterritorializing forces associated with markets, transnational social forces, cyberspace, demographic and environmental pressures, and urbanism" (Falk, 1999:35).

THE STATE: THE INDICTMENT

In rough division, there are two main lines of reasoning by those scholars who foresee or advocate the decline, perhaps the demise, of states as principal actors on the world stage. One contention is that states are obsolete; a second argument is that states are destructive (Lugo, 1996).

States Are Obsolete

The argument that states are obsolete begins with the premise that they were created in the middle of the last millennium as utilitarian political organizations to meet security, economic, and other specific needs and replaced the feudal and other forms of political organization that no longer worked effectively. "The nation-state is a rough and ready mechanism for furnishing a set of real services," one scholar writes. The problem, he continues, is that "the relation between what a state is supposed to do and what it actually does is increasingly slack" (Dunn, 1995:9). There is an interesting line of reasoning that suggests that states are too large to do the small things people want and need and too little to do the big things.

States Are Too Large   Some scholars believe that the claim of states to be sole legitimate international representatives of their citizens may be weakening because of the feeling of many people that their interests are ignored or subverted by states and other mega-organizations (such as big corporations) of the modern world. Political minorities are especially likely to feel powerless. This sense of loss of individual and group power and people's concern about their diversity being homogenized into a bland monoculture intensify when talk about world or regional government and a uniculture in the global village begins. This may lead to the Tribalism tendency and propel people to join or identify with movements or organizations that are more accessible and that share their values.

States Are Too Small   It may also (or alternatively) be that states are too limited to deal with the greatest problems facing humankind (Cusimano, 1998). As one study puts it, "the separate nation-states have become ever more impotent in dealing on their own... with material and political realities that are increasingly threatening the safety and well-being of their citizens" (Brown, 1998:3).

Providing physical safety is one key role of the state. Yet the ability of states to protect their citizens is limited at best (Betts, 1998; Keller & Rothchild, 1996). If we date the sovereign-state system to its symbolic beginning in 1648 with the Treaty of Westphalia, it is possible to argue that the record that states have of protecting their people is horrendous and getting worse. Since the mid-1600s, as shown in Figure 12.1 on page 332, there have been almost 600 wars that have killed around 144 million people. Moreover, the victim totals have risen rapidly through the centuries as humankind "improved" its killing capabilities. Therefore, the question is, in an era of nuclear, chemical, and biological weapons of mass destruction, against which there is little or no defense, does the state protect people or simply define them as targets for other states in an anarchical international system?

Providing economic prosperity is a second key role of the state. The same genre of questions applies to the economic functions of a state. The tidal wave of trade and capital that moves across national borders means that states are increasingly less able to provide for the prosperity of their residents. Jobs are won or lost depending on a variety of factors, such as where transnational corporations decided to set up manufacturing, over which national governments have little or no control.

Providing for the general welfare is a third key role of the state. Health is one such concern, and states as independent entities are finding themselves increasingly unable to contain the spread of disease in an era when people and products that may carry the threat of disease with them move quickly and in massive numbers around the globe.

AIDS has become the greatest transnational health disaster since the bubonic plague epidemic, commonly called the Black Death, spread throughout Europe. Beginning in 1347 and over the next several years, the plague killed 25 million people, about one-third of Europe's population. AIDS, thought to have its origins in Africa, threatens people everywhere. According to *AIDS Epidemic Update, December 2001*, a report issued jointly by the UN and the World Health Organization, more than 60 million people have been infected by the HIV virus and nearly one-third of those have died of AIDS-related diseases since the epidemic began. The morbid statistics are getting worse. In 2001, 40 million people were HIV positive, about 5 million new cases were reported that year, and 3 million people died. Such statistics prompted the Clinton administration to declare in 2000 that AIDS was a threat to national security. "The heart of the security agenda is protecting lives," explained Vice President Al Gore, "and we now know that the number of people who will die of AIDS in the first decade of the twenty-first century will rival the number that died in all the wars in all the decades of the twentieth century."[14]

Some observers argue that states are too limited to address such global problems as nuclear weapons, environmental degradation, economic interdependence, and the worldwide spread of diseases. AIDS is one such transnational disease, and the global approach that many advocate is represented here by the AIDS Ribbon unveiled at the beginning of the XIII International AIDS Conference, which met in Durban, South Africa, during July 2000.

Whether it is AIDS or another microbial enemy, the reality, according to a U.S. physician, is that "Today, in 30 hours, you can literally travel to the other side of the world. And likewise, while you are there, you can pick up a germ or a micro-organism that may not exist on this side of the globe and within 30 hours you can have that back in the United States."[15] National borders provide increasingly scant protection to these globally transportable diseases, which, if they are to be contained, must be attacked through an international effort.

States Are Destructive

The essence of the sovereign state is to pursue its interests. Those interests clash. There is little in the system other than power to determine which states' interests will prevail. Therefore, the argument continues, states too often use economic coercion or military force to settle disputes. Critics of the state system contend that whatever the wins and losses for states, the most likely losers are average citizens, who bear the brunt of war and economic sanctions to a far greater degree than do leaders.

To make matters worse, states are often perpetrators of violence on those they are supposed to protect (Burgess, 1998). "Political regimes—governments—have probably murdered nearly 170 million of their own citizens and foreigners in this century—about four times the number killed in all international and domestic wars and revolutions," one scholar charges (Rummel, 1995:3).

THE STATE: THE DEFENSE

While those who predict or advocate the diminishment or demise of the state as a primary political organization are able to make a strong case, it is hardly an open-and-shut case leading to a verdict against the state.

First, as we noted in chapter 6, nationalism has proven resilient, and its political vehicle, the state, still has many resources at its disposal. This leads some analysts to doubt the substantial weakening, much less the disappearance, of states as sovereign actors. As two such scholars write, "Reports of its demise notwithstanding, sovereignty appears to us to be prospering, not declining.... It still serves as an indispensable component of international politics" (Fowler & Bunck, 1995:163). Another scholar observes that while borders are becoming less and less meaningful as barriers to economic interchange, the flow of information, and some other transnational functions, "states are responding to globalization by attempting to restore meaning to national borders, not as barriers to entry, but as boundaries demarcating distinct political communities" (Goff, 2000:533).

Second, it may be possible that states can adjust to the new realities by learning to cooperate and live in peace with other countries. Analysts who hold this view point to the increasing creation of and membership in numerous IGOs, like the WTO, as evidence that states are willing to give up some of their sovereignty in return for the benefits provided by free trade and other transnational interactions.

Third, states are arguably being strengthened as increasingly complex domestic and international systems create new demands for services. From this perspective, globalization and the strength of states "may be mutually reinforcing rather than antagonistic" (Weiss, 1998:204). "Empirical evidence demonstrates that the roles of the state are changing rather than diminishing," according to two scholars. "The state remains crucially involved in a wide range of problems," they continue, and "in each of these areas, specific initiatives may make state policies more efficient... as the roles of the nation-state continue to evolve" (Turner & Corbacho, 2000:118–119).

Fourth, sovereignty has always been a relative, not an absolute principle and a dynamic, rather than static concept (Sorensen, 1999). States and their leaders have long violated the principle when it suited their interests in what one scholar terms "organized hypocrisy" (Krasner, 1999). This leads some analysts to conclude that states will survive by adapting the parameters of sovereignty to international norms.

Fifth, it is possible to defend sovereign states as better than the other forms of political organization. States do provide some level of defense, and some states have been relatively effective at shielding their citizens from the ravages of war. Sometimes, as with the United States, that is a matter of power. But in other cases, it is related to geography, diplomatic skill, or a simple resolution not to take sides under almost any circumstances. Sweden and Switzerland, for example, managed to avoid becoming involved in any war, including either world war, during the twentieth century.

Sixth, it is yet to be proven that international governmental organizations (IGOs) provide an effective alternative to the state. Peacekeeping by the United Nations and other IGOs has had successes, but also notable failures. The WTO and other economic IGOs are under attack for benefiting rich countries, corporations, and individuals at the expense of less developed countries, small businesses, and workers. It may well be, as we will discuss in the next chapter, that IGOs can prove to be more effective and just instruments of governance as they evolve. That remains an open question, though.

THE STATE: THE VERDICT

For now, the jury is still out on whether states will and should continue to dominate the political system and be the principal focus of political identity. States continue to exercise great political strength and most of them retain the loyalty of most of their citizens. Yet it is also true that the state exists in a rapidly changing political environment that is creating great pressures, whether they be those of Tribalism or McWorld. The state will not survive based on its record or on residual loyalties. Instead, as one scholar notes, "history sides with no one.... [The] lesson to be drawn [from the rise and evolution of states] is that all institutions are susceptible to challenges." Therefore, the sustainability of states depends in substantial part on whether or not they provide "efficient responses to such challenges" (Spruyt, 1994:185).

Where does this leave the future of sovereign states at the dawn of the twenty-first century? The answer that most political scientists would probably give is that "although the system of sovereign states is likely to continue [in the foreseeable future] as the dominant structure in world politics, the content of world politics is changing" (Keohane & Nye, 1999:118). Those changes are well captured in the view of one scholar that "a new epoch is evolving. It is an epoch of multiple contradictions:... States are changing, but they are not disappearing. State sovereignty has eroded, but it is still vigorously asserted. Governments are weaker, but they can still throw their weight around.... Borders still keep out intruders, but they are also more porous. Landscapes are giving way to ethnoscapes, mediascapes, ideoscapes, technoscapes, and financescapes, but territoriality is still a central preoccupation for many people" (Rosenau, 1998:18).

Chapter Summary

1. States are the most important political actors. States as political organizations have these defining characteristics: sovereignty, territory, population, diplomatic recognition, internal organization, and domestic support.

2. The sovereign territorial state is a relatively modern form of political organization. States emerged in the West in the aftermath of the decline of the local authority of the feudal system and the universalistic authority of the Roman Catholic Church and the Holy Roman Empire.

3. There are various authoritarian and democratic theories of governance that shape the state as a core political organization.

4. Monarchism, theocracy, communism applied politically, and fascism are four forms of authoritarian governance. The percentage of countries ruled by authoritarian regimes has declined, but dictatorial governments are still common.

5. Democracy is a complex concept. Different procedural and substantive standards serve as a basis to determine whether or not a political system is democratic.

6. There are also disputes over when it is possible or advisable to press all countries to quickly adopt democratic forms of government.

7. Democratic theorists and societies also disagree over the proper balance between individualism and communitarianism in a democracy.

8. Democratic peace theory argues that democracies are unlikely to enter into conflict with one another. Why democracies do not fight one another remains disputed among scholars, with explanations given from institutional, normative, and interest perspectives.

9. There are many types of interests—national, state, governmental, global, and individual—and it is important to distinguish among them. National interest has been and is the traditional approach to determining international activity, but there are some people who contend that national interest is synonymous with destructive self-promotion and should be diminished or even abandoned.

10. The future of the state is a hotly debated topic among scholars of international relations.

11. Some analysts predict the demise of states as principal actors, claiming that states are obsolete and destructive.

12. Other analysts of nationalism contend that the state is durable and has many resources at its disposal. These analysts doubt that the states will weaken substantially or disappear as sovereign actors.

13. One key question that will help determine the fate of states is whether they can cooperate to address global problems, such as environmental degradation.

14. A second key question that will help determine the fate of states is whether they can remain at peace in an era of nuclear arms and other weapons of mass destruction.

Chapter 9

International Organization: The Alternative Structure

Friendly counsel cuts off many foes.

Shakespeare, *Henry VI, Part 1*

[The United Nations is] group therapy for the world.

Antonio Montiero, Portuguese ambassador to the UN

No nation needs to face or fight alone the threats which this organization was established to diffuse.

UN secretary-general Kofi Annan

Chapter Objectives

After completing this chapter, you should be able to:

- Examine the nature and development of international organization as an alternative form of organizing and conducting international relations.
- Characterize the roots of international organization as a primarily modern phenomenon.
- Trace the growth of intergovernmental organizations and nongovernmental organizations during the twentieth century.
- Summarize the traditional goals and activities of international organizations.
- Examine and discuss the current and expanding roles of IGOs.
- Discuss the concept of world and regional government.
- Explain the prospect of effective supranational organizations for international governance, making reference to the evolution of the European Union.
- Describe IGO structure by evaluating the experience of the United Nations.
- Identify the promotion of international peace and security as the primary IGO activity, as exemplified by the United Nations.
- Outline major social, economic, environmental, and other roles of intergovernmental organizations.
- Speculate regarding the shape of international organization in the future.

The sovereign state has been the primary actor in world politics and the essential building block of the state-based international system. Indeed, it is hard to conceive of any other form of organizing and conducting international relations. Yet there are alternatives.

International organization is one of these alternatives. Some analysts are convinced that basing global relations on self-interested states operating in an anarchical international system is outmoded and even dangerous. As an alternative, these observers believe that international organizations can and should begin to regulate the behavior of states, and that working through these organizations is the best way to address world problems. Those who take this view would join in the counsel given by Shakespeare in *Henry VI, Part III*: "Now join your hands, and with your hands your hearts." Such advice may be right. It is just possible that ongoing organizations will serve as prototypes or building blocks for a future, higher form of political loyalty and activity.

Surrendering some of your country's sovereignty to an international organization may seem unsettling. But it is neither inherently wrong, nor unheard of in today's world. In fact, the growth in the number, functions, and authority of international organizations is one of the most important trends in international relations. To explore this change in governance, this chapter takes up international organizations. The European Union, as a regional organization, and the United Nations, as a global organization, will be given particular attention to illustrate what is and what might be. Shakespeare tells us in *Hamlet* that "we know what we are, but not what we can be." Perhaps he was correct in saying that we cannot know for sure what we can be, but we surely can imagine what we might be if we keep our minds open to new ideas.

The Origins, Growth, and Roles of International Organization

The concept of international organization is not a new one, although the practice of having a continuous international organization is a relatively recent advance in the conduct of international relations. Now there are a growing number of permanent international organizations. They can be divided geographically into global or regional organizations and grouped by functions into general or specialized international organizations, as shown in Table 9.1. Whatever their specifics, though, all the organizations that we will discuss in this chapter share the fact that their memberships consist of national governments. Therefore, they are termed international **intergovernmental organizations (IGOs)**. They are distinct from the transnational (or international) **nongovernmental organizations (NGOs)**, whose members consist of private individuals or groups.

Table 9.1 Types and Examples of IGOs

	Purpose	
Geography	General	Specialized
Global	United Nations	World Trade Organization
Regional	European Union	Arab Monetary Fund

International intergovernmental organizations (IGOs) can be classified according to whether they are general purpose, dealing with many issues, or specialized, dealing with a specific concern. Another way of dividing IGOs is into global and regional organizations.

The Peace Conferences held at The Hague, the Netherlands, in 1899 and 1907 marked the first step toward establishing a global organization that evolved through the League of Nations to the current United Nations. The conferences were attended by the United States, and this photo shows some of the American delegates who had just arrived in Rotterdam, the Netherlands.

THE ORIGINS OF IGOs

IGOs are primarily a modern phenomenon. Nearly all of them were created in the last 50 years or so. Yet the origins of IGOs extend far back in history to three main sources.

Belief in a Community of Humankind

The origins of IGOs are rooted in part in a universalistic concept of humankind that extends back to 300 B.C. and the Stoics, as discussed in chapter 7. Philosophers such as William Penn (1644–1718) and Immanuel Kant (1724–1804) argued that the way to create a community of humankind was through general international organizations (Pagden, 1998; Bohman & Lutz-Bachmann, 1997). The first example of an IGO based on this goal was the **Hague system**, named for the 1899 and 1907 peace conferences held at that city in the Netherlands (Best, 1999). The 1907 conference was more comprehensive, with 44 European, North American, and Latin American states participating. Organizationally, the Hague system included a rudimentary general assembly and a judicial system. The conferences also adopted a series of standards to limit the conduct of war.

The next step on the path was the creation of the **League of Nations** after World War I. The League had a more developed organizational structure than that of the Hague system. It was intended mainly as a peacekeeping organization, although it did have some elements aimed at social and economic cooperation. Unfortunately, the League could not survive the turbulent post–World War era that included the Great Depression and the rise of militant fascism. After only two decades of frustrated existence, the League died in the rubble of World War II.

The **United Nations (UN)** is the latest, and most advanced, developmental stage of universal concern with the human condition. Like the League of Nations, the UN was established mainly to maintain peace. Nevertheless, it has increasingly become involved in a broad range of issues that encompasses almost all the world's concerns. In addition, the UN and its predecessor, the League, represent the coming together of all the root systems of international organizations. They are more properly seen as the emergent saplings of extensive cooperation and integration.

Big-Power Peacekeeping

IGOs also evolved from the idea that powerful countries have a special responsibility to cooperate and preserve peace. Hugo Grotius, the "father of international law," suggested as early as 1625 in his classic *On the Law of War and Peace* that the major Christian powers cooperate to mediate or arbitrate the disputes of others or even, if required, to compel warring parties to accept an equitable peace.

This idea first took on substance with the Concert of Europe. This informal coalition of the major European powers and the following balance-of-(big)-power diplomacy managed generally to keep the peace for the century between the fall of Napoleon in 1815 and the outbreak of World War I in 1914.

The philosophy of big-power responsibility (and authority) carried over to the Council of the League of Nations. It had authority (Covenant Article 4) to deal "with any matter within the sphere of activity of the League or affecting the peace of the world." Significantly, five of the nine seats on the council were permanently assigned to the principal victors of World War I. The council was thus a continuation of the Concert of Europe concept.

When the United Nations succeeded the League of Nations, the special status and responsibilities of the big powers in the League were transferred to the UN Security Council (UNSC). Like the Council in the League, the UNSC is the main peacekeeping organ and includes permanent membership for five major powers (China, France, Great Britain, Russia, and the United States), an arrangement that is a conceptual descendant of the Concert of Europe.

Pragmatic Cooperation

Sheer necessity has also driven the evolution of IGOs. An increasingly complex and intertwined world has necessitated the creation of specialized agencies to deal with specific economic and social problems. The six-member Central Commission for the Navigation of the Rhine, established in 1815, is the oldest surviving IGO, and the International Telegraphic (now Telecommunications) Union (1865) is the oldest surviving IGO with global membership. As detailed below, the growth of specialized IGOs and NGOs has been phenomenal. This aspect of international activity is also reflected in the UN through the 20 specialized agencies associated with the world body.

THE GROWTH OF IGOs

The twentieth century saw rapid growth in the number of all types of IGOs. Just in terms of sheer quantity, the number of well-established IGOs increased sevenfold from 37 in 1909 to 251 in 2000, according to the Union of International Associations. Indeed, about one-third of all major IGOs in 2000 were younger than the average American, whose age in 2000 was 35.

Even more important than the quantitative growth of IGOs is the expanding roles that they play. More and more common governmental functions are being dealt with by IGOs. Indeed, there are now few if any major political issues that are not addressed at the international level by one or more IGOs. In some cases, existing IGOs take up new roles. Just as the U.S. government and other national governments have assumed new areas of responsibility over the years as problems arose, so has the United Nations moved to create units to deal with terrorism, biological warfare, environmental degradation, and a range of issues that were not part of the UN's realm when it was founded.

At other times, new areas of global concern are dealt with by creating new IGOs. For example, the development of satellites and the ability to communicate through them and the need to coordinate this capability led to the establishment of the International Mobile Satellite Organization (IMMARSAT) in 1979.

Theories of IGO Growth

A first step in analyzing the growth in the number of IGOs and the expansion of their roles is to look at two ideas about how IGOs do and should develop. These two schools of thought are functionalism and neofunctionalism.

Functionalism The term **functionalism** represents the idea that the way to global cooperation is through a "bottom-up," evolutionary approach that begins with limited, pragmatic cooperation on narrow, nonpolitical issues. One such issue was how to deliver the mail internationally. To solve that problem, countries cooperated to found the Universal Postal Union in 1874. Each such instance of cooperation serves as a building block to achieve broader cooperation on more and more politically sensitive issues. Plato's description of "necessity" as "the mother of invention" in *The Republic* (ca. 380 B.C.) might well serve as a motto for modern functionalists.

Functionalists support their view about how global cooperation has been and is being achieved by pointing to hundreds, even thousands, of IGOs, multilateral treaties, NGOs, and other vehicles that have been pragmatically put in place to deal with specific international concerns. Functionalists further hold that by cooperating in specific, usually nonpolitical areas, countries and people can learn to trust one another. This, in turn, will lead to ever broader and ever higher levels of cooperation on the path to comprehensive cooperation or even global government.

Neofunctionalism The "top-down" approach to solving world problems is called **neofunctionalism**. Its advocates are skeptical about the functionalist belief that nonpolitical cooperation can, by itself, lead eventually to full political cooperation and to the elimination of international conflict and self-interested state action. Neofunctionalists also worry that the functionalists' evolutionary approach will not move quickly enough to head off many of the world's looming problems. Therefore, neofunctionalists argue for immediately establishing IGOs and giving them enough independence and resources so that they can address political issues with an eye to fostering even greater cooperation.

Reasons for Growth

The twentieth century's rapid growth of international organizations, both in number and in scope of activity, is the result of a number of both functionalist and neofunctionalist forces. Those forces were summarized by two scholars who examined why states act through international organizations (IOs). Their conclusion was that "by taking advantage… of IOs, states are able to achieve goals that they cannot accomplish [alone]" (Abbot & Snidal, 1998:29). In other words, the growth of international organizations has occurred because countries have found that they need them and that they work. We can note six specific causes for this expansion:

Increased international contact is one cause. The revolutions in communications and transportation technologies have brought the states of the world into much closer contact. These interchanges need organizational structures in order to become routine and regulated. The International Telegraphic Union, founded over a century ago, has been joined in more modern times by the IMMARSAT and many others.

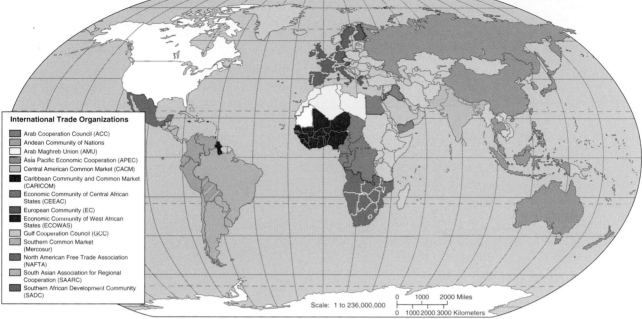

International Trade Organizations

- Arab Cooperation Council (ACC)
- Andean Community of Nations
- Arab Maghreb Union (AMU)
- Asia Pacific Economic Cooperation (APEC)
- Central American Common Market (CACM)
- Caribbean Community and Common Market (CARICOM)
- Economic Community of Central African States (CEEAC)
- European Community (EC)
- Economic Community of West African States (ECOWAS)
- Gulf Cooperation Council (GCC)
- Southern Common Market (Mercosur)
- North American Free Trade Association (NAFTA)
- South Asian Association for Regional Cooperation (SAARC)
- Southern African Development Community (SADC)

Scale: 1 to 236,000,000

0   1000   2000 Miles
0 1000 2000 3000 Kilometers

Pragmatic necessity is one reason for the rapid growth of many types of IGOs. One response to the fast expansion of global trade has been the establishment of a large number of regional trade organizations. None of these existed fifty years ago; now virtually every country is in at least one of them. The term "national economy" is rapidly becoming outmoded.

Increased global interdependence, particularly in the economic sphere, is a second factor that has fostered a variety of IGOs designed to deal with this phenomenon (Diehl, 1997). The International Monetary Fund (IMF) and the World Bank are just two examples. Regional trade and monetary organizations, cartels, and, to a degree, multinational corporations are other examples.

The expansion of transnational problems that affect many states and require solutions that are beyond the resources of any single state is a third cause of the growth of international organizations. One such issue (and its associated IGO) is nuclear proliferation (International Atomic Energy Agency).

The failure of the current state-centered system to provide security is a fourth incentive for the expansion of IGOs. The agony of two world wars, for instance, convinced many that peace was not safe in the hands of nation-states. The United Nations is the latest attempt to organize for the preservation of peace. The continuing problems in health, food, human rights, and other areas have also spurred the organization of IGOs.

The effort of small states to gain strength through joint action is a fifth factor. The concentration of military and economic power in a handful of countries has led less powerful actors to join coalitions in an attempt to influence events. Vulnerability has thus motivated countries to come together in such organizations as the 113-member Nonaligned Movement (NAM) and the Group of 77, a now-132-member organization of less developed countries (LDCs) interested in promoting economic cooperation and development. In some ways the end of the cold war has increased this vulnerability. As a Western diplomat attending a NAM meeting commented, "A lot of these tiny nations are praying the movement and organizations like it can survive and advocate on their behalf.... No one pays attention to them any more."[1]

The successes of international organizations is a sixth reason for their expansion. People and countries have learned that they can sometimes work together internationally, and this has created even more IGOs and NGOs to help address an ever greater range of transnational issues.

ROLES THAT IGOs PLAY

Given the expanding number and importance of international organizations, we should ask ourselves what it is that we want IGOs to do. So far, IGOs have mostly played limited, traditional roles. There are, however, a range of more far-reaching activities that some people believe IGOs can and should take up. It is possible to arrange these roles along a scale that measures how close each is to the traditional road or to the alternative road of international politics. Starting at the traditional end of the scale and moving toward the alternative end, the four roles are: interactive arena, creator and center of cooperation, independent international actor, and supranational organization.

Interactive Arena

The most common use of IGOs is to provide an interactive arena in which member-states pursue their individual national interests. This approach is rarely stated openly, but it is obvious in the struggles within the UN and other IGOs, where countries and blocs of countries wage political struggles with a vengeance. For example, research on the UN General Assembly since the end of the cold war indicates that its principal dimension of conflict is between the dominant West, led by the United States, and a "counterhegemonic" bloc of countries (Voeten, 2000:185).

The use of IGOs to gain national advantage is somewhat contradictory to the purpose of these supposedly cooperative organizations and has disadvantages. One negative factor is that it sometimes transforms IGOs into another scene of struggle rather than utilizing them to enhance cooperation. Furthermore, countries are apt to reduce or withdraw their support from an international organization that does not serve their narrow national interests.

The use of IGOs as an interactive arena does, however, have advantages. One is based on the theory that international integration can advance even when IGOs are the arena for self-interested national interaction. The reasoning is that even when realpolitik is the starting point, the process that occurs in an IGO fosters the habit of cooperation and compromise.

A second advantage is that sometimes, as in the case of reversing Iraq's aggression against Kuwait in 1990, using the IGO to authorize action makes it politically easier to take. Third, debate and diplomatic maneuver may even provide a forum for diplomatic struggle. This role of providing an alternative to the battlefield may promote the resolution of disputes without violence. As Winston Churchill put it once, "To jaw-jaw is better than to war-war."[2]

Creator and Center of Cooperation

A second role that IGOs perform is to promote and facilitate cooperation among states and other international actors. Secretary-General Kofi Annan has observed correctly that the UN's "member-states face a wide range of new and unprecedented threats and challenges. Many of them transcend borders. They are beyond the power of any single nation to address on its own."[3] Therefore, countries have found it increasingly necessary to cooperate to address physical security, the environment, the economy, and a range of other concerns. The Council of the Baltic Sea States, the International Civil Aviation Organization, and a host of other IGOs were

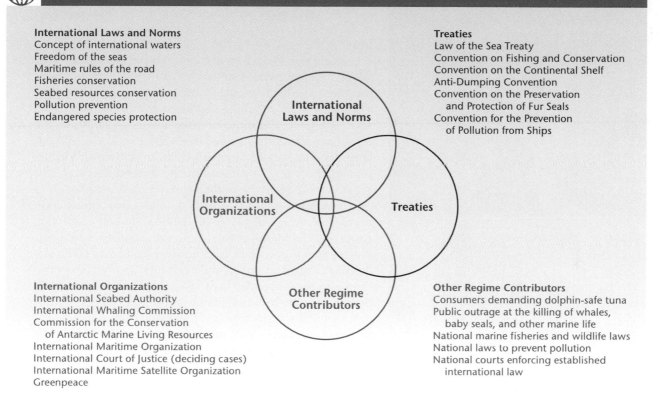

Figure 9.1 **Regimes for Oceans and Seas**

International Laws and Norms
Concept of international waters
Freedom of the seas
Maritime rules of the road
Fisheries conservation
Seabed resources conservation
Pollution prevention
Endangered species protection

Treaties
Law of the Sea Treaty
Convention on Fishing and Conservation
Convention on the Continental Shelf
Anti-Dumping Convention
Convention on the Preservation
   and Protection of Fur Seals
Convention for the Prevention
   of Pollution from Ships

International Organizations
International Seabed Authority
International Whaling Commission
Commission for the Conservation
   of Antarctic Marine Living Resources
International Maritime Organization
International Court of Justice (deciding cases)
International Maritime Satellite Organization
Greenpeace

Other Regime Contributors
Consumers demanding dolphin-safe tuna
Public outrage at the killing of whales,
   baby seals, and other marine life
National marine fisheries and wildlife laws
National laws to prevent pollution
National courts enforcing established
   international law

Entries are only a sample of all possibilities.

The concept of an international regime represents the nexus of a range of laws and actors that regulate a particular area of concern. This figure shows some of the elements of the expanding regime for oceans and seas.

all established to address specific needs and, through their operations, to promote further cooperation.

Regime Theory What sometimes occurs is that narrow cooperation expands into more complex forms of interdependence. International regimes are one such development (Hasenclever & Mayer, 1997). A regime is not a single organization. Instead, a **regime** is a collective noun that designates a complex of norms, rules, processes, and organizations that, in sum, have evolved to help to govern the behavior of states and other international actors in an area of international concern such as the use and protection of international bodies of water (Cortell & Davis, 1996). Some regimes may encompass cooperative relations within a region. Other regimes are global, and we will use one of these, the regime for oceans and seas, as an example.

The Regime for Oceans and Seas The regime that is currently evolving to govern the uses of the world's oceans and other bodies of international water is represented in Figure 9.1. Note the regime's complex array of organizations, rules, and norms that promote international cooperation in a broad area of maritime regulation. Navigation, pollution, seabed mining, and fisheries are all areas of expanded international discussion, rule-making, and cooperation. The Law of the Sea Treaty proclaims that the oceans and seabed are a "common heritage of mankind," to be shared according to "a just and equitable economic order." To that end, the treaty

Activists with Greenpeace, an environmentalist NGO, are trying to prevent the Japanese whaler *Nishin Maru* from hoisting a minke whale carcass aboard. Greenpeace is a part of a complex group of international and national actors, treaties, international norms, and other elements that make up the regime for oceans and seas, as illustrated in Figure 9.1.

contains provisions for increased international regulation of mining and other uses of the oceans' floors. It established (as of 1994) the International Seabed Authority, headquartered in Jamaica, to supervise the procedures and rules of the treaty.

In addition to the Law of the Sea Treaty, the regime of the oceans and seas extends to include many other organizations and rules. The International Maritime Organization has sponsored agreements regarding safeguards against oil spills in the seas. As a result, the annual average volume of spills into the oceans and seas during the late 1990s fell over 80 percent from what it had been in the early 1970s. The International Whaling Commission, the Convention on the Preservation and Protection of Fur Seals, the Commission for the Conservation of Antarctic Marine Living Resources, and other efforts have begun the process of protecting marine life and conserving resources. The Montreal Guidelines on Land-Based Pollution suggest ways to avoid fertilizer and other land-based pollutants from running off into rivers and bays and then into the oceans. Countries have expanded their conservation zones to regulate fishing. The South Pacific Forum has limited the use of drift nets that indiscriminately catch and kill marine life. NGOs such as Greenpeace have pressed to protect the world seas. Dolphins are killed less frequently because many consumers only buy cans of tuna that display the "dolphin safe" logo. The list of multilateral lawmaking treaties, IGOs, NGOs, national efforts, and other programs that regulate the use of the seas could go on. The point is that while each activity and organization is separate, they are, in combination, an ever-expanding network that constitutes a developing regime of the seas. Gradually, what swims in the sea, what lies under it, the availability of international waters as a dumping ground, the conduct of ships on the seas, and myriad other matters that were once the focus of international struggles over sovereign utilization are falling within the regime for oceans and seas.

Independent International Actor

The third of the existing and possible IGO roles is that of an independent international actor. This role is located toward the alternative end of the traditional-alternative scale of IGO activities. Technically, what any IGO does is controlled by the wishes and votes of its members. In reality, many IGOs develop strong, relatively permanent administrative staffs. These individuals often identify with the organization and try to increase its authority and role. Global expectations—such as "the UN should do something"—add to the sense that an IGO may be a force unto itself. Soon, to use an old phrase, the whole (of the IGO) becomes more than the sum of its (member-country) parts. We will explore this role more fully when we discuss the United Nations later in the chapter. But insofar as IGOs do play an independent role, proponents of this approach argue that it should be one mainly of mediation and conciliation rather than coercion. The object is to teach and allow, not to force, states to work together.

To a degree, organizational independence is intended and established in the charters of various IGOs. The International Court of Justice (ICJ) was created to act independently. The UN Charter directs that the secretary-general and his or her staff "shall not seek or receive instructions from any government or from any other authority external to the organization." And the European Parliament is a unique example of an IGO assembly whose representatives are popularly elected rather than appointed and directed by national governments.

Supranational Organization

It may also be possible for IGOs to play a fourth role: **supranational organization**. This means that the international organization has authority over its members, which, therefore, are subordinate units. Theoretically, some IGOs possess a degree of supranationalism and can obligate members to take certain actions. In reality, supranationalism is extremely limited. Few states concede any significant part of their sovereignty to any IGO. But there are some signs that this is giving way to limited acceptance of international authority. As we will see in chapter 11 on international law, for instance, countries normally abide by some aspects of international law, even at times when it conflicts with their domestic law or their immediate interests.

The extreme limits on supranationalism now does not mean, however, that the authority of IGOs cannot expand. There are many people who believe that the world is moving and should continue to move toward a more established form of international government. Such supranational government could be regional or global in scope.

World Government The most far-reaching alternative to the current state-based international system is the possibility of a **world government** that governs a global political system (Zolo, 1997). One argument in favor of such an idea is that the current system based on sovereign states is destructive because of the continuance of military, economic, and diplomatic rivalries among states in an anarchical system. Advocates of world government also contend that a world divided among almost 200 sovereign states is inadequate to address the environmental threat, international global terrorism, the regulation of multinational corporations, and a range of other global problems.

There is also strong opposition to the one-world idea. Critics argue that, first, there are practical barriers to world government. The assumption here is that nationalism has too strong a hold and that neither political leaders nor masses would be willing to surrender independence to a universal body (Taylor, 1999). Are we ready to "pledge allegiance to the United States of the World"? Second, critics of the world government movement pose political objections. They worry about the concentration of power that would be necessary to enforce international law and to address the world's monumental economic and social problems. A third doubt is whether any such government, even given unprecedented power, could succeed in solving world problems any better than states can. Fourth, some skeptics further argue that centralization would inevitably diminish desirable cultural diversity and political experimentation in the world. A fifth criticism of the world government movement is that it diverts attention from more reasonable avenues of international cooperation, such as the United Nations and other existing IGOs.

Gradually through history our primary political loyalty has shifted from smaller units such as tribes and villages to larger units, especially countries. Some people believe that this trend should continue and that a world government should be established. The image of children starting out their day by saying "I pledge allegiance to the flag of the United States of the World" may seem strange, but a global government may evolve.

Regional Government The idea of **regional government** meets some of the objections to global government. Regions would still have to bring heterogeneous peoples together and overcome nationalism, but the regional diversity is less severe than is global heterogeneity. Moreover, regional governments would allow for greater cultural diversity and political experimentation than would a global government. Some proponents of regional governments also suggest that they might serve as a stepping-stone toward world government.

Structuring a World or Regional Government Global government might take one of three forms based on the degree of power sharing between the central government and the subunits. *Centralized government* is one structure. In such a system, countries would be nonsovereign subunits that serve only administrative purposes. *Federal government* would be a less dramatic alternative. A federal government is one in which the central authority and the member units share power. Models of federalism include the relations between the United States and its 50 states and between Canada and its 10 provinces. *Confederal government* is the least centralized of the three arrangements. In a confederal government, members are highly interdependent and join together in a weak directorate organization while retaining all or most of their sovereign authority. The European Union provides a current example of what is, or at least approaches, a **confederation**.

Whatever one's views about whether international governance should occur at the regional or global level—or at all, for that matter—the reality is that there is movement toward supranational organization. To further explore the current and expanding roles of IGOs, we can break them down into two groups, regional IGOs and global IGOs, with a focus on the most prominent regional IGO, the European Union, and the most important global IGO, the United Nations.

Regional IGOs: Focus on the European Union

The growth of regional IGOs has been striking (Mansfield & Milner, 1999; Mace & Therien, 1996). Prior to World War II there were no prominent regional IGOs. Now there are many. Most of these are relatively specialized, with regional economic IGOs, such as the Arab Cooperation Council, the most numerous. Other regional IGOs are general purpose and deal with a range of issues. These include, for example, the Organization of African Unity (OAU) and the Organization of American States (OAS).

Another noteworthy development regarding regional IGOs is that some of them are transitioning from specialized to general purpose organizations. The Association of Southeast Asian Nations (ASEAN) was founded in 1967 to promote regional economic cooperation. More recently, though, ASEAN has begun to take on a greater political tinge, and, in particular, may serve as a political and defensive counterweight to China in the region (Ahmad & Ghoshal, 1999). A more obvious change in role is evident for the Economic Community of West African States (ECOWAS). It was established in 1975 to facilitate economic interchange, but in the 1990s ECOWAS took on a very different function when it intervened in the civil wars raging in Liberia and Sierra Leone.

Beyond any of these examples of regional IGOs, the best example of what is possible is the regionalism in Europe. There, the European Union, with its 15 member-countries, has moved toward full economic integration. It has also traveled in the direction of considerable political cooperation (McCormick, 1999).

THE ORIGINS AND EVOLUTION OF THE EUROPEAN UNION

The **European Union (EU)** has evolved through several stages. One way to keep track of the changes in the structure and purpose of the EU described in the following paragraphs is to note the changes in the names of the successive organizations. "What's in a name?" you might ask, echoing Shakespeare's heroine in *Romeo and Juliet*. As she discovered, the names Capulet and Montague proved important. So too, the name changes leading up to the current EU are important in the tale they tell.

Economic Integration

The organizational genesis of the EU dates back to 1952 when Belgium, France, (West) Germany, Italy, Luxembourg, and the Netherlands joined together to create a common market for coal, iron, and steel products called the European Coal and Steel Community (ECSC). It proved so successful that in 1957 the six countries signed the Treaties of Rome that created the **European Economic Community (EEC)** to facilitate trade in many additional areas and the European Atomic Energy Community (EURATOM) to coordinate matters in that realm. Both new communities came into being on January 1, 1958.

Interchange among the 6 countries expanded rapidly, and they soon felt that they should coordinate their activities even further. Therefore, the 6 created the **European Communities (EC)**, which went into operation in 1967. Each of the three preexisting organizations became subordinate parts of the EC. Success brought new members, as detailed in Figure 9.2 on page 237. Most of the other countries of Europe have expressed interest in joining the EU, and as of early 2002 negotiations were under way between the EU and 13 applicants (Bulgaria, Cyprus, the Czech Republic, Estonia, Hungary, Latvia, Lithuania, Malta, Poland, Romania, Slovakia, Slovenia, and Turkey).

The eventual, if not quite stated, goal of the EU is to encompass all the region's countries. Jacques Santer, president of the European Commission (1995–1999), insisted that no country that met the EU economic and political standards should be kept out. "There will be no such things as 'in countries' and 'out countries'; rather there will be 'ins' and 'pre-ins'," he said.[4] He might have added that within a decade or two, all the countries of Europe may well be "ins."

For about 30 years, the integrative process in Europe focused on economics. Members of the EC grew ever more interdependent as economic barriers were eliminated. In 1968 the members of the EC abolished the last tariffs on manufactured goods among themselves and established a common EC external tariff. The EC also began to bargain as a whole with other countries in trade negotiations. On another economic front, members agreed in 1970 to fund the EC with a virtually independent revenue source by giving it a share of each country's value-added tax (VAT, similar to a sales tax) and all customs duties collected on imports from non-EC countries. The last major step in the pre-EU evolution toward economic integration was the Single European Act (SEA) of 1987. The SEA amended the basic EC agreement and committed the EC to becoming a fully integrated economic unit.

Political Integration

There comes a point in economic integration when pressure builds to take steps toward political integration. One reason this occurs is that it is impossible to reach full economic integration among sovereign states whose domestic and foreign political policies are sometimes in conflict. Moreover, as the people unite economically, it is easier to think of becoming one politically.

Europe entered a new, more political phase of integrative evolution in 1993 when the far-reaching Treaty on European Union (known as the **Maastricht Treaty**) went into effect. The treaty had important provisions to increase the EU's economic integration even further. Of greater importance were the political changes that began under the treaty. The concept of European citizenship was expanded. Citizens of EU countries can now travel on either an EU or a national passport, and citizens of any EU country can vote in local and European Parliament elections in another EU country in which they live. In addition, the EU acts increasingly as a political unit (Piening, 1997; Rhodes, 1997). The Maastricht Treaty called for the eventual creation of a common foreign and defense policy and common policy relating to such issues as crime, terrorism, and immigration. Gradually, such ideas have begun to become reality. The EU and the United States exchange ambassadors.

Since the adoption of the Maastricht Treaty, EU integration and expansion has moved forward through other treaties including the **Treaty of Amsterdam (1997)** and the Treaty of Nice (2000, still awaiting full ratification). The Amsterdam treaty creates yet stronger political integration of the EU and strengthens the powers of the president of the EU Commission and the European Parliament (EP). The Treaty of Nice is primarily devoted to easing the way for the further expansion of the EU's membership by detailing political arrangements—such as the distribution of seats or votes in the EP, the Commission, and the Council of Ministers—after several new members are admitted, perhaps as early as 2004.

THE GOVERNMENT OF EUROPE: A PROTOTYPE

The EU's organizational structure is extremely complex, but a brief look at it is important to illustrate the extent to which a regional government has been created (Hix, 1999; Peterson & Bomberg, 1999). As with all governments, the structure and the authority of the various EU units play an important part in determining how policy is made and which policies are adopted (Meunier, 2000). Figure 9.2 gives a brief overview of this structure. The EU's government can be divided for analysis into the political leadership, the bureaucracy, the legislature, and the judiciary (Richardson, 1997).

Political Leadership

Political decision making occurs within the Council of the European Union, usually called the **Council of Ministers**. The council meets twice a year as a gathering of the prime ministers and other heads of government and decides on the most important policy directions for the EU. The council meets more often with lesser ministers (often finance ministers) in attendance to supplement the prime ministerial meetings. Most sessions are held in Brussels, Belgium, which is the principal site of the EU administrative element. Decisions are made by a weighted-vote plan (termed "qualified majority voting"). Under this plan the larger EU countries have more votes on some matters. There are a total of 87 votes, with each country's allocation ranging from 10 votes for France, Germany, Great Britain, and Italy to 2 votes for Luxembourg. Unanimity is often required, but 62 of the 87 votes are sometimes sufficient to make policy.

Bureaucracy

Bureaucracy in the EU is organized within the **European Commission**. The 20-member commission administers policy adopted by the council. Individual commissioners are selected from the member-states on the basis of two each from France, Germany, Great Britain, Italy, and Spain and one commissioner from each of the other members. The commissioners are not, however, supposed to represent the viewpoint of their country. They serve five-year terms and act as a cabinet for the EU, with each commissioner overseeing an area of administrative activity. One of the commissioners is selected by the Council of Europe to be the commission president.

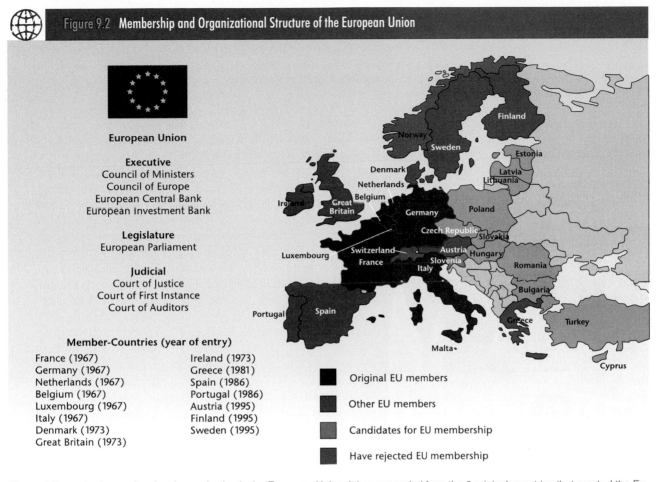

Figure 9.2 Membership and Organizational Structure of the European Union

European Union

Executive
Council of Ministers
Council of Europe
European Central Bank
European Investment Bank

Legislature
European Parliament

Judicial
Court of Justice
Court of First Instance
Court of Auditors

Member-Countries (year of entry)

France (1967)	Ireland (1973)
Germany (1967)	Greece (1981)
Netherlands (1967)	Spain (1986)
Belgium (1967)	Portugal (1986)
Luxembourg (1967)	Austria (1995)
Italy (1967)	Finland (1995)
Denmark (1973)	Sweden (1995)
Great Britain (1973)	

- Original EU members
- Other EU members
- Candidates for EU membership
- Have rejected EU membership

The world's most advanced regional organization is the European Union. It has expanded from the 6 original countries that created the European Community in 1967 to 15 countries today. Thirteen others await admission. The EU's focus is primarily economic, but it is also involved in a variety of political, social, and environmental issues and reflects a greater level of integration than can be found in any other region.

This official serves as the EU's administrative head and is the overall director of the EU bureaucracy headquartered in Brussels (Cini, 1997; Nugent, 1997).

The post of **President of the Commission** has evolved into one of the most significant in the EU, arguably something like a president of the European Union. A great deal of that evolution can also be attributed to Jacques Delors, a French national who served as president from 1985 through 1994 and who became known as "Mr. Europe" because of his strong advocacy of European integration. Delors and his staff created a core structure, informally referred to as "Eurocracy," which has a European point of view, rather than a national orientation.

Delors's aggressive stance caused a negative reaction in some countries, and when he stepped down the British and some others pressed for the election of a president who would be more restrained. This led the Council of Europe to choose Luxembourg's prime minister, Jacques Santer, who took a lower profile than did Delors. Santer's successor, Romano Prodi of Italy, has followed suit. Nevertheless, the size and power of the EU bureaucracy mean that anyone serving as its president will be a person of significant influence.

Yet another indication of the importance of the commission, as well as the political integration of Europe, is the emergence of an ever larger, more active, and more powerful EU infrastructure. The EU's administrative staff has almost quintupled since 1970 to about 29,000 today. The number of EU regulations, decisions, and directives from one or the other EU body has risen from an annual 345 in 1970 to over 600. The EU's 2002 budget is about $86 billion, raised from tariff revenues, from contributions based on each member's gross domestic product, and from part of each member's VAT.

Legislative Branch

The **European Parliament (EP)** serves as the EU's legislative branch and meets in Strasbourg, France. It has 626 members, apportioned among the EU countries on a modified population basis and elected to five-year terms. The most populous country (Germany) has 99 seats; the least populous country (Luxembourg) has 6 seats. Unlike most international congresses, such as the UN General Assembly, the EP's members are elected by voters in their respective countries. Furthermore, instead of organizing themselves within the EP by country, the representatives have tended to group themselves by political persuasion. The 1999 elections, for example, resulted in the moderately conservative coalition, called the European People's Party (EPP), winning 223 seats and the moderately liberal coalition, the Socialist Party of Europe (SPE), winning 179 seats. It was the first time in the EU's history that the EPP had gained more seats than the SPE. The remaining seats were scattered among seven identifiable groupings of legislators and a few dozen unaffiliated members.

The EP has had mostly advisory authority, but it is struggling to carve out a more authoritative role. That goal was advanced under the Treaty of Amsterdam, which extends the EP's "co-decision" authority with the Council of Ministers to a greater number of matters. The EP can also veto some regulations issued by the commission and it confirms the President of the Commission. A key power, albeit one that is so far little used, is the EP's ability to accept or reject the EU budget proposed by the commission.

One indication that the European Parliament is slowly gaining legal authority within the European Union is the upsurge of people pressing the EP to favor their causes. In this photograph, the issue is animal rights, and Chrissie Hynde of the rock band The Pretenders is among the demonstrators protesting an EU policy that allows testing chemicals on beagles like the one on the placard and other animals. The EU flag is visible in the background on the upper right side of the picture.

Judicial Branch

The **Court of Justice** is the main element of the judicial branch of the EU (Alter, 1998; Garrett, Kelemen, & Schulz, 1998; Mattli & Slaughter, 1998). The 15-member court hears cases brought to it by member-states or other EU institutions and sometimes acts as a court of appeals for decisions of lower EU courts. The combined treaties of the EU are often considered its "constitution." Like the EU's other institutions, the courts have gained authority over time. In one illustrative case, the Court of Justice ruled that certain VAT exemptions in Great Britain violated EU treaties and would have to be eliminated. The ruling prompted some members of the British Parliament to grumble that it was the first time since Charles I's reign (1625–1649) that the House of Commons had been compelled to raise taxes. Another bit of evidence of the mounting influence of the court is that its workload became so heavy that the EU created a new, lower court, the Court of First Instance, which hears cases related to the EU brought by corporations and individuals.

THE FUTURE OF THE EU

There is in Europe both a sense that the EU should continue to press economic and political integration forward and a hesitancy to move toward becoming the United States of Europe (Wallace, 1999). This duality was evident in a recent speech by France's president Jacques Chirac to Germany's parliament: "Those countries that want to proceed further with integration, on a voluntary basis and in specific areas, must be allowed to do so without being held back," he declared. But, he added, his image was of a "united Europe of states rather than a United States of Europe."[5] How much further and how fast the EU proceeds down the road of integration and expansion rests on a number of factors (Gabel, 1998; Cafruny & Lankowski, 1997; Landau & Whitman, 1997).

Popular Support for EU Integration The level of public support for EU integration is one factor that will determine the EU's future. A poll, the Eurobarometer, that tracks opinion in Europe finds somewhat mixed signals about how Europeans feel about the EU.[6] For example, popular support for their country's membership in the EU can be viewed in two ways. From one perspective, only about half of Europeans voice support. But only 12 percent voice opposition, with others uncertain. Over time, average support increased from about 50 percent in the early 1980s to approximately 70 percent during 1989–1991, then dropped back to about 50 percent in 2000 and 2001.

There are numerous indications, however, that Europeans support EU integration, want it to proceed further, and want it to proceed faster. For instance, people are relatively comfortable with EU governance of at least some areas once exclusively the realm of national governments. The Eurobarometer finds 66 percent of the EU's population supporting the principle of a common foreign policy, and 73 percent in favor of a common security policy. Support for EU decision making in domestic policy areas is lower. There is only 34 percent support, for instance, for an EU role in setting education policy.

Polls also indicate that about two-thirds favor a European Union constitution. To that end, the Convention on the Future of Europe convened in Brussels, Belgium, in February 2002. Chaired by former French president Valery Giscard d'Estaing the meeting is commonly referred to as Europe's "constitutional convention" and is scheduled to work for a year to draft an EU constitution. Speaking to the delegates at the opening ceremony, Giscard d'Estaing told them that the complexity of treaties that currently govern the EU have rendered its decision-making structures "complex to the point of being unintelligible to the general public," threatening to create an inertia toward integration that he termed "euro-sclerosis." "So let us dream of Europe!" the former president exclaimed. "Let us imagine a continent... freed of its barriers and obstacles, where history and geography are finally reconciled, allowing all the states of Europe to build their future together after following their separate ways, East and West."[7] In sum, although he was careful enough politically not to say it, Giscard d'Estaing challenged the delegates to create a federal United States of Europe.

The EU Economy The degree of economic prosperity of EU members and their citizens is a second factor that influences the course of EU integration. Whether Europeans feel that the EU is beneficial is based in part on their perceptions of its impact on their prosperity. During the 1980s, the average annual growth of the EU's GDP was 2.2, and on average 55 percent of poll respondents said that their country benefited from EU membership. During the 1990s the EU's average annual GDP growth dropped off to 1.7 percent, and that was reflected in a drop to 48 in the average percentage of those saying that their country benefited from EU membership.

The European Union's new currency, the euro, entered general use in 2002, replacing French francs, German marks, Italian lira, and many other familiar national currencies in all but three of the EU's member-countries. It is a sign of the advancement of European political as well as economic integration that most Europeans did not resist giving up the use of their national currencies and readily adapted to the much more efficient use of the euro.

While the potential for the European economy is immense, there are numerous possible obstacles to overcome. One is economic disparity. The original six members were relatively close in their economic circumstances. The addition of new countries has changed that and will continue to do so. As it stands, the average annual per capita GDPs of EU countries range from Luxembourg's $44,340 to Greece's $11,960. Adding East European countries, such as Poland ($4,200), which have applied to join the EU, will further complicate the integration of the EU's diverse economies.

Just as expanding EU membership has potential pluses and minuses, so does the implementation of the euro as the official currency and the abolishment of the German mark, French franc, Italian lira, and the other national currencies of the EU members (McKay, 1999; Overturf, 1997). Having a common currency is necessary to achieve full economic integration and to move further toward political integration. Still, the introduction of the euro has created major issues as the EU struggles to resolve longstanding national differences over fiscal policy. Three EU countries (Denmark, Great Britain, and Sweden) are not in the "euro zone," that is, they will not substitute the euro for their national currencies. Moreover, the currency was not received with confidence in the world financial markets. When put into circulation on January 1, 1999, it was pegged at 1 euro = $1.17. From that point, the euro's exchange rate fell 24 percent to 1 euro = $0.89 when euro coins and bills went into general circulation on January 1, 2002. Among other negative effects, the falling value of the euro spurred European exports, but it also had the effect of driving up the price of petroleum and other imported products.

Satisfaction with EU Institutions The degree to which the EU's rule-making and administrative institutions function effectively is a third factor that will affect the future of EU integration. Some European voters oppose expansion of EU functions because of their sense that so-called Eurotaxes are too high and that the EU bureaucracy, the "Eurocracy," is too powerful, unresponsive, and even corrupt. Some of the tales of Eurocratic excess that circulate are related in the box, When Is a Banana a Banana?

Polls taken in late 2001 showed a marked increase in the public's trust of EU's institutions, but that spike was almost surely a reaction to the fear of terrorism in the aftermath of the 9-11 attacks on the United States. The increase to 53 percent in trust in the EU was paralleled by similar jumps in the degree to which Europeans trusted their national governments and the UN. There was a similar upsurge of trust in the U.S. government by Americans. What is likely is that in time, the level of trust in the EU's institutions will ebb to the usual range of 40 percent. This does not mean, however, that Europeans are any more skeptical of the EU than of their national governments. Indeed, Europeans trust them even less by a margin of about 3 percent.

This feeling was substantiated in March 1999 when all 20 members of the European Commission, including its president, Jacques Santer, resigned amid allegations of mismanagement and cronyism and were replaced by a new set of commissioners headed by Italy's Romano Prodi.

(Continued on page 241)

WHEN IS A BANANA A BANANA?

Many people consider Europe the epicurean center of the world, and the EU's "food fights" bear out the intensity of that continent's decision makers toward gastronomical policy.

During one discussion in the Council of Ministers in 2002 over a proposal to locate the new EU food safety agency in Finland, Italy's Prime Minister Silvio Berlusconi argued that it should be put in Parma, Italy, on the grounds that "Parma is synonymous with good cuisine. The Finns don't even know what prosciutto is." Prime Minister Guy Verhofstadt of Belgium pointed out reasonably that "the gastronomic attraction is not argument for the allocation of an EU agency." And President Jacques Chirac of France asked aloud, "How would it be if Sweden got an agency for training models, since [it has such] pretty women?" Berlusconi was unpersuaded. "My final word is no," he proclaimed, and the conferees put off the decision until after lunch.[1]

The many tales of attempts by EU bureaucrats to regulate everything, which have become part of the political lore of Europe, have also often included skirmishes over what food can be called.

Many Europeans reacted with bemusement, for example, at the EU's banana contretemps. The details are slippery, but it all stemmed from a bunch of regulations promulgated by the EU bureaucracy that, among other things, specified that imported bananas had to be at least 5.5 inches long and 1.1 inches wide, and could not be abnormally bent. Great Britain, where archeologists uncovered the remains of a banana skin dating back to the mid-1400s, was especially offended. "Brussels bureaucrats proved yesterday what a barmy bunch they are—by outlawing curved bananas. The crazy laws were drawn by thumb-twiddling EU chiefs who spent thousands on a yearlong study," protested the British newspaper, the *Sun*. An EU spokesperson replied that while, indeed, bananas of an abnormal shape could not be imported, that "in no sense" meant that EU regulation banned "curved bananas because a curve is a normal shape for a banana."[2]

Once the Europeans agreed on what a banana was, they also agreed to impose lower tariffs on ba-

nanas from their former colonies than on bananas from other places. That drove Americans bananas because many of those other places were Caribbean and Central American countries with close ties to the United States. Washington then butted heads with the EU by threatening to retaliate by barring cashmere and other EU products. This got the goat of Scottish cashmere producers. In the end, the two economic superpowers were able to escape the horns of this dilemma by agreeing that the EU would gradually end its preferences for its bunch of favored countries and equally admit the bananas from the U.S.-favored bunch of countries.

The reputation of the Eurocracy was further darkened by the chocolate imbroglio. Having decided that bananas could indeed be bent, at least somewhat, and in the right places, EU policymakers turned to the sticky issue of what constitutes chocolate. The battle line was drawn between the eight EU countries that require chocolate to consist entirely of cocoa butter and the other seven EU members that allow up to 5 percent vegetable oil in chocolate. Representing the purists, the head of the Belgian chocolate company Godiva proclaimed that only "100 percent chocolate should be called... chocolate." Answering back for the nondoctrinaire chocolatiers, a representative of Great Britain's largest chocolate maker, Cadbury, urged, "Let's celebrate Europe's regional diversity and recognize that there are different ways of making chocolate." The purists won the first round when the European Parliament voted 306 to 112 in favor of their position. But the war was not over, for the European Council of Ministers had to make the final gooey decision. "Whatever we do will be attacked from one side or the other," an EU spokesperson has complained. Compromise was the sweet solution. An early 2000 ruling declared that chocolate with vegetable oil could be shipped throughout the EU. Moreover it could be labeled chocolate, but only in the seven nonpurist countries. In the purist eight, it would have to be labeled "family milk chocolate." Not that it has anything to do with families or milk. Ah well, as Forrest Gump mused, "Life is like a box of chocolates."

Political Identity How Europeans identify politically is a fourth factor that will impact EU integration (Zielonka, 1998). It will be necessary for Europeans to shift their political loyalties away from their national states and toward the EU for integration to proceed much further.

Recent polls give some evidence that this is occurring. While almost no one considers themselves, politically, a North American or an African, 52 percent of people in the EU countries indicated they see themselves, at least partly, as European. But the sense of Euronationalism is also limited in several ways. Only 10 percent of EU citizens see themselves as simply European or as more European than national.

Nationalism-based resistance is especially evident in the newer EU members, but it is an important emotion in even the original six EU members. "Our nations are the source of our identities and of our roots," President Chirac of France recently proclaimed, "The diversity of our political traditions, cultures and languages is one of the strengths of the union. In the future, our nations will stay the first reference point for our people."[8]

Perceptions of Germany   Wariness of Germany is a fifth factor that impinges on EU integration. Germany accounts for 21 percent of the EU's population, 25 percent of the GDP, and 22 percent of total EU merchandise exports. One survey of British, French, German, and Italian citizens asked which country, if any, "will become the dominant power" in the EU. A majority of the British, French, and Italians, and even a plurality of the Germans, replied "Germany." When asked if they liked the idea of Germany dominating, 91 percent of the British, 73 percent of the French, and 71 percent of the Italians said no.[9]

Furthering the disquiet in some, Germany has been a leading proponent of ever greater economic and political integration. In May 2000 German foreign minister Joschka Fischer commented in a speech that the current EU structure was too cumbersome to achieve a fully integrated Europe and should be replaced by "nothing less than a European Parliament and a European government which really do exercise legislative and executive power within [a]... federation."[10] In short, Fischer proposed creating a more powerful European government and a federal United States of Europe. Reaction was swift and sharp. "There is a tendency in Germany to imagine a federal structure for Europe which fits in with its own model," warned France's interior minister, Jean-Pierre Chevènement. "Deep down, [Germany] is still dreaming of the Holy Roman Empire. It hasn't cured itself of its past derailment into Nazism."[11] Fischer later protested he was speaking as an individual, not as German foreign minister, and Chevènement apologized for his undiplomatic reference to Germany's Nazi past. Still, the incident reflected a concern that is not far below the surface in Europe.

Expanded Membership   Popular willingness to accept new members into the EU is a sixth pivotal issue in the future of the EU and is also related to nationalism. Support for integration does not necessarily mean support for expansion, and the latter is being limited by the recent upsurge in antiforeigner sentiment in Europe. As a result, public support for the enlargement of the EU is mixed. Support for expansion can muster only a weak plurality of 43 percent among EU citizens, while 35 percent are opposed to it, and 22 percent are unsure.

In sum, the evolution of the EU has been one of the remarkable events of the past half century. It does not take much imagination to foresee a day when the once antagonistic states of Europe are forged into a United States of Europe. That is just one possibility, however, and what is certain is that the progress of the EU toward further economic and political integration, whether or not it leads to true federation, will be difficult.

Global IGOs: Focus on the United Nations

The growing level and importance of IGO activity and organization at the regional level is paralleled by IGOs at the global level. Of these, the United Nations is by far the best known and most influential (Ryan, 2000). Therefore, we will focus in this

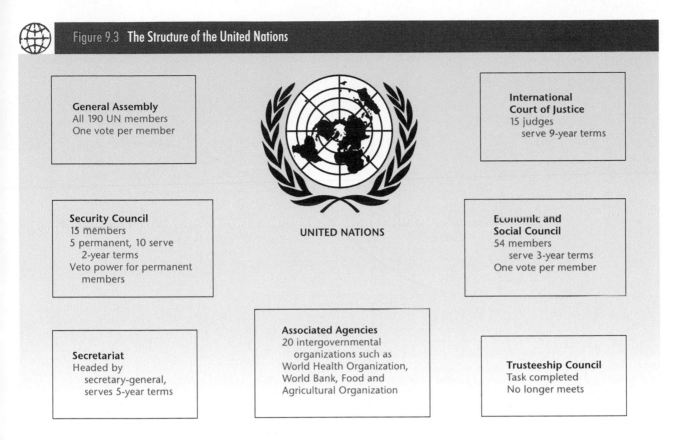

Figure 9.3 The Structure of the United Nations

General Assembly
All 190 UN members
One vote per member

International Court of Justice
15 judges
        serve 9-year terms

Security Council
15 members
5 permanent, 10 serve
    2-year terms
Veto power for permanent
    members

UNITED NATIONS

Economic and Social Council
54 members
        serve 3-year terms
One vote per member

Secretariat
Headed by
    secretary-general,
    serves 5-year terms

Associated Agencies
20 intergovernmental
    organizations such as
World Health Organization,
World Bank, Food and
Agricultural Organization

Trusteeship Council
Task completed
No longer meets

The United Nations is a complex organization. It has 6 major organs and 20 associated agencies.

section on the UN, both as a generalized study of the operation of IGOs and as a specific study of the most prominent member of their ranks.

IGO ORGANIZATION AND RELATED ISSUES

Many people assume that the study of organizational structure is dry and meaningless, but the contrary is true. Constitutions, rules of procedure, finance, organization charts, and other administrative details are often crucial in determining political outcomes. It is, for example, impossible to understand how the UN works without knowing that 5 of its members possess a veto in the Security Council and the other 185 do not. An outline of the UN's structure is depicted in Figure 9.3.

Organizational structure is also important because it must reflect realities and goals and have the flexibility to change if it becomes outmoded. "Clearly we cannot meet the challenges of the new millennium with an instrument designed for the very different circumstances of the middle of the twentieth century," the UN's secretary-general, Kofi Annan, points out.[12] To examine structure and rules, the following discussion of IGOs will take up matters relating to general membership, the structure of representative bodies, voting formulas, the authority of executive leadership, and the bureaucracy. Then we will turn to the matter of IGO finance.

General Membership

Theoretically, membership in most IGOs is open to any state that is both within the geographic and/or functional scope of that organization and subscribes to the principles

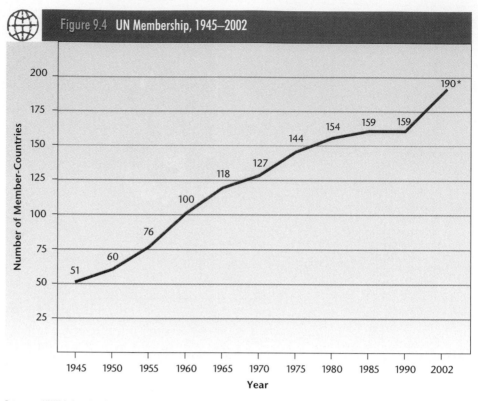

Figure 9.4   UN Membership, 1945–2002

Data source: UN Web site at: http://www.un.org, and author.

*Switzerland has applied for membership and will almost certainly be admitted as the UN's 190th member for the General Assembly session beginning in fall 2002. If, as expected, East Timor, which gained independence in May 2002, also applies and is admitted, it would be the 191st member.

Membership in the United Nations has risen rapidly. The 373 percent rise in UN membership is an indication of the increased number of states in existence and also of the UN's nearly universal membership.

and practices of that organization. In practice, a third standard, politics, often becomes a heavy consideration in membership questions. Today the UN has grown to nearly universal membership, as Figure 9.4 shows, but that was not always the case.

Standards for admitting new members is one point of occasional controversy. One instance occurred in 1998 when the General Assembly gave the Palestinians added legitimacy by voting overwhelmingly to give them what amounts to an informal associate membership. The Palestinians cannot vote, but they can take part in debates in the UN and perform other functions undertaken by states.

Successor state status can also sometimes be a political issue. With little fanfare, the UN agreed to recognize Russia as the successor state to the Soviet Union. This meant, among other things, that Russia inherited the USSR's permanent seat and veto on the Security Council. Taking the opposite approach, the UN in 1992 refused to recognize the Serbian-dominated government in Belgrade as the successor to Yugoslavia once that country broke apart. Instead, the General Assembly required Yugoslavia to (re)apply for admission. Once dictator Slobodan Milosevic was toppled, Yugoslavia did reapply, and it was (re)admitted in 2000.

Withdrawal, suspension, and expulsion is another membership issue. Nationalist China (Taiwan) was, in effect, ejected from the UN when the "China seat" was transferred to the mainland. In a move close to expulsion, the General Assembly refused between 1974 and 1991 to accept the credentials of South Africa's delegate because that country's apartheid policies violated the UN Charter. The refusal to recognize

Yugoslavia in 1992 as a successor state was, in effect, an expulsion of that country based on its bloody repression of Bosnians, Croats, and others.

Representative Bodies

There are important issues that relate to how to structure the representative bodies of international organizations. Most IGOs have a **plenary representative body** that includes all members. The theoretical basis for plenary bodies is the mutual responsibility of all members for the organization and its policies. The **UN General Assembly (UNGA)** is the UN's plenary organ, but in other IGOs it may be termed a council, a conference, a commission, or even a parliament. These plenary bodies normally have the authority to involve themselves in virtually all aspects of their organizations. Thus, in theory, they are the most powerful elements of their organizations. In practice, however, the plenary organization may be secondary to the administrative structure or some other part of the organization.

A second type of representative organization body is a **limited membership council**. The theory here is that some members have a greater stake, responsibility, or capacity in a particular area of concern. The **UN Security Council (UNSC)** has 15 members. Ten are chosen by the UNGA for limited terms, but 5 are permanent members. These 5 (China, France, Russia, the United Kingdom, and the United States) were the leading victorious powers at the end of World War II and were thought to have a special peacekeeping role to play. These 5 countries have served continuously since 1945 as permanent members on the Security Council; more than half of the other 185 members have never served on the Council (Russett, 1997).

The special status enjoyed by the five permanent members of the UNSC is a simmering issue in the UN. The existing membership has never been fully realistic and is becoming less so as time goes by. One issue, as the German mission to the UN puts it, is, "The Security Council as it stands does not reflect today's world which has changed dramatically since 1945."[13] Reflecting current realities, Germany, India, Japan, and some other powerful countries have begun to press for permanent seats for themselves.

Another issue is geographic and demographic imbalance. Geographically, Europe and North America have four of five permanent seats, and those four permanent members are also countries of predominantly Eurowhite heritage. African countries are offended that their continent has no permanent seat on the Council. Giving voice to that view, the president of Zambia has declared that the Council "can no longer be maintained like the sanctuary of the Holy of Holies with only the original members acting as high priests, deciding on issues for the rest of the world who cannot be admitted."[14]

A third issue is the equity of the veto for any country. Speaking in 2001 during debates in the General Assembly, a delegate from Ethiopia called the Security Council "feudal in nature and undemocratic in character." And a diplomat representing Venezuela described the veto, even if "justified in the past" as "an anti-democratic practice nowadays" and "not in accordance with the principle of the sovereign equality of States."[15]

Whatever may be just, however, change will be hard to achieve. One difficulty is that any Charter revision must be recommended by a two-thirds vote of the UNSC (where each of the five permanent members has a veto), adopted by a two-thirds vote of the UNGA, and ratified by two-thirds of the members according to their respective constitutional processes. The permanent UNSC members are opposed to surrendering their special status. It will also be difficult to arrive at a new formula that satisfies the sensitivities of other countries and regions. For example, the thought of India having a permanent seat alarms Pakistan, whose UN representative

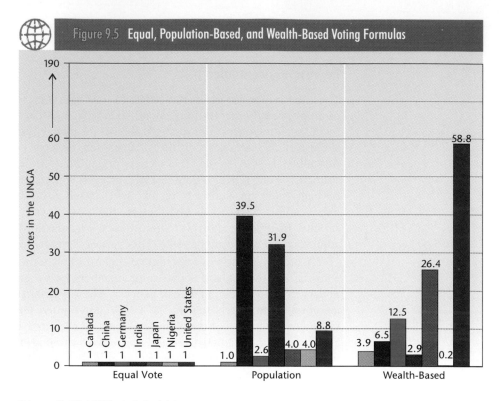

Figure 9.5   Equal, Population-Based, and Wealth-Based Voting Formulas

Data source: World Bank (2002) and author's calculations.

To see the impact of various voting formulas, imagine that the current 190 votes in the UNGA were allocated on three different bases: equality, population, and wealth. Voting power would vary widely. For example, the United States would have one vote under equal voting, 8.8 votes under population-based voting, and 58.8 votes under wealth-based voting. Nigeria would gain votes under population and lose votes under wealth. Canada would lose under population and gain under wealth. Are any of these formulas fair? What would be a fair formula?

has characterized those seeking permanent status as motivated by "an undisguised grab for power and privilege."[16] Therefore, the prospects for reform remain dim. As an Italian diplomat has noted, "The only matter that we would seem to have agreed on is that we are in profound disagreement on how to enlarge the Council."[17]

Voting Formulas

One of the difficult issues that any international organization faces is its formula for allocating votes (Bohman, 1999). Three major alternatives as they exist today are majority voting, weighted voting, and unanimity voting. The implications of various voting formulas are evident in Figure 9.5.

Majority voting is the most common formula used in IGOs. This system has two main components: (1) each member casts one equal vote, and (2) the issue is carried by either a simple majority (50 percent plus one vote) or, in some cases, an extraordinary majority (commonly two-thirds). The theory of majoritarianism springs from the concept of sovereign equality and the democratic notion that the will of the majority should prevail. The UNGA and most other UN bodies operate on this principle.

The problem with the idea of equality among states is that it does not reflect some standards of reality. Should Costa Rica, with no army, cast an equal vote with the powerful United States? Should San Marino, with a population of thousands, cast the same vote as China, with its more than 1 billion people? It might be noted, for example, that in the UNGA, some 126 states, whose combined populations are less than 15 percent of the world's population, account for two-thirds of members and, thus, the available votes. By contrast, the 10 countries with populations over 100 million (Bangladesh, Brazil, China, India, Indonesia, Japan, Nigeria, Pakistan, Russia, and the United States), which combine for 60 percent of the world's population, have just 5 percent of the available votes in the General Assembly.

Weighted voting, or a system that allocates unequal voting power on the basis of a formula, is a second voting scheme. Two possible criteria are population and wealth. As noted earlier, the European Parliament provides an example of an international representative body based in part on population. A number of international monetary organizations base voting on financial contributions. Voting in the World Bank and the International Monetary Fund is based on member contributions. The United States alone commands about 17 percent of the votes in the IMF, and it and France, Germany, Great Britain, and Japan together can cast almost 40 percent of the votes in that IGO. This "wealth-weighted" voting is especially offensive to LDC states, which contend that it perpetuates the system of imperial domination by the industrialized countries.

Unanimity voting constitutes a third scheme. This system requires the assent by all, although sometimes abstaining from a vote does not block agreement. The Organization for Economic Cooperation and Development (OECD) and some other IGOs operate on that principle. Unanimity preserves the concept of sovereignty but can easily lead to stalemate.

The voting formula in the UNSC by which any of the 5 permanent members (the P5) can **veto** proposals while the other 10 members cannot is an unusual variation on the unanimity scheme (O'Neill, 1997). Vetoes were cast frequently during the cold war, but have been infrequent since 1990. Nevertheless, the power remains important. First, a veto is still sometimes cast. China in 1999 forced an end to the UN peacekeeping mission in Macedonia by vetoing a continuing resolution. Second, the threat of a veto can sometimes forestall action. For example, most Security Council members favored recommending Secretary-General Boutros-Ghali for reapppointment in 1996. The United States did not, though, and it had the unilateral ability to block a second term. "We hope that Boutros-Ghali will, will decide that he needs to step down," a U.S. State Department spokesperson commented. "If that does not happen, if he does force it to a vote, we will use our veto."[18] Faced with the inevitable, Boutros-Ghali chose to retire rather than face the embarrassment of being rejected formally.

Voting formulas are important politically because they have a major impact on who will be powerful, who will not, and what policies will be adopted (Holloway & Tomlinson, 1995). Furthermore, how to apportion representation in the parliamentary bodies of such IGOs as the UN will become increasingly important and contentious as the IGOs become more powerful, especially if and when they begin to have true supranational power to compel states to act in certain ways. As noted, one way to think further about the ramifications of various voting schemes is to examine Figure 9.5. It shows the number of votes each of six countries would have in the current 190-vote UNGA using equality, population, or wealth as the determinant.

Political Leadership

It is difficult for any organization to function without a single administrative leader, and virtually all IGOs have a chief executive officer (CEO). The UN's administrative structure is called the **Secretariat**, and the secretary-general is the CEO. In this section we will take up the selection and role of the UN secretary-general and other CEOs of IGOs. Then, in the next section, we will address the bureaucratic understructure of IGO secretariats (Barnett & Finnemore, 1999).

(Continued on page 248)

MUCH ADO ABOUT SOMETHING

The argument that IGOs are marginal to world politics is belied by the frequent conflict over who will head them. Clearly, there must be much ado about something. There are several reasons that battle lines have sometimes been drawn over the appointment or reappointment of the UN secretary-general or the head of some other IGO.

The selection of Boutros Boutros-Ghali (1992–1996) began with African discontent that no one from that continent had yet been secretary-general. The United States and some other countries were dubious about the political orientation of a secretary-general from sub-Saharan Africa, but also did not want to alienate Africa by being "the 900-pound gorilla," in the words of one U.S. official.[1] In this atmosphere, Boutros-Ghali, an Egyptian and the only non-sub-Saharan African candidate, was an ideal compromise. He was the most Westernized of all the African candidates, spoke several languages, and had been a professor of international law in Egypt and a Fulbright scholar at Columbia University. Any possible alarm that Boutros-Ghali was an Arab was eased by the fact that he is a Coptic Christian, not a Muslim, and his wife, Leah, is Jewish.

Boutros-Ghali proved to be an assertive, sometimes acerbic secretary-general who often rankled some members, especially the United States. Washington was particularly piqued by his criticism of the Eurowhite-dominated Security Council for what he saw as a racially tinged tendency to pay more attention to some matters (such as the Balkans crisis in Europe) than others (such as the crises in Somalia and Rwanda in Africa). Whatever the validity of such charges, the result was that the United States tacitly vetoed a second term for Boutros-Ghali.

Since Boutros-Ghali had been appointed to remedy the fact that there had been no previous secretary-general from Africa, and since most recent secretaries-generals have served two terms, the African countries felt that it was still their "turn." Washington did not want to offend Africa, but also worried about the political views of potential African candidates. After extensive maneuvering, the final choice for the seventh secretary-general was Kofi Annan, a career UN diplomat from Ghana. He had a reputation as a capable and moderate diplomat and administrator, and his personal history (a B.A. degree in economics from Macalaster College in St. Paul, Minnesota, M.A. in management from MIT) helped assuage Washington's concern that a secretary-general from black Africa might prove too radical. Annan is married to Nane Lagergren, a Swedish lawyer, who is a niece of Raoul Wallenberg, the heroic Swedish diplomat noted for trying to save Jewish lives during World War II.

The often sharp political contests that are waged when picking UN secretaries-general underlines the importance of that office. This standard can also be applied to the heads of other IGOs. For example, there have been spirited contests each time there has been a leadership change at the World Trade Organization. During the most recent round in 1999, the struggle featured a determined effort by the LDCs to break the EDCs' monopoly on the top jobs in the leading financial IGOs. The result was a compromise: an EDC national, Mike Moore of New Zealand, was selected with the understanding that in 2002 he would step down in favor of Thailand's Supachi Panitchpakdi, who would serve until 2005.

There have been similar contests over who would become president of the Commission of the European Union, the World Bank, the International Monetary Fund, and other IGOs in recent years, but recounting these dramas is not necessary to make the basic point that the jostling among the major powers to appoint one of their own or someone of their liking to the top jobs indicates how important these IGOs are. All that sound and fury must signify something.

Selection The UN secretary-general is nominated by the UNSC, then elected by the General Assembly for a five-year term. This simple fact does not, however, adequately emphasize the political considerations that govern the appointment of administrators. One sign of the importance of IGOs is that who will head them has often been, and seems increasingly to be, the subject of intense struggle among member-countries. This is taken up in the box, Much Ado About Something.

Role: Activism Versus Restraint An issue that swirls around IGO executives is their proper role. The role orientations of the UN secretary-general and other IGO leaders can range between activism and restraint. For the most part, the documents that established IGOs anticipated a restrained role. In the UN Charter, for example, the Secretariat is the last major organ discussed. That placement indicates the limited, largely administrative role that the document's drafters intended for the secretary-general.

Whatever was intended, the first two secretaries-general, Trygve Lie of Norway (1946–1953) and Dag Hammarskjöld of Sweden (1953–1961), were activists who steadily expanded the role of their office. Hammarskjöld argued that he had a "responsibility" to act to uphold the peace "irrespective of the views and wishes of the various member governments" (Archer, 1983:148). Hammarskjöld's approach was epitomized during the civil war that followed the independence of the Belgian Congo in 1960. The secretary-general aggressively used UN military forces to try to restore peace. It is somehow sadly fitting that he died in the area when his plane crashed after reportedly being shot down by one of the warring factions.

The Soviets were so upset at the activist and what they saw as a pro-Western stance of Hammarskjöld that they pressed for successors with more restrained conceptions of the role of secretary-general. Over time, however, secretaries-general have once again tended toward activism. The sixth secretary-general, Egypt's Boutros Boutros-Ghali (1992–1996), believed that "if one word above all is to characterize the role of the secretary-general, it is independence. The holder of this office must never be seen as acting out of fear or in an attempt to curry favor with one state or groups of states."[19] Just as Hammarskjöld's activism had led him into disfavor, so to did Boutros-Ghali's views. As a result, as related in the box Much Ado About Something, Boutros-Ghali was forced from office after one term.

In the aftermath of his ouster, the Security Council nominated and the General Assembly elected Kofi Annan of Ghana as the UN's seventh secretary-general. Annan is the first secretary-general to have spent almost his entire career as a UN diplomat rather than as a diplomat for his country. He joined UN service at age 24 and served in a variety of positions, including undersecretary-general for peacekeeping. As also related in the box Much Ado About Something, Annan was chosen because of Washington's view that he would be a cautious bureaucrat, and this coupled with his quiet demeanor led many observers to speculate that he would not act independently.

Those predictions were inaccurate. Since taking office in 1997, Annan has demonstrated a willingness to exercise leadership and even differ with the United States. He has done so more diplomatically, however, than the sometimes sharp-tongued Boutros-Ghali. This has earned Annan generally smooth relations with Washington and other major capitals, and he was easily reappointed for a second term beginning in 2002. Certainly he is soft-spoken; but that does not mean soft. Annan strongly supports the idea that the UN and its secretary-general should act with independence when necessary. During a commencement speech at the Massachusetts Institute of Technology (MIT), Annan told graduates that his years at MIT had given him "not only the analytical tools but also the intellectual confidence... to be comfortable in seeking the help of colleagues, but not fearing, in the end, to do things my way."[20]

Since coming to office in 1997, Secretary-General Kofi Annan of Ghana has shown himself to be a skilled and assertive leader. The UN secretary-general and the heads of many other international organizations are more than mere administrators; many of them are important diplomatic figures in their own right.

Early in this tenure, Annan had the opportunity to demonstrate his willingness to live up to his words about doing it "my way" if necessary. A crisis boiled up in early 1998 over Iraq's refusal to allow UN weapons inspectors free access to some sites. Both Baghdad and Washington seemed to be spoiling for a fight. Annan worked with the Security Council members to derive a UN position, but the United States let it be known that it would oppose Annan's intervention unless the UNSC position was acceptable to Washington. The Clinton administration's position was too obdurate, in the view of some, and Annan forced the issue by indicating that he would go to Iraq with or without U.S. approval. Sounding much like Dag Hammarskjöld might have in a similar situation, Annan avowed, "I had a constitutional duty to avert this kind of tragedy [renewed war with Iraq] if I could." When asked whether the maneuvering that forced the U.S. hand had been unintended, the secretary-general laughed softly and replied, "To some extent, no, it wasn't."[21]

Whatever the reaction of Washington or other capitals to any of Annan's specific actions, the overall reaction has been one of acclaim. He was accorded a high honor when in June 2001 on unanimous recommendation of the Security Council, the General Assembly voted without dissent to reappoint him to a second term as secretary-general beginning in January 2002. Then in October 2001 he received the Nobel Peace Prize for his work toward making "a better organized and more peaceful world." All in all, as a classic Frank Sinatra tune goes, "It was a very good year." And one senses that when his time as secretary-general is over, Annan will leave softly humming another famous Sinatra refrain, "I did it my way."

Similar tensions over the role of top officials exist in other IGOs; they are in substantial part a struggle between the traditional approach versus the alternative approach to world politics. Traditionally, national states have sought to control IGOs and their leaders. As IGOs and their leaders have grown stronger, however, they have more often struck out independently down the alternative path. As Secretary-General Annan has commented, he and his predecessors have all carried out their traditional duties as chief administrative officer, but they have also assumed another, alternative role: "an instrument of the larger interest, beyond national rivalries and regional concerns."[22] Presidents and prime ministers are finding, comments one U.S. diplomat, that "you can't put the secretary-general back in the closet when it's inconvenient."[23]

Bureaucracy

The secretary-general appoints the other principal officials of the Secretariat, but he must be sensitive to the desires of the dominant powers in making these appointments and must also pay attention to the geographic and, increasingly, to the gender composition of the Secretariat staff. Controversies have occasionally arisen over the distributions, but in recent years the focus of criticism has been the size and efficiency of the staffs of the UN headquarters in New York and its regional offices (Geneva, Nairobi, and Vienna). In this way, the UN is like many other IGOs and, indeed, national governments, whose allegedly bloated, inefficient, and unresponsive bureaucracies have made them a lightning rod for discontent with government.

Certainly, as with almost any bureaucracy, it is possible to find horror stories about the size and activities of IGO staffs. It is also the case, however, that the charges that the UN and its associated agencies are a bureaucratic swamp need to be put in perspective.

For instance, the UN Secretariat has trimmed its staff over 25 percent, from 12,000 in 1985 to 8,700 in 2002. Some perspective on such data can also be gained by comparing the UN bureaucracy to local governments and to companies. The city of New Orleans (pop. 485,000), for instance, employs more people (10,100) than does the UN (pop. 6,100,000,000). Even if one were to count all 64,700 employees of the UN and its 29 affiliated agencies (like the World Health Organization), they would only be roughly equal in number to the municipal employees of Baltimore and San Francisco combined, and just slightly more than the combined workers at Disney World and Disneyland. Indeed, McDonald's has more than five times as many employees devoted to serving the world hamburgers, french fries, and shakes than the UN has people devoted to serving the world's needs for peace, health, dignity, and prosperity.

IGO FINANCING AND RELATED ISSUES

All IGOs face the problem of obtaining sufficient funds to conduct their operations. National governments must also address this issue, but they have the power to impose and legally collect taxes. By contrast, IGOs have very little authority to compel member-countries to support them.

The United Nations Budget The United Nations is beset by severe and controversial financial problems. There are several elements to the extended UN budget. The first is the *core budget* for headquarters operations and the regular programs of the major UN organs. Second, there is the *peacekeeping budget* to meet the expenses of operations being conducted by the Security Council. These two budgets were, respectively, $1.2 billion and $2.9 billion in FY2003. Supporting the UN budgets respectively cost each American $4.25 and $10.28, for a total of $14.53, on the often incorrect assumption that the United States fully paid its share of UN costs. The third budget element is called the *voluntary contributions budget*, which funds a number of UN agencies such as the United Nations Children's Fund (UNICEF) and the United Nations Environment Programme (UNEP). The combined FY2003 expenditures of these agencies are about $3.5 billion.

The UN is almost entirely dependent on the assessment it levies on member-countries to pay its core and peacekeeping budgets. This assessment is fixed by the UNGA based on a complicated formula that reflects the ability to pay. According to the UN Charter, which is a valid treaty binding on all signatories, members are required to meet these assessments and may have their voting privilege in the General Assembly suspended if they are seriously in arrears. There are nine countries that each have assessments of 2 percent of the budget or higher. They and their percentages of the core budget assessment are: the United States (22.0 percent), Japan (19.6 percent), Germany (9.8 percent), France (6.5 percent), Great Britain (5.6 percent), Italy (5.1 percent), Canada (2.6 percent), Spain (2.5 percent), and Brazil (2.2 percent). There are another nine countries that pay between 1 and 2 percent. At the other end of the financial scale, about 70 percent of the UN's members are assessed below .01 percent, including about 20 percent paying the minimum assessment of 0.001 percent. The "target" voluntary budget payments are the same as the core budget. Because of their special responsibility (and their special privilege, the veto), permanent UNSC members pay a somewhat higher assessment for peacekeeping, with the U.S. share at 25 percent.

The assessment scheme is criticized by some on the grounds that while the 18 countries with assessments of 1 percent or higher collectively pay 90 percent of the UN budget, in FY1999 they cast just 9 percent of the votes in the UNGA. One result of the gap between contributions and voting power has been disenchantment with the organization by a number of large-contributor countries who sometimes find themselves in the minority on votes in the UNGA.

Such numbers are something of a fiction, however, because some countries do not pay their assessment. In early 2002 member-states were in arrears by $3.4 billion. As a result, the UN's financial situation constantly teeters on the edge of crisis at the very time it is being asked to do more and more to provide protection and help meet other humanitarian and social needs. "It is," said a frustrated Boutros-Ghali just before he stepped down, "as though the town fire department were being dispatched to put out fires raging in several places at once while a collection was being taken to raise money for the fire-fighting equipment."[24] The analogy between the UN's budget and fire fighting is hardly hyperbole. During FY2003, for example, the UN's peace-keeping budget is only about half the public safety (police and fire departments) budget of New York City.

The United States and the UN Budget The key to the UN's financial difficulties is the United States, which is the largest debtor. In early 2002, it owed $1.4 billion to the UN, accounting for 38 percent of the UN deficit. About one-third of that arrearage is for the core budget, about two-thirds for the peacekeeping budget. The build-up of the U.S. debt began in the late 1970s and was caused by a variety of factors. These included the general disinclination of the United States to fund inter-national relations needs other than military affairs, some loss of U.S. influence as many new countries took seats in the General Assembly, charges that the UN is wasteful, and opposition because it supports programs (especially abortion) that are opposed by some members of Congress and presidents Reagan, G. H. W. Bush, and G. W. Bush.

The U.S. refusal to pay evoked mounting criticism, even from Washington's allies. "We are growing tired of UN bashing," Prime Minister Jean Chrétien of Canada reproved, "and it is especially irritating when it comes from those who are not paying their bills." And, in a line that British diplomats had been waiting for over 200 years to deliver, the British foreign secretary said that for Americans to continue to vote in the UN without paying their assessment was tantamount to "represen-tation without taxation."[25]

Finally, with the United States facing a loss of its vote in the UN for nonpayment of its obligations, Congress in 1999 authorized gradually paying off the arrearage if the United Nations instituted a series of reforms, such as cutting the size of its staff, and dropping the U.S. assessments: from 25 percent to 22 percent for the core budget and from 30 percent to 25 percent for the peacekeeping budget. These steps were taken by the UN in 2000, and Congress has authorized some extra funding beyond the yearly assessment. Unanticipated peacekeeping expenditures have meant that the total U.S. debt has not decreased, but at least it is not rising as it had been.

IGO ACTIVITIES AND RELATED ISSUES

The most important aspects of any international organization are what it does, how well this corresponds to the functions we wish it to perform, and how well it is per-forming its roles. The following pages will begin to explore these aspects by exam-ining the scope of IGO activity, with an emphasis on the UN. Much of this discussion will only begin to touch on these activities, which receive more attention in other chapters.

Promoting International Peace and Security

The opening words of the UN Charter dedicate the organization to saving "suc-ceeding generations from the scourge of war, which… has brought untold sorrow to mankind." The UN attempts to fulfill this goal by creating norms against violence, by providing debate as an alternative to fighting, by intervening diplomatically to avert the outbreak of warfare or to help restore peace once violence occurs, by insti-tuting diplomatic and economic sanctions, by dispatching UN military forces to repel aggression or to act as a buffer between warring countries, and by promoting arms control and disarmament.

There are many people who hope that the UN will continue to become a more comprehensive and more powerful actor on the world stage. Others, including these two protesters in La Verkin, Utah (pop. 2,000), believe that the UN is at the forefront of an international conspiracy to rob them of their liberty. On July 4, 2001, the La Verkin town council enacted an ordinance that bans giving aid to the United Nations with town funds and displaying UN symbols on town property. The law also prohibits the "involuntary servitude" of any resident in UN peacekeeping and requires any residents who might work for the UN to file annual reports of their activities.

Creating Norms Against Violence One way that the United Nations helps promote international peace and security is by creating norms (beliefs about what is proper) against aggression and other forms of violence. To accomplish this, the UN works in such areas as promoting the concept of nuclear nonproliferation through the International Atomic Energy Agency, limiting chemical and biological weapons, and promoting rules for the restrained conduct of war when it occurs.

Countries that sign the Charter pledge to accept the principle "that armed force shall not be used, save in the common interest" and further agree to "refrain in their international relations from the threat or the use of force except in self-defense." Reaffirming the Charter's ideas, the UN (and other IGOs) have condemned Iraq's invasion of Kuwait, Serbian aggression against its neighbors, and other such actions. These denunciations and the slowly developing norm against aggression have not halted violence, but they have created an increasing onus on countries that strike the first blow. When, for example, the United States decided in 1989 to depose the regime of Panama's strongman, General Manuel Noriega, it acted unilaterally. Noriega was toppled, but Washington's action was condemned by both the UN and the OAS. Five years later, Washington again decided to overthrow the regime of a small country to its south. But before U.S. troops landed in Haiti, Washington took care to win UN support for its action.

Providing a Debate Alternative A second peace-enhancing role for the United Nations and some other IGOs is serving as a passive forum in which members publicly air their points of view and privately negotiate their differences. The UN thus acts like a safety valve, or perhaps a sound stage where the world drama can be played out without the dire consequences that could occur if another "shooting locale" were chosen. This grand-debate approach to peace involves denouncing your opponents, defending your actions, trying to influence world opinion, and winning symbolic victories. The British ambassador to the UN has characterized it as "a great clearing house for foreign policy," a place where "We talk to people... whom we don't talk to elsewhere because we have fraught relations with them."[26]

Diplomatic Intervention International organizations also regularly play a direct role in assisting and encouraging countries to settle their disputes peacefully. Ideally this occurs before hostilities, but it can take place even after fighting has started. The United Nations and other IGOs perform the following functions: (1) *Inquiry*: Fact-finding by neutral investigators; (2) *Good Offices*: Encouraging parties to negotiate; acting as a neutral setting for negotiations; (3) *Mediation*: Making suggestions about possible solutions; acting as an intermediary between two parties; (4) *Arbitration*: Using a special panel to find a solution that all parties agree in advance to accept; and (5) *Adjudication*: Submitting disputes to an international court such as the ICJ. These activities do not often capture the headlines, but they are a vital part of maintaining or restoring the peace.

It is possible, even probable, that renewed fighting between Iraq and the United States and some other countries was averted in early 1998 because of Secretary-General Annan's personal mediation and his ability to fashion a solution acceptable to all. According to the UN ambassador at the time, "Annan's personal diplomacy coupled with a formula that only he, through his stature, could sell to the Iraqis" was the difference between war and peace.[27]

Sanctions The increased interdependence of the world has heightened the impact of diplomatic and economic sanctions. In recent years, these have been applied by the UN, the OAS, and other IGOs on such countries as Haiti, Iraq, Libya, South Africa, and Yugoslavia. As we will see in chapter 15, sanctions are controversial and often do not work. But there have been successes. Sanctions against South Africa helped ease apartheid there; they helped force Iraq to grudgingly give up some of its hidden remaining arms and arms production facilities and to allow UN military inspectors to search for other violations; and they were a factor in finally persuading Yugoslavia to turn over former president Slobodan Milosevic to the UN-sponsored tribunal in The Hague to be tried for war crimes.

Peacekeeping The United Nations additionally has a limited ability to intervene militarily in a dispute. Other IGOs, such as the OAS, have also occasionally undertaken collective military action. In the UN, this process is often called peacekeeping. It is normally conducted under the auspices of the UNSC, although the UNGA has sometimes authorized action.

Peacekeeping as a form of international security is extensively covered in chapter 13, but a few preliminary facts are appropriate here. Through mid-2000, the United Nations had mounted 55 peacekeeping operations that had utilized about 800,000 military and police personnel from 118 countries. These operations ranged from very lightly armed observer missions, through police forces, to full-fledged military forces. Never before have international forces been so active as they are now. The number of UN peacekeeping operations has risen markedly in the post–cold war era, as shown in Figure 9.6. In early 2002 , there were 16 UN peacekeeping forces of varying sizes in the field at locations throughout the world. These forces totaled about 46,000 troops and police. As the UN took on more missions, peacekeeping costs rose sharply from $235 million in FY1987 to about $3.5 billion for FY1996. From there they fell off for the next two years, but an upsurge of turmoil in East

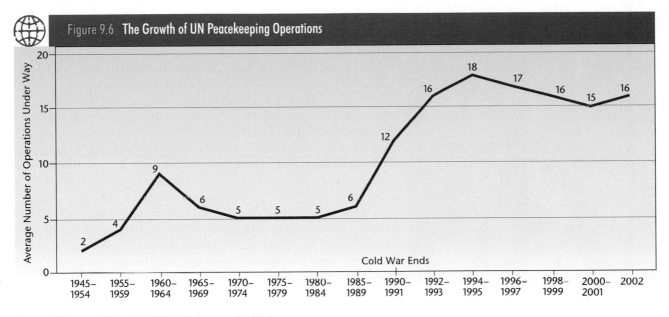

Figure 9.6 **The Growth of UN Peacekeeping Operations**

Data source: UN, Department of Peacekeeping Web site, http://www.un.org/depts/dpko/.

The end of the cold war and its standoff between the United States and the Soviet Union in the Security Council has allowed the UN to mount a significantly increased number of peacekeeping operations since the early 1990s.

Timor, Afghanistan, Ethiopia, Eritrea, and other trouble spots led the UN to project a $2.95 billion peacekeeping budget for FY2003.

United Nations peacekeeping seldom involves a stern international enforcer smiting aggressors with powerful blows. Few countries are willing to give any IGO much power and independence. Rather, UN peacekeeping is usually a "coming between," a positioning of a neutral force that creates space and is intended to help defuse an explosive situation. This in no way lessens the valuable role that the UN has played. It has, for example, been a positive force in helping East Timor first escape the violence inflicted on it when it was seeking independence from Indonesia and then helping the East Timorese transition during the period between the final withdrawal of Indonesia's troops to the date of the country's independence in May 2002. Fortunately, UN peacekeeping forces have suffered relatively few casualties, but almost 1,700 have died in world service. For these sacrifices and contributions to world order, the UN peacekeeping forces were awarded the 1988 Nobel Peace Prize.

Arms Control and Disarmament Promoting arms control and disarmament is another international security function of IGOs. The International Atomic Energy Agency, an affiliate of the UN, helps promote and monitor the nonproliferation of nuclear weapons. The UN also sponsors numerous conferences on weapons and conflict and has also played an important role in the genesis of the Chemical Weapons Convention and other arms control agreements.

Social, Economic, Environmental, and Other Roles

In addition to maintaining and restoring the peace, IGOs engage in a wide variety of other activities. During its early years, the United Nations' emphasis was on security. This concern has not abated, but it has been joined by social, economic, environmental, and other nonmilitary security concerns. This shift has been a result of the ebb and eventual end

Did You Know That:
The UN and its associated agencies, such as UNICEF, annually have about 81 cents per human to spend on economic and social development. The world defense ministries have about $135 per human for military expenditures.

These Chinese police seen in Dili, the capital of East Timor, were part of the UN peacekeeping civilian police force that helped keep the country stable until it achieved full independence in 2002. To date most UN forces have been small and lightly armed, and they have not always succeeded in maintaining or restoring the peace. But in East Timor the UN was instrumental in restoring the peace after the brutal effort by the Indonesian army to halt East Timor's drive for self-determination.

of the cold war, the growing number of LDCs since the 1960s, realization that the environment is in danger, and changing global values that have brought an increased focus on human and political rights. "Peacekeeping operations claim the headlines," Secretary-General Annan has observed astutely, "but by far the lion's share of our budget and personnel are devoted to the lower-profile work of... helping countries to create jobs and raise standards of living; delivering relief aid to victims of famine, war and natural disasters; protecting refugees; promoting literacy; and fighting disease. To most people around the world, this is the face of the United Nations."[28] This effort has recently included the UN's sponsorship of a conference of aid donors to coordinate assistance to rebuild Afghanistan; coordination of the delivery of humanitarian relief to its people; and the repatriation of hundreds of thousands of Afghanis who had fled the country into Pakistan and other neighboring countries.

It would be impossible to list here, much less fully describe, the broad range of endeavors in which the UN and other IGOs are involved. Suffice it to say that they cover most of the issues that humans address at all levels of government. Many of these activities will be highlighted in subsequent chapters, so this discussion is limited to a few of the programs and successes of the United Nations and other IGOs.

IGOs and Economic Development The United Nations Development Programme (UNDP), the World Bank, and a significant number of other global and regional IGOs work to improve the economic well-being of those who are deprived because of their location in an LDC, gender, or some other cause. The UNDP alone supports more than 5,000 projects globally with a budget of $1.3 billion. The UN Development Fund for Women (UNIFEM) focuses on the betterment of women in LDCs.

IGOs and Human Rights Beginning with the Universal Declaration of Human Rights in 1948, the UN has actively promoted dozens of agreements on political, civil, economic, social, and cultural rights. The UN Commission on Human Rights has used its power of investigation and its ability to issue reports to expose abuses of human rights and to create pressure on the abusers through a process that one scholar has termed the "mobilization of shame" (Weisband, 2000). Currently, for example, the UN is at the heart of the global effort to free the estimated 250 million children who are forced to work instead of being sent to school, to end the sexual predation of children that is big business in some parts of the world, and to eliminate other abuses that mock the meaning of childhood.

IGOs and the Environment Beginning with the UN Conference on Environment and Development (dubbed the Earth Summit) in 1992, the UN has sponsored several global meetings on the environment. These have resulted in the initiation of programs that will slow down, stop, or begin to reverse the degradation of the environment. IGOs are increasingly also requiring that environmental impact statements accompany requests for economic development aid, and in some cases refusing to finance projects that have unacceptable negative impacts on the biosphere.

IGOs and International Law and Norms An important and increasing role of the UN and other IGOs is defining and expanding international law and international norms of cooperation. International courts associated with IGOs help establish legal precedent. Also, the signatories to the UN Charter and other IGO constitutions incur obligations to obey the principles of these documents. International organizations additionally sponsor multinational treaties, which may establish the assumption of law. Over 300 such treaties have been negotiated through the UN's auspices. As one scholar sees the norm-building function of IGOs, "The procedures and rules of international institutions create information structures. They determine what principles are acceptable as a basis for reducing conflicts and whether governmental actions are legitimate or illegitimate. Consequently, they help shape actors' expectations" (Keohane, 1998:91).

IGOs and the Quality of Human Existence More than 30 million refugees from war, famine, and other dangers have been fed, given shelter, and otherwise assisted through the UN High Commissioner for Refugees. A wide variety of IGOs also devote their energies to such concerns as health, nutrition, and literacy. For example, UNICEF, WHO, and other agencies have undertaken a $150 million program to develop a multi-immunization vaccine. This vaccine program is designed to double the estimated 2 million children who now annually survive because of such international medical assistance. The Food and Agriculture Organization (FAO) has launched a program to identify, preserve, and strengthen through new genetic techniques those domestic animals that might prove especially beneficial to

This Afghani woman is begging in the streets of Kabul outside a UN office for humanitarian aid in late 2001. The United Nations is coordinating a massive effort to give humanitarian assistance to Afghanis, and one hopes it will soon help to ease the desperation of this woman.

LDCs. Western breeds of pigs, for example, usually produce only about 10 piglets a litter; the Taihu pig of China manages 15 to 20. The FAO hopes to use the latter and other appropriate animals to increase protein availability in the LDCs.

IGOs and Independence Yet another role of IGOs has been to encourage national self-determination. The UN Trusteeship Council once monitored numerous colonial dependencies, but the wave of independence in recent decades steadily lessened its number of charges. Then, in October 1994, the United States and Palau notified the council that, as Kuniwo Nakamura, Palau's president, put it, "We have made our own decision that we are ready to embark on the journey of independence with confidence."[29] Inasmuch as Palau was the last trust territory, the announcement meant that the Trusteeship Council's mission was fulfilled and, while it continues to exist technically, it no longer meets.

EVALUATING IGOs AND THEIR FUTURE

The United Nations has existed for more than fifty years. Most other IGOs are even younger. Have they succeeded? The answer depends on your standard of evaluation.

Ultimate goals are one standard. Article 1 of the UN Charter sets out lofty goals such as maintaining peace and security and solving economic, social, cultural, and humanitarian problems. Clearly, the world is still beset by violent conflicts and by ongoing economic and social misery. Thus, from the perspective of meeting ultimate goals, it is easy to be skeptical about what the UN and other IGOs have accomplished.

One has to ask, however, whether the meeting of ultimate goals is a reasonable standard. There is, according to one diplomat, a sense that "failure was built into [the UN] by an extraordinary orgy of exaggerated expectations."[30]

Progress is a second standard by which to evaluate the UN and other IGOs. The question is, Is the world better off for their presence? That is the standard Kofi Annan appeals for when he implores people to "Judge us rightly… by the relief and refuge that we provide to the poor, to the hungry, the sick and threatened: the peoples of the world whom the United Nations exists to serve."[31] Between its 40th and 50th anniversaries, the United Nations surpassed all previous marks in terms of numbers of simultaneous peacekeeping missions, peacekeeping troops deployed, and other international security efforts. During the 1990s alone, the UN sponsored 12 conferences on such diverse topics as the environment (Rio de Janeiro, 1992), women's issues (Beijing, 1995), and food (Rome, 1996). This activity has continued apace, with conferences on racism (Durban, 2001), aging (Madrid, 2002), and sustainable development (Johannesburg, 2002) among those held in the first two years of the new century. These meetings have all focused attention on global problems and have made some contribution to advancing our knowledge and to enhancing our attempts to deal seriously with a wide range of economic, social, and environmental global challenges. Moreover, the people of the world tend to recognize these contributions. A survey of people in many countries around the world found that 60 percent of the respondents evaluated the UN as "very" or "somewhat" satisfactory. More than 80 percent of respondents in Africa, the world's most troubled region, gave the UN positive marks.[32] Thus, by the standard of progress, the UN and other IGOs have made a contribution.

What is possible is a third standard by which to evaluate the UN and other IGOs. Insofar as the UN does not meet our expectations, we need to ask whether it is a flaw of the organization or the product of the unwillingness of member-states to live up to the standards that countries accept when they ratify the Charter. Simply paying their assessments regularly and on time is one thing more countries could do. The UN will also work better if countries try to make it effective. It is a truism, as Kofi

Annan put it, that there is a "troubling asymmetry between what the member-states want of the [UN] and what they actually allow it to be."[33]

Whether alternatives exist is a fourth standard by which to evaluate the UN and other IGOs. One must also ask, If not the UN and other international organizations, then what? Can the warring, uncaring world continue unchanged in the face of nuclear weapons, persistent poverty, an exploding population, periodic mass starvation, continued widespread human rights violations, resource depletion, and environmental degradation? Somehow the world has survived these plagues, but one of the realities that this book hopes to make clear is that we are hurtling toward our destiny at an ever-increasing, now exponential speed. In a rapidly changing system, doing things the old way may be inadequate and may even take us down a road that, although familiar, will lead the world to cataclysm. At the very least, as Secretary of State Madeleine Albright noted, "The United Nations gives the good guys—the peacemakers, the freedom fighters, the people who believe in human rights, those committed to human development—an organized vehicle for achieving gains."[34] This returns us to the question, If not the UN, then what? In reply, there may be considerable truth in the view of the British ambassador to the UN that "it's the UN, with all its warts, or it's the law of the jungle."[35] It is through this jungle that the road more familiar has passed, and following it into the future may bring what Shakespeare was perhaps imagining when he wrote in *Hamlet* of a tale that would "harrow up thy soul, [and] freeze thy young blood."

To repeat an important point, the UN and other IGOs are, in the end, only what we make them. They do possess some independence, but it is limited. Mostly their successes and failures reflect the willingness or disinclination of member-countries to cooperate and use them to further joint efforts. Kofi Annan urged support of the UN by quoting what Winston Churchill said to Franklin Roosevelt in 1941: "Give us the tools and we will do the job."[36] In the same vein, Dag Hammarskjöld aptly predicted, "Everything will be all right—you know when? When people, just people, stop thinking of the United Nations as a weird Picasso abstraction and see it as a drawing they made themselves."[37]

Whether that occurs is uncertain. What is clear is that critics of IGOs are too often narrowly negative. They disparage the organizations without noting their contributions or suggesting improvements. IGOs hold one hope for the future, and those who would denigrate them should make other, positive suggestions rather than implicitly advocate a maintenance of the status quo. There is a last bit of Shakespeare's wisdom, found in *Julius Caesar*, that is worth pondering. The playwright counsels us that:

> There is a tide in the affairs of men
> Which, taken at the flood, leads on to fortune;
> Omitted, all the voyage of their life
> Is bound in shallows and in miseries.

Chapter Summary

1. One sign of the changing international system is the rapid rise over the last century in the number of intergovernmental organizations (IGOs).
2. There are many classifications of international organizations, including global, regional, and specialized IGOs.
3. Current international organization is the product of three lines of development: the idea that humans should live in peace and mutual support, the idea that the big powers have a special responsibility for maintaining order, and the growth of specialized international organizations to deal with narrow nonpolitical issues.

4. The rapid growth of all types of international organizations stems from increased international contact among states and people, increased economic interdependence, the growing importance of transnational issues and political movements, the inadequacy of the state-centered system for dealing with world problems, small states attempting to gain strength by joining together, and successful IGOs providing role models for new organizations.

5. There are significant differences among views on the best role for international organizations. Four existing and possible roles of IGOs are: providing an interactive arena, acting as a center for cooperation among states, evolving into an independent national actor, and becoming a supranational organization.

6. Some observers argue that international organizations are best suited to promoting cooperation among states rather than trying to replace the state-centered system. Still others contend that international organizations should concentrate on performing limited functional activities with the hope of building a habit of cooperation and trust that can later be built upon. Finally, many view international organizations as vehicles that should be manipulated to gain national political goals. The UN serves as an example of how current IGOs are organized and operate.

7. Some observers favor moving toward a system of supranational organization, in which some form of world government, or perhaps regional governments, would replace or substantially modify the present state-centered system.

8. The EU provides an example of the development, structure, and roles of a regional IGO. The EU has evolved considerably along the path of economic integration. The movement toward political integration is more recent and is proving more difficult than economic integration.

9. The United Nations provides an example of the development, structure, and roles of a global IGO.

10. There are several important issues related to the structure of international organizations. One group of questions relates to membership and criteria for membership.

11. Voting schemes to be used in such bodies are another important issue. Current international organizations use a variety of voting schemes that include majority voting, weighted voting, and unanimity voting.

12. Another group of questions concerns the administration of international organizations, including the role of the political leaders and the size and efficiency of IGO bureaucracies. The source of IGO revenue and the size of IGO budgets are a related concern.

13. There are also a number of significant issues that relate to the general role of international organizations. Peacekeeping is one important role. Others include creating norms against violence, providing a debate alternative, intervening diplomatically, imposing sanctions, and promoting arms control and disarmament.

14. Other roles for the UN and other international organizations include promoting international law, promoting arms control, bettering the human condition, promoting self-government, and furthering international cooperation.

15. However one defines the best purpose of international organization, it is important to be careful of standards of evaluation. The most fruitful standard is judging an organization by what is possible, rather than setting inevitably frustrating ideal goals.

Chapter 10

National Power and Diplomacy: The Traditional Approach

Then, everything includes itself in power,
Power into will, will into appetite.

Shakespeare, *Troilus and Cressida*

Bid me discourse, I will enchant thine ear

Shakespeare, *Venus and Adonis*

We thought, because we had power, we had wisdom.
Stephen Vincent Benét, *Litany for Dictatorships*, 1935

All politicians make their decisions on the basis of national or political
interest and explain them in terms of altruism.
Former Israeli diplomat Abba Eban, 1996

Chapter Objectives

After completing this chapter, you should be able to:

- Characterize diplomacy as an activity conducted by a state to further its interests.
- Understand power as the foundation of diplomacy.
- Analyze the characteristics of power.
- Understand the major elements of a country's power.
- Explain the functions of diplomacy.
- Describe the various settings of diplomacy.
- Summarize the evolution of diplomacy from ancient Greece to nineteenth-century Europe.
- Describe and characterize diplomatic practice in the modern era.
- Explain the increase in high-level, leader-to-leader diplomacy.
- Consider the growing importance of public diplomacy in world politics.
- Explain the art of diplomacy and the importance of choosing among various options in its practice.
- Consider the various rules of diplomacy.
- Identify various diplomatic alternatives.

Once upon a time," began a fable told by the great British diplomat and prime minister Winston Churchill, "all the animals in the zoo decided that they would disarm." To accomplish that laudable goal, the animals convened a diplomatic conference, where, Churchill's tale went:

> The Rhinoceros said when he opened the proceeding that the use of teeth was barbarous and horrible and ought to be strictly prohibited by general consent. Horns, which were mainly defensive weapons, would, of course, have to be allowed. The Buffalo, the Stag, the Porcupine, and even the little Hedgehog all said they would vote with the Rhino, but the Lion and the Tiger took a different view. They defended teeth and even claws, which they described as honourable weapons of immemorial antiquity. The Panther, the Leopard, the Puma, and the whole tribe of small cats all supported the Lion and the Tiger. Then the Bear spoke. He proposed that both teeth and horns should be banned and never used again for fighting by animals. It would be quite enough if animals were allowed to give each other a good hug when they quarreled. No one could object to that. It was so fraternal, and that would be a great step toward peace. However, all the other animals were very offended by the Bear, and the Turkey fell into a perfect panic. The discussion got so hot and angry, and all those animals began thinking so much about horns and teeth and hugging when they argued about the peaceful intentions that had brought them together, that they began to look at one another in a very nasty way. Luckily the keepers were able to calm them down and persuade them to go back quietly to their cages, and they began to feel quite friendly with one another again.[1]

Sir Winston's allegory is instructive, as well as colorfully entertaining. It touches on many aspects of diplomacy discussed in this chapter. *Power* is the first thing we will explore. It remains an essential element of diplomacy in a system based on self-interested sovereignty. In our world, like the zoo, the actors that possess the power to give rewards or inflict punishment are able to influence other actors. Power has many forms. Physical strength is one, and the rhino and the lion were both powerful in this way. Skill is another aspect of power. The turkey had little tangible strength, but perhaps it possessed guile and other intangible diplomatic skills to persuade the other animals to adopt its views. Economic power is also important in diplomacy. The zookeepers controlled the food supply, and may have used food as a positive incentive (more food) or negative sanction (less or no food) to persuade the animals to return to their cages.

The general nature of diplomacy is a topic that naturally follows our exploration of the power foundations of diplomacy. This topic involves the overall system, the setting in which modern diplomacy occurs. The zoo was the system in which the animals negotiated. Like the current international system, the zoo system was based on self-interest, with each group of animals selecting goals that were advantageous to itself with little thought about how they affected others. The zoo system also apparently allowed some potential for fighting and thus based success in part on the Darwinian law of the jungle. Yet it is the case that the animals were also partly constrained by the zookeepers with, perhaps, some protection afforded by cages.

Modern diplomacy is the third major topic in this chapter, and we will look at how it has evolved and at some of its characteristics. Multilateral diplomacy, for example, has become a much more prominent part of diplomacy than it once was. In Churchill's story, the animals conducted multisided negotiations instead of bilateral diplomacy between, say, just the rhino and the tiger. Those two animals might have made a bilateral agreement that both horns and fangs were acceptable; once hedgehogs, turkeys, and others became involved, the diplomatic dynamic changed greatly. In such a circumstance, diplomatic coalition building is one aspect of support gathering. It may well have been that, before the conference, the rhino had met with the buffalo, stag, porcupine, and hedgehog to convince them that they should support the rhino's position that horns were defensive weapons, while teeth and claws were offensive weapons.

Options in the conduct of diplomacy make up the fourth and final part of this chapter. Direct negotiation is one method, and the animals were engaged in that. Signaling is another method. This occurred when the animals "began to look at each other in a very nasty way." Public diplomacy to win the support of public opinion is another diplomatic method, and it is possible to see in Churchill's story how a clever diplomatic proposal can create an advantage. One can imagine the bear's proposal emblazoned in the *Zoo News* headline the next day: "Bear Proposes Eliminating All Weapons. Suggests Hugging as Alternative to Fighting." World opinion might have rallied to the bear; this would have put pressure on the other negotiators to accede to a seemingly benign proposal to usher in a new world order based on peace, love, and hugging.

Before proceeding, we should take a moment to put this chapter in context. It is the first of two chapters that look at the traditional and the alternative bases for establishing what policies will prevail in the world. The traditional approach involves countries' practicing national diplomacy by applying power in the pursuit of their self-interest. This approach does not mean that might makes right, but it surely means that might usually makes success. The alternative approach, discussed in chapter 11, is to apply the standards of international law and justice to the conduct of international relations so that right, rather than who is mightiest, will more often determine who prevails.

National Power: The Foundation of National Diplomacy

"Until human nature changes, power and force will remain at the heart of international relations," a top U.S. foreign policy adviser commented.[2] Not everyone would agree with such a gloomy realpolitik assessment, but it underlines the crucial role that power plays in diplomacy. When the goals and interests of states conflict, states often struggle to determine whose interests will prevail. The resolution rests frequently on who has the most power. In the aftermath of the 9-11 terrorist attacks, the United States demanded that Afghanistan turn over Osama bin Laden and other al-Qaeda members whom Washington blamed for the attacks. The Taliban government in Kabul demanded proof of the U.S. allegations, and declared, "If there is no evidence and proof, we're not prepared to give up Osama bin Laden." President Bush's response was, "The Taliban must act and act immediately. They will hand over the terrorists or they will share in their fate."[3] The Taliban refused to act, and they soon shared al-Qaeda's fate as U.S. bombs rained down on them.

THE NATURE OF POWER

Social scientists struggle to define and measure power and to describe exactly how it works. Harvard University dean and former top U.S. Defense Department official Joseph Nye (2000:55) writes that power "is like the weather. Everyone talks about it, but few understand it." Alluding to an even greater mystery, Nye confides that power is "like love… easier to experience than to define or measure." He also warns that if we

The success of a country's diplomacy rests at least in part on its power. The ultimatum that President George Bush gave to Afghanistan in 2001 to surrender al-Qaeda terrorists was backed up by American arms. When the Taliban government in Kabul refused to give in, bombs rained down from U.S. warplanes such as this B-1B Lancer bomber.

always try to intimidate others, "we may be as mistaken about our power as was the fox who thought he was hurting Brer Rabbit when he threw him into the briar patch." Weather, love, briar patches? Yes, power is perplexing! If its intricacies can throw a Harvard dean and assistant secretary of defense into such a morass of mixed metaphors and similes, then how can we understand power? The first step is to define the way this text uses the word, so that we can proceed from a common point.

Power as an Asset

Power can be understood to equal national capabilities. Power is a political resource, which encompasses the sum of the various attributes of a state that enable it to achieve its goals even when they clash with the goals of other international actors. Power is multifaceted. It includes tangible elements, such as numbers of weapons; it also includes intangible elements, such as public morale.

One way to comprehend power is to think about *power as money*, as a sort of political currency. Equating power and money is helpful because both are assets that can be used to acquire things. Money buys things; power causes things to happen. Like money, power is sometimes used in a charitable way. But also like money, power is more often used for self-interest. It is also true that acquiring money and power both often require sacrifices. Furthermore, those who use their financial or power assets imprudently may lose more than they gain. As with any analogy, however, you should be wary of overusing the comparison. There are differences between money and power. One is that political power is less liquid than money; it is harder to convert into things that you want. A second difference is that power, unlike money, has no standard measurement that allows all parties to agree on the amount involved.

As with money, one of the confusions about power is whether it is an asset (an end, goal) that you try to acquire and maintain or a tool (a means, instrument) that you use. It is both. Countries seek both to acquire power and to use it in international politics. While this chapter concentrates on power as an asset, it is important to realize that countries sometimes treat power as a goal.

One important issue about any asset is, "How much is enough?" If you think about money as a physical object, it is pretty useless. It is inedible, you cannot build anything useful out of money, and it will not even burn very well if you need to keep warm. Yet some people are obsessed with having money for its own sake. For them, acquiring money is an end in itself. Literature is full of such stories, ranging from Moliére's *The Miser* to Dickens's classic *A Christmas Carol* and its tragic tale of Ebenezer Scrooge. The misers give up love, friendships, and other pleasures to get and keep money only to discover, in the end, that their money becomes a burden. Similarly, some people believe that countries can become fixated on acquiring power, especially military power, beyond what is prudently needed to meet possible exigencies. This, critics say, is unwise because power is expensive, it creates a temptation to use it, and it spawns insecurity in others.

Measuring Power

At a general level, it is possible to measure or at least estimate power. There can be no doubt, for example, that China is more powerful than Mongolia. Beyond such broad judgments, however, scholars and policy makers have not been successful at anything approaching precise measurements of power. One problem is creating a formula that allocates realistic relative weights to military might, economic capacity, leadership capability, and other factors in the power equation. This was well illustrated by a study that reviewed four attempts by various scholars to devise formulas to measure national power (Taber, 1989). There were numerous disagreements based on the imprecise ability to measure power. Two studies rated the Soviet Union the most powerful. One each rated the United States and China most powerful. One ranked China only seventh. Brazil ranked number three in one study, and India ranked number four in another study; yet two studies did not place either country in the top ten. The list need not go on to make the point that different formulas for measuring power yielded very different results.

A second problem with measuring power precisely is a result of the fact that many aspects of power are difficult to quantify. Gathering data on some aspects of power (such as number of weapons, GDP, or population) is easy. Quantifying other aspects of power, such as leadership, borders on the impossible.

Does this mean that we should abandon trying to estimate national power? No, it does not. To repeat a point, there are clearly differences in national power. Ignoring them would be foolish, but it would also be a mistake to ignore the complexity and fluidity of power and to underestimate or overestimate the power of others based on one or more simple calculations.

Characteristics of Power

Power is not a simple and stable phenomenon. Indeed, it is very much a political chameleon, constantly changing even while it remains the same. The last task of this section is to explore the impact of the various characteristics of power.

Power Is Dynamic Even simple measurements show that power is constantly in flux. Economies prosper or lag, arms are modernized or become outmoded, resources are discovered or are depleted, and populations rally behind or lose faith in their governments. The USSR was a superpower; it collapsed; its successor state, Russia, is far from a superpower status.

Adding to the dynamism of power, some scholars believe that its very nature is changing. They contend that military and other assets that contribute to **coercive power** (also called "hard power," the ability to make another country do or not do something) are declining in importance as military force and economic sanctions become more costly and less effective. Simultaneously, according to this view, **persuasive power** (also called "soft power," assets such as moral authority or technological excellence that enhance a country's image of leadership) is increasing in importance (Nye, 2000; Hall, 1999).

Some scholars even believe that war has become so destructive that it is a fading phenomenon, especially among economically developed countries (EDCs). That thought is given some credence by the fact that the 1990s were not a time of interstate warfare, with the major exception of Iraq's invasion of Kuwait and a few relatively minor border clashes. Perhaps coercive diplomacy will sometime become a relic of humankind's barbaric past, but that day, if it comes at all, is probably far in the future for two reasons. First, as one study notes, the incidence of violence during the 1990s was so high and so often sparked outside intervention that conflict was a "growth industry" (Bloomfield & Moulton, 1997:34). Second, there are still times when force or the threat of force is needed to resolve an international crisis. After an agreement that averted war in 1998 over Iraq's refusal to allow continued UN arms inspections, Iraqi foreign minister Tarik Aziz and UN secretary-general Kofi Annan held a joint press conference. Aziz contended that it was "diplomacy that reached this agreement, not the saber-rattling." To which Annan chimed in, "You can do a lot with diplomacy, but of course you can do a lot more with diplomacy backed up by firmness and force."[4]

Did You Know That:
Frederic the Great, the king of Prussia (1712–1786), once commented, "Diplomacy without arms is like music without instruments."

Power Is Both Objective and Subjective We have seen on several occasions that international politics is influenced both by what is true and by what others perceive to be true. **Objective power** consists of assets that you objectively possess and that you have both the capacity and the will to use. As such, it is a major factor in determining whose interests prevail, as Afghanistan found out in 2001 in its war with the U.S.-led coalition of forces.

Subjective power is also important. It is common to hear politicians argue that their country cannot back down in a crisis or get out of an ill-conceived military action because the country's reputation will be damaged. Research shows that concern to be overdrawn (Mercer, 1996). Still, a country's power is to a degree based on others' perceptions of its current or potential power or its reputation for being willing (or not willing) to use the power it has. Sometimes the perception that a country is not currently powerful can tempt another country. When asked for his evaluation of the U.S. military in 1917, a German admiral replied, "Zero, zero, zero." Based on this perception of U.S. power, Germany resumed the submarine warfare against U.S. merchant shipping, a move that soon led to war with the United States.

Power Is Relative Power does not exist in a vacuum. Since power is about the ability to persuade or make another actor do or not do something, calculating power is of limited use except to measure it against the power of the other side. When assessing capabilities, then, **relative power**, or the comparative power of national actors, must be considered. We cannot, for example, say that China is powerful unless we specify in comparison to whom. Whatever Beijing's power resources may be, China's relative power compared to another major power, such as Japan, is less than is China's relative power compared to a smaller neighbor, such as Vietnam.

A related issue is whether power is a **zero-sum game**. If a gain in power of one actor inevitably means a loss of power for other actors, the game is zero-sum. If an actor can gain power without the power of other actors being diminished, then the game is non–zero-sum. Realists tend to see power as zero-sum; idealists usually portray it as non–zero-sum. Without delving too far into this controversy, we can say that the relative nature of power implies that sometimes, especially between antagonists, power approaches zero-sum. When China's Asian rival India tested nuclear weapons in 1998, it decreased China's relative power compared to India and arguably reduced China's influence in the countries to its southwest. Yet India's advance in power was non–zero-sum relative to another of its regional rivals, Pakistan, because that country tested its own nuclear weapons almost simultaneously with India. When the nuclear dust settled, India and Pakistan were in the same relative power position vis-à-vis one another as they had been before the blasts.

Power Is Situational A country's power varies according to the situation, or context, in which it is being applied. A country's **situational power** is often less than the total inventory of its capabilities. Military power provides a good example. If we agree that, even if provoked, India is unlikely to use nuclear weapons against Sri Lanka no matter what occurs there in the civil war between the majority Buddhist Sinhalese and the minority Hindu Tamils, then India's becoming a nuclear weapons state has not affected the Sri Lanka/India power relationship.

Power Is Multidimensional Power is multifaceted. Therefore, to analyze power well it is important to consider *all* the dimensions of power *and* to place them in their proper relative and situational contexts. Only then can we begin to answer the question of who is powerful and who is not. To help with that process, our next step is to identify the various determinants of national power.

The Elements of Power

There are many ways to categorize the multitudinous elements of power. One common way that we have mentioned is to distinguish between objective (easily measurable, tangible) elements of power and subjective (hard-to-measure, intangible) facets of power. Another approach is to group both the tangible and the intangible power assets into various functional categories. Two such categories, the national core and the national infrastructure, are central to the power of all countries because they serve as a foundation for the more utilitarian categories of national power, specifically military power and economic power. We will, in the following sections, analyze these two central categories of national power; military and economic power will be discussed in chapters 12 and 15 respectively.

THE NATIONAL CORE

The national state forms the basis of this element of power. The essence of a state can be roughly divided into three elements: national geography, people, and government.

National Geography

Shakespeare's King Henry VI proclaimed:

> Let us be backed with God and with the seas
> Which He hath given for fence impregnable,…
> In them and in ourselves our safety lies.

It is not clear what, if anything, God has done for England over the centuries, but King Henry's soliloquy reminds us that the English Channel has helped save England from European conquest for nine centuries. The country's most important physical characteristic is being separated from the continent by a narrow expanse of water. Without it the British might have been conquered by Napoleon in the early 1800s or by Hitler's army in 1940. Geographic factors include location, topography, size, and climate.

The *location* of a country, particularly in relation to other countries, is significant. The Chinese army's significance as a power factor is different for the country's relations with the United States and with Russia. The huge Chinese army can do little to threaten the United States, far across the Pacific Ocean. By contrast, Russia and China share a border, and Chinese soldiers could march into Siberia. Location can be an advantage or a disadvantage. Spain was able to avoid involvement in either world war partly because of its relative isolation from the rest of Europe. Poland, sandwiched between Germany and Russia, and Korea, stuck between China and Japan, each has a distinctly unfortunate location. The Israelis would almost certainly be better off if their promised land were somewhere—almost anywhere—else. And the Kuwaitis probably would not mind moving either, providing they could take their oil fields with them.

Geography can add or detract from a country's power. Afghanistan's high and rugged mountains and its frigid winters have long been an ally against military operations by outsiders. That was true for the U.S.-led forces that entered the country after the 9-11 attacks. The steep, snow-covered mountains visible behind the U.S. Army CH-47 Chinook helicopter illustrate the daunting weather and terrain American forces have had to face.

A country's *topography*—its mountains, rivers, and plains—is also important. The Alps form a barrier that has helped protect Switzerland from its larger European neighbors and spared the Swiss the ravages of both world wars. The rugged mountains of Afghanistan bedeviled British and Soviet invaders in the past, and in 2001 and 2002 they frequently frustrated the efforts of U.S. and other coalition troops to corner and capture or kill remnants of the al-Qaeda and Taliban forces.

Topography can also work against a country. The broad European plain that extends from Germany's Rhine River to the Ural Mountains in central Russia has been an easy invasion avenue along which the armies of Napoleon, Kaiser Wilhelm II, and Hitler have marched.

A country's *size* is important. Bigger is often better. The immense expanse of Russia, for example, has repeatedly saved it from invasion. Although sometimes overwhelmed at first, the Russian armies have been able to retreat into the interior and buy time in exchange for geography while regrouping. By contrast, Israel's small size gives it no room to retreat.

A country's *climate* can also play a power role (Eichengreen, 1998). The tropical climate of Vietnam, with its heavy monsoon rains and its dense vegetation, made it difficult for the Americans to use effectively much of the superior weaponry they possessed. At the other extreme, the bone-chilling Russian winter has allied itself with Russia's geographic size to form a formidable defensive barrier. Many of Napoleon's soldiers literally froze to death during the French army's retreat from Moscow, and 133 years later Germany's army, the *Wehrmacht*, was decimated by cold and ice during the sieges of Leningrad and Stalingrad. In fact the Russian winter has proved so formidable that Czar Nicholas I commented, "Russia has two generals we can trust, General January and General February."

People

A second element of the national core is a country's human characteristics. Tangible demographic subcategories include number of people, age distribution, and such quantitative factors as health and education. There are also intangible population factors such as morale.

Population As is true for geographic size, the size of a country's population can be a positive or a negative factor. Because a large population supplies military personnel and industrial workers, sheer numbers of people are a positive power factor. It is unlikely, for instance, that Tonga (pop. 104,000) will ever achieve great-power status. A large population may be disadvantageous, however, if it is not in balance with resources. India, with 1 billion people, has the world's second-largest population, yet because of the country's poverty ($460 per capita GNP), it must spend much of its energy and resources merely feeding its people.

Age Distribution It is an advantage for a country to have a large number and percentage of its population in the productive years (15–64 by international reporting standards). Some countries with booming populations have a heavy percentage of children who must be supported. In other countries with limited life expectancy, many people die before they complete their productive years. Finally, some countries are "aging," with a geriatric population segment that consumes more resources than it produces.

Worldwide, 30 percent of the Earth's population in 2000 was less than 15 years old; 7 percent was 65 or over; 63 percent was in the working-age years (15–64). Figure 10.1 (p. 270) shows the age distributions of several countries, which you should compare. The figure also shows the dependency ratio of young and old people combined compared to the working-age population. Many analysts would contend that South Korea is relatively advantaged by its large working-age population, while Uganda, with numerous children, and Italy, with a high percentage of senior citizens, are relatively disadvantaged.

Countries like Italy that have such low birthrates that they are in a zero or even a negative population growth pattern are also disadvantaged in that they may experience economic difficulty because of future labor shortages. A growing geriatric population also means that the cost of providing pensions and other services to retired citizens will strain a country's capacity. By 2025, for instance, an estimated 28 percent of Japan's population will be age 65 and older, and by 2050 fully a third of all Japanese will be of retirement age. Most European countries will also have increasingly higher percentages of retirees. Although the proportion of retired Americans will be somewhat less (13 percent currently, 19 percent in 2025, 21 percent in 2050) than in most other economically developed countries (EDCs), the U.S. social security and health care systems will face a formidable challenge.

Education An educated population is important to national power. Although there are education variations among all countries, LDCs are especially disadvantaged compared to EDCs, as illustrated by the contrasts between Canada and Senegal in Table 10.1 (p. 272). It will be hard, for example, for LDCs to create educational programs that will close the gap in research and development (R&D) scientists and technicians, who number 41 per every 10,000 people in the EDCs and only 4 per 10,000 people in the LDCs. To make matters worse for LDCs, many of them suffer a substantial "brain drain," an "outflow of highly educated individuals," to EDCs, where professional opportunities are better (Carrington & Detragiache, 1999:1).

The quality of a country's education system is also important. For example, almost all Americans are literate, yet, there is growing concern that the U.S. educational system is not adequately preparing students to meet the requirements of the modern world. It may be that the basic 3 Rs—reading, 'riting, and 'rithmetic—that

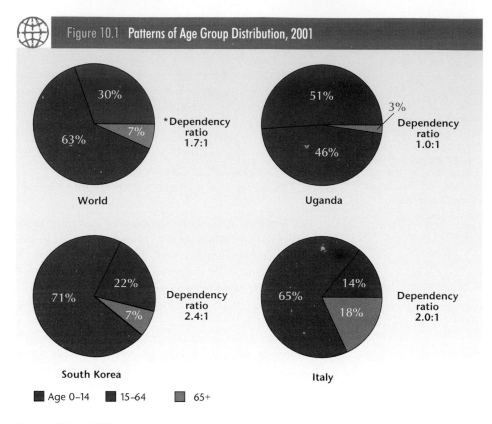

Figure 10.1 Patterns of Age Group Distribution, 2001

World — *Dependency ratio 1.7:1 — 30%, 63%, 7%

Uganda — Dependency ratio 1.0:1 — 51%, 46%, 3%

South Korea — Dependency ratio 2.4:1 — 22%, 71%, 7%

Italy — Dependency ratio 2.0:1 — 14%, 65%, 18%

■ Age 0–14   ■ 15–64   ■ 65+

Data source: U.S. Census (2002).

*Dependency ratio is a World Bank calculation of the ratio of the working-age population (15–64) to the dependent population (age 14 and under plus age 65 and older). Generally, the higher the ratio, the more economically advantaged a country is.

Most economically less developed countries (LDCs), like Uganda, are disadvantaged because their population has a high percentage of children. These youngsters add little to their country's economic vitality. While investing in them is wise policy, children consume resources for their education and general care that they will only begin to "repay" the system in terms of productivity and taxes when they become adults. A high percentage of senior citizens, as in Italy, is also suboptimal economically.

once served to train a workforce will no longer suffice in the twenty-first century. Instead, the requirements will be more like the 3 Cs—computers, calculus, and communications.

There are growing questions about how well American students are being educated in mathematics, science, technology, and other advanced areas, and that could negatively affect U.S. power in the long term. A recent study showed that for general mathematics competence, American high school seniors finished behind those in 13 other countries, equal to seniors in 4 countries, and ahead of seniors only in Cyprus and South Africa. General physics yielded about the same results, with American students far behind most of their contemporaries and, again, only ahead of those in Cyprus and South Africa.

Expenditure on education is just one factor in determining national achievement. There are some countries, such as Japan, that spend considerably less of their GDP on education than does the United States and yet have students that score better than U.S. students. One clue as to why this occurs may be in Figure 10.2, which shows that American students during their four years of high school spend an average of less than 1,500 hours in classes dealing with core

Did You Know That:

A survey taken in 2000 asked seniors at 55 top U.S. universities to answer 34 multiple-choice questions drawn from high school history exams. The average score was 53 percent. Only 23 percent could pick out James Madison as the "father of the Constitution," and only 34 percent could select George Washington as the victorious general at the Battle of Yorktown. But 99 percent knew that Bevis and Butt-Head were "television cartoon characters," and an equally impressive 98 percent correctly identified Snoop Doggy Dog as a "rap singer."

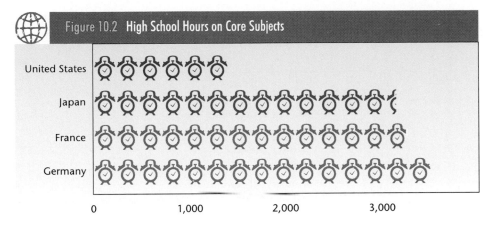

Figure 10.2 **High School Hours on Core Subjects**

Data source: "Prisoners of Time," The Report of the National Education Commission on Time and Learning, at http://www.ed.gov/pubs/PrisonersOfTime/.

The graph above indicates the number of hours students spend on core academics in their four years of high school.

An educated populace is a key element of a country's infrastructure. American students, compared to students in many other countries, score lower on mathematics and some other academic achievement tests. One possible cause is that U.S. students spend fewer hours on these core subjects than do students in many other countries.

subjects. This contrasts with the 3,000 to 3,500 hours spent on core subjects during average four-year curriculums in Japan, France, and Germany.

Yet another way to break down general educational statistics is to see how well a country trains various segments of its population. Most countries limit their power potential by underutilizing major elements of their population. For example, sexism limits the possible contribution of women in virtually all countries. In Bangladesh, 42 percent more male than female teenagers are enrolled in secondary school. Racial, ethnic, and other bases of discrimination add to this failure to maximize a population's potential. The fact that among adults over age 24 in the United States, just 15 percent of African Americans and 11 percent of Latino/as, compared to 25 percent of whites, have completed college means that the potential of a significant number of these disadvantaged people has been lost to the country.

Health Health problems can also sap a country's power. The health gap between Canada and Senegal shown in Table 10.1 can be supplemented by such information as the specific health problems that some countries face. AIDS is a worldwide scourge, but it is particularly devastating in Africa. About 50 percent of the world's 40 million HIV-infected people live in Africa. With less than a 2 percent HIV-infection rate, Senegal is relatively lucky compared to 16 other countries in the region, where more than 10 percent of their population between 15 and 49 are infected with HIV. The toll on the region is immense. The disease is killing more than 2 million people a year there, and there are some 11 million AIDS orphans, some of whom are themselves infected and will meet an early death.

The disease is also having a profound economic impact on the continent. According to a recent UN report, "AIDS has become the biggest threat to the continent's development and its quest to bring about an African Renaissance" as several countries lose many of their "small number of highly skilled personnel in important areas of public management and core social services… to AIDS," and as these countries deplete their already meager resources trying to deal with the epidemic.[5]

Alcohol and other attacks on health are devastating Russia and some other countries. Chain smoking, a deficient diet, and the ravages of alcohol are decimating Russia's male population. Two-thirds of all adult Russian males smoke (2.5 times the

	Canada	Senegal
Table 10.1 Health and Education in Canada and Senegal		
Health Spending	$1,824	$23
Life Expectancy	79	52
Children Dying Before Age 5	0.5%	12%
Population per Physician	476	10,000
Education Spending	$1,186	$19
Adult Literacy	99%	64%
Secondary School Enrollment	97%	16%

Public spending for health and education is per capita; life expectancy is years; secondary school enrollment is the percentage of youths in that age group.

Data source: World Bank (2002).

Canada's power is enhanced by its educated and healthy population, especially relative to Senegal's disadvantaged population.

U.S. rate), and there are estimates that the average Russian adult male drinks almost two quarts of vodka a week. "Sobriety is no longer the moral norm in Russia," says one health official there.[6]

The attitude of Russian men, President Boris Yeltsin once explained, is "What kind of Russian man are you if you cannot drink?"[7] One answer is a healthy man, because a huge number of the estimated 60 percent of Russian men who do drink to excess die from alcohol-related diseases and accidents. Others kill themselves in despair, with Russian males having the world's highest reported annual suicide rate (73 per 100,000 males). This compares to a rate of 14 for Russian women and 28 for American men. As a result, the longevity of Russian males has actually declined substantially, and now only 59 percent of them (compared to 79 percent of Russian women) live to age 65. Indeed a smaller percentage of Russian males reach retirement age than do males in profoundly poor Bangladesh. The threat to Russia's national strength is so palpable that one Russian government study calls it "the clearest possible threat to national security."[8]

Did You Know That:
Vodka has long undermined Russia's power. According to the *Washington Post*, the Russians lost a battle in 1373 to the Tartars because the czar's forces were too inebriated to fight. The defeated Russians were thrown into a nearby river, which was then dubbed the Reka Pianaya (the Drunk River).[1]

Morale A final factor that affects the population element of national power is the morale of a country's citizens. World War II demonstrated the power of strong civilian morale. Early in the war, Great Britain and the Soviet Union reeled under tremendous assaults by the Nazi forces. Yet the Allies hung on. Winston Churchill proclaimed in Parliament on October 9, 1940, during the darkest days of the war, that for the British people, "Death and sorrow will be the companions of our journey; hardship our garment; constancy and valor our only shield. We must be united, we must be undaunted, we must be inflexible." The British answered Sir Winston's call. They remained undaunted; they held; they prevailed.

Conversely, the collapse of national morale can bring about civil unrest and even the fall of governments. The end of the USSR in 1991 provides an example. The normally gloomy Russian outlook, which novelist Fyodor Dostoyevsky (1821–1881) described as "almost a Russian disease," has spawned dark humor, such as the joke in which one Russian meets another and asks, "How are things?" The comrade replies, "Well, it appears I've hit rock bottom," to which the first Russian says, "Ah, you always were an optimist" (Javeline, 1999). Even by Russian standards, however, the populace in 1990 was disheartened, with 90 percent believing that the country's economic situation was dire, and 57 percent expressing no confidence in the future. This profound pessimism led to an almost total collapse of support for the government of Soviet president Mikhail Gorbachev and, indeed, the country's political system. On December 25, 1991, President Mikhail Gorbachev resigned and dissolved the Soviet Union. The "evil empire," as President Reagan called it, had been brought down by a vacuum of public support, not by the opposing superpower.

Government

The quality of a country's government is a third power element associated with the national core. The issue is not what form of government, such as a democracy or an authoritarian system, a country has. Instead the issue is *administrative competence*: whether a state has a well-organized and effective administrative structure to utilize its power potential fully. The collapse of the Soviet Union stemmed in part from its massive and inefficient bureaucratic structure, and Russia continues to struggle under poor governance. President Vladimir Putin candidly told the Duma in July 2000 that "government lies have become the norm," and that earlier pledges to build a strong state had proven "hollow." Putin went on to warn the legislators that Russia was at risk of becoming a "derelict nation.... We have created islands, separate islets of government, but we have not built any bridges to them." Among the other impacts of this ineptitude, he added, was continued economic disarray, creating a "growing gap between the advanced nations and Russia [that] is pushing us into the group of Third World countries."[9]

Leadership skill also adds to a government's strength. Leadership is one of the most intangible elements of national power. Yet it can be critical, especially in times of crisis. For example, Prime Minister Winston Churchill's sturdy image and his inspiring rhetoric well served the British people during World War II. By contrast, the presidency of Boris Yeltsin, which had begun with heroics as he faced down tanks in the streets of Moscow, dissolved into incompetence as the ailing, often inebriated Yeltsin became an increasingly sad caricature of his former self.

THE NATIONAL INFRASTRUCTURE

Another group of elements that form the foundation of state power is related to a country's infrastructure. The infrastructure of a state might roughly be equated with the skeleton of a human body. For a building, the infrastructure would be the foundation and the framing or girders. To examine the infrastructure of the state as an element of national power, the following sections will discuss technological sophistication, transportation systems, and information and communications capabilities. Each of these factors strongly affects any country's capacity in the other elements of power.

Technology

"Everything that can be invented has been invented," intoned Charles H. Duell, commissioner of the U.S. Office of Patents in 1899.[10] Commissioner Duell was obviously both in error and in the wrong job. Most of the technology that undergirds a great deal of contemporary national power has been invented since his shortsighted assessment. Air conditioning modifies the impact of weather, computers revolutionize education, robotics speed industry, synthetic fertilizers expand agriculture, new drilling techniques allow for undersea oil exploration, microwaves speed information, and lasers bring the military to the edge of the Luke Skywalker era. Thus, technology is an overarching factor and will be discussed as part of all the tangible elements.

One source of U.S. strength is the considerable money that its government, corporations, and universities spend on research and development (R&D). During

Information and communications capabilities are a key element of a country's power. Contrary to the incongruous image of this Samburu warrior talking on a cell phone, his native Kenya and other less developed countries are hampered by a lack of sophisticated and extensive information and communications technology.

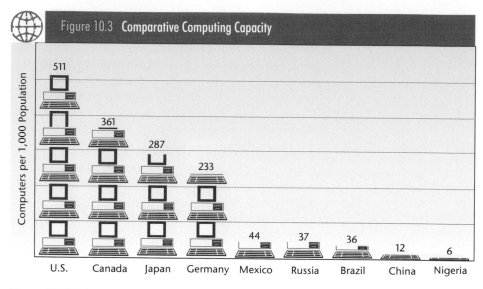

Figure 10.3 **Comparative Computing Capacity**

Data source: World Bank (2002).

Computer capacity is a key element of a country's technological infrastructure. As this figure shows, there is a huge gap, called the "global digital divide," in global computing power.

2000 the United States spent $254 billion. That was more than the combined spending of $249 billion of the next five highest countries (Japan, Germany, France, Great Britain, and Italy). Another good measure of technological sophistication and capability is computing capacity. Needless to say, the business, education, science, and other key elements of national power depend on computers, and, as Figure 10.3 shows, there is a vast disparity in national capabilities.

Transportation Systems

The ability to move people, raw materials, finished products, and sometimes the military throughout its territory is another part of a country's power equation. For example, one of the major hurdles that Russia must overcome to invigorate its economy is its relatively limited and decrepit transportation systems. As one standard, for every 1,000 square miles of its territory, Russia has but 84 miles of paved roads and 14 miles of railroad track. The United States has 1,049 miles of paved roads and 45 miles of railroad track for the same amount of territory. Inadequate transportation systems are also a problem for LDCs. Nigeria, for one, has just 213 miles of paved roadway and only 6 miles of railroad track for each 1,000 square miles.

Information and Communications Systems

A country's information and communications capabilities are becoming increasingly important (Rothkopf, 1998). The advent of satellites and computers has accelerated the revolution begun with radio and television. Photocopying machines, then fax machines, and now the Internet have dramatically changed communications. Enhanced communications technology increases the ability of a society to communicate within itself and remain cohesive. It also increases efficiency and effectiveness in industry, finance, and the military.

Here again, the gap between LDCs and EDCs is wide. There are, for example, approximately 3 times more television sets, 8 times more radios, 8 times more telephones, 49 times more fax machines, and 34 times more Internet users per capita in the United States than in China.

🌐 The Nature of Diplomacy

Now that we have explored the core and infrastructure elements of the power foundation on which much of national diplomacy rests, we can turn to the conduct of national diplomacy. At its core, diplomacy is a basic human activity. As one study notes, "The desire to resolve problems amicably pervades all arenas of social organization. It is the function of negotiation to provide a channel for peaceful dispute resolution" (Starkey, Boyer, & Wilkenfeld, 1999:1). To see how this occurs and to provide a level of continuity in our discussion of diplomacy, this chapter will make frequent, although not exclusive, use of illustrations from five diplomatic events (1) the U.S.-North Korea nuclear crisis of 1993 and 1994, (2 and 3) the two crises between China and Taiwan in 1996 and in 2000, (4) the U.S.-Iraq inspection crisis of 1997–1998, and (5) the U.S-Afghanistan crisis of 2001.

The U.S.-North Korea nuclear crisis of 1993 and 1994 occurred when the United States moved to force North Korea (the Democratic People's Republic of Korea, DPRK) to give up its alleged nuclear weapons program. Alarm that North Korea was developing a nuclear bomb rang out in 1993 when North Korea announced its withdrawal from the Nuclear Non-Proliferation Treaty (NPT). Adding to the concern, the CIA reportedly believed that the DPRK probably had one or two nuclear weapons. The image of a nuclear-armed North Korea created grave concerns because of the possibility of a nuclear nightmare occurring on the ever-tense Korean peninsula and because, in the estimate of former U.S. defense secretary Harold Brown, "A few nuclear weapons in North Korea could have a significant effect on the possibility of nuclear programs in Japan, South Korea, and Taiwan."[11]

What followed was a series of diplomatic moves and countermoves during a 19-month-long confrontation that focused on persuading North Korea (1) to allow the resumption of inspections by the UN-associated International Atomic Energy Agency (IAEA) and (2) to dismantle those nuclear reactors that the DPRK had or was building that were capable of producing nuclear weapons-grade uranium or plutonium. The confrontation escalated to the point that between April and June 1994 there were dire threats, military moves, and an open discussion of the possibility of war in the capitals of Pyongyang, North Korea; Seoul, South Korea; and Washington, D.C.

Then diplomacy lowered the flame of crisis. All the parties eased their stands to facilitate agreement. North Korea agreed to suspend work on the nuclear reactors it had under construction, to dismantle its current nuclear energy program over 10 years, and to allow the IAEA inspections to resume. The United States and its allies pledged that they—principally Japan and South Korea—would spend approximately $4 billion to build in North Korea two nuclear reactors that were not capable of producing plutonium for bomb building. The West also agreed to help meet North Korea's energy needs by annually supplying it with about 138 million gallons of petroleum until new reactors are on line. The issue resurfaced in 1998 when U.S. intelligence agencies discovered what they charged was a massive effort by North Korea to build an underground nuclear facility. That proved false, however, and implementation of the accord has proceeded.

The crises between China and Taiwan in 1996 and in 2000, which featured diplomatic interplay between China and the United States during the periods just before Taiwan's two most recent presidential elections, were detailed in the chapter 4 box, To Be or Not To Be, on pages 94–95.

The U.S.-Iraq inspection crisis of 1997–1998 was sparked by Iraq's refusal to live up to its agreement (at the end of the Persian Gulf War of 1991) to allow UN inspectors to ensure that the Iraqis had destroyed all their nuclear, biological, and chemical weapons capabilities. Over the years there was frequent friction between Iraq and the UN inspection team, and this escalated to crisis level when, in late 1997,

The U.S. crisis with Afghanistan related to its complicity in the 9-11 terrorist attacks is one event used herein to illustrate diplomacy. President Bush demanded that Afghanistan surrender Osama bin Laden and other al-Qaeda leaders. The Taliban's ambassador to Pakistan, Mullah Abdul Salam Zaeef, is seen here speaking at a news conference in Islamabad explaining why his government was refusing to comply and indicating that if the United States attacked, there would be a "showdown of might."

Iraq refused to allow the inspectors access to large facilities that Baghdad claimed were presidential palaces.

Like the crisis on the Korean peninsula four years before, the confrontation with Iraq teetered on the edge of war. Finally, however, the diplomatic maneuvering again avoided war. The crisis subsided after a trip by UN secretary-general Kofi Annan to Baghdad, where he negotiated an agreement acceptable to both sides. Among other things, Saddam Hussein agreed to let the UN inspectors enter the supposed presidential palaces and Annan held out the hope that the long-standing economic sanctions on Iraq would be eased, perhaps even ended. As with the North Korean nuclear issue and many other sagas of diplomacy, the agreement in early 1998 was not the end of the story. Later in the year, perhaps trying to take advantage of President Clinton's embroilment in the Monica Lewinsky affair, Iraq again defied UN inspectors. Once again the world sought a solution somewhere between acquiescence and war.

The crisis between Afghanistan and the United States followed the terrorist attacks in September 2001 on the United States. Washington soon became convinced that the attacks had been directed by al-Qaeda, a terrorist organization that was based in Afghanistan under the leadership of Osama bin Laden. President George W. Bush demanded that bin Laden and the rest of the leadership of al-Qaeda be turned over; the Taliban government in Kabul under the leadership Mullah Mohammad Omar refused.

THE FUNCTIONS OF DIPLOMACY

National diplomats serve as communication links between their country and the rest of the world. As one scholar puts it, "Diplomats not only seek to represent their states to the world, but also seek to represent the world back to their respective states, with the objective of keeping the whole ensemble together" (Sharp, 1999:53).

Traditionally, diplomacy has focused on the national interest. Writing in the 1400s, Venetian ambassador Ermolao Barbaro asserted that "the first duty of an ambassador is… to do, say, advise, and think whatever may best serve the preservation and aggrandizement of his own state" (Craig & George, 1995). More sardonically, Sir Henry Wotton, the English ambassador to Venice, wrote in *Reliquae Wottonianae* (1651) that "an ambassador is an honest man sent to lie abroad for the commonwealth [state]." Whether it is conducted with honor or deceit, diplomacy is carried on by officials with a variety of titles such as president, prime minister, ambassador, or special envoy, and it is worthwhile to explore the roles that these officials and other diplomats play in promoting the national interest (Berton, Kimura, & Zartman, 1999).

Observer and reporter is one role. A primary diplomatic role has always been to gather information and impressions and to analyze and report these back to the home office. This information comes from activities that range from formal meetings to the day-to-day contacts that an ambassador and other diplomats have with officials and the general public in another country. Many embassies also contain a considerable contingent of intelligence officers who are technically attached to the diplomatic service. Whatever the method, it is important for policy makers to know both the facts and the mood of foreign capitals, and the embassy is a primary source.

The value of this function is especially evident when it is absent. The intentions of North Korea, for example, are more difficult to ascertain because many countries, including the United States, do not have embassies in Pyongyang, and travel within the country is highly restricted for the few foreigners who are there. One U.S. official noted that "compared with North Korea, the Soviet Union was a duck-soup intelligence target."[12] This lack of good information was particularly worrisome during the events of 1993 and 1994 that involved North Korea's nuclear program. "The fact of the matter is that we don't really understand what they are doing," a U.S. official commented at one point.[13]

For all of this continued value, the importance of the ambassador as an observer and reporter has declined. Countries are also far less isolated from one another than they once were, and there are many new ways, using advanced technology, to gather information about other countries. The result is that diplomatic reports compete with many other sources of information. This frustrates diplomats. As one U.S. official put it, "There is a diminished value in classical diplomatic reporting. If you had a choice between reading the [diplomatic] cables in your box and tuning in to CNN three times a day, you'd tune in to CNN."[14]

Negotiator is a second important role of a diplomat. Negotiation is a combination of art and technical skill that attempts to find a common ground among two or more divergent positions (Hopmann, 1996). For all of the public attention given to meetings between national leaders, the vast bulk of negotiating is done by ambassadors and other such personnel. The early negotiations between U.S. and North Korean diplomats resembled two boxers feeling each other out in the early rounds. "The whole idea is to test the proposition that the North Koreans are willing to deal," observed the chief American negotiator, Assistant Secretary of State Robert L. Gallucci. "And I always put it in terms of 'test the proposition' because I don't have... high confidence that we actually can resolve this through negotiations."[15]

Here again though, and especially during crises, the negotiating role of ambassadors has declined. In the immediate aftermath of the terrorist attacks on the United States in September 2001, the personal contacts among world leaders was intense. Within weeks of the attack, President Bush met in Washington with, among others, the prime ministers of France, Great Britain, Canada, Japan, Belgium; the German chancellor; the king of Jordan; the emir of Qatar; the secretary-general of NATO, and the president of Mexico. Bush spoke by phone with the president of China and, on several occasions, with the president of Russia. President Bush also met with these two leaders, as well as many others, during the annual Asia-Pacific Economic Cooperation meeting in Shanghai, China, in mid-October.

Policy representative is a third role of a diplomat. This function includes explaining and defending the policies of the diplomat's country. Misperception is dangerous in world politics, and the role that diplomats play in explaining their countries' actions and statements to friends and foes alike is vital to accurate communications.

Substantive representation can also mean carrying messages from the diplomat's home government. For very powerful countries, it can also mean making demands. When, in 1972, South Vietnam resisted the U.S.-negotiated settlement, President Nixon cabled President Thieu that "all military and economic aid will be cut off... if an agreement is not reached" and that "I have... irrevocably decided to proceed... to sign [the agreement]. I will do so, if necessary, alone [and] explain that your government obstructs peace." As the United States' chief diplomat, Nixon was being distinctly undiplomatic. "Brutality is nothing," he told Kissinger. "You have never seen it if this son-of-a-bitch doesn't go along, believe me" (Kissinger, 1979:1420, 1469). Thieu went along.

A bit less dramatically, the United States made many specific demands on countries around the world to join in the fight against terrorism in the aftermath of the 9-11 attacks. President Bush has a penchant for charts that can be checked off, and he asked the State Department to construct a "What We Expect" matrix with country names and three columns: what we expect them to do, what they are doing, and who is responsible for ensuring they do it. Soon, the chart became so complex that the staff dubbed it the "mother of all matrixes."[16]

THE DIPLOMATIC SETTING

The nature of diplomacy and how it is carried out are also affected by its setting. The setting can be roughly divided into three parts: the international system, the diplomatic environment, and the domestic connection.

The International System

One aspect of the setting is the system. As we have noted many times, the nature of the anarchical international system creates a setting in which self-interested actors pursue their diplomatic goals by, if necessary, using power to ensure that their goals prevail over the goals of others. That emphasis on national interest is why this chapter discusses national diplomacy and national power.

When China, Taiwan, and the United States found themselves embroiled in the two crises that arose over China's attempt to influence Taiwan's 1996 and 2000 presidential elections, Taipei and Washington could only look to themselves to forestall any military attempt by Beijing to reincorporate Taiwan. China was similarly limited to self-reliance. In the current system, the only recourse for China if Taiwan were to declare its independence would be to try to reincorporate Taiwan militarily. Thus, when tension occurred, the actors had little choice but to rely on their own power to protect their divergent national interests.

The Diplomatic Environment

A second part of the diplomatic setting is determined by the relationships among the various actors who are involved in a particular matter. This part of the setting can be subdivided into four diplomatic environments: hostile, adversarial, coalition, and mediation diplomacy.

Hostile Diplomacy Where one or more countries are engaged in armed clashes or when there is a substantial possibility that fighting could result, diplomacy is conducted in a hostile environment. The maneuvering surrounding the U.S. demand on Afghanistan that it surrender those responsible for the 9-11 terrorist attacks fell distinctly within the range of **hostile diplomacy**. Almost immediately, the United States moved to deploy a massive Navy flotilla centered around the aircraft carriers *Enterprise*, *Carl Vinson*, and *Theodore Roosevelt* to the Indian Ocean. On September 16, Bush also instructed, "The secretary of state should issue an ultimatum against the Taliban today warning them to turn over bin Laden and his al-Qaeda or they will suffer the consequences." If the Taliban do not comply, Bush instructed his advisers, "We'll attack with missiles, bombers, and boots on the ground.... We are going to rain holy hell on them."[17]

Adversarial Diplomacy An environment of **adversarial diplomacy** occurs at a less confrontational level when two or more countries' interests clash but when there is little or no chance of armed conflict. A great deal of diplomacy involving economic issues occurs in adversarial circumstances as countries press other countries to accede to their wishes. Russia and the United States have disagreed strongly about the proposals of President George W. Bush to abandon the Anti-Ballistic Missile (ABM) Treaty of 1972 in order to try to build a ballistic missile defense system. Russia's president Putin tried to head off the Bush move by arguing it would upset deterrence and also by attempting to enlist the support of the European members of NATO, many of whom have doubts about the U.S. move. Russia's weakness left little that it could do when Bush formally announced in December 2001 that he would go ahead. Putin's comments were moderate, but other Russian leaders expressed anger. A former Russian ambassador to Washington complained that "the U.S. used our enormous help to conduct the anti-terrorist operation in Afghanistan.... [then] announces its position on ABM. It's a sign, and a bad sign at that." And a leader of one of the party's in the Russian parliament called the move proof that the United States is "a superpower that is trying to dictate its rules to the world."[18]

At other times, adversarial diplomacy addresses less critical issues. President Bush in early 2002 ordered tariff increases of up to 30 percent on foreign steel imports. Washington claimed the move was to offset unfair pricing by foreign competitors to the U.S. steel industry; critics charged the move was more about giving Republicans a political boost in big steel-producing states. Whatever the cause, Russia and other countries that export steel to the United States struck back. With Russia's lost revenues estimated at $750 million a year, Moscow announced that it was barring U.S. poultry imports, which amounted in 2001 to about $800 million, because of health concerns. With tongue in beak, the press quickly dubbed the contretemps the "cold chicken war." To the diplomats involved, however, it was serious. The American ambassador to Russia termed the dispute, "the number one problem in U.S.-Russia relations in the past month," and he indicated that so many feathers had flown that diplomacy had "engaged at least five cabinet ministers on my side, and even President George W. Bush, who has spoken to President Putin directly about this."[19] At this writing the adversarial diplomacy of the chicken war continues in an attempt to find where in the pecking order of U.S.-Russia relations the trade in steel and chickens stands.

Coalition Diplomacy

When a number of countries have similar interests, often in opposition to the interest of one or more other countries, then **coalition diplomacy** becomes a significant aspect of international activity. National leaders spend a good deal of time and effort to build coalitions that will support the foreign policy initiatives of their country or of other international actors that they support. When, for instance, Iraq invaded Kuwait in August 1990, President George Bush spent much time and effort in rounding up international support for military action against Iraq. During the first four days of the crisis Bush made 23 phone calls to a dozen foreign leaders, and personally flew to Colorado to consult with British prime minister Margaret Thatcher, who was coincidentally speaking at a conference there.

When President George W. Bush entered the White House, he favored a more unilateralist approach to diplomacy, and was less interested in building coalitions than his father had been. The complexities of combating global terrorism provided the son a lesson that his father had learned earlier. The younger Bush found that he could not succeed without building a broad coalition in support of U.S. goals. In addition to a high volume of phone calls to heads of government around the world, a presidential adviser speaking in January 2002 indicated that "Since September 11, Mr. Bush has met personally with nearly 80 foreign leaders, using each session to elicit whatever backing the other nation was willing to give."[20]

Mediation Diplomacy Unlike hostile, adversarial, or coalition diplomacy, the use of **mediation diplomacy** occurs when a country that is not involved directly as one of the parties tries to help two or more sides in conflict resolve their differences. The United States has been involved for decades in an attempt to mediate the conflict between Israel and its Arab neighbors, especially the Palestinians, as told in the box, Palestinians: A Nation Without a State, in chapter 6 on pages 152–153.

In April 2002, the mounting crisis in the Middle East led the United States to once again intervene in an attempt to mediate at least a surcease in the violence marked by multiple terror attacks in Israel by Palestinian suicide bombers and a full-scale Israeli invasion of the Palestinian-controlled areas of the West Bank and Gaza. Fear grew that the fighting could destabilize neighboring Jordan and perhaps Egypt and might even lead to yet another general Arab-Israeli war. In this tense atmosphere, President Bush used the tranquil setting of the White House Rose Garden to declare, "The storms of violence cannot go on. Enough is enough."[21] On the diplomatic front, Bush dispatched Secretary of State Colin Powell to the area to upgrade the ongoing mediation attempt of special envoy Anthony Zinni. Bush also was unusually blunt in his public remarks to and about both Israeli prime minister Ariel Sharon and Palestinian leader Yasser Arafat. In a direct and well-reported phone call to Sharon, Bush told him that he "meant what he said" in his public call for Israel to begin to withdraw without delay, and that "without delay means immediately." Bush also said openly that he had "lost trust" in Arafat and called on him to "order an immediate effective cease-fire and to crack down on terrorists."[22]

By early May, the fighting had subsided, and Prime Minister Sharon had traveled to Washington to discuss the future with President Bush. Then, literally when the two leaders were meeting, they received news that a suicide bomber had destroyed a crowded recreation hall near Tel Aviv, killing at least 15 people and wounding more than 50 others. Sharon cut his visit short to hurry back to Israel, and the violence threatened to escalate anew.

The Domestic Connection

Domestic politics provide the third part of the diplomatic setting. The concept of **two-level game theory**, discussed in chapter 4, holds that to be successful a country's diplomats must find a solution that is acceptable to both the other country at the international level and, at the domestic level, to the political actors (legislators, public opinion, interest groups) in the diplomat's own country. From this perspective, the diplomatic setting exists at the domestic as well as at the international level, and is influenced by the interplay of the two levels when leaders try to pursue policies that satisfy the actors at both levels (Trumbore, 1998; Peterson, 1996).

During the Taiwan crises, the leaders of China and the United States not only had to find a point of agreement between themselves, they also had to fend off domestic forces that were pushing to escalate the crisis. Prior to the 1996 crisis, President Jiang Zemin told the U.S. ambassador, "Any leader who lets this [Taiwan's independence] pass would be overthrown."[23] Similarly, during the crisis in 2000, the domestic political issue for the leadership in Beijing, one political scientist explained, was the worry that Taiwan would evolve gradually into a recognized state without Beijing being able to stop it. "It has become imperative," the scholar continued, "not only to not be the leader who lost Taiwan, but not to be the leader who allowed this slow drift [toward independence] to continue."[24]

President Clinton also had to deal with strong domestic forces. In 1996 House Republicans urged Clinton to commit the United States "to the defense of Taiwan."[25] Keeping the pressure up in 2000, Republican Senate leader Trent Lott condemned the "threats emanating from Beijing" and suggested that the Clinton "administration should worry more about protecting and promoting Taiwan's democracy than offending the communist dictators in Beijing."[26] To ensure that Clinton did not ignore their views, GOP legislators introduced the Taiwan Security Enhancement Act, to substantially increase the U.S. commitment to Taiwan. "There is a lot of pent-up frustration about the administration's policy approach to China," a GOP aide noted.[27] The GOP did not push that bill to passage, but it served notice of the strong support of Taiwan in Congress.

The Evolution of Diplomacy

Diplomacy is an ancient art. Because of the economic and political world dominance of Europe and European-heritage countries for the past several centuries, a great deal of modern diplomatic practice can be traced through its evolution in Western practice. Still, diplomacy predates the West.

EARLY DIPLOMACY

Diplomatic records in the Eastern Mediterranean region around the Tigris and Euphrates river valleys date back almost four millennia, and records from what appear to be embassies can be found from as far back as the time of the great Babylonian emperor, Hammurabi (1792–1750 B.C.). Somewhat later, ancient Greece and Rome originated many of the practices used in modern diplomacy. Diplomatic missions are described in Homer's *Iliad* (about 850 B.C.), and the Greeks, followed by the Romans, wrote treaties, established the rudiments of international law, and used ambassadors to negotiate disputes. The Byzantine Empire, which flourished after Rome's collapse, added further to the evolution of diplomacy by specifically training negotiators and by establishing the first department of foreign affairs.

Did You Know That:
The oldest surviving diplomatic document is a cuneiform tablet written about 2,500 B.C. It is a message sent by Ibubu, chief minister to the king of Ebla (in modern Lebanon), to King Zizi of Hamazi (in modern Iran), some 1,200 miles away. In it Ibubu pledges goodwill, relates that he is sending Zizi a quantity of rare wood, and says that he wants him to "give me good mercenaries. Please send them" (Cohen, 1996:2).

The diplomacy of the Italian city-states beginning in the fifteenth century contributed to the evolution of diplomacy through the establishment of the first permanent diplomatic missions in modern times. Italians also introduced summit meetings as a diplomatic practice and became particularly known for diplomatic artifice. Indeed, the unflattering adjective, Machiavellian, is an eponym after Niccolò Machiavelli of Florence, who counseled in *The Prince* (1532) that it was best to be as powerful as a lion and as sly as a fox, and who summed up his estimation of human nature with the observation that one "must start with assuming that all men are bad and ever ready to display their vicious nature whenever they may find occasion for it."

The French system is the direct predecessor of modern diplomacy. Cardinal Richelieu, who served as chief minister (1624–1642) to King Louis XIII, was the first to see diplomacy as an ongoing process rather than as an expedience, and he consolidated all foreign affairs functions under one ministry. Later, during the reign (1643–1715) of Louis XIV, the minister of foreign affairs became a member of the king's cabinet, and permanent embassies were established in all the major capitals, with lesser-ranked missions in minor capitals. It was also at the end of this era that the first diplomatic manual, *On the Manner of Negotiating with Sovereigns* (1716), was written by François de Callierres.

In general, the old diplomacy that developed mostly in Europe had several traits. *Elite domination* was one. "*L'état c'est moi*" (I am the state), Louis XIV supposedly proclaimed with some justification, and true to that assertion, foreign policy was almost exclusively dominated by the monarch and ministers and diplomatic corps recruited from the nobility and gentry. Secrecy was a second trait of early diplomacy. Negotiations were normally conducted in secret, and even treaties were often secret. *Bilateral diplomacy* was a third trait. Although there were a few multilateral conferences, such as the Congress of Vienna (1815), **bilateral diplomacy** (direct negotiations between two countries) was the normal form of negotiation.

MODERN DIPLOMACY

The World War I (1914–1918) era serves as a benchmark in the transition to modern diplomacy. It was the beginning of the end of European world dominance. It also marked the fall of the German, Austrian, Ottoman, and Russian emperors. Nationalistic self-determination stirred strongly in Europe and other parts of the world. New powers—the United States, Japan, and China—began to assert themselves and they joined or replaced the declining European countries as world powers. The "old diplomacy" did not vanish, but it changed substantially. The "new diplomacy" includes seven characteristics: expanded geographic scope, multilateral diplomacy, parliamentary diplomacy, democratized diplomacy, open diplomacy, leader-to-leader diplomacy, and public diplomacy. These new practices have been greeted as "reforms," but many also have drawbacks.

Expansion of Geographic Scope

Modern diplomacy has been marked by expansion of its geographic scope. The two Hague Conferences (1899, 1907) on peace, particularly the second, with its 44 participants, included countries outside the European sphere. President Wilson's call for national self-determination foreshadowed a world of almost 200 countries. Today, the United Nations, with its nearly universal membership, symbolizes the truly global scope of diplomacy.

Multilateral Diplomacy

The use of conferences involving a number of nations has expanded greatly in the modern era (Best, 1999). Woodrow Wilson's call for a League of Nations symbolized the rise of **multilateral diplomacy**. There are now a number of permanent world and regional international organizations. Ad hoc conferences and treaties are also more apt to be multilateral. Before 1900, for example, the United States attended an average of one multilateral conference per year. Now, the United States is a member of scores of international organizations and American diplomats participate daily in multilateral negotiations.

Multilateral diplomacy has increased for several reasons. One is that advances in travel and communications technology allow faster and more frequent contacts among countries. Second, many global concerns, such as the environment, cannot be solved by any one country or through traditional bilateral diplomacy alone. Instead, global cooperation and solutions are required. Third, diplomacy through multilateral organizations is attractive to smaller countries as a method of influencing world politics beyond their individual power.

A fourth factor promoting multilateral diplomacy is the rise of expectations that important international actions, especially the use of military force, will be taken within the framework of a multilateral organization. President Bush said in 2001 that he would act alone if necessary against Afghanistan, but he was also careful to engage in the multilateral diplomacy necessary to win both UN and NATO support for the U.S.-led campaign.

Parliamentary Diplomacy

Another modern practice is **parliamentary diplomacy**. This includes debate and voting in international organizations and sometimes supplants negotiation and compromise.

The maneuvering involved in parliamentary diplomacy was strongly evident in the UN with regard to North Korea during 1993 and 1994. The United States had to proceed cautiously with threats of UN-endorsed sanctions against North Korea because both China and Russia were averse to sanctions and each possessed a veto. "What will the Chinese do?" Assistant Secretary Gallucci rhetorically asked reporters at a briefing. "Will you be able to pass a sanctions resolution? If there is anybody in this room who knows things they know, if they are willing to give me odds, and I do not care in which direction, I'll take them. I do not know what the Chinese are going to do."[28]

Despite the reluctance of China and Russia to act, parliamentary diplomacy did eventually play a role in putting pressure on North Korea. In May 1994, the five permanent members of the Security Council issued a joint statement calling on North Korea to provide evidence that it was not reprocessing spent nuclear reactor fuel rods into plutonium for weapons. Among other benefits, this statement signaled to Pyongyang that the five permanent members (P5) of the Security Council were united in opposition to a North Korean nuclear-weapons capability and that even Chinese and Russian patience was not inexhaustible.

Democratized Diplomacy

The elite and executive-dominant character of early diplomacy has changed in several ways. One change brought about by **democratized diplomacy** is that diplomats are now drawn from a wider segment of society and, thus, are somewhat more representative of their nations, rather than just the rulers of their state.

A second democratic change is the rise of the roles of legislatures, interest groups, and public opinion. Executive leaders still dominate the foreign policy–making process, but it is no longer their exclusive domain. Now, as discussed in the earlier section on the domestic setting, national executives often must conduct two-level diplomacy by negotiating with domestic actors as well as other countries to find a mutually agreeable solution to outstanding issues.

Third, the democratization of diplomacy has promoted the conduct of public diplomacy aimed at influencing not just leaders, but also the legislatures, interest groups, and public opinion in other countries. UN secretary-general Kofi Annan has said, "If I can't get the support of governments, then I'll get the support of the people. People move governments."[29]

Open Diplomacy

Woodrow Wilson in his Fourteen Points called for "open covenants, openly arrived at." As such, Wilson would have approved of the fact that, much more than before, diplomacy and even international agreements are now widely reported and documented. One advantage of **open diplomacy** is that it fits with the idea of democracy. Secret diplomacy more often than not is used by leaders to "mislead the populations of their own countries" rather than to keep information from international opponents (Gibbs, 1995:213).

COME ABROAD TO SEE THE WORLD

To the outsider, the thought of being a president or prime minister engaged in world diplomacy seems pretty attractive. Your personal plane flies you to interesting places where you meet important people. You stay in the best hotels or official residences and are the host or the guest at lavish banquet after lavish banquet. Not a bad deal, most people would say.

Amazingly, though, leaders often complain bitterly about the rigors of travel and ceremony. Tight schedules and jet lag are often so exhausting that, to cite one example, Ronald Reagan once fell asleep while listening to a speech by the pope.

Then there is the culinary challenge. Dining can be a delicious part of diplomacy, but there are many hazards to what has been waggishly labeled "meal-politik" and "gravy-boat diplomacy." One peril is having to eat odd things to avoid injuring local sensitivities. President Bush dined on boar's penis soup while visiting China in 1989. One American at the dinner recalls hoping that there had been a translation error, but finding out it was "what everyone thought it was."[1] Only slightly more palatable were the moose lips that appeared on Bill Clinton's presidential plate during a 22-course dinner hosted by President Boris Yeltsin in Russia. "This was not a chocolate dessert," joked one American official.[2] Even if the food is not exotic, the hectic pace can lead to gastric distress. One victim was Jimmy Carter, who was felled in Mexico City by what he undiplomatically called Montezuma's revenge. And while in Tokyo,

George H. W. Bush was so indisposed that he threw up on the Japanese prime minister, then fainted. It is no wonder, then, that presidents may often think of Shakespeare's *Comedy of Errors* and the lament of Dromio, "For with long travel I am stiff and weary."

Of all presidents, Bill Clinton holds the record as most traveled. Indeed, as one critic put it, Clinton acted "like the Energizer Bunny, he has continued to keep on going, and going and going."[3] During his eight years in office, Clinton made 54 trips abroad, visiting 133 countries and spending 229 days, or almost 8 percent of his presidency, outside the United States.

Despite the fact that President Clinton averaged about one month a year abroad, it is almost certainly political rhetoric to charge that paying attention to Moscow, Russia, and Athens, Greece, means that the president is paying too little attention to Moscow, Idaho, and Athens, Georgia. A bit more substantive, however, are concerns about the cost of presidential travel abroad.

President Clinton's 10-day trip to China in 1998 provides a case in point. Accompanying the president were his wife and daughter, 5 cabinet secretaries, 6 members of Congress, 86 senior aides, 150 civilian staff (doctors, lawyers, secretaries, valets, hairdressers, and so on), 150 military staff (drivers, baggage handlers, snipers, and so on), 150 security personnel, several bomb-sniffing dogs, and many tons of equipment, including 10 armored limousines and the "blue goose," Clinton's bulletproof lectern.

There are, however, advantages to secret diplomacy. Most scholars and practitioners agree that public negotiations are difficult. Early disclosure of your bargaining strategy will compromise your ability to win concessions. Public negotiations are also more likely to lead diplomats to posture for public consumption. Concessions may be difficult to make amid popular criticism. In sum, it is difficult to negotiate (or to play chess) with someone kibitzing over your shoulder. Indeed, domestic opposition to dealing with an adversary may be so intense that it may be impossible to negotiate at all.

Soon after the 9-11 terrorist attacks on the United States, the Bush administration made a series of demands on Pakistan that, in Washington's view, were crucial to the success of the U.S. response. Secretary of State Powell and Deputy Secretary of State Richard Armitage drew up a list of seven demands. Many of these, such as the right to use Pakistani military bases, were difficult for the government in Islamabad to accept because of the large number of militant Muslims in the country and the connection between Pakistani Pashtuns and their ethnic brethren who made up the bulk of the Taliban ranks in Afghanistan. Nevertheless, the requirements were presented strongly. "We're talking to Pakistanis in a way we've never talked to them before," one U.S. official commented.[30] Among other exchanges, Secretary Powell called Pakistan's president, General Pervez Musharraf, and told him, "As one

The cost of the expedition was almost $19 million dollars according to the U.S. General Accounting Office.[4] This figure represents what is called "incremental costs," that is, costs in addition to the salaries of the federal employees who accompanied the president and the costs of planning the trip. The reported costs also did not include the expense of protecting the president, a figure that is classified for national security reasons.

The bulk of costs accrue to the Defense Department (DOD), which some critics charge is an unwise way to spend the country's defense dollars. To get the presidential entourage and its vast array of equipment to China and back, the Air Force flew 36 airlift missions using Boeing 747, C-141, and C-5 (the largest transport, with a capacity of 145 tons of cargo) aircraft. The cost to DOD of the China trip was $14 million. Indeed, operating Air Force One alone costs over $34,000 an hour.

Presidents George H. W. Bush and Bill Clinton represented a clear break with predecessors in terms of their zeal for foreign travel. Their seven immediate predecessors (Presidents Eisenhower through Reagan) spent a collective average of 13 days a year abroad, with no one of them away for more than 17 days annually. Bush and Clinton averaged 27 days annually overseas, a jump of 59 percent.

It is too early to tell if the current President Bush will display the wanderlust of his father and President Clinton. One sign that he might is that the newly inaugurated president took less than a month in 2001 to depart on this first foreign journey, a trip to Mexico to meet with President Vicente Fox. In all, during 2001 Bush took six trips, visited 11 countries and spent 18 days away. It may be that this relatively limited travel reflects his well-known pre-presidency penchant for staying close to home. But Clinton made only two trips for 8 days abroad during his first year, and it may be that like Clinton and most other presidents, the number of trips Bush takes annually will tend to increase during his presidency.

Why do presidents and other leaders travel so much? Certainly there is a value to leader-to-leader diplomacy, whether it be a dramatic breakthrough or the ability to meet other leaders and, as one scholar puts it, to "see how they talk, how they laugh... if they laugh."[5] It is also the case that presidents can escape the voracious press at home. The percentage of time President Clinton spent overseas increased markedly during the time he was immersed in the Monica Lewinsky scandal toward the end of his presidency. Finally, visiting foreign capitals provides a relief from the difficulty of working with a cantankerous Congress and bureaucratic barons. Clinton once explained that foreign policy was more "fun" because he could make policy "with less interference and static in Congress," whereas in domestic policy even the president was but "one of a zillion decision makers."[6] Thus, like Petruchio in Shakespeare's *Taming of the Shrew*, presidents outward bound on Air Force One may muse to themselves:

Crowns in my purse I have and goods at home,
And so am come abroad to see the world.

general to another, we need someone on our flank fighting with us. Speaking candidly, the American people would not understand if Pakistan was not in this fight with the United States."[31] The demands and the pressure were all applied in secret, however, because open diplomacy might have caused such a reaction among Pakistanis that Musharraf might have been forced to reject the U.S. requirements or might have been toppled from power if he accepted them.

Leader-to-Leader Diplomacy

Modern transportation and communications have spawned an upsurge of high-level diplomacy (Dunn, 1996). National leaders regularly hold bilateral or multilateral summit conferences, and foreign ministers and other ranking diplomats jet between countries, conducting shuttle diplomacy. One hundred thirty years of American history passed before a president (Woodrow Wilson) traveled overseas while in office. George W. Bush departed on his first state visit only 27 days after his inauguration, and presidents now travel frequently, as the box, Come Abroad to See the World, discusses. The once-rare instances of leader-to-leader diplomacy meetings between heads of state have become so common that in some cases they have become routine, as for example, the annual meetings of the leaders of the Group of Eight (G-8, the largest industrialized countries plus Russia).

The advent of globe-trotting, leader-to-leader diplomacy, or **summit meetings**, and the increased frequency of telecommunications diplomacy are mixed blessings. There are several *advantages*. The first is that meetings between leaders can demonstrate an important symbolic shift in relations. One of the most significant moments in the more than 50 years since the outbreak of the Korean War occurred in June 2000, when the presidents of North and South Korea met for the first time. Some agreements were reached during the meeting in Pyongyang, but their importance paled compared to the symbolic televised image of the two shaking hands, smiling, bantering, and drinking champagne. "Maybe nothing dramatic will happen right away," a clerk in Seoul noted wisely, "but most people would agree that a surprising amount of progress and understanding has been achieved already."[32]

Second, leaders can sometimes make dramatic breakthroughs. The 1978 Camp David accords, which began the process of normalizing Egyptian-Israeli relations after decades of hostility and three wars, were produced after President Carter, Egyptian president Sadat, and Israeli prime minister Begin isolated themselves at the presidential retreat in Maryland. A third advantage is that rapid diplomacy can help dispel false information and stereotypes. President G. H. W. Bush lauded the telephone as a helpful tool. "If [another leader] knows the heartbeat a little bit from talking [with me]," the president explained, "there's less apt to be misunderstanding."[33]

A fourth advantage of personal contact among leaders is that mutual confidence or even friendships may develop. It is probable that adversarial diplomacy that marks much of U.S.-Russian relations will be somewhat easier in the near future than might otherwise have been the case because Presidents Bush and Putin seem to have struck up a friendship. After the two presidents and their wives spent a night at the Bush's Prairie Chapel ranch in Crawford, Texas, in November 2001, the leaders "seemed like real good buddies" to one local resident.[34] According to a news report, the two had a "lovefest of backslapping and wisecracking" that included commiserating with one another about the travails of having teenage daughters and jesting about which is worse: Texas in the heat of August or Siberia in the frigid winter. Putin jokingly complained that Bush wanted him to "join a plus-40 [years of age] club who jog when it is 110°F and more," and Bush kidded him about serving him guacamole, catfish, and cornbread, delicacies unknown in Moscow.[35]

A bit more seriously, Bush gushed, "A lot of people never really dreamed that an American president and a Russian president could have established the friendship that we have."[36] "The best diplomacy starts with getting to know each other," Bush added. "I knew that President Putin was a man with whom I could work to transform the relationship between our two countries."[37]

Clear vision and good feelings are laudable, but there are *disadvantages* to leader-to-leader diplomacy. One problem is that it may lead to misunderstandings. There are numerous instances where leaders have made and reached what each thought was a mutual understanding, only to find to their equally mutual surprise and anger that they had misunderstood one another. Furthermore, as tricky as personal contacts may be, the telephone may present even greater difficulties. Henry Kissinger, for example, argues that "the telephone is generally made for misunderstanding. It is difficult to make a good record. You can't see the other side's expressions or body language."[38]

Second, while mistakes made by lower-ranking officials can be disavowed by their superiors, a leader's commitments, even if not well thought out, cannot be easily retracted. "When Presidents become negotiators no escape routes are left," Kissinger (1979:12) warns. "Concessions are irrevocable without dishonor."

Third, specific misunderstanding and general chemistry can work to damage working relations between leaders instead of improving them. Kissinger (1979:142), who should know, has observed that most world leaders are characterized by a

The ease of travel and the frequency with which some leaders meet has made how well they interact one factor in the success or failure of diplomacy. Many analysts believe U.S.-Russian relations were enhanced by President Bush's invitation to President Putin to visit Bush's Crawford, Texas, ranch in November 2001. Bush took Russia's leader for a ride in his pickup, fed him some "down-home" cooking such as catfish, and held a news conference at the local high school. The two presidents can be seen here at the press conference joking with one another in front of a representation of the state's "lone star" flag. Just six months later, Bush traveled to Moscow, and the two signed a major new nuclear arms control treaty. Bush and Putin's cordiality was not why the treaty was signed, but their goodwill probably helped them agree.

"healthy dose of ego," and when two such egos collide, "negotiations can rapidly deteriorate from intractability to confrontation."

Public Diplomacy

The communications revolution has placed leaders and other diplomats in public view more than ever before, and their actions have an impact on world opinion that is often distinct from their negotiating positions. Among other things, this means that diplomacy is often conducted under the glare of television lights and almost everything that officials say in public is heard or read by others. Additionally, a country's overall image and the image of its leaders have become more important because of the democratization of the foreign policy process discussed above.

These changes have meant that international relations are also increasingly conducted through **public diplomacy**. The concept of public diplomacy can be defined as a process of creating an overall international image that enhances a country's ability to achieve diplomatic success. This is akin to propaganda. Public diplomacy includes traditional propaganda, but goes beyond that: it also includes what is

"EL PASO" POWELL

It helps to ease international negotiations if diplomats can establish some level of cordiality and relax a bit as they strut and fret their hours on the diplomatic stage. As one way to achieve this, a tradition that has developed during the annual Association of Southeast Asian Nations (ASEAN) foreign ministers conference to stage an off-the-record talent show. The 2001 event held in Hanoi, Vietnam, featured such top acts as the Australian delegation, complete with surfboard, belting out an enthusiastic, if inexpert, rendition of the Beach Boys' number, "Kokimo." The Russian foreign minister reportedly starred in a skit in which a slightly deranged Russian czar had an imaginary phone conversation with former U.S. secretary of state Madeleine Albright, affectionately called "Mad." Among her lines, "Colin Powell will not have the guts to go on stage."[1]

Accusations of being chicken were too much for the former chairman of the Joint Chiefs of Staff.

Wearing a blue denim shirt and a red bandana and brandishing a toy six-gun, Secretary of State Powell took center stage to perform his rendition of the Marty Robbins country-and-western classic, "El Paso." Powell not only sang, he acted out the lyrics, which tell the story of a cowboy who shoots a rival over the love of a "Mexican maiden," Feleena (played by Japan's foreign minister, Makiko Tanaka), and is then gunned down by a posse (made up of U.S. State Department officials). From all reports, the performance drew mixed reviews. One staff member wisely characterized his boss's singing as "O.K.," but also conceded, "There is no danger of him losing his day job." Perhaps, but the crowd was apparently brought to its feet at the last line of the song when Colin "El Paso" Powell got his "One little kiss and Feleena [Makiko], goodbye." Bring down the curtain; bring up the lights. Applause!

actually said and done by political figures, practices of national self-promotion that are much the same as advertising, and other forms of public relations that are utilized by business. In practice, as we shall see, propaganda and public diplomacy overlap substantially. One scholar's concept of public diplomacy envisions a "theater of power" that is a "metaphor for the repertoire of visual and symbolic tools used by statesmen and diplomats." As players in the theater of power, leaders "must be sensitive to the impression they make on observers.... They surely [are] subject to the same sort of 'dramatic,' if not aesthetic, criticism of other kinds of public performances" (Cohen, 1987:i-ii). There are even times when the symbolic theater becomes real theater, as explained in the box, "El Paso" Powell.

There is also an element of public diplomacy that goes beyond presenting one's best face and that involves distortions through propaganda and even outright lying. *Propaganda* is an attempt to influence another country through emotional techniques rather than logical discussion or presentation of empirical evidence. It is a process of appealing to emotions rather than minds by creating fear, doubt, sympathy, anger, or a variety of other feelings. Although the use of propaganda is as old as history, advances in communication, democratization, and the understanding of psychology have made propaganda increasingly important. In essence, if you cannot persuade another country's leaders through force or diplomacy, you can try to affect policy by persuading its people through propaganda.

By any standard, propaganda is big business. The United States, for one, operates or sponsors the Voice of America, Radio Free Europe/Radio Liberty, and Radio Martí. The U.S. Information Agency also produces Worldnet, a television service available globally, provides Web sites, and has other modern communications capabilities. Still, the end of the cold war has dealt harshly with most such efforts. Radio Free Europe/Radio Liberty, for example, has just 200 employees, down from 1,700 in the 1980s.

This does not mean that propaganda is dying. It is not. A plan proposed by the U.S. Defense Department in 2001 would have created an Office of Strategic Information, reportedly in order "to provide news items, possibly even false ones, to foreign media organizations as part of a new effort to influence public sentiment and policy-makers in both friendly and unfriendly countries."[39] The plan to spread what is euphemistically called **disinformation** was quickly killed once it became public, but it is unclear whether it was rejected because of the U.S. aversion to such tactics, as the Bush administration claimed, or because of the uproar it caused in the domestic and foreign press.

The Conduct of Diplomacy

Diplomacy is a complex game of maneuver in which the goal is to get other players to do what you want them to do. The players can number from two, in bilateral diplomacy, to many, in multilateral diplomacy. The rules of diplomacy are, at best, loose, and there is not just one mode of play. Instead, like all the most fascinating games, diplomacy is intricate and involves considerable strategy that can be employed in several ways. Thus, while diplomacy is often portrayed by an image of somber negotiations over highly polished wooden tables in ornate rooms, it is much more than that. Modern diplomacy is a far-ranging communications process.

Even hostile diplomacy requires some level of communications. This photograph of an Israeli soldier in front of a poster of Palestinian leader Yasser Arafat in the West Bank's Jenin refugee camp after Israeli troops entered the city in April 2002 symbolizes the nearly total breakdown in Israeli-Palestinian communications. Soon after this picture was taken, the United States tried to ease the fighting by becoming more active in the realm of mediation diplomacy.

DIPLOMACY AS A COMMUNICATIONS PROCESS

In essence, diplomacy is a communications process. It involves communicating to one or more other countries or other actors what your goal, demands, request, and other objectives are. Diplomacy also includes persuading other actors to support or comply with your objectives by communicating either the logic or morality of your point of view or by communicating the power that you can utilize to press for conformance with your goal, whether or not the other actor agrees. The diplomatic communication process has three elements: negotiation, signaling, and public diplomacy.

Negotiation When two or more parties are communicating with one another, either directly or indirectly through an intermediary, negotiations are occurring. It is very difficult to accomplish anything unless the two or more sides are talking. When the United States moved to quell the violence in the Middle East in early 2002, a major objective of Secretary of State Powell was to get the leadership of Israel and the leadership of the Palestinians back into negotiations with one another. Other than extremists in the Middle East, perhaps, no one disagreed with Powell's assessment that "the world is in agreement that the solution will not be produced by terror or a response to terror—this is not going to get us there. What will get us there are political discussions and the sooner we can get them the better."[40]

Signaling Conveying signals entails saying or doing something with the intent of sending a message to another government. When leaders make bellicose or conciliatory speeches, when military forces are deployed or even used, when trade privileges are granted or sanctions invoked, or when diplomatic recognition is extended or relations are broken, these actions are, or at least should be, signals of attitude and intent to another country.

The U.S. invasion of Afghanistan in response to the 9-11 terror attacks was meant in part as a signal beyond the immediate issue. At more than one point in the aftermath of the attacks, President Bush expressed worry about potential opponents of the United States doubting the resolve of Americans. Bush told the press, "I do believe there is the image of America out there that we are so materialistic, that we're almost hedonistic, that we don't have values, and that when struck, we won't fight back. It is clear," the president argued, "that bin Laden felt emboldened and didn't feel threatened by the United States."[41] Returning to this theme at another point, Bush told an audience, "They thought we would cower in the face of terror. And my, my, are they wrong."[42] It was this sense of the U.S. image overseas that urged Bush and his advisers to look for a response that not only dealt with the perpetrators of the terrorist attacks but also served as a signal to others beyond those immediately involved. "Let's hit them hard," Bush told the chairman of the Joint Chiefs of Staff when he directed the general to send ground troops as well as warplanes and missiles against Afghanistan. "We want to signal this is a change from the past," the president explained. "We want to cause other countries like Syria and Iran to change their views [about supporting terrorism]."[43]

Public diplomacy, as we noted earlier, involves the modern practice of trying to gain influence by appealing beyond another government to a wider audience, including public opinion in another country or throughout the world.

Once it would have been unthinkable for Soviet or Chinese leaders to have direct television access to Americans or for U.S. leaders to have reciprocal access. Now it is not uncommon. President Clinton treated visits to Russia and China as something akin to campaign stops. His trip to China in 1998, for example, was a tour de force of public diplomacy. He spoke to crowds on several stops, engaged in a question-and-answer session with students at Beijing University, and, most importantly, held a joint press conference with President Jiang that was broadcast live on China's state television. During the press conference, the two leaders exchanged views on such sensitive topics as Taiwan, Tibet, U.S.-China economic relations, and human rights in China. It was the first time that the Chinese had seen their government's policies openly criticized on national television, not to mention their president debating those policies.

THE RULES OF EFFECTIVE DIPLOMACY

Delineating the three modes of diplomatic communications is easy. Utilizing them effectively is hard. There is no set formula that will ensure victory. There are, however, several considerations that affect the chances of diplomatic success. We can examine some of these considerations by looking, in this section, at the rules of effective diplomacy, then, in the next section, by turning to the various options available for playing the great game of diplomacy. Some basic rules of effective diplomacy are:

Be realistic. It is important to have goals that match your ability to achieve them. "The test of a statesman," Kissinger (1970:47) has pointed out, "is his ability to recognize the real relationship of forces." Being realistic also means remembering that the other side, like yours, has domestic opponents. During discussions with North Korea in 1994, U.S. negotiator Robert Gallucci avoided pressing for nonvital, albeit desirable, concessions that, he said, "we recognized [as] serious [domestic] issues for [North Korea, but which] needed not be undertaken immediately."[44] When critics charged that the Clinton administration was being too soft, a U.S. official noted pragmatically that making some concession was "better than [going to] war."[45]

Be careful about what you say. The experienced diplomat plans and weighs words carefully. The first draft of the speech to the nation that President Bush gave on September 20, 2001, contained the sentence, "We will make no distinction between the terrorists who committed these [9-11] acts and those who harbor them." Several top advisers thought that the words were too strident, and favored language that would give countries a chance to change policy and would not seem, as Secretary of State Colin Powell reportedly thought, as if "the United States would be declaring war on everybody." This view led to the insertion of the words "continue to" before "harbor them" to distinguish between past and future behavior.[46]

At other times, President Bush's words seemed less well chosen. When he called for a "crusade" against terrorism, the association of the word with Christian-Muslim clashes in the past made many diplomats wince and set off a negative reaction in Muslim countries that made it difficult for them to cooperate with Washington. "We have to avoid a clash of civilizations at all costs," French foreign minister Hubert Vedrine said, and he urged Washington "to avoid falling into this huge trap, this monstrous trap" of having the war on terrorism portrayed as one of largely Christian countries against largely Muslim ones.[47]

Seek common ground. Finding common ground is a key to ending disputes peacefully. A first step to seeking common ground is to avoid seeing yourself as totally virtuous and your opponent as the epitome of evil. As a study of how peace is made and maintained, puts it, "Wars are seldom a struggle between total virtue and vice.... But when so conceived, they become crusades that remove the possibility of finding common ground after the battles are over" (Kegley & Raymond, 1999:249).

Understand the other side. There are several aspects to understanding the other side. One is to appreciate an opponent's perspective even if you do not agree with it. Just four months after Ronald Reagan was inaugurated and began an arms buildup, the Soviet leader, Leonid Brezhnev, wrote to his American counterpart to protest the military expansion "aimed against our country." "Try, Mr. President," Brezhnev asked Reagan, "to see what is going on through our eyes" (Kriesberg, 1992:12). It was good advice. As a corollary, it is also wise to make sure that thine enemy knows thee. Errors that result from misperceptions based on cultural differences and the lack of or wrong information are a major cause of conflict.

Be patient. It is also important to bide your time. Being overly anxious can lead to concessions that are unwise and may convey weakness to an opponent. As a corollary, it is poor practice to set deadlines, for yourself or others, unless you are in a very strong position or you do not really want an agreement. Throughout the negotiations with North Korea, which were frustrating and included many setbacks, the Clinton administration was patient and used gradual offers of rewards and threats of punishments. Critics called for stronger action. The steady course eventually carried the day.

Leave avenues of retreat open. It is axiomatic that even a rat will fight if trapped in a corner. The same is often true for countries. Call it honor, saving face, or prestige; it is important to leave yourself and your opponent an "out." Ultimatums, especially public ones, often lead to war. During the crisis with Iraq in 1998, Secretary-General Kofi Annan sought face-saving compromises that would allow Iraq to back away from its refusal to let inspectors into so-called presidential palaces. "Talk to some of your Arab friends," he suggested to a journalist. "Ask them to talk about dignity. It's like Chinese losing face—it's that important. It's not a joke. The sense of humiliation or losing your dignity or losing face—they would die or go to war over that."[48]

OPTIONS FOR CONDUCTING DIPLOMACY

While the above rules are solid guidelines to effective diplomacy, the practice is still more art than science. Therefore, effective diplomacy must tailor its approach to the situation and the opponent. To do this, diplomats must make choices about the channel, level, visibility, type of inducement, degree of precision, method of communication, and extent of linkage that they will use (Feron, 1997).

Direct or Indirect Negotiations

One issue that diplomats face is whether to negotiate directly with each other or indirectly through an intermediary. *Direct negotiations* have the advantage of avoiding the misinterpretations that an intermediary third party might cause. As in the old game of "Gossip," messages can get garbled. Direct negotiations are also quicker. An additional plus is that they can act as a symbol.

Indirect negotiations may also be advisable. Direct contact symbolizes a level of legitimacy that a country may not wish to convey. Israel, for instance, long refused to openly and directly negotiate with the PLO. Indirect diplomacy can also avoid the embarrassment of a public rebuff by the other side. During the opening moves in 1970, exploring diplomatic relations, the United States and China sent oral messages through the "good offices" (friendly intermediaries) of Pakistan and Romania, and written messages were exchanged on photocopy paper with no letterheads or signatures.

High-Level or Low-Level Diplomacy

The higher the level of contact or the higher the level of the official making a statement, the more seriously will a message be taken. It implies a greater commitment, and there will be a greater reaction. Therefore, a diplomat must decide whether to communicate on a high or a low level.

High-level diplomacy has its advantages. Verbal and written statements by heads of government are noted seriously in other capitals. As the violence between Israelis and Palestinians mounted in 2001, Muslim states became increasingly worried and angered by what they saw as a combination of an unwillingness of the United States to use its hegemonic status to mediate and by a bias against the Palestinians. At one point when President Bush criticized Palestinian leader Yasser Arafat, the de facto leader of Saudi Arabia, Crown Prince Abdullah ibn Abdulaziz, "just went bananas," according to a Saudi official. The crown prince called his ambassador in Washington and told him to tell President Bush that "Saudi Arabia could not accept" the U.S. position, which seemed to the crown prince to include an "extraordinary, un-American bias whereby the blood of an Israeli child is more expensive and holy than the blood of a Palestinian child."[49] Therefore, the ambassador was instructed to tell Bush, "Starting from today,... you go your way, I go my way."

Such strident language from an important ally and key Arab state was a powerful message. It brought a rapid response from Bush in the form of a letter that outlined a balanced approach to the issues in the region, including Bush's endorsing the idea of establishing a Palestinian state. This high-level, written response quelled Saudi ire, at least for the moment. A Saudi official called the letter "groundbreaking" and indicated, "Things in it had never been put in writing."[50]

Low-level diplomacy is wiser at other times. Communications at a low level avoid overreaction and maintain flexibility. Dire threats can be issued as "trial balloons" by cabinet officers or generals and then, if later thought unwise, disavowed by higher political officers. During the Taiwan crisis of 2000, the principal leaders tended to avoid military threats, leaving that role to lesser officials. For example, an editorial in the Chinese military's newspaper, *Liberation Army Daily*, was far enough removed from official policy makers to warn provocatively that China would "spare no effort in a blood-soaked battle" if Taiwan declared independence.[51] From a position safely distant from the pinnacle of U.S. authority in the Oval Office, Undersecretary of Defense for Policy Walter Slocombe growled back that China would face "incalculable consequences" if it attacked Taiwan.[52]

Sometimes it is even prudent to use a representative who is not in the government at all. During the 2000 crisis it was diplomatically difficult for China and Taiwan officials to meet face-to-face, so, apparently, Jeremy Stone, president of the American Federation of Scientists and a close friend of Taiwan's new president, was used as an intermediary. Stone, who also has a diplomatic background in arms control, visited President-elect Chen in Taiwan. He then flew to Beijing as an "unofficial representative of Taipei," according to one Chinese official. "What we're trying to do is find ways to communicate," explained a Taiwanese source.[53]

Using Coercion or Rewards to Gain Agreement

Yet another diplomatic choice is whether to brandish coercive sticks or proffer tempting carrots. To induce an opponent to react as you wish, is it better to offer rewards or to threaten punishment?

Coercive diplomacy can be effective when you have the power, will, and credibility to back it up. Verbal threats and military maneuvering were central to the diplomatic interplay among the United States, North Korea, and the other countries embroiled in the 1993–1994 confrontation. Perhaps because it was the weaker side, North Korea was particularly bombastic. Its main newspaper, *Rodong Sinmum*, declared that if "war breaks out," the "reactionaries" would be "digging their own grave."[54] Given the long and bloody Korean War (1950–1953) and North Korea's considerable military might, such rhetoric was believable. There was a consensus, one Pentagon source put it, that "it's going to be a bloody, bloody mess if [war] happens. A real tragedy."[55] The United States and its allies also practiced coercive diplomacy. They threatened economic sanctions and at least refused to rule out military action. After Pyongyang refused to allow inspections, a stern U.S. official announced, "This time the North went too far. There are no more carrots."[56]

There are also a number of drawbacks to coercive diplomacy. If it does not work, then those who have threatened force face an unhappy choice. On the one hand, not carrying out threats creates an image of weakness that may well embolden the opponent in the crisis at hand. Opponents in other ongoing and future confrontations may also be encouraged. On the other hand, putting one's military might and money where one's mouth is costs lives and dollars and is not necessarily successful either. Even if coercion does work, it may entail a long-term commitment that was not originally planned or desired. The war with Iraq ended in February 1991, but U.S. forces have remained enmeshed in the region, have been on the verge of renewed war with Iraq on several occasions, and have spent many billions of dollars patrolling the region.

There are many times when *offers of rewards* may be a more powerful inducement than coercion. Threats may lead to war, with high costs and uncertain results. It may also be possible to "buy" what you cannot "win." One song in the movie *Mary Poppins*

SCHOT
ALGEMEEN DAGBLAD
Rotterdam
NETHERLANDS

$.....
DONOR AID

PRICE TAG

CARTOONISTS & WRITERS SYNDICATE http://CartoonWeb.com

Economic incentives are one diplomatic tool. This Dutch editorial cartoon of former Yugoslavian president Slobodan Milosevic wearing prison garb and being hanged by "donor aid" represents the widely held, and probably accurate, assumption that the decision of Yugoslavia's government to extradite him was taken in part to get international financial aid. Within hours of Milosevic's departure under guard for trial in the Netherlands in June 2001, Western donor countries offered $1.28 billion in aid to Belgrade.

includes the wisdom that "a spoonful of sugar helps the medicine go down," and an increase in aid, a trade concession, a state visit, or some other tangible or symbolic reward may induce agreement.

Often, the best diplomacy mixes carrots and sticks (O'Reilly, 1997). Economic sanctions and other diplomatic sticks helped topple the regime of Slobodan Milosevic in October 2000. The new government refused, however, to turn him over for trial by the war crimes tribunal sitting in The Hague. What seemingly turned the trick was proffering an exceptionally attractive bunch of carrots to Belgrade. In an unspoken but obvious deal, the Yugoslav government extradited Milosevic in June 2001, and within hours, the United States, the European Union, and other donor countries and organizations (such as the World Bank) meeting in Brussels pledged $1.28 billion in aid to the country.

Being Precise or Being Intentionally Vague

Most diplomatic experts stress the importance of being precise when communicating. There are times, however, when purposeful vagueness may be in order.

Precision is a hallmark of diplomacy. Being precise in both written and verbal communications helps avoid misunderstandings. It can also indicate true commitment, especially if it comes from the national leader.

Vagueness may at times be a better strategy. Being vague may paper over irreconcilable differences. "The Saudis have a nice way of doing things" when they do not wish to agree, says one U.S. official. "They say, 'we'll consider it.' It is not their style to say no."[57] Lack of precision also can allow a country to retreat if necessary or permit it to avoid being too provocative. During the Taiwan elections in 1996 and 2000, the United States accomplished both goals by refusing to say exactly what it would do if China attacked Taiwan. When in 1996 a reporter asked Secretary of State Warren Christopher what would occur, he pushed aside the possibility of a Sino-American war as mere "operational details."[58]

Communicating by Word or Deed

Diplomacy utilizes both words and actions to communicate. Each method has its advantages.

Oral and written communications, either direct or through public diplomacy, are appropriate for negotiations and also can be a good signaling strategy. They can establish positions at a minimum cost and are more apt to maintain flexibility than active signaling. Sometimes communications can even be indirect signals. The dismay that Saudi Arabia felt in 2001 with the policy of President Bush toward the Israeli-Palestinian crisis was not only expressed in the direct criticism of U.S. policy conveyed from Crown Prince Adbullah to President Bush. The Saudis further underlined their ire by taking the very drastic diplomatic step of deriding Bush personally in the form of indirectly questioning his basic competency. According to one official, they saw Bush as "goofy." That view led to an op-ed piece by the Saudi ambassador to Great Britain in an English-language Arab paper published in London that portrayed the U.S. president as a lightweight governed by "complexes." "In a few months," the diplomat wrote, "this man created enemies for America to an extent making him worthy of a new prize, to be called the prize for transforming friends into adversaries, effortlessly."[59]

Signaling by action is often more dramatic than verbal signaling and it has its uses. Some signals can be fairly low level. Crown Prince Abdullah further indicated Saudi distress with the U.S. position in the Middle East crisis by canceling an annual review of Saudi-U.S. military relations scheduled to occur in Washington, D.C., in August 2001. The Saudi military chief of staff had already arrived in the United

States for the high-level talks when Abdullah ordered him to return home. "You don't cancel visits like this on the day before. It was a big, big event," a senior aide to the crown prince noted correctly. Both sides downplayed the event, but the Pentagon reportedly was "shocked" by the cancellation, and the signal drove home the message of Saudi discontent.[60]

Other actions can be stronger, but they are perilous because it is harder to retreat from dramatic deeds than from words or even subtle acts. When, in 1961, the East Germans and Soviets threatened to blockade Berlin, President John F. Kennedy took the risky step of going there and, before a throng of West Berliners, proclaimed himself a symbolic fellow citizen. "*Ich bin ein Berliner*," Kennedy's words rang out. Both sides understood the import of the president's putting his personal honor on the line, and the crisis eased. Germans on both sides of the Wall also got a good chuckle, because the president's speech writers had made a minor grammatical error. "*Ich bin Berliner*" (I am a Berliner) is what he had wanted to say. By adding the "*ein*," however, Kennedy had inadvertently changed the meaning of Berliner from citizen to jelly doughnut, locally called a *berliner*. Thus what the leader of the free world actually declared was "I am a jelly doughnut."[61]

Various military actions, ranging from alerting forces, through deploying them, to limited demonstrations of force, can also be effective (albeit perilous) signals. Such maneuvers were especially evident during the Taiwan imbroglio in 1996. Just before the election in Taiwan, Beijing announced that it was going to "conduct joint ground, naval, and air exercises in and over a sea area near Taiwan."[62] This demonstration of military might included, among other things, China's firing six powerful missiles into the seas near Taiwan's two major ports, Kaohsiung and Keelung. Chinese television showed the launch of the M-9 and M-11 missiles, which can carry nuclear or conventional warheads. As breathlessly described by the Chinese narrator, "Milky-white missiles were seen deployed, nested in a mountain range. Officers and men were in full battle array. In the middle of the night, the command post issued the orders of operation. Amid the uproar of the launch came the reports: 'The first missile hits the target, the second missile hits the target.'"[63]

For its part, the United States responded to the implied Chinese threat by utilizing its aircraft carriers. President Clinton ordered a major naval flotilla, centered around the carriers USS *Nimitz* and USS *Independence*, into the waters off Taiwan. The commanding admiral of the U.S. Seventh Fleet explained that "we do not want to see an escalation. China has said [it is] not going to attack Taiwan, and that's exactly what we want to see happen."[64]

Linking Issues or Treating Them Separately

A persistent dispute is whether a country should deal with other countries on an issue-by-issue basis or link issues together as a basis for a general orientation toward the other country. Advocates of *linking issues* argue that it is inappropriate to have normal relations on some matters with regimes that are hostile and repressive. Those who favor *treating issues separately* claim that doing so allows progress on some issues and keeps channels of communications and influence open.

During the crisis in 2000, China's stand on Taiwan became enmeshed with the fate of China's permanent normal trade relations with the United States and with China's admission to the WTO. A Chinese foreign ministry official objected that his country "firmly opposes any attempt to link these issues," and claimed that China's stand on Taiwan and "the issue of normal trade relations [are] two entirely separate issues."[65] That protest was in vain, however, and the issues remained tied together.

On a more general basis, linkage remains an ongoing and inconsistent issue in U.S. foreign policy. President Clinton argued that China's poor human rights record and authoritarian form of government should not be linked to China's trade status. One reason to delink the issues, according to Clinton, was that regular interaction would be a "force for change in China, exposing China to our ideas and ideals." The president also argued that "our engagement with China serves American interests… [by promoting] stability in Asia, preventing the spread of weapons of mass destruction, combating international crime and drug trafficking, [and] protecting the environment."[66] Not mentioned, but a factor, were the billions of dollars in U.S. exports and investments that go to China.

Cuba has been another matter, though, and delinking issues has not extended to that country. There are a number of U.S. measures, including the Helms-Burton Act (1996), that institute economic sanctions on Cuba and foreign companies doing business with Cuba in an attempt to weaken the government of President Fidel Castro. Why delinking would promote change in China and not in Cuba remains unexplained.

Maximizing or Minimizing a Dispute

Diplomats face a choice over whether to put a confrontation in a broad or narrow context. The advantage of *maximizing a dispute* by invoking national survival, world peace, or some other major principle is that it increases credibility. During the 1996 Taiwan Strait crisis, China maximized the stakes by having the country's second-ranking official, Premier Li Peng, publicly depict the matter as a "core principle" involving China's "territorial integrity and the cause of reunification."[67] Similarly, President Bush in 2001 sought to put the U.S. response to the 9-11 terrorist attacks in very broad terms. The goal of al-Qaeda "is remaking the world—and imposing its radical beliefs on people everywhere," Bush told Congress, the nation, and the world. He also elevated al-Qaeda to the level of the Nazis and others in the pantheon of evil by denouncing Osama bin Laden and his followers as "the heirs of all the murderous ideologies of the twentieth century." From this perspective of epic, global evil, Bush could then argue, "This is not… just America's fight…. This is the world's fight. This is civilization's fight. This is the fight of all who believe in progress and pluralism, tolerance and freedom."[68]

The advantages of *minimizing a dispute* were evident in both the Taiwan crises. To ease the crisis in 2000, Chinese officials in March seemed to disavow a policy paper issued in February that escalated tension by declaring for the first time that "all drastic measures" would be used if Taipei refused "indefinitely" to rejoin the mainland. Responding to the furor, China's deputy prime minister reassuringly said on television that the document merely "reiterates the government's consistent stance" and that, "some foreign media have regarded China as making a major change to its policy on the Taiwan issue. This is incorrect."[69]

The United States also sought to minimize the dispute. "We will continue to insist that the Taiwanese… not seek independence," Secretary of Defense William S. Cohen told reporters during the confrontation in 2000.[70] Washington was also careful to downplay any U.S. military threat to China. "Our decision to deploy naval forces to the region was one with the intent to defuse tension, not to raise tension," a senior White House official publicly assured China and the world in 1996.[71]

A final note is that despite the recitation of diplomatic rules and analysis of the advantages and disadvantages of various diplomatic options in the preceding two sections, there is no substitute for skill and wisdom. Understanding how the game ought to be played does not always produce a win on the playing field of sports or a success at the negotiating table of diplomacy. Certainly you are advantaged if you know the fundamentals, but beyond that, individual capacity and field savvy provide the margin of victory.

🌐 Chapter Summary

1. National diplomacy is the process of trying to advance a country's national interest by applying power assets to attempt to persuade other countries to give way.

2. Power is the foundation of diplomacy in a conflictual world. National power is the sum of a country's assets that enhance its ability to get its way even when opposed by others with different interests and goals.

3. Measuring power is especially difficult. The efforts to do so have not been very successful, but they do help us see many of the complexities of analyzing the characteristics of power. These characteristics include the facts that power is dynamic, both objective and subjective, relative, situational, and multidimensional.

4. The major elements of a country's power can be roughly categorized as those that constitute (1) its national core, (2) its national infrastructure, (3) its national economy, and (4) its military. The core and infrastructure are discussed here and form the basis for economic and military power, which are analyzed in later chapters.

5. The national core consists of a country's geography, its people, and its government.

6. The national infrastructure consists of a country's technological sophistication, its transportation system, and its information and communications capabilities.

7. The functions of diplomacy include advancing the national interest through such methods as observing and reporting, negotiating, symbolically representing, intervening, and propagandizing.

8. Diplomacy does not occur in a vacuum. Instead it is set in the international system, in a specific diplomatic environment (hostile, adversarial, coalition, and mediation diplomacy), and in a domestic context.

9. Diplomacy is an ancient art, and some of the historical functions of diplomacy are still important. Diplomacy, however, has also changed dramatically during the past century. Seven characteristics describe the new approach to diplomacy: expanded geographic scope, multilateral diplomacy, parliamentary maneuvering, democratized diplomacy, open diplomacy, leader-to-leader communications through summit meetings, and public diplomacy.

10. These changes reflect the changes in the international system and in domestic political processes. Some of the changes have been beneficial, but others have had negative consequences. At the least, diplomacy has become more complex with the proliferation of actors and options. It has also become more vital, given the possible consequences should it fail.

11. Diplomacy is a communication process that has three main elements. The first is negotiating through direct or indirect discussions between two or more countries. The second is signaling. The third is public diplomacy.

12. Good diplomacy is an art, but it is not totally freestyle, and there are general rules that increase the chances for diplomatic success. Among the cautions are to be realistic, to be careful about what you say, to seek common ground, to try to understand the other side, to be patient, and to leave open avenues of retreat.

13. There are also a wide variety of approaches or options in diplomacy. Whether contacts should be direct or indirect, what level of contact they should involve, what rewards or coercion should be offered, how precise or vague messages should be, whether to communicate by message or deed, whether issues should be linked or dealt with separately, and the wisdom of maximizing or minimizing a dispute are all questions that require careful consideration.

Chapter 11

International Law and Morality: The Alternative Approach

Which is the wiser here, Justice or Iniquity?

Shakespeare, *Measure for Measure*

The law hath not been dead, though it hath slept.

Shakespeare, *Hamlet*

I establish law and justice in the land.

Hammurabi, king of Babylon, circa 2100 B.C.

Power not ruled by law is a menace.

Arthur J. Goldberg, U.S. Supreme Court justice

Chapter Objectives

After completing this chapter, you should be able to:

- Discuss the dynamic nature of law by addressing the concept of a primitive but evolving legal system.
- Evaluate the effectiveness of international law.
- Distinguish between the different sources of international law.
- Discuss the role of morality in the international system and in international law.
- Understand the four essential elements of the international legal system.
- Identify and examine the roots and characteristics of international law.
- Discuss adherence to international law.
- Describe the process of adjudication in international law.
- Enumerate problems in applying international law to different cultures.
- Identify the international legal issues that developed during the twentieth century and explain how changes in the world system have affected these issues.
- Illustrate how and why international law has been applied increasingly to individuals rather than only to states.
- Examine issues of morality in the modern international legal system and the role of morality in a future system.

This chapter focuses on the possibility of placing greater emphasis on international law and morality in the conduct of world politics. This is an alternative approach to the power-based diplomatic pursuit of self-interest discussed in the last chapter. It would be naive to ignore the reality that most actors, whether they are individuals and groups in domestic political systems or states in the international system, emphasize their own welfare. There are differences, however, in how domestic and international systems work. What is of interest here is the way domestic systems place greater restraints on the pursuit of self-interest than the international system does.

Legal systems are one thing that helps limit the role of pure power in a domestic system. The Fourteenth Amendment to the U.S. Constitution, for example, establishes "the equal protection of the laws" as a fundamental principle. Certainly, powerful individuals and groups have distinct advantages in every domestic system. Rules are broken and the guilty, especially if they can afford a high-priced attorney, sometimes escape punishment. Still, laws in the United States cannot overtly discriminate, and an attorney is provided to indigent defendants in criminal cases. Thus, the law somewhat evens the playing field.

Morality is a second thing that restrains the role of power in domestic systems. We are discussing what is "right" here, not just what is legal. Whether the word is moral, ethical, fair, or just, there is a greater sense in domestic systems than there is in the international system that appropriate codes of conduct exist, that the ends do not always justify the means, and that those who violate the norms should suffer penalties. Surely, there is no domestic system in which everyone acts morally toward everyone else. Yet the sense of morality and justice that citizens in stable domestic systems have does have an impact on their behavior.

Most importantly, what all this means is that politics does not have to work just one way. There are alternatives. *Idealists* envision and prescribe a system of international law that covers more and more aspects of international interchange and that contains strong mechanisms to resolve disputes and enforce the law. *Realists* do not believe that this goal is attainable and suspect that national states will follow the dictates of national interest, ignore the law, and act in a self-serving way, especially on national security and other vital matters. Idealists reply that they are not so foolish as to imagine a perfect world, only a better one.

Fundamentals of International Law and Morality

What actors may and may not legitimately do is based in both international and domestic law systems on a combination of expectations, rules, and practices that help govern behavior. We explore the fundamental nature of these legal systems and moral codes by looking first at the primitive nature, growth, and current status of international law; then by turning to issues of morality (Ku & Diehl, 1998).

THE PRIMITIVE NATURE OF INTERNATIONAL LAW

No legal system, domestic or international, emerges full blown. Each one grows, advancing from a primitive level to ever more sophisticated levels. As such, any legal system can be placed on an evolutionary scale ranging from primitive on one end to modern on the other. Note that modern does not mean finished; people in the future may shake their heads in disbelief over how rudimentary current legal systems are.

This is speculative, but what is certain is that the concept of a *primitive but evolving legal system* is important to understanding international law.

The current international legal system falls toward the primitive end of the evolutionary scale of legal systems. First, as a primitive law system, the international system does not have a formal rule-making, or legislative, process. Instead, codes of behavior are derived from custom or from explicit agreements among two or more societal members or groups. Second, there is little or no established authority to judge or punish violations of law. Primitive societies, domestic or international, have no police or courts. Moreover, a primitive society is often made up of self-defined units (such as kinship groups), is territorially based, primarily governs itself, and resorts to violent "self-help" in relations with other groups.

Viewing international law as a primitive legal system has two benefits. One is that we can see that international law does exist, even if it is not as developed as we might wish. The second benefit is that it encourages us with the thought that international society and its law may evolve to a higher order.

THE GROWTH OF INTERNATIONAL LAW

The beginning of international law coincides with the origins of the state. As sovereign, territorial states arose, they needed to define and protect their status and to order their relations. Gradually, along with the state-based political system, elements of ancient Jewish, Greek, and Roman practice combined with newer Christian concepts and also with custom and practice to form most of the rudiments of the prevailing international system of law (Van Dervort, 1997).

A number of important theorists built on this foundation. The most famous of these was the Dutch thinker Hugo Grotius (1583–1645), whose study *De Jure Belli et Pacis* (On the Law of War and Peace) earned him the title "father of international law." Grotius and others discussed and debated the sources of international law, its role in regulating the relations of states, and its application to specific circumstances such as the justification and conduct of war and the treatment of subjugated peoples. From this base, international law expanded and changed slowly over the intervening centuries, as the interactions between the states grew and the expectations of the international community became more sophisticated.

It has been during the last century or so, however, that the most rapid expansion by far of concern with international law and its practical importance has occurred. Increasing international interaction and interdependence have significantly expanded the need for rules to govern a host of functional areas such as trade, finance, travel, and communications (Armstrong, 1999). Similarly, our awareness of our ability to destroy ourselves and our environment, and of the suffering of victims of human rights abuses, has led to lawmaking treaties on such subjects as genocide, nuclear testing, use of the oceans, and human rights. Even the most political of all activities, war and other aspects of national security, have increasingly become the subject of international law. Aggressive war, for example, is outside the pale of the law. The UN's response of authorizing sanctions and then force against Iraq after it invaded Kuwait reflected, in part, a genuine global rejection of aggression (Linklater, 1999).

THE PRACTICE OF INTERNATIONAL LAW

One of the charges that realists make against international law is that it exists only in theory, not in practice. As evidence, critics cite ongoing, largely unpunished examples of "lawlessness" such as war and human rights abuses. The flaw in this argument is that it does not prove its point. In the first place, international law is effective in many areas. As one scholar notes, "the reality as demonstrated through their behavior is that states do accept international law as law, and, even more significant, in the vast majority of instances they... obey it" (Joyner, 2000:243). Furthermore, the fact that law does not cover *all* problem areas and that it is not *always* followed does not disprove its existence. There is, after all, a substantial crime rate in the United States, but does that mean there is no law?

International law is *most effective* in governing the rapidly expanding range of transnational **functional relations**. Functional interactions are those that involve "low politics," a term that designates such things as trade, diplomatic rules, and communications.

International law is *least effective* when applied to "high-politics" issues such as national security relations between sovereign states. When vital interests are involved, governments still regularly bend international law to justify their actions rather than alter their actions to conform to the law.

This does not mean, however, that the law never influences political decisions. To the contrary, there is a growing sensitivity to international legal standards, especially insofar as they reflect prevailing international norms. Both international law and world values, for instance, are strongly opposed to states unilaterally resorting to war except in self-defense. Violations such as Iraq's invasion of Kuwait still occur, but they are met with mounting global condemnation and even counterforce. Now even countries as powerful as the United States regularly seek UN authorization to act in cases such as Afghanistan in 2001, when not long ago they would have acted on their own initiative.

THE FUNDAMENTALS OF INTERNATIONAL MORALITY

As with international law, it would be equally erroneous to overestimate the impact of morality on the conduct of states or to dismiss the part that morality plays. As one scholar notes, "Contrary to what the skeptics assert, norms do indeed matter. But norms do not necessarily matter in the ways or often to the extent that their proponents have argued" (Legro, 1997:31).

Concepts of moral behavior may stem from religious beliefs, from secular ideologies or philosophies, from the standard of equity (what is fair), or from the practice of a society. We will see in our discussion of roots of international law that what a society considers moral behavior sometimes becomes law. At other times, legal standards are gradually adopted by a society as moral standards. Insofar as moral behavior remains an imperative of conscience rather than law, we can consider morality in a broad sense. There are distinctions that can be made between moral, ethical, and humanitarian standards and behavior, but for our purposes here, the three terms—morals, ethics, and humanitarianism—are used interchangeably.

It would be madness—given recurring war, gnawing human deprivation, persistent human rights violations, and debilitating environmental abuse—to imagine that morality is a predominant global force. Yet moral considerations do play a role in world politics (Frost, 1996). Even more important, there is a growing body of ethical norms that help determine the nature of the international system. Progress is slow and inconsistent, but it exists. The UN-authorized force did not drop nuclear weapons on Iraq in 1991, even though it arguably could have saved time, money, and the lives of Americans and their allies by doing so. Many countries give foreign aid to less developed countries. National leaders, not just philosophers and clergy, regularly discuss and sometimes even make decisions based on human rights. Consumers have rallied to the environmentalist cause to protect dolphins by purchasing only cans of tuna on which dolphin-safe logos are featured.

The reality is that world politics operates neither in a legal vacuum nor in a moral void. To understand the current course of world interactions and events we

The ideals of international law and morality are slowly beginning to have greater application in the real world. It is almost certainly painful memories that bring tears to this Bosnian Muslim woman, Fatima Begovic, as she watches former Yugoslavian president Slobodan Milosevic on television during his trial before the UN tribunal in The Hague, the Netherlands, in February 2002. All the male members of her family were among the 7,000 Bosnian Muslims massacred by the Serbs in Srebrenica in July 1995. Now Milosevic is on trial for giving support to those who committed the atrocity and many other war crimes against non-Serbs in Kosovo, Croatia, and Bosnia.

will turn in the following pages to an examination of the international legal system and then to a discussion of the application of law and morality in the international system.

The International Legal System

International law, like any legal system, is based on four critical considerations: the philosophical roots of law, how laws are made, when and why the law is obeyed (adherence), and how legal disputes are decided (adjudication).

THE PHILOSOPHICAL ROOTS OF LAW

Before considering the mechanics of the legal system, it is important to inquire into the roots of law. Ideas about what is right and what should be the law do not spring from thin air. Rather, they are derived from sources both external and internal to the society that they regulate.

External Sources Some laws come from sources external to a society. The idea here is that some higher, metaphysical standard of conduct should govern the affairs of humankind. An important ramification of this position is that there is or ought to be one single system of law that governs all people.

Those who believe in the external sources can be subdivided into two schools. The **ideological/theological school of law** is one. This school of thought holds that law is derived from an overarching ideology or theology. For instance, a substantial part of international legal theory extends back to early Western proponents of international law who relied on Christian doctrine for their standards. The writings of Saint Augustine and Saint Thomas Aquinas on the law of war are examples. There are also elements of long-standing Islamic, Buddhist, and other religions' law and scholarship that serve as a foundation for just international conduct.

The **naturalist school of law** relies on a second source of external principles. This view holds that humans, by nature, have certain rights and obligations. The English philosopher John Locke argued in *Two Treatises of Government* (1690) that there is "a law of nature" that "teaches all mankind, who will but consult it, that all [people] being equal and independent [in the state of nature], no one ought to harm another in his life, health, liberty, or possessions." Since countries are collectives of individuals, and the world community is a collective of states and individuals, natural law's rights and obligations also apply to the global stage and form the basis for international law.

Critics of the theory of external sources of law contend that standards based on ideology or theology can lead to oppression. The problems with natural law, critics charge, are both that it is vague and that it contains such an emphasis on individualism that it almost precludes any sense of communitarian welfare. If a person's property is protected by natural law, then, for instance, it is hard to justify taking any individual's property through taxes levied by the government without the individual's explicit agreement.

Internal Sources Some legal scholars reject the idea of divine or naturalist roots and, instead, focus on the customs and practices of society. This is the **positivist school of law**, which advocates that law reflects society and the way people want that society to operate. Therefore, according to positivist principles, law is and ought to be the product of the codification or formalization of a society's standards.

Critics condemn the positivist approach as amoral and sometimes immoral, in that it may legitimize immoral, albeit common, beliefs and behavior of a society as a whole or of its dominant class. These critics would say, for instance, that slavery was once widespread and widely accepted, but it was never moral or lawful, by the standards of either divine principle or natural law.

HOW INTERNATIONAL LAW IS MADE

Countries usually make domestic law through a constitution (constitutional law) or by a legislative body (statutory law). In practice, law is also established through judicial decisions (interpretation), which set guidelines (precedent) for later decisions by the courts. Less influential sources of law are custom (common law), and what is fair (equity).

Compared to its domestic equivalent, modern international lawmaking is much more decentralized. There are, according to the Statute of the International Court of Justice, four sources of law: international treaties, international custom, the general principles of law, and judicial decisions and scholarly legal writing. Some students of international law would tentatively add a fifth source: resolutions and other pronouncements of the UN General Assembly. These five rely primarily on the positivist approach but, like domestic law, include elements of both external and internal sources of law.

International Treaties Treaties are the primary source of international law. A primary advantage of treaties is that they **codify**, or write down, the law. Agreements between states are binding according to the doctrine of **pacta sunt servanda** (treaties are to be served/carried out). All treaties are binding on those countries that are

(Continued on page 305)

CORRUPTION AND INTERNATIONAL LAW

The growing global movement against corruption is one way to see the sources and evolution of positivist international law. The growth of economic interdependence has made corruption increasingly intolerable to those doing business across international borders. International financial agencies such as the World Bank are also critical of corruption because it hinders development (Elliot, 1997). Studies indicate, for example, that there is an inverse relationship between the degree of corruption and annual gross domestic product (GDP) growth. Other research indicates that because corruption short-circuits both growth and the dispersal of money in an economy, the more corrupt a country is the higher the level of that country's income inequality. Corrupt countries also have higher levels of illiteracy, child mortality, and other indications of social ills because bribe-taking and other forms of corruption siphon off money that might otherwise be spent on education, health, and other social services.

At the heart of the movement against corruption is a relatively new international nongovernmental organization (NGO) called Transparency International (TI). It was founded in 1993, has its headquarters in Berlin, Germany, and has national chapters in 80 countries. The organization's budget (nearly $4 million in 2001), is financed mainly by governmental agencies (like the U.S. Agency for International Development, USAID), and by corporations (such as General Electric). The Advisory Council of TI includes such luminaries as former president of Costa Rica and Nobel Peace Prize laureate Oscar Arias Sánchez and former U.S. president Jimmy Carter. According to its Web page (www.transparency.org), TI "is a non-governmental organization dedicated to increasing accountability and curbing both international and national... corruption."

Perhaps TI's most effective public relations tool is the annual Corruption Perception Index that it began publishing in 1994. According to TI chairman, Peter Eigen, a former World Bank official, the index measures "how business people around the globe perceive levels of corruption."[1] The results of the 2001 index, which scored 91 countries from 0 ("highly corrupt") to 10 ("highly clean"), found Bangladesh (0.4) to be the world's most corrupt country. Finland finished best in 2001 with a near perfect 9.9. Canada (8.9) was seventh, and the United States (7.6) came in sixteenth.

TI has been able to move the issue of corruption

One result of economic globalization in the area of law has been the increased effort of governments, international governmental organizations, and international nongovernmental organizations, such as Transparency International, to end corruption. This photograph shows a protester defacing a billboard of President Joseph Estrada of the Philippines promoting his administration's campaign against graft and corruption. Ironically, what had angered the protester was Estrada's arrest for taking more than $80 million in bribes. He was forced from office and in early 2002 went on trial for "plundering" and other crimes that could carry the death penalty.

onto the international political and legal agenda. For example, the Organization for Economic Cooperation and Development (OECD), which includes the world's economically developed countries (EDCs) and a number of other countries, adopted in 1997 the Convention on Combating Bribery of Foreign Public Officials in International Business Transactions. The 21 countries that have ratified the treaty so far agree to a number of steps, such as passing national laws to, among other things, end the ability to take tax deductions for bribes paid in international business transactions. There is also now a biennial International Anti-Corruption Conference. The 2001 meeting, which was held in Prague, Czech Republic, drew over 1,300 delegates from 143 countries and the 2003 meeting is scheduled to convene in Seoul, South Korea.

It is too early to predict exactly the degree to which corrupt practices will become the subject of international law, but the activities of TI are arguably part of the genesis of turning what not long ago was an exclusive concern of national law into a matter of international law.

party to them (have signed and ratified or otherwise given their legal consent). Moreover, it is possible to argue that some treaties are also applicable to nonsignatories. Multilateral treaties, those signed by more than two states, are an increasingly important source of international law. When a large number of states agree to a principle, that norm begins to take on system-wide legitimacy. The 1948 Convention on the Prevention and Punishment of the Crime of Genocide, for example, has been ratified by most states. Some would argue, therefore, that genocide has been "recognized" and "codified" as a violation of international law and that this standard of conduct is binding on all states regardless of whether or not they have formally agreed to the treaty. Now people are being tried, convicted, and sentenced for genocide, as we shall discuss presently.

International Custom The second most important source of international law is custom. The old, and now supplanted, rule that territorial waters extend three miles from the shore grew from the distance a cannon could fire. If you were outside the range of land-based artillery, then you were in international waters. Maritime rules of the road and diplomatic practice are two other important areas of law that grew out of custom. Sometimes, long-standing custom is eventually codified in treaties. An example is the Vienna Convention on Diplomatic Relations of 1961, which codified many existing rules of diplomatic standing and practice.

General Principles of Law The ancient Roman concept of *jus gentium* (the law of peoples) is the foundation of the general principles of law. By this standard, the International Court of Justice (ICJ) applies "the general principles of law recognized by civilized nations." Although such language is vague, it has its benefits. It encompasses "external" sources of law, such as the idea that freedom of religion and freedom from attack are among the inherent rights of people. More than any other standard, it is for violating these general principles that Slobodan Milosevic, the former president of Yugoslavia, was brought to trial in 2002 at the international tribunal in the Netherlands. According to the United Nations, the charges against Milosevic included nine counts of violating a specific treaty, the 1949 Geneva Conventions. But the indictment was also based on *jus gentium*, including "13 counts of violations of the laws or customs of war," such as "murder; torture; cruel treatment; [and] wanton destruction of villages... not justified by military necessity;" and "10 counts of crimes against humanity," such as "persecutions on political, racial or religious grounds; extermination; murder; imprisonment; torture; [and]; inhumane acts (forcible transfers)."[1]

Judicial Decisions and Scholarly Writing In many domestic systems, legal interpretations by courts set precedent according to the doctrine of *stare decisis* (let the decision stand). This doctrine is specifically rejected in Article 59 of the Statute of the International Court of Justice, but as one scholar points out, "The fact is that all courts... rely upon and cite each other [as precedent] abundantly in their decisions" (Levi, 1991:50). Thus, the rulings of the ICJ, other international tribunals, and even domestic courts when they apply international law, help shape the body of law that exists. Judicial review is another possible role of international judicial bodies, and one that is exercised by many domestic courts. This is a court's authority to rule on whether the actions of the executive and legislative branches violate the constitution or other charter under which the court operates. The European Court of Justice has exercised that authority, and some scholars believe that the ICJ is moving cautiously toward a similar stand.

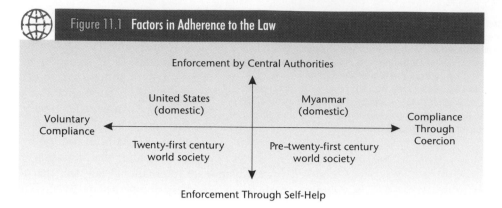

Figure 11.1 Factors in Adherence to the Law

Two crucial factors in international law are how the law is enforced and what encourages compliance. These factors differ over time and for different societies.

International Representative Assemblies The preceding four sources of international law are generally recognized. The idea that laws can come from the UN General Assembly or any other international representative assembly is much more controversial. Clearly, to date, international law is nonlegislative. The General Assembly cannot legislate international law the way that a national legislature does. Yet, UN members are bound by treaty to abide by some of the decisions of the General Assembly and the Security Council, which makes these bodies quasi-legislative. Some scholars contend that those resolutions that are approved by over-whelming majorities of the General Assembly's nearly universal membership constitute international law. The reasoning here is that such votes reflect international custom and/or the general principles of law and, therefore, they subtly enter the stream of international law. We may, then, be seeing the beginnings of legislated international law, but, at best, it is in its genesis. Certainly, UN resolutions and mandates are often not followed, but some would argue that this means that the law is being violated rather than that the law does not exist.

ADHERENCE TO THE LAW

Adherence to the law is a third essential element of any legal system. What makes the law effective in any legal system is a mixture of compliance and enforcement. As Figure 11.1 represents, people obey the law because of a mixture of voluntary and coerced compliance, and they enforce the law through a mixture of enforcement by central authorities and enforcement through self-help (Hurd, 1999).

Compliance Obedience in any legal system—whether it is international or domestic, primitive or sophisticated—is based on a mix of voluntary compliance and coercion. *Voluntary compliance* occurs when the subjects obey the law because they accept its legitimacy. This means that people abide by rules because they accept the authority of the institution that made the rules (say, a legislature or a court) and/or agree that the rules are necessary to the reasonable conduct of society. *Coercion* is the process of gaining compliance through threats of violence, imprisonment, economic sanction, or other punishment.

Any society's legal system can be placed somewhere along the compliance scale between complete reliance on voluntary compliance and complete reliance on coercion. Voluntary compliance is usually more important, but the mixture of it and coercion varies widely among societies. Americans tend to obey the law voluntarily;

in Myanmar (Burma) obedience to the laws of the country's military junta is primarily a function of force.

The overall degree of compliance to the law is lower in the international system than in most domestic systems, but insofar as adherence to international law has grown, it has been based more on voluntary compliance than on coercion. Legitimacy, based primarily on pragmatism, is the key to international voluntary compliance. Countries recognize the need for a system that is made predictable by adherence to laws. As we saw earlier, functional international law governing day-to-day relations between states has expanded rapidly because of their need to regulate complex international interactions such as trade, finance, communications, and diplomacy. Legitimacy based on norms is less well established, but it has also grown. Aggression, violation of human rights, and other unacceptable practices still occur, but they increasingly meet with widespread international and domestic condemnation. Unilateral military action is, for example, becoming ever more difficult for a country to launch without meeting severe criticism. The unilateral U.S. invasion of Panama in 1989, for example, was condemned by the United Nations and the Organization of American States as a violation of international law and the UN Charter. American leaders have also found that the public increasingly is averse to unilateral military action. Since then, U.S. presidents have repeatedly found it politically prudent to avoid unilateral action and, instead, act within the context of a multilateral force sanctioned by an international organization. This desire to gain UN authorization for a response to even a direct attack was demonstrated in 2001 when the United States sought UN Security Council (UNSC) support for the U.S.-led response to the 9-11 terrorist attacks. Among other provisions, UNSC Resolution 1373, which was unanimously passed on September 12, declared terrorists "a threat to international security and affirmed the U.S. right to exercise individual or collective self-defense."

Enforcement In all legal systems, enforcement relies on a combination of *enforcement by central authorities* and *enforcement through self-help*. In more sophisticated legal systems, most enforcement relies on a central authority such as the police. Still, even advanced legal systems recognize the legitimacy of such self-help doctrines as self-defense. Primitive societies rely primarily on self-help and on mediation to enforce laws and norms. As a primitive society evolves, it begins to develop enforcement authorities. Domestic systems have done this, and the international system is now just beginning to take this evolutionary path.

In the primitive international legal system, enforcement by central authorities has been slow to develop. Domestic societies rely on central authorities to provide law enforcement organizations (usually the police) and sanctions (fines, prison) to compel compliance with the law. Neither law enforcement organizations nor sanctions are well developed at the international level, but both have begun to evolve. International law continues to rely mainly on self-help to enforce adherence, as reflected in the UN Charter's recognition of national self-defense. There have been, however, instances of enforcement and the number is growing. War criminals were punished after World War II, and indictments have been handed down for war crimes in Bosnia. Economic and diplomatic sanctions are becoming more frequent and are sometimes successful. Armed enforcement by central authorities is even less common and sophisticated. The UN-authorized military action against Iraq (1991) and the NATO intervention in Kosovo in 1999 were more akin to an Old West sheriff authorizing posses to chase the outlaws than true police actions, but they did represent a step toward enforcement of international law by central authorities.

The International Court of Justice (ICJ)

J   Countries with judges on the ICJ in 2002: Brazil, China, Egypt, France, Germany, Hungary, Japan, Jordan, Madagascar, the Netherlands, Russia, Sierra Leone, the United Kingdom, the United States, and Venezuela.

Countries involved in cases brought to, decided by, or pending before the ICJ, 1993–2002: Australia, Bahrain, Belgium, Bosnia-Herzegovina, Botswana, Burundi, Cameroon, Canada, Chad, Colombia, Congo (Kinshasa), Croatia, Denmark, France, Germany, Guinea, Guinea-Bissau, Honduras, Hungary, Indonesia, Iran, Italy, Libya, Liechtenstein, Malaysia, Namibia, Nauru, New Zealand, Nicaragua, Nigeria, Norway, Portugal, Qatar, Rwanda, Senegal, Slovakia, Spain, Uganda, the United Kingdom, the United States, and Yugoslavia.

Countries with ICJ judges in 2002, also involved in ICJ cases: France, Germany, Hungary, the United Kingdom, and the United States.

The International Court of Justice (ICJ), which sits in The Hague, the Netherlands, draws both its judges and its caseload from around the world. This map shows the home countries of the ICJ's 15 judges and the 41 countries involved in one or more cases before the ICJ from 1993 to 2002.

ADJUDICATION OF THE LAW

How a political system resolves disputes between its actors is a key element in its standing along the primitive-to-modern evolutionary scale. As primitive legal systems become more sophisticated, the method of settling disputes evolves from (1) primary reliance on bargaining between adversaries, through (2) mediation/conciliation by neutral parties, to (3) **adjudication** (and the closely related process of arbitration) by neutral parties. The international system of law is in the early stages of this developmental process and is just now developing the institutions and attitudes necessary for adjudication (Roht-Arriaza, 1999).

International Courts There are a number of international courts in the world today. The genesis of these tribunals extends back less than a century to the Permanent Court of International Arbitration established by the Hague Conference at the turn of the century. In 1922 the Permanent Court of International Justice (PCIJ) was created as part of the League of Nations, and in 1946 the current **International Court of Justice (ICJ)**, which is associated with the UN, evolved from the PCIJ. The ICJ, or so-called World Court, sits in The Hague, the Netherlands, and consists of 15 judges, who are elected to nine-year terms through a complex voting system in the UN. By tradition, each of the five permanent members of the UN Security Council has one judge on the ICJ, and the others are elected to provide regional representation, as is evident in the map on page 308.

In addition to the ICJ, there are a few regional courts of varying authority and levels of activity, including the European Court of Justice (ECJ), the European Court of Human Rights, the Inter-American Court of Human Rights, the Central American Court of Justice, and the Community Tribunal of the Economic Community of West African States. None of these has the authority of domestic courts, but like the ICJ, the regional courts are gaining more credibility. In 2000, for example, Tanja Kreil, a 23-year-old German woman, brought a case to ECJ seeking to overturn a German law that bars women from holding combat positions in the military. Germany argued that it was within its sovereign discretion to determine the composition of its armed forces, and Great Britain and Italy filed briefs supporting Germany's position.

In the end, it was Fräulein Kreil who prevailed. The court ruled that the German "national authorities could not... adopt the general position that the composition of all armed units in the Bundeswehr had to remain exclusively male."[2] The court also found historic discrimination against women in hiring and promotion stemming "from deep-rooted prejudices and from stereotypes" and declared that Germany must "restore the balance."[3] "It was... a very good discovery, the existence

International courts are beginning to have greater importance. When Germany refused to allow Tanja Kreil to serve in an army combat position, she sued for sex discrimination in the European Court of Justice. The court found in Kreil's favor in January 2000. This picture of Private Jessica Müller in full combat gear during German army maneuvers in January 2001 is a direct result of that ruling. It marked the first time that female German soldiers joined a military exercise in combat units and were permitted to handle weapons.

of this European court," said Kreil, after the decision. "I used to think of myself as German. Now I feel a little European, too."[4]

Also, as with domestic courts, the mere existence of international courts sometimes has an impact by making people or governments change their behavior rather than face an adverse ruling. In one such instance, Great Britain established the age of consent at 16 for heterosexuals and 18 for homosexuals. A 17-year-old British homosexual sued in the ECJ, arguing that the differentiation of two years was discriminatory. Rather than contest a case the British would probably have lost, and despite polls showing two-thirds of them opposed to the change, Prime Minister Tony Blair persuaded the House of Commons to lower the age of consent for homosexuals to 16. Great Britain's upper house of Parliament, the House of Lords, blocked the measure. One opponent, the Earl of Longford, reasoned, "A girl is not ruined for life by being seduced. A young fellow is." This logic escaped many. "Lord Longford is 92," wrote a columnist in the *Observer* of London, "but he acts like a man twice his age."[5] The legal stalemate was ended in late 2000 when the prime minister, for only the fourth time since World War I, used provisions of the Parliament Act to have Commons once again approve the change and have it declared law despite the continued opposition of the House of Lords.

> **Did You Know That:**
> When a lesbian couple recently sued the British government of Prime Minister Tony Blair in the European Court of Justice on the grounds of gender discrimination in the workplace, the plaintiffs' lawyer was Cherie Booth, Prime Minister Blair's wife. The court dismissed the complaint, ruling that the issue was not gender discrimination, which is against European Union law, but sexual-orientation discrimination, which is not barred.

Jurisdiction Although the creation of international tribunals during this century indicates progress, the concept of sovereignty remains a potent barrier to adjudication. The authority of the ICJ extends in theory to all international legal disputes. There are two ways that cases come before the ICJ. One is when states submit legal disputes between them. The second is when one of the organs or agencies of the UN asks the ICJ for an advisory opinion.

From 1946 through the present, the court has annually taken up only about two new contentious cases submitted by states or advisory cases involving issues submitted by organs of the United Nations. This is obviously relatively few cases, given the ICJ's broad jurisdiction and the number of issues facing the world and its countries. More than any other factor, the gap between the court's jurisdiction and its actual role is a matter of the willingness of states to submit to decisions of the ICJ. First, states must agree to be subject to the ICJ. Although all UN member-countries are technically parties to the ICJ statute, they must also sign the so-called *optional clause* agreeing to be subject to the compulsory jurisdiction of the ICJ. About two-thirds of all countries have not done so.

Second, irrespective of their agreement to accept ICJ jurisdiction, countries can reject it or the court's decisions in specific cases. When, in 1984, Nicaragua filed a case with the ICJ charging that U.S. support of the Contra rebels and its mining of Nicaraguan harbors violated international law, the United States argued that the charges were political and, therefore, that the court had no jurisdiction.

Third, countries can withdraw their agreement to the optional clause. When the ICJ ruled that it did have jurisdiction in the case brought by Nicaragua, the Reagan administration in 1985 withdrew U.S. consent to the optional clause.

Fourth, even if countries are signatories of the optional clause, they can attach "reservations" to their agreement. Approximately 75 percent of the signatory countries had done so. For example, before the United States withdrew from the optional clause, it reserved the right to reject ICJ jurisdiction in any "domestic matter... as determined by the United States." This is an extremely broad disclaimer and, in effect, means that the United States can reject ICJ jurisdiction on virtually any issue.

Before leaving the matter of the ability of countries to reject or limit ICJ jurisdiction under the optional clause, it should be noted that the ability to do so does not mean that such countries are entirely exempt from ICJ jurisdiction. It is common for treaties to have a clause that commits the signatories to submit disputes arising under the treaty to the ICJ. For instance, the United States is not a signatory to the optional clause, yet it was a party to an ICJ case brought against it by Germany in 1999. Germany accused the United States of violating the provisions of the Vienna Convention on Consular Relations (1963), which the United States has ratified, and which also committed its signatories to settling disputes through the ICJ. Therefore the United States was bound to recognize the ICJ's jurisdiction, despite the U.S. rejection of the optional clause. The case involved two German nationals who were executed that year by Arizona after being convicted for murder. Under the provisions of the convention, U.S. authorities should have notified the accused at the time of their arrest of their right to contact German diplomatic officials in the United States. The ICJ found in Germany's favor and directed the United States to ensure that procedures were followed. While the ICJ ruling could not undo the fate of the two Germans, it may provide greater protections for future foreign nationals arrested in the United States.

Use and Effectiveness of International Courts There are some important limits on the impact of the ICJ and other international courts. One is the real limits on their jurisdiction. The second is the fact that such courts have little ability to enforce their decisions. All courts rely heavily on the willingness of those within their jurisdiction to comply voluntarily or, when that fails, on a powerful executive branch to enforce court decrees. Effective domestic courts have these supports. By contrast, countries are often reluctant to follow the decisions of international courts, and the UN Secretariat, which is the ICJ executive branch, does not have the authority or power to enforce ICJ rulings.

Given these limitations on international courts, it is tempting to write them off as having little more than symbolic value. Such a judgment would be in error. The ICJ, for instance, does play a valuable role. Its rulings help define and advance international law. Furthermore, the court can contribute by giving countries a way, short of war, to settle a dispute once diplomacy has failed. The current ICJ case between Nicaragua and Colombia over their maritime border provides a good example. In its complaint to the ICJ in 2001, Nicaragua contested Colombia's control of a number of Caribbean islands and their surrounding territorial seas, including any possible undersea resources, such as petroleum and natural gas. Throughout history, many land and maritime border disputes have resulted in failed diplomacy, in each side seizing the other's people and property, and in war. Without an ICJ to appeal to, that might have been the outcome of the boundary dispute between Nicaragua and Honduras. With an ICJ there is an alternative option that may well lead to a peaceful settlement.

Even when countries reject ICJ jurisdiction, the court's decisions may have some effect. In the 1984 *Nicaragua versus United States* case, discussed earlier, the court heard the case anyway and ruled in Nicaragua's favor. This decision gave a black eye to the United States in the court of world opinion and strengthened the U.S. domestic opponents of the Reagan administration's policy. The United States stopped mining Nicaragua's harbors.

The ICJ's advisory opinions also help resolve issues between IGOs and may even help establish general international law. In separate actions, the UN General Assembly and the World Health Organization each asked the ICJ to rule on the legality of using nuclear weapons (Matheson, 1997). The court ruled in 1996 that "the threat or use of nuclear weapons would generally be contrary to the rules of

One benefit of the International Court of Justice is that it allows countries to seek a judicial solution to disputes. In this photograph, Colombian soldiers patrol a beach on the San Andres Islands in the Caribbean Sea days after Nicaragua laid claim to a number of the islands in December 2001. Fortunately, the soldiers were not needed. Nicaragua chose to sue Colombia in the International Court of Justice instead of going to war.

international law applicable in armed conflict," but went on to say that it was unable to "conclude definitively whether the threat or use of nuclear weapons would be lawful or unlawful in an extreme circumstance of self-defense, in which the very survival of a state would be at stake."[6] While the ICJ's ruling was not as all-encompassing as some antinuclear advocates hoped, the decision does put any leader considering the use of nuclear weapons except in extremis on notice that he or she could wind up the defendant in some future war crimes trial.

Finally, there is evidence that the willingness of countries to utilize the ICJ, the ECJ, and other international courts and to accept their decisions is slowly growing. The map of the ICJ's justices and cases on page 308 shows that countries around the world serve on the court and are party to its cases. Now more than 60 countries, including Canada, India, and the United Kingdom, adhere to the optional clause giving the ICJ compulsory jurisdiction over their international legal disputes. It is true that the international judicial system is still primitive, but each of the more than 150 opinions issued by the PCIJ and the ICJ since in 1922 is one more than the zero instances of international adjudication in previous centuries.

Applying International Law and Morality

Law and morality are easy to support in the abstract, but it is much more difficult to agree on how to apply them. To examine this, we will look at issues of cultural perspective, issues of applying international law and standards of morality equally to states and individuals, and issues of prudence.

LAW AND HUMAN RIGHTS: CULTURAL PERSPECTIVES

As primitive political systems evolve and expand to incorporate diverse peoples, one problem that such legal systems encounter is the "fit" between differing culturally based concepts of law and morality. The evolving international system of law faces the same difficulty. Most of international law and many of the international standards of morality that currently exist and influence world politics are based on the concepts and practices of the West. This is a result of U.S. and European dominance, though, and does not mean that Western concepts are superior to those held in other parts of the world. Now, in a changing international system, Africans, Asians, Latin Americans, and other non-Westerners are questioning and sometimes rejecting law based on Western culture.

Law and Cultural Perspectives

There are numerous points on which Western and non-Western precepts of law and morality differ. The *Western view* of law is based on principles designed to protect the long-dominant power of this bloc of states. Order is a primary point, as is sovereignty. Closely related is the theory of property, which holds that individuals (and states) have a "right" to accumulate and maintain property (wealth). This is a major philosophical underpinning of capitalism. Western law also relies heavily on the process and substance of law rather than on equity. Thus, there is an emphasis on courts and what the law is rather than on what is fair. One current controversy that touches on both property rights and "law versus fairness" involves HIV/AIDS and patents held by Western pharmaceutical firms. Patent drugs, which can be as much as 50 times more expensive than generic equivalents, are beyond the financial means of most less developed countries (LDCs). They argue that their right to try to respond to the epidemic is more important than the Western emphasis on property rights and also that it is unfair, whatever the law may be, that the poor have to suffer untreated because they cannot afford drugs that, in essence, are only available to wealthy individuals and countries.

The *non-Western view* of international law is influenced by the different cultural heritage of non-Western states, by the recent independence of those states, and by the history of exploitation their people have often suffered at the hands of the West. The newer, mostly non-Western, and mostly less developed countries (LDCs) claim that since they had little or no role in determining the rules that govern the international system, they are not necessarily bound by preexisting agreements, principles, or practices that work to their disadvantage. These countries support sovereignty and reject aspects of international law that they claim are imperialistic abridgments of that principle. They insist on noninterference, which, for example, led many LDCs to oppose NATO's intervention in Kosovo in 1999. Whatever their sympathies with the plight of the Kosovars, many LDCs are aware that humanitarian interventions can violate sovereignty and they worry that claims of human rights abuses could at times become an excuse for outside interference in the internal affairs of the LDCs.

Expressing this view, Premier Zhu Rongji of China told a Canadian newspaper that the "Kosovo question is an ethnic problem which of course is an internal matter.... Questions like this exist in many countries, you in Canada have the question of Quebec, the United Kingdom has the Northern Ireland question, and for China there is the question of Tibet." Zhu went on to say that outside interference to solve such matters was "very bad precedent" and wondered whether intervention in Kosovo also justified "foreign powers... [taking] military actions against Canada, the UK and China over ethnic issues of Quebec, Northern Ireland and Tibet."[7]

The LDCs also reject weighted voting schemes, such as those in the UN Security Council, the World Bank, and the International Monetary Fund, that favor the rich and powerful. The LDCs often emphasize equity over the substance and process of law. For them, the important standard is fairness, especially in terms of economic maldistribution.

Human Rights and Cultural Perspectives

Western and non-Western perspectives also differ considerably on the *rights of the individual* versus the *rights of the community*. This divergence of thought affects how human rights are defined. Imagine a scale that ranges, on one end, from a value system in which the rights of an individual are always more important than those of the community to, at the other end, a value system in which the good of the community always takes precedence over the good of the individual. Western states would generally fall toward the individualistic end of the scale; non-Western states would generally fall farther toward the communitarian end of the scale. There is, for example, a long list of rights afforded in the United States to individuals accused and even convicted of crimes. Non-Western cultures tend to think this practice gives the society too little protection; they therefore favor a more communitarian approach to ordering their society. That perspective was expressed succinctly by Singapore's foreign minister, Shanmugam Jayakumar, who defended what Americans might see as draconian laws by explaining, "We believe that the legal system must give maximum protection to the majority of our people. We make no apology for clearly tilting our laws and policy in favor of the majority."[8]

What constitutes a human rights abuse and what is merely a matter of clashing cultural values has been a particular sore point between the United States and China. American criticism of China on a wide range of rights issues is reflected in the annual U.S. State Department's review of global human rights. Typically, the report issued in 2002 characterized China as an "authoritarian state" in which citizens lack most civil rights and liberties and in which the government committed "numerous human rights abuses."[9]

China rejects such criticisms. In reality, one spokesperson contends, such human rights criticisms "arise largely from the fact that East and West have different conceptions of human rights. For Asians," the official continued, "human rights do not mean the privileges of the few but of the many."[10] Using its more communitarian standards, China also accuses the United States of its own range of human rights violations. "Human rights protection provided by the U.S. Constitution is very limited," a Chinese government report asserts. It notes, for instance, that in the United States there is no right to "food, clothing, shelter, education, work, rest, and reasonable payment." The report also criticizes widespread racism as "the darkest abyss in American society" and points out that democracy is limited because "running for office requires large sums of money."[11]

The individualism that marks American political culture demands that even convicted murderers receive many constitutional protections. China's more communitarian political culture emphasizes the common good more than the individual. Trials and even executions serve as object lessons to deter crime. In a scene common in China, six convicted drug traffickers are being escorted out of a stadium after being publicly tried and sentenced to death. The United States marked the UN's Anti-Drug Day, June 26, 2000, with speeches and television ads warning about the perils of drug use. China marked the day by executing 57 drug dealers, including these men. Appeals are almost unheard of in China. Whereas it takes years for a death sentence to be carried out in the United States, the six men were probably shot before the end of the day. Is this cruel and unusual punishment that violates human rights, or is it merely a reflection of China's political culture?

APPLYING INTERNATIONAL LAW AND MORALITY IN A MULTICULTURAL WORLD

Given the differences in perspective between cultures, the question arises as to whether it is reasonable to try to apply the standards of law and morality at all. Those who deny that any common principles exist contend that no single standard does (or, they suspect, can) exist, at least not without global cultural homogenization, and imposing that would be **cultural imperialism**. It is easy from a Western perspective to dismiss as self-serving claims of cultural imperialism by China and other countries that we see as human rights abusers. That would be too easy, though, and there are many analysts in the West who, without supporting the specifics of any alleged abuse, do find the fundamental argument meritorious. One American scholar writes, for instance, "We must understand and learn from other traditions while seeing them as historically conditioned—and this includes our own tradition. What we must not do... is elevate our own tradition to the status of 'universalism'. This is just rehashed cultural imperialism and has its roots in the dogmatic religious outlooks of the past and present." In sum, he argues, "We should realize that we create our own values, reacting to the times and climes, and rational people can disagree on what these values are."[12]

Others reject such claims of cultural imperialism as poor attempts to justify the unjustifiable. President Chandrika Kumaratunga of Sri Lanka, for one, has expressed the opinion that "of course, every country has its own national ethos, but... when people talk about a conflict of values, I think it is an excuse that can be used to cover a multitude of sins" (Franck, 1997:627). Seconding this view, Secretary-General Kofi Annan told an audience in Iran, there is "talk of human rights being a Western concept,... [but] don't we all suffer from the lack of the rule of law and from arbitrariness? What is foreign about that? What is Western about that? And when we talk of the right [of people]... to live their lives to the fullest and to be able to live their dreams, it is universal."[13]

APPLYING INTERNATIONAL LAW AND MORALITY TO STATES

Traditionally, the application of international law and of standards of moral behavior in the international system has focused primarily on states. The actions of individuals have not been subject to judgment. Now that is changing rapidly, as we shall see presently. This section will deal with states and, with regard to them, the first thing to address is whether states and individuals can be held to the same standards of law and morality. Then we can look at the specific issues of law and morality as they relate to states.

Should States Be Held to the Same Standards as Individuals?

It is common for states to act legitimately in ways that would be reprehensible for individuals. Imagine if as a private person you were having a dispute with your neighbors, and you laid siege to your neighbors' houses and somehow managed to significantly reduce their ability to feed their children and buy them medicine. As a result, some of your neighbors' children died. Would any dispute justify such actions? Most people would think not and would consider you a heinous criminal.

In a somewhat analogous situation, the United States and other countries have for more than a decade continued UN-authorized economic sanctions against Iraq. Whatever the cause of the sanctions, though, one impact, studies show, is that the lack of food, medicine, and other basics have contributed to the deaths of several hundred thousand more Iraqi children than would have otherwise died. Surely those sanctions are at least partly the result of the obdurate refusal of the regime in Baghdad to grant access to UN arms inspectors. But does that settle the question? It is hard to conceive of a circumstance where we as individuals could legally or morally take action against a person that would injure that person's children. Is it moral, should it be legal, that we—as the collective of states in the UN—assail the Iraqi children to punish Iraq's regime?

Of course, we recognize differences between justifiable and inexcusable actions, but where do you draw the line? Some have argued that the state cannot be held to individual moral standards. Realist philosopher and statesman Niccolò Machiavelli wrote in *The Prince* (1517) that a ruler "cannot observe all those things which are considered good in men, being often obliged, in order to maintain the state, to act against faith and charity, against humanity, and against religion."

Proponents of state morality disagree and argue that neither national interest nor sovereignty legitimizes immoral actions. A philosopher and statesman who took this view was Thomas Jefferson. While secretary of state (1789–1793), Jefferson argued that since a society is but a collection of individuals, "the moral duties which exist between individual and individual" also form "the duties of that society toward any other; so that between society and society the same moral duties exist as between the individuals composing them" (Graebner, 1964:55).

States and Issues of Law and Morality

Traditionally, international law has concerned itself with the actions and status of states. Some of the most prominent issues are sovereignty, war, the biosphere, and human rights.

Issues of Sovereignty Sovereignty continues to be a cornerstone of the state system, but sovereignty is no longer a legal absolute. Instead, it is being chipped away by a growing number of law-creating treaties that limit action. Sovereignty is also being slowly restricted by the international community's growing intolerance of human rights abuses and other ills inflicted by governments on their people. As Secretary-General Annan puts it, sovereignty "was never meant as a license for governments to trample on human rights and human dignity. Sovereignty implies responsibility, not just power."[14] Views such as this led, for instance, to international action that ended apartheid in South Africa (1993) and forced the military junta in Haiti to flee (1994), and to the NATO bombardment of Yugoslavia until it ceased its ethnic cleansing policy in Kosovo (1999).

Issues of War Most of the early writing in international law was concerned with the law of war, and this issue continues to be a primary focus of legal development. In addition to issues of traditional state-versus-state warfare, international law now attempts also to regulate revolutionary and internal warfare and terrorism.

To illustrate these diverse concerns, we can focus on the long debate on when and how war can morally and legally be fought. "Just war" theory has two parts: the cause of war and the conduct of war. Western tradition has believed in *jus ad bellum* (just cause of war) in cases where the war is (1) a last resort, (2) declared by legitimate authority, (3) waged in self-defense or to establish/restore justice, and (4) fought to bring about peace. The same line of thought maintains that *jus in bello* (just conduct of war) includes the standards of proportionality and discrimination. Proportionality means that the amount of force used must be proportionate to the threat. Discrimination means that force must not make noncombatants intentional targets (Barry, 1998).

As laudable as limitations on legitimate warfare may seem, they present problems. One difficulty is that the standards of when to go to war and how to fight it are rooted in Western-Christian tradition. The parameters of *jus in bello* and *jus ad bellum* extend back to Aristotle's *Politics* (ca. 340 B.C.) and are especially associated with the writings of Christian theological philosophers Saint Augustine (Aurelius Augustinus, A.D. 354–430) and Saint Thomas Aquinas (1226–1274). As a doctrine based on Western culture and religion, not all the restrictions on war are the same as those derived from some of the other great cultural-religious traditions, including Buddhism and Islam.

Another difficulty with the standards of just war, even if you try to abide by them, is that they are vague. What, for example, is proportionally in line with *jus in bello*? Almost everyone would agree, for instance, that France, Great Britain, and the United States would not have been justified in using their nuclear weapons against Yugoslavia in 1999 to force it to withdraw from Kosovo or against Afghanistan in 2001 for refusing to surrender the al-Qaeda terrorists. But what if Iraq had used chemical weapons against the forces of those three countries during the Persian Gulf War in 1991? Would they have been justified if they had retaliated with nuclear weapons? Some people even argue that using nuclear weapons under any conditions would violate the rule of discrimination and would thus be immoral.

The *jus in bello* standard of discrimination also involves matters of degree rather than clear lines. The U.S. preference for using aerial bombardment rather than first risking ground combat troops (or at all in some cases) has raised troublesome issues of discrimination for some observers. With respect to the U.S.-led actions in Kosovo in 1999, for example, one retired U.S. Marine colonel has charged that an American "willingness-to-kill-but-not-to-die" attitude led to a bombing campaign that caused unnecessary civilian casualties. What occurred, in the colonel's view, was that "the allies' resolve was greater than the resources [troops] they were willing to commit to the action." Therefore, the colonel concludes, "Immorality resided in the mismatch" (DeCamp, 2000:43).

Although a few U.S. special forces were sent to Afghanistan in the early days of military operations against that country, the overall pattern of U.S. military action once again favored heavy aerial bombardment. White House and Pentagon representatives went to great lengths to give assurances that all efforts were being made to avoid unnecessary civilian casualties, but when those occurred and criticism arose, the stance of Secretary of Defense Donald H. Rumsfeld was, "We did not start this war. So understand, responsibility for every single casualty in this war, whether they're innocent Afghans or innocent Americans, rests at the feet of the al-Qaeda and the Taliban."[15] Not everyone agreed. Based on "the principle of discrimination, non-killing of civilians is at the heart of *jus in bello*," one American scholar suggested, but, "Because of their methods, neither the September 11 terrorists nor the U.S. response in Afghanistan honored that principle." He went on to maintain, "Both could argue that the killing of innocent people was secondary effect. Both were aware their action would kill civilians, and that awareness made the action unacceptable to Islamic or Christian morality, as well as by international law."[16]

As these examples illustrate, the law and morality of war remain highly controversial. Most observers would support neither of the two polar views: that the United States could not be held responsible for any level of civilian casualties; that knowingly taking actions that would kill any civilians violates the standards of *jus in bello*. It is, however, easier to question two extreme views than to clearly define the right balance.

Still, progress has been made in setting down rules. The Hague Conferences (1899, 1907) and the Geneva Conventions of 1949 set down some rules about *jus in bello* regarding impermissible weapons, the treatment of prisoners, and other matters. Other treaties have banned the possession and use of biological and chemical weapons, and the ICJ has ruled that in most circumstances the use of nuclear weapons would be illegal. *Jus ad bellum* is addressed by the UN Charter, by which members agree that the only legitimate reasons to resort to interstate violence

The international law of war requires that care be taken to discriminate as much as possible between legitimate military targets and noncombatants. Almost inevitably, U.S. air strikes against Afghanistan injured civilians, purportedly including this child who is waiting for medical treatment. This picture and others like it were broadcast to the Muslim world by Qatar's Al-Jazeera satellite network. Taliban leaders and others accused the United States of committing war crimes. Whatever the validity of that charge, the images made a powerful impression on many already alienated Muslims.

are (1) in self-defense and (2) as part of a UN or regional military effort. Violating this standard has brought condemnation and sometimes action, as Iraq found out when it was expelled from Kuwait by a force authorized by the global community through the UN. Also in the realm of *jus ad bellum*, individuals are now sometimes held accountable for war crimes. That happened after World War II and, as related later, it is occurring once again for the horrendous violations of international law that were committed in Bosnia and Rwanda. The treaty establishing the new International Criminal Court, which will be discussed presently, is the most recent step in codifying the law of war and furthering the principle of individual responsibility.

Issues of the Biosphere   Another important and growing area of international law addresses the obligation of states and individuals to use the biosphere responsibly on the theory that it belongs to no one individually and to everyone collectively. This area of law is aptly illustrated by the law of the sea.

The status of the world's oceans is a long-standing subject of international law. The international maritime rules of the road for ships have long had general acceptance. The extension of a state's territorial limits to 3 miles into the ocean was another widely acknowledged standard based, as noted, on international custom.

In recent years, the resource value of the seas has grown because of more sophisticated harvesting and extraction technology, and this has created uncertainty and change. Undersea oil exploration, in particular, is the source of serious dispute among a number of countries. As early as 1945, the United States claimed control of the resources on or under its continental shelf. In 1960 the Soviet Union proclaimed the extension of its territorial waters out to 12 miles, a policy that has been imitated by others, including the United States as of 1988. Several Latin American countries claimed a 200-mile territorial zone, and the United States not only established a

Table 11.1 Eight Important Multilateral Human Rights Treaties

Multilateral Treaty	Year	Countries* (2002)
Convention on the Prevention and the Punishment of the Crime of Genocide	1949	130
Convention Relating to the Status of Refugees	1951	136
International Convention on the Elimination of All Forms of Racial Discrimination	1965	161
International Covenant of Civil and Political Rights	1976	148
International Covenant on Economic, Social, and Cultural Rights	1976	145
Convention on the Elimination of All Forms of Discrimination Against Women	1979	168
Convention Against Torture and Other Cruel, Inhuman, or Degrading Treatment or Punishment	1984	128
Convention on the Rights of the Child	1989	191

*Indicates number of countries that have ratified or otherwise agreed to abide by the treaty.

Data source: United Nations Treaty Collection at: http://untreaty.un.org/English/treaty.asp.

Most countries have signed a variety of multilateral treaties, thereby agreeing to abide by the treaties' various human rights standards. Even though not all countries have signed every treaty, and while there have also been numerous violations, many analysts argue that such treaties take on the characteristic of international law once they have been ratified by the preponderance of the world's states. As such, the standards set in these treaties may be used in a number of ways, including through international courts and tribunals, to judge the cases of states and individuals.

200-mile "conservation zone" in 1977 to control fishing but in 1983 extended that control to all economic resources within the 200-mile limit.

In an ambitious attempt to settle and regulate many of these issues, the Law of the Sea Convention (1982) defines coastal zones, establishes the International Seabed Authority (ISB) to regulate nonterritorial seabed mining, provides for the sharing of revenue from such efforts, and establishes the International Tribunal for the Law of the Sea to settle disputes. As of 2002, 138 countries had ratified the convention. The United States has not signed, much less ratified, the treaty amid concerns about the possible transfer of control over offshore activities (such as oil drilling) and their revenues from Washington to the ISB, through decisions of the International Seabed Authority. The absence of a few countries—even a few powerful ones—should not take away from the growing body of law that protects the oceans and seas.

Issues of Human Rights International law is developing affirmatively in the area of defining human rights. International attention to the law of human rights has grown because of many factors, including the horror of the images of abuses that television reveals, the expanding efforts of individuals and organizations that promote human rights, and the growing awareness that human rights violations are a major source of international instability.

The UN Charter supports basic rights in a number of its provisions. This language was expanded in 1948 when the UN General Assembly passed the Universal Declaration of Human Rights. No country voted against the declaration, although a few did abstain. Since then, the growth of global human rights has also been enhanced by a number of important global multilateral treaties. The most important of these treaties are listed in Table 11.1. In addition to global treaties, there have been a number of regional multilateral treaties, such as the Helsinki Accords (1977), which address European human rights, and the African Charter on Human and Peoples' Rights (1990).

Some people doubt whether all the world's diverse cultures can agree on one system of international law. It will be difficult, but in some areas there is growing agreement on at least fundamental principles. One such area is human rights. Most of the world's countries have agreed to the Universal Declaration of Human Rights.

Much, however, remains to be done. Canada and several other countries have signed all the human rights treaties found in Table 11.1; many other countries have not. There are also many countries, including the United States, whose legislatures have not ratified some of the treaties because of fears that they might be used as platforms for interfering in domestic affairs or for pressing demands for certain international policy changes, such as a redistribution of world economic resources. For instance, the Convention on the Prevention and Punishment of the Crime of Genocide (1949) awaited U.S. ratification for almost 40 years before the Senate acted in 1988. The Senate still has not consented to the Convention on the Elimination of All Forms of Discrimination Against Women (signed 1979).

The gap between existing legal standards and their application is the area of greatest concern. Gross violations of the principles set down in the multilateral treaties continue to occur. And the record of international reaction to violation of the standards and enforcement of them through sanctions and other means is very sporadic and often weak. "We have not traveled as far or as fast as we had hoped," UN deputy secretary-general Margaret J. Anstee has commented on the convention to protect women.[17] To varying degrees, this could be said about all human rights treaties. Yet their existence provides a constant reminder that most of the world considers certain actions to be reprehensible. The treaties also serve, in the view of many, as a standard of international law and conduct for which states and individuals can be held accountable. Thus, the growth of human rights law has just begun. The acceptance of the concept of human rights has gained a good deal more rhetorical support than practical application, and enforcement continues to be largely in the hands of individual states with a mixed record of adherence. For all these shortcomings, though, human rights obligations are now widely discussed, and world opinion is increasingly critical of violations.

APPLYING INTERNATIONAL LAW AND MORALITY TO INDIVIDUALS

International law has begun recently to deal with the actions of individuals. A series of precedents in the twentieth century marked this change. It is possible to divide these developments into four topics: Post–World War II Tribunals, the National Enforcement of International Law, Current International Tribunals, and the International Criminal Court (Beigbeder, 1999).

Post–World War II Tribunals

The first modern instances of individuals being charged with crimes under international law came in the aftermath of the horrors of World War II. In the Nuremberg and Tokyo war crimes trials, German and Japanese military and civilian leaders were tried for waging aggressive war, for war crimes, and for crimes against humanity. Nineteen Germans were convicted at Nuremberg; 12 were sentenced to death. Similar fates awaited convicted Japanese war criminals. Seven were hanged. Many Germans and Japanese also went to prison. Some important precedents were established. One was that those who ordered criminal acts or under whose command the acts occurred were just as liable to punishment as those who actually carried out the crimes. Another important precedent was that obeying orders was not a defense for having committed atrocities (Osiel, 1999).

There were efforts in the UN as early as 1948 to establish a permanent international tribunal to deal with genocide and other criminal affronts to humankind. Little came of the effort, however, and there were no subsequent war crimes tribunals for almost the next half-century.

National Enforcement of International Law

The lack of international tribunals did not mean that crimes went completely unpunished. Although trials have been unusual, a number of states have used their national courts to try those accused of crimes under international law.

One reason that countries began capturing and trying individuals for crimes that had occurred in another country was the inability of the international system to bring such criminals to justice. Germans who eluded prosecution immediately after the war were a special target for prosecution. Perhaps the most famous incident was Israel's abduction from Argentina of a top Nazi, Adolf Eichmann. He was charged, tried, convicted, and hanged in 1962 by Israel for crimes that not only had not occurred in Israel, but for crimes committed before Israel even existed. More recently, Germany tried and convicted two Serbs for committing war crimes in Bosnia. Both men were arrested in Germany after having unwisely fled there, and the German courts rejected the claim of the accused that Germany had no jurisdiction over what they might have done in another country.

Taking yet a further step, there have been a small, but growing number of actions taken in recent years by individual countries to extradite and try former heads of state. Of the cases of third-country extradition attempts in recent years, the most well-known one occurred in 1999 when a Spanish court sought the extradition of former Chilean dictator (1973–1989) General Augusto Pinochet from Great Britain, where he was receiving treatment for cancer. The Spanish judge charged that Pinochet not only had ordered the murders of Spanish citizens in Chile, but also had committed crimes against humanity through the murder and torture of British, American, and Chilean citizens. It is important to see the implications of the charges for the traditional sovereign immunity of current or former heads of state. Another aspect of the case with great importance for international law was the effort to bring to trial in Spain a former Chilean president for crimes committed in Chile against, among others, Chileans.

During more than a year of legal maneuvering, British legal officials agreed to extradite Pinochet. His British lawyers then argued that their client was too ill with cancer to stand trial. Perhaps in recognition of the immense implications of an extradition order, the British government accepted this maneuver and ordered the general out of the country and back to Chile. The government revoked Pinochet's immunity and moved to try him for his alleged crimes (Weller, 1999). The general unsuccessfully appealed his loss of immunity to Chile's Supreme Court but was finally able to escape trial in 2001, when a court ruled that Pinochet, who was by then 85 years old, was suffering from dementia and mentally unfit to stand trial.

Going even beyond the implications of the Pinochet case, Belgium moved in 2001 to extradite and try Prime Minister Ariel Sharon of Israel for war crimes that he allegedly committed against Palestinians in 1982 while he was defense minister. The attempted prosecution was to take place under Belgian law, which permits its courts to try suspected war criminals even if the alleged crime did not take place in Belgium or involve Belgian nationals. That effort was forestalled in early 2002 when the International Court of Justice (ICJ) ruled on an earlier case involving the efforts by Belgium to try a foreign minister from the Democratic Republic of Congo over the 1998 killings of hundreds of ethnic Tutsi refugees from Rwanda (a former Belgian colony). The ICJ ruled that there is "no exception under international law to the rule establishing immunity from criminal process before foreign national courts," and that the Belgian "investigating judge was not entitled to hold himself competent in respect of the offenses in question relying on a universal jurisdiction not recognized by international law."[18] Arguably, the ICJ ruling ended the recent trend in national courts to prosecute leaders of other countries for crimes committed elsewhere, but whatever the long-term impact of the ICJ's decision, the fact that it had to be made at all is an indication of how far the attack has progressed on the sovereign immunity of leaders for acts taken while in office.

Current International Tribunals

After languishing for nearly 50 years, the idea of international tribunals to deal with criminal violations of international law was resurrected by the atrocities that occurred in Bosnia and in Rwanda during the 1990s. In both places, people on all sides were abused, injured, and killed; in Bosnia it was the Muslims who were the principal victims and the Serbs who inflicted the most death and degradation between 1990 and 1995, and in Rwanda the Hutus were the murderous aggressors in 1994 and the Tutsis the victims of genocide.

The atrocities in Bosnia and Rwanda shocked the conscience of the world and made it obvious, as a former UN official put it, that "a person stands a better chance of being tried and judged for killing one human being than for killing 100,000."[19] This jarring reality led to the establishment in 1994 of a tribunal for Bosnia and another for Rwanda to prosecute those who committed atrocities. The tribunal for the Balkans sits in The Hague, the Netherlands. The Rwanda tribunal is located in Arusha, Tanzania. In 1999, the authority of the Balkans tribunal was expanded to include war crimes in Kosovo.

The Hague tribunal has indicted over 100 individuals as war criminals, and almost 70 have been arrested. Of the 32 individuals whose trials had been completed by mid-2002, 27 were convicted and 5 were acquitted of committing crimes such as genocide, murder, rape, and torture. Sentences have ranged up to 46 years in prison, and the convicted war criminals have been transferred from their cells in the Netherlands to other countries in Europe to serve their time.

The most important of the trials in The Hague began mid-2001 when Slobodan Milosevic, the former president of Yugoslavia, was extradited to The Hague to stand trial for crimes against Bosnian Muslims and Croats in the early 1990s and against Muslim Kosovars in the late 1990s. During pretrial hearings, Milosevic declared both the court and the indictment illegal, telling the court, "The aim of this tribunal is to justify the crimes committed in Yugoslavia. That is why this is a false tribunal, an illegitimate one." Given his view that "the whole world knows this is a political trial," Milosevic further reasoned, "I have no need to appoint counsel" and refused to enter a plea of guilty or not guilty.[20] Unfazed, the court entered not guilty pleas to all charges, and the prosecutors began presenting their case in February 2002 in a trial that could well last a year.

The Rwanda tribunal has made headway more slowly than its counterpart in The Hague, but an important step occurred in 1998 when the tribunal obtained its first conviction. Former Rwandan prime minister Jean Kambanda pleaded guilty to genocide and was sentenced to life in prison. Through mid-2002, the tribunal had convicted 8 people and was holding another 42 people suspected of inciting or committing genocide. Hutu civilian and military leaders have made up most, but not all, of the convicted and accused. For instance, a Belgian-born Italian citizen, Georges Henry Joseph Ruggiu, who was a radio journalist in Rwanda, was sentenced in June 2000 to 12 years in prison for inciting genocide. Among the many other chilling calls to mayhem he broadcast in 1994: "You [Tutsi] cockroaches must know you are made of flesh.... We will kill you."[21]

For those accused of committing atrocities, sovereignty is increasingly no defense against being brought to justice before an international tribunal. While the tribunal for the Balkans, which sits in The Hague, the Netherlands, has received the most media attention, the tribunal for Rwanda is also at work. Sitting in Arusha, Tanzania, the tribunal is dealing with the genocide committed in Rwanda in 1994. In this April 2002 photograph, Judge Lloyd Williams of Saint Kitts and Nevis presides during the trial of four Rwandan Hutu army officers accused of crimes against humanity for the slaughter of Rwandan Tutsis.

Attempts have been make to create other such tribunals. A long effort to create a joint Cambodian-United Nations tribunal to bring to justice some of the former Khmer Rouge officials responsible for the death of upwards of 1.5 million Cambodians in the late 1970s finally ended when the government of Cambodia and the UN could not agree on a range of legal issues. A similar effort to establish a war crime tribunal for Sierra Leone has been more successful, with the tribunal scheduled to begin operation in late 2002. In that afflicted country, rebels killed and mutilated many thousands of noncombatants in an attempt to terrorize the population. The rebels' favorite gruesome tactic was to hack off part of one or more of their victims' limbs so that the maimed individuals would serve as living reminders not to oppose the Revolutionary United Front. The RUF leader, Foday Sankoh, is in custody and will almost certainly be one of the first to face the bar of international justice.

International Criminal Court

The advent of ad hoc international tribunals and the enforcement of international law by national courts have signaled that those who commit war crimes are at peril. But the world has also begun to recognize, as President Clinton said, that "the signal will come across even more loudly and clearly if nations all around the world... establish a permanent international court to prosecute... serious violations of humanitarian law."[22]

To that end, a UN-sponsored conference that included most of the world's countries convened in 1998 to create a permanent International Criminal Court

(ICC). During the 1998 conference, a bloc of about 50 countries, with Canada as its informal leader, favored establishing a court with broad and independent jurisdiction. Secretary-General Kofi Annan supported this position, calling on the delegates in Rome to "not flinch from creating a court strong and independent enough to carry out its tasks. It must be an instrument of justice, not expediency."[23]

Other countries, including the United States, wanted a much weaker ICC. The crux of U.S. opposition to a strong ICC rested on the fear that U.S. leaders and military personnel might become targets of politically motivated prosecutions. "The reality is that the United States is a global military power and presence.... We have to be careful that it does not open up opportunities for endless frivolous complaints to be lodged against the United States as a global military power," explained the chief U.S. delegate to the talks.[24]

The U.S. stand drew strong criticism. Canada's foreign minister accused the United States of wanting only a facade, "a Potemkin village," and an Italian diplomat expressed disbelief "that a major democracy... would want to have an image of insisting that its soldiers be given license never to be investigated."[25]

In the end, some of the reservations of the United States and some other countries were met, but the conference opted to create a relatively strong court by a vote of 120 for to 7 against (including China, India, and the United States), and 21 abstentions. Secretary-General Annan told the delegates in Rome, "Two millennia ago one of this city's most famous sons, Marcus Tullius Cicero, declared that 'in the midst of arms, law stands mute.' As a result of what we are doing here today, there is real hope that that bleak statement will be less true in the future than it has been in the past."[26]

The treaty gives the ICC jurisdiction over genocide and a range of other "widespread and systematic" crimes committed as part of "state, organization, or group policy," during international and internal wars. National courts will remain the first point of justice, and the ICC will be able to try cases only when they fail to do so. The UNSC can delay a prosecution for up to a year, but the vote to delay will not be subject to veto.

The ICC became a reality on April 12, 2002, when 10 countries notified the UN of their ratification of the treaty. That brought the number of formal accessions to 66, more than the minimum required for the ICC treaty to take effect. "The long-held dream of a permanent international criminal court will now be realized," Secretary-General Annan proclaimed.[27] The creation of the court means, added French president Jacques Chirac, that, "Starting now, all those who might be inclined to engage in the madness of genocide or crimes against humanity will know that nothing will be able to prevent justice."[28] The timetable for the ICC to become operational remained to be set, but it is probable that the court will be seated in The Hague and begin its operations in 2003, and it will have jurisdiction over war crimes committed after July 1, 2002.

There is little doubt that the creation of the ICC represented "an extremely significant moment in world history," as David Scheffer, the U.S. negotiator for the treaty during the Clinton administration commented.[29] Still, how effective it will be is the key question about the court, and the U.S. attitude is the most critical component of that question. Also of importance are the future attitudes of China, Russia, and some other major powers that have also not agreed to the treaty. Just before leaving office, President Clinton directed a U.S. representative to sign the Rome Treaty. That was done, however, as a legal maneuver to ensure continued U.S. participation in discussions of possible revisions of the treaty, and Clinton also recommended that his successor, George Bush, not submit the treaty to the Senate for ratification unless revisions were made. That was superfluous advice for Bush, who has repeatedly expressed his opposition. "The level of U.S. cooperation with the ICC in the future is a matter of speculation," a Bush administration spokesperson commented. "But what I can say," he added, "is that our intention is to be divorced from the process and play no role in it." [30] For a time Bush also threatened to veto all UN peacekeeping operations unless U.S. troops were specifically given immunity from possible prosecution before the ICC. This issue was resolved when the Security Council in July 2002 voted to give U.S. peacekeepers one year's exemption from prosecution by the ICC.

That posture may have played well for much of the U.S. domestic audience, but it also brought international criticism from many quarters, including some of the closest and most important U.S. allies. "International established law should also apply to large nations. For this reason it is unacceptable that the United States... [is] still standing apart," is how Germany's minister of justice put it.[31]

LAW AND MORALITY: ISSUES OF PRUDENT JUDGMENT AND APPLICATION

In a perfect world, everyone would act morally, obey the law, and insist that others conduct themselves in the same way. Moreover, what is legal and what is not, and what is moral and what is not, would be clear. Finally, our choices would be between good and evil, rather than between greater and lesser evils. In our imperfect world, standards and choices are often much murkier, which leads to several questions regarding the prudence of applying our standards of law and morality.

Can Ends Justify Means? One conundrum is whether an act that by itself is evil can be justified if it is done for a good cause. Some believe that ends never justify means. The philosopher Immanuel Kant took a position of **moral absolutism** in his *Groundwork on the Metaphysics of Morals* (1785) and argued that ends never justify means. He therefore urged us to "do what is right though the world should perish."

There are others who, at least in practice, maintain that what they consider to be lofty goals do justify acts that most other people would condemn as morally abhorrent. Terrorism is a case in point. For example, the Middle East terrorist group Hamas issued a statement in December 2001 justifying suicide bombings against Israeli civilians on the grounds that the "heroic martyrdom operations... represent the sole weapon" available to the Palestinian people. The statement went on to argue that "denying the Palestinian people the right of self-defense and describing this as terrorism, which should have been linked with the occupation [of Palestinian lands by Israel], violates all laws and norms which granted the peoples the right of self-defense" and that "considering the Palestinian resistance as a terrorist act and an outlaw legitimizes occupation because it de-legitimizes its resistance."[32]

Would you kill this baby? Imagine you have been transported back to early 1890 and you are standing just out of this picture. No one but you and the child are present. The baby in this picture is Adolf Hitler, about a year after his birth on April 20, 1889, in Braunau, Austria. Given your knowledge of the horrors of World War II and the Holocaust, would you kill baby Adolf? Would the end justify the means? This and other issues are raised if one attempts to apply moral standards to the formation and conduct of foreign policy.

In practice, the primitive international political system can make applying strong moral principles strictly, adhering to international law, and other such altruistic acts unwise and even dangerous. Clearly, most of us do not adhere to such an absolute position. Nor do we practice **amorality**. Instead, most people adhere to **moral relativism**. They believe that actions must be placed in context. For example, most Americans explicitly or implicitly accept capital punishment and the atomic bombings of Hiroshima and Nagasaki as somehow justified as retaliation or even as an unfortunate necessity to a better end. The problem, again, is where to draw the line. How about assassination? Think about this innocent baby photograph of Adolf Hitler. What if you had a time machine? Would you be justified in traveling back to 1890 and killing the baby Hitler in order to prevent World War II and the genocide that killed 6 million Jews, and other people deemed undesirable?

Should We Judge Others by Our Own Standards? The issue about whether to judge others morally rests on two controversies. The first, which we have already addressed, is whether it is supportable to apply standards of international law and morality given the divergent values of a multicultural world. Some claim that doing so is cultural imperialism; others believe that at least some universal standards exist.

The second objection to any country's or even the UN's imposing sanctions or taking any other action based on another country's supposed morality or lack thereof is that it violates the sovereignty of the target country. Many Americans have few qualms about criticizing the human rights record of other countries, but they become outraged when others find American standards lacking. Capital punishment is legal and on the rise in most U.S. states, but many other countries find the practice abhorrent. Therefore they refuse to extradite accused criminals to the United States if there is a possibility of capital punishment. This has included statements by a number of countries in the aftermath of the 9-11 attacks that they would not transfer suspected terrorists to the United States if the accused faced the death penalty. Belgium was one of the countries that did so. As its foreign minister Marc Verwilghen explained, "We always have said in the European Union that the execution of the death penalty is not an option."[33]

The opposition to capital punishment is intensified by the belief that there are demographic injustices in who gets executed. The UN Commission on Human Rights (UNCHR) passed a resolution in 1998 calling for a moratorium on executions because, in part, of a UNCHR report that found that in the United States "race, ethnic origin and economic status appear to be key determinants of who will and will not receive a sentence of death."[34] Americans have regularly rejected such refusals to extradite and questioning of fairness as gross outside interference.

Is It Prudent to Apply Moral and Legal Standards? Another objection to trying to apply moral principles is based on self-interest. Realists maintain that national interest sometimes precludes the application of otherwise laudable moral principles. They further contend that trying to uphold abstract standards of morality casts a leader as a perpetual Don Quixote, a pseudo knight-errant whose wish "To dream the impossible dream; To fight the unbeatable foe;… [and] To right the unrightable wrong" while appealing romantically, is delusional and perhaps dangerous. One danger is that you waste your reputation, your wealth, and the lives of your soldiers trying to do the impossible. A second peril springs from the reality that since not all states act morally, those who do are at a disadvantage: "Nice guys finish last."

Those who disagree with this line of reasoning contend that it fails the test of courageously standing up for what is right. They might even recall the remonstration of President John Kennedy, who, evoking Dante Alighieri's *The Divine Comedy* (1321), commented, "Dante once said that the hottest places in hell are reserved for those who in a period of moral crisis maintain their neutrality."[35]

More pragmatically, advocates of applying principles of law and morality contend that greater justice is necessary for world survival. This argument deals, for example, with resource distribution. It contends that it is immoral to maintain a large part of the world both impoverished and without self-development possibilities. The inevitable result, according to this view, will be a world crisis that will destroy order as countries fight for every declining resource.

One way out of the dilemma about when and how great a degree of law, morality, and other principles to apply to foreign policy may be to begin with the observation that it is not necessary to choose between moral absolutism and amorality. Instead, there is a middle ground of moral relativism that relies on **moral prudence** as a guiding principle. There is a secular prayer that asks for the courage to change the wrongs one can, the patience to accept the wrongs that one cannot change, and the wisdom to know the difference. From this perspective, a decision maker must ask, first, whether any tangible good is likely to result from a course of action and, second, whether the good will outweigh negative collateral consequences.

By the first standard, taking high-flown principled stands when it is impossible or unlikely that you will affect the situation is quixotic. By the second standard, applying morality when the overall consequences will be vastly more negative also fails the test of prudence. But not taking action when change is possible and when the good will outweigh the bad fails the test of just behavior.

The Future of International Law and Morality

The often anarchic and inequitable world makes it easy to dismiss talk of conducting international relations according to standards of international law and morality as idealistic prattling. This view, however, was probably never valid and certainly is not true now. An irreversible trend in world affairs is the rapid acceleration of states and people interacting in almost all areas of endeavor. As these interactions have grown, so has the need for regularized behavior and for rules to prescribe that behavior. For very pragmatic reasons then, many people have come to believe, as one analyst notes, that "most issues of transnational concern are best addressed through legal frameworks that render the behavior of global actors more predictable and induce compliance from potential or actual violators" (Ratner, 1998:78). The growth of these rules in functional international interactions has been on the leading edge of the development of international law. Advances in political and military areas have been slower, but here too there has been progress. Thus, as with the United Nations, the pessimist may decry the glass as only half full, whereas, in reality, it is encouraging that there is more and more water in the previously almost empty glass.

All the signs point to increasing respect for international law and a greater emphasis on adhering to at least rudimentary standards of morality. Violations of international standards are now more likely to draw criticism from the world community. It is probable, therefore, that international law will continue to develop and to expand its areas of application. So too will moral discourse have increasing impact on the actions of the international actors. There will certainly be areas where growth is painfully slow, and there will also be those who violate the principles of law and morality and who sometimes get away with their unlawful and immoral acts. But, just as surely, there will be progress.

Chapter Summary

1. International law can be best understood as a primitive system of law in comparison with much more developed domestic law. There are only the most rudimentary procedures and institutions for making, adjudicating, and enforcing international law. This does not mean, however, that international law is impotent, only that it is in an earlier stage of development than domestic law.

2. As a developing phenomenon, international law is dynamic and has been growing since the earliest periods of civilization. This growth accelerated in the twentieth century because the increasing level of international interaction and interdependence required many new rules to govern and regularize contacts in trade, finance, travel, communication, and other areas. The possible consequences of war have also spurred the development of international law.

3. Thus far, international law is most effective when it governs functional international relations. International law works least well in areas of "high politics," where the vital interests of the sovereign states are at stake. Even in those areas, though, international law is gradually becoming more effective.

4. Morality is another factor in establishing the rules of the international system. It acts as a guide to action and as the basis for some international law.

5. The international legal system has four essential elements: its philosophical roots, lawmaking, adherence, and adjudication.

6. The roots of law for any legal system may come from external sources, such as natural law, or from within the society, such as custom.

7. Regarding lawmaking, international law springs from a number of sources, including international treaties, international custom, general principles of law, and international representative assemblies. Some scholars argue that resolutions and other pronouncements of the UN General Assembly should be included as a significant influence.

8. Regarding adherence, international law, again like primitive law, relies mainly on voluntary compliance and self-help. Here again, though, there are early and still uncertain examples of enforcement by third parties, a feature that characterizes more advanced systems.

9. The fourth essential element of a legal system, adjudication, is also in the primitive stage in international law. Although there are a number of international courts in the world today, jurisdiction and the use and effectiveness of these courts are limited. The existence of the International Court of Justice and other such international judicial bodies represent an increasing sophistication of international law in this area as well.

10. In a still culturally diverse world, standards of international law and morality have encountered problems of fit with different cultures. Most current international law and many concepts of morality, such as the stress on individualism, are based on Western ideas and practices, and many states from the South object to certain aspects of international law as it exists.

11. The changes in the world system in this century have created a number of important issues related to international law. Among these are status of sovereignty, the legality of war and the conduct of war, rules for governing the biosphere, and observing and protecting human rights.

12. International law has been interpreted as applying to states. Now it is also concerned with individuals. Primarily, it applies to the treatment of individuals by states, but it also has some application to the actions of individuals. Thus people, as well as countries, are coming to have obligations, as well as rights, under international law.

13. It is not always possible to insist on strict adherence to international law and to high moral standards, yet they cannot be ignored. One middle way is to apply principles prudently.

National Security: The Traditional Road

[W]hen the blast of war blows in our ears,
Then imitate the tiger:
Stiffen the sinews, conjure up the blood,
Disguise fair nature with hard-favour'd rage;
Then lend the eye a terrible aspect.

Shakespeare, *King Henry V*

We make war that we may live in peace.
Aristotle, *Nichomacean Ethics*, circa 325 B.C.

An eye for an eye only winds up making the whole world blind.
Mohandas K. (Mahatma) Gandhi

Chapter Objectives

After completing this chapter, you should be able to:

• Identify reasons for studying war and summarize the human record of war, including the incidence, death toll, frequency, and severity.
• Discuss the causes of war by applying the three levels of analysis: system, state, and individual.
• Understand force as a political instrument and its limitations.
• Explain the escalating use of a country's military power, from intimidation to attack.
• Analyze the effectiveness of the threat and use of force in the international system.
• Consider how the nature of war has changed as a result of nationalism and technology.
• Describe the destinations, sources, motives, and impact of international arms transfers.
• Characterize covert intervention and terrorism and distinguish between them.
• Define and describe the goals and conduct of war.
• Discuss limited nuclear-biological-chemical war as part of a battlefield strategy.
• Examine the major issues surrounding strategic nuclear war.
• Summarize strategic nuclear weapons and strategy as ongoing factors in international politics.

War is an enigma. We bewail its existence and consequences while we regularly battle with exhilaration. Those who have fought and seen war often speak of its tragedy. "I am tired and sick of war," General William Tecumseh Sherman told military cadets in 1879. "Its glory is all moonshine. It is only those who have neither fired a shot nor heard the shrieks and groans of the wounded who cry aloud for more blood, more vengeance, more desolation. War is hell!" General of the Army Dwight David Eisenhower agreed with his historical comrade in arms: "I hate war as only a soldier who has lived it can, as only one who has seen its brutality, its futility, its stupidity." From their experience, the generals would have surely agreed with the lament of English poet Wilfred Owen in 1914:

> War broke: and now the Winter of the world
> With perishing great darkness closes in.

War may be hell, but we are too often attracted to it like moths to the flame. "I have loved war too much," King Louis XIV of France confessed in 1710. "It is well that war is so terrible—we should grow too fond of it," General Robert E. Lee wrote similarly in 1862. More than a century later, President George Bush paced the White House grounds, carrying a handheld television to follow live reports from the Persian Gulf War. When miniature images flickered on the screen of U.S. warplanes attacking Iraqi targets, "Bush jabbed his index finger at each target on the screen as though silently declaring 'Gotcha!'" as "smart bombs" obliterated buildings and bodies.[1] Perhaps, then, there is something to Henry Ward Beecher's observation in *Proverbs From Plymouth Pulpit* (1887): "It is not merely cruelty that leads men to war, it is excitement."

War and World Politics

Whether one considers war a tale of tragedy or a saga of heroism, there is resonance to scholar Max Weber's (1864–1920) classic observation: "The decisive means for politics is violence. Anyone who fails to see this is... a political infant" (Porter, 1994:303). Realists would agree that war is an inherent part of politics. Idealists would rejoin that humans can learn to live without war. Whoever is right, the fact for now is that countries continue to rely on themselves for protection and sometimes use threats and violence to further their interests. Thus, it is important to examine military power and to grasp the role that force plays in the conduct of international politics.

WAR: THE HUMAN RECORD

War is as ancient as humanity (Cioffi-Revilla, 1996). There are varying estimates of the number of wars that have occurred throughout history, but there can be little doubt that the number is high. One reasonable number, as shown in Figure 12.1, is that there were almost 1,000 wars during the millennium that just ended. Looking even farther back, it is possible to see that the world has been totally free of significant interstate, colonial, or civil war in only about 1 out of every 12 years in all of recorded human history.

The data also shows that war is not a tragic anachronism waged by our less civilized ancestors. To the contrary, political violence continues. Two ways to gauge this are frequency and severity.

Frequency provides bad news. Over the last ten centuries, as Figure 12.1 on page 332 shows, wars have become more frequent, with some 30 percent occurring in just

WAR IS HELL!

War is hell! Burned in a misdirected American napalm attack on the pagoda in which she had sought refuge, 9-year-old Phan Thi Kim Phuc (right) flees in terror near the town of Trang Bang, South Vietnam. Over half of the girl's body was charred by third-degree burns from the jellied-gasoline inferno; her two little brothers were instantly incinerated and a third brother also suffered excruciating burns. War is hell!

Nick Ut, the photographer who took this Pulitzer Prize–winning picture, rushed the girl to a hospital and may have saved her life. But it has not been an easy life. Kim Phuc spent over a year in the hospital recovering from her immediate wounds, and she still has massive scars over most of her upper body. Most of her oil and sweat glands were also burned away, and she continues to be assailed by migraine headaches, diabetes, breathing difficulty, and chronic pain associated with her trauma.

Some 24 years after the searing napalm attack, Ms. Kim Phuc came to lay a wreath at the Vietnam Veterans Memorial in Washington, D.C. She sought reconciliation, not recrimination, and hugged American veterans. "I have suffered a lot [of] physical and emotional pain. Sometimes I could not breathe. But God saved my life and gave me faith and hope," she told the audience to several standing ovations. "Even if I could talk face to face with the pilot who dropped the bomb," she went on, "I would tell him, 'We cannot change history, but we should try to do good things for the present and for the future to promote peace.'" Said one tearful American Vietnam veteran, "It's important to us that she's here, part of the healing process. We were just kids doing our job. For her to forgive us personally means something." Kim Phuc said that she also had accepted the invitation by a Vietnam Veterans group to speak at the memorial in order to tell the world that "behind that picture of me [at age 9], thousands and thousands of people suffered more than me. They died. They lost part of their bodies. Their whole lives were destroyed, and nobody took [their] picture."[1] War is hell!

the last two centuries. It is true that the frequency of war in the 1900s declined somewhat from the horrific rate in the 1800s, but it is also the case that the number of civil wars increased. This means that the overall incidence of interstate and intrastate warfare remains relatively steady (Pickering & Thompson, 1998).

Severity is the truly terrible news. Again as evident in Figure 12.1, over 147 million people died during wars since the year 1000. Of the dead, an astounding 75 percent perished in the twentieth century and 89 percent since 1800. Not only do we kill more soldiers, we also now kill larger numbers of civilians. During World War I, six soldiers died for every civilian killed (8.4 million soldiers and 1.4 million civilians). World War II killed two civilians for every soldier (16.9 million troops and 34.3 million civilians). The worst news may lie ahead. President John F. Kennedy observed in 1961 that "mankind must put an end to war, or war will put an

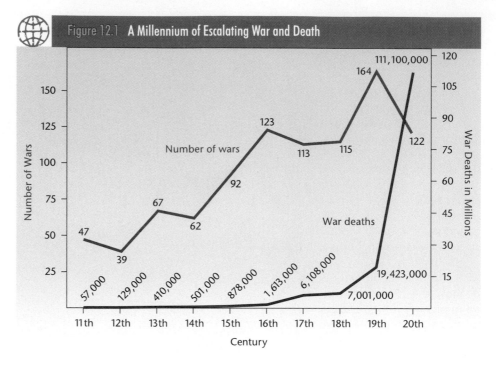

Figure 12.1 A Millennium of Escalating War and Death

Data sources: Eckhardt (1991); author. Eckhardt defines a war as a conflict that (1) involves a government on at least one side and (2) accounts for at least 1,000 deaths per year of the conflict.

This figure shows the long-term trend in the rise of both the frequency and severity of war. Beginning in the year 1000, the number of wars in each century has usually increased. The soaring death toll of the twentieth century's wars, which accounted for 75 percent of the millennium's total, is a truly alarming figure.

end to mankind." A nuclear war would escalate the casualty count from millions per year to millions per minute, and Kennedy's cataclysmic characterization could literally come to pass.

THE CAUSES OF WAR: THREE LEVELS OF ANALYSIS

Why war? This question has challenged investigators over the centuries (Geller & Singer, 1998). Philosophers, world leaders, and social scientists have many theories. It may be that further research can identify a single root cause of war, but it is more likely that there is no single reason why people fight. Given this, one way to discuss the multiple causes of war is to classify them according to the three levels of analysis: system-level analysis, state-level analysis, and individual-level analysis detailed in chapters 3, 4, and 5.

System-Level Causes of War

Wars may be caused by a number of factors related to the general nature of the world's political system (Cashman, 1999; Rosecrance & Lo, 1996). To illustrate that here, we can touch on four system-level variables.

The distribution of power. Recall from chapter 3 that some analysts believe that the propensity for warfare to occur within the international system is related to factors such as the system's number of poles (big powers), their relative power, and whether the poles and their power are stable or in flux (Maoz, 1996; Walt, 1996a). When, for example, a system is experiencing significant power transitions (that is, when some powers are rising and others are declining or even vanishing), power vacuums often occur. These can cause conflict, as opposing powers move to fill the void. Postwar alliances that concentrate power by bringing victorious, major countries together have also been found to be "war prone" (Gibler & Vasquez, 1998:805).

The anarchical nature of the system. Some systems analysts argue that wars occur because there is no central authority to try to prevent conflict and to protect countries. Unlike domestic societies, the international society has no effective system of law creation, enforcement, or adjudication. This causes insecurity, and, therefore, countries acquire arms in part because other countries do, creating a tension-filled cycle of escalating arms →tensions →arms →tensions.

System-level economic factors. The global pattern of production and use of natural resources is one of the system-level factors that can cause conflict. This was evident when Iraq in 1990 endangered the main sources of petroleum production by attacking Kuwait and threatening Saudi Arabia. A U.S-led coalition of countries dependent on petroleum rushed to defend the Saudis and liberate the Kuwaitis (and their oil), and the 1991 Persian Gulf War broke out. The global gap between wealthy and poor countries is another system-level factor. Some analysts are concerned that the highly uneven distribution of wealth between countries and regions could spark conflict along the North-South axis as the resentment of the relatively poor countries rises. From this perspective, some observers point to the "wealth gap" as one reason that a great deal of the terrorism is rooted in the South.

System-level biosphere stress. Overconsumption of biosphere resources is yet another possible system-level cause of conflict. Water provides one example. This basic resource is becoming so precious in many areas that, as you will see in chapter 18, there are growing concerns that countries might soon go to war with one another over disputes about water supplies. According to one scholar, "When the empire of man over nature can no longer be easily extended, then the only way for one people to increase its standard of living is by redistributing the sources or fruits of industry from others to themselves. The surest way to do this is by extending man's empire over man" (Orme, 1998:165).

State-Level Causes of War

War may also result from the very nature of states (Auerswald, 1999; Dassel, 1998). There are also several theories of war that have to do with the internal processes and conditions of countries (Morgan & Anderson, 1999; Fordham, 1998).

Militarism. Some scholars believe that states inherently tend toward militarism. One such analyst writes that "it is impossible to understand the nature of modern politics without considering its military roots" (Porter, 1994:xix). The argument is that as warfare required more soldiers and more increasingly expensive weapons, it created a need for political units with larger populations and economies. This gave rise to the state.

Externalization of internal conflict. Sometimes governments engage in war to rally the populace and divert its attention from domestic problems. This ploy is called diversionary war or the externalization of internal conflict. Evidence indicates, for instance, that revolutionary regimes will attempt to consolidate their power by fomenting tension with other countries (Snyder, 1999). It is also the case that countries are more likely to go to war while they are experiencing times of economic distress (Gelpi, 1997; Wang, 1996). Just as occurred in the movie *Wag the Dog*, starring Dustin Hoffman, analysts believe that when leaders fear they may lose power, they are tempted "to engage in international crises" (Smith, 1996:147).

Type of country. There are analysts who believe that some types of countries, because of their political structure (democratic, authoritarian) or their economic resources and wealth, are more aggressive than others. Chapter 8 discusses, for example, the democratic peace theory, the conclusion of most analysts that democratic countries are not prone to fighting with one another.

Political culture. Some scholars believe that a nation's political culture is correlated to warlike behavior. No nation has a genetic political character. Nations, however, that have had repeated experiences with violence may develop a political culture that views the world as a hostile environment (Ember & Ember, 1996). It is not necessary for the list to go on to make the point that how states are organized and how they make policy can sometimes lead to conflict and war among them.

Individual-Level Causes of War

It may be that the causes of war are linked to the character of individual leaders or to the nature of the human species. "In the final analysis," one scholar writes, "any contemplation of war must return to… the nature of humanity, which yet stands as the root cause of war and the wellspring of History's inestimable tragedy" (Porter, 1994:304).

Those who have this perspective believe that although it is clear that human behavior is predominantly learned, there are also behavioral links to the primal origins of humans. Territoriality, which we examined in chapter 5, is one such possible instinct, and the fact that territorial disputes are so frequently the cause of war may point to some instinctual territoriality in humans (Huth, 1996; Vasquez, 1996). Another possibility, some social psychologists argue, is that human aggression, individually or collectively, can stem from stress, anxiety, or frustration. The reaction of the German society to its defeat and humiliation after World War I is an example. A sociopsychological need for power is yet another possibility. At least some leaders have a power drive that may cause aggressive behavior. While discounting some of the more strident characterizations of Saddam Hussein as a madman, most personality analyses of Iraq's leader characterize him as driven to seek power and to dominate.

National Military Power

For good or ill, military power adds to a country's ability to prevail in international disputes. Therefore, it is appropriate to first consider the nature of military power that provides the sword for policy makers to wield. Military power is based on an array of tangible factors, such as spending and weapons levels, and intangible factors, such as leadership, morale, and reputation. Military power is not free, though. To the contrary, acquiring it and using it can be costly in many direct and indirect ways.

LEVELS OF SPENDING

One of the largest categories in any nation's budget is the amount spent on national security. In times of peril, the amount may account for more than half of all government spending. Global military spending soared during the tense years of the cold war. Then, with the conclusion of that era, defense spending dropped significantly during the 1990s. Global arms spending during the last half of the 1990s averaged about $730 billion, a decrease of more than 25 percent in current dollars and even more in real dollars (value controlled for inflation) from spending levels a decade earlier. Spending, however, began to inch higher during 1999 and 2000, and the massive increases in the U.S. defense budget sparked by the 9-11 terrorist attacks will almost certainly push global military spending sharply upward, at least during the next few years. Given the fact that U.S. defense expenditures account for more than one-third of the world's total military spending, the 30 percent U.S. increase

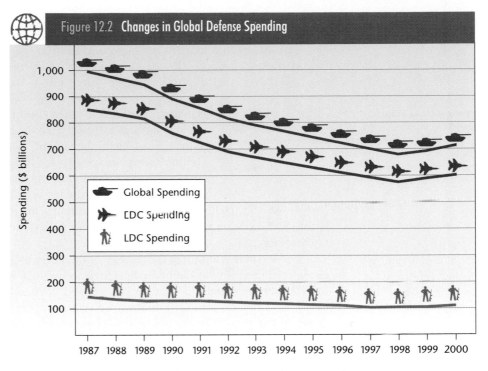

Figure 12.2 Changes in Global Defense Spending

Legend:
- Global Spending
- LDC Spending
- LDC Spending

Expenditures are calculated in billions of 1991 dollars.

Data sources: U.S. Arms Control and Disarmament Agency at http://dosfan.lib.uic.edu/acda; Stockholm International Peace Research Institute (SIPRI) 2002.

There are two ways to look at global defense spending. One way is that it has dropped off significantly since 1987. The other way is that the world's countries still spend huge amounts on weapons and soldiers, and that after a long decline in spending, it is again on the rise.

from $305 billion in 2001 to $396 billion (current dollars) in 2003, will almost surely drive global expenditures upward by more than 10 percent to levels approximately those at the end of the cold war. Data through 2000 is shown in Figure 12.2.

Within Figure 12.2 it is also worth focusing on the indications that military spending (in real dollars) of the world's economically less developed countries (LDCs) have declined only marginally overall since the cold war ended and have turned upward since 1998. The LDCs spent over $250 billion (current dollars) on their militaries in 2000. The amount was equivalent to nearly 4 percent of their collective GNPs compared to an average of about 3 percent of their GNPs that LDCs spend on health and education combined. This means that without the need for military forces, these developing countries could substantially increase spending to create a healthier, more educated population.

A final troubling point is that the military budgets of some regions and countries have increased amid the general global decline in military spending. Military expenditures in South and East Asia increased about 25 percent in the 1990s, and there is an escalating arms race in the region, with China, India, and Pakistan the main contenders. China's defense spending measured in real dollars increased 65 percent from 1995 through 2000, and India's spending escalated 48 percent during the same period.

Did You Know That:
The 2002 U.S. defense budget ($343 billion) accounted for about 35 percent of world military spending. The U.S. population is about 5 percent of the world population.

WEAPONRY: QUANTITY VERSUS QUALITY

Very often when you see a comparison of two countries' or alliances' military might, you see a map with an overlay of small figures representing troops, tanks, planes, and other weapons. Such graphics emphasize quantity, and it always seems as if the other side's figures far outnumber your own.

Quantity is an important military consideration, but the relative value of these figures must be modified by the cost and quality of the weapons and troops. The West, especially the United States, has tended to favor acquiring fewer but superior high-technology weapons. By contrast, China and other countries, because of their technology lag and preferences, have favored masses of weapons. There is a general agreement that most important Western military weapons systems are technologically superior to any other country's weapons. The war in the Persian Gulf was, for example, a showcase for high-technology warfare. In that war, U.S. main battle tanks maneuvered at nearly highway speeds and coalition pilots used laser guidance systems to maneuver "smart bombs" to their targets.

> **Did You Know That:**
> The world's smallest army is the Vatican's 100-man Swiss Guard. The original force was formed from Swiss mercenaries who had defended Pope Clement VII during the sacking of Rome in 1527 by, oddly, Charles V, the Holy Roman Emperor.

The seeming triumph of technology in the Persian Gulf War must, however, be considered carefully. In the first place, high technology is very expensive. Just after the 9-11 terrorist attacks, President Bush vowed, "When I take action, I'm not going to fire a $2 million [cruise] missile at a $10 empty tent [in Afghanistan] and hit a camel in the butt."[2] Yet he did use B-2 bombers, which cost $2.1 billion each, to drop munitions on the rudimentarily armed Taliban and al-Qaeda forces. Indeed, the cost of a single B-2 is more than the yearly defense budgets of about two-thirds of the world's countries.

Second, it is difficult to calculate precisely the relative worth of a greater number of lower technology weapons versus fewer, more sophisticated, weapons. The newest U.S. fighter, the F-22, is a technological marvel that can defeat any other fighter. One has to wonder, though, whether one $127 million F-22 could defeat, say, four Russian-built SU-30 fighters (available for $34 million), which are being supplied to China, North Korea, Iran, and a variety of other countries with which U.S. relations are often strained.

Third, high-technology weapons are also less durable and are more difficult to fix under battle conditions than are low-tech weapons. The $2.1 billion B-2 bomber cannot be left outside in the rain. The GAO reports that the warplane "must be sheltered or exposed to [only] the most benign environments—low humidity, no precipitation, moderate temperatures," because even mildly adverse weather makes the plane's skin, which is made of thermoplastic-composite material, deteriorate and lose the qualities that supposedly make the B-2 invisible to radar. Even the Air Force has had to admit that "it would be difficult to operate the B-2 from a deployed location," meaning near where the war is.[3]

It should also be remembered that the effectiveness of soldiers and military hardware is very situational. Therefore, a country's military systems need to be appropriate to the challenges they will face. American technology easily overwhelmed the Iraqis in the relatively open terrain near the Persian Gulf but was not able to prevail during the war in densely forested Vietnam against an even less sophisticated opponent than Iraq.

MILITARY MORALE AND LEADERSHIP

Morale is a key element of military power. An army that does not fight well cannot win. Historian Stephen Ambrose, who served as a consultant for the film *Saving Private Ryan*, reflects that "in the end success or failure on D-Day [came] down to a relatively small number of junior officers, noncoms, and privates." According to Ambrose, "If the men coming in over the beaches [had] flopped down behind the seawall and

Military morale is one of the intangible aspects of a country's power. Russia's military power has been undermined by the poor pay and living conditions of its armed forces and the unpopularity of the seemingly endless and fruitless attempts by Moscow to suppress the rebellion of the Chechens. This dispirited Russian soldier on duty in Grozny, Chechnya's capital, symbolizes the sagging morale in his country's military.

refused to advance, if the noncoms and junior officers [had] failed to lead their men up and over the seawall… in the face of enemy fire—why, then, the Germans would [have won] the battle and thus the war."[4]

Morale, of course, is not inherent. Russian soldiers fought with amazing valor during World War II despite conditions that, in many cases, were far worse than those that American troops faced. Yet in more recent times, the morale of Russia's soldiers has been sapped by being left poorly paid, housed, equipped, and trained. "My heart aches for our hungry soldiers, for our officers who do not receive their pay on time, for their families roaming about for years with nowhere to live," Russia's president told a radio audience.[5] Such heartaches have left the once-vaunted Soviet/Russian army a dispirited shell. What should be an overpowering Russian force has not been able to batter the outnumbered, outgunned Chechen rebels into submission in a war that has dragged on since 1996. One reason is the poor morale of Russia's troops. As one Chechen rebel said of his opponents, "They have very strong weapons—but not very strong spirits."[6]

Military leadership, in the form of both inspirational and tactical skills, plays a significant role (Taylor & Rosenbach, 1996). It is difficult, for instance, to understand the long resistance of the U.S. Southern Confederacy to the overwhelming numerical superiority of the Union unless the brilliant generalship of Robert E. Lee is considered. By contrast, French generals in this century made a series of classic errors. Marshal Ferdinand Foch, who commanded Allied forces on the Western Front during World War I, was of the opinion that "airplanes are interesting toys, but of no military value."[7] Continuing this old mindset into the 1930s, French generals relied on the fortified, but static, Maginot Line and were routed in 1940 by the Germans, who did not think their Stuka dive bombers were toys and who created a highly mobile and mechanized army with air support. In 1954, still relying on a static defense, the French garrison at Dien Bien Phu in Indochina was surrounded and decimated by Vietnamese forces under the command of the able General Giap.

MILITARY AND POLITICAL REPUTATION

Another power consideration is a country's reputation. Whatever real power a country may possess, its ability to influence others will depend partly on how those others perceive its capacity and will. National leaders commonly believe that weakness tempts their opponents, while a reputation for strength deters them. "Real leadership requires a willingness to use military force," argues one former White House aide.[8]

Some analysts believe, as one French general put it, that Americans want "zero-dead wars," as demonstrated by U.S. withdrawals in the face of casualties in Lebanon in 1983 and Somalia in 1993.[9] This reputation, the analysts say, is undermining U.S. power because opponents often do not take American threats seriously. "The nature of American society makes it impossible for the United States to bear tens of thousands of casualties," Saddam Hussein calculated when he invaded Kuwait.[10]

President Bush was adamant about "putting boots on the ground" (committing ground forces) in 2001 because of his belief that U.S. power was being harmed by the image abroad that Americans were "flaccid" and "wouldn't fight back." Still, the actual use of U.S. troops was generally limited in favor of using Afghani forces. This led to some criticism that a reluctance to expose U.S. troops to casualties for fear of endangering public support of the war let Osama bin Laden and other top al-Qaeda and Taliban leaders and many of their armed supporters escape being captured or killed.

MILITARY POWER: THE DANGERS OF OVEREMPHASIS

Given the importance of military power as a tool of national defense and diplomacy, it is not uncommon for people to assume that the phrase "too much military power" must be an oxymoron. Exactly how much is enough is a complex question, but it is certain that there are clear dangers associated with overemphasizing military power. Three such perils deserve special mention. They are insecurity, temptation, and expense.

Military power creates insecurity. One result of power acquisition is the "spiral of insecurity." This means that our attempts to amass power to achieve security or gain other such ends are frequently perceived by others as a danger to them. They then seek to acquire offsetting power, which we see as threatening, causing us to acquire even more power… then them… then us, ad infinitum, in an escalating spiral. As evident in chapter 13's review of disarmament, the arms race is a complex phenomenon, but the interaction of one country's power and other countries' insecurity is an important factor in world politics.

Military power creates temptation. A second peril of amassing excess military power is the temptation to use it in a situation that is peripheral to the national interest. The United States went to war in Vietnam despite the fact that President Lyndon Johnson derided it as a "raggedy-ass fourth-rate country." One reason Americans intervened in Vietnam was because of a so-called arrogance of power. Had U.S. military power been more modest, the United States might have emphasized diplomacy or maybe even acquiesced to the reunification of North and South Vietnam. One can never be sure, but it is certain that it is hard to shoot someone if you do not own a gun.

Military power is expensive. A third problem with acquiring power for its own sake is that it is extremely expensive. Beyond short-term budget decisions about spending (domestic or defense programs) and how to pay the bills (taxes or deficits), there is a more general, longer-range concern. One scholar who studied the decline of great powers between 1500 and the 1980s concluded that "imperial overstretch" was the cause of their degeneration (Kennedy, 1988). Kennedy's thesis is that superpowers of the past poured so many resources into military power that, ironically, they weakened the country's strength by siphoning off resources that should have been devoted to maintaining and improving the country's infrastructure. Kennedy's study did not include the Soviet Union, but it is arguable that the collapse of the USSR followed the pattern of overspending on the military, thereby enervating the country's economic core. Declinists warn that the United States is also guilty of imperial overstretch and could go the way of other great powers that rose, dominated, then fell from the pinnacle of power.

The **imperial overstretch thesis** has many critics (Knutsen, 1999). At the strategic level, some critics argue that far more danger is posed by a "lax Americana" than by any effort to create a "pax Americana." The reasoning is that if the United States does not exercise certain leadership as hegemon, then the international system is in danger of falling into disorder.[11] Similarly, some scholars warn that a rush to peace is only slightly less foolish than a rush to war. One study that reviewed the sharp cuts in U.S. military spending after World War II, the Korean War, and the Vietnam War concluded, "In each case the savings proved only temporary, as declining defense budgets eroded military readiness and necessitated a rush to rearm in the face of new dangers abroad" (Thies, 1998:176).

Critics of Kennedy's thesis also say that it is wrong about the economic cause of decline. These critics agree with Kennedy that *overconsumption* (spending that depletes assets faster than the economy can replace them) at the expense of reinvestment (spending that creates infrastructure assets) causes decline. Whereas

The drawing of Uncle Sam reaching beyond his grasp illustrates the view that U.S. power is declining because of "imperial overstretch," whereby the country spends too much on military power in an effort to become and remain a superpower. Other observers argue that any decline that has occurred is the result of overspending on what they see as economically unproductive programs such as care for the elderly. This might be called "social overstretch."

Kennedy argues that excessive military spending causes overconsumption, his critics say that the villain is too much social spending. This might be termed the **social overstretch thesis**. "Whether in the form of bread and circuses in the ancient world or medical care for the lower classes and social security for the aged in the modern world," the argument goes, it is social spending on the least productive elements of a society that financially drains a society (Gilpin, 1981:164). It is a harsh judgment, but its advocates believe that the economic reality is that such altruistic programs may leave our spirits enriched but our coffers depleted. Consider, for example, Figure 12.3. It shows that U.S. military spending has declined while spending on social programs has increased steadily as a percentage of the U.S. budget. It is also the case, however, that U.S. military spending accounts for about one-third of all military spending in the world. Which, if either, category would you cut to increase spending on education, transportation, communications, and other infrastructure programs?

Force as a Political Instrument

It may be that future social scientists will be able to write of war in the past tense, but for the present we must recognize conflict as a fact of international politics. For this reason, having discussed the human record and causes of war, we should also consider levels of violence, the diplomatic and military effectiveness of force, the changing nature of warfare, and the classification of wars.

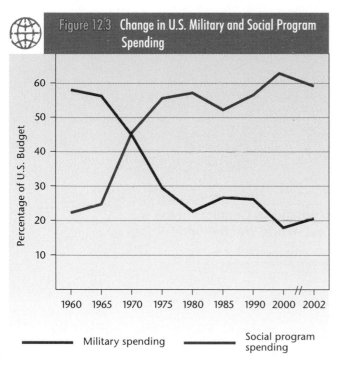

Figure 12.3 Change in U.S. Military and Social Program Spending

Military spending ———

Social program spending ———

Social spending does not include education. Military spending includes Department of Defense, Department of Energy nuclear weapons programs, and veterans' programs. The 2002 budget includes defense spending increases added after the 9-11 attacks.

Data sources: U.S. Bureau of the Census (2002) and for FY 2002 data, U.S. General Accounting Office Web site: http://w3.access.gpo.gov/usbudget/fy2002/pdf/blueprnt.pdf.

Many analysts agree that a country's power declines if it does not invest in its infrastructure, but they disagree about what diverts funds from that investment. Imperial overstretch theory argues that defense spending is the drain; social overstretch theory contends that appropriations for welfare, elderly care, and other such programs are sapping the economy. This figure shows the relative changes in U.S. military and social spending, but it does not answer whether either or both are too high, too low, or about right.

LEVELS OF VIOLENCE: FROM INTIMIDATION TO ATTACK

A country's military power may be used in several escalating ways. These range from serving as a diplomatic backdrop that creates perceived power to direct use of military forces to defeat an opponent. It also should be noted that the options provided by the five levels of violence form a multiple menu. That is, they are often exercised concurrently.

Diplomatic backdrop. Military power does not have to be used or even overtly threatened to be effective. Its very existence establishes a diplomatic backdrop that influences other countries (Freedman, 1998). "Diplomacy without force is like baseball without a bat," one U.S. diplomat has commented.[12] One obvious role of military strength is to persuade potential opponents not to risk confrontation. Military power also influences friends and neutrals. One reason why the United States has been, and remains, a leader of the West is because massive U.S. conventional and nuclear military power creates a psychological assumption by both holder and beholder that the country with dominant military power will play a strong role. This reality is what led the U.S. ambassador to China to put a photograph of a U.S. aircraft carrier on his office wall with the caption, "90,000 tons of diplomacy."[13]

Overt threats. A step up the escalation ladder is overtly threatening an opponent. That is what President

(Continued on page 342)

International Conflicts in the Post–World War II World

War is a continuing reality in the international system. The conflicts since World War II have been less cataclysmic than that global conflagration, but the ongoing use of force means that the world cannot be sure that World War III does not lie in the future. The possibility of conflict also means that the military instrument is used in many ways, ranging from an intimidating diplomatic backdrop to a full-scale assault on an opponent.

	Conflict[1]	Start Date	Major Belligerents [2] (in alphabetical order)	
1	Palestine	1948	Egypt Iraq Israel	Jordan Lebanon Syria
2	Korean	1950	China & North Korea South Korea United Nations: 　United States and 　other countries	
3	Soviet-Hungarian	1956	Hungary	Soviet Union
4	Sinai	1956	Egypt France	Israel United Kingdom
5	Sino-Indian	1962	China	India
6	Kashmir	1965	India	Pakistan
7	Vietnam	1965	Australia North Vietnam South Korea	South Vietnam United States
8	Six-Day	1967	Egypt Israel	Jordan Syria
9	Soviet-Czech	1968	Czechoslovakia	Soviet Union
10	Football	1969	El Salvador	Honduras
11	Indo-Pakistani	1971	India	Pakistan
12	Yom Kippur	1973	Egypt Israel	Syria
13	Cyprus	1974	Cyprus	Turkey
14	Ogaden	1977	Ethiopia	Somalia
15	Cambodian-Vietnamese	1978	Cambodia China	Vietnam
16	Ugandan-Tanzanian	1978	Tanzania	Uganda
17	Afghanistan	1979	Afghanistan	Soviet Union
18	Persian Gulf	1980	Iran	Iraq
19	Angola	1981	Angola Cuba	South Africa
20	Falklands	1982	Argentina	United Kingdom
21	Saharan	1983	Chad	Libya
22	Lebanon	1987	France Israel Lebanon	Syria United States
23	Panama	1989	Panama	United States
24	Persian Gulf	1990	Iraq United Nations: 　United States and 7 other 　countries	
25	Yugoslavia	1990	Bosnia-Herzegovina	Croatia Serbia
26	Peruvian-Ecuadorian	1995	Ecuador	Peru
27	Albania	1995	Albania	Yugoslavia (Serbia-Montenegro)
28	Rwanda	1995	Burundi	Rwanda
29	East Timor	1995	Indonesia	New Guinea insurgency
30	Cameroon	1996	Cameroon	Nigeria
31	Northern Iraq	1996	Iraq	Kurdish insurgency
32	Eritrea	1997	Eritrea	Yemen
33	Iraq	1998	Great Britain Iraq	United States
34	Kosovo	1999	Albania NATO	Yugoslavia
35	Democratic Republic of the Congo	1998	Angola Chad Congo	Namibia Sudan Zimbabwe
36	Chechnya	1999	Chechnya	Russia
37	"War on Terrorism"	2001	Afghanistan (Taliban) al-Qaeda organization Great Britain	United States Others

[1] "Conflict" implies at least 1,000 battle deaths.
[2] "Belligerent" implies combatants supplied at least 5% of the combat troops in the conflict.

International Conflicts in the Post–World War II World

✦ Area of conflict

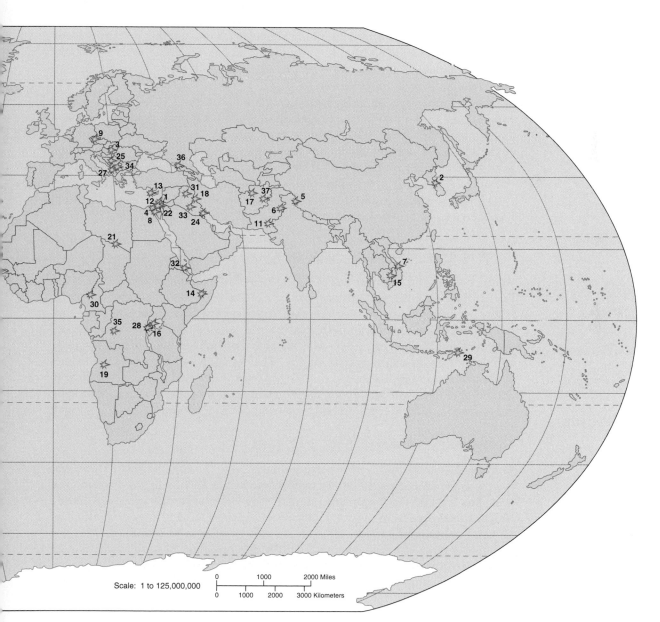

Scale: 1 to 125,000,000

0   1000   2000 Miles

0   1000   2000   3000 Kilometers

Bush did in his address to Congress on September 20, 2001, when he declared, "The Taliban must act and act immediately. They will hand over the terrorists, or they will share in their fate." The Taliban refused and, as Bush predicted, they shared a similar fate. The president also, if a bit less precisely, threatened other countries when he vowed, "From this day forward, any nation that continues to harbor or support terrorism will be regarded by the United States as a hostile regime."

Indirect intervention. There are a number of techniques that can be used to apply military power while avoiding a commitment of your armed forces to direct combat. One approach is supplying arms and other military material or training and advisers to another government or to dissident forces. A second form of indirect intervention is sending military forces or nonuniformed operatives into another country secretly to conduct clandestine operations. Such operations can involve terrorism when the weapons supplied or the operatives sent in are involved in attacking targets beyond those that are of clear military utility.

Limited demonstration. A further escalation involves overtly wielding restrained conventional force to intimidate or harass rather than defeat an opponent. In 1996, for example, the United States attacked Iraqi military installations with about 30 cruise missiles in an effort to persuade Baghdad to end its military operations against Kurdish areas in the northern part of Iraq.

Direct action. The most violent option involves using full-scale force to attempt to defeat an opponent. Within this context, the level of violence can range from highly constrained conventional conflict to unrestricted nuclear war.

THE EFFECTIVENESS OF FORCE

Another aspect of the threat and use of force is the question of whether or not it works in a utilitarian way. It does, and one of the reasons that weapons and war persist in the international system is that they are sometimes successful. This continuing use of force is evident in the map of international conflicts between the end of WW II and 2002 on pages 340–341. The threat of violence may successfully deter an enemy from attacking you or an ally. The actual use of force also sometimes accomplishes intended goals. Given these realities, we should ask ourselves how to determine if force will be effective by utilitarian standards. Answering this question necessitates looking at measurements and conditions for success.

Measurement

Cost/benefit analysis is one of two ways of measuring the effectiveness of war. War is very expensive. There is no accurate count of the deaths in the Persian Gulf War, but 100,000 is a reasonable estimate. The UN-coalition countries spent $60 billion to oust Iraq from Kuwait. Estimates of the costs to both sides (including the physical destruction and lost oil revenues) are as high as $620 billion. Were the results worth the loss of life, human anguish, and economic destruction? Although such trade-offs are made in reality, it is impossible to arrive at any objective standards that can equate the worth of a human life or political freedom with dollars spent or territory lost.

Goal attainment is the second way to judge the effectiveness of force. Generally, the decision to initiate a war is not irrational because leaders usually calculate, accurately or not, their probability of successfully achieving the goals that the use of force is intended to accomplish (Nevin, 1996). This calculation is called the "expected utility" of war. In the words of one study, "Initiators [of war] act as predators and are likely to attack [only] target states they know they can defeat" (Gartner & Siverson, 1996:4). Of course, as Miguel de Cervantes noted in *Don Quixote* (ca. 1615), "There is nothing so subject to inconsistency of fortune as war." Leaders often miscalculate and, as Saddam Hussein did in 1990, start a war they ultimately lose.

Even given the costs and the risks, the utilitarian rationality of threatening or using force is supported by the fact that it sometimes does work. The military destruction of the Taliban regime and most of al-Qaeda's infrastructure in Afghanistan provides an apt example. The expected utility of force is especially apt to be positive when a major power starts the war. One study found that from 1495 to 1991, great powers that initiated wars won 60 percent of them (Wang & Ray, 1994). What is more, the initiators' success rate is going up. During the first three centuries (1495–1799), the initiators won 59 percent of the wars they fought. But during the last two centuries (1800–1991), the success rate increased, with the initiators winning 75 percent of the wars.

Conditions for Success

The next question, then, is, When does force succeed and when does it fail to accomplish its goals? There is no precise answer, but it is possible to synthesize the findings of a variety of studies and the views of military practitioners (see the Explanatory Notes section on page 572) to arrive at some rudimentary rules for the successful use of military force, especially in cases of intervention when a country has not been directly attacked. In cases of intervention, success is most likely when a country's use of military force is:

1. Taken in areas where it has a clearly defined, preferably long-standing, and previously demonstrated commitment.
2. Supported firmly and publicly by the country's leaders.
3. Supported strongly by public opinion.
4. Used to counter other military force, not to try to control political events.
5. Applied early and decisively, rather than by extended threatening and slow escalation.
6. Meant to achieve clear goals and does not change or try to exceed them.

These correlations between military action, political circumstances, and success are only preliminary and do not guarantee success. They do, however, indicate some of the factors that contribute to successful use of the military instrument.

THE CHANGING NATURE OF WAR

Warfare has changed greatly over the centuries (Lawrence, 1998). Three factors are responsible: technology, nationalism, and strategy.

Technology has rapidly escalated the ability to kill. Successive "advances" in the ability to deliver weapons at increasing distances and in the ability to kill ever more people with a single weapon have resulted in mounting casualties, both absolutely and as a percentage of soldiers and civilians of the countries at war.

Nationalism has also changed the nature of war. Before the nineteenth century, wars were generally fought between the houses of nobles with limited armies. The French Revolution (1789) changed that. War began to be fought between nations, with increases in intensity and in numbers involved. France proclaimed military service to be a patriotic duty and instituted the first comprehensive military draft in 1793. The idea of patriotic military service coupled with the draft allowed France's army to be the first to number more than a million men (Avant, 2000).

As a result of technology and nationalism, the scope of war has expanded. Entire nations have become increasingly involved in wars. Before 1800, no more than 3 of 1,000 people of a country participated in a war. By World War I, the European powers called 1 of 7 people to arms. Technology increased the need to mobilize the population for industrial production and also increased the capacity for, and the rationality of, striking at civilians. Nationalism made war a movement of the masses, increasing their stake and also giving justification for attacking the enemy nation. Thus, the lines between military and civilian targets have blurred.

Strategy has also changed. Two concepts, the power to defeat and the power to hurt, are key here. The **power to defeat** is the ability to seize territory or overcome enemy military forces and is the classic goal of war. The **power to hurt**, or coercive violence, is the ability to inflict pain outside the immediate military sphere. It means hurting some so that the resistance of others will crumble. The power to hurt has become increasingly important to all aspects of warfare because the war effort depends on a country's economic effort and, often, the morale of its citizens. Perhaps the first military leader to understand the importance of the power to hurt in modern warfare was General William Tecumseh Sherman during the U.S. Civil War. "My aim was to whip the rebels, to humble their pride, to follow them to their inmost recesses, and [to] make them fear and dread us," the general wrote in his memoirs.[14]

Traditionally wars were fought with little reference to hurting. Even when hurting was used, it depended on the ability to attack civilians by first defeating the enemy's military forces. During the American Revolution, for example, the British could have utilized their power to hurt—to kill civilians in the major cities they controlled—and they might have won the war. Instead they concentrated on defeating the American army (which they could not catch, then grew too strong to overpower), and they lost.

In the modern era, the power to defeat has declined in importance relative to the power to hurt. Terrorism, guerrilla warfare, and nuclear warfare all rely extensively on the power to hurt to accomplish their ends. Even conventional warfare sometimes uses terror tactics to sap an opponent's morale. The use of strategic bombing to blast German cities during World War II is an example.

CLASSIFYING WARS

The changing nature of war, the increased power of weapons, and the shifts in tactics have all made classifying warfare more difficult. Studies of war and other uses of political violence divide these acts into a variety of categories. Whatever the criteria for these categories, though, the exact boundaries between various types of wars or other political phenomena are imprecise. Therefore, you should be concerned mostly with the issues involved in planning for and fighting wars. With recognition of their limits, this chapter divides international conflict into three categories: unconventional warfare, conventional warfare, and weapons of mass destruction warfare.

Unconventional Warfare

Of our three categories of force, **unconventional force** is the one that usually has the most limited geographical scope and involves the least powerful weapons. It is possible to use a variety of the instruments of violence at this level. Three ways for an outside country to apply its military power in local conflict are through (1) arms transfers, (2) special operations, and (3) terrorism.

ARMS TRANSFERS

The international supply of arms is big business, involving tens of billions of dollars annually. There are several motivations to export arms that we will explore. Whatever the cause, however, the global flow of arms can be properly considered as a form of intervention because, whether intended or not, it has an impact on events within countries and between countries (other than the supplier). Moreover, arms transfers frequently either supply dissidents using unconventional warfare to battle a government, or they supply a government battling dissidents. In such scenarios, the international flow of weapons is an indirect way to intervene abroad, and it also promotes unconventional military action.

Arms Transfers: Destinations and Sources

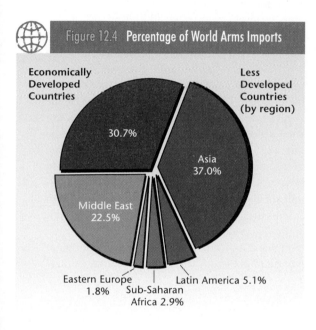

Figure 12.4 Percentage of World Arms Imports

Economically Developed Countries — 30.7%

Less Developed Countries (by region):
Asia 37.0%
Middle East 22.5%
Eastern Europe 1.8%
Sub-Saharan Africa 2.9%
Latin America 5.1%

Data source: Stockholm International Peace Research Institute (SIPRI) Web site at: http://projects.spiri.se/armstrade/atfproj.html.

World arms imports in 2001 came to about $29 billion. LDCs buy most of the weapons; a similar pie chart of exports would show that EDCs sell most of the arms.

The export and import of arms has long been important economically and politically, but it reached new heights during the cold war as the two hostile superpowers struggled for influence. World arms exports during the 1980s alone amounted to $490 billion. The arms that flowed in the world during the cold war came largely from the superpowers, with the United States and Soviet Union accounting for about two-thirds of all arms transfers. The LDCs were the destination of about two-thirds of the flow of weaponry.

Once the cold war ended, the arms trade declined about 45 percent. During the 1990s, overall, annual world arms transfers (sales and military aid) ranged between $19 billion and $25 billion (measured in constant 1990 dollars). Transfers in 2000 were an unusually low $15.3 billion (in 1990 dollars; about $28 billion in current dollars). Whether that sharp drop of 25 percent after 1999 was an aberration or marked the beginning of declining arms sales remains uncertain. Whatever the case, the movement of arms that continues is substantial. Figure 12.4 shows the percentage of arms imports of various global regions. The most worrisome region is Asia, with the arms imports of East Asia increasing nearly 40 percent during the decade.

As for arms exports, the United States is by far the world's leading arms merchant. During the period 1996–2000, U.S. arms transfers accounted for 47.3 percent of the market. Other countries with more than 5 percent are Russia (15.0 percent), France (10.3 percent), Great Britain (6.8 percent), and Germany (5.4 percent). Just these five countries were the source of 84.8 percent of all the major conventional military weaponry transfers for the five-year period.

Arms Transfers: Motives

There are several motives that prompt countries to sell and give weapons to other countries or to insurgent groups. *Supporting allies* during peacetime is one motive. *Intervening in a conflict* is a second reason countries supply weapons. The decades of conflict among various groups in Afghanistan have been possible in substantial part because India, Iran, Pakistan, Russia/the USSR, the United States, and other countries have supplied huge quantities of weapons and other military material to the many factions in that beleaguered country.

Striving for diplomatic influence over the recipient by befriending it or by creating a dependency relationship is a third motive for supplying arms. Sometimes the strategy works, but often it does not. The United States is a major supporter of Israel's armed capabilities, extending over $2 billion in military aid to Israel in 2002. Yet the repeated demands by President Bush during April 2002 that Israel withdraw its forces from the West Bank and Gaza brought only a limited and reluctant response from the government of Ariel Sharon.

Preserving the defense production infrastructure is a fourth motive for selling weapons. Declining military budgets lead to the closing of defense plants and the movement of scientists, engineers, and skilled plant workers into other fields. Arguably, this loss of capacity weakens a country because it will be difficult to replace if necessary in the future, especially if it is needed quickly. One way to have both a low defense budget and continued weapons production capability is to keep the weapons industry and its workers busy making arms for other countries and groups.

National economic benefit is a fifth, and now perhaps the predominant, motive behind arms exports. This is especially true for the world's leading arms merchant, the United States. The sale of F-16 fighters is crucial to the economic well-being of Lockheed Martin Company and the approximately 12,000 workers at its Fort Worth, Texas, plant. A majority of the more than 4,200 F-16s produced or ordered since the fighter first flew in 1976 have gone to other countries. Moreover, foreign sales are increasingly important. The U.S. Air Force ordered just a dozen F-16s in 2000, while foreign governments placed contracts for 222 of the warplanes. Thus, the economic welfare of Texas is not just linked to U.S. military needs; it also depends in part on the thousands of F-16s that have been sold to over 20 countries around the world.

Other countries are also eager to sell their military wares, and for some, foreign sales are a critical part of their exports. Arms are North Korea's leading export, and it has been developing such missiles as the Taepodong, with a 2,000-to-3,000-mile range, more to market them than for Pyongyang's own use. "Our military exports are aimed at obtaining foreign money we need at present," the official Korean Central News Agency has candidly admitted.[15]

Arms Transfers: Drawbacks

It is worth belaboring the obvious to point out that selling or giving arms to other countries is not like other trade and aid transfers. There can be little doubt that countries have legitimate defense needs and that sometimes arms transfers help stabilize situations. It is also true, however, that the massive flow of arms entails drawbacks to both the importing and to the exporting countries.

Cost is one danger of the weapons trade. As noted earlier, countries, especially poorer ones, face classic "guns or butter" budget decisions about whether to spend on defense or domestic programs. At least some of the billions of dollars that LDCs spend annually on arms imports could be devoted to domestic infrastructure or social programs.

Increased violence is a second problem. Many scholars believe that the arms flow increases the level and perhaps the frequency and intensity of violence between countries and within countries. One recent study concludes that the consequences of the flow of weapons, especially to the LDCs, are "likely to be severe.... Third World countries now possess the capacity to conduct wars of greater intensity, duration, and reach." The study notes that "while no one can predict that the growing availability of modern weapons will lead to an increased frequency of armed conflict, there is a high correlation between the growing diffusion of war-making material and the increased tempo of global violence" (Klare & Lumpe, 2000:173; Parker, 1999; Sanjian, 1999; Hashim, 1998).

One of the drawbacks of selling weapons abroad is that allies sometimes become enemies and a country's soldiers may have to face weapons their own country sold to what have become opposing forces. The United States supplied hundreds of Stinger surface-to-air missiles to the Afghani fighters who were battling the Soviets in the 1980s. When U.S. forces attacked Afghanistan in 2001, there was considerable concern that Stinger missiles, shown here being readied by Taliban soldiers near Kandahar, Afghanistan, would be used to shoot down U.S. planes and helicopters.

Moral corruption is a third peril of the weapons trade. According to some critics, it is immoral to supply weapons that are used to kill others. Whether or not you agree with that, it is hard not to give some credence to the view of one analyst that "one doesn't have to subscribe to the 'merchants of death' theory" to agree that "flooding the world with more efficient killing tools does not make it a safer place."[16]

Another troubling moral issue is based on the fact that supplying arms to an oppressive government sometimes helps it to stay in power. Although studies show that human rights factors do play a role in determining whether or not the United States will supply another country with weapons, it is also true that "a nondemocracy still has roughly a [50 percent] chance of receiving U.S. arms" (Blanton, 1998:15).

Facing one's own weapons is a fourth peril that may occur. During the 1980s, the United States supplied $2 billion worth of weapons, including sophisticated, shoulder-fired Stinger surface-to-air missiles, to the Afghan rebels seeking to oust the Soviet Union from their country. Those missiles had created havoc for Soviet helicopters and warplanes. More than a decade after the last Soviet soldier had departed, it was invading American troops that had to worry about the 100 or more Stinger missiles that intelligence sources indicated were in Taliban hands. Secretary of Defense Donald Rumsfeld worried publicly about a "nontrivial Stinger population" in Afghanistan. Certainly, U.S. pilots had to be wary. "Our air crews are still flying prudently, because there still are surface-to-air, man-portable weapons that are being fired into the air," a Pentagon spokesperson commented. "I don't know the numbers of what might be a Stinger or what might be a Russian variant of that, or what might even be just a rocket-propelled grenade. But they're shooting at [our] aircraft," he said.[17]

Hypocrisy is a fifth problem associated with the arms trade. However laudable you think your goals are, it is hard to persuade others not to do what you are doing. One effort by Washington to prevent the sale of weapons to Iran by the Czech Republic left a Czech official fuming that the Americans "are preaching that we drink water while they drink wine. I consider it hypocritical."[18]

SPECIAL OPERATIONS

Not all military action involves the use of large numbers of uniformed troops against other organized military forces in classic battle scenarios. In addition to this type of force, there are approaches to violence that fall under the heading of special operations.

Special operations include overtly or covertly sending one's own special operations forces, intelligence operatives, or paramilitary agents into another country to conduct such small-unit activites as commando operations and intelligence gathering. When these actions are aimed at an opponent1's armed forces or other military targets, then the activity falls under the general heading of special operations warfare.

The use of special operations forces and techniques as a form of military intervention has increased in recent decades for several reasons. First, there has been an increase in civil strife within countries. Second, attempts to topple governments or to create separatist states are now usually waged using guerrilla tactics, rather than the conventional tactics that were usually used in the past. More than any single reason, this change in tactics has occurred because the preponderance of high-tech weapons available to government forces makes it nearly suicidal for opposition forces to fight conventionally. Third, covert intervention avoids the avalanche of international and, often, domestic criticism that overt interventions set off. Fourth, clandestine operations allow the initiating country to disengage more easily, if it wishes, than would be possible if it overtly committed regular military forces.

Covert operations also have drawbacks. Escalating involvement can be a major problem. Interventions can begin with supplying weapons. If the arms flow does not bring victory, then the next step may be to send in advisers and special operations forces. Even if the supplier country has its doubts about wanting to commit its own armed forces, the process of intervention often causes that country's prestige to become associated with the fate of the recipient country or rebel group that is being supported. Therefore, if things continue to go badly for the recipient, then the supplier may be tempted to engage in limited combat support, and, finally, to commit to a full-scale military intervention with its own troops. This is how the United States waded ever deeper into the quagmire in Vietnam and how the Soviet Union fell into the abyss in Afghanistan.

Some observers worry that the policies followed by President George W. Bush to wage war on terrorism threaten to snare the United States into escalating commitments, much as occurred in Vietnam. For example, approximately 650 U.S. troops, including 160 members of the U.S. Special Operations Command Pacific, were sent in January 2002 to the Philippines to "advise" that country's army in the war against Abu Sayyaf, a Muslim rebel group. According to Filipino sources, the U.S. troops will be armed, will accompany Philippine units on operations, and will be able to use their weapons "in self-defense." That, according to one critic, "is another name for combat."[19]

Abu Sayyaf, which has at most 1,000 fighters, has had some links to Osama bin Laden, and a U.S. military spokesperson has characterized the group as "an international terrorist group that poses as much of a threat to the U.S. as to the Philippines." That description is disputed by some American analysts. According to one, "There is no national-security justification for American involvement. The group's ties to al-Qaeda are tangential at best.... The group operates more like criminals than terrorists."[20]

TERRORISM

When a survey taken in 1999 asked Americans to spontaneously name two or three top foreign policy concerns, terrorism was mentioned by only 12 percent of respondents. Indeed the percentage of people worried about terrorism substantially trailed the 21 percent of respondents who could not think of anything in the foreign policy realm that concerned them (Rielly, 1999).

In some ways this low level of worry about terrorism was not surprising. It is true that terrorism has become a persistent and nasty reality in global politics and that prior to 1999 there had been terrorist attacks in the United States. But the worst of those, the 168 lives lost in the 1995 bombing of the Federal Building in Oklahoma City, was perpetrated by Americans. The World Trade Center had been shaken when foreign nationals detonated a bomb in its garage in 1993, but with only 6 people killed, the incident soon faded from most people's minds. There had been other attacks on Americans, but the most sensational of these, such as the destruction of Pan Am Flight 103 over Lockerbie, Scotland, in 1988 and the bombing of the U.S. embassies in Kenya and Tanzania in 1998, had occurred overseas. This relatively carefree sense held by Americans of being safely remote from terrorism crashed on the morning of September 11, 2001, amid the rubble of the World Trade Center and the Pentagon.

The Nature and Limits of Terrorism

One of the challenges of examining terrorism is that there is no widely accepted definition. The difficulty of coming to a common understanding of what is and is not terrorism has been underlined by the inability of the United Nations in the aftermath of the 9-11 attacks to move forward with a proposed Comprehensive Convention Against Terrorism. "The simple fact is that terrorism means different things to different people," one diplomat explained. "We couldn't find common political ground on several issues—despite the fact that the entire world is preoccupied with international terrorism."[21]

Therefore it is important to establish how the word is used here. To that end, **terrorism** is defined as: (1) a form of political violence that (2) is carried out by individuals, by nongovernmental organizations, or by relatively small groups of covert government agents; that (3) specifically targets civilians; and that (4) uses clandestine attack methods, such as car bombs and hijacked airliners.

What this definition stresses is that terrorism relies exclusively on the power to hurt, that is, harming some people in order to create fear in others. Terrorists target civilians and facilities or systems (such as transportation) on which civilians rely. The objective of terrorists is not the people they kill or physical material they destroy. Instead the true target of terrorism is the emotions of those who see or read about the act of violence and become afraid.

It is important to note that not everyone would agree with this definition. The two main divisions involve whether noble ends can justify terrorist means and whether actions taken by uniformed military force can be classified as terrorism.

The ultimate goal of the terrorist who blew up himself and destroyed this blazing bus was not the deaths of the 18 Israelis he killed or wounded in Netanya, Israel, in September 2001. Instead, the object was to create publicity for the terrorist's cause and instill fear among the surviving Israelis.

Can noble ends justify terrorist means? Some critics proffer the old adage, "One man's terrorist is another man's freedom fighter," to make the point that what is terrorism to some is legitimate action to others. For instance, one barrier to agreeing on language for the UN's Comprehensive Convention Against Terrorism is the insistence of many LDCs that there be wording to indicate that an armed struggle for national liberation, against occupation, or against a racist regime should not be considered terrorism. The problem with both the adage and the LDC position is that it rests on the assumption that ends can justify means, an issue discussed in chapter 11. The view here is that noble goals cannot justify reprehensible actions, and that an attack that specifically targets noncombatants is an act of terrorism.

Can actions taken by uniformed military force can be classified as terrorism? Another possible criticism of the definition of terrorism used herein is that it generally excludes uniformed military personnel and government officials from being classified as terrorists. Critics of this view question why a civilian dissident who detonates a car bomb in a market, killing numerous noncombatants, is a terrorist and a military pilot who drops a bomb that kills numerous noncombatants near the target is not a terrorist.

There are two replies to this objection. The first is that intent is important. The terrorist intends to kill noncombatants. With rare exception, uniformed personnel attack military or hostile targets. Noncombatant casualties may occur, but they are not the object of the attack.

Second, it must be stressed that not all military actions are acceptable. When they are not, however, they are properly classified as war crimes under the principles of *jus in bello* (just conduct of war) discussed in chapter 11. When war crimes occur, the perpetrators should be and sometimes are brought to justice. The trial of Slobodan Milosevic, the former president of Yugoslavia, for numerous crimes committed during the 1990s in his official capacity serves as an example. It should be noted, though, that Milosevic is charged with genocide, forceful deportation, and a variety of other war crimes, not with terrorism.

A final note is that not all attacks categorized as terrorism by the United States fall within the definition of terrorism used here. For example, Washington condemned as terrorism the October 12, 2000, attack on the guided missile destroyer USS *Cole* while it was refueling in Aden. Yet despite the fact that it was suicide bombers operating a small boat laden with explosives that mangled the ship and killed 17 crew members, the fact that the target was a military vessel puts the act beyond the definition of terrorism used here.

Sources of Terrorism

There are two sources of political terrorism that concern us here. One is state terrorism. The second is transnational terrorism. As we shall see, they are closely linked.

State Terrorism To argue that most acts, even if horrific, committed by uniformed military tactics are not properly regarded as terrorism does not mean that countries cannot engage in terrorism. They can through **state terrorism**. This is terrorism carried out directly by an established government's clandestine operators or by others who have been specifically encouraged and funded by a country.

From the U.S. perspective, the State Department has repeatedly listed Cuba, Iran, Iraq, Libya, North Korea, Sudan, and Syria as countries guilty of state terrorism.[22] Each of these countries vehemently denies being involved in terrorism, and some of the U.S. allegations would fall outside the definition of terrorism used here. Not all acts would, though. For example, the International Court of Justice sitting in the Netherlands overturned appeals and in 2002 committed Abdel Basset al-Megrahi to prison for his role as the agent of Libya's intelligence service in the bomb destruction of Pan Am Flight 103 over Lockerbie, Scotland, in 1989 and the death of 270 people on board and on the ground.

There have been many other accusations of state terrorism, including some against the United States. "We consider the United States and its current administration as a first-class sponsor of international terrorism, and it along with Israel form an axis of terrorism and evil in the world," a group of 126 Saudi scholars wrote in a joint statement issued in April 2002.[23]

Most, but not all, such charges fall outside the definition of terrorism used here. Questions have been raised, for example, about Washington's complicity in the alleged state terrorism practiced internally by some U.S. client states, especially during the anticommunist fervor of the cold war. A secret document declassified in 1999 records the anguished views of an American diplomat in Guatemala regarding U.S. support of the Guatemalan army against Marxist guerrillas and their civilian supporters. After detailing a long list of atrocities committed by the army, the American diplomat told his superiors in the State Department that "We have condoned counter-terror... even... encouraged and blessed it.... Murder, torture, and mutilation are all right if our side is doing it and the victims are Communists."[24]

Transnational Terrorism The changes in the world that have given rise to a rapid increase in the number of international nongovernmental organizations have also expanded the number of terrorist groups that are organized and operate internationally committing **transnational terrorism**. As chapter 3 relates, the U.S. State Department's "2001 Report on Foreign Terrorist Organizations" lists 28 such groups, including al-Qaeda, and there are dozens of other such organizations that one source or another label as terrorist.[25]

Al-Qaeda is surely the most famous of these, and its origins and operations provide a glimpse into transnational terrorism. According to U.S. sources, al-Qaeda (the Base) was founded by Osama bin Laden, the son of a wealthy Saudi family, in the late 1980s to support Arabs fighting in Afghanistan against the Soviet Union. Once the Soviets were driven from Afghanistan in 1989, bin Laden's focus shifted to the United States. He was outraged by the presence of U.S. forces in Saudi Arabia near Mecca and Medina, the two holiest cities of Islam, and by American support of what he saw as Israel's oppression of Palestinian Muslims. Reflecting this view, he issued a *fatwa*, a religious call, in 1998 entitled "Jihad Against Jews and Crusaders," which proclaimed that "to kill the Americans and their allies—civilians and military—is an individual duty for every Muslim who can do it in any country in which it is possible to do it."[26]

American officials charge that prior to the attacks on the World Trade Center and the Pentagon, bin Laden and his followers masterminded a number of other terrorist attacks. Among these were the bombings in August 1998 of the U.S. embassies in Nairobi, Kenya, and Dar es Salaam, Tanzania, that killed more than 300 people and injured thousands of others.

From 1991 to 1996 bin Laden was based in Sudan. He moved the headquarters of al-Qaeda to Afghanistan in 1996 after international pressure forced the government of Sudan to expel him. Beyond the countries in which bin Laden found support, investigators have discovered links to al-Qaeda operatives, bank accounts, and activities in more than 50 countries. There is no accurate count of how many individuals al-Qaeda included, but it and other closely associated extremist groups had and probably still have several thousand members. In addition to al-Qaeda's own members, it trained many thousands of terrorists for other groups in its camps in Afghanistan and elsewhere. They derived their funding in part from bin Laden's vast personal wealth, in part from contributions from sympathizers around the world, and perhaps in part from donations from sympathetic governments. Al-Qaeda also established a sophisticated global network of bank accounts and other financial vehicles that allowed them to move money easily around the world.

The Causes and Record of Terrorism

Although the attacks of September 11, 2001, brought terrorism to the front of the international agenda, it has long existed. Understanding the causes of terrorism and its recent record are important parts of combating it.

The Causes of Terrorism Untangling the causes of terrorism is much like trying to understand why war occurs. As noted earlier in this chapter, there also appear to be many causes of terrorism that are rooted at each level of analysis. At the *system level of analysis*, it is possible to argue that such political violence is in part a product of the global unequal distribution of wealth, with a minority of countries possessing significant wealth and a majority of the world's people and countries relatively impoverished and, as a result, angry. *State-level analysis* of the 9-11 attacks might cite the policies of Israel toward the Palestinians and the general U.S. support of Israel as causal factors. On the *individual level of analysis*, one looks into the psychological drives of terrorists ranging from Osama bin Laden to the numerous suicide bombers who have blown themselves to pieces attacking Israelis in cafés, shops, and meeting rooms. Like general war, there is little agreement among analysts about the causes of terrorism along these dimensions.

It is possible, however, to explain that terrorism occurs because, like war, it is effective. To begin with, there is wide agreement among serious analysts that it is misleading to treat terrorism as the irrational acts of crazed fanatics. To the contrary, terrorism occurs because many of those who use it consider it a necessary, legitimate, and effective tool to rid themselves of what they consider oppression. It is necessary, its proponents say, because it may be the only way for an oppressed group to prevail against a heavily armed government.

The effectiveness of terrorism has been further enhanced by modern conditions. First, these have increased the power of the weapons that terrorists can use. Explosives have become more deadly, huge airliners can be made into piloted missiles, and there is an increasing danger of terrorists having access to the material and means to launch a biological, chemical, or nuclear attack.

Second, there is an ever-greater number of tempting targets for terrorists. Urbanization brings people together so that they are more easily attacked. With eerie premonition, a U.S. senator warned in March 1999 that "there is a real opportunity for a handful of zealots to wreak havoc on a scale that hitherto only armies could attain." The legislator went on to warn that targets might be "selected for their symbolic value, like the World Trade Center in the heart of Manhattan."[27] Third, modern communications have also made terrorism more efficacious because the goal of the terrorist is not to kill or injure, as such. Instead, the aim of terrorism is to gain attention for a cause and to create widespread anxiety that will, in turn, create pressure on governments to negotiate with terrorists and accede to their every demand. Without the media to transmit the news of their acts, terrorists would affect only their immediate victims, which would not accomplish the terrorists' goals.

In the end, terrorism, like most forms of violence, exists because terror tactics sometimes do accomplish their goals (Guelke, 1998; Reich, 1998). As one leading expert puts it, "Terrorism has proved a low cost, low risk, cost-effective and potentially high yield means of winning useful tactical objectives for its perpetrators, such as massive publicity, securing the release of large numbers of terrorist prisoners from jail, and the extortion of considerable sums to finance the purchase of more weapons and explosives and the launching of a wider campaign."[28]

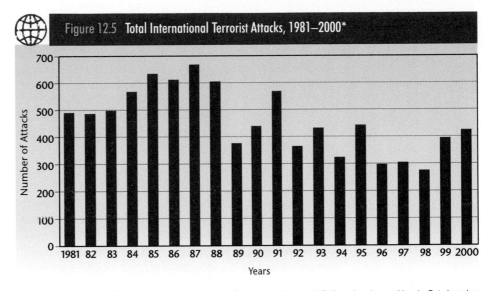

Figure 12.5 Total International Terrorist Attacks, 1981–2000*

*The data is based on the U.S. definition of terrorism, which varies somewhat from the definition otherwise used herein. Data based on other definitions would yield somewhat different results.

Data source: U.S. Department of State, Patterns of Global Terrorism-2000 on the Web at: http://www.state.gov/s/ct/rls/pgtrpt/2000/2451.htm.

Terrorism is a constant in the world. It spiked upward in the mid-1980s, then generally declined through 1998, only to rise again. What has changed is the degree to which terrorists are organized globally and their increased ability to inflict horrendous damage and suffering.

Terrorism: The Recent Record International terrorism has also become a regular occurrence (Enders & Sandler, 1999). Official U.S. data extending through 2000 indicates that the number of attacks rose from 165 in 1968 to peak at 666 in 1987. Then terrorist attacks became less frequent. The years 1996–1998, with an average of 291 attacks annually, were the least violent three-year period in more than two decades. Violence turned sharply upward in 1999 (392 terrorist incidents) and 2000 (423 attacks). Complete data for 1981 through 2000 is displayed in Figure 12.5. During the period 1994 through 2000, international terrorist attacks injured over 20,600 people worldwide, of whom over approximately 2,500 died. The data for 2001 is not yet complete, but, of course the year included the horrific terrorist attacks unleashed on September 11, which claimed more lives than all the acts of terrorism combined over the previous six years.

Geographically, international terrorism has been widespread, with all regions other than North America suffering frequent terrorist attacks. Thus Americans had been largely spared until the 9-11 attacks, with no fatalities in the United States due to international terrorism between the bombing of the World Trade Center in New York City that killed 6 people in 1993 and the attack on it and the Pentagon eight years later. Indeed, from 1995 through 2000, only 77 Americans were killed and 751 injured by international terrorism. Those relatively low numbers changed dramatically on September 11, 2001. The 2001 attack on the World Trade Center was the worst single terrorist event in history. With the attack on the Pentagon and the crash of the plane in Pennsylvania that did not reach its target, the death toll was more than 3,000 people.

Terrorist Weapons and Tactics

The explosions that tore apart the World Trade Center and Pentagon and buried their victims under tons of rubble, the mangled remains of Israeli civilians in a bomb-shattered bus, the hollow stares of hostages held as pawns in the macabre game that terrorists play—these are the images of terrorism that have too often gripped us. For all the ghastly history of terrorism using conventional weapons, future possibilities are even more disturbing. Now there is a new, more terrible threat—radiological, nuclear, biological, and chemical terrorism (Gurr & Cole, 2000; Tucker, 2000). As the U.S. National Intelligence Estimate released in 2002 described the situation, for the first time "U.S. territory is more likely to be attacked" with radiological, biological, or chemical weapons using "ships, trucks, airplanes or other means" than by weapons of mass destruction from another country using its military missiles or bombers.[29]

Conventional Weapons Terrorism With relatively few exceptions, most terrorist attacks have used bombs, guns, and other conventional weapons. Data compiled by the U.S. State Department for 2000 indicates, for example, that of 200 Americans injured by international terrorist attacks, bombing was responsible for 179 of the casualties, with firebombing, arson, gunfire, knives, and kidnapping accounting for the balance of the 21 injuries. Even the attacks on the World Trade Center and Pentagon, as horrific as they were, would fall under the category of a conventional weapons terrorist attack.

Radiological Terrorism. An initial point is that there is a difference between nuclear and radiological weapons. The extraordinary difficulty of creating a nuclear chain reaction and the security surrounding existing nuclear weapons make it unlikely (but not impossible) in the foreseeable future that terrorists could acquire or construct and detonate a mini version of a military nuclear weapon. There is a much greater possibility of terrorists being able to construct and use a so-called dirty bomb that would use conventional explosives to disperse radioactive material over a large area. A related approach would be to destroy a nuclear power plant, spewing radioactivity into the surrounding air and water. Such scenarios would result in very few immediate or near-term deaths. Rather the danger would be from increased levels of radiation causing future cancers, pregnancy complications, and other medical risks. There is also the potential for significant economic damage, since a radiological attack could render parts of a city or an important facility (such as a port) unsafe for perhaps years. Thus, as one expert characterized the impact of a dirty bomb to Congress, "The effects are not instantaneous. You have long-term potential health hazards, and you also have longer-term psychological, social, and political impacts that can go on weeks, months, maybe years."[30]

The concern over the possibility of terrorists acquiring the material to fashion a radiological weapon has grown in recent years as authorities in Europe and elsewhere have seized several small (up to 12 ounces) shipments of plutonium and several larger quantities (up to 6 pounds) of uranium-235 (Cameron, 1999). There are literally hundreds of places around the world where terrorists could obtain radioactive material. Of all possible sources, however, Russia is the most likely. That country is dismantling many of its nuclear weapons, and it needs to store tons of plutonium and uranium. Adding to that problem is Russia's desperate economic condition. There is concern that impoverished Russian military and scientific officials might be willing to sell radioactive material to terrorist groups or states. Additionally, the partial breakdown of governmental functions throughout the former Soviet republics (FSRs) creates the possibility that the material to make a radiological bomb could be stolen. Concern arose in 2002, for example, about the security and even location of some, perhaps many, of the hundreds of small radiothermal power generators (RTGs) that the Soviets had placed in remote areas to power communications systems and other devices. Each contains cesium or strontium with the radioactive equivalent of more than an ounce of plutonium. These RTGs "would be easy targets for a terrorist attack," a Russian commission reported. "The consequences," it added with considerable understatement, "could be extremely serious."[31]

Chemical and Biological Terrorism The existing possibility of chemical or biological attack came into sharp focus after the 9-11 attacks. There was alarm when it was learned that one of the suicide hijackers, Mohammad Atta, had made repeated trips to rural airports to learn about crop dusters. Anxiety was further heightened by the spread of anthrax through the U.S. mail to postal facilities, news organizations, and congressional offices. The resulting atmosphere spawned a spate of doomsday images of chemical and biological attacks that would leave millions dead. Most experts consider such scenarios overdrawn, and it is important to have a balanced understanding of the possibilities of chemical or biological attack and the impact of such attacks.

Causes for Concern. There surely are worrisome realities. The tons of chemical weapons and agents seized from Iraq after the Persian Gulf War bear testimony to the amount of such weapons in the world and the proliferation of the ability to produce them. The possibilities of a terrorist chemical attack became a reality in 1995 when a Japanese cult, Aum Shinrikyo (Supreme Truth), used nerve gas in an attack on a Tokyo subway station that killed 12 people and injured 5,000.

Biological weapons are also a threat. A truly scary report by the U.S. Office of Technology Assessment (OTA) worries about the possibility of terrorists spreading plague, botulism, or anthrax. The OTA anticipates that on a calm night, a light plane flying over Washington, D.C., and releasing just 220 pounds of anthrax spores using a common crop sprayer could deliver a fatal dose to 3 million people.[32]

The lack of adequate preparations for a chemical or biological attack reasonably adds to concerns. An exercise dubbed Dark Winter was conducted in June 2001 and simulated a biological attack using smallpox virus. The gloomy finding, said one evaluator, was that the government "was not capable of dealing with an incident." The exercise estimated that two weeks after the initial simulated attack more than 1,000 people would have died and another 15,000 people would have become infected (of which between 1,500 and 6,000 would later die, depending on the strain of virus).

Calls for Calm. As unnerving as the possibilities of chemical and biological attack are and as unprepared as society has been to meet them, the threat also has to be kept in perspective. Providing that perspective, one scientist testifying before Congress detailed the significant difficulties of amassing enough of a chemical or biological agent to cause widespread death and injury and told legislators, "When one retreats from the hyperbole and examines the intricacies involved in executing a mass casualty attack with [biological or chemical] agents, one is confronted with technical obstacles so high that even terrorists that have had a wealth of time, money, and technical skill, as well as a determination to acquire and use these weapons [would have difficulty doing so]."[33]

While it is impossible to rule out a biological or chemical attack that takes tens-of-thousands of lives, it is probably more realistic to see the likelihood of such an attack as remote. Given the problems of manufacturing and delivering substantial quantities of biological and chemical weapons, the greatest possibility of a massive attack would be the result of state terrorism, with a murderous government either launching a direct attack or supplying a transnational terrorist organization with the means to do so. The possibility of such an organization acting independently is much more limited. On balance then, the impact of a chemical or biological terrorist attack is most likely to be similar to a radiological attack. The psychological impact will far outweigh the actual casualties. This is what occurred during the anthrax incidents in the United States in late 2001, which caused only five deaths and about a dozen other infections, but which virtually closed down Congress for a time and frightened millions.

It is also the case that the United States and other countries have begun to take the threat of terrorism much more seriously, and the increased vigilance and improved security measures will make it harder for terrorists to strike. Domestically, the United States has created the Office of Homeland Security, the FBI is devoting at least 25 percent of its agents to counterterrorism, armed air marshals are on most flights, and numerous other actions are being taken. Internationally, there has been a massive effort to track down and destroy the international financial networks of al-Qaeda and other terrorist organizations, and the CIA and other national intelligence agencies in the United States and other countries are devoting even more of their considerable technological and human intelligence assets to monitor, intervene, and disrupt terrorist groups.

Conventional Warfare

The most overt form of coercive intervention is for a country to dispatch its own forces to another country. That intervention can range from such limited demonstrations of power as the numerous U.S. aerial and cruise attacks on Iraq since 1991 to the global warfare seen during World War I and World War II. With the exceptions of the U.S. atomic attacks on Hiroshima and Nagasaki in 1945 and some use of chemical weapons, wars have been waged using conventional weapons.

The **conventional warfare** that has been the norm throughout most of history is distinguished from other types of warfare by the tactics and weapons used. The overt use of uniformed military personnel, usually in large numbers, is what separates conventional tactics from special operations and terrorism. As for weapons, it is easier to indicate what conventional weapons are not than what they are. Generally, conventional weapons are those that rely on explosives or impact but are not nuclear/radiological, biological, or chemical weapons.

GOALS AND CONDUCT

The classic statement on the proper goal of war was made by German strategist Carl von Clausewitz in *On War* (1833). He argued that "war is not merely a political act, but also a political instrument, a continuation of political relations, a carrying out of the same by other means." Note that Clausewitz's point implies three principles that civilian and military decision makers should keep in mind.

War is a part of diplomacy, not a substitute for it, is the first principle. Therefore, channels of communication to the opponent should be kept open in an attempt to limit the conflict and to reestablish peace.

Wars should be governed by political, not military, considerations, is the second principle. Often commanders chafe under restrictions, as General Douglas MacArthur did during the Korean War (1950–1953) over his lack of authority to attack China. When generals become insubordinate, as MacArthur did, they ought to be removed from command, as he was.

War should be fought with clear political goals, is the third principle that Clausewitz advocated. When goals are not established or are later ignored, disaster looms. The stated U.S. goal at the beginning of the Korean War in 1950 was to drive North Korea's forces out of South Korea. That was soon accomplished, but instead of declaring victory, an emboldened President Truman ordered U.S. forces to move northward to "liberate" North Korea from communism. That brought China into the war. As a result, a war that arguably had already been won dragged on in stalemate for two more years and cost tens of thousands more lives. For all the later criticism of George H. W. Bush for not driving on to Baghdad and unseating Saddam Hussein, the U.S. president should get credit for not repeating Truman's mistake. The stated UN goal in 1991 was to liberate Kuwait. When that was accomplished, Bush halted hostilities. In so doing, he ended the killing and stayed within the legal confines of the UN resolution that authorized the action.

The fact that most wars are fought within limits does not mean that those boundaries are never violated. **Escalation** occurs when the rules are changed and the level of combat increases. Increasing the scope and intensity of a war, however, has always been dangerous, and it is particularly so in an era of nuclear, biological, and chemical (NBC) weapons. Not long after their entry into the war in Vietnam in the mid-1970s, Americans began to realize that continuing the war within the limits it was being fought offered little chance of victory and carried a heavy cost in lives and economics. Escalating the war by invading North Vietnam might have brought China into the war and increased the cost monumentally. Also, many Americans were sickened by the human cost to both sides; if the war had been continued or escalated, there would have surely been an increase of deep divisions within the United States. Ultimately, the United States could have achieved a military victory by "nuking" North Vietnam and killing everyone there. Americans finally accepted, though, that victory was not the only thing. American troops began to withdraw from Vietnam in 1969; all U.S. troops were gone by 1973; Vietnam was reunited under Hanoi's control in 1975.

AVOIDING UNCHECKED ESCALATION

The dangers of escalation and the prudence of keeping limited wars limited make it important to understand how to avoid unchecked escalation. As with most things political, there is no set formula. There are, however, a few useful standards.

Keep lines of communication open. The basic principle is that escalation (or de-escalation) should be a deliberate strategy used to signal a political message to the enemy. Accordingly, it is also important to send signals through diplomatic or public channels so that the opponent will not mistake the escalation as an angry spasm of violence or misconstrue the de-escalation as a weakening of resolve.

Limit goals. Unlimited goals by one side may evoke unlimited resistance by the other, so limiting goals is another way to avoid unchecked escalation. It is usually appropriate, for instance, that a goal should fall short of eliminating the opponent as a sovereign state! Even where unconditional victory is the aim, obliteration of the enemy population is not an appropriate goal.

Restrict geographical scope. It is often wise to limit conflict to as narrow a geographical area as possible. American forces refrained from invading China during the Korean War. Similarly, the Soviets passed up the temptation to blockade Berlin in 1962 in response to the U.S. blockade of Cuba.

Observe target restrictions. Regional wars can be controlled by limiting targets. Despite their close proximity, the Arabs and Israelis have never tried to bomb each other's capitals. Iraq's launch of Scud missiles against Tel Aviv and other Israeli cities in 1991 was, by contrast, a serious escalation.

Limit weapons. Yet another way to keep war limited is to adhere to the principle that the level of force used should be no greater than the minimum necessary to accomplish war aims. The stricture on weapons has become even more important in an era when there is such a great potential for the use of limited, on-the-battlefield

NBC weapons. In addition to moral issues, even the limited use of NBC weapons might well set off a serious escalation that could lead to strategic nuclear war or massive biological and chemical attacks.

Weapons of Mass Destruction Warfare

The world's history of waging war primarily with conventional weapons does not guarantee a continuation of that restraint. Science and technology have rapidly increased the ability of countries to build, deploy, and potentially employ **weapons of mass destruction**. These nuclear, biological, and chemical weapons in the amounts and potencies that are available to national militaries can cause horrific levels of death and injury to enemy forces or civilian targets. In the pages that follow, we will deal briefly with biological and chemical weapons, then turn to a more extensive examination of nuclear weapons and strategy.

BIOLOGICAL WEAPONS

Many historians trace the use of biological warfare to 1763 when, during an Indian uprising, the British commander in North America, Sir Jeffrey Amherst, wrote to subordinates at Fort Pitt, "Could it not be contrived to send the smallpox among those disaffected tribes of Indians?"[34] As it turns out, Sir Jeffrey's prompting was unnecessary. Soldiers at the fort had already given disease-infected blankets to members of the Shawnee and Delaware tribes.

Although the 1972 Biological Weapons Convention bans their production, possession, and use, germ-based *biological weapons* continue to be a threat. For example, Russia's deputy foreign minister admitted in 1992 that "the Soviet Union was violating [the BW] convention and was running a program in the sphere of offensive biological research and development" from 1946 until 1992 and had amassed 20 tons of smallpox.[35] The UN-led inspections of Iraq since the Persian Gulf War indicate that the country also had a germ warfare program that had, at minimum, produced 132,000 gallons of anthrax and botulism toxins. According to one expert, "it's far more likely than not" that, in addition to Russia, such countries as Iran, Iraq, and North Korea also have biological weapons.[36]

CHEMICAL WEAPONS

Of the three components of NBC warfare, chemical weapons are the most prevalent because they are relatively easy and inexpensive to produce. Indeed, they have earned the sobriquet of "the poor man's atomic bomb." As CIA director John M. Deutch told Congress, "Chemicals used to make nerve agents are also used to make plastics and [to] process foodstuff. Any modern pharmaceutical facility can produce biological warfare agents as easily as vaccines or antibiotics."[37]

Most ominously of all, chemical weapons have been used recently. Both Iran and Iraq used them during their grueling war (1980–1988), and Iraq used them to attack rebellious Kurds in its northern provinces. The UN inspections in Iraq after the Persian Gulf War also discovered huge stores of chemical weapons, including over 105,000 gallons of mustard gas; 21,936 gallons of tabun, sarin, and other nerve gases; and over 453,000 gallons of other chemicals associated with weapons. Some of this supply was contained in munitions, such as 12,786 artillery shells filled with mustard gas and 18 warheads or bombs filled with nerve agents. There is no evidence that any chemical weapons were used during the war, but traces of mustard gas and sarin were detected on the battlefield. These may have been released inadvertently when the allied attacks destroyed Iraqi weapons depots, and some analysts

The good news is that this October 2001 picture of rescue workers shows only a drill, as they practice their responses during an "antinuclear, biological, and chemical" weapons training exercise in Osaka, Japan. The bad news is that terrorists may have increasing access to such weapons and that photographs like this could one day be "for real."

suspect that exposure to these chemicals may be the cause of Gulf War Syndrome, which has afflicted many veterans of the war.

THE POTENTIAL FOR NUCLEAR WAR

The Bible's Book of Revelation speaks of an apocalyptic end to the world: A "hail of fire mixed with blood fell upon the earth; and… the earth was burnt up…. The sea became blood… and from the shaft rose smoke like the smoke of a great furnace and the sun and the air were darkened." Revelation laments, "Woe, woe, woe to those who dwell on earth," for many will die a fiery death, and the survivors "will seek death and will not find it; they will long to die, and death will fly from them." Whatever your religious beliefs, such a prophecy is sobering. We now have the capability to sound "the blast of the trumpets" that will kill the living and make those who remain wish to die.

Nuclear Weapons States

The world joined in a collective sigh of relief when the Soviet Union collapsed and the cold war between the two great nuclear powers ended. Almost overnight, worry about the threat of nuclear war virtually disappeared from the media and general political discussion. Unfortunately, the perception of significantly greater safety is illusory. It is certainly true that the number of strategic nuclear weapons has declined since the end of the cold war. Nevertheless, there remains a huge number of extremely powerful nuclear weapons.

As the next chapter discusses, the number of nuclear weapons in the world has decreased significantly. Moreover,

Did You Know That:
There were 18 Japanese who survived both the atomic attack on Hiroshima and (three days later) the atomic blast in Nagasaki, where they and others had sought safety after the first mushroom cloud.

whether the decrease in the number of nuclear weapons means that the chances of nuclear war have also lessened is very debatable. The United States and Russia remain the nuclear Goliaths. In mid-2002, the U.S. deployed strategic (intercontinental-range) arsenal included 6,480 nuclear warheads and bombs and 1,097 missiles and bombers to carry them to destinations anywhere in the world. Russia's deployed strategic inventory was approximately 5,600 weapons and 1,100 delivery vehicles. Each country also has thousands of nuclear devices in storage. Additionally, the United States has 1,600 deployed tactical (shorter-range, battlefield) nuclear weapons, and Russia has some 3,600.

China, France, Great Britain, India, and Pakistan all openly have nuclear weapons, and Israel and (perhaps) North Korea have undeclared nuclear weapons, adding another 1,300 or so nuclear devices to the volatile mix of over 19,000 deployed tactical and strategic nuclear devices. There are another 10,000 or so such weapons in U.S. and Russian reserve inventories. The largest of the warheads has an explosive power equal to 50 times that of the bombs dropped on Japan in 1945. Additionally, several countries have or are suspected of having nuclear weapons development programs, and another 30 countries have the technology base needed to build nuclear weapons.

Given this reality, it would be unwise to discount the continuing impact of nuclear weapons on world politics. One role that nuclear weapons play is to be a part of the "backdrop" of power and influence. There can be little doubt that the continuing importance of Russia, despite its tremendous travails, rests in part on its still immense nuclear arsenal. Deterrence is a second role played by nuclear weapons. Whether or not nuclear weapons will always deter conventional or nuclear attack is uncertain, but they have at least sometimes been and remain a restraining factor that deters an opponent from attacking in the first place or that limits an opponent's weapons or tactics. It is not unreasonable to conjecture, for instance, that the nuclear option that the United States, France, and Great Britain all had in the Persian Gulf War may have helped deter Saddam Hussein from using his chemical weapons. Actual use is a third role for nuclear weapons. The atomic attacks on Hiroshima and Nagasaki demonstrate that humans have the ability and the will to use weapons of mass destruction. Therefore, it is naive to imagine that nuclear war cannot happen. To the contrary, there are several ways that a nuclear war could break out.

The United States and Russia still have by far the largest arsenal of nuclear weapons and strategic-range missiles. But China's inventory is growing, as symbolized in this photo of a People's Liberation Army soldier contemplating a display of Chinese missiles in Beijing. The end of the cold war may have eased the threat of nuclear war, but it did not eliminate it.

How a Nuclear War Might Start

For all its potential horror, nuclear war is within the realm of possibility. Strategic analysts envision many possible scenarios.

Irrational leader. A leader who is fanatical, deranged, drunk, or otherwise out of control is one possible cause of nuclear war. What if Adolf Hitler had had the bomb? Were Russia's weapons safe under the control of the country's hard-drinking president, Boris Yeltsin? According to reports, worried Russian generals told the Duma in secret that they were unsure of what could be expected of their often drunken president during a crisis.[38] It is also possible that a berserk military officer might try to use nuclear weapons, although there are numerous safety devices such as the "dual key" system and electronic "permissive action links" designed to limit such a possibility.

Calculated attack. A "bolt out of the blue" nuclear attack could also happen. This might occur if one country felt that it could deliver a first strike that would disable all or most of its opponent's strategic forces. Such an attack could come if a country believed that, combined with defensive measures, the strike would result in a victory with "acceptable losses." An unprovoked nuclear attack could also come as a result of a nuclear country attacking a nonnuclear country, especially if that country used chemical or biological weapons against the nuclear country.

Last gasp. Nuclear war could come as a final attempt to fend off conventional defeat. One scenario with real possibilities is to imagine a beleaguered Israel, its vaunted conventional forces finally overwhelmed by numerically superior Arab invaders, launching a last-gasp strike against Egyptian, Jordanian, and Syrian armies pounding the last Israeli defensive positions in Jerusalem near the Wailing Wall on Temple Mount, the holiest place of the Jewish people.

Inadvertent nuclear war. Of the various triggers of a nuclear war, misperception is one of the two most likely causes. The limits of rationality in decision making mean that those who command nuclear weapons can make mistakes. False intelligence that a nuclear attack is imminent or even under way, for example, might cause a leader to inadvertently strike first.

In 1995, for example, Russian radar detected what appeared to be an incoming missile fired over the Norwegian Sea. Russian forces prepared to launch a retaliatory strike on the United States. Only at the last moment was it determined that the radar blip was an outgoing Norwegian scientific rocket, not an incoming U.S. D-5 missile. "For a while," said a Russian defense official, "the world was on the brink of nuclear war."[39] This was neither the first nor last such close call.

The time for American and Russian leaders to make decisions in a nuclear crisis is short enough, at most 30 minutes given the flight time of a nuclear missile between the two countries. Leaders of countries close to one another, like Pakistan and India, would have much, much less time to respond. This will decrease the time to confirm reports that a nuclear attack has been launched or is about to be launched. It will also vastly increase the chances of erroneously launching what a leader sees as a counterstrike, but what, in fact, is a first strike.

Escalation. A deadly spiral is a final, not unlikely, single path to nuclear war. History has demonstrated that leaders are willing to risk nuclear war even when there is no immediate and critical threat to national security. Perhaps the closest the world has ever come to nuclear war was during the 1962 Cuban missile crisis, when the Soviets risked nuclear war by placing missiles with nuclear warheads in Cuba, and the United States risked nuclear war by threatening to invade Cuba and attack the Russian forces guarding the missiles unless Moscow withdrew them.

This roiling red nuclear cloud captures a hint of the menace inherent in nuclear weapons. Notice the height of the mushroom cloud in this photograph, which was taken sometime in the 1950s. It is more than one mile high, as you can tell from the size of the surrounding islets below that form Bikini Atoll, where the blast took place. For an interactive look at the implications of a nuclear attack in your area, go to the Web URL: http://www.pbs.org/wgbh/amex/bomb/sfeature/mapablast.html.

NUCLEAR WEAPONS, DETERRENCE, AND STRATEGY

The reality that nuclear weapons exist and could be used make it important that we briefly examine strategic nuclear weapons and strategy. There are issues of what a country's nuclear arsenal and doctrines should be that seldom enter the public debate, but that are crucial to an effective and stable arsenal. Furthermore, the post–cold war changes have brought on new challenges in strategic planning. As one expert has noted, within the declared nuclear weapons countries, it "is clear that there is a great debate… over who is the enemy and what is the target."[40] Within the debate, the two main issues are (1) how to minimize the chance of nuclear war and (2) how to maximize the chance of survival if a nuclear exchange does occur. It is not possible here to review all the factors that impinge on these issues, but we can illustrate the various concerns by examining deterrence and then several specific issues about weapons systems and strategy.

Weapons

One way to divide up a discussion of nuclear weapons is to distinguish between delivery vehicles and explosive devices. It is also important to differentiate between long-range strategic nuclear weapons and shorter-range tactical nuclear weapons. Strategic range is defined by treaty as more than 5,500 kilometers (3,416.8 miles).

Strategic delivery vehicles. The United States and the Soviet Union, now Russia, have both long relied on a triad of delivery vehicles. These include (1) submarine-launched ballistic missiles (SLBMs) carried aboard ballistic missile nuclear submarines (SSBNs), (2) land-based intercontinental ballistic missiles (ICBMs), and (3) bombers. Most ICBMs are located in silos, Russia's road-mobile SS-25 being the exception. The number of warheads that any given model of ICBM or SLBM carries ranges from one to ten. Multi-warhead missiles have multiple independent reentry vehicle (MIRV) capability, meaning that each warhead will attack a different target. Bombers can deliver explosive devices either by gravity bomb, air-launched cruise missile, or short-range missiles.

Tactical delivery vehicles. These can also be launched from the air, land, and sea. There are a number of warplanes, such as the U.S. F-16s, in the arsenals of various countries that are "nuclear-weapons capable." Also, numerous countries have tactical-range missiles capable of delivering nuclear warheads. India and Pakistan, for example, both have missiles that can reach one another's capitals. The United States, Russia, and Israel have sea-launched cruise missile capability. The United States and Russia once had a range of battlefield nuclear weapons, including nuclear land mines, but these are no longer deployed by either.

Strategic and tactical explosive devices. There is a wide array of nuclear weapons, as discussed in part in the box Mini- and Maxi-Nukes. The largest single explosive currently deployed is mounted on Russian SS-18 ICBMs, each of which carries 10 MIRV 750 kiloton warheads. The United States's largest entry weapons are 475 kiloton MIRV warheads, eight of which are carried on D-5 SLBMs. The explosive power of tactical weapons can be as low as the 0.3 kiloton yield of a U.S. B-61 bomb.

Deterrence

The concept of deterrence has been and remains at the center of the strategy of all the nuclear powers. **Deterrence** is persuading an enemy that attacking you will not be worth any potential gain. Deterrence is based on two factors: capability and credibility.

Capability. Effective deterrence requires that you be able to respond to an attack or impending attack on your forces. This capability is what India claimed it was seeking when it openly tested nuclear weapons in 1998. "Our problem is China,"

MINI- AND MAXI-NUKES

The smallest nuclear weapon ever deployed was the W54 warhead. It was fired from an antiarmor weapon, the Davy Crockett recoilless rifle, had a range of about 2.5 miles, and was deployed with U.S. forces from 1964 to 1989. The W54 warhead weighed only 51 pounds, and it had an explosive power of 0.01 kilotons (10 tons of TNT), approximately three times as powerful as the ammonium nitrate bomb that destroyed the Federal Building in Oklahoma City on April 19, 1995.

The USSR produced the largest nuclear weapon ever. Nicknamed the Tsar Bomb, it was built in the early 1960s. The explosive power of this maxi-nuke was 100 megatons (100 million tons of TNT), making it some 6,500 times more powerful than the atomic bomb dropped on Hiroshima in 1945 and 10 million times more powerful than the W54 mini-nuke.

said an Indian official. "We are not seeking [nuclear] parity with China.... What we are seeking is a minimum deterrent."[41] Just having weapons, however, is not enough. Since there is no way to defend against a missile attack once it is launched, deterrence requires that you have enough weapons that are relatively invulnerable to enemy destruction so that you can be assured that some will survive for a counter-attack. Of all the strategic delivery systems, SLBMs are the least vulnerable; ICBMs in silos are the most vulnerable.

Credibility. It is also necessary for other states to believe that you will actually use your weapons. Perception is a key factor. The operational reality will be determined by what the other side believes rather than by what you intend. We will see, for example, that some analysts believe that relying on a second-strike capability may not always be credible.

This two-part equation for deterrence sounds simple enough on the surface, but the question is how to achieve it. The debate can be roughly divided into two schools of nuclear strategy. They are characterized by the bizarrely colorful acronyms of **MAD (Mutual Assured Destruction)** and **NUT (Nuclear Utilization Theory)**.

Those who favor the mutual assured destruction strategy (the MADs) believe that deterrence is best achieved if each nuclear power's capabilities include (1) a sufficient number of weapons that are (2) capable of surviving a nuclear attack by an opponent and then (3) delivering a second-strike retaliatory attack that will destroy that opponent. MADs believe, in other words, in *deterrence through punishment*. If each nuclear power has these three capabilities, then a mutual checkmate is achieved. The result, MAD theory holds, is that no power will start a nuclear war because doing so will lead to its own destruction (even if it destroys its enemy).

Those who favor nuclear utilization theory (the NUTs) contend that the MAD strategy is a mad gamble because it relies on rationality and clear-sightedness when, in reality, there are other scenarios (discussed earlier in the section "How a Nuclear War Might Start") that could lead to nuclear war. Therefore, NUTs prefer to base deterrence partly on *deterrence through damage denial* (or limitation), in contrast to the punishment strategy of MADs. This means that NUTs want to be able to destroy enemy weapons before the weapons explode on one's own territory and forces. One way to do this is to destroy the weapons before they are launched.

Nuclear Strategy

The rapid reconfiguration of the political world and nuclear weapons inventories has muted the MAD-NUT debate, but there are still echoes in current weapons and strategy issues. To illustrate these issues, we can examine two weapons systems: first-strike weapons and missile-defense systems.

(Continued on page 366)

PRESIDENT BUSH AND NUT STRATEGY

Beginning in the 1950s, the Peter Paul Candy Company ran a well-known advertising jingle that started, "Sometimes you feel like a nut, sometimes you don't," to feature its Almond Joy candy bar, which had nuts, and its Mounds candy bar, which did not. That jingle might well have been applied to the choice American voters had in 2000 between the nuclear policy views of George Bush and Al Gore. Bush distinctly leans toward the NUT (nuclear utilization theory) approach to nuclear weapons and strategy. In line with the policies of the Clinton White House, Gore does not and would be better classified as MAD (mutual assured destruction) in his view.

During most of the nuclear era, U.S. strategy has generally, but not exclusively, conformed to MAD doctrine. President Ronald Reagan shifted strategy somewhat toward a NUT orientation when in 1981 he signed National Security Decision Directive 13 (NSDD), which ordered a shift in nuclear planning away from emphasizing deterrence toward one that also included a strategy to prevail in a nuclear war that might last up to six months. Of all Reagan's policies, none reflects his NUT orientation better than his advocacy of the Strategic Defense Initiative (SDI), a plan to build a comprehensive defense against a ballistic missile attack.

Reagan's SDI goal proved unreachable. American nuclear strategy has been a mix of MAD and NUT strategies and weapons since then. Now, President George W. Bush has shifted the U.S. nuclear posture several degrees further toward the NUT end of the MAD-NUT continuum.

One step that the Bush administration has taken is to devote $10 million to attempting to modify current warheads so that they can penetrate deep into the ground to attack underground targets. These so-called burrowing nukes would, among other things, be especially effective at rooting out such targets as the bunkers developed by Iraq's leadership. The problem with such a program from the MAD point of view is, in the words of one U.S. senator, that it broadcasts a "signal to the world that there is a new and broader range of contingencies in which the United States would consider using nuclear weapons."[1]

The distinct inclination of President Bush toward nuclear utilization theory has also been evident in his directives to the Pentagon to further increase the targeting of Iran, Iraq, North Korea, and other "rogue states." From the MAD perspective, according to one analyst, the targeting change instituted in 2002 "confirms that the Bush administration is seeking to increase, not decrease, the role of nuclear weapons in U.S. foreign and military policy."[2]

President Bush's most important decision to move toward a NUT orientation has been his strong support of building a ballistic missile defense (BMD) system, or National Missile Defense (NMD) system, as it is currently termed. It is perhaps the most significant defense initiative Bush has taken, but building a BMD system is also very controversial. There are three elements to the debate: cost, technical feasibility, and whether a BMD system would enhance or detract from national (and global) national security. NUTs argue it will; MADs are certain it will worsen the situation.

Cost. Predicting the cost of any future weapons system, especially one as monumentally complex as a BMD system, is very difficult. Given the fact that the Bush administration is already spending about $8 billion a year on research and development, it is reasonably conservative to estimate that the final cost of deploying a system could top $100 billion, and there are estimates far beyond that. Is cost important? Arguably not. Certainly $100 billion sounds like a staggering amount. It is also, however, only a bit more than the $91 billion Americans spent in 2000 on alcoholic beverages or the $86 billion they spent purchasing carcinogenic tobacco products to smoke or chew. Thus, if the $100 billion could, indeed, buy safety, it is hard to argue that it would not be worth the country giving up drinking or smoking for one year to pay for it.

Technical feasibility. A more cogent question centers on whether the system can work. What can be agreed upon is that the technical hurdles are formidable. Shooting down an incoming warhead traveling 15,000 miles per hour, hundreds of miles above the Earth, is often said to be like "shooting a bullet with a bullet." The answer to whether it is possible to do that with high reliability depends on who is doing the evaluating.

The NMD program evolves a number of subprograms aimed at various types of missile threats. Of these, the most expensive, complex, and important is the effort to destroy attacking warheads in midflight. The warheads would be destroyed by an "exoatmospheric kill vehicle" (EKV), a 55-inch-long, 120-pound canister full of sensors, explosives, and rocket thrusters initially launched by a U.S. missile. Testing of the EKV since 1999 has yielded mixed results. Some EKVs have intercepted their targets; others have not. After a successful test in March 2002, a Defense Department official boasted, "I think what we can say is that our test program is proceeding and showing some quite impressive success."[3] Critics disagree. They charge that the tests are done under ideal conditions, not realistic scenarios, and that a significant number of test failures under these optimal conditions

The most important consideration regarding building a national missile defense (NMD) system is whether it will create greater safety or will destabilize deterrence. This photograph of the vapor trail of an outgoing missile carrying a test antimissile weapon over Victorville, California, forms something of a question mark in the sky. Implicit in that ? is the uncertainty of the wisdom of building an NMD system.

underscores the unreliability of the BMD system, even under conditions meant to maximize the possibility of success. Not atypically after one failure, one detractor commented, "You have to consider this a very serious setback for missile defense programs, because it shows that even the simple stuff is difficult."[4]

Impact on National Security. The most important debate about the proposed NMD system is whether it will improve or harm national security. President Bush and many others believe it will enhance safety. In a major policy address in May 2001, Bush pointed to programs of North Korea and other "rogue states" to build weapons of mass destruction and the missiles to deliver them. Using language very much in line with NUT doctrine, Bush told his audience, "We need new concepts of deterrence that rely on both offensive and defensive forces. Deterrence can no longer be based solely on the threat of nuclear retaliation.... [We need] effective missile defenses that can protect the United States, our deployed forces, our friends and our allies."[5] The president also called for the abrogation of the Anti-Ballistic Missile Treaty of 1972, arguing that

it "enshrines the past. No treaty that prevents us from addressing today's threats, that prohibits us from pursuing promising technology to defend ourselves... is in our interests or in the interests of world peace." Seven months later, Bush formally notified Russia that the United States was withdrawing from the treaty.

There are many analysts who condemn these actions. Critics charge that canceling the ABM Treaty and deploying the NMDs would harm national security by putting all other arms reduction treaties in jeopardy and setting off an arms race. Particularly worrisome for other countries would be a scenario in which the United States launched a first strike to destroy much of the other country's retaliatory system, then was able to use the NMD system to neutralize the country's much-diminished retaliatory strike. With "mutual," "assured," and "destruction" all undermined, countries may well dramatically increase the number of missiles and warheads they have in order to have enough to overwhelm U.S. defense. Other countries will also be pressed, according to one U.S. expert, "to keep large numbers of ICBMs on hairtrigger alert."[6]

Commentary from officials in Russia, China, and elsewhere confirm this concern. Russia's foreign minister has taken this view, pointing out that "the prevailing system of arms control agreements is a complex and quite fragile structure." Therefore, he has argued, "Once one of its key elements has been weakened, the entire system is destabilized. The collapse of the ABM Treaty would, therefore, undermine the entirety of disarmament agreements concluded over the last 30 years."[7] On behalf of China, its director general for arms control has commented that the NMD system would destroy the "balance of terror" that has arguably deterred nuclear war for decades. "We will not sit on our hands," he told U.S. diplomats. Instead, he said, "To defeat your defenses we'll have to spend a lot of money, and we don't want to do this. But otherwise, the United States will feel it can attack anyone at any time, and that isn't tolerable. We hope you'll give this up. If not, we'll be ready."[8]

It is tempting, but unwise, to easily write off these views of past and potential U.S. enemies. There is a curious logic to nuclear weapons strategy that argues that the best defense is no defense. MADs believe that to be true, and they argue that the assurance of destruction in a nuclear war has kept everyone from starting one. Bush and other NUTs doubt that logic ever worked, and, even if it did, are sure that the proliferation of weapons of mass destruction has created a new reality that requires a ballistic missile defense system. It is a debate of literally earth-shattering potential.

First Use One long-standing debate is when, if ever, to be the first to use nuclear weapons, especially to escalate from nonnuclear to nuclear warfare. The NATO alliance long held that it might launch a nuclear strike to destroy oncoming, overwhelming Soviet ground forces. More recently, President G. H. W. Bush reportedly warned Saddam Hussein that if Iraq used biological or chemical weapons in the impending Persian Gulf War, Iraq faced U.S. nuclear retaliation. Similarly, President Clinton issued Presidential Decision Direction 60 (PDD-60) that anticipates the possible use of nuclear weapons in the face of biological or chemical attack. If some nation were to attack the United States with chemical weapons, the secretary of defense said, "we could make a devastating response without the use of nuclear weapons, but we would not forswear the possibility."[42] This first-strike option was furthered in 2002, as related in the box, President Bush and NUT Strategy.

MAD advocates are very leery of first-use, warning that using nuclear weapons against a nuclear power could lead to uncontrolled escalation. Their worry is that using nuclear weapons against a nonnuclear power could undermine the norm against nuclear warfare and make it easier in the future for other nuclear powers to use their weapons against still other nonnuclear powers (Tannenwald, 1999). NUT advocates argue that, just like nuclear weapons, biological and chemical weapons are weapons of mass destruction and, therefore, deterring their use along with nuclear weapons is valid.

First-Strike Weapons Another controversy centers on first-strike weapons. These are warheads and delivery systems designed to destroy an enemy's "hardened" targets such as missile silos and command centers, thereby making it impossible for an opponent to attack or counterattack. Weapons with first-strike potential include some very powerful ICBMs and SLBMs. One such weapon is the D-5 missile, which is carried on Ohio-class U.S. nuclear ballistic missile submarines (SSBNs). Each such SSBN carries 24 D-5 missiles, each of which contains 8 warheads, with an explosive power of 475 kilotons apiece. This means that each such submarine can fire nuclear warheads with a combined explosive power equal to some 6,080 of the 15-kiloton-yield atomic bombs dropped on Japan. There is no need to have such powerful warheads to erase cities and other "soft" targets. Instead, such huge warheads are most valuable for "hard-target kill" capability that is most advantageous during a first strike.

NUTs favor first-strike weapons as part of a damage-denial strategy. They believe that one path to safety is to be able to destroy enemy missiles, bombers, and leadership capabilities before an attack occurs. MADs disagree. They claim that first-strike weapons dangerously undermine mutual assured destruction by threatening to destroy an opponent's retaliatory system, thereby creating instability. MADs oppose such weapons on two grounds: they create a temptation to strike first and they also create instability by making the ability of other nuclear powers to launch a counterattack less than assured.

Missile Defense Systems Another long-standing controversy in the area of nuclear planning is whether or not to build a ballistic missile defense (BMD) system. There were some thoughts of mounting such an effort in the 1960s, but high costs and technical unfeasibility led the United States and the Soviet Union to sign the Anti-Ballistic Missile (ABM) Treaty in 1972, largely banning the testing and development of such a system. Ronald Reagan renewed the controversy when he proposed building the Strategic Defense Initiative (SDI), also labeled "Star Wars" by its critics. Reagan's vision of a comprehensive shield from missile attack was abandoned as too expensive and technically infeasible.

Advances in technology and concern about future possible nuclear attacks by "rogue states" such as North Korea once raised the issue of building a BMD system in the late 1990s. President Clinton was ambivalent, and while he devoted funds to research, the program moved slowly. Among other impediments was that testing would violate the Anti-Ballistic Missile (ABM) Treaty that Washington and Moscow had signed in 1972. That effort has been greatly speeded up by his successor, President Bush, who is a firm advocate of a BMD system. Whether or not a BMD system can or should be deployed remains controversial, however, and that debate is related in the box, President Bush and NUT Strategy.

As the box indicates, NUTs favor building a BMD system because it fits in with the damage-denial strategy by, perhaps, allowing you to destroy all or some of your opponent's weapons in flight. NUTs also argue that if your opponent believes that its weapons may not get through, the opponent is less likely to launch them and risk retaliation. MADs adamantly oppose BMD capability as dangerously destabilizing. They argue that a defensive system detracts from assured retaliatory destruction, since second-strike missiles would be destroyed in flight. MADs also worry that a BMD system might tempt its possessor into a first strike, since the BMD system would be most effective against a reduced retaliatory strike rather than a full-scale first strike by an opponent. This double-edged element of a BMD, its critics say, means that it would inevitably push other nuclear powers to develop a massive number of new nuclear delivery devices capable of overwhelming any defensive system.

 Chapter Summary

1. War is organized killing of other human beings. Virtually everyone is against that. Yet war continues to be a part of the human condition, and its incidence has not significantly abated. Modern warfare affects more civilians than it traditionally did; the number of civilians killed during war now far exceeds that of soldiers.

2. The study of force involves several major questions. When and why does war occur? When it does happen, how effective is it, what conditions govern success or failure, and what options exist in structuring the use of force?

3. Although much valuable research has been done about the causes of war, about the best we can do is to say that war is a complex phenomenon that seems to have many causes. Some of these stem from the nature of our species, some from the existence of nation-states, and some from the nature and dynamics of the world political system.

4. Military power is both tangible and intangible. Tangible elements of power, such as tanks, are relatively easy to visualize and measure. Intangible elements of military power, such as morale and reputation, are much more difficult to operationalize.

5. Acquiring military power also has drawbacks. It creates the temptation to use it, it makes others insecure, and it is costly. Some people argue, and others disagree, that spending too many resources on military power is a major factor in the decline of once-mighty countries. Another argument debates whether quantity or quality provides the best defense.

6. Force can be used, threatened, or merely exist as an unspoken possibility. When it is used, its success requires much planning and skill. Studies have determined the ideal conditions for successful use of military force. If force is to be used, it should be employed as a means, or tool, rather than, as sometimes happens, as an end in itself.

7. Force does not have to be used to have an impact. The possession of military power creates a backdrop to diplomacy, and the overt threat of force increases the psychological pressure even more. The tools of force can be applied through arms sales and other methods of intervention. When it is used, force can range from a very limited demonstration to a full-scale nuclear attack.

8. The nature of war is changing. Technology has enhanced killing power; nationalism has made war a patriotic cause. As a result, the scope of war has expanded, which has also changed the strategy of war. The power to defeat is a traditional strategy of war, while the power to hurt has increased in significance and incidence.

9. Warfare can be classified into three categories: unconventional warfare (including arms transfers, special operations, and terrorism), conventional warfare, and weapons of mass destruction warfare (including nuclear, biological and chemical weapons.)

10. For each type of conflict examined in this chapter, we looked at a variety of factors, such as weapons and strategy. The MAD versus NUT debate, for instance, involves how to structure nuclear weapons systems and doctrines. We also saw that the ability to conduct war is continuing to change as new technology develops new weapons.

Chapter 13

International Security: The Alternative Road

Weapons! arms! What's the matter here?

Shakespeare, *King Lear*

He's mad that trusts in the tameness of a wolf.

Shakespeare, *King Lear*

As the bomb fell over Hiroshima and exploded, we saw an entire city disappear. I wrote in my log the words: "My God, what have we done?"

Capt. Robert Lewis, U.S. Army Air Corps,
copilot of the *Enola Gay*

A world without nuclear weapons would be less stable and more dangerous for all of us.

British prime minister Margaret Thatcher

Chapter Objectives

After completing this chapter, you should be able to:

- Think about the issue of security by considering what insecurity means.
- Discuss limited self-defense as an approach to security.
- Characterize arms control as an approach to achieving security by limiting the numbers and types of weapons that countries have.
- List major events and themes in the history of arms control.
- Explain the limitation and reduction of arms as important aspects of arms control.
- Discuss limits on arms transfers, focusing on the issues of proliferation and nonproliferation of weapons, including biological, chemical, and conventional weapons.
- Summarize and evaluate political, technical, and domestic barriers to arms control.
- Describe the role that international security plays in world politics.
- Consider the abolition of war as an approach to security, focusing on disarmament and pacifism.

Security is the enduring yet elusive quest. "I would give all my fame for a pot of ale, and safety," a frightened boy cries out before a battle in Shakespeare's *King Henry V.* Alas, Melpomene, the muse of tragedy, did not favor the boy's plea. The English and French armies met on the battlefield at Agincourt. Peace—and perhaps the boy—perished. Today most of us similarly seek security. Yet our quest is tempered by the reality that while humans have sought safety throughout history, they have usually failed to achieve that goal for long.

Thinking About Security

Perhaps one reason that security from armed attack has been elusive is that we humans have sought it in the wrong way. The traditional path has emphasized national self-defense by amassing arms to deter aggression. Alternative paths have been given little attention and fewer resources. From 1948 through 2002, for example, the world states spent about 1,300 times as much on their national military budgets (about $38 trillion) as on UN peacekeeping operations (about $29 billion). It just may be, then, that the first secretary-general of the United Nations, Trygve Lie, was onto something when he suggested that "wars occur because people prepare for conflict, rather than for peace."[1]

The aim of this chapter is to think anew about security from armed aggression in light of humankind's failed effort to find it. Because the traditional path has not brought us to a consistently secure place, it is only prudent to consider alternative, less-traveled-by, paths to security. These possible approaches include limiting or even abandoning our weapons altogether, creating international security forces, and even adopting the standards of pacifism.

A TALE OF INSECURITY

One way to think about how to increase security is to ponder the origins of insecurity. To do that, let us go back in time to the hypothetical origins of insecurity. Our vehicle is a parable. Insecurity may not have started exactly like this, but it might have.

A Drama and Dialogue of Insecurity

It was a sunny, yet somehow foreboding, autumn day many millennia ago. Og, a caveman of the South Tribe, was searching for food. It had been a poor season for hunting and gathering, and Og fretted about the coming winter and his family. The urge to provide security from hunger for his family carried Og northward out of the South Tribe's usual territory and into the next valley.

It was the valley of Ug of the North Tribe. The same motivations that drove Og also urged Ug on, but he had been luckier. He had just killed a large antelope. Ug, then, was feeling prosperous as he used his large knife to clean his kill. At that moment, Og, with hunting spear in hand, happened out of the forest and came upon Ug. Both the hunters were startled, and they exchanged cautious greetings. Ug was troubled by the lean and hungry look of the spear-carrying stranger, and he unconsciously grasped his knife more tightly. The tensing of his ample muscles alarmed Og, who instinctively dropped his spear point to a defensive position. Fear was the common denominator. Neither Og nor Ug wanted a confrontation, but they were trapped. Their disengagement negotiation went something like this (translated):

Ug: You are eyeing my antelope and pointing your spear at me.

Og: And your knife glints menacingly in the sunlight. But this is crazy. I mean you no harm; your antelope is yours. Still, my family is needy and it would be good if you shared your kill.

Ug: Of course I am sympathetic, and I want to be friends. But this is an antelope from the North Tribe's valley. If there is any meat left over, I'll even give you a little. But first, why don't you put down your spear so we can talk more easily?

Og: A fine idea, Ug, and I'll be glad to put down my spear, but why don't you lay down that fearful knife first? Then we can be friends.

Ug: Spears can fly through the air farther.... You should be first.

Og: Knives can strike more accurately. You should be first.

And so the confrontation continued, with Og and Ug equally unsure of the other's intentions, with each sincerely proclaiming his peaceful purpose, but unable to convince the other to lay his weapon aside first.

Critiquing the Drama

Think about the web of insecurity that entangled Og and Ug. Each was insecure about providing for himself and his family in the harsh winter that was approaching. Security extends further than just being safe from armed attacks. Ug was a "have" and Og was a "have-not." Ug had a legitimate claim to his antelope; Og had a legitimate need to find sustenance. Territoriality and tribal differences added to the building tension. Ug was in "his" valley; Og could not understand why unequal resource distribution meant that some should prosper while others were deprived. The gutting knife and the spear also played a role. But did the weapons cause tension or, perhaps, did Ug's knife protect him from a raid by Og?

We should also ask what could have provided the security to get Og and Ug out of their confrontation. If Og's valley had been full of game, he would not have been driven to the next valley. Or if the region's food had been shared by all, Og would not have needed Ug's antelope. Knowing this, Ug might have been less defensive. Assuming, for a moment, that Og was dangerous—as hunger sometimes drives people to be—then Ug might have been more secure if somehow he could have signaled the equivalent of today's 911 distress call and summoned the region's peace-keeping force, dispatched by the area's intertribal council. The council might even have been able to aid Og with some food and skins to ease his distress and to quell the anger he felt when he compared his ill fortune with the prosperity of Ug.

The analysis of our parable could go on and be made more complex. Og and Ug might have spoken different languages, worshipped different deities, or had differently colored faces. That, however, would not change the fundamental questions regarding security. Why were Og and Ug insecure? More important, once insecurity existed, what could have been done to restore harmony?

SEEKING SECURITY: APPROACHES AND STANDARDS OF EVALUATION

Now bring your minds from the past to the present, from primordial cave dwellers to yourself. Think about contemporary international security. The easiest matter is determining what our goal should be. How to do that is, of course, a much more challenging question.

Security is partly a state of mind. Like this man in Argentina who is being held hostage in a kidnapping that ultimately failed, an individual in domestic societies can suddenly fall victim to a violent crime. Yet most people do not carry guns, because they feel safe in their domestic system with its law enforcement system and norms against violence. By contrast, the anarchical international system relies mostly on self-protection, which is why most countries are heavily armed.

Approaches to Security

There are, in essence, four possible approaches to securing peace. The basic parameters of each is shown in Table 13.1. As with many, even most matters in this book, which approach is best is part of the realist-idealist debate.

Unlimited self-defense, the first of the four approaches, is the traditional approach of each country being responsible for its own defense and amassing weapons it wishes for that defense. The thinking behind this approach rests on the classic realist assumption that humans have an inherent element of greed and aggressiveness that promotes individual and collective violence. This makes the international system, from the realists' perspective, a place of danger where each state must fend for itself or face the perils of domination or destruction by other states.

Beyond the traditional approach to security, there are three alternative approaches: *limited self-defense* (arms limitations), *international security* (regional and world security forces), and *abolition of war* (complete disarmament and pacifism). Each of these will be examined in the pages that follow. Realists do not oppose arms control or even international peacekeeping under the right circumstances. Realists, for instance, recognize that the huge arsenals of weapons that countries possess are dangerous and, therefore, there can be merit in carefully negotiated, truly verifiable arms accords. But because the three alternative approaches all involve some level of trust and depend on the triumph of the spirit of human cooperation over human avarice and power-seeking, they are all more attractive to idealists than to realists.

Standards of Evaluation

Now that we have identified the approaches to seeking security, the question is which one of them offers the greatest chance of safety. There is no clear answer, so it is important to consider how to evaluate the various possibilities.

To evaluate the approaches to security, begin by considering the college community that you are living in while taking the course for which this book is being used. The next time you are in class, look around you. Is anyone carrying a gun? Are you? Probably not. Think about why you are not doing so. The answer is that you feel relatively secure.

The word "relatively" is important here. There are, of course, dangerous people in your community who might steal your property, attack you, and perhaps even kill you. There were 15,530 homicides, 89,110 reported rapes, and 1,326,050 other violent crimes in the United States during 1999. Criminals committed another 10,204,500 burglaries, car thefts, and other property crimes. Thus, with one crime for every 22 Americans, it is clear that you are not absolutely secure. Yet most of us feel secure enough to forgo carrying firearms.

The important thing to consider is why you feel secure enough not to carry a gun despite the fact that you could be murdered, raped, beaten up, or have your property stolen. There are many reasons. *Domestic norms* against violence and stealing are one reason. Most people around you are peaceful and honest and are unlikely, even if angry or covetous, to attack you or steal your property. Established *domestic collective security forces* are a second part of feeling secure. The police are

Table 13.1 Four Approaches to Security

Security Approach	Sources of Insecurity	World Political System	Armaments Strategy	Primary Peacekeeping Mechanism	Strategy
Unlimited Self-Defense	Many; probably inherent in humans	State-based; national interests and rivalries; fear	Have many and all types to guard against threats	Armed states, deterrence, alliances, balance of power	Peace through strength
Limited Self-Defense	Many; perhaps inherent, but weapons intensify	State-based; limited cooperation based on mutual interests	Limit amount and types to reduce capabilities, damage, tension	Armed states; defensive capabilities, lack of offensive capabilities	Peace through limited offensive ability
International Security	Anarchical world system; lack of law or common security mechanisms	International political integration; regional or world government	Transfer weapons and authority to international force	International peacekeeping/peacemaking force	Peace through law and universal collective defense
Abolition of War	Weapons; personal and national greed and insecurity	Various options from pacifistic states to libertarian global village model	Eliminate weapons	Lack of ability; lack of fear; individual and collective pacifism	Peace through being peaceful

Concept source: Rapoport (1992).

The path to peace has long been debated. The four approaches outlined here provide some basic alternatives that help structure this chapter on security.

on patrol to deter criminals, and if anyone does attack you or steal your property, you can call 911; criminal courts and prisons deal with convicted felons. *Domestic disarmament* is a third contributor to your sense of security. Most domestic societies have disarmed substantially, shun the routine of carrying weapons, and have turned the legitimate use of domestic force beyond immediate self-defense over to their police. *Domestic conflict-resolution mechanisms* are a fourth contributor to security. There are ways to settle disputes without violence. Lawsuits get filed, and judges make decisions. Indeed, some crimes against persons and property are avoided because most domestic political systems provide some level of social services to meet human needs.

To return to our stress on relative security, it is important to see that for all the protections and dispute-resolution procedures provided by your domestic system, and for all the sense of security that you usually feel, you are not fully secure. Nor are countries and their citizens secure in the global system. For that matter, it is unlikely that anything near absolute global security can be achieved through any of the methods offered in this chapter or anywhere else. Therefore, the most reasonable standard by which to evaluate approaches to security is to compare them and to ask which makes you more secure.

Limited Self-Defense Through Arms Control

The first alternative approach to achieving security involves limiting the numbers and types of weapons that countries possess. This approach, commonly called **arms control**, aims at lessening military (especially offensive) capabilities and lessening the damage even if war begins. Additionally, arms control advocates believe that the decline in the number and power of weapons systems will ease political tensions, thereby making further arms agreements possible (Gallagher, 1998).

METHODS OF ACHIEVING ARMS CONTROL

There are a number of methods to control arms in order to limit or even reduce their number and to prevent their spread. These methods include numerical restrictions; research, development, and deployment restrictions; categorical restrictions; and transfer restrictions. Several of the arms control agreements that will be used to illustrate the restrictions are detailed in the following section on the history of arms control, but to familiarize yourself with them quickly, it would be wise to peruse the agreements listed in Table 13.2.

Numerical Restrictions. Placing numerical limits above, at, or below the current level of existing weapons is the most common approach to arms control. This approach specifies the number or capacity of weapons and/or troops that each side may possess. In some cases the numerical limits may be at or higher than current levels. For example, both the first and second Strategic Arms Limitations Talks treaties, the two Strategic Arms Reduction Treaties, and the Treaty at Moscow (2002) have combined to significantly reduce the number of American and Russian nuclear weapons.

Categorical Restrictions. A second approach to arms control involves limiting or eliminating certain types of weapons. The Intermediate-Range Nuclear Forces Treaty (INF) eliminated an entire class of weapons—intermediate-range nuclear missiles. The START II Treaty will erase multiple-independent-reentry-vehicle (MIRV) warhead ICBMs from the nuclear arsenals. The new Anti-Personnel Mine Treaty (APM) will make it safer to walk the Earth.

Development, Testing, and Deployment Restrictions. A third method of limiting arms involves a sort of military birth control that ensures that weapons systems never begin their gestation period of development and testing or, if they do, they are never deployed. The advantage of this approach is that it stops a specific area of arms building before it starts. For instance, the countries that have ratified the Nuclear Non-Proliferation Treaty (NPT) and that do not have such weapons agree not to develop them. A related approach for weapons that have already been developed is to prohibit their deployment in certain geographic areas. The deployment of military weapons in Antarctica, the seabed, space, and elsewhere is, for example, banned.

Transfer Restrictions. A fourth method of arms control is to prohibit or limit the flow of weapons and weapons technology across international borders. Under the NPT, for example, countries that have nuclear weapons or nuclear weapons technology pledge not to supply weapons or the technology to build them to non-nuclear states.

This review of the strategies and methods of arms control leads naturally to the question of whether they have been successful. And if they have not been successful, why not? To address these questions, we will, in the next two sections, look at the history of arms control, then at the continuing debate over arms control.

THE HISTORY OF ARMS CONTROL

Attempts to control arms and other military systems extend almost to the beginning of written history. The earliest recorded example occurred in 431 B.C. when Sparta and Athens negotiated over the length of the latter's defensive walls. Prior to the beginning of the twentieth century, however, arms control hardly existed. Since then there has been a buildup of arms control activity. Technology, more than any single factor, spurred rising interest in arms control. The escalating lethality of weapons sparked a growing sense that an apocalypse awaited the world if humans could not restrain their ability to slaughter one another. It is possible to explore the growth of arms control activity over the last century or so in three parts. The first will cover arms control to 1990. Then the subsequent history will be divided into a discussion

(Continued on page 375)

Table 13.2 Selected Arms Control Treaties

Treaty	Provisions	Date Signed	Number of Signatories
Geneva Protocol	Bans using of gas or bacteriological weapons	1925	125
Limited Test Ban	Bans nuclear tests in the atmosphere, space, or under water	1963	123
Non-Proliferation Treaty (NPT)	Prohibits selling, giving, or receiving nuclear weapons, materials, or technology for weapons	1968	187
Biological Weapons	Bans the production and possession of biological weapons	1972	131
Strategic Arms Limitation Talks Treaty (SALT I)	Limits U.S. and USSR strategic weapons	1972	2
Anti-Ballistic Missile Treaty (ABM)	U.S.-USSR pact limits anti-ballistic missile testing and deployment	1972	2
Threshold Test Ban	Limits U.S. and USSR underground tests to 150 kt	1974	2
SALT II	Limits U.S. and USSR strategic weapons	1979	2
Intermediate-Range Nuclear Forces (INF)	Eliminates U.S. and USSR missiles with ranges between 500 km and 5,500 km	1987	2
Missile Technology Control Regime (MTCR)	Limits transfer of missiles and missile technology	1987	25
Conventional Forces in Europe Treaty (CFE)	Reduces conventional forces in Europe.	1992	20
Strategic Arms Reduction Treaty (START I)	Reduces U.S. and USSR/Russian strategic nuclear forces	1991	2
START II	Reduces U.S. and Russian strategic nuclear forces	1993	2
Chemical Weapons Convention (CWC)	Bans the possession of chemical weapons after 2005	1993	165
Comprehensive Test Ban Treaty (CTBT)	Bans all nuclear weapons tests	1996	165
Anti-Personnel Mine Treaty (APM)	Bans the production, use, possession, and transfer of land mines.	1999	122
Treaty of Moscow	Reduces U.S. and Russian strategic nuclear forces	2002	2

Notes: The United States withdrew from the ABM Treaty in 2001; START II was only conditionally ratified by Russia's Duma; the MTCR is a negotiated understanding, not a treaty; the NPT was renewed and made permanent in 1995; the CTBT is open for ratification and was rejected by the U.S. Senate.

Data sources: Numerous news and Web sources, including the United Nations Treaty Collection at: http://untreaty.un.org/.

Progress toward controlling arms has been slow and often unsteady, but each agreement listed here represents a step down the path of restraining the world's weapons.

of attempts to control **weapons of mass destruction (WMD):** nuclear, biological, and chemical weapons) and a discussion of controlling conventional weapons.

Arms Control Through the 1980s

The modern history of arms control began with the Hague Conferences (1899, 1907). These multilateral arms negotiations did nothing about general arms levels, but some restrictions were placed on poison gas and the use of other weapons (Croft, 1997). The horror of World War I further increased world interest in arms control. The Washington Naval Conference (1921–1922) established a battleship tonnage ratio among the world's leading naval powers and, for a time, headed off a naval arms buildup. There were a number of other bilateral and multilateral arms negotiations and agreements in the 1920s and 1930s, but they all had little impact on the increasing avalanche of aggression that culminated in World War II.

Arms control efforts were spurred even more by the unparalleled destruction wrought by conventional arms during World War II and by the atomic flashes that leveled Hiroshima and Nagasaki in 1945. One early reaction was the creation in 1946 of what is now called the International Atomic Energy Agency (IAEA), to limit the use of nuclear technology to peaceful purposes.

The intensity of the cold war blocked arms control during the 1950s, but by the early 1960s worries about nuclear weapons began to overcome even that impediment. The first major step occurred in 1963, when most countries agreed to cease testing nuclear weapons in the atmosphere. Between 1945 and 1963, there were on average 25 above-ground nuclear tests each year. After the treaty was signed, such tests (all by nonsignatories) declined to about three a year, then ended in the 1980s. Thus, the alarming threat of radioactive fallout that had increasingly contaminated the atmosphere was largely eliminated. Later in the decade, the multilateral nuclear **Non-Proliferation Treaty (NPT)** of 1968 pledged its signatories to avoid taking any actions that would add to the number of countries with nuclear weapons.

During the 1970s, with cold war tensions beginning to relax substantially, and with the U.S. and Soviet nuclear weapon inventories each passing the 10,000 mark, the pace of arms control negotiations picked up. The **Anti-Ballistic Missile Treaty (ABM)** of 1972 put stringent limits on U.S. and Soviet efforts to build a ballistic missile defense (BMD) system, which many analysts believed could destabilize nuclear deterrence by undermining its cornerstone, mutual assured destruction (MAD). President George W. Bush notified Russia in 2001 that the United States was withdrawing from the treaty in order to pursue the development and deployment of BMD systems. This controversial step is discussed in the box, President Bush and NUT Strategy, in chapter 12.

The 1970s also included important negotiations to limit the number, deployment, or other aspects of weapons of mass destruction. The most important of these with regard to nuclear weapons were the **Strategic Arms Limitation Talks Treaty I (SALT I)** of 1972 and the **Strategic Arms Limitation Talks Treaty II (SALT II)** of 1979. Each put important caps on the number of Soviet and American nuclear weapons and delivery vehicles, as illustrated in part in Figure 13.1. Moscow and Washington, already confined to underground nuclear tests by the 1963 treaty, moved to limit the size of even those tests to 150 kilotons in the Threshold Test Ban Treaty (1974).

Another important advance in the realm of controlling WMDs occurred with the conclusion of the **Biological Weapons Convention** of 1972, which virtually all countries subsequently signed and ratified. Those countries with biological weapons agreed to destroy them, and all signatories agreed not to manufacture new ones.

The 1980s were a decade when arms control momentum picked up even more speed as the cold war began to wind down, reversing the trend of earlier decades when the destructive power of WMDs and the number of countries possessing them had continued to grow. The **Missile Technology Control Regime (MTCR)** was established in 1987 to restrain the proliferation of missiles. The odd designation "regime" is because, according to the U.S. State Department, the MTCR is an "informal political arrangement" through which signatory countries pledge not to transfer missile technology or missiles with a range greater than 300 kilometers.[2] The

Did You Know That:
Pakistan's Ghauri missile is named after Mohammed Ghauri, the 12th-century leader who began the Muslim conquest of Hindu India. India's Agni missile bears the name of the Hindu god of fire.

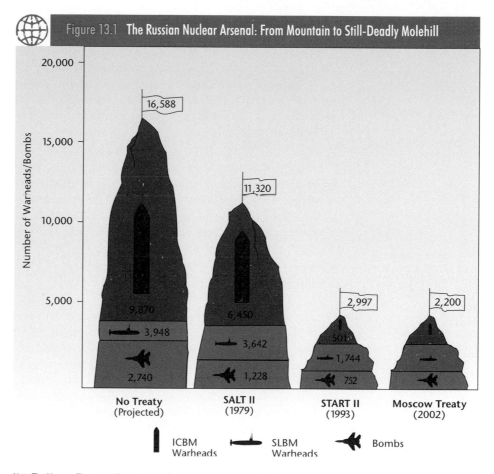

Figure 13.1 The Russian Nuclear Arsenal: From Mountain to Still-Deadly Molehill

No Treaty (Projected): 16,588 — ICBM 9,870, SLBM 3,948, Bombs 2,740

SALT II (1979): 11,320 — ICBM 6,450, SLBM 3,642, Bombs 1,228

START II (1993): 2,997 — ICBM 501, SLBM 1,744, Bombs 752

Moscow Treaty (2002): 2,200

ICBM Warheads | SLBM Warheads | Bombs

Note: The Moscow Treaty specifies only total delivery systems and does not limit the subcategories of delivery systems within that overall total.

Data source: Official treaty figures and author's calculations.

You can see the impact of arms control efforts by comparing the data from the projection of what Russia's nuclear forces might have become without any arms control treaties, through the SALT II Treaty and START II, to the projected totals of the Treaty of Moscow concluded in 2002.

MTCR has not stopped the spread of missiles but has certainly slowed it down. The countries with the most sophisticated missile technology all adhere to the MTCR, and they have brought considerable pressure to bear on China and other missile-capable countries that do not.

A second important agreement was the U.S-Soviet **Intermediate-Range Nuclear Forces Treaty (INF)** of 1987. Because it eliminated an entire class of nuclear delivery vehicles (missiles with ranges between 500 and 5,500 kilometers), the treaty was the first pact to actually reduce the globe's nuclear arsenal. The deployment of such U.S. missiles to Europe and counter-targeting by the Soviet Union had put Europe at particular risk of nuclear war.

WMDs and Arms Control Since 1990

The years since 1990 have been by far the most important in the history of the control WMDs, especially nuclear weapons. The most significant arms control during the 1990s involved efforts to control nuclear arms (Larsen & Rattray, 1996). To review the changes and the controversy associated with them, we can examine three treaties to reduce strategic-range nuclear weapons: the renewal of the NPT, the efforts to ban all nuclear testing, and the treaty on chemical weapons.

Strategic Arms Reduction Treaty I After a decade of negotiations, Presidents George Bush and Mikhail Gorbachev signed the first **Strategic Arms Reduction Treaty I (START I)** in 1991. The treaty mandated significant cuts in U.S. and Soviet strategic-range (over 5,500 kilometers) nuclear forces. Each country was limited to 1,600 delivery vehicles (missiles and bombers) and 6,000 strategic explosive nuclear devices (warheads and bombs). Thus, the START I Treaty began the process of reducing the U.S. and Soviet strategic arsenals, each of which contained more than 10,000 warheads and bombs.

Treaty of Moscow Presidents Boris Yeltsin and George Bush took a further step toward reducing the mountain of nuclear weapons when they signed the second **Strategic Arms Reduction Treaty II (START II)** in 1993. The impact of this change of direction is evident in Figure 13.1. Under START II, Russia and the United States agreed that by 2007 they would reduce their nuclear warheads and bombs to 3,500 for the United States and 2,997 for Russia. The treaty also has a number of clauses relating to specific weapons, the most important of which is the elimination of all multiple-warhead ICBMs.

Strategic Arms Reduction Treaty III Presidents Bill Clinton and Boris Yeltsin agreed in 1997 on the broad principles for a third round of START aimed at further cutting the number of nuclear devices mounted on strategic-range delivery systems by one-third of the START II Treaty limits. Their preliminary goal was to reduce the number of such weapons to between 2,000 and 2,500. That goal took on greater substance in May 2002 when President George Bush met with President Vladimir Putin in Moscow and the two leaders signed what many had expected to be called the third Strategic Arms Reduction Treaty (START III), but which the two leaders dubbed the **Treaty of Moscow**. Under the provisions of the treaty, the two countries agree to cut their nuclear arsenals of nuclear warheads and bombs to no more than 2,200 by 2012. Unlike START I and START II, there are no provisions relating to delivery vehicles.

Most observers hailed the new agreement, but many also voiced caution because of some of the treaty's clauses. For one, there is no schedule of reductions from START II levels as long as they are completed by 2012. Second, the treaty expires that year if the two sides do not renew it. Third, either country can withdraw with just 90-days notice. And fourth, both countries will be able to place dismantled weapons in reserve, which would allow them to be rapidly reinstalled on missiles and deployed.

Such concerns should not cause one to lose track of the fact that when the START agreements are fully implemented they will have accomplished a remarkable reduction of more than 80 percent of nuclear warheads and bombs that existed before the treaties, as illustrated in Figure 13.1. Even now the silos at several former U.S. ICBM sites are completely empty, and some of the bases have even been sold. Perhaps they will be reverted to farming, bringing to fruition the words from the Book of Isaiah (2:4), "They shall beat their swords into plowshares, and their spears into pruning hooks."

The Nuclear Non-Proliferation Treaty Renewal The stark fact is that nuclear weapons are proliferating, as indicated in the map on the next page. Less than 60 years ago there were no countries with nuclear arms. Now there are seven countries that openly possess nuclear weapons, one country (Israel) whose nuclear arsenal is an open secret, and one country (North Korea) that may well have nuclear weapons. Several other countries such as Iran and Iraq have or recently had active programs to develop nuclear weapons.

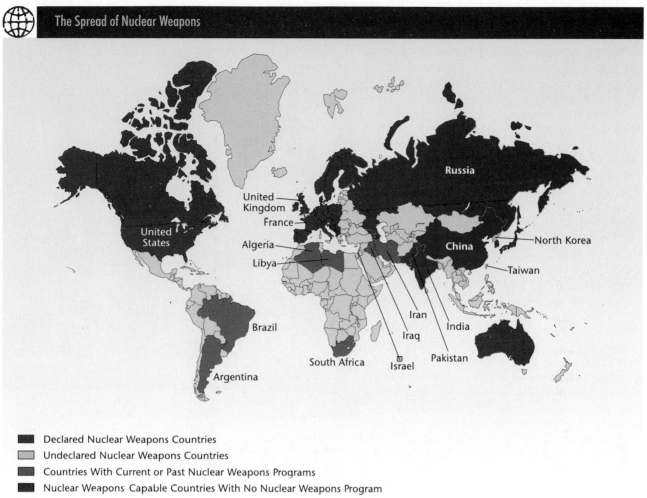

The Spread of Nuclear Weapons

- ■ Declared Nuclear Weapons Countries
- ▨ Undeclared Nuclear Weapons Countries
- ■ Countries With Current or Past Nuclear Weapons Programs
- ■ Nuclear Weapons Capable Countries With No Nuclear Weapons Program
- ▨ Countries With Neither Nuclear Weapons nor the Capability to Build Them

Efforts such as the Nuclear Non-Proliferation Treaty have slowed, but not stopped, the proliferation of nuclear weapons. There are now nine declared and undeclared nuclear weapons countries. Numerous other countries have the ability and, in some cases, the desire to acquire nuclear weapons.

The cornerstone of the effort to control the spread of nuclear weapons is the Nuclear Non-Proliferation Treaty (NPT). The treaty was originally signed in 1968; it was renewed and made permanent in 1995, and it has now been signed by more than 85 percent of the world's countries. The signatories agree not to transfer nuclear weapons or in any way to "assist, encourage, or induce any nonnuclear state to manufacture or otherwise acquire nuclear weapons." Nonnuclear signatories of the NPT also agree not to build or accept nuclear weapons and to allow the IAEA to establish safeguards to ensure that nuclear facilities are used exclusively for peaceful purposes. These efforts have been successful insofar as there are many countries with the potential to build weapons that refrain from doing so, but for all its contributions, the NPT is not an unreserved success.

At least some of the reasons that proliferation is hard to stop were evident during the negotiations preceding the NPT's renewal in 1995. Many nonnuclear countries resisted renewal unless the existing nuclear-weapons countries set a timetable for dismantling their arsenals. Malaysia's delegate to the conference charged, for instance, that without such a pledge, renewing the treaty would be "justifying nuclear states for eternity" to maintain their monopoly.[3] Gradually, however, the

(Continued on page 380)

CHAINED TO THE NUCLEAR ROCK

There are many mythological tales warning against hubris, the arrogance of seeking godlike power. In one such Greek myth, the Titan Prometheus stole fire from the gods and gave it to humankind. An angry Zeus chained Prometheus to a rock and each day sent an eagle to tear open his abdomen. To punish humans for receiving the fire, Zeus created the deceitful Pandora. He gave her a box containing all the travails that could plague humankind and sent her to live in the household of the brother of Prometheus. There Pandora succumbed to the human trait of seeking the unknown despite its risks. She opened the box; evil escaped to bedevil the world.

There are echoes of this fable in the saga of atomic weapons. It is a tragic tale about the folly and hubris that led humans to develop the atomic fire that has given them the godlike power to destroy the Earth and all of its creatures and that has left the world unable to escape the nuclear rock that could be the site of humanity's final agony. In the modern replay of the hubris and agony of Prometheus and the folly of Pandora, the box was opened with the first atomic blast at Alamogordo, New Mexico, on July 16, 1945. Humankind now possessed the atomic fire; humankind has arguably been chained to the rock of potential nuclear destruction ever since.

After that first detonation, the number of tests, like the ominous cloud that symbolizes them, kept mushrooming, peaking in 1962 at 171 blasts. Then the flood tide of testing began to ebb in response to the negotiation of a number of treaties restricting testing (see Table 13.2), a declining need to test, and unilateral restraints.

By the early 1990s, the number of nuclear weapons tests had declined to the point where they were unusual. Moreover, when tests did occur, they were greeted with rancor. France detonated four underground nuclear blasts in 1995 on uninhabited atolls in the South Pacific and set off an explosion of criticism. "An act of stupidity," thundered

When Mumtaz Mahal, wife of the great Mughal emperor Shah Jahan, died during childbirth in 1630, the bereft monarch ordered a magnificent mausoleum to be built as a "symbol of eternal love," an inscription there relates. Many people consider the resulting monument, the Taj Mahal, to be the world's most beautiful building. Perhaps with a sense of ironic contrast between the sublime structure and the dark portent of nuclear weapons, the NGO Greenpeace flew this hot air balloon around the Taj Mahal in Agra, which is near New Delhi, India. Greenpeace was protesting the fact that India and Pakistan had chained themselves to the nuclear rock in 1998 by testing nuclear weapons, thereby placing not only the Taj Mahal but also the more than 1 billion people who live in the two countries at nuclear risk.

the prime minister of Australia, making one of the milder comments.[1]

The following year China, contending that it, too, needed tests to modernize its weapons, exploded two bombs at its test facility under Lop Nor. They were the

objections were overcome. One important factor was a pledge by the nuclear-weapons states to conclude a treaty to ban all nuclear testing. As we shall see in the next section, the United States reneged on that pledge.

It is also worth noting that neither India nor Pakistan agreed to the NPT, and the two countries acquired the dubious distinction of joining the nuclear club when they each tested nuclear weapons in 1998. This fact and the continued interest of several countries in acquiring nuclear weapons makes it easy to deride the NPT as a failure. That judgment is, however, probably too facile. For every country like India and Pakistan that can develop nuclear weapons and has, there world's 2,045th and 2,046th nuclear weapons tests. Once again, the world was dismayed.

The total rose to 2,051 after India conducted five underground tests in May 1998. Like countries before it, India argued that it needed the atomic fire for national security. Critics charged that the urge to nuclear power was a derivative of nationalist and chauvinistic aggressive impulses. "Made with Viagra," is how one editorial cartoon in India labeled the bomb.[2]

Whatever the reasons for India's decision to acquire nuclear weapons, it is debatable whether India's security improved. One U.S. expert commented that Asia "is a nuclear powder keg, and India just lit the fuse."[3] That fuse flared when, on May 28, 1998, Pakistan began its own series of tests. "Today, the flames of the nuclear fire are all over.... We have jumped into these flames without thinking through our minds... but going into a decision made by our heart, the decision of courage," Prime Minister Nawaz Sharif declared.[4] Dispensing with thought in favor of emotion notched up the infamous total of nuclear tests to 2,056.

What comes next is extremely important. One scenario includes more tests, more countries with nuclear arms, and, perhaps, nuclear war. Secretary of Defense William S. Cohen was almost certainly correct when soon after India's tests he told a U.S. Senate committee that "there will be other countries that see this [testing] as an open invitation to try to acquire [nuclear weapons] technology. We have a real proliferation problem that's taking place globally."[5]

The other scenario, escaping the nuclear rock—if that is what humans wish to do—will be difficult. Some believe that one key to unlocking the chains is to forswear further testing of nuclear weapons by agreeing to the Comprehensive Test Ban Treaty (CTBT) and for eternity leaving the final total at 2,056.

To go into effect, however, the 1996 treaty requires the ratification of all countries with nuclear reactors. The countries with nuclear weapons are particularly important, and of these, only France, Great Britain, and Russia have ratified the treaty. China, Israel, and the United States signed the CTBT, but have not rat-

ified it. India and Pakistan have not even signed it.

Because of the global leadership of the United States, the absence of its ratification of the CTBT is arguably the most important barrier to the treaty becoming fully legal. When the CTBT was opened for signature, President Clinton called it "the longest-sought, hardest-fought prize in arms control history" and predicted that it would "immediately create an international norm against nuclear testing even before the treaty formally enters into force."[6] The Republican-controlled U.S. Senate did not share Clinton's enthusiasm, and it rejected the treaty in 1999. "I assure you the fight is far from over," a resolute Clinton told treaty supporters. "When all is said and done," he predicted, "the United States will ratify the treaty."[7] Perhaps, but his successor, President Bush, has expressed opposition to the treaty on the grounds that the CTBT is not verifiable and that some testing may be necessary to ensure the reliability of U.S. nuclear weapons.

There the matter stands. The Bush administration has maintained an informal moratorium on nuclear testing. "Any country that has nuclear weapons has to be respectful of the enormous lethality and power of those weapons, and has a responsibility to see that they are safe and reliable," Secretary of Defense Donald Rumsfeld explained. "To the extent that can be done without testing, clearly that is the preference. And that is why the president has concluded that, thus far, that is the case."[8]

But the Bush administration also remains unwilling to adhere to the CTBT or otherwise forswear future tests. Moreover, it continues to contemplate building new types of nuclear weapons, such as a low-yield weapon that can penetrate deep underground to attack command bunkers and other hardened sites, and low-yield nuclear weapons to destroy incoming warheads, as part of the national missile defense system. Such programs would almost certainly require testing to ensure they work, which could lead the United States to being the country that increases the current total of nuclear tests to 2,057 and beyond.

are many other technologically advanced countries that have remained nonnuclear. These countries adhere to the NPT, which is both an expression of their animus toward proliferation and a confirmation for the treaty that supports their determination to remain without nuclear weapons.

The Comprehensive Test Ban Treaty Another important effort toward arms control has involved the drive to ban the testing of nuclear warheads. Soon after the NPT was renewed, the permanent UN Conference on Disarmament in Geneva attempted to agree on a treaty, but the negotiations were derailed by the opposition of several countries, most notably India, which was moving toward its own nuclear weapons test program (Walker, 1998; Arnett, 1997).

This setback shifted the negotiations to the UN General Assembly, which in 1996 endorsed the **Comprehensive Test Ban Treaty (CTBT)** by the overwhelming vote of 158 to 3 (India, Libya, and Nepal; 24 other countries abstained or were absent) and opened it to signature and ratification. Even though the CTBT has been signed by 165 countries and ratified by 91 of those, it has not gone into force. The reason is that it does not become operational until all 44 countries that had nuclear reactors in 1996 ratify it, and several have not. Thus, for now, the treaty remains in legal limbo, leaving the world Chained to the Nuclear Rock, as the title of the accompanying box puts it.

Chemical Weapons Convention Nuclear weapons were not the only WMDs to receive attention during the 1990s. Additionally, the growing threat and recent use of chemical weapons led to the **Chemical Weapons Convention (CWC)** in 1993. The signatories pledge to eliminate all chemical weapons by the year 2005; to "never under any circumstance" develop, produce, stockpile, or use chemical weapons; to not provide chemical weapons, or the means to make them, to another country; and to submit to rigorous inspection (Price, 1997).

As with all arms control treaties, the CWC represents a step toward, not the end of, dealing with a menace. One issue is that Iraq, Libya, North Korea, Syria, and several other countries with demonstrated or suspected chemical weapons programs did not sign the treaty. Not all these refusals were necessarily sinister. Some nonnuclear states view chemical weapons as a way to balance the nuclear weapons of other countries. Some Arab nations, for instance, are reluctant to give up chemical weapons unless Israel gives up its nuclear weapons.

A second problem with implementing a chemical weapons treaty is that many common chemicals also have weapons applications. Furthermore, some chemicals are deadly in such minute quantities that verification is extremely difficult. Perfluoroisobutene, for one, is a gas that causes pulmonary edema (the lungs fill with fluid). The chemical is clear and odorless and therefore hard to detect, has a toxic effect when dispersed in minute levels, and can be formed from the same chemical (polytetrafluoroethene) used to make nonstick frying pans.

Conventional Weapons and Arms Control Since 1990

Arms control efforts in the decades following the advent of nuclear weapons in 1945 focused mostly on restraining these awesome weapons and, to a lesser degree, the other WMDs (biological and chemical weapons). In the 1990s, the world also began to pay more attention to conventional weapons inventories and to the transfer of conventional weapons.

Conventional Weapons Inventories The virtual omnipresence of conventional weapons and their multitudinous forms makes it more difficult to limit conventional weapons than nuclear weapons (Pierre, 1997). Still, progress has been made.

One major step is the **Conventional Forces in Europe Treaty (CFE)**. After 17 years of wrangling between the countries of NATO and the Soviet-led Warsaw Treaty Organization (WTO), the two sides concluded the CFE Treaty in 1990. The treaty, which has been reaffirmed by the various former Soviet Republics (FSRs), cuts conventional military forces in Europe from the Atlantic to the Urals (the ATTU region). This geographic focus excludes forces in the United States and Canada and also does not affect FSR forces in Asia (east of the Ural Mountains).

The arms reductions under the CFE Treaty have been impressive. By mid-1997, forces in the ATTU region had been reduced by approximately 53,000 units of the covered weapons systems (artillery tubes, tanks, other armored vehicles, combat helicopters, and fixed-wing combat aircraft).

A supplementary step was taken in 1992 when 29 countries at the Helsinki, Finland, meeting of the Organization for Security and Cooperation in Europe (OSCE) signed a nonbinding, but still important, agreement that established the goal of reducing their troop strengths in the ATTU region. For the larger countries, the troop limits in the ATTU region now are: France (325,000), Germany (345,000), Great Britain (260,000), Russia (1,450,000), Ukraine (450,000), and the United States (250,000). The agreement, said chief U.S. negotiator Lynn Hansen, is "unprecedented in the history of Europe, [or] as far as I know, anywhere"[4]

An additional step in conventional weapons arms control came in 1997 when most of the world's nations signed the **Anti-Personnel Mine Treaty (APM)** during ceremonies in Ottawa, Canada. The treaty, which has been ratified by more than 120 countries, prohibits the making, using, possessing, or transferring of land mines. The details of the danger of land mines and the impact of the APM can be found in the box, Adopt a Minefield.

Conventional Weapons Transfers Another thrust of conventional arms control in the 1990s and beyond has been and will be the effort to limit the transfer of conventional weapons. To that end, 31 countries in 1995 agreed to the Wassenaar Arrangement on Export Controls for Conventional Arms and Dual-Use Goods and Technologies. Named after the Dutch town where it was organized, the "arrangement" is an agreement directing its signatories to limit the export of some types of weapons technology and to create an organization to monitor the spread of conventional weapons and **dual-use technology** that has both peaceful and non-peaceful applications.

An even more recent attempt to control conventional weapons is exemplified in the work of the United Nations Conference on the Illicit Trade in Small Arms and Light Weapons in All Its Aspects, which convened in July 2001. Speaking to the delegates from more than 170 countries, Secretary-General Kofi Annan commented, "Four years ago, the International Campaign to Ban Land Mines took the world by storm, and with remarkable speed and compelling logic mobilized the world against these instruments of death. Equally deadly and even more pervasive," Annan continued, "are small arms such as revolvers and rifles, machine guns and mortars, hand grenades, anti-tank guns and portable missile launchers. They should be the next focus of urgent global attention"[5] To that end, the conference called on states to curb the illicit trafficking in light weapons through such steps as ensuring that manufacturers mark weapons so that they can be traced and tightening measures to monitor the flow of arms across borders. The program is non-binding, but it does represent a first step toward regulating and stemming the huge volume of weapons moving through the international system.

THE BARRIERS TO ARMS CONTROL

Limiting or reducing arms is an idea that most people favor. Yet arms control has proceeded slowly and sometimes not at all. The devil is in the details, as the old maxim goes, and it is important to review the continuing debate over arms control to understand its history and current status. None of the factors that we are about to discuss is the main culprit impeding arms control. Nor is any one of them insurmountable. Indeed, important advances are being made on a number of fronts. But together, these factors form a tenacious resistance to arms control.

ADOPT A MINEFIELD

A common sight driving throughout the United States are roadside adopt-a-highway signs that indicate one or another civic organization or business has pledged to keep a section of the road clear of litter. Fortunately for Americans, a discarded beer can or fast-food wrapper is likely to be the about the worst thing they might see or step on while walking along the country's roadways or in its fields and forests.

The fields of Cambodia, the paths of Angola, the hills of Afghanistan, and the countryside in dozens of other countries contain a much greater danger. In those places land mines wait with menacing silence and near invisibility. They are patient, often waiting for many years to claim a victim. Land mines are also nondiscriminatory; they care not whether their deadly yield of shrapnel shreds the body of a soldier or a child. Cambodian farmer Sam Soa was trying to find his cow in a field near his village when he stepped on a mine. "It knocks you down," he remembers. "I didn't realize what had happened, and I tried to run away."[1] Sam Soa could not run away, though; the bottom of his left leg was gone.

It is impossible to know exactly how many land mines lie in wait around the world, but a U.S. State Department report issued in 1998 put the figure at 60 to 70 million in 60 countries.[2] Data on casualties is also imprecise, but the International Red Cross estimated in 1995 that 24,000 people a year were injured by mines, with between a third and a half of those victims being killed. Most of the victims are not soldiers. According to UNICEF, 75 percent of mine victims in El Salvador are children.

The ghastly toll of mines spurred the formation of the International Campaign to Ban Land Mines (ICBL), an NGO alliance of more than 1,000 citizen-groups from 60 countries. The effort of the ICBL and supportive countries such as Canada eventually led to banning the production, use, or sale of land mines through the Anti-Personnel Mine Treaty (APM) (1997). The treaty became effective on March 1, 1999, six months after the 40th country had ratified it. By mid-2002, some 122 countries had ratified the APM Treaty, but 3 key countries (China, Russia, and the United States) were among those that had not. When the treaty was signed, the U.S. military adamantly opposed it, arguing that mines were still necessary along the border between North and South Korea. "I can't afford a breach with the Joint Chiefs," Clinton told the audience to explain why he refused to sign the treaty.[3]

The opposition of the United States and a few other countries was not enough to stem the momentum. Whatever her president may have thought, American Jody Williams was among those celebrating in Ottawa at the signing ceremony. The Vermont native was a cofounder of the ICBL and in 1997 the recipient of the Nobel Peace Prize for her work to rid the world of mines. "Together we are a superpower," Williams said to the national and NGO representatives in Ottawa. "It's a new definition of superpower. It's not one of us, it's everyone."[4]

Whatever the position of Beijing, Moscow, and

Security Barriers

Security concerns constitute perhaps the most formidable barrier to arms control. Those who hold to the realist school of thought have strong doubts about whether countries can maintain adequate security if they disarm totally or substantially. Realists are cautious about the current political scene and about the claimed contributions of arms control.

The Possibility of Future Conflict Some analysts argue, "Serious military threats to U.S. security have diminished dramatically since the end of the cold war."[6] Others see the world situation very differently, and argue for keeping defenses up. Testifying before the House Armed Services Committee in 2002, Secretary of Defense Donald Rumsfeld contended that, "When the Cold War ended.... a defense drawdown took place that went too far—overshooting the mark by a wide margin. Hindsight is 20/20," he continued, "and the truth is that we spent much of the 1990s living off of the investments made during the Cold War, instead of making the new investments needed to address the fast-approaching threats of this new century." The secretary went on to lay out the Bush administration's request for a $48 billion,

Most arms control treaties have dealt with weapons of mass destruction, but conventional weapons are increasingly being addressed. Jody Williams, a resident of Vermont and a founder of an NGO called the International Campaign to Ban Landmines, is speaking here at a March 2001 rally in Washington, D.C., to protest the fact that the United States has refused to join the vast majority of countries that have agreed to the Anti-Personnel Mine Treaty of 1999. The young woman just behind Williams is Song Kosal, who in 1988 at age 4 had her right leg torn off when she stepped on a mine in Cambodia while walking in a field with her mother. Williams won the Nobel Peace Prize in 1997 for her efforts to make the world a safer place for children and others to walk.

Washington, the APM Treaty and the associated effort to rid the world of existing mines has had an important impact. According to the report of the 1991 meeting, of the countries that are party to the treaty, 30 countries have destroyed their stockpiles of land mines, and another 17 countries are in the process of doing so. Furthermore, under the coordination of the UN Mine Action Service, approximately $220 million raised through donor countries and through NGOs is being used to fund the expensive and dangerous effort to clear existing land mines and to educate local populations about how to avoid danger.[5] No precise data exists on the number of mines that have been cleared, but many are being removed and most sources report that the casualty rate is slowly declining.

Much remains to be done. Tens of millions remain, and mines continue to be newly deployed by countries such as India and Pakistan (along their mutual border). Certainly the efforts of individual countries and the UN and other IGOs will be important. But individuals can also get involved if they wish through NGOs such as such as the ICBL, Landmine Action, and Adopt-a-Minefield. Jody Williams decided to play a role, and she won the Nobel Peace Prize. There is one note of caution: If you do decide to adopt a minefield, let the experts pick up the explosives.

15 percent budget increase. "The message is clear," Rumsfeld told legislators. "We must invest so our country can deter and defend against the now clear new threats—against those who might wish to attack and kill our people."[7]

Doubts About the Value of Arms Control Those who have doubts about arms control are also skeptical about its supposed benefits. They tend to disbelieve the often heard arguments that arms races occur and that reducing arms will increase security. The skeptics therefore reject the idea that arms control agreements necessarily represent progress (Kydd, 2000).

Arms control advocates argue that weapons create insecurity and tensions that can lead to war. Arms control skeptics doubt it. Instead, a classic tenet of realpolitik is that humans arm themselves and fight because the world is dangerous, as represented by Theory A in Figure 13.2. Given this view, realists believe that political settlements should be achieved before arms reductions are negotiated. Idealists, by contrast, agree with Homer's observation in the *Odyssey* (ca. 700 B.C.) that "the blade itself incites to violence." This is represented by Theory B in Figure 13.2.

While the logic of arms races seems obvious, empirical research has not confirmed that arms races always occur (Koubi, 1999; Li, 1996). Similarly, it is not clear

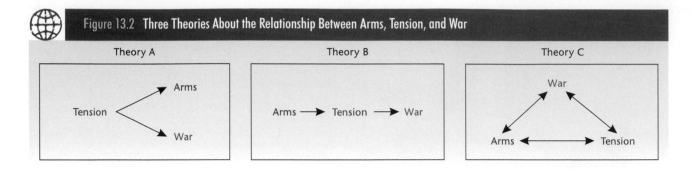

Figure 13.2 Three Theories About the Relationship Between Arms, Tension, and War

Theory A approximates the realist view, and Theory B fits the idealist view of the casual relationship between arms, tension, and use. Theory C suggests that there is a complex causal interrelationship between arms, tension, and war in which each of the three factors affects the other two.

whether decreases in arms cause or are caused by periods of improved international relations. Instead, a host of domestic and international factors influence a country's level of armaments. What this means is that the most probable answer to the chicken-and-egg debate about which should come first, political agreements or arms control, lies in a combination of these theories. That is, arms, tension, and wars all promote one another, as represented in Theory C of Figure 13.2.

There are even arms control skeptics who argue that more weapons equal greater strength. This line of thought was evident in President Ronald Reagan's mantra, "Peace through strength." From this perspective, it is even possible that nuclear arms have increased security. Early in the atomic age, Winston Churchill observed that "it may be that we shall by a process of sublime irony" come to a point "where safety will be the sturdy child of terror and survival the twin brother of annihilation" (Nogee & Spanier, 1988:5). His point was that nuclear weapons may have made both nuclear war and large-scale conventional war between nuclear powers too dangerous to fight. There are also scholars whose work supports this view. One study suggests that, "peace… may depend on the maintenance of credible deterrent policies.… Consequently, the great powers… should not… undermine the potency of their nuclear deterrent" (Huth, Gelpi, & Bennett, 1993:619). If such views are correct, then eliminating or perhaps even substantially reducing nuclear weapons levels could make war more possible and decrease security (Feaver & Niou, 1996; Cimbala, 1995).

While these suspicions about the supposed value of arms control merit consideration, you should be chary of too easily accepting them. One caution is that such conclusions are disputed by other studies and even by some of those who commanded nuclear weapons. For example, 57 retired generals and admirals from various nuclear weapons countries issued a manifesto in 1996, proclaiming that nuclear weapons are now "of sharply reduced utility," and that "the ultimate objective… should be the complete elimination of nuclear weapons from all nations" (Schultz & Isenberg, 1997:87).

Verification Barriers

The problem is simple. Countries suspect that others will cheat. This worry was a significant factor in the rejection of the CTBT by the U.S. Senate. Majority Leader Trent Lott characterized the treaty as "ineffectual because it would not stop other nations from testing or developing nuclear weapons, but it could preclude the United States from taking appropriate steps to ensure the safety and reliability of the U.S. nuclear arsenal." Furthermore, Lott continued, "That it is not effectively verifiable is made clear by the intelligence community's inability to state unequivocally the purpose of activities under way for some number of months at the Russian nuclear test site.... The CTBT simply has no teeth."8

Possible cheating can be divided into two levels: *break-out cheating* and *creep-out cheating*. A violation significant enough by itself to endanger your security would constitute a break-out. This possibility worries skeptics of arms control. Some are also hesitant about arms control because they believe there might be a reluctance to respond to creep-out cheating. In this scenario, no single violation would be serious enough by itself to create a crisis or warrant termination of the treaty. Yet the impact of successive and progressive violations might seriously upset the balance of forces.

There have been great advances in verification procedures and technologies. The most important recent procedural advance is increased **on-site inspection (OSI)**. Countries are increasingly willing to allow others to inspect their facilities. Yet as the problems UN inspectors have had in Iraq illustrate, even OSI is not foolproof, especially if the other side is not cooperative. **National technical means (NTM)** of verification using satellites, seismic measuring devices, and other equipment have also advanced rapidly. These have been substantially offset, however, by other technologies that make NTM verification more difficult. Nuclear warheads, for example, have been miniaturized to the point where 10 or more can fit on one missile and could literally be hidden in the back of a pickup truck or even in a good-sized closet. Therefore, in the last analysis, virtually no amount of OSI and NTM can ensure absolute verification.

Because absolute verification is impossible, the real issue is which course is more dangerous: (1) coming to an agreement when there is at least some chance that the other side might be able to cheat or (2) failing to agree and living in a world of unrestrained and increasing nuclear weapons growth? Sometimes, the answer may be number 2. Taking this view while testifying in 1996 before the U.S. Senate about the pending Chemical Weapons Convention, former secretary of state James A. Baker III counseled, "The Bush administration never expected the treaty to be completely verifiable and had always expected there would be rogue states that would not participate." Nevertheless, Baker urged the Senate to ratify the treaty on the grounds that "the more countries we can get behind responsible behavior around the world..., the better it is for us."9

Domestic Barriers

As chapter 4 discusses, all countries, and especially democracies, are complex decision-making organizations. Even if they favor arms control, leaders have numerous other powerful domestic political actors that they must work with or, perhaps, overcome in the policy-making process. Some of the opposition that leaders face when they try to restrain or reduce arms comes from the ideological differences and policy doubts expressed above. In addition to these security and technical issues, other domestic opposition to arms control often stems from national pride and from the interrelationship among military spending, the economy, and politics.

National Pride The Book of Proverbs tells us that "pride goeth before destruction," and this statement is equally applicable to modern arms acquisitions. Whether we are dealing with conventional or nuclear arms, national pride is a primary drive behind their acquisition. For many countries, arms represent a tangible symbol of strength and sovereign equality. EXPLOSION OF SELF-ESTEEM read one newspaper headline in India after that country's nuclear tests in 1998.10 LONG LIVE NUCLEAR PAKISTAN read a Pakistani newspaper headline soon thereafter. "Five nuclear blasts have instantly transformed an extremely demoralized nation into a

THE CRUSADE TO SAVE THE CRUSADER

Somewhat like the knights that it was named after, the Crusader is an armored behemoth designed to put its enemies to flight. The issue is whether the Crusader will save the day or has been rendered obsolete even before it is deployed. The Crusader is a 46-ton self-propelled artillery system that can fire a dozen 155 mm shells per minute, with a range of more than 25 miles. The projected cost of development and planned units is $11 billion. The U.S. Army claims that adding the Crusader to its inventory is vital to ensure battlefield superiority in the years ahead. President George Bush and Secretary of Defense Donald Rumsfeld think that the Crusader is too expensive and too heavy; a holdover concept from the cold war that should be scrapped.

One might think that a weapons system opposed by the president and the secretary of defense would be dead, but that is not necessarily how Washington works. Even when Rumsfeld announced in May 2002 that the Pentagon would not request funds for the new artillery system, the battle had just begun as the military-industrial-congressional complex went to battle stations.

The military, in this case the Army, has worked assiduously both publicly and behind the scenes to convince Congress that it should insist that the exec-

The battle over whether to deploy the U.S. Army's Crusader advanced field artillery system, a 155-mm self-propelled howitzer, pits President George W. Bush, who opposes the Crusader, against the military-industrial-congressional complex, which favors it. Presidents have often lost such battles, and Bush may also be bested. Here we can see the howitzer being test-fired at the Yuma Proving Ground in Arizona.

utive branch continue to develop and eventually deploy the system. Among other actions, the office of

self-respecting proud nation… having full faith in their destiny," the accompanying article explained.[11]

Military Spending, the Economy, and Politics Supplying the military is big business, and economic interest groups pressure their governments to build and to sell weapons and associated technology (Keller & Nolan, 1997). Furthermore, cities that are near major military installations benefit from jobs provided on the bases and from the consumer spending of military personnel stationed on the bases. For this reason, defense related corporations, defense plant workers, civilian employees of the military, and the cities and towns in which they reside and shop are supporters of military spending and foreign sales. Additionally, there are often bureaucratic elements, such as ministries of defense, in alliance with the defense industry and its workers. Finally, both interest groups and bureaucratic actors receive support from legislators who represent the districts and states that benefit from military spending. This alliance between interest groups, bureaucracies, and legislators forms a military-industrial-congressional complex that has been termed the iron triangle. Just one story of the power of the **iron triangle** is told in the box, The Crusade to Save the Crusader.

🌐 International Security Forces

The idea of forming international security forces to supplement or replace national military forces is a second approach to seeking security on the road less traveled by. This approach would enhance, not compete with, the first approach, arms control.

the Secretary of the Army, who technically works for Rumsfeld, sent a series of "talking points" to sympathetic members of Congress that implied that the secretary of defense's desire to eliminate the Crusader "puts ground forces and American soldiers at risk.... Studies show the Crusader... reduces American casualties by 30 percent."[1]

Industry was also a powerful actor in this budget drama. The corporation developing the Crusader is United Defense Industries (UDI), which is a subdivision of the Carlyle Group. The parent company is headed by Frank C. Carlucci, a defense secretary under President Ronald Reagan. Moreover, the Carlyle Group numbers among its directors and executives an extraordinarily well-connected group of former top federal officials, including former secretary of state James Baker and two retired top Army generals: J.H. Binford Peay III, a former commander-in-chief of Central Command and John M. Shalikashvili, a former chairman of the Joint Chiefs of Staff (JCS). The corporation also was spending over $1 million annually to employ high-powered lobbyists such as former U.S. senator Dan Coats.

In addition to lobbying, UDI made campaign contributions in 2000 ranging up to $10,000 each to 50 members of Congress, including 15 on the House Appropriations Committee and 26 on the House Armed Services Committee. The employees of UDI added another $180,000 in contributions to legislators' campaign funds.

Congress, the third side of the iron triangle, also posed obstacles to Rumsfeld's plan to kill the Crusader. The weapons system would be primarily produced in Oklahoma, and that brought opposition from Representative Rep. J. C. Watts, chairman of the House Republican Conference, and other Oklahoma representatives and senators. Oklahoma senator James M. Inhofe proclaimed the Crusader the "crown jewel of our Army modernization program," and Representative Watts vowed he would employ "the full force and every resource of my office to make sure our soldiers have the tools needed to win—not just to play a good game."[2]

During the political battle that followed, the House approved the fiscal 2003 defense authorization bill containing the funding to continue to develop the Crusader, and the Senate Armed Services Committee also supported retaining the Crusader money. Certainly as of this writing, the struggle is not over. Perhaps the president and secretary of defense can overcome the iron triangle. But their victory is far from assured. "There's a lot of power out there," a former member of the JCS commented about the Army's crusade to save the Crusader. "When you say, 'I'm going to stop a program,'" the general added, "the political-military-industrial complex rolls in there and says, 'No you aren't.'"[3]

Organizing for international security would emphasize international organizations and de-emphasize national defense forces. Thus, the creation of international security forces and the first approach, arms control, are mutually supportive.

INTERNATIONAL SECURITY FORCES: THEORY AND PRACTICE

The idea of seeking security through an international organization is not new. Immanuel Kant foresaw the possibility over two centuries ago in *Idea for a Universal History From a Cosmopolitan Point of View* (1784). "Through war, through the taxing and never-ending accumulation of armament... after devastations, revolutions, and even complete exhaustion," Kant predicted, human nature would bring people "to that which reason could have told them in the beginning": that humankind must "step from the lawless condition of savages into a league of nations" to secure the peace. These ideas have evolved into attempts to secure the peace through such international structures as the Concert of Europe, the League of Nations, and the United Nations. An increased UN peacekeeping role has been especially evident, and other international governmental organizations (IGOs) also have occasionally been involved in international security missions (Roberts, 1996). The far-reaching language in the UN Charter related to peacekeeping can be found in the box, The UN Charter and International Security on page 391.

An important point is that while our discussion here will focus on the UN as a global organization, much of what is said is also applicable to regional IGOs and their security forces. The **North Atlantic Treaty Organization (NATO)** is providing

Although Pakistan and India are desperately poor countries, they both spent huge sums of money to develop nuclear weapons and the missiles to deliver them. Whatever their rational reasons might be, it is also true that emotional national pride played a role in the decisions of Islamabad and New Delhi to build nuclear weapons. That pride is evident in these Pakistanis brandishing a replica of a Shaheen (Eagle) short-range ballistic missile (SRBM) capable of delivering a nuclear warhead. The Pakistanis, who are also burning an effigy of India's prime minister, are expressing their anger during the May 2002 crisis between Pakistan and India over Kashmir.

international security forces in Bosnia-Herzegovina and in Macedonia. Also in Europe, the **Organization for Security and Cooperation in Europe (OSCE)** has taken on some functions of a regional security structure. Established in 1973, the OSCE now has 55 members, including almost all the countries of Europe, Kazakhstan and several other states in Central Asia, and Canada and the United States (Flynn & Farrell, 1999). Operationally, it has begun limited field activities to, in the words of the OSCE, "work 'on the ground' to facilitate political processes, prevent or settle conflicts, and inform the OSCE community."[12] These efforts primarily involve sending monitors and other personnel to try to resolve differences, and as of mid-2002, OSCE missions were operating in Albania, Bosnia, Macedonia, and more than a dozen other countries or hotspots. The largest OSCE peacekeeping effort involved the dispatch of 6,000 troops from eight countries to Albania in April 1997 when that country's political system collapsed into anarchy amid factional fighting.

Beyond Europe, troops from the **Economic Community of West African States (ECOWAS)** helped return Liberia to some semblance of normalcy after a particularly horrendous civil war and were also able in 1998 to restore a measure of unfortunately temporary peace in Sierra Leone (Love, 1996). And in the Western Hemisphere, the Organization of American States (OAS) has advanced peace on a number of fronts, including helping to settle the long and seemingly intractable border dispute between Ecuador and Peru. The potential cause of war was eliminated in October 1998 when the presidents of the two countries met in Brazil to sign the Acta de Brasilia demarcating their border and establishing Argentina, Brazil, Chile, Spain, and the United States as the guarantors of the pact.

To organize our discussion of global and regional international security forces, we can examine the theory and practice of their use according to three essential concepts: collective security, peacekeeping, and peacemaking.

THE UN CHARTER AND INTERNATIONAL SECURITY

The fundamental idea of international security is contained in the UN Charter. Article 1 commits all members "to maintain international peace and security, and to that end, to take effective collective measures" to preserve or restore the peace. Article 24 gives to the Security Council the "primary responsibility for the maintenance of international peace and security," and by Article 25 members "agree to accept and carry out the decisions" of the council. Article 42 gives the Security Council the authority to "take such action by air, sea, or land forces as may be necessary to main-

tain or restore international peace and security." Key language in Article 43 requires members to "undertake to make available to the Security Council, on its call... armed forces... necessary for the purposes" of peace maintenance. The forces are subject to "special agreements" between the UN and member-countries, but the article (as written in 1945) states that the "agreements shall be negotiated as soon as possible." If you think about the implications of this language, clauses to which virtually all countries are bound legally, it is very powerful.

Collective Security

One theory behind use of international security forces through the UN and other IGOs is the concept of collective security. This idea was first embodied in the Covenant of the League of Nations and is also reflected in the Charter of the United Nations. **Collective security** is based on three basic tenets. First, all countries forswear the use of force except in self-defense. Second, all agree that the peace is indivisible. An attack on one is an attack on all. Third, all pledge to unite to halt aggression and restore the peace by supplying to the UN or other IGOs whatever material or personnel resources are necessary to deter or defeat aggressors and restore the peace.

This three-part theory is something like the idea that governs domestic law enforcement. First, self-defense is the only time an individual can use force legally. Second, acts of violence are considered transgressions against the collective. If one person assaults another in, say, Ohio, the case is not the victim versus the aggressor but the society (Ohio) versus the aggressor. Third, domestic societies provide a collective security force, the police, and jointly support this force through taxes.

Collective security, then, is not only an appealing idea but one that works—domestically, that is. It has not, however, been a general success on the international scene. In part, applying collective security is limited by problems such as how, in some cases, to tell the aggressor from the victim. But these uncertainties also exist domestically and are resolved. The more important reason that collective security fails is the unwillingness of countries to subordinate their sovereign interests to collective action. Thus far, governments have generally maintained their right to view conflict in terms of their national interests and to support or oppose UN action based on their nationalistic points of view. Collective security, therefore, exists mostly as a goal, not as a general practice. Only the UN-authorized interventions in Korea (1950–1953) and in the Persian Gulf (1990–1991) came close to fulfilling the idea of collective security.

Peacekeeping

What the United Nations has been able to do more often is implement a process commonly called **peacekeeping**. Apart from using military force, peacekeeping is quite different from collective security. The latter identifies an aggressor and employs military force to defeat the attacker. Peacekeeping takes another approach and deploys an international military force under the aegis of an international organization such as the UN to prevent fighting, usually by acting as a buffer between

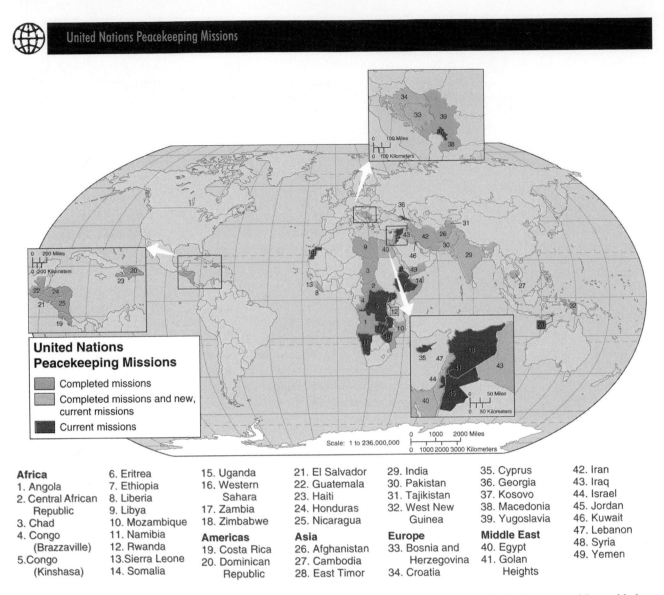

United Nations Peacekeeping Missions

United Nations Peacekeeping Missions

Completed missions

Completed missions and new, current missions

Current missions

Scale: 1 to 236,000,000

Africa
1. Angola
2. Central African Republic
3. Chad
4. Congo (Brazzaville)
5. Congo (Kinshasa)
6. Eritrea
7. Ethiopia
8. Liberia
9. Libya
10. Mozambique
11. Namibia
12. Rwanda
13. Sierra Leone
14. Somalia
15. Uganda
16. Western Sahara
17. Zambia
18. Zimbabwe

Americas
19. Costa Rica
20. Dominican Republic
21. El Salvador
22. Guatemala
23. Haiti
24. Honduras
25. Nicaragua

Asia
26. Afghanistan
27. Cambodia
28. East Timor
29. India
30. Pakistan
31. Tajikistan
32. West New Guinea

Europe
33. Bosnia and Herzegovina
34. Croatia
35. Cyprus
36. Georgia
37. Kosovo
38. Macedonia
39. Yugoslavia

Middle East
40. Egypt
41. Golan Heights
42. Iran
43. Iraq
44. Israel
45. Jordan
46. Kuwait
47. Lebanon
48. Syria
49. Yemen

The United Nations has played a valuable peacekeeping and collective security role. This map shows the locations around the world where UN forces have been or are active. The 1988 Nobel Peace Prize was awarded to the soldiers who have served, some of whom have been wounded or lost their lives, in the interest of international peace.

combatants. The international force is neutral between the combatants and must have been invited to be present by at least one of the combatants.

Some of the data regarding the use of UN peacekeeping forces and observer groups to help restore and maintain the peace are given in chapter 9 but bear repeating briefly here. During its first 55 years (1945 through mid-2000), the United Nations sent over 8,900,000 soldiers, police officers, and unarmed observers from more than 120 countries to conduct 54 peacekeeping or truce observation missions. Over 1,760 of these individuals have died in UN service. The frequency of such UN missions has risen sharply, as can been seen in Figure 9.6 on page 255. In mid-2002, there were 16 UN peacekeeping forces of varying size, totaling 46,000 troops and police drawn from 87 countries in the field in Africa, Asia, the Caribbean, Europe, and the Middle East. The cost of these operations was about $3 billion in 2002.

Did You Know That:
The U.S. assessment for UN peacekeeping operations in 2002 cost each American about $2.65. The U.S. defense budget that year amounted to about $1,200 per American.

Several characteristics of UN peacekeeping actions can be noted. First, most have taken place in LDC locations, as evident in the map. Second, UN forces have generally utilized military contingents from smaller or nonaligned powers. Canada and Fiji have contributed personnel to virtually all peacekeeping efforts, and the Scandinavian countries and Ireland have also been especially frequent participants. The end of the cold war has made it possible for the troops of larger powers to take a greater part in international security missions, and in 2002, American, British, Chinese, French, German, and Russian troops and police personnel were in the field as UN peacekeepers.

Peacemaking

For all the contributions that UN peacekeeping efforts have made, they have sometimes been unable to halt fighting quickly (or even at all) or to keep the peace permanently. The numerous reasons for the limited effectiveness of UN forces can be boiled down to two fundamental and related problems: First, countries frequently do not support UN forces politically or financially. Second, it is often difficult to get the self-interested UN Security Council members, especially the five, veto-wielding permanent members, to agree to authorize a UN mission. Even when the mission is authorized, it is often given a very narrow scope of authority to act and few troops. When the UN initially sent forces to the Balkans, the secretary-general asked for 35,000 peacekeepers. He got only 7,000, and their lack of heavy weapons and lack of authority to take strong action led, at one point, to UN troops being taken hostage and chained to potential targets to deter threatened action by NATO forces.

> **Did You Know That:**
> Countries with 1,000 or more troops/police serving with the UN in mid-2002 were: Bangladesh (6,008), Pakistan (5,449), India (4,507), Nigeria (3,491), Ghana (2,490), Jordan (1,870), Kenya (1,830), Australia (1,689), Nepal (1,091), Uruguay (1,064), and Poland (1,020).

Peacemaking: Support Surges The mounting frustrations with the reactive, passive peacekeeping approach of UN forces led to an upsurge of support for the idea of proactive **peacemaking**. This new role would involve heavily armed UN forces with the authority to restore and maintain the peace. Such UN units would not only intervene where fighting had already broken out. They could also be deployed to imperiled countries before trouble starts, thereby putting an aggressor in the uncomfortable position of attacking UN forces as well as national defense forces. The UN Security Council called on the secretary-general to examine such a possibility by suggesting ways, including a permanent UN force, to strengthen the UN's capacity for "preventative diplomacy, for peacemaking and for peacekeeping."[13]

Secretary-General Boutros Boutros-Ghali soon responded in a 1992 report entitled "Agenda for Peace" that, among other things, asked for the establishment of a $1 billion contingency fund that would allow the UN to dispatch forces to troubled areas quickly. To create such a force, Boutros-Ghali requested member-states to commit a total of 100,000 troops that could be deployed by the UN as a rapid-response force to intervene early during crises in the hopes of containing them.

Initially, the international response was positive. Numerous countries, including the United States, indicated a willingness to have their units train with units from other countries so that they could rapidly join in a UN force. Within two years, 15 countries had pledged 54,000 troops for a rapid-response force. The goal was not to create a standing UN army. Instead, the units of participating countries would have specialized training that would enable them to assemble quickly and operate effectively as a UN force. As such, according to one analyst, the ready force would be a half-step toward a standing UN force "in the hopes [that] countries get half-pregnant with the idea of committing forces to the UN."[14] Whatever the strategy, however, the gestation is proving to be long and difficult.

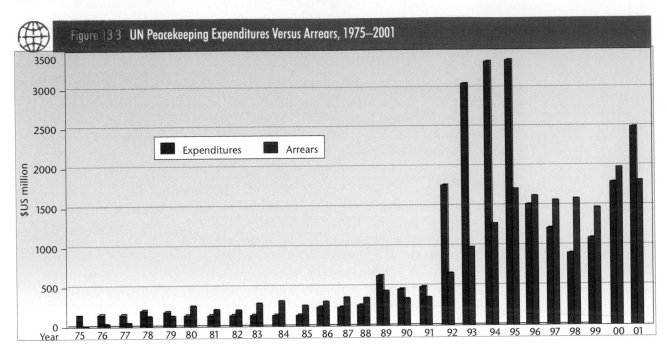

Figure 13.3 UN Peacekeeping Expenditures Versus Arrears, 1975–2001

Data source: Global Policy Forum at the Web site: http://www.globalpolicy.org/finance/tables/chart12.htm. Reprinted by permission of the Global Policy Forum.

One of the key reasons the United Nations has not been more successful in its mission to create a world of peace has been a shortage of funds. Many countries are in arrears of payment of their dues, and as this figure shows, UN expenses continue to mount with the increased demand for UN security operations. The amount owed is less than what the world spends collectively each day on national defense.

Peacemaking: Support Wanes Soon, however, the momentum lost steam. One damper was the variety of barriers, especially nationalism and sovereignty, to an expanded UN role. As one analyst explained, "Robust peace enforcement is beyond the capacity of the United Nations. The Security Council does not have the stomach for it, contributing countries don't want to put their troops under other commanders and then have to answer questions at home when their troops get killed."[15]

Additionally, as discussed in chapter 9, the UN has continued to be hobbled by the unwillingness of many countries to pay their assessments. In mid-2002 member-states were in arrears on their peacekeeping obligations by $1.9 billion. The United States was the largest debtor, with a shortfall of over 40 percent of the total. Moreover, all indications are that the deficit will get worse. There have been increasing demands for UN security operations, and as you can see from Figure 13.3, as the cost of UN operations go up, the level of arrears also rises because countries do not meet their assessments.

Peacemaking: Humanitarian Intervention or Neocolonialism? Doubts about a more aggressive UN military role are not just based on nationalism and other such factors. There is also a concern that creating a more powerful, proactive UN will undermine the sovereignty of the smaller LDCs and that the UN will become a neocolonial tool of the big powers. The chaos and abuses that engulf weak countries sometimes render them mere legal fictions that have no coherent government, and they are considered so-called failed states. In such a situation, other states may have powerful emotional and political incentives to intervene, either to alleviate the suffering or to take political advantage of the turmoil. One observer notes, for example, that "the new rule whereby human rights outrank sovereignty must still prevail, because the old rule is simply dead." The problem, the analyst continues, is the "places where this new rule could be applied all too easily: weak states" (Luttwak, 2000: 61). That, arguably allows powerful states like China to continue to abuse human rights while small countries may be "invaded" by international security forces and have their sovereignty abridged.

Other commentators worry that once the barrier of sovereignty is breached, the powerful countries will have license through the UN to impose their will on weaker countries. That suspicion is not voiced only from within LDCs, it also receives support from a recent review of UN peacekeeping activity. The analysis of the record from 1945 to 1990 led the scholar to conclude that the "interests that have been served by UN peacekeeping are those of the Western states whose interests are served by the status quo and a few non-Western states that lay claim to some prestige in international affairs through their UN activities." This use of the UN, the scholar continues, may "amount to Western interventionist foreign policy bordering on imperialism. The recent expansion of UN peacekeeping activities may indeed signal an era in which sovereignty is eroded, but only for non-Western states" (Neack, 1995:194).

INTERNATIONAL SECURITY AND THE FUTURE

What does the future hold for international security? While there are certainly many impediments on the path to international security, it would be foolish to dismiss the idea as impossible. First, it is in almost everyone's interest to prevent or contain crises, and there is a growing recognition that cooperation through the use of an international security force may often be a more effective way to maintain or restore peace than is continued reliance on unlimited national self-defense in a world capable of producing and using nuclear, biological, and chemical weapons. As such, the existence of peacekeeping has been largely a functional response to an international problem, and the increased number of missions, whether by the UN or one of the regional organizations, is evidence that the international security efforts are necessary and almost certainly have become a permanent part of world politics.

Second, it is important to see that many of the shortcomings of previous international security missions have not been due to an inherent failure of the UN (Wesley, 1997). Certainly the UN has problems, as any large political and bureaucratized organization does (Jett, 2000). The central problem, at least in Kofi Annan's view, is that the UN has "been asked to do too much with too little."[16]

Efforts to create the nucleus of a UN ready force continue but remain controversial (Rosenblatt & Thompson, 1998; Ratner, 1996). Events in the first years of the new millennium somewhat revived interest in strengthening UN forces and giving them more proactive authority. As has occurred too often, UN forces, this time in Sierra Leone in 2000, were outnumbered and outgunned by hostile forces and suffered other problems inherent in trying to deploy an army made up of various national contingents with little ability to work as a unified force. The worst moment came when several dozen Kenyan and Zambian soldiers serving with the UN force were taken hostage by rebels. In the aftermath of this humiliation, the Security Council augmented UN forces in the country from the 6,000 initially authorized in 1999 to 17,500 and gave the forces broader authority to initiate action against the rebels. These improvements in the UN position played an important role in creating conditions of stability to allow for elections in May 2002.

Another approach for the immediate future may be to distinguish types of international security efforts, including peacekeeping and peacemaking missions, and to handle them differently (Mockaitis, 1999; Diehl, Druckman, & Wall, 1998). The UN's undersecretary-general for peacekeeping has contended that "peace enforcement and serious peace restoration campaigns will... be the responsibility of a coalition of interested countries using their own forces but with a green light from the Council."[17] This

Those who disparage UN peacekeeping forces as weak and ineffective ignore the successes that they are able to achieve. International peacekeepers helped restore order in Sierra Leone after a long, especially gruesome, civil war. The new stability permitted the country's first election in years in May 2002. As part of that process, the UN troops stood guard around the country to protect candidates and voters. Here peacekeepers are on guard in the country's capital, Freetown, near a poster of Johnny Paul Koroma, the presidential candidate for the Peace and Liberation Party. He finished a distant second to Ahmad Tejan Kabbah, who was peacefully sworn in as president.

model is much like the NATO-led interventions in Bosnia in 1995 and in Kosovo in 1999 and the International Force in East Timor (INTERFET). This Australian-led multinational force moved to restore stability in East Timor beginning in September 1999 before handing over responsibility for the territory to the UN. According to this model, peacemaking would be up to heavily armed regional forces and peacekeeping to lightly armed UN contingents. As one U.S. diplomat explains it, "There has to be a peace to keep before the blue helmets are put on the ground."[18] In the case of East Timor, at least, the model worked well. Peace was restored and protected, and the UN established a transitional administration that prepared East Timor for full independence in May 2002.

This model also resembles the intervention in Afghanistan beginning in 2001. The initial action was taken under UN authority by a U.S.-led coalition of forces that routed al-Qaeda and toppled the Taliban government. Then in December 2001, the UN Security Council authorized the International Security Assistance Force (ISAF). Made up of about 4,500 forces from such countries as Britain, France, Germany, Italy, and Turkey, and commanded first by a British general, followed in May 2002 by a Turkish general, the ISAF focused on providing security in Kabul in support of the efforts of the interim government to begin the reconstruction of the country's physical and political structures.

Whatever the model, talk of an international security force may sound outlandish, but this is one of those junctures when it is important to remember the events during the life of Dominica's Elizabeth Israel. When she was born in 1875, the Hague Conferences, the League of Nations, and the United Nations were all in the future. When she reached 65, retirement age for many, talk of international peacekeeping forces in Bosnia, Cyprus, Haiti, and other far-flung places would have been greeted with incredulous shakes of the head. Yet all these things exist today. The world needed them. Some say the world also needs an international security force.

Abolition of War

The last of the four approaches to security that we will examine in this chapter looks toward the abolition of war. For our purposes, we will divide the discussion into two parts: complete disarmament and pacifism.

COMPLETE DISARMAMENT

The most sweeping approach to arms control is simply to disarm. The principal argument in favor of disarmament is, as noted, the idea that without weapons people will not fight. This rests in part on sheer inability. **General and complete disarmament (GCD)** might be accomplished either through unilateral disarmament or through multilateral negotiated disarmament.

In the case of *unilateral disarmament*, a country would dismantle its arms. Its safety, in theory, would be secured by its nonthreatening posture, which would prevent aggression, and its example would lead other countries to disarm also. Unilateral disarmament draws heavily on the idea of pacifism, or a moral and resolute refusal to fight. The unilateral approach also relies on the belief that it is arms that cause tension rather than vice versa.

Negotiated disarmament between two or more countries is a more limited approach. Advocates of this path share the unilateralists' conviction about the danger of war. They are less likely to be true pacifists, however, and they believe one-sided disarmament would expose the peace pioneer to unacceptable risk.

The GCD approach has few strong advocates among today's political leaders. Even those who do subscribe to the ideal also search for intermediate arms limitation steps. Still, the quest goes on. The UN Disarmament Committee has called for GCD, and the ideal is often a valuable standard by which to judge progress as "real."

PACIFISM

The second war-avoidance approach, pacifism, relies on individuals. As such, it very much fits in with the idea that people count and that you can affect world politics if you try. Unlike other approaches to security, **pacifism** is a bottom-up approach that focuses on what people do rather than a top-down approach that stresses government action.

Pacifism begins with the belief that it is wrong to kill. Leo Tolstoy, the Russian novelist and pacifist, told the Swedish Peace Conference in 1909 that "The truth is so simple, so clear, so evident… that it is only necessary to speak it out completely for its full significance to be irresistible." That truth, Tolstoy went on, "lies in what was said thousands of years ago in four words: *Thou Shalt Not Kill.*"

Beyond this starting point, pacifists have varying approaches. There are *universal pacifists*, who oppose all violence; *private pacifists*, who oppose personal violence but who would support as a last resort the use of police or military force to counter criminals or aggressors; and *antiwar pacifists*, who oppose political violence but would use violence as a last resort for personal self-defense.

The obvious argument against pacifism is that it is likely to get one killed or conquered. Those who support pacifism make several counter-contentions. One is that there is a history of pacifism's being effective. As one scholar points out, "Nonviolence is as old as the history of religious leaders and movements." The analyst goes on to explain that "traditions embodied by Buddha and Christ have inspired successful modern political movements and leaders [such as]… the Indian struggle for independence under the leadership of [Mohandas K.] Gandhi [in India] and the struggle of the American Blacks for greater equality under the leadership of Martin Luther King Jr." (Beer, 1990:16).

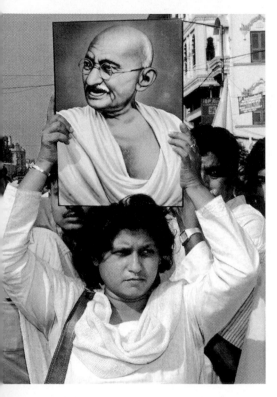

Pacifism, simply refusing to fight physically, is one way to halt violence. The success of Mohandas K. Gandhi, who used nonviolent resistance to free present India, Bangladesh, and Pakistan from British colonial rule in 1947, undermines the argument that pacifists are hopelessly idealistic. Gandhi's image is being used here in March 2002 by a woman in Calcutta, India, protesting the violence between Muslims and Hindus in the northwest areas of the country.

Gandhi was the great Indian spiritual leader (Burrowes, 1996). He began his career as a London-trained attorney earning what was then an immense sum of £5,000 annually practicing in Bombay. Soon, however, he went to South Africa, where, earning £50 a year, he defended Indian expatriates against white legal oppression. Gandhi returned to India in 1915 to work for its independence. He gave up Western ways for a life of abstinence and spirituality. Gandhi believed that the force of the soul focused on, to use the Hindi, *satyagraha* (truth seeking) and *ahimsa* (nonviolence) could accomplish what a resort to arms could not. He developed techniques such as unarmed marches, sit-downs by masses of people, work stoppages, boycotts, and what might today be called "pray-ins," whereby *satyagrahi* (truth seekers) could confront the British nonviolently. "The sword of the satyagrahi is love," he counseled the Indian people (Lackey, 1989:14). Gandhi became known as Mahatma (great soul) and was the single most powerful force behind Great Britain's granting of independence to India in 1947. The Mahatma then turned his soul toward ending the hatred and violence between Hindus and Muslims in independent India. For this, a Hindu fanatic, who objected to Gandhi's tolerance, assassinated him in 1948. Earlier, after the United States had dropped atomic bombs on Japan, Gandhi was moved to write that "mankind has to get out of violence only through nonviolence. Hatred can be overcome only by love. Counter-hatred only increases the surface as well as the depth of hatred." One has to suspect that had he been able to, Gandhi would have repeated this to the man who shot him.

Pacifists, especially antiwar pacifists, would also make a moral case against the massive, collective violence that is war. They would say that no gain is worth the loss. This view, they would argue, has become infinitely more compelling in the nuclear age. Consider the description of Nagasaki filed by the first reporter who flew over the city after a U.S. bomber dropped an atomic bomb, killing at least 60,000 people. "Burned, blasted, and scarred," he wrote, "Nagasaki looked like a city of death." It was a scene, he continued, of "destruction of a sort never before imagined by a man and therefore is almost indescribable. The area where the bomb hit is absolutely flat and only the markings of the building foundations provide a clue as to what may have been in the area before the energy of the universe was turned loose" (Lackey, 1989:112). Pacifists contend that even by the standards of just war conduct (jus in bello) adopted by nonpacifists, any nuclear attack would be unconscionable.

A final point about pacifism is that it is not an irrelevant exercise in idealist philosophy. There are some countries, such as Japan, where at least limited pacifism represents a reasonably strong political force. Moreover, in a changing world, public opinion, economic measures, and other nonviolent instruments may create what is sometimes called a "civilian-based defense." Indeed, there are efforts, such as the Program on Nonviolent Sanctions in Conflict and Defense at Harvard University's Center for International Affairs, that are working to show that those who favor nonviolence should not be considered "token pacifists" who are "tolerated as necessary to fill out the full spectrum of alternatives, with nonviolent means given serious considerations only for use in noncritical situations" (Bond, 1992:2). Instead, advocates of this approach believe that the successes of Gandhi, King, and others demonstrate that proactive techniques, including nonviolent protest and persuasion, noncooperation, and nonviolent intervention (such as sit-ins), can be successful (Bock & Young, 1999).

It is true that pacifists are unlikely to be able to reverse world conflict by themselves. They are a tiny minority everywhere. Instead, pacifism may be part of a series of so-called "peace creation" actions. It is an idea worth contemplating.

🌐 Chapter Summary

1. The goal of the chapter is to discuss alternative paths to security. Security is not necessarily synonymous with either massive armaments or with disarmament. There are four approaches to security: unlimited self-defense, limited self-defense, international security, and abolition of war. The first was the subject of the last chapter. This chapter investigates the other three.

2. There are four possible approaches to ensuring security. They involve restrictions on the number of arms; their development, testing, and deployment; restrictions on certain types of weapons; and the transfer of weapons. Additionally, the standards of evaluation are determined by domestic norms, domestic collective security forces, domestic disarmament, and the established domestic conflict-resolution mechanism. Despite all of the protections and dispute-resolution procedures provided by a domestic system, security is a relative term, thus making full security impossible.

3. There are some people who believe that, because of the nature of humans and the nature of the international system, unlimited self-defense is the prudent policy. Advocates of this approach are suspicious of arms control.

4. Limited self-defense is one means of alternative security. People who favor limited self-defense would accomplish their goals through various methods of arms control.

5. From the standpoint of pure rationality, arms control, or the lack of it, is one of the hardest aspects of international politics to understand. Virtually everyone is against arms; virtually everyone is for arms control; yet there are virtually no restraints on the explosive arms escalation in which we are all trapped. It is a story that dates back far into our history, but unless progress is made, we may not have a limitless future to look forward to.

6. There are many powerful arguments against continuation of the arms race. Arms are very costly, in direct dollars and in indirect impact on the economy. Arms are also very dangerous and add to the tensions that sometimes erupt in violence.

7. During the 1990s, efforts increased to regulate arms. Several START treaties, renewal of the Nuclear Nonproliferation Treaty (NPT), the Comprehensive Test Ban Treaty (CTBT), conventional weapons inventories, conventional weapons transfer regulation, and biological and chemical arms control are among the efforts made. There are heavy domestic pressures from the military-industrial-congressional complex and sometimes from the public against arms control.

8. There are a number of ways to implement approaches to arms control, including arms reductions, limits on the expansion of arms inventories, and prohibitions against conventional arms transfers and nuclear proliferation.

9. Some people favor trying to achieve security through various international security schemes. Collective security, peacekeeping, and peacemaking are among the most significant attempts of an international security effort. The most likely focus of this approach would be the United Nations with a greatly strengthened security mandate and with security forces sufficient to engage in peacemaking, rather than just peacekeeping.

10. Abolition of war is a fourth approach to security. One way to avoid war is through general and complete disarmament. This makes violence difficult and may also ease tensions that lead to violence. Individual and collective pacifism is another way to avoid violence. Pacifists believe that the way to start the world toward peace is to practice nonviolence individually and in ever-larger groups.

Chapter 14

The International Economy: A Global Road Map

O, behold, the riches of the ship is come onshore.

Shakespeare, *Othello*

They are sick that surfeit with too much, as they that starve with nothing.

Shakespeare, *The Merchant of Venice*

You don't make the poor richer by making the rich poorer.

Winston Churchill

If we make the average of mankind comfortable and secure, their prosperity will rise through the ranks.

Franklin D. Roosevelt

Chapter Objectives

After completing this chapter, you should be able to:

- Explain why politics and economics are intertwined aspects of international relations.
- Understand international political economy (IPE).
- Discuss the economic nationalist doctrine.
- Discuss the economic internationalist approaches to IPE.
- Discuss the economic structuralist approaches to IPE.
- Analyze the economic elements that form the base of the North-South axis.
- Consider the three explanations offered for the existence of the economic gap between the North and South.
- Understand the history of IPE while focusing on the effect of changes during the last 50 years.
- Discuss how the expansion of IPE continues to be dominated by the North.
- Note the growth of trade, rapid expansion of international financial ties, and economic importance of monetary relations.
- Analyze the effect of increasing economic interdependence on both countries and individuals.
- Discuss the arguments for and against free international economic interchange.

Given the degree to which this text has already discussed the interplay of politics and economics, you have probably concluded correctly that, to a significant extent, economics is politics and vice versa. This chapter and the two that follow it will continue to explicate how economics and politics intertwine. The subject of this chapter is the general nature of **international political economy (IPE)**, including IPE theories, and the situation of the **economically developed countries (EDCs)** of the North and the **less developed countries (LDCs)** of the South. Chapter 15 examines the traditional political path of national economic competition. Finally, chapter 16 discusses the alternative path of international economic cooperation.

It is important before delving into the subject to familiarize yourself with the distinctions between gross national product (GNP) and gross domestic product (GDP), between either of those adjusted for purchasing power parity (GNP/PPP, GDP/PPP), and between **current dollars** and **real dollars**. It is also important that you understand how to read graphs (including 100-as-baseline graphs) and that you gain a sense of the origin and reliability of economic statistics. To do so, go to Explanatory Notes on page 571, and review "Economics: Technical Terms and Sources."

Theories of International Political Economy

Before getting into the details of current global economic conditions, it is appropriate to examine the broad theories about the connection between economics and politics (Burch & Denemark, 1997; Pettman, 1996). As chapter 1 discusses, many political scientists believe that economic forces and conditions are the key determinants of the course of world politics. One scholar observes, "Clearly, a state perceives its international economic interests on the basis of a set of ideas or beliefs about how the world economy works and what opportunities exist within it" (Woods, 1995:161).

There are numerous schools of thought related to IPE. They can be roughly divided into economic nationalist, economic internationalist, and economic structuralist approaches. The three approaches are descriptive, in that they all purport to describe how and why conditions occur. The three approaches are also prescriptive, in that they make arguments about how policy should be conducted. These descriptions and prescriptions are summarized in Table 14.1 on page 402. You should further note that economic nationalism is a realpolitik school of IPE, while economic internationalism and, especially, economic structuralism are idealist schools.

ECONOMIC NATIONALISM

The core of **economic nationalism** is the belief that the state should use its economic strength to further national interests. By extension, economic nationalists also advocate using a state's power to build its economic strength. Epitomizing this view, the first U.S. secretary of the treasury, Alexander Hamilton, argued that "The interference and aid of [the U.S.] government are indispensable" to protect American industry and to build U.S. economic strength (Balaam & Veseth, 1996:23).

Economic nationalists are realists who believe that conflict characterizes international economic relations and that the international economy is a zero-sum game in which one side can gain only if another loses. As Hamilton asked rhetorically in *The Federalist Papers* (1787), "Have there not been as many wars founded upon commercial motives since that has become the prevailing system of nations, as were before occasioned by the cupidity of territory or dominion?"[1] From the economic

Table 14.1 Approaches to International Political Economy

	Economic Nationalism	Economic Internationalism	Economic Structuralism
Associated terms	Mercantilism, economic statecraft	Liberalism, free trade, free economic interchange, capitalism, laissez-faire	Marxism, dependencia, neo-Marxism, neoimperialism, neocolonialism
Primary economic actors	States; alliances	Individuals, multinational corporations, IGOs	Economic classes (domestic and state)
Current economic relations	Competiton and conflict based on narrow national interest; zero-sum game	National competition but cooperation increasing; non–zero-sum game	Conflict based on classes of countries; wealthy states exploit poor ones; zero-sum game
Goal for future	Preserve/expand state power, secure national interests	Increase global prosperity	Eliminate internal and international classes
Prescription for future	Follow economic policies that build national power; use power to build national economy	Eliminate/minimize role of politics in economics; use politics	Radically reform system to end divisions in wealth and power between classes of countries
Desired relationship of politics and economics	Politics controls economic policy	Politics used only to promote domestic free markets and international free economic interchange	Politics should be eliminated by destruction of class system
View of states	Favorable; augment state power	Mixed; eliminate states as primary economic policy makers	Negative; radically reform states; perhaps eliminate states
Estimation of possibility of cooperation	Impossible; humans and states inherently seek advantage and dominance	Possible through reforms within a modified state-based system	Only possible through radical reform; revolution may be necessary
Views on development of LDCs	No responsibility to help. Also could lose national advantages by creating more competition, higher resource prices	Can be achieved through aid, loans, investment, trade, and other assistance within current system. Will ultimately benefit all countries	Exploitation of countries must be ended by fundamentally restructuring the distribution of political and economic power

Conceptual sources: Balaam & Veseth (1996); Gilpin (1996); author.

Analysts take very different approaches in describing how the international political economy works and in prescribing how it should work.

nationalist perspective, political goals should govern economic policy because the aim is to maximize state power in order to secure state interests.

To accomplish their ends, economic nationalists rely on a number of political-economic strategies. These include:

Imperialism and neoimperialism are one set of economic nationalist practices. Imperialism is the direct control of another land and its people for national economic gain. It was this motive that propelled Europeans outward to conquer and build the great colonial empires that dominated so much of the world until recent decades. Direct colonial control has largely died out, but many observers charge that neoimperialism (indirect control) continues to be a prime characteristic of the relationship that exists, or that EDCs try to achieve, between themselves and LDCs.

Economic incentives and disincentives provide a second set of economic nationalist practices. Countries that offer economic carrots, such as foreign aid and favorable trade policies, or that use economic sticks, such as sanctions, to promote the state's national interests are practicing economic nationalism. For example, a State Department official justified what he depicted as putting "pressure on the Cuban government through the embargo and [other economic measures]" on the

Economic nationalists believe that it is appropriate for countries to use trade and other forms of international interchange as tools to pursue political goals. President Bush is a strong adherent to this approach to international political economy. Here, with a Cuban flag as a backdrop, he is telling Cubans at an anti-Castro celebration of Cuban Independence Day in Miami, Florida, on May 20, 2002, that he will continue the U.S. trade embargo against Cuba until President Fidel Castro allows free elections and improves his human rights record.

grounds that "economic sanctions can be and are a valuable tool for… protecting our national interests."[2]

Protectionism and domestic economic support are a third set of tools that economic nationalists believe should be used to promote national power. "I use not porter [ale] or cheese in my family, but such as is made in America," George Washington once avowed.[3] From this perspective, economic nationalists are suspicious of economic interdependence on the grounds that it undermines state sovereignty and weakens the national economic strength. Economic nationalists would prefer that their respective countries use trade barriers, economic subsidies, and other policies to protect national industries, especially those with military value.

ECONOMIC INTERNATIONALISM

A second major theoretical and policy approach to IPE is **economic internationalism**. This approach is also associated with such terms as capitalism, laissez-faire, economic liberalism, and free trade. Economic internationalists are idealists. They believe that international economic relations should and can be conducted cooperatively because, in their view, the international economy is a non–zero-sum game in which prosperity is available to all.

Economic internationalists contend that the best way to create prosperity is by freeing economic interchange from political restrictions. Therefore, economic internationalists (in contrast to economic nationalists) oppose tariff barriers, domestic subsidies, sanctions, and any other economic tool that distorts the free flow of trade and investment capital.

The origins of economic liberalism lie in the roots of capitalism. In one of the early expositions of capitalist theory, *The Wealth of Nations* (1776), Adam Smith wrote that "it is not from the benevolence of the butcher, the brewer, or the baker, that we expect our dinner, but from their regard to their own interest." Smith believed that this self-interest constituted an "invisible hand" of competition that created the most efficient economies. Therefore, he opposed any political interference with the operation of the invisible hand, including political meddling in trade. It was Smith's contention that, "If a foreign country can supply us with a commodity cheaper than we ourselves can make it, better buy it of them with some part of the produce of our own industry, employed in a way in which we have some advantage."

The pure capitalism advocated by Smith has few adherents today. Instead, most modern economic liberals favor using the state to modify the worst abuses of capitalism by ensuring that monopolies do not form and by taking other steps to ensure that the competition and unequal distribution of wealth inherent in capitalism is not overly brutal. Writing in the 1930s, the British economist John Maynard Keynes found classic capitalism "in many ways objectionable" but believed that "capitalism, wisely managed, can probably be made more efficient for attaining economic ends than any alternative system" (Balaam & Veseth, 1996:49).

At the international level, Keynesian economics has influenced economic internationalists and the changes they advocate to traditional economic nationalist policies. They are moderate reforms, though, which would alter, but not radically change, either capitalism or the state-based international system. For example, the efforts in the 1940s to set up organizations such as the International Monetary Fund (IMF) and to promote trade through the General Agreement on Tariffs and Trade (GATT) reflect the Keynesian idea of using intergovernmental organizations (IGOs) and agreements to promote and, when necessary, to regulate international economic interchange. Modern liberals also favor such government interference as foreign aid and, sometimes, concessionary trade agreements or loan terms to assist LDCs to develop.

In sum, modern economic liberals generally believe in the capitalist approach of eliminating political interference in the international economy. They are modified capitalists, though, because they also favor using IGO and national government programs for two ends: (1) to ensure that countries adopt capitalism and free trade and (2) to ease the worst inequities in the system so that future competition can be fairer and current LDCs can have a chance to achieve prosperity. Thus economic liberals do not want to overturn the current political and economic international system.

ECONOMIC STRUCTURALISM

The third major approach to IPE is called **economic structuralism**. Like the other two approaches, economic structuralism has both descriptive and prescriptive elements.

Economic structuralists believe that economic structure determines politics. That is, the conduct of world politics is based on the way that the world is organized economically. Structuralists contend that the world is divided between have and have-not countries and that the "haves" (the EDCs) work to keep the "have nots" (LDCs) weak and poor in order to exploit them. To change this, economic structuralists favor a radical restructuring of the economic system designed to end the uneven distribution of wealth and power.

Economic structuralists can be divided into two major camps: Marxist theorists and dependencia theorists. Marxists see the state and capitalism as inherent sources of economic evil; dependencia analysts do not necessarily share this view. Instead, they advocate fundamental reforms to end economic oppression. Both types of economic structuralists believe that significant changes have to be made in the way international politics works in order to promote LDC development, but they disagree about how radical the change must be. Marxists believe that the entire capitalist-based system must be overturned and replaced with domestic and international socialist systems before economic equity can be achieved. Less radical economic structuralists stress reform of the current market system.

Marxist Theory

Marxism is perhaps the best-known strand of structuralist thought. Communist ideology, associated with Karl Marx, maintains that the economic order determines political and social relationships. Thus the distribution of wealth and the struggle between the propertied and powerful *bourgeoisie* and the poor and oppressed *proletariat* is the essence of politics. The first Soviet Communist Party chief, V. I. Lenin, applied **Marxism** to international politics. He argued in *Imperialism: The Highest Stage of Capitalism* (1916) that capitalist, bourgeois leaders had duped their proletariat workers into supporting the exploitation of other proletariat peoples through imperialism. Thus, the class struggle also included an international class struggle between bourgeois and proletariat countries and peoples.

GOMAA
AL AHRAM WEEKLY
Cairo
EGYPT

Poverty Line

This Egyptian editorial drawing captures the view of economic structuralists, who believe that the world's wealthier countries want the world's less developed countries to remain poor in order to dominate and exploit them.

Dependencia Theory

A second variation of structuralist thought is **dependencia theory**, which is also referred to as neo-Marxist theory and economic radical theory. Dependencia theorists argue that the exploitation of the LDCs by the EDCs is exercised through indirect control and is driven by the EDCs' need for cheap primary resources, external markets, profitable investment opportunities, and low-wage labor. The South produces low-cost, low-profit **primary products** such as agricultural products and raw materials. These help supply the EDCs' production of high-priced, high-profit **manufactured goods**, some of which are sold to the LDCs. It is, therefore, in the interest of capitalist exploiters to keep LDCs dependent. For this reason, economic structuralists say, **neocolonialism** (neoimperialism), which operates without colonies but is nevertheless imperialistic, has created a hierarchical structure in which the rich states in the center of the world economic system dominate the LDCs on the periphery of the system. The dependency of LDCs is maintained in a number of ways, such as structuring the rules and practices of international economics to benefit the North. The economic structuralists further contend that neoimperial powers corrupt and co-opt the local elite in LDCs by allowing them personal wealth in return for the governing of their countries to benefit the North in such ways as keeping wages low for MNCs and ensuring low prices for the primary products needed by the EDCs .

An economic radical would argue, for example, that the U.S. role in the Persian Gulf region dating back to World War II epitomizes neoimperialism. The devil's bargain, in the view of structuralists, is this: The United States protects or tries to protect the power of obscenely rich, profoundly undemocratic rulers of oil-rich states, such as Saudi Arabia and Kuwait, as it did in 1991. In return, the king and emir keep the price of oil down, which benefits the economies of the United States and the other oil-importing EDCs. Crude oil sold for an average of about $23 a barrel (equal to 42 gallons) in 1990. During the decade after the Persian Gulf War, oil seldom sold above $20 per barrel. And while the price recently spiked up and by mid-2002 was at about $27 a barrel (current dollars), that amounted to a decreased price, about $20 in real (1990) dollars. It is possible to argue that the bargain basement price of petroleum has been based on supply and demand. Structuralists would differ, though, and argue that those market forces have been manipulated through a greedy conspiracy between capitalist oil consumers and despotic oil producers.

Two Economic Worlds: North and South

Whether or not you subscribe to economic nationalist, internationalist, or structuralist theory, it cannot be denied that the world is generally divided into two economic spheres: a wealthy North made up of EDCs and a less wealthy South composed of LDCs. The two geographical designations result from the fact that most EDCs lie to the north in North America and Europe and most LDCs are farther to the south in Africa, Asia, and Central and South America. There are exceptions, however, and what is important is that the North and the South are distinguished from each other by economic and political factors more than by their geographical position.

TWO ECONOMIC WORLDS: ANALYZING THE DATA

The economic factor is the most objective distinction between North and South. The **North** is much wealthier than the **South**, as can be ascertained by examining countries (and the 2000 per capita GNP of each). That year the two dozen wealthiest countries had an average per capita GNP of $27,680; the South's average per capita GNP was $1,230. The structure of the economy is another factor that generally differentiates EDCs from LDCs. The countries of the North tend to have more diverse economic bases that rely for their income on the production of a wide variety of manufactured products and the provision of diverse and sophisticated services. The countries of the South usually depend on fewer products for their income; these are often agricultural produce or raw materials, such as minerals. In 2000, for example, agriculture accounted for 12 percent of the GNPs of the South and only 2 percent of the GNPs of the North.

It is important to note that these two classifications and the overall numbers contain some difficulties. One is that, as with most attempts to categorize the world's political and economic divisions, the classifications are imprecise and subject to change. On the sole basis of per capita GNP, for example, the World Bank divides countries into four economic groups: low-income ($755 or less), lower-middle-income ($756–$2,995), upper-middle-income ($2,996–$9,265), and high-income (more than $9,266). These groupings are illustrated in the accompanying map.

These two classifications (North-South, and the four World Bank income groups) generally coincide, but not completely. One difference is that six countries (Brunei, Israel, Kuwait, Qatar, Singapore, and the United Arab Emirates), which are usually classified as part of the South, fall into the high-income group. It is also important to note that some LDCs have moved a significant distance toward achieving a modern economic base. The **newly industrializing countries (NICs)** are still usually placed in the South by analysts, but countries such as South Korea ($8,920) and Argentina ($7,460) could be classified as developed market economies. The NICs are also sometimes referred to as NIEs (newly industrializing economies) to accommodate the inclusion of Taiwan ($11,200).

A second issue of classifying countries economically relates to how to treat Russia, the other former Soviet republics (FSRs), and the former communist region of Eastern Europe. The World Bank designates these countries as transition economies (from communism to capitalism). They are also referred to as **countries in transition (CITs)**. Some of these transition economies have a reasonable industrial base, although all of them have experienced significant economic difficulties during the transition. Of them, only one, Slovenia ($10,050), falls in the high-income group.

Classifying countries economically is complex. We are used to thinking of Russia as an industrialized country, yet by some objective economic criteria, it is a less developed country. The dire economic condition of many Russians is captured in this 2001 photo of a boy begging in Moscow. The sign reads, "Help me. I want to eat."

Others, such as Hungary ($4,710), fall into the upper-middle-income group, but most CITs, including Russia ($1,660), are in the lower-middle-income group, and five of the Asian FSRs are all in the low-income category. Of this group of FSRs, Tajikistan ($180) is the poorest. Given the economic data, all these countries except Slovenia are treated here as LDCs.

A third concern centers on the difficulty of measuring and reporting economic data. All the statistics are only an approximation. If, for instance, you have ever had an odd job babysitting or raking leaves, have been paid for it, and have not reported your income to the government, then the GDP for your country is slightly lower

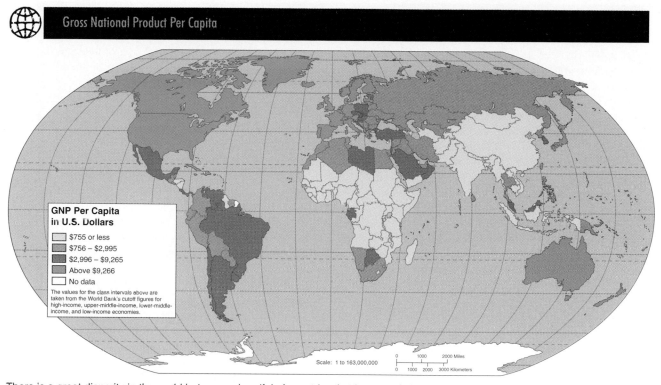

Gross National Product Per Capita

GNP Per Capita in U.S. Dollars

- $755 or less
- $756 – $2,995
- $2,996 – $9,265
- Above $9,266
- No data

The values for the class intervals above are taken from the World Bank's cutoff figures for high-income, upper-middle-income, lower-middle-income, and low-income economies.

Scale: 1 to 163,000,000

0   1000   2000 Miles
0   1000   2000   3000 Kilometers

There is a great disparity in the world between a handful of countries that have a relatively small percentage of the world population but possess a huge proportion of global wealth (measured here in per capita GNP) and everyone else. The dollars that the legend uses to divide countries into economic categories do not truly convey the impact of the differences in economic circumstance. Especially if you are living in one of the poorest countries, you are much more likely to be illiterate, ill-housed, malnourished, and ill, and to die earlier than your contemporaries in the wealthy countries.

than it should be. All countries, especially LDCs, have significant unrecorded economic activity. For this reason, major differences in economic circumstances, economic trends, and other macroeconomic indicators are more important than specific dollar figures.

Fourth, the cost of many items varies tremendously from country to country, undermining part of the relevance of some data, such as GNP. This issue is explored in the box, GNP-PPP: The Big Mac Standard.

For all of these difficulties, the classification of the world into a North and a South is still useful. One reason is that the classification anomalies do not disguise the fact that, as a rule, the countries of the South are poorer and less industrialized than those of the North. The data can be dry to read, but the reality behind the data is that, on average, the conditions of life for the citizens in the countries of the industrialized North are dramatically better than the living standards of the relatively deprived people who reside in the LDCs of the South.

Economic vulnerability is a second factor that unites most of the South and distinguishes it from the North. Even many upper-middle-income countries of the South have a shaky economic base that relies on one or a few products. For example, those LDCs that rely on petroleum production and export are at substantial risk when the price of oil is exceptionally low, as it was throughout most of the 1990s.

Common political experiences of the LDCs are a third reason that the North-South distinction continues to be applicable. Most LDCs share a history of being directly or indirectly dominated by the EDCs of Europe and North America or, in the case of the former communist countries, by Russia.

GNP-PPP: THE BIG MAC STANDARD

The existence of over 180 national currencies and their fluctuation in values against one another make it difficult to evaluate any country's financial status by using standard measures, such as gross national product (GNP). Using the U.S. dollar as a base to calculate exchange rates, some countries' 2000 per capita GNPs were: United States ($34,380), South Africa ($3,020), and Switzerland ($38,140). These figures might lead you to conclude that the average Swiss citizen is somewhat better off economically than the average American, who, in turn, is more than 10 times better off than the average South African. This analysis, however, would not be totally accurate.

Many economists argue that these figures do not present an accurate picture because they do not reflect the prices for commonly consumed local products such as housing, public transportation, movies, and fast food. One way that some analysts keep track of these relative factors is by using the ubiquitous Big Mac as a standard to measure relative prices. According to data on 30 countries compiled by the *Economist* (a leading financial journal), the average 2000 Big Mac cost $2.54 in the base-price United States, and ranged from $0.97 in South Africa to $3.98 in Switzerland.[1]

To adjust GDP to reflect the actual cost of living in various countries, the World Bank and other financial institutions use GNP adjusted for **Purchasing Power Parity (PPP)**. This measure uses a "market basket" of items "not traded on international markets" (that is, like Big Macs, locally produced and consumed) to help compare standards of living. By this standard (and again using the United States as the base), the above countries' per capita GNP-PPPs in 2000 were: United States ($29,340), South Africa ($9,400), and Switzerland ($28,769). Note that when using per capita GNP-PPP instead of just per capita GNP, the Swiss were worse, not better, off than Americans, and the South Africans were nowhere near as badly off compared to the Americans.

It is important to see that neither the standard GNP nor the newer GNP-PPP is a fully accurate measure. GNP does not take prices of locally produced and consumed items into account. But GNP-PPP misses the fact that many items we all consume come through international trade, and the price of a barrel of imported petroleum, an imported Toyota, or an imported Mac—in this case the computer—is pretty much the same, whether you are paying for it in U.S. dollars, South African rand, or Swiss francs.

TWO ECONOMIC WORLDS: HUMAN CONDITIONS

Sensationalism is not the aim of this book. Still, it is hard to recount conditions of impoverishment in neutral, academic terms. Approximately 85 percent of the world's people live in the South, yet they produce only 23 percent of the global GNP. Far outpacing the fortunes of those who reside in LDCs, the 15 percent of the people who are fortunate enough to reside in the North produce 77 percent of the world's measurable GNP. Another telling calculation is that on a per capita basis, the richest 15 percent of the world's citizens produce $67 for every $1 produced by the 40 percent of the world's population who live in the poorest countries (the low-income or **least developed countries, LLDCs**). Perhaps worse, this 67:1 ratio has doubled from a 30:1 ratio in 1960. As stark as these statistics are, their true meaning is in their social impacts. Compared with those who live in an EDC, a person who lives in an LLDC is:

Did You Know That:
Worldwatch Institute estimates that 1.2 billion people around the world are underfed and undernourished. It also reports that during 1999, some 400,000 Americans underwent liposuction procedures to siphon excess fat from their bodies.

- 24 times more likely to be illiterate if adult.
- 16 times more likely to die before age 5.
- 27 times more likely not to have access to basic sanitation services.
- 18 times more likely to have to work full-time as a child.
- 13 times more likely to die during childbirth.
- 19 years earlier in the grave.

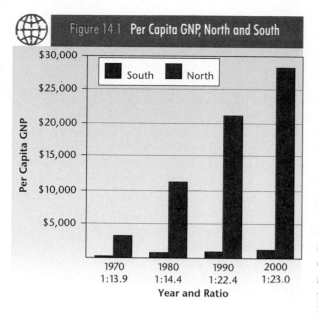

Figure 14.1   Per Capita GNP, North and South

Year	1970	1980	1990	2000
Ratio	1:13.9	1:14.4	1:22.4	1:23.0

Year and Ratio

Data source: World Bank (2002).

The economic gulf that divides the wealthy countries of the North and the poorer countries of the South has expanded 65 percent. In 1970, the average citizen in the North earned 13.9 times the average earnings of the average citizen in the South. That gap expanded to 23 times the average earnings in the South by 2000.

The scope of the deprivation that many in the South suffer also boggles the mind when the total number of humans affected is calculated. More than 1 billion people in the LDCs live on less than $1 a day. Literacy and education are beyond the dreams of many. There are 842 million illiterate adults and 80 million children in the South who are not in school. The perils to health are everywhere. Some 2.5 billion people in LDCs do not have access to safe water and sanitary sewer facilities. Food supplies are often inadequate, with more than 150 million children in the LDCs suffering from malnutrition. Medical facilities in the South are overwhelmed. Each physician in the LLDCs is responsible for about 2,000 people, compared to only 360 people for a physician in the North; hundreds of millions of people in the South have no access to any kind of health care. These conditions lead to disease and death on a wide scale. Infants die at a scandalously high rate, as do women during childbirth, and just 57 percent of the people in LLDCs (compared to 86 percent of the people in EDCs) live to age 65.

Nor is the future bright for many in the South in spite of some improving indicators of social conditions. Overall, though, the economic gap between North and South is widening. This increasing disparity is evident in Figure 14.1.

The worst news is that conditions are declining in some countries. Sub-Saharan Africa is a particularly depressed region. The combined per capita GNP of the region's countries declined by an annual average of –0.2 percent between 1965 and 2000. Even though the United States and sub-Saharan Africa have approximately equal populations, the U.S. total GDP is 23 times larger than that of sub-Saharan Africa. A horrific 46 percent of its population lives on less than $1 a day. The region has the world's highest birthrate, and the rapidly rising population is outpacing agricultural production. Only 55 percent of the region's population has access to basic sanitation; there is but one physician for every 10,000 people; adult illiteracy is 39 percent; life expectancy is only 47 years. It is unnecessary to recite more grim statistics in order to document that—relatively speaking and, in some cases, absolutely—the rich are getting richer and the poor are getting poorer.

The Growth and Extent of International Political Economy

Economic interchange between politically separate people predates written history. Trading records extend back to almost 3000 B.C., and archaeologists have uncovered evidence of trade in the New Stone Age, or Neolithic period (9000–8000 B.C.). Since then, economics has become an ever more important aspect of international relations. This is evident in expanding trade and the resulting increased interrelationship between international economic activity and domestic economic circumstances. We can see this by examining trade, investment, and monetary exchanges and by looking at both the general expansion of each of these factors and the uneven pattern of each.

TRADE

Before beginning our discussion of the historical growth and the current extent of trade, it is necessary to note the two elements that compose trade: goods and services.

Merchandise trade is what people most frequently associate with imports and exports. These goods are tangible items and are subdivided into two main categories: primary goods (raw materials) and manufactured goods. **Services trade** is less well known but also important. Services include things that you do for others. When American architects receive pay for designing foreign buildings, when U.S. insurance companies earn premiums for insuring foreign assets or people, when American movies and other intellectual properties earn royalties abroad, when U.S. trucks carry goods in Mexico or Canada, the revenue they generate is payment for the export of services. These services are a major source of income for countries, amounting to more than $1.5 trillion, or 20 percent of the entire flow of goods and services across international borders.

The trade in services can also have a significant impact on a country's balance of trade. The United States in 2000 had a merchandise-trade deficit of $427 billion. This was somewhat offset by an $80 billion services-trade surplus, which reduced the overall U.S. trade deficit by 19 percent. It is also worth pointing out that exported services do not have to be performed overseas. American colleges and universities, for example, are one of the country's largest exporters of services. More than 515,000 foreign students spent over $10 billion for tuition, room, and board at U.S. institutions of higher learning and about another $4 billion on other aspects of college life ranging from textbooks to pepperoni pizzas.

Did You Know That:
The early economic and military empire of Assyria extended between the Black, Caspian, and Mediterranean Seas. At the empire's height under Ashurbanipal (669–633 B.C.), it welded vassal states into a single monetary system that facilitated trade. The recent excavation of the Philistine vassal-city of Ekron in modern Israel revealed 105 olive-oil pressing sites capable of producing 290,000 gallons annually for the empire.

A General Pattern of Expanding Trade

Trade is booming, and the international flow of goods and services is a vital concern to all world states (Moon, 1996). World trade in 1913 totaled only $20 billion. In 2001 world trade stood at over $7.5 trillion. Even considering inflation, this represents a tremendous jump in world commerce. Figure 14.2 depicts the rise in the dollar volume of trade. Trade growth has been especially rapid during the

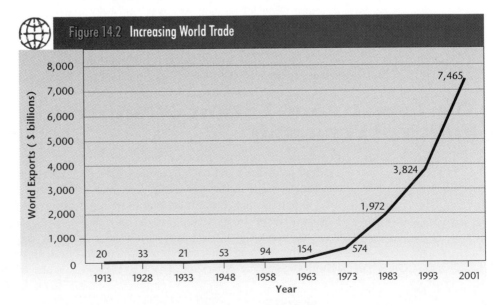

Figure 14.2 Increasing World Trade

Data source: IMF, World Economic Outlook, May 2002, on the Web at: http://www.imf.org/.

Trade, measured here in current dollar exports, has grown meteorically during recent decades. This growth is one sign of the vastly increased importance of international economic relations to the individual countries and their citizens.

post–World War II era of significant tariff reductions. During the 1913 to 1948 period of world wars, depression, and trade protectionism, trade increased at an average annual rate of only 0.8 percent. The postwar period has seen average annual increases at a rate of approximately 9 percent. The rapid growth of trade has been caused by a number of supply and demand factors and the implementation of a free trade philosophy.

Supply: Productive Technology The industrial revolution, which began in eighteenth-century Europe, is one factor behind increased trade. As productivity increased, so did the supply of goods. From 1705 to 1780, prior to industrialization, world industrial production increased only slowly at an annual rate of only 1.5 percent. Mechanization of industry boosted that average annual rate of increase to 2.6 percent in the four decades that followed, and to 3.3 percent between 1820 and 1860 (Rostow, 1978). As production rates sped up, the manufactured goods saturated local markets, and manufacturers increasingly had to seek markets for their surplus goods farther away and even across national borders. Thus, the greater volume of manufactured goods formed the supply side of trade development.

Demand: Resource Requirements Industrialization also affected the "demand" side of international trade. During the nineteenth century and through World War II, importation of raw materials by the industrialized European countries was a primary force in trade as manufacturing needs both increased demand for raw materials and outstripped domestic resource availability. During the late 1800s, for example, raw materials accounted for well over half of the goods moving across international borders. This level declined steadily during the twentieth century for several reasons, one of which is that synthetic materials became an ever larger part of the manufacturing process. Currently primary products account for only about 20 percent of all goods in international trade; that percentage, although it seems small, equals about $1.2 trillion dollars in primary products.

Demand: Materialism The rise in the world's standard of living, especially in the industrialized countries, has also contributed to "demand" pressure on international trade. More workers entered the wage-producing sector, and their "real" (after inflation) wages went up. The real wages of English craftspersons held relatively steady between 1300 and 1800, for instance, but beginning in 1800, after the industrial revolution, more than doubled by the 1950s.

This trend has continued into the current era. The workers of the wealthier countries have especially enjoyed increased real wages. The average real wage in the industrialized countries, for example, rose 1.7 percent annually between 1980 and 2000. This strengthens demand because individuals have more wealth with which to purchase domestic and imported goods.

Supply and Demand: Transportation Technology has also increased our ability to transport goods: to carry the supply of manufactured goods and to meet the demand for them. The development of railroads and improvements in maritime shipping were particular spurs to trade. They both increased the volume of trade that was possible and decreased per-unit transportation costs. Less than two centuries ago, all exported products were carried abroad in sailing ships or in wagons. Now foreign commerce is carried around the world by about 28,000 oceangoing merchant vessels and a vast number of trains and trucks; in just the United States, it is delivered by over 1 million large trucks and by more than 19,000 locomotives pulling almost 1.3 million freight cars.

Free Trade Philosophy The central idea of economic internationalists, that free trade will enhance overall prosperity, is rooted in the writings of capitalist economists that date back as far as the 1600s. These are reviewed later in this chapter. Whatever their validity, such theories did not come to the center stage until they captured the attention of national policy makers in the wake of the global trauma occasioned by the great economic depression of the 1930s and World War II in the early 1940s. One cause for these miseries, it was said, was the high tariffs that had restricted trade and divided nations. To avoid a recurrence, the United States took the lead in reducing barriers to international trade. The General Agreement on Tariffs and Trade (GATT) came into being in 1947 when countries accounting for 80 percent of world commerce agreed to work to reduce international trade barriers. As a result of this and a series of related efforts, world tariff barriers dropped dramatically. American import duties, for example, dropped from an average of 60 percent of a product's wholesale price in 1934, to 25 percent in 1945, to a current level of less than 4 percent. The tariffs of other EDCs have similarly dropped. Tariffs, as we will soon see, are not the only trade barrier, but their sharp reductions have greatly reduced the cost of imported goods and have strongly stimulated trade.

Uneven Patterns of Trade: North and South

The historical growth of trade, it is important to note, has not occurred evenly throughout the world. Instead, three facts about the patterns of international commerce stand out. First, as depicted in Figure 14.3, trade is overwhelmingly dominated by the EDCs in the North. These countries amass 76 percent of the exports in goods and services combined. The percentage of world trade shared by the LDCs is relatively small, especially in per capita figures.

A second, and related, pattern of world trade is that only a small percentage of global commerce occurs among LDCs. The merchandise trade among LDCs in 2000 accounted for a scant 15 percent of the world total. Moreover, the handful of EDCs bought 59 percent of all LDC exports. This pattern of trade leaves the LDCs heavily dependent on the EDCs for export earnings and, thus, in a vulnerable position.

A third important trade pattern involves types of exports. Merchandise exports account for 82 percent of what EDCs sell abroad; primary products make up only 18 percent. For LDCs a higher 34 percent of their exports are primary products, such as food, fibers, fuels, and minerals. For the poorest countries, the LLDCs, that figure is 48 percent. The United States and Chile provide a good comparison. Of all U.S. goods exported, manufactured products account for 82 percent and primary products for 18 percent. Chile's exports are just about the opposite, with manufactured goods at 17 percent and primary products at 83 percent. To make matters worse, just one primary product, copper, accounts for about 40 percent of Chile's exports. This dependence on primary products for export earnings leaves the LDCs in a disadvantaged position because the prices of primary products increase more slowly than those of manufactured goods and also because the prices for primary products are highly volatile. In this case, Chile's economy in the late 1990s was rocked by the plummeting price of copper, which was $1.33 a pound in 1995, sank to $0.66 a pound in 1999, and had only risen to $0.75 a pound in mid-2002.

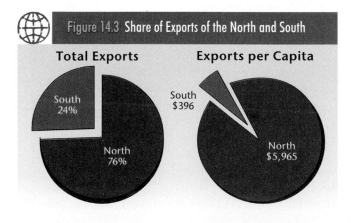

Figure 14.3 Share of Exports of the North and South

Total Exports

South 24%
North 76%

Exports per Capita

South $396
North $5,965

Data source: World Bank (2002).

The pattern of world trade is very uneven. The North exports more than 3 times as much in goods and services as does the South in overall dollars and 22 times as much on a per capita basis.

INTERNATIONAL INVESTMENT

Trade has not been the only form of international economic activity that has grown rapidly. There also has been a parallel expansion of international financial ties. This flow of investments can be examined by reviewing types of foreign investments and multinational corporations.

Foreign Direct and Portfolio Investment

One aspect of increased financial ties is the growth of investment in other countries. When Americans invest in British or Nigerian companies, or when Canadians invest in U.S. corporations, a web of financial interdependency is begun. Such international investment has long existed but has accelerated greatly since World War II. In 1950 U.S. direct investment abroad was $11.8 billion. By 2000 that figure had skyrocketed to $2.6 trillion. Investors in other industrialized countries and a few investors from LDCs have added to the international flow of investment capital. Currently, total world **foreign direct investment (FDI)**, buying a major stake in foreign companies or real estate, is well over $11 trillion, including $2.8 trillion in direct investments in the United States. **Foreign portfolio investment (FPI)** in stocks and bonds that does not involve the control of companies and real estate is measured in the trillions. For the United States alone, foreign investors hold just over $2.5 trillion in such U.S. assets, and Americans own over $2.6 trillion in foreign portfolio investment.

Like most areas of international economics, the movement of investment in the world is not evenly distributed. Since few investors are from the South, the flow of profits from investment mostly benefits the North. Certainly, the flow of investment capital has benefits for recipient countries, but even here the distribution is mixed. About three-quarters of all FDI, and an even greater percentage of FPI, is made in EDCs. Furthermore, the NICs and a few other countries such as China receive most of the investment capital, and most LDCs receive little or none.

The flow of investment capital into and out of countries is an important factor in their economic well-being. FDI and, to a degree, FPI helps support and expand local businesses. For example, foreigners hold about $3.1 trillion in U.S. debt instruments (mostly U.S. federal and corporate bonds), and these loans to Americans help finance the U.S. government and American businesses. Foreign investments also create earnings for investors. Americans and U.S. corporations earned $105 billion in 2000 alone from their foreign direct investments.

International Investment and Multinational Corporations

To understand the flow of international investment, it is especially important to analyze the growth and practices of **multinational corporations (MNCs)**. These firms, also called transnational corporations (TNCs), are at the forefront of the international movement of investment capital and private loans among countries.

An MNC is a private enterprise that includes subsidiaries operating in more than one state. This means more than merely international trading. Rather, it implies ownership of manufacturing plants and/or resource extraction and processing operations in a variety of countries. Additionally, MNCs conduct businesses abroad that supply services, such as banking, insurance, and transportation. Many observers therefore contend that MNCs are transnational organizations with operations that transcend national boundaries (Pauly & Reich, 1997).

The roots of modern MNCs extend back to Europe's great trading companies, beginning with the Dutch East India Trading Company in 1689. The level of multinational enterprise grew slowly, then expanded more quickly along with the increased European industrialization in the nineteenth century. By the end of that century, burgeoning American industry began to be a force, and it was not long after Henry Ford began building Model T's that his corporation had its first subsidiary in Europe. Indeed, as early as 1902 one British author wrote a book, *The American Invaders*, warning against the takeover of the European economy by such American predators as Singer Sewing Machine, Otis Elevator, and General Electric.

Then, after World War II, the development of MNCs truly accelerated. Since 1945 direct private investment in international ventures has increased, on average, about 10 percent annually, and it is currently expanding at over $200 billion a year. In the process, modern MNCs became economic goliaths that account for a growing percentage of trade and other forms of international commerce.

There are now tens-of-thousands of MNCs operating in more than one country. Not only are MNCs numerous; they also pack enormous economic muscle. The so-called Global 500, the world's 500 largest corporations measured in terms of earnings, had a combined gross corporate product in 2000 of $9.2 trillion, or about 30 percent of the entire economic production of the world (the global GDP). They employ tens of millions of workers and have assets worth trillions of dollars. Moreover these companies are growing quickly. Total gross corporate profits (GCP) in real dollars for the Global 500 increased by 6.9 percent in 1999; world GDP grew a less robust 4.7 percent. Moreover, the size of some individual MNCs is immense. Using a company's GCP as a standard, the biggest manufacturing MNC in 2000 was ExxonMobil with a GCP of $210 billion and over 100,000 employees. If ExxonMobil's GCP counted as its GDP, the company would have been the world's twenty-first largest economy.

> **Did You Know That:**
> There are 57 multinational corporations that employ 100,000 or more people. Wal-Mart is the MNC with the largest number of employees. There are 61 countries whose populations are smaller than Wal-Mart's 1,383,000 employees.

It is also worth noting that the MNCs are overwhelmingly based in the North. Therefore they contribute to the wealth and economic power of the EDCs at, some analysts would say, the expense of the South. Of the top 500 MNCs, about 95 percent are based in the North, with only a few of the biggest corporations in LDCs.

MONETARY RELATIONS

The increased flow of trade and capital means that **monetary relations**, including exchange rates, interest rates, and other monetary considerations, have become an increasingly significant factor in both international and domestic economic health. This has always been true, but as trade and other economic relations have expanded, the importance of monetary interchange has increased proportionately. To begin to explore the complex area of monetary relations here and in later chapters, we can look at the evolution of the monetary system, how exchange rates work, and the calculation and impact of the balance of payments.

The Globalization of the Monetary System

The dramatic growth of world trade, international investment, and other aspects of international economic interchange already detailed in this chapter have necessarily been accompanied by a globalization of the monetary system. We can examine that by looking at the globalization of money, the globalization of financial services, North-South patterns of money and banking, and the international regulation of money.

The Globalization of Money Increased trade, investment, and other factors have set off a torrent of money moving in international channels. The amount of currency exchange has reached such a point that it is impossible to calculate very accurately, but it is not unreasonable to estimate that the currency flow is at least $1.5 trillion a day, or

The international flow of currency is so immense that there is no truly accurate count. But at least $1.5 billion a day are converted from one currency to another, and the rise and fall of exchange rates has a significant impact on the economies of all countries and their citizens.

$548 trillion a year. About two-thirds of this moves through the banking centers in just four countries: Germany, Japan, the United Kingdom, and the United States. With just these four leading banking centers exchanging at least $1 trillion a day, this represents a phenomenal increase from the 1989 levels of $550 billion a day, or $201 trillion a year, in currency exchanges. Central banks use their monetary reserves (foreign currencies and gold) to try to control exchange rates by buying or selling currency. The problem is that these reserves amount to only about two days' worth of global currency transactions. This limits the ability of the central banks to control currency fluctuations, thereby endangering monetary exchange stability and, by extension, economic prosperity.

The Globalization of Financial Services To accommodate the globalization of money, there has been a parallel globalization of banking and other financial services. In a relatively short period of time, banks have grown from hometown to national to multinational enterprises. Another indicator of increased international financial ties is the level of international lending by private banks. Many multinational banks are members of the Global 500. Just the top 50 multinational banks controlled assets of nearly $20 trillion in 2000, giving them immense financial power in the global economy.

It is also worth noting that many MNCs are merging into immense, multi-purpose financial service conglomerates. The merger in 1998 of Citicorp and Travelers Group into Citigroup is one example. Citicorp included Citibank, the second largest U.S. bank, which operates in nearly 100 countries, and Global Consumer Business, the world's largest issuer of credit cards (about 60 million). The Travelers Group included the insurance company and such subsidiaries such as Primerica Financial Services and the now-merged major brokerage houses, Salomon Brothers and Smith Barney. The trend, then, is toward multipurpose financial MNCs that have a major impact on the global economy based on to whom they lend their money, for what purposes they lend it, and what interest rates they charge.

Did You Know That:
Citigroup was the largest multinational bank in 2000 with $902 billion in assets.

North-South Patterns of Money and Banking In line with the general pattern of global economic power, the control of money and banking is largely dominated by the North and little influenced by the South. The world's largest banks, like most MNCs, are almost all headquartered in EDCs. Indeed, of the top 50 largest multinational banks, none were headquartered in LDCs. The 13 percent of the countries that are EDCs hold 42 percent of all foreign reserves. With the exception of a few offshore banking havens controlled by the North, the banks of the LDCs hold only 5 percent of all foreign deposits and have made only about 3 percent of all foreign loans.

The International Regulation of Money As trade, transnational investing, and other forms of international economic interchange increased during the twentieth century, it became clear that some mechanisms needed to be created to help regulate the rapidly expanding flow of currencies across borders. The most pressing problem was, and still is, how to stabilize the values of currencies against one another. To that end, there have been a number of regional and global efforts to keep exchange rates stable and to otherwise ensure that currency issues do not impede economic activity.

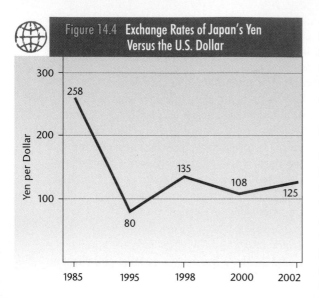

Figure 14.4 **Exchange Rates of Japan's Yen Versus the U.S. Dollar**

The changes in the yen/dollar exchange rate illustrate currency fluctuations.

The most advanced efforts have been in the European Union, which has the European Central Bank and now a common currency, the euro. At the global level, the International Monetary Fund, which is detailed in chapter 16, has the primary responsibility for attempting to maintain monetary stability.

Exchange Rates

Of all the facets of international economic relations, one of the least understood is the importance of the ebb and flow of the world's currencies. **Exchange rates** are, very simply, the values of two currencies in relation to each other—for example, how many U.S. dollars per Japanese yen and vice versa. Exchange rates are important because they affect several aspects of the balance of payments and the health of domestic economies. Fundamentally, a decline in the exchange rate of your country's currency in relation to another country's currency means that things you buy in or from that country will be more expensive and things that the other country buys in or from you will be less expensive. If your country's currency increases in value, things you buy in or from that country will be less expensive and things that the other country buys in or from you will be more expensive. For a fuller explanation of this, see the entry "How Exchange Rates Work" in the Explanatory Notes on page 571.

One example of the dramatic change in the value of a currency involves the exchange rate of the U.S. dollar versus Japan's yen (¥) since 1985, as shown in Figure 14.3. In January of that year, one dollar was worth 258 yen ($1 = ¥258). From that point, the yen fluctuated as low as $1 = ¥80 in 1995 and stood at $1 = ¥125 in mid-2002. The normal way of discussing this change would be to say that the U.S. dollar in 1995 was 68 percent weaker versus the yen than it was in 1985 and in 2002 was 56 percent stronger than it was in 1995. Does weak equal bad and strong equal good, though? That depends.

If you are an American, a relatively strong dollar versus the yen is good news if you are going to buy a Japanese automobile. It will cost less. But if you are a U.S. worker producing cars, you may get laid off because relatively inexpensive foreign cars cut into the domestic market. If you are a traveler and the dollar is strong, going to Japan will be less costly because your dollar will be worth more there. If you are in the American tourist industry, however, you will be harmed by the strong dollar since fewer Japanese will visit the United States because their yen will be worth less there. The list need not go on to make the point that currency fluctuations are a two-edged sword that have both financial benefits and drawbacks no matter which way it swings.

On a more general level, if your national currency is strengthening, inflation will probably go down in your country because the foreign products you buy will be less expensive. Also, your standard of living may go up because you can buy more imported goods to improve your material well-being.

If, on the other hand, you are a U.S. manufacturer trying to sell something to the Japanese, the dollar's rise is bad news because your product's price will rise in those countries and you will probably export less. If you work for one of those companies, your standard of living could plummet if you are laid off. A declining currency, then, benefits businesses that export and may also translate into more jobs as factories expand to meet new orders.

Balance of Payments

Along with exchange rates, another complicated aspect of international political economy that is central to understanding a country's overall health in the global economy is that country's balance of payments. Many of the matters that we have already discussed, including exports and imports, the ebb and flow of investment capital and investment returns, and international borrowing and other financial flows, combine to determine a country's **balance of payments**, a figure that represents the entire flow of money into and out of a country—that is, credits minus debits.

It is important to understand the components of the overall balance of payments to determine whether a country has a net inflow or a net outflow of financing. The United States has since 1989, when it had a balance-of-payments surplus of $15.3 billion, steadily amassed larger and larger balance-of-payments deficits, reaching $446 billion in 2001. The primary cause has been the mounting U.S. merchandise trade deficit, which grew from $101 billion in 1990 to $426 billion in 2001. Payments on the national debt are a second factor in the growing U.S. balance-of-payments deficit. With an accumulated federal debt over $5 trillion, the annual interest payment for FY2001 came to $206 billion. Of that, about one-third went to foreign bondholders.

What is even more worrisome than the dollar amounts of the U.S. deficit is the rising percentage of the national economy that it represents (Krugman, 1998). In the 1970s and 1980s, there was a surplus. For most of the 1990s, the United States economy took in between 1 percent and 2 percent less than it spent. That shot up to 3.5 percent in 1999, was over 4 percent in 2000 and 2001, and is projected by the IMF to remain over 4 percent during 2002 and 2003. That worries analysts. They ask, "How much longer can the United States continue to spend more than it earns and support the resumption of global growth?" The answer is that "At some point... the United States' [current account deficit]... will become too great a burden on the U.S. economy," touching off severe financial repercussions.[4]

It is also worth noting that a positive balance of payments does not automatically mean prosperity. Beset by lagging domestic demand, poor banking practices, and other problems, Japan's economy has been stagnant, growing only a weak 0.8 percent annually during the period 1993–2002, despite a balance-of-payments surplus for the same period that averaged over $105 billion annually and equaled 2 percent of the country's GDP. Still, a chronic deficit or one that is a high percentage of GDP eventually depletes a country's financial strength (Lincoln, 1998).

GLOBALIZATION AND INTERDEPENDENCE: DEBATING THE FUTURE

There is no doubt that the expansion of world trade, investment, and currency exchange has profoundly affected countries and their citizens. Economic **interdependence** has inexorably intertwined personal, national, and international prosperity (El-Agraa, 1997; Macesich, 1997). Domestic economics, employment, inflation, and overall growth are heavily dependent on foreign markets, imports of resources, currency exchange rates, capital flows, and other international economic factors. Globalization is a reality.

What is in doubt is how much further economic interdependence will or should proceed. Indeed, there is a crucial debate being held across the world in government councils, academic circles, the media, and elsewhere about the advantages and disadvantages of economic globalization. Supporting globalization, President Clinton told the World Economic Forum (WEF), which brings together many of the globe's business and political leaders, "Those who wish to roll back the forces of globalization because they fear its disruptive consequences... are plainly wrong. Fifty years of experience shows that greater economic integration and political cooperation are positive forces."[5] Others are opposed to or very cautious about globalization. "Our global village has caught fire, from where we do not know," President Hosni Mubarak of Egypt told the same conclave. "In the emerging world," Mubarak continued, "there is a bitter sentiment of injustice, a sense that there must be something wrong with a system that wipes out years of hard-won development because of changes in market sentiment."[6]

The issue of the impact of globalization on the average citizen and, even more, on the poor (both countries and individuals) has caused a sharp increase in protest movements and demonstrations at meetings of the World Bank, the World Trade Organization (WTO), the IMF, WEF, and other organizations identified with promoting the agenda of free economic interchange. For example, when the WTO held its annual summit meeting in Quebec City, Canada, in 2001, it was greeted by throngs of protesters whom one press report characterized as "baffling: Some are dressed as endangered sea turtles or genetically modified tomatoes. There are mad cows and sad hawks, Zapatistas and Sandinistas, giant Uncle Sams and stylized Grim Reapers. This is the anti-globalization movement. Sprawling, disparate, powerful. A political force unto itself that, given its international scope and staggering number of participants, is unprecedented in history." In terms that reflect the sentiments of many of the protesters, one asserted, "If you were to land on Earth today, you would see a world of tremendous inequality. The vast majority of people on this planet are living in poverty and without access to the wonderful technological, medical, informational and scientific advances that humanity has achieved. And that is what this is all about." Taking a very different view of what it is all about, Mike Moore, the director-general of the WTO exclaimed angrily, "The people that stand outside [our meeting] and say they work in the interests of the poorest people... they make me want to vomit. Because the poorest people on our planet, they are the ones that need us the most."[7]

The main points of that debate are reviewed in the following two sections that outline the case for and against free economic interchange. Think about these points as you read them and decide which view is closer to your own.

The Case for Free Economic Interchange

Advocates of free economic interchange argue from a series of economic and political propositions. Some of these involve trade or some other single aspect of international economic exchange. Other arguments are more general.

General Prosperity The most general economic argument is that trade and other forms of free economic exchange promote prosperity. Especially since the mid-twentieth century, trade has accounted for a rapidly growing share of the world's economic activity. Trade in 1960 equaled 25 percent of the collective GDPs of the world's countries. That share grew to 43 percent in 2000. The meaning of these numbers is that trade consumes more and more of what

Proponents of free economic interchange argue that one of its advantages is that it helps bring technology and other forms of development to LDCs. Illustrating this idea, U.S. Secretary of Commerce Don Evans greets Chinese children at a kindergarten in Beijing in April 2002. He was leading a delegation of 15 U.S. business leaders seeking new commercial opportunities in China soon after it joined the World Trade Organization. The children are looking at one of the computers donated as part of a program sponsored by IBM.

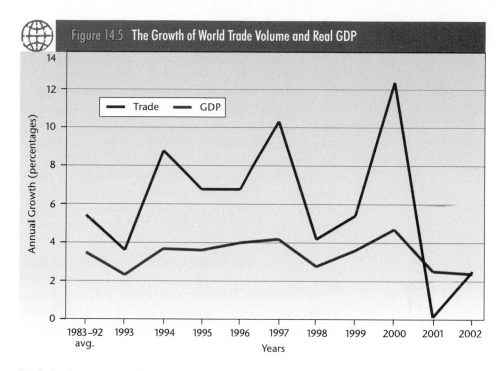

Figure 14.5 **The Growth of World Trade Volume and Real GDP**

Note: Trade volume is a measure of inflation, exchange rates, and unit prices.

Data source: IMF, World Economic Outlook, on the Web at: http://www.imf.org/.

As it long has, the growth of trade continued to outpace the growth of national economies measured in GDP since the early 1980s. This means that more and more of what countries produce is sold abroad. Therefore, national economic prosperity is ever more dependent on trade.

countries and their workers produce. Without trade, then, or with a marked decline in trade, national economies would slow, perhaps stall, or might even decline. Figure 14.5 demonstrates that trade growth helps drive economic expansion by comparing the growth of two inflation-adjusted measures: the volume of trade (exports) and real GDP.

Benefits of Specialization One economic theory supporting free trade holds that each country should efficiently do what it does best. Free trade theory dates back at least to Edward Misselden's *Free Trade or the Means to Make Trade Flourish*, published in England in 1632. Free trade theory is also associated with Adam Smith who in *The Wealth of Nations* (1776) held that political interference in commerce created ineffi- ciences that harmed prosperity. This belief that free trade is economically beneficial was further propounded by the English economists David Ricardo in *On the Principles of Political Economy and Taxation* (1817) and John Stuart Mill in *Principles of Political Economy* (1848). Ricardo developed the theory of "competitive advantage," which held that everyone would benefit if each country produced and exported its most cost- efficient products. Based on this view, Mill argued that trade's "advantage consists in a more efficient employment of the productive forces of the world."

The Cost of Protectionism The reverse side of specialization is the cost of protec- tionism to the country erecting barriers. Tariffs and other types of trade barriers result in higher prices. This occurs because the tariff cost is passed on to consumers or because consumers are forced to buy more expensive domestically produced goods. A study that examined 21 protected U.S. industries with annual sales of more than $1 billion in the United States found that the protectionism added an average of

35 percent to the prices of the products of those industries. The protection saved an estimated 191,000 jobs but cost American consumers $170,000 per job saved. Even when the cost of unemployment, other payments to displaced workers, lost taxes from unemployed workers, and lost tariff revenues were deducted from the $170,000, the net loss per job saved was still $54,000.[8]

Moreover, the economists found that the benefits from protection did not principally aid the workers. The average hourly pay in the 21 protected industries was only $7.76. One of the economists used the sugar industry, which is one of the most heavily protected in the United States, to illustrate this point. "If protection were a boon to low-skill workers," he asked rhetorically, "how is it that we have extremely bad working conditions and low pay in sugar plantations in Florida and Louisiana?" Answering his own question, the economist argued that "basically, if protection helps anybody, it's the owners. It doesn't trickle down."[9]

Promotion of Competition A third economic free trade argument focuses on competition (Crystal, 1998). Without foreign competition, domestic manufacturers have a captive market. However, a variety of ill effects, from price fixing to lack of innovation, may occur, especially if one corporation dominates its field or if there is monopolistic collusion among supposed competitors. American automakers seemingly refused to offer U.S. consumers well-built, inexpensive, fuel-efficient small cars until pressure from foreign competition forced them to reshape their product and modernize their production techniques. Competition has also spurred American manufacturers to modernize and streamline their operations to boost productivity, reduce costs, and improve competitiveness. There can be little doubt that the beating that U.S. manufacturers took at the hands of their foreign competitors, especially during the 1970s and 1980s, forced Chrysler, Ford, and General Motors to be more efficient and to offer better products.

Providing Development Capital Fourth, those who are in favor of free economic interchange contend that the flow of investment capital is an important source of development capital for LDCs. The IMF calculates that during the 1990s, more than $1.3 trillion in net foreign direct and portfolio investment flowed into the LDCs to bolster their economic development. It is also the case that MNC-directed investments provide EDCs with a wide variety of economic benefits. Jobs are one example. Foreign-owned MNCs employ 4.9 million people in the United States, or about 4 percent of the U.S. workforce. They pay those workers over $200 billion a year and contribute tens of billions of dollars in U.S. federal, state, and local taxes. At least some of these jobs would not have existed without foreign investment.

World Cooperation A fifth, and this time political, argument claims that free economic interchange promotes world cooperation. Functionalism argues that cooperating in certain specific functions, such as trade, can lead to cooperation in more political areas. If countries can trade together in peace, the interactions will bring greater contact and understanding. Cooperation will then become the rule rather than the exception, and this, it is thought, will lead to political cooperation and interaction. The move toward the political integration of Europe, which began with economic cooperation, is the most frequently cited example.

By a similar logic, supporters of free economic interchange also contend that the flow of investment capital around the world through MNCs promotes transnational cooperation and additionally serves the function of bringing people together through regular contact, cooperation, familiarity, and friendship.

Conflict Inhibition A sixth, and again political, argument for free economic interchange is that it restrains conflict by promoting interdependence, which makes fighting more difficult and more unlikely (Mott, 1997). In the words of one study, "Higher levels of economically important trade… are associated with lower incidences of militarized interstate disputes and war" (Oneal & Russett, 1997:288). One link between peace and trade is the contention that a high degree of interdependence among countries may dissuade or even prevent them from fighting. If oil and iron are necessary to fight, and if Country A supplies Country B's oil, and B supplies A's iron, then they are too enmeshed to go to war.

Much the same case is made for international investment as a restraint on conflict. Arguably, the more we own of each other, the more self-damaging it is to engage in economic or other sorts of aggression. For example, the nearly $200 billion in foreign direct and portfolio investment that the Americans and Japanese each staked in the other's country has given rise to the somewhat grim joke that goes, If the Japanese were ever again to attack Pearl Harbor, they would be blowing up their own property, and if the Americans retaliated, Wall Street would be as devastated as the Japanese roadways that were bombed.

Promoting Democracy A seventh, and once more political, argument advanced by some advocates of economic liberalization is that the openness required for free economic exchange promotes democracy. During the past few years, such NICs as South Korea, Taiwan, and Mexico have had their first truly democratic elections either ever or in many decades. The collapse of the repressive regime of President Suharto in Indonesia in 1998 and the country's first democratic elections in 1999 were, in the view of some observers, a result of the country's exposure to the liberalizing dictates of free trade and capital movements. Suharto had ruled as a despot for 30 years; in 2000 he was ordered to stand trial for looting his country's economy. In short, a South Korean political scientist explains, "Corrupt, authoritarian governments cannot adjust to the demands of the new globalized world, where you have to have a more transparent, competitive, and rational economic structure."[10]

The Case Against Free Economic Interchange

There are also several political and economic arguments for economic nationalism. Some of these involve trade or some other single aspect of international economic exchange; other arguments are more general (Greider, 1997).

Protecting the Domestic Economy The need for economic barriers to protect threatened domestic industries and workers from foreign competition is a favorite theme of domestic interest groups and politicians (Milner & Rosendorff, 1997). "I'm not a free trader," a U.S. secretary of commerce once confessed. "The goal," he said, "is to nurture American workers and industry. It is not to adhere to some kind of strict ideology."[11] An associated argument seeks protection for new or still small, so-called infant industries. This is an especially common contention in LDCs trying to industrialize, but it is also heard worldwide. Many economists give the idea of such protection some credibility but argue that supposedly temporary protection too often becomes permanent.

Opponents of the free flow of investment capital also argue that the positive impact of creation or preservation of jobs by the inflow of investment is offset by the loss of jobs when MNCs move operations to another country or when MNCs create new jobs in another country rather than in their own home country. American MNCs, for example, employ about 500,000 more workers in other countries than foreign MNCs employ American workers in the United States. Furthermore, these

Opposition to globalization has increased markedly during the last decade. This photograph shows riot police charging antiglobalization protesters, who wear life vests, motorcycle helmets, and other protective gear during a recent meeting of the Organization for Economic Cooperation and Development in Bologna, Italy. The picture could, however, have been taken at virtually any one of the recent meetings of leaders of the IMF, World Bank, or other international economic organizations, because almost all of them have met with large, angry protests.

opponents say, forcing well-paid workers in the United States and elsewhere to compete with poorly paid workers in LDCs depresses the wages and living conditions in EDCs. As a general statement the statistics show that this is not the case, but some types of workers, such as those in manufacturing that directly competes with foreign sources, are especially hard hit. The U.S. apparel industry, for one, has been devastated. The U.S. government estimates that from 1983 to 2005, the number of textile and garment workers will decline from 1.9 million to 1.3 million. For the regions in the U.S. South, where these plants are concentrated, the consequences are especially serious.

Lost jobs and wages must also be measured in terms of the ripple effect that multiplies each dollar several times. A worker without a job cannot buy from the local merchant, who in turn cannot buy from the building contractor, who in turn cannot buy from the department store, and so on, rippling out through the economy. Displaced workers also collect unemployment benefits and may even wind up on public assistance programs. These costs are substantial, and although some economists find that they are less than the cost of protecting jobs, the economic costs of unemployment diminish the gains derived from free trade. Finally, there is the psychological damage from being laid off and from other forms of economic dislocation that cannot be measured in dollars and cents.

Diversification Another economic nationalist argument holds that economic diversification should be encouraged. Specialization, it is said, will make a country too dependent on a few resources or products; if demand for those products falls, then economic catastrophe will result. In reality, no modern, complex economy will become that specialized, but the argument does have a simplistic appeal.

Compensating for Existing Distortions Yet another economic nationalist argument is that real-world trade distortions exist that are unaccounted for by pure economic theory. When the oil-producing countries set prices, authoritarian governments control exports and imports (state trading), protectionist countries erect NTBs, and governments subsidize producers of export items or items that compete with imports, then, the argument goes, nice-guy free-traders will finish last.

Free trade advocates reply that the answer to such distortions is to correct them rather than to retaliate. There has been, for example, progress made through negotiations between the United States and Japan to remedy the informal barriers in Japan that Americans have long complained about. Still, many existing distortions (such as consumer attitudes) are difficult to remedy by governmental action. It is also fatuous to imagine that countries will not control trade at least to some degree for economic, strategic, or domestic political reasons. Therefore, many argue that it is prudent to continue to compensate for existing distortions and that it is imprudent to take too far a lead in free trade and suffer negative consequences while others hold back.

Social, Economic, and Environmental Protection The chairman of Dow Chemical Company once confessed, "I have long dreamed of buying an island owned by no nation and establishing the world headquarters of the Dow company on… such an island, beholden to no nation or society" (Gruenberg, 1996:339). Critics of MNCs claim that such statements confirm their suspicions that these global enterprises use their ability to move operations around the globe to undercut protections relating to child labor, minimum wages, employment benefits, the ability of workers to organize, and many other socioeconomic standards (Rodrik, 1998). In the estimate of one analyst, "National governments have lost much of their power to direct their own economies because of the power of capital to pick up and leave." The result of the "quantum leap in the ability of transnational corporations to relocate their facilities around the world," he continues, is to make "all workers, communities and countries competitors for these corporations' favor." This competition, he worries, has set off "a 'race to the bottom' in which wages and social and environment conditions tend to fall to the level of the most desperate" (Brecher, 1993:685).

Critics of globalization also charge that, among other evils, the race to the bottom will mean gutting desirable social programs. Europe has built an extensive social welfare support system through government programs and mandates on industries (such as health insurance for workers, paid vacations, and other benefits). Such programs and benefits are costly, however, and European economies are struggling to meet them while also keeping the price of their products low enough to be competitive in the world markets or even at home compared to imported goods and services.

National Sovereignty One of the fastest-growing sources of sentiment against free economic interchange is the realization of many people that the process is eroding their country's national sovereignty. Many people are shocked to find that sometimes their country's laws and regulations must give way when they clash with rules of the WTO or some other international organization or agreement.

A closely related phenomenon involves the fear that foreign investors will gain control of your country's economy and will be able to influence your political processes and your culture (Bartlett & Seleny, 1998). In the 1960s U.S. investment capital seemed ready to engulf other countries' economies; Jean-Jacques Servan-Schreiber's best-seller, *The American Challenge* (1968), called on Europeans to resist foreign domination. Then, in the second half of the 1980s, when the value of the dollar plunged, the tide of foreign investment reversed, and the United States was seemingly flooded with foreign investors. During the late 1980s, foreigners invested nearly $200 billion more in U.S. assets than Americans invested in foreign assets. Foreign investors acquired quintessential American brand names. The British controlled Capitol Records; Canadians ran Roy Rogers; the Germans directed Alka-Seltzer; the Japanese acquired the 7–11 stores. Cries rang out that the British, among others, were coming. One member of Congress fretted that "for the first time since the Revolution, Americans are being subjected to decisions and dictates from abroad."[12]

Then, in the ceaseless ebb and flow of international finance, the tide turned again. Through the early and mid-1990s changes in the global economy resulted in a flood tide of American direct investment (FDI) abroad once again outpacing FDI coming into the United States. A sort of slack tide occurred in 1996 with the net inflows and outflows even at just over $100 billion each, followed by a new and continuing ebb tide, with more FDI being invested in the United States than being invested abroad by Americans.

The ebb and flow of FDI and the fears occasioned by foreign ownership have to be put in some perspective. For a country as large as the United States, the economy is so huge that foreign investment is still a minor aspect of the overall economic enterprise. Total foreign investment is just .02 percent (two one-hundredths) of the estimated $24 quadrillion worth of privately held tangible U.S. assets. Also, foreign investment is spread broadly among many countries. In 2000, the British were the largest direct investors in the United States with $230 billion in assets, and the Japanese were second with $163 billion in FDI. All totaled, though, there were 30 countries with $1 billion or more FDI in the United States. With such diversity, control by any outside country is impossible. It must also be remembered that Americans control more of other people's assets than others hold in U.S. assets. Maybe the British are coming, as the worry goes, with $230 billion worth of control in the United States, but the Yanks are also going, with their $233 billion FDI beachhead in the British economy.

National Security A related political economic nationalist argument involves national defense. The contention is somewhat the reverse of the "conflict inhibition," pro–free trade argument made earlier. Protectionists stress that the country must not become so dependent on foreign sources that it will be unable to defend itself. In recent years, the U.S. government has acted to protect industries ranging from specialty steels to basic textiles, partly in response to warnings that the country was losing its ability to produce weapons systems and uniforms.

Also under the rubric of national security, there is the issue of what can be called strategic trade. The question is how far a country should go in restricting trade and other economic interchanges with countries that are or may become hostile. Currently, the primary focus of the strategic trade debate is on dual-use technology that has peaceful uses but also has military applications.

Trying to maintain the U.S. lead in the multibillion dollar global computer market, the Bush administration in 2001 raised the level above which individual licenses for computer exports to potentially hostile countries (such as China and

Russia) are required from 85,000 millions of theoretical operations per second (MTOPS) to 190,000 MTOPS. While the move will help preserve the dominance of U.S. computer manufacturers in the global marketplace, it also creates concerns about how those computers will be used in countries such as China. At about the same time as the Bush administration allowed increasingly more sophisticated computers to be sold without restriction to China, the prestigious Rand Institute issued a report on the potential of a conflict with China, commenting that China was "able to take advantage of various new technologies that are commercially available. They [the Chinese] can't compete with the U.S. military across the board," the report continued, "but if they can pick niche areas, they can make life more difficult for us." From a U.S. policymaking perspective, one staff member in Congress commented that "the Rand report underscores.... the serious undermining of U.S. national security due to relaxed restrictions on export of dual-use technologies. The Chinese threat of a 'high-tech Pearl Harbor' is well within their reach."[13]

The issue well illustrates the tug of selling billions of dollars of aircraft and other equipment abroad versus the pull of supplying a less than friendly country with the capacity to increase the sophistication of its military equipment. "The U.S. faces excruciating trade-offs," observed one former ranking U.S. trade official. "On the one hand, we have overwhelming commercial goals. On the other, we have to be careful about transferring technology, first because there could be unintended military consequences, and secondly because we could be transferring our competitiveness."[14]

Policy Tool A seventh economic nationalist argument maintains that trade is a powerful political tool that can be used to further a country's interests. The extension or withdrawal of trade and other economic benefits also has an important—albeit hard-to-measure—symbolic value. Clearly, economic tools can be used to promote a country's political goals and free economic interchange necessarily limits the availability of economic tools to pursue policy.

A current example is the U.S. embargo on most trade with and travel to Cuba, which has existed since 1960. The debate over the wisdom of continuing the sanctions on the regime of Fidel Castro came to the fore in May 2002 when former president Jimmy Carter visited Cuba and, in a televised address, expressed his hope that the Bush administration would "soon act to permit unrestricted travel between the United States and Cuba, establish open trading relationships, and repeal the embargo." Carter went on to say that "the embargo freezes the existing impasse, induces anger and resentment, restricts the freedoms of U.S. citizens, and makes it difficult for us to exchange ideas and respect."[15]

President Bush saw things very differently. As he told a convention of Cuban Americans in Florida just five days later, "Well-intentioned ideas about trade will merely prop up this dictator, enrich his cronies, and enhance the totalitarian regime. It will not help the Cuban people. With real political and economic reform, trade can benefit the Cuban people and allow them to share in the progress of our times."[16]

The Debate in Perspective

To return to the point with which we began this section, the clash between the forces that favor the advancement of free economic interchange and those that oppose it, will be one of the most pivotal struggles in the years ahead. Secretary-General Kofi Annan is correct in his observation that while the world has moved toward ever greater globalism, "we have underestimated its fragility. The problem is this: The spread of markets far outpaces the ability of societies and their political systems to adjust to them let alone guide the course they take. History teaches us that such imbalances between the economic, social and political realms can never be sustained for very long."[17]

Economic nationalism, the traditional path in world politics, remains the prevailing approach to the global economy. But there has also been great change. The countries of the world have adopted a vast array of policies, have concluded numerous economic agreements, and have created many international organizations to promote and facilitate free economic interchange. These policies, agreements, and organizations all represent an alternative approach to the international political economy, and this newer path is mapped out in chapter 15.

Chapter Summary

1. Economics and politics are closely intertwined aspects of international relations. Each is a part of and affects the other. This interrelationship has become even more important in recent history. Economics has become more important internationally because of dramatically increased trade levels, ever-tightening economic interdependence between countries, and the growing impact of international economics on domestic economics.

2. The study of international political economy (IPE) examines the interaction between politics and economics.

3. There are many technical aspects to explaining and understanding the international political economy, and those not familiar with economic terms and methods should review the listing called "Economics: Technical Terms and Sources" found in the section toward the end of the book entitled Explanatory Notes on pages 571–572.

4. The approaches to IPE can be roughly divided into three groups: economic nationalism (mercantilism), economic internationalism (liberalism), and economic structuralism.

5. The core of the economic nationalist doctrine is the realist idea that the state should harness and use national economic strength to further national interest. Therefore, the state should shape the country's economy and its foreign economic policy to enhance state power.

6. Economic internationalists are idealists who believe that international economic relations should and can be harmonious because prosperity is available to all and is most likely to be achieved and preserved through cooperation. The main thrust of economic internationalism is to separate politics from economics, to create prosperity by freeing economic interchange from political restrictions.

7. Economic structuralists hold that world politics is based on the division of the world into have and have-not countries, with the EDCs keeping the LDCs weak and poor in order to exploit them. There are two types of economic structuralists. Marxists believe that the entire capitalist-based system must be replaced with domestic and international socialist systems before economic equity can be achieved. Less radical economic structuralists stress reform of the current market system by ending the system of dependencia.

8. Whether or not you subscribe to economic structuralist theory, it is clear that the world is generally divided into two economic spheres: a wealthy North and a much less wealthy South. There are some overlaps between the two spheres, but in general the vast majority of the people and countries of the South are much less wealthy and industrially developed than the countries of the North and their people. The South also has a history of direct and indirect colonial control by countries of the North.

9. The history of international economics is ancient, but a change that has occurred since the second half of the twentieth century is that the level of eco-

nomic interchange (trade, investments and other capital flows, and monetary exchange) has increased at an exponential rate.

10. Within the overall expansion of the international economy, there is, however, a pattern in which most of the trade, investment, and other aspects of international political economy are dominated by the North and work to its advantage.

11. Trade in goods and services is booming, having grown 2,600 percent from $20 billion in 1913 to nearly $7.5 trillion in 2000. There has also been a rapid expansion of international financial ties. This flow of investment can be examined by reviewing types of foreign investments and multinational corporations.

12. The increased flow of trade and capital means that monetary relations, including exchange rates, interest rates, and other monetary considerations, are a significant economic factor. It is not unreasonable to estimate that the daily currency flow is $1.5 trillion, or some $548 trillion a year.

13. The expansion of world trade and investment has profoundly affected countries and their citizens. Economic interdependence has inexorably intertwined national and international economic health.

14. There are significant arguments on both sides of the question of whether or not to continue to expand free international economic interchange. Advocates of doing so contend that it results in greater efficiency and lower costs and that international commerce promotes world cooperation and inhibits conflict. Opponents argue that economic barriers are needed to protect domestic industry, that relying on other countries is dangerous for national security reasons, and that trade can be a valuable policy tool.

Chapter 15

National Economic Competition: The Traditional Road

I greatly fear my money is not safe.

Shakespeare, *The Comedy of Errors*

Having nothing, nothing can he lose.

Shakespeare, *Henry VI, Part III*

No one can… love his neighbor on an empty stomach.
Woodrow Wilson, speech, May 23, 1919

As the images of life lived anywhere on our globe become available to all, so will the contrast between the rich and the poor become a force impelling the deprived to demand a better life from the powers that be.
Nelson Mandela, to a joint session of the U.S. Congress, October 7, 1994

Chapter Objectives

After completing this chapter, you should be able to:

- Explain why politics and economics are intertwined aspects of international relations.
- Describe how economics has taken on a more important role in international relations.
- Understand the source of economic power.
- Analyze the use of economic statecraft.
- Describe the economies of the North and their current political issues.
- Describe the economies of the South and their current political issues.
- Discuss the sources of hard currency.
- Consider the effects of debt crisis on the global financial community and the role of loans.
- Discuss LDCs' need for investment capital and the difficulty in acquiring it.
- Understand the role of foreign aid in the global political community.
- Analyze the demand for a New International Economic Order.
- Describe the various impediments to free trade.
- Discuss the arguments for and against free international economic interchange.

Economic nationalism—the state-centric approach to international political economy—is the traditional road that countries have long followed. While it is true that there has been considerable movement toward liberalizing international economic relations in recent decades, economic nationalism remains the dominant practice in global economic affairs for two reasons: First, states remain the principal actors on the world stage. Second, these states most often use economic tools and formulate economic policy to benefit themselves, not the global community. This chapter will explore the economic nationalist approach, including discussions of national economic power assets and the ways that countries utilize their economic power (Milner, 1998).

National Economic Power: Assets and Utilization

The use of political power to achieve national economic goals and the reciprocal use of economic power to gain national political goals is at the core of economic nationalism. This orientation, which is also called "economic statecraft" or "mercantilism," remains in one form or another the basic approach of states to international political economy in the current state-based, quasi-anarchical system. The reason states take this self-serving approach is understandable. Each state is largely responsible for its own economic well-being. Certainly there is foreign aid, and other forms of financial assistance are available from states and from international governmental organizations (IGOs), such as the United Nations, the International Monetary Fund (IMF), and the World Bank. Such assistance, however, is neither guaranteed nor munificent. Thus, as is true for military security, economic security is based mostly on self-help.

NATIONAL ECONOMIC POWER

It is axiomatic that to pursue economic statecraft effectively, a country needs to possess considerable economic power. Chapter 10 has already reviewed the national infrastructure (technological sophistication, transportation systems, information and communications capabilities) that provides part of the basis for building a powerful economy. To these factors this chapter will add as determinants of national power the following: financial position, natural resources, industrial output, and agricultural output.

Financial Position

The center of any country's economic power is its basic financial position. To think about that, consider Table 15.1 and the six criteria of financial strength detailed there for the United States and Russia. Neither country has an enviable record on all points. Still, the United States is in vastly better financial shape than is Russia. The U.S. economy is huge, has experienced moderate growth and low inflation, and the American dollar is backed by substantial international reserves. In 2000, the United States had both a negative balance of payments and a budget deficit, but they were relatively small as a percentage of the GNP. Since then, the U.S. budget has again lapsed into deficit spending, and Russia's deficit has narrowed. Still the U.S. fiscal position remains much better.

Russia is weak financially—especially compared to the United States. The most recent data shows that Russia's GNP was relatively small and had declined steadily since the Soviet Union dissolved. Russia had scant international reserves and a gaping budget deficit. With the Russian government virtually broke and with

Table 15.1 **Measures of National Financial Power**					
Country	2000 GNP ($ billions)	GNP Growth 1993–2002	Annual Inflation 1993–2002	International Reserves, 2001 ($ billions)	Balance of Payments as % of GNP, 2001	Government Budget Balance as % of GNP, 2000
Russia	$338	−2.7%	94%	$12	−0.3	−1.5
United States	$7,921	+2.8%	1.9%	$136	−4.3	+1.7

Note: GNP growth rate is calculated in real, not current, monetary terms; budget balance is for the central government.
Data Sources: World Bank (2002)

Every country's power rests in part on its financial strength. Notice the U.S. and Russian comparative data for each column. In each, except balance of payments, the U.S. financial situation is considerably stronger than is Russia's position.

industry staggering, many workers remain unpaid. Soaring inflation during the 1990s wiped out much of the purchasing power of people's savings and the fixed pensions of retired Russians. The salaries of those who did get paid often did not keep up with inflation. Rampant corruption has made a bad situation much worse. The result is that about one-third of all Russians are living in poverty.

A weak financial position makes it difficult for an economy to provide the solid infrastructure required for prosperity or to provide adequately for national defense, as illustrated recently in Argentina. Plagued by a variety of economic woes and unable to meet its international debts, in 2001 the government of Argentina's President Fernando de la Rua introduced a series of stringent budget cuts to try to correct the situation. Those cuts, however, drastically reduced social welfare payments, government employment, and a number of other programs important to large segments of Argentina's citizenry. Riots broke out across the country, and de la Rua was forced to resign in December.

He was soon replaced by Eduardo Duhalde. No new president could quickly fix the country's underlying economic weakness. Nor could Duhalde rapidly reverse the damage that had been done to the value of Argentina's currency, the peso. It collapsed in early 2002, with its value versus the U.S. dollar falling 71 percent between January 1 and May 31, from US$1 = 1 peso to $1 = 3.45 pesos. This drove up the price of imported products, which in turn increased the demand for local products, thereby also sending those prices spiraling upward. The annual inflation rate in mid-2002 stood at about 120 percent, with the prices of some items moving upward at a much faster pace. During the first five months of 2002, the price increases of cooking oil, flour, eggs, and vinegar ranged from 107 percent to 161 percent, laundry detergent was up 122 percent and toothpaste crested at 111 percent. Other big price jumps included rice (97 percent), chicken (82 percent), and milk (67 percent). As Argentina's currency went into a tailspin, the rest of the economy staggered. Construction fell 50 percent, and unemployment neared 20 percent by midyear. To pay civil servants, some bankrupt provinces resorted to printing

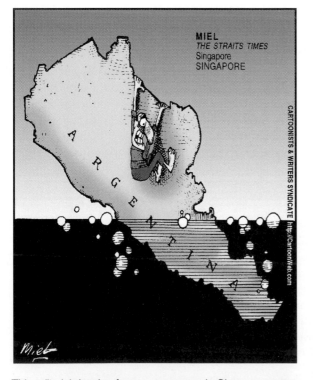

MIEL
THE STRAITS TIMES
Singapore
SINGAPORE

CARTOONISTS & WRITERS SYNDICATE http://CartoonWeb.com

This editorial drawing from a newspaper in Singapore represents the rampant inflation, high unemployment, and other dire financial conditions that have undermined Argentina's economy and its national power since late 2001.

their own currency, including one note with a picture of Evita Peron that became known as an "evita." Conditions in mid-2002 were gloomy; the economy was in deep recession, and inflation was wiping out the savings of the middle class and leaving retirees and others on fixed incomes unable to live on their devalued incomes. Unemployment was high, and of those with jobs some were being paid by ad hoc provincial currencies and others in pesos that bought little.

Financial weakness also saps a country's diplomatic influence. Since the collapse of the Soviet Union, Russia has objected to the expansion of NATO, the intervention in Kosovo, the U.S. plans to build a national missile defense system, and a number of other initiatives taken by the United States and its allies. There has only been so far Moscow could go in opposition, though, because it has needed infusions of cash from the West-dominated IMF to keep the Russian economy from total collapse.

Natural Resources

The possession, or lack, of energy, mineral, and other natural resources has become an increasingly important power factor as industrialization and technology have advanced. Natural resources affect power in four related ways: (1) The greater a country's self-sufficiency in vital natural resources, the greater its power. (2) Conversely, the greater a country's dependency on foreign sources for vital natural resources, the less its power. (3) The greater a country's surplus (over domestic needs) of vital resources needed by other countries, the greater its power.

Each of these three related points plays a key role in determining international relationships. Self-sufficiency and dependency are inexorably linked. The United States, for example, depends on imports for a least half, and in some cases 100 percent, of all 11 minerals designated by the U.S. government as "federal strategic and critical minerals." By contrast, there are some countries, such as Russia and Canada, that are relatively more resource sufficient. Still other countries are almost totally dependent on foreign sources for their natural resource requirements. Japan, for one, imports virtually all of its primary energy supplies (oil, natural gas, and others) and 90 percent or more of most critical minerals.

The key here is not just production; it is production compared to consumption. With less than 5 percent of the world population, the United States produces about 8 percent of world's crude petroleum, putting U.S. output third in the world behind Russia and Saudi Arabia. That would seem advantageous, but it is not because the United States consumes 26 percent of global petroleum production. As a result, the United States in 2001 had to import approximately 10.6 million barrels (or 445.2 million gallons) of petroleum each day. One concern is that the U.S. petroleum dependency makes the country vulnerable to disruptions of the flow of oil that it needs to maintain prosperity. Second, the dependency causes a huge outflow of financial resources. Imported petroleum cost Americans about $24.50 per barrel in 2001, which means that they were spending nearly $260 million dollars a day (or $95 billion a year) importing oil.

Possessing a surplus of a vital resource is a third power factor. As is evident in Figure 15.1, the global imbalance of oil production has dramatically underlined this point. Oil resources have been the chief source of export revenue for many countries in the Middle East and, despite the depressed oil market during most of the 1990s, so-called black gold has allowed some of that region's countries to amass huge financial reserves. In 2001, for example, Saudi Arabia earned $50 billion from petroleum products. Oil has also increased the global political focus on the petroleum-producing countries and on their diplomatic power, especially

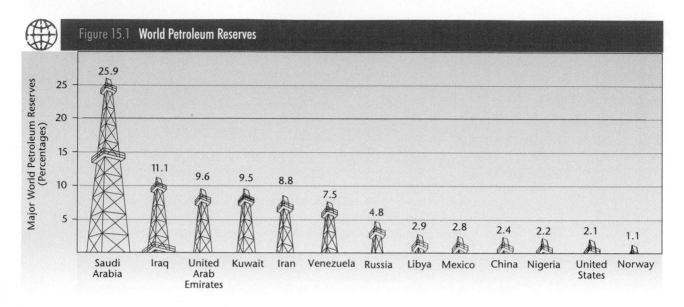

Figure 15.1 **World Petroleum Reserves**

Data source: World Almanac (2002).

There are only 13 countries that have 1 percent or more of the world's oil reserves. The concentration of oil, espeically in the Middle East, which has about two-thirds of the world's oil reserves, enhances the political importance and power of those countries that export oil.

the countries in the Middle East, which account for about two-thirds of world petroleum reserves.

Industrial Output

Even if a country is bountifully supplied with natural resources, its power is limited unless it can convert those assets into industrial goods. On a global basis, industrial production is highly concentrated. The European Union, Japan, and North America (the United States and Canada) alone produce over 45 percent of the world's total steel output. Vehicle production is another indication of industrial concentration, as indicated in Figure 15.2. It shows that the three biggest vehicle manufacturers (Germany, Japan, and the United States) made 51 percent of the global total. Another 11 countries combined for 39 percent, with a mere 10 percent manufactured by 14 other countries. About 85 percent of the world's countries (including all those in Africa) produce no, or only a negligible number of, vehicles.

Agricultural Output

It is not common to equate food production with power. Yet a country's agricultural capacity is an important factor. Self-sufficiency varies widely in the world. The United States is basically able not only to supply its own needs but to earn money from agricultural exports. With less than 5 percent of the world's population, it produces 16 percent each of the world's cereal grains and meat. Other countries are less fortunate. Some have to use their economic resources to import food. Yet others have insufficient funds to buy enough food and face widespread hunger. Many parts of Africa are in particularly desperate shape.

Another significant agricultural factor is the percentage of economic effort that a country must expend to feed its people. Countries are relatively disadvantaged if they have larger percentages of their workforce in agriculture (and thus not available for the manufacturing and service sectors), if they have to spend a

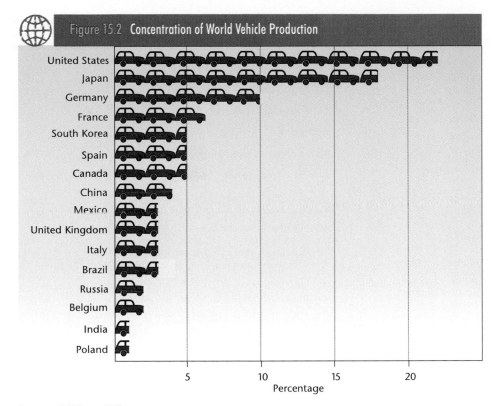

Figure 15.2 **Concentration of World Vehicle Production**

Data source: World Almanac (2002).

Global industry is highly concentrated. The 16 countries that produced 1 percent or more of the 57.8 million vehicles manufactured in 2000 accounted for 93 percent of the world's production. The biggest three producers combined for half of all the cars and trucks produced.

great deal of their economic effort (measured as a percentage of GDP) to feed their people, and if they have to import food. Table 15.2 on page 434 contrasts the agricultural efficiency of an EDC (Canada) to that of an LDC (Pakistan). On each measure Pakistan is disadvantaged agriculturally. Compared to Canadians, Pakistanis devote much more of their economic effort and workforce to agriculture. Those workers are inefficient because they have so little farm machinery. As a result, the value of the products of each Pakistani farm worker is only about 2 percent that of a Canadian agricultural worker. Moreover despite its efforts, Pakistan is unable to feed its population. It has to spend its meager capital to finance the $1 billion net deficit in its annual food trade, while Canada enjoys an $18 billion agricultural **net trade** surplus.

Pakistan devotes 27 percent of its economic activity and 44 percent of its workforce to this task. Canada expends a relatively tiny percentage of its economic effort and workforce to feed itself. Among the most important reasons that Canadian agriculture is so much more efficient than Pakistan's is that Canada can afford to enhance its yield by equipping its workers with more agricultural machinery and by using more fertilizers.

METHODS OF MANIPULATING ECONOMIC INTERCHANGE

Economic nationalists, as detailed in chapter 14, believe that a state's political, military, and economic powers are inextricably linked. Therefore, economic nationalists advocate harnessing all aspects of a government's economic policy, including its foreign economic relations, to enhance the state's power. From this perspective, the

Table 15.2 Agricultural Effort of Canada and Pakistan		
Agricultural Effort	Canada	Pakistan
Agriculture as % of GDP	4	27
% of workforce in agriculture	3	44
Tractors per 1,000 agricultural workers	1,678	12
Value of agricultural output per worker	$34,922	$626
Net food trade (exports – imports)	+$18 billion	–$1.2 billion

Data Source: World Bank (2001)

Like Pakistan, many LDCs spend an inordinate amount of their economic effort and their workforce to feed themselves and yet are unable to do so. Many EDCs spend little economic effort and few workers on agriculture, yet because of mechanization are able not only to produce enough food for domestic use but also to earn revenues by being net agricultural exporters.

movement of goods, services, investments, and other forms of economic interchange into and out of the country should be manipulated in the interest of state power by barriers and domestic support.

Barriers to Merchandise Trade

There are numerous ways that countries can restrict trade. **Tariffs** are the most familiar trade barrier. While these are generally low, tariff hikes are still occasionally either threatened or used. Most often this occurs over economic issues. Not long ago, for example, the United States threatened to impose 100 percent tariffs on some Chinese goods if Beijing did not end the piracy of U.S. intellectual property (copyrights and

The lack of tractors and other mechanical farm equipment in the economically less developed countries means that they have to utilize an inordinate amount of their labor force simply to feed themselves. These Albanian farmers and their team of oxen are struggling to till their field and plant their crop, but there is only so much they can do. The farmers would have preferred to use a 65-horsepower John Deere 5420 farm tractor. But given the small tractor's $26,000 price tag, it would take the average Albanian 28 years to earn enough money to buy one.

patents) by Chinese manufacturers. China pledged to crack down on those producing bootleg copies of music and video compact discs and other violators. The practices continue, however, and the tariff club remains in the U.S. closet.

Nontariff barriers (NTBs) are a less-known but more common and important way of restricting trade. These NTBs are sometimes reasonable regulations based on health, safety, or other considerations. More often they are simply protectionist.

Import and export prohibitions based on political sanctions, such as the ban against importing Iraqi oil, is another method. At the extreme, trade embargoes, such as the one that the United States has imposed on Cuban goods, may totally bar trade.

Quotas that limit the number of units that can be shipped are one form of NTB. Some quotas are imposed by importing countries; others are self-imposed by exporting countries in preference to facing imposed restrictions. One reason Japanese auto manufacturers built plants in the United States was the threat of U.S. quotas on the importation of Japanese vehicles.

Pricing limits are another way to restrain trade. Once NAFTA came into being, some U.S. growers complained that they were unable to compete with Mexican imports. During the 1996 election campaign, President Clinton responded in a way meant to please Florida tomato farmers by successfully pressuring the Mexican government to keep the price of tomatoes exported to the United States at a minimum of 20.86 cents per pound. The pressure on Mexico violated the spirit of NAFTA, but, one U.S. official commented, "This was Mexico's moment to pay [Clinton] back for the bailout" of the Mexican economy after the peso collapse. Besides, the official said, "the math was pretty simple. Florida has 25 electoral votes, and Mexico doesn't."[1]

Technical restrictions, such as health and safety regulations, are sometimes really meant to bar imports or increase their cost considerably. Even though NAFTA allows the trucks of its member-countries to carry goods across borders, many Mexican trucks are barred from the United States because they do not meet the stricter U.S. safety regulations. Subsidization allows a domestic producer to undersell foreign competition at home. Many governments, for instance, heavily subsidize their agriculture industries. Efforts to reduce agricultural subsidies have met with fierce domestic resistance in France, Japan, and elsewhere.

Barriers to the Trade in Services and to Investment

Just as there are a wide array of merchandise trade barriers, so too, there are multitudinous ways to restrict the trade in services and the flow in investment. Of the few that we can sample here, licensing requirements are one way to make it difficult for foreign professionals and companies to provide services in another country. Many countries license architects, engineers, insurance agents, stock and bond traders, and other professionals. Majority ownership requirements are a way to bar the foreign ownership of businesses within a country. India, for example, requires that all companies located in India have at least 51 percent Indian ownership.

Domestic Support of Trade

Countries can also attempt to gain an unfair advantage in the international marketplace. These practices all violate international trade agreements and sometimes national law, but they are hard to eliminate completely. Conducting economic espionage, providing domestic subsidies, and encouraging dumping are just three of the many ways governments can interfere in free trade.

Economic espionage is an ongoing problem. This practice involves the theft of trade secrets from a country's companies by both friendly and hostile foreign governments (as well as private companies and individuals). The country doing the spying can then use the stolen trade secrets to build products that compete both domestically and internationally with the products of the companies that have been victimized. These activities became such a concern to U.S. economic prosperity and national power that Congress enacted the Economic Espionage Act of 1996. The protection of U.S trade secrets is assigned to the Office of the National Counterintelligence Executive (ONCE), a joint undertaking of the FBI, CIA, and other U.S. intelligence agencies. The continuing concern is illustrated in ONCE's 2001 report, which indicated, "As the world's leading industrial power and leader in technology development, the United States continues to be a prime target of foreign economic collection and industrial espionage. The United States pays a high financial price for economic espionage." The report continued, "The business community estimates that, in calendar year 2000, economic espionage cost from $100 to 250 billion in lost sales. The greatest losses to U.S. companies involve information concerning manufacturing processes and research and development."[2]

Domestic subsidies include various forms of financial support that a government gives to a company to allow it to compete unfairly in the marketplace. For example, if a country gives a company tax breaks when it produces merchandise for export, then that company can profitably sell its products both at home and abroad for less than it otherwise would be able to. This promotes exports and discourages imports. In addition to tax incentives, domestic subsidies come in many forms, including direct payments to producers, providing cheap or below-cost services to producers (such as energy or transportation), and providing research and development assistance. When, for example, in May 2002 President Bush signed a bill that will give billions of dollars annually in support to U.S. agribusiness, many foreign countries complained that it would give U.S. agricultural exports an unfair advantage in the world marketplace. For one, Teofisto Guingona, the foreign minister of the Philippines, objected to the subsidies as a violation of World Trade Organization (WTO) rules. Speaking in June 2002 at the UN's World Food Summit being held in Rome, Guingona protested, "We are poor. You are rich. Level the playing field!"[3]

Dumping is yet another way to seek an unfair trade advantage. Dumping occurs when a company, sometimes with the support of its national government, sells its goods abroad at a price lower than what it sells them for at home. Mexico, for example, recently placed an added duty of 1,105 percent on Chinese shoes after finding that China was dumping them on the Mexican market.

APPLYING ECONOMIC POWER

States possess a variety of economic tools. It is possible to divide the economic instruments available to countries into economic incentives and economic sanctions.

Economic Incentives

States regularly offer economic incentives to induce other states to act in a desired way. Incentives include providing foreign aid, giving direct loans or credits, guaranteeing loans by commercial sources, reducing tariffs and other trade barriers, selling or licensing the sale of sensitive technology, and a variety of other techniques. Not all incentives are successful in changing another country's behavior, but they certainly do work some of the time. For example, to help persuade Pakistan to cooperate in the attack on Afghanistan in the fall of 2001, the United States ended the economic sanctions that it had imposed on Pakistan after its nuclear weapons tests in 1998. To further sweeten the pot, Washington provided $100 million in immediate economic assistance, rescheduled or forgave $900 million in debt owed by Pakistan, and offered a longer term aid package that will provide over $400 to help Pakistan purchase U.S. goods and services. Additionally, at U.S. urging, the World

Bank in October 2001 approved a $300 million loan for Pakistan and indicated its willingness to favorably consider yet another $300 million loan, and the IMF extended a $1.3 billion credit line to help Pakistan keep its currency stable during the crisis.

Economic Sanctions

Countries and alliances can use their economic power in a negative way by applying sanctions. Research indicates that countries are especially likely to do so "if there are expectations of frequent conflict with the target" (Drenzer, 1998:728). Methods include raising trade barriers, cutting off aid, trying to undermine another country's currency, and even instituting blockades.

The History of Sanctions The use of economic sanctions dates back to at least 432 B.C. when the city-state of Athens embargoed all trade with another city-state, Megara. Then, like now, sanctions were acts of hostility, and the Megarian Decree was one of the causes of the Peloponnesian War (431–404 B.C.), in which Megara was part of the Peloponnesian League led by Sparta in its conflict with the Athenian Empire and its allies.

The point of this story is that the use of economic instruments to promote policy is ancient. In more modern times, sanctions are becoming more frequent policy tools. There were only 8 incidents of economic sanctions (0.3 per year) from 1914 through 1939. This increased to 44 incidents of sanctions (1.5 per year) between 1940 and 1969, and the number rose again to 71 incidents (3.6 per year) during the two decades of the 1970s and 1980s (Rothgeb, 1993). The increased use of sanctions has occurred, in part, because people are more aware of events in the world around them and more intent on influencing how other governments act both domestically and internationally. Sanctions are also more frequent because economic interdependence makes target countries more vulnerable to sanctions. The increased use of sanctions additionally reflects the search for ways to pressure other countries without going to war (Doxey, 1996).

Before leaving the history of sanctions, it should be noted that they are used by international organizations as well as by individual countries. The 1990s saw sanctions imposed by the UN on Libya and the Sudan for supporting terrorism; on Yugoslavia for aggression in the Balkans; on Iraq for aggression against Kuwait and for failing to live up to the cease-fire agreement of 1991; on Haiti for toppling its democratic government and substituting a military regime; and, for the first time, on a rebel group, UNITA, in Angola (Cortright & Lopez, 2000; Brown, 1999).

The Effectiveness of Sanctions Economic sanctions are a blunt instrument that attempts to economically bludgeon a target country into changing some specific behavior. As such, the effectiveness of sanctions is mixed. Sometimes they can be effective. Sanctions cost South Africa tens of billions of dollars and helped push the country's white leadership to end the apartheid system. The harsh sanctions on Yugoslavia arguably helped cause the downfall of President Slobodan Milosevic in October 2000.

It is also the case, though, that, more often than not, sanctions fail to accomplish their goal. Some analysts place their success rate as low as 5 percent (Kaempfer & Lowenberg, 1999; Elliott, 1998; Pape, 1997). Given this paltry success rate, a reasonable question is, When do they accomplish their goals? Sanctions are most likely to be effective in certain circumstances (Drezner, 2000; Shambaugh, 2000; Brawley, 1996). These include instances where (1) "the goal is relatively modest," thereby minimizing the need for multilateral cooperation; (2) "the target is politically unstable, much smaller than the country imposing sanctions, and economically weak"; (3) "the sender and target are friendly toward one another and conduct substantial trade"; (4) "the sanctions are imposed quickly and decisively to maximize impact"; and (5) "the sender avoids high costs to itself," such as the loss of substantial export revenue (Elliott, 1993:34).

Whatever the evidence, sanctions remain a regularly used tool. They are especially prevalent in U.S policy, which in 2001 had sanctions in place against 75 countries for what one new report described as "offenses ranging from mislabeling cans of tuna... to engaging in egregious human rights violations and narcotics trafficking." This common U.S. use of sanctions is all the more curious given the view of Secretary of State Colin Powell that using them so broadly "shows a degree of American hubris and arrogance that may not, at the end of the day, serve our interests all that well."[4] "Therein is the great paradox," says one expert on sanctions. "While unilateral embargoes are less and less of an effective force in an integrated world economy, American enthusiasm for them has not diminished."[5] There are a number of possible explanations for this paradox. One is that tangible success is not the only standard by which to measure sanctions. They also have a symbolic value that has nothing to do with whether they actually cause another country to change its behavior. Simply put, just as you might choose not to deal with an immoral person, so too, countries can express their moral indignation by reducing or severing their interactions with an abhorrent regime (Baldwin, 2000).

The Drawbacks of Sanctions Especially given the high failure rate of sanctions, countries that apply them must be wary of the negative impact of sanctions on unintended victims. One such difficulty is that sanctions may harm economic interests other than those of the intended target. The UN sanctions imposed on Iraqi oil exports have cost Jordan and Turkey many millions of dollars by way of lost revenues that they would have earned for the use of pipelines that run from Iraq through them and on to ports from which the oil is shipped.

Another drawback is that threatening or implementing sanctions can damage those who impose them. For instance, USA Engage, a lobby organization supported by nearly 700 U.S. corporations that favors fewer sanctions, has estimated that current U.S. sanctions cost the country up to $19 billion in lost trade revenue and more than 200,000 jobs.[6]

A third criticism of sanctions is that they are often the tool used by EDCs to continue their dominance of LDCs. Of the 71 incidents of sanctions applied during the 1970s and 1980s, 49 of the cases (69 percent) involved EDCs placing sanctions on LDCs (Rothgeb, 1993). A fourth charge against sanctions is that they can dismay countries that do not support them. Continuing U.S. sanctions against Cuba are viewed as particularly offensive by many U.S. allies and other countries.

A fifth criticism is that sanctions often harm the very people whom you want to assist. President Fidel Castro of Cuba has called sanctions "noiseless atomic bombs" that "cause the death of men, women, and children."[7] Iraq provides a good example of Castro's point. There, persistent UN sanctions and a defiant government in Baghdad have had a brutal impact. Scant supplies of food and medicine for the civilian population are among the hardships. The effects are especially devastating for children. Various studies by the UN, Harvard University's School of Public Health, and others have all found that the sanctions have caused (beyond normal expectations) over 1 million Iraqi children to be malnourished and upwards of 500,000 to have died. The sanctions have been relaxed in recent years to allow Iraq to sell some oil and, under supervision, to use the proceeds to buy food and medicine. Still, serious human

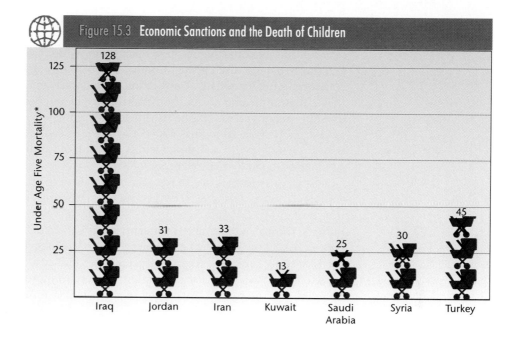

Figure 15.3 **Economic Sanctions and the Death of Children**

* The number of children who die before age five per 1,000 children born.

Data source: World Bank (2001).

One objection to economic sanctions is that they often have the most deleterious impact on those who have the least responsibility for the actions of their government. There is little doubt that the economic sanctions that were imposed on Iraq beginning in 1990 have caused many young children to die. The average death rate of small children for Iraq's six neighbors dropped markedly from 83 in 1990 to 30 in 2000, while Iraq's rate rose from 95 to 128.

damage continues. This deleterious effect is evident in Figure 15.3, which compares the child mortality rate in Iraq to that of its neighbors.

Now, having reviewed national economic assets and the use of the economic instrument, we can turn to specific national economic concerns and policies. This discussion will be divided into two parts: the national economic issues and policies of the North and the national economic issues and policies of the South.

The North and International Political Economy

By many standards, the economic position of the North is enviable. Its 2000 per capita GNP was $27,680 compared to $1,230 each for the people of the South. Between 1980 and 2000, the combined GDPs of the EDCs jumped from $8 trillion to $24 trillion. That was monumental compared with a rise in the combined GDPs of the LDCs from $3.1 trillion to $6.1 trillion. Yet all is not well in the North.

THE NATIONAL ECONOMIES OF THE NORTH

The fundamental cause of concern among EDCs is that the North's economic growth rate has slowed somewhat from its earlier high levels. The average annual real GDP growth rate of the EDCs during the 1980s was 3.4 percent; during the 1990s that declined to 2.3 percent. The number of new jobs being created in the North increased an annual average of 1.3 percent in the 1980s; during the 1990s average job growth was but 0.7 percent.

There are many reasons for the deceleration of the North's economy. One is the beginning of competition from a few newly industrializing countries (NICs) of the South in the manufacturing, industrial, and service sectors. Also, the post–cold war drop in defense spending has caused some dislocation.

Yet another adjustment for the EDCs involves their entering a period that some analysts call the postindustrial economy. What this means is that through the use of robotics and other techniques, fewer and fewer workers are needed to produce more and more manufactured goods. Companies need to reduce their workforces to stay competitive internationally. Downsizing is a relatively new, and unwelcome, word in the economic vocabulary of the North. Many of the displaced workers are either unemployed or find jobs in the usually lower-paying service sector. Indeed, the shift away from manufacturing has added a whole new class of economies, service economies, to such traditional designations as primary product (agriculture, minerals) economies and industrialized economies.

Service economies are those countries that derive at least a plurality of their earnings from performing services (such as banking, education, insurance, and transportation). For most countries, domestic services (everything from flipping burgers, through almost all government activity, to acting in movies) are already the biggest part of their internal economic activity. Such services make up 71 percent of the U.S. GDP, compared to just 24 percent for industry, and 5 percent for primary products. Services are also becoming a more important part of exports and, therefore, the international economy. The services that Americans exported in 1980 were just 17 percent of all U.S. exports; in 2000 that percentage was up to 28 percent. Thus other countries increasingly import what Americans know and do, rather than just what they harvest, mine, and make.

At the beginning of the first decade of the twenty-first century, the overall economic numbers for the North are good, but much of the rosy picture stems from the longest and one of the most robust periods of American economic expansion in history. Other parts of the North are having a more difficult time. Japan's economy is stagnant, with GDP growth for 1998–2002 at –0.2 percent. The growth rate for the European Union (EU) was 2.5 percent, compared to 3.2 percent for the United States. Unemployment in the EU (8.1 percent in 2000) was more than twice the rate in the United States (4.0 percent). As for Japan, its unemployment rate nearly doubled to 4.7 percent between 1990 and 2000, and for the first time in decades exceeded the U.S. rate. Germany's economy also lagged. Unemployment, which averaged 7.3 percent in the 1980s, stood at 8.5 percent during the last half of the 1990s. For the same two periods, Germany's annual average per capita GDP real growth rate fell from 5.1 percent to 1.8 percent.

In sum, the economy of the North is not in immediate trouble, but it is not as healthy as it could be or has been. Moreover, the slowdown in the U.S. economy during 2001, the steep declines in the U.S. stock market that year, the scandal associated with the collapse of Enron (the Houston-based energy trading company), and the general uncertainty that have made American consumers and investors cautious since the 9-11 terror attacks make it uncertain how quickly and to what degree the U.S. economy will recover. A positive view, as reflected in the title of an optimistic 1998 analysis, "A Second American Century," is that the United States will soon resume its strong growth. That article predicted, "If anything, American business should widen its lead over the rest of the world. France had the seventeenth century, Britain the nineteenth, and America the twentieth. It will also have the twenty-first" (Zuckerman, 1998:31). It is also possible to argue that another, less rosy look into the future, also written that year, will prove more accurate. That article, "America the Boastful," cautioned, "The current sense that the United States is on the top of the world is based on a huge exaggeration of the implications of a few good years here and a few bad years elsewhere.... Future historians will not record that the twenty-first century belonged to the United States" (Krugman, 1998:45).

Whatever the future may hold, the record of the North since 1990 has accentuated the concern of each EDC with its own economy and has sometimes strained economic relations within the North. It is to these concerns and policies that we now turn our attention.

NATIONAL ECONOMIC ISSUES AND POLICIES OF THE NORTH

Because they make up such an overwhelming percentage of the world's economic enterprise, the economic issues and policies of the North are a key determinant of the course of the global economy. For an extended period after World War II, the EDCs enjoyed good growth and were generally united politically with the United States and under its leadership. Now, with both economic and political factors changing, tensions among the EDCs are increasing.

Changes in the Economic and Political Climate in the North

The 1990s were a time of significant shifts in the international economic relations and policies of the countries of the North. There were several causes of these shifts. One, as noted, was the unsteady economic fortunes of the North. During the decades of booming prosperity following World War II, the rapidly expanding international economy minimized any pressures for economic rivalry among the developed countries. Now, in a less robust economic climate, there is increased protectionist sentiment.

A second factor is the end of the cold war. The resulting changes in the international system have lessened the need for strategic cooperation among the industrialized Western allies. With no common enemy to bind them together, the long-standing trade disputes among the so-called trilateral countries (Japan, the United States/Canada, Western Europe) that had once been suppressed in the name of allied unity have become more acrimonious.

A third and related factor that has further complicated matters is that central direction has declined in the North. The United States once provided that direction. But with an upsurge in economic rivalries among the EDCs and with the American people less willing to support U.S. internationalism, Washington has lost some of its ability to lead. Japan's ongoing economic woes have prevented it from taking up any of the leadership slack. By contrast, the expansion has increased political as well as economic integration of the European Union and has created an economic bloc that rivals the size of the U.S. economy, and Europeans are increasingly willing to challenge U.S. hegemony on a range of political, economic, and social issues. "There is a rhythm of global dominance, and no country remains the first player forever," Romano Prodi, the EU's president, has observed. "Maybe [U.S. dominance] won't last. And who will be the next leading player? Maybe next will be China. But more probably, before China, it will be the united Europe," Prodi predicted. "Europe's time is almost here."[8]

There are efforts to create greater coordination through such vehicles as the **Group of Seven (G-7)**. This is an informal directorate of the economically powerful Western countries (Canada, France, Germany, Great Britain, Italy, Japan, and the United States) that has met annually since 1975. In 1998 the G-7 created the **Group of Eight (G-8)**, when the G-7 leaders added Russia as a member for political matters. The G-7 still exists, therefore, because the G-7 continues to meet without Russia at the finance minister level on economic issues. To avoid confusion, the groups will be referred to as the G-8 in all their activities. The EDCs also attempt to coordinate their efforts through the World Bank and IMF, which the G-8 largely control. These programs and processes are examined more fully in chapter 16.

Despite such efforts, however, the reality is that the EDCs continue to act with a sort of dual personality in the realm of international economic affairs. There is one set of forces within most EDCs that has pressed with significant success for the continued expansion of **free economic interchange** among nations. The EU has continued to integrate; Canada, Mexico, and the United States joined together in the North American Free Trade Agreement (NAFTA); and the world extended and enhanced the General Agreement on Tariffs and Trade (GATT) and created the World Trade Organization (WTO) to administer it. All these efforts in the 1990s toward economic cooperation will be discussed in the next chapter.

Simultaneously, however, protectionism remains a powerful countervailing force, and there has been increased pressure within countries to follow economic nationalist policies. This pressure has been occasioned by the sagging economies of the North, by increased economic competition not only from other EDCs but also from NICs, and by a gnawing sense of economic insecurity among many people of the North. When the American public was presented with a list of policy options and asked which they thought were important, 80 percent said that "protecting the jobs of American workers should be a very important U.S. foreign policy goal" (Rielly, 1999). Only 45 percent of American leaders gave job protection a high priority. It follows, then, that public attitudes have pushed national leaders to follow policies of economic nationalism (Cohen, 2000).

The result of these countervailing internationalist and nationalist economic pressures within the EDCs gives something of a schizophrenic pattern to the foreign economic policies of the North's countries. They profess support of the further internationalization of the world economy while at the same time trying to promote and protect their own national economies.

Economic Disputes Among the EDCs

Trade relations among the EDCs have become more difficult in the past decade. One source of tension is that some countries have chronic trade surpluses, while others regularly run trade deficits. Japan and the United States are the two countries at the opposite ends of the scale. During the period 1993–2002, Japan accumulated a global goods and services trade surplus of just over $689 billion, while the U.S. trade balance was a staggering $2 trillion deficit. Although trade is but one aspect of a country's overall international balance of payments, it is an important one. This is reflected in Japan having a cumulative balance-of-payments surplus of $1.1 trillion during 1993–2002, and the United States amassing a total $2.3 trillion deficit in its balance of payments for the same period.

The more unilateralist approach of the administration of President George W. Bush to trade policy has also created some friction between Washington and its major trading partners. Bush's decision to put a 30 percent tariff on steel imports into the United States to offset alleged dumping of the product at below cost prices brought a sharp retort from Japan and the European Union. An official of Japan's Ministry of Economics, Trade and Industry called the U.S. tariffs a "clear-cut violation of the WTO rules" and announced that Japan would impose retaliatory tariffs on U.S. steel.[9] Similarly, the EU's trade commissioner objected that "The U.S. decision to go down the route of protectionism is a major setback for the world trading system."[10] The EU began to prepare a case to present to the WTO charging that Bush had violated its rules. EU trade officials also moved to compile a target list for retaliatory tariffs designed to reduce U.S. exports to the EU by about $2.1 billion annually, about the same amount as projected losses of EU steel exports to the United States. The suspicion that the move to protect steel was at least partly related to boosting Republican 2002 electoral chances in Pennsylvania, Ohio, and other steel producing states reportedly led the EU to choose its targets with politics in mind. One target was orange juice, an important export product in Florida, where the president's brother, Governor Jeb Bush, was campaigning for reelection in 2002.

Protest: American steelworkers and their supporters can be seen here near the White House in February 2002 demanding that President Bush increase the tariff on imported steel. The protesters claimed that other countries were dumping their steel on the U.S. market for below cost, and the illegal practice was costing U.S. workers their jobs.

Counterprotest: When President Bush met the demands of the people in the picture to the left and raised the steel tariff, the move set off demonstrations by steelworkers in many other countries, who accused Bush of illegal protectionism. In this March 2002 photograph, steelworkers in Concepción, Chile, are protesting against the U.S. tariff hike.

How well the EDCs will be able to cooperate and to avoid making conflictive economic decisions in the future remains to be seen. The record in recent decades has been relatively good, but it is also the case that these years have been ones of relative prosperity. There have been economic downturns, but none has been severe or prolonged. Whether governments could avoid the domestic pressure to resort to protectionism and other forms of economic nationalism in the midst of a sharp, extended financial recession is uncertain. President Bush during his trip to Western Europe and Russia in May 2002 was referring specifically to the trade disputes between the United States and the EU when he told German legislators, "The magnitude of our shared responsibilities makes our disagreements look so small. And those who exaggerate our differences play a shallow game and hold a simplistic view of our relationship."[11] History will be the judge of that optimistic assessment.

The South and International Political Economy

The economic goals of the North and South are very much alike but also very different. They are alike in that both the EDCs' and the LDCs' goals have to do with prosperity. They are different in that the North's goal is to preserve and enhance prosperity; the South's goal is to achieve it.

To further understand the economic position, goals, and policies of the LDCs, the following sections will examine economic development by looking first at the LDCs' sources of development capital and then by turning to the perspective of the LDCs on development issues. Before taking up these matters, though, it is important to look at the status of LDC development.

DEVELOPMENT IN THE SOUTH: STATUS

There can be little doubt that on many statistical bases there has been improvement in the socioeconomic development of the South. Over the last few decades, the infant mortality rate has been cut by 40 percent; the percentage of people with access to safe water has grown 70 percent; the adult literacy rate is up 35 percent; and people live an average of 16 percent longer. Between 1983 and 2002, the real GDP of the South grew an annual average of 5.1 percent. Annual real per capita GDP growth was a slower 3.1 percent, but it did advance (Dickson, 1997; Hoogvelt, 1997).

The progress in the South, however, has also had its drawbacks. What these averages disguise is a highly variegated pattern of development in the South.

Development: A Mixed Pattern

The diverse pattern and disparity in development in the South has occurred both between and within countries.

Disparity between countries is one characteristic of uneven economic growth in the South. Although it is possible to show, for example, that for LDCs the aggregate manufacturing output, GDP, and some other factors have expanded considerably during the last 25 years, these averages are misleading. This is because much of the progress was confined to a relatively few **newly industrializing countries (NICs)**. During 2000 these NICs (Argentina, Brazil, China, Malaysia, Mexico, Singapore, South Korea, Taiwan, and Thailand) accounted for 53 percent of all the goods exported by all LDCs as well as 52 percent of the South's combined GDPs. Excluding China, the NICs also had an average per capita GDP that is much greater than that of the average LDC.

For most LDCs, by comparison, development has been much slower. While LDCs generally have a positive growth rate in per capita GDP, about 20 percent of the LDCs had a negative growth rate between 1965 and 2000. Another 20 percent grew during the period at less than half the average annual 2.4 percent growth rate of the EDCs. The point is that a few LDCs (the NICs) are making progress economically; most LDCs are either nearly static or actually experiencing long-term economic decline.

Disparity within countries is a second characteristic of LDC economic development. Economic class, sometimes based on race or ethnicity, is one division. Within the South there are cities with sparkling skyscrapers and luxuriant suburbs populated by well-to-do local entrepreneurs who drive Mercedes-Benzes and splash in marble pools. For each such scene, however, there are many more of open sewers, contaminated drinking water, distended bellies, and other symptoms of rural and urban human blight. In short, the scant economic benefits that have accrued in the South are not evenly distributed.

Figure 15.4 shows the percentage of income earned by the wealthiest and poorest 20 percent of income earners in an LDC (Brazil), an EDC (Austria), and the world's largest economy (the United States). Notice how unevenly Brazil's income is distributed, especially relative to Austria's; the wealthiest Austrians make only 3.2 times as much as the country's poorest citizens. In Brazil the top 20 percent of income earners make 24 times what the poorest 20 percent of Brazilians receive. When Pope John Paul II visited Brazil, he spoke of "the contrasts between the two Brazils: one is highly developed, strong, and launched on the path of progress and riches; the other is seen in untold zones of poverty, suffering, illiteracy, and marginalization."[12]

If all countries could have been crammed into Figure 15.4, you would have seen that while they all have income distribution disparities, the gaps tend to be larger in the South than in the North. It might be noted, however, that the U.S. disparity is greater than that of any other major industrialized economy and approaches the difference one would expect to find in an LDC rather than in an EDC.

Gender is another basis of economic disparity within countries. Women make up 59 percent of those people living

Did You Know That:
Between 1989 and 2001, the number of billionaires in the world increased from 157 to 497. The net wealth of this exclusive club was about $1.54 trillion. That equaled about 50 percent more than the combined GNPs of the 64 LLDCs.

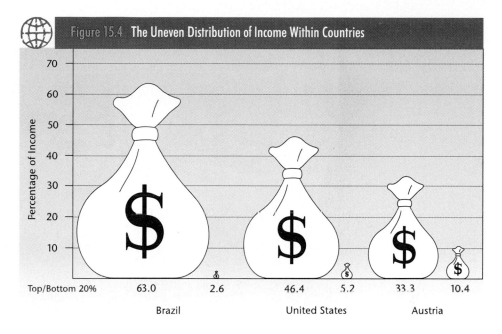

Figure 15.4 The Uneven Distribution of Income Within Countries

Top/Bottom 20%	63.0	2.6	46.4	5.2	33.3	10.4
	Brazil		United States		Austria	

Data source: World Bank (2001).

The figure shows one comparative indication of the uneven distribution of wealth within countries. The money bags represent the incomes of the wealthiest 20 percent of a country's income-earners and the poorest 20 percent in Brazil (which has one of the greatest disparities), the United States (the largest economy), and Austria (which has one of the narrowest gaps). All countries have disparities, but they tend to be much wider in the LDCs.

in absolute poverty in the LDCs. One reason is that women comprise only 39 percent of the wage earners in LDCs. Adding to the disparity, data shows that women perform many more hours of unpaid household labor than do men. If this labor is included, women do 62 percent of the total work and (if salaries were equal, which they are not) receive only 32 percent of the wages.

Modernization: A Mixed Blessing

The LDCs have benefited from advances in medicine, communications technology, and other aspects of modernization. It has been a mixed blessing, however, which has had several negative side effects for the South.

Explosive population growth has occurred as a result of medical advances that have decreased infant mortality and increased longevity. The population of sub-Saharan Africa, for instance, rose 290 percent from 210 million in 1960 to 605 million in 2000, and the region is expected to reach 866 million people by 2015.

Rapid urbanization has also beset the South, as the hope of finding jobs and better health, sanitation, and other social services has set off a mass migration from rural areas to cities in the South. Between 1965 and 2000 the percentage of the South's population living in urban areas grew from 22 to 41 percent, and it is projected to reach 53 percent in the year 2020. There are now a total of approximately 175 cities in LDCs with populations over 1 million. Tokyo is the world's largest urban area (the core city and its suburbs) with 26.4 million people. Mexico City; Mumbai (Bombay), India; and São Paulo, Brazil, are the most populous LDC urban areas, with about 18 million inhabitants each. Fifteen of the 19 urban areas with populations above 10 million are in LDCs.

This rapid urbanization process has created a host of problems. One is the weakening of social order. Older tribal, village, and extended-family loyalties are being

Modernization has proven to be a mixed blessing for many less developed countries. Rapid urbanization is one by-product, and the LDCs have not been able to expand housing, water supply, sewerage, and services fast enough to keep up. The outcome is that this picture of a shantytown outside Mexico City is typical of the hovels in many of the burgeoning cities in the LDCs. The population of Mexico City doubled from 9 million to 18 million people between 1970 and 2000.

destroyed, with few new offsetting values and other social support systems to take their place. Second, the hope of employment is often unfulfilled, and unemployment and poverty in many cities is staggering. Third, struggling LDC governments are often unable to meet the sanitary, housing, and other needs of the flood of people moving to or being born in the cities. More than a quarter of the South's urban population is living in what the World Bank terms "absolute poverty," with nutritional, sanitary, and housing conditions below the minimum standard for health. At least a third of all urban dwellings in sub-Saharan Africa have no running water, toilets, or electricity. By one count, only 8 of India's 3,000 large towns and cities have sewage treatment facilities capable of handling all the effluents of the population.

Industrial and environmental dangers have also been undesirable by-products of development. The impact of development on the environment is detailed in chapter 18, but some brief note of the dangers is appropriate here. One problem is deforestation. This is especially critical in the South, where increased demand for wood, expanding farm and ranch acreage, and general urban growth are rapidly depleting the forests. Loss of these forests increases soil erosion, decreases oxygenation of the air, lessens rainfall, and has numerous other deleterious effects. It is also the case that LDC industrial development is adding to air, water, and soil pollution. This is a problem of industrialization in general, but pollution growth is especially acute in developing countries, which often cannot afford the expensive processes to cleanse emissions and dispose of waste.

DEVELOPMENT IN THE SOUTH: CAPITAL NEEDS

Whatever the problems and drawbacks of industrialization, the LDCs are justifiably determined to increase their development. Because of their poor economic base, most LDCs find it difficult to raise capital internally. Incomes are so low in India, for example, that less than 1 percent of the country's people pay income taxes. Many things can be accomplished with domestic resources and drive, but the LDCs also need massive amounts of **development capital** in order to expand and diversify their economies. "Uganda needs just two things," says its president, Yoweri Museveni. "We need infrastructure and we need foreign investment. That is what we need. The rest we shall do ourselves."[13]

Obtaining these resources is difficult. The LDCs are constrained by limited financial reserves, especially **hard currency**. American dollars are the standard currency of international exchange. Japanese yen, European Union euros, and a handful of other currencies are also widely convertible. Guatemalan quetzals, Malaysian ringgits, and Nigerian nairas are another story. They and most LDC currencies are not readily accepted in international transactions. Since most of the world's hard-currency reserves are concentrated in the EDCs, the LDCs struggle to purchase needed imports.

A primary issue for LDCs, then, is the acquisition of hard-currency development capital. Four main sources of convertible currencies are available: loans, investment, trade, and aid. Unfortunately, there are limitations and drawbacks to each. Unless significant changes are made to increase the flow of development capital to the LDCs and to distribute it more broadly among all LDCs, the majority of them are destined for the foreseeable future to remain relatively poor.

Loans

One source of hard currency is loans extended by private or government sources. Based on a number of economic factors, the LDCs in the 1970s moved to finance their development needs by borrowing heavily from EDC banks, other private lenders, national governments, and international organizations. The upshot was that by 1982 LDC international debt had skyrocketed to $849 billion (equal to $1.6

The ability of many less developed countries to develop economically is being hindered by their heavy foreign debt. These countries use such a high percentage of what they take in from exports and other external sources of capital to pay the principal and interest on their debt that they have insufficient funds remaining to invest in the development of their economies. The debt crisis has eased somewhat in the past few years, but the debt burden remains a major problem for many LDCs.

billion in real 2000 dollars). While the rate of increase has eased, the total debt owed by the LDCs has continued to grow and stood at $2.1 trillion in 2000. Banks and other private institutional and individual bondholders are the largest creditors, followed by IGOs (such as the IMF and World Bank) and governments.

A Debt Crisis Breaks Out Most countries borrow money. During the 1800s when the United States was developing, it and its major enterprises (such as railroads) borrowed heavily from abroad to help finance expansion. More recently, the United States borrowed over a trillion dollars from foreigners to help pay for the budget deficit that persisted for thirty years. Thus, the recent borrowing by LDCs is neither remarkable nor necessarily irresponsible.

Both borrowers and lenders must manage money carefully, however, and in the 1980s, as evident in Figure 15.5, an unwise spiral of lending and borrowing occurred. The reasons are complex, but suffice it to say that LDCs were in dire need of funds and the lenders in the EDCs had surplus capital, which they urged the LDCs to borrow. Then a global economic downturn undercut the LDCs' ability to repay their loans. At its 1987 peak, debt was nearly twice the total of the LDCs' export earnings, and the LDCs had to pay 26 percent of all their export earnings just to meet the annual principal and interest payments.

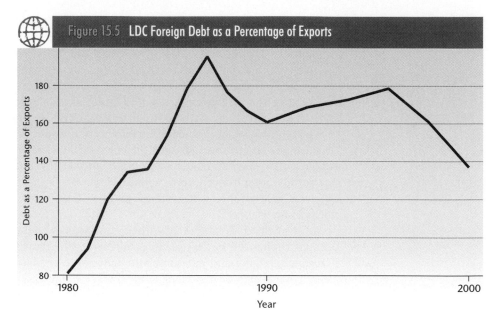

Figure 15.5 LDC Foreign Debt as a Percentage of Exports

Data sources: World Bank (2001) and IMF (2002).

Export earnings are a key source of capital that LDCs use to pay debt. This ability was severely strained during the 1980s as the LDCs' debt as a percentage of export earnings soared. Financial cooperation between the LDCs and EDCs along with an improved global economy have eased the crunch since its peak in 1987. Still, the 2000 level of debt at 137 percent of export earnings remains too high.

Argentina, Brazil, Mexico, Nigeria, and several other LDCs verged on the edge of bankruptcy and faced a seemingly lose-lose choice. They could either halt payments and thereby ruin their credit. Or they could continue to try to meet their **debt service** (principal and interest payments) even though that meant an annual outflow of $100 billion that the LDCs desperately needed to provide domestic services and to develop their economies.

The North was also threatened. Banks and other creditors faced potential losses of hundreds of billions of dollars that might have driven some huge banks into insolvency. That would have cost the governments of the EDCs billions, as they intervened to fend off bank failures or to repay depositors under government insurance plans.

The Debt Crisis Eases The mutual danger of the debt crisis to both the North and South led them to search for solutions. The details are complex, but a plan proposed in 1989 by U.S. secretary of the treasury Nicholas Brady began to ease the debt crisis. Under the Brady Plan during the 1990s, banks forgave over $100 billion of what the LDCs owed, lowered interest rates, and made new loans. In return, the governments of the EDCs, the IMF, and the World Bank guaranteed the loans and have increased their own lending to the LDCs. The Brady Plan has also required that the LDCs meet fiscal reform requirements negotiated with the IMF and other lenders.

The Current Debt Situation The immediate LDC debt crisis has abated, but the debt situation remains troublesome. One concern is that the LDCs still have a towering debt. Earnings from exports are one source of revenue to service debt, and the 2000 debt as a percentage of export earnings was a burdensome 137 percent. Among other things, this meant that the LDCs paid out $348 billion (22.5 percent of their annual export earnings) that year to meet their principal and interest obligations.

While the debt service is below its 30 percent peak in 1985, it still represents a loss of much-needed capital for the LDCs.

The ever-present possibility that the debt issue can rapidly become a debt crisis was evident in 2001 and into 2002 when a combination of Argentina's monetary policies, its faltering economy, and its nearly $150 billion in foreign debts caused a political and financial crisis that collapsed the value of the peso, as described earlier in this chapter. One result was that in January 2002 Argentina suspended payments of its debt service. In the months that followed, the government of Eduardo Duhalde, the country's fifth president within six months, struggled to reach an agreement with the IMF that would bring financial support to Argentina. As a condition of making the needed loans, the IMF demanded that Argentina undertake a series of tough financial reforms, such as reducing government employment. The IMF argued that the changes were needed to correct the underlying weakness of Argentina's financial structure; President Duhalde's view was that the IMF's conditions would make the desperate situation in Argentina even worse and might plunge it into violent political chaos. In late April, Duhalde agreed to try to institute the reforms, but some parts were rejected by Argentina's national legislature and many provincial governors also refused to cooperate. This stalemate left Argentina in crisis and the lending sources in the EDCs facing huge losses from the country's continuing debt default.

Private Investment

A second source of capital for LDCs is private investment through foreign direct investment (FDI) and foreign portfolio investment (FPI), as discussed in chapter 14. The flows of FDI and FPI are growing in importance as capital sources for the LDCs. Figure 15.6 shows that the combined net FDI and FPI in the LDCs skyrocketed during the 1990s. Although there is an upward trend in the proportion of global FDI that LDCs receive, with the LDCs' proportion of FDI increasing from 16 percent in 1990 to 27 percent in 1998, most funds are still being invested in EDCs.

There are several factors that temper the developmental impact of the rising flow of investment capital. First, most investment capital goes to only a handful of LDCs. During 2000, for example, China and Brazil alone received almost 39 percent of the FDI flow to the LDCs, and those two and another six countries (Argentina, Chile, South Korea, Mexico, Singapore, and Thailand) took in 77 percent of the available FDI capital. By contrast, Africa received only 4.3 percent of the capital. Second, as evident in Figure 15.6, FPI is volatile. Third, the net flow of FPI can turn sharply negative. Mexico in 1995, much of Asia in the late 1990s, and Argentina in 2001 and 2002 suffered serious financial shocks when nervous foreign investors created net outflows of investment capital.

Trade

Export earnings are a third possible source of development capital. In light of the vast size of the world market, and because earnings from trade can be utilized by LDCs according to their own wishes, trade is theoretically the optimal source of hard currency for LDCs. Yet, in reality, the LDCs are severely disadvantaged by the pattern and terms of international trade.

There are several sources of LDC trade weakness. First, they command only 24 percent of the world goods and services export market. Second, as noted earlier, just a few NICs account for a lion's share of all the goods exported by the South. Third, most LDCs suffer a chronic trade deficit. Only a handful of the 64 least developed countries (LLDCs), that is, the poorest LDCs, had a positive trade balance in 1998.

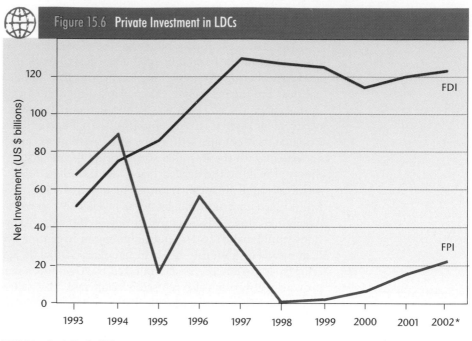

Figure 15.6 Private Investment in LDCs

*2002 data estimated by the IMF.

Data source: IMF (2002).

Foreign direct investment and foreign portfolio investment are important sources of development capital for LDCs. Notice that, compared to FDI, the flow of FPI is relatively unstable and, thus, less desirable as a source of external financing. The sharp decline in net FPI beginning in 1995 and, after a brief recovery, through the rest of the 1990s was a reaction first to Mexico's currency crisis in late 1994, then to the onset in 1997 of the Asian and Russian financial crises, which made investors wary. The first years of the new millennium, however, have brought a welcome, if still uncertain, upswing in net investment flows.

Many of the other LLDCs had staggering trade deficits that debilitated their national economies. For example, Mozambique's imports were 280 percent of its exports.

Fourth, LDC trade weakness stems from the heavy dependence of these countries on the export of primary products, including fibers, foodstuffs, fuels, and other minerals and raw materials. A general rule of thumb is that the more dependent a country is on the export of primary products other than petroleum, the poorer that country is likely to be. This is illustrated by the fact that 48 percent of the LLDC merchandise exports are primary products, compared to 32 percent of the middle-income LDC exports and 18 percent of the high-income EDC export. Trade conditions are even worse for the many LDCs that are export-dependent on one or just a few primary products. Dependency on a few products, especially primary products, for export earnings leaves LDCs disadvantaged because of several factors.

Product instability is one factor. Countries that rely on fish and other marine foodstuffs for export are endangered by the declining fish stocks in the world's oceans. When a freeze damages Colombia's coffee crop, a drought devastates the groundnut crops that Ghana relies on, or floods wipe out the Bangladesh jute crop, then trade of those countries suffers greatly.

Market and price weaknesses are also common for primary products. A downturn in world demand can decimate markets. During the past decades, world trade in products such as cotton, sisal, jute, wool, and other natural fibers has been harmed by the development of synthetics. Sugar sales have been undercut by artificial substitutes and by dietary changes. Minerals such as tin and lead have also experienced market declines. Despite its recent rise, even the oil market was

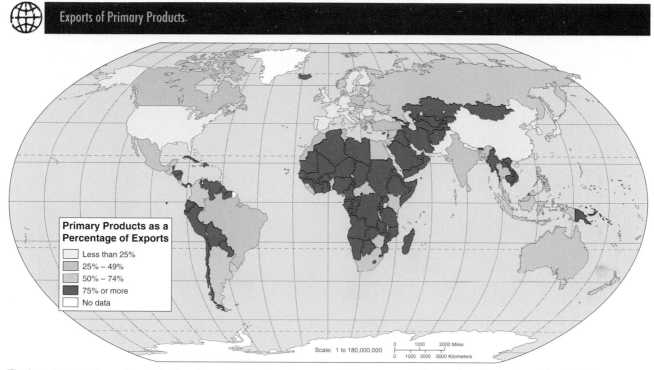

Exports of Primary Products.

Primary Products as a Percentage of Exports

- Less than 25%
- 25% – 49%
- 50% – 74%
- 75% or more
- No data

Scale: 1 to 180,000,000

The less developed countries of the South are disadvantaged compared to the economically developed countries of the North. One reason is that the LDCs are much more reliant on primary products for export earnings. The dependency is a disadvantage because the demand for and price of primary products is unstable. Also, over the long term the value of primary products rises more slowly than manufactured products. Therefore most LDCs have increasing difficulty earning the foreign capital needed for economic development. This map shows the distribution of countries according to the percentage of their exports accounted for by primary products.

depressed during most of the 1990s. That leaves even what seems to be a wealthy country like Saudi Arabia vulnerable, because in 2001 its petroleum and natural gas sales made up 90 percent of the country's exports, accounted for 32 percent of the kingdom's GDP, and provided 75 percent of government revenue.

Price weakness for primary products is the response to the classic economic relationship of too much supply and too little demand. According to the World Bank, the real dollar price of most primary products declined between 1990 and 2000, while the real dollar value of manufactured goods increased sharply. Figure 15.7 shows price changes in absolute terms and also gives you some sense of the even more dramatic relative change caused by primary products going down in price while the price of manufactured goods is going up. The net result is that the primary products that LDCs export are increasingly less valuable compared to the manufactured products and the services that these countries need to import.

The use of trade, then, to acquire capital and to improve economic conditions has not been highly effective for most LDCs. Their pattern of merchandise trade deficits, over-reliance on primary product exports, and market and price weaknesses are all disadvantages for LDCs in their trade relations with the EDCs.

Foreign Aid

A fourth possible external source of capital for LDCs is foreign aid (Hook, 1996). In some ways the flow of official development assistance (ODA) to LDCs has been impressive, amounting to over half a trillion dollars since World War II. Official ODA for 2001 was $51.4 billion. Currently, almost all foreign aid that is given comes from the 22 EDCs that are members of the Development Assistance Committee

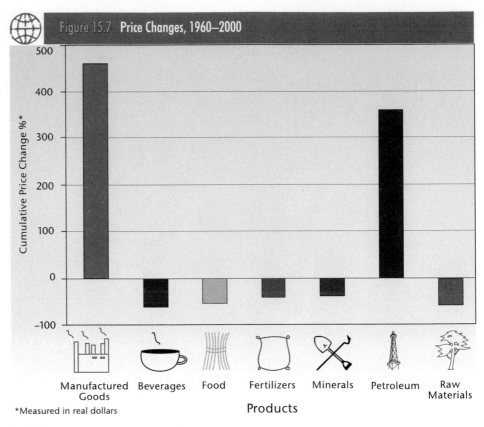

Figure 15.7 Price Changes, 1960–2000

*Measured in real dollars

Products

Data sources: World Bank (2001) and author's calculations.

When the real price changes of primary products and of manufactured goods are compared between 1960 and 2000, it is evident that the value of almost all primary products has declined while the value of manufactured goods has risen. This means that LDCs that rely in substantial part on primary products for export earnings have an increasingly difficult time earning enough foreign capital through trade to modernize their economies. Even the price of petroleum, the one primary product that has seen its real price increase since 1960, has not kept up with the cost of manufactured goods.

(DAC) of the Organization for Economic Cooperation and Development (OECD). Most assistance is extended through **bilateral aid** (country to country), with a smaller amount being channeled through **multilateral aid** (via the United Nations, the World Bank, and other IGOs).

Limitations on the Impact of Aid

Without disparaging the value or intent of past or current efforts, aid is neither a story of undisguised generosity nor one of unblemished success (Katada & McKeown, 1998; Schraeder, Hook, & Taylor, 1998). Factors that reduce the impact of aid include political considerations, the military content of aid, recipient per capita aid, donor aid relative to wealth, and aid application.

Political considerations are one factor that limits the effectiveness of aid. The bilateral aid that makes up the bulk of all foreign aid is often given more on the basis of political-military interest than to meet economic needs or to promote human rights. For example, about 40 percent of all U.S. bilateral foreign aid during 2001 went to just two countries: Israel ($2.7 billion) and Egypt ($1.9 billion). By contrast, the countries in sub-Saharan Africa received only 10 percent of U.S. bilateral aid.

Military content is another factor that limits the impact of the aid figures that are sometimes reported (Blanton, 2000). Egypt certainly needs aid, but of the total

Table 15.3	Recipient Foreign Aid Data, 1998		
Recipient	Received ($ millions)	% of GNP	Per Capita ($)
Bangladesh	1,171	2.6	9.15
Cambodia	398	9.1	33.85
Ghana	609	8.0	32.43
Guatemala	264	1.6	22.18
All LLDCs	12,052	8.5	19.02

Note: LLDCs are the least developed countries—those with per capita GNPs under $756.

Data Source: OECD Web site at. http://www.oecd.org.

It is impressive to talk about foreign aid in the tens of billions of dollars; it is less impressive when aid is measured on a recipient per capita basis. For example, Bangladesh, one of the world's poorest countries, received per capita aid of only $9.15, not quite enough in the United States for a large cheese pizza.

U.S. aid to that country in 2001, more than two-thirds was military aid. Indeed, over 25 percent of all American bilateral assistance that year was military aid.

Measuring recipient per capita aid, rather than gross aid, is also useful to gain a truer picture of the impact of economic foreign aid. In 2001 the LLDCs received about $19 per person. Some representative aid recipients are shown in Table 15.3.

Donor aid relative to wealth is another analytical approach that lessens the seeming significance of aid figures. This compares aid given to the donor's wealth. Overall, aid as a percentage of EDCs' total GNP has been steadily declining for a quarter century. In 1965 aid equaled 0.46 percent of the OECD's total GNP. That percentage declined to 0.22 in 2001. Americans are particularly apt to think that their country is a sort of Santa Claus, beneficently sending massive amounts of foreign aid down the chimneys of deserving LDCs in an act of self-sacrifice that unmercifully burdens American taxpayers (perhaps portrayed as elves in the stage version). The image is a delusion. It is true that the $10.4 billion in U.S. bilateral and multilateral economic aid for 2001 ranked first among the EDC countries. But, from the perspective of U.S. wealth, American aid was truly paltry. It equaled a tiny eleven one-hundredths of 1 percent (0.11 percent) of the U.S. GDP. As Figure 15.8 shows, this placed the United States dead last among the EDCs in terms of generosity measured against wealth. The UN recommends that each EDC use 0.7 percent of its GNP for economic assistance. As evident in the figure, however, only 5 of the 22 countries meet or exceed that standard. If they had all given the recommended 0.7 percent, economic aid in 2001 would have risen to $163 billion, with a U.S. share at $69 billion.

The way aid is applied is a final factor that limits its impact (Koehn & Ojo, 1999). Too often in the past aid has been used to fund highly symbolic but economically unwise projects such as airports and sports arenas. Inefficiency and corruption have also sometimes drained off aid. There is criticism, too, on the grounds that aid is used to maintain the local elite, does not reach the truly poor, and, therefore, continues the dependencia relationship between North and South. In fact, some critics argue that aid can actually retard growth, contending, for example, that giving poor people food reduces their incentive to farm. These charges are not universally accurate, but aid donors and recipients have moved to address problems that do exist. Among other changes, donors are now working to ensure that the aid is used wisely. "For too long development cooperation has

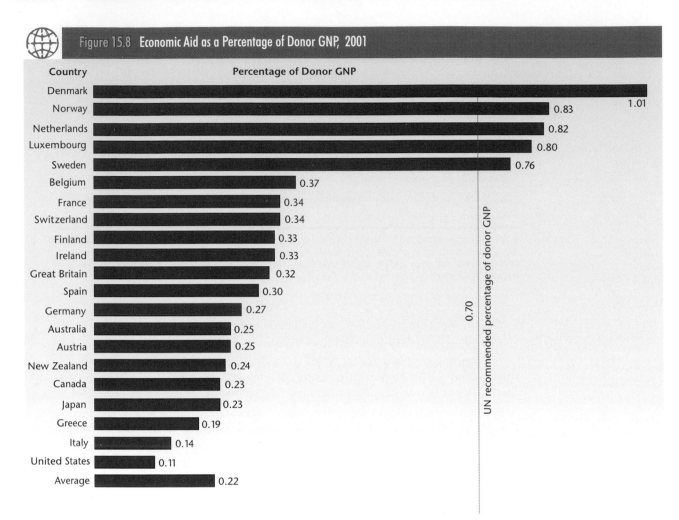

Figure 15.8   Economic Aid as a Percentage of Donor GNP, 2001

Country	Percentage of Donor GNP
Denmark	1.01
Norway	0.83
Netherlands	0.82
Luxembourg	0.80
Sweden	0.76
Belgium	0.37
France	0.34
Switzerland	0.34
Finland	0.33
Ireland	0.33
Great Britain	0.32
Spain	0.30
Germany	0.27
Australia	0.25
Austria	0.25
New Zealand	0.24
Canada	0.23
Japan	0.23
Greece	0.19
Italy	0.14
United States	0.11
Average	0.22

0.70 — UN recommended percentage of donor GNP

Data source: OECD Web site at: http://www.oecd.org/EN/document/0,,EN-document-15-nodirectorate-no-12-29438-15,00.html.

The UN recommends that the EDCs allocate 0.7 percent of their GNPs to economic aid. Only four EDCs meet that mark. The U.S. percentage of its wealth devoted to foreign economic aid is by far the lowest.

focused on the economy and not the polity," the head of United Nations Development Programme (UNDP) has conceded. "Without a functioning political system and effective governance, the best-lain economic plans are not going to succeed."[14] To address this issue, aid is now being aimed at what is called "capacity building." This means creating a political and business structure to use aid more effectively to build a recipient's economic infrastructure.

DEVELOPMENT IN THE SOUTH: LDC PERSPECTIVES AND POLICIES

While the gap in wealth between the North and South has long existed, relations between the two economic spheres have not been static. The LDCs are now asserting with mounting intensity the proposition that they have a right to share in the world's economic wealth. They have acted on a number of fronts to enhance their own economic situations and to pressure the EDCs to redistribute part of their wealth. We will examine these views and efforts in terms of the LDCs' expectations, organizational movement, demands, and actions.

Development of the LDC Movement

One of the most important developments in the last half of the twentieth century was the independence movement among LDCs. Dozens of colonies in Africa and Asia demanded and won political sovereignty. Even after independence, though, many LDCs remained in an economically subservient and disadvantaged position in relation to their former colonial masters or to other dominant EDCs. Most people in LDCs are not willing to accept such manipulation, and increasingly during the last 50 years, the LDCs have joined together to demand what they believe to be a more equitable distribution of financial resources and political power.

The developing identity of the South first took the form of political non-alignment. In 1955, 29 African and Asian countries convened the Bandung Conference in Indonesia to discuss how to hasten the independence of colonial territories and how to be nonaligned in the cold war. Most of the colonies are now independent, and the cold war is over. But the Bandung Conference remains an important mark of the ongoing sense of identity among the LDCs.

The South's concerns soon also turned to economic development. Political demands for an end to colonialism provided a role model for similar economic assertiveness. A coalition of disadvantaged countries, the Group of 77, emerged and called for creation of the first United Nations Conference on Trade and Development (UNCTAD), which met in Geneva in 1964. This conference and the Group of 77 (which has grown to 133 members) evolved into an ongoing UNCTAD organization. UNCTAD, which has 190 members, has served as a vehicle for the LDCs to discuss their needs and to press demands on the North.

LDC Demands

The development of LDC consciousness and assertiveness has led to a series of demands on the industrialized North. These came together in the Declaration on the Establishment of a **New International Economic Order (NIEO)**, which was drafted by UNCTAD and adopted as a resolution by the UN General Assembly in 1974. The NIEO declaration began by protesting the North's domination of the existing economic structure and the maldistribution of wealth. To remedy this situation, the declaration called for a number of reforms. These changes have regularly been reiterated, refined, and expanded by UNCTAD and other LDC organizations, but none of the reforms have been truly implemented. Indeed the onward march of globalization has in many ways sharpened the demands for what UN secretary-general Annan has termed a "Global New Deal" for the LDCs, one in which "large parts of the world are [no longer] excluded from the benefits of globalization."[15] Speaking to global business magnates as well as political leaders at the World Economic Forum in early 2002, Annan bluntly characterized the perceptions of the LDCs. "The reality is that power and wealth in this world are very, very unequally shared, and that far too many people are condemned to lives of extreme poverty and degradation," he told his audience. "The perception among many is that this is all the fault of globalization and that globalization is driven by a global elite, composed of, at least represented by, the people who attend this gathering." Annan concluded.[16]

Perhaps the best recent exposition of the views of the LDCs occurred at the South's first ever general summit meeting, which occurred at the Group of 77 conference held in Havana, Cuba, during April 2000. The leaders adopted a joint declaration entitled the "Havana Program of Action" that declared, "Rather than be passive witnesses of a history not of our own making, we in the South will exert every effort to shape the future through the establishment of a world order that will reflect our needs and interests."[17] That future, the document asserted, should include:

Cartoonists and Writers Syndicate
http://cartoonWeb.com

As this editorial cartoon from France suggests, the people of the economically less developed countries of the South are demanding that they receive a greater share of the world's wealth, which is largely possessed by a minority of people who live in the economically developed countries of the North.

The countries of the South consider economic sanctions to be an attempt by the countries of the North to exercise neoimperial control over them, and they are demanding an end to most sanctions, especially unilateral sanctions. This viewpoint is evident in this 2001 photograph taken in Monrovia, Liberia, showing the reaction to sanctions imposed by the UN on Liberia because its government was allegedly supporting rebels in Sierra Leone and Guinea. Critics of sanctions say they are more apt to hurt the average citizen, such as the men who are repairing shoes in the makeshift shop underneath the billboard, than the government that is supposedly being penalized.

1. *Trade reforms.* The LDCs are pressing to secure improved and stabilized markets for their products. In the words of the Havana declaration, "It is necessary to adopt measures that improve access, for all products of export interest to developing countries, to the markets of developed countries by means of reducing or eliminating tariff and non-tariff barriers."

2. *Monetary reforms.* The LDCs wish to create greater stability in exchange rates and the ebb and flow of FDI and FPI. "As the recent financial crisis has illustrated," the Havana declaration noted, "financial liberalization including speculative and volatile financial flows, over which the developing countries have little controls, in the absence of adequate institutional arrangements to manage the processes, has generated significant instability in the international economies," with specially disastrous results for the developing countries.

3. *Institutional reforms.* The LDCs have long demanded greater LDC participation in the decision making of the IMF, the World Bank, and other such international financial agencies. "There is an increasing need for the reform of the international financial architecture," the Havana declaration asserted. "In this context, we should seek to ensure a more democratic and fair ordering [of decision making in financial IGOs] … in order to increase the effective participation of developing countries in the management of the international economy."

4. *Economic modernization.* The LDCs, from the 1974 NEIO resolution through the Havana UNCTAD summit, have called on the North to assist the South in

modernizing the economies of the South through technology transfers and assistance in increasing industrial production. The LDCs gathered in Havana called on the North to assist with "measures that support capacity-building for production and export in our countries" and to "facilitate the access to, dissemination and transfer of technologies on concessional and preferential terms from developed to developing countries."

5. *Political and economic sovereignty.* The South asserts the right of each of its countries to choose its own form of government, its own economic system, and to otherwise exercise sovereign control over its internal affairs. This includes the right to control its own resources and to regulate the activities of MNCs. "We stress that every state has the inalienable right to choose political, economic, social and cultural systems of its own, without interference in any form by another state," the leaders in Havana wrote. "We also reaffirm the principle of permanent sovereignty of peoples under foreign occupation over their natural resources."

6. *Greater labor migration.* The LDCs seek greater freedom for their workers to seek employment in the more prosperous EDCs. The Havana declaration noted that, "while the capital markets have been opened, including in developing countries, there has hardly been any movement in opening of the labour market in developed nations."

7. *Elimination of economic coercion.* The South tends to see sanctions as a tool used by the EDCs to punish and control LDCs. For this reason, the Havana meeting called on "developed countries to eliminate … unilateral economic coercive measures, inconsistent with the principles of international law" and urged "the international community to exhaust all peaceful methods before resorting to sanctions, which should only be considered as a last resort."

8. *Economic aid.* The meeting in Havana expressed the view that "The post–cold war period with its promise of a peace dividend has not fulfilled the hopes and expectations of the developing world. Instead, we have witnessed a weakening of the commitment of the developed countries to international cooperation in support of development." The declaration called for working toward meeting the UN's foreign aid "target of 0.7 percent of GNP of developed countries by the end of the first decade of the twenty-first century." Only five EDCs now meet that standard, as detailed in Figure 15.8 on page 454. There are also calls for more nonpolitical multilateral aid to be given through the World Bank and other such IGOs.

9. *Debt relief.* The LDCs believe that the EDCs, the World Bank, and the IMF should "Work towards outright cancellation of unsustainable debt of developing countries, and reaffirm the need of a just and lasting solution to the problem of the foreign debt of developing countries, which considers the structural causes of indebtedness and prevents the recurrence of this phenomenon in the future."

LDC Action

The LDCs have not waited passively for the EDCs to respond to their demands. They have instead taken action on a number of fronts. Not all these moves have succeeded, but they indicate the South's growing assertiveness.

Early LDC Development Policy Nationalizing MNCs, a process by which countries take over foreign corporations operating within their borders, was one early LDC approach. The oil-producing countries, for example, made Western producers surrender all or majority control of their fields and processing facilities. Many LDCs reasoned that if they controlled an industry it would operate in their interest rather than in the interest of foreign companies, investors, and governments. Perhaps, but these drastic measures caused considerable backlash and dried up the inflow of new investment money. As a result, the practice of nationalization has largely been abandoned.

Establishing cartels was a second tactic that LDCs tried initially. A **cartel** is an international trading agreement among producers who hope to control the supply and price of a primary product. The first cartel was established in 1933 to regulate tea, but the decade of the 1960s, when 18 came into existence, was the apex of cartel formation. They ranged in importance from the Organization of Petroleum Exporting Countries (OPEC) to the Asian and Pacific Coconut Community.

Cartels, however, have proven generally unsuccessful. Even OPEC, which controls a primary product that is vital to the economic prosperity of the North, has not been able utilize that position as effectively as might be imagined. It is the case, as Figure 15.7 on page 452 indicates, that petroleum prices have done better over recent decades than most other primary products, but as the figure also indicates, even the price of oil has lagged the price of manufactured goods. There are a number of reasons that have limited the ability of OPEC to dominate. First, the cartel only produces about 40 percent of the world's oil. Second, it has been difficult for OPEC to cooperate on producing and pricing when many of the members (such as Iraq, Iran, and Kuwait) have strong political differences and have even gone to war with one another. Third, the consumer countries have been able to use measures such as conservation, releasing petroleum reserves, and developing other sources of energy (such as nuclear power) to decrease demand (Lynn, 1999; Morse, 1999).

Protectionism was a third, and now also rapidly declining, thrust of early LDC activity. The temptation and domestic political pressure for developing countries to use tariff and nontariff barriers to protect infant industries are strong and may, in the earliest stages, even have some merit. It is also understandable, given the common fear, as one Indian economist explains, "that the foreigners will exploit, dominate, and control us."[18] Protectionist policies, however, have numerous drawbacks. Most important, there is evidence that protectionism does not work for LDCs and that economic growth is positively associated with eliminating trade impediments. Moreover, whether protectionism works or not, EDCs are less willing to tolerate it and have used a variety of approaches to entice or coerce the LDCs to open their markets.

More Recent LDC Development Policy With nationalization, cartels, and protectionism not helping, and even proving counterproductive, and under pressure from the United States, the IMF, and other bastions of free-market advocacy, many LDCs have turned toward trying to compete with the EDCs on their own terms. Even most of the few remaining communist countries, such as China and Vietnam, have succumbed to capitalism. Moreover, there have been some remarkable success stories, as our earlier discussion of NICs indicates. Singapore's per capita GNP is the ninth-highest in the world, and South Korea's is just short of the World Bank's "high-income" category.

Yet for the LDCs, including the countries in transition (CITs, the former communist countries) that are struggling to develop their economies, the capitalist path to development has several negative by-products. One is control. To a degree, some LDCs have achieved development by suppressing democracy in favor of the political stability that outside investors favor. Second, some LDCs have also followed anti–labor union practices and other policies in order to keep wages low so that export prices can be kept down. A third drawback is that some LDCs have attracted foreign investment by having lax environmental, safety, and other regulations. Some LDCs are among the world's most polluted countries. Japan, for instance, produces 4.6 times more manufactured goods than does China; yet China's industrial emissions of carbon dioxide are 2.8 times higher than are Japan's.

Fourth, CITs and even those, such as China, that remain officially communist have found that capitalism and international economic liberalism have negative social consequences. China once stressed socioeconomic equality. Now some Chinese drive imported Mercedes, while others live in the shantytowns that have sprung up around Chinese cities. The wealthiest 20 percent of Chinese now take in 47 percent of the country's income; the poorest 20 percent make only 6 percent of the national income. That is about the same income disparity as the quintessential capitalist country, the United States.

The Future of National Economic Policy

There can be no doubt that the economic story of the last half-century has been marked by two important and related trends. The first has been the almost complete triumph of **capitalism** over competing economic models, especially Marxism and socialism. One measure of this change is the Index of Economic Freedom, which has been calculated since 1995 by the Heritage Foundation, a conservative think tank. The index measures 50 variables, including the absence of government interference, corruption, and other factors that would distort a free economy.[19] By 1995 the movement toward capitalism was well under way, but even since then, there has been a noticeable shift in the economic orientation of countries. As evident in Figure 15.9, the percentage of countries in the economically "free" category (1–1.99) and the "mostly free" category (2–2.99) increased a combined 6 percent. According to the 2002 survey, Singapore (1.55) was the freest economy, North Korea (5.00) the least free. The United States garnered a rating of 1.80, with high taxes the main "negative" in the index's rating system.

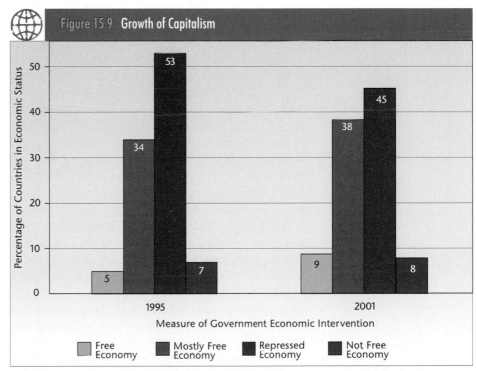

Figure 15.9 Growth of Capitalism

Data source: Gerald P. O'Driscoll Jr., Kim R. Holmes, & Mary Anastasia O'Grady, The 2002 Index of Economic Freedom, Heritage Foundation Web site at: http://www.heritage.org/index/2002/#Contents.

A significant change in the past few decades had been a surge in the capitalist approach to national economic management and a decline in the prevalence of other models, particularly Marxism and socialism. The shift is evident in this figure based on data from the Heritage Foundation. Notice especially the shift in percentages from the Repressed Economy category to the Mostly Free Economy category.

The second important trend has been a steady movement toward ever greater economic interdependence based on an increasingly free exchange of trade, investment, and other financial activity. An array of statistics presented in this and the preceding chapter show conclusively that the movement of goods, services, investment capital, and currencies across borders has expanded exponentially. Furthermore, as we shall take up in the next chapter, the international system has created the EU, IMF, NAFTA, World Bank, WTO, and numerous global and regional organizations and arrangements to facilitate and promote free international economic interchange.

For all this evidence, it would be erroneous to conclude that the world is on a path to inevitable economic integration and the eclipse of economic nationalism. Indeed, there are powerful arguments against and forces opposed to globalization. "We have sunlight, but we have shadows, too," the head of the WTO commented.[20] Those shadows are cast, according to one analyst, by the fact that "today many people think that globalization is going to destroy their life as they know it. We have gotten used to the idea that globalization will inevitably succeed, but I am not so sure anymore."[21]

Whether or not globalization is to continue and to succeed without alienating the majority of LDCs, who believe they are being left behind, depends on the degree to which greater international cooperation can be achieved. The history, current status, and future of that effort are explored in chapter 16.

 # Chapter Summary

1. Economics and politics are closely intertwined aspects of international relations. Each is a part of and affects the other. This interrelationship has become even more important in recent history. Economics has become more important internationally because of dramatically increased trade levels, ever-tightening economic interdependence between countries, and the growing impact of international economics on domestic economics.

2. The stronger role played by international economics means that political relations between countries have increasingly been influenced by economic relations. Conversely, politics also significantly affects economic relations. Domestic political pressures are important determinants of tariff policies and other trade regulations. Trade can also be used as a diplomatic tool.

3. Economic strength is a key element of every country's overall power. Economic power is based on financial position, natural resources, industrial output, agricultural output, and international competitiveness.

4. Countries use their economic power through a mixture of positive incentives and negative sanctions. While each approach is sometimes successful, both incentives and, particularly, sanctions are difficult to apply successfully and have numerous drawbacks.

5. There are a variety of barriers to the unimpeded international movement of trade and capital that countries use to pursue economic nationalism. These include such barriers as tariffs, nontariff barriers, and licensing requirements.

6. The economies of the North are prosperous compared to those of the South. With the end of the cold war and with a variety of changing economic circumstances, however, the situation has changed greatly. The EDCs are experiencing a number of economic difficulties, including the pressure of entering into a period of postindustrial economy, and economic tensions among them have increased.

7. The economies of the South are relatively weak compared to those of the North. Also, in the South there is great disparity in wealth among and within countries. A few NICs have expanding and modernizing economies. There is also, in most LDCs, a small wealthy class of people and a much larger class of impoverished people.

8. The LDCs need hard currency capital to buy the goods and services that will allow them to develop their economies. There are four basic sources of hard currency: loans, foreign investment, trade, and foreign aid. There are, however, problems with each of these sources.

9. Loans are unsatisfactory because of high repayment costs. The debt crisis has eased, but LDC debt is growing once again and could threaten the global financial community.

10. Investment capital has grown in amount and importance in recent years. Still, investment capital flows mostly into just a few LDCs.

11. The catch-22 of trade is that the primary products that LDCs mainly produce do not earn them enough capital to found industries to produce manufactured goods that would earn more money.

12. Foreign aid is minor compared with world needs and is often given on the basis of political expediency rather than economic necessity.

13. In recent years, the countries of the South have begun to make greater demands for economic equity to press the North to join in establishing a New International Economic Order.

Chapter 16

International Economic Cooperation: The Alternative Road

The gods sent not
Corn for the rich men only.

Shakespeare, *Coriolanus*

Happy are they that can hear their detractions, and can put them to mending.

Shakespeare, *Much Ado About Nothing*

If a house be divided against itself, that house cannot stand.

Mark 3:25

The Lord so constituted everybody that no matter what color you are you require the same amount of nourishment.

Will Rogers, *The Autobiography of Will Rogers*

Chapter Objectives

After completing this chapter, you should be able to:

- Explain why economic cooperation and integration will prove to be pivotal determinants of future international relations.
- Describe the specialized cooperative efforts currently at work on the world stage.
- List and describe the most significant development agencies involved in granting loans and aid to less developed countries.
- Discuss the reasons leading to growing international monetary cooperation, giving special attention to the International Monetary Fund.
- Evaluate how the European Union exemplifies efforts at international or regional economic integration.
- Trace the evolution of the North American Free Trade Agreement and assess its effects on the region and the world.
- Describe efforts at regionalism that have emerged at least partly in response to the economic integration occurring in Europe and North America.

This chapter is the third of three that examine international political economy. Chapter 14 the first of the trio, laid out the global economic road map. Chapter 15 took up economic nationalism, which is characterized by self-interested economic competition among and between the states of the North and of the South. Economic nationalism persists and, in some aspects, is on the rise. It may even eventually provide prosperity to all states and peoples.

There are, however, economic internationalists and structuralists who condemn the harvest that we reap from this nationalist economic strategy. They believe that the global economic future will be better if countries cooperate economically, or even integrate their economies. Whereas chapter 15 explores the economic nationalist path, this chapter assesses the alternative route of greater international cooperation. This assessment will first examine global cooperation then turn its attention to regional efforts. As you will see, one aspect of cooperation is continuing the relative prosperity of the economically developed countries (EDCs) of the North. An arguably even more important goal of economic cooperation is to improve the circumstances of the less developed countries (LDCs) of the South, and we will pay particular attention to economic development programs. With these broader topics, this chapter will also deal with a variety of more specific issues, such as child labor and the puzzle of how to continue to grow economically while simultaneously protecting the environment from the negative by-products of economic expansion.

Global Economic Cooperation: Background

The thought of moving toward a very different way of dealing with the international economy is more than theory. It is a process that has made substantial progress and one that many scholars, practitioners, and other analysts think can and should become the dominant paradigm in the future. At the global level, it is appropriate to first look at the background of economic cooperation. Then we will turn to detailing the most important international economic institutions.

THE ORIGINS OF ECONOMIC COOPERATION

Economic nationalism has long been the prevailing reality, but it is also true that economic cooperation and regulation have become increasingly commonplace, albeit still limited, elements of national and international economics. The liberal idea of creating a global economy based on free economic interchange and interdependence dates back several hundred years, as elaborated in chapter 14. This view was slow to take hold, though, and did not begin to shape international economic relations to any great extent until the 1930s and 1940s. A combination of the strife that had marked the twentieth century to that point and the Great Depression that was gripping the world in the 1930s led an increasing number of leaders to agree with the view of the longest-serving U.S. secretary of state (1933–1944), Cordell Hull, that "international commerce is not only calculated to aid materially in the restoration of prosperity everywhere, but it is the greatest civilizer and peacemaker in the experience of the human race" (Paterson, Clifford, & Hagan, 2000:121).

While the tensions that led to World War II kept international economic reform on the political back burner for a decade, the war added to the impetus to change the structure and course of world politics. With the United States leading the anti-Axis alliance and then the anticommunist West, the capitalist EDCs moved during the years 1943–1948 to create the foundation for a new international economic order. The EDCs created a number of global and regional intergovernmental organizations (IGOs) to reduce national economic barriers and to otherwise handle a range of economic interactions across national boundaries. The most prominent of these IGOs are the World Bank, the International Monetary Fund (IMF), the General Agreement on Tariffs and Trade (GATT, both a treaty and an organization; the organization was renamed the World Trade Organization, WTO), and the United Nations, with its numerous economic agencies and responsibilities, which was brought into existence by the U.S.-led victors at the end of World War II. Although the UN was created to address a broad range of global issues, it had and continues to have an important economic role.

Thus began the current era of enhanced global and regional economic cooperation. Trade and the flow of international capital grew rapidly. These successes and the need to further regulate the increased economic interchanges led to yet more agreements and IGOs dedicated to still further reductions of national economic barriers. The European Union (EU) and the North American Free Trade Agreement (NAFTA) are just two of the more recent IGOs or treaties that facilitate and further the free flow of goods, services, and capital. We will examine them by first taking up global efforts, then by turning to regional ones.

GLOBAL ECONOMIC COOPERATION: EDC PROSPERITY

The United States and other countries that in the 1940s initiated the movement toward greater economic cooperation were all EDCs, and their goal was to renew and maintain their prosperity. Initially, little attention was paid to the South, much of which was still in a colonial status. Economic cooperation has come to include efforts to develop the South, but there remains an important dimension of cooperation among countries of the North to maintain their prosperity.

In addition to creating the IMF, World Bank, and WTO to help ensure their post–World War II economic health, the EDCs also later founded other institutions and processes designed specifically to foster cooperation among the EDCs. The **Organization for Economic Cooperation and Development (OECD)** was the first of these. It was originally created in 1948 by several European countries as the Organization for European Economic Cooperation, to coordinate the foreign aid that the United States extended to Europe under the Marshall Plan. In 1960 the member-countries agreed to ask the United States and Canada to join the organization, to change its name to OECD, and to reorient its mission to coordinating economic policy among the Western EDCs. This led to the subsequent admission of Japan and most other EDCs and, thus, to the OECD's becoming known as a "rich man's club."

This has begun to change slightly. Although the OECD remains primarily an organization of EDCs fostering cooperation among themselves, it has begun to also deal with the LDCs and their development. Symbolic of the shift, Mexico in 1994 became the OECD's first new member in 21 years and the first LDC member. Mexico's admission came in light of its link to the United States and Canada under NAFTA. Since then, two other LDCs (South Korea and Turkey) and several countries in transition (CITs, including the Czech Republic, Hungary, Poland, and Slovakia) have also been admitted to join the 23 EDCs that make up the bulk of the OECD's membership.

If the OECD is something of an exclusive club of prosperous member-countries, the **Group of Eight (G-8)** is equivalent to the executive board. The G-8 does not have a formal connection to the OECD, but it does represent the pinnacle of economic power. The G-8 began in 1975 as the **Group of Seven (G-7)**, which included the seven most economically powerful Western countries (Canada, France, Germany, Great Britain, Italy, Japan, and the United States). The group's annual meeting in 1997 expanded membership for political matters to include Russia. The group officially became the Group of Eight (G-8) the following year. In some sense, however, the G-7 continues to exist because the original seven agreed they would meet as the G-7 without Russia on financial issues and with the Russian president as the G-8 on political issues. To avoid confusion, the group will be referred to as the G-8 in all its activities.

Whatever the G-number, the most important issue is the impact of the process. There are numerous G-8 meetings at the ministerial level, but the apex is the annual summit meeting. Canada hosted the twenty-eighth G-8 summit in Kananaskis, a resort area 55 miles west of Calgary, Alberta, in June 2002. The remote location was chosen largely to try to avoid the large contingents of antiglobalism protesters that besieged the 2001 meeting in Genoa, Italy. While the G-8 remains primarily devoted to economic coordination among the leading EDCs, it has also expanded the scope of its meetings. This shift was reflected by the comment of Canada's premier that the 2002 summit focused on "strengthening global economic growth,... fighting terrorism, and... working with African countries on key development issues."[1]

Many analysts conclude that the annual summits play a positive, if not always clear-cut role. As one scholar writes, the member-countries "do comply modestly with the decisions and consensus generated [at the annual economic summit meetings]. Compliance is particularly high in regard to agreements on international trade and energy." The analyst also points out that the meetings provide "an important occasion for busy leaders to discuss major, often complex international issues, and to develop the personal relations that help them" both to "respond in an effective fashion to sudden crises or shocks" and to "shape the international [economic] order more generally."[2] Also, the group takes up political and social issues.

There are other analysts who fault the G-8 for not achieving more concrete results and cite this as a reason why the meetings of the G-8, which were once major news stories, have more recently been far from front-page news. To return to the forefront, two scholars observe, "the group needs to show that its initiatives are not spinning into oblivion, leaving behind only lengthy communiqués."[3]

GLOBAL ECONOMIC COOPERATION: LDC DEVELOPMENT

Documenting the plight of the South is easier than agreeing on the causes or the remedies. An initial question is, Why did the gap between North and South develop? One factor was circumstance. The industrial revolution came first to Europe and, by extension, to North America. Industrialization brought the North both wealth and technology that, in part, could be turned into sophisticated weapons that overpowered the more rudimentarily armed people of the South. The need for primary products to fuel the North's factories and the search for markets in which to sell those products led to increased direct colonization and indirect domination. Nationalism intensified this process as countries also sought colonies to symbolize their major-power status. As a result of all these factors, Asians, Africans, Latin Americans, and others were exploited to benefit the industrialized, imperialist countries. This pattern existed for a century and in some cases much longer. Politically, most of the LDCs achieved independence in the decades following World War II. Economically, though, the South remains disadvantaged in its relationship with the North. In many ways that we will explore later, the international economic system remains stacked against the LDCs. What can and should be done? More specifically, what can and should the countries of the North do to assist the countries of the South? The three fundamental approaches to international political economy (IPE) detailed in chapter 14 give very different answers to these questions.

The Economic Nationalist Approach Economic nationalists operate from a realpolitik orientation and believe that each country should look out for itself first and

Some of the debate about political economy relates to this representation of the sinking of the *Titanic* and the dilemma faced by those in the lifeboats: How many of the unfortunate souls in the water could be saved without swamping the lifeboat and drowning everyone? Some economic nationalists make an analogy between a lifeboat and the world economic situation. They fear that if the less populous economically developed countries (which are safely in the lifeboat of prosperity) too selflessly try to save the tide of humanity in the less developed countries (struggling in sea of poverty), then the entire lifeboat will be lost. Others reject the analogy and maintain that for good or ill, we are all on the SS *World* together.

foremost. Therefore, economic nationalists argue that an EDC should be governed by its own national interest when formulating trade, investment, and aid policies toward the South. Furthermore, economic nationalists suspect that the South's calls for greater equity are, in essence, attempts to change the rules so that the LDCs can acquire political power for themselves.

Economic nationalists view the political economy as a zero-sum game in which gains made by some players inevitably mean losses for other players. It is a perspective that leads economic nationalists to worry that extensive aid to LDCs may be counterproductive for both the donor and the recipient. This reasoning often uses a **lifeboat analogy**. This image depicts the world as a lifeboat that can support only so many passengers. The people of the EDCs are in the boat. The billions of poor are in the sea, in peril of drowning, and clamoring to get aboard. The dilemma is that the lifeboat is incapable of supporting everyone because there are not enough resources. Therefore, if everyone gets in, the lifeboat will sink and all will perish. The answer, then, is to sail off with a sad but resolute sigh, saving the few at the expense of the many in the interest of common sense. An extension of this logic, economic nationalists suggest, is that providing food and medicine to the already overpopulated LDCs only encourages more childbearing, decreases infant mortality, and increases longevity, and thereby worsens the situation by creating more people to flounder and drown in the impoverished sea.

The Economic Internationalist Approach Economic internationalist theorists believe that development can be achieved within the existing international economic structure. This belief is related to the idealist approach to general world politics. Economic internationalists believe that the major impediments to the South's development are its weakness in acquiring capital, its shortage of skilled labor, and some of its domestic economic policies, such as centralized planning and protectionism. These difficulties can be overcome through free trade and foreign investment supplemented by loans and foreign aid and through reduced government interference in the economy. Such policies, economic internationalists believe, will allow unimpeded international economic exchange among states, which will eventually create prosperity for all. Thus, for economic internationalists, the global economy is not a zero-sum game. They believe it is possible to integrate LDCs into the world economic system by eliminating imperfections in the current system while maintaining the system's basic structure and stability.

As for the lifeboat analogy, economic internationalists contend that we are not in (or out of) a lifeboat at all. Instead, they say, we are all inescapably sailing on the same vessel, perhaps the *SS World*, to a common destiny. From this perspective, we can all reach the home port of prosperity, or we can all suffer the fate of the *Titanic*, which struck an iceberg and sank in the North Atlantic in 1912. The 1,513 passengers who drowned came from both luxurious first-class and steerage accommodations, but they found in death the equality inherent in all humans. Commenting in this vein about Brazil, one reformer noted that the country, with its gulf between rich and poor, "is like a huge ocean liner that has been slowly sinking. The elite are in the top cabins, so they haven't been noticing as the rest of us have been going under water. But now the water is beginning to tickle their feet and they see that they're on the same sinking ship."[4]

The Economic Structuralist Approach Scholars of the structuralist school of thought believe that the political-economic organization of the world's patterns of production and trade must be radically altered for the LDCs to develop. In terms of the lifeboat analogy, economic structuralists believe that not only should the poor be allowed into the boat, but that they should also at least share command with, and perhaps supplant, the wealthy captains who have been sailing the vessel in their own interests and at the expense of others. Marxists would not shun a peaceful change of command if that were possible, but they are not averse to a mutiny if necessary.

Incentives and Resistance to Development

It is obvious that the three different IPE approaches to the general conduct of global economic affairs and to North-South relations present markedly different descriptions of, and even more dramatically different prescriptions for, the conduct of political-economic relations. To help decide which of the three contains the greatest element of truth, it is appropriate to turn to an examination of the current status of incentives to getting more LDCs in the lifeboat and the resistance to that goal.

Incentives to Assist the Development of the South There are several incentives for the North to try to assist the South. One of these is moral; the others are pragmatic.

Humanitarian compassion is one reason to assist the South. The concept that each domestic society has an obligation to provide at least a minimally acceptable level of existence for its people has taken firm hold throughout most of the world. This has led all countries, especially the wealthy ones, to adopt a wide range of economic and social programs to help those in need. National borders have created a sense of boundaries relating to whom a country does or does not have a moral responsibility to help, but as chapters 6 and 8 relate, those borders are artificial creations that are increasingly less relevant in today's interconnected world.

Decreased international violence is one of the pragmatic ways that the North will benefit from increased prosperity in the South, according to aid advocates. This view

Since the 9-11 attacks, there has been much greater acknowledgment that the abject poverty in many parts of the world engenders the kind of anger and frustration in people that sometimes leads to terrorism. The boys driving the donkey cart in this photograph are part of the *zabaleen*, or "garbage people," of Egypt who live and scavenge among the city's garbage dumps hoping to recover items they can use, consume, or sell. One wonders how these boys will see justice in the world when they are young men.

contends that the poor are becoming increasingly hostile toward the wealthy. Modern communications have heightened the South's sense of relative deprivation—the awareness of a deprived person (group, country) of the gap between his or her circumstances and the relatively better position of others. Research shows that seeing another's prosperity and knowing that there are alternatives to your own impoverished condition cause frustration and a sense of being cheated that often lead to resentment and sometimes to violence.

Perhaps it was the 9-11 attacks that provided the wake-up call, but when world leaders met in Monterrey, Mexico, in March 2002 to discuss LDC development, a constant theme was the connection between poverty and violence. "Poverty in all its forms is the greatest single threat to peace [and] security," the head of the WTO, told delegates. "No one in this world can feel comfortable, or safe, while so many are suffering and deprived," was the way the UN secretary-general Kofi Annan, put it. The president of the UN General Assembly, Han Seung-Soo, depicted poverty as "the breeding ground for violence and despair," and President Alejandro Toledo of Peru told the conference, "To speak of development is to speak also of a strong and determined fight against terrorism."[5]

Increased economic prosperity for the EDCs is another benefit that many analysts believe will result from the betterment of the LDCs. This view maintains that it is in the North's long-term economic interest to aid the South's development. After World War II, the United States launched the Marshall Plan, which gave billions of dollars to Europe. One motivation was the U.S. realization that it needed an economically revitalized Europe with which to trade and in which to invest. Europe recovered, and its growth helped drive the strong growth of the American economy. In the same way, according to many analysts, helping the South toward prosperity would require an immense investment by the North. In the long run, though, that investment would create a world in which many of the 1.3 billion Chinese could purchase Fords, more of India's 1 billion people could afford to travel in Boeing airplanes, and a majority of the 124 million Nigerians and 168 Brazilians could buy Dell personal computers. It is true that a developed South will compete economically with the North, but economic history demonstrates that increased production and competition bring more, better, and cheaper products that increase the standard of living for all.

Resistance to Development However pragmatic the benefits of increasing LDC prosperity may seem, the North has been slow to respond to the development needs of the South. Traditional narrow self-interest has been strengthened recently by the rising global economic competition among, and economic uncertainty within, the EDCs. One indication of this trend, as we have noted, is that bilateral foreign economic aid-giving by the EDCs has dropped off both in real dollars and as a percentage of their productive wealth.

Efforts to bring the North and South together directly to marshal resources and coordinate programs have also shown very limited results. The initial UN-sponsored meeting that brought the leaders of the North and South together was held in 1981. This meeting and a number of others on development that have followed have helped increase international awareness among the policymakers of the North about

Table 16.1 Official Development Aid: 1985 and 2001 Compared			
	France	United States	All DAC* donors
1985 aid (current $billions)	3.080	9.057	28.443
1985 aid (real 1985 $billions)	3.080	9.057	28.443
2001 aid (current $billions)	4.290	10.880	51.354
2001 aid (real 1985 $billions)	2.622	6.649	31.383
1985 aid (% of GNP)	0.62	0.24	0.34
2001 aid (% of GNP)	0.34	0.11	0.22

*DAC is the Development Assistance Committee, the principal official development aid (ODA) donors of the Organization of Economic Cooperation and Development (OECD).

Data source: OECD at: http://www.oecd.org.

The data in this table casts doubt on whether the EDC leaders who have pledged more foreign aid can meet that goal. Notice that for both France and the United States there has been a decline in both the amount that they give in real dollars and the percentage of their respective GNP that they donate. Using the United States as an example, the current dollar growth from $9.057 billion in 1985 to $10.880 billion appears to be a 20 percent increase. In real (1985) dollars, the change is actually a 27 percent decrease to $6.649 billion. For the DAC donors overall, real dollar spending did increase slightly (from $28.433 billion to $31.383 billion), but the percentage of their collective GNP declined.

the need for development, have elicited expressions of concern, and have even brought some financial support. Still, the outcome has been that the North has been unwilling to take the actions needed to rapidly advance the South's development.

An example of the continuing gap between rhetoric and reality, between what is needed to address development and what is offered, was provided by the most recent of the North-South meetings, the **International Conference on Financing for Development (ICFD)**, which was held in March 2002 in Monterrey, Mexico. The conference was attended by 50 heads of government, ranging from George Bush to Fidel Castro, the leaders of the World Bank, IMF, and other top financial IGOs, representatives of numerous NGOs (such as Focus on the Global South, headquartered in Thailand), and representatives of the Institute of Canadian Bankers and other business entities.

The challenge to the conference was put forth by UN secretary-general Kofi Annan. "All serious studies concur that we cannot achieve [our development goals] without at least $50 billion a year of additional official aid," he told the delegates. "The clearest and most immediate test of the Monterrey spirit," Annan continued, "is whether the donor countries will provide that aid." He went on to recognize that "some donors may still be skeptical, because they are not convinced that aid works," but added, "To them, I say, 'look at the record.' There is abundant evidence that aid does work."[6]

To some degree, the leaders of the EDCs were responsive. France's President Jacques Chirac proposed meeting the long-standing UN goal of "allocating 0.7 percent of the wealth of the industrialized countries to development of the poor countries." The European Union pledged to add $7 billion a year by 2006 to the aid that its members collectively contribute, and President Bush announced that he would ask Congress to increase U.S. economic aid by 50 percent to about $15 billion by 2005.

Such promises need to be put in perspective: They are unlikely to be fulfilled and, even if they are, may fall short of the 0.7 percent standard and the additional $50 billion. As presidents of democratic countries, both Chirac and Bush must convince their respective national legislatures to appropriate the funds they indicated as a goal. The fact, as Table 16.1 indicates, that foreign aid measured in both real dollars and as a percentage of donor countries' respective GNPs has been going down creates skepticism that Chirac, Bush, or other EDC presidents will be able to win large aid increases. For France to meet the 0.7 percent goal, its aid ($4.2 billion) would have to double from its 2001 level of 0.34 percent of its GNP. A $5 billion increase for the United States, while still doubtful, is possible, but even that would only increase the percentage of the U.S. aid to 0.16 percent of its GNP, well short of the 0.7 percent basis. Similarly, the EU's pledge of an additional $7 billion increase in its donations may be politically impossible to achieve, and even it does occur, it would increase aid from 0.33 percent of its annual GNP to only 0.39 percent, again far short of the goal of 0.7 percent. In sum, one does not want to be unduly pessimistic, but meeting the goals of the Monterrey conference and adequately funding development in the South will require a substantial change in the recent historical trends among the recalcitrant rich.

Global Economic Cooperation: The Institutions

The most obvious manifestation of the move toward economic cooperation and globalization that began in earnest in the 1940s is the array of global and regional IGOs that have been created to try to regulate and enhance the world economy. Of the global IGOs, the most important are the UN, the WTO, the IMF, and the World Bank.

THE UNITED NATIONS AND ECONOMIC COOPERATION

The UN serves as a global umbrella organization for numerous agencies and programs that deal with economic issues through the UN General Assembly (UNGA), the United Nations Economic and Social Council (UNESCO), and other UN divisions and associated agencies. The economic focus of the UN can be roughly divided into two categories: global economic regulation and the economic development of the South.

The UN and Global Economic Regulation

The UN is involved in a number of areas related to global economic cooperation. The regulation of transnational (or multinational) corporations (TNCs/MNCs) is one such area. The need to regulate business first became apparent at the national level. As a result, the sometimes predatory practices of capitalist corporations have been partially restrained by domestic laws enacted over the past century or so. In the United States, for instance, the Progressive Era of the late 1800s and early 1900s led to efforts to rein in the so-called robber barons of big business through the passage of such legislation as the Sherman Antitrust Act (1890) and the establishment of such agencies as the Federal Trade Commission (1914).

Now, some people worry that internationalization has allowed business to escape regulation. These critics, therefore, favor creating global regulations and oversight ("watchdog") agencies similar to those in most EDCs. "Are we really going to let the world become a global market without any laws except those of the jungle?" President François Mitterrand of France once asked a UN-sponsored economic conference. "Should we leave the world's destiny in the hands of those speculators who in a few hours can bring to nothing the work of millions of men and women?"[7] In response to such concerns, the UN's Center for Transnational Corporations was established as part of the effort to create global standards and regulations to limit the inherently self-serving practices of capitalist corporations.

Creating global labor standards is a related area of economic regulation. At the national level, for example, it was during the American Progressive Era that workers

The UN and associated agencies are slowly moving to institute economic regulations to end corruption, labor abuses, and other problems. Child labor is one such concern, with the International Labor Organization a leader in the effort to create a world where scenes such as the one pictured here cease to exist. This young girl is at work carrying bricks at a construction site in Myanmar rather than going to school and playing, as she should be. Bricks such as the eight this girl is carrying weigh between 3 and 4 kilos each, meaning that the total weight pressing down on her neck and spine is somewhere between 53 and 71 pounds.

began to organize widely into unions. The American Federation of Labor, for one, was established in 1886. The U.S. government also began to regulate labor through such statutes as the Federal Child Labor Law (1916) and to create agencies such as the Department of Labor (1913) to promote the welfare of workers. Similarly, the UN is trying to make progress on labor conditions at the international level through such affiliated specialized agencies as the United Nations Children's Fund (UNICEF) and the International Labor Organization (ILO).

Child labor is one of the principal current concerns of the ILO. It estimates that 13 percent (73 million) of the world's children between the ages of 10 and 13 go to work, not to school. Furthermore, "this is only part of the picture," reports an ILO official, because "no reliable figures" exist on the "significant" numbers of child workers under 10 or the even larger number of 14- and 15-year-olds who must work. "If all of these could be counted and if proper account were taken of the domestic work performed full-time by girls," says the official, "the total number of child workers around the world today might well be in the hundreds of millions."[8]

Such abuses have long existed, but it is only in the past few years that the world community has turned more seriously to addressing the issue. For example, an ILO-sponsored international conference meeting in 1999 led to an agreement known as the Worst Forms of Child Labour Convention. The convention bars countries from inflicting on children any form of compulsory labor similar to slavery (including being forced to become a child soldier), using children for illicit activities (prostitution, pornography, drug trafficking), and having children do work that is inherently dangerous. As of late 2001, the treaty had been ratified by 113 countries and was well on its way to becoming part of international law.

The UN and the Economic Development of the South

The second focus of UN economic activity has been on the economic development of the LDCs. One role that the UN plays is providing a forum where world leaders from North and South occasionally come together. During the Millennium Summit sponsored by the UN in September 2000, one lunch table included Nigeria's president, Olusegun Obasanjo, U.S. president Bill Clinton, UN secretary-general Kofi Annan, China's president Jiang Zemin, British prime minister Tony Blair, and several other leaders. "The wishes of the developing world are simple," President Obasanjo told President Clinton and Prime Minister Blair. "We are all living in the same house, whether you are developed or not developed... [But some of us] are living in superluxurious rooms; others are living in something not better than an unkempt kitchen where pipes are leaking and where there is no toilet. We [in the South] are saying," Obasanjo continued, "Look... let [those] living in the superluxurious rooms pay a bit of attention to those who are living where the pipes are leaking, or we'll all be badly affected. That's the message."[9] The Millennium Summit also agreed that in two years the leaders of North and South should meet again, and that gathering came to pass in the form of the UN-sponsored International Conference on Financing for Development held in Monterrey, Mexico.

The UN also has numerous programs to promote development. Many of the UN's programs began during the mid-1960s in response to the decolonization of much of the South and the needs and demands of the new countries. The General Assembly, for example, created the **UN Development Programme (UNDP)** in 1965 to provide both technical assistance (such as planning) and development funds to LDCs. The UNDP's budget of just over $2.2 billion is obtained through voluntary contributions from the member-countries of the UN and its affiliated agencies. With offices in 132 LDCs, the UNDP especially focuses on grassroots economic development, such as promoting entrepreneurship, supporting the Development Fund for Women, and transferring technology and management skills from EDCs to LDCs.

Another important UN organization, the **UN Conference on Trade and Development (UNCTAD)**, was founded in 1964 to address the economic concerns of the LDCs. With 191 members, UNCTAD has virtually universal membership. There is an UNCTAD summit conference every four years, with the tenth and most recent conference held in Bangkok, Thailand, in 2000. The organization has a small budget of about $70 million. Its primary functions are to gather information and, even more importantly, to serve as a primary vehicle for the formation and expression of LDC demands for reforms in the structure and conduct of the international political economy, as discussed in chapter 15. For example, at the UNCTAD gathering in Thailand, the group concentrated on the theme that globalization could not serve just the interests of the EDCs. That view was captured in the report of UNCTAD's secretary-general, Rubens Ricupero. "It is not the amount and pace of international integration that counts, but its quality," he commented. "A world economic system that fails to offer poorer countries, and the poorer parts of the populations within them, adequate and realistic opportunities to raise their living standards will inevitably lose its legitimacy in much of the developing world," Ricupero warned. "And without this legitimacy, no world economic system can long endure."[10]

While UNCTAD itself includes virtually universal membership and addresses general issues of trade and LDC development, the organization spun off a closely associated bloc called the **Group of 77 (G-77)**, named after the LDCs that issued the Joint Declaration of the Seventy-Seven Countries at the end of the first UNCTAD conference. Since then the G-77 has expanded to include 133 members. In 2000, as detailed in chapter 15, the leaders of the G-77 countries gathered in Havana, Cuba, for the organization's first summit meeting since the initial one that founded it in 1964. Much like the UNCTAD meeting in Bangkok, the Havana summit stressed the need to narrow the economic gap between the few EDCs and the many LDCs. In particular, the meeting called for debt relief.

TRADE COOPERATION: THE GATT AND THE WTO

While the UN addresses the broad range of global economic issues, there are a number of IGOs that focus on one or another specific area of economic interchange. One of the most prominent of these specialized economic IGOs on the global level is the **General Agreement on Tariffs and Trade (GATT)**. It was founded in 1947 to promote free trade. For most of its existence, the name GATT was the source of considerable confusion because it was both the name of a treaty and the name of the organization headquartered in Geneva, Switzerland. That confusion has now ended. The GATT treaty was amended to create the **World Trade Organization (WTO)**, which superseded the GATT organization as of January 1, 1995. Therefore, references to the organization (even before 1995) will use WTO; the treaty will be referred to as the GATT. Whatever its name, the organization's initial membership of 23 countries has expanded to 144 members. Russia and Saudi Arabia are the only countries of significant economic note that are not WTO members, but they and 24 other countries have applied for WTO membership. Moreover, it is probable that Russia will be admitted to the WTO sometime in 2002. The trade of the full members accounts for approximately 90 percent of all world trade. The GATT and the WTO have played an important role in promoting the meteoric expansion of international trade. The organization has sponsored a series of trade negotiations that have greatly reduced tariffs and nontariff barriers (NTBs), such as import quotas.

The Latest Revisions of the GATT: The Uruguay Round The eighth, and most recent round of negotiations to revise the GATT in order to further reduce trade barriers was convened in Punta del Este, Uruguay, in 1986. The **Uruguay Round** proved to be the most difficult in GATT history, and it was not completed until 1994.

The GATT revisions related to reducing economic barriers are complex. They address the nature and trade details of some 10,000 products and myriad businesses and other commercial interchanges. There are, for example, four paragraphs on the importation of "soft-ripened cow's milk cheese" and how to distinguish that kind of cheese from other kinds of cheese.

What is important, though, is that, overall, the countries that signed the Uruguay Round document agreed to reduce their tariffs over a 10-year period by an average of one-third. According to U.S. estimates, these cuts are designed to reduce tariffs globally by $744 billion over 10 years. Agricultural tariffs were included in the GATT for the first time, and the agreement also further reduced or barred many NTBs. Japan will have to end its ban on rice imports, for example; the United States will have to end its import quotas on peanuts, dairy products, sugar, textiles, and apparel. The signatories also agreed to institute within five years effective protection of intellectual property, such as patents, copyrights, trade secrets, and trademarks.

The Structure and Role of the WTO

To deal with the complexities of the GATT and to deal with the disputes that will inevitably arise, the Uruguay Round also created the WTO. It is headquartered in Geneva, Switzerland, and currently headed by Director-General Supachai Panitchpakdi, a former deputy prime minister of Thailand, who took office on September 1, 2002.

Countries can file complaints against one another for violation of the GATT. The WTO has the power to enforce the provisions of the GATT and to assess trade penalties against countries that violate the accord. While any country can withdraw from the WTO by giving six months' notice, that country would suffer significant economic perils because its products would no longer be subject to the reciprocal low tariffs and other advantages WTO members accord one another. When one country charges another with a trade violation, a three-judge panel under the WTO hears the complaints. If the panel finds a violation, the WTO may impose sanctions on the offending country. Each country will have one vote in the WTO, and sanctions may be imposed by a two-thirds vote. This means, among other things, that domestic laws may be disallowed by the WTO if they are found to be de facto trade barriers.

Did You Know That:
Symbolic of the complexity of modern trade negotiations, the 1994 GATT revision is some 26,000 pages long and weighs 385 pounds.

Despite grumbling by critics about the loss of sovereignty, the WTO judicial process has been busy. From 1995 through January 2002, the WTO handled 236 cases. The first case in 1995 involved a complaint by Singapore against Malaysia related to its prohibition of imports of polyethylene and polypropylene. Case number 236 filed in late 2001 resulted from a charge that the United States was discriminating against the importation of softwood (such as pine) lumber from Canada. The United States was the country most frequently involved in the process. It has brought more than 50 complaints to the WTO and has had to answer more than 25 complaints by other countries. Most of these issues are settled "out of court," but of the cases actually decided by the WTO, the United States prevailed more often than it lost.

The operation and value of the WTO hearing process was evident in the global dispute that flared up in 2002, after the United States dramatically hiked steel tariffs to protect the U.S. steel industry from what the Bush administration claimed was the below-cost dumping of foreign steel into U.S. markets. Dumping is illegal under the GATT. Furthermore, Washington moved to file a complaint with the WTO about the alleged practice. The countries that were being accused of dumping and whose steel industries would be harmed by the increased U.S. tariffs also sought relief from the WTO. Meeting at the WTO headquarters in April 2002, representatives of the EU, Japan, South Korea, China, Switzerland, and Norway issued a joint statement that charged, "the protectionist measures of the U.S. violate… WTO requirements" and called upon the United States to "terminate the WTO incompatible [tariffs] without delay." They indicated that failure to do so would cause them "to proceed to request a WTO panel."[11]

As related in chapter 15, Japan, the EU, and others also moved to institute retaliatory tariffs against U.S. products. This led Washington to object that those violated WTO rules. Two weeks after the joint statement by the EU, Japan, and others, the Office of the U.S. Trade Representative (USTR) asserted that the WTO rules mandated that countries follow the organization's dispute-settlement procedures before they could impose retaliatory tariffs. "Taking unilateral action will encourage other WTO members to ignore the dispute-settlement process, which both Europe and Japan have vigorously defended in dispute-settlement cases before the WTO," the USTR contended in a press release.[12] Who is right is not the point here. Rather it is that both sides recognized the validity of the WTO's rules and its dispute-resolution process; each side accused the other of violating the rules by filing appeals, and both appealed to the WTO. Even more importantly, it was a war of words, rather than a war of bullets, which past trade disputes have sometimes caused.

The Future of the GATT and the WTO

Although the WTO has gotten off to a promising start, its future is not clear. There are a number of potential problems areas.

The Tension Between Sovereignty and Global Governance One issue is what will happen if one or more member-countries, especially powerful ones, refuse to abide by the WTO rules and reject the findings of the judicial process. So far, when Washington and the EU have lost a case, they have quietly given way, as they almost certainly will if the steel tariff dispute of 2002 has to be resolved by a WTO panel. What remains to be seen, however, is the reaction when a highly sensitive case is brought before the WTO.

Criticism of the WTO as an Agent of Globalization A second and related issue for the WTO involves globalization, which the WTO epitomizes, and the strengthening movement against it. When the WTO member-countries held an annual summit meeting in Seattle, Washington, in December 1999, President Clinton applauded the progress achieved through the GATT and the WTO, but he also cautioned the conclave that, "for 50 years, trade decisions [have been] largely the province of trade ministers, heads of government and business interests. But now, what all those people in the street tell us is that they would also like to be heard, and they're not so sure that this deal is working for them."[13] The people in the streets that Clinton mentioned were the throngs of protesters who had gathered outside the convention center where he was speaking. Their views were captured in two protest placards. One asked,

There is a growing debate over whether globalization is a positive or negative trend. The World Trade Organization is one prominent symbol of globalization, and this editorial cartoon negatively portrays those who protested and, in some cases, rioted against globalization during the WTO meeting in Seattle, Washington, in December 1999. To this political cartoonist, the protesters are like Ebenezer Scrooge from Charles Dickens's *Christmas Carol* (1843), who snorted, "Bah, humbug," at the thought of a beneficent Christmas spirit.

This political cartoon takes the opposite view from the one to your left. Here we see global business, vaguely resembling the World Wrestling Entertainment's 250-pound bad guy Stone Cold Steve Austin mauling a hapless victim, in this case workers' rights. Just like the WWE matches, the referee stands by passively while flagrant fouls are committed. The turtle that the wrestler is wielding is a reference to a WTO decision that disallowed U.S. trade penalties on countries whose fishing practices harmed sea turtles and other endangered marine species.

"When Did We Elect the WTO?" The other urged, "Resist Corporate Tyranny. Ban the WTO. The People Have Spoken."[14] These criticisms have continued unabated, and, as one reaction, the WTO has created a part of its Web presence that has a slight feel of David Letterman's late night "top ten reasons" segment. The WTO Web site has a page featuring "Top 10 Reasons to Oppose the World Trade Organization?" with an added line: "Criticism, yes… misinformation, no!"[15]

Disagreements Over Revising the GATT A third issue facing the WTO is whether to begin a new, general round of trade negotiations to further the revisions to the GATT made during the Uruguay Round. The United States and some other countries favor that, but there is opposition. The LDCs argue that a new round should not begin because the current agreement is not being fully implemented, and they are facing too many barriers to trade with the EDCs. The LDCs also contend that the focus of a new round should be on development, while some EDCs favor a more across-the-board approach to a new round. Moreover, even if a new round is begun, there will be very difficult issues to resolve.

Agriculture is one area of dispute. In the area of agriculture, the United States and some other countries have pressed for a reduction of subsidies, while the EU, Japan, South Korea, and some other countries oppose such measures. They cite food security, among other concerns, contending that an overreliance on imported food could put them in peril if a hostile country were able to cut off their food supply.

Patent rights are also controversial. The discontent about patents is based on LDCs' belief that EDCs have adopted excessively long periods of patent protection for new medicines, technology, and other innovations the LDCs need desperately but cannot afford to pay for. The charge is that the EDCs want to profit from patents at the expense of the LDCs and also to use these patents to continue their neocolonial domination of the LDCs.

Social and Environmental issues are also divisive. The EU, for one, urges that a new round of talks include negotiations about how to structure trade policy to enhance the protection of the environment, consumer and worker rights, and public health. In a curious alliance, the LDCs and United States are among the countries that maintain that such matters are adequately dealt with by the current GATT and that social and environmental regulations could in some cases be used as an excuse to practice protectionism.

Labor standards are yet another point of controversy. The EU is among those advocating the inclusion on standards for the protection of workers in any new revision of the GATT. The United States seems ambivalent on this matter, and the LDCs worry that the EDCs could evoke labor standards to weaken the competitiveness of goods from the South by driving up its labor costs.

MONETARY COOPERATION: THE IMF

As trade and the level of other international financial transactions have increased, the need to cooperate internationally to facilitate and stabilize the flow of dollars, marks, yen, pounds, and other currencies has become vital. To meet this need, a number of organizations have been founded. The **International Monetary Fund (IMF)** is the most important of these.

Early Monetary Regulation

The formation of the IMF stemmed in part from the belief of many analysts that the Great Depression of the 1930s and World War II were both partly caused by the near-chaotic international monetary scene that characterized the years between 1919 and 1939. Wild inflation struck some countries. Many countries suspended the convertibility of their currencies, and the North broke up into rival American, British, and French monetary blocs. Other countries, such as Germany, abandoned convertibility altogether and adopted protectionist monetary and trade policies. It was a period of open economic warfare—a prelude to the military hostilities that followed.

As part of postwar planning, the Allies met in 1944 at Bretton Woods, New Hampshire, to establish a new monetary order. The **Bretton Woods system** operated on the basis of "fixed convertibility into gold." The system relied on the strength of the U.S. dollar, which was set at a rate of $35 per ounce of gold.

The delegates at Bretton Woods also established the IMF and several other institutions to help promote and regulate the world economy. Thus, like the GATT, the IMF was created by the West, with the United States in the lead, as part of the liberalization of international economic interchange. The specific role of the IMF in attempting to provide exchange rate stability will be discussed in the next section.

The Bretton Woods system worked reasonably well as long as the American economy was strong, international confidence in it remained high, and countries accepted and held dollars on a basis of their being "as good as gold." During the 1960s and the early 1970s, however, the Bretton Woods system weakened, then collapsed. The basic cause was the declining U.S. balance-of-payments position and the resulting oversupply of dollars held by foreign banks and businesses. Countries were less willing to hold surplus dollars and increasingly redeemed their dollars for gold. U.S. gold reserves fell precipitously, and in 1971 this forced the United States to abandon the gold standard. In place of fixed convertibility, a new system, one of "free-floating" currency relations, was established. The conversion from a fixed standard to floating exchange rates in the international monetary system increased the IMF's importance even more because of the potential for greater and more rapid fluctuations in the relative values of the world's currencies.

In the initial period after the end of the Bretton Woods system, international money managers assumed that exchange rates among the EDCs would fluctuate slowly and within narrow boundaries. This has not been true. Instead, the exchange rates of most currencies have fluctuated greatly. Figure 14.4 on page 416 and the associated discussion of the fluctuation of the Japanese yen (¥) versus the U.S. dollar illustrate this volatility. In January 1985, one dollar equaled 258 yen ($1 = ¥258). A decade later the yen value had changed 68 percent, and stood at $1 = ¥80 in 1995. Then it moved in the opposite direction by 56 percent and in mid-2002 was $1 = ¥125.

Such large fluctuations occur because governments have frequently had difficulty managing international monetary exchange rates. To do so, a country's central bank, for example, may choose to create demand by buying its own currency if it wishes to keep its price up. The price goes up because of increased demand for a limited supply of currency. Conversely, a central bank that wishes to lower the value of its currency may create a greater supply by selling its currency. Governments sometimes even cooperate to control any given currency by agreeing to buy or sell it if it fluctuates beyond certain boundaries. Given the more than $1.5 trillion in currency exchanges each day, however, even the wealthiest countries with the largest foreign reserves often find themselves unable to adequately regulate the rise and fall of their currencies.

The Role of the IMF

The IMF began operations in 1947 with 44 member-countries. Since then the IMF has grown steadily, and in 2002 membership stood at 183. Indeed, about the only countries not in the IMF are those few (such as Nauru, which uses the Australian dollar) that do not have their own currency and have adopted the currency of a larger neighbor. The IMF's headquarters are in Washington, D.C. The managing director of the IMF since May 2000 is Horst Köhler, a German and former president of the European Bank for Reconstruction and Development.

The IMF's primary function is to help maintain exchange-rate stability by making short-term loans to countries with international balance-of-payments problems because of trade deficits, heavy loan payments, or other factors. In such times, the IMF extends a country a line of credit that the country can use to draw upon IMF funds in order to help meet debt payments, to buy back its own currency (thus maintaining exchange-rate stability by balancing supply and demand), or take other financial steps.

The IMF receives its usable funds from hard currency reserves ($265 billion in 2002) placed at its disposal by wealthier member-countries and from earnings that it derives from interest on loans made to countries that draw on those reserves. The IMF also holds more than $100 billion in reserves in LDC currencies, but they do not trade readily in the foreign exchange markets and, therefore, are of little practical use.

To help stabilize national currencies, the IMF has **Special Drawing Rights (SDRs)** that serve as reserves on which central banks of needy countries can draw. SDR value is based on an average, or market basket, value of several currencies, and SDRs are acceptable as payment at central banks. In April 2002, one SDR equaled about 1.25 U.S. dollars (SDR = $1.25). A country facing an unacceptable decline in its currency can borrow SDRs from the IMF and use them in addition to its own reserves to counter the price change. As of the end of February 2002, the IMF had SDR 61.7 billion ($77.1 billion) in loans and credit lines outstanding to 88 countries. The growth of total outstanding IMF lending from 1992 through 2002 is shown in Figure 16.1.

While SDRs have helped, they have not always been sufficient to halt instability. One problem is that the funds at the IMF's command are paltry compared to the immense daily flow of about $1.5 trillion in currency trading. Also, monetary regulation is difficult because countries often work at odds with one another.

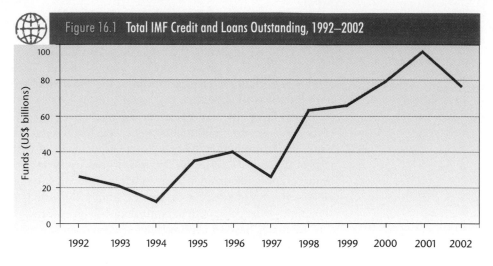

Figure 16.1 Total IMF Credit and Loans Outstanding, 1992–2002

Sources express data in SDRs; conversion to dollars by author using average SDR rate for each year. Data for 2002 as of April 15, 2002.

Data sources: IMF (2002) and IMF Web site at: http://www.imf.org/external/index.htm.

The rapid growth of the world economy and the need to keep currencies stable in a free-floating exchange rate environment have led to increasing importance for the IMF. Almost all of the IMF's funds go to developing and transitional economies to support the value of their currencies.

The IMF Focus on LDCs and CITs The IMF typically lends countries money to support their currency or to stabilize their financial situation by refinancing their debt. Over the last two decades, the IMF has especially concentrated on loans to LDCs and to CITs, with virtually all of the IMF's funds going to those countries. Russia, with $10.6 billion in loans and credit, was the IMF's biggest client as of late 2001. Indonesia was second, with its $10 billion outstanding credits and loans.

Controversy About the IMF

Although the IMF has played a valuable role and has many supporters, it has not been above criticism (Feldstein, 1998; Hale, 1998). Indeed, in recent years the IMF has been one focus of struggle over globalization. It is possible to divide the controversies regarding the IMF into two categories: voting and conditionality.

Voting The first issue centers on the formula that determines voting on the IMF board of directors. Voting is based on the level of each member's contribution to the fund's resources. On this basis, the United States (17.2 percent), Japan (6.2 percent), Germany (6.0 percent), France (5.0 percent) and Great Britain (5.0 percent), which combine to make up 2.7 percent of the IMF membership, cast more than 39 percent of the votes on the board. By a slightly different grouping, the combined votes of the EU countries (30.1 percent), the United States, and Japan are enough to form a majority of 53.5 percent. This wealth-weighted system has two ramifications. One is that the formula gives the small percentage of the world's people who live in EDCs a solid majority of the votes. This apportionment has led to LDC charges that the fund is controlled by the North and is being used as a tool to dominate the LDCs.

Conditionality The second criticism of the IMF is that it imposes unfair and unwise conditions on countries that use its financial resources. Most loans granted by the IMF to LDCs and CITs are subject to **conditionality**. This refers to requirements that the borrowing country take steps to remedy the situations that, according to the IMF, have caused the recipient's financial problems.

Foreign banks and other sources of external funding also base their decisions on the degree to which an applicant country has met the IMF's terms. The IMF's conditions press the LDCs to move toward a capitalist economy by such steps as privatizing state-run enterprises, reducing barriers to trade and to the flow of capital (thus promoting foreign ownership of domestic businesses), reducing domestic programs in order to cut government budget deficits, ending domestic subsidies or laws that artificially suppress prices, and devaluing currencies (which increase exports and make imports more expensive).

For example, Argentina's economy fell into turmoil that reached a crisis stage in December 2001. In the months that followed, the government in Buenos Aires sought a $9 billion credit line from the IMF to support the exchange rate of the Argentine peso, to help it meet the debt service on its immense foreign debt and to otherwise stem the economy's free fall. The IMF, which had long been extending credit to Argentina, offered to help, but only if the country took a number of steps, such as drastically reducing the spending of both the national and provincial governments, to correct the problems that the IMF saw as the cause of the economic difficulty. On the surface such conditions sound prudent, but in reality they have their drawbacks.

Violates sovereignty. First, LDCs charge that the IMF conditions *violate sovereignty* by interfering in the recipients' policy-making processes. In Argentina, most provincial governors resisted the demand by the IMF that they slash their budget deficits. The IMF "should go to hell," growled Alfredo Avelín, governor of San Juan province. "The only thing lacking is for us to pull down the Argentine flag and replace it with the IMF's," he continued. Taking a similar view after a top IMF official had visited the country to stress organization's conditions, Senator Rodolfo Terragno characterized the deference to the official as "like paying homage to a viceroy." It must be added that not everyone, including in Argentina, agreed with such complaints. Economist Marcelo Lascano of the University of Buenos Aires rejoined that the IMF official acted "as a viceroy" because Argentina needed outside direction. "The problem doesn't lie with [the IMF], but with the Argentine leadership," Lascano said.[16]

Promotes neocolonialism. Second, some critics have contended that conditionality intentionally or unintentionally maintains the *dependencia relationship*. Reacting to the conditions laid down by the IMF in 1997 and 1998 to assist Asia's faltering economies, *Matichon*, a daily newspaper in Thailand, editorialized that the conditions amounted to "economic colonialism."[17] Taking a similar view, President Eduardo Duhalde of Argentina blamed part of his country's crisis on "domination" by the industrialized world.[18] Other Argentines blame the IMF for pumping money into the country during the presidency of Carlos Menem (1989–1999), who, in the words of one critic, "sold off our valuable [state-owned] industries [to foreign investors] for nothing and then pocketed all the international loans he got for hugging up to the IMF." The critic also blamed the IMF for "lending money to Menem, a government that was so corrupt that any fool could see he was robbing the country."[19]

Imposes harmful conditions. Third, critics charge that sometimes the IMF *harms economies* in LDCs and CITs rather than helps them by requiring "cookbook" plans of fiscal austerity and other stringent conditions and by not sufficiently tailoring plans to the circumstances of individual countries. Harvard economist Jeffrey Sachs has argued, "Even though Argentina is, in the last analysis, mainly responsible for its fate, the IMF is not helping." In Sachs's view, the IMF "continues to pound on one theme alone: that Argentina's economic crisis is the result of fiscal profligacy, the result of a government living beyond its means. So it emphasizes the need for Argentina to cut budget expenditures." The problem with this remedy, according to Sachs, is that the cuts in government spending increase unemployment and otherwise depress Argentina's economy. Yet, he continues, "as Argentina's crisis worsens, the IMF keeps asking for [still] deeper cuts." Sachs compares this approach to "the 18th-century medical practice in which doctors 'treated' feverish patients by drawing blood from them, weakening the patients further and frequently hastening their deaths." Finally, Sachs argues that "this IMF approach was abandoned in rich countries about 70 years ago during the Great Depression" in favor of deficit spending to stimulate the economy during economic downturns.[20]

Destabilizes governments. Critics charge that while a stable government is a key factor during times of financial trouble, the reforms that the IMF demands are often so politically difficult to institute that they undermine the very government that the IMF needs to work with and that needs to remain viable in order to deal with the crisis. Reflecting that concern in Argentina, one observer commented, "The IMF has the wrong idea if they think Duhalde or any president can immediately make the kinds of reforms they are demanding and still be left standing in the morning."[21]

Undermines social welfare. Yet another line of criticism aimed at the IMF contends that it pushes countries to adopt fiscal reforms that strengthen the economic elite of the recipient country while ignoring the welfare of workers and others. According to critics, this leads the IMF to demands that force recipient LDC governments to harm the quality of life of their citizens by reducing economic growth and by cutting social services in order to maintain a balanced budget. Often it is the poorest people that are hurt the most, and civil unrest is not uncommon.

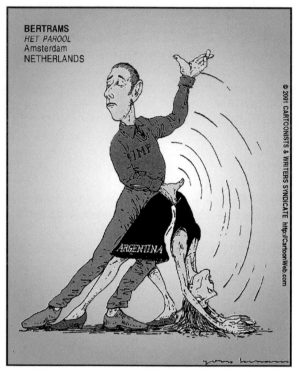

BERTRAMS
HET PAROOL
Amsterdam
NETHERLANDS

© 2001 CARTOONISTS & WRITERS SYNDICATE http://CartoonWeb.com

This editorial drawing from a Dutch newspaper picks up the theme of the tango, for which Argentina is famous, to depict the relationship between the International Monetary Fund and that country during its financial crisis. The IMF is demanding that the swooning Argentina make difficult economic changes in order to receive help; Argentina is resisting the IMF's urgings. As the old line goes, "It takes two to tango."

Many Argentines blamed their financial plight on the Menem government's decisions taken in the 1990s at the behest of the IMF and on the general pressures of globalism to privatize state-owned industry, reduce protectionist trade barriers, and otherwise adopt capitalist free economic interchange. During one of the numerous riots that have marked Argentina's time of turmoil, an unemployed textile worker who was looting a grocery store told a reporter that he was compelled to criminality; he had lost his job two years earlier when the shirt company where he worked closed because it could not compete with cheaper imports. "I can't feed my children and I can't find work—I will not watch my family go hungry at Christmas. It is time for all of this cruel madness to stop, and for the people to live in dignity," he exclaimed angrily. Waving a national flag, the displaced worker called for an "Argentine revolution" and shouted, "The free-market model is over; today is the beginning of the end."[22]

The Defense of the IMF Accusations are not equivalent to a guilty verdict, and it is important to understand the justifications for the ways in which the IMF operates. With respect to the *voting formula*, the reply to inequality is that since it is the EDCs that provide the funds, they should have a proportionate share of the say in how they are invested. Defenders say that a formula based, for example, on one vote for every member-country would mean that it would be the countries in financial difficulty, the borrowers, and not the countries supplying the loan money to the IMF, who would decide what the IMF's policies should be. That, IMF defenders say, would not work with domestic bank loans, and it would be an ill-advised policy for the IMF or any other financial institution.

As for *conditionality*, the IMF acknowledges that its demands often cause hardship. But it argues that the required reforms are necessary to correct the problems that led the borrower country into financial difficulty in the first place. Without reform, IMF defenders contend, there would be an unsupportable continuing cycle of crisis and loans, crisis and loans that would constitute "throwing good money after bad," as the phrase goes. Reflecting this view during Argentina's economic meltdown, Horst Köhler, the head of the IMF, argued, "What Argentina needs now is growth and growth requires savings, investment, and a working banking system." As for the bitter side-effects of following the IMF's prescribed regimen, Köhler, stated, "One also must recognize that without pain, it won't get out of this crisis, and the crisis—at its root—is homemade." Others, including U.S. national security adviser Condoleezza Rice, agreed. "We [in the Bush administration] truly believe that if they [the Argentines] can just do the things that the IMF is requesting that they do, we believe that they can find a way back to sustainable growth," Rice said. She indicated that the U.S. position "is not an unwillingness to have international assistance go to Argentina. It is an understanding that the conditions have to be right so that those resources actually make a difference."[23]

Before concluding our discussion of the IMF, it is important to note that there are several other monetary IGOs that make contributions. On a global scale, the oldest and largest (founded in 1930) is the Bank for International Settlements (BIS). The BIS has 45 members, including all the major EDCs and a number of economically important LDCs such as China and Saudi Arabia. The BIS serves several functions. One is as a meeting ground where its members' central banks discuss global monetary issues. Second, the BIS provides expertise to assist the central banks of those LDCs and other countries that are struggling with fiscal stability. Third, the BIS has assets ($149 billion in 2001) deposited by the central banks of its members, and it uses these funds for purposes such as maintaining currency exchange stability. Finally, there are a number of regional monetary policies and institutions, such as the European Central Bank and the Arab Monetary Fund, that are affiliated with larger regional organizations.

DEVELOPMENT COOPERATION: THE WORLD BANK GROUP

A third type of multilateral economic cooperation involves granting loans and aid for the economic development of LDCs. The most significant development agency today is the World Bank Group, which is commonly referred to simply as the World Bank. The word "group" relates to the fact that it has four agencies, which are detailed below.

World Bank Operations

Like the IMF and GATT/WTO, the World Bank was established in the World War II era to promote the postwar economic prosperity of the United States and its allies, especially those in Western Europe. In line with that purpose, the World Bank's first loan ($250 million) went to France in 1947 for postwar reconstruction.

Over time, the World Bank's priorities have shifted more and more to assisting the development of the South. To highlight just two examples, the World Bank according to its 2001 annual report increased funding to Africa, especially "to respond to the HIV/AIDS crisis, postconflict situations, and oil price shocks." The second increase was "to provide deeper, broader, and faster debt relief to some of the world's poorest countries, many of them in Africa, under the... Heavily Indebted Poor Countries (HIPC) initiative."[24] According to the World Bank, the HIPC program was able to decrease the debt service compared to exports of participating countries from 19 percent in 1999 to 9 percent at the end of 2001.

The *International Bank for Reconstruction and Development (IBRD)*. Of the four World Bank agencies, the IBRD was established first (1946) and has lending policies that most closely resemble those of a commercial bank. The bank applies standards of creditworthiness to recipients and the projects they wish to fund, and charges some interest. In 2001, the IBRD drew on the funds donated by its 183 members to make loans of $10.5 billion to fund 91 projects in 36 countries.

The *International Development Association (IDA)*. This arm of the World Bank was created in 1960 and has a separate pool of funds drawn from member contributions. It has 162 members, and it focuses on making loans at no interest to the very poorest countries to help them provide to better basic human services (such as education, health care, safe water, and sanitation), to improve economic productivity, and create employment. During 2001, the IDA extended $6.8 billion in loans to fund 134 projects in 57 countries. Given its focus on the LDCs, about a third of all IDA money went to sub-Saharan Africa, whereas very few loans of the slightly more commercial IRBD went to countries in that region.

The *International Finance Corporation (IFC)*. This part of the World Bank was established in 1956 and has 175 members. The IFC makes loans to companies in LDCs and guarantees private foreign or domestic investment aimed at establishing or improving companies in LDCs. This contrasts with the IBRD and the IDA, which mostly make loans to governments for public projects. Because of its goal of enhancing capitalism, the IFC, more than any of the other multilateral banks, has been favorably received in the United States. The IFC's loans for 2001 came to $3.9 billion to 205 companies in 74 countries. Because of the risky business climates in many countries, many of the IFC's projects are hazardous. But the philosophy at the agency, according to one of its officials, is that "the IFC needs to be ahead of the curve—we need to go where angels fear to tread. As it turns out, angels and devils tread everywhere now."[25]

The *Multilateral Investment Guarantee Agency (MIGA)*. The fourth and newest of the World Bank Group agencies, having been established in 1988, is the MIGA. The agency specializes in promoting the flow of private development capital to LDCs by providing guarantees to investors against part of any losses they might suffer due to noncommercial risks (such as political instability). The agency in 2001 issued $2 billion in guarantees on approximately five times the amount of private capital invested in LDCs. Like the IFC, the MIGA, with 154 members, is autonomous from the World Bank, but draws on the bank's administrative, analytical, and other services.

Controversy About the World Bank Group

Like the IMF, the agencies that make up the World Bank Group do a great deal of good, but they have also been the subject of considerable controversy. One point of criticism involves the North's domination of the South. An American runs the World Bank, a New Zealander has headed the WTO until mid-2002, and a German directs the IMF. Exemplifying these leaders is the ninth and current (since June 1995) head of the World Bank, James D. Wolfensohn. He holds MBA and J.D. degrees and has been an attorney, a Wall Street investment officer, and a consultant on international investing to more than 30 multinational corporations. As evidence of the North's domination, critics also point out that the World Bank Group, like the IMF, has a board of directors with a voting formula that gives the majority of the votes to the handful of EDCs. Therefore, as is the case for the IMF, the United States, the countries of the European

Union, and Japan control a majority of the votes. What all this means, from the perspective of the LDCs, is that the leaders of the World Bank Group and many other financial agencies do not truly understand the development needs of the South. A more dire interpretation of the dominance of the financial IGOs by the North is that they are vehicles for neoimperialist control of the LDCs by the EDCs. For example, Martin Kohr, a Malaysian economist who heads an NGO called Third World Network, charges, "Economically speaking, we are more dependent on the ex-colonial powers than we ever were. The World Bank and the IMF are playing the role that our ex-colonial masters used to play."[26]

A second complaint about the World Bank is simply that it provides too little funding. Figures such as $23.2 billion in total World Bank commitments to or guarantees of projects in 2001 sound impressive. But they are less so in light of the fact that lending has declined somewhat. In 2001, for example, IBRD and IDA lending combined was 13 percent less than it had been, measured in current dollars, and 19 percent less measured in real dollars (adjusted for inflation). The terms of the loans are a third sore spot. The World Bank is caught between the North's concentration on "businesslike," interest-bearing loans and the South's demands that more loans be unconditionally granted to the poorest countries at low rates or with no interest at all. While the IDA made 50 percent of its loans in 2001 to Africa, the more "commercial" IBRD did not grant any loans to that economically besieged continent. The IFC and MIGA only finance projects that meet with the Western, capitalist model.

Such criticisms and the more general uneasiness about globalization have made the World Bank, like the WTO and IMF, the target of massive street protests. When the World Bank had its annual meeting in April 2000, up to 20,000 demonstrators clogged the streets around its Washington, D.C., headquarters demanding that LDC debt be canceled and that the World Bank take other steps to alleviate poverty. "It was impossible not to be affected," bank president James Wolfensohn said soon thereafter; "I come to work every day with 10,000 colleagues who think that they are doing what we are being criticized for [not doing]." It would be too strong to say that such protests have an immediate dramatic effect, but they do add to the pressure that affects policy. That is evident in recent shifts in the World Bank and other global financial IGOs toward a greater willingness to support social programs. At the 2000 meeting, for instance, Wolfensohn announced that the bank would commit "unlimited money" to fight AIDS in the LDCs.[27]

Regional Economic Cooperation

For all the far-reaching economic cooperative efforts at the global level, the degree of activity and economic cooperation and integration at the regional level is even more advanced (El-Agraa, 1999). There are a dozen regional development banks. In terms of loan commitments in 1999, the largest regional banks (and their loans) were the 46-member Inter-American Development Bank ($5.3 billion), the 57-member Asian Development Bank ($5.3 billion), and the 58-member European Bank for Reconstruction and Development ($2.4 billion), which focuses on projects in the European CITs. Many other regional banks are much more limited in their funding. The annual loans of the poorly funded African Development Bank, for example, amount to less than $1 billion, despite its region's pressing needs, and the Caribbean Development Bank manages under $200 million in loans annually to the distressed countries in its region.

There are also a large and growing number of regional organizations that promote free trade and other forms of economic interchange. Table 16.2 provides just one index of the interest in regional economic interchange. Note the global diversity of the regional organizations. Some, in truth, are little more than shell organizations

Table 16.2 Regional Trade Organizations and Agreements		
Name	Founded	Membership
European Union and antecedents	1958	15
Latin American Integration Association	1960	11
Central American Common Market	1961	5
Council of Arab Economic Unity	1964	11
Central African Customs and Economic Union	1966	6
Association of Southeast Asian Nations	1967	10
Andean Community of Nations	1969	5
Caribbean Community and Common Market	1973	14
Economic Community of West African States	1975	16
Gulf Cooperation Council	1981	6
Economic Community of Central African States	1983	11
Arab Cooperation Council	1989	4
Arab Maghreb Union	1989	5
Asia-Pacific Economic Cooperation	1989	21
Black Sea Economic Cooperation Zone	1992	11
North American Free Trade Agreement	1992	3
South African Development Community	1992	14
Southern Common Market (Mercosur)	1995	6
Free Trade Area of the Americas	1995	34

The geographically diverse, growing number of regional trade organizations testifies to the belief of most countries that they are better able to achieve or preserve prosperity through relatively free trade than through protectionism.

that keep their goals barely alive. Yet the very existence of each organization represents the conviction of its members that, compared to standing alone, they can achieve greater economic prosperity by working together through economic cooperation or even economic integration.

Economic cooperation is a process whereby sovereign states cooperate with one another bilaterally or multilaterally through IGOs (such as the IMF) or processes (such as the G-8 meetings). *Economic integration* means such a close degree of economic intertwining that, by formal agreement or informal circumstance, the countries involved begin to surrender some degree of sovereignty and act as an economic unit. There is no precise point when economic cooperation becomes economic integration. It is more a matter of moving along a continuum ranging from economic isolation, through mercantile policy, then to economic cooperation, and finally to economic integration. The countries of the EU have moved far along this continuum toward integration; the three countries of NAFTA are just beginning this journey. It is also worth noting that the process of economic integration is not the result of a single strand of activity. Rather, integration is a complex phenomenon that results from the interaction and mutual strengthening of transnational trade and finance, of IGOs and NGOs, and of transnational values and international law.

One discussion of transnational economic activity divides economic integration into five different levels (Feld, 1979). These levels (ranging from the least to the most integrated) are (1) a *free trade area*, which eliminates trade barriers for goods between member-countries; (2) a *customs union*, which adds common tariff and non-tariff barriers adopted against external countries; (3) a *common market*, which increases integration further by eliminating barriers among members to the free flow of labor, capital, and other aspects of economic interchange; (4) an *economic union*, which proceeds to harmonize the economic policies (such as tax and social welfare policies) of members; and (5) a *monetary union*, which adopts a common currency, a common central bank, and other aspects of financial integration. Feld (p. 272) comments that once monetary union is achieved, "the member states might be very close to political unification." He adds the caveat that this final step "might not really be possible without the unification of political institutions." This comment has proven to be the case for the EU, as we shall explore presently.

To give our discussion of economic integration additional substance, we can now turn our attention to the progress that has been made along the continuum toward integration. This will entail an examination of regional integration in Europe, North America, and the Pacific region.

EUROPE

The European Union is by far the most extensive regional effort. This Western European organization of 15 member-countries has moved substantially toward full economic integration. It has also traveled in the direction of considerable political cooperation. The evolution of the EU's economic integration since the early 1950s and its organizational structure and political development are all discussed in chapter 9. Given this background, it is possible to make a few summary points about the current status and future of the EU's progress toward economic and political integration that reflect the earlier discussion.

One such point is that the EU took a huge stride forward when its new common currency, the euro, went into general circulation on January 1, 2002, and began to replace the German mark, French franc, Italian lira, and the other national currencies of most of the other EU members. In addition to the monetary union that a common currency will bring to the EU, there is a great deal of political symbolism in the willingness of the French, Germans, Italians and other to give up their respective national currencies, which are visible representations of the state and sovereignty.

Another event with great portent was the convening of the Convention on the Future of Europe in Brussels, Belgium, in February 2002. With former French president Valery Giscard d'Estaing, a strong advocate of EU political integration, presiding, Europe's so-called constitutional convention is scheduled to work for a year to draft an EU constitution. As chapter 9 discusses, there are numerous potential pitfalls on the road to greater EU integration, and it would be extraordinarily premature to predict the creation of a true United States of Europe in the near future. Still, anyone who 50 years ago would have predicted the degree of EU integration that exists today—or even its existence—would have been considered a naïve visionary.

A third observation is that the 15-member EU is destined to expand. Currently, its 293 million citizens slightly outnumber Americans (278 million). The GNP of the EU at over $7.8 trillion (2000) is slightly smaller than that of the United States ($8.9 trillion), but the EU accounts for 36 percent of all the world's goods and services exports compared to the U.S. share of 14 percent. There are 13 other countries that have applied for EU membership, and it would be surprising if all or virtually all of them were not part of the EU by 2010. Given the additional economic mass and population this expansion will almost certainly add to the EU, this regional organization, especially if political integration proceeds, will rival the United States economically and perhaps even politically.

Europe has achieved a degree of economic and even political cooperation that would have been unimaginable not too long ago. This is illustrated by the introduction of the euro, which has now taken the place of previous, long-existing national currencies of most of the countries in the European Union.

THE WESTERN HEMISPHERE

Economic cooperation in the Western Hemisphere does not yet rival the level found in Europe, but the process is under way. The origins of hemispheric distinctiveness and a U.S. consciousness of its connection to the hemisphere date back many years. The United States proclaimed the Monroe Doctrine in 1823. Often that meant gunboat diplomacy: heavy-handed, unilateral U.S. intervention in the region, a practice that continued through the 1989 invasion of Panama. But, slowly, the idea that the United States should help and cooperate with its hemispheric neighbors took hold. The first hemispheric conference met in 1889. A U.S. proposal to establish a customs union was thwarted by the other 17 countries that attended, but they did create the first regional organization, the International Bureau of American Republics. That later became the Pan-American Union, then, by the Rio Treaty of 1948, the Organization of American States (OAS). President Franklin Delano Roosevelt announced the Good Neighbor Policy. John F. Kennedy announced the Alliance for Progress. The first summit of most of the hemisphere's heads of government occurred in Punta del Este, Uruguay, in 1967.

These events and trends have recently led to two important trade efforts. The first was the creation of the North American Free Trade Agreement. The second was a commitment by the hemisphere's countries to create a hemisphere-wide free trade area by the year 2005.

The North American Free Trade Agreement

For good or ill, the United States is the economic hegemon of the Western Hemisphere, and regional integration only truly began when the Americans moved to forge free trade agreements with other countries in the region. That effort began with the formation of the **North American Free Trade Agreement (NAFTA)**, which encompasses much of the northern half of the hemisphere.

The Evolution and Provisions of NAFTA The first step toward creating NAFTA was the U.S-Canada Trade Agreement (1988) to eliminate most economic barriers between the two signatories by 1999. Four years later, Mexico was added to the free trade zone when the leaders of the three countries signed the NAFTA documents. After considerable debate, especially in Canada and the United States, each of the countries' legislatures ratified NAFTA, and the treaty went into effect on January 1, 1994.

The agreement, which takes up more than 2,000 pages, established schedules for reducing tariff and nontariff barriers to trade over a 5-to-10-year period in all but a few hundred of some 20,000 product categories. By 2003, almost all U.S. and Canadian tariffs and about 92 percent of all Mexican tariffs on one another's merchandise will have vanished, with all tariffs eliminated by 2009. Also under NAFTA, many previous restrictions on foreign investments and other financial transactions among the NAFTA countries will end, and investments in financial services operations (such as advertising, banking, insurance, and telecommunications) will flow much more freely across borders. This is particularly important for Mexico, which, for example, has not heretofore allowed foreign direct investment in its petroleum industry. Beginning in 2000, American banks, which had been virtually banned from operating in Mexico before NAFTA, were able to hold 15 percent of the Mexican market. Intra-NAFTA transportation has also become much easier. Truck and bus companies now have largely unimpeded access across borders, and starting in 2000, U.S. trucking firms were allowed to become majority owners of Mexican trucking companies. There is a standing commission with representatives from all three countries to deal with disputes that arise under the NAFTA agreement.

The Growth of Intra-NAFTA Trade The greatest change under NAFTA is that it allows a much freer flow of goods, services, and investment among the three member-countries. Trade among them was extensive even before NAFTA and has grown even more since then, as can be seen in the data on merchandise trade in Figure 16.2. Mexico is the most dependent on intra-NAFTA trade, with 91 percent of its exports going to, and 75 percent of its imports coming from, Canada and the United States. Canada's level of intra-NAFTA trade is not much less, with 88 percent of exports going to, and 66 percent of its imports coming from, its NAFTA partners. Another index of the importance of NAFTA is that total U.S.-Canada trade of $375 billion is the world's largest two-way commercial relationship. The United States is least dependent, albeit still heavily so, on NAFTA trade, with 37 percent of U.S. exports going to Canada and Mexico and 31 percent of U.S. imports coming from them.

NAFTA is certainly less advanced than the EU, but it is a no less portentous example of regional integration. Indeed, NAFTA is an economic unit that, with 400 million people, a combined 2000 GDP of $11.1 trillion, and 20 percent of all world goods exports, rivals the EU.

There is little doubt that NAFTA has increased trade among the three partners as a percentage of each of the partners' trade with the rest of the world. Beyond trade expansion, it is difficult to be precise about specific impacts. There was and, to a degree, still is, a vigorous debate going on inside each of the three countries about the pros and cons of NAFTA.

Nationalism is the basis of one set of concerns that makes some Americans, Canadians, and Mexicans wary. Canadians and Mexicans are concerned about the possibility of being overwhelmed by American dollars and culture. Sharing the continent

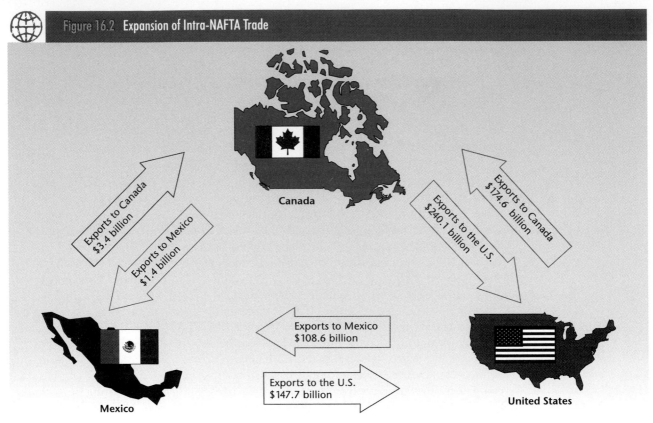

Figure 16.2 Expansion of Intra-NAFTA Trade

Canada

Exports to Canada
$3.4 billion

Exports to Mexico
$1.4 billion

Exports to Canada
$174.6 billion

Exports to the U.S.
$240.1 billion

Exports to Mexico
$108.6 billion

Exports to the U.S.
$147.7 billion

Mexico

United States

Total Intra-NAFTA Trade for 2001: $675.8 billion

Data source: IMF (2001).

The North American Free Trade Agreement has accounted for a rapid rise in trade among Canada, Mexico, and the United States since the treaty went into effect in 1994. There are now plans for a Western Hemisphere free trade zone, the Free Trade Area of the Americas.

with the United States was once likened by a prime minister to "sleeping with an elephant. No matter how friendly and even-tempered the beast... one is affected by every twitch and grunt" (Duchacek, 1975:146). Many Mexicans were even more worried than Canadians about the behemoth on their border. This concern is captured in the oft quoted, if perhaps apocryphal, sigh of a Mexican leader, "Poor Mexico so far from God, so close to the United States." Already, U.S. products and business ventures are flooding Mexico. A Mexico City billboard tells those passing by that "It's Time for a Domino's Pizza." Traditional, donkey-shaped piñatas have lost favor to Mutant Ninja Turtle and McDonald's "Hamburglar" piñatas. In an odd cultural twist, the American-owned chain, Taco Bell, is opening franchises in Mexico! "The Mexican economy is becoming Americanized, the culture to a great extent, too," lamented writer Homero Aridjis. "Many Mexicans are becoming aliens in their own country," he continued. "When I ask the question, 'What is going to happen to the tortilla culture?' nobody has an answer."[28]

The economic impact of NAFTA on the consumers, workers, and business of the three partners engenders both optimism and pessimism in each of the three countries. A joint study was done by the Centre for Policy Alternatives in Canada, the Economic Policy Institute in the United States, and the Mexican Institute of Labour Studies and Investigation and released in 1991. It found a net shift of jobs to Mexico due to NAFTA, with that country gaining 1.2 million jobs, while the United States lost 766,000 jobs and Canada lost 276,000.[29] Such figures have to be taken with care, though. For example, unemployment in the United States averaged 6.8 percent in the decade before NAFTA went into effect, but fell to 4.9 percent in the following nine years (1994–2002). For the same periods, Canada's unemployment rate fell from 9.8 percent to 8.4 percent.

Arguably, one cause of the seeming contradiction of job losses and falling unemployment may be that the availability of lower priced goods from Mexico lowered the cost of living of Americans and Canadians, giving them more money to spend on domestic products and services, thereby stimulating their own economies and creating new jobs to replace those that had been lost.

These lower priced goods have mostly come from areas in Mexico just to the south of the U.S. border, from factories known as *maquiladoras* (Carr, 1999). These factories are owned not only by major U.S. corporations, but also by MNCs of many other countries, including Sony, Sanyo, Samsung, Hitachi, and Philips, all taking advantage of Mexico's low labor costs and the region's proximity to the U.S. market. Free trade under NAFTA has dramatically boosted these plants. Prior to NAFTA there were about 2,000 maquiladoras; now there are nearly 4,000, employing nearly 1.3 million workers and annually producing approximately $7 billion dollars worth of products, about 80 percent of which are shipped to the United States.

In sum, whatever the effect on the overall economies of each of the three participating countries may be, it is certain that some businesses and types of workers will benefit; others will be harmed. It is also clear that NAFTA reduced the sovereignty of each signatory. So do all trade agreements and, indeed, all international treaties. It is equally sure, though, that Canada and Mexico are not about to become the 51st and 52nd American states. Political integration at some point in the future is not impossible, but it will be many mañanas before that occurs, if it ever does.

The Free Trade Area of the Americas

It is possible that NAFTA may also be another step toward integration of all or most of the Western Hemisphere. Trade cooperation in the hemisphere moved toward a new, higher level in 1994 with the beginning of an effort to create what has been tentatively named the **Free Trade Area of the Americas (FTAA)**.

The Origins of FTAA Proposals for a free trade area date back to the 1880s, as noted. The reality of trade zones is more recent. Seven of the regional trade groups listed in Table 16.2 on page 484 are in the Western Hemisphere, and the momentum behind trade cooperation has steadily built up since the early 1990s. The most specific precursor of the current efforts to found a hemispheric trade zone occurred in 1990 when President George H. W. Bush advocated such a goal in response to the general integration of the global economy.

The Summit of the Americas Preliminary negotiations over the next few years culminated in 1994 when the heads of 34 countries met at the Summit of the Americas in Miami, Florida. Only Cuba was excluded. The conference agreed to aim at the creation of a free trade zone in the hemisphere within 10 years. The leaders also agreed to a series of more than 100 specific political, environmental, and economic programs and reforms. "We pushed very, very hard" said one U.S. official, to get a document in which the signatories pledged, among other things, to "strive to make our trade liberalization and environmental policies mutually supportive" and to "secure the observance and promotion of worker rights."[30]

The conference ended in near-euphoria. "The atmosphere was splendid," said José Angel Gurria, Mexico's secretary of foreign affairs. "We now have a flight plan that will keep us busy for years to come."[31] "When our work is done, the free trade area of the Americas will stretch from Alaska to Argentina," said President Clinton. "In less than a decade, if current trends continue, this hemisphere will be the world's largest market."[32]

The Future of FTAA If it proceeds as planned, the FTAA will link the Western Hemisphere in a single market that in 2005 will have an estimated 850 million people producing $13 trillion worth of goods and services. The bargaining over the details will be difficult. As excited as they are about access to the U.S. markets, the hemisphere's LDCs are equally as nervous about dropping their protections and being drowned in a tidal wave of American imports, services, and purchases of local businesses and other property. Many Americans are just as sure their jobs will wind up in the hands of an underpaid Bolivian, Honduran, or perhaps Uruguayan worker. President Clinton was fond of recalling an image used often by John Kennedy in which JFK would observe, "As they say on my own Cape Cod, a rising tide lifts all boats. And a partnership, by definition, serves both partners." Another possibility, Prime Minister Owen Arthur of Barbados told President Clinton in Miami, is that "a rising tide can... overturn small boats."[33] Yet for all the difficulty ahead, the momentum in the direction of creating FTAA will probably carry the day. One is tempted to say that the leaders who gathered in Miami did not so much begin the task of creating a regional trade area as to recognize and organize a process that was already under way.

Yet the exact future of the FTAA remains unclear (Wrobel, 1998). When in 1998 the second FTAA summit meeting convened in Santiago, Chile, and the third met in Quebec City, Canada, in 2001, the mood at each was a good deal more sober than it had been in Miami. Expanding trade under U.S. leadership has faltered on several fronts. For example, Congress in 1997 refused to renew the president's "fast-track authority" to rapidly negotiate trade treaties, a process under which legislators could accept or reject, but not amend a trade treaty. It thus became less clear to the other FTAA countries that the U.S. administration could assure acceptance of a trade treaty even if one could be negotiated successfully. Progress to restoring fast-track authority to the president had been made by mid-2002, but President Bush and the Congress were at odds over the exact provisions, with Senate Democrats threatening to kill the restoral unless Bush accepted some limits and Bush threatening to veto the legislation if limits were included.

The countries of the hemisphere have also been dismayed by what they perceive as a gap between the rhetoric and reality of the Bush administration's trade policies. At the Quebec conference in 2001, Bush not only expressed his support for the FTAA but also indicated a desire to explore the idea of a free trade deal with Costa Rica, Honduras, Guatemala, El Salvador, and Nicaragua. Yet he has also dismayed U.S. trading partners by such protectionist measures as dramatically hiking steel tariffs, a shift that especially threatened the steel industry of Brazil, and by signing a bill to provide billions of dollars to U.S. agribusinesses, thereby disadvantaging the agricultural producers and exporters in other countries.

The fate of Argentina has also increased the pressures in Brazil and other of the region's countries to step away from the principle of free economic interchange to such a degree that Bush felt constrained to warn at a meeting of the Organization of the American States in 2002 that "Argentina—and nations throughout the hemisphere—need to strengthen [their] commitment to market-based reform, not weaken it."[34]

Finally, the movement toward completing an FTAA has become embroiled in the more general backlash against globalism. There were large protests during the Quebec conference sparked by such groups as Stop the FTAA, whose Web site

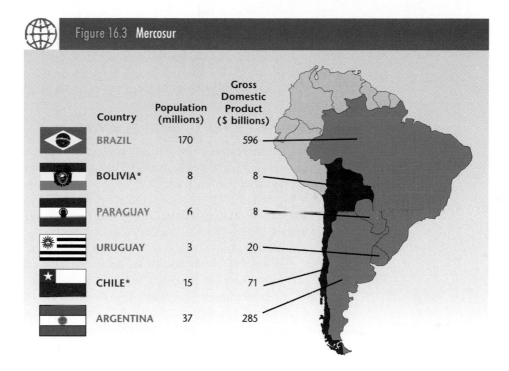

Figure 16.3　Mercosur

Country	Population (millions)	Gross Domestic Product ($ billions)
BRAZIL	170	596
BOLIVIA*	8	8
PARAGUAY	6	8
URUGUAY	3	20
CHILE*	15	71
ARGENTINA	37	285

*associate members

Data source: World Bank (2002)

The Southern Common Market (Mercosur) is an example of one of the several important and growing regional free trade organizations. A key issue for the future of the Western Hemisphere is whether it will unite into a single free trade organization, the Free Trade Area of the Americas (FTAA), or whether the hemisphere will be divided into two rival trade blocs, Mercosur and the North American Free Trade Agreement (NAFTA).

begins with the statement, "The Free Trade Area of Americas (FTAA) is an international business deal, disguised as a proposed treaty."[35]

At the Quebec summit, the gathered leaders issued a statement, "We direct our Ministers to ensure that negotiations of the FTAA Agreement are concluded no later than January 2005 and to seek its entry into force as soon as possible thereafter, but in any case, no later than December 2005."[36] That, to use an old phrase, will be much easier said than done.

Mercosur

Whatever the disposition of the new U.S. president and the Congress that took office in January 2001, a number of countries have undertaken or continued efforts to establish or expand their own trade treaties. The **Southern Common Market (Mercosur)** is of particular note. Mercosur was established in 1995 by Argentina, Brazil, Paraguay, and Uruguay. Chile and Bolivia became associate members in 1996 and 1997, respectively. They are negotiating full membership, and Colombia, Ecuador, Peru, and Venezuela have evinced interest in joining Mercosur. Including just its four full members, Mercosur is a market of 216 million people with a combined GDP of $909 billion. Adding in associate members Bolivia and Chile increases that number to nearly $1 trillion, as shown in Figure 16.3.

Whether, like NAFTA, Mercosur is a building block toward the FTAA is uncertain. As the president of Argentina explained the relationship between the FTAA's uncertain future and the expansion of Mercosur, "I don't want to rule out the [FTAA],... but charity begins at home."[37] This had led some observers to worry that an expanded Mercosur might even derail the FTAA and compete with NAFTA. Another analyst's more optimistic scenario is that it would be easier to form a hemispheric union after several smaller regional pacts had "ironed out" their problems. The wise advice of this analyst: "I suggest that everybody take a deep breath and calm down. A hemispheric trade agreement is going to take a while."[38]

ASIA, THE PACIFIC, AND ELSEWHERE

The impulse for regional ties has not been confined to Europe and the Americas. Other regions have also begun to form their own groups. There are four Arab and seven sub-Saharan African trade groups. The three Slavic FSRs (Belarus, Russia, and Ukraine) agreed in 1993 to negotiate cooperation agreements with an eye to a future economic union. Adding to that, Belarus and Russia agreed in 1994 to move to unify their monetary systems based on the Russian ruble.

Even more portentous than these efforts is the trend toward regionalism in the Pacific. The **Association of Southeast Asian Nations (ASEAN)** was established in 1967 and now includes Brunei, Cambodia, Indonesia, Laos, Malaysia, Myanmar (Burma), the Philippines, Singapore, Thailand, and Vietnam. The ASEAN countries have a combined population of over 500 million, a GDP of approximately $750 billion, and total exports of about $355 billion. As discussed in chapter 9, ASEAN, like some other trade organizations, is also working to forge greater political cooperation among its members and to try to bargain as a group (as the EU does) with external countries and other trade organizations.

More recently, the **Asia-Pacific Economic Cooperation (APEC)**, an oddly named structure, began in 1989 and may be evolving toward becoming a regional trade organization. The 21-member organization includes most of countries of the greater Pacific Ocean region. The members range in the eastern Pacific from Russia in the north, through Southeast Asia, to Australia in the south. On the other side of the Pacific, members extend from Canada in the north, through Mexico, to Chile in the south. The APEC members account for slightly over 40 percent of the world population, about 60 percent of the global GDP, and half of all merchandise trade. APEC has a small secretariat based in Singapore, but it is symbolic of APEC's still-tentative status that it has not added a word such as "organization" or "community" to the end of its name.

The first of what have become annual summit meetings of the APEC leaders took place in Seattle, Washington, in 1993. The United States hoped for an agreement in principle to move toward a free trade zone, an Asia-Pacific Community. That effort was forestalled because, as one Japanese diplomat put it, "there are a variety of concerns, especially among the developing nations, that we proceed with some caution." Delegates from the other countries also doubted U.S. sincerity in light of the bruising battle in Congress over the ratification of NAFTA that was then under way. "If there was this much debate on NAFTA, imagine the debate you would have in America over a free trade area with the whole Pacific," South Korea's foreign minister pointed out cogently.[39]

Progress toward further APEC integration has been slow. There have been agreements in principle, for example, to achieve "free and open trade and investment" in the Asia-Pacific region. Japan and the United States are to remove all their barriers by the year 2010, with the rest of the APEC members achieving a zero-barrier level by 2020. Whether this will occur, given such factors as China's already rising trade surplus with the United States and Japan's faltering economy, remains very unclear. Beyond this, few specific agreements have resulted from these summits, but they are part of a process of dialogue that helps keep lines of communications open.

Beyond Asia, regional trade pacts are even less developed. The various efforts to give life to them in the Middle East have fallen prey to the region's political problems, to the fact that many of the oil production-dependent economies have little to trade with one another, and to other problems. Similarly, Africa's regional trade groups have languished in the face of the continent's poverty and frequent political turmoil.

THE FUTURE OF REGIONALISM

The precise role that regional trading blocs will play on the world stage is unclear. Some observers believe that such groupings will help integrate regions, improve and strengthen the economic circumstances of the regions' countries and people, and provide a stepping-stone to world economic integration, just as the EEC was part of the genesis of the EU and just as NAFTA led to the FTAA agreement. Other analysts are worried. Economist Jagdish Bhagwati believes that "the revival of regionalism is unfortunate."[40] While regional blocs (no matter what their level of integration) must still adhere to the GATT rules with respect to trade with other blocs and countries, Bhagwati is still afraid that the regions will become increasingly closed trading areas and that competition among the blocs will cause a breakdown of the GATT and the construction of higher trade barriers among the blocs.

Such concerns are not far-fetched, given the impetus that is partly responsible for the current rapid regionalization that the world is undergoing. Whatever the organization, it is clear that part of the motivation to get together is the urge to defend against the possibility of predatory and protectionist trade practices by other economic blocs. The EU's integration is being driven in part by such fears. From Europe's point of view, competing with the United States alone is unnerving; competing with NAFTA, much less with the newly forming FTAA, is truly alarming. A modern European advocate of unity might echo Benjamin Franklin's warning to the revolutionary American colonies that if we do not all hang together, we will all hang separately, and today's equivalent of Paul Revere might gallop through the European night crying, "NAFTA is coming, NAFTA is coming!" Some Europeans, as one Dutch scholar explained, "want a united Europe out of fear more than out of love."[41]

Similarly, NAFTA and FTAA are in part a response to the EU. "My fear," a U.S. Chamber of Commerce official told Congress, "is that, as European governments seek to balance political interests among [themselves], the legitimate interests of outsiders will be the first to be traded off. 'Fortress Europe' may not be a realistic outcome, but selected protectionism... will be defended as necessary" (Olmer, 1989:133). This concern led the United States to use the threat and reality of regional trade associations to pressure Europe, Japan, and others to open their markets. During the FTAA summit in Miami, Mickey Kantor, the U.S. trade representative, observed that one benefit of the meeting was that "the Europeans will be encouraged, to use a delicate word, to be more open in a number of areas we have been concerned about. And Asians will also be encouraged to go in this direction, or they too will be left behind."[42] Like the regional trends in North America and Europe, the Southeast Asian effort is partly defensive. Explained Prime Minister Goh Chok Tong of Singapore, "Unless ASEAN can match the other regions," it will lose out. By contrast, the free trade agreement would make ASEAN a "strong player in the new world order."[43]

While these defensive reactions and counter-reactions are understandable, they also contain a danger. Instead of promoting global economic cooperation, the regional organizations that exist or are being created may one day become economic-political-military rivals that are as bitterly locked in contest as individual countries once were. There are already signs that regionalization, rather than global-ization, is determining where the investors from various countries put their FDI.

The majority of all American FDI in LDCs now goes to Latin America and the Caribbean. Similarly, the majority of Japan's FDI in LDCs is in East Asia and the Pacific; the French put the majority of their FDI investment in the LDCs and CITs of Eastern Europe and Central Asia. In George Orwell's novel *1984* there is an image of the world divided into three hostile blocs—East Asia, Eurasia, and Oceania. It is a vision with an unsettling geographical resemblance to a possible ASEAN-EU-FTAA tripolar system. Just as it is much too early to predict a merging of the various trade regions into a global free trade economy, so is it premature to assume an Orwellian future. The most likely path lies somewhere between the two extremes, yet either of them is possible (Hanson, 1998).

Chapter Summary

1. This chapter discusses the global and regional attempts of countries to cooperate to address the economic issues that face them and to find common interests and solutions.

2. A wide variety of general intergovernmental organizations (IGOs) and efforts are devoted to economic cooperation. The UN maintains a number of efforts aimed at general economic development, with an emphasis on the less developed countries (LDCs).

3. Many specialized intergovernmental organizations (IGOs) are also involved in economic cooperation; some examples are the Organization for Economic Cooperation and Development and the Group of Eight.

4. Economic nationalists, economic internationalists, and economic structuralists all offer different explanations of why the relative deprivation of the South exists. The three schools of thought also have varying prescriptions about what, if anything, to do to remedy the North-South gap in economic development.

5. Trade cooperation has grown through the new General Agreement on Tariffs and Trade (GATT) and its administrative structure, the World Trade Organization (WTO), and great strides have been taken toward promoting free trade.

6. Among monetary institutions, the International Monetary Fund is the primary organization dedicated to stabilizing the world's monetary system. The IMF's primary role in recent years has been to assist LDCs and CITs to prosper by reducing their foreign debt.

7. The IMF, however, attaches conditions to its assistance, and this practice has occasioned considerable criticism, especially regarding voting formula, conditionality, capitalism, and social justice.

8. There are a number of international organizations established to provide developmental loans and grants to countries in need. The best known of these is the World Bank Group, which consists of several interrelated subsidiaries. These organizations also primarily extend aid to EDCs, but, like the IMF, some analysts criticize the conditions they attach.

9. There are also several regional efforts aimed at economic integration. The European Union and the North American Free Trade Agreement are the most important of these.

10. By far the most developed is the European Union. The EU has been experiencing some sharp difficulties but has also showed great resilience. Whether the EU can integrate its national monetary systems and convert to a single European currency, the euro, is the next great hurdle facing the organization.

11. The new NAFTA regional free trade area will rival the EU in population and combined GDP. The Free Trade Area of the Americas, Mercosur, the Association of Southeast Asian Nations, and the Asia-Pacific Economic Cooperation forum are on the horizon as even larger regional organizations.

Chapter 17

Preserving and Enhancing Human Rights and Dignity

The sun with one eye vieweth all the world.

Shakespeare, *Henry VI, Part I*

And your true rights be term'd a poet's rage.

Shakespeare, "Sonnet XVII"

Recognition of the inherent dignity and of the equal and inalienable rights of all members of the human family is the foundation of freedom, justice, and peace in the world.

Preamble to the Universal Declaration of Human Rights, 1948

Chapter Objectives

After completing this chapter, you should be able to:

- Understand the two types of human rights.
- Evaluate the global problems related to population growth and food shortages, and assess international efforts to address them.
- Evaluate the global problems related to health and assess international efforts to address them.
- Discuss the role of education in achieving human rights and the organizations developed to improve levels of education.
- Examine the two types of individual rights.
- Discuss the prevalence of human rights abuses and the ideological justification for those abuses.
- Identify the focus of modern international efforts to ease human rights abuses.
- Analyze the political barriers to human rights efforts and the progress that has been made.

As we near the end of this survey of world politics, it is appropriate to pause momentarily to remember that, amid all the sound and fury, politics ought to be about maintaining or improving the quality of life of people. We have been exploring whether the traditional state-based international system that operates on self-interested competition can best protect and enhance humanity or whether the alternative of global cooperation in an international system with reduced sovereignty will lead to a more felicitous future. This and the next chapter continue that inquiry by addressing the human rights and social dignity of the world's people and the condition of the biosphere that they inhabit. First, this chapter will address preserving and enhancing human rights and dignity by looking at efforts to provide for the human body and spirit. Then chapter 18 will take up environmental concerns and programs.

⊕ The Biosphere and Its Inhabitants: The Essence of Politics

It is important to stress that while the discussions of the human condition and the environment are divided into two chapters, the two subjects are intrinsically intertwined. The size of the globe's population and the need to feed people and supply their material needs is putting tremendous pressure on the capacity of the biosphere to provide resources and to absorb waste. Indeed, the intersection of people and their environment and the combined impact of the two on the social and economic future are so strong that the World Bank has devised a new way to measure the *comprehensive wealth* of countries. The traditional method relies exclusively on economic production measured by either per capita gross national or domestic product (GNP, GDP). The alternative method introduced by the World Bank in 1995 and dubbed "green accounting" starts with manufactured wealth (products) and adds estimates of "natural capital" and "human capital." Natural capital is divided into two subcategories. One is "land" and includes factors such as the acreage available for farming. The second is "resources," and measures available water, minerals, and other related factors. Human capital measures education, health, and other such criteria. Estimating natural and human capital is even more difficult than arriving at GDP figures, but the results are valuable. Nobel Prize–winning economist Robert M. Solow contends that the new method is more comprehensive because "what we normally measure as capital is a small part of what it takes to sustain human welfare." Therefore, adds another economist, green accounting "is a valuable thing to do even if it can only be done relatively crudely."[1]

Changing the emphasis away from mere production helps us to focus on the economic reality that any economic unit needs to add to its national core and infrastructure in order to remain prosperous. If, for example, the owner of a farm devotes all of the farm's financial and human resources to producing crops, does not take care to avoid depleting the soil and water supplies, and does not devote resources to keeping the workers healthy and to training them in the latest farm methods, then, even though production may soar in the short term, the farm's long-term prospects are not good. Similarly, countries that do not preserve and, when possible, replenish their natural and human capital may face an increasingly bleak future. As one observer put it, such "countries are [inflating] income by selling off the family jewels."[2]

Figure 17.1 helps visualize the different results for six countries derived from calculating only GDP and, alternatively, from calculating comprehensive wealth (production, natural capital, and human capital). Notice, for example, that Australia's percentage of the sum of the six countries' per capita comprehensive wealth

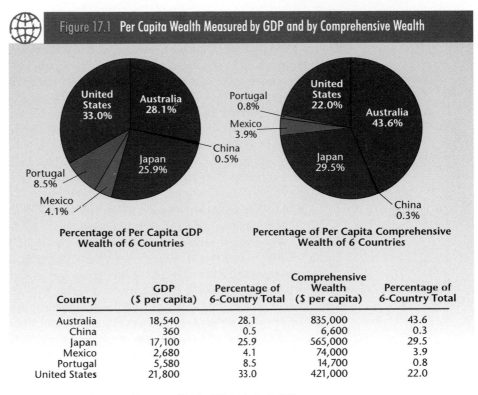

Figure 17.1   Per Capita Wealth Measured by GDP and by Comprehensive Wealth

Percentage of Per Capita GDP
Wealth of 6 Countries

Percentage of Per Capita Comprehensive
Wealth of 6 Countries

Country	GDP ($ per capita)	Percentage of 6-Country Total	Comprehensive Wealth ($ per capita)	Percentage of 6-Country Total
Australia	18,540	28.1	835,000	43.6
China	360	0.5	6,600	0.3
Japan	17,100	25.9	565,000	29.5
Mexico	2,680	4.1	74,000	3.9
Portugal	5,580	8.5	14,700	0.8
United States	21,800	33.0	421,000	22.0

The World Bank data is for 1990 and, for comparability, the GDP data is also for 1990.

Data sources: New York Times, September 19, 1995, for comprehensive wealth; *World Almanac* (1993) for GDP; percentage calculations by author.

The traditional way of calculating a country's per capita wealth is by GDP. The absolute and relative wealth of countries can change significantly when natural and human resources are added to production to calculate wealth.

is much greater than its share of the combined per capita GDPs. This is primarily because of the estimated value that the World Bank places on Australia's land resources. Japan is also advantaged because of the high value of its human capital. By contrast, the U.S. share of the six countries' per capita comprehensive wealth is much less than the U.S. share of their combined per capita GDPs. The United States produces a great deal, but the World Bank calculates that U.S. per capita resources are low and that U.S. human wealth is below par for such a wealthy country. Of the six countries, Portugal fares worst in percentage of comparative wealth compared to GDP because of its paucity of natural capital.

The complexities of this green-accounting approach to measuring wealth should not obscure its basic message that the richness or impoverishment of the human condition is an amalgam of the human rights people enjoy or are denied and the biosphere's bounty or exhaustion. As noted, we will address human rights in this chapter, and then turn to the environment in the next.

The Nature of Human Rights

Before moving to a detailed discussion of human rights, it is important to explain the broad concept of human rights used here. We are used to thinking about human rights in terms of *individual human rights*, that is, freedom from specific abuses or restrictions, especially by governments. The U.S. Bill of Rights, for example, prohibits (except in extreme cases) the government from abridging individual Americans' right to exercise their religion or free speech, from discriminating against citizens based on race and other demographic traits, from long-imprisoning citizens without a trial, and from commiting a variety of other abuses. Gradually, these constitutional prohibitions have been extended to restrict actions by U.S. state and local governments and even, in some cases, by individuals.

There is a more comprehensive concept of rights. This broader view holds that people and groups not only have the right not to be specifically abused, but that they also have *collective human rights* to a quality of life that, at minimum, does not detract from their human dignity (Felice, 1996). One scholar suggests that the most fruitful way to think about human rights is to begin with the idea that "ultimately they are supposed to serve basic human needs." These basic human needs, which generate corresponding rights, include, among others (Galtung, 1994:3, 72):

- "Survival needs—to avoid violence": The requisite to avoid and the right to be free from individual and collective violence.
- "Well-being needs—to avoid misery": The right to adequate nutrition and water; to movement, sleep, sex, and other biological wants; to protection from diseases and from adverse climatological and environmental impacts.
- "Identity needs—to avoid alienation": The right to self-expression; to realize your potential, to establish and maintain emotional bonds with others; to preserve cultural heritage and association; to contribute through work and other activity; and to receive information about and maintain contact with nature, global humanity, and other aspects of the biosphere.
- "Freedom needs—to avoid repression": The right to receive and express opinions, to assemble with others, to have a say in common policy; and to choose in such wide-ranging matters as jobs, spouses, where to live, and lifestyle.

Few, if any, people would argue that these rights are absolute. As the classic formulation about free speech goes, for example, freedom of speech does not include the right to shout "fire!" in a crowded theater. It is also the case that the legal rights granted and recognized by countries largely include only protections from specific abuses of individuals and groups and do not include the right to certain qualitative standards of life. But it is also arguable that the very nature of being human means that people have the right to exist in at least tolerable conditions as well as the right to be merely free from specific abuses. It is also appropriate to say a bit about the origins of human rights. Recall from chapter 11 that there is an ancient debate about the basis of human rights. Universalists represent one school of thought; relativists represent the other.

Universalists believe that human rights are derived from sources external to society. Depending on the universalist, the source may be one or another theological or ideological doctrine or it may be natural rights. This last concept holds that the fact of being human carries with it certain rights that cannot be violated or can only be violated in extremis. Universalists therefore believe that there is a single, prevailing set of standards of moral behavior on which human rights are based.

Relativists argue from a positivist point of view and claim that rights are the product of a society's contemporary values. Positivists therefore contend that in a world of diverse cultures, no single standard of human rights exists or is likely to exist short of the world becoming completely homogenized culturally. Those who believe in the cultural relativism of rights also tend to view attempts to impose standards of rights by one culture on another as cultural imperialism.

It is not uncommon to hear those in the non-Western world argue that many of the rights asserted in such international documents as the Universal Declaration of Human Rights, which was adopted in 1948 by an overwhelming vote of the UN General Assembly, are based on the values of the politically dominant West. Positivists contend that many of these Western values, such as individualism and democracy, are not held as strongly in other cultures, and that no matter how high-minded the intent, Western attempts to impose them are imperialist. There are, however, leaders in non-Western cultures who reject these assertions of cultural relativism. Burmese political activist and 1991 Nobel Peace Prize winner Aung San Suu Kyi writes that claims about "the national culture can become a bizarre graft of carefully selected historical incidents and distorted social values intended to justify the policies and actions of those in power." She goes on to argue that, "It is precisely because of the cultural diversity of the world that it is necessary for different nations and peoples to agree on those basic human values which will act as a unifying factor." As for the cultural imperialism argument, Suu Kyi contends that "when democracy and human rights are said to run counter to non-Western culture, such culture is usually defined narrowly and presented as monolithic." To avoid this, she counsels, it is possible to conceive of rights "which place human worth above power and liberation above control" (Suu Kyi, 1995:14, 15, 18). The power and control she wishes to subordinate are not just those of government, but also those of one ethnic group, race, religion, sex, or other societal faction over another.

It must be said that differences over what constitutes a human right are not only matters of Western and non-Western philosophies. There are also vigorous disputes between countries of similar cultural heritage. For example, many countries have taken the same position and will not extradite people accused of capital crimes unless assured that the death penalty will not be invoked. In one case, Italy's Constitutional Court cited the alleged barbarity of executions and blocked the extradition of an Italian wanted for first-degree murder in Florida, which has a death penalty. A U.S. Department of Justice official called the Italian court's decision "a bad omen"; Giovanni Leone, a former president of Italy, called the decision "one of historic character that does honor to Italy."[3]

Such views have increased worldwide as the number of executions in the United States has risen, as evident in Figure 17.2. A total of 85 inmates were put to

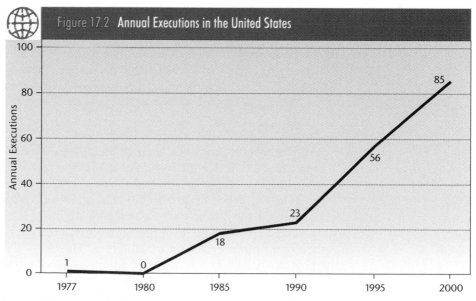

Figure 17.2 **Annual Executions in the United States**

Data source: U.S. Census Bureau (2001).

The U.S. Supreme Court in 1976 declared that executing prisoners was not "cruel and inhuman punishment," thereby reinstating the death penalty after a four-year moratorium. One prisoner was executed (by firing squad) in 1977. Through 2000 another 682 individuals had been put to death. Many countries and such groups as Amnesty International consider the death penalty to be a violation of human rights. What do you think?

death in U.S. prisons in 2000, and 3,527 other prisoners were under sentence of death. Of these, 85 had been sentenced to death for crimes they had committed as children (under the age of 18). The U.S. record stands in sharp contrast to the trend worldwide, where the number of countries that prohibit the execution of prisoners increased from 8 in 1948 to 90 in 2000. This difference was one factor that led the UN in late 1997 to name a monitor to report on potential human rights violations by the United States in light of (1) its relatively high rate of executions (third in the world in 2000 after China and Saudi Arabia); (2) the execution of individuals for crimes they committed as children; and (3) the high percentage of those executed who are from minority groups (42 percent of all those executed in 2000 were African Americans; adding Latinos, for whom separate data is not compiled, would certainly push the minority rate over 50 percent).

The two matters of whether rights protect only against specific abuses or extend to quality of life criteria and whether rights are culture-based or universal are addressed further in the box, A Global Bill of Rights on page 502. See if you agree with the range of individual and group rights that the UN General Assembly adopted.

Human Rights: Quality of Life Issues and Progress

One set of pressing problems for the world community involves preserving and enhancing human dignity by protecting and improving the physical condition of humans (Lauren, 1998). These issues are, in part, economic in nature and are being addressed by the international economic cooperation efforts discussed in chapter 16. There are also, however, specific efforts to deal with such concerns as living conditions and human rights. Note that many of these issues have a strong environmental factor. It is not facile to say that how people are treated has a great deal to do with the way that they treat one another and the ecosphere they share. It is also the case that, in the view of many, food, health, and the other quality of life matters included in this section fall under the rubric of human rights (Speth, 1998). For example, the UN-sponsored World Food Summit that met in 1996 reasserted the principle found in many international human rights documents that there is a "right to adequate food and the fundamental right of everyone to be free from hunger."[4]

FOOD

Just over two centuries ago, Thomas Malthus predicted in *Essay on the Principle of Population* (1798) that the world's population would eventually outpace the world's agricultural carrying capacity. For the two centuries since Malthus's essay, human ingenuity has defied his predictions. The question is whether it can continue to do so, given the rapidly increasing global population.

There are two basic food problems. One is the *short-term food supply*. Regional shortages inflict real human suffering. Hunger—indeed, starvation—is most common in Africa, where many countries face a severe shortage of food. In addition to the multitudes that have died from starvation or diseases stemming from malnutrition, agricultural insufficiency has a host of negative economic impacts that range from sapping the vigor of the population to consuming development funds for food relief. The UN's Food and Agricultural Organization (FAO) estimates that around the globe there are nearly 800 million people who are undernourished; some 15 million a year die from outright starvation or from diseases brought on by malnutrition.

The *long-term adequacy* of the food supply is also a significant concern. A combination of population control and agricultural development is necessary to ensure that the world's appetite does not outstrip its agriculture. There is, in essence, a race under way between demand and supply. The growing population and the efforts to increase the calorie, protein, and other nutrient intake of chronically underfed people is rapidly increasing demand. On the supply side, food production must rise 75 percent over the next 30 years to meet this escalating demand. Whether that standard can be met is, however, uncertain.

One critical determinant will be crop yields. On the positive side, yields have grown over 50 percent since 1970 due to the "green revolution" (the development and widespread introduction of high-yielding rice, wheat, and other grains), the increased use of fertilizers and pesticides, and other agricultural advances. On the negative side, the annual rate at which yields are increasing has been dropping steadily from about 5 percent annually in the 1970s, to about 2 percent annually in the 1990s, to what the FAO is projecting will be about 1 percent in the first decade of the twenty-first century. At 1 percent, the food supply is expanding more slowly than the world population. This decline and uncertainty in the food supply is compounded by the loss of land available for farming. Only about 11 percent of the world's land surface was well suited for agriculture to begin with. Some new farmland has been added through irrigation and other methods, but even more has been lost to urbanization, to poor environmental practices that cause erosion, to soil-nutrient exhaustion, to salinization, and to other degradations. The FAO calculates that 38 percent of the world's original cropland (some 2.1 million square miles, almost two-thirds the area of the United States) has been lost to agriculture, and that a combination of increasing population and loss of arable land has cut the world's cultivated land to six-tenths of an acre per mouth to feed.

Causes of the Food Problem

There are several causes of hunger. *Population growth* is one. Production cannot keep up with population in many areas of the world. The result is that LDC per capita food production is barely expanding from its poverty base, and there is the constant threat of calamity. There are 38 countries whose per capita food production declined during the 1990s. Cuba had the worst record, with an average annual drop of 6.5 percent in its per capita production.

Maldistribution of food is a second problem. In 2000 the world produced enough food to allow for 2,757 calories per person in the world. Thus, for now at least, the world has the agricultural capacity to feed everyone adequately. Resources and consumption, however, are concentrated in relatively few countries. In the EDCs, daily food consumption averages a waist-expanding 3,240 calories a day. In significant segments of the South calorie intakes were at belt-tightening low levels. The sub-Saharan countries of Africa, for example, averaged only 2,183 calories per capita daily.

Nutritional content represents a third, and even greater gap between the ability of the North and South to meet dietary needs. Protein deficiency is particularly common in the LLDCs. Most people in Africa, for instance, consume less than 60 grams of protein per day per capita and in some countries they average as little as 30 grams. The recommended daily intake is about 55 grams for sedentary individuals, which means that in the LLDCs, where manual labor is the norm, protein deficiency is also the norm. The lack of protein is especially detrimental to children because of the role it plays in developing both healthy bodies and brain tissue, and there are over 300 million children in LDCs who suffer from stunted growth, poor cognitive development, and other ills due to protein malnutrition. Vitamin A deficiency, also

(Continued on page 504)

A GLOBAL BILL OF RIGHTS

It is easy to assert that people have, or ought to have, rights, especially when we think ours are being violated. It is much harder to agree on what rights all people (regardless of place, status, or demographic trait) should have and which, therefore, we and our governments should respect and protect.

The following list of rights is drawn in close paraphrase from almost all of the clauses of the Universal Declaration of Human Rights. This declaration was adopted in 1948 by the UN General Assembly with no dissenting votes (albeit with abstentions by the Soviet bloc countries, Saudi Arabia, and South Africa). The rights that the UN membership recognized with near-unanimity illustrate two of the important controversies about rights. One is the matter of cultural relativism. The Universal Declaration of Human Rights (UNDHR) in its preamble implicitly rejects the positivist concept that rights are culture-based by recognizing the existence of "inalienable rights of all members of the human family." The second contro-

versy is whether rights involve only prohibitions on governments, and perhaps people, against specific abuses (such as abridging free speech), or whether rights extend to quality of life criteria (such as health and economic condition). You will note that beginning with number 20, the rights enumerated by the Universal Declaration include several quality of life standards.

One thing that you can do with this list, in your class or with your friends, is to constitute yourselves as the World Constitutional Convention, debate the various clauses of the UNDHR, and decide whether to ratify or reject each one of them. You might also decide to open them up for amendment. Finally, take note of clause 27 and ponder whether it provides too much of an escape clause that potentially allows governments to violate rights and to assert that doing so is necessitated by "the just requirements of morality, public order, and the general welfare in a democratic society."

How say you to the propositions that:

1. Everyone has the right to life, liberty, and security of person.   Ratify_____ Reject_____

2. No one shall be held in slavery or servitude; slavery and the slave trade shall be prohibited in all their forms.   Ratify_____ Reject_____

3. No one shall be subjected to torture or to cruel, inhuman, or degrading treatment or punishment.   Ratify_____ Reject_____

4. All are equal before the law and are entitled without any discrimination to equal protection of the law.   Ratify_____ Reject_____

5. No one shall be subjected to arbitrary arrest, detention, or exile.   Ratify_____ Reject_____

6. Everyone charged with a penal offense has the right to be presumed innocent until proved guilty according to law in a public trial [and to have] all the guarantees necessary for his [or her] defense.   Ratify_____ Reject_____

7. Everyone has the right to freedom of movement and residence within the borders of each state.   Ratify_____ Reject_____

8. Everyone has the right to leave any country, including his own, and to return to his country.   Ratify_____ Reject_____

9. Everyone has the right to seek and to enjoy in other countries asylum from persecution.   Ratify_____ Reject_____

10. No one shall be arbitrarily deprived of his nationality nor denied the right to change his nationality.   Ratify_____ Reject_____

11. Adults, without any limitation due to race, nationality, or religion, have the right to marry or not to marry and to found a family. They are entitled to equal rights both during marriage and at its dissolution.

Ratify_____ Reject_____

12. Everyone has the right to own property alone. No one shall be arbitrarily deprived of his property.

Ratify_____ Reject_____

13. Everyone has the right to freedom of thought, conscience, and religion; to change religion or belief; and in public or private to manifest that religion or belief in teaching, practice, worship, and observance.

Ratify_____ Reject_____

14. Everyone has the right to freedom of opinion and expression; this includes freedom to hold opinions without interference and to seek, receive, and impart information and ideas through any media and regardless of frontiers.

Ratify_____ Reject_____

15. Everyone has the right to freedom of peaceful assembly and association.

Ratify_____ Reject_____

16. No one may be compelled to belong to an association.

Ratify_____ Reject_____

17. Everyone has the right to take part in the government of his country, directly or through freely chosen representatives.

Ratify_____ Reject_____

18. Everyone has the right to equal access to public service in his country.

Ratify_____ Reject_____

19. The will of the people shall be the basis of the authority of government; this will shall be expressed in periodic and genuine elections which shall be by universal and equal suffrage and shall be held by secret vote or by equivalent free voting procedures.

Ratify_____ Reject_____

20. Everyone has the right to work, to free choice of employment, to just and favorable conditions of work, and to protection against unemployment.

Ratify_____ Reject_____

21. Everyone, without any discrimination, has the right to equal pay for equal work.

Ratify_____ Reject_____

22. Everyone has the right to form and to join trade unions for the protection of his interests.

Ratify_____ Reject_____

23. Everyone has the right to a standard of living adequate for the health and well-being of himself and of his family, including food, clothing, housing and medical care, and necessary social services, and the right to security in the event of unemployment, sickness, disability, widowhood, old age, or other lack of livelihood in circumstances beyond his control.

Ratify_____ Reject_____

24. Motherhood and childhood are entitled to special care and assistance. All children, whether born in or out of wedlock, shall enjoy the same social protection.

Ratify_____ Reject_____

25. Everyone has the right to education. Education shall be free, at least in the elementary and fundamental stages. Elementary education shall be compulsory. Technical and professional education shall be equally accessible to all on the basis of merit.

Ratify_____ Reject_____

26. Parents have a prior right to choose the kind of education that shall be given to their children.

Ratify_____ Reject_____

27. In the exercise of his rights and freedoms, everyone shall be subject only to such limitations as are determined by law solely for the purpose of securing due recognition and respect for the rights and freedoms of others and of meeting the just requirements of morality, public order, and the general welfare in a democratic society.

Ratify_____ Reject_____

OVERABUNDANCE AND SCARCITY

The world is a place of dietary overabundance as well as scarcity. Many in the North die early because they eat too much in general and have fat intakes way beyond what is healthy. Many people in the South die too early or never develop to their full potential because they eat too little and have other nutritional deficiencies. The people with the highest daily per capita caloric intake are the Americans (3,699). Somalis (1,566) have the lowest calorie consumption. For fat, which is a problem when too much or too little is consumed, the French, whose daily per capita intake is 165 grams, are most in need of watching their diets. The people of Mozambique, who consume just 35 grams of fat daily, are the most deprived. Protein, which is critical for muscle and brain development and maintenance, is also most abundant in France, where people consume 114 grams a day. The people of Burundi suffer the greatest protein deficiency, consuming just 12 grams a day.

common in LLDCs, is the cause of visual impairment in over 100 million children a year. Adding to the nutritional woes of the South, there are 740 million people who suffer from disorders such as mental retardation, delayed motor skill development, and stunting caused by iodine deficiency, even though this can be cheaply remedied by the use of iodized salt. Some dietary comparisons for specific countries are detailed in the box, Overabundance and Scarcity.

Political strife is a fourth problem. In many countries with severe food shortages, farms have been destroyed, farmers displaced, and food transportation disrupted by internal warfare. Rwanda is one of the recent tragic examples and now produces 19 percent less food than the already meager supply it managed to provide in 1990 before it was overtaken by strife between the Hutus and Tutsis.

The International Response to the Food Problem

A number of international efforts are under way. Some deal with food aid to meet immediate needs, while others are dedicated to increasing future agricultural productivity.

Sometimes the UN's World Food Programme (WFP) is all that stands between life and death for starving people in countries suffering from food emergencies. This photograph shows a WFP worker talking to a child who was one of the 400,000 people in Nicaragua whom the agency helped feed during a recent drought that had devastated the country's agriculture.

Emergency Food Aid Supplying food aid to areas with food shortages is a short-term necessity to alleviate malnutrition and even starvation (Belgrad & Nachmias, 1997). By UN standards there were 33 countries in 2001 suffering food emergencies. Grains constitute about 95 percent of food aid. About 10 million tons of grains and more limited amounts of other foodstuffs are donated each year, of which about 65 percent comes from the United States. Some of the aid is given bilaterally, but a good deal of the assistance goes through a number of multilateral food aid efforts. The UN's World Food Programme (WFP) is the largest. It distributes food in crisis situations, feeding 77 million people in 82 countries during 2001. About three-quarters of WFP aid goes to countries that have experienced massive crop failures or natural disasters; another 25 percent goes to feed refugees and other displaced persons. In 2001, the WFP received $4.3 billion in grains and other foodstuffs. While these contributions are laudable, they meet only about two-thirds of the emergency food needs identified by the WFP and amounted in 2001 to only about $72 per individual whom the WFP tried to sustain. There are also a variety of NGOs, such as Food for the Hungry International, that are active in food aid.

Agricultural Development The development of agricultural techniques and capabilities is crucial if there is to be any hope of future self-sufficiency. This is particularly important to the 8 countries that suffer what the FAO labels critical food security (all sources of supply are less than 65 percent of need) and to another 20 countries that have low food security (supply is 65 to 75 percent of need).

On a bilateral basis, many countries' programs include agricultural development aid. There is also a multilateral effort. The oldest agricultural IGO is the FAO. Founded in 1945, it has 183 members and an annual budget of approximately $650 million. The FAO supplies food aid and technical assistance to LDCs. The agency has been criticized for a variety of its policies, including putting too much emphasis on short-term food aid and not enough effort into long-range agricultural growth. This, in addition to the growing recognition of the food problem, has led to the establishment of several other global food efforts.

One of these is the International Fund for Agricultural Development (IFAD), a specialized UN agency. IFAD began operations in 1977 and is particularly dedicated to environmentally sustainable agricultural development projects in the poorest LDCs. The agency raises its funds through the voluntary contributions of its 161 member-countries, and disburses about $300 million annually to support projects in agriculturally struggling countries. These efforts are supplemented by several UN-associated organizations involved in various donor, investment, and research efforts in agriculture. Finally, there are a variety of regional and specialized organizations that address agricultural issues.

World Food Conferences A key event in both the area of short-term aid and especially agricultural development effort was the 1974 World Food Conference held in Rome. Among its other actions, the conference sponsored the creation of IFAD and various structures associated with the UN Economic and Social Council to monitor the global food supply and its delivery to needy countries and people.

A second global conference, the 1996 World Food Summit, met at FAO headquarters in Rome and was attended by the heads of more than 80 governments and representatives from more than 100 other governments. Reflecting the declining commitment of the EDCs to foreign aid, though, the leaders of most of the industrialized countries were not present. The United States, for example, was represented by only its secretary of agriculture. The tone of the meeting was set by the first plenary speaker, Pope John Paul II, who called on the world's countries to "eliminate the specter of hunger from the planet" and to "jointly seek solutions so that never again will there be hungry people living side by side with people in opulence.... Such contrasts between poverty and wealth cannot be tolerated."[5]

Without the strong support of the EDCs, though, there was little of immediate substance that the summit could accomplish. It did, however, establish the goal of reducing the number of undernourished people from 800 million to 400 million by 2015. It also reaffirmed the UN's traditional standard that the EDCs should devote 0.7 percent of their respective GDPs to development aid, including food and agricultural assistance. Third, in a move that rankled Washington and some other capitals, the conference resolved that "food should not be used as an instrument for political and economic pressure."[6] This swipe at economic sanctions came just days after the

UN General Assembly voted overwhelmingly to urge the United States to end its embargo against Cuba.

The continuing problems with supplying adequate calories and nutrition to a large number of LDCs occasioned a review of the efforts since the 1996 conference. The World Food Summit—Five Years Later conference, organized by the FAO, was held in Rome during June 2002. The fifth year review was necessary, in the estimation of Jacques Diouf, the FAO's director-general, because little progress was being made toward achieving the goal to cut the number of malnourished people in half, set by the 1996 conference. "There is very little evidence," according to Diouf, "of the large-scale purposive action needed to get to grips with the underlying causes of hunger."[7]

HEALTH

The state of medical care, sanitation, and other conditions related to health in some areas of the world is below a level imaginable by most readers of this book. The EDCs spend on average $2,702 per citizen annually on health care, of which about two-thirds is paid for through public funds or private (usually employer-supported) health insurance. By comparison, the countries and the citizens of the South (which have scant public funds and very limited private health insurance) can afford to spend annually an average of just $73 per capita on health care. The amount for LLDCs is a mind-boggling $21. By another measure, there are 6 times as many physicians per person and 11 times as many hospital beds per capita in the EDCs as there are in the LLDCs. The health of people within these countries is an international concern for reasons beyond personal well-being. A healthy population is vital to economic growth because healthy people are economically productive and because unhealthy people often consume more of a society's resources than they produce.

The fate of children is one way to think about health care. In LDCs, 18 percent of all children born have low birth weights (less than 5.5 pounds), which is one reason why children under age 5 die in the South at a rate 10 times higher than children in the North. The reality that proper medical care, sanitation, and nutrition could reduce the infant mortality rate in the LDCs to that of the EDCs means that each year about 6 million children in LDCs die needlessly from malnutrition. Another 6 million perish from curable or preventable diseases, with acute respiratory and infectious intestinal (diarrheal) diseases being the most common. Overall, some 41 percent of deaths in the LDCs, compared to just 1 percent of deaths in the EDCs, result from such infectious and parasitic diseases. As the director of the UN Children's Fund (UNICEF) has lamented, "No famine, no flood, no earthquake, no war has ever claimed the lives of this many children a year."[8]

As grim as these figures are, they were once much worse. An infant born in an LDC is now 31 percent more likely to live to age 1 than an infant born in 1980. As recently as 1974, only 5 percent of all children in LDCs received any vaccinations; now 78 percent receive protection against diphtheria, whooping cough, and polio. As a result, the health of children in LDCs has improved dramatically. According to UNICEF, 90 percent of the children in LDCs live in countries that are making progress in the area of children's health. This means that about 2.5 million fewer children now die needlessly and almost a million fewer children will be disabled, blinded, crippled, or mentally handicapped than a decade ago.

Much of the credit for these advances goes to the **World Health Organization (WHO)**. Headquartered in Geneva, Switzerland, the UN-affiliated WHO was created in 1946. It has 191 members and an annual budget of about $2 billion from the UN and from other sources. The crusade against smallpox provides a heartening example of WHO's contributions. Smallpox was a scourge throughout human history. There were over 131,000 cases worldwide in 1976 when WHO began a 10-year campaign to eradicate the disease. By 1987 smallpox was confined to a single case in Somalia; no case has been reported since 1989. Polio is another disease whose death may be imminent. The annual global incidence has been cut from 350,000 reported cases in 125 countries during 1988 to 2,882 cases in 10 countries during 2001. Moreover, WHO hopes to have all children vaccinated by 2005. Among other notable achievements in that quest was the immunization against polio of some 80 million children under age 5 living in 16 West African countries during the week of October 19–26, 2001. "Victory of total eradication of polio is at hand," Rimah Salah, the regional director for UNICEF, exultantly proclaimed. "We are on the verge of eradicating this debilitating disease."[9]

Optimism based on progress is offset by continuing problems and new threats. For all the progress made, far too many people in the South suffer and die from diseases, nutritional deficiencies, and even starvation. Also, diseases once thought to be on the decline can reassert themselves catastrophically. Tuberculosis is one such disease. WHO declared in 1993 that TB had resurged, and there were 34 million people suffering from TB in 2000. Indeed, TB has become the leading cause of death from a single infectious agent and, in WHO's estimate, will kill more than 35 million people between 2000 and 2020.

New problems add to these old worries. The worldwide AIDS epidemic, for one, is a global killer. At the beginning of 2002, one of every 150 people, about 40 million people, worldwide were HIV-positive. That was a net annual increase of 3 million cases, a grim statistic derived from subtracting the 2 million people who died from AIDS-related causes from the 5 million new HIV-positive people. Some countries are truly devastated. More than 10 percent of the populations of 14 sub-Saharan countries are HIV-positive, with Botswana having an especially disturbing 36 percent infection rate. Perhaps the most tragic victims are the 2.7 million children under age 15 who are HIV-positive. A total of 580,000 of them died in 2001, and were sadly replaced by 800,000 new cases. Other children will fall victim to AIDS in a different way. In Botswana, nearly 40 percent of pregnant women were HIV-positive in 2000. The UN estimates that by the end of the decade well over 10 million children will lose their mothers to AIDS. As one WHO physician explains the grim logic, "As more women die of AIDS, the number of orphans will rise exponentially."[10]

Yet other horrific emerging diseases lurk in the shadows and threaten to spread, as AIDS has, to a world with few or no natural or manufactured immunological defenses. The mosquito-transmitted West Nile virus began in 1999 to alarm Americans in the Northeast, but its effects are minor compared to such horrors as the Ebola virus. It was discovered in 1976 and is named for a river in Zaire where it was first detected. The most recent outbreak of the disease was in Gabon and the neighboring Republic of the Congo in 2002. Through May, there were 97 confirmed cases, including 73 deaths. The source of the Ebola virus in nature remains unknown, but monkeys, like humans, are susceptible to infection and may serve to transmit the disease. The virus causes a hemorrhagic fever, beginning with fever and chills, and then usually progressing to vomiting, diarrhea, and other acute symptoms. Finally, the victim's blood fails to clot, and he or she dies from internal bleeding from the gastrointestinal tract and other internal organs. So far local medical personnel aided by WHO and other international agencies have contained outbreaks of new and recurring horrors such as the bubonic plague, Ebola, monkeypox, and o'nyong-nyong fever. Still, one WHO physician cautions, "There are almost certainly diseases out there waiting to get us. What is happening is that human beings are invading territories where no human beings have been before. We're cutting down forests; we're going to areas to develop agriculture where there wasn't any before. Human beings are coming into contact with animals and insects they never met before."[11]

This man, whom a child is leading by a stick, is one of the many people in Liberia who suffer from onchocerciasis, or river blindness. The disease is caused by a parasite carried by black flies that breed most prolifically near rivers. When in 1986 the World Heath Organization and other international agencies began a program to try to eradicate river blindness in 11 countries in West Africa, 2.4 million people in that region (and 20 million worldwide) were infected by the parasite and 100,000 of them had lost their sight. Now new cases are rare; 1.25 million people have been cured of their onchocerciacal infection, and 100,000 have been prevented from going blind. All this has been accomplished at a cost of about $1 per person in affected areas in the 11 countries.

What makes these diseases even more of a world problem than they once were is the flow of humans and their products around the globe, which means that diseases can be spread very quickly from continent to continent. A person who contracts an exotic disease in one place can board an airplane and, 12 hours later, be stifling a sneeze while sitting next to you in a restaurant. Therefore, the work of WHO has become increasingly pivotal to combating new and persistent diseases worldwide.

EDUCATION

Education, like health, affects more than just the quality of life. Education is also a key to increased national and international productivity, population control, and other positive social goals. Promotion of education remains primarily a national function, but there are a number of international efforts. For one, the United Nations Educational, Scientific, and Cultural Organization (UNESCO) sponsors several programs. These national and international efforts are slowly paying off. In the 1950s less than 30 percent of all children in LDCs ever attended any school; now almost all children begin the first grade and more than half go on to begin secondary school. Overall, the level of adults with at least rudimentary literacy has increased to about 75 percent in the LDCs. The data is even more encouraging if younger people (age 15–24) are considered. Of this group in LDCs, 80 percent are literate.

The increasing percentages should not disguise the crying needs that still exist. More than 1 billion adults are still illiterate, and their personal and societal

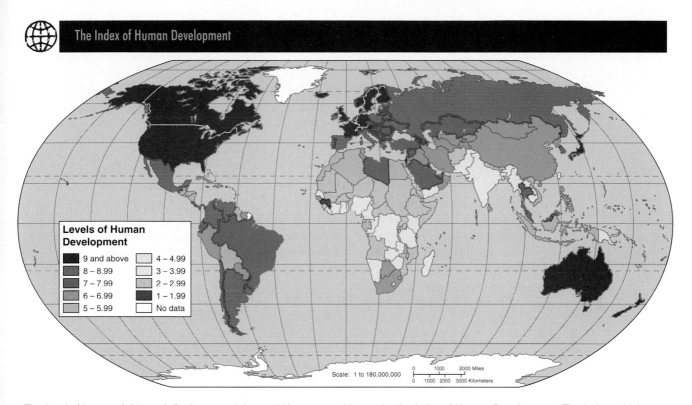

The Index of Human Development

Levels of Human Development

- 9 and above
- 8 – 8.99
- 7 – 7.99
- 6 – 6.99
- 5 – 5.99
- 4 – 4.99
- 3 – 3.99
- 2 – 2.99
- 1 – 1.99
- No data

Scale: 1 to 180,000,000

The level of human rights and dignity around the world is measured in part by the Index of Human Development. The index, which was developed by the United Nations Development Programme, includes such gauges as health, literacy, income, and education. As you can see, the level of development that people enjoy or endure, as they case may be, varies greatly.

productivity is limited. There is also a gender gap in education, especially in LDCs, where males are 14 percent more likely to be literate than females. An optimistic note is that the gap is only 8 percent among people aged 15 to 24. The averages also tend to disguise regional areas of profound educational deprivation. In sub-Saharan Africa, adult illiteracy is 39 percent.

The statistics showing an increase of literacy in LDCs also tend to cloud the fact that most children receive just a few years of primary education. Only about 59 percent of the relevant age groups of children in LDCs are in secondary school; that figure drops off to 46 percent in the LLDCs. The postsecondary school level is attained by only 10 percent of LDC students, compared with 62 percent of students in EDCs. Expenditures on education also vary widely between LDCs and EDCs, which annually spend 27 times as much per student than the LDCs can manage. In our technological age, the lack of advanced training is a major impediment to development. In the North there are nearly 10 times as many scientists and technicians per capita as there are in the South. That imbalance is 80 times as many per capita for the LLDCs.

Human Rights Issues Regarding Abuses of Individuals and Groups

The human condition depends on more than food security, level of education, and degree of health, on the individual level or collectively. There is also a range of rights having to do with the treatment of specific groups or individuals within a society, whether domestic or global, that are subject to abuse. Some legal scholars distinguish between two types of such rights. *Civil rights* involve a positive obligation on the part of governments to ensure that all people and groups are treated equally by the government and perhaps by everyone. The Fourteenth Amendment to the U.S. Constitution, which provides to all people in the country "the equal protection of the laws," is a quintessential statement of civil rights. *Civil liberties* involve restraints, and include those negative things that the government (and perhaps anyone) cannot, or should not, be able to do. Examples would include restricting the freedom of religion, speech, and assembly of individuals or groups.

HUMAN RIGHTS ABUSES: DIVERSE DISCRIMINATION AND OPPRESSION

Intolerance and the abuses that stem from it are ancient and persistent. They also are global and demographically diverse. Whether the focus is race, ethnicity, gender, sexual orientation, religious choice, or some other trait, there are few human characteristics or beliefs that have not been the target of discrimination and abuse somewhere in the world.

The hatred of other humans based on what they are, rather than on what they have done, extends as far back into history as we can see. Genocide is a modern term, but the practice is ancient. The Roman philosopher and statesman Seneca (ca. 8 B.C.–A.D. 65) wrote in *Epistles* that Romans were "mad, not only individually, but nationally" because they punished "manslaughter and isolated murders" but accepted "the much vaunted crime of slaughtering whole peoples."

In the intervening years, attitudes on racial or other forms of demographic superiority have often played a powerful, and always destructive role in history. Many of today's divisions and problems are, for example, a legacy of the racism that combined with political and economic nationalism to rationalize oppression. The ideas of biologist Charles Darwin in *The Origin of Species* (1859) were thoroughly corrupted to allow the exploitation of the "unfit" (nonwhites) by the "fit" (whites). Whites in this context (as used here) means European-heritage whites (Eurowhites) and does not extend to Arabs, Persians, most of the people of India, and other Caucasians. Racism also joined with religion to build a case in the Western mind that subjugation was in the interest of the uncivilized and pagan—that is, nonwhite, non-Christian societies. Symbolic of this racist self-justification is Rudyard Kipling's "White Man's Burden," penned in 1899 to urge Americans to seize the Philippines:

Take up the White Man's burden— Take up the White Man's burden—
Send forth the best ye breed— And reap his old reward:
Go bind your sons to exile The blame of those ye better
To serve your captives' need; The hate of those ye guard—
To wait in heavy harness The cry of hosts ye humor
On fluttered folk and wild— (Ah, slowly!) toward the light:—
Your new-caught, sullen peoples, "Why brought ye us from bondage,
Half devil and half child. Our beloved Egyptian night?"

This sort of bastardized **social Darwinism** also reared its head in such brutally repressive ideologies as Italian fascism and the related German credo, National Socialism. The *führer* proclaimed that war and conquest were "all in the natural order of things—for [they make] for the survival of the fittest." Race was a particular focus of conflict because, Hitler asserted in *Mein Kampf* (1925), "all occurrences in world history are only expressions of the races' instinct of self-preservation." This racist social theory became a key part of the Nazi *weltanschauung* (worldview) and of Hitler's foreign policy.

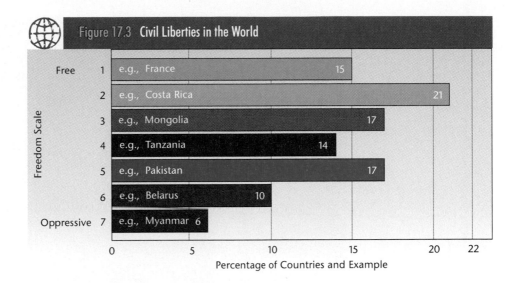

Figure 17.3 **Civil Liberties in the World**

Freedom Scale		Percentage of Countries and Example
Free	1	e.g., France — 15
	2	e.g., Costa Rica — 21
	3	e.g., Mongolia — 17
	4	e.g., Tanzania — 14
	5	e.g., Pakistan — 17
	6	e.g., Belarus — 10
Oppressive	7	e.g., Myanmar — 6

Note: Percentages do not add to 100 due to rounding.

Data source: Freedom House, *Freedom in the World, 1999–2000,* on the Web at: http://www.freedomhouse.org/survey/2000/method.html.

Oppression of civil liberties remains common. Freedom House evaluates countries for freedom of speech, religion, association, and other aspects of civil liberties and assigns each country a score of 1 (free) to 7 (oppressive) on the freedom scale. Only 36 percent of all countries fall into the most laudable 1 and 2 categories; most countries have a mixed score; and 16 percent fall into the very oppressive 6 and 7 categories.

It must be added that while genocidal attacks are often blamed on leaders who whip their former and otherwise peaceful followers up to murderous frenzy, it is also the case that ordinary common people are often all too willing to join the attacks. For example, Daniel Goldhagen argues in *Hitler's Willing Executioners: Ordinary Germans and the Holocaust* (1996), that the reason "the most committed anti-Semites in history" were able to come to power in Germany and turn a grotesque "private fantasy into the core of the state," was because German culture was "pregnant with murder" and rendered psychopathic by "hallucinatory anti-Semitism." This, Goldhagen concludes, led Germans in general to "believe [that] what they were doing to Jews was the right thing."[12]

The point is to not delude ourselves into thinking that the doctrine of superiority based on ethnic, racial, religious, or other differences died with the Third Reich or that it is always forced on unwilling populations by a few satanic leaders. Instead, hatred remains virulently alive. The many persistent forms of intolerance and oppression have been discussed earlier and will be encapsulated in the next section.

Oppression is also, of course, the tool of dictators, and the degree to which it is all too common is evident in data from one survey that ranked countries' respect for civil liberties on a scale of 1 (free) to 7 (oppressive). Civil liberties include freedoms such as speech, belief, and association that enable individuals to make choices about their lives. Political freedoms involve the right to vote and other factors that contribute to a democratic political process. Figure 17.3 illustrates that civil liberties are still moderately to severely restricted in most of the world's countries.

It is likely that you, like most of the people who read this book, live in the United States, Canada, or some other country that has attained a ranking of 1 on the Freedom House civil liberties scale and where civil rights, while far from ideal, have progressed over time. Indeed, it is hard for those of us fortunate enough to live in such countries to imagine how widespread and how harsh oppression can be. It is tempting to describe lurid tales of repression, and it would be easy to do so, for there are many. It will suffice, however, to review briefly the many types of oppression and

Domestic violence against women is a global human rights crisis that the world network of IGOs, such as the UN Fund for Women (UNIFEM), and NGOs, such as Women Against Violence, are bringing to the attention of national and international leaders. This shocking photograph shows two victims of domestic abuse, Nusrat Parveen (right) and Tasneen Bibi in a Pakistani hospital. Parveen had her nose cut off by her husband, and Bibi had acid thrown in her face by her in-laws. Parveen's husband, enraged when she complained about his bad temper, tied her to her bed, cut off her hair to humiliate her, then sliced off her nose. When she was able to escape, she went to the police, but they refused to press charges after Parveen's husband denounced her as an evil woman. Bibi's in-laws offered no explanation other than that she had displeased her husband. The burns were so serious that one operation had to be done to separate her cheek from her shoulder after the acid had fused her skin. Like Parveen's husband, Bibi's in-laws were not prosecuted.

the diversity of victims that have suffered from it by examining some of the human rights issues and violations regarding women, children, ethnic and racial groups, religious groups, indigenous people, and refugees and immigrants.

Women

In our discussion of the plight of a diversity of demographic groups, it is appropriate that we begin with the largest of all minority groups, women. Females constitute about half the world's population, but they are a distinct economic-political-social minority because of the wide gap in societal power and resources between women and men. Compared to men, women are much less likely to have a job that pays money, are much less likely to hold a professional position, are much more likely to be illiterate, and are much more likely to be living below the poverty line (Rhein, 1998).

The relative disadvantages of women are, of course, nothing new, but what has changed is that the issues of women's rights and circumstances have moved much higher on the global agenda. For example, it was not until 1994 that the U.S. State Department's annual report on global human rights focused for the first time on the status of women. "Its findings are grim," one news analysis related. "In painstaking detail the report… paints a dreary picture of day-to-day discrimination and abuse."[13] The common theme found in virtually every discussion of women's economic, political, and social status is that females suffer because of their gender. We have noted that women work longer hours than men but earn less; that women are afforded fewer opportunities than men to go to school; and that there is or has recently been a pattern of sexual and other physical assaults, including politically directed rape in Bosnia, forced prostitution in Thailand, bride-burning in India, sexual mutilation in many countries, and wife-beating almost everywhere.

Women in many countries are sold or forced by poverty to go into de facto slavery in their own countries or abroad. These domestic servants are often mistreated. The sale of young women and even girls (and young men and boys) into heterosexual or homosexual slavery is also relatively common in some places. In Pakistan, girls between 8 and 10 years old reportedly brought bids of $397 to $529 at one auction. According to the director of social welfare in Pakistan's Sind province, many men there believe that "since a woman is no better than a dumb, driven chattel, who cares what happens to her? She can be sold, purchased, transferred and bargained off like cows, sheep, goats or some other property."[14] So many women from Russia have been forced, physically or by poverty, into prostitution in other countries that this sad trafficking in women has become known as the "Natasha trade" (Hughes, 2000).

Other assaults on women arguably constitute a form of genocide. UNICEF reports, "In many countries, boys get better care and better food than girls. As a result, an estimated 1 million girls die each year because they are born female."[15] Not only that, but medical advances mean that more female than male fetuses are being terminated by abortion. A UN Population Fund (UNFPA) study of India concluded that the spread of ultrasound technology, by which sex can be determined, has resulted in increased abortions of female fetuses. "It is generally recognized," the report said, "that [the] adverse sex ratio occurs not because fewer girls are born (or conceived) but because fewer are allowed to be born or to survive." This has led some groups in India and elsewhere to campaign against procedures such as ultrasound. "We want to make these sex determination tests illegal," explained a representative of the All-India Democratic Women's Association; "we think it is an attack on the existence of women."[16] The groups in India have not been successful, but China, which has the same problem, has banned sex-determination tests.

Sometimes the abuses are sanctioned by law, but more often the rights of women are ignored because male-dominated governments turn a blind eye. In some cases, there are also economic incentives for governments to ignore abuses. Prostitution is a huge business in Southeast Asia, as elsewhere, and the females—often poor girls and women who are forced or duped into sexual slavery—bring in billions of dollars. The UN has estimated, for example, that Thailand's sex tourism and other aspects of the illicit sexual trade is equal to about 15 percent ($18 billion in 2000) of Thailand's officially reported GDP. According to the UN report "The Sex Sector: The Economic and Social Bases of Prostitution in Southeast Asia," the "revenues [the sex trade] generates are crucial to the livelihoods and earning potential of millions of workers beyond the prostitutes themselves."[17]

Most often, civil law and social strictures reinforce one another. This is so in Saudi Arabia, where women are treated as second-class citizens. Women cannot live independently; they are not permitted to drive, and there is widespread gender segregation in schools, universities, and workplaces. Saudi women are disadvantaged compared to men in matters of marriage, divorce, and child custody. All women are required to wear a black scarf to cover their head and an *abaya* (robe) that completely covers them except for their eyes, hands, and feet. If they fail to do so, they are subject to harassment, or even physical punishment, by the so-called religious police, the government-funded Committee for the Propagation of Virtue and the Prevention of Vice. Women's rights organizations do not exist in the country, nor does any woman have a role of importance in the government.

A bizarre and tragic example of the power of this religious police force, known as the *mutaween*, occurred in March 2002 when a fire broke out in a middle school housing 800 girls aged 12 to15 in Mecca. The religious police prevented many of the girls from fleeing the blazing building because they were not dressed modestly enough, and 15 died. One witness told reporters that the mutaween were "beating

ASYLUM

Fauziya Kassindja arrived at the U.S. border on December 17, 1994, and presented herself to customs officials. The 17-year-old from Togo asked for asylum. She was fleeing her country, she said, to avoid those who wanted "to scrape my woman parts off."[1]

What terrorized Kassindja was female genital mutilation (FGM), or, euphemistically, female circumcision. This traditional rite of puberty is performed widely in central and northern Africa and involves a clitoridectomy (the excision of the clitoris), which deprives a woman of all or most sexual sensation. Sometimes, more drastically, FGM extends to infibulation, the cutting away of all of a female's external genitalia and labial tissue. The UN estimates that as many as 130 million girls and women in the world today have suffered FGM and that each year another 2 million girls are subjected to the knife, shears, or razor blade. The practice is extremely painful. A woman who performs the rite in Togo explains that "young, weak girls are held down by four women. Stronger ones require five women, one to sit on their chests and one for each arm and leg."[2]

Aside from the psychic scars, FGM can be dangerous when carried out, as it usually is, by people who are not medically trained and who operate in unsanitary conditions. Infections and other complications are common; death can result. When a journalist asked the patriarch (senior male) of the Kassindja family in Togo about the danger, he conceded, "There are some girls who die." Still, he insisted, "To me it is not the excision that caused the death." When the reporter asked him what did cause the death, he merely shrugged.[3]

Supporters defend FGM on two grounds. One is tradition. "Since our forefathers' time, this is the law," a village elder said.[4] The second rationale is that it supposedly ensures chaste behavior by girls and women. "Am I supposed to stand around while my daughter chases men?" one African father asked incredulously. "So what if some infidel doctor says it is unhealthy?" he went on. "Banning it would make women run wild like those in America," added another man to reporters.[5]

It should be noted that some women favor FGM. "During the ceremony they find out if you are a virgin," one Togolese woman explained. "If you are a virgin the man will pay more dowry and your family will be honored by the husband." Other women are merely resigned to their fate and that of their daughters. "I have to do what my husband says," one woman commented. "It is not for women to give an order.... I remember my suffering. But I cannot prevent it for my daughter."[6]

Shielded by her family, Kassindja was able for a time to avoid the rite. But then, at age 15, she was betrothed to 45-year-old man. He demanded that she undergo a clitoridectomy. Rather than face mutilation, Kassindja fled from Togo to Ghana, and through a circuitous route, she eventually tried to use a fake passport to enter the United States, where she had a relative. There she was initially treated as a criminal, and was subjected to treatment that must have made her wonder whether her flight had been from one purgatory to another. "What I hate is when they put 20 or 30 people in a room," Kassindja has recalled. "They strip all of us together. They tell us to turn around, open your legs, squat. They stand looking at you. Sometimes they laugh."[7]

Kassindja's plight gained increasing attention of the national press, however, and in April 1996 she was released after nearly 16 months in prison to await the resolution of her appeal for asylum. The following year, a U.S. court finally granted asylum to Kassindja on the grounds that immigration law allows asylum for those who can show that they have a well-founded fear of persecution because of their race, religion, nationality, political opinions, or membership in a social group. The court found that Kassindja's membership in the Tchamba-Kunsuntu tribe, as a social group, made her subject to persecution. In

young girls to prevent them from leaving the school because they were not wearing the abaya." A Saudi newspaper quoted other witnesses as saying that the mutaween had shouted, "It is sinful to approach [the girls]" and had prevented male bystanders from trying to rescue the girls.[18]

Saudi Arabia ratified the Convention on the Elimination of All Forms of Discrimination Against Women in 2000, but that had little or no impact on the status of women in the kingdom. Indeed, the Saudi minister of the interior, Prince Nayef Ibn Abdul Aziz, commented at a press conference in April 2001, that a public debate on women's rights was "out of the question." As for allowing women to drive, the

Seventeen-year-old Fauziya Kassindja (center) fled Togo to avoid ritual genital mutilation. When she entered the United States using a fake passport to join a relative who had agreed to shelter her, she asked for asylum. Instead she was arrested. The relief she felt on being released after 15 months in prison is evident in this picture of Kassindja and some of the women whose support had helped free her, pending an appeal of the decision to deny her application for asylum. She was finally granted asylum, giving hope to other women who wish to escape FGM.

instead of 14 or 15. The reason for that change, a male village elder explained, is, "We don't want to let them grow up before we do it because they can run away."[9]

The larger implication of Kassindja's refusal to submit is that it highlights and symbolizes the determination of many people to eradicate the practice of FGM. About a third of the countries where FGM is performed have made it illegal, but these laws have only begun to reduce the incidence of FGM. Some advances have been made by individual countries. The ability to seek refuge is clear in Canada, which, like a few other countries, has enacted a law that makes FGM and other acts of gender abuse grounds for asylum. The U.S. court decision in Kassindja's case should have made it easier for other women to claim asylum, but that has not occurred. For example, Adelaide Abankwah, who fled from Ghana to escape FGM, spent two years in a U.S. jail before she was finally granted asylum in 1999.

There is also a determined international effort to end FGM by such global organizations as the International Planned Parenthood Federation and the World Health Organization. Perhaps most prominently, this campaign is represented by Waris Dirie, a women's rights activist, fashion model, and victim of FGM at age 5. One of her contributions has been to publicize her ordeal in an effort to educate others about FGM. Dirie's (1998) story, *Desert Flower*, was published as a book and excerpted in *Reader's Digest*. She also serves as special ambassador for the elimination of female genital mutilation of the United Nations Population Fund. Ambassador Dirie, a native of Somalia, lived through her ordeal, but a sister and several of her cousins did not. Then at age 13, betrothed to a 60-year-old man and facing even more radical FGM, Dirie fled, as Kassindja had, to safety in another country. "Because women and girls are not valued equally as human beings, they are treated as less than such," Dirie charges. "Female genital mutilation is one example of this that has got to be stopped."[10]

support, the court quoted an Immigration and Naturalization Service report that commented, "It remains particularly true that women have little legal recourse and may face threats to their freedom, threats of acts of physical violence, or social ostracization for refusing to undergo this harmful traditional practice."[8]

While Kassindja left the courtroom a free and whole woman, other women have not been and will not be so fortunate. Reportedly, the girls in Kassindja's home village are now being cut at age 4 to 7

prince, seemingly unaware that women drive competently throughout most of the world, said of granting licenses to Saudi women, "It is not possible, and there are no studies on the subject at all." Overall, the prince was of the opinion that Saudi Arabia's international pledge to end discrimination against women "in no way means an end to women's modesty or to exposing them to unveiling, anything shameful, or any violation of Islamic law."[19]

The defense of such policies toward females on the grounds of compliance with the *Shari'a* raises the point of cultural relativism, which is frequently used to justify the differences between how women and men are treated in some Muslim and other societies (Howland, 1999). Cultural relativism is also the crux of debate over another ancient practice—genital mutilation. The story of this African practice and the reaction of U.S. officials to a young woman who fled from Togo to avoid it is told in the box, Asylum.

Children

Children are not commonly considered a minority group. But insofar as they are dominated and sometimes abused by others, children fall well within the range of the groups that suffer because of their lack of economic and political power and because they are often denied rights accorded to the dominant segments of society.

Besides conditions such as lack of adequate nutrition that deny to a vast number of children any opportunity for a fulfilling life, there are a variety of abuses that children endure. Being forced to work is one of them. According to the 2000 data of the International Programme for the Elimination of Child Labour (IPEC), a division of the International Labor Organization (ILO), there are 186 million children aged 5 to 14 in LDCs who go to work, not to school, each day. This includes 29 percent of the children in Africa, 19 percent of the children in Asia, and 16 percent of the children in Latin America and the Caribbean. Only about 2 percent of children in EDCs work.

Even more disturbing than children in the general labor pool is the fate of the estimated 8.4 million children who are in what IPEC terms "unconditional worst forms of child labor." This includes children in four categories (and the number of children in each): forced and bonded labor (5.7 million), armed conflict (so-called boy soldiers, 0.3 million), prostitution and pornography (1.8 million) and illicit activities (such as drug sales, 0.6 million).[20] Child prostitution is especially prevalent in Southern Asia and Latin America. "Brazil may be the worst in the world, but nobody really knows," says a UN representative in Brazil.[21] There are many reasons—ranging from abuse at home to economic desperation—why children turn to prostitution; it is also the case that many children are sold by their families or kidnapped by sex-slavers to supply the multibillion-dollar sex trade. An astronomical rate of AIDS and other sexually transmitted diseases are among the myriad dangers these children face.

Children are even put in the position of killing or being killed as boy soldiers. These children, usually small boys, are persuaded or forced to fight or serve as support workers for one rebel group or another. For example, during Liberia's grueling civil war (1989–1997), one faction created a fighting force called the Small Boy Unit. Samuel Bull joined it when he was eight years old. He later recalled being given Valium tablets before battles, and he admits to killing many people, including one woman whom he machine-gunned because "I liked the sound of the gun." Sam entered a UN rehabilitation program, but observers were worried that he and the others who have been turned into killers before puberty are scarred for life. At the UN compound, Sam discovered that someone had taken a pair of his socks. "The next time someone comes into my sock drawer, I'll take my knife and kill him," Sam snarled. "I knew he meant it," a UN social worker shuddered.[22]

The treatment of children is certainly the proper concern of national governments, but it is also an international issue. It is estimated that 10 to 12 million men travel each year internationally as "sex tourists" to exploit children. Clothes, shoes, and other products manufactured by children are sold in international trade; you may be wearing one of these products even as you read these words. The wars and civil strife that ruin the lives of boy soldiers and other children are often rooted in world affairs.

As hard as it is to believe in our "modern" world, these children are slaves. The boys pictured here near Khartoum, Sudan, are among the 132 women and children that the Swiss-based NGO Christian Solidarity International bought from a slave trader for $13,200 in order to obtain their freedom. Improving the human rights of children is the primary goal of UNICEF and a number of other international agencies.

Ethnic and Racial Groups

Strife and oppression based on ethnicity and race are still unsettlingly common. Until international pressure through economic sanctions and other actions finally compelled South African whites to surrender political power in 1994, racism persisted officially through the apartheid system that permitted 6.5 million whites to dominate the other 29 million black, Asian, and "colored" (mixed-race) people. Also in 1994 the slaughter of Tutsis by Hutus in Rwanda and the recurring violence between these two groups in Burundi and Rwanda provided a terrible example of racial/ethnic hate politics. Throughout the 1990s, various ethnic groups in what was Yugoslavia beset one another, with the Serbs the main perpetrators, and the Muslim Bosnians and, more recently, the Muslim Kosovars, the main victims. The previous descriptions, especially in chapter 6, of these ethnic and racial tensions mean that here it is only necessary to reiterate that ethnic and racial identification are a key component of the tensions and conflict that make nationalism one of, if not the most, divisive elements of human politics.

Religious Groups

Strife and oppression based all or in part on religion is also common on the world stage, as the conflict in Northern Ireland, the conflict in Sudan between the Muslim government and non-Muslim rebels, the earlier-mentioned slaughter of Bosnian Muslims and Kosovars by Orthodox Bosnian Serbs, and other conflicts attest. There are also, as detailed in chapter 7, numerous efforts by religious fundamentalists in India, Israel, Northern Ireland, several Muslim countries, and elsewhere to align the legal codes and religious laws of their respective countries and to force everyone, regardless of their personal beliefs, to follow those theocratic laws. Even in countries where there is no move to supplant civil with theocratic law, religious intimidation is not uncommon.

Racism, anti-Semitism, and other disturbing forms of hatred are also on the rise in Europe. Russia and Eastern Europe have witnessed the reemergence of overt and not infrequent verbal and physical assaults on Jews. Public opinion surveys in some countries reveal that many negative images of Jews persist. One poll found 59 percent of Russians agreeing with the statement, "Jews have too much power in the world of business" (ADL, 1999:21). Giving voice to that sort of xenophobia, Gennadi Zyuganov, the leader of the still powerful communists in Russia's parliament, has charged that Russia and the rest of Christian civilization was separated from its moral foundations by Jews who "traditionally controlled the financial life of the continent."[23]

Other former communist countries in Europe are also seeing more overt anti-Semitism. A survey in Poland found that one-third of all respondents thought Jewish influence "too great" in the country, and 31 percent admitted to being somewhere between "extremely" and "slightly" anti-Semitic. When the movie *Schindler's List*, depicting the horrors in the Polish ghettos and in the concentration camps, played in Germany, some Germans charged that the movie overdramatized events, and a poll found that 39 percent of the Germans surveyed agreed with the statement, "Jews are exploiting the Holocaust for their own purposes."[24]

Indigenous People

The history of the world is a story of mass migrations and conquests that have often left the indigenous people of a region as a minority in national political systems imposed on their traditional tribal or other political structures. The most familiar of these groups to many readers probably are the numerous native peoples of North and South America commonly lumped together as "Indians," or more contemporarily referred to by such designations as Native Americans and Mezo-Americans. The Eskimos or Inuits of Canada and Alaska (as well as Greenland and eastern Siberia), and native Hawaiians in that U.S. state are also indigenous peoples.

The efforts of various indigenous groups in Central and South America have also become increasingly well known. The unrest in the southern area of Chiapas in Mexico is associated in part with the alienation of the impoverished Mayan and other indigenous people of that region from the Mexican government. This feeling of oppression is supported by UN data that finds that on the UNDP's Human Development Index, the level of development of the Mexican people is 27 percent higher than that of the country's indigenous people. This relative poverty, even in what used to be called **Third World** countries, has led to the term **Fourth World** to designate indigenous people collectively.

One of the particular efforts of indigenous people in recent years has been their effort to protect their traditional home areas politically and environmentally from the incursion of the surrounding cultures. The spread of people and commercial activities such as logging and mining into the vast interior areas of the Amazon River system has increasingly degraded the health, environment, and other aspects of the life of the indigenous people of that region. The Yanomami people of Brazil and Venezuela provide an example. The Yanomami (the word means "human being") had little contact with outsiders before the mid-1980s when the lure of gold brought prospectors and miners far up Brazil's river and into the Yanomami's forest retreats. The invasion has left the Yanomami devastated by the diseases and by mercury and other toxins brought by the miners, and, on occasion, by violence aimed at forcing the tribe off its lands. Their numbers have shrunk since the mid-1980s by about 10 percent, to 19,000.

Beyond the Amazon basin, similar stories are common. Representatives of the Khwe people of Botswana traveled to the annual UN Commission on Human Rights convention in Geneva, Switzerland, to seek help in fending off their threatened expulsion from the Kalahari Desert to make way for tourism facilities. "We came without any promise of getting anything done," said John Hardbattle, leader of the First People of the Kalahari organization. "We felt that if we can't get help at the UN, then we won't get it anywhere else."[25] As Hardbattle recognized, the ability of aboriginal groups to resist the hunger of powerful outside forces for resources and land is limited. They depend in part on gaining world attention and help. That has just begun, as we will see later.

Refugees and Immigrants

Many commentators have accurately noted the rise of ethnic and racial strife, religious fundamentalism, and other xenophobic movements in recent years. One clear indication of that nativist tendency is evident in the upsurge in negative feeling in many quarters of the world toward immigrants and refugees. The post–cold war spasm of civil wars and other internal violence, added to the economic desperation of many people, has set off a flood of refugees. "Migration is the visible face of social change," as a report by UNFPA puts it.[26] According to the United Nations High Commissioner for Refugees, there were 11.5 million refugees living outside of their native countries at the beginning of 2000. Additionally, there were another 4 million internally displaced persons who, while still living in their own country, had been forced to flee their homes, villages, and cities.

In addition to the people who are overt refugees, there are millions of people who have legally or illegally entered other countries to find work. The tide of refugees and immigrants, legal and illegal, has been met with increasing resistance in the EDCs. Europe, in particular, has seen a rise of anti-immigrant xenophobia, as discussed in chapter 6. During 2002, for example, there were repeated demonstrations of intolerance in Europe. In France, Jean-Marie Le Pen, the candidate of the right-wing National Front, finished second among 18 candidates for the presidency of France after campaigning on an unabashed anti-immigrant platform. "They are taking our jobs, our peace, our space, our customs," Le Pen told audiences before ending with his mantra, "France for the French."[27] Italy to the south also has increasingly displayed anti-immigrant sentiments, and those are echoed in 2002 by Prime Minister Silvio Berlusconi, who warned Italians about the danger of being "thrown out of our own country by the mass arrivals of clandestine immigrants."[28] Elsewhere in Europe, the right wing recorded important electoral gains during 2002 in Belgium, the Netherlands, and other countries. Several governments passed legislation raising the age level when immigrants could marry above the age for citizens, and Germany and Austria adopted legislation increasing the requirement to learn German in order to remain in those countries.

These and many other attitudes and actions led to a report from the British Institute on Race Relations in 2002 that highlighted the reality that European attitudes are related to the fact that most Europeans are Eurowhites and most immigrants are not. "We are entering a new era in domestic race policy, where old, discredited ideas of monoculturalism and assimilation into the dominant white, European Christian culture are once again in the ascendant," the report warned.

The United Nations Commission on Human Rights (UNCHR) estimates that there are over 21 million refugees in the world who have been displaced by war, famine, and other causes. The conditions shared by many of these refugees is represented in this January 2002 photograph of an Afghan refugee child walking between snow-covered plastic tents in a camp in Pakistan. The UNCHR and a wide range of other public and private international organizations are working to try to meet the immediate human needs of the ceaseless waves of refugees and also to promote the protection of their human rights.

That view was seconded by the European Union's Monitoring Centre on Racism and Xenophobia, which urged the political leaders of member-countries to "be more active in countering the racist threat in Europe," and by a UN official concerned with refugees who decried what he described as a "no-holds-barred... targeting asylum-seekers as a political issue."[29]

Coping with refugees and economically driven illegal immigrants is costing the North many billions of dollars each year. Billions are spend to assist refugees overseas, and many countries are also spending vast sums on their border patrols and on other domestic programs to stem the influx of refugees and undocumented immigrants, to assist those who are admitted or who slip in, and to return to their country of origin some of those who do arrive.

Whatever the impact of programs to lessen the inflow of refugees and immigrants may be, it is certain that they are not only expensive, but that they will be unending as long as people in some countries are subject to endemic violence and poverty. The Kevin Costner movie *Field of Dreams* revolved around the line, "If you build it, they will come." To those who daily face death, disease, and hunger, the EDCs' societies of relative peace and material wealth represent a field of dreams. And people in danger and destitution will come.

> **Did You Know That:**
> The United States admitted a total of just 2.1 million refugees between 1980 and 1998, accounting for less than 12 percent of total immigrants allowed to enter the country. During the period 1980–1998, the U.S. immigration rate of 3.3 (immigrants per 1,000 citizens) was well below half of what it was (8.0) during the first two decades of the 1900s.

One way to avoid perpetually spending vast sums on aid, immigration control, and other programs, some say, is to help the South develop quickly, to at least build a field that meets minimum needs of sustenance and safety. It is arguable that if Mexico's standard of living were to increase substantially, many of its citizens would no longer undergo the dislocation and risk the physical danger that leaving home and slipping into the United States entails. "We have a good argument now, a very concrete one," for helping the LDCs, the prime minister of Denmark told a UN conference, "which is, if you don't help the Third World..., then you will have these poor people in your society."[30]

THE INTERNATIONAL RESPONSE TO INDIVIDUAL AND GROUP HUMAN RIGHTS ISSUES

It would be naive to argue that the world has even begun to come close to resolving its numerous individual and group human rights issues; it would be equally wrong to deny that a start has been made (Moravcsik, 2000). The way to evaluate the worth of the efforts that we are about to discuss is to judge their goals and to see them as the beginnings of a process that only a few decades ago did not exist at all. Whatever country you live in, the protection of human rights has evolved over an extended period and is still far from complete. The global community has now embarked on an effort similar to your country's effort. It will, however, take time and will be controversial.

The United Nations is at the center of global human rights activity (Pace, 1998). The basis for concern is the UN's charter, which touches on human rights in several places (Eide, 1998; Korey, 1998). More specific is the Universal Declaration of Human Rights (1948), which includes numerous clauses discussed in the earlier box, A Global Bill of Rights. These are proclaimed as a "common standard... for all peoples and all nations." Many of the rights contained in the Universal Declaration are also included in two other multilateral treaties: the International Covenant on Civil and Political Rights (1966) and the International Covenant on Economic, Social and Cultural Rights (1966). Most countries have agreed to all three of these pacts. A notable addition to these ranks came in 1998 when China signed the treaty on civil and political rights. In addition, there are 19 other UN-sponsored covenants that address children's rights, genocide, racial discrimination, refugees, slavery, stateless persons, women's rights, and other human rights issues (Kent, 1999). These agreements and human rights in general are monitored by the United Nations Commission on Human Rights (UNCHR).

It would be foolish to imagine that when China or any other country adopts one or another of these treaties, doing so ends abuses. That has not happened in China, which agreed to become a signatory to the civil and political rights covenant in order to head off the yearly ritual of a U.S.-led move to censure China in the UN. In return for China's agreement and its release of some political prisoners, the United States ended the censure effort. "China still has an enormous way to go," one U.S. official explained, "but in light of these steps, we have decided not to sponsor the resolution [of censure]."[31] It is easy to decry such decisions as cover-ups, but the desire of China to avoid censure and its willingness to formally sign the human rights treaty are also evidence of the impact of changing global norms.

There are also a number of regional conventions and IGOs that supplement the principles and efforts of the UN. The best developed of these are in Western Europe and include two human rights covenants. These are adjudicated by the European Court of Human Rights and by the Commission on Human Rights. Additionally, there are a substantial number of NGOs, such as Amnesty International and Human Rights Watch, which are concerned with a broad range of human rights. These groups work independently and in cooperation with the UN and regional organizations to further human rights. They add to the swell of information about, and criticisms of, abuses. They help promote the adoption of international norms that support human rights (Clark, 1996).

The impact of IGOs and NGOs and general progress in the human rights arena have, as noted, been mixed. Political selectivity and national domestic political concerns are two of the factors that impede the growth of human rights observance and enforcement on the international stage. Both these factors were discussed in chapter 8 and thus merit only brief recapitulation. Political selectivity disposes all countries to be shocked when opponents transgress against human rights and to ignore abuses by themselves, by their allies, and by countries that they hope to influence. Nationalism and the standard of sovereignty continue to be used by some countries to reject outside interference of domestic abuses, and by other countries as a reason for ignoring those abuses. An associated issue is the claim that cultural standards are different, and, therefore, what is a human rights violation in one country is culturally acceptable in another.

These and other impediments should not cloud the human rights contributions of the UN, Amnesty International, and other IGOs and NGOs. The frequency and horror of the abuses that they highlight increasingly are penetrating the international consciousness and disconcerting the global conscience. The 1993 UN-sponsored World Conference on Human Rights (WCHR) held in Vienna, Austria, provides an example. As is true for international forums on most issues, the WCHR witnessed political fissures along several lines. Some Asian, Muslim, and other countries resisted broad declarations of human rights based on what they see as Western-oriented values. This charge of cultural imperialism also led them to oppose the appointment of a high commissioner for human rights to head the UNCHR and give it more impact. In the end, though, some advances were made in both defining global human rights and creating and empowering a high commissioner. To clarify human rights, the WCHR declared that "all human rights are universal and indivisible and interdependent and interrelated," while adding that "the significance of national and regional particularities and various historical, cultural, and religious backgrounds must be kept in mind" when defining rights and identifying and condemning abuses (Burk, 1994:201). Those who advocated appointing a high commissioner were able

The UN and other international agencies have played an important role in raising the consciousness of women around the world and helping them to establish a transnational advocacy network that promotes women's rights and the betterment of their circumstances. Providing a glimpse of the global women's movement, this photograph shows (from left to right), Theresa Garuba from Nigeria, Wendy Mwandia from Kenya, Jariatu Sesay from Sierra Leone, Kumbi Sonaike from Nigeria, and Gail Wright Sirmans from the United States gathered at the UN in New York City in March 2002, for a conference being held on International Women's Day.

to overcome the roadblocks erected at the WCHR by subsequently bringing the issue before the UN General Assembly, which created the post.

To give a bit more detail on the efforts of the UN, other IGOs, and NGOs in the area of human rights, we can turn to their activities with respect to women, children, ethnic and racial groups, religious groups, indigenous people, and refugees and immigrants.

Women A great deal of the human rights attention and some of the most vigorous international human rights efforts in recent years have focused on women. The most significant progress has been made in the realm of identifying the treatment of women as a global problem, identifying some of the causes and worst abuses, and defining women's rights. This has placed the issue of women solidly on the international agenda. For example, the UN General Assembly's Third Committee, which specializes in social, cultural, and humanitarian issues, spent less than 2 percent of its time discussing women's rights from 1955 to 1965. That percentage had risen almost sevenfold by the mid-1980s, and, indeed, has become the second most extensively discussed issue (after racial discrimination) in the Third Committee.

A major symbolic step occurred with the UN declaration of 1975 as International Women's Year and the kickoff of a Decade for Women. Numerous conferences brought women together to document their status. Funding for projects to benefit women was begun through the establishment of such structures as the UN Fund for Women (UNIFEM, after its French initials). The adoption of the Convention on the Elimination of All Forms of Discrimination Against Women in 1979 was a pathbreaking step in defining women's rights on an international level. As of mid-2002, 69 countries had agreed to the treaty, but the United States remained among the absent. Progress on women's issues also occurred at the 1993 WCHR. The plan adopted by the conference urged universal adoption of the 1979 treaty and urged the

THE ROAD TO BEIJING AND BEYOND

The most recent, well-publicized effort to advance women's rights globally was the fourth World Conference on Women (WCW) that convened in Beijing in September 1995. Building on the third conference, held in Nairobi in 1985, and also on other events such as the 1994 UN Conference on Population and Development (UNCPD) held in Cairo, the WCW had three "priority themes": equality (especially equal pay for equal work), development (with an emphasis on population, nutrition, and health factors), and peace (particularly eradicating societal and family abuse of women).

The 188-page report that emerged from the WCW declared that women have the right to decide freely on all matters related to their sexuality and childbearing. This included a condemnation of forced sterilizations and abortions. The final document denounced rape in wartime as a war crime and called on national governments to intervene to prevent the genital mutilation of girls, bride burning, and all spousal abuse. The conference also called for the economic empowerment of women. To this end, it demanded an end to sexual harassment at work. The document further called for public and private lending organizations to extend credit to low-income women for establishing small businesses and other economic betterment projects and for an end of forbidding women to inherit their husband's property (Scott, 1996).

There were, of course, controversies. The ongoing sensitivities of some Roman Catholic, Muslim, and other countries to the issue of abortion led to language in the final document that was not as strong as some abortion-rights advocates wished. Lesbian rights were debated internationally for the first time, but no language was included in the report.

In many ways, though, the specifics about what the conference said are less important than the fact that it happened and that it voiced the concerns of women and presented their goals to a global audience. The official conference at Beijing was attended by some 3,000 delegates from 180 countries. The U.S. delegation was headed by first lady Hillary Rodham Clinton; UN ambassador and future U.S. secretary of state Madeleine Albright was the deputy head of the delegation. There was also a huge parallel conference for NGOs at nearby Huairou, which drew 30,000 delegates representing some 2,000 NGOs. In short, the meetings in China constituted the largest conclave of women in history. Not only could women meet and strengthen their already formidable network of women's groups, but their collective voice was carried outward by the 2,500 reporters who covered the conferences.

While the Beijing conference's platform of action was not binding on states, it set a standard that has already begun to have an impact. In June 1996, for example, the Hague tribunal on war crimes in Bosnia declared for the first time in history that rape in war is a war crime by indicting eight Bosnian Serb soldiers for the rape of Bosnian Muslim women. "This is a landmark indictment because it focuses exclusively on sexual assaults, without including any other charges," noted a tribunal spokesperson.[1]

The meetings in China also strengthened the resolve of women to campaign against cultural sexism. Mahnaz Afkhami, an Iranian exile who heads an NGO, the Sisterhood Is Global Institute, and who is a leader of the effort to establish a Muslim women's movement, was able to meet with women from Iran. "The Iranian women were under enormous constraint," she noted, but she also found that while "they may have had to wear the chador (traditional full-cover garment),... they didn't have a conservative line.... That kind of interaction is very important."[2]

UNCHR to create the post of special rapporteur on violence against women. The commission complied in early 1994, naming a Sri Lankan jurist to the post.

This rise in the level of consciousness also led to a number of other institutional changes at the UN. The organization created the Division for the Advancement of Women, which is responsible for addressing women's issues and promoting their rights. In this role, the division administratively supports both the Commission on the Status of Women (CSW), which is the main UN policy-making body for women, and the Committee on the Elimination of Discrimination Against Women (CEDAW), which monitors the implementation of the 1979 convention on women's rights. The division has also organized four UN world conferences on women.

Of these, the most important was the fourth World Conference on Women (WCW), which convened in Beijing in 1995. During the planning for the conference, its chairwoman urged that "the road to Beijing must be paved with vision and commitment" (Burk, 1994:239). It was, and the story of that conference is told in the box, The Road to Beijing and Beyond.

Finally, there have been advances in other contexts to further the rights of women. One notable stride occurred through the treaty that created the International Criminal Court (ICC). It specifies in Article 7 (Crimes Against Humanity) that such crimes "when committed as part of a widespread or systematic attack directed against any civilian population, with knowledge of the attack," include, among others, acts of "rape, sexual slavery, enforced prostitution, forced pregnancy, enforced sterilization, or any other form of sexual violence of comparable gravity." There are currently war criminals being prosecuted at the existing tribunals in The Hague (for the Balkans) and in Tanzania (for Rwanda) for such depravities, and the world has now served notice that rape and related abuses are war crimes. The ICC treaty gained enough ratifications by April 2002 to go into effect and to put in motion the process for establishing the court, which is likely to be seated in The Hague, the Netherlands and begin its operations in 2003. Indicative of the progress toward supporting women's rights that the ICC represents, MADRE, a U.S.-based women's rights NGO, issued a press release indicating that it, "celebrates the creation of the International Criminal Court as a critical new tool in the defense of human rights for women and their families around the world."[32]

There is also evidence that the rising international condemnation of the abuse of women is having some impact on norms and practices within countries. Egypt provides a case study. The country has long been one in which the genital mutilation of women was common. Then its health ministry banned the practice in 1996, setting off a legal struggle. The following year, an Egyptian court overturned the law as a usurpation of power by the government. That ruling was, however, reversed by Egypt's highest court, which held that "circumcision of girls is not an individual right under the Shari'a. There is nothing in the Koran that authorizes it."[33] Egypt has also changed its divorce laws, and women now have the ability to file for divorce, an option men alone had formerly possessed.

Children Serious international efforts to protect the rights of children have only recently begun, but there have already been worthwhile steps. UNICEF is the most important single agency, but it is supported by numerous other IGOs. The efforts of UNICEF are also supported and supplemented by a wide range of NGOs, such as End Child Prostitution in Asian Tourism, which was established in 1991 by child welfare groups in several Asian countries. Their common goal, in the words of UNICEF's executive director, is to "ensure that exploitive and hazardous child labor becomes as unacceptable in the next century as slavery has become in this. Children should be students in school, not slaves in factories, fields, or brothels."[34]

One noteworthy advance is the Convention on the Rights of the Child (Mower, 1997). Work on it began in 1979, which was designated by the UN as the International Year of the Child. A treaty was adopted unanimously by the UN General Assembly in 1989 and made available for signature and ratification by the world's countries. The convention outlines a wide range of collective and individual rights for all persons under the age of 18. If all countries and people abided by the convention, the sexual exploitation of children, the use of boy soldiers, the diversion of children from their education to work, and many other abuses would end.

It is a mark of hope that the convention garnered enough ratifications to go into force in less than a year and also quickly became the most widely ratified human rights treaty in history. Indeed, as of mid-2002, of the 191 countries, every country in the world save the United States, the failed state Somalia, and brand new East

Slowly, progress is beginning to be made to protect children globally through the efforts of UNICEF, the International Labor Organization, and other agencies and through the adoption of international agreements, such as the Convention on the Rights of the Child. Ending child labor is part of the campaign to improve the lives of children. The boy carrying a giant soccer ball had been a worker in a soccer ball factory in India. He was participating in a demonstration in New Delhi organized by the Global March Against Child Labor in May 2002. The goal, as the message on the ball says, is to "Kick Child Labor Out of the World!"

Timor was a party to the treaty. Among other concerns in the United States was whether the convention would abridge the possibility in some U.S. states that minors convicted of capital crimes can be executed once they reach age 18.

A second important effort on behalf of children was the World Congress Against Commercial Sexual Exploitation of Children, which met in Stockholm, Sweden. The 1996 conference was attended by representatives of 122 national governments, the UN and other IGOs, and 471 NGOs. The authority of such international meetings is severely limited, but they do serve a valuable function by focusing attention on issues. As the congress's general rapporteur, Vitit Muntarbhorn of Thailand, noted, "There can be no more delusions—no one can deny that the problem of children being sold for sex exists, here and now, in almost every country in the world."[35]

Despite the near impossibility of opposing children's rights in theory, the effort to protect them in practice, like most international human rights programs, runs into the problems of nationalism and parochialism. Countries resist being told what to do, and they are better able to see what others should do than what they themselves should do. India's representative to the UNCHR in Geneva reacted to criticism of the number of children being exploited in her country by lashing out at "finger pointing" by other countries and recounting that when India had tried to garner support for a global ban on sex tourism, the effort had met resistance from Germany, Japan, Korea, and the Netherlands. Displaying ads in German magazines offering "boys of any color, size, or age," the delegate from India related that other countries had told her, "We are not willing to ban promotion of sex tours."[36]

Ethnic, Racial, and Religious Groups The global effort to combat intolerance has also been furthered by a series of international conferences to highlight the problem and seek solutions. The first two met in Geneva, Switzerland, in 1978 and 1983. The third, the World Conference against Racism, Racial Discrimination, Xenophobia and Related Intolerance (WCAR) convened in Durban, South Africa, in 2001. The meeting brought together official delegations from 160 countries. Like most UN conferences, there was also an unofficial parallel conference that brought together representatives of hundreds of NGOs ranging alphabetically from ABC Ulwazi (South Africa) to the Zoroastrian Women's Organization (Iran).

Unfortunately for the future of a united struggle against intolerance, the Durban conference fell into acrimonious debate over what some saw as an undiplomatic truculence (and others viewed as justified candor) on the part of delegations from the South. This was captured in the comments of the host, South African president Thabo Mbeki. Opening the conference, he told the assembly, "It became necessary that we convene in Durban because together we recognized the fact there are many in our common world who suffer indignity and humiliation because they are not white." Therefore, he continued, "Their cultures and traditions are despised as savage and primitive and their identities denied.... To those who have to bear the pain of this real world, it seems the blues singers were right when they decried the world in which it was said, 'If you're white you're alright; if you are brown, stick around; if you are black, oh brother! get back, get back, get back!'"[37]

Wrangling between North and South particularly focused on two issues raised in preliminary resolutions. One was the demand by African countries that the countries of Western Europe and the United States that long ago were involved in the slave trade apologize and perhaps pay reparation.

The other sore point centered on Israel and the Palestinians. Draft language favored by Muslim countries labeled Israel a "racist apartheid state" and demanded an end to the "ongoing Israeli systematic perpetration of racist crimes, including war crimes, genocide and ethnic cleansing."[38]

Even before the meeting, this strident stand caused Canada, Great Britain, the United States and a number of other Western countries to downgrade their delegation. Then when the attack on Israel persisted, the U.S. delegation withdrew altogether. "I have taken this decision with regret," Secretary of State Colin Powell said. "[But] I know that you do not combat racism by conferences that produce declarations containing hateful language," he concluded.[39]

While the conference expanded and strengthened the **transnational advocacy network (TAN)** against intolerance, the image that it projected abroad was one of "all the wrong news," as one delegate put it.[40] As the conference drew to a close, UN Human Rights Commissioner Mary Robinson optimistically told the delegates, "We have not been deterred from making a breakthrough here in Durban." Probably more accurate was the evaluation of an Australian representative, who lamented, "Far too much of the time at the conference was consumed by bitter divisive exchanges on issues which have done nothing to advance the cause of combating racism."[40]

More positively, efforts to define the rights of ethnic, racial, and religious groups have been part of the major human rights documents such as the International Covenant on Economic, Social, and Cultural Rights and the Convention on the Prevention and Punishment of the Crime of Genocide. There have also been some specific agreements, such as the International Convention on the Elimination of all Forms of Racial Discrimination (1969). It is a step forward that 165 countries have been willing to agree to this document, which, among other things, proclaims that its signatories are "convinced that any doctrine of superiority based on racial differentiation is scientifically false, morally condemnable, socially unjust and dangerous, and that there is no justification for racial discrimination, in theory or in practice, anywhere."[41]

These efforts have been supplemented by some levels of enforcement. The earlier international pressure on South Africa to end legal racism was an important step. The international tribunals investigating and trying war crimes committed in the Balkans and in Rwanda are further evidence that persecution based on ethnicity, race, or religion are increasingly considered an affront to the global conscience.

Indigenous People The UN General Assembly proclaimed 1993 to be the International Year of the Indigenous Peoples (Pritchard, 1998). The following year, as part of that year's UNCHR meeting, representatives of the more than 5,000 indigenous peoples agreed to an International Covenant on the Rights of Indigenous Nations and made it available for signature and ratification by the world's countries. The efforts of indigenous people have also been furthered by numerous NGOs, including the International Indian Treaty Council, the World Council of Indigenous Peoples, the Inuit Circumpolar Conference, and the Unrepresented Nations and Peoples' Organization. The causes of indigenous people were also furthered when the Nobel Peace Prize Committee made its 1992 award to Rigoberta Menchú of

While the UN, other IGOs, and NGOs have only begun to address the vast range of human needs in the world, their efforts have played a crucial role in improving the lot of countless people. As testament to that work is this January 2002 photograph of Daut, a six-year-old Afghani boy, hugging a sack of wheat donated by Finland and distributed by the World Food Programme.

Guatemala in recognition of her efforts to advance the rights of her Mayan people in her country and to further the welfare of indigenous people globally.

Refugees and Immigrants International efforts on behalf of refugees provide very mixed results. There have been a number of efforts to define the status and the rights of both international and internal refugees. An early effort was the 1951 Convention Relating to the Status of Refugees (1951). This document charged the UN with providing assistance to people who were being persecuted in their countries or who feared persecution if returned to their home countries. The convention also defined the basic rights of refugees and minimum standards for their treatment and has served, among other things, as a foundation for subsequent efforts on behalf of refugees. It is also true, though, that it is one of the least widely ratified of the UN's major human rights treaties. Because of concerns that they might be required to open their borders to refugees or extend rights to those that managed to arrive unbidden, only 140 countries have signed and ratified it, with the United States among those missing countries.

Aid to refugees, while scant compared to their actual need, presents a somewhat brighter picture. The effort on behalf of displaced persons in the early 1950s led to the creation of the UN High Commissioner for Refugees in 1951 with wide responsibility for refugee rights and needs. Also formed that year was the International Organization for Migration (IOM), a body specifically concerned with the movement of refugees either to new homes or back to their former homes, as appropriate. Additionally, there are a number of IGOs, such as the International Red Cross (and its Muslim counterpart, the International Red Crescent), Oxfam, and others, which are involved in providing food, clothes, shelter, and other necessities.

Did You Know That:
The word *Eskimo* is probably derived from the word *assimew*, which means "she laces a snowshoe" in Montagnais, the Algonquin language of eastern Canada, and from the related Objibwa word for snowshoe, *askime*.

⊕ Chapter Summary

1. This chapter discusses two types of human rights. Individual human rights consist of freedom from specific abuses or restrictions, especially by governments. Collective human rights include the right to a quality of life, including adequate nutrition; reasonable health care; and educational opportunity that, at minimum, does not detract from human dignity.

2. Population growth, the underproduction of food, and the maldistribution of the food that is produced means that there are many people who do not receive adequate nutrition. International organizations, such as the Food and Agriculture Organization, attempt to provide short-term food relief and long-term agricultural assistance to countries facing nutritional shortages.

3. Many people in LDCs face diseases and lack of medical care to degrees that boggle the minds of most people in EDCs. Some of the diseases, such as AIDS, can become a world health threat. The World Health Organization, other IGOs, and many NGOs are attempting to bring better health care to people globally.

4. The ability of individuals to achieve a higher quality of life and the ability of countries to develop economically depend in substantial part on education. More than 1 billion adults are still illiterate, many more have only the most rudimentary education, and the personal and societal productivity of these people is limited. The United Nations Educational, Scientific, and Cultural Organization is one of many international organizations working to improve education in the LDCs.

5. There are two types of individual rights. Civil rights include standards, such as equal standing in the courts, that must exist to ensure that all people and groups are treated equally. Civil liberties are those things, like exercising free speech, which individuals cannot be prevented from doing.

6. Human rights abuses are widespread. They spring from intolerance, authoritarianism, and other causes and are often rationalized by pseudoscientific theories, such as social Darwinism, and by repressive ideologies, such as fascism.

7. The discussion of human rights abuses and the efforts to ease them focuses on women, children, ethnic and racial groups, religious groups, indigenous people, and refugees and immigrants.

8. The area of human rights is one of the most difficult to work in because violations are usually politically based. Therefore, efforts to redress them are often resented and rejected by target countries. The greatest progress has been made in adopting a number of UN declarations, such as the Universal Declaration of Human Rights, and multilateral treaties that define basic human rights. The enforcement of human rights is much less well developed, but the rising level of awareness and of disapproval of violations on a global scale is having a positive impact. There are also many IGOs, such as the UN Human Rights Commission, and NGOs, such as Amnesty International, that work to improve human rights.

Chapter 18

Preserving and Enhancing the Global Commons

Comfort's in heaven, and we are on the earth.

Shakespeare, *Richard II*

Dear earth, I do salute thee with my hand.

Shakespeare, *Richard II*

Over the long haul of life on this planet, it is the ecologists, and not the book-keepers of business, who are the ultimate accountants.

Stewart L. Udall, U.S. secretary of the interior

Only in the last moment of human history has the delusion arisen that people can flourish apart from the rest of the living world.

Edward O. Wilson

Chapter Objectives

After completing this chapter, you should be able to:

- Explain the concept of sustainable development and consider whether it is possible or desirable.
- Understand the debate regarding environmental degradation and possible solutions.
- Describe the world's growing population and efforts to control population growth.
- Evaluate the global problems related to population and industrialization, including their causes.
- Discuss current efforts toward international environmental cooperation and speculate about their future role.

This chapter deals with ecological concerns and cooperation, but in many ways it is an extension of the human rights issues in chapter 17. One connection between the two chapters is the normative question, Should we care? Clearly, the view in this text is that we all should care. Self-interest compels us to attend to issues of the world's expanding population, the depletion of natural resources, the increase of chemical discharges into the environment, and the impact of these trends on the global biosphere. You will see that new approaches are needed because solutions attempted by single countries will be insufficient to solve the problems we humans face collectively. The issues discussed in this chapter are transnational problems. Therefore, their solution requires transnational programs achieved through international cooperation (Zurn, 1998; Bellany, 1997).

🌐 Toward Sustainable Development

Before taking up specific issues, it is helpful to understand how they are related. To do this, we will discuss two overarching controversies. One debate concerns the *ecological state of the world*. You will see presently that some analysts are truly alarmed about the future. Other observers believe that worries about the ecosphere are frequently overwrought. The second overarching controversy focuses on **sustainable development**. The issue is whether (or perhaps, *how*) the world can continue simultaneously to sustain development *and* to protect its environment. Another important term is **carrying capacity**, which is the largest number of humans that the Earth can sustain indefinitely at current rates of per capita consumption of natural resources.

THE ECOLOGICAL STATE OF THE WORLD

There is a book, *The State of the World*, published annually by the Worldwatch Institute.[1] Just as the U.S. president delivers an annual State of the Union address to Congress, each year this study assesses the ecological state of the world. We should follow its lead and regularly take stock of the Earth we all live on.

A good place to start is by considering the value of Earth's ecological systems. About $33 trillion was the figure one group of scientists came up with. Of course, it is impossible to measure precisely the financial value of the world's ecosystems. Still, there is some food for thought in the estimates of these 13 scientists, who assigned a dollar value to 17 different natural functions (such as water supply, soil formation, oxygen generation by plants) based on either the economic value they supply or what it would cost to replicate them artificially.[2] The estimates ranged from $16 trillion to $54 trillion, with $33 trillion as a median figure. This amount was about twice the size of the world GDP at the time the estimates were made. Whatever the exact amount, the key point is that in sheer dollars and cents, the globe's ecological systems are extraordinarily valuable.

A second preliminary point about the state of the world's ecological systems is to ask how important they are to us, irrespective of monetary value. The answer is that we cannot get along unless they are in reasonably good working order. Using medical analogies, one scientist refers to the biosphere as "the planet's life-support system," and another scientist called it humankind's "umbilical cord." He added, "Common sense and what little we have left of the wisdom of our ancestors tells us that if we ruin the Earth, we will suffer grievously."[3]

There is no controversy over the immense financial value of the biosphere and our dependence on it. Consensus ends, however, when we turn to the question of the current and future ecological state of the world. Here the range of opinions can be roughly divided into two camps: the environmental pessimists and the environmental optimists.

Environmental pessimists aptly describes one group of analysts who assess the state of the world. They believe that human activity is causing serious, in some cases irreversible, damage to the environment. The pessimists further worry that the environmental damage will increasingly cause human suffering: severe and devastating storms due to global warming, skin cancer due to ozone layer depletion, warfare over scarce natural resources, and other problems. This school of thought charges that those who ignore the environmental degradation that is already occurring and hope that new energy supplies and other scientific and technological innovation will make strong conservation unnecessary are akin to the proverbial ostrich that keeps its head planted firmly in the sand so that it can avoid seeing trouble.

Those who contribute to the annual *State of the World* volume are among the environmental pessimist group. The book warns (p. 3) that the alarming indications of environmental decline "are no less riveting than the drama of a surprise [terrorist] attack. Yet they alert the world to a danger less visible than terrorism but over the long term more serious." The commentary recognizes steps that have been made to address the situation, but it characterizes them as "too small, too slow, or too poorly rooted [in government policy]." UN Secretary-General Kofi Annan's commentary in his foreword to the *State of the World* places him among the ranks of environmental pessimists, as he tells readers (p. xvii) that ecologically "unsustainable approaches to economic progress remain pervasive" and warns of the "perilous state of our world" environment.

Some pessimistic analysts even foresee "environmental scarcities" as the cause of future warfare among states desperate to sustain their economies and quality of life. According to one study, scarcities of renewable resources are already causing some conflict in the world, and there may be "an upsurge of violence in the coming decades... that is caused or aggravated by environmental change" (Homer-Dixon, 1998:342).

Environmental optimists reject this gloomy view of the world and its future. Indeed, some optimists believe that the pessimists resemble Chicken Little, the protagonist in a children's story who was hit on the head by a shingle that had fallen off the barn roof. Convinced that he had been struck by a piece of the sky, Chicken Little panicked and raced around the barnyard crying, "The sky is falling, the sky is falling," thereby creating unfounded pandemonium. For example, one optimist chastises the ecology movement for promoting "green guilt" by "scaring and shaming people" and falsely contending that there is "little that we in the industrial world... do that... [is not] lethal, wicked, or both."[4]

Optimists say that the sky remains safely in its traditional location and that with reasonable prudence there is no need to fear for the future. They argue that we will be able to meet our needs and continue to grow economically through conservation, population restraints, and, most importantly, through technological innovation. They believe that new technology can find and develop oil fields. Synthetics can replace natural resources. Fertilizers, hybrid seeds, and

Environmental optimists charge that environmental pessimists are like Chicken Little, running around in a panic because of the false belief that the sky is falling. Environmental pessimists reply that the optimists are like the proverbial ostrich that sticks its head in the sand to avoid seeing danger. Until you are fully informed, perhaps the best approach is to be a wise environmental owl who carefully considers all the arguments and evidence. These particular owls were gathered in Banff, Alberta, Canada, in April 2002 to urge a meeting of the G-8 environment ministers (who were preparing for the G-8 summit meeting in June) to take steps to protect spotted owls.

(Continued on page 534)

World Ecological Regions

The world has many ecological areas. There is one issue that all these diverse areas share: the environmental health of each of them has been degraded and continues to be further threatened by human activity. Without international cooperation, it is improbable that the conundrum of sustainable development can be successfully resolved.

World Ecological Regions

Arctic and Subarctic Zone

- Ice Cap
- Tundra Province: moss-grass and moss-lichen tundra
- Tundra Altitudinal Zone: polar desert (no vegetation)
- Subarctic Province: evergreen forest, needleleaf taiga; mixed coniferous and small-leafed forest
- Subarctic Altitudinal Zone: open woodland; wooded tundra

Humid Temperate Zone

- Moderate Continental Province: mixed coniferous and broadleaf forest
- Moderate Continental Altitudinal Zone: coastal and alpine forest; open woodland
- Warm Continental Province: broadleaf deciduous forest
- Warm Continental Altitudinal Zone: upland broadleaf and alpine needleleaf forest
- Marine Province: lowland, west-coastal humid forest
- Marine Altitudinal Zone: humid coastal and alpine coniferous forest
- Humid Subtropical Province: broadleaf evergreen and broadleaf deciduous forest
- Humid Subtropical Altitudinal Zone: upland, subtropical broadleaf forest
- Prairie Province: tallgrass and mixed prairie
- Prairie Altitudinal Zone: upland mixed prairie and woodland
- Mediterranean Province: sclerophyll woodland, shrub, and steppe grass
- Mediterranean Altitudinal Zone: upland shrub and steppe

Humid Tropical Zone

- Savanna Province: seasonally dry forest; open woodland; tallgrass savanna
- Savanna Altitudinal Zone: open woodland steppe
- Rain Forest Province: constantly humid, broadleaf evergreen forest
- Rain Forest Altitudinal Zone: broadleaf evergreen and subtropical deciduous forest

Arid and Semiarid Zone

- Tropical/Subtropical Steppe Province: dry steppe (short grass), desert shrub, semidesert savanna
- Tropical/Subtropical Steppe Altitudinal Zone: upland steppe (short grass) and desert shrub
- Tropical/Subtropical Desert Province: hot, lowland desert in subtropical and coastal locations; xerophytic vegetation
- Tropical/Subtropical Desert Altitudinal Zone: desert shrub
- Temperate Steppe Province: medium to shortgrass prairie
- Temperate Steppe Altitudinal Zone: alpine meadow and coniferous woodland
- Temperate Desert Province: midlatitude rainshadow desert; desert shrub
- Temperate Desert Altitudinal Zone: extreme continental desert steppe; desert shrub, xerophytic vegetation, shortgrass steppe

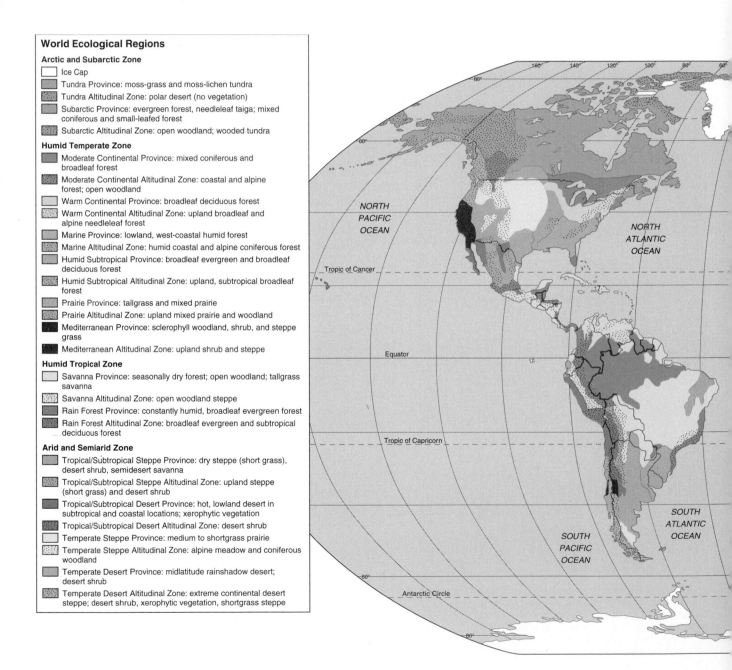

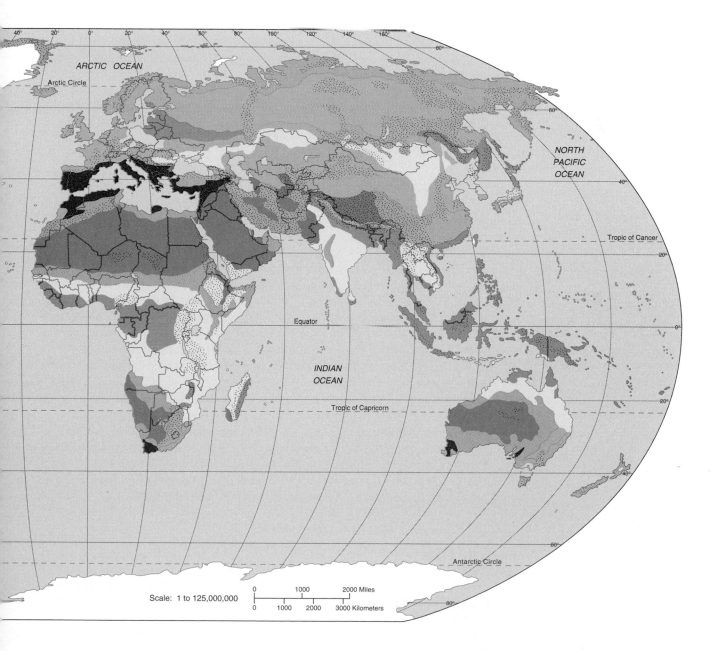

ARCTIC OCEAN

Arctic Circle

NORTH
PACIFIC
OCEAN

Tropic of Cancer

Equator

INDIAN
OCEAN

Tropic of Capricorn

Antarctic Circle

Scale: 1 to 125,000,000

0   1000   2000 Miles

0   1000   2000   3000 Kilometers

mechanization can increase acreage yields. Desalinization and weather control can meet water demands. Energy can be drawn from nuclear, solar, thermal, wind, and hydroelectric sources. In sum, according to one of the best-known optimists, economist Julian Simon (1994:297), not only do the scientific facts indicate that "the current gloom-and-doom about a 'crisis' of our environment is all wrong," but "almost every economic and social change or trend points in a positive direction." In fact Simon was so sure of his view, that in 1980 he made a $1,000 bet with an equally convinced pessimist, biologist Paul Ehrlich, author of *The Population Bomb*, about the prices of five basic metal ores in 1990. Ehrlich wagered that population demands would drive the prices up; Simon bet they would not. A decade and nearly a billion people later, the prices were all down. Ehrlich sent Simon a check.

It is important to note that most optimists do not dismiss the problems that the world faces. "Progress does not come automatically," Simon wrote (p. 306); "and my message is not complacency. In this I agree with the doomsayers—that our world needs the best efforts of all humanity to improve our lot." That effort will be provided, he continued, expressing his profound optimism, by our "ultimate resource... people—especially skilled, spirited, and hopeful young people... who will exert their wills and imaginations for their own benefit, and so inevitably they will benefit not only themselves but the rest of us as well."

SUSTAINABLE DEVELOPMENT

Industrialization and science have been two-edged swords in their relationship to the environment and the quality of human life. On the positive side, industrialization has vastly expanded global wealth, especially for the economically developed countries (EDCs). Science has created synthetic substances that enhance our lives; medicine has dramatically increased our chances of surviving infancy and has extended adult longevity. Yet, on the negative side, industry consumes natural resources and discharges pollutants into the air, ground, and water. Synthetic substances enter the food chain as carcinogens, refuse to degrade, and have other baleful effects. Decreased infant mortality rates and increased longevity have been major factors behind the world's skyrocketing population growth.

All these phenomena and trends, however, are part of modernization and are unlikely to be reversed. The dilemma is how to protect the biosphere and, at the same time, advance human socioeconomic development. This conundrum overarches specific issues such as population, habitat destruction, and pollution.

Pessimists would certainly see this concern as immediate and critical, but even most optimists would concede that the challenge would be vastly compounded if you were to increase the industrial production and standard-of-living levels of the 5.2 billion people who live in less developed countries (LDCs) in the South up to the levels enjoyed by the less than 1 billion people who reside in the North.

The Conundrum of Sustainable Development

Here is the problem you should ponder as you read the rest of this chapter: If the minority of the world's population who live in EDCs use most of the resources and create most of the pollution, how can the South develop economically without accelerating the ecological deterioration that already exists? Think about what consumption would be like if China were economically developed and the Chinese per capita consumption of petroleum and minerals and per capita CO_2 emissions were equal to that of Americans. Figure 2.3 on page 50 illustrates this. Given the fact that China's population is about four times that of the United States, a fully developed China with a per capita consumption equal to the current U.S. level would more than triple the two countries' combined petroleum consumption and their combined CO_2 emissions and it would more than quadruple their combined mineral consumption. Furthermore, if you were to bring the rest of the LDCs up to the U.S. level of resource use and emissions discharge, then you would hyperaccelerate the depletion of natural resources and the creation of pollution even more. Clearly, this is not acceptable.

Options for Sustainable Development

The question is, What to do? Apart from doing little or nothing and hoping for the best, there are two options. One option is to restrict or even halt economic development. The second option is to make the cooperative political and financial commitment to develop in the most environmentally safe way possible.

Severely Restricting Development Preserving the environment by consuming less is the first option. What is necessary, according to one analyst, is to institute "an integrated global program to set permissible levels" for consumption and emission, to mobilize huge financial resources for resource conservation and pollution control, and to create "effective international institutions with legally binding powers... to enforce [the] agreed-upon standards and financial obligations" (Johansen, 1994:381).

Objections to such solutions leap to mind. Are we, for instance, to suppress LDC development? If the Chinese do not acquire more cars, if Indians are kept in the fields instead of in factories, and if Africans continue to swelter in the summer's heat without air conditioners, then accelerated resource use and pollution discharges can be partly avoided. As we saw in chapter 15, however, the LDCs are demanding a global "New Deal," as Secretary-General Annan has called it, that will allow them to develop industrially and technologically.[5] The EDCs cannot "try to tell the people of Beijing that they can't buy a car or an air-conditioner" because they pollute, said one Chinese energy official; "it is just as hot in Beijing as it is in Washington."[6]

Another possible answer is for the people of the North to use dramatically fewer resources and to take the steps needed to reduce pollution drastically. Polls show that most people favor the theory of conservation and environmental protection. Yet practice indicates that, so far, most people are also unwilling to suffer a major reduction in their own conveniences or standards of living. Efforts to get more Americans to use mass transit, for example, have had very little success. Proposals to raise U.S. gasoline taxes (thereby reducing consumption and raising environmental protection revenue) have met with strong political opposition. Laws could be passed mandating compact cars, but Americans, it is generally agreed, would vote anyone out of office who threatened their SUVs and pickup trucks.

Those who advocate stringent programs believe that, eventually, we will be better off if we make the sacrifices necessary to restrain development and preserve the environment. In the end, one advocate asserts, "accepting and living by sufficiency rather than excess" will allow people to return to nonmaterialistic values "that give depth and bounty to human existence."

Paying the Price for Environmentally Responsible Development A second option is to pay the price to create and distribute technologies that will allow for a maximum balance between economic development and environmental protection. Without modern technology and the money to pay for it, China, for example, poses a serious environmental threat. China now stands second behind the United States in terms of national production of carbon dioxide emissions. A primary reason is that China generates most of its commercial power by burning coal, which is very polluting. In 2000, China consumed almost 1.2 billion tons of coal, nearly one-third of the world total. That, combined with the country's economic development, is a major reason why China's per capita CO_2 emission more than doubled between 1980 and 2000.

There are choices, such as generating more power by burning petroleum or utilizing hydroelectric energy. Each option, however, has trade-offs, which are often win-lose scenarios. For China, consuming more oil would require vastly expensive imports, which could affect the country's socioeconomic development. Increased oil consumption at the level China would need would also accelerate the depletion of the world's finite petroleum reserves. Moreover, the new oil fields that are being found often lie offshore, and drilling endangers the oceans.

A second possibility is using hydroelectricity to provide relatively nonpolluting energy. This requires the construction of dams that flood the surrounding countryside, displace its residents, and spoil the pristine beauty of the river valley downstream. China, for example, is trying to ease its energy crunch and simultaneously develop clean hydroelectric power by building the massive Three Gorges Dam and hydroelectric project on the Yangtze River. The engineering project rivals the Great Wall of China in scope. It is officially projected to cost $24 billion, but most analysts place the real cost at as much as three times that figure. When completed, the project will vastly increase the availability of electric power to rural provinces by generating 18,200 megawatts of electricity without burning highly polluting coal. The dam will also help stem floods that have often caused catastrophic damage downstream. To accomplish these benefits, however, the dam will create a reservoir almost 400 miles long, thereby flooding 425 square miles of fertile land, inundating 1,500 factories, some 160 towns, 16 archaeological sites, and submerging what many consider one of the most scenic natural areas in the world. The huge reservoir that will eventually be created is expected to force an estimated 1.1 million people from their homes. Moreover, a collapse of the dam from structural failure, earthquake or other natural disaster, or military attack could cause a flood of unimaginable proportions. Adding a bit of reality to this horrific possibility are worries about the quality of concrete and other materials being used by cash-poor China and the discovery in 2001 of cracks in parts of the dam that have been completed. Thus, the Three Gorges project is an almost perfect illustration of the difficulty of sustainable development. Even though the project will ease some environmental problems (in this case, coal burning) it will also have an adverse impact on people and on the environment.

Even if you can cut such Gordian knots, you will encounter other problems: the short-term costs of environmental protection in terms of taxes to pay for government programs; the high costs of products that are produced in an environmentally acceptable way and that are themselves environmentally safe; and the expense of disposing of waste in an ecologically responsible manner.

Moreover, since the LDCs are determined to develop economically, yet must struggle to pay the costs of environmentally sound progress, the North will have to extend significant aid to the South to help it develop in a relatively safe way. Money is needed to create nonpolluting energy resources, to install pollution control devices in factories, and to provide many other technologies. The costs will be huge, approaching, in some estimates, $20 billion a year. Billions more are needed each year to help the LDCs stem their—and the world's—spiraling population.

Is the North willing to pay this price? Polls show that people in many countries are concerned about global warming, ozone layer destruction, deforestation, wildlife destruction, and acid rain. Cross-national polls also regularly find that a majority of respondents say that their governments should do more to protect their country's environment and also to be involved in the global environmental effort. Yet surveys additionally find that a majority of citizens think that their tax burdens are already too heavy and are unwilling to support large expenditures on environmental programs.

China is trying to achieve sustainable development by building the immense Three Gorges Dam project to meet the country's energy needs and improve its poor environmental conditions. When complete in 2009, the project will be capable of generating 18,200 megawatts of electric power, more than enough to supply power to New York City and Long Island combined. Yet it has many drawbacks. More than 1 million people are being relocated, often against their will. Also the 370-mile-long, nearly 600-foot deep reservoir behind the dam will inundate part of an archeological area that is the cradle of Chinese civilization and will also fill up the three gorges, which are considered by many to be some of the world's most beautiful scenery. It is possible to get a glimpse of that natural splendor in this photograph of a small boat on the Yangtze River in the Wu Xia Gorge, the middle gorge of the three.

One illustrative poll asked Americans if they would pay $200 in extra taxes to clean up the environment. A laudable 70 percent said "yes." That was the limit of the majority's financial commitment, though. When the next question raised the cleanup bill to an extra $500, only 44 percent said "yes." This resistance will work against any attempt to amass the funds that need to be spent internationally to help the LDCs simultaneously develop and protect the environment.[7]

The Sustainable Development Debate: What to Believe "Help!" you might exclaim at this point. "Is it necessary to live in unheated tents and abandon our cars to keep the sky from falling?" Fortunately, the answer is "Probably not." Unfortunately, that does not get us off the hook, because the problems will not disappear if we ignore them. Addressing any problem requires two basic steps. The first is recognizing that there is an issue. That has been accomplished. The convening by the UN of two "Earth Summits," in 1992 and 2002, is one indication of a general agreement that sustainable development must be addressed. The second step is to decide what to do. The answers are not easy. Indeed, sustainable development is "a Herculean task," as Canadian diplomat Maurice Strong, the secretary-general of the 1992 Earth Summit, put it.[8] Some of the impediments to progress that Ambassador Strong faced in 1992 and that also confronted the delegates to Earth Summit II in 2002 are addressed in the accompanying box, The Earth Summits and Sustainable Development.

We will now turn our attention to the specific issues surrounding the state of the biosphere and its inhabitants, and the possibility of achieving international cooperation toward sustainable development. We will first consider population. Then we

THE EARTH SUMMITS AND SUSTAINABLE DEVELOPMENT

The convening in 1992 of the UN Conference on Environment and Development (UNCED) meeting in Rio de Janeiro symbolized the growing concern with the environment and how to achieve sustainable development. Popularly dubbed the Earth Summit, the conference was attended by 178 countries and 115 heads of state. Some 8,000 journalists covered the proceedings, and 15,000 representatives of NGOs and national citizens' groups flocked to Brazil (Willets, 1996). By its end, the conference produced Agenda 21 (an 800-page document covering 112 topics that constitute a nonbinding blueprint for sustainable development in the twenty-first century) and two treaties (the Biodiversity and the Global Warming Conventions).

Beyond this simple recounting of the facts, the Earth Summit illustrates the often-divisive politics of environmental protection (Porter & Brown, 1996). In particular, the North and the South were at odds on many issues. The EDCs objected to and were able to defeat efforts by the LDCs to force the EDCs to set binding timetables to cut down on the use of fossil fuels and to reduce emissions of carbon dioxide and other gases that contribute to global warming.

For its part, the South resisted and was able to defeat restrictions on the use of forest resources proposed by the North. "Forests are clearly a sovereign resource—not like atmosphere and oceans, which are a global commons," said Malaysia's chief negotiator. "We cannot allow forests to be taken up in global forums."[1]

Funding was another issue that split North and South. Many environmental programs are expensive, and estimates at the time were that the LDCs would annually need $125 billion for new environmental programs. The South pressed for the North to make a substantial commitment to meeting that need; the North resisted. "We do not have an open pocketbook," President George H. W. Bush observed.[2] In the end, EDCs committed to an additional $2 billion in extra funding in theory, but the reality four years after the conference was that aid earmarked for environmental program had increased only about $1 billion.

In the end, 153 countries signed both the Biodiversity and the Global Warming Conventions, and other countries signed one or the other (Swanson, 1999). Even though neither treaty created legally binding mandates, President George H. W. Bush attached a reservation to his signature of the Global Warming Convention, saying that the United States would not be bound by the timetables for reducing greenhouse gas emissions. He also refused to sign the Biodiversity Convention on the grounds that it did not protect intellectual property rights in biotechnology. Less than a year later, a new U.S. president, Bill Clinton, marked the annual Earth Day, April 21, by signing the biodiversity pact and rescinding the U.S. reservation to the timetables in the Global Warming Convention. He was succeeded, however, by George W. Bush, and in the spirit of "like father, like son," the younger Bush has taken a skeptical view of global warming treaties that

will turn to concerns over such resources as minerals, forests, wildlife, and water. Last, the chapter will take up environmental issues, including pollution of the ground, water, air, and upper atmosphere.

Sustainable Development: Issues and Cooperation

Throughout history, humans have taken their world for granted. We have assumed that it will always be here, that it will yield the necessities of life, and that it will absorb what is discarded. For several millennia this assumption proved justifiable. The Earth was generally able to sustain its population and replenish itself.

Now, the exploding human population and technology have changed this. Not only are there five times as many people as there were just a little more than 150 years ago, but our technological progress has multiplied our per capita resource consumption and our per capita waste and pollutant production. Technological wizardry may bring solutions, as the optimists predict, but such solutions are uncertain; for now the reality is that the world faces a crisis of carrying capacity—the potential has no doubt made his father proud. A further discussion of President G. W. Bush and global warming is in the box, From Kyoto to Johannesburg and Beyond.

Was the Earth Summit a success? At the time, Norway's prime minister observed, "We owe the world to be frank about what we have achieved in Rio." That is, she said, "progress in many fields, too little progress in most fields, and no progress at all in some fields."[3] Certainly, it is important to note that the Earth Summit was a step forward. Not long ago, no one paid any attention to the environment, much less did anything about it. In June 1992 representatives of almost every country on Earth gathered to affirm their support of sustainable development. Principles were established on many issues and a few commitments were made.

The lack of sufficient commitments has equaled a lack of sufficient progress, and that occasioned a move to hold a second Earth Summit. As Secretary-General Kofi Annan (2002) explained it, "The... conceptual breakthrough achieved at Rio has not... proved decisive enough to break with business as usual. As the global community prepares for the World Summit on Sustainable Development in Johannesburg in September 2002," he continued, "it is too late... to avoid the conclusion that there is a gap between the goals and the promises set out in Rio and the daily reality [of what has been accomplished.]"

The conference, dubbed Earth Summit II, was predicted to be the largest UN gathering ever, with more than 100 heads of government present, and with 60,000 delegates attending either the official conference or the parallel NGO gathering. Preliminary indications were that the meeting would find itself embroiled in the same North-South disputes that bedeviled Earth Summit I. For their parts the United States and some other EDCs were unwilling to commit to what they saw as lofty rhetoric and attempts to obligate the governments of the North to vast amounts of aid. Instead, the U.S. representative called for more local efforts and for developing programs by seeking private investment capital for environmental improvement. As the U.S. delegate to preparatory talks in Bali, Indonesia, put it, "Johannesburg... should produce compelling results, not merely high-sounding rhetoric. The world community does not need to negotiate new goals or create new global bureaucracies." Instead, she continued, the best approach is through "effective domestic policies" achieved by "building and nurturing local, national, and international public-private partnerships. Through this approach, sustainable development can be achieved in a way that benefits both developing and developed nations."[4]

Others disagree with this somewhat "do-it-yourself" approach to sustainable development. "It's a battle, a conflict of interest between developed and developing countries," observed Emil Salim, the former Indonesian environment minister who chaired the Bali talks. NGO representatives were less diplomatic. "The U.S. and its friends might as well come from Mars for all they care about the future of our planet," complained the head of one such NGO.[5]

of no longer being able to sustain its population in an adequate manner or being able to absorb its waste. To put this as an equation:

$$\text{Exploding population} \times \text{Spiraling per capita resource consumption} \times \text{Mounting waste and pollutant production} = \text{Potential catastrophe}$$

POPULATION ISSUES AND COOPERATION

Identifying the population problem is simple: There are too many of us, and we are reproducing too quickly. Here are some amazing and, to most people, disturbing, statistics. Stop and think about what they mean for the future.

On Tuesday, October 12, 1999, the population of the world passed the 6 billion mark. That is a stunning number. It took all of human history before 1804 for the population to reach 1 billion. Adding the next billion people took just 123 years. Now we are expanding by 1 billion people about every 13 years. Of all the people who have ever lived, an incredible 10 percent are alive right now. One country, China, with its 1.3 billion inhabitants, has more people than there were humans in the entire world less than 200 years ago. And just since the birth in 1875 of the world's oldest living person, Elizabeth "Ma Pampo" Israel of Dominica, the world population has nearly quadrupled. At its current growth rate of 78 million per year, the world is annually adding a number of people equal to the combined populations of Argentina, Belgium, and Canada. In only the time it takes you to complete this course, assuming a 15-week semester, the world's population expansion equaled the number of people in Finland. Indeed, by tomorrow the number of new people in the world will be larger than the current populations of more than a dozen of the world's smaller countries. Almost thirty percent of the world population is less than 16 years old. Most of these children will soon become adults and become parents.

Projections of future population trends are not reassuring either. According to the United Nations Population Fund (UNFPA), the world population will reach the 10 billion mark in 2071 and will not stabilize until it reaches about 10.7 billion people in 2200. Thus the population continues to expand rapidly, and the 1999 milestone of 6 billion people means a doubling of the Earth's population in less than 40 years. Such numbers have convinced the executive director of the UNFPA that population growth is a "crisis" that "heightens the risk of future economic and ecological catastrophe."[9]

To the extent that anything in the UNFPA data and estimates can be considered good news, it is that the rate of growth has slowed somewhat. As recently as 1994, the population was expanding at 94 million a year, and the UN was estimating that it would reach 11.6 billion by 2150. Even this bit of good news about the decline in the overall growth rate is dampened, however, by the fact that the fastest population increases are occurring in the very poorest countries (the least developed countries, LLDCs), which often are not able to adequately support their people, and whose economic development is further retarded by the burden of the increased population. Moreover, as one demographer commented about the easing of the population growth rate, "The difference is comparable to a tidal wave surging toward one of our coastal cities. Whether the tidal wave is 80 feet or 100 feet high, the impact will be similar."[10] Population increases are shown in Figure 18.1 and the following map.

Causes of the Population Problem

There are several causes of the rapidly expanding population. *Fewer deaths* is one. Infant mortality has decreased; adult longevity has increased. These two factors combine to mean that even in areas where the birthrate declines, the population growth rate sometimes continues to accelerate. For example, the birthrate in the LLDCs declined from 45 births per 1,000 population in 1960 to 29 in 2000. But during the same period, advances in health and other conditions decreased the crude death rate (annual death of people per thousand) from 22 to 11. Children were more likely to live, with the child mortality rate (annual deaths per thousand children through age 5) dropping from 242 to a better, if still tragic, 115. Moreover, life expectancy rose from 44 years to 59 years. The net result is that the rapidly declining death rates have more than offset the more slowly declining birthrates and resulted in an annual population growth of 2.7 percent. This means that the population of the LLDCs jumped 250 percent, from 1 billion in 1960 to 2.5 billion in 2000.

The huge population base of 6.3 billion is another reason for the alarming population growth. This problem is one of mathematics. Although the average woman has 45 percent fewer babies now than in 1970, there are so many more women in their childbearing years that the number of babies born continues to go up. During the next decade, some 3 billion women will enter their childbearing years. At the current fertility rate, these women will have 8.1 billion children, of which 7.5 billion

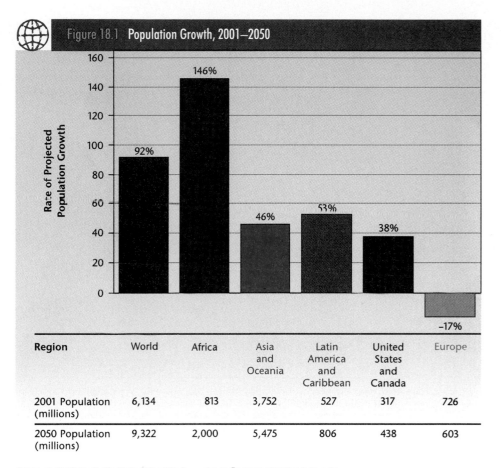

Figure 18.1 Population Growth, 2001–2050

Region	World	Africa	Asia and Oceania	Latin America and Caribbean	United States and Canada	Europe
2001 Population (millions)	6,134	813	3,752	527	317	726
2050 Population (millions)	9,322	2,000	5,475	806	438	603

Data source: The State of the World's Population at http://www.unfpa.org. Percentage calculations by the author.

World population growth is not even. The burden of additional people will fall most heavily on the regions with a predominance of less developed countries, which have scant resources to support their burgeoning populations.

will live to at least age 5. Happily, most of this tidal wave of children will grow up. When they do, most of them will also one day become parents. That will be a more joyous event for them, but it will not be a blessed event for the embattled ecosphere.

There is a clear relationship between poverty and birthrates. Ninety-five percent of global population growth is in the LDCs. In 2000, the fertility rate in EDCs was 1.7. In the LDCs it was 70 percent higher at 2.9. The rate in the poorest countries is even higher. The fertility rate in sub-Saharan Africa is 5.3, more than triple the EDC rate. With a fertility rate of 3.1, India alone accounted for more than 20 percent of the world's population growth between 1980 and 2000, and at current rates will surpass the population of China (fertility rate: 1.9) by 2040 with about 1.5 billion people.

How does one explain the link between population and poverty? One commonly held view is that overpopulation causes poverty. This view reasons that with too many people, especially in already poor countries, there are too few resources, jobs, and other forms of wealth to go around. Perhaps, but that is only part of the problem, because it is also true that poverty *causes* overpopulation (Catley-Carlson & Outlaw, 1998). The LLDCs tend to have the most labor-intensive economies, which means that children are economically valuable because they help their parents farm or, when they are somewhat older, provide cheap labor in mining and manufacturing processes. As a result, cultural attitudes in many countries have come to

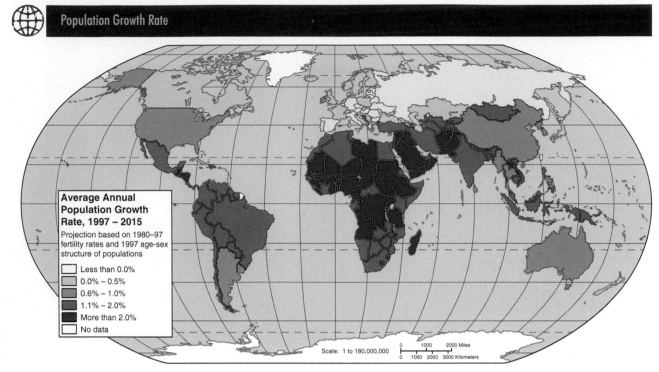

Average Annual Population Growth Rate, 1997 – 2015

Projection based on 1980–97 fertility rates and 1997 age-sex structure of populations

- Less than 0.0%
- 0.0% – 0.5%
- 0.6% – 1.0%
- 1.1% – 2.0%
- More than 2.0%
- No data

Scale: 1 to 180,000,000

0   1000   2000 Miles

0   1000   2000   3000 Kilometers

The world's population approximately quadrupled during the twentieth century. We continue to strain the Earth's resources by adding about 1 billion people every 15 years. Although Figure 18.1 and this map use slightly different data parameters, they are complementary. What you can see in this map is a graphic representation that the growth of population is not evenly spread around the globe. The most rapid growth is in less developed countries of the South, which will struggle to house, educate, feed, and otherwise care for their burgeoning populations. At the same time, many of the economically developed countries of the North are near or even below the zero population growth rate. For these countries, an aging population will present a different set of challenges than face the LDCs with their massive number of children.

reflect economic utility. Having a large family is also an asset in terms of social standing in many societies with limited economic opportunities.

Furthermore, women in LDCs have fewer opportunities to limit the number of children they bear. Artificial birth control methods and counseling services are less readily available in these countries. Another fact is that women in LDCs are less educated than are women in EDCs. It is therefore harder to convey birth control information, especially written information, to women in LDCs. Additionally, women in LDCs have fewer opportunities than do women in EDCs to gain paid employment and to develop status roles beyond that of motherhood. The inadequacies in financial, educational, and contraceptive opportunities for women are strongly correlated to high fertility rates. One way to see relationships is to consider Figure 18.2, which compares Malawi and the United States.

The International Response to the Population Problem

The world has generally concluded that something must be done to stem population growth. The only option, other than letting disproportionate numbers of poor children die in infancy and allowing impoverished adults to die in their forties and fifties, is to lower the average fertility rate. That has already begun, with the average global rate down from 4.9 in 1970 to 2.7 in 1998. The goal is 2.1, which is considered the stable replacement rate, although as infant mortality and crude death rates continue to drop, it may even be necessary to reach 2.0 or slightly lower to stabilize the population.

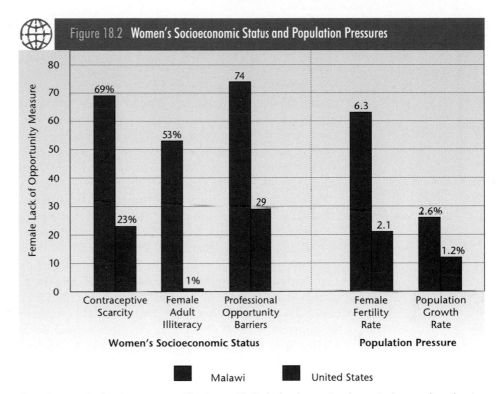

Figure 18.2   Women's Socioeconomic Status and Population Pressures

Malawi   United States

Notes: Contraceptive Scarcity: percentage of females age 15–49 who (or whose partners) are not using some form of contra-ception; Female illiteracy: percentage of age 15 or more; Professional Opportunity Barriers: degree of lack of equality in political, professional, and economic opportunities that make up the gender empowerment measure (GEM) of the UNDP; Female Fertility Rate: number of children the average woman will have during her childbearing years; Growth Rate: annual growth population data on scale and converted to a 100 base for comparison.

Data sources: World Bank (2001); UNDP (1999, 2001).

There is a strong relationship between the lack of availability to women of contraceptive programs, ed-ucation, and professional and other economic opportunities (represented by the three categories to the left) and upward population pressures (represented by the two categories to the right.) Notice that compared to the United States, the measures for Malawi related to the lack of opportunities for women in the three left categories are reflected by greater upward population pressures in the two categories on the right. The evidence indicates that the best way to control population growth is to enhance wom-en's opportunities.

While the population problem has been building up momentum for almost two centuries, efforts to deal with the issue through international cooperation are relatively recent. The growth of cooperative efforts is symbolized by the establishment of numerous international governmental and nongovernmental organizations (IGOs, NGOs) concerned with the issue, and by a series of world conferences on population.

Unfortunately, not all the news about the effort to constrain population growth is good. Funding to keep programs going is vital, and the downtrend in the foreign aid offered by many EDCs is imperiling population programs. The U.S. Congress, for example, cut or held up funding to IGOs in an attempt to make the Clinton adminis-tration agree to include language that would bar any of the appropriated funds going to any agency that supports abortions overseas or counsels women about their avail-ability. Once President Bush took office in 2001, Congress no longer had to pressure a pro-choice president. Only three days after taking office in 2001, President Bush signed an executive order barring the payment of U.S. funds to the UNFPA or another other IGO involved in family planning if they "perform or actively promote" abortions. "It is my conviction that taxpayer funds should not be used to pay for abortions or advocate or actively promote abortion, either here or abroad," Bush explained.[11] As for UNFPA, it takes the position that it does not encourage abortions as part of family planning, but that it does want to ensure that women who make that choice can do so safely. As Thoraya Ahmed Obaid, the Saudi Arabian executive director of the agency puts it, "The basic right is for women not to die while they are having a baby."[12]

International Organizations and the Population Problem   The effort to control global population growth is led appropriately by the United Nations. There are a number of associated organizations and programs within the UN's purview. Of these, the UNFPA, a subsidiary organ of the UN General Assembly, is the largest. The agency began operations in 1969 and focuses on promoting family planning services and improving reproductive health in LDCs. During its three decades of operation, the UNFPA has provided a total of over $4.6 billion to support population programs in the vast majority of the world's countries. The organization is funded through voluntary contributions, and in 2000 had a budget of $256 million donated by about 95 countries. This aid currently accounts for about 12 percent of the world's population assistance to LDCs. Beyond that, the agency helps coordinate the programs of other efforts by IGOs, NGOs, and national governments.

Within the UN group of associated agencies, the work of the UNFPA is supported by the United Nations Children's Fund (UNICEF), the World Health Organization (WHO), and other IGOs. These efforts are further supplemented by and often coordinated with NGOs such as the International Planned Parenthood Federation (IPPF). This British-based organization, which was founded in 1952, operates its own international family planning programs and also links the individual planned parenthood organizations of about 150 countries. The IPPF is funded by these national organizations, by private contributions, and by donations from approximately 20 countries. Like a number of other IGOs in the population control and reproductive health area, the IPPF has consultative status with the UN.

World Population Conferences   The rapidly rising global population also led the UN to begin the World Population Conference series to focus world attention on the issue, to seek agreement on solutions, and to galvanize international cooperative efforts to address the issue. There have been three conferences, the first two of which met in Bucharest (1974) and in Mexico City (1984). The most recent of these, the 1994 **United Nations Conference on Population and Development (UNCPD)** met in Cairo, Egypt. It was organized by UNFPA, and brought together delegates from over 170 countries and a large number of NGOs. The session focused on population control and on reproductive health. Each year, for example, about 413,000 women (99 percent of whom live in LDCs) die from complications of pregnancy and childbirth.

Abortion presents a particularly emotional issue for both its supporters and opponents. Only about 2 percent of all countries ban abortion to protect a woman's life, but beyond that, whether and under what circumstances abortions are legal varies greatly. Abortions to protect a women's physical or mental heath are legally available in 90 percent of the EDCs but in only about 50 percent of LDCs. Among the LDCs, China and India both permit abortions, giving about 75 percent of the world's women access to abortion.

Abortions that are unsafe, either in countries where abortion is illegal or severely restricted or in countries with an inadequate health care system, are a major threat to women's health. The World Health Organization estimates that at least 75,000 women a year die due to unsafe abortions, accounting for about 13 percent of the maternal mortality rate. There are estimates that in some countries, which both restrict abortions and are exceptionally poor, over half of all maternal mortality is the result of illegal abortions.

Such harsh realities turned the attention of the 1994 conference to a third focus, which was, in the words of the executive director on UNFPA, "gender equality and empowering women to control their lives, especially their reproductive lives."[13] As such, an important, if informal, role of the UNCPD was to bring women together internationally and to promote a shared consciousness of gender as a transnational focus of political identity and activity. "Women have dreams at every level," commented a Pakistani delegate; "when an opportunity [such as the Cairo conference] comes, they take it." A Chinese delegate agreed that she had become more aware that "women all over the world have a lot of things in common."[14]

While the related goals of restraining population growth, improving reproductive health, and empowering women were hardly debatable, how to achieve these ends sparked considerable controversy at the conference. The dispute centered on the charge that the conference was moving toward supporting social and even legal pressure on people to limit the number of children they had, advocating abortion, and promoting other practices to which the critics objected. Several predominantly Muslim countries refused to attend the conference, and the Sudanese government charged that it would result in "the spread of immoral and irreligious ideas."[15]

The Roman Catholic Church was also critical. Following the conference, Pope John Paul II wrote to the head of the UNFPA that "parenthood must be free from social and legal coercion" and asserted that the "Cairo draft document ignores the rights of the unborn." The pope additionally emphasized his opposition to methods of "finality," such as sterilization and abortion, calling them a "violation of human rights, especially [those] of women." As an alternate approach, the pontiff contended that the world would be better off if societies promoted development that improved the lot of families, rather than denying the right to be born.

The Vatican's view drew furious criticism. For one, Prime Minister Gro Harlem Brundtland of Norway, who has since become head of WHO, charged that "morality becomes hypocrisy if it means accepting mothers' suffering or dying in connection with unwanted pregnancies and illegal abortions and unwanted children."[16]

The result of all this was a series of compromises. The document's language on promoting safe abortion was qualified by adding the phrase, "in circumstances in which abortion is legal," and it specified, "In no case should abortion be promoted as a method of family planning." The 1994 Cairo conference unanimously approved a "Program of Action" calling for spending $5.7 billion annually by the year 2000 on international programs to foster family planning. As has been the case with many such calls to action and financial commitment, the funds have not met the goals. At first, funding increased nicely, rising from $1.3 billion in 1993, the year before the conference, to $2 billion in 1996. Then progress stopped. Funding moved little in current dollars and fell in real dollars (adjusted for inflation), leaving the $2.2 billion spent in 2000 some 61 percent short of the goal set in 1994. Nevertheless, the conference, and even the objections of the pope and others, served at the very least to heighten awareness and to initiate a global debate about how to address the population problem and the closely associated issue of women's reproductive health.

Whether the programs being developed are engendered by IGOs and NGOs or by global conferences such as the UNCPD, there are two basic approaches to reducing the birthrate. One is social, the other is economic.

Did You Know That:
A British birth-control advocacy group outraged many in France by offering low-cost vasectomies to Frenchmen. Because of France's law barring "self-mutilation" and cultural attitudes, only 1 percent of men there are sterilized. The Paris metro and French newspapers refused to carry ads for the service, and some press stories treated it as one more Anglo-Saxon attempt to neuter France. Word got out anyway, and the first Frenchman to take advantage of the offer reported, "I feel great."

Social Approaches to Reducing the Birthrate One approach to reducing the birthrate involves social programs such as providing information about birth control and encouragement to practice it. The social approach also involves making birth control devices and pills, sterilization, and, in some cases, abortion programs available. At the national level, many LDCs have made strong efforts, given their limited financial resources. In Thailand, for instance, 72 percent of all couples practice contraception (the contraceptive prevalence rate).

These national efforts are supported by the UNFPA, other IGOs, and NGOs, and their combined efforts have had an impact. During the early 1960s, the contraceptive prevalence rate in the LDCs was only 9 percent. Now about 49 percent of couples in LDCs practice birth control. This contraceptive prevalence rate falls off drastically in the least developed countries (LLDCs), where it is only 23 percent. There are at least 15 countries in which the rate is a mere 10 percent or less.

Economic Approaches to Reducing the Birthrate Population growth can also be slowed through economic approaches. The evidence that poverty causes population increases means that if the poverty gap both between countries and within countries is narrowed, then declining birthrates will be among the benefits. Therefore, efforts must be made to develop the LDCs and to equalize income distribution within countries if population is to be controlled. One economic approach to population control is to improve the status of women, because women who are more fully and equally employed have fewer children.

Those who study population dynamics have found that advancing the economic and educational opportunities available to women needs to be an integral part of population control. This realization was one of the factors that led the UN to designate 1975 as International Women's Year and to kick off the Decade for Women. That year the UN also convened the first World Conference on Women (WCW). These initiatives were followed in 1976 by the establishment of the UN Development Fund for Women (UNIFEM, after its French acronym). The Fund works through 10 regional offices to improve the living standards of women in LDCs by providing technical and financial support to improve the entry of women into business, scientific, and technical careers, and other key areas. UNIFEM also strives to incorporate

Perhaps the best way to decrease population growth is to provide women with increased educational and occupational opportunities. The international effort to promote these is symbolized by this picture of a Palestinian woman in Gaza reading *We Mean Business*, by Susan Norman (Boston: Longman Publishing, 1993). The woman is in a facility run by the White Ribbon Alliance, a UN-affiliated NGO that works to make pregnancy and childbirth safe for all women and infants.

women into the international and national planning and administration of development programs and to ensure that the issues of particular concern to women such as food, security, human rights, and reproductive health are kept on the global agenda. The UN also established the International Research and Training Institute for the Advancement of Women with the task of carrying out research, training, and information activities related to women and the development process. Headquartered in the Dominican Republic, the institute conducts research on the barriers that impede the progress of women in social, economic, and political development.

RESOURCE ISSUES AND COOPERATION

Recent decades have witnessed increased warnings that we are using our resources too quickly. Most studies by individual analysts, governmental commissions, and private organizations have concluded that the rates at which humans are depleting energy, mineral, forest, land, wildlife, fishery, and water resources are matters calling for a level of concern ranging from caution to serious alarm.

Petroleum, Natural Gas, and Minerals

The supply of oil, gas, and mineral resources is one area of concern. At the forefront of these worries are the cost and supply of energy resources. The energy issue has such immense economic and environmental ramifications that it set off a war when Iraq invaded Kuwait in 1990.

World energy needs are skyrocketing. Global commercial energy production increased roughly 33 percent between 1980 and 2000. The burning of fossil fuels (coal, oil, gas) accounts for about 85 percent of output. There has been a growth of geothermal and hydroelectric power generation, but together they still account for only 8 percent of world energy production, with nuclear power plants producing the remaining 7 percent of all commercial energy. Of the various sources, nuclear energy production by far increased the most rapidly, growing more than tenfold over the last two decades.

At one time the world had perhaps 2.3 trillion barrels of oil beneath its surface. More than half of that has already been consumed. Projections of future use are tricky, as are estimates for the discovery of future reserves. Still, it is clear that the supply of petroleum is running out. Current estimates of all known crude oil reserves amount to about 1 trillion barrels. The current rate of global consumption, about 25 billion barrels a year, means that the supply will be exhausted in approximately 40 years.

The story for natural gas is nearly the same. New discoveries, enhanced extraction methods, and other factors may have a peripheral impact on the timing, but the bottom line is that by mid-century, the supplies of petroleum and natural gas will have been depleted.

Coal is another and abundant energy source that will last almost 500 years at current consumption rates, but it is a major pollutant if not controlled by expensive technology. The development of hydroelectric power is attractive in some ways, but it is expensive (albeit increasingly less so) to develop. Moreover, as noted earlier, damming rivers creates environmental and social problems. Nuclear power is yet another alternative, and some countries have become reliant on it. France and Lithuania lead in this category, each generating about 75 percent of its commercial electricity by nuclear power. They are exceptions, however. Only 32 countries generate nuclear power, and on average it amounts to only 27 percent of their total commercial energy production. Additionally, there are high costs and obvious hazards to nuclear power. Some people advocate developing wind, solar, geothermal, and other such sources of power. So far, though, cost, production capacity, and other factors

Did You Know That:
The world's first oil well was drilled in 1959 in Titusville, Pennsylvania. Depending on its quality as a lubricant, oil in those days sold for between $20 to $30 a barrel, which was still about its average price in the 1990s. Adjusted for inflation, the 1859 price is approximately equal to $2,000 a barrel today.

have limited the application of these energy sources and will continue to do so unless there are major technological breakthroughs.

Dealing with the supply and demand for energy also requires understanding of use patterns. The vast majority of all energy is used by the EDCs. Most of the growing demand for energy, by contrast, is a result of increased needs by the countries of the South. During the period 1980–1998, the energy consumption of EDCs increased 26 percent, while the LDCs' energy use increased 47 percent. Among other things, this means that LDC development without proper energy conservation and other environmental safeguards is a serious concern.

The supply of fossil fuel resources has the highest political profile, but there are also many other minerals being rapidly depleted. Based on world reserves and world use, some minerals that are in particularly short supply (and estimates of the year that the Earth's supply will be exhausted) include copper (2056), lead (2041), mercury (2077), tin (2053), and zinc (2042). Moreover, "current use" may well skyrocket as current LDCs develop, and that eventuality would considerably decrease the projected depletion years listed here.

The resource puzzle, as mentioned, is how, all at the same time, to (1) maintain the industrialized countries' economies and standards of living, (2) promote economic development in the South (which will consume increased energy and minerals), and (3) manage the problems of resource depletion and environmental damage involved in energy and mineral production and use. If, for instance, we were able to develop the South to the same economic level as the North, if the LDCs' energy-use patterns were the same as the North's currently are, and if the same energy resource patterns that exist now persisted, then petroleum reserves would soon be dry. Natural gas and many other minerals would quickly follow oil into the museum of geological history.

Forests and Land

For many who will read this book, the trees that surround them and the very land on which they stand will hardly seem like natural resources and will certainly not seem to be endangered. That is not the case. There are serious concerns about the depletion of the world's forests and the degradation of the land.

Forest Depletion The depletion of forests and their resources concerns many analysts. Data compiled by the UN Food and Agriculture Organization (FAO) and other sources indicates that the increase in world population and, to a lesser degree, economic development are destroying the world's forests. Some 1 billion people depend on wood as an energy source, and many forests have disappeared because of such domestic needs as cooking and heating. Forests are also being cleared to make room for farms and grazing lands. Forests and woodland still cover about 25 percent of the Earth's land area. Once, however, they occupied 48 percent of the land area, and tree cover is declining by about one percent every three years. The annual global trade in lumber is about $110 billion, and poor countries are cutting their trees and exporting the wood to earn capital to pay off their international debt and to finance economic development. Forests are also being drowned by hydroelectric projects and being strip-mined for minerals. Acid rain and other environmental attacks increase the toll on trees. Whatever the cause, the result is that some 40,000 square miles of forest are being lost every year. This is a loss roughly equivalent to clear-cutting both Belgium and Ireland. Reforestation replaces only about 10 percent of the loss.

Some areas have already suffered almost total devastation. Madagascar has lost 90 percent of its original vegetation; significant stretches of China, East Africa, Malaysia, and Brazil have been nearly denuded of their forests. The tropical forests,

Each year the world's forests shrink as trees are cut and land is cleared. It is easy to decry this and to advocate a halt to forest destruction, but what does one say to this poor Indonesian farmer standing amid the ruins of the forest he burned to start his farm? "There's no other way of clearing the land," he said. "I've got to grow crops," he might have added, "so that I can earn a living and support my family."

which account for over 80 percent of all forest losses, are of particular concern. Fifty years ago, 12 percent of the Earth's land surface was covered by tropical forest; now just 6 percent is. The Amazon River Basin's tropical forest in Brazil and the surrounding countries is an especially critical issue. This ecosystem is by far the largest of its kind in the world, covering 2.7 million square miles, about the size of the 48 contiguous U.S. states. The expanding populations and economic needs of the region's countries have exerted great pressure on the forest. For example, the Amazon Basin has recently been losing 25,000 square miles (an area about the size of West Virginia) of forest every two years, a rate of more than 15 acres a minute.

Even worse, the FAO projects that harvesting trees for fuel, paper, and wood products will increase 53 percent from 4.3 billion tons in 1990 to 6.6 billion tons in 2010. Clearing land for agriculture will take a further toll on the world's trees. Overall, the FAO estimates that 39 percent of the Earth's remaining relatively pristine "frontier forests" are in severe to moderate danger from agriculture, logging, mining, and other threats. It is easy to blame the LDCs for allowing their forests to be overcut, but many in those countries ask what alternative they have. "Anyone, American, Dutch or whatever, who comes in and tells us not to cut the forest has to give us another way to live," says an official of Suriname (a former Dutch colony). "And so far they haven't done that." Instead, what occurs, charges the country's president, is "eco-colonialism" by international environmental organizations trying to prevent Suriname from using its resources.[17]

Deforestation has numerous negative consequences. One is global warming, which we will discuss in a later section. Another ill effect of forest depletion is that with a shrinking supply of wood and an increased demand for cooking and heating, the cost of wood goes up and may swallow a third of a poor family's income in some African cities. In some rural areas, wood is so scarce that each family must have at least one member working nearly full-time to gather a supply for home use. The devastation of the forests is also driving many forms of life into extinction. A typical

4-square-mile section of the Amazon Basin rain forest contains some 750 species of trees, 125 kinds of mammals, 400 types of birds, 160 different kinds of reptiles and amphibians, and perhaps 300,000 insect species. The loss of biodiversity has an obvious aesthetic impact, and there are also pragmatic implications. Some 25 percent of all modern pharmaceutical products contain ingredients originally found in plants. Extracts from Madagascar's rosy periwinkle, for example, are used in drugs to treat children's leukemia and Hodgkin's disease. A drug called taxol, derived from the Pacific yew, is a promising treatment for breast and ovarian cancer. Many plants also contain natural pesticides that could provide the basis for the development of ecologically safe commercial pesticides to replace the environmental horrors (such as DDT) of the past.

Land Degradation Not only are the forests in trouble, so too is the land. Deforestation is one of the many causes of soil erosion and other forms of damage to the land. Tropical forests rest on thin topsoil. This land is especially unsuited for agriculture, and it becomes exhausted quickly once the forest is cut down and crops are planted or grazing takes place. With no trees to hold soil in place, runoff occurs, and silt clogs rivers and bedevils hydroelectric projects. Unchecked runoff can also significantly increase the chances of down-river floods, resulting in loss of life and economic damage.

Honduras is one of the many countries that environmental scientists had identified as endangered by deforestation. As one study relates, "They were right. In October 1998, Hurricane Mitch slammed into the Gulf [of Mexico] coast of Central America and stalled there for four days. Nightmarish mudslides obliterated entire villages," the study continues; "half the population of Honduras was displaced, and the country lost 95 percent of its agricultural production.... And in the chaos and filth of Mitch's wake, there followed tens of thousands of additional cases of malaria, cholera, and dengue fever" (Bright, 2000:23).

Since 1950, according to the United Nations Environmental Programme (UNEP), 4.6 million square miles of land have suffered mild to extensive soil degradation. This is an area about equal to the combined size of India and China. At its worst, *desertification* occurs. More of the world's surface is becoming desert-like because of water scarcity, timber cutting, overgrazing, and overplanting. The desertification of land is increasing at an estimated rate of 30,600 square miles a year, turning an area the size of Austria into barren desert. Moreover, that rate of degradation could worsen, based on UNEP's estimate that 8 billion acres are in jeopardy. Some areas are in particular trouble. "All regions of the world suffer from desertification and drought," Arthur Campeau, Canada's ambassador for environment and sustainable development, points out, "but the African nations are the most vulnerable and the least able to combat these problems."[18]

Wildlife

The march of humankind has driven almost all the other creatures of the Earth into retreat and, in some cases, into extinction. Beyond the impact of deforestation, there are many other by-products of human civilization, ranging from urbanization to pollution, that destroy wildlife habitat. Whatever its cause, a decrease in the planet's wildlife will be an immeasurable loss to humans. The drug Capoten, which is used to control high blood pressure, is derived from the venom of the Brazilian pit viper. And the American Heart Association has identified an anti–blood-clotting drug based on substances found in bat saliva that is effective in preventing heart attacks in humans.

The Convention on the International Trade in Endangered Species has provided some relief to many endangered species by banning the international sale of live wildlife or wildlife products, such as skins. This picture shows the confiscated pelts of a tiger and leopard being burned by custom officials at Mumbai (Bombay) international airport. The blaze was meant to send out a signal to those engaged in the illegal wildlife trade that India's government is serious about protecting endangered wildlife. Still, saving the tiger and other species is difficult because of their monetary value to poachers. A tiger skin can fetch $900, a canine tooth goes for $125, and each claw brings $10. Other parts of the big cat are used in traditional medicines. Men hoping to improve their virility pay $800 for a potion made from a tiger penis, and tiger bones, which are said to relieve rheumatism, sell for $180 a pound.

Many endangered species have no known immediate pragmatic value. Nevertheless, a world without giant pandas, hooded cranes, Plymouth red-bellied turtles, and Chinese river dolphins will be a less diverse, less appealing place.

Unfortunately, some species do have economic value: The trade in feathers, pelts, ivory, and other wildlife products is endangering indigo macaws, snow leopards, black rhinoceroses, and many other species. During the 1980s, for example, legal hunters and illegal poachers seeking ivory, which sold for up to $120 per pound, slaughtered some 650,000 elephants in Africa, reducing their number by half. Humans further add to the destruction of wildlife through pollution. When, for example, an Ecuadorian tanker ran aground in January 2001 off the Galápagos Islands, 800,000 gallons crude oil spilled into the sea causing the death of more than 60 percent of the world's marine iguanas, a species unique to these Pacific Ocean islands 500 miles off Ecuador's coast.

It should be noted that on the issue of wildlife, like many other of the matters discussed in this chapter, there are optimists who believe that the problem is being grossly overstated. According to Julian Simon, "a fair reading of the available data suggests a rate of extinction not even one one-thousandth as great as the one the doomsayers scare us with." Simon was careful to say that he was not suggesting, "that we should ignore possible dangers to species." He contended, though, "we should strive for a clear and unbiased view of species' assets so as to make sound judgments about how much time and money to spend on guarding them."[19]

Human food requirements bring increasing pressure on the ocean's fish, mollusks, and crustaceans. The importance of marine life as food plus the demands of a growing world population have combined to increase the marine (salt-water) catch by a third between 1985 and 1999, to 92 million metric tons. The FAO estimates that the sustainable annual yield of Earth's oceans is somewhere between 69 and 96 million tons, which means that the most optimistic interpretation is that fishing is at full capacity. For the most commercially desirable species, the story is worse. According to FAO data, 69 percent of the commercial species of marine life are being fully fished or overfished. Taking fish, crustaceans, and mollusks faster than they can replenish themselves will lead to a progressive decline of the catch, and that could pose a health threat to countries that rely on fish for vital protein supplies. Especially imperiled would be Asia and Africa, where fish contribute over 20 percent of the protein in the diet of the regions' inhabitants.

Water

The final resource that we will examine here is perhaps the most basic of all. Along with oxygen, water is an immediate need for almost all life forms. Seventy-one percent of the Earth's surface may be covered by water, but 96.5 percent is salt-water, and 2.4 percent is in the form of ice or snow. This leaves just 1.1 percent readily available for human consumption. A significant part of this is polluted, and drinking it poses serious health risks. Moreover, this scarce drinkable water supply is threatened, and the cry "Water, water, everywhere/Nor any drop to drink" of

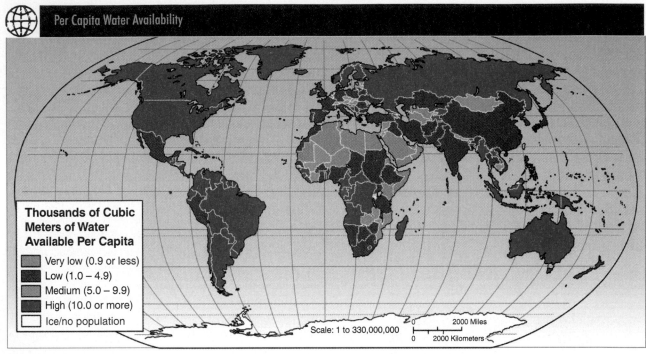

Per Capita Water Availability

Thousands of Cubic Meters of Water Available Per Capita

- Very low (0.9 or less)
- Low (1.0 – 4.9)
- Medium (5.0 – 9.9)
- High (10.0 or more)
- Ice/no population

Scale: 1 to 330,000,000

0   2000 Miles
0   2000 Kilometers

Data source: World Resources Institute, 2002.

A report by the United Nations Commission on Sustainable Development warns that 1.2 billion people live in countries facing "medium-high to high water stress."

Samuel Taylor Coleridge's Ancient Mariner may foreshadow the shortages of the future. Increased agricultural and industrial use, pollution, and other factors are depleting or tainting water supplies. Freshwater use, after tripling between 1940 and 1975, has slowed its growth rate to about 2 to 3 percent a year. Much of this is due to population stabilization and conservation measures in the developed countries. Still, because the population is growing and rainfall is a constant, the world needs to use an additional 7.1 trillion gallons each year just to grow the extra grain needed to feed the expanding population.

Complicating matters even more, many countries, especially LDCs, have low per capita supplies of water, as you can see in the map above. The world per capita average availability is 7,044 cubic meters. There are currently 25 countries with an annual availability of less than 1,000 cubic meters of water per person. Given the fact that Americans annually use 1,677 cubic meters of water per capita, the inadequacy of less than 1,000 cubic meters is readily apparent.

To make matters worse, the water usage in the LDCs will increase as they develop their economies. These increases will either create greater pressure on the water supply or will limit a country's growth possibilities. Globally, most freshwater is used for either agriculture (70 percent) or industry (21 percent), with only 9 percent for domestic (personal) use. Industrialized countries, however, use greater percentages for industry and more water per capita overall than LDCs. It follows then, that as the LDCs industrialize, their water needs will rise rapidly. China provides an example: Water use for industry, which amounted in 1980 to 46 billion cubic meters, increased 107 percent to 95 billion cubic meters in 1999. Adding to the problem in many countries, a great deal of the water needed for drinking is being contaminated by fertilizer leaching, industrial pollution, human and animal wastes, and other discharges. China, for one, daily discharges 18.7 million pounds of organic pollutants into its rivers, lakes, and coastal waters. This leaves one of every

THE DEATH OF A SEA

There are few stories better than that of the sad fate of the Aral Sea to illustrate humankind's abuse of the environment and its devastating consequences. The inland sea is located between Kazakhstan to the north and Uzbekistan to the south. In 1960, when those countries were still part of the Soviet Union, the sea was the fourth-largest inland body of water, covering 26,300 square miles, an area about the size of Belgium and the Netherlands combined.

Then, beginning in the 1960s, Soviet agriculture demands and horrendous planning began to drain water from the sea and from the two great rivers that feed it (the Amu Darya from the north and the Syr Darya from the south) faster than the water could be replenished.

The sea started to shrink rapidly. As it did, the level of its salinity rose, and by 1977 the catch from the once-important fishery had declined by over 75 percent. Still the water level continued to fall, as the sea provided irrigation for cotton fields and for other agricultural production. The same Soviet planning that brought the world the Chernobyl nuclear plant disaster in Ukraine stood by paralyzed as the Aral Sea began to disappear before the world's eyes.

Now, in reality, the geographical name Aral Sea is a fiction, because it has shrunk in size and depth so much that a land bridge separates the so-called

This man and his fishing boat have been left high and dry by the environmental mismanagement that has drained the Aral Sea of 75 percent of its water. Exactly where it lies now, the boat was once tied to a pier in the Aral Sea port of Munak, Uzbekistan. Now the shore is 50 miles away.

Greater Sea to the north from the Lesser Sea to the south. What was a single sea has lost 75 percent of its water and 50 percent of its surface area in the past 40 years. That is roughly equivalent to draining Lake Erie and Lake Ontario. The Uzbek town of Munak was once the Aral Sea's leading port, with its fishermen harvesting the sea's abundant catch. Now there are few fish, but even if there were many, it would not help the people of Munak. The town is now in the middle of a desert; the shoreline of the Lesser Sea is 50 miles away.

four Chinese without access to safe drinking water, but they fare favorably compared to people in many other countries. For instance, 70 percent of Cambodians do not have access to safe drinking water.

Overall, UNEP predicts, "if present consumption patterns continue, two out of every three persons on Earth will live in water-stressed conditions by the year 2025."[20] The result of such a projection coming to pass could lead to a competition for water and to international tensions. There are, for example, 19 countries that get 20 percent or more of their fresh water from rivers that originate outside their borders. The security of these countries would be threatened if upstream countries diverted that water for their own purposes or threatened to limit it as a political sanction. Such possibilities have led some analysts to suggest that in the not-too-distant future the access to water supplies could bring "thirsty" countries to and over the brink of war.

Before leaving this unhappy catalog of types of environmental abuse and turning to the happier topic of resource conservation, it is worth noting that damage to one aspect of the environment can also adversely affect others. This is readily obvious in the box, The Death of a Sea, which details the impact of poor water conservation. Fishery stock depletion, desertification, and salinization are among other disasters that have befallen the Aral Sea and the countries and people on its shrinking shores.

RESOURCE CONSERVATION: THE GLOBAL RESPONSE

While pessimists and optimists disagree about how serious the problems are and how immediate and drastic remedies need to be, it is certain that mineral, forest, wildlife, and water resources must be more carefully managed and conserved. After several millennia of unchecked resource use, people are now beginning to act with some restraint and to cooperate in conservation causes. All the various individual and organized efforts cannot be mentioned here, but a few illustrative examples will serve to demonstrate the thrust of these activities.

Land and Wildlife

Desertification is one area in which the international community has begun to act. Some 100 countries signed the Convention on Desertification in 1994 to coordinate efforts for land preservation and reclamation projects. Sri Kamal Nath, India's environment minister, commented that desertification "is as much of a threat to the planet and civil society as war, and we have to combat it with as much vigor."[21] More recently, 122 countries agreed in 2000 to a treaty that will eventually ban 12 so-called "dirty dozen" pollutants, such as PCBs and dioxins, that have been linked to birth defects and other genetic abnormalities.

Progress is also being made in the preservation of forest and wildlife resources. Membership in environmental groups has grown dramatically. In several European countries and in the European Parliament, Green parties have become viable political forces. In Germany the green party, *Bündnis 90/Die Grünen* (Alliance 90/The Greens), became part of the governing coalition of Chancellor Gerhard Schröder, with party leader Joschka Fischer serving as foreign minister. The growing interest in flora and fauna is also increasing the so-called ecotourist trade, and many countries are beginning to realize that they can derive more economic benefit from tourists shooting pictures than from hunters shooting guns or loggers wielding chain saws.

Although the world's list of endangered species is still growing, these threatened species are also now gaining some relief through the Convention on the International Trade in Endangered Species (CITES). Elephants were added in 1989 to the CITES list of endangered species, and the legal ivory trade has dropped from 473 tons in 1985 to zero. Wild cats have also found greater refuge, with the international sale of their skins declining from 192,000 in 1985 to 22,000 in 1997. During the same period, the number of reptile skins traded plummeted from 10.5 million to 2.9 million. The global trade in live primates, birds, and reptiles has seen similar decreases.

Individual countries have also acted. In 1994, for example, the United States imposed trade sanctions on Taiwan in retaliation for its refusal to halt the sale of tiger bones and rhinoceros horns. The sanctions were limited, but they were also, as President Clinton noted, "the first time any country has acted on the international call for trade sanctions to protect endangered species."[22]

The Seas and Fisheries

One major step at the international level came in 1994 when the United States, after a decade of opposition, signed the UN's Law of the Sea Treaty. The treaty, which soon thereafter went into effect, gives countries full sovereignty over the seas within

12 miles of their shores and control over fishing rights and oil- and gas-exploration rights within 200 miles of their shores. That should help improve conservation in these coastal zones. Additionally, an International Seabed Authority, with its headquarters in Jamaica, has been established. It will help regulate mining of the seabed in international waters and will receive royalties from those mining operations to help finance ocean-protection programs.

National and international efforts are also being taken in other areas. A 64 percent decline between the mid-1980s and the mid-1990s in the catch of demersal fish (such as cod, flounder, and haddock) in the northwest Atlantic prompted both Canada and the United States to limit severely or temporarily ban catches in rich fishing grounds such as the Grand Banks and the Georges Bank off their North Atlantic coasts. Canada has also reached an agreement with the European Union to regulate fishing in and near these rich fisheries. On an even broader scale, 99 countries, including all the major fishing countries, agreed in 1995 to an international treaty that will regulate the catch of all the species of fish (such as cod, pollock, tuna, and swordfish) that migrate between national and international waters. "The freedom to fish on the high seas no longer exists as it once did. It is no longer a free-for-all situation," explained the elated chairman of the conference, Satya Nandan of Fiji.[23]

At the global level, the International Whaling Commission (IWC) regulates whaling. An average of 30,000 whales a year were killed between 1925 and 1975, and worry about their number led to the creation of the IWC in 1946 and, finally, to a ban on commercial whaling in 1986. That did not end the killing of whales, but it did reduce the number of whales killed annually to about 2,000. Japan, under the guise of scientific study (permitted under IWC rules), continues to allow its ships to hunt the marine mammal. For 2002, Tokyo authorized its whaling fleet to kill 700 whales. After what Japan calls scientific study, the meat is sold to the public under a Japanese law that forbids waste. Norway is more up-front with its whaling. It rejected the IWC ban and allowed its whalers to harpoon 671 whales in 2002. The IWC allows approximately 400 whales to be taken for what it terms "aboriginal subsistence whaling" by indigenous people in various areas.

At the 2002 meeting of the IWC in Shimonoseki, Japan, both Norway and Japan proposed an end to the commercial whaling ban. They claim that the whale population will sustain a limited harvest and that whales eat so much other marine life that the expanding number of whales threatens the fisheries. Much of the scientific community rejected these arguments, as did the IWC.

It may be, in a very ironic twist, that pollution will add to the protection of whales provided by the IWC. Research done at the University of Hokkaido in Japan has found that whale meat contains so much mercury that those who eat it are at risk of brain damage or poisoning their unborn children, Samples of whale liver contained 370 micrograms of mercury per gram of liver, about 700 percent of the weekly mercury intake that the World Health Organization considers safe. Given that there are more than 28 grams in an ounce, the researchers were being absolutely literal when they warned, "Acute intoxication could result from a single [bite]."[24]

It is important to note, whatever one's view of whaling, that the overall numbers of most whale species and other marine wildlife are recovering. For one, the Pacific gray whale population has doubled since conservation began, and it is no longer on the U.S. endangered species list. It is also true, though, that other species, such the right whale, with only 400 surviving animals, remain at the edge of extinction. And while Galápagos fur seals, once at the edge of extinction, now have viable population, a marine oil spill off the Galápagos Islands in 2000 wiped out 60 percent of the marine iguanas that live there and nowhere else. Thus, what has been accomplished is the beginning, rather than the culmination, of conservation efforts.

When the International Whaling Commission held its 2002 meeting in Japan's southwestern port city of Shimonoseki, a traditional whaling port, the Japanese government pressed its effort to have the ban on commercial whaling eased by sponsoring whale-tasting events at the convention hall and around the country. This photo shows two Japanese college students sampling deep-fried whale meat. Prime whale meat sells for almost $150 a pound in Japan. The gastronomic approach failed; the IWC did not loosen the restrictions.

Faced with adverse public opinion and economic boycotts, known in the tuna canning industry as the "Flipper factor," Starkist and all other major U.S. tuna canners now display logos, such as the one above, to assure their consumers that the tuna are not taken using nets that kill dolphins.

One of the themes of this book is the role that you as an individual can play on the world stage, and the protection of marine mammals provides one more example of that. For example, public pressure, which the industry refers to as the "Flipper" factor (after the 1960s TV series), forced U.S. tuna canners to demand that suppliers use dolphin-safe methods of netting to save dolphins. That was followed in 1990 by a U.S. law banning the importation of tuna caught without dolphin-safe methods. Other governments have followed suit. Concern over an increase in the number of dolphins dying as a result of fishing by European fleets led the European Union in 2002 to station observers on fishing boats that are suspected of using methods that do not minimize the chances of dolphins being killed. NGOs are also involved. The Inter-American Tropical Tuna Commission sponsors a program in which a monitor is onboard all large tuna vessels. The result is that the number of dolphins killed annually has dropped from over 200,000 before 1990 to an estimated 20,000 in 2001.

ENVIRONMENTAL ISSUES

The state of the biosphere is related to many of the economic and resource issues we have been examining. Like the concerns over those issues, international awareness and activity are relatively recent and are still in their early stages. Several concerns that have an environmental impact, such as desertification, deforestation, and biodiversity loss, have already been discussed. The next sections will look at ground pollution, water pollution, air pollution, global warming, and ozone layer depletion.

Ground Pollution

The pollution of the land is a significant problem, but the territorial dominance of states renders this issue primarily domestic and, therefore, outside the realm of international action. Exporting solid waste for disposal does, however, have an international impact. With their disposal sites brimming and frequently dangerous, EDCs annually ship millions of tons of hazardous wastes to LDCs. Financial considerations have persuaded some countries to accept these toxic deliveries. The practice is widely condemned on the grounds that, as one Nigerian diplomat put it, "international dumping is the equivalent of declaring war on the people of a country."[25] Nevertheless, a UN investigation has found that "the volume of transboundary movements of toxic wastes has not diminished." Even more alarmingly, the report went on to warn, "The wastes are sent to poor countries lacking the infrastructure for appropriate treatment. They are usually dumped in overpopulated areas in poor regions or near towns, posing great risks to the environment and to the life and health of the poorest populations and those least able to protect themselves."[26] A closely associated international aspect of ground pollution is that it is often caused by waste disposal by multinational corporations (MNCs), which may set up operations in LDCs because they have fewer environmental regulations.

Water Pollution

There are two water environments: the marine (saltwater) environment and the freshwater environment. Water pollution is damaging both.

Marine pollution has multiple sources. Spillage from shipping, ocean waste dumping, offshore mining, and oil and gas drilling activity taken together account for 23 percent of the pollutants that are introduced into the oceans, seas, and other international waterways. Petroleum is a particular danger. Of the 940 million gallons of petroleum discharged each year into the marine environment, almost half comes from transportation spillage. Municipal and industrial waste discharges account for another 36 percent of the total. Offshore drilling is a rising threat, with the production of petroleum from marine drilling steadily rising.

Another 44 percent of the marine pollution is carried by the rivers, which serve as highways that carry human sewage, industrial waste, pesticide and fertilizer runoff, petroleum spillage, and other pollutants into the seas. One of the worst sources are fertilizers, and their global use has grown from about 40 million metric tons a year in 1960 to some 156 million metric tons annually in the late 1990s. Another major source is the exploding world population, which creates ever more intestinal waste. Many coastal cities are not served by sewage treatment facilities. Sewage is the major polluter of the Mediterranean and Caribbean Seas and the ocean regions off East Africa and Southeast Asia. Industrial waste is also common.

Of these pollutants, the influx of excess nitrogen into the marine system is especially damaging. Human activities, such as using fertilizers and burning fossil fuels, add about 210 million metric tons to the 140 million metric tons generated by natural processes. Excess nitrogen stimulates eutrophication, the rapid growth of algae and other aquatic plants. When these plants die in their natural cycle, the decay process strips the water of its dissolved oxygen, thereby making it less and less inhabitable for aquatic plants, fish, and other marine life. To make matters worse, some algae blooms are toxic, and take a heavy toll on fish, birds, and marine mammals. The Baltic Sea, Black Sea, the Caribbean, Mediterranean Sea, and other partly enclosed seas have been heavily afflicted with eutrophication, and even ocean areas such as the northeast and northwest coasts of the United States have seen a significant increase in the number of algae blooms in the last quarter century.

Inasmuch as 99 percent of all commercial fishing is done within 200 miles of continental coasts, such pollution is especially damaging to fishing grounds.

Freshwater pollution of lakes and rivers is an international as well as a domestic issue. The discharge of pollutants into lakes and rivers that form international boundaries (the Great Lakes, the Rio Grande) or that flow between countries (the Rhine River) is a source of discord. Freshwater pollution is also caused by acid rain and other contaminants that drift across borders.

Air Pollution

The world's air currents ignore national boundaries, making air pollution a major international concern (Soroos, 1997). To illustrate the many sources of, and problems associated with, air pollution, we will explore the acid rain issue.

Acid rain is caused by air pollutants that contaminate water resources and attack forests through rainfall. Sulfur dioxide (SO_2) and nitric acids from the burning of fossil fuels and from smelting and other industrial processes are the major deleterious components of acid rain. The damage done by acid rain has followed industrialization. The United States, Canada, and Europe were the first to suffer. Especially in the northern part of the United States and in Canada there has been extensive damage to trees, and many lakes have become so acidified that most of the fish have been killed.

Europe has also suffered extensive damage. About a quarter of the continent's trees have sustained moderate to severe defoliation. The annual value of the lost lumber harvest to Europe alone is an estimated $23 billion. The tourist industry in once verdant forests around the world is also in danger, imperiling jobs. The death of trees and their stabilizing root systems increases soil erosion, resulting in the silting-up of lakes and rivers. The list of negative consequences could go on, but that is not necessary to make the point that acid rain is environmentally and economically devastating.

The good news is that pollution control in the EDCs has substantially reduced new air pollution. Annual EDC sulfur dioxide emissions, for instance, have declined dramatically. As one example, U.S. emissions dropped from about 31,000 tons in 1970 to under 19,000 tons in 1999. The bad news is that the improvement in the EDCs is being more than offset by spiraling levels of air pollution in the LDCs. This is particularly true in Asia. There, rapid industrialization combined with the financial inability to spend the tens of billions of dollars needed to control SO_2 emissions is expected to more than triple annual SO_2 emissions from 34 million tons in 1990 to about 115 million tons in 2020.

Air pollution from sulfur dioxide, nitrogen dioxide, and suspended particles (such as dust and soot) cause about 500,000 deaths a year according to the World Health Organization. The majority of those are in Asia, where most of the major cities exceed WHO guidelines for suspended particles. China's cities provide an example. Shanghai's air pollution is 246 percent above the WHO standard, and Beijing's 419 percent over that mark. The 1.7 million people of the industrial city of Lanzhou in northwest China daily gasp in air that is 859 percent dirtier than what WHO thinks is healthy.

The idea of oxygen bars where people can escape the choking air seems like something out of a bad science-fiction story. Yet they are real, as proven by this 2002 picture of police officers in Bangkok, Thailand, trying to clear their lungs in one of the city's oxygen bars. Bangkok's air quality level of suspended particulates (such as soot) is 247 percent above the maximum level considered safe by the World Health Organization. Patrons receive 20 minutes of "oxygen therapy" for about $5; as a civic gesture, the bar offered it for free to police officers.

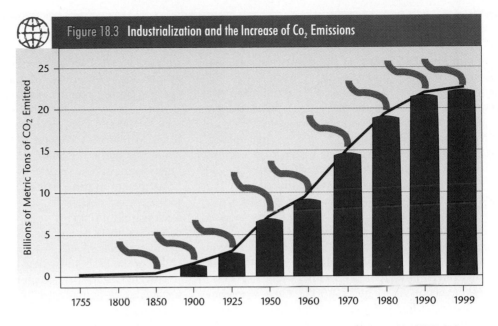

Figure 18.3   Industrialization and the Increase of CO_2 Emissions

Data sources: U.S. Department of Energy Web site at: http://www.eia.doe.gov/; Worldwatch Web site at: http://www.worldwatch.org/alerts/990727a.html.

Since the industrial revolution began in Great Britain in the mid-1700s, the discharge of carbon dioxide (CO_2) into the air by the industrial burning of coal, gas, oil, and other fossil fuels has rapidly increased. The majority of scientists who study this believe that these emissions are creating a global warming effect that is significantly altering the Earth's climate.

Global Warming

Many scientists believe that we are experiencing a gradual pattern of global warming. The reason, according to these scientists, is the greenhouse effect, which is caused by carbon dioxide (CO_2) from fossil fuel burning and from discharges of other chemical gases. The CO_2 accumulates in the upper atmosphere and creates a blanket effect, trapping heat and preventing the nightly cooling of the Earth. Other gases, especially methane and chlorofluorocarbons (CFCs), also contribute heavily to creating the thermal blanket.

There is controversy about the existence, causes, and impact of the greenhouse effect. We will begin with a brief synopsis of what is known and what is in dispute. Then we will turn to the key issue: What to do.

Global Warming: What We Know Two things are known for sure. First, both global emissions of CO_2 and other gases and the level of these gases in the atmosphere have increased. Second, the Earth is getting warmer.

This rise in global emissions is associated with the industrial revolution and the surge in the world population. For example, annual global CO_2 emissions have nearly quadrupled since 1950. Now more than 22 billion tons of CO_2 are discharged annually, and they are joined by 270 million tons of methane and 400,000 tons of CFCs. Since these gases linger in the atmosphere for 50 to 200 years, the cumulative effect is also worth considering. Scientists estimate that at the beginning of the industrial revolution in the mid-1700s there were about 55 million tons of CO_2 in the atmosphere. Since then, more than an additional 1 trillion billion tons have been discharged, and a great deal of that CO_2 remains trapped in the atmosphere. About 80 percent of these emissions come from the burning of coal, gas, petroleum, and other fossil fuels during industrial activity. This connection between industrialization and CO_2 emissions is evident in Figure 18.3.

BAD MATH AND SUSTAINABLE DEVELOPMENT

The rapid global increase in the number of gasoline-powered vehicles and the rapid decrease in the world's number of trees add to the buildup of carbon dioxide (CO_2) in the atmosphere. As a mathematical equation, this environmental formula might be written as (+vehicles) + (− trees) = + CO_2. The problem with this equation is, many scientists worry that this "bad math" is contributing to global warming.

The elements of the equation are not complex. The number of vehicles in the world has risen from about 70 million in 1945 to about 650 million. Analysts predict that there will be 1 billion vehicles on the world's roads in 2025. Most of this increase will come as the LDCs improve their standard of living. There are in the United States about 750 vehicles for every 1,000 people. By contrast, for every 1,000 people, China has only 8 vehicles and India just 7. If the people of China and India were as well off today as the average American, there would be another 1.6 billion cars (+246 percent) on the road. The Chinese and Indians are, of course, a long way from the American standard of living, but the future may hold a car—or several cars—in every Chinese and Indian driveway and garage.

The 650 million vehicles being driven today emit an immense amount of CO_2. According to the U.S. Environmental Protection Agency (EPA), a small, fuel-efficient Geo Metro emits 9,200 pounds of CO_2 a year (based on 15,000 miles). A Ford F-150 pickup truck emits 18,500 pounds of CO_2, and a Dodge Durango, one of the popular sport utility vehicles, discharges 21,100 pounds of CO_2 annually.

Trees are another part of the equation. They are the environmental antithesis of gasoline-powered vehicles in that they convert CO_2 to oxygen. Unfortunately for the atmosphere, the number of trees has been decreasing as vehicles have been increasing. As noted earlier in this chapter, the forests that remain today are only about half the size of the forests that once were. Inasmuch as a large tree can absorb and convert up to 48 pounds of CO_2 into oxygen annually, the loss of billions of trees has vastly diminished the ability of the Earth to cleanse itself of excess CO_2.

How to balance the equation, that is, how to achieve sustainable development without degrading the environment, is complex. Yet there may be some relatively simple guidelines available by plugging numbers into the equation. To wit, in terms of CO_2 conversion to oxygen per tree, 1 Geo Metro = 200 trees. Similarly, 1 Ford F-150 = 385 trees, and 1 Dodge Durango = 440 trees. Sustainable development, then, requires less vehicles (or vehicles that are less polluting), or more trees, or some combination thereof. The current trend of more vehicles and less trees leads to a bad result. Rewriting the equation to say (−vehicles) + (+less polluting vehicles) + (+trees) yields a better result for our future.

Deforestation also contributes to increased levels of CO_2 in the atmosphere. By destroying a multitude of trees, which are nature's method of converting CO_2 into oxygen, humans over the centuries have added more than 4.1 billion tons of CO_2 to the atmosphere. Some of that is CO_2 that would have otherwise been absorbed by the vanished trees; some of it is CO_2 discharged into the atmosphere by burning the trees and underbrush to clear the land. A third certainty is that emissions and deforestation have caused atmospheric CO_2 concentrations to rise, at first slowly, then more rapidly, from 277 parts per million (ppm) in 1750, to 280 ppm in 1850, 315 ppm in 1958, and 370 ppm in 2000. During the 1990s, the average annual rate of increase of CO_2 concentrations was 1.2 ppm, with each added 1 ppm the result of retaining an additional 2.13 billion tons of CO_2 in the atmosphere. The problem is discussed further in the box, Bad Math and Sustainable Development.

Did You Know That:
The first warning about global warming was issued in 1896 by Swedish chemist Svante Ahrrenius, who wrote that "we are evaporating our coal mines into the air."

There is also no doubt that the global temperature is rising. Scientists estimate that over the last century the Earth's average temperature rose 0.5° C/1.1° F. In fact, 1998 was the warmest year in recorded history, 2001 was the second-warmest on record, and nine of the ten warmest years since global record keeping began in 1856 have occurred since 1981. Those two years and 1983, 1987, 1988, 1990, 1995, 1996, 1997, and 1999 were the ten warmest years.

Global Warming: What Is in Dispute Two things about global warming are controversial. One is whether global warming is caused by humans or is a natural phenomenon. As one atmospheric scientist accurately notes, "I don't think we're arguing over whether there's any global warming. The question is, What is the cause of it?"[27] The second issue is whether global warming will have dire consequences or an impact that will in some cases be beneficial and in other cases can be addressed using modern technology.

Environmental pessimists contend that humans are causing global warming. A report of the UN-sponsored Intergovernmental Panel on Climatic Change (IPCC) argued that the buildup of CO_2 and the climatic changes over the last few decades are "unlikely to be entirely due to natural causes." Instead, the report stated, "A pattern of climatic response to human activities is identifiable in the climatological record."[28]

Environmental pessimists are also alarmed about the impact of global warming. The IPCC report concluded that, given current trends, the world's average temperature could increase 1° F to 6° F by the year 2100. For comparison, the temperature increase since the last ice age is estimated to be 5° F to 9° F. The pessimists believe that rainfall, wind currents, and other climatic patterns will be dramatically, and sometimes dangerously, altered. The polar ice caps will melt more quickly, and sea levels will rise. There is some evidence that the process has already begun in earnest. A report issued in 1999 by the Goddard Space Science Institute estimated that the Arctic ice cover had thinned by 45 percent over the previous 40-year period, with the size of the ice cover shrinking by about 14,000 square miles, an area larger than Delaware and Maryland combined.

The result of such melting, the IPCC report estimated, is that up to 118 million people could be displaced by rising seas over the next century. Satellite-generated sea measurements indicate, according to one scientist, that "the mean annual rise in sea level will probably be something like one or two millimeters a year."[29] This is a small annual rise, but over time it can be significant. The sea level particularly affects island countries, 37 of which have formed the Alliance of Small Island States. The question, President Maumoon Abdul Gayoom of the Maldives, an Indian Ocean island country, told the world leaders gathered at the UN Millennium Summit in September 2000 is, "When the UN meets [in 2100] to usher in yet another century, will the Maldives and other low-lying nations be represented here?" Noticing that his five-minute time limit had elapsed, President Gayoom finished with the thought, "My time at the podium is up. But I pray that that of my country is not."[30]

Violent weather caused by rapid evaporation, the buildup of atmospheric heat, and other factors that would create higher winds also worries the pessimists. The head of the IPCC notes that the 1980s and early 1990s were remarkable for their "frequency and intensity of extremes of weather and climate."[31] Insurance industry data shows, for example, that the number of hurricanes and other types catastrophic windstorms in the world have more than tripled since the 1960s. Pointing out the obvious danger, the head of the U.S. Federal Emergency Management Agency noted, "Fifty to 58 percent of the [U.S.] population is on the eastern coastline. That's an awful lot of people at higher risk."[32]

Did You Know That:
La Niña is marked by unusually cold water in the mid-Pacific; El Niño is marked by unusually warm water in the same region. The term El Niño originated with South American fishermen who noticed that unusually warm water would appear some years near Christmas. This led to the name, which means "little boy" and refers to the Christ child. Since La Niña is something of the opposite of El Niño, that name soon came into use.

Adding to the possible woes, the UN has warned that global warming "could have a wide range of impacts on human health, most of which would be adverse."[33] Scientists predict, for example, that warming could increase the number and range of mosquitoes, with a resulting annual increase of 80 million malaria cases. Cholera, dengue fever, and other hemorrhagic diseases associated with warm climates could also spread northward and southward.

Environmental optimists treat the pessimists as alarmists. First, the optimists point out, the Earth has natural warming and cooling trends, and the optimists believe that a good part of the observed temperature rise is due to this natural cycle, rather than human activity. They note that the Earth cooled somewhat in the 1950s and 1960s, and some predict that the cooling trend will resume over the next few decades. Other environmental optimists do not believe that increases will be huge, either because they will not occur in any significant way or because offsetting factors, such as increased cloudiness, will ease the effect. One scientist labels CO_2 "an unlikely candidate for causing any significant worldwide temperature change."[34] And only slightly less optimistically, another scientist comments, "The prospects for having a modest climate impact instead of a disastrous one are quite good."[35]

Optimists also down play the damage from global warming. "It should be pretty clear," says one, "that warming to date didn't demonstrably dent health and welfare very much." There is no reason, he added, "to expect a sudden [greater danger] in the next 50 years."[36] Moreover, the optimists predict that some areas could benefit and most could adapt to the changes brought on by global warming (Moore, 1998). Drought in the lower and middle latitudes would ruin some present agricultural areas, the logic goes, but new ones would be created and would prosper at higher latitudes. Farmers in colder regions might have their growing seasons and bounty increased. Moreover, a U.S. National Academy of Science study concluded that while global warming was occurring, people could adapt and that "we mustn't get into the state of mind that… [leads us to] think the world is going to vaporize."[37]

Global Warming: What to Do The key issue in the global warming debate is what to do. Economic cost is one factor. Those who recommend caution in responding to demands that global warming be halted also point out that significantly reducing CO_2 emissions will not be easy. It might well require substantial lifestyle changes in the industrialized countries. "To stabilize carbon dioxide concentrations at even twice today's levels… over the next 100 years can be attained only [if] emissions eventually drop substantially below the 1990 levels," the IPCC has calculated.[38] To do that "will require a degree of bureaucratic control over economic affairs previously unknown in the West," predict two scholars who oppose such a course.[39] Costs would also be enormous. The Union of Concerned Scientists, for instance, has concluded that a program to cut CO_2 emissions by 70 percent over a 40-year period would cost the U.S. economy $2.7 trillion. The organization argues, however, that the loss would be more than offset by a $5 trillion savings in fuel costs. Additionally, the economy would be stimulated by programs to create and provide alternative, environmentally safe technologies.

In the end, what can be said for certain, then, is that climatic warming is occurring, but, in the words of one scientist, "we have no means of knowing, actually" how much, if any, of that is due to atmospheric emissions.[40] Do you bet trillions in economic costs that emissions-driven global warming is occurring, or do you bet the atmosphere that it is not? Given the fact that CO_2 stays in the atmosphere for centuries and that, if it is having a climatic effect, it will take several lifetimes to begin to reverse significantly, a U.S. national research agency recommends betting the money. "Despite the great uncertainties," it counsels, "greenhouse warming is a potential threat sufficient to justify action now."[41]

Ozone Layer Depletion

In contrast to the debate over global warming, there is little doubt about the depletion of the ozone layer and the damage that it causes. Atmospheric ozone (O_3)

absorbs ultraviolet (UV) rays from the sun, and, without the ozone layer 10 to 30 miles above the planet, human life could not exist. The ozone layer is being attacked by the emission of chlorofluorocarbons (CFCs), a chemical group that gasifies at low temperatures, releasing chlorine atoms. These attack ozone and turn it into atmospheric oxygen (O_2), which does not block ultraviolet rays. Each chlorine atom can repeat this transformation up to 100,000 times.

Because of their low gasification point, CFCs are good refrigerants and insulators and are therefore used in refrigerators and air-conditioners and in products such as styrofoam. CFCs are also found in many spray can propellants, fire extinguishers, and industrial solvents. Some 400,000 metric tons are spewed into the atmosphere annually. The most dramatic depletion, according to a report by the World Meteorological Organization, is occurring over Antarctica, where a 3.86-million-square-mile hole—about the size of Europe and with as much as a 70 percent depletion of atmospheric O_3—occurs annually. Ozone levels over the rest of the world have declined less, but they are still down about 10 percent since the 1950s.

Emissions of CFCs create several problems. One is that they add to the greenhouse effect, as noted above. More to the point here, the thinning of the ozone layer increases the penetration through the atmosphere of ultraviolet-B (UV-B) rays, which cause cancers and other mutations in life forms below. Scientists estimate that each 1 percent decrease in the ozone layer will increase UV-B penetration 1.3 percent. This can increase the rate of various types of skin cancer from 1 to 3 percent. The impact of this on Americans was noted in chapter 1. Australia and New Zealand have measured temporary increases in UV-B radiation of as much as 20 percent, and light-skinned Australians have the world's highest skin cancer rate. Another possible deleterious effect of increased UV-B bombardment came to light when a study of the water surrounding Antarctica found evidence of a 6 to 12 percent decline in plankton organisms during the period of the annual ozone hole. Such losses at the bottom of the food chain could restrict the nutrition and health of fish and eventually humans farther up the food chain. Also, scientists from Oregon State University, studying the inexplicably rapid drop in the number of frogs around the world, have concluded that UV-B radiation may be killing the eggs before they hatch into mosquito larvae-consuming tadpoles.

ENVIRONMENTAL PROTECTION: THE INTERNATIONAL RESPONSE

Like many of the other issues discussed in this chapter, environmental problems have been slowly growing for centuries. They have accelerated rapidly in this century, however, and in some cases they have reached hypervelocity growth rates. Only recently has widespread public and governmental concern been sparked. The result is that programs are just beginning. Most of the work that has been done has had a national focus, and there have been many advances. In a great part of the developed world, where the problems were most acute and where the resources to fund programs were available, water is cleaner, acid rain is being curbed, trees are being planted, toxic wastes are being dealt with better, recycling is under way, and a host of other positive programs have stemmed and have sometimes even reversed the flood tide of pollution. Because many forms of pollution spread internationally, the national programs have been beneficial.

There has also been progress at the international level (Meyer, Frank, & Tuma, 1997; Caldwell, 1996). There are many IGOs and NGOs that focus on one or more environmental programs. The UN has been involved in a number of environmental efforts. These began with the 1972 Conference on the Human Environment in Stockholm, which led to the establishment of the United Nations Environmental Programme (UNEP). The work of the many IGOs that are concerned with preserving

FROM KYOTO TO JOHANNESBURG AND BEYOND

The Earth Summit in Rio de Janeiro (1992) laid out a hopeful path. The economically developed countries (EDCs) that signed the Global Warming Convention agreed to voluntarily stabilize emissions at their 1990s levels by the year 2000. They also resolved to reconvene in Japan after five years to review their progress in restraining the emission of carbon dioxide (CO_2) and other gases that most scientists believe are contributing to global warming.

Like many paths paved with good intentions, the journey to Kyoto did not fulfill its promise. Many of the EDCs had made no progress toward meeting the goals set in 1992. Also, many of the economically less developed countries (LDCs) had generated increasing levels of greenhouse gases.

Virtually all countries agreed that the EDCs had to cut emissions. Various proposals were offered aiming for the EDCs to cut emissions between 12 and 15 percent below their 1990 levels by no later than 2012. The EDCs did not expect the LDCs to meet the same stringent targets as the EDCs, but they did want some upper limits on future emissions. As President Clinton put the U.S. position, there had to be "meaningful participation by key developing nations."[1] To this, Mark Mwandosya of Tanzania, who headed the LDC caucus in Kyoto, rejoined, "Very many of us are struggling to attain a decent standard of living for our people. Any yet we are constantly told that we must share in the effort to reduce emissions so that industrialized countries can continue to enjoy the benefits of their wasteful lifestyle."[2]

The negotiations at Kyoto were intense, as the negotiators tried to balance the pressure to address the environment with their own country's economic interests. Cost estimates varied widely, with projections of the funds needed globally to stabilize CO_2 concentrations in the atmosphere ranging from $3 trillion to $10 trillion. The LDCs wanted promises of massive aid to help them stem pollution; the EDCs were reluctant to make specific commitments.

Almost inevitably, the environmental and economic cross-pressures led to a compromise. The treaty concluded in Kyoto requires the EDCs to reduce greenhouse gas emissions by about 7 percent below their 1990 levels by 2012. The treaty also allows the EDCs to trade emissions quotas among themselves. If, say, the United States fails to meet its goal, it can buy emissions quota units from an EDC that has exceeded its goal. To the disappointment of strong environmentalists, no sanctions for failure to meet standards were set. Furthermore, the LDCs were exempted from binding standards. The negotiators decided that the treaty will go into effect when ratified by at least 55 countries representing at least 55 percent of the world's emissions of greenhouse gases.

Supporters greeted the compromise with faint praise. "This is a modest step forward in what will be a long-term battle to protect the Earth's climate system," said a representative of the Union of Concerned Scientists.[3] Scientists also pointed out that, even if it was fully implemented, the treaty would not stop global warming. First, even though in 2012 the EDCs planned to produce 30 percent less than they would have without restraints, the emissions will still add greenhouse gases to the atmosphere faster than the Earth can eliminate them. Second, LDC emissions will continue to go up. Therefore, the Kyoto limits will only slow the increase, not reverse the tide.

Other observers were caustic in their denunciations. A representative of a U.S. business-lobbying group denounced the treaty as "unilateral economic disarmament [by the EDCs]. It is a terrible deal, and the president should not sign it." Republican leaders in the U.S. Congress also rushed to denounce the treaty. The Senate GOP leader declared that Congress "will not ratify a flawed treaty."[4] The Speaker of the House called the treaty an "outrage" that would cripple the U.S. economy.[5]

President Clinton defended the treaty, but he also maneuvered to keep the treaty from becoming a political issue during the 2000 presidential campaign by declining to sign it himself and instead relegating the task to a relatively obscure diplomat. He also did not send the treaty to the Senate for ratification. During

and enhancing the biosphere is supplemented by a vast host of NGOs dedicated to the same purpose (Haas & McCabe, 1996; Wapner, 1996). It is also increasingly common for trade treaties, such as the North American Free Trade Agreement, and other international pacts to include environmental protection clauses (Audley, 1997). Additionally, there are countless local organizations and even individuals involved in international environmental activism (Lipschutz & Mayer, 1996).

President George W. Bush's rejection of the Kyoto Treaty on global warming has drawn the ire of environmentalists world-wide. Here a demonstrator holds up a protest poster in June 2001, outside the U.S. Embassy in Brussels, Belgium, where Bush was attending a NATO summit meeting.

the presidential election contest the treaty did not emerge as a major issue, but the Republican candidate George W. Bush did make his views clear. "I oppose the Kyoto [treaty]," he told reporters; "It is ineffective, inadequate, and unfair to America because it exempts 80 percent of the world, including major population centers such as China and India, from compliance."[6]

It was no surprise then, that as president, Bush directed in 2001 that the United States withdraw as a signatory of the Kyoto Treaty. That set the stage for supporters of the treaty to press to meet the required 55–55 rule (at least 55 ratifications, by industrialized countries emitting 55 percent of the CO_2, including the EDCs, Russia, and Eastern Europe) before the Earth Summit II conference convened in Johannesburg in September 2002. In June 2002, representatives of the EU deposited the ratifications of all of its 15 members with the UN. Japan also ratified the treaty that month. Thus three months before Earth Summit II, 74 countries had ratified the Kyoto Treaty, meeting the first part of the 55–55 rule, and the ratifi-

cations equaled more than 40 percent of the industrialized countries' emissions, which meant that the second 55 percent standard was also nearing fulfillment. If U.S. emissions were added in, the total would reach 48 percent of the needed total. Without the United States, it will be important for Russia (6 percent) and Canada (5 percent) to ratify the treaty. Given President Putin's request in April 2002 to Russia's Duma to ratify the treaty, that country's accession seemed likely.

The pressure on President Bush increased even further as a result of a report issued in early June 2002 by the U.S. Environmental Protection Agency. "The changes observed over the last several decades are likely mostly due to human activities," the report said. It added that despite some scientific uncertainties, "There is general agreement that the observed warming is real and has been particularly strong within the past 20 years."[7] Supporters of the Kyoto treaty were quick to seize on the report to criticize the president's anti-treaty position, but he seemed unfazed. He characterized the findings as a "report put out by the bureaucracy," and reiterated his stance. "The Kyoto treaty would severely damage the United States's economy, and I don't accept that," Bush told reporters. Placing himself squarely in the camp of environmental optimists, he expressed his belief that "we can grow our economy and, at the same time, through technologies, improve our environment."[8] There the matter rested, as the global community readied itself for Earth Summit II. It was not exactly Bush versus the world, but it was pretty close to that.

What is also clear is that the path from Kyoto to Johannesburg and beyond goes somewhere, whatever the decisions in the world's capitals are. The road favored by environmental pessimists involves taking strong measures to reduce greenhouse emissions even if they are costly or alter people's lifestyles. The alternative path favored by environmental optimists involves relying on technology to provide solutions without requiring sacrifices. The destination of that path evokes the ancient Chinese adage that tells us, "If you continue on the road you are on you will get to where it leads."

Protecting the Ozone Layer Among its other accomplishments, the UNEP sponsored a 1987 conference in Montreal to discuss protection of the ozone layer. There, 46 countries agreed to reduce their CFC production and consumption by 50 percent before the end of the century. Subsequent amendments to the Montreal Convention at quadrennial conferences, the last of which was held in Vienna in 1995, resulted in multilateral treaties requiring a complete phase out of CFC production by EDCs by 1996 and LDCs by 2010.

As a result, there is relatively good news on ozone depletion. The annual buildup of CFC concentrations reversed itself from 5 percent in the 1980s to a slight decline beginning in 1994, only seven years after the Montreal Convention. Somewhat modifying this good news is the CFC buildup had increased so rapidly in the years before 1987 that, in the estimate of one scientist, "We might be back to 1979 [CFC concentration] levels sometime around 2050 or so."[42]

The scientist might have added, "If we are lucky" to that prediction because there are uncertainties. The most important of these has to do with sustainable development and the economic advancement of the LDCs. The substitutes for CFCs in refrigerants and other products are expensive, and the estimates of phasing out CFCs worldwide range up to $40 billion. Therefore LDCs will be hard-pressed to industrialize and provide their citizens with a better standard of living while simultaneously abandoning the production and use of CFCs. For example, refrigerators, which not long ago were rare in China, are becoming more and more commonplace, and, as one researcher put it, "simply allowing every Chinese family to have a refrigerator… will swamp" efforts in the developed countries to limit CFCs.[43] Representatives of LDCs resist having to give up their progress, especially without help from the EDCs to develop the often more expensive alternative technologies. As a former environment minister of India asked, "Is it fair that the industrialized countries who are responsible for the ozone depletion should arm-twist the poorer nations into bearing the cost of their mistakes?"[44]

Easing Global Warming Progress on dealing with global warming has been more limited. The reduction of CFCs will have a positive impact because of their role in global warming. The significant reduction of CO_2 discharges will be more difficult. There is increased recognition of the need to act, however, and a UNEP-sponsored World Climate Conference convened in Geneva in 1990 with the CO_2 problem as a major focus. At that meeting of 130 countries, most EDCs pledged to stabilize or reduce greenhouse gas emissions by the year 2000. The United States, however, declined to join in because of concern about the cost and the negative domestic economic impact. The global effort to reduce greenhouse gas emissions was reconfirmed in the Global Warming Convention signed at the 1992 Earth Summit. Further progress occurred when President Clinton agreed to drop the U.S. reservation to that treaty's suggested timetables for reducing emissions.

Progress on that treaty will, however, be difficult to put into effect. The next major effort to give practical application to the goal of easing the threat of global warming came in Kyoto, Japan, in 1997. The events leading up to the conference, its outcome, and the implications are related in the box, From Kyoto to Johannesburg and Beyond, on pages 564–565.

Addressing Other Environmental Concerns There has also been progress on a range of other environmental concerns, such as international dumping. The 1989 Convention on the Control of Transboundary Movements of Hazardous Wastes and Their Disposal (the Basel Convention), signed by 105 countries in Switzerland, limits such activity. In 1991 almost all African states signed the Bamako Convention in Mali banning the transboundary trade in hazardous wastes on their continent. The limits in the Basel Convention were stiffened further in reaction to the continued export of hazardous wastes under the guise of declaring that the materials were meant for recycling or as foreign aid in the form of recoverable materials. Great Britain alone exported 105,000 tons of such toxic foreign aid in 1993 to 65 LDCs, a practice that one British opposition leader called the "immoral… dumping of our environmental problems in someone else's backyard."[45] As of January 1, 1998, all such shipments for recycling and recovery purposes were banned.

Marine pollution has also been on the international agenda for some time, and progress has been made. One of the first multilateral efforts was the International Convention for the Prevention of Pollution From Ships. More recently, 43 countries, including the world's largest industrial countries, agreed in 1990 to a global ban on dumping industrial wastes in the oceans. It went into effect in 1995. The countries also agreed not to dispose of nuclear waste in the oceans. These efforts make a difference. For example, during 1976–1980, there was an annual average of 23 large (over 66,000 gallons) oil spills; the number came down to an average of 5 spills during 1996–2000, with a resulting decrease of 88 percent in amount of the oil dumped into the marine environment.

After reading this chapter and the chapters on international law, international organization, arms control, and economic cooperation, it is easy to be discouraged. The problems are immense and complex; barriers to cooperation are formidable; failure to find solutions carries potentially dire consequences. And sometimes when you begin to think that you are making progress, as the world has in recent years, a setback occurs. Still, the world must and does continue to try to preserve and improve the condition of the Earth and its people. It is true that the current level of cooperation, when compared with the problems, seems woefully inadequate, but that does not mean that we should despair.

The message here is to avoid the extremes of either unguarded optimism or hopeless pessimism. It is equally unwise to take the rosy "It's darkest before the dawn" approach or the gloom-and-doom approach represented by comedian Eddie Murphy's observation that "Sometimes it's darkest before the light goes out completely."

Don't sell the early efforts that we have discussed in this chapter and elsewhere too short. It is only during the last century, and really since World War II, that the need to cooperate has penetrated our consciousness and our conscience. The intervening years have been a microsecond in human history. In that sense, much has been done. Yet, much remains to be done to secure the future, and the microseconds keep ticking by.

This book began its discussion of the alternative nationalist and internationalist approaches to world politics by using Robert Frost's poem about two roads diverging in a wood. The choice of which road to take is yours to make individually, as well as a group choice for all of humankind. Your present and, more important, your future will be determined by which road you follow. It will be hard to turn back. So, as Shakespeare tells us in *Richard III*, "Go, tread the path that thou shalt ne'er return."

Less developed countries are becoming more adamant about not accepting toxic wastes from industrialized countries. At the same time, these latter countries are closing their own dumps. The question is, Where will the oil-soaked rags, the soiled Pampers, and the rest of humanity's waste products go?

🌐 Chapter Summary

1. This chapter deals with international ecological concerns and cooperation. Self-interest, some people would say self-survival, compels us to attend to issues concerning the world's expanding population, the depletion of natural resources, the increase of chemical discharges into the environment, and the impact of these trends on the global biosphere.

2. A key concept and goal is sustainable development. The question is how to continue to develop industrially and otherwise while simultaneously protecting the environment. Given the justifiable determination of the LDCs to develop economically, the potential for accelerated resource depletion and pollution production is very high.

3. There is a wide range of views about how great the environmental threats are and what can and should be done to address them.

4. Population is a significant problem facing the world, with the global population surpassing the 6 billion mark. The 1994 UN Conference on Population and

Development in Cairo marked the latest step in the effort to control population and the associated attempts to improve women's reproductive and other rights. There are also numerous international organizations, such as the United Nations Population Fund, working in the area. The most effective way to control population is to improve the educational and economic status of women and to make contraceptive services widely available.

5. Increasing population and industrialization have rapidly increased the use of a wide range of natural resources. It is possible, using known resources and current use rates, to project that petroleum, natural gas, and a variety of minerals will be totally depleted within the present century. The world's forests, its supply of freshwater, and its wildlife are also under population and industrialization pressure. There are many international governmental nongovernmental organizations and efforts, symbolized by the 1992 Earth Summit, to address these problems.

6. Population growth and industrialization are also responsible for mounting ground pollution, water pollution, air pollution, global warming, and ozone layer depletion due to atmospheric pollution. Work in other areas, such as reducing CO_2 emissions, has only just begun and is difficult because of the high costs.

7. The efforts at international cooperation in the areas discussed in this chapter return us to the question of standards of judgment. It is easy to view the vast extent of the problems facing the globe, to measure the limited effort being made to resolve them, and to dismiss the entire subject of international cooperation as superficial. It is true that not nearly enough is being done. But it is also true that only a very few decades ago nothing was being done. From that zero base, the progress made since World War II is encouraging. The only question is whether or not we will continue to expand our efforts and whether or not we will do enough, soon enough.

An Epilogue to the Text/ A Prologue to the Future

Where I did begin, there I shall end.

Shakespeare, *Julius Caesar*

So here it is some months later, and we are at the end of this book and this course. Finals await, and then, praise be, vacation. That well-deserved break from your academic labors brings you to an implicit point of decision about what to do with this text, the other course readings, and the knowledge you have gained from your instructor. One option is to sell what books you can back to the bookstore and forget the rest. I can remember from my undergraduate days how attractive an idea that sometimes seems.

But then, again, is that really the best option? Probably not. We began our semester's journey with the idea that we are all inescapably part of the world drama. There may be times when we want to shout, "Stop the world, I want to get off," but we cannot. We have also seen that we are both audience and actors in the global play's progress. At the very least, we are all touched by the action in ways that range from the foreign designer jeans that we wear to, potentially, our atomized end.

We can leave it at that, shrug our shoulders, and complain and mumble at the forces that buffet us. But we also can do more than that. We do not have to be just passive victims. We can, if we want and if we try, help write the script. The plot is ongoing and improvisational. The final scene is yet unwritten. We are not even sure when it will occur. It could be well into the far distant future—or it could be tomorrow. This, more than any particular point of information, is the most important message. You are not helpless, and you owe it to yourself and your fellow humans to take an active role in your life and in the world's tomorrows.

The world is beset by great problems. War continues to kill without cessation. The specter of terrorism increasingly haunts many people as they go about their daily lives. A billion-dollar diet industry prospers in many countries of the North due to the fact that many of its citizens are overweight, while in the South, infants and the elderly starve to death in the dry dust. As if localized malnutrition were too slow and selective, we globally attack our environment with the waste products of our progress, and the human population tide threatens to overwhelm the Earth's ability to sustain the people who live on it. Of even more immediate peril, an expanse of nuclear mushroom clouds could instantly terminate our biosphere's more evolutionary decay.

To face these problems, we have, at best, a primitive political system. Sovereignty strengthens nationalities but divides the world. Frontier justice is the rule. As in a grade-B western, most of the actors carry guns on their hips and sometimes shoot it out. The law is weak, and the marshals have more authority in theory than in practice.

There are few anymore who really try to defend the system of assertive sovereignty as adequate for the future. Clearly, it is not. What is less certain is what to do next and how to do it. Cooperation, humanitarianism, enlightenment, and other such words provide easy answers, but they are vague goals. Real answers are difficult to come by. They may involve tough choices; we may be asked to give up some things now so that they will not be taken later, to curb our lifestyle, to risk arms control in the hope of avoiding nuclear war, and to think of the world in terms of "we."

At every step there will be those who urge caution, who counsel self-preservation first, who see the world as a lifeboat. Maybe they will be right—but probably not. We *have* begun to move toward a more rational order. The last five chapters clearly show this. But they also show how limited and fragile this progress has been. This is where you come in. Your job is to work to make the world the place you want it to be. It is your job to consider the problems, to ponder possible solutions, to reach informed opinions, and to act on your convictions. Think? Yes, of course. But also DO!! That is what is really important.

We began this study with the thought from Shakespeare's *Henry V* that "the world [is] familiar to us and [yet] unknown." My hope is that this text and the course you have just about completed have made the world more familiar, less unknown to you. What you do with what you have learned is now the issue. Will you treat this moment as an end? Or is it a beginning? Heed, if you will, the counsel of Shakespeare's King Lear:

Be governed by your knowledge and proceed.

Explanatory Notes

Page 45. **Some matters of terminology: EDC/LDC.** The use of the acronym EDC for economically developed country is not common in the literature. I am using "economically developed" here instead of simply "developed" in order to stress the economic factor and to avoid the all-too-common stereotype of the countries of the South as culturally or otherwise inferior. Indeed, the designation LDC, or less developed country, is misleading in the same way. Less economically developed country (LEDC) would be preferable, and politically and economically disadvantaged country (PEDC) would be better still, because these terms would recognize that the countries are in a relatively weak international political and economic position. The acronym LDC, however, is so common that I will continue to use it. The South is also referred to frequently as the Third World, although this term is rapidly becoming outmoded. It has been used somewhat inconsistently, but it generally has meant LDCs, especially those not aligned with either of the two superpowers in the East-West Axis. It may seem odd to refer to Third World countries when we do not refer to Second World ones, but the term has been useful to designate those countries that are not only politically and economically disadvantaged but that have invariably suffered through or are still undergoing a direct or an indirect colonial experience. It would be reasonable therefore to classify many of the former Soviet republics as Third World countries. Poor, mostly Muslim Uzbekistan, for example, was until recently something of a colony of the Russian-dominated Soviet state. The point is that such countries, many of which have had unfortunate experiences with politically and militarily powerful EDCs, share similar views of EDCs and their alleged role in causing and maintaining the LDCs' unjust economic and politically disadvantaged status. Finally, some analysts have used the words "core" and "periphery" to designate, respectively, those countries with power as being at the center of the political system and those without much power on the margins. These nuances need not concern us here. Therefore, the terms North, EDC, developed country, and core country all mean about the same thing; as do South, LDC, Third World, and periphery country.

Page 92. **Names in non-Western Cultures.** Names in many parts of the world do not follow the format familiar to Americans, Canadians, and others whose names are most likely to follow the European tradition of a first (given) name followed by a family name (surname). In China, the Koreas, Vietnam, and many other countries in Asia, the custom is to place the surname first, followed by the given name. Thus, Zhu Rongji would be addressed formally as Premier Zhu. Given the greater formality followed in China (and most of the rest of the world) compared to the United States, only Zhu's family and very close friends would call him Rongji. Japan presents something of a twist on this practice. Like most other North and East Asian people, the Japanese in their own usage place the surname first. But the very externally oriented Japanese have long practiced putting the given name first in all communications with the outside world. Thus internally in Japanese characters, the Japanese would refer to their prime minister as Mori (surname) Yoshiro (given name). Externally in English or other languages, he would be designated Yoshiro Mori. There are also countries in which only one name is used. Najibullah is the entire name of the Soviet-backed president of Afghanistan overthrown by U.S.–backed rebels in 1992. In somewhat the same way, the familiar name of President Saddam Hussein of Iraq creates some confusion. Originally, he was given his father's name (Hussein) coupled with what could be construed as a surname, al-Takrit, after the Takrit region of his home in Iraq. The designation "Saddam" is not a name as such. Rather it is an adopted political appellation meaning "one who confronts." In this way, he is President Hussein, but his familiar name is also Hussein. Finally, Spanish-heritage surnames often have longer and shorter versions that relate to family and origin. The full name of the Mexican president elected in 2000 is Vicente Fox Quesada, who succeeded President Ernesto Zedillo Ponce de León. After the first long form, they would be referred to as Presidents Fox and Zedillo. In the same way, former Costa Rican president and 1987 Nobel Peace Prize winner Oscar Arias Sanchez is President Arias.

Page 343. **The Conditions for Military Success.** Elements for success are those of George, Hall, and Simons (1971), which include (1) strong U.S. determination, (2) a less determined opponent, (3) clear U.S. goals, (4) a sense of urgency to accomplish these goals, (5) adequate domestic political support, (6) usable military options, (7) fear of U.S. escalation by the opponent, and (8) clarity concerning terms of the peaceful settlement. Other elements of success have been provided by Blechman and Kaplan (1978) and include (1) the opponent finds the threat credible, (2) the opponent is not yet fully committed to a course of action, (3) the goal is maintaining the authority of a particular regime abroad, (4) force is used to offset force by an opponent, (5) the goal is to have an opponent continue current behavior, that is, to deter a change in behavior, (6) the action is consistent with prior policy, (7) there has been previous U.S. action in the area, (8) U.S. involvement begins early in the crisis, (9) military action is taken rather than threatened, and (10) strategic forces become involved, thus signaling seriousness of purpose. Caspar Weinberger's six criteria included (1) vital U.S. interests must be at stake, (2) there must be a clear intention of winning, (3) political and military objectives must be clearly defined, (4) sufficient military force must be employed to gain the objective, (5) there must be reasonable congressional and public support, and (6) combat should be a last resort. General Colin Powell's comments, made during a press interview, were not as easily enumerated as Weinberger's, but they generally agreed with the criteria of the then–secretary of defense. Powell's views can be found in the *New York Times*, September 29, 1992, p. A1.

Page 45. **Economics: Technical Terms and Sources.** The terms *gross national product* (GNP) and *gross domestic product* (GDP) are similar but not interchangeable. GNP measures the sum of all goods and services produced by a country's nationals whether they are in the country or abroad. Thus GNP includes data such as the profits of a country's MNCs. Some sources, such as the World Bank, use the term "gross national income" (GNI) to refer to GNP. By the same logic, GNP does not include profits from production in one's country by foreign MNCs. GDP includes only income within a country (by both nationals and foreigners) and excludes foreign earnings of a country's nationals. The fact that some countries report only GNP and others report only GDP creates slight statistical comparison anomalies.

The most recent change in calculating a country's production of wealth is the addition of "purchasing power parity" (PPP) to the calculation. Because GDP or GNP is expressed in a single currency, usually the U.S. dollar, it does not fully account for the difference in prices for similar goods and services in different countries. Some countries are more expensive than the United States. Refer to the box GNP-PPP on page 397 for a complete explanation of GNP-PPP. There is certainly value to PPP adjustments, but this book uses unadjusted figures. Using both adjusted and unadjusted figures would created more confusion than clarity, and the reason for using the unadjusted GDP/GNP is that since many of the industrial and technological products that LDCs wish to acquire come from abroad, the cost to the LDC is not affected by PPP. A U.S. tractor that costs $50,000, costs $50,000 whether you buy it in the United States or Kenya. Therefore, PPP masks the gap in international purchasing power between LDCs and EDCs and inflates the economic position of LDCs compared to EDCs in the world economy.

All monetary values in this book are in current U.S. dollars (US$), unless otherwise noted. There are two ways to express monetary values. One is in current dollars, which means the value of the dollar in the year reported. Because of inflation, using current dollars means that, for example, the percentage increase in *value* of exports will rise faster than the percentage increase in the *volume* of exports over any period. The second way to express monetary value is in *real dollars*, or uninflated dollars. This means that the currency is reported in terms of what it would have been worth in a stated year. In this book, monetary value is in current U.S. dollars except where noted. Therefore, you could say either that a car in 2000 cost $15,395 or that (assuming a 4 percent inflation rate) it cost $10,000 in real 1989 dollars. Note that you figure inflation by compounding the rate, that is, multiplying $10,000 by 1.04 x 1.04 x 1.04.... The number 100 is used as a baseline in many of the figures in this and other chapters. It is used to show relative change. This number is an abstraction and has no value as such. It simply allows comparisons of later growth or decline. It is used instead of zero to avoid pluses and minuses before subsequent data. For example, if you earned $5,000 in 1989 and a friend earned $7,000, and you wished to compare later earning growth, you would make 1989 earnings for both of you equal to 100. Then, if in 2000 you earned $8,000, but your friend earned only $4,000 (using increments of 10 to equal each $1,000), your earnings would be expressed as 130 and your friend's earnings would be 70. You may find that the data, such as trade expressed in dollars, used in this book for any given year or period varies somewhat from what is cited by another source. Most of the data is based on extensive compilations and complex calculations completed by the sources cited or by the author. But the reporting organizations, such as the U.S. government, the United Nations, the IMF, the World Bank, and GATT all use slightly different assumptions and inputs in calculating their final figures. Most of the major sources used herein include careful discussion of exactly how they arrive at their conclusions. You may refer to these if you wish a detailed explanation of their methodologies. The key, then, usually is not to focus too much on specific numbers, especially if they come from different sources. Rather it is best to concentrate on patterns, such as the rate of growth or decline of trade over a period of years. Unless specifically noted, this chapter relies on the following sources for financial, trade, and other economic data: International Monetary Fund (2001–2002), *Direction of Trade Statistics*, Washington, DC; IMF (2002), *International Financial Statistics*; IMF (2002), *World Economic Outlook*; IMF (2002), *IMF Survey*; U.S. Central Intelligence Agency (CIA) (2001), *The World Factbook, 2001–2002*; (U.S.) Bureau of the Census and U.S. Economics and Statistics Administration (2002), *Statistical Abstract of the United States, 2000*; *World Almanac, 2002*; World Bank (2002), *World Development Report, 2002*; World Resources Institute (2002), *World Resources, 2001–2002*. In addition to these sources, five newspapers—the *Financial Times* (London), the *Hartford Courant* (Hartford, Connecticut), the *New York Times* (New York), the *Washington Post* (Washington, D. C.), and the *Wall Street Journal* (New York)—were used as sources herein. Several further comments on these sources are appropriate. One is that many are periodic publications. The most current year used is shown, but historical data may also be drawn from various issues in the current or earlier years. Second, some sources of historical data are not shown because of the sheer mounting volume of citation that would be necessary through multiple editions of this study. Where it is not cited herein, historical data sources are cited in earlier editions of *International Politics on the World Stage*. Third, full bibliographic citations for most of the sources listed here can be found in this volume's bibliography.

Page 416. **How Exchange Rates Work.** To begin to understand the mysteries of how exchange rates work and the impact of their fluctuation, consider the following two scenarios: the first with the dollar ($) equal to the post–World War II high of 258 yen (¥), which was the case in early 1985; and the second with the dollar equal to the 2000 value of ¥108. For illustration, assume that one automobile costs ¥3,096,000 to manufacture in Japan and another costs $18,000 to build in Detroit. Let us further suppose that an average Japanese worker makes ¥1,806 an hour; an American makes $10 an hour. Manufacturing costs and wages are not directly affected by exchange rates and, therefore, remain constant.

Automobile Imports at a ¥258 = $1 Exchange Rate
• At ¥258 to the dollar, the equivalent cost is $12,000 for the Japanese car (¥3,096,000 ÷ ¥258) and ¥4,644,000 for the U.S. car ($18,000 × ¥258).
• It will take the Japanese worker earning ¥1,806 ($7) an hour a total of 1,714 work hours (¥3,096,00 ÷ ¥1,806) to buy the Japanese car and 2,571 work hours (¥4,644,000 ÷ ¥1,806) to buy the U.S. car. The Japanese worker will probably buy the Japanese car.
• It will take the American worker earning $10 (¥2,580) an hour a total of 1,200 work hours (¥3,096,000 ÷ ¥2,580) to

buy the Japanese car and 1,800 work hours ($18,000 ÷ $10) to buy the U.S. car. The American worker will probably buy the Japanese car.

•With both the Japanese and the American worker buying Japanese cars, Japanese automobile exports to the United States will rise and U.S. exports to Japan will decline.

•**Automobile Imports at a ¥108 = $1 Exchange Rate**

•At ¥108 per dollar, the equivalent cost is $28,667 for the Japanese car (¥3,096,000 × ¥108) and ¥1,944,000 for the U.S. car ($18,000 × ¥108).

•It will take the Japanese worker earning ¥1,806 ($17) an hour a total of 1,714 work hours (¥3,096,000 ÷ ¥1,806) to buy the Japanese car and 1,076 work hours (¥1,944,000 ÷ ¥1,806) to buy the U.S. car. The Japanese worker will probably buy the U.S. car.

•It will take the American worker earning $10 (¥1,080) an hour a total of 2,867 work hours (¥3,096,000 ÷ ¥1,080) to buy the Japanese car and 1,800 work hours ($18,000 ÷ $10) to buy the U.S. car. The American worker will probably buy the U.S. car.

•With both the Japanese and the American worker buying U.S. cars, exports from Japan will decline and U.S. exports will rise.

Endnotes

CHAPTER 1

1. *New York Times*, December 28, 1997, p. A10.
2. *New York Times*, November 28, 1997, p. A28.
3. Korb is quoted in Anthony Lewis, "The Defense Anomaly," *New York Times*, January 22, 1996, p. A15.
4. *Hartford Courant*, May 18, 1992, p. A5.
5. Gallup Poll, January 4, 2002, on the Web at: http://www.gallup.com/poll/releases/pr020104.asp.
6. State of the Union address of President G. W. Bush, January 29, 2002.
7. *New York Times*, November 28, 1995, p. A14.
8. *New York Times*, August 14, 1992, p. A15.
9. *New York Times*, July 29, 1996, p. A17.

BOX, "The End of Illusion," p. 4

1. Robert J. Samuelson, "End of Illusion," *Washington Post National Weekly Edition*, September 17–23, 2001, p. 27.

Box, "The Financial Toll of 9-11," p. 7

1. The estimate of damages relies heavily on International Monetary Fund, *World Economic Outlook* (December 2001), pp. 14–33; and Peter Navarro and Aron Spencer, "September 11, 2001: Assessing the Costs of Terrorism," *Milken Institute Review* (Fourth Quarter, 2001), pp. 16–30, located on the Web at http://www.milken-inst.org.
2. *Washington Post*, January 25, 2002, p. 1.

BOX, "Cindy Beaudoin," p. 14

1. *Hartford Courant*, May 24, 1992.

CHAPTER 2

1. Speech of December 20, 2001, found on the Web site of the External Relations Commissioner of the European Union at http://europa.eu.int/comm/external_relations/news/patten/sp01_643.htm.
2. The scholar is Larry Goodson of Bentley College giving an address, "Post-Taliban Afghanistan: Reconstructing a Failed State" at the Hoover Institution, November 19, 2001, found at the Web site of Hoover Institution at http://www-hoover.stanford.edu/homepage/news/112601.html.
3. The analyst is Charles V. Peña, Senior Defense Policy Analyst, Cato Institute, from a paper, "A Bigger Military Is Not the Solution to Terrorism," October 1, 2001, found on the Web site of the Council for a Livable World at http://www.clw.org/sept11/pena.html.
4. State of the Union message, January 29, 2002.
5. Colin Powell's comments were voiced on the *Newshour with Jim Lehrer*, Public Broadcasting Service, September 13, 2001.
6. State of the Union message, January 29, 2002.

7. U.S. Government, White House, "A National Security Strategy For A New Century," released January 5, 2000, and found on the Web at: http://usinfo.state.gov/regional/ar/natsec2k.htm#4
8. *Time*, June 1, 1992, p. 43.

BOX, "The 6 Billionth Baby," p. 47

1. Carol Bellamy, "The Progress of Nations 1999: The Roll of the Dice," UNICEF, at: http://www.unfpa.org/modules/6billion/facts.htm.

CHAPTER 3

1. *New York Times*, October 6, 1995, p. B10.
2. *International Herald Tribune*, April 30, 2001, found on the Web at: http://www.iht.com/articles/18441.htm
3. *Hartford Courant*, September 10, 1995, p. A7.
4. U.S. State Department Web site: http://www.state.gov/s/ct/rls/rpt/fto/2001/5258.htm
5. Federation of American Scientists Web site: http://www.fas.org/irp/world/para
6. *New York Times*, February 15, 1999.
7. Gallup Poll, May 1999, found on the Public Agenda Online Web site at: http://www.publicagenda.org/issues/nation_divided_detail.cfm?issue_type=americas_global_role&list=5.
8. *Time*, November 16, 1992, p. 78.
9. *Washington Post*, January 28, 2002.
10. Haass's quote is taken from Gaddis Smith, "Saddle Up," a review of Haass's book in the *New York Times Review of Books*, August 3, 1997, p. 20.
11. *Hartford Courant*, September 1, 1995, p. A1.
12. *Time*, November 27, 1995, p. 4.
13. *New York Times*, March 17, 1996, p. D1.
14. *New York Times*, February 12, 1995, p. E5.
15. *New York Times*, February 15, 1999.
16. BBC News, 12 February, 12, 2002, from the Web at http://news.bbc.co.uk/hi/english/world/europe/newsid_1816000/1816395.stm.
17. The quotes from Michael Williams of the International Institute for Strategic Studies in London and David Owen are both from the *Hartford Courant*, December 15, 1995, p. A1.
18. *New York Times*, May 27, 1994, p. A8.
19. *New York Times*, May 5, 1994, p. A11.
20. *Newsday*, October 14, 2001.
21. *Congressional Quarterly Weekly Report*, September 1, 1990, p. 2778.
22. *Time*, September 12, 1991, p. 53.

BOX, "World's Top Cop," p. 58

1. U.S. Department of State press release found on the Web at http://usinfo.state.gov/topical/pol/terror/01121107.htm.

BOX, "THE New NATO Marches East," pp. 60–61

1. The Washington Summit, Fact Sheets: "NATO Summit: NATO's Newest Members," on the U.S. White House Web site at: http://www.whitehouse.gov/WH/New/NATO/fact1.html.
2. *Washington Post*, June 16, 2001.

BOX, "Balance of Power," p. 68

1. From Kissinger's 1994 book, *Diplomacy*, quoted in *Newsweek*, April 11, 1994, p. 42.

BOX, "Japan: A Rising Sun?" pp. 70–71

1. Poll by the newspaper *Asahi Shimbun*, found on the Web at http://www.kanzaki.com/jpoll/2001/#P20011001.
2. *Newsweek*, November 22, 1993, p. 38.
3. *Asahi Shimbun* Poll, March 1997, on the Kanzaki Web site at: http://www.kanzaki.com/jpoll/poll.html#P970317.
4. *Washington Post*, August 14, 2001.
5. CNN report, August 15, 2001, on the Web at http://asia.cnn.com/2001/WORLD/asiapcf/east/08/14/koizumi.reaction/.
6. The view of Professor Yasuaki Onuma, University of Tokyo, *Far Eastern Economic Review*, August 15, 2001, found at its Web site: http://www.feer.com/articles/2001/0108_16/p022region.html.
7. *Christian Science Monitor*, February 28, 1990.
8. *Hartford Courant*, December 11, 1991.
9. *Time*, December, 2, 1991, p. 71.
10. All quotes from *Newsweek*, October 5, 2001, Web edition at http://www.msnbc.com/news/638697.asp.
11. *New York Times*, June 10, 1992, p. A7.
12. *New York Times*, April 21, 1996, p. E5.
13. *Hartford Courant*, January 6, 1992, p. 49.

CHAPTER 4

1. *New York Times*, November 9, 1999.
2. Gallup Polls of October 9, 1998 and February 2, 1999.
3. CBS News/*New York Times* Poll, September 20–25, 1991.
4. *Guardian Unlimited Observer Poll*, September 25, 2001 on the Web at: http://www.observer.co.uk/waronterrorism/story.
5. *Christian Science Monitor*, April 30, 1999, reporting on public opinion in Kosovo and previous U.S. military actions.
6. *New York Times*, December 1, 1991.
7. *Washington Post*, March 1, 2002.
8. BBC News on the Internet, "World: Asia-Pacific Tension Rises over Spratly Islands," February 13, 1999, at: http://news.bbc.co.uk/hi/english/world/asia-pacific/newsid_278000/278359.stm.
9. Henry A. Kissinger, "China: The Deadlock Can Be Broken," *Washington Post*, March 28, 1994, quoted in "U.S.-China Trade," *CQ Researcher*, Vol. 4. No. 14 (April 15, 1994), p. 319.
10. *Time*, March 25, 1995, p. 39.
11. All quotes are from the *Washington Post*, February 2, 2002.
12. *Washington Post*, November 9, 1999.
13. Letter from the President to the Speaker of the House of Representatives and the President Pro Tempore of the Senate, October 9, 2001, State Department Web site at http://usinfo.state.gov/topical/pol/terror/01100909.htm.

14. The member in the first quote was Representative Robert Portman. The second quote was anonymous. Both quotes are from the *Washington Post National Weekly Edition*, October 1–7, 2001.
15. Transcript of joint press conference, October 21, 2001 found on the White House Web site at http://www.whitehouse.gov/news/releases/2001/10/20011021-3.html.
16. *New York Times*, September 17, 1995, p. A26.
17. *Washington Post*, February 1, 2002.
18. CNN news item, "Shelton: British General Refused Order from NATO Commander in Kosovo," September 9, 1999, found at the CNN.Com Web site at: http://www.cnn.com/US/9909/09/shelton.nato/.
19. *New York Times*, April 21, 2000.
20. *New York Times*, April 13, 2000.
21. *Hartford Courant*, November 25, 1999, p. A28.
22. *New York Times*, April 18, 2000.
23. Associated Press, November 24, 1998, on Nando Media Web site at: http://www.nando.com/.
24. National Farmers Union Submission to the Standing Committee on Foreign Affairs and International Trade on the effects of the WTO and FTAA negotiations on farmers' orderly marketing agencies, safety nets, and agricultural programs, April 27, 1999, NFU Web site at: http://www.nfu.ca/.
25. *New York Times*, January 12, 1998, p. D1.
26. Princeton Survey Research/*Newsweek* survey, October 1999, on the Public Agenda Online Web site at: http://www.publicagenda.org/.
27. *Washington Post*, January 28, 2002.
28. *Washington Post*, February 1, 2002.

BOX, "Taiwan: To Be or Not to Be," pp. 94–95

1. *New York Times*, June 26, 1994, p. A8.
2. *New York times*, February 22, 2000.
3. *Washington Post*, February 2, 2002.
4. CNN, April 25, 2001, found on the Web at http://www.cnn.com/2001/ALLPOLITICS/04/24/bush.taiwan.abc/.
5. *New York Times*, January 31, 1996, p. A2.

BOX, "The Lone Dissenter," p. 102

1. This exchange was reported in the *Washington Post*, January 28, 2002.
2. Statement found on Representative Lee's congressional home page at http://www.house.gov/lee/votes.htm.
3. The commentator was David Horowitz in "The Enemy Within," *FrontPage*, September 19, 1991 found at the magazine's Web site http://www.frontpagemag.com/horowitzsnotepad/2001/hn09-19-01.htm.
4. *Congressional Record*, August 14, 1964.

CHAPTER 5

1. *Washington Post*, January 27, 2002.
2. *Washington Post*, January 29, 2002.
3. Interview of Robert McNamara, circa 1997, as part of the CNN "Cold War Experience" series at: http://cnn.com/SPECIALS/cold.war/episodes/11/interviews/mcnamara/.
4. *Washington Post*, February 12, 2002.
5. *Hartford Courant*, June 18, 1998, p. A13.
6. *New York Times*, June 1, 1998, p. S3.

7. *Hartford Courant*, June 18, 1998, p. A13.
8. *South China Morning Post*, September 16, 1996, p. 1.
9. The adviser was Arthur Goldberg, and the quote is from Robert Dallek, *Flawed Giant: Lyndon Johnson and His Times, 1961–1973* (New York: Oxford University Press, 1998) as reproduced in a review of the book, Sean Wilentz, "Lone Starr Setting," *New York Times Book Review*, April 12, 1998, p. 6.
10. *Hartford Courant*, February 4, 1990, p. C4.
11. All quotes from *Washington Post*, January 27, 2002.
12. *Washington Post*, January 27, 2002.
13. Quotes from *Washington Post*, February 3, 2002.
14. Lloyd Etheredge, "Will the Bush Administration Unravel," June 2001, on the Web at http://www.policyscience.net/.
15. The psychiatrist is Fritz C. Redlich, professor emeritus at UCLA and former dean of the Yale School of Medicine. His comments are in the *Hartford Courant*, March 22, 1992, p. A2.
16. *New York Times*, June 17, 1991, p. A10.
17. *New York Times*, January 8, 1997, p. A3.
18. President Bush speaking on the USS Enterprise, December 7, 2001, on the Web at http://www.whitehouse.gov.
19. *U.S. News & World Report*, February 8, 1993, p. 39.
20. Colin Powell, PBS Frontline series, The Gulf War: An Oral History, on the Web at http://www.pbs.org/wgbh/pages/frontline/gulf/oral/powell/5.html.
21. *Washington Post*, January 29, 2002.
22. *Time*, November 30, 1987, p. 18.
23. Press conference, October 11, 2001, on the Web at http://www.whitehouse.gov.
24. All quotes are from the *Christian Science Monitor*, September 27, 2001.
25. CNews, May 18, 2001, on the Web at http://www.canoe.ca/CNEWSMideast0105/08_mid-ap.html.
26. Comments at the World Conference Against Racism, Durban, South Africa, quoted in the *Hartford Courant*, August 31, 2001.
27. George C. Herring, "Cold Blood: LBJ's Conduct of Limited War in Vietnam," Harmon Memorial Lecture #33, 1990, United States Air Force Academy on the Web at www.usafa.af.mil/dfh/Harmon33.doc.
28. *Washington Post*, January 28, 2002.

BOX, "Why Do They Hate Us?" pp. 116–117

1. The commentator was Fareed Zakarian in *Newsweek*, October 15, 2001, on the Web at http://www.msnbc.com/news/639057.asp.
2. Gallup Poll Web site at http://www.gallup.com/poll/summits/islam.asp.
3. These and other quotes of Osama bin Laden are taken from transcripts of his tape printed in the *New York Times*, December 28, 2001, and the *Washington Post*, December 29, 2001.
4. *Christian Science Monitor*, September 27, 2001.
5. Cairo Press Review, on the Web at http://www.sis.gov.eg/pressrev/html/pv240921.htm.
6. Lawrenge Eagleberger quoted in *Time*, July 5, 1993.
7. Quoted in the *Christian Science Monitor*, September 27, 2001.

CHAPTER 6

1. *New York Times*, October 6, 1995, p. B10.
2. *New York Times*, June 8, 1994, p. A16.
3. From "Patrie" in *Dictionnaire Philosophique*, 1764.
4. *New York Times*, August 2, 1994, p. C1. The anthropologist was Eugene Hammel.
5. *New York Times*, April 10, 1994, p. E1.
6. Statement in "Report of the Secretary-General on the Work of the Organization," quoted in the *Hartford Courant*, September 9, 1999.
7. *Time*, March 12, 1990, p. 50.
8. *Toronto Star*, August 31, 2001, on the Web at http://www.ekos.com/media/files/torstar_31-aug-2001c.html.
9. *Hartford Courant*, March 12, 2000.
10. *Hartford Courant*, April 8, 1994, p. A8.
11. *New York Times*, May 11, 1998, p. A6.
12. Wilson's speech to Congress was on February 11, 1918.
13. Both quotes are from the *New York Times*, December 10, 1995, p. A3.

BOX, "The Chechens: Death or Freedom," p. 145

1. Quoted on the Web site of Consortiumnews.com, February 7, 2000, at: http://www.consortiumnews.com.
2. Solzhenitsyn is quoted in Edward Kline, "ASF Chechnya Brief," on the Web site of the Andrei Sakharov Foundation at: http://www.wdn.com/asf/.
3. CNN.com, January 11, 2002, on the Web at http://www.cnn.com/2002/WORLD/europe/01/11/chechnya/.

BOX, "Palestinians: A Nation Without a State," pp. 152–153

1. Poll conducted by Birzeit University on the Web at www.birzeit.edu/dsp/).
2. *Jerusalem Post* Poll, December 17, 2001, found on the Web at http://www.gamla.org.il/english/poll/index.htm.
3. U.S. State Department press bulletin, October 2, 2001, on the Web at http://usinfo.state.gov/regional/nea/summit/1002bush.htm.
4. Gallup/Ma'ariv poll of April 2000, found on the Web at http://www.us-israel.org/jsource/Politics/ispopal.html.
5. ABC News, March 29, 2002, on the Web at http://abcnews.go.com/sections/world/DailyNews/middleeastviolence_010329.html.

Box Afghanistan: Fact or Fiction, pp. 156–157

1. *Washington Post*, February 21, 2002.
2. *Washington Post*, February 2, 2002.
3. The expert was Martha Brill Olcott of the Carnegie Endowment for International Peace, quoted in the *Kansas City Star*, November 26, 2001, found on the National Geographic Society Web site at http://news.nationalgeographic.com/news/2001/11/1126_wireafghan.html.

"Did You Know That," p. 158

1. *New York Times*, July 23, 1996, p. A10.

CHAPTER 7

1. Pauline Maier, "No Sunshine Patriot." A review of *Tom Paine: A Political Life* (Boston: Little, Brown, 1995) in the *New York Times Book Review*, March 12, 1995, 1–*et. seq.*
2. Richard M. Nixon, *Beyond Peace* (New York: Random House, 1994), excerpted in *Time*, May 2, 1994, p. 33.

3. Both quotes are from the *New York Times*, August 3, 1992, p. A9.
4. *New York Times*, January 23, 1996, p. A7.
5. *New York Times*, October 21, 1993, p. A1.
6. *Los Angeles Times*, February 27, 2002.
7. CNN, February 1, 2002, on the CNN Web site http://www.cnn.com/2002/US/02/01/cheney.al.jazeera/.
8. *Chicago Tribune*, October 11, 2001, found on the Web at http://www.chicagotribune.com/news/nationworld/chi-0110110260oct11.story?coll=chi-news-hed.
9. *New York Times*, January 26, 2000.
10. *Time,* June 15, 1996, p. 54.
11. *Hartford Courant*, September 10, 1995, p. A7.
12. *New York Times*, March 8, 1998, p. A15. The scholar was Charlotte Bunch, executive director, Center for Women's Global Leadership, Rutgers University.
13. *New York Times*, June 13, 2000.
14. *Daily Star*, June 12, 2000, the paper's Web site at: http://dailystar.com.lb/features/12_06_00.htm.
15. *Hartford Courant*, July 10, 1992, p. A1.
16. Colin Powell, *My American Journey* (New York, Random House, 1995), excerpted in *Time*, September 18, 1995, p. 69, and quoted in the *New York Times*, September 17, 1995, p. A26.
17. Survey in the *New York Times*, June 7, 2000.
18. "Women 2000," final unedited document at: http://www.un.org/womenwatch/daw/followup/reports.htm.
19. *New York Times*, September 16, 1995, p. A5.
20. *New York Times*, January 28, 1998.
21. *New York Times*, April 10, 1995, p. A1.
22. *New York Times*, April 10, 1995, p. A1.
23. *New York Times*, August 24, 1994, p. E5.
24. *New York Times*, June 9, 1996, p. E5.
25. *New York Times*, November 7, 1995.
26. *Washington Post*, February 22, 2002.
27. Former Syrian prime minister Maaruf al-Dawalibi, quoted in the *New York Times*, June 2, 1993, p. A3.
28. *New York Times*, February 27, 1998, p. A8.
29. Gallup Poll Web site at http://www.gallup.com/poll/releases/pr020308.asp.
30. *USA Today*-CNN-Gallup Poll, reported in the *Arizona Republic*, March 5, 2001, on the Web at http://www.arizonarepublic.com/news/articles/0305poll05.html.
31. *USA Today*-CNN-Gallup Poll, reported in the *Arizona Republic*, March 5, 2001, on the Web at http://www.arizonarepublic.com/news/articles/0305poll05.html.
32. Sheik Abdalah bin Biyah, a member of the Supreme Council of Mosques and a professor of theology at King Abdelziz University in Jidda, Saudi Arabia, quoted in the *New York Times*, June 2, 1993, p. A3.
33. *New York Times*, April 14, 1996, p. D1.
34. *Washington Post*, January 29, 2000.
35. *BusinessWeek* Online, 8/13/01 at http://www.businessweek.com/magazine/content/01_33/b3745009.htm.
36. *New York Times*, October 21, 1994, p. A4.
37. *Hartford Courant*, September 19, 1999.
38. *Sydney Morning Herald*, November 30, 1999, on the SMH Web site at: http://www.smh.com.au/news/9911/30/world/world9.html.
39. *Hartford Courant*, March 7, 1996, p. E4.
40. *New York Times*, March 15, 1994, p. A1.
41. *New York Times*, July 11, 1992, p. A3.
42. *New York Times*, April 14, 1996, p. D1.
43. David Shenk of the Columbia University Freedom Forum Media Studies Center, quoted in the *New York Times*, April 14, 1996, p. D1.
44. *New York Times*, June 4, 1996, p. C1.
45. The scholar was political theorist Michael Sandel of Harvard University, quoted in the *New York Times*, March 18, 1996, p. A21.

BOX, "India, Pakistan, Religion, and the Bomb," p. 182–183

1. *Newsweek*, June 8, 1998, p. 25.
2. *New York Times*, February 16, 1998.
3. *New York Times*, May 16, 1998, p. A1.
4. *Washington Post*, February 28, 2002.

BOX, "And Never the Twain Shall Meet: Until Now," p. 192

1. *New York Times*, April 24, 1992, p. A4.
2. The analyst was Tom McCarthy, chief executive officer of the Asian Basketball Confederation. On the Web at http://www.gluckman.com/NBA.html.
3. *New York Times*, February 24, 1996, p. D7.

"Did You Know That," p. 172

1. CNN, January 22, 2002, on the Web at http://www.cnn.com/2002/WORLD/africa/01/22/blackhawk.screening/.

CHAPTER 8

1. *New York Times*, July 1, 2001. The advocate is Kenneth Roth, executive director of Human Rights Watch.
2. *Washington Post*, August 22, 2001. The senator is Larry E. Craig of Idaho.
3. Representative Ron Paul, *Congressional Record*, July 17, 2001, p. H4022.
4. *New York Times*, February 26, 1992, p. A6.
5. *The Internet Encyclopedia of Philosophy*, on the Web at: http://www.utm.edu/research/iep/d/donoso.htm.
6. InterPress Service World News, September 20,1998, on the Web at http://www.oneworld.org/ips2/sept98/12_34_035.html. The official was Maurice Glele-Ahanhanzo, UN Special Rapporteur of the Commission on Human Rights.
7. Anti-Defamation League (ADL) Web site at: http://www.adl.org/backgrounders/joerg_haider.html.
8. *Le Monde*, May 1998 at: http://www.monde-diplomatique.fr/en/1998/05/08igou.
9. *Chicago Tribune*, September 28, 2001, on the Web at http://www.chicagotribune.com/news/nationworld/chi-0109280210sep28.story?coll=chi-newsnationworld-utl.
10. *Hartford Courant*, February 25, 1994, p. A4.
11. *Newsweek*, June 6, 1994, p. 37.
12. *New York Times*, September 19, 1994, p. A10.
13. *Newsweek*, September 19, 1994, p. 37.
14. *New York Times*, March 22, 2002.
15. CNN.com, April 30, 2000 at: http://www.cnn.com/2000/HEALTH/AIDS/04/30/aids.threat.03/index.html.
16. CNN.com, April 20, 2000, at: http://www.cnn.com/2000/HEALTH/04/26/emerging.infections/index.html.

BOX, "The Wisdom of Patience," pp. 202–203

1. CNN, May 23, 2001 on the CNN Web site at http://www.cnn.com/2001/WORLD/asiapcf/east/05/23/dalai.bush.02/.
2. The White House, Office of the Press Secretary, Statement by the Press Secretary on the Meeting With the Dalai Lama, May 23, 2001, on the Web at http://usembassy.state.gov/tokyo/wwwhse0181.html.
3. Quotation found on the Web at http://www.geocities.com/Tokyo/Pagoda/6828/quote/all.html.

BOX, "Russia: Precarious Democracy," pp. 214–215

1. Romir Research Group Web site at: http://www.romir.ru/eng/default.htm. The survey was taken in 1999.
2. *Pravda*, June 13, 2001, on the Web at http://english.pravda.ru/politics/2001/06/13/7586.html.
3. Freedom House Web site at: www.freedomhouse.org/research/nattransit.htm.
4. *Washington Post*, January 3, 2000.
5. *Washington Post*, January 23, 2002. The commentator was Yevgeny Yasin, a liberal economist.
6. Interview of Professor Michael McFaul on Voice of America, no date, on the Web at http://www.voa.gov/thisweek/library/archive/jul00/putin.htm.

"Did You Know That," p. 211

1. Reuters press dispatch, January 21, 2002, found on the Web at http://ca.news.yahoo.com/020121/5/hhsj.html.

CHAPTER 9

1. *New York Times*, September 7, 1992, p. A5.
2. Churchill made the widely quoted statement on June 26, 1954, while visiting the United States. Various papers printed it the next day.
3. Address to the General Assembly, July 16, 1997, UN Doc. SG/SM/6284/Rev.2.
4. *Manchester Guardian Weekly*, July 27, 1997, p. 4.
5. *New York Times*, June 28, 2000.
6. Data is from the latest relevant poll taken by the Eurobarometer. The Web site is: http://europa.eu.int/comm/dg10/epo/.
7. Speech by President V. Giscard d'Estaing to the Convention on the Future of Europe, February 26, 2002, at: http://european-convention.eu.int/discours.asp?lang=EN.
8. *New York Times*, June 28, 2000.
9. *World Opinion Update*, March 1997, p. 33.
10. Speech by Joschka Fischer at the Humboldt University in Berlin, May 12, 2000, on the Web at: http://www.auswaertiges-amt.de/6_archiv/2/r/r000512b.htm.
11. *Wall Street Journal Europe*, May 5, 2000, on the Web at: http://www.nejtillemu.com/chevenement.htm.
12. Address to the Council on Foreign Relations, New York, April 22, 1997, UN document SG/SM/6218.
13. Permanent Mission of Germany to the United Nations Web site at: http://www.germany-info.org/UN/un_reform.htm.
14. President Frederick J. T. Chiluba of Zambia, both quoted in the *New York Times*, October 23, 1995, p. A8.
15. Fifty-sixth General Assembly, November 1, 2001, on the UN Web site at: http://www.un.org/News/Press/docs/2001/ga9945.doc.htm.
16. UN Press Release GA/9692, December 20, 1999.
17. Ambassador Francisco Paolo Fulci, quoted in the *New York Times*, November 15, 1995, p. A9.
18. PBS Online NewsHour inteview with U.S. State Department official Nicholas Burns, June 20, 1996, on the PBS Web site at: http://www.pbs.org/newshour/bb/middle_east/june96/boutros-ghali_6-20.html.
19. *New York Times*, March 6, 1995, p. A6.
20. Address to commencement at the Massachusetts Institute of Technology, Cambridge, June 5, 1997. UN Document SG/SM/6247.
21. James Traub, "Kofi Annan's Next Test," *New York Times Magazine*, March 29, 1998, p. 49.
22. Address to the Council on Foreign Relations, New York, January 19, 1999, UN document SG/SM/6865.
23. James Traub, "Kofi Annan's Next Test," *New York Times Magazine*, March 29, 1998, p. 80.
24. *New York Times*, September 12, 1995, p. A1.
25. *Time*, October 30, 1995, p. 74.
26. *New York Times*, December 16, 1996, p. A8.
27. James Traub, "Kofi Annan's Next Test," *New York Times Magazine*, March 29, 1998, p. 49.
28. Address to "Empower America," Washington, D.C., October 16, 1998, UN Document SG/SM/6754.
29. *New York Times*, November 6, 1994, p. A11.
30. *Time*, October 30, 1995, p. 74.
31. *New York Times*, July 17, 1997, p. A1.
32. Gallup International Millennium Survey, on the Web at: http://www.gallup-international.com/survey8.htm.
33. Address at Princeton University, November 24, 1997, UN document SG/SM/6404.
34. *New York Times*, January 8, 1997, p. A3.
35. *New York Times*, September 18, 1994, p. A16.
36. Kofi Annan, "The Unpaid Bill That's Crippling the UN," an op-ed piece, *New York Times*, March 9, 1998, p. A19.
37. Hammarskjöld's widely quoted statement is attributed to the *New York Times*, June 27, 1955.

BOX, "When Is a Banana a Banana?" p. 241

1. Reuters press dispatch, January 12, 2002.
2. *New York Times*, October 6, 1994, p. A16.

BOX, "Much Ado About Something," p. 248

1. *Time*, December 2, 1991, p. 28.

CHAPTER 10

1. Churchill told this story in a speech on October 24, 1928, and it can be found, among other places, in Robert Rhodes James, ed., *Winston S. Churchill: His Complete Speeches: 1897–1963*, Vol. 5 (1974), p. 5421.
2. *New York Times*, March 7, 1996, p. A10.
3. *Los Angeles Times*, September 22, 2001.
4. *New York Times*, February 24, 1998, p. A1.
5. Joint United Nations Programme on HIV/AIDS (UNAIDS) and World Health Organization (WHO), *AIDS Epidemic Update December 2001*, p. 16.

6. Andrei Memin, president of the Public Health Association, quoted in the *Hartford Courant*, November 24, 1995, p. A27.
7. *New York Times*, May 10, 1996, p. A10.
8. *New York Times*, June 8, 1997, p. E1.
9. *Washington Post*, July 9, 2000.
10. *Time*, July 15, 1996, p. 54.
11. *Time*, April 11, 1994, p. A10.
12. *Time*, June 13, 1994, p. 32.
13. *New York Times*, May 29, 1994, p. A1.
14. *Washington Post*, April 13, 1990, p. A7.
15. *New York Times*, August 28, 1994, p. E7.
16. *Washington Post*, February 3, 2001.
17. *Washington Post*, February 1, 2002.
18. MSNBC report, December 13, 2001, on the Web at: http://www.cdi.org/russia/johnson/5598-7.cfm.
19. BBC News 31 March, 2002, at http://news.bbc.co.uk/hi/english/world/europe/newsid_1903000/1903908.stm.
20. CBS News, January 20, 2002, at http://www.cbsnews.com/ stories/2002/01/20/politics/main324986.shtml.
21. *Washington Post*, April 5, 2002.
22. *Washington Post*, April 7, 2002.
23. The quote is Ambassador J. Stapleton Roy's recollection of what Jiang said, *New York Times*, July 3, 1995, p. E3.
24. *New York Times*, February 27, 2000.
25. *New York Times*, March 7, 1996, p. A1.
26. *New York Times*, April 19, 2000.
27. *New York Times*, February 27, 2000.
28. *New York Times*, May 6, 1994, p. A6.
29. *New York Times*, March 3, 1998, p. E3.
30. *Washington Post*, January 28, 2002.
31. *Washington Post*, January 29, 2002
32. *New York Times*, June 15, 2000.
33. *Time*, April 9, 1990, p. 39.
34. BBC report, November 15, 2001, on the BBC Web site: http://news.bbc.co.uk/hi/english/world/americas/newsid_1659000/1659048.stm.
35. Reuters dispatch, November 15, 2001, on the Web at: http://www.cdi.org/russia/johnson/5549-1.cfm.
36. BBC report, November 15, 2001, on the BBC Web site: http://news.bbc.co.uk/hi/english/world/americas/newsid_1659000/1659048.stm.
37. Reuters dispatch, November 15, 2001, on the Web at: http://www.cdi.org/russia/johnson/5549-1.cfm.
38. *New York Times*, February 3, 1996, p. A11.
39. *New York Times*, February 19, 2001.
40. *Washington Post*, April 11, 2002.
41. *Washington Post*, January 28, 2002
42. *Washington Post*, February 1, 2002.
43. *Washington Post*, February 1, 2002.
44. *Hartford Courant*, September 18, 1994, p. A4.
45. *Hartford Courant*, October 14, 1994, p. A9.
46. *Washington Post*, February 2, 2002.
47. *Wall Street Journal*, September 19, 2001.
48. *New York Times Magazine*, March 29, 1998, p. 50.
49. *Washington Post*, February 10, 2002.
50. *Washington Post*, February 10, 2002.
51. *New York Times*, March 6, 2000.
52. *New York Times*, February 27, 2000.
53. *Washington Post*, April 1, 2000.
54. *Hartford Courant*, March 17, 1994, p. A6.
55. *Time*, June 13, 1994, p. 32.

56. *New York Times*, March 17, 1994, p. A10.
57. *New York Times*, October 4, 1994, p. A1. The official was Assistant Secretary of Defense Joseph Nye.
58. *USA Today*, March 11, 1996, p. A7.
59. *Washington Post*, February 10, 2002.
60. *Washington Post*, February 10, 2002.
61. *New York Times*, April 30, 1988, p. 31.
62. *New York Times*, March 16, 1995, p. A5.
63. *New York Times*, March 16, 1995, p. A5. Some words added to smooth out the poor translation quoted in the *Times*.
64. Vice Admiral Archie Ray Clemins, quoted in the *New York Times*, March 17, 1996, p. D1.
65. *Washington Post*, February 25, 2000.
66. *New York Times*, June 6, 1998, p. A1.
67. *New York Times*, August 19, 1995, p. A1.
68. President George W. Bush address to joint session of Congress, September 20, 2001, on the White House Web site at: http://www.whitehouse.gov/news/releases/2001/09/20010920-8.html.
69. *New York Times*, March 1, 2000.
70. *New York Times*, March 11, 2000.
71. Chief of Staff Leon Panetta, quoted in the *New York Times*, March 18, 1996, p. A3.

BOX, "Come Abroad to See the World," pp. 284–285

1. *New York Times*, June 28, 1998.
2. *New York Times*, August 4, 1998.
3. Representative Larry Craig, October 5, 1998, *Congressional Record*, p. S11405.
4. U.S. General Accounting Office report GAO/NSAID-99-164 (Presidential Travel).
5. Charles Jones, quoted in the *Christian Science Monitor*, November 21, 1997.
6. *Time*, October 31, 1994, p. 36.

BOX "'El Paso' Powell," p. 288

1. Report and quotes, other than from the song "El Paso," are from the *New York Times*, July 27, 2001.

"Did You Know That," p. 272

1. *Washington Post*, July 2, 2001.

CHAPTER 11

1. UN Web site at: http://www.un.org/icty/glance/milosevic.htm.
2. European Court of Justice Case C-285/98, January 11, 2000, paragraph 29.
3. *New York Times*, November 12, 1997, p. A7.
4. *New York Times*, January 14, 2000.
5. *New York Times*, August 4, 1998, p. A4.
6. *New York Times*, July 9, 1996, p. A6.
7. *World Tribune*, April 26, 1999, on the Web at: http://www.worldtribune.com/mz04-26-99.html.
8. *New York Times*, May 5, 1994, p. A11.
9. U.S. State Department, Bureau of Democracy, Human Rights, and Labor, Country Reports on Human Rights

Practices, 2001, released March 4, 2002, on the Web: http://www.state.gov/g/drl/rls/hrrpt/2001/eap/8289.htm.

10. *Newsweek*, November 29, 1993, p. 47.

11. *New York Times*, March 5, 1997, p. A8.

12. Thomas Riggins, "Why Humanists Should Reject The Social Contract," March 20, 2001, Corliss Lamont Chapter of the American Humanist Association Web site at:http://www.corliss-lamont.org/hsmny/contract.htm. Professor Riggins teaches the history of philosophy at the New School for Social Research and at New York University.

13. Address at the University of Tehran on Human Rights Day, December 10, 1997, UN document SG/SM/6419.

14. Address at Ditchley Park, United Kingdom, June 26, 1998, UN document SG/SM/6313.

15. Statement of December 4, 2001, quoted in Nicholas J. Wheeler, "Protecting Afghan Civilians From the Hell of War," Social Science Research Council Web site: http://www.ssrc.org/sept11/essays/wheeler_text_only.htm.

16. The quote is by Professor Ken Brown, Director, Peace Studies, Manchester College, Indiana, writing on February 22, 2002, to the *Chronicle of Higher Education* on its Web site at: http://chronicle.com/colloquy/2002/letter/15.htm.

17. *New York Times*, January 24, 1990, p. A1.

18. *Jerusalem Post*, February 15, 2002, on the Web at: http://www.jpost.com/Editions/2002/02/15/News/News.43505.html.

19. Taken from the Web at: http://worldnews.miningo.com/msub.12.htm.

20. BBC, July 4, 2001, on the Web at: http://www.cnn.com/2001/WORLD/europe/07/03/milosevic.court/.

21. CNN, June 1, 2000, at: http://www.cnn.com/2000/LAW/06/01/tanzania.rwandatribun.ap/.

22. Remarks by President Bill Clinton, University of Connecticut, October 15, 1995, available at: http://www.pub.whitehouse.gov/uri-res/I2R?urn:pdi://oma.eop.gov.us/1995/10/17/10.text.1.

23. *New York Times*, June 16, 1998, p. A6.

24. *New York Times*, August 13, 1997, p. A10.

25. *New York Times*, June 10, 1998, p. A6, and June 15, 1998, p. A8, respectively.

26. Annan speech was found on the Web at: http://un.org/icc.

27. NewsMax, April 12, 2002, on the Web at: http://www.newsmax.com/archives/articles/2002/4/11/144333.shtml.

28. *Washington Post*, April 12, 2002.

29. NewsMax, April 12, 2002, on the Web at: http://www.newsmax.com/archives/articles/2002/4/11/144333.shtml.

30. *Washington Post*, April 12, 2002.

31. *Washington Post*, April 12, 2002.

32. Statement of the Islamic Resistance Movement, Hamas-Palestine, issued December 17, 2001, in reaction to the speech of President Arafat, on the Web at: http://www.jmcc.org/new/01/dec/hamasstate.htm.

33. Associated Press release, October 8, 2001, on the Web at: http://www.deathpenaltyinfo.org/Terr-APExtradition.html.

34. *New York Times*, April 7, 1998, p. A17.

35. Kennedy's remark was on June 24, 1963, and can be found in the *Public Papers of the President of the United States: John F. Kennedy, 1963*.

BOX, "Corruption and International Law," p. 304

1. *New York Times*, August 13, 1997, p. A3.

CHAPTER 12

1. *Time*, January 28, 1991, p. 33.

2. *Newsweek*, September 24, 2001.

3. *New York Times*, August 23, 1997, p. A5.

4. *Newsweek*, July 13, 1998, p. 59.

5. *New York Times*, July 28, 1997, p. A1.

6. *Time*, September 9, 1996, p. 17.

7. *Time*, July 15, 1996, p. 54.

8. Richard Haas, quoted in *Time*, November 27, 1995, p. 49.

9. *Newsweek*, November 26, 1994, p. 36.

10. *Time*, October 1, 1990, p. 54.

11. Jacob Heilbrunn and Michael Lind, "The Third American Empire," an op-ed piece in the *New York Times*, January 2, 1996, p. A15.

12. The diplomat was Charles H. Thomas II, former U.S envoy to Bosnia, quoted in the *New York Times*, November 29, 1995, p. E2.

13. *Washington Post*, April 13, 2001.

14. Gary W. Gallagher, "At War With Himself," a review of Michael Fellman, *Citizen Sherman: A Life of William Tecumseh Sherman* (New York: Random House, 1995) in the *New York Times Review of Books*, October 22, 1995, p. 24.

15. *New York Times*, June 17, 1998, p. A5.

16. Nicholas Berry, senior analyst, Center for Defense Information, on the CDI Web site at: www.cdi.org.

17. Agence France Presse story, December 4, 2001, on the Web at: http://www.globalsecurity.org/org/news/2001/011204-attack01.htm.

18. *New York Times*, February 13, 1994, p. A12. The official was Vladimir Diouhy, Czech minister of industry and trade.

19. *World Press Review*, Feb. 19, 2002, on the Web at: http://www.worldpress.org/Asia/401.cfm.

20. Doug Bandow, "Our War Against Bandits?" May 2002, Cato Institute Web site at: http://www.cato.org/current/terrorism/pubs/bandow-020118.html.

21. Interpress Service World News, November 29, 2001, on the Web at: http://www.oneworld.org/ips2/oct01/01_13_005.html.

22. 2001 Report on Foreign Terrorist Organizations, at http://www.state.gov/s/ct/rls/rpt/fto/2001/5258.htm.

23. *Washington Post*, April 24, 2002.

24. *Hartford Courant*, March 12, 1999.

25. U.S. State Department Web site: http://www.state.gov/s/ct/rls/rpt/fto/2001/5258.htm.

26. World Islamic Front Statement, "Jihad Against Jews and Crusaders," February 23, 1998, on the Web site of the Federation of American Scientists at: http://www.fas.org/irp/world/para/docs/980223-fatwa.htm.

27. *Washington Post National Weekly Edition*, October 1–7, 2001. The senator was Pat Robert of Kansas.

28. Paul Wilkenson, "The Strategic Implications of Terrorism," on the Web site of the Center for the Study of Terrorism and Political Violence at: http://www.st-and.ac.uk/academic/intrel/research/cstpv/publications1d.htm.

29. *Washington Post*, January 11, 2002.

30. ABC News report, March 6, 2002, on the Web at: http://abcnews.go.com/sections/wnt/DailyNews/WNT_

dirtybombs_020306.html. The expert was John Pike, director of the Global Security Organization testifying before the U.S. Senate Committee on Foreign Relations.

31. *Washington Post*, March 18, 2002.
32. *World Press Review*, September 1996, p. 42.
33. Amy Smithson on the Web site of the Henry L. Stimson Center at: http://www.stimson.org/cbw/?SN=CB2001121259; and testifying before the U.S. House Committee on Energy and Commerce, on the congressional Web site at: http://energycommerce.house.gov/107/hearings/10102001Hearing390/Smithson622.htm.
34. Elizabeth A. Fenn, "Biological Warfare, Circa 1750," an op-ed piece in the *New York Times*, April 11, 1998, p. A11.
35. *Hartford Courant*, September 15, 1992, p. A10.
36. *Hartford Courant*, April 2, 2000. The expert was Alan Zellicoff of Sandia National Laboratories.
37. *New York Times*, February 25, 1996, p. A8.
38. Colonel General Lev Rokhlin, quoted in *Time*, June 3, 1996, p. 48.
39. *Time*, May 19, 1997, p. 47.
40. *New York Times*, October 26, 1994, p. A10.
41. *New York Times*, July 7, 1998, p. A7.
42. Washington Post, March 12, 2002, quoting Defense Secretary William Perry's 1996 statement.

BOX, "War Is Hell!" p. 331

1. All quotes are from the *New York Times*, November 12, 1996, p. A1.

BOX, "President Bush and NUT Strategy," pp. 364–365

1. *Washington Post*, March 15, 2002.
2. *Washington Post*, March 12, 2002, quoting Darryl Kimball, director of the Arms Control Association.
3. *Washington Post*, March 17, 2002. The official was Deputy Secretary of Defense Paul Wolfowitz.
4. *Washington Post*, December 15, 2001. The critic was Joseph Cirincione of the Carnegie Endowment for International Peace.
5. George Bush, May 1, 2001, address at the National Defense University, on the White House Web site at: http://www.whitehouse.gov/news/releases/2001/05/20010501-10.html.
6. *Washington Post*, December 16, 2001. The expert was John Rhinelander, an arms control negotiator in the Nixon administration.
7. *New York Times*, April 26, 2000.
8. *New York Times*, May 11, 2000.

CHAPTER 13

1. *Labor*, September 6, 1947.
2. U.S. Department of State Web site at: http://www.state.gov/www/global/arms/np/mtcr/mtcr96.html.
3. *New York Times*, May 12, 1996, p. A1.
4. *Hartford Courant*, July 7, 1992, p. A6.
5. United Nations Department of Disarmament Affairs Web site at: http://www.un.org/Depts/dda/CAB/smallarms/sg.htm.
6. Ivan Eland, "Tilting at Windmills: Post–Cold War Military Threats to U.S. Security," Cato Institute, February 1999, available through the Columbia Working Papers on

the Web: http://wwwc.cc.columbia.edu/sec/dlc/ciao/wpsfrm.html.
7. U.S. House of Representative Armed Services Committee Web site: http://www.house.gov/hasc/openingstatementsandpressreleases/107thcongress/02-02-05rumsfeld.html.
8. *Congressional Record*, October 13, 1999, p. S12549.
9. *New York Times*, September 12, 1996, p. A9.
10. *Newsweek*, May 25, 1998, p. 32B.
11. *New York Times*, May 31, 1998, p. A1.
12. Organization for Security and Cooperation in Europe Web site at: http://www.osce.org/field_activities/field_activities.htm.
13. *New York Times*, December 20, 1995, p. A9.
14. *New York Times*, January 31, 1992, p. A9.
15. *New York Times*, May 10, 2000. The analyst was J. Stephen Morrison, the director of Africa programs at the Center for Strategic and International Studies in Washington.
16. *New York Times*, January 6, 1995, p. A3.
17. New York Times, May 4, 1997, p. 12.
18. *New York Times*, October 3, 1999.

BOX, "Chained to the Nuclear Rock," pp. 370–371

1. *Time*, September 18, 1995, p. 85.
2. *Newsweek*, May 25, 1998, p. 32B.
3. *New York Times*, May 17, 1998, p. WK2. The scholar was Joseph Cirincione, director of the Nonproliferation Project of the Carnegie Endowment.
4. ABC News, May 28, 1998, on the ABC Web site at: http://abcnews.go.com/sections/world/DailyNews/pakistan_missiles980528.html.
5. *New York Times*, May 17, 1998, p. WK2.
6. *New York Times*, September 25, 1996, p. A1.
7. *New York Times*, October 14, 1999.
8. *Washington Post*, January 7, 2002.

BOX, "Adopt a Minefield," pp. 384–385

1. *New York Times*, May 1, 1996.
2. U.S. Department of State report, "Hidden Killers: The Global Landmine Crisis," 1998, on the Web at: http://www.state.gov/www/global/arms/rpt_9809_demine_toc.html.
3. *New York Times*, June 17, 1997.
4. *New York Times*, September 4, 1997.
5. United Nations Web site at: http://disarmament.un.org/MineBan.nsf.

BOX, "The Crusade to Save the Crusader," pp. 388–389

1. *Washington Post,* May 3, 2002.
2. Government Executive, May 14, 2002, online edition http://www.govexec.com/dailyfed/0502/051402db.htm.

CHAPTER 14

1. *Federalist Number 6* found on the Web at: http://memory.loc.gov/const/fed/fedpapers.html.
2. U.S. Congress, House of Representatives., Hearings before the Subcommittee on Trade of the Committee on Ways and Means, May 7, 1998. Michael Ranneberger was the official.

3. Quoted in Michael Lind, "Why Buy American?" a review of Alfred E. Eckes Jr., *U.S. Foreign Trade Policy since 1776* (Chapel Hill: University of North Carolina Press, 1995), in the *New York Times Book Review*, October 29, 1995, p. 42.
4. Catherine L. Mann, "Is the U.S. Current Account Deficit Sustainable?" *Finance & Development* (a quarterly magazine of the IMF), March 2000, 37/1, on the IMF Web site at: http://www.imf.org/external/pubs/ft/fandd/2000/03/mann.htm.
5. Clinton's remarks were made on January 29, 2000, and can be found on the Web: http://www.usembassy-mexico.gov/et000131WEF.html.
6. *New York Times*, February 1, 1999.
7. *Toronto Star*, July 29, 2001, on the Web at: http://www.organicconsumers.org/corp/antiglobalization080101.cfm. The protest leader was Joshua Karliner, executive director of CorpWatch.
8. Data supplied by economist Gary Hufbauer and Kimberly Elliott to the *New York Times*, November 12, 1993, p. D1.
9. *New York Times*, November 12, 1993, p. D1.
10. *New York Times*, May 28, 1998, p. A10.
11. *New York Times*, November 2, 1996.
12. Representative Joseph Gaydos in the *Congressional Record*, April 13, 1988, p. A1613.
13. All quotes are from Charles R. Smith, "Rand Report Warns of Conflict With China," June 20, 2001, on the NewsMax Web site at: http://www.newsmax.com/archives/articles/2001/6/19/205940.shtml. The congressional staff member was Al Santoli, national security adviser to Representative Dana Rohrabacher.
14. *New York Times*, October 30, 1996, p. A1.
15. *Washington Post*, May 15, 2002.
16. From the White House Web site, May 20, 2002, at http://www.whitehouse.gov/news/releases/2002/05/200205201.html.
17. *New York Times*, February 1, 1999.

BOX, "GNP-PPP: The Big Mac Standard," p. 406

1. The Big Mac Standard can be found in several places on the Web including http://www.oanda.com/products/bigmac/bigmac.shtml.

CHAPTER 15

1. *New York Times*, October 12, 1996, p. A1.
2. Office of the National Counterintelligence Executive. Annual Report to Congress on Foreign Economic Collection and Industrial Espionage, 2001, on the Web at: http://www.ncix.gov/pubs/reports/fy01.htm#a.
3. *Washington Post*, June 12, 2002.
4. *Los Angeles Times*, June 22, 2001.
5. Economist Gary C. Hufbauer, quoted in the *New York Times*, September 11, 1996, p. D1.
6. See the USA Engage Web site at: www.usaengage.org.
7. *New York Times*, October 23, 1995, p. A8.
8. *Washington Post*, May 22, 2002.
9. *Washington Post*, May 18, 2002.
10. Press release, March 5, 2002, on the European Union Web site at: http://www.eurunion.org/news/press/2002/2002011.htm.
11. *Washington Post*, May 23, 2002.
12. *New York Times*, April 4, 1991, p. A6.

13. *New York Times*, March 2, 1997, p. A39.
14. *New York Times*, April 7, 1996, p. E5.
15. BBC News, February 12, 2000, on the Web at: http://news2.thls.bbc.co.uk.
16. *New York Times*, February 5, 2002.
17. This and the following quotes related to the G-77 summit are from the "Havana Program of Action," April 14, 2000, found on the UNCTAD Web site at: http://www.g77.org/main/docs.htm.
18. *Time*, September 19, 1995, p. 92.
19. The 2002 Index to Economic Freedom can be found on the Heritage Foundation's Web site at: http://www.heritage.org/index/2002.
20. *New York Times*, June 25, 1996, p. A1.
21. Klaus Schwab, director of the Davos Forum, quoted in Thomas L. Friedman, "Revolt of the Wannabes," a column in the *New York Times*, February 7, 1996, p. A19.

CHAPTER 16

1. Government of Canada's G-8 summit site at: http://www.g8.gc.ca/summitintro-e.asp.
2. John Kirton of the University of Toronto's G-7 Research Group, "What Is the G-7?" document on the Web on November 10, 1996, at: http://unl1.library.utoronto.ca/www/g7/what_is_g7.html.
3. *Hartford Courant*, July 23, 2000. The two scholars were William Anhholis and Daniel Benjamin.
4. Emerson Kapaz of São Paulo, quoted in the *Wall Street Journal*, June 21, 1991, p. A11.
5. BBC News, March 22, 2002, on the Web at: http://news.bbc.co.uk/hi/english/world/newsid_1886000/1886617.stm.
6. Address on March 22, 2002, International Conference on Financing for Development Web site at: http://www.un.org/esa/ffd/.
7. *Hartford Courant*, March 12, 1995, p. A1.
8. ILO report, "Child Labour Today: Facts and Figures, Geneva, June 10, 1996," taken from the Web at: http://www.ilo.org.
9. *New York Times*, September 7, 2000.
10. Web site for UNCTAD's tenth meeting at: http://www.unctad-10.org/index_en.htm.
11. Joint press release, April 15, 2002, found on the European Union Web site at: http://www.eurunion.org/news/press/2002/2002018.htm.
12. Press release, April 29, 2002, the Office of the U.S. Trade Representative (USTR) found on the Web: http://www.useu.be/Categories/Trade/Steel/.
13. Speech by President Bill Clinton at the WTO meeting in Seattle, Washington, December 1, 1999, on the U.S. State Department Web site at: http://usinfo.state.gov/topical/econ/wto99/pp1201l.htm#reform.
14. Associated Press photo APA4141750 (2GRSM), December 1, 1999, on the AP proprietary Web site at: http://photoarchive.ap.org.
15. WTO Web site: http://www.wto.org/english/thewto_e/minist_e/min99_e/english/misinf_e/04envir_e.htm.
16. All quotes in this paragraph from Inter Press Service News Agency, April 17, 2002, on the Web at: http://www.ipsnews.net/interna.asp?idnews=9119.
17. *New York Times*, February 17, 1998, p. A1.
18. *Washington Post*, January 15, 2002.

19. *Washington Post*, December 21, 2001. The critic was Cristina Lopez, a government official.
20. Jeffrey D. Sachs, "IMF 'Cure' Is Adding to Crisis in Argentina," op-ed piece in the *Irish Times*, May 4, 2002. On the Web at: http://www.ireland.com/newspaper/world/2002/0504/1301835165FR04WVIEW.html.
21. *Washington Post*, May 3, 2002. The observer was Artemio Lopez, chief economist for EquisResearch.
22. *Washington Post*, December 21, 2001.
23. *Washington Post*, April 30, 2002.
24. World Bank, *Annual Report 2001*, on the Web: http://www.worldbank.org/annualreport/2001/overview.htm#fig1.1.
25. *New York Times*, November 11, 1995, p. A37.
26. Comments in a speech, January 22, 1999, on the Web at: http://www.oneworld.net/guides/imf_wb/front.shtml.
27. *New York Times*, April 18, 2000.
28. *Hartford Courant*, November 1, 1992, p. F7.
29. *Toronto Star*, April 11, 2001.
30. *New York Times*, December 8, 1994, p. A14.
31. *New York Times*, December 12, 1994, p. A8.
32. *New York Times*, December 11, 1994, p. A1.
33. Both quotes are from the *New York Times*, December 12, 1994, p. A8.
34. *Washington Post*, January 17, 2002.
35. Stop the FTAA Web site at: http://www.stopftaa.org/.
36. Declaration of Quebec City, April 22, 2001, on the Web site of the Organization of the American States at: http://www.sice.oas.org/ftaa/quebec/declara_e.asp.
37. *New York Times*, September 18, 1997, p. A7.
38. *New York Times*, April 19, 1998, p. A10.
39. All quotes are from the *New York Times*, November 19, 1993, p. A1.
40. *New York Times*, August 23, 1992, p. F5.
41. Jans Kerkhofs of Louvain University, quoted in *Time*, December 9, 1991, p. 40.
42. *New York Times*, December 12, 1994, p. A8.
43. *New York Times*, January 29, 1992, p. D2.

CHAPTER 17

1. Both quotes, the second by Robert Repetto of the World Resources Institute, are from the *New York Times*, September 19, 1995, p. C1.
2. Paul Portney of Resources for the Future, quoted in the *New York Times*, September 19, 1995, p. C1.
3. *New York Times*, February 28, 1996, p. A3.
4. Final document of the World Food Summit, November 17, 1996, taken from the World Wide Web at: http://www.fao.org/wfs/final/rd-e.htm.
5. CNN news item, November 13, 1996, taken from the World Wide Web.
6. Final document of the World Food Summit, November 17, 1996, taken from the World Wide Web at: http://www.fao.org/wfs/final/rd-e.htm.
7. United Nations Chronicle Web site, 1991, Issue 3, at http://www.un.org/Pubs/chronicle/2001/issue3/0103p12.html.
8. *Hartford Courant*, December 17, 1992, p. A1.
9. World Health Organization press release, October 19, 2001, on the Web at: http://www.who.int/inf-pr-2001/en/pr2001-45.html.
10. *New York Times*, November 28, 1996, p. A10.
11. CNN news report of October 18, 1995, taken from the World Wide Web.
12. The quotes are from an interview of Goldhagen, not from his book, and are found in the *New York Times*, April 1, 1996, p. C11.
13. *New York Times*, February 3, 1994, p. A12.
14. *Hartford Courant*, December 13, 1991, p. A1.
15. *Hartford Courant*, December 17, 1992, p. A1.
16. The previous two quotes are from the *New York Times*, December 13, 1991, p. A13.
17. *New York Times*, August 20, 1998, p. A11.
18. BBC News, March 15, 2002, on the BBC Web site at: http://news.bbc.co.uk/hi/english/world/middle_east/newsid_1874000/1874471.stm.
19. All quotes from Human Rights Watch, "Human Rights in Saudi Arabia: A Deafening Silence," December 2001, on the Human Rights Watch Web site at: http://hrw.org/backgrounder/mena/saudi/#Discrimination against Women.
20. International Programme for the Elimination of Child Labour, "Every Child Counts," 2002, in the International Labor Organization Web site at: http://www.ilo.org/public/english/standards/ipec/simpoc/others/globalest.pdf.
21. Toronto *Globe and Mail*, August 26, 1996, reproduced in the *World Press Review*, November 1996, p. 10.
22. *Newsweek*, August 13, 1995, pp. 44–46.
23. Quoted in Adrian Karatnycky, "The Real Zyuganov," an op-ed piece in the *New York Times*, March 5, 1996, p. A23.
24. The poll, commissioned by the American Jewish Committee, was reported in the *Hartford Courant*, March 30, 1994, p. A11.
25. *New York Times*, March 31, 1996, p. A8.
26. *Hartford Courant*, July 7, 1993, p. A1.
27. *World Press Review* online, April 30, 2002, http://www.worldpress.org/Europe/584.cfm
28. *The Australian*, May 08, 2002, on the Web at: http://www.theaustralian.news.com.au/common/story_page/0,5744,4278379%255E21207,00.html.
29. All quotes from *The Australian*, May 08, 2002, on the Web at: http://www.theaustralian.news.com.au/common/story_page0,5744,4278379%255E21207,00.html.
30. *New York Times*, March 11, 1995, p. A5.
31. *New York Times*, March 4, 1998, p. A1.
32. MADRE press release, April 12, 2002, on the Web at: http://www.madre.org/criminalcourt.html.
33. *New York Times*, December 29, 1997, p. A3.
34. *Hartford Courant*, December 12, 1996, p. A8.
35. Report on the World Congress against Commercial Sexual Exploitation of Children, taken in December 1996 from the UNICEF Web site at: http://www.childhub.ch/webpub/csechome/.
36. Quoted in Barbara Crossette, "Snubbing Human Rights," *New York Times*, April 28, 1996, p. E3.
37. *Guardian Unlimited*, September 1, 2001, on the Web at: http://www.guardian.co.uk/unracism/story/0,1099,545232,00.html.
38. *Guardian Unlimited*, September 3, 2001, on the Web at: http://www.guardian.co.uk/unracism/story/0,1099,546042,00.html.

39. State of Secretary of State Powell on the State Department Web site at: http://www.state.gov/p/io/uncnf/wcar/.
40. *Hartford Courant*, September 8, 2001.
41. BBC September 8, 2001 on the Web at: http://news.bbc.co.uk/hi/english/world/africa/newsid_1530000/1530976.stm.

BOX, "Asylum," pp. 512–513.

1. *New York Times*, April 15, 1996.
2. *New York Times*, September 11, 1996, p. B7.
3. *New York Times*, September 11, 1996, p. B7.
4. *New York Times*, September 11, 1996, p. B7.
5. *New York Times*, August 8, 1996, p. A3.
6. Both quotes are from the *New York Times*, September 11, 1996, p. B7.
7. *New York Times*, April 15, 1996, p. A1.
8. *New York Times*, June 14, 1996, p. A1.
9. *New York Times*, September 11, 1996, p. B7.
10. UNFPA press release, September 18, 1997, on the UNFPA Web site at: http://www.unfpa.org/news/pressroom/1997/dirie.htm.

BOX, "The Road to Beijing and Beyond," p. 521

1. *New York Times*, June 28, 1996, p. A1.
2. *New York Times*, May 12, 1996, p. A3.

CHAPTER 18

1. The *State of the World* series is an annually published project of the Worldwatch Institute, with articles by a group of analysts on a variable agenda of issues related to the environment. The 2002 project director was Hilary French. The series is published by W. W. Norton in New York City.
2. *New York Times*, May 20, 1997, p. C1.
3. *New York Times*, May 20, 1997, p. C1.
4. Theodore Roszak, "Green Guilt and Ecological Overload," an op-ed piece published in the *New York Times*, June 9, 1992, p. A27. Roszak is on the faculty of California State University, Hayward.
5. Annan's comments can be found in the *Washington Post*, February 12, 2000.
6. *New York Times*, November 29, 1995, p. A1.
7. *Time*, December 12, 1990, p. 48.
8. *Time*, June 1, 1992, p. 42.
9. *New York Times*, April 30, 1992, p. A12.
10. *New York Times*, December 31, 1997, p. A6.
11. CBS News, January 23, 2001, on the CBS News Web site at: http://www.cbsnews.com/stories/2001/01/11/politics/main263530.shtml.
12. *Newsday*, March 7, 2002, on the Web at: http://www.commondreams.org/views02/0307-08.htm. Dr. Obaid became executive director in early 2001; earlier references (prior to 2001) to the UNFPA executive director in this and other sections refer to Nafis Sadik.
13. *Time*, September 5, 1994, p. 52.
14. The Pakistani delegate, Said Khawar Mumtaz of Punjab University, and the Chinese delegate, Wang Jiaxaing of Beijing Foreign Studies University, were quoted in the *New York Times*, September 2, 1994, p. A3.
15. *New York Times*, August 31, 1994, p. A9.
16. *New York Times*, September 6, 1994, p. A1.
17. All quotes are from the *New York Times*, September 4, 1995, p. A2.
18. *New York Times*, December 12, 1993, p. A5.
19. Julian Simon, "Environmentalists May Cause the Truth to Become Extinct," an op-ed piece in the *Hartford Courant*, June 15, 1992, p. C11.
20. UNEP Web site at: http://www.indev.org/news/1jan02.html.
21. *New York Times*, August 23, 1998, p. A19.
22. *New York Times*, April 12, 1994.
23. *Hartford Courant*, August 4, 1995, p. A9.
24. *Sydney Morning Herald*, June 7, 2002. http://www.smh.com.au/articles/2002/06/06/1022982747801.html.
25. *Time*, January 2, 1989, p. 47.
26. UN Human Rights Commission, Document E/CN.4/1998/10. "Adverse Effects of the Illicit Movement and Dumping of Toxic and Dangerous Products and Wastes on the Enjoyment of Human Rights," January 20, 1998. On the Web at: http://www.hri.ca/fortherecord1998/documentation/commission/e-cn4-1998-10.htm#Introduction.
27. *New York Times*, February 29, 2000.
28. *New York Times*, September 10, 1995, p. A1.
29. *New York Times*, December 20, 1994, p. C4. The scientist was R. Steven Nerem of NASA.
30. *New York Times*, September 6, 2000.
31. *New York Times*, May 24, 1994, p. C1. The IPCC head is John Houghton.
32. *Hartford Courant*, May 11, 2000.
33. *New York Times*, July 8, 1996, p. A2.
34. *New York Times*, September 14, 1993, p. C1. The scientist was Dixy Lee Ray, author of a 1993 book, *Environmental Overkill: Whatever Happened to Common Sense?*
35. *New York Times*, August 19, 2000.
36. *New York Times*, February 29, 2000.
37. *Hartford Courant*, September 22, 1991, p. A1. Statement by Paul Waggoner, who headed the academy's study panel.
38. *Hartford Courant*, September 16, 1994, p. A8.
39. *New York Times*, September 14, 1993. The scholars are Ben W. Bolch and Harold Lyons of Rhodes College, authors of *Apocalypse Not: Science, Economics and Environmentalism*.
40. *New York Times*, May 24, 1994. This scientist was John Houghton, head of the IPCC and author of *Global Warming: The Complete Briefing*.
41. *New York Times*, September 14, 1993, p. C1.
42. NASA's Marshall Space Flight Center, *Science@NASA* article, September 17, 2001, found on the Web at: http://www.southpole.com/headlines/y2001/ast17sep_1.htm. The scientist was Paul Newman of the Goddard Space Flight Center.
43. *New York Times*, December 18, 1990, p. C1.
44. *New York Times*, December 18, 1990, p. C1.
45. *Manchester Guardian Weekly*, March 20, 1994, p. 10. The opposition leader was Chris Smith, environment spokesman for the Labour Party.

BOX, "Earth Summits and Sustainable Development," pp. 538–539

1. *New York Times*, June 12, 1992, p. A9.
2. *Hartford Courant*, June 8, 1992, p. A2.

3. *Hartford Courant*, June 15, 1992, p. A1.
4. Web site of the U.S. Embassy in Indonesia at http://
www.usembassyjakarta.org/press_rel/wssd_bali4.html .
The U.S. delegate was Under Secretary of State for Global
Affairs Paula Dobriansky.
5. All quotes from a Reuters wire story, June 7, 2002, on the
Web at: http://www.miami.com/mld/miami/news/world/
3418504.htm.

**BOX, "From Kyoto to Johannesburg and Beyond,"
pp. 562–563**

1. *New York Times*, December 12, 1997, p. A1.
2. *New York Times*, November 20, 1997, p. A7.
3. *Hartford Courant*, December 11, 1997, p. A1.
4. *Hartford Courant*, December 11, 1997, p. A1.
5. *New York Times*, December 12, 1997, p. A1.
6. *New York Times*, December 13, 1997, p. A7.
7. *Washington Post*, June 4, 2002.
8. *Washington Post*, June 5, 2002.

Glossary

Adjudication   The legal process of deciding an issue through the courts. 308

Adversarial diplomacy   A negotiation situation where two or more countries' interests clash, but when there is little or no chance of armed conflict. 279

Amorality   The philosophy that altruistic acts are unwise and even dangerous, or that morality should never be the absolute guide of human actions, particularly in regard to international law. 325

Anarchical political system   An anarchical system is one in which there is no central authority to make rules, to enforce rules, or to resolve disputes about the actors in the political system. Many people believe that a system without central authority is inevitably one either of chaos or one in which the powerful prey on the weak. There is, however, an anarchist political philosophy that contends that the natural tendency of people to cooperate has been corrupted by artificial political, economic, or social institutions. Therefore, anarchists believe that the end of these institutions will lead to a cooperative society. Marxism, insofar as it foresees the collapse of the state once capitalism is destroyed and workers live in proletariat harmony, has elements of anarchism. 29

Anti-Ballistic Missile Treaty   A treaty signed by the United States and the Soviet Union (now Russia) in 1972 that barred the two countries from developing and deploying a system to shoot down ballistic missiles. The United States withdrew from the treaty in 2001 in order to pursue the development and deployment of a national missile defense system. 376

Anti-Personnel Mine Treaty   A treaty signed in 1997 and effective in 1999 that commits its adherents not to product, stockpile, or transfer antipersonnel land mines, to destroy any current inventory of mines, and to remove all mines they have planted. The United States is among the handful of countries that is not in agreement to the treaty. 383

Appeasement policy   A policy advocated by the British and French toward the Germans following World War I. The hope was to maintain peace by allowing Hitler to annex the Sudentenland part of Czechoslovakia. 36

Arms control   A variety of approaches to the limitation of weapons. Arms control ranges from restricting the future growth in the number, types, or deployment of weapons; through the reduction of weapons; to the elimination of some types of (or even all) weapons on a global or regional basis. 373

Asia-Pacific Economic Cooperation (APEC)   A regional trade organization founded in 1989 that includes 18 countries. 492

Association of Southeast Asian Nations (ASEAN)   A regional organization that emphasizes trade relations, established in 1967; now includes Brunei, Cambodia, Indonesia, Laos, Malaysia, Myanmar (Burma), the Philippines, Singapore, Thailand, and Vietnam. 492

Asymmetrical warfare   A strategy by which a national military or other armed force, including a terrorists organization, that is relatively small and lightly equipped attacks a militarily stronger opponent by using unconventional means, such as terrorism, or with limited unconventional weapons, such as nuclear explosives and material, biological agents, or chemical agents. 43

Authoritarian government   A political system that allows little or no participation in decision making by individuals and groups outside the upper reaches of the government. 85, 209

Authoritarianism   A type of restrictive governmental system where people are under the rule of an individual, such as a dictator or king, or a group, such as a party or military junta. 211

Balance of payments   A figure that represents the net flow of money into and out of a country due to trade, tourist expenditures, sale of services (such as consulting), foreign aid, profits, and so forth. 417

Balance of power   A concept that describes the degree of equilibrium (balance) or disequilibrium (imbalance) of power in the global or regional system. 34, 67

Beijing + 5 Conference   A meeting held at the UN in New York City in 2000 to review the progress made since the fourth World Conference on Women held in 1995. 175

Bilateral diplomacy   Negotiations between two countries. 282

Bilateral (foreign) aid   Foreign aid given by one country directly to another. 452

Biological Weapons Convention   A multilateral treaty concluded in 1972. The parties to the treaty agree not to develop, produce, stockpile, or acquire biological agents or toxins "of types and in quantities that have no justification for prophylactic, protective, and other peaceful purposes" and to destroy any such material that they might have. 376

Biopolitics   This theory examines the relationship between the physical nature and political behavior of humans. 115

Bipolar system   A type of international system with two roughly equal actors or coalitions of actors that divide the international system into two poles. 66

Bretton Woods system The international monetary system that existed from the end of World War II until the early 1970s; named for an international economic conference held in Bretton Woods, New Hampshire, in 1944. 476

Bureaucracy The bulk of the state's administrative structure that continues even when leaders change. 99

Capitalism An economic system based on the private ownership of the means of production and distribution of goods, competition, and profit incentives. 459

Carrying capacity The number of people that an environment, such as Earth, can feed, provide water for, and otherwise sustain. 530

Cartel An international agreement among producers of a commodity that attempts to control the production and pricing of that commodity. 458

Chemical Weapons Convention (CWC) A treaty that was signed and became effective in 1995 under which signatories pledge to eliminate all chemical weapons by the year 2005; to submit to rigorous inspection; to never develop, produce, stockpile, or use chemical weapons; and to never transfer chemical weapons to another country or assist another country to acquire such weapons. 382

Clash of civilizations Samuel P. Huntington's thesis (1996, 1993) that the source of future conflict will be cultural. 167

Coalition diplomacy A negotiation situation where a number of countries have similar interests, which are often in opposition to the interests of one or more other countries. 279

Codify To write down a law in formal language. 303

Coercive diplomacy The use of threats or force as a diplomatic tactic. 293

Coercive power "Hard power" such as military force or economic sanctions. 265

Cognitive decision making Making choices within the limits of what you consciously know. 112

Cold war The confrontation that emerged following World War II between the bipolar superpowers, the Soviet Union and the United States. Although no direct conflict took place between these countries, it was an era of great tensions and global division. 37

Collective security The original theory behind UN peacekeeping. It holds that aggression against one state is aggression against every member and should be defeated by the collective action of all. 391

Communism An ideology originated in the works of Friedrich Engels and Karl Marx that is essentially an economic theory. As such, it is the idea that an oppressed proletariat class of workers would eventually organize and revolt against those who owned the means of production, the bourgeoisie; a political system of government applied in the Soviet Union, China, and elsewhere, wherein the state owns the means of production as a system to expedite Engels and Marx's economic theory. 210

Communitarianism The concept that the welfare of the collective must be valued over any individual rights or liberties. 213

Comprehensive Test Ban Treaty A treaty that bans all testing of nuclear weapons. The treaty was signed in 1996 but will not go into force until ratified by the major nuclear weapons powers. The United States Senate rejected ratification in 2001. 382

Conditionality A term that refers to the policy of the International Monetary Fund, the World Bank, and some other international financial agencies to attach conditions to their loans and grants. These conditions may require recipient countries to devalue their currencies, to lift controls on prices, to cut their budgets, and to reduce barriers to trade and capital flows. Such conditions are often politically unpopular, may cause at least short-term economic pain, and are construed by critics as interference in recipient countries' sovereignty. 478

Confederation A group of states that willingly enter into an alliance to form a political unit for a common purpose, such as economic security or defense; it is highly interdependent, but has a weak directorate organization thus allowing the individuals states to maintain a fairly high degree of sovereignty. 234

Containment doctrine U.S. policy that sought to contain communism, during the cold war. 37

Conventional Forces in Europe Treaty (CFE) A treaty negotiated between the countries in NATO and the (now defunct) Soviet-led Warsaw Pact that placed numerical limits on a range of conventional "heavy" weapons, including tanks and other armored combat vehicles, artillery, and fix-wing and rotary combat aircraft permitted in the so-called Atlantic-to-the-Urals Zone (ATTU) region. 382

Conventional warfare The application of force by uniformed military units usually against other uniformed military units or other clearly military targets using weapons other than biological, chemical, or nuclear weapons. 356

Council of Ministers The Council of the European Union involved in political decision making. 236

Countries in transition (CITs) Former communist countries such as Russia whose economies are in transition from socialism to capitalism. 406

Court of Justice The most important court in the European Union. 238

Crisis situation A circumstance or event that is a surprise to decision makers, that evokes a sense of threat (particularly physical peril), and that must be responded to within a limited amount of time. 90

Cultural imperialism The attempt to impose your own value system on others, including judging others by how closely they conform to your norms. 315

Current dollars   The value of the dollar in the year for which it is being reported. Sometimes called inflated dollars. Any currency can be expressed in current value. *See also* real dollars. 401

Debt service   The total amount of money due on principal and interest payments for loan repayment. 448

Decision making   The process by which humans choose which policy to pursue and which actions to take in support of policy goals. The study of decision making seeks to identify patterns in the way that humans make decisions. This includes gathering information, analyzing information, and making choices. Decision making is a complex process that relates to personality and other human traits, to the sociopolitical setting in which decision makers function, and to the organizational structures involved. 112

Decision-making analysis   A means of investigating how countries make policy choices. 84

Democracy/democratic government   The most basic concept describes the ideology of a body governed by and for the people; also the type of governmental system a country has, in terms of free and fair elections and levels of participation. 85, 209

Democratic peace theory   The assertion that as more countries become democratic, the likelihood that they will enter into conflict with one another decreases. 216

Democratized diplomacy   The current trend in diplomacy where diplomats are drawn from a wider segment of society, making them more representative of their nations. 283

Dependencia theory   The belief that the industrialized North has created a neocolonial relationship with the South in which the less developed countries are dependent on and disadvantaged by their economic relations with the capitalist industrial countries. 405

Détente   A cold war policy involving the United States, the Soviet Union, and China, which sought to open relations among the countries and ease tensions. 38

Deterrence   Persuading an opponent not to attack by having enough forces to disable the attack and/or launch a punishing counterattack. 362

Development capital   Monies and resources needed by less developed countries to increase their economic growth and diversify their economies. 447

Direct democracy   Policy making through a variety of processes, including referendums, by which citizens directly cast ballots on policy issues. 109

Disinformation   False stories that are given to the media, placed on the Internet, or otherwise broadcast as part of a propaganda effort to undermine a country, leader, or organization. 288

Dual-use technology   Technology that has peaceful uses but also has military applications. 383

East-West Axis   A term used to describe the ideological division between hemispheres following World War II. The East was associated with communism, while the West was associated with democracy. 37

Economic Community of West African States (ECOWAS)   A regional group of 15 countries founded in 1975. Its mission is to promote economic integration, and it has also taken on some peacekeeping activities through its nonpermanent function called Economic Community's African States Monitoring Group (ECOMOG). 390

Economic internationalism   The belief that international economic relations should and can be conducted cooperatively because the international economy is a non–zero-sum game in which prosperity is available to all. 403

Economic nationalism   The belief that the state should use its economic strength to further national interests, and that a state should use its power to build its economic strength. 401

Economic structuralism   The belief that economic structure determines politics, as the conduct of world politics is based on the way that the world is organized economically. A radical restructuring of the economic system is required to end the uneven distribution of wealth and power. 401

Economically developed country (EDC)   An industrialized country mainly found in the Northern Hemisphere. 45, 401

Environmental optimists   Those analysts who predict that the world population will meet its needs while continuing to grow economically through conservation, population restraints, and technological innovation. 562

Environmental pessimists   Those analysts who predict environmental and ecological problems, based on current trends in ecology and population pressure. 561

Escalation   Increasing the level of fighting. 357

Ethnonational group   An ethnic group in which a significant percentage of its members favor national self-determination and the establishment of a nation-state dominated by the group 80, 139

Ethology   The comparison of animal and human behavior. 115

European Commission   A 20-member commission that serves as the bureaucratic organ of the European Union. 236

European Communities (EC)   Established in 1967, the EC was a single unit whose plural name (Communities) reflects the fact that it united the European Coal and Steel Community, the European Economic Community, and the European Atomic Energy Community under one organizational structure. The EC evolved into the European Union beginning in 1993. 235

European Economic Community (EEC)   The regional trade and economic organization established in

Western Europe by the Treaty of Rome in 1958; also known as the Common Market. 235

European Parliament   The 626-member legislative branch of the European Union. Representation is determined by population of member-countries, and is based on five-year terms. 238

European Union (EU)   The Western European regional organization established in 1983 when the Maastricht Treaty went into effect. The EU encompasses the still legally existing European Community (EC). When the EC was formed in 1967, it in turn encompassed three still legally existing regional organizations formed in the 1950s: the European Coal and Steel Community (ECSC), the European Economic Community (EEC), and the European Atomic Energy Community (EURATOM). 234

Eurowhites   A term to distinguish the whites of Europe and of Australia, Canada, New Zealand, the United States, and other countries whose cultures were founded on or converted to European culture from other races and ethnic groups, including Caucasian peoples in Latin America, the Middle East, South Asia, and elsewhere. 32

Event data analysis   A study of interactions, called events, and subsequent events used to analyze the reactions and counter-reactions of countries. 84

Exchange rate   The values of two currencies relative to each other—for example, how many yen equal a dollar or how many lira equal a pound. 416

Failed states   Countries in which all most of the citizens give their primary political loyalty to an ethnic group, a religious group, or some other source of political identity. Such states are so fragmented that no one political group can govern effectively and, thus, are more legal entities than functioning governments. 42, 156

Fascism   An ideology that advocates extreme nationalism, with a heightened sense of national belonging or ethnic identity. 210

Feudal system   Medieval political system of smaller units, such as principalities, dukedoms, baronies, ruled by minor royalty. 204

Foreign direct investment (FDI)   Buying stock, real estate, and other assets in another country with the aim of gaining a controlling interest in foreign economic enterprises. Different from portfolio investment, which involves investment solely to gain capital appreciation through market fluctuations. 413

Foreign portfolio investment (FPI)   Investment in the stocks and the public and private debt instruments (such as bonds) of another country below the level where the stock- or bondholder can exercise control over the policies of the stock-issuing company or the bond-issuing debtor. 413

Formal powers   Authority to act or to exert influence that is granted by statutory law or by the constitu-

tion to a political executive or to another element of government. 98

Fourth World   A term used to designate collectively the indigenous (aboriginal, native) people of the countries of the world. 518

Fourth World Conference on Women (WCW)   The largest and most widely noted in a series of UN conferences on the status of women. This international meeting took place in Beijing, China, in 1995. 173

Free economic interchange   The absence of tariffs and nontariff barriers in trade between countries. 442

Free Trade Area of the Americas (FTAA)   The tentative name given by the 34 countries that met in December 1994 at the Summit of the Americas to the proposed Western Hemisphere free trade zone that is projected to come into existence by the year 2005. 489

Frustration-aggression theory   A psychologically based theory that frustrated societies sometimes become collectively aggressive. 115

Functional relations   Relations that include interaction in such usually nonpolitical areas as communication, travel, trade, and finances. 301

Functionalism   International cooperation in specific areas such as communications, trade, travel, health, or environmental protection activity. Often symbolized by the specialized agencies, such as the World Health Organization, associated with the United Nations. 228

Fundamentalism   Religious traditionalism and values incorporated into secular political activities. 181

Gender opinion gap   The difference between males and females along any one of a number of dimensions, including foreign policy preferences. 87

General Agreement on Tariffs and Trade (GATT)   The world's primary organization promoting the expansion of free trade. Established in 1947, it has grown to a membership of over 100. 472

General and complete disarmament (GCD)   The total absence of armaments. 397

Government   A type of governing political body, such as the democratic system in Canada or the authoritarian system in China; also the specific regime in power, such as the government of a particular leader. 55

Gross domestic product (GDP)   A measure of income within a country that excludes foreign earnings. 8

Gross national product (GNP)   A measure of the sum of all goods and services produced by a country's nationals, whether they are in the country or abroad. 46, 61

Group of Eight (G-8)   The seven economically largest, free market countries plus Russia (a member on political issues since 1998). 441, 464

Group of Seven (G-7)   The seven economically largest free market countries: Canada, France, Great Britain, Italy, Japan, the United States, and Germany. 441, 464

Group of 77 (G-77) The group of 77 countries of the South that cosponsored the Joint Declaration of Developing Countries in 1963 calling for greater equity in North-South trade. This group has come to include more than 120 members and represents the interests of the less developed countries of the South. 472

Groupthink How an individual's membership in an organization/decision-making group influences his or her thinking and actions. In particular there are tendencies within a group to think alike, to avoid discordancy, and to ignore ideas or information that threaten to disrupt the consensus. 122

Hague system Name given to the peace conferences held in the Netherlands in 1899 and 1907. This serves as the first example of an international attempt to improve the condition of humanity. 226

Hard currency Currencies, such as dollars, marks, francs, and yen, that are acceptable in private channels of international economics. 447

Hegemonic power A single country or alliance that is so dominant in the international system that it plays the key role in determining the rules and norms by which the system operates. It dominates the system and has a central position in both making and enforcing the norms and modes of behavior. Hegemon is a synonym for a hegemonic power. 40, 64

Heuristic devices A range of psychological strategies that allow individuals to simplify complex decisions. Such devices include evaluating people and events in terms of how well they coincide with your own belief system ("I am anticommunist; therefore all communists are dangerous"), stereotypes ("all Muslims are fanatics"), or analogies ("appeasing Hitler was wrong; therefore all compromise with aggressors is wrong"). 114

Holy Roman Empire The domination and unification of a political territory in Western and Central Europe that lasted from its inception with Charlemagne in 800 to the renunciation of the imperial title by Francis II in 1806. 204

Horizontal authority structure A system in which authority is fragmented. The international system has a mostly horizontal authority structure. 54

Hostile diplomacy A situation where negotiation takes place in an environment where one or more countries are engaged in armed clashes or when there is a substantial possibility that fighting could result. 278

Idealists Analysts who reject power politics and argue that failure to follow policies based on humani-

tarianism and international cooperation will result in disaster. 17

Ideological/theological school of law A set of related ideas in secular or religious thought, usually founded on identifiable thinkers and their works, that offers a more or less comprehensive picture of reality. 302

Idiosyncratic analysis An individual-level analysis approach to decision making that assumes that individuals make foreign policy decisions and that different individuals are likely to make different decisions. 124

Imperial overstrech thesis The idea that attempting to maintain global order through leadership as a hegemon, especially through military power, is detrimental to the hegemon's existence. 338

Imperialism A term synonymous with colonization, meaning domination by Northern Eurowhites over Southern nonwhites as a means to tap resources to further their own development. 32

Incremental decision making The tendency of decision makers to treat existing policy as a given and to follow and continue that policy ("policy inertia") or make only marginal changes in the policy. 123

Individualism The concept that rights and liberties of the individual are paramount within a society. 213

Individual-level analysis An analytical approach that emphasizes the role of individuals as either distinct personalities or biological/psychological beings. 25

Industrial revolution The development of mechanical and industrial production of goods that began in Great Britain in the mid-1700s and then spread through Europe and North America. 32, 205

Informal powers Authority to act or to exert influence that is derived from custom or from the prestige within a political system of either an individual leader or an institution. 98

Interdependence The close interrelationship and mutual dependence of two or more domestic economies on each other. 44, 417

Interest group A private (nongovernmental) association of people who have similar policy views and who pressure the government to adopt those views as policy. 104

Intergovernmental organizations (IGOs) International/transnational actors that are composed of member-countries. 56, 225

Intermediate-Range Nuclear Forces Treaty (INF) (1987) A treaty between the United States and Soviet Union signed in 1987 that pledged the two countries to destroy all their ground-launched ballistic and cruise missiles with ranges of between 500 and 5,500 kilometers. 377

Intermestic The merger of *inter*national and d*omestic* concerns and decisions. 4, 91

International Conference on Financing for Development (ICFD) A UN-sponsored conference on development programs for the South that met in Monterrey, Mexico, during March 2002. Fifty heads of state or government, as well as over 200 government cabinet ministers, leaders from NGOs, and leaders from the major IGOs attended the conference. 469

International Court of Justice (ICJ)   The world court, which sits in The Hague with 15 judges and is associated with the United Nations. 309

International Monetary Fund (IMF)   The world's primary organization devoted to maintaining monetary stability by helping countries to fund balance-of-payment deficits. Established in 1947, it now has 170 members. 476

International political economy (IPE)   An approach to the study of international relations that is concerned with the political determinants of international economic relations and also with the economic determinants of international political relations. 401

International organization   Organizations that conduct business across national boundaries and have members from or units operating in more than one country. International organizations whose members are countries are called intergovernmental organizations. International organizations whose membership consists of individuals or private groups are called nongovernmental organizations. 225

International system   An abstract concept that encompasses global actors, the interactions (especially patterns of interaction) among those actors, and the factors that cause those interactions. The international system is largest of a vast number of overlapping political systems that extend downward in size to micropolitical systems at the local level. *See also* System-level analysis. 28

Iron triangle   An alliance between interest groups, bureaucracies, and legislators that forms a military-industrial-congressional complex. 388

Irredentism   A minority population's demand to join its motherland (often an adjoining state), or when the motherland claims the area in which the minority lives. 154

Issue areas   Substantive categories of policy that must be considered when evaluating national interest. 91

Jus ad bellum   The Western concept meaning "just cause of war," which provides a moral and legal basis governing causes for war. 316

Jus in bello   The Western concept meaning "just conduct of war," which provides a moral and legal basis governing conduct of war. 316

Leader-citizen opinion gap   Differences of opinion between leaders and public, which may have an impact on foreign policy in a democratic country. 87

League of Nations   The first, true general international organization. It existed between the end of World War I and the beginning of World War II and was the immediate predecessor of the United Nations. 226

Least developed countries (LLDCs)   Those countries in the poorest of economic circumstances. In this book, this includes those countries with a per capita GNP of less than $400 in 1985 dollars. 408

Less developed countries (LDCs)   Countries, located mainly in Africa, Asia, and Latin America, with economies that rely heavily on the production of agriculture and raw materials and whose per capita GDP and standard of living are substantially below Western standards. 45, 401

Levels of analysis   Different perspectives (system, state, individual) from which international politics can be analyzed. 25

Lifeboat analogy   An image that compares global economic circumstances to that of a lifeboat which can safely accomodate only so many people. Therefore those fortunate enough to be in the boat will be endangered if they try to rescue too many of those still in the water, whatever their peril. This anology represents the view that the world has only so much "carrying capacity" (such as natural resources) and that economic competition creates a zero-sum game, one in which the betterment of one player or groups of players can only come at the expense of others. 466

Limited membership council   A representative organization body of the UN that grants special status to members who have a greater stake, responsibility, or capacity in a particular area of concern. The UN Security Council is an example. 245

Limited unipolar system   An international system in which there is one dominant power, but that power is reluctant to act, or a system in which second-rank powers are strong enough that the dominant power cannot be termed a true hegemon. Some analysts believe that the power and role of the United States are strong enough to make the current international system a limited unipolar system. 40

Maastricht Treaty   The most significant agreement in the recent history of the European Union (EU). The Maastricht Treaty was signed by leaders of the EU's 12 member-countries in December 1991 and outlines steps toward further political-economic integration. 235

macrolevel   At the broadest possible level. For example, system-level analysis is macrolevel analysis, while human level analysis is microlevel analysis. 203

MAD (Mutual Assured Destruction)   A situation in which each nuclear superpower has the capability of launching a devastating nuclear second strike even after an enemy has attacked it. The belief that a MAD capacity prevents nuclear war is the basis of deterrence by punishment theory. 363

Majority voting A system used to determine how votes should count. The theory of majoritarianism springs from the concept of sovereign equality and the democratic notion that the will of the majority should prevail. This system has two main components: (1) each member casts one equal vote, and (2) the issue is carried by either a simple majority (50 percent plus one vote) or, in some cases, an extraordinary majority (commonly two-thirds). 246

Manufactured goods Items that required substantial processing or assembly to become usable. Distinct from primary products, such as agricultural and forestry products, that need little or no processing. 405

Marxism The philosophy of Karl Marx that the economic (material) order determines political and social relationships. Thus, history, the current situation, and the future are determined by the economic struggle, termed dialectical materialism. 404

McWorld This concept describes the merging of states into an integrated world. Benjamin Barber coined this term to describe how states are becoming more globalized, especially with the growth of economic interdependence. 41

Mediation diplomacy A negotiation situation where a country that is not involved directly as one of the parties tries to help two or more conflicting sides to resolve their differences. 280

Merchandise trade The import and export of tangible manufactured goods and raw materials. 410

Micronationalism The tendency partially evident in the current political system for individuals to give their primary political loyalty to seemingly ever smaller ethnonational groups and to seek territory over which the group can exercise sovereignty. Micronationalism involves the fragmentation of political identities. 164

Microstate A country with a small population that cannot economically survive unaided or that is inherently so militarily weak that it is an inviting target for foreign intervention. 158

Mirror image perception The tendency of two countries or individuals to see each other in similar ways, whether positive or negative. 131

Missile Technology Control Regime (MTCR) A series of understandings that commits most of the countries capable of producing extended-range missiles to a ban on the export of ballistic missiles and related technology and that also pledges MTCR adherents to bring economic and diplomatic pressure to bear on countries that export missile-applicable technology. 376

Monarchism A political system that is organized, governed, and defined by the idea of the divine right of kings, or the notion that because a person is born into royalty, he or she is meant to rule. 210

Monetary relations The entire scope of international money issues, such as exchange rates, interest rates, loan policies, balance of payments, and regulating institutions (for example, the International Monetary Fund). 414

Moral absolutism A philosophy based on the notion that the ends never justify the means, or that morality should be the absolute guide of human actions, particularly in regard to international law. 325

Moral prudence The idea that there is a middle ground between amorality and moral absolutism that acts as a guide to human actions, particularly in regard to international law. 326

Moral relativism A philosophy that human actions must be placed in context as a means to inform international law. 325

Multilateral diplomacy Negotiations among three or more countries. 282

Multilateral (foreign) aid Foreign aid distributed by international organizations such as the United Nations. 452

Multinational corporations (MNCs) Private enterprises that have production subsidiaries or branches in more than one country. 61, 413

Multinational states Countries in which there are two or more significant nationalities. 150

Multipolar system A world political system in which power primarily is held by four or more international actors. 34, 67

Multistate nation A nation that has substantial parts of its people living in more than one state. 151

Munich analogy A belief among post–World War II leaders, particularly Americans, that aggression must always be met firmly and that appeasement will only encourage an aggressor. Named for the concessions made to Hitler by Great Britain and France at Munich during the 1938 Czechoslovakian crisis. 127

Munich Conference A meeting between France, Germany, Great Britain, and Italy in 1938, during which France and Great Britain, unwilling to confront Hitler, acquiesced with Germany's decision to annex the Sudetenland (part of Czechoslovakia). This appeasement of Germany became synonymous with a lack of political will. 36

Nation A group of culturally and historically similar people who feel a communal bond and who feel they should govern themselves to at least some degree. 55, 137

National technical means (NTM) An arms control verification technique that involves using satellites, seismic measuring devices, and other equipment to identify, locate, and monitor the manufacturing, testing, or deployment of weapons or delivery vehicles, or other aspects of treaty compliance. 387

Nationalism The belief that the nation is the ultimate basis of political loyalty and that nations should have self-governing states. *See also* Nation-state. 35, 139

Nation-state A politically organized territory that recognizes no higher law, and whose population politically identifies with that entity. *See also* State. 139

Naturalist school of law Those who believe that law springs from the rights and obligations that humans have by nature. 303

Nature-versus-nurture debate A dispute regarding whether gender differences are the result of biological factors or socialization factors. 120

Neocolonialism The notion that EDCs continue to control and exploit LDCs through indirect means, such as economic dominance and co-opting the local elite. 405

Neofunctionalism The top-down approach to solving world problems. 228

Net trade The difference between exports and imports, either overall or for specific commodities. For example, if a state exports $10 billion in agricultural products and imports $8 billion dollars in agricultural products, that country has a net agricultural trade surplus of $2 billion. 433

New International Economic Order (NIEO) A term that refers to the goals and demands of the South for basic reforms in the international economic system. 455

Newly industrializing countries (NICs) Less developed countries whose economies and whose trade now include significant amounts of manufactured products. As a result, these countries have a per capita GDP significantly higher than the average per capita GDP for less developed countries. 45, 406, 444

Nongovernmental organizations (NGOs) International (transnational) organizations with private memberships. 59, 225

Nontariff barrier (NTB) A nonmonetary restriction on trade, such as quotas, technical specifications, or unnecessarily lengthy quarantine and inspection procedures. 435

Norms A principle of right action that is binding on members of a group and that serves to regulate the behavior of the members of that group. The word is based on the Latin *norma*, which means a carpenter's square or an accurate measure. Norms are based on custom and usage and may also become part of formal law. Norms are recognized in international law under the principle of *jus cogens* (just thought), which states that a standard of behavior accepted by the world community should not be violated by the actions of a state or group of states. In domestic systems, "common law" is equivalent to norms in the international system. 48, 78

North The economically developed countries including those of Western Europe, the United States and Canada in North America, Japan in Asia, and Australia and New Zealand in Oceania. The term North is synonymous with economically developed countries (EDCs). 405

North American Free Trade Agreement (NAFTA) An economic agreement among Canada, Mexico, and the United States that went into effect on January 1, 1994. It will eliminate most trade barriers by 2009 and will also eliminate or reduce restrictions on foreign investments and other financial transactions among the NAFTA countries. 487

North Atlantic Treaty Organization (NATO) An alliance of 19 member-countries, established in 1949 by Canada, the United States, and most of the countries of Western Europe to defend its members from outside, presumably Soviet-led, attack. In the era after the cold war, NATO has begun to admit members from Eastern Europe and has also expanded its mission to include peacekeeping. 389

North-South Axis The growing tension between the few economically developed countries (North) and the many economically deprived countries (South). The South is demanding that the North cease economic and political domination and redistribute part of its wealth. 34

Non-Proliferation Treaty (NPT) A multilateral treaty concluded in 1968, then renewed and made permanent in 1995. The parties to the treaty agree not to transfer nuclear weapons or in any way to "assist, encourage, or induce any nonnuclear state to manufacture or otherwise acquire nuclear weapons." Nonnuclear signatories of the NPT also agree not to build or accept nuclear weapons. 376

NUT (Nuclear Utilization Theory) The belief that because nuclear war might occur, countries must be ready to fight, survive, and win a nuclear war. NUT advocates believe this posture will limit the damage if nuclear war occurs and also make nuclear war less likely by creating retaliatory options that are more credible than massive retaliation. 363

Objective power Assets a country objectively possesses and has the will and capacity to use. 266

On-site inspection (OSI) An arms control verification technique that involves stationing your or a neutral country's personnel in another country to monitor weapons or delivery vehicle manufacturing, testing, deployment, or other aspects of treaty compliance. 387

Open diplomacy The public conduct of negotiations and the publication of agreements. 283

Operational code A perceptual phenomenon that describes how an individual acts and responds when faced with specific types of situations. 132

Operational reality The process by which what is perceived, whether that perception is accurate or not, assumes a level of reality in the mind of the beholder and becomes the basis for making an operational decision (a decision about what to do). 132

Organization for Economic Cooperation and Development (OECD) An organization that has existed since 1948 (and since 1960 under its present name) to facilitate the exchange of information and otherwise to promote cooperation among the economically developed countries. In recent years, the OECD has started accepting a few newly industrializing and former communist countries in transition as members. 464

Organization for Security and Cooperation in Europe (OSCE) Series of conferences among 34 NATO, former Soviet bloc, and neutral European countries that led to permanent organization. Established by the 1976 Helsinki Accords. 390

Organizational behavior An individual-level analysis approach to decision making that assumes that group dynamics, group interaction, and group and organization structure influence how decisions are made. 121

Pacificism A bottom-up approach to avoidance of war based on the belief that it is wrong to kill. 397

Pacta sunt servanda Translates as "treaties are to be served/carried out" and means that agreements between states are binding. 303

Parliamentary diplomacy Debate and voting in international organizations to settle diplomatic issues. 283

Peacekeeping The use of military means by an international organization such as the United Nations to prevent fighting, usually by acting as a buffer between combatants. The international force is neutral between the combatants and must have been invited to be present by at least one of the combatants. *See also* Collective security. 391

Peacemaking The restoration of peace through, if necessary, the use of offensive military force to make one or all sides involved in a conflict cease their violent behavior. 393

Perceptions The factors that create a decision maker's images of reality. 129

Persuasive power "Soft power" such as moral authority or technological excellence. 266

Plenary representative body An assembly, such as the UN's General Assembly, that consists of all members of the main organization. 245

Political culture A concept that refers to a society's general, long-held, and fundamental practices and attitudes. These are based on a country's historical experience and on the values (norms) of its citizens. These attitudes are often an important part of the internal setting in which national leaders make foreign policy. 91

Political executives Those officials, usually but not always in the executive branch of a government, who are at the center of foreign policy making and whose tenures are variable and dependent on the political contest for power. 98

Political identification The connections in the mind of an individual between how that person defines herself or himself and an organization, group, philosophy or other reference point. Nationalism is the dominant political identity of most people, but others do exist as primary identifications and are becoming more common. 164

Politics of identity A view that national identity will be less important in the future than other subnational identities. 81

Popular sovereignty A political doctrine that holds that sovereign political authority resides with the citizens of a state. According to this doctrine, the citizenry grant a certain amount of authority to the state, its government, and, especially, its specific political leaders (such as monarchs, presidents, and prime ministers), but do not surrender ultimate sovereignty. 29, 141

Positivist school of law Those who believe that law reflects society and the way that people want the society to operate. 303

Postinternationalism A concept that extends from postmodernism and holds that in a turbulent world, people have begun to change their political identity and may give much greater weight to subnational political identities, such as ethnic group, or transnational political identities, such as gender. 166

Postmodernism This theory holds that reality does not exist as such. Rather, reality is created by how we think and our discourse (writing, talking). As applied to world politics, postmodernism is the belief that we have become trapped by stale ways of conceiving of how we organize and conduct ourselves. Postmodernists wish, therefore, to "deconstruct" discourse. 166

Power The totality of a country's international capabilities. Power is based on multiple resources, which alone or in concert allow one country to have its interests prevail in the international system. Power is especially important in enabling one state to achieve its goals when it clashes with the goals and wills of other international actors. 264

Power pole An actor in the international system that has enough military, economic, and/or diplomatic strength to often have an important role in determining the rules and operation of the system. Power poles, or simply poles, have generally been either (1) a single country or empire or (2) a group of countries that constitute an alliance or bloc. 37, 64

Power to defeat The ability to overcome in a traditional military sense—that is, to overcome enemy armies and capture and hold territory. 344

Power to hurt The ability to inflict pain outside the immediate battle area; sometimes called coercive violence. It is often used against civilians and is a particular hallmark of terrorism and nuclear warfare. 344

President of the Commission   Comparable to being president of the European Union (EU), this person is the director of the 20-member European Commission, the policy-making bureaucratic organ of the EU. 237

Primary products   Agricultural products and raw materials, such as minerals. 405

Procedural democracy   A form of democracy that is defined by whether or not particular procedures are followed, such as free and fair elections or following a set of laws or a constitution. 212

Protestant Reformation   The religious movement initiated by Martin Luther in Germany in 1517 that rejected the Catholic Church as the necessary intermediary between people and God. 206

Public diplomacy   A process of creating an overall international image that enhances your ability to achieve diplomatic success. 287

Purchasing Power Parity (PPP)   A measure of the relative purchasing power of different currencies. It is measured by the price of the same goods in different countries, translated by the exchange rate of that country's currency against a "base currency," usually the U.S. dollar. 408

Rally effect   The tendency during a crisis of political and other leaders, legislators, and the public to give strong support to a chief executive and the policy that leader has adopted in response to the crisis. 98

Real dollars   The value of dollars expressed in terms of a base year. This is determined by taking current value and subtracting the amount of inflation between the base year and the year being reported. Sometimes called uninflated dollars. Any currency can be valued in real terms. *See also* Current dollars. 401

Realists   Analysts who believe that countries operate in their own self-interests and that politics is a struggle for power. 17

Realpolitik   Operating according to the belief that politics is based on the pursuit, possession, and application of power. 35

Regime   A complex of norms, treaties, international organizations, and transnational activity that orders an area of activity such as the environment or oceans. 231

Regional government   A possible middle level of governance between the prevalent national governments of today and the world government that some people favor. The regional structure that comes closest to (but still well short of) a regional government is the European Union. 233

Relative power   Power measured in comparison with the power of other international actors. 266

Relativists   A group of people who subscribe to the belief that human rights are the product of cultures. 498

Renaissance   A period of cultural and intellectual rebirth and reform following the Dark Ages from approximately 1350 to 1650. 206

Role   How an individual's position influences his or her thinking and actions. 121

SALT I   The Strategic Arms Limitation Talks Treaty signed in 1972. 376

SALT II   The Strategic Arms Limitation Talks Treaty signed in 1979 but withdrawn by President Carter from the U.S. Senate before ratification in response to the Soviet invasion of Afghanistan. 376

Secretariat   The administrative organ of the United Nations, headed by the secretary-general. In general, the administrative element of any IGO, headed by a secretary-general. 247

Self-determination   The concept that a people should have the opportunity to map their own destiny. 158

Services trade   Trade based on the purchase (import) from or sale (export) to another country of intangibles such as architectural fees; insurance premiums; royalties on movies, books, patents, and other intellectual properties; shipping services; advertising fees; and educational programs. 410

Situational power   The power that can be applied, and is reasonable, in a given situation. Not all elements of power can be applied to every situation. 267

Social Darwinism   A social theory that argues it is proper that stronger peoples will prosper and will dominate lesser peoples. 510

Social overstretch thesis   The idea that spending money on altruistic social welfare programs to support the least productive people in society financially drains that economy. 339

South   The economically less developed countries, primarily located in Africa, Asia, and Latin America. The term South is synonymous with economically less developed countries (LDCs). 405

Southern Common Market (Mercosur)   A regional organization that emphasizes trade relations, established in 1995 among Argentina, Brazil, Paraguay, and Uruguay, with Chile (1996) and Bolivia (1997) as associate members. 491

Sovereignty   The most essential characteristic of an international state. The term strongly implies political independence from any higher authority and also suggests at least theoretical equality. 29, 197

Special drawing rights (SDRs)   Reserves held by the International Monetary Fund that the central banks of member-countries can draw on to help manage the values of their currencies. SDR value is based on a "market-basket" of currencies, and SDRs are acceptable in transactions between central banks. 477

Special operations   The overt or covert use of relatively small units of troops or paramilitary forces, which conduct commando/guerrilla operations, gather intelligence, and perform other specialized roles. Special operations forces in the U.S. military include such units as the U.S. Green Berets, Seals, and Delta Force; Great Britain's Special Air Services (SAS), and Russia's Special Purpose Force (SPETSNAZ). 347

Sphere of influence A region that a big power claims is of special importance to its national interest and over which the big power exercises special influence. 96

State A political actor that has sovereignty and a number of characteristics, including territory, population, organization, and recognition. 55, 197

State building The process of creating both a government and other legal structures of a country and the political identification of the inhabitants of the country with the state and their sense of loyalty to it. 138

State terrorism Terrorism carried out directly by, or encouraged and funded by, an established government of a state (country). 350

State-centric system A system describing the current world system wherein states are the principal actors. 55

State-level analysis An analytical approach that emphasizes the actions of states and the internal (domestic) causes of their policies. 25

Stateless nation A nation that does exercise political control over any state. 154

Strategic Arms Reduction Talks Treaty I (START I) A nuclear weapons treaty signed by the Soviet Union and the United States in 1991 and later re-signed with Belarus, Kazakhstan, Russia, and Ukraine that will limit Russia and the United States to 1,600 delivery vehicles and 6,000 strategic explosive nuclear devices each, with the other three countries destroying their nuclear weapons or transferring them to Russia.378

Strategic Arms Reduction Talks Treaty II (START II) A nuclear weapons treaty signed by the Soviet Union and the United States in 1993, which establishes nuclear warhead and bomb ceilings of 3,500 for the United States and 2,997 for Russia by the year 2003 and that also eliminates some types of weapons systems. As of February 1997 the treaty had not been ratified by the Russian parliament and, therefore, the treaty is not legally in effect.378

Subjective power A country's power based on other countries' perception of its current or potential power. 266

Subnational actors Institutions and other elements of a country's political structure, including the political leadership, legislature, bureaucracy, interest groups, political opposition, and the public. 97

Substantive democracy A form of democracy that is defined by whether qualities of democracy, such as equality, justice, or self-rule, are evident. 212–213

Summit meetings High-level meetings for diplomatic negotiations between national political leaders. 285

Superpower A term used to describe the leader of a system pole in a bipolar system. During the cold war, the Soviet Union and the United States were each leaders of a bipolar system pole. 37

Supranational organization An organization that is founded and operates, at least in part, on the idea that international organizations can or should have authority higher than individual states and that those states should be subordinate to the supranational organization. 57, 233

Sustainable development The ability to continue to improve the quality of life of those in the industrialized countries and, particularly, those in the less developed countries while simultaneously protecting the Earth's biosphere. 50, 530

System-level analysis An analytical approach that emphasizes the importance of the impact of world conditions (economics, technology, power relationships, and so forth) on the actions of states and other international actors. 25, 54

Tariff A tax, usually based on percentage of value, that importers must pay on items purchased abroad; also known as an import tax or import duty. 434

Terrorism A form of political violence conducted by individuals, groups, or clandestine government agents that attempts to manipulate politics by attacking noncombatants and nonmilitary targets in order to create a climate of fear. 349

Terrorist groups Groups of individuals that are not officially part of a government but attack nonmilitary targets using bombs and other methods to inflict pain on an opponent rather than defeat that opponent in a traditional military sense. Many terrorist groups draw individuals from more than one country and operate across national boundaries. 62

Theocracy A political system that is organized, governed, and defined by spiritual leaders and their religious beliefs. 209

Third World A term once commonly used to designate the countries of Asia, Africa, Latin America, and elsewhere that were economically less developed. The phrase is attributed to French analyst Alfred Sauvy, who in 1952 used *tiers monde* to describe neutral countries in the cold war. By inference, the U.S.–led Western bloc and the Soviet-led Eastern bloc were the other two worlds. But since most of the neutral countries were also relatively poor, the phrase had a double meaning. Sauvy used the older *tiers*, instead of the more modern *troisième*, to allude to the pre-Revolutionary (1789) third estate (*tiers état*), that is, the underprivileged class, the commoners. The nobility and the clergy were the first and second estates. Based on this second meaning, Third World came most commonly to designate the less developed countries of the world, whatever their political orientation. The phrase is less often used since the end of the cold war, although some analysts continue to employ it to designate the less developed countries. 518

Transnational actors Organizations that operate internationally, but whose membership, unlike IGOs, is private. 59

Transnational advocacy networks (TANs) IGOs, NGOs, and national organizations that are based on shared values or common interests and exchange information and services. 59, 526

Transnational corporations (TNCs) Transnational corporations are business enterprises that conduct business beyond just selling a product in more than one country. Companies with factories in several countries are TNCs, as are banks with branches in more than one country. The businesses are also referred to as multinational corporations (MNCs). The two terms are synonymous; TNC is used herein based on UN usage. 61

Transnational political identity A focus of political identification that an individual has and uses to define his or her views and loyalties, which transcends the traditional boundaries of the nation and territorial state and causes the individual to define themselves politically in reference to a larger, nonterritorial unit, such as a religion. 164

Transnational terrorism Terrorism carried out either across national borders or by groups that operation in more than one country. 351

Transnationalism Extension beyond the borders of a single country; applies to a political movement, issue, organization, or other phenomena. 164

Treaty of Amsterdam (1997) The most recent agreement in a series of treaties that has further integrated the economic and political sectors of the European Union. 236

Treaty of Moscow A treaty signed in 2002 by President George W. Bush and President Vladimir Putin. Under the treaty's provisions, the United States and Russia agree to reduce their nuclear arsenals of nuclear warheads and bombs to no more than 2,200 by 2012. When Presidents Bill Clinton and Boris Yeltsin had earlier committed to the general levels established in the treaty, they had referred to the potential accord as the third Strategic Arms Reduction Treaty (START III), but that name was abandoned by Bush and Putin. 378

Treaty of Westphalia The treaty that ended the Thirty Years' War (1618–1648). The treaty signals the birth of the modern state system and the end of the theoretical subordination of the monarchies of Europe, especially those that had adopted Protestantism, to the Roman Catholic Church and the Holy Roman Empire. While the date of 1648 marked an important change, the state as a sovereign entity had begun to emerge earlier and continues to evolve. 28, 206

Tribalism A term used by scholar Benjamin Barber

to decribe the internal pressure on countries that can lead to their fragmentation and even to their collapse. 42

Tripolar system A type of international system that describes three roughly equal actors or coalitions of actors that divide the international system into three poles. 67

Two-level game theory The concept that in order to arrive at satisfactory international agreements, a country's diplomats actually have to deal with (at one level) the other country's negotiators and (at the second level) legislators, interest groups, and other domestic forces at home. 98, 280

UN Conference on Population and Development (UNCPD) A UN-sponsored conference that met in Cairo, Egypt, in September 1994 and was attended by delegates from more than 170 countries. The conference called for a program of action to include spending $17 billion annually by the year 2000 on international, national, and local programs to foster family planning and to improve the access of women in such areas as education. 544

UN Conference on Trade and Development (UNCTAD) A UN organization established in 1964 and currently consisting of all UN members plus the Holy See, Switzerland, and Tonga, which holds quadrennial meetings aimed at promoting international trade and economic development. 472

UN Development Programme (UNDP) An agency of the UN established in 1965 to provide technical assistance to stimulate economic and social development in the economically less developed countries. The UNDP has 48 members selected on a rotating basis from the world's regions. 472

UN General Assembly (UNGA) The main representative body of the United Nations, composed of all 190 member-states. 245

UN Security Council The main peacekeeping organ of the United Nations. The Security Council has 15 members, including 5 permanent members. 245

Unanimity voting A system used to determine how votes should count. In this system, in order for a vote to be valid, all members must agree to the proposed measure. Abstention from a vote may or may not block an agreement. 247

Unconventional force The application of force using the techniques of guerrilla warfare, covert operations, and terrorism conducted by military special forces or by paramilitary groups. Such groups frequently rely on external sources for funds and weapons. Unconventional warfare is sometimes waged against nonmilitary targets and may use conventional weapons or weapons of mass destruction. 344

Unipolar system A type of international system that describes a single country with complete global hegemony. 64

United Nations (UN)   An international body created with the intention to maintain peace through the co-operation of its member-states. As part of its mission, it addresses human welfare issues such as the environment, human rights, population, and health. Its headquarters are located in New York City, and it was established following World War II to supersede the League of Nations. 226

United Nations Conference on Population and Development (UNCPD)   The most recent (1994) world conference held in Cairo, Egypt, that focused on the issue of population control and reproductive health. 544

Universalists   A group of people who subscribe to the belief that human rights are derived from sources external to society, such as from a theological, ideological, or natural rights basis. 498

Uruguay Round   The eighth, and latest, round of GATT negotiations to reduce tariffs and nontariff barriers to trade. The eighth round was convened in Punta del Este, Uruguay, in 1986 and its resulting agreements were signed in Marrakesh, Morocco, in April 1994. 473

Vertical authority structure   A system in which subordinate units answer to higher levels of authority. 54

Veto   A negative vote cast in the UN Security Council by one of the five permanent members; has the effect of defeating the issue being voted on. 247

Vietnam analogy   An aversion to foreign armed intervention, especially in conflicts in less developed countries involving guerrillas. This attitude is especially common among political leaders and other individuals who were opposed to the U.S. war in Vietnam or who were otherwise influenced by the failed U.S. effort there and the domestic turmoil that resulted. 128

Weapons of mass destruction   Generally deemed to be nuclear weapons with a tremendous capability to destroy a population and the planet, but also include some exceptionally devastating conventional arms, such as fuel-air explosives, as well as biological, and chemical weapons. Weapons of mass destruction warfare refers to the application of force between countries using biological, chemical, and nuclear weapons. 358, 375

Weighted voting   A system used to determine how votes should count. In this system, particular votes count more or less depending on what criterion is deemed to be most significant. For instance, population or wealth might be the important defining criterion for a particular vote. In the case of population, a country would receive a particular number of votes based on its population, thus a country with a large population would have more votes than a lesser-populated country. 247

West   Historically, Europe and those countries and regions whose cultures were founded on or converted to European culture. Such countries would include Australia, Canada, New Zealand, and the United States. The majority of the populations in these countries are also "white," in the European, not the larger Caucasian, sense. After World War II, the term West took on two somewhat different but related meanings. One referred to the countries allied with the United States and opposed to the Soviet Union and its allies, called the East. The West also came to mean the industrial democracies, including Japan. *See also* Eurowhites. 32

Westernization of the international system   A number of factors, including scientific and technological advances, contributed to the domination of the West over the international system that was essentially created by the Treaty of Westphalia (1648). 32

World Bank Group   Four associated agencies that grant loans to LDCs for economic development and other financial needs. Two of the agencies, the International Bank for Reconstruction and Development (IBRD) and the International Development Association (IDA), are collectively referred to as the World Bank. The other two agencies are the International Finance Corporation (IFC) and the Multilateral Investment Guarantee Agency (MIGA). 481

World government   The concept of a supranational world authority to which current countries would surrender some or all of their sovereign authority. 66, 233

World Health Organization (WHO)   A UN-affliated organization created in 1946 to address world health issues. 506

World Trade Organization (WTO)   The organization that replaced the General Agreement on Tariffs and Trade (GATT) organization as the body that implements GATT, the treaty. 472

Xenophobia   Fear of others, "they-groups." 146

Zero-sum game   A contest in which gains by one player can only be achieved by equal losses for other players. A non–zero-sum game is a situation in which one or more players, even all players, can gain without offsetting losses for any other player or players. 266

Zionism   The belief that Jews are a nation and that they should have an independent homeland. 152

Abbreviations

The following abbreviations are used in the text:

ABM	Anti-Ballistic Missile
APEC	Asia-Pacific Economic Cooperation
APM	Anti-Personnel Mine
ASEAN	Association of Southeast Asian Nations
ATTU	Atlantic to the Urals (region)
BIS	Bank for International Settlement
BMD	Ballistic Missile Defense
BWT	Biological Weapons Treaty
CEDAW	Committee on the Elimination of Discrimination Against Women
CFE	Conventional Forces in Europe (treaty)
CIS	Commonwealth of Independent States
CIT	Country in Transition
CITES	Convention on the International Trade in Endangered Species
CSW	Commission on the State of Women
CTBT	Comprehensive Test Ban Treaty
CWC	Chemical Weapons Convention
EC	European Community
ECB	European Central Bank
ECJ	European Court of Justice
ECOSOC	Economic and Social Council
ECOWAS	Economic Community of West African States
ECSC	European Coal and Steel Community
EDC	Economically Developed Country
EEC	European Economic Community
EMS	European Monetary System
EMU	European Monetary Union
EP	European Parliament
EPA	Environmental Protection Agency
EPP	European People's Party
EU	European Union
EURATOM	European Atomic Energy Community
FAO	Food and Agriculture Organization (United Nations)
FDI	Foreign Direct Investment
FIS	Front for Islamic Salvation
FPI	Foreign Portfolio Investment
FSR	Former Soviet Republic
FTAA	Free Trade Area of the Americas
GATT	General Agreement on Tariffs and Trade
GCD	General and Complete Disarmament
GCP	Gross Corporate Product
GDP	Gross Domestic Product
GEF	Global Environmental Facility
GNP	Gross National Product
GPS	Global Positioning System
HDI	Human Development Index
IAEA	International Atomic Energy Agency
IBRD	International Bank for Reconstruction and Development
ICBM	Intercontinental Ballistic Missile
ICJ	International Court of Justice
IDA	International Development Association
IFAD	International Fund for Agricultural Development
IFC	International Finance Corporation
IFOR	International Force
IGO	Intergovernmental Organization
ILO	International Labor Organization
IMF	International Monetary Fund
INF	Intermediate-Range Nuclear Forces
IOM	International Organization for Migration
IPCC	International Panel on Climatic Change
IPE	International Political Economy
IPPF	International Planned Parenthood Federation
IWC	International Whaling Commission
JCS	Joint Chiefs of Staff
LDC	Less Developed Country
LLDC	Least Developed Country
MAD	Mutual Assured Destruction
MAI	Multilateral Agreement on Investment
MFN	Most-Favored-Nation
MIGA	Multilateral Investment Guarantee Agency

MIRV	Multiple-Independent-Reentry-Vehicle
MNC	Multinational Corporation
MTCR	Missile Technology Control Regime
NAFTA	North American Free Trade Association; North American Free Trade Agreement
NAM	Non-Aligned Movement
NATO	North Atlantic Treaty Organization
NBC	Nuclear-Biological-Chemical
NGO	Nongovernmental Organization
NIC	Newly Industrializing Country
NIEO	New International Economic Order
NPT	Non-Proliferation Treaty
NSC	National Security Council
NTB	Nontariff Barrier
NTM	National Technical Means
NUT	Nuclear Utilization Theory
OAS	Organization of American States
OAU	Organization of African Unity
ODA	Official Development Aid
OECD	Organization for Economic Cooperation and Development
OPEC	Organization of Petroleum Exporting Countries
OSCE	Organization for Security and Cooperation in Europe
OSI	On-Site Inspection
P5	Permanent 5
PCIJ	Permanent Court of International Justice
PLA	People's Liberation Army (China)
PLO	Palestine Liberation Organization
PNA	Palestine National Authority
PNTR	Permanent Normal Trade Relations
SALT	Strategic Arms Limitation Talks
SDF	Self-Defense Force (Japan)
SDI	Strategic Defense Initiative
SDR	Special Drawing Right
SEA	Single European Act
SLBM	Sea-Launched Ballistic Missile
SPE	Socialist Party of Europe
START	Strategic Arms Reduction Talks
TAN	Transnational Advocacy Network
THAAD	Theater High Altitude Area Defense
TI	Transparency International
TNC	Transnational Corporation
UN	United Nations
UNCED	United Nations Conference on Environment and Development
UNCHR	United Nations Commission on Human Rights
UNCPD	United Nations Conference on Population and Development
UNCTAD	United Nations Council on Trade and Development
UNDHR	Universal Declaration of Human Rights
UNDP	United Nations Development Programme
UNEP	United Nations Environment Program
UNESCO	United Nations Educational, Scientific, and Cultural Organization
UNFPA	United Nations Population Fund
UNGA	United Nations General Assembly
UNICEF	United Nations Children's Fund
UNIDO	United Nations Industrial Development Organization
UNIFEM	UN Development Fund for Women
UNSC	United Nations Security Council
VAT	Value-Added Tax
WEDO	Women's Environment and Development Organization
WCHR	World Conference on Human Rights
WCW	World Conference on Women
WEU	Western European Union
WFC	World Food Council
WHO	World Health Organization
WTO	World Trade Organization

References

Abbott, Kenneth W., and Duncan Snidal. 1998. "Why States Act Through Formal International Organizations." *Journal of Conflict Organization*, 42:3–32.

Ackerman, Peter, and Christopher Kruegler. 1993. *Strategic Nonviolent Conflict: The Dynamics of People Power in the Twentieth Century*. Westport, CT: Praeger.

ADL (Anti-Defamation League). 1999. *Highlights from a September 1999 Anti-Defamation League Survey on Anti-Semitism and Societal Attitudes in Russia*. New York: Martilla Communications Group. Also available at the ADL Website: http://www.adl.org/frames/front_israel.html.

Ahmad, Zakaria Haji, and Baladas Ghoshal. 1999. "The Political Future of ASEAN After the Asian Crisis." *International Affairs*, 75:759–778.

Allulis, Joseph, and Vickie Sullivan, eds. 1996. *Shakespeare's Political Pageant: Essays in Politics and Literature*. Boulder, CO: Rowman & Littlefield.

Alter, Karen J. 1998. "Who Are the 'Masters of the Treaty'?: European Governments and the European Court of Justice." *International Organization*, 52:121–148.

Amadife, Emmanuel N. 1999. *Pre-Theories and Theories of Foreign Policy–Making*. Lanham, MD: University Press of America.

Ambrose, Stephen E. 1991. *Nixon: The Triumph of a Politician, 1962–1972*. New York: Simon & Schuster.

Annan, Kofi. 2002. "Foreword." In *State of the World 2002*. Christopher Flavin, Hilary French, Gary Gardner et. al. New York: W. W. Norton.

Apodaca, Clair, and Michael Stohl. 1999. "United States Human Rights Policy and Foreign Assistance." *International Studies Quarterly*, 43:185–198.

Archer, Clive. 1983. *International Organizations*. London: Allen & Unwin.

Arend, Anthony Clark, and Robert J. Beck. 1994. *International Law and the Use of Force*. New York: Routledge.

Armstrong, David. 1999. "Law, Justice and the Idea of a World Society." *International Affairs*, 75:563–598.

Arnett, Eric. 1997. *Military Capacity and the Risk of War: China, India, Pakistan and Iran*. Oxford, UK: Oxford University Press.

Astorino-Courtois, Allison. 1998. "Clarifying Decisions: Assessing the Impact of Decision Structures on Foreign Policy Choices During the 1970 Jordanian Civil War." *International Studies Quarterly*, 42:733–754.

Attali, Jacques. 1997. "The Clash of Western Civilization: The Limits of the Market and Democracy." *Foreign Policy*, 107:54–64.

Audley, John J. 1997. *Green Politics and Global Trade: NAFTA and the Future of Environmental Politics*. Washington, DC: Georgetown University Press.

Auerswald, David. P. 1999. "Inward Bound: Domestic Institutions and Military Conflicts." *International Organization*, 53:469–504.

Avant, Deborah. 2000. "From Mercenaries to Citizen Armies: Explaining Change in the Practice of War." *International Organization*, 54: 41–73.

Bacchus, William I. 1997. *The Price of American Foreign Policy: Congress, The Executive, and International Affairs Funding*. University Park: University of Pennsylvania Press.

Balaam, David N., and Michael Veseth. 1996. *Introduction to International Political Economy*. Upper Saddle River, NJ: Prentice Hall.

Baldwin, David A. 2000. "The Sanctions Debate and the Logic of Choice." *International Security*, 24/3:80–107.

Barber, Benjamin R. 1995. *Jihad vs. McWorld*. New York: Times Books/Random House.

Barber, Benjamin R. 1996. *Jihad vs. McWorld: How Globalism and Tribalism Are Reshaping the World*. New York: Ballantine Books, Inc.

Barber, Charles T. 1996. "UN Security Council Representation: The First 50 Years and Beyond." Paper presented at the International Studies Association convention, San Diego.

Barber, James David. 1985. *Presidential Character*, 3rd ed. Englewood Cliffs, NJ: Prentice Hall.

Barkey, Karen, and Mark von Hagen, eds. 1997. *After Empire: Multi-Ethnic Societies and Nation-Building*. Boulder, CO: Westview.

Barnett, Michael N., and Martha Finnemore. 1999. "The Politics, Power, and Pathologies of International Organizations." *International Organization*, 53:699–732.

Barrington, Lowell W. 1997. "Nation and 'Nationalism': The Misuse of Key Concepts in Political Science." *PS: Political Science & Politics*, 30:712–724.

Bartlett, David, and Anna Seleny. 1998. "The Political Enforcement of Liberalism: Bargaining, Institutions, and Auto Multinationals in Hungary." *International Studies Quarterly*, 42:319–338.

Barry, James A. 1998. *The Sword of Justice: Ethics and Coercion in International Politics*. Westport, CT: Praeger.

Beer, Francis A. 1990. "The Reduction of War and the Creation of Peace." In *A Reader in Peace Studies*, ed. Paul Smoker, Ruth Davies, and Barbara Munske. New York: Pergamon.

Beer, Francis A., and Robert Harriman, eds. 1996. *Post-Realism: The Rhetorical Turn in International Relations*. Ann Arbor: University of Michigan Press.

Beigbeder, Yves. 1999. *Judging War Criminals: The Politics of International Justice*. New York: St. Martin's.

Beiner, Ronald, ed. 1999. *Theorizing Nationalism*. Albany: State University of New York Press.

Beitz, Charles R. 1999. *Political Theory and International Relations*. Princeton: Princeton University Press.

Belgrad, Eric A., and Nitza Nachmias. 1997. *The Politics of International Humanitarian Aid Operations*. Westport, CT: Praeger.

Bellany, Ian. 1997. *The Environment in World Politics: Exploring the Limits*. Lyme, NH: Edward Elgar.

Bennett, D. Scott. 1996. "Security, Bargaining, and the End of Interstate Rivalry." *International Studies Quarterly*, 40:157–184.

Bennett, D. Scott. 1997. "Testing Alternative Models of Alliance Duration, 1816–1984." *American Journal of Political Science*, 41:846–878.

Bernstein, Richard, and Ross Munro. 1997. "The Coming Conflict with China." *Foreign Affairs*, 76/2:18–32.

Berry, Nicholas. 2001. "China Is Not an Imperialist Power." *Strategic Review*, 29/1:4–10.

Berton, Peter, Hiroshi Kimura, and I. William Zartman. 1999. *International Negotiation: Actors Structure/Process, Values*. New York: St. Martin's.

Best, Geoffrey. 1999. "Peace Conferences and the Century of Total War: The 1899 Hague Conference and What Came After." *International Affairs*, 75:619–634.

Betts, Richard K. 1998. "The New Threat of Mass Destruction." *Foreign Affairs*, 77/1:26–45.

Blanton, Shannon Lindsey. 1996. "Images in Conflict: The Case of Ronald Reagan and El Salvador." *International Studies Quarterly*, 40:23–44.

Blanton, Shannon Lindsey. 1998. "U.S. Arms Transfers and the Promotion of Global Order." Paper presented at the International Studies Association convention, Minneapolis.

Blanton, Shannon Lindsey. 2000. "Promoting Human Rights and Democracy in the Developing World: U.S. Rhetoric versus U.S. Arms Exports." *American Journal of Political Science*, 44:123–133.

Bloomfield, Lincoln P., and Allen Moulton. 1997. *Managing International Conflict: From Theory to Policy*. New York: St. Martin's Press.

Bobrow, Davis B., and Mark A. Boyer. 1998. "International System Stability and American Decline: A Case for Muted Optimism." *International Journal*, 53:285–305.

Bock, Peter, and Nigel Young. 1999. *Pacifism in the Twentieth Century*. Syracuse, NY: Syracuse University Press.

Bohlen, Charles E. 1973. *Witness to History*. New York: W. W. Norton.

Bohman, James. 1999. "International Regimes and Democratic Governance: Political Equality and Influence in Global Institutions." *International Affairs*, 75:499–514.

Bohman, James, and Matthias Lutz-Bachmann, eds. 1997. *Perpetual Peace: Essays on Kant's Cosmopolitan Ideal*. Cambridge, MA: MIT Press.

Bond, Doug. 1992. "Introduction." In *Transforming Struggle: Strategy and the Global Experience of Nonviolent Direct Action*. Cambridge, MA: Program on Nonviolent Sanction in Conflict and Defense, Center for International Affairs, Harvard University.

Borawski, John and Thomas-Durell Young. 2001. *NATO After 2000: Future of the EURO-Atlantic Alliance*. Westport, CT: Greenwood.

Bouton, Marshall M. 1998. "India's Problem Is Not Politics." *Foreign Affairs*, 77/3:80–94.

Boyer, Mark A. 1993. *International Cooperation and Public Goods: Opportunities for the Western Alliance*. Baltimore: Johns Hopkins University Press.

Boyer, Mark A. 1996. "Political System and the Logic of Two-Level Games: Moving Beyond Democracies in the Study of International Negotiation." Paper presented at the International Studies Association Northeast convention, Boston.

Bozdogan, Sibel, and Resat Kasaba, eds. 1997. *Rethinking Modernity and National Identity in Turkey*. Seattle: University of Washington Press.

Brandes, Lisa C. O. 1994. "The Liberal Feminist State and War." Presented at the annual meeting of the American Political Science Association, New York.

Brawley, Mark. 1996. "Economic Coercion by a Power in Relative Decline: Why Sanctions May Be More Effective as Hegemonic Leadership Ebbs." Paper presented at the International Studies Association convention, San Diego.

Brecher, Jeremy. 1993. "Global Village or Global Pillage." *The Nation*, December 6.

Brecher, Michael, and Jonathan Wilkenfeld. 1997. *A Study of Crisis*. Ann Arbor: University of Michigan Press.

Breuning, Marijke. 1996. "Nationalist Parties and Foreign Policy Assistance." Paper presented at the International Studies Association convention, San Diego.

Bright, Chris. 2000. "Anticipating Environmental 'Surprise,'" In *State of the World 2000*, ed. Lester R. Brown, et al. New York: W. W. Norton.

Brooks, Stephen G. 1997. "Dueling Realisms." *International Organization*, 51:445–478.

Brown, Sarah Graham. 1999. *Sanctioning Saddam: The Politics of Intervention in Iraq*. New York: St. Martin's.

Brown, Seyom. 1992. *International Relations in a Changing Global System*. Boulder, CO: Westview.

Brown, Seyom. 1998. "World Interests and the Changing Dimension of Security." In *World Security: Challenges for a New Century*, 3rd ed., ed. Michael T. Klare and Yogesh Chandran. New York: St. Martin's.

Bueno de Mesquita, Bruce. 2002. "Domestic Politics and International Relations." *International Studies Quarterly*, 46:1–10.

Bueno de Mesquita, Bruce J., and James D. Morrow. 1999. "Sorting Through the Wealth of Nations." *International Security*, 24/2:56–73.

Bueno de Mesquita, Bruce J., and Randolph M. Siverson. 1993. "War and the Survival of Political Leaders: A Comparative Analysis." Presented at the annual meeting of the American Political Science Association, Washington, DC.

Bull, Hedley, and Adam Watson. 1982. *The Expansion of International Society*. London: Oxford University Press.

Bunch, Charlotte, and Roxana Carillo. 1998. "Global Violence against Women: The Challenge to Human Rights and Development." In *World Security: Challenges for a New Century*, 3rd ed., ed. Michael T. Klare and Yogesh Chandran. New York: St. Martin's.

Burch, Kurt, and Robert A. Denemark, eds. 1997. *Constituting International Political Economy: International Political Economy Yearbook, vol. 10*. Boulder, CO: Lynne Rienner.

Bureau of the Census. *See* (U.S.) Bureau of the Census.

Burgess, Stephen F. 1998. "The Limits of Westphalia Sovereignty and Genocide in Africa." Paper presented at the International Studies Association convention, Minneapolis.

Burk, Erika. 1994. "Human Rights and Social Issues." In *A Global Agenda: Issues Before the 49th General Assembly*, ed. John Tessitore and Susan Woolfson. Lanham, MD: University Press of America.

Burrowes, Robert J. 1996. *The Strategy of Nonviolent Defense*. Albany: State University of New York Press.

Cafruny, Alan W., and Carl Lankowski, eds. 1997. *Europe's Ambiguous Unity: Conflict and Consensus in the Post-Maastricht Era.* Boulder, CO: Lynne Rienner.

Caldwell, Lynton Keith. 1996. *International Environmental Policy: From the Twentieth to the Twenty-First Century.* Durham, NC: Duke University Press.

Calleo, David P. 2001. *Rethinking Europe's Future.* Princeton, NJ: Princeton University Press.

Cameron, Gavin. 1999. *Nuclear Terrorism: A Threat Assessment for the Twenty-First Century.* New York: St. Martin's.

Caplan, Richard, and John Feffer, eds. 1996. *Europe's New Nationalism: States and Minorities in Conflict.* New York: Oxford University Press.

Caprioli, Mary. 1998. "Why Democracy?" In *Taking Sides: Clashing Views on Controversial Issues in World Politics,* 8th ed., ed. John T. Rourke. Guilford, CT: Dushkin/McGraw-Hill.

Caprioli, Mary. 2000. "The Myth of Women's Pacifism." In *Taking Sides: Clashing Views on Controversial Issues in World Politics,* 9th ed., ed. John T. Rourke. Guilford, CT: McGraw-Hill\Dushkin.

Cardús, Salvador, and Joan Estruch. 1995. "Politically Correct Anti-Nationalism." *International Social Science Journal,* 144:347–352.

Carment, David. 1994. "The Ethnic Dimension in World Politics: Theory, Policy, and Early Warning." *Third World Quarterly,* 15:551–579.

Carrington, William J., and Enrica Detragiache. 1999. "How Extensive Is the Brain Drain?" *Finance & Development,* 36/2:108.

Carruthers, Susan L. 1998. "Not like the US? Europeans and the Spread of American Culture." *International Affairs,* 74:883–892.

Carter, Jimmy. Speech, December 6, 1978. *Department of State Bulletin,* January 1979.

Cashman, Greg. 1999. *What Causes War? An Introduction to Theories of International Conflict.* Lanham, MD: Lexington Books.

Catley-Carlson, Margaret, and Judith A.M. Outlaw. 1998. "Poverty and Population Issues: Clarifying the Connections." *Journal of International Affairs,* 52:233–252.

Cederman, Lars-Erik. 1994. "Emergent Polarity: Analyzing State-Formation and Power Politics." *International Studies Quarterly,* 38:501–533.

Cederman, Lars-Erik. 1997. *Emergent Actors in World Politics: How States and Nations Develop and Dissolve.* Princeton, NJ: Princeton University Press.

Center for Defense Information. *The Defense Monitor,* 28/1 (1999).

Central Intelligence Agency. *See* U.S. (CIA).

Chafetz, Glenn. 1995. "The Political Psychology of the Nuclear Nonproliferation Regime." *Journal of Politics,* 57:743–775.

Chafetz, Glenn, Michael Spirtas, and Benjamin Frankel, eds. 1999. *Origins of National Interests.* Essex, U.K.: Frank Cass.

Chan, Stephen. 1997. "In Search of Democratic Peace: Problems and Promise." *Mershon International Studies Review,* 41:59–92.

Chan, Stephen, and Jarrod Weiner, eds. 1998. *Twentieth Century International History.* New York: St. Martin's.

Chase-Dunn, Christopher, and Thomas D. Hall. 1997. *Rise and Demise: Comparing World-Systems.* Boulder, CO: Westview Press.

Chen, Martha Alter. 1995. "Engendering World Conferences: The International Women's Movement and the United Nations." *The Third World Quarterly,* 16:477–495.

China, People's Republic of. 1993. *China's Foreign Policy.* Beijing: New Star Publishers.

Chittick, William O., and Lee Ann Pingel. 2002. *American Foreign Policy: History, Substance and Process.* New York: Seven Bridges Press.

Christensen, Thomas J., and Jack Snyder. 1997. "Progressive Research on Degenerative Alliances." *American Political Science Review,* 4:919–922.

Chrystal, Jonathan. 1998. "A New Kind of Competition: How American Producers Respond to Incoming Foreign Direct Investment." *International Studies Quarterly,* 42:513–543.

CIA. *See* U.S. (CIA).

Cimbala, Stephen J. 1995. "Deterrence Stability With Smaller Forces: Prospects and Problems." *Journal of Peace Research,* 32:65–78.

Cini, Michelle. 1997. *The European Commission: Leadership, Organization and Culture in the EU Administration.* New York: Manchester University Press.

Cioffi-Revilla, Claudio. 1996. "Origins and Evolution of War and Politics." *International Studies Quarterly,* 40:1–22.

Cioffi-Revilla, Claudio. 2000. *Origins of the International System: Mesopotamian and West Asia Politics, 6000 B.C. to 1500 B.C.* Denver: Long-Range Analysis of War Project, University of Colorado.

Clapham, Christopher. 1999. "Sovereignty and the Third World State." *Political Studies,* 47:522–537.

Clark, Ann Marie. 1996. "The Contribution of Non-Governmental Organizations to the Creation and Strengthening of International Human Rights Norms." Paper presented at the International Studies Association convention, San Diego.

Clark, Ann Marie, Elisabeth J. Friedman, and Kathryn Hochstetler. 1998. "The Sovereign Limits of Global Civil Society: A Comparison of NGO Participation in UN World Conferences on the Environment, Human Rights, and Women." *World Politics,* 51:1–35.

Cohen, Raymond. 1987. *Theater of Power: The Art of Diplomatic Signaling.* Essex, U.K.: Longman.

Cohen, Raymond. 1996. "Reflection on the New Global Diplomacy: Statecraft 2500 B.C.–A.D. 2000." Paper presented at the International Studies Association convention, San Diego.

Cohen, Stephen D. 2000. *The Making of United States International Economic Policy,* 5th ed. Westport, CT: Praeger.

Conley, Richard S. 1997. "Sovereignty or the Status Quo: The 1995 Pre-Referendum Debate in Québec." *Journal of Commonwealth & Comparative Politics,* 35:67–92.

Constantinou, Costas M. 1996. "Representation of Sovereignty in the Himalayas." Paper presented at the International Studies Association convention, San Diego.

Cooper, Leo. 1999. *Russia and the World: New State-of-Play on the International Stage.* New York: St. Martin's.

Cortright, David, and George A. Lopez, eds. 1996. *Economic Sanctions: Panacea or Peacebuilding in a Post–Cold War World?* Boulder, CO: Westview.

Cortright, David, and George A. Lopez. 2000. *The Sanctions Decade: Assessing UN Strategies in the 1990s.* Boulder, CO: Lynne Rienner.

Cox, Robert W., ed. 1997. *The New Realism: Perspectives on Multilateralism and World Order.* New York: St. Martin's.

Craig, Gordon A., and Alexander L. George. 1995. *Force and Statecraft: Diplomatic Problems of Our Time*, 3rd ed. New York: Oxford University Press.

Croft, Stuart. 1997. *Strategies of Arms Control: A History and Typology.* New York: St. Martin's.

Culter, A. Claire, Virginia Haufler, and Tony Porter, eds. 1999. *Private Authority and International Affairs.* Albany: State University of New York Press.

Cusimano, Maryann, ed. 1998. *Beyond Sovereignty: Issues for a Global Agenda.* New York: St. Martin's.

Dassel, Kurt. 1998. "Civilians, Soldiers, and Strife: Domestic Sources of International Aggression." *International Security*, 23:107–140.

Dassel, Kurt, and Eric Reinhardt. 1999. "Domestic Strife and the Initiation of Violence at Home and Abroad." *American Journal of Political Science*, 43:56–85.

Dawisha, Karen. 1997. "Russian Foreign Policy in the Near Abroad and Beyond." In *Annual Editions, World Politics 97/98.* Guilford, CT: Dushkin/McGraw-Hill.

de la Garza, Rodolfo, and Harry Pachon, eds. 2000. *Latinos and U.S. Foreign Policy: Representing the "Homeland"?* Landover, MD: Rowman & Littlefield.

DeCamp, William T. 2000. "The Big Picture: A Moral Analysis of Allied Force in Kosovo." *Marine Corps Gazette*, 84/2:42–44.

Deibert, Ronald. 1997. *Parchment, Printing, and Hypermedia: Communication and World Order Transformation.* New York: Columbia University Press.

DeRouen, Karl R., Jr. 1995. "The Indirect Link: Politics, the Economy, and the Use of Force." *Journal of Conflict Resolution*, 39:671–695.

Dickson, Anna K. 1997. *Development and International Relations: A Critical Introduction.* Cambridge, U.K.: Polity Press.

DiClerico, Robert E. 1979. *The American President.* Englewood Cliffs, NJ: Prentice Hall.

Diehl, Paul F., ed. 1997. *The Politics of Global Governance: International Organizations in an Interdependent World.* Boulder, CO: Lynne Rienner.

Diehl, Paul F., Daniel Druckman, and James Wall. 1998. "International Peacekeeping and Conflict Resolution: A Taxonomic Analysis with Implications." *Journal of Conflict Resolution*, 42:33–55.

Dirie, Waris, with Cathleen Miller. 1998. *Desert Flower: The Extraordinary Journey of a Desert Nomad.* New York: William Morrow.

Downs, Erica Strecker, and Philip C. Saunders. 1999. "Legitimacy and the Limits of Nationalism: China and the Diaoyu Islands." *International Security*, 23/3:114–246.

Doxey, Margaret P. 1996. *International Sanctions in Contemporary Perspective.* New York: St. Martin's.

Drezner, Daniel W. 1998. "Conflict Expectations and the Paradox of Economic Coercion." *International Studies Quarterly*, 42:709–732.

Drezner, Daniel W. 2000. "Bargaining, Enforcement, and Multilateral Sanctions: When is Cooperation Counterproductive?" *International Organization*, 54:73–102.

Druckman, Daniel. 1994. "Nationalism, Patriotism and Group Loyalty: A Social Psychological Perspective." *Mershon International Studies Review*, supplement to *International Studies Quarterly*, 38:43–68.

Duchacek, Ivo D. 1975. *Nations and Men.* Hinsdale, IL: Dryden.

Dunn, David H., ed. 1996. *Diplomacy at the Highest Level: The Evolution of International Summitry.* New York: St. Martin's.

Dunn, John. 1995. "Introduction: Crisis of the Nation State." In *Contemporary Crisis of the Nation State*, ed. John Dunn. Oxford, U.K.: Blackwell.

Ebenstein, Alan O., William Ebenstein, and Edwin Fogelman. 1994. *Today's Isms: Socialism, Capitalism, Fascism, and Communism.* Englewood Cliffs, NJ: Prentice Hall.

Ehrenreich, Barbara, and Katha Pollitt, 1999. "Fukuyama's Follies." *Foreign Affairs*, 78/1:118–129.

Eichengreen, Barry. 1998. "Geography as Destiny." *Foreign Affairs*, 77/2:128–139.

Eide, Asbjorn. 1998. "The Historical Significance of the Universal Declaration." *International Social Science Journal*, 50: 475–498.

El-Agraa, Ali M., ed. 1997. *Economic Integration Worldwide.* New York: St. Martin's.

Eley, Geoff, and Ronald Grigor Suny. 1996. *Becoming National.* New York: Oxford University Press.

Elliott, Kimberly Ann. 1993. "A Look at the Record." *Bulletin of the Atomic Scientists*, November.

Elliot, Kimberly Ann, ed. 1997. *Corruption and the Global Economy.* Washington, DC: Institute for International Economics.

Elliott, Kimberly Ann. 1998. "The Sanctions Glass: Half Full or Completely Empty?" *International Security*, 23:50–65.

Elman, Colin. 1996. "Why Not Neorealist Theories of Foreign Policy?" *Security Studies*, 6:7–53.

Elman, Colin, and Miriam Fendius Elman. 1997. "Diplomatic History and International Relations Theory: Respecting Difference and Cross Boundaries." *International Security*, 22:5–21.

Elman, Colin, and Miriam Fendius Elman. 1997. "Lakatos and Neorealism: A Reply to Vasquez." *American Political Science Review*, 4:923–926.

Ember, Carol R., and Melvin Ember. 1996. "War, Socialization, and Interpersonal Violence." *Journal of Conflict Resolution*, 38:620–646.

Enders, Walter, and Todd Sandler. 1999. "Transnational Terrorism in the Post–Cold War Era." *International Studies Quarterly*, 43:145–167.

Enriquez, Juan. 1999. "Too Many Flags." *Foreign Policy*, 116:30–49.

Esposito, John L., ed. 1997. *Political Islam: Revolution, Radicalism, or Reform?* Boulder, CO: Lynne Rienner.

Etzioni, Amitai. 1993. "The Evils of Self-Determination." *Foreign Policy*, 89:21–35.

Faksh, Mahmud A. 1997. *The Future of Islam in the Middle East: Fundamentalism in Egypt, Algeria, and Saudi Arabia.* Westport, CT: Praeger.

Falk, Richard. 1999. "World Prisms: The Future of Sovereign States and International Order." *Harvard International Review*, 21/3:30–35.

(FAO) Food and Agricultural Organization. 1995. "Forest Resources Assessment 1990: Global Synthesis." *FAO Forestry Paper 124.* Rome: FAO.

Farnen, Russell, ed. 1994. *Nationalism, Ethnicity, and Identity: Cross-National and Comparative Perspectives.* New Brunswick, NJ: Transaction.

Farrell, Robert H. 1998. *The Dying President: Franklin D. Roosevelt, 1944–1945.* Columbia: University of Missouri Press.

Farsoun, Samih. 1997. *Palestine and the Palestinians.* Boulder, CO: Westview.

Feaver, Peter D., and Emerson M. S. Niou. 1996. "Managing Nuclear Proliferation: Condemn, Strike, or Assist?" *International Studies Quarterly,* 40:209–234.

Feld, Werner J. 1979. *International Relations: A Transnational Approach.* New York: Alfred Publishing.

Feldstein, Martin. 1998. "Refocusing the IMF." *Foreign Affairs,* 77/2:46–71.

Felice, William F. 1996. *Taking Suffering Seriously: The Importance of Collective Human Rights.* Albany: State University of New York Press.

Feron, James D. 1997. "Signaling Foreign Policy Interests." *Journal of Conflict Resolution,* 41:68–90.

Finn, James, ed. 1997. *Freedom in the World: The Annual Survey of Political and Civil Liberties, 1996–1997.* New York: Freedom House.

Fitzsimons, David M. 1995. "Thomas Paine's New World Order: Idealistic Internationalism in the Ideology of Early American Foreign Relations." *Diplomatic History,* 19:569–582.

Flavin, Christopher. 1996. "Facing up to the Risks of Climate Change." In *State of the World 1996,* ed. Lester R. Brown. New York: W. W. Norton.

Flynn, Gregory, and Henry Farrell. 1999. "Piecing Together the Democratic Peace: The CSCE and the 'Construction' of Security in Post–Cold War Europe." *International Organization,* 53:505–535.

Fordham, Benjamin. 1998. "The Politics of Threat Perception and the Use of Force: A Political Economy Model of U.S. Uses of Force, 1949–1994." *International Studies Quarterly,* 42:567–590.

Fowler, Michael Ross, and Julie Marie Bunck. 1995. *Law, Power, and the Sovereign States: The Evolution and Application of the Concept of Sovereignty.* University Park: University of Pennsylvania Press.

Foyle, Douglas C. 1997. "Public Opinion and Foreign Policy: Elite Beliefs as a Mediating Variable." *International Studies Quarterly,* 41:141–170.

Franck, Thomas M. 1997. "Is Personal Freedom a Western Value?" *American Journal of International Law,* 91:593–627.

Fraser, Arvonne S. 1999. "Becoming Human: The Origins and Development of Women's Human Rights." *Human Rights Quarterly* 21:853–906.

Freedman, Lawrence. 1998. "Military Power and Political Influence." *International Affairs,* 74:36–49.

Freedom House. 1997. *Freedom in the World: The Annual Survey of Political Rights & Civil Liberties, 1996–1997.* New Brunswick, NJ: Transaction.

Frost, Mervyn. 1996. *Ethics in International Relations.* New York: Cambridge University Press.

Fukuyama, Francis. 1989. "The End of History?" *National Interest,* 16:3–18.

Fukuyama, Francis. 1998. "Women and the Evolution of Politics." *Foreign Affairs,* 77/5:24–40.

Fuller, Graham E., and Rend Rahim Francke. 2000. *The Arab Shi'a: The Forgotten Muslims.* New York: St. Martin's.

Fursenko, Aleksandr, and Timothy Naftali. 1997. *One Hell of a Gamble: Khrushchev, Castro, and Kennedy, 1958–1964.* New York: W. W. Norton.

Gabel, Matthew. 1998. "Public Support for European Integration: An Empirical Test of Five Theories." *Journal of Politics,* 60:333–355.

Gaenslen, Fritz. 1997. "Advancing Cultural Explanations." In *Culture and Foreign Policy,* ed. Valerie M. Hudson. Boulder, CO: Lynne Rienner.

Gallagher, Nancy W., ed. 1998. *Arms Control: New Approaches to Theory and Policy.* Newbury Park, U.K.: Frank Cass.

Galtung, Johan. 1994. *Human Rights in Another Key.* Cambridge, U.K.: Polity Press.

Garrett, Geoffrey, R. Daniel Kelemen, and Heiner Schulz. 1998. "The European Court of Justice, National Governments, and Legal Integration in the European Union." *International Organization,* 52:149–176.

Gartner, Scott Sigmund, and Randolph M. Siverson. 1996. "War Expansion and War Outcome." *Journal of Conflict Resolution,* 40:4–15.

Gartzke, Erik. 1998. "Kant We All Just Get Along? Opportunity, Willingness, and the Origins of the Democratic Peace." *American Journal of Political Science,* 42:1–27.

Gayton, Jeffrey T. 1997. "From Here to Extraterritoriality: The United States Within and Beyond Borders." Paper presented at the International Studies Association convention, Toronto, Canada, March 1997. On the Web at: http://www.polisci.wisc.edu/~jtgayton/papers/.

Geller, Daniel S. 1993. "Power Differentials and War in Rival Dyads." *International Studies Quarterly,* 37:173–193.

Geller, Daniel S., and J. David Singer. 1998. *Nations at War: A Scientific Study of International Conflict.* Cambridge, U.K.: Cambridge University Press.

Gellner, Ernest. 1995. "Introduction." In *Notions of Nationalism,* ed. Sukumar Periwal. Budapest: Central European University Press.

Gelpi, Christopher. 1997. "Democratic Diversions." *International Studies Quarterly,* 41:255–282.

Genest, Marc A. 1994. "Realism and the Problem of Peaceful Change." *Perspectives on Political Science,* 23:70–78.

George, Alexander L. 1994. "Some Guides to Bridging the Gap." *Mershon International Studies Review,* 39:171–172.

Gerner, Deborah J. 1995. "The Evolution of the Study of Foreign Policy." In *Foreign Policy Analysis,.* ed. Laura Neack, Jeane A. K. Hey, and Patrick J. Haney. Englewood Cliffs, NJ: Prentice Hall.

Geva, Hehemia, and Alex Mintz, eds. 1997. *Decisionmaking on War and Peace: The Cognitive-Rational Debate.* Boulder, CO: Lynne Rienner.

Gibbs, David N. 1995. "Secrecy and International Relations." *Journal of Peace Research,* 32:213–238.

Gibler, Douglas M., and John A. Vasquez. 1998. "Uncovering the Dangerous Alliances, 1495–1980." *International Studies Quarterly,* 42:785–810.

Gibney, Matthew J. 1999. "Liberal Democratic States and Responsibilities to Refugees." *American Political Science Review,* 93:169–182.

Gilbert, Alan. 1999. *Must Global Politics Constrain Democracy? Great-Power Realism, Democratic Peace, and Democratic Internationalism.* Princeton, NJ:Princeton University Press, 1999.

Gilpin, Robert. 1981. *War and Change in World Politics.* Cambridge, U.K.: Cambridge University Press.

Glad, Betty. 1989. "Personality, Political and Group Process Variables in Foreign Policy Decision Making: Jimmy Carter's Handling of the Iranian Hostage Crisis." *International Political Science Review,* 10:35–61.

Gleditsch, Nils Petter, and Håvard Hegre. 1997. "Peace and Democracy: Three Levels of Analysis." *Journal of Conflict Resolution,* 41:283–310.

Gleijeses, Piero. 1995. "The CIA and the Bay of Pigs." *Journal of Latin American Studies,* 27:18–42.

Gochman, Charles S., and Aaron M. Hoffman. 1996. "Peace in the Balance? A Matter of Design." *International Studies Notes,* 21/2 (Spring):20–25.

Goff, Patricia M. 2000. "Invisible Borders: Economic Liberalization and National Identity." *International Studies Quarterly,* 44:533–62.

Goldstein, Melvyn C. 1997. *The Snow Lion and the Dragon: China, Tibet and the Dalai Lama.* Berkeley: University of California Press.

Graebner, Norman, ed. 1964. *Ideas and Diplomacy.* New York: Oxford University Press.

Grant, Rebecca, and Kathleen Newland, eds. 1991. *Gender and International Relations.* Bloomington: Indiana University Press.

Grantham, Bill. 1998. "America the Menace: France's Feud With Hollywood." *World Policy Journal,* 15/2:58–66.

Gray, Colin S. 1994. "Force, Order, and Justice: The Ethics of Realism in Statecraft." *Global Affairs,* 14:1–17.

Green, Michael. 1996. *Arming Japan: Defense Production, Alliance Politics, and the Post-War Search for Autonomy.* Baltimore: Johns Hopkins University Press.

Greenfeld, Liah. 1992. *Nationalism: Five Roads to Modernity.* Cambridge, MA: Harvard University Press.

Greider, William. 1997. *The Manic Logic of Global Capitalism.* New York: Simon & Schuster.

Griffin, Roger, ed. 1995. *Fascism.* New York: Oxford University Press.

Gruenberg, Leon. 1996. "The IPE of Multinational Corporations." In *Introduction to International Political Economy,* ed. David N. Balaam and Michael Veseth. Upper Saddle River, NJ: Prentice Hall.

Guelke, Adrian. 1998. *The Age of Terrorism and the International Political System.* New York: St Martin's.

Guibernau, Montserrat. 1996. *Nationalisms: The Nation-State and Nationalism in the Twentieth Century.* Cambridge, U.K.: Polity Press.

Gurr, Nadine, and Benjamin Cole. 2000. *The New Face of Terrorism : Threats From Weapons of Mass Destruction.* New York: St. Martin's.

Gurr, Ted Robert. 2000. *Peoples Versus States.* Washington, DC; United States Institute of Peace Press.

Gurr, Ted Robert. 2000a. "Ethnic Warfare on the Wane." *Foreign Affairs,* 79/3:52–64.

Gurr, Ted Robert, and Michael Haxton. 1996. "Minorities Report (1). Ethnopolitical Conflict in the 1990s: Patterns and Trends." Paper presented at the International Studies Association convention, San Diego.

Gurr, Ted Robert, Monty G. Marshall, and Deepa Khosla. 2001. *Peace and Conflict 2001: Armed Conflicts, Self-Determination Movements, and Democracy.* College Park Maryland: Integrated Network for Societal Conflict Research at the University of Maryland. Available on the Web at http://www.bsos.umd.edu/cidcm/peace.htm.

Haas, Peter M., and David McCabe. 1996. "International Institutions and Social Learning in the Management of Global Environmental Risks." Paper presented at the International Studies Association convention, San Diego.

Hagen, Joe D. 2001. "Does Decision Making Matter: Systemic Assumptions vs. Historical Reality in International Theory." *International Studies Review,* 3:2 (summer): 5–46.

Hall, John. 1995. "Nationalism, Classified and Explained." In *Notions of Nationalism,* ed. Sukumar Periwal. Budapest: Central European University Press.

Hall, Rodney Bruce. 1999. *National Collective Identity: Social Constructs and International Systems.* New York: Columbia University Press.

Hannum, Hurst. 1999. "The Specter of Secession." *Foreign Affairs,* 77/2:13–19.

Harbour, Frances V. 1998. *Thinking About International Ethics: Moral Theory and Cases From American Foreign Policy.* Boulder, CO: Westview.

Harnisch, Sebastian. 2001. "The Hegemon and the Demon": U.S. Nuclear Learning vis-à-vis North Korea." unpublished paper on the Web at http://www.uni-trier.de/uni/fb3/politik/liba/harnisch/Pubs/Hegemon-Demon-Final.pdf.

Hart, Paul, and Eric K. Stern, eds. 1997. *Beyond Groupthink: Political Group Dynamics and Foreign Policy Making.* Ann Arbor: University of Michigan Press.

Hasenclever, Andreas, and Peter Mayer. 1997. *Theories of International Regimes.* Cambridge, U.K.: Cambridge University Press.

Hashim, Ahmed S. 1998. "The Revolution in Military Affairs Outside the West." *Journal of International Affairs,* 51:431–446.

Hashmi, Sohail H., ed. 1997. *State Sovereignty: Change and Persistence in International Relations.* University Park: Pennsylvania State University Press.

Hawkins, Darren. 1999. "Transnational Activists as Motors for Change." *International Studies Review,* I/1:119–122.

Heberer, Thomas. 1995. "The Tibet Question as a Problem of International Politics." *Aussen Politik,* 46:299–309.

Helleiner, Eric. 1998. "Electronic Money: A Challenge to the Sovereign State?" *Journal of International Affairs,* 51:387–410.

Henderson, Earl Anthony. 1999. "The Democratic Peace through the Lens of Culture, 1820–1989." *International Studies Quarterly,* 42/3:461–484.

Henry, Charles P., ed. 2000. *Foreign Policy and the Black (Inter)National Interest.* Albany: State University of New York Press.

Herek, Gregory M., Irving L. Janis, and Paul Huth. 1987. "Decision-Making During International Crises: Is the Quality of Progress Related to the Outcome?" *Journal of Conflict Resolution,* 31:203–236.

Hermann, Margaret G. 1998. "One Field, Many Perspectives: Building the Foundations for Dialogue." *International Studies Quarterly,* 42/4:605–620.

Hermann, Margaret G. 2001. "How Decision Units Shape Foreign Policy: A Theoretical Framework." *International Studies Review*, Special Issue, "Leaders, Groups, and Coalitions: Understanding the People and Processes in Foreign Policy Making" :47–82

Hermann, Margaret G., and Joe D. Hagan. 1998. "International Decision Making: Leadership Matters." *Foreign Policy*, No. 110 (Spring):124–137.

Hermann, Margaret B., Thomas Preston, Baghat Korany, & Timothy M. Shaw. 2001. "Who Leads Matters; The Effects of Powerful Individuals." *International Studies Review*, Special Issue, "Leaders, Groups, and Coalitions: Understanding the People and Processes in Foreign Policy Making," 83–132.

Heymann, Philip B. 2002. "Dealing With Terrorism: An Overview." *International Security*, 26/3:24–38.

Higgins, Rosalyn. 1994. *Problems and Process: International Law and How We Use It*. New York: Oxford University Press.

Hirst, Paul, and Grahame Thompson. 1996. *Globalization in Question: The International Economy and the Possibilities of Governance*. Cambridge, U.K.: Polity Press.

Hix, Simon. 1999. *The Political System of the European Union*. New York: St. Martin's.

Hobbes, Heidi H., ed. 2000. *Pondering Postinternationalism: A Paradigm for the Twenty-First Century*. Albany, NY: State University of New York Press.

Hobsbawm, Eric J. 1990. *Nations and Nationalism Since 1780: Programme, Myth, Reality*. Cambridge, U.K.: Cambridge University Press.

Hobsbawm, Eric. 2001. "Democracy Can be Bad for You." *New Statesman* 14/626 (March 5, 2001): 25–28.

Hoffmann, Stanley. 1995. "The Crisis of Liberal Internationalism." *Foreign Policy*, 98:159–179.

Hoffmann, Stanley. 1998. *World Disorders: Troubled Peace in the Post–Cold War Era*. Lanham, MD: Rowman & Littlefield.

Holloway, Steven K., and Rodney Tomlinson. 1995. "The New World Order and the General Assembly: Block Realignment at the UN in the Post–Cold War World." *Canadian Journal of Political Science*, 28:227–254.

Holsti, Ole R. 1997. *Public Opinion and American Foreign Policy*. Ann Arbor: University of Michigan Press.

Homer-Dixon, Thomas. 1998. "Environmental Scarcity and Intergroup Conflict." In *World Security: Challenges for a New Century*, 3rd ed., ed. Michael T. Klare and Yogesh Chandran. New York: St. Martin's.

Hoogvelt, Ankie. 1997. *Globalization and the Postcolonial World: The New Political Economy of Development*. Baltimore, MD: Johns Hopkins University Press.

Hook, Steven W. 1996. *Foreign Aid Toward the Millennium*. Boulder, CO: Lynne Rienner.

Hopf, Ted. 1991. "Polarity, the Offense-Defense Balance, and War." *American Political Science Review*, 85:475–493.

Hopmann, P. Terrence. 1996. *The Negotiation Process and the Resolution of International Conflicts*. Columbia: University of South Carolina Press.

Hout, Will. 1997. "Globalization and the Quest for Governance." *Mershon International Studies Review*, 41:99–106.

Howard, Michael, George J. Andreopoulos, and Mark R. Shulman, eds. 1994. *The Laws of War*. New Haven, CT: Yale University Press.

Howland, Courtney, ed. 1999. *Religious Fundamentalism and the Human Rights of Women*. New York: St. Martin's.

Hudson, Valerie M., ed. 1997. *Culture and Foreign Policy*. Boulder, CO: Lynne Rienner.

Hufbauer, Gary Clyde, and Jeffrey J. Schott. 1994. *Western Hemisphere Economic Integration*. Washington, DC: Institute for International Economics.

Hughes, Donna M. 2000. "The 'Natasha' Trade: The Transnational Shadow Market of Trafficking in Women." *Journal of International Affairs*, 53:625–652.

Huntington, Samuel. 1993. "The Clash of Civilizations." *Foreign Affairs*, 72(3):56–73.

Huntington, Samuel P. 1996. *The Clash of Civilizations and the Remaking of World Order*. New York: Simon & Schuster.

Huntington, Samuel P. 1999. "The Lonely Superpower." *Foreign Affairs*, 78/2 (March/April 1999):35–49.

Huntley, James Robert. 1998. *Pax Democratics: A Strategy for the Twenty-First Century*. New York: St. Martin's.

Hurd, Ian. 1999. "Legitimacy and Authority in International Politics." *International Organization*, 53:379–408.

Huth, Paul K. 1996. *Standing Your Ground: Territorial Disputes and International Conflict*. Ann Arbor: University of Michigan Press.

Huth, Paul K., Christopher Gelpi, and D. Scott Bennett. 1993. "The Escalation of Great Power Militarized Disputes: Testing Rational Deterrence Theory and Structural Realism." *American Political Science Review*, 87:609–623.

IMF (International Monetary Fund). 1999. *World Economic Outlook*. October 1999. On the IMF Web site at: http://www.imf.org/external/pubs/ft/weo/1999/02/index.htm.

IMF (International Monetary Fund). 1999a. *International Capital Markets*. Washington, DC: IMF.

IMF (International Monetary Fund). 2000. *World Economic Outlook*. May 2000. On the IMF Web site at: http://www.imf.org/external/pubs/ft/weo/2000/01/index.htm.

Iriye, Akira. 1997. *Cultural Internationalism and World Order*. Baltimore, MD: Johns Hopkins University Press.

Ishiyama, John T., and Marijke Breuning. 1998. *Ethnopolitics in the "New" Europe*. Boulder, CO: Lynne Rienner.

Iyer, Pico. 1996. "The Global Village Finally Arrives." In *Annual Editions: Global Issues 96/97*. Guilford, CT: Dushkin/McGraw-Hill.

Jackson, Robert. 1999. "TI Sovereignty in World Politics: A Glance at the Conceptual and Historical Landscape." *Political Studies*, 47:431–56.

James, Alan. 1999. "The Practice of Sovereign Statehood in Contemporary International Society." *Political Studies*, 47: 457–573.

James, Patrick, and Frank Harvey. 1992. "The Most Dangerous Game: Superpower Rivalry in International Crises, 1948–1985." *The Journal of Politics*, 54:25–53.

James, Patrick, and Jean-Sebastain Rioux. 1998. "International Crises and Linkage Politics: The Experiences of the United States, 1953–1994." *Political Research Quarterly*, 51/3: 781–812.

Jaquette, Jane S. 1997. "Women in Power: From Tokenism to Critical Mass." *Foreign Policy*, 108:23–97.

Javeline, Debra. 1999. "Protest and Passivity: How Russians Respond to Not Getting Paid." Davis Center for Russian Studies, Harvard University. Published on the Web at: http://data.fas.harvard.edu/~javeline/draft1.htm.

Jervis, Robert. 1999. "Realism, Neoliberalism, and Cooperation: Understanding the Debate." *International Security*, 24:42–63.

Jett, Dennis C. 2000. *Why Peacekeeping Fails*. New York: St. Martin's.

Jewett, Aubrey W., and Marc D. Turetzky. 1998. "Stability and Change in President Clinton's Foreign Policy Beliefs, 1993–96," *Presidential Studies Quarterly*, 28:638–676.

Johansen, Robert C. 1994. "Building World Security: The Need for Strengthened International Institutions." In *World Security: Challenges for a New Century*, ed. Michael T. Klare and Daniel C. Thomas. New York: St. Martin's.

Johnson, Bryan T. 1991. "The World Bank: Promoting Stagnation." *The World & I*, February.

Johnson, James Turner. 1997. *The Holy War Idea in Western and Islamic Traditions*. University Park: Pennsylvania State University Press.

Johnston, Alastair I., and Robert S. Ross, eds. 1999. *Engaging China: The Management of an Emerging Power*. New York: Routledge.

Jones, Howard. 1988. *The Course of American Diplomacy*, 2nd ed. Chicago: Dorsey.

Jones, R. J. Barry. 1999. "Globalization and Change in the International Political Economy." *International Affairs*, 75/2: 357–369.

Joyner, Christopher C. 2000. "The Reality and Relevance of International Law in the Twenty-First Century." In *The Global Agenda: Issues and Perspectives*, ed. Charles W. Kegley, Jr. and Eugene R. Wittkopf. Boston: McGraw-Hill.

Kaempfer, Willliam H., and Anton D. Lowenberg. 1999. "Unilateral Versus Multilateral International Sanctions: A Public Choice Perspective." *International Studies Quarterly*, 43:37–58.

Kane, Thomas. 2001. "China's Foundations: Guiding Principles of Chinese Foreign Policy." *Comparative Strategy*, 20:45–55.

Kaplan, Robert D. 1994. "The Coming Anarchy." *The Atlantic*, February.

Kaplan, Robert D. 1999. "Was Democracy Just a Moment?" In *Stand: Contending Issue and Opinion, World Politics*, ed., Marc Genest. Boulder, CO: Coursewise Publishing.

Karatnycky, Adrian. 1997. *Freedom in the World: The Annual Survey of Political Rights & Civil Liberties*. New York: Freedom House.

Karl, Terry Lynn. 1999. "The Perils of the Petro-State: Reflections on the Paradox of Plenty." *Journal of International Affairs*, 53:31–51.

Karmel, Solomon. 2000. *China and the People's Liberation Army: Great Power or Struggling Developing State?* New York: St. Martin's.

Katada, Saori N., and Timothy J. McKeown. 1998. "Aid Politics and Electoral Politics: Japan, 1970–1992." *International Studies Quarterly*, 42:591–600.

Kateb, George. 2000. "Is Patriotism a Mistake?" *Social Research*, 67:901–923.

Katzenstein, Lawrence. 1997. "Change, Myth, and the Reunification of China." In *Culture & Foreign Policy*, ed. Valerie M. Hudson. Boulder, CO: Lynne Rienner.

Kaufman, Stuart J. 1997. "The Fragmentation and Consolidation of International Systems." *International Organization*, 51:755–776.

Keane, John. 1994. "Nations, Nationalism, and Citizens in Europe." *International Social Science Journal*, 140:169–184.

Keating, Michael. 1996. *Nations against the State: The New Politics of Nationalism in Quebec, Catalonia, and Scotland*. New York: St. Martin's.

Keck, Margaret E., and Kathryn Sikkink. 1998. *Activists beyond Borders: Advocacy Network in International Politics*. Ithaca, NY: Cornell University Press.

Kegley, Charles W., Jr., and Gregory A. Raymond. 1999. *How Nations Make Peace*. New York: St. Martin's.

Keller, Edmund J., and Donald Rothchild, eds. 1996. *Africa in the New International Order: Rethinking State Sovereignty and Regional Security*. Boulder, CO: Lynne Rienner.

Keller, William W. 1995. *Arm in Arm: The Political Economy of the Global Arms Trade*. New York: Basic Books.

Keller, William W., and Janne E. Nolan. 1997. "The Arms Trade: Business As Usual?" *Foreign Policy*, 109:113–125.

Kelman, Herbert C. 2000. "The Role of the Scholar-Practitioner in International Conflict Resolution." *International Studies Perspective*, 1:273–288.

Kennedy, Paul. 1988. *The Rise and Fall of the Great Powers*. New York: Random House.

Kent, Ann. 1999. *China, the United Nations, and Human Rights: The Limits of Compliance*. Philadelphia: University of Pennsylvania Press.

Keohane, Robert O. 1998. "International Institutions: Can Interdependence Work?" *Foreign Policy*, 110:82–96.

Keohane, Robert O., and Lisa L. Martin. 1995. "The Promise of Institutionalist Theory." *International Security*, 20/1:39–51.

Keohane, Robert O., and Joseph S. Nye, Jr. 1999. "Globalization: What's New? What's Not? (And So What?)." *Foreign Policy*, 114:104–119.

Keylor, William. 1996. *The Twentieth Century World*. New York: Oxford University Press.

Kim, Samuel S. 1997. "China as a Great Power." *Current History*, 96:246–251.

Kimura, Masato, and David A. Welch. 1998. "Specifying 'Interests': Japan's Claim to the Northern Territories and Its Implications for International Relations Theory." *International Studies Quarterly*, 42:213–244.

Kissinger, Henry A. 1970. "The Just and the Possible." In *Negotiation and Statecraft: A Selection of Readings*, U.S. Congress, Senate Committee on Government Operations, 91st Cong., 2nd sess.

Kissinger, Henry A. 1979. *The White House Years*. Boston: Little, Brown.

Kissinger, Henry A. 1994. *Diplomacy*. New York: Simon & Schuster.

Klare, Michael T., and Yogesh Chandrani, eds. 1998. *World Security: Challenges for a New Century*, 3rd ed. New York: St. Martin's.

Klare, Michael T., and Lora Lumpe. 2000. "Fanning the Flames of War: Conventional Arms Transfers in the 1990s." In *World Security: Challenges for a New Century*, 3rd ed., eds. Michael T. Klare and Yogesh Chandrani. New York: St. Martin's.

Klotz, Audie. 1997. *Norms in International Relations: The Struggle Against Apartheid*. Ithaca, NY: Cornell University Press.

Knutsen, Torbjorn L. 1999. *The Rise and Fall of World Orders*. New York: St. Martin's.

Kocs, Stephen A. 1995. "Territorial Disputes and Interstate War, 1945–1987." *Journal of Politics*, 57:159–175.

Koehn, Peter H., and Olatunde J. B. Ojo. 1999. *Making Aid Work: Innovative Approaches for Africa at the Turn of the Century*. Lanham, MD: University Press of America.

Koll, Steven. 1997. *Americans on Expanding NATO: A Study of U.S. Public Attitudes*. College Park, MD: Center for the Study of Policy Attitudes and Center for International and Security Studies.

Korbin, Stephen. 1996. "The Architecture of Globalization: State Sovereignty in a Networked Global Economy." In *Globalization, Governments and Competition*. Oxford, U.K.: Oxford University Press.

Korey, William. 1998. *NGOs and the Universal Declaration of Human Rights: The Curious Grapevine*. New York: St. Martin's.

Koubi, Vally. 1999. "Military Technology Races." *International Organization*, 53:537–565.

Krasner, Stephen D. 1999. *Sovereignty: Organized Hypocrisy*. Princeton, NJ: Princeton University Press.

Krause, Keith, and W. Andy Knight, eds. 1995. *State, Society, and the UN System: Perspectives on Multilateralism*. Tokyo: United Nations University Press.

Kriesberg, Louis. 1992. *International Conflict Resolution*. New Haven, CT: Yale University Press.

Krosnick, Jon, and Shibley Telhami. 1995. "Public Attitudes Toward Israel: A Study of the Attentive and Issue Publics." *International Studies Quarterly*, 39:535–554.

Krugman, Paul. 1998. "America the Boastful." *Foreign Affairs*, 77/3:32–45.

Ku, Charlotte, and Paul F. Diehl. 1998. *International Law: Classic and Contemporary Readings*. Boulder, CO: Lynne Rienner.

Kubalkova, Vendulka, Nicholas Onuf, and Paul Kowert, eds. 1998. *International Relations in a Constructed World*. Armonk, NY: M. E. Sharpe.

Kugler, Jacek, and Douglas Lemke, eds. 1996. *Parity and War: Evaluations and Extensions of the War Ledger*. Ann Arbor: University of Michigan Press.

Kunihiro, Masao. 1997. "The Decline and Fall of Pacifism." *Bulletin of the Atomic Scientists*, 36 (January/February): 35–39.

Kurth, James. 1994. "The *Real* Clash." *National Interest*, 37:3–15.

Kuttner, Robert. 1998. "Globalism Bites Back." *American Prospect*, 37 (March-April, 1998):6–8.

Kydd, Andrew. 2000. "Arms Races and Arms Control: Modeling the Hawk Perspective." *American Journal of Political Science*, 44:228–244.

Lackey, Douglas. 1989. *The Ethics of War and Peace*. Englewood Cliffs, NJ: Prentice Hall.

Landau, Alice, and Richard Whitman, eds. 1997. *Rethinking the European Union: Institutions, Interests, and Identities*. New York: St. Martin's.

Lapid, Yosef, and Friedrich Kratochwil. 1996. *The Return of Culture and Identity in IR Theory*. Boulder, CO: Lynne Rienner.

Larsen, Jeffrey A., and Gregory J. Rattray, eds. 1996. *Arms Control: Toward the Twenty-First Century*. Boulder, CO: Lynne Rienner.

Latham, Robert. 1997. *The Liberal Moment: Modernization, Security, and the Making of the Postwar International World*. New York: Columbia University Press.

Lauren, Paul Gordon. 1998. *The Evolution of International Human Rights*. Philadelphia: University of Pennsylvania Press.

Lawrence, Philip K. 1998. *Modernity and War: The Creed of Absolute Violence*. New York: St. Martin's.

LeDuc, Lawrence. 2000. "Referendums and Elections: Do Voters Behave Differently? When and How?" Paper presented at the International Political Science Association World Congress, Quebec, Canada, August 1–6, 2000.

Lefebvre, Jeffrey A. 1996. "Middle East Conflicts and Middle Level Power Intervention in the Horn of Africa." *Middle East Journal*, 50:387–404.

Legro, Jeffrey W. 1996. "Culture and Preferences in the International Cooperation Two-Step." *American Political Science Review*, 90:118–137.

Legro, Jeffrey W. 1997. "Which Norms Matter: Revisiting the 'Failure' of Internationalism." *International Organization*, 51:31–63.

Legro, Jeffrey W., and Andrew Moravcsik. 1999. "Is Anybody Still a Realist?" *International Security*, 24/ 2:5–55.

Legro, Jeffrey W. and Andrew Moravcsik. 2001. "Faux Realism: Spin Versus Substance in the Bush Foreign-Policy Doctrine." *Foreign Policy* 125:80–82.

Lemke, Douglas, and Suzanne Warner. 1996. "Power Parity, Commitment to Change, and War." *International Studies Quarterly*, 40:235–260.

Lensu, Maria, and Jan-Sefan Fritz, eds. 1999. *Value Pluralism, Normative Theory, and International Relations*. New York: St. Martin's.

Lepgold, Joseph. 1998. "Is Anyone Listening? International Relations Theory and the Problem of Policy Relevance." *Political Science Quarterly*, 113:43–63.

L'Etang, Hugh. 1970. *The Pathology of Leadership*. New York: Hawthorne Books.

Levi, Werner. 1991. *Contemporary International Law*, 2nd ed. Boulder, CO: Westview.

Lewis, Bernard. 1996. *The Middle East: A Brief History of the Last 2,000 Years*. New York: Scribner.

Li Chien-pin. 1996. "Fear, Greed, or Garage Sale: The Analysis of Defense Spending in East Asia." Paper presented at the International Studies Association convention, San Diego.

Liddle, William, and Saiful Mujani. 2000. "The Triumph of Leadership: Explaining the 1999 Indonesian Vote." Paper presented at the International Political Science Association convention, August 2000, Quebec, Canada.

Lincoln, Edward J. 1998. "Japan's Financial Mess." *Foreign Affairs*, 77/3:57–66.

Lind, Michael. 1994. "In Defense of Liberal Nationalism." *Foreign Affairs*, 73(3):87–99.

Lindsay, James M. 1994. "Congress, Foreign Policy, and the New Institutionalism." *International Studies Quarterly*, 38:281–304.

Linklater, Andrew. 1999. "The Evolving Spheres of International Justice." *International Affairs*, 75:473–482.

Lipschutz, Ronnie D., and Judith Mayer. 1996. *Global Civil Society and Global Environmental Governance: The Politics of Nature from Place to Planet*. Albany: State University of New York.

Litfin, Karen T. 1994. *Ozone Discourses: Science and Politics in Global Environmental Cooperation.* New York: Columbia University Press.

Locher, Birgit and Elizabeth Prügl. 2001. "Feminism and Constructivism: World Apart or Sharing the Middle Ground?" *International Studies Quarterly,* 45:111–129.

Lopez, George A., Jackie G. Smith, and Ron Pagnucco. 1995. "The Global Tide." *Bulletin of the Atomic Scientists,* 51/6 (July/August):33–39.

Love, Herbert. 1996. "Lessons of Liberia: ECOMOG and Regional Peacekeeping." *International Security,* 21:145–176.

Lugo, Luis E. 1996. *Sovereignty at the Crossroads? Morality and International Politics in the Post–Cold War Era.* Lanham, MD: Rowman & Littlefield.

Lustick, Ian S. 1997. "The Absence of Middle Eastern Great Powers: Political 'Backwardness' in Historical Perspective." *International Organization,* 51:653–684.

Luttwak, Edward. 2000. "Kofi's Rule: Humanitarian Intervention and Neocolonialism." *The National Interest* 58 (Winter): 57–62.

Mace, Gordon, and Jean-Philippe Therien, eds. 1996. *Foreign Policy and Regionalism in the Americas.* Boulder, CO: Lynne Rienner.

Macesich, George. 1997. *World Economy at the Crossroads.* Westport, CT: Praeger.

MacIver, Don. 1999. *The Politics of Multinational States.* New York: St. Martin's.

Macridis, Roy C., and Mark L. Hulliung. 1996. *Contemporary Political Ideologies.* New York: Harper-Collins.

Mahbubani, Kishore. 1994. "The Dangers of Decadence." *Foreign Affairs,* 72/4 (September/October):10–14.

Manning, Robert A. 1998. "The Nuclear Age: The Next Chapter." *Foreign Policy,* 109:70–84.

Mansbach, Richard W. 1996. "Neo-This and Neo-That: Or, 'Play It Sam' (Again and Again)." *Mershon International Studies Review,* 40:90–95.

Mansbach, Richard W., and Edward Rhodes, eds. 2000. *Global Politics in a Changing World.* Boston: Houghton Mifflin.

Mansfield, Edward D., and Rachel Bronson. 1997. "Alliances, Preferential Trading Arrangements, and International Trade." *American Political Science Review,* 91:94–106.

Mansfield, Edward D., and Helen V. Milner. 1999. "The New Wave of Regionalism." *International Organization,* 53: 589–628.

Margulis-Ohnuma, Zachary. 1999. "The Unavoidable Correlative: Extraterritorial Power and the United States Constitution." *Journal of International Law & Politics* 32:147–203.

Maoz, Zeev. 1996. *Domestic Sources of Global Change.* Ann Arbor: University of Michigan Press.

Marshall, Monty G. 1999. *Third World War: System, Process, and Conflict Dynamics.* Lanham, MD: Rowman & Littlefield.

Matheson, Michael J. 1997. "The Opinions of the International Court of Justice on the Threat or Use of Nuclear Weapons." *American Journal of International Law,* 91:417–436.

Mattli, Walter, and Anne-Marie Slaughter. 1998. "Revisiting the European Court of Justice." *International Organization,* 52:177–210.

Mattox, Gale A., and Arthur R. Rachwald, eds. 2001. *Enlarging NATO: The National Debates.* Boulder, CO: Lyne Rienner.

May, Ernest R. 1994. "The 'Great Man' Theory of Foreign Policy." Review of Henry Kissinger. *Diplomacy. New York Times Book Review,* April 3.

May, Greg. 1998. "China and the World." *The World & I* (October):52–57.

Mayall, James. 1999. "Sovereignty, Nationalism, and Self-Determination." *Political Studies,* 47/3:474–502.

Maynes, Charles William. 1998. "The Perils of (and for) an Imperial America." *Foreign Policy,* 111:503–521.

McCormick, John. 1999. *Understanding the European Union.* Boulder, CO: Westview Press.

McKay, David. 1999. "The Political Sustainability of European Monetary Union." *British Journal of Political Science,* 29: 463–486.

McKim, Robert, and Jeff McMahan. 1997. *The Morality of Nationalism.* New York: Oxford University Press.

Mearsheimer, John J. 1995. "The False Promise of International Institutions." *International Security,* 19/3:5–49.

Menon, Rajan. 1997. "The Once and Future Superpower." *Bulletin of the Atomic Scientists,* 36 (January/February): 29–34.

Mercer, Jonathan C. 1996. *Reputation and International Politics.* Ithaca, NY: Cornell University Press.

Metselaar, Max, and Bertjan Verbeek. 1996. "Bureau-Politics. Decisional Conflicts, and Small Group Dynamics." Paper presented at the International Studies Association convention, San Diego.

Meunier, Sophie. 2000. "What Single Voice? European Institutions and EU-US Trade Negotiations. *International Organization,* 54/2:103–135.

Meyer, John W., David John Frank, and Nancy Brandon Tuma. 1997. "The Structuring of a World Environmental Regime, 1870–1990." *International Organization,* 51:623–652.

Meyer, Mary K., and Elisabeth Prügel, eds. 1999. *Gender Politics in Global Governance.* Lanham, MD: Rowman & Littlefield.

Midlarsky, Manus. 1999. "Democracy and Islam: Implications for Civilizational Conflict and the Democratic Peace." *International Studies Quarterly,* 42:485–512.

Miller, Benjamin. 1995. *When Opponents Cooperate: Great Power Conflict and Collaboration in World Politics.* Ann Arbor: University of Michigan Press.

Miller, David. 1995. *On Nationality.* Oxford, U.K.: Clarendon Press.

Miller, Marian A. L. 1995. *The Third World in Global Politics.* Boulder, CO: Lynne Rienner.

Milner, Helen V. 1997. *Interests, Institutions, and Information: Domestic Politics and International Relations.* Princeton, NJ: Princeton University Press.

Milner, Helen V. 1998. "International Political Economy: Beyond Hegemonic Stability." *Foreign Policy,* 110:112–123.

Milner, Helen V., and B. Peter Rosendorff. 1997. "Democratic Politics and International Trade Negotiations." *Journal of Conflict Resolution,* 412:117–146.

Mirsky, Georgiy I. 1997. *On Ruins of Empire: Ethnicity and Nationalism in the Former Soviet Union.* Westport, CT: Greenwood.

Mo, Jongryn. 1994. "The Logic of Two-Level Games With Endogenous Domestic Coalitions." *Journal of Conflict Resolution*, 38:402–422.

Mockaitis, Thomas R. 1999. *Peace Operations and Interstate Conflict: The Sword or the Olive Branch*. Westport, CT: Praeger.

Modelski, George, and William R. Thompson. 1998. "The Long and the Short of Global Politics in the Twenty-First Century: An Evolutionary Approach." Paper presented at the International Studies Association convention, Minneapolis.

Moller, Bjorn. 1995. *Dictionary of Alternative Defense*. Boulder, CO: Lynne Rienner.

Moon, Bruce E. 1996. *Dilemmas of International Trade*. Boulder, CO: Westview.

Moore, Gale. 1998. *Climate of Fear: Why We Shouldn't Worry About Global Warming*. Washington, DC: Cato Institute.

Moore, Margaret. 1997. "On National Self-Determination." *Political Studies*, 45:900–915.

Moran, Theodore H. 1990. "The Globalization of America's Defense Industries: Managing the Threat of Foreign Dependence." *International Security*, 15:57–99.

Moravcsik, Andrew. 1997. "Taking Preferences Seriously: A Liberal Theory of International Politics." *International Organization*, 51:513–554.

Moravcsik, Andrew. 2000. "The Origin of Human Rights Regimes: Democratic Delegation in Postwar Europe." *International Organization*, 54:217–252.

Morgan, T. Clifton, and Christopher J. Anderson. 1999. "Domestic Support and Diversionary External Conflict in Great Britain, 1950–1992." *Journal of Politics*, 61:799–814.

Morgenthau, Hans W. 1973, 1986. *Politics among Nations*. New York: Knopf. Morgenthau's text was first published in 1948 and periodically thereafter. Two sources are used herein. One is the fifth edition, published in 1973. The second is an edited abstract drawn from pp. 3–4, 10–12, 14, 27–29, and 31–35 of the third edition, published in 1960. The abstract appears in Vasquez 1986:37–41. Pages cited for Morgenthau 1986 refer to Vasquez's, not Morgenthau's, book.

Morse, Edward L. 1999. "A New Political Economy of Oil?" *Journal of International Affairs*, 53:1–30.

Mortimer, Edward, and Robert Fine. 1999. *People, Nation, and State: The Meaning of Ethnicity and Nationalism*. New York: St. Martin's.

Mott, William H., IV. 1997. *The Economic Basis of Peace: Linkages Between Economic Growth and International Conflict*. Westport, CT: Greenwood.

Mower, A. Glenn, Jr. 1997. *The Convention of the Rights of the Child: International Law Support for Children*. Westport, CT: Greenwood.

Murray, A. J. H. 1996. "The Moral Politics of Hans Morgenthau." *The Review of Politics*, 58:81–109.

Murray, Geoffrey. 1998. *China: The Next Superpower: Dilemmas in Change and Continuity*. New York: St. Martins.

Murray, Shoon Kathleen. 1997. *Anchors Against Change: American Opinion Leaders' Beliefs After the Cold War*. Ann Arbor: University of Michigan Press.

Musgrave, Thomas D. 1997. *Self Determination and National Minorities*. Oxford, U.K.: Clarendon.

Namkung, Gon. 1998. *Japanese Images of the United States and Other Nations: A Comparative Study of Public Opinion and Foreign Policy*. Doctoral dissertation. Storrs, CT: University of Connecticut.

Nathan, Andrew. 1998. *China's Transition*. New York: Columbia University Press.

Neack, Laura. 1995. "UN Peace-Keeping: In the Interest of Community or Self?" *Journal of Peace Research*, 32:181–196.

Neuman, Stephanie. 1998. *International Relations Theory and the Third World*. New York: St. Martin's.

Neumann, Iver B., and Ole Weaver, eds. 1997. *The Future of International Relations: Masters in the Making*. New York: Routledge.

Nevin, John A. 1996. "War Initiation and Selection by Consequences." *Journal of Peace Research*, 33:99–108

Noël, Alain, and Jean-Philippe Thérien. 1996. "Political Parties, Domestic Institutions, and Foreign Aid." Paper presented at the International Studies Association convention, San Diego.

Nogee, Joseph L., and John Spanier. 1988. *Peace Impossible—War Unlikely: The Cold War Between the United States and the Soviet Union*. Glenville, IL: Scott, Foresman.

Norman, Richard. 1995. *Ethics, Killing, and War*. Cambridge, U.K.: Cambridge University Press.

Nugent, Neill, ed. 1997. *At the Heart of the Union: Studies of the European Commission*. New York: St. Martin's.

Nye, Joseph. 2000. *Understanding International Conflicts*, 3rd ed. New York: Longman.

O'Leary, Brendan. 1997. "On the Nature of Nationalism: An Appraisal of Ernest Gellner's Writings on Nationalism." *British Journal of Political Science*, 27:191–222.

Olmer, Lionel H. 1989. "Statement on EC 1992 and the Requirement for U.S. Industry and Government Partnership." *Europe 1992*. Hearings before the U.S. Congress, House of Representatives, Sub-committee on Trade of the Committee on Ways and Means. March 20.

Oneal, John R., and Bruce M. Russett. 1997. "The Classical Liberals Were Right: Democracy, Interdependence, and Conflict, 1950–1985." *International Studies Quarterly*, 41:267–294.

Oneal, John R., and Bruce Russett. 1999. "The Kantian Peace: The Pacific Benefits of Democracy, Interdependence, and International Organizations, 1885–1992." *World Politics*, 52: 1–37.

O'Neill, Barry O. 1997. "Power and Satisfaction in the Security Council." In *The Once and Future Security Council*, ed. Bruce Russett. New York: St. Martin's.

Opello, Walter C., Jr., and Stephen Rosow. 1999. *The Nation-State and Global Order: A Historical Introduction to Contemporary Politics*. Boulder, CO: Lynne Rienner.

O'Reilly, Marc J. 1997. "'Following Ike': Explaining Canadian-U.S. Co-operation during the 1956 Suez Crisis." *Journal of Commonwealth & Comparative Studies*, 35/3:75–107.

Orme, John. 1998. "The Utility of Force in a World of Scarcity." *International Security*, 22/3:138–167.

Osiander, Andreas. 1998. "Rereading Early Twentieth-Century IR Theory: Idealism Revisited." *International Studies Quarterly*, 42:409–432.

Osiel, Mark. 1999. *Obeying Orders: Atrocity, Military Discipline, and the Law of War*. New Brunswick, NJ: Transaction.

Ostrom, Charles W., and H. J. Aldrich. 1978. "The Relationship Between Size and Stability in the Major Power International System." *American Journal of Political Science*, 22:743–771.

Pace, John P. 1998. "The Development of Human Rights Law in the United Nations, Its Control and Monitoring Machine." *International Social Science Journal*, 50:499–512.

Pagden, Anthony. 1998. "The Genesis of 'Governance' and Enlightenment Conceptions of the Cosmopolitan World Order." *International Social Science Journal*, 50:7–16.

Papayoanou, Paul A. 1997. "Economic Interdependence and the Balance of Power." *International Studies Quarterly*, 41:113–140.

Pape, Robert A. 1997. "Why Economic Sanctions Do Not Work." *International Security*, 22:90–136.

Pape, Robert A. 1998. "Why Economic Sanctions Still Do Not Work." *International Security*, 23:66–77.

Park, Bert Edward. 1994. *Ailing, Aging, Addicted: Studies of Compromised Leadership*. Lexington, KY: University Press of Kentucky.

Parker, Christopher S. 1999. "New Weapons for Old Problems: Conventional Proliferation and Military Effectiveness in Developing States." *International Security*, 23/4:119–147.

Paterson, Thomas G. J., Garry Clifford, and Kenneth J. Hagen. 2000. *American Foreign Relations: A History. Vol. II: Since 1945*, 5th ed. Boston: Houghton Mifflin.

Pauly, Louis W., and Simon Reich. 1997. "National Structures and Multinational Corporate Behavior: Enduring Differences in the Age of Globalization." *International Organization*, 51:1–30.

Peterson, John, and Elizabeth Bomberg. 1999. *Decision-Making in the European Union*. New York: St. Martin's.

Peterson, M. J. 1997. "The Use of Analogies in Developing Outer Space Law." *International Organization*, 51:245–274.

Peterson, Susan. 1996. *Crisis Bargain and the State: The Domestic Politics of International Conflict*. Ann Arbor: University of Michigan Press.

Pettman, Ralph, ed. 1996. *Understanding International Political Economy, With Readings for the Fatigued*. Boulder, CO: Lynne Rienner.

Phan, Chau T. 1996. "International Nongovernmental Organizations, Global Negotiations, and Global Activist Networks: The Emergence of INGOs as Partners in the Global Governance Process." *International Organization*, 51:591–622.

Philpott, Daniel. 1999. "Westphalia, Authority, and International Society." *Political Studies*, 47/3:566–589.

Pickering, Jeffrey, and William R. Thompson. 1998. "Stability in a Fragmenting World: Interstate Military Force, 1946–1988." *Political Research Quarterly*, 51:241–264.

Piening, Christopher. 1997. *Global Europe: The European Union in World Affairs*. Boulder, CO: Lynne Rienner.

Pierre, Andrew J., ed. 1997. *Cascade of Arms: Managing Conventional Weapons Proliferation*. Washington, DC: Brookings Institution.

Pollins, Brian M. 1996. "Global Political Order, Economic Change, and Armed Conflict: Coevolving Systems and the Use of Force." *American Political Science Review*, 90:103–117.

Porter, Bruce D. 1994. *War and the Rise of the State*. New York: Free Press.

Porter, Gareth, and Janet Welsh Brown. 1996. *Global Environmental Politics*, 2nd ed. Boulder, CO: Westview.

Posen, Barry R. "The Struggle Against Terrorism: Grand Strategy, Strategy, and Tactics." *International Security* 26/3:39–55.

Poulton, Hugh. 1997. *Top Hat, Grey Wolf and Crescent: Turkish Nationalism and the Turkish Republic*. New York: New York University Press.

Powell, Robert. 1996. "Stability and the Distribution of Power." *World Politics*, 48:239–267.

Powlick, Philip. J. 1995. "The Sources of Public Opinion for American Foreign Policy Officials." *International Studies Quarterly*, 39:427–52.

Powlick, Philip J., and Andrew Z. Katz. 1998. "Defining the American Public Opinion/Foreign Policy Nexus." *Mershon International Studies Review*, 42/1:29–62.

Preston, Christopher. 1998. *Enlargement and Integration in the European Union*. New York: Routledge.

Price, Richard M. 1995. "A Genealogy of the Chemical Weapons Taboo." *International Organization*, 49:73–104.

Price, Richard M. 1997. *The Chemical Weapons Taboo*. Ithaca, NY: Cornell University Press.

Pritchard, Sarah, ed. 1998. *Indigenous Peoples, the United Nations, and Human Rights*. New York: St. Martin's.

Rabkin, Jeremy. 1994. "Threats to U.S. Sovereignty." *Commentary*, 97(3):41–47.

Ramet, Sabrina P. 2000. "The So-Called Right of National Self-Determination and Other Myths." *Human Rights Review*, 2:84–103.

Rapoport, Anatol. 1992. *Peace: An Idea Whose Time Has Come*. Ann Arbor, MI: University of Michigan Press.

Ratner, Steven R. 1996. *The New UN Peacekeeping: Building Peace in Lands of Conflict After the Cold War*. New York: St. Martin's.

Ratner, Steven R. 1998. "International Law: The Trials of Global Norms." *Foreign Policy*, 110:65–81.

Raustiala, Kal. 1997. "State, NGOs, and International Environmental Institutions." *International Studies Quarterly*, 41:719–770.

Razavi, Shahra. 1999. "Seeing Poverty Through a Gender Lens." *International Social Science Journal*, 51:473–483.

Reardon, Betty A. 1990. "Feminist Concepts of Peace and Security." In *A Reader in Peace Studies*, ed. Paul Smoker, Ruth Davies, and Barbara Munske. Oxford, U.K.: Pergamon Press.

Reich, Walter, ed. 1998. *Origins of Terrorism : Psychologies, Ideologies, Theologies, States of Mind*. Princton, N.J.: Woodrow Wilson Center Press.

Renan, Ernest. 1995. "Qu'est-ce Qu'une Nation?" In *Nationalism*, ed. John Hutchinson and Anthony D. Smith. New York: Oxford University Press.

Renshon, Stanley A. 1995. "Character, Judgment, and Political Leadership: Promise, Problems, and Prospects of the Clinton Presidency." In *The Clinton Presidency: Campaigning, Governing, and the Psychology of Leadership*, ed. Stanley Renshon. Boulder, CO: Westview.

Renshon, Stanley A. 2000. "After the Fall: The Clinton Presidency in Psychological Perspective." *Political Science Quarterly*, 115: 41–66.

Reynolds, Andrew. 1999. "Women in the Legislatures and Executives of the World: Knocking at the Highest Glass Ceiling." *World Politics*, 514: 547–569.

Rhein, Wendy. 1998. "The Feminization of Poverty: Unemployment in Russia." *Journal of International Affairs*, 52:351–367.

Rhodes, Carolyn, ed. 1997. *The European Union in the World Community*. Boulder, CO: Lynne Rienner.

Richards, Diana. 1993. "A Chaotic Model of Power Concentration in the International System." *International Studies Quarterly*, 37:55–72.

Richardson, Jeremy, ed. 1997. *European Union: Power and Policy-Making*. New York: Routledge.

Riddell-Dixon, Elizabeth. 1996. "Canada and the Fourth UN Conference on Women: NGO-Government Relations." Paper presented at the International Studies Association convention, San Diego.

Rielly, John E. 1995. "The Public Mood at Mid-Decade." *Foreign Policy*, 82:79–96.

Rielly, John E. 1999. "Americans and the World: A Survey at Century's End." *Foreign Policy*, 114:97–113.

Ripley, Brian. 1995. "Cognition, Culture, and Bureaucratic Politics." In *Foreign Policy Analysis*, ed. Laura Neack, Jeane A. K. Hey, and Patrick J. Haney. Englewood Cliffs, NJ: Prentice Hall.

Roberts, Adam. 1996. "From San Francisco to Sarajevo: The UN and the Use of Force." *Survival*, 37/4 (Winter):7–28.

Robertson, Charles L. 1997. *International Politics Since World War II: A Short History*. Armonk, NY: M. E. Sharpe.

Robinson, Glenn E. 1997. *Building a Palestinian State: The Incomplete Revolution*. Bloomington: Indiana University Press.

Rodrik, Dani. 1998. *Has Globalization Gone Too Far?* Washington, DC: Institute for International Economics.

Rogers, J. Phillip. 1987. "The Crisis Bargaining Code Model: A Cognitive Schema Approach to Crisis Decision-Making." Presented at the International Studies Association convention, April, Washington, DC.

Roht-Arriaza, Naomi. 1999. "Establishing a Framework." *Journal of International Affairs*, 52:473–492.

Rose, Gideon. 1998. "Neoclassical Realism and Theories of Foreign Policy." *World Politics*, 51:144–169.

Rosecrance, Richard, and Chih-Cheng Lo. 1996. "Balancing, Stability, and War: The Mysterious Case of the Napoleonic International System." *International Studies Quarterly*, 40:479–500.

Rosenau, James N. 1990. *Turbulence in World Politics: A Theory of Change and Continuity*. Princeton, NJ: Princeton University Press.

Rosenau, James N. 1997. *Along the Domestic-Foreign Frontier: Exploring Governance in a Turbulent World*. Cambridge, U.K.: Cambridge University Press.

Rosenau, James N. 1998. "The Dynamism of a Turbulent World." In *World Security: Challenges for a New Century*, 3rd ed., ed. Michael T. Klare and Yogesh Chandran. New York: St. Martin's.

Rosenau, James N., and Mary Durfee. 1995. *Thinking Theory Thoroughly*. Boulder, CO: Westview.

Rosenblatt, Lionel, and Larry Thompson. 1998. "The Door of Opportunity: Creating a Permanent Peacekeeping Force." *World Policy Journal*. 15:36–47.

Rostow, Walt W. 1978. *The World Economy*. Austin: University of Texas Press.

Rothgeb, John M., Jr. 1993. *Defining Power: Influence and Force in the Contemporary International System*. New York: St. Martin's.

Rothkopf, David J. 1998. "Cyberpolitik: The Changing Nature of Power in the Information Age." *Journal of International Affairs*. 51:325–360.

Rourke, John T. 1990. *Making Foreign Policy: United States, Soviet Union, China*. Pacific Grove, CA: Brooks/Cole.

Rourke, John T. 1993. *Presidential Wars and American Democracy: Rally 'Round the Chief*. New York: Paragon.

Rourke, John T., Ralph G. Carter, and Mark A. Boyer. 1996. *Making American Foreign Policy*, 2nd ed. Guilford, CT: Brown & Benchmark/Dushkin.

Rourke, John T., Richard P. Hiskes, and Cyrus Ernesto Zirakzadeh. 1992. *Direct Democracy and International Politics*. Boulder, CO: Lynne Rienner.

Rummel, R. J. 1995 "Democracy, Power, Genocide, and Mass Murder." *Journal of Conflict Resolution*, 39:3–26.

Rusk, Dean, as told to Richard Rusk. 1990. *As I Saw It*. New York: W. W. Norton.

Russett, Bruce, ed. 1997. *The Once and Future Security Council*. New York: St. Martin's.

Russett, Bruce. 2000. "How Democracy, Interdependence, and International Organizations Create a System for Peace." In *The Global Agenda: Issues and Perspectives*, ed. Charles W. Kegley, Jr. and Eugene R. Wittkopf. Boston: McGraw-Hill.

Ryan, Stephen. 2000. *The United Nations and International Politics*. New York: St. Martin's.

Sachs, Jeffrey. 1998. "International Economics: Unlocking the Mysteries of Globalization." *Foreign Policy*, 110:97–111.

Saideman, Stephen M. 1997. "Explaining the International Relations of Secessionist Conflicts: Vulnerability Versus Ethnic Ties." *International Organization*, 51:721–754.

Saideman, Stephen M. 2001. *The Ties That Divide: Ethnic Politics, Foreign Policy, and International Conflict*. New York: Columbia University Press.

Sanjian, Gregory S. 1998. "Cold War Imperatives and Quarrelsome Clients: Modeling U.S. and USSR Arms Transfers to India and Pakistan." *Journal of Conflict Resolution*, 42:97–127.

Sanjian, Gregory. 1999. "Promoting Stability or Instability? Arms Transfers and Regional Rivalries, 1950–1991." *International Studies Quarterly*, 43:641–670.

Sazanami, Yoko, Shujiro Urata, and Hiroki Kawai. 1994. *Measuring the Costs of Protectionism in Japan*. Washington, DC: Institute for International Economics.

Schafer, Mark, and Scott Crichlow. 2002. "The Process-Outcome Connection in Foreign Policy Decision Making: A Quantitative Study Building on Groupthink." *International Studies Quarterly*, 46:45–68.

Schampel, James H. 1996. "A Preponderance of Conflict over Peace: A Dialogue With Charles Gochman and Aaron Hoffman." *International Studies Notes*, 21/2 (Spring):26–27.

Schmidt, Brian C. 1997. *The Political Discourse of Anarchy*. Albany: State University of New York Press.

Schmidt, Brian C. 1998. "Lessons From the Past: Reassessing the Interwar Disciplinary History of International Relations." *International Studies Quarterly*, 42:433–460.

Schraeder, Peter J., Steven W. Hook, and Bruce Taylor. 1998. "Clarifying the Foreign Aid Puzzle: A Comparison of American, Japanese, French, and Swedish Aid Flows." *World Politics*, 50:294–324.

Schubert, James N. 1993. "Realpolitik as a Male Primate Strategy." Presented at the annual meeting of the International Studies Association, Acapulco, Mexico

Schultz, Kathryn R., and David Isenberg. 1997. "Arms Control and Disarmament." In *A Global Agenda: Issues Before the 52nd General Assembly of the United Nations*, ed. John Tessitore and Susan Woolfson. Lanham, MD: Rowman & Littlefield.

Schultz, Kenneth A. 1999. "Do Democratic Institutions Constrain or Inform? Contrasting Two Institutional Perspectives on Democracy and War." *International Organization*, 53:233–266.

Schulzinger, Robert D. 1989. *Henry Kissinger: Doctor of Diplomacy*. New York: Columbia University Press.

Schweller, Randall L. 1997. "New Realist Research on Alliances: Refining, Not Refuting, Waltz's Balancing Proposition." *American Political Science Review*, 4:927–930.

Schweller, Randall L. 1998. *Deadly Imbalances: Tripolarity and Hitler's Strategy of World Conquest*. New York: Columbia University Press.

Schweller, Randall L., and David Priess. 1997. "A Tale of Two Realisms: Expanding the Institutions Debate." *Mershon International Studies Review*, 41:1–32.

Scott, Catherine V. 1996. *Gender and Development: Rethinking Modernization and Dependency Theory*. Boulder, CO: Lynne Rienner.

Sen, Amartya. 1999. *Development as Freedom*. New York: Alfred A. Knopf.

Setala, Maija. 1999. *Referendums and Democratic Government*. New York: St. Martin's.

Seymour, Michel. 2000 "Quebec and Canada at the Crossroads: A Nation Within a Nation." *Nations and Nationalism*, 6:227–256.

Shaheed, Farida. 1999. "Constructing Identities: Culture, Women's Agency and the Muslim World." *International Social Science Journal*, 51:61–75.

Shambaugh, George E., IV. 1996. "Dominance, Dependence, and Political Power: Tethering Technology in the 1980s and Today." *International Studies Quarterly*, 40:559–588.

Shambaugh, George E. 2000. *States, Firms, and Power: Successful Sanctions in United States Foreign Policy*. Albany, NY: State University of New York Press.

Sharp, Paul. 1999. "For Diplomacy: Representation and the Study of International Relations." *International Studies Review*, 1:33–58.

Sharp, Paul. 2001. "Making Sense of Citizen Diplomats: The People of Duluth, Minnesota, as International Actors." *International Studies Perspective*, 2:131–150.

Sherill, Robert. 1979. *Why They Call It Politics*. New York: Harcourt Brace Jovanovich.

Shevchenko, Arkady. 1985. *Breaking With Moscow*. New York: Alfred A. Knopf.

Shlaim, Avi. 1999. *The Iron Wall: Israel and the Arab World*. New York: W. W. Norton.

Simmons, Beth A. 1993. "Why Innovate? Founding the Bank for International Settlements." *World Politics*, 45:361–405.

Simmons, Geoff. 1998. *Vietnam Syndrome: Impact on U.S. Foreign Policy*. New York: St. Martin's.

Simon, Julian L. 1994. "More People, Greater Wealth, More Resources, Healthier Environment." In *Taking Sides: Clashing Views on Controversial Issues in World Politics*, 6th ed., ed. John T. Rourke. Guilford, CT: Dushkin.

(SIPRI) Stockholm International Peace Research Institute. Annual Editions. *SIPRI Yearbook*. Oxford, U.K.: Oxford University Press.

Smith, Alastair. 1996. "Diversionary Foreign Policy in Democratic Systems." *International Studies Quarterly*, 40:133–153.

Smith, Steve. 1984. "Groupthink and the Hostage Rescue Mission." *British Journal of Political Science*, 15:117–126.

Snyder, Robert S. 1999. "The U.S. and Third World Revolutionary States: Understanding the Breakdown in Relations." *International Studies Quarterly*, 43:265–290.

Somit, Albert, and Steven A. Peterson. 1997. *Darwinism, Dominance, Democracy: The Biological Bases of Authoritarianism*. Westport, CT: Greenwood.

Sorensen, George. 1999. "Sovereignty: Change and Continuity in a Fundamental Institution." *Political Studies*, 47:590–609.

Soroos, Marvin S. 1997. *The Endangered Atmosphere: Preserving a Global Commons*. Norman: University of Oklahoma Press.

Spanier, John, and Eric M. Uslaner. 1993. *American Foreign Policy Making and the Democratic Dilemmas*, 6th ed. New York: Macmillan.

Spegele, Roger D. 1996. *Political Realism in International Theory*. Cambridge, U.K.: Cambridge University Press.

Speth, James Gustave. 1998. "Poverty: A Denial of Human Rights." *Journal of International Affairs*, 52:277–292.

Spruyt, Hendrik. 1994. *The Sovereign State and Its Competitors: An Analysis of Systems Change*. Princeton, NJ: Princeton University Press.

Starkey, Brigid, Mark A. Boyer, and Jonathan Wilkenfeld. 1999. *Negotiating a Complex World*. Lanham, MD: Rowman & Littlefield.

Sterling-Folker, Jennifer. 2002. *Theories of International Cooperation and the Primacy of Anarchy: Explaining U.S. International Monetary Policy-Making After Bretton Woods*. Albany: State University of New York Press.

Sterling-Folker, Jennifer. 1996. "Realist Environment, Liberal Process, and Domestic-Level Variables." Paper presented at the International Studies Association convention, San Diego.

Sterling-Folker, Jennifer. 1997. "Realist Environment, Liberal Process, and Domestic-Level Variables." *International Studies Quarterly*, 41:1–26.

Stoessinger, John G. 1998. *Why Nations Go to War*, 7th ed. New York: St. Martin's.

Strange, Susan. 1997. *The Retreat of the State: The Diffusion of Power in the World Economy*. New York: Cambridge University Press.

Suu Kyi, Aung San. 1995. "Freedom, Development, and Human Worth." *Journal of Democracy*, 6/2 (April):12–19.

Swanson, Timothy. 1999. "Why Is There a Biodiversity Convention? The International Interest in Centralized Development Planning." *International Affairs*, 75:307–331.

Taber, Charles S. 1989. "Power Capability Indexes in the Third World." In *Power in World Politics*, ed. Richard J. Stoll and Michael D. Ward. Boulder, CO: Lynne Rienner.

Talbott, Strobe. 2000. "Self-Determination in an Interdependent World." *Foreign Policy*, 118 (Spring 2000):152–163.

Tamir, Yael. 1995. "The Enigma of Nationalism." *World Politics*, 47:418–440.

Tammen, Ronald L., et al. 2000. *Power Transitions: Strategies for the Twenty-First Century*. New York: Chatham House/ Seven Bridges Press.

Tannenwald, Nina. 1999. "The Nuclear Taboo: The United States and the Normative Basis of Nuclear Non-Use." *International Organization*, 53:433–468.

Taras, Ray, and Rajat Ganguly. 1998. *Understanding Ethnic Conflict: The International Dimension*. New York: Longman.

Tarrow, Sidney. 2001. *Rethinking Europe's Future*. Princeton, NJ: Princeton University Press.

Taylor, Andrew J., and John T. Rourke. 1995. "Historical Analogies in the Congressional Foreign Policy Process." *Journal of Politics*, 57:460–468.

Taylor, Paul. 1999. "The United Nations in the 1990s: Pro active Cosmopolitanism and the Issue of Sovereignty." *Political Studies*, 47: 538–565.

Taylor, Robert L., and William E. Rosenbach. 1996. *Military Leadership: In Pursuit of Excellence*. Boulder, CO: Westview.

Tehranian, Majid. 1999. *Global Communication and World Politics: Domination, Development, and Discourse*. Boulder, CO: Lynne Rienner.

Thies, Wallace J. 1998. "Deliberate and Inadvertent War in the Post–Cold War World." In *Annual Editions, American Foreign Policy 98/99*, ed. Glenn P. Hastedt. Guilford, CT: Dushkin/McGraw-Hill.

Thompson, James C., Jr. 1989. "Historical Legacies and Bureaucratic Procedures." In *Major Problems in American Foreign Policy*, Vol. 2, ed. Thomas G. Paterson. Lexington, MA: D. C. Heath.

Thompson, Kenneth W. 1995. *Fathers of International Thought: The Legacy of Political Theory*. Baton Rouge: Louisiana State University Press.

Tibi, Bassam. 1997. *Arab Nationalism: Between Islam and the Nation-State*. New York: St. Martin's.

Tickner, J. Ann. 1997. "You Just Don't Understand: Troubled Engagements Between Feminists and IR Theorists." *International Studies Quarterly*, 41:611–632.

Trumbore, Peter F. 1998. "Public Opinion as a Domestic Constraint in International Negotiations: Two-Level Games in the Anglo-Irish Peace Process." *International Studies Quarterly*, 42:545–565.

Tucker, Jonathan B. 2000. *Toxic Terror: Assessing Terrorist Use of Chemical and Biological Weapons*. Cambridge, MA: MIT Press.

Turner, Frederick C., and Alejandro L. Corbacho. 2000. "New Roles for the State." *International Social Science Journal*, 163:109–120.

UN, Department of Economic and Social Affairs, Population Division. 1999. *World Population 1998* at: http://www. undp.org/popin/wdtrends/p98/p98.htm.

(UN, UNICEF) United Nations Children's Fund. Annual editions. *State of the World's Children 1998*. New York: Oxford University Press.

(UNDP) United Nations Development Programme. Annual editions. *Human Development Report*. New York: Oxford University Press.

United Nations. *See* (UN).

(U.S.) Bureau of the Census. Annual editions. *Statistical Abstract of the United States*. Washington, DC.

U.S. (CIA) Central Intelligence Agency. Annual editions. *World Fact Book*. Washington, DC: GPO.

Van Dervort, Thomas R. 1997. *International Law and Organization*. Thousand Oaks, CA: Sage.

Vandenbroucke, Lucien. 1991. *Perilous Options: Special Operations in U.S. Foreign Policy*. Unpublished dissertation, The University of Connecticut. A manuscript based on Vandenbroucke's revised dissertation was published in 1993 under the same title by Oxford University Press.

Vasquez, John A. 1995. "Why Do Neighbors Fight? Proximity, Interaction, or Territoriality." *Journal of Peace Research*, 32:277–293.

Vasquez, John A. 1996. "Distinguishing Rivals That Go to War From Those That Do Not: A Quantitative Comparative Case Study of the Two Paths to War." *International Studies Quarterly*, 40:531–558.

Vasquez, John A. 1997. "The Realist Paradigm and Degenerative Versus Progressive Research Programs: An Appraisal of Neotraditional Research on Waltz's Balancing Proposition." *American Political Science Review*, 4:899–912.

Vertzberger, Yaakov Y. I. 1994. "Collective Risk Taking: The Decisionmaking Group and Organization." Presented at the annual meeting of the International Studies Association, Washington, DC.

Vertzberger, Yaakov Y. I. 1998. *Risk Taking and Decision Making: Foreign Military Intervention Decisions*. Palo Alto, CA: Stanford University Press.

Vlahos, Michael. 1998. "Entering the Infosphere." *Journal of International Affairs*, 51:497–526.

Voeten, Erik. 2000. "Clashes in the Assembly." *International Organization*, 54:185–216.

Volgy, Thomas J., and Lawrence E. Imwalle. 1995. "Hegemonic and Bipolar Perspective on the New World Order." *American Journal of Political Science*, 39:819–834.

Walker, Stephen G., Mark Schafer, and Michael D. Young. 1998. "Systematic Procedures for Operational Code Analysis: Measuring and Modeling Jimmy Carter's Operational Code." *International Studies Quarterly*, 42:175–189.

Walker, William. 1998. "International Nuclear Relations after the Indian and Pakistani Test Explosions." *International Affairs*, 74:505–528.

Wallace, William. 1999. "The Sharing of Sovereignty: The European Paradox." *Political Studies*, 47:503–521.

Walt, Stephen M. 1996. "Alliances: Balancing and Bandwagoning." In *International Politics*, 4th ed., ed. Robert J. Art and Robert Jervis. New York: HarperCollins.

Walt, Stephen M. 1996a. *Revolution and War*. Ithaca, NY: Cornell University Press.

Walt, Stephen M. 1997. "Building up New Bogeymen: Review of Huntington's *The Clash of Civilizations and the Remaking of World Order*." *Foreign Affairs*, 76/3:132–139.

Walt, Stephen M. 1997a. "The Progressive Power of Realism." *American Political Science Review*, 4:931–935.

Waltz, Kenneth N. 1997. "Evaluating Theories." *American Political Science Review*, 4:913–918.

Wang, Kevin H. 1996. "Presidential Responses to Foreign Policy Crises: Rational Choice and Domestic Politics." *Journal of Conflict Resolution*, 40:68–97.

Wang, Kevin H., and James Lee Ray. 1994. "Beginnings and Winners: The Fate of Initiators of Interstate Wars Involving Great Powers Since 1495." *International Studies Quarterly*, 38:139–154.

Wapner, Paul. 1996. *Environmental Activism and World Civic Politics*. Albany: State University of New York.

Wapner, Paul, and Lester Edwin J. Ruiz, eds. 2000. *Principled World Politics: The Challenge of Normative International Relations at the Millennium.* Lanham, MD: Rowman & Littlefield.

Watson, James L. 2000. "China's Big Mac Attack." *Foreign Affairs*, 79/3:120–142.

Weber, Peter. 1994. "Safeguarding the Oceans." In *The State of the World, 1994*, ed. Lester R. Brown et al. New York: W. W. Norton.

Weigel, George. 1995. "Are Human Rights Still Universal?" *Commentary*, 99/2 (February):41–45.

Weisband, Edward. 2000. "Discursive Multilateralism: Global Benchmarks, Shame, and Learning in the ILO Labor Standards Monitoring Regime." *International Studies Quarterly*, 44:643-666.

Weiss, Linda. 1998. *The Myth of the Powerless State.* Ithaca, NY: Cornell University Press.

Weller, Marc. 1999. "On the Hazards of Foreign Travel for Dictators and Other International Criminals." *International Affairs*, 75:599–618.

Wesley, Michael. 1997. *Casualties of the New World Order: The Causes of Failure of UN Missions to Civil Wars.* New York: St. Martin's.

Wilcox, Clyde, Lara Hewitt, and Dee Allsop. 1996. "The Gender Gap in Attitudes Toward the Gulf War: A Cross-National Perspective." *Journal of Peace Research* 33:67–82.

Wilhelm, Alfred D. 1994. *The Chinese at the Negotiating Table.* Washington, DC: National Defense University Press.

Willets, Peter. 1996. "From Stockholm to Rio and Beyond: The Impact of the Environmental Movement on the United Nations Consultative Arrangements for NGOs." *Review of International Studies*, 22:57–80.

Wittkopf, Eugene R. 1990. *Faces of Internationalism: Public Opinion and American Foreign Policy.* Durham, NC: Duke University Press.

Wittkopf, Eugene R. 1994. "Faces of Internationalism in a Transitional Environment," *Journal of Conflict Resolution*, 38:376–401.

Wohlforth, William C. 1999. "The Stability of a Unipolar World." *International Security*, 24/1:5–41.

Woods, Ngaire. 1995. "Economic Ideas and International Relations: Beyond Rational Neglect." *International Studies*, 39:161–180.

World Almanac and Book of Facts. Annual editions. New York: Funk & Wagnalls.

World Bank. 2000a. *World Development Indicators 2000.* Washington, DC: World Bank.

World Bank. Annual editions. *World Development Report.* New York: Oxford University Press.

World Resources Institute. Annual editions. *World Resources.* New York: Oxford University Press.

Yost, David S. 1999. *NATO Transformed: The Alliance's New Roles in International Security.* Washington, DC: United States Institute of Peace Press.

Yu Quanyu. 1994. "Human Rights: A Comparative Study Between China and the U.S." Presented at the Sino-American Relations Conference, cosponsored by the China Institute of Contemporary International Relations and the Washington Institute for Values in Public Policy, Beijing, China.

Zakaria, Fareed. 1993. "Is Realism Finished?" *National Interest*, 32:21–32.

Zakaria, Fareed. 1996. "Speak Softly, Carry a Veiled Threat." *New York Times Magazine*, February 18.

Zhang, Ming, and Ronald N. Montaperto. 1999. *A Triad of Another Kind.* New York: St. Martin's.

Zielonka, Jan. 1998. *Explaining Euro-Paralysis: Why Europe Is Unable to Act in International Politics.* New York: St. Martin's.

Zolo, Danilo. 1997. *Cosmopolis: Prospects for World Government.* Cambridge, MA: Blackwell.

Zuckerman, Mortimer B. 1998. "A Second American Century." *Foreign Affairs*, 77/3:13–31.

Zurn, Michael. 1998. "The Rise of International Environmental Politics: A Review of Current Research." *World Politics*, 50:617–649.

Index

Page numbers in boldface refer to glossary terms.

Credits

Evolution of the World Political System

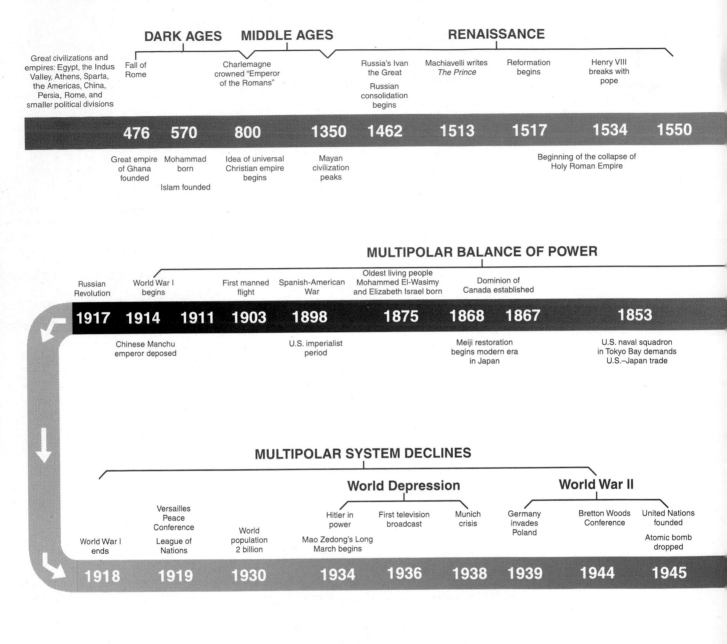

DARK AGES   **MIDDLE AGES**   **RENAISSANCE**

Great civilizations and empires: Egypt, the Indus Valley, Athens, Sparta, the Americas, China, Persia, Rome, and smaller political divisions

Fall of Rome

Charlemagne crowned "Emperor of the Romans"

Russia's Ivan the Great

Russian consolidation begins

Machiavelli writes *The Prince*

Reformation begins

Henry VIII breaks with pope

| 476 | 570 | 800 | 1350 | 1462 | 1513 | 1517 | 1534 | 1550 |

Great empire of Ghana founded

Mohammad born

Islam founded

Idea of universal Christian empire begins

Mayan civilization peaks

Beginning of the collapse of Holy Roman Empire

MULTIPOLAR BALANCE OF POWER

Russian Revolution

World War I begins

First manned flight

Spanish-American War

Oldest living people Mohammed El-Wasimy and Elizabeth Israel born

Dominion of Canada established

| 1917 | 1914 | 1911 | 1903 | 1898 | 1875 | 1868 | 1867 | 1853 |

Chinese Manchu emperor deposed

U.S. imperialist period

Meiji restoration begins modern era in Japan

U.S. naval squadron in Tokyo Bay demands U.S.–Japan trade

MULTIPOLAR SYSTEM DECLINES

World Depression   ### World War II

Versailles Peace Conference

League of Nations

World population 2 billion

Hitler in power

Mao Zedong's Long March begins

First television broadcast

Munich crisis

Germany invades Poland

Bretton Woods Conference

United Nations founded

Atomic bomb dropped

World War I ends

| 1918 | 1919 | 1930 | 1934 | 1936 | 1938 | 1939 | 1944 | 1945 |

NEW INTERNATIONAL SYSTEM EVOLVING

International Criminal Court treaty adopted

Earth Summit II

Bush in power

9-11 terrorist attack

UN Millennium Summit

World population 6 billion

Putin in power

India and Pakistan conduct nuclear tests

Kyoto Global Warming Conference

Peace in Bosnia

4th World Conference on Women

UN's 50th anniversary

Cairo Population Conference

Genocide in Rwanda

NAFTA ratified

European Union begins

Clinton in power

Yeltsin in power

| 2002 | 2001 | 2000 | 1999 | 1998 | 1997 | 1996 | 1995 | 1994 | 1993 | 1992 |

Switzerland joins UN

War in Afghanistan

NATO intervenes in Kosovo

Kofi Annan becomes UN secretary-general

World Trade Organization begins

Summit of the Americas

START II

Earth Summit

Chaos in Bosnia